Revisioning Curriculum in Higher Education

Edited by
Jennifer Grant Haworth
Loyola University Chicago
and
Clifton F. Conrad
University of Wisconsin-Madison

ASHE READER SERIES
Barbara Townsend, Series Editor

SIMON & SCHUSTER
CUSTOM PUBLISHING

10 9 8 7 6 5 4 3 2 1

ISBN 0–536–58848–1
BA 1487

SIMON & SCHUSTER CUSTOM PUBLISHING
160 Gould Street/Needham Heights, MA 02194
Simon & Schuster Education Group

COPYRIGHT ACKNOWLEDGMENTS

Contents

PART III   CONSTRUCTING CURRICULA: PLANNING AND IMPLEMENTATION

viii

PART IV   LEARNING FROM PARTICIPANTS' EXPERIENCES: CURRICULUM-IN-PRACTICE

Acknowledgments

While this book represents a collaborative effort between Jennifer Grant Haworth and Clifton F. Conrad, both editors gratefully acknowledge that this book would not have been nearly as rich or comprehensive without the candid input of members from our advisory board. These individuals—many of whom teach or conduct research in the areas of curriculum, teaching and learning, or program planning and evaluation—unselfishly contributed their expertise to the development of this volume. Besides providing helpful comments on the book's initial conceptualization, they recommended numerous articles for inclusion and helped us to choose from among them the most representative and highest-quality pieces.

Additionally, the editors would like to express their sincere appreciation to Barbara Townsend (Series Editor) and Kathleen Kourian (Senior Acquisitions Editor, Simon & Schuster Custom Publishing) for their generous advice and conscientious assistance in the preparation of this book.

Advisory Board

Marcia Baxter Magolda
John Braxton
Judith Glazer
Patricia Gumport
Julie Caplow
Anna Neumann
Gary Rhoades
Joan Stark
William Tierney
Susan Twombly
Barbara Townsend

The ASHE Reader Series

The ASHE Reader Series presents a collection of high quality readers on topics of sweeping interest in today's higher education scene. The books are designed to be used as supplementary text material in courses in the field of higher education or as reference. They reflect the collective ideas of those who teach in particular areas.

NEW TEACHING AND LEARNING IN THE COLLEGE CLASSROOM

Edited by Kenneth A. Feldman and Michael B. Paulsen

A comprehensive review of classic and recent research in the area, TEACHING AND LEARNING IN THE COLLEGE CLASSROOM addresses issues from diverse theoretical and philosophical perspectives. Each section includes quantitative and qualitative research, a separate introductory essay, research reports, literature reviews, theoretical essays, and practitioner-oriented articles. It emphasizes teacher-student and student-student interaction. It considers multicultural and gender issues and contains practical teaching strategies based on research.

Paperbound 704 pages ISBN 0-536-58535-0

NEW ASSESSMENT AND PROGRAM EVALUATION

Edited by Joan S. Stark and Alice Thomas

This reader effectively provides the broad perspective necessary for the study of assessment by consolidating articles from a wide range of sources, some not easily obtained. By addressing such topics as the historical and philosophical context and ethical issues, this volume will help readers develop the necessary assessment skills, attitudes and knowledge to conduct and supervise studies and program reviews or to be informed clients inside or outside the academic environment.

Paperbound 832 pages ISBN 0-536-58586-5

COMMUNITY COLLEGES

Edited by James L. Ratcliff

This updated edition includes new information on the diversity of the student population and features a special focus on community college scholarship and faculty renewal. It will give you and your students a review of the current community college systems in American history, philosophy, and purpose: organization, administration, and finance; programs and services; students; professional staff; and the social role.

Paperbound 503 pages ISBN 0-536-58571-7

QUALITATIVE RESEARCH IN HIGHER EDUCATION:
Experiencing Alternative Perspectives and Approaches

Edited by Clifton E. Conrad, Anna Neuman, Jennifer Grant Haworth, and Patricia Scott

Designed to help students and teachers prepare for, enter into, participate in, reflect on, and give voice to the experience of doing qualitative research. Organized around six topics: Explicating Frames of Reference, Approaching Inquiry, Doing Fieldwork, Interacting with Self and Other, Creating a Text, Reading a Text.

Paperbound 600 pages ISBN 0-536-58417-0

WOMEN IN HIGHER EDUCATION: A Feminist Perspective

Edited by Judith Glazer, Estela Bensimon, and Barbara Townsend

Essays representing the best of feminist scholarship in the field of higher education on four main themes: Theoretical and Research Perspectives, Context Historical, Social, and Professional, Institutional, Women in Academe: As Student, Faculty, Administrators, and Trustees, and The Transformation of Knowledge: Circular Change and Feminist Pedagogy.

Paperbound 600 pages ISBN 0-536-58351-0

FOUNDATIONS OF AMERICAN HIGHER EDUCATION

Edited by James L. Bess

A comprehensive introduction to the basics of American higher education—45 articles by some of today's most respected leaders in the field, in six parts: The Scope of Higher Education in American Society, The Participants, The Conduct of Education and Research, The Management of the College or University, Innovation, Change, and the Future, The Study and Practice of Higher Education Administration.

Paperbound 772 pages ISBN 0-536-58013-8

THE HISTORY OF HIGHER EDUCATION

Edited by Lester E. Goodchild and Harold S. Wechsler

Included are an introductory essay on American higher education historiography; introductory overviews of each of the five chronological periods of higher education; in-depth scholarly analyses from journal articles, book chapters, and essays; and the use of primary readings to capture the flavor and meaning of important issues for each period.

Paperbound 675 pages ISBN 0-536-57566-5

ORGANIZATION AND GOVERNANCE IN HIGHER EDUCATION, Fourth Edition

Edited by Marvin W. Peterson, with Associate Editors Ellen E. Chaffee and Theodore H. White

The selections not only reflect the changing views of colleges and universities as organizations, but also highlight the areas of literature applied to higher education that need to be addressed. The text is divided into three parts: Organization Theory and Models, Governance and Management Processes, and Leadership Perspectives.

Paperbound 475 pages ISBN 0-536-57981-4

FINANCE IN HIGHER EDUCATION

Edited by Dave Breneman, Larry L. Leslie and Richard E. Anderson

Practical and theoretical, the selections look at the financial management of colleges and universities, higher education economies, and federal and state policies, and represent a number of divergent perspectives and opinions.

Paperbound 450 pages ISBN 0-536-58352-8

UPCOMING TITLES IN THE SERIES:

MINORITIES IN HIGHER EDUCATION: A HISTORY

Edited by Caroline Turner, Mildred Garcia, Laura Rendon, and Amaury Nora

ISBN 0-536-59003-6

COLLEGE STUDENTS

Edited by Frances Stage, Guadelupe Anaya, John Bean, Don Hossler, and George D. Kuh

To Order:

To order copies of these titles for your class, please contact your campus bookstore and provide them with the quantity and ISBN. You can receive a complimentary desk copy with an order of 10 or more copies.

To order copies for yourself, simply call Simon & Schuster Custom Publishing at 800-428-4466 (or 617-455-7000 in Massachusetts and Canada) from 8:30 to 5:00 EST.

PART I
(RE)VIEWING PERSPECTIVES: FRAMES OF REFERENCE ON CURRICULUM

Introduction

What is curriculum? What perspectives have been brought to bear on the idea of curriculum? How has curriculum been defined in colleges and universities? In this section, we invite you—the reader—to explore and reflect on the different ways in which scholars have made sense of curriculum in higher education. Specifically, we have chosen articles that provide five frames of reference on curriculum: rationalist (structural), cultural, critical, nonfoundational and post-modern. As you read these selections, we encourage you to relate these views to your own perspectives on and experiences with curriculum and, in so doing, to (re)view the concept of curriculum in higher education from a more critical and holistic standpoint.

All of us have schooling, life, and cultural experiences that shape our understandings and perceptions of reality and define our sphere of knowledge (as well as the tacit assumptions upon which we determine "what counts" as knowledge and how we "come to know what we know"—assumptions upon which most views of curriculum are grounded). Indeed, the contexts that inform our daily realities—our families, work environments, neighborhoods, religious and social communities, political and economic milieus—have an enormous influence on how we make sense of the world around us and, in turn, how we construct our interpretations of college and university curriculum, schooling, teaching and learning.

We bring these constructions of reality to our reading of this text. As you read the selections in Part One, you might find it helpful to examine your tacit assumptions about what "curriculum is or should be" by asking yourself the following: What is my view of curriculum? What assumptions animate my view? Do my assumptions provide insights into how I define what counts as legitimate knowledge?

The readings included in this section of the text offer a variety of perspectives on curriculum. Like all of us, these writers have constructed views of curriculum that reflect their understandings of what curriculum is and should be. In their essay, for instance, Francis Hunkins and Patricia Hammill outline two frames of reference on curriculum: the rational (i.e., structuralist) and the post-modern. The former provides a view of curricula in which knowledge is considered relatively unchanging and, therefore, can be structured in any number of ways to achieve the stated purposes of a particular college or university. As such, the curriculum is conceived primarily as a mechanical structure for organizing de-contextualized, authoritative knowledge in light of pre-determined goals. In contrast, a post-modern perspective on curriculum emphasizes the dynamic interplay between teachers and students in the rediscovery, construction, and generation of knowledge. For those embracing a post-modern view, the curriculum becomes less a goal-driven structural entity and more a dialectical community in which participants constantly challenge assumptions, grapple with anomalies and paradoxes, reflect on multiple layers of meaning, and through dialogue, seek to build relations between knowledge, themselves, and their society.

The rational and post-modern perspectives provide only a glimpse of the many frames of reference that scholars have developed to explain curriculum in higher education. For example, William Tierney views the curriculum as a socially-constructed, ideological artifact of a college or university's culture. Kenneth Bruffee defines the curriculum as a "nonfoundational" knowledge community in which students and faculty dialogically question, interpret, and justify their own beliefs as well as the beliefs of their various disciplinary communities.

Whether reading Doll or Tierney or Bruffee, we believe that the selections in this section raise a number of evocative but not easily answered questions. Among others, these include: Is the curriculum only what is taught? Can our understandings of curriculum be separated from our assumptions about knowledge? Is curriculum best conceptualized as a rational plan for learning, an institutional system, a mirror of an institution's or society's culture, or a discursive community? Is there such a thing as "the" curriculum? We encourage you to analyze and reflect upon each author's view of curriculum by asking yourself these and other questions. In so doing, we urge you to examine critically how each author justifies his or her view of curriculum and the assumptions upon which it is based.

Frederick Rudolph once quipped that "an elementary caution on the way to understanding the curriculum may be to assume . . . that maybe there is no such thing as the curriculum." In our view, developing critical and holistic understandings of what curriculum is or should be requires us to view curriculum from many different perspectives and to probe the assumptions upon which they are constructed. We need to complement our personal knowledge by interacting with and listening carefully to how others (published authors and classmates alike) have made sense of curriculum. Only then will we begin to develop more robust responses to the question, "What is curriculum, anyhow?"

Frames of Reference

Frederick Rudolph

There is no way to make a history of the American college and university curriculum read like an account of the winning of the West or the collapse of the Old South. Martin Duberman's study of the history of sexuality in America, three years in the offing, has something going for it that curricular history does not. Even so, a puckish inspiration to entitle this book *The Harvard-Yale Game and Other Major Rivalries* was not altogether misleading. For the curriculum has been an arena in which the dimensions of American culture have been measured, an environment for certifying an elite at one time and for facilitating the mobility of an emerging middle class at another. It has been one of those places where we have told ourselves who we are. It is important territory.

There have been times and places where the curriculum was not taken seriously or should not have been. A little over 100 years ago fewer than two of every 100 Americans between the ages of eighteen and twenty-one were serious enough about it to enroll in a college or university, and many of those who did enroll were not serious. The approximately 700 pages of catalogue material required to describe the undergraduate courses of study for 1975 at Cornell are impressive evidence that Ezra Cornell did indeed, as he promised, "found an institution where any person can find instruction in any study." But can we take all 700 pages seriously?

Thinking about the curriculum historically presents many problems and requires a willingness to accept surprise, ambiguity, and a certain unavoidable messiness. If the world does not always make sense, why should the curriculum? George W. Pierson, coming up for air after being long submerged in the history of Yale, gasped, "One is appalled at the incoherence of American higher education"[2] The inability of colleges to take common action, to speak or act with authority and a common voice, is surely more than a manifestation of the competitive nature of American life, but this inability or even unwillingness is a challenge to anyone who would view the curriculum with clarity. An elementary caution on the way to understanding the curriculum may be to assume, at the beginning anyway, that maybe there is no such thing as *the* curriculum.

An argument can be made for thinking of the curriculum as being about what students learn or about the body of organized knowledge at the command of teachers or about the courses that try to make some effective connection between learning and teaching. Certainly the curriculum cannot be understood without paying attention to all the elements that give it life—students, knowledge, teachers, and the courses where everything either falls together or falls apart. Also, the curriculum is both structure and substance, subject to measurement and judgment. In describing its structure, we compute courses, semesters, lectures, departments, majors, and so forth. In exploring the substance of the curriculum, the stuff of which the learning and teaching is made, we are in the presence of quality, whether good or bad.[3]

Judging quality requires some notion of what the curriculum is expected to do. If the design is to turn out clergymen and the performance delivers businessmen, has something gone wrong with the curriculum, or has society changed its mind? Even if it is easy to agree with William

James's suggestion that the curriculum is intended to "help you know a good man when you see him," a few more particulars would be helpful. Because higher education is the habitat of the more verbal among us, there is, however, no shortage of particulars. A president of Smith College clarified curricular expectations with these demands: "Make a man or woman wiser, more sensitive, more compassionate, more responsible, more useful, and happier." A university professor may have been more or less saying the same thing when he assigned to the college the responsibility for developing in its students "such general attributes as freedom from prejudice, depth of interest, a humanized conscience, and eagerness for continued learning."[4] In any case, the curriculum is also a locus and transmitter of values.

Values change and so does the curriculum, as the more than 300 years since the founding of Harvard College clearly say. Since that time long ago, when a peculiarly self-demanding band of alienated Englishmen got themselves a college almost before they had built themselves a privy, change in the course of study has been constant, conscious and unconscious, gradual and sudden, accidental and intentional, uneven and diverse, imaginative and pedestrian. An earlier historian of the curriculum, writing in 1907, decided that "the process of alteration from the colonial type of curriculum to that of modern date has everywhere proceeded by cautious amalgamation and well-considered deliberation."[5] If that is so, the curriculum is the only institutional expression of social purpose to pass so gently through the dynamic and explosive decades of the nineteenth century. But of course it did not.

Patience is not one of the essential qualities of a reformer, and it must be from the collective frustration of curricular reformers that there has developed the "academic truism that changing a curriculum is harder than moving a graveyard."[6] The reasons for curricular rigidity are many, some simply being a function of organization. Assemble a cluster of professors in a country town, surround them with scenic grandeur, cut them off from the world beyond, and they will not have much trouble congratulating themselves into curricular torpor. Let someone knock at the door with a vision of change, he will discover that access is blocked by those within the gate. Let him argue in behalf of some perceived need or desire of the students, and he will soon discover his mistake: The institution is really not for the students, after all, but for the professors. Besides, that is not the way it is done, nor is the particular purpose or goal, however worthy, the only one that must be considered.

These are barriers to change in all institutions. Colleges and universities in addition have had some that are particularly characteristic. Their intentions are conservative—to preserve and to transmit that which has survived. Their friends and supporters are mostly among the more comfortable classes, those with an investment in stability. Colleges and universities are also in a way trapped between the schools that send them students and the graduate and professional schools to which they send their own graduates; the curriculum is necessarily responsive to and limited by these relationships. And then there are the professors, a highly organized and narrowly self-selected guild of professionals, each something of a law unto himself, collectively suspicious of efficiency and expert at obstruction. Each of these rather special academic barriers to change has a history of its own. Because the American "system" of education developed downward rather than upward, with the founding of colleges before there were schools sufficient to supply them, standards of all kind—including curricular standards—were from the beginning difficult to establish. On the other hand, social change has sometimes been more rapid than the capacity of the colleges to respond, and on occasion they have found themselves almost without any friends at all. And professors have not always been as firmly in charge of the curriculum as they now are. The changing fortunes of these characteristic sources of academic inertia are ingredients in the shaping of curricular history.[7]

Also, as life developed in British America in the years after the founding of Harvard College in 1636, a whole new set of social and economic expectations that had not been anticipated by the country's first settlers intruded themselves into defining what a curriculum could be. The college as an environment for the general education of a small governing elite found itself losing ground in the nineteenth century, as it became increasingly apparent that the new nation was going to be a country in which getting rich would be a good deal easier than at any time and any place elsewhere in human history. The consequences for the college course of study would be staggering. When the goal of worldly wealth and ease finally collided, as it did, with the more ascetic traditions of New England—traditions by then stretched across the country in hundreds of little colleges bearing the imprint of Yale and Princeton—the explosion was resounding. By 1900 the sons of the rich, the clumsy, awkward rich, were going to Yale for quite different reasons from those that had guided young men to Yale two centuries before, and the curriculum was required to acknowledge the difference.

The universities that were redefining the course of study in the late nineteenth and early twentieth centuries were recording more than the arrival on their campuses of sons and daughters of a confident bourgeoisie. The curricular remedies they developed—sometimes grossly utilitarian, sometimes purely scientific, occasionally romantically cultural—would make defining the American college and university curriculum forever after an exercise in intellectual juggling.[8]

Yale and Harvard really did wage a major battle over what that curriculum should be. The presidents of Harvard and Princeton engaged in public debate. The presidents of eight New England colleges placed themselves before the Harvard corporation as opponents of the Harvard president. By the time when these encounters took place, the curriculum as a focus of universal concern could not rival the football field, but great talent and great wisdom and sometimes great blindness were engaged. The friends of pure science and of scholarly research who identified the enemy as undergraduate teaching and utilitarian values; the friends of liberal learning who identified the enemy as the scientists, both pure and applied; and the friends of the useful for whom the enemy was everyone else—all were very much aware that the stakes were high and that if the consequences were not of great popular interest they were of tremendously greater importance than the outcome of all the football games ever played.

"The curriculum is the battlefield at the heart of the institution," JB Lon Hefferlin concluded after an exhaustive study of academic reform. "Complaints of institutional irrelevance, obscurantism, and ossification all aim here. . . . To leave the curriculum to its own devices and try to improve its periphery . . . is, in the vernacular of the religious fundamentalists, to whitewash the sepulcher."[9] Those who would understand the history of the college and university curriculum must, among everything else, see the sepulcher as a battleground.

The battle in which the contenders over the curriculum have been engaged in a sense has known no beginning and no ending, in large part because the curriculum is a remarkably vital organism, containing within itself and its environment seeds of change that only intuition might reveal. In 1848 Philip Lindsley, the brilliant young president of the college at Nashville, defined the ideal product of the curriculum: "Our graduates . . . betray no arrogance, pride or vanity. . . . They seem to think their education only just begun. . . . They do not think more highly of themselves than they ought to think. . . . To bring youth to this point—to this modest correct self-appreciation . . . is the crowning glory of a university education. . . ."[10] Who could have imagined, hearing Lindsley in that year when Europe was racked with revolution and his own country was playing at war with Mexico, that only a half century later a whole new vocabulary would be required by one college alumnus to describe the process that formed the graduate in 1901? "The history of the Yale curriculum," wrote John C. Schwab of the class of 1886, "is the story of a medieval workshop, with its limited range of simple tools, all of which the apprentice learned to master, developing into a modern factory, well equipped with a large stock of tools and machinery, no two of them alike in their construction or use, many of them delicate and complicated, and few of them fully understood and manipulated by all the employees of the shop."[11] Of course there were some in 1848 who made the imaginative leap to 1901, as there were some in 1901 who could make the no less difficult leap to 1848 or to any other moment in the past or future. But it was not easy. So much changed.

All kinds of assumptions and certainties turned out to be perilously unstable. If one generation found guidance in the stern morality of the Old Testament, another found a softer style in the love and fellowship of the New Testament. Could a curriculum that was appropriate for young men named Jedidiah, Ephriam, and Israel be passed without change to their sons with names like Matthew, Mark, Luke, and John? Wide as the Atlantic was, even before the American Revolution it was no barrier to the importation of disruptive ideas: A parcel of books threw eighteenth-century Yale into curricular disarray. A changed view of human nature threw Latin out of Yale's requirements for the bachelor's degree 200 years later: The difficult, disciplinary, testing study of impractical Latin may have been appropriate for a world that lived with the reality of Hell, but in a world oozing with natural goodness Latin became an abomination.[12] Even the origin of truth changed in the history of the curriculum, from book (one book, at that) to process. Human psychology itself was finally recognized as a bed of shifting sands.

The best way to misread or misunderstand a curriculum is from a catalogue. It is such a lifeless thing, so disembodied, so unconnected, sometimes even intentionally misleading. Because the curriculum is a social artifact, the society itself is a more reliable source of curricular illumination. In his inaugural address as president of Harvard in 1869, Charles Willion Eliot stated the relationship clearly: "The university must accommodate itself promptly to significant changes in the character of the people for whom it exists. The institutions of higher education . . . are always a faithful mirror in which are sharply reflected the national history and character." In 1907 Louis Franklin Snow, pioneer historian of the curriculum, agreed: "The ideals of the community have become the ideals of the college. . . . That college becomes most truly national which reflects and reproduces, in its curriculum, the national ideal."

More recently a historian of Indiana University went as far as to describe the relationship between the curriculum and society as a one-way connection: "The curriculum reflects the society . . . it does not significantly affect or change that society." On the other hand, a young historian of higher education sees the relationship in quite different terms: "The university has exerted a formative influence upon society: as the matrix within which the culture of professionalism matured; as the center to which practitioners trace the theoretical basis of knowledge upon which they establish authority; as the source of a usable history, economics, political science, and sociology for individuals who in the course of rapid movement require instant ideas." And as if that were not enough, "The university contained and structured the culture of ideas in American life, as college football stadiums contained and structured the culture of spectator recreation, and home economics the culture of good housekeeping."[13] The traffic between the society and the curriculum may essentially have been all or mostly in one direction, whichever direction that was, but by any useful definition of culture, the traffic necessarily flowed in both directions, the curriculum responding to the society and in turn shaping that society, the relationship being sufficiently subtle sometimes even to defy detection.

But it takes no great investigative imagination to see in the proliferation of colleges during the Jacksonian era at the same time that their classical course of study was under wide public attack the reflection of a consistency rather than a conflict in Jacksonian society. The Jacksonian temper was friendly to college founding as an act of corporate enterprise and unfriendly to the course of study as a manifestation of class privilege. Nor should there be any mistake about whether a new social demand was about to be placed upon the curriculum in the late nineteenth century, when Chauncey M. Depew observed that he had met many millionaires but none "who did not feel in the presence of cultured people a certain sense of mortification which no money paid for."[14]

The absence of a strong federal interest or control in higher education in no way denied society's recognition of the college as a social necessity. Society's claims and expectations were large, although the federal interest was weak: The 1802 act that provided two townships of federal land for the endowment of a university in each new state carved out of the national land holdings was an act to promote settlement, not education, and the Morrill Land-grant Act in 1862, which endowed the beginnings of agricultural and mechanical colleges in all the states, was an act as much for getting rid of land as for supporting education.[15] At one time the burden of the curriculum was to facilitate the production of what society defined as a cultured gentleman; eventually a professional career in the United States would be unthinkable without benefit of the college course, although in an earlier day, when most college graduates went into the learned professions, most who practiced these professions were not college graduates. Not until the twentieth century—and well into it—was the professional education of a majority of doctors, lawyers, and clergymen a postcollegiate experience. Most professionals in those fields in the nineteenth century entered practice by way of apprenticeship or education in professional schools that were coequal with the colleges, just as the elementary school for teachers for a growing public school movement were trained in normal schools that were coequal with academies and high schools. The shifting technological focus of society, from steam to electricity, from the railroad to the dynamo, also meant a corresponding shift in the curriculum.

But if no course of study was as vulnerable as the American curriculum to social demand, nowhere else in the world (a 1911 Carnegie Foundation report pointed out) did colleges compete for students, nowhere else was education treated as a commodity.[16] Was there a moment in the history of the curriculum when the individual overtook society as the client? Did the college, as an extension of the society's agencies of value formation and nurture, withdraw, concede, regroup, and reorganize, and then fulfill a whole new set of demands that may have served individuals well but society poorly? The curriculum may have undergone some such experience between the Civil War and World War I.

Status was socially defined; the status of teaching was one determinant of what a curriculum was. In a society that respected and valued its professors the curriculum was not the same as in a society that was indifferent to professors. Moreover, the professors, whatever their status, if their concern was primarily intellectual rather than moral, thought of the course of study as serving the needs of an intellectual community as opposed to the needs of individual clients. But society's purpose cannot be denied, and in recent years, as society has redefined higher education from being a privilege to being a right and a duty, it has moved in on colleges and universities in a way that has made university and society almost inseparable. The California system of higher education *is* California. But even as universal access fulfills the democratic promise of American life and reshapes the course of study accordingly, at a place such as Harvard, since World War II extracurricular achievement has been no substitute in the status race among Harvard undergraduates for winning out "in the major meritocratic contest of the curriculum."[17] Who would resist the verdict of one historian, who concluded that the curriculum is "as irrational and confusing as society itself"?[18]

By 1960, 2,452 different kinds of degrees had been conferred by American institutions of higher education, 832 of which had been abandoned, casualties of changing academic fashion, curricular consolidation, or a revision of standards. Of the 1,620 degrees still being awarded in 1960, 43 percent were various kinds of bachelor degrees for four years' study in specific fields and 8 percent were associate degrees, generally for the work of two years in a junior or community college. Bachelor of arts degrees (108 varieties) and bachelor of science degrees (426 varieties) were being earned in agriculture, architecture, dentistry, education, forestry, nursing, public administration, social work, and almost any other vocation for which an organized body of knowledge existed. In addition, such degrees as bachelor of music, bachelor of music education, bachelor of fine arts, and bachelor of education revealed both the proliferation of knowledge and the disintegration of a common body of learning since the day in 1642 when Harvard awarded to nine young men the first American bachelor of arts degrees.[19] It is one thing to describe the curriculum under which Harvard for decade after decade awarded nothing but the B.A; it is almost an affront to the imagination to be expected to make sense of the 200 different degrees offered by the University of Illinois in 1960. Yet some sense must be made, for those degrees recorded, among other things, an explosion of knowledge, an accumulation of technical learning and scholarship that burst on the world in the nineteenth century as a result of the gathering prestige of empirical thought.

In the nineteenth century the great German universities were the centers from which spread a gargantuan appetite for research and scholarship as well as a profound regard for the scientific ethos that defined it. The consequences have generally and appropriately been described as both profoundly inventive and overwhelmingly destructive. The creation of new knowledge seeking a place in the course of study, the specialization of various areas of academic endeavor, the consequent tendency to view all subject matter as equal, and the disestablishment of "the conception of a liberal education as a definite body of knowledge"—these may be thought of as curricular fallout from the knowledge explosion.[20] While making room for new knowledge, therefore, became a baffling challenge for those responsible for the course of study as the nineteenth century progressed, the nature of knowledge and of the society in whose service it was created also led to the abandonment of substantial portions of the curriculum. Some knowledge that had appeared in the colonial curriculum as innovative and practical, such as navigation and surveying, lost utility. Some knowledge, such as Latin and Greek, could not be made popular, a fatal flaw for knowledge in the kind of country the United States was developing into. Some knowledge, such as arithmetic, English grammar, geography, and algebra, could be shoved into the secondary schools by brave colleges willing to raise their admissions standards as one way of making room for new knowledge. Some knowledge instead of being abandoned found new life by being synthesized into a new field of study; the biology and social science that became ecology may even be thought of as having benefited from blood transfusions.[21]

About some curricular developments it is never possible to be certain, but if professors became interested enough in something to focus their research on it, almost certainly that research would make its way into the course of study—as new subjects, new courses, or simply new lectures and texts; the extracurriculum played a similar role in being responsive to undergraduate interests and has even on occasion anticipated and guided the formal curriculum. The simplicity and sanctity of the old course of study were irreparably violated by the explosion of knowledge, but some of the dismay and unhappiness with the consequences that have been registered by curricular critics has bordered on the hysterical. The so-called Germanic influence has been a favorite target for those who needed a villain to explain what happened to the tightly ordered course of liberal studies with which Harvard College began. The Germans did not really ignite the knowledge explosion, an event that in no way could have been avoided. They did know what to do with it, and the example they set was much needed by an untried new nation tied to two charming but absurd conceits—the jack-of-all-trades and the self-made man.

The curriculum was in many ways whatever students made of it. Were they more responsive to "the rich financial reward of an early mastery of some practical branch of knowledge" than to "the advantage of a mental culture which they are too immature to appreciate"?[22] Were they to think of themselves, in the presence of the curriculum, as children with duties or as citizens with rights?[23] Were they mature or assumed to be? Did their chronological and psychophysical ages harmonize with the course of study or had they fallen out of balance? The answers to these and similar questions will clarify what the curriculum was at any given time. What could go on in an American college—contrasted with a German university—was in part a function of the entering age, which was much lower in the United States, and in part a function of the absence of a driving student motivation that, in Germany, recognized the vital relationship between university studies and the state-administered examinations that opened the way to professional careers. The openness of American society for a very long time militated against the importance of a college education and helped to undercut efforts to support a high level of intellectual rigor and achievement. Perhaps not until after World War II, in an environment that for the first time permitted colleges in any number to be selective in their admissions policies, were students who represented "the academic culture"—the curriculum, the intellectual life—setting the tone of undergraduate society, instead of that traditional turned-off or indifferent majority who found their purpose in the extracurriculum.[24]

Around 1900, college rooms all over the country were decorated with posters bearing the admonition: "Don't let your studies interfere with your education."[25] This motto placed constraints not only on what the curriculum could do but also on what it could be. What faculty could be expected to develop a course of study that treated students like young men and women when they insisted on behaving like boys and girls? And what faculty possessed the collective imagination to recognize the extent to which their students were often learning from life itself what was being denied in the classroom? Was there a classroom in the United States in 1845 that was advanced enough in the teaching of sociology and psychology to match the experience described that year by a student at Indiana University in a letter to his mother:

> On last Saturday evening . . . I went into a house and tried to make peace between a man and his wife. The man had been whipping her brutally. I tried to defend her, and she turned on me, and at length run me out of the house with some boiling water; but not until I had knocked her husband down with my cane. . . . She says since that she was very glad I came to her assistance, but she says she could not stand by and see me knock her husband down without throwing some hot water on me.[26]

Much can be made of the invigorating new directions in which the curriculum turned as induction and empiricism created new scientific studies—economics, sociology, political science—out of what had sometimes almost been only Biblical exegesis. It did sometimes seem as if real life, the real world, was not allowed access to the course of study until the late nineteenth and early twentieth centuries. Until then, however, and long after, students derived from the extracurricular fabric of clubs, athletics, libraries, and fraternities a kind of instruction and experience that anticipated their needs and their futures. If much that was first extracurricular in time became curricular—English literature, American history, fine arts, music—for a considerable period the intellectual and vocational interests of students were supported by the extracurriculum. The institutionalization of the extracurriculum gave students a source of strength in the academic power structure; it also both usurped some of the prerogatives and responsibilities of the caretakers of the curriculum, the professors, and gave them excuses for resisting curricular innovation.

The extracurriculum complemented the curriculum quite as much as it subverted it. The intensity of some students' attachment to the former was certainly subversive to the latter, but in another sense the extracurriculum was a kind of laboratory for nascent practical and vocational interests. On the curricular battlefields, for three centuries, one contender or the other has insisted on being recognized as the friend of the practical in the course of study. When both contenders knew what they were doing, both were claiming the practical label, for it should never be thought that any curricular reform was really ever advocated or any curriculum defended, at least on this side of the Atlantic, as being other than practical. The famous Yale Report of 1828 has been thought of as a dramatic last stand in defense of the impractical studies, but the Yale faculty in the report argued for the practicality of what others considered impractical.

The president of Bowdoin was making a point in his attack on elective studies in 1802, but he did not expect to be taken seriously when he said: "I declare . . . that in my opinion a youth had better be four years employed . . . in diligently doing what would be utterly useless to him in life, than in light reading which requires no thinking." And the president of the University of Alabama displayed a spectacular failure of imagination when, relying on the durability of the apprentice system in a craft society, he resisted demands in 1855 for a more vocational emphasis in the course of study: "While time lasts, the farmer will be made in the field, the manufacturer in the shop, the merchant in the counting room, the civil engineer in the midst of the actual operation of his science." The Hamilton College president who as late as 1904 insisted that his college educated "man, and not blacksmiths and farmers" did not really say what he meant; what he meant was that Hamilton College educated businessmen, clergymen, and lawyers, and not blacksmiths and farmers. For the course of study had always to some degree—except perhaps at St. John's since the 1930s and for a time at the University of Chicago—been relevant to the practical affairs of men, intentionally oriented toward social utility.[27]

There is something perniciously misleading about the interpretation of the American experience with the curriculum that argues that "only students who could afford to be unconcerned about their eventual employment and its economic rewards have been able to enjoy an exclusively cultural or nonutilitarian higher education."[28] Nothing could have been more cultural or nonutilitarian than the Harvard education that was being experienced by the student who responded to Henry Adams's question as to why he was at Harvard: "The degree of Harvard College is worth money to me in Chicago."[29] An exclusively cultural or nonutilitarian education is a concept contrary to experience. As Christopher Jencks and David Riesman put it, "The question always has been *how* an institution mixed the academic with the vocational, not *whether* it did so."[30] And the question has also been how much value society attached to the academic, the cultural, and supposedly nonutilitarian.

The students who designed the extracurriculum as a testing ground for skills and aspirations ignored by the curriculum were, on the other hand, complementing the course of study as an instrument of personality development. The language might not have been understood by the founders of Harvard College but, in appropriate translation, they would have agreed with the judgment of the psychologist Nevitt Sanford that "all curricula either favored or hamper personality regardless of whether they were designed with such development in mind."[31] It is instructive that in the era when recitation, the testing of memorized texts, dominated the college classroom, the extracurriculum correspondingly dominated student life; the classroom style was hostile to imagination; literary societies and fraternities supported personality development by freeing the imagination. And the students knew it.

The curriculum was a record of how the American people faced such matters as who were to be their leaders, whether the society was to be governed by an elite, and how far the concept of equality was to be carried in the provision of courses of study appropriate not just for the few but for the many. These questions agitated the academic community in the United States long before they were recognized as pertinent to the concerns of higher education elsewhere in the Western world. By progressive steps the American people enlarged their commitment to mass education, on the primary level in the first half of the nineteenth century, on the secondary level in the first half of the twentieth century, and increasingly since World War II on the level not only of higher education[32] but also of that more accessible network of opportunities known as "postsecondary education."

The commitment to mass higher education was not made automatically; if it was implicit in the Declaration of Independence and the Constitution, even Thomas Jefferson, who designed an educational system for Virginia that would sift the talented from "the rubbish," did not know it. As late as 1845 in the democratic atmosphere of Jacksonville, Illinois, Julian M. Sturtevant, the president of the struggling little college there, argued for the appropriateness of a common school education for the majority and a college education for the minority. In Indiana nearly a decade later a professor at the state university made an extraordinary—and unheeded—plea: "Could my voice prevail with our American colleges I would say, 'Cut down your numbers without fear and thereby increase your power; sift, select, separate, purge out until you have only men, though but a select few—men who are fitted to do the highest work of society!'"[33]

Such intentions could be better fulfilled on the eastern seaboard than at a western college or university, and especially at both Johns Hopkins under Daniel Coit Gilman and Harvard under Charles William Eliot, where the course of study and the arrangements that implemented it were designed with regard for what Eliot called "the cravings of the select few as well as the needs of the average many." Gilman and Eliot were building for leadership, for an intellectual aristocracy, for, in Eliot's words, an "elite . . . those who, having the capacity, prove by hard work that they have also the necessary perseverance and endurance."[34]

But what was possible, or even worth trying, in one part of the United States was out of question in another. The problem was illustrated by the grading systems adopted at the University of Michigan and at Harvard in the late nineteenth century. Both were designed to encourage standards, but Michigan, sensitive to the need to avoid more "undemocratic" distinctions than necessary, provided in 1879 for a system that divided obvious failures into those who passed, those who were conditioned, and those whose work was incomplete. Ten years later Harvard adopted a system of degrees that encouraged distinctions and grades of superiority—an ordinary degree plus three degrees of distinction: *cum laude, magna cum laude*, and *summa cum laude*.[35] The curriculum for nurturing an elite would necessarily differ from a curriculum for everyone, even if only in expectations and standards. Could the United States choose between an elite and the mass? Could it have both? Could it make up its mind? Who should go to college? "I grow weary of the expression so often on the lips of men who call themselves educators that too many men and women go to college," said the president of the University of South Carolina in 1925. "Every potential leader . . . and no one else . . . should go to college," said the president of Oberlin College in 1927.[36]

In 1872 Richard Owen, son of Robert Owen, was elected the first president of Purdue. His "Plan of Education" presented to the board of trustees in 1873 omitted all reference to how the curriculum was to be organized, but it did recommend that "the free use of pork, meats, fried grease, rich pastry, and the like be avoided as being highly injurious to those having more work of the brain than of the muscle." Owen resigned in 1874, before Purdue opened, perhaps because the trustees wanted a curriculum *and* pork. Owen's importance is symbolic. He is a reminder of the extent to which eccentricity and diversity entered into the construction of the course of study. "How different might the teaching of French be with exclusive use of four rooms designed and furnished in Renaissance, Louis XIV, Louis XV, and Empire styles respectively!" fantasized a

Wesleyan University professor in 1948. But these were deviations that did not occur. An important one that did was the persistence of the Catholic colleges in resisting curricular change, in standing outside the main curricular movements until well into the twentieth century. The 1905 catalogue at Holy Cross resembled Yale's catalogue for 1828.[37]

If eccentricity could be a characteristic of the curriculum, so could a flexibility of style and purpose that hid change even from its perpetrators. Thomas LeDuc has pointed out that geology and the classics were taught in the colleges for over a hundred years "for various purposes and with various results." Edward Hitchcock taught geology at Amherst in 1840 as a demonstration of divine benevolence, the geological state of the world being so "well adapted to a state of probation." Geology was still being taught at Amherst a hundred years later. Edward Hitchcock would have been shocked by what was going on.[38]

Purposes and results varied from time to time and place to place, but there was a consistent thread of concern with values and character, even, it might be said, at those institutions in the twentieth century that were willing to say that values and character were not their concern. In the early eighteenth century the Yale College laws put the matter directly: "Every student shall consider the main end of his study to wit to know God in Jesus Christ and answerably to lead a Godly sober life."[39]

The history of the American college curriculum may be the history of how a people departed from such a goal, but it is also a history of how the course of study has been laced with a concern for values, character, personality, a concern so enmeshed with everything else that was going on that, leaving aside the question of what happened to God, one asks without expectation of finding the answer, "What happened to man?" Such questions, however they are answered, chart the career of values in the curriculum. To evaluate the effectiveness of the college's concern with values is to assess the private and public lives of the American college and university graduate; that surely is another book, a book that might not go beyond the wisdom of William James's observation that "there is not a public abuse for which some Harvard advocate may not be found."[40] Be that as it may, in 1959 over half of Harvard's undergraduates professed to having had their political values changed while at Harvard, over a half of them by lectures and course reading.[41] Colleges also taught values absentmindedly. Can there be any question about whether Princeton was teaching values by not admitting black students until World War II?

Some young professor once said of the possibilities of curricular reconstruction at his institution: "The progress of this institution . . . will be directly proportional to the death rate of the faculty."[42] The professor was an optimist. College faculties by the late nineteenth and early twentieth centuries had developed an authority that made the course of study a jealously guarded compound of special interests. By then it seldom mattered who died. What the curriculum was has depended in greater measure on whether the institution has been an autocracy or a bureaucracy, the former being likely—at least in the hands of a reformer like Eliphalet Nott at Union—to be more innovative and receptive to change than a bureaucracy of self-serving, jealous, single-purposed, departmentalized professors. An experimental college at Fordham was possible because of the autocratic nature of the institution; on the other hand, autocracy, in the form of a president who was suspicious of psychology, delayed the development of that subject as a field of study at Notre Dame.[43]

When Eliot was in the process of reforming Harvard—it should not be forgotten that it took him forty years—an obstructionist faculty was remarkably adept at advancing "good" reasons for protecting its own interests: Electives would be too expensive, they would encourage attendance by students with base motives, they would require the appointment of inexperienced young instructors. Eliot prevailed in part because, knowing that his reforms were expensive, he raised enough money to keep everyone happy.[44]

The faculty stranglehold on the curriculum was a function of intellectual specialization and academic professionalization: With the Ph.D. went a kind of competence and authority and power that an earlier academic community did not have. With the explosion of knowledge that created the generations of trained professionals, there developed a curriculum that was a compound of courses subject to change, but to change that derived from faculties increasingly unable to make up their minds about how much election, how much prescription, how strong a major, how general an education there should be. What they could make up their minds about was what would advance or retard the interests of their own academic departments.

The curriculum was subject to accident, peculiarities of time and place, delayed reaction, and singularity of style. Western colleges often resounded with echoes of practices long since abandoned in the East, memories carried westward by graduates who grew up to be successful and adept at founding colleges. In 1888 a replica of an earlier New England college was opened at Pomona in California; extracurricular literary societies were withering away in the East when Euphronia and Nestoria announced their presence on the opening of Stanford. As late as 1931 at Tusculum College, a small Presbyterian institution in Tennessee, the curriculum was required to adjust itself to Monday holidays, instituted to avoid the preparation of classes on Sundays.[45]

In any given state or region or locality the question of which institution or institutions shouldered the major curricular responsibility of training high school teachers—the state university, the land-grant college, the normal schools, or the liberal arts colleges—depended on political and socioeconomic considerations that defy simple generalization.

In the twentieth century, as college enrollments dramatically mounted, more and more thousands of young men and women went off to college to experience something called "freshman year." Esther Raushenbush described how different those freshman experiences were: Some courses of study were almost a repeat of senior year in secondary school; some were a mystifying and shattering embarkation into a curriculum for which students were in no way prepared; others were an invitation to intellectual excitement and growth. Every college and university delivered a freshman year appropriate to its own history; higher education in the United States necessarily delivered a whole range of freshman years.[46]

President Millar Upton of Beloit once said that "when a college is on the verge of oblivion, there is no problem in its achieving instant curricular revision." He could have been thinking of Brown in 1850, Antioch in 1921, and St. John's in 1937, where radical curricular transformations were necessary for survival. Each of these transformations can be identified with the dedicated advocacy of an inspired reformer. The imprint of creative and imaginative reformers has been so indelible that a kind of perverseness is required to think of the University of Virginia without Thomas Jefferson, Johns Hopkins without Daniel Coit Gilman, the University of Chicago without William Rainey Harper or Robert Maynard Hutchins.[47]

The takeover of Harvard by the Unitarians in 1805 has been considered a significant contribution to "the advance of a free intellectual climate at Harvard." The Unitarians were not of a sort to have designs on other colleges, with the result that the fresh air of inquiry and the hostility to intellectual parochialism with which they blessed Harvard were not generally shared during the first half of the nineteenth century. Harvard's Unitarian era may greatly explain why there was but one Harvard, why in 1910 an undergraduate socialist club could petition—with three hundred signatures—for a course on socialism and get it, and why early in the 1970s another student generation could apply pressure that led to the appointment of a Marxist professor and the inclusion of Marxist materials in economics courses.[48]

In an earlier time businessmen had as easy a time of it, even at Harvard, where, partly in response to pressure from Boston merchants and Massachusetts manufacturers, the course of study was redesigned to accommodate orthodox economics, the natural sciences, and the useful social sciences. At Union College in 1894 an expanded curriculum in electrical engineering was a gift of the General Electric Company.[49]

More subtle influences shaped the curriculum. Concern for university prestige and image called forth a rivalry in which university presidents used professorships and academic departments as part of the weaponry; competition meant expansion, growth, and curricular standardization.[50] At Yale in the 1930s and 1940s anti-Semitism in professional appointments restricted the development and health of scientific and humanistic study; the absence of a comparable anti-Semitism caused the sciences to flourish at Columbia and Princeton.[51] Humanistic studies were strengthened by the enrollment of women in the colleges, but there is no way of knowing what the curriculum would have been had women been welcomed into a more creative role in its shaping.

The curriculum was also sometimes a creature of convenience. Early in the twentieth century the University of Illinois, cramped for space, suddenly made all junior and senior courses elective in order "not to block the graduation of men who could not be given laboratory space" in previously required courses.[52]

The writing of curricular history runs the risk of making the irrational rational, of overlooking the significant while stressing the dramatic, and of emphasizing subject matter at the expense of style. It may even take itself too seriously or not seriously enough.

Surely there was nothing unique about the officers of Yale College, who have been described by one historian as "not always sure what they believed, or agreed when they were sure, or able to blend the varied things on which they did agree." The verdict of Christopher Jencks and David Riesman would be difficult to refute: "American educators have seldom been able to give coherent explanations for what they were doing."[53] The curriculum makers and the curriculum itself were no more rational than the rest of us, and a history about them should not make them so.

The dramatic commands attention—a bold curricular statement such as distributed by the Yale faculty in 1828, Ezra Cornell's fantasy brought to life in Ithaca, William Rainey Harper's everything university in Chicago—but basically learning, change, the new moved slowly, surreptitiously, silently into the curriculum. As Edmund Morgan said of Ezra Stiles's Yale: "You could not close down the college while you retooled for the new model of learning." Change in the teaching of physics at Yale between 1701 and 1739 did not announce itself with new course titles but was registered by the abandonment of an out-of-date Aristotelian manuscript developed from 1688 Harvard class notes and its replacement by a "disguised Newtonian" treatise. A recent student of academic change has concluded: "Accretion and attrition are the most common means of academic change, primarily because they are the most simple."[54] That should not be news, but it often is.

"One cannot tell anything about the character of the training given by a certain course from its name or department," Edwin E. Slosson wrote in 1910. "Whether a study trains the eye, cultivates the memory, stimulates the imagination, improves the taste, or inspires the soul depends not so much on the subject matter as upon the way it is taught."[55] His stress on the style and spirit of instruction as being of more importance in the definition of what the curriculum was up to than subject matter itself has been widely shared. It found expression in Charles William Eliot's Harvard inaugural address in 1869, although he may not really have meant it. President Arthur Twining Hadley of Yale may have been apologizing for a deliberately sluggish course of study when he bluntly declared: "It does not matter so much what you teach as how you teach it." Eliot and Hadley have been echoed down the halls so long and so often that what may have been a sort of public relations defense for university and college presidents embroiled in curricular reform has now become more or less scientific truth. The ultimate dismissal of subject matter must have been James A. Garfield's celebrated aphorism: "The ideal college is Mark Hopkins on one end of a log and a student on the other." Laurence Veysey, whose understanding of the American university may be equaled by a few of his contemporaries but not surpassed by any, has concluded that while "the precise nature of the curriculum seems to be rather unimportant," what has been important is its "flavor and texture."[56]

There is supporting evidence. A 1957 survey of college graduates in the employ of General Electric gave subject matter a mere 2 percent edge over teaching personalities as the more long-term influence—and this among graduates of largely vocationally oriented courses of study. (The respondents listed engineering as the third most useful subject and as the third least useful subject.) David Riesman, a senior statesman on the frontier of figuring out what the curriculum is all about, has decided that "Harvard can make its greatest contribution to undergraduate teaching, less by revision of the undergraduate curriculum than by more serious efforts to introduce graduate students to problems of teaching as a regular part of their training."[57] Riesman's preference for better teaching rather than curricular reform has a long tradition; it may even be purely sentimental, but in 1977 it sounds revolutionary.

Antidotes to a posture of excessive solemnity toward the curriculum have rarely appeared in the literature, and, when they have, they have even more rarely been recognized. The great educational foundations had hardly begun their work, however, before one observer sensed how close to the edge of the ridiculous the curriculum could be urged: "If some educational revolutionist were to arise and assert that the whole curriculum should be inverted, that we should begin with metaphysics and ethics and end with geography and arithmetic, nobody could prove him a fool, and if he were given a few millions and a free hand, he might prove that he was not."[58] And today nothing is more sobering than a trip through the history of a great state university: A history of the University of California is not, cannot, be a curricular history, it has to be so much else; a curricular history of the University of California would be an excursion beyond reality; the University of California is a way of life, a multiversity, but it is not a curriculum.[59]

The intentions of *this* curricular history, as of all those that have come before it, are serious, but it does not intend to make more claims for the curriculum than the record allows. Who would reject the suggestion that "the paperback revolution did far more to improve academic quality in this country . . . than any curricular innovation of the last seventy years"?[60] Who would dispute the promoters of higher education in late nineteenth-century Colorado who, directing attention to malaria in Indiana and tuberculosis in the East, stressed the salutary role of the Colorado climate to a degree that left the impression that a Colorado college was not a curriculum but a sanitarium?[61] Who would deny the uncalculated influence of television in changing the perceptions and skills of students and in subtly challenging the primacy of the written word?

The curriculum began as an import, arriving in the intellectual baggage of the settlers of Massachusetts Bay. Over three hundred years of change have given it a thoroughly American character, reflecting the diversity and flexibility of the culture around it, lending itself to society's major purposes.

The shaping of the curriculum has had its heroes, perhaps even its villains. Were Jeremiah Day at Yale and James McCosh at Princeton, determined to hold the future at bay until the colleges could digest the changes being forced on them by a rapidly moving world, heroes or villains? Had the bottom dropped out of the world or of American democracy, or simply of Yale, or not even that, when a freshman might arrive in New Haven without entrance Greek and be welcomed? Did Samuel Eliot Morison take leave of his historical senses when he accused his distant cousin, Charles William Eliot, of "the greatest educational crime of the century against American youth—depriving him of his classical heritage"?[62] In the problem-oriented history curriculum of the 1940s and 1950s there existed a pamphlet text that asked, "John D. Rockefeller: Robber Baron or Industrial Statesman?"[63] Should William Rainey Harper, who staffed the University of Chicago by raiding the vulnerable faculties of eastern and midwestern universities, be subjected to similar treatment?

Curricular history is American history and therefore carries the burden of revealing the central purposes and driving directions of American society. As the curriculum has moved across time from being wholly prescribed to greatly elective, the loss of philosophic purpose and neatness has been repeatedly but unsuccessfully countered by structural devices designed to support some coherent, defensible general education. In the meantime the curriculum, in response to social demand and the financial support necessary to underwrite that demand, has been burdened with larger purpose than the provision of a general education for the native governing elite of a few frontier colonies of the British Empire. By the 1960s, indeed, the American college and university had arrived at a position of awesome power in the culture, having achieved—without quite knowing it—a near monopoly over entry to social and economic success. Except for skilled trades, entertainment, art, and professional athletics (and less so even there), a college education had become a necessity for all those seeking such success.[64] It may well be, as Christopher Jencks and David Riesman have argued, that "the majority of those who enter college are plainly more concerned with accumulating credits and acquiring licenses than with learning any particular skill while enrolled."[65] In this view the purpose of the curriculum is not education but certification. According to Clark Kerr, there is no organic university, as such, only a gathering of functions and discrete schools for carrying them out.[66] Perhaps there is no curriculum either, only an assumption of burdens and discrete programs for carrying them out: an accidental compromise between the only partially understood past and the unanticipated future.

Beyond Tyler and Taba: Reconceptualizing the Curriculum Process

FRANCIS P. HUNKINS AND PATRICIA A. HAMMILL

Introduction

These are dynamic times in the realm of curriculum. As we near the next century, we are asking ourselves if we finally should rid ourselves of our technological rationality and assume a new posture. A rising cacophony of voices is demanding that we detach ourselves from our techno-logical-modern past and form a new paradigm—a post-modern perspective. We are being urged to purge ourselves of our adherence to the Tyler rationale, to get beyond Tyler and Taba.

Many critics of Tyler and scientist-modernism appear to be urging us to wipe clear our slate of the past. However, as Toulmin (1990) states, the idea of starting again with a clean slate is a myth. And it is folly to assume that we must destroy all that was before in order to nurture a new start. To accept a new paradigm, to move beyond Tyler and Taba, does not require destroying our very past and discrediting these two curriculum thinkers. There is no new starting line where we can assemble and then advance into our futures with certainty. Indeed, such thinking is part of the very modernity that many of us wish to leave. All that we can do is to begin where we discover ourselves, and at the time in which we find ourselves. These are times of excitement and uncertainty, not times in which we can advance a "self-sustaining, tradition-free intellectual system" (Toulmin, 1990, p. 1979).

All realms of scholarship are immersed in these times in forming not just a new paradigm, but paradigms. To assume that there is only one paradigm is to assume that we can attain a new certainty, which really is anathema to being postmodern in perspective. Postmodernism is essentially a *metaparadigm* encompassing all realms of thinking and action (Kung cited in Doll, 1993). While postmodernism has spawned new avenues of investigation and ways of conceptualizing physics, chemistry, biology, and mathematics, as well as the arts, it has not—and indeed cannot by its very posture—furnish us with a consensus on what it really is or whether it will be the dominant mode of our thinking in the 21st century.

As Doll (1993) asserts, the implications of a postmodern perspective for the reality of educa-tion and curriculum in particular are staggering, while remaining for many frustratingly fuzzy. We currently do not know how this urging of a shift to postmodernism will play out within the curriculum realm. We should take pleasure, however, in the fact that we will be involved in the shaping of our own immediate and distant futures. We can recognize that we are in an evolving system, moving toward the edge of chaos, and that this place is the zone where new ideas are generated, new paradigms are formulated, and new questions are posed (Lewin, 1992).

To recognize an edge we must have some vision of the total area from whence we have come. We cannot fully grasp a paradigm shift to postmodernism if we fail to understand our history of modernism. We cannot accept modernism as a thing of the past unless we have a sense of our past.

The Legacy

Modernism or modernity is not synonymous with contemporaneousness (Selznick, 1992). If that were the case, all societies would be modem in their time period. Rather, modernism refers to those attributes of technology that advanced societies have developed since the 18th century. Some would place the beginning date with Newton. The hallmark of modernism is a society in which emphasis is placed on the rational, the impersonal or objective, and the fragmentation of thought and action. It is a society of prizing and accepting certainty, a society privileging a mechanical view of the world. It is a society that employs the rational, the scientific, in addressing the problems of human life and society (Toulmin, 1990).

Bobbitt and Modernism

Modernism achieved its pinnacle in this century. In the early decades, increasing numbers of educators eagerly accepted the tenets of modernism and the approach called *scientism*. Many believed that by employing the rational, the precise, and the mechanistic, they would be able to address the problems of human life and society. Education, looked at as a mechanical system, could be quantified and managed. In being modern, one could bring efficiency and effectiveness to the schools and their curricula.

Bobbitt is credited with bringing the scientism or modernism message to education and to the field of curriculum in particular. His book, *The Curriculum*, published in 1918, is often considered the first book devoted specifically to the curriculum and to consider curriculum as a science. Bobbitt believed that it was possible to be precise in determining just what the curriculum should contain. It was the responsibility of the curriculum decision maker to outline what knowledge was important for each subject, and to identify the objectives that would be appropriate for those subjects. Once done, one then had to develop those activities that would enable the learner to master the content.

While in looking back we may think Bobbitt was "wrong-headed," we must recognize that he was essentially engaged in embracing an existing paradigm that had not been employed within educational thinking. Bobbitt's view about the use of scientism in curriculum activity greatly affected the field of curriculum. He was most influential in developing principles of curriculum-making that involved determining aims, objectives, the needs of students, and learning experiences. He noted that the objectives of the curriculum could be derived from the study of needs, something still being advocated today. Perhaps his greatest contribution is his argument that the process of curriculum-making is not specific to any particular content, but rather cuts across subject matter. As Cornbleth (1990) points out, although not relating her comments to Bobbitt, the process of curriculum development was decontextualized both conceptually and operationally. It set the stage for conceptualizing curriculum development as precise and predictable, resulting in a tangible product. The entire process and its resultant product were seen as separate from curriculum policymaking, design, practice, and even evaluation (Cornbleth, 1990).

Bobbitt, and later Tyler, did their work well—so well that the approach to curriculum development and thinking about curriculum is still very much in evidence, even with all of the dialogue about paradigm shifts to postmodern ways of thinking about the field. Indeed, the foundation that Bobbitt laid down is still the mainstream view regarding curriculum development in today's schools. This view is most difficult to budge, for the very nature of what we are being urged to employ in the place of modernism commands no consensus. There is no precise new system by which we can finally overturn the work of Bobbitt and later Tyler and Taba. This is not surprising since we do not want to deal with "mists"; we want to know specifics. We measure the worth of suggestions by their specificity rather than their heuristic value of making us challenge the details and assumptions of our thinking, of our ways.

Ralph Tyler, Prime Technocrat

Tyler was greatly influenced by Bobbitt and others similarly oriented. His book *Basic Principles of Curriculum and Instruction*, published in 1949, epitomized modernism. It has come to have an enormous influence on the field of curriculum. Despite all the criticism of Tyler, his thinking is still dominant in schools across the nation.

If we are to move beyond Tyler we must first recognize that we could not be at this juncture, debating the merits of a new paradigm for curriculum development, if Tyler had not written his 128-page book and presented four basic questions to the field: (a) What educational purposes should the school seek to attain? (b) What educational experiences can be provided that are likely to attain these purposes? (c) How can these educational experiences be effectively organized? (d) How can we determine whether these purposes are being attained?

These four questions have become known as the Tyler rationale for creating curriculum. These questions and the method implicit in dealing with them have such appeal because they appear to be so reasonable. Even Doll (1993) acknowledges that they are reasonable, but only if we accept a modernist, linear, cause-effect framework. We would argue that the continuing popularity of Tyler at the level of schools and school districts, and perhaps even on a few university campuses (despite all the rhetoric at national curriculum conferences), is due to the very reasonableness and workability of the rationale, regardless of one's context. Educators in classrooms and on local curriculum committees feel a sense of comfort knowing that curriculum is essentially a plan composed of identifiable components (objectives, subject matter, methods, and materials). Likewise, they feel a sense of calm knowing that the procedures for creating such a curriculum are knowable and predetermined in a manner that will assure an efficient and orderly creating and control of the curriculum. The procedures for creating curriculum, taking this viewpoint, are essentially value neutral (Cornbleth, 1990). Certainly, we exhibit values as to what content we wish to include, and perhaps even the experiences we wish students to have, but many assert that we at least can relax a bit in knowing that the procedures by which we bring curricula into existence are essentially beyond argument. We know what to do!

To even suggest that educators reflect on the assumptions behind their actions is to be somewhat confrontational. Even many not disturbed by such confrontation feel that we are asking them to forsake a professionalism that has been won only after much effort. The entire push for being scientific was an attempt to bring not only precision to curricular action, but a professionalism to the field itself. We borrowed management by objectives from the field of business. We looked to the various scientific management movements throughout this century to furnish us with ideas as to how to go about our business.

Tyler gave us a techno-speak that enabled us to be part of the modernism of this century. In a very real sense, the Tyler Rationale gave us slogans and shared ideals and views of curriculum and its creation. We could share common visions; we could communicate with a shared language. As Cornbleth (1990) notes, this technological orientation enabled us to have a sense of community gaining comfort in knowing that we were following the right path. We were exhibiting an aura of curriculum expertise that was exportable to any and all who wished to be involved in creating programs. We could identify the problems that needed to be addressed, we could determine the objectives, we could select the necessary experiences, and we could assure people that we had, indeed, obtained what we had set out to do. And administrators could take pride that their staffs had indeed been efficient in carrying out their curricular responsibilities. In those instances where this was not the case, administrators knew that there were outside experts who could be brought in to do the job of determining goals and objectives, and outlining the means to attain them. It could all be mapped out in linear fashion. In a sense, all we had to do was connect the dots and the outline of the program would become evident. Then our task was just to color within the lines and the curriculum would be covered.

Tyler's message, perhaps, would not now be so dominant if he had been a voice crying in the wilderness. But Tyler had company, and he still has. Hilda Taba was a colleague of Tyler's who gave an added boost to his rationale for the curriculum world.

Hilda Taba

Taba's thinking regarding curriculum and curriculum development also reflected the modernism-scientistic tradition. In her seminal book on curriculum development, *Curriculum Development: Theory and Practice* (1962), she argued that there was a definite order to curriculum development, and that pursuing such order would result in a more thoughtful and dynamically conceived curriculum. Like Tyler, she noted that all curricula are composed of certain elements. She accepted the assumption of componentiality. Not only could we define things in terms of their components, we could actually take these components apart and put them back together again. These units were essential to all the curricula, and in identifying them we could manage them in ways that would make them predictable (Berger, Berger, & Kellner, cited in Cornbleth, 1990).

In the procedure that Taba advanced for creating curricula, Tyler's modernism influence is evident. The model has definite steps, each to be engaged in one at a time such that a curriculum plan for teaching would result, addressing the objectives created at the outset of the process. Taba did differ from Tyler and others of the scientific bent in that she believed that teachers should have an active role in the procedure for creating curricula.

Her seven-step model of curriculum development gives even more detail to the process than do Tyler's questions.

1. Diagnosis of needs. The teacher or curriculum designer begins the process by identifying the needs of students for whom the curriculum is to be planned.

2. Formulation of objectives. Here the teacher or curriculum designer selects those specific objectives that require attention in light of the needs identified. These objectives, perceived actually as ends, allow a precision to the process and enable curriculum makers to view learning as an observable outcome that could be measured.

3. Selection of content. From the objectives selected, one can determine the subject matter of the curriculum.

4. Organization of content. While Tyler dealt rather broadly with the organization of educational experiences, Taba was more specific, actually separating the organization of content from the selection and organization of experiences. Again, this step made it clear to teachers or curriculum designers the components of the content and how they were to be organized to attain expected results.

5. Selection of learning experiences. Taba was explicit in noting that selecting learning experiences was a different component in the curriculum development process. Experiences could only be selected after the content or subject matter had been determined.

6. Organization of learning experiences. Once the experiences were selected, they needed to be placed into a sequence to optimize students' learning. Again, the assumption is that this sequence could be determined prior to the students actually becoming engaged in their learning.

7. Evaluation and means of evaluation. Like Tyler, Taba's final step engaged the curriculum planner in determining just what objectives had been accomplished. Actually, in the approach, the means of evaluation are determined prior to the actual implementation of the curriculum.

There have been variations of Tyler's and Taba's approaches to curriculum development, but most of the models extant today draw heavily on this technocratic mentality. Most are presented as if there is total agreement as to approach; most appear to be decontextualized from their social context; and most give the illusion that there is a timeless precision to the process.

In arguing that we should go beyond Tyler and Taba, we are asking educators to reflect on the assumption of scientism-modernism, and perhaps to challenge basic tenets that have guided educators' actions for most of this century. It is not to suggest that we generate a specific plan to replace Tyler and Taba. It is not to purport that we know where we have moved or even to suggest toward what we should be moving. At this juncture, perhaps we only should realize that some of us are in the process of moving. As to our destination, we cannot say.

Challenges, Transitions, Transformations

Arguing getting beyond Tyler and Taba is not so much to criticize their work and their times as it is to recognize that we are in different times—times that challenge us to think in novel ways about our realities and how to generate curricula within them. Tyler and Taba reflected a view of modernism: that life could be viewed as mechanical, that there existed a stable-state universe, that the process of curriculum development could be compartmentalized and decontextualized, that goals could be separated from the experiences designed to address those goals.

Currently, we are realizing with increasing sophistication that life is organic, not mechanical; the universe is dynamic, not stable; the process of curriculum development is not passive acceptance of steps, but evolves from action within the system in particular contexts; and that goals emerge oftentimes from the very experiences in which people engage. Curriculum gains life as it is enacted (Cornbleth, 1990). We are in a time that is encouraging the projection of new meanings, and suggesting ways to organize these myriad interpretations. The times, being identified as postmodern, are encouraging the achievement and employment of multiple awarenesses (Giroux, 1991).

Post-modernism is not just a one-world movement. It involves the thinking and actions of myriad scholars from diverse disciplines. The very crossing of these disciplinary lines has generated new ideas and practices—has triggered hybrid subject matter and invited a most heterogeneous audience to dialogue. The focus of the dialogue is to contest knowledge and to critique a total view, the primacy of reason, and the universality of general knowledge (Jencks, 1992).

The prime challenge is to query meta-narratives and accepted "stories" of the way things are in the world, and to reject the notion that we can bracket our reality. In many ways, the post-modernist is behaving in ways similar to those persons delving into the science of complexity. These individuals are convinced that through creative questioning and inventing of paradigms, they can come to understand more fully the spontaneous self-organizing dynamics of the world in ways never before imagined (Waldrop, 1992).

In rejecting grand narratives about ways to create curriculum and to generate paradigms, curricularists can address—even celebrate—the complexity of curricular deliberations and educational programs. Accepting post-modern views as well as those of complexity, curricularists can realize that what are called for at this juncture in time are plural codings of reality and actions, and multiple communications of the phenomena we are attempting to engage (Jencks, 1992). There is an attempt to assert differences in thinking, to distance ourselves from homogeneous thinking about curriculum and its development. Post-modernism asserts that there is indeed no structure or master narrative in which we can wrap ourselves for comfort (Hutcheon, 1992). There is no master curriculum plan that we can generate for all times. Master plans are illusions.

A stretch to the edges actually pushes us to the limits of possibility. It challenges us to engage in experiencing the limits—the limits of our language, our subjectivity, our identities, our views, and our systematization of approaches to curricular action. Such challenge demands a rethinking of the bases upon which we function (Hutcheon, 1992). It invites us to play with forms emerging in dynamic shadows.

Emerging Forms of Dynamic Shadows

Suggesting we go beyond Tyler and Taba is more than recommending that we follow new rules. As Lyotard (1992) submits, we are invited to play the game *without* rules, and from the very playing, to invent new rules. We are enticed to play with emerging forms in dynamic shadows of thinking, trying to put shape to what has previously been unimaginable and unpresentable.

In urging that curricularists play in these shadows, we are saying that we need to create, to conceive, curricula without the direction of pre-established rules. We need to gain excitement from engaging in the curricular game without what Lyotard calls the solace of good forms, the consensus of a taste that would enable us to share collectively a common vision. In a real sense, going beyond Tyler and Taba is engaging in action that is seeking the formulation of new rules, the shaping of forms emerging in the mist of the edge of our thinking. We are asked to create new metaphors to guide our dealings with the world. Our challenge is not that of supplying a clear reality, but inventing allusions to the conceivable and engaging ourselves in the dynamics of the system (Lyotard, 192).

To play with forms emerging from dynamic shadows places our focus on forms and wholes, in contrast to segments, parts, and their arrangements. To get beyond Tyler and Taba is to suggest that we engage in a holistic approach to conceptualizing the curriculum and its creation. If we consider the whole, we will be immersed in considering the dynamics of the system. We will come to realize that order will emerge from such dynamics (Lewin, 1992).

This new thinking within the realm of post-modern and complexity denies the validity and usefulness of the mechanical notion of the universe. We are urged to reject the clock metaphor to explain our worlds and come to apply biology as a more useful paradigm. It is more productive for curricularists to think of curricula as comprising ecological systems. In employing the language of biology within a post-modern framework, we recognize that diversity and differentiation are the commonplace, not the exceptional (Toulmin, 1990). Getting away from traditional thinking, in our case Tyler's and Taba's, we manifest more discriminating and discerning means of processing curriculum questions. No master narrative or rationale directs our curriculum actions.

The biology metaphor enables us to consider the curriculum and its creation as comprising a living system. Instead of looking at an external manipulation of distinct parts, we accept that we are viewing worlds, immersed within the on-going behavior of an ecological entity. We celebrate curricula as living systems that never really settle down. There is a perpetual novelty (Waldrop, 1992). The systems contain internal dynamics that make them both complex and adaptive, allowing for an immense realm of possibilities.

In a dynamic world, we need approaches to curriculum development and to curriculum itself that are adaptive under conditions of constant change and unpredictability. We need for these and anticipated times curricular systems that enable us to process perpetual novelty, that privilege the notion of emergence (Waldrop, 1992). We want emergence of forms, emergence of actions, emergence of systems, and emergence of results (Lewin, 1992).

Further, we need to realize that we are not outsiders who create and manage these systems. We are integral parts of the very systems and views we generate. The ways in which we engage in curriculum development and the conceptions we formulate of curriculum emerge from our engagement with these procedures and notions. Our involvement within the social contexts, both large and small, will influence and shape our curriculum formulations. Our actions over time cause us to realize, even celebrate, the increase in complexity within the total realm of the curriculum field. Our willingness to immerse ourselves and others in curriculum deliberations and dialogue is testimony to our faith that we will be able from our actions to add memory and information from times past, times present, and anticipated times in ways that will increase our collective curricular wisdom (Waldrop, 1992).

Post-Modern Curriculum Development

It is much easier to indicate where we have been than to indicate where we are going. As humans, we want purposefulness; the desire is part of being human (Doll, 1993). We want specifics; we judge the quality of dialogue by the number of specifics we can glean. We possess a need for action that leads to closure, to resolving our problems, to defining our actions. In taking this stance, we derive understanding and management of our worlds. If we are to go beyond Tyler and Taba, what will we specifically put in their place?

The procedures that Tyler and Taba advocated were predicated on a positivistic certainty (Doll, 1993). There were distinct points in the process that had definite purpose. In post-modern curriculum development, we are suggesting that the stress is not on the specific steps of action, but on the relations that result when people get together for the purpose of creating curricula. Rather than bring certainty to the process, there is a pragmatic doubt that results from realizing that decisions are not based on some privileged meta-narrative, but rather on the dynamics of human experiences within the local milieu.

One of the surprises of post-modernism is its acceptance of the chaotic, the emergent currents of change. Harvey (1992) quotes from Foucalt that we should "develop action, thought, and desires by proliferation, juxtaposition, and disjunction. We should prefer what is positive and multiple, difference over uniformity, flows over unities, mobile arrangements over systems. Believe that what is productive is not sedentary but nomadic."

Curriculum development in the post-modern vein would stress play rather than certain purpose; chance over certain design; process and performance over a static, finished work; participation of players over distance of players from the process; a dispersal of ideas over a centering of ideas; a combination of ideas over a narrow selection, action driven by desire rather than symptom; and a system characterized by indeterminacy rather than determinacy (Hassan, cited in Harvey, 1992).

Accepting the post-modern stance, we recognize that there can be no one way of creating curricula. There is no one meta-narrative or meta-theory through which we can generate curricula. There are no rules for creating programs that can be considered universal or having the posture of truths. Going beyond Tyler and Taba is going into the realm of thought and action in which we have a plurality of procedures or language games for discourse about curriculum development. There is no permanence—all is fluid, but from fluid motions come patterns. In curriculum development, we need to utilize the motion, the ferment, to develop the curriculum. How we actually engage in such creative curriculum development is unclear: "It is a problem we will need to live with for generations" (Doll, 1993, p. 148).

As we live with this idea of dynamic patterns emerging from being engaged, from considering curriculum development as an ongoing social activity molded by myriad contextual influences, we will begin to see patterns of necessary curricular actions. The modern paradigm of Tyler and Taba will take time to be replaced by a post-modern paradigm (Doll 1993). We now know, however, that curriculum development is not the algorism that has been central to much of modernist thinking. Rather curriculum development is more of a playful dance—a process in which the dancers (both teachers and students) engage in a dialogue of motions (goal setting, content selection, experience design), and are thus transformed in ways influenced by the dynamics of the local "dance" situation (Doll, 1993).

Initial attempts to get beyond modernism in curriculum development are sure to appear rather slight. Perhaps it is more the attempt to move on than the actual results of such moving that should be our focus. For instance, Cornbleth (1990) cites Goodman's work on critical curriculum design, noting that his five phases of curriculum development (developing curriculum themes, exploring resources, developing learning activities, pupil evaluation, and unit evaluation) do sound conventional. But it is in discussing these stages that we see that he is attempting to get us beyond Tyler and Taba. Rather than ask what content students can learn for specific purposes, Goodman raises questions as to what topics would enrich children's lives and expand their learning horizons. Also, he raises questions that address not the pieces of knowledge, but the holistic nature of knowledge. There is an emphasis on the uncertainty, ambiguity, and dynamism of knowledge, rather than a false sense of precision (Cornbleth, 1990). Central to the process of curriculum development is a perpetual, deep questioning of the "dance," the dancers themselves, and their locales.

An Example

There is danger in setting to paper a curriculum development model that will get us beyond Tyler and Taba. That danger is that the model suggested may be interpreted with the modernism mentality. Doll (1993) has suggested an alternative to the Tyler rationale. While his suggestions are not dealing exactly with how one actually creates a curriculum, we do get an idea as to how one might "dance" through the implied process. Doll presents four criteria for a curriculum designed to foster a postmodern view: Richness, Recursion, Relations, and Rigor. We consider these four criteria to be fluid points of reference in the creation of the curriculum. These criteria seem to imply different questions for teachers and students to pose when developing curricula.

In dealing with *richness*, curriculum designers—and we think it important to note that these players are teachers, students, and interested parties from the wider community—query themselves as to the depth of the curriculum that can be experienced so that students' lives are enriched. What layers of meaning can be arranged for students; what variety of interpretations can be selected or encouraged? At this juncture, involved parties ask themselves what is the "'right amount' of indeterminacy, anomaly, inefficiency, chaos, disequilibrium, dissipation, lived experienced" (Doll, 1993, p. 176). It is this right amount that cannot be predetermined, as would have been the case in determining scope within a modern framework of thinking. The right amount is an issue to be continually negotiated among students, teachers, and text. But, Doll asserts, one thing that cannot be negotiated is the fact that the curriculum must have some disturbing qualities. It is this very nature of the post-modern curriculum, celebrating an unstable order, that allows this means of curriculum planning to foster the creation of a rich and, it is hoped, transforming curriculum.

The second criterion for a post-modern curriculum, *recursion*, suggests to curriculum developers that they are to participate in a development process that has both stability and change. The general categories of knowledge may be the same, but the particulars addressed will vary. As people think about aspects of the curriculum, their thoughts will continually cycle back to previous thoughts and be changed and enriched in the process. Having the curriculum development process be recursive encourages the participants to engage in reflective interaction with all the players. The very act of curriculum development not only enables a listing of curricular possibilities for students to experience, but also creates a culture for all the players.

Doll (1993) notes that in creating a curriculum that is recursive, there is no fixed beginning or ending. All seeming endings are new beginnings. The components of the curriculum being designed are not perceived as disconnected units or even connected units. Rather, what is suggested for the curriculum is perceived as differing series of opportunities for students and teachers to engage in reflection, in constructing meaning. Everything suggested to be done leads to other things to be done, considered. The curriculum is designed to allow for continually going back to and then incorporating previous points and insights into a growing sense of understanding.

The third criterion, *relations*, suggests that in designing a post-modern curriculum, we need to think more about the relations between the parts of the curriculum than centering our attention on the parts. It is important that content selected encourage individuals to relate to it and to other students also experiencing said content. The emphasis on relations brings students and teachers into dialogue. It suggests that the resulting curriculum essentially cannot arise outside the school and classroom. It cannot be generated by persons who create educational materials. Certainly, it cannot be created by textbook authors. The criteria of relations makes evident that curriculum construction is a social activity being played out within particular frameworks; it is a human activity full of surprises, and we must allow for the surprises in our actions (Cornbleth 1990). This differs from the technical modern approach of listing steps with the cannon of no surprises.

The frameworks within which the relations exist make clear that what people bring to the dialogue, to the conversations, to the teaching and teaming, is influenced by the contexts they are experiencing. The process of creating curricula is interactive. We have people participating in a type of ecological system, able to be adaptive and self-regulatory.

Rigor is the fourth criterion that Doll presents for a post-modern curriculum. While rigor is not a step in the process, it is a criterion to consider as one engages in curriculum development. Rigor demands that curriculum creators constantly question their actions and the results of their actions. It is being aware of (a) the assumptions one brings to the curriculum "dance" and (b) the fact that these assumptions contain values that influence the very process. It means getting beneath the surface appearances—challenging claims (Cornbleth, 1990).

Another aspect of rigorously creating a curriculum is realizing the impossibility of being certain that one has attained the correct answer. The search must go on with individuals striving for new combinations, interpretations, and patterns (Doll, 1993). Indeed, contrary to the scientific heritage in creating curricula, one seeks to enrich the imagination. In many ways, the scientific heritage, in stressing the one correct answer, has served to impoverish the imagination. Approaching curriculum development from a post-modern stance means addressing the paradox of imagination (Postman, 1993). Being scientific or modern in curriculum development has led to the weeding-out of the proliferation of new ideas. In contrast, being post-modern is to cultivate new ideas and novel ways of dealing with them.

It appears that the model of curriculum development implied by Doll has the features of being self-organizing as opposed to mechanistic, of being non-linear in action compared to linear, of being conducive to creativeness and openness as opposed to being deterministic, and drawing its essence from chaos theory as opposed to Newtonian mechanics (Jencks, 1992). Curriculum development in a post-modern posture beyond Tyler and Taba is ecological in view, holistic and interconnected, interrelated and semi-autonomous, and heterarchical rather than hierarchical.

However, despite much heated debate, this new "model" is not the antithesis of the modern. As Jencks argues, post-modern is a complexification and hybridization of the modern. In going beyond Tyler and Taba, it appears that this is exactly what we are doing. Rather than denying our Tylerian past, we are adding needed complexity and creativity— imagination, if you will—to our heritage. We are transforming, rather than overturning, what Tyler and Taba urged us to consider.

Our adherence to the modern has served as a safe harbor. It is time to take the educational ship and ourselves with it out of safe harbor, into the challenges, uncertainties, and dynamics of a chaotic ocean. We are invited to sail uncharted waters, discover and create new worlds, and to share stories of adventure so as to establish new educational communities.

References

Bobbitt, E. (1918). *The Curriculum.* New York: Arno Press.

Cornbleth, C. (1990). *Curriculum in context.* London: The Falmer Press.

Doll, W., Jr. (1993). *A post-modern perspective on curriculum.* New York: Teachers College Press.

Giroux, H. A. (Ed.). (1991). *Postmodernism, feminism, and cultural politics.* Albany: State University of New York Press.

Harvey, D. (1992). The condition of postmodernity. In C. Jencks (Ed.), *The post-modern reader* (pp 299–316). New York: St. Martin's Press.

Hutcheon, L. (1992). Theorizing the postmodern. In C. Jencks (Ed.), *The post-modern reader* (pp. 76–93). New York: St. Martin's Press.

Jencks, C. (Ed.). (1992). *The post-modern reader.* New York: St. Martin's Press.

Lewin, R. (1992). *Complexity.* New York: Macmillan.

Lyotard, J. E. (1992). What is postmodernism. In C. Jencks (Ed।., *The post-modern reader* (pp. 138–150). New York: St. Martin's Press.

Postman, N. (1993). *Technopoly.* New York: Alfred A. Knopf.

Selznick, P. (1992). *The moral commonwealth.* Berkeley: The University of California Press.

Taba, H. (1962). *Curriculum development: Theory and practice.* New York: Harcourt, Brace, & World.

Toulmin, S. (1990). *Cosmopolis.* Chicago: The University of Chicago Press.

Tyler, R. W. (1949). *Basic principles of curriculum and instruction.* Chicago: University of Chicago Press.

Waldrop, M. M. (1992). *Complexity.* New York: Simon & Schuster.

A Nonfoundational Curriculum

Kenneth A. Bruffee

College and university education should help students renegotiate their membership in the knowledge communities they come from while it helps them reacculturate themselves into the academic communities they have chosen to join. The communities they have chosen to join are represented on campus by their teachers. What college and university teachers do when they design a curriculum, therefore, is choose the communities that they want their students to join.

How, then, should college and university teachers approach designing a curriculum that assumes a nonfoundational social constructionist understanding of knowledge and in which the goal is to induct students into knowledge communities where human interdependence is understood to be the norm? The answer is best described as a generalization of the discussion of collaborative learning tasks seen in Chapter 2. The point of departure in designing such a nonfoundational curriculum is not any knowledge community's common ground, a liberal education "core," or some canon of treasured texts. It is the notion of "knowledge communities" itself and the ways in which human beings negotiate and renegotiate knowledge within and among those communities. The goal would be to help students understand their academic studies—of mathematics, chemistry, sociology, English, whatever—as reacculturation, and specifically as reacculturation into communities in which knowledge is a construct of the community's constituting language or form of discourse. Along with this basic expertise in the workings of language and other symbolic systems, furthermore, would necessarily go basic expertise in how people live and work well together.

Such a curriculum would, first, help students recognize that they are already members in good standing of many communities of knowledgeable peers; second, help them discover which of their own and their classmates' beliefs have been socially justified, and in what ways; and third, help them explore the historical, sociolinguistic nature of knowledge.

In accordance with Stanley Fish's notion that teaching begins by identifying "knowledge with something that [students] are already doing" (discussed in Chapter 11), at each point in a curriculum of this kind teachers would select examples to be studied from the knowledge communities that students were currently members of as well as from the academic and professional disciplinary communities that teachers are members of. They would present this disciplinary subject matter and methodology as examples of how highly complex, self-aware communities of knowledgeable peers construct knowledge by justifying their beliefs socially and of how subject matter and methodology change when a community's consensus changes. These principles apply equally to courses in the sciences (discussed in Chapter 9) and courses in the humanities and social sciences.

The curriculum sketch that follows draws on my own understanding of knowledge as a sociolinguistic construct and of learning as a social, negotiated, consensual process. Its goal is to help students come to terms with cultural pluralism by demonstrating that knowledge is not a universal entity but a local one, constructed and maintained by local consensus and subject to endless conversation. The chapter ends with a nonfoundational critique of the nonfoundational curricular suggestions the chapter offers.

First, a curriculum based on a nonfoundational social constructionist understanding of knowledge would try to *help students recognize that they are already members in good standing of many communities of knowledgeable peers.* Students would consider the possibility that, as a consequence of joining new communities of college- and university-educated people, they may have to negotiate quite new relationships with the communities they come from.

To help students take these first steps in self-awareness, teachers would ask them to identify, in nonevaluative ways, their own beliefs and the beliefs of the overlapping and nested local, religious, ethnic, national, supranational, and special-interest communities they belong to. Protestant students from Kansas, Jewish students from Atlanta, Catholic students from Boston, Vietnamese from Michigan, Polish-Americans from Toledo, African-Americans from Chicago, Chicanos from Los Angeles; Southerners, Northerners, Easterners, Midwesterners, blacks and whites, women and men, middle class and poor; bridge addicts, hockey fans, oboe players, parents, police officers, balletomanes: people from potentially every conceivable community would become more aware of the beliefs held by the members of their own communities and the beliefs held by the members of other communities with whom, as it happens, they are being educated. They would try to discover what distinguishes beliefs of their own communities from those of other communities and in what respects, if any, the beliefs of most of those communities are nearly identical.

From the beginning, the curriculum would help students discover how a knowledge community defines and characterizes, and in some cases (as we noticed in Chapter 1) circumscribes, dominates, and suppresses, the lives of its members. It would provide linguistic tools that would help students diversify, individualize, and free themselves collaboratively. It would also help students learn how beliefs affect the ways in which community members and outsiders interact. The curriculum would help students make these discoveries in part through collaborative analysis and in part through self-conscious efforts to join the several disciplinary communities whose representatives are college and university teachers. Meanwhile it would give college and university teachers an opportunity to demonstrate the relationships that always exist between "popular culture" and the treasured texts of the Western or any other tradition.

It may not be easy at first to imagine undergraduate students undertaking any of this. The process may seem artificial, baroque in its complexity, and stressful. One reason it may seem so is that, in most colleges and universities today, conversation does not yet exist in which the analytical terms involved are the norm. Traditional academic study tends either to suppress or to sublimate the origins and extraacademic alliances of both students and teachers, in favor of the prevailing academic culture. This curriculum would not necessarily reverse that tendency. But it would understand communities of all kinds, academic and nonacademic, as similar in their constitution and goals.

Many colleges and universities have taken a step in this direction by finding a place on their campus and in their curriculum for peer tutoring (Chapter 5) and by including in the curriculum nontraditional cultures such as women's studies and ethnic studies: African-American, Italian-American, Hispano-American, Native American, and so on. Each of these nontraditional programs, besides being a protodiscipline with distinct community characteristics of its own, serves the valuable purpose of providing a cultural critical mass, a support group for community members, both students and faculty.

The most important difference between these nontraditional programs and the nonfoundational curriculum I am outlining here is the internal cultural coherence that the former provide. In most such programs currently, students learn to represent and speak for the community they belong to, primarily to other members of that community. Their admirable goal, as I pointed out in Chapter 11, is to provide new access to treasured texts and artifacts outside the Western cultural mainstream. But (again as pointed out in Chapter 11) these programs make the same cognitive assumptions that the Western liberal humanist curriculum makes. They assume that we understand other cultures, peoples different from ourselves, through empathy: imaginative engagement with other people, trying to "see the world as they see it."

The curriculum I am describing here, making nonfoundational assumptions of the sort that I attribute in Chapter 11 to Clifford Geertz, has a different goal. It creates conditions in which students learn to represent and speak for the communities they come from without immediate access to a familiar cultural critical mass for support. Unlike a women's studies or ethnic studies curriculum, its goals are not necessarily to provide students with the means to develop cultural identity by sharing familiar texts and artifacts with others like themselves and to defend themselves against prejudicial assaults by outsiders, however worthwhile these goals may be. Its goal is to help students examine their own and their peers' cultural attachments comparatively.

The process has some drawbacks. For example, membership in some communities (Little League, Girl Scouts, subscribers to *Field and Stream*) would be easier to speak for and analyze than membership in others (mothers, Secret Service agents, any religion, the Inuit nation). Membership in still other communities, antisocial in tendency (the KKK, child pornographers, crack dealers, inside traders) might be impossible for almost anyone to speak for and analyze.

But this goal of a nonfoundational curriculum is worth the effort, as Greg Sarris discovered in his work teaching Native American students in southern California and central Canada. Sarris uses fictional narratives chosen from American Indian literature to help his students "explore unexamined assumptions by which . . . [we] frame the texts and experiences of members of another culture." In doing this, he demonstrates in practical terms the educational value, as well as the difficulty, of trying to escape "the old and still pervasive misconception of critical thinking as something devoid of cultural and historical contexts," the "perceived split between life experience and critical thought."[1]

Besides being stressful, the introductory process that students will have undergone so far would be necessarily superficial. The second and third goals of a curriculum devised on nonfoundational social constructionist assumptions deepen the process considerably by considering some of the complexities of community composition and the relationships among communities. The *second goal* would be to *help students discover which of the beliefs that they and their classmates hold have been socially justified and in what ways.* To achieve this goal, students would examine not only their own local communities but also the communities relevant to college and university education, both the academic disciplines such as chemistry, philosophy, and classics, and the larger, encompassing community of the college- or university-educated public, writers of standard written English, and so on. Studying the natural sciences as an interpretive, pragmatic intellectual tradition (discussed in Chapter 9) becomes especially relevant in meeting this goal.

Students would approach the justification of belief in three phases. In the first phase they would learn to distinguish between justified and unjustified beliefs. They would learn to distinguish beliefs that are justifiable in the terms of the subject community from those that are not. They would learn to ask if the members of that community hold any beliefs that remain unjustified, and, if so, why and how. The process would be something like the one Stanley Fish describes: shifting students' attention from what "texts" mean to what they "do," making the text "an *event* something that *happens* to, and with the participation of, the readers "Texts," of course, can include anything from a slogan, a few sentences, a novel, an article in *Nature* or Bach's partitas and Picasso's Blue Period paintings, to Boolean algebra, BASIC, or graphs representing results of research in the natural or social sciences.

For example, some ninety-nine percent of all Americans and Western Europeans believe that people have walked on the moon. What do we do to justify that belief, and by what assumptions? What does it do for us and to us as a community to justify that particular belief in that particular way? There may also be one percent or so of us who believe that people have never walked on the moon. Is that belief socially justifiable? If so, how? What assumptions are necessary in order to justify it? What does justifying it do for or to those who believe it? Moreover, by what processes do chemists justify their beliefs? Philosophers? Sociologists? Classicists? What, in each community, is regarded as evidence? Would a sociologist's criteria in examining evidence be accepted by a physicist? Do biologists, historians, geometricians, and English teachers all mean the same thing when they use the term "describe"? If not, why not, and what are the implications of their not doing so?

The second phase would generalize the first. Students would learn to distinguish what might be called genres of justification, typical ways in which members of various communities justify their beliefs. Can any belief be justified socially by explaining it logically? If so, by the logic of which community? What are the rules of logic as they are known in the West? Are "the universals of sound reasoning" really universal? If more than (or something other than) logic and sound reasoning are necessary for justifying beliefs socially in any community, what exactly is required and how does it work?

To return to our example, what would it take to convince the dissenting one percent that people really did walk on the moon? What would it take to convince the assenting ninety-nine percent that they did not? What part does metaphor play in justification, and how does that work? Which of the facts of the "hard sciences" depend for their conceptualization on metaphor? What role do terms such as "quark" and "charm" play in physicists' attempts to identify and character- ize the "basic building blocks" of nature? For that matter, what does that commonplace metaphor, "building blocks," do for those attempts, and to them?

In the third phase, students would learn and practice the techniques of discursive justification of belief and the critical analysis thereof as practiced in the large, encompassing community they are joining—the culture of people educated in the West or educated elsewhere according to Western educational principles and values. The point is not just that students would learn to write unified, coherent, readable prose, although that is certainly part of the point. They would learn, as Vincent Leitch puts it, that "writing produces all our knowledge." And since all writers are their own first readers, students would learn to read effectively in order to learn to write well and contribute in that way to the construction of knowledge. They would acquire an "active suspicion of all language formations," of every "system governing meaning," and of "the forms (in) which" they are taught.[3].

Here, the study of "the rhetoric of inquiry" might play a role. A collection of essays edited by John S. Nelson et al., entitled *The Rhetoric of the Human Sciences* offers a number of persuasive examples of the use of rhetorical analysis for understanding the constituting languages of profes- sional and academic communities: for example, Charles Bazerman on psychology, Philip J. Davis and Reuben Hersh on mathematics, Misia Landau on human paleontology, Allan Megill and Donald N. McCloskey on history, and Renato Rosaldo on anthropology.

An example of the kind of teaching that the second goal may yield is Albert D. Hutter's effort to help his students overcome "mistaken and confining assumptions, inculcated by their medical education." Hutter teaches M.D.s in training to become psychoanalysts. To help them begin to understand writing as constructing knowledge by learning to justify in writing their diagnoses and other beliefs they form about their patients, he teaches them not just to "write better" but also to "reconceptualize the nature of all writing."[4]

Another example of teaching relevant to the curriculum sketched here, seemingly at the other end of the professional spectrum from Hutter's but actually closely allied with it, is Susan Wells's work with technical writers in corporations that manufacture computers and large, complex machines. Hutter and Wells both want their students to understand the "mistaken and confining assumptions" involved in all attempts "to describe complex human behavior by 'objective' and 'complete' accounts." Wells's students write manuals that tell workers how to operate compli- cated machinery. She teaches them to become aware in doing so of the "authority claim" made in technical writing and to analyze the "interests" involved both in "producing knowledge [and] in our employment of it." Thus the interests of Hutter and Wells are also closely related to Sarris's attempt to overcome the "split between life experience and critical thought" perceived by his Native American undergraduates. In each case, the teacher leads students to examine their own and others' beliefs with the goal of discovering how community members justify those beliefs to each other.[5]

The *third curricular goal* of college and university education based on understanding knowl- edge as socially justified belief would be to *help students explore the historical sociolinguistic nature of knowledge.* This goal would be approached in four phases. First, students would return to the question of what constitutes a knowledge community and examine it in greater detail. They would ask such questions as, What diverse sorts of social divisions might conceivably be described as knowledge communities? Is a Boy Scout troop a knowledge community? Is a family a knowledge community? What about the Mormon Church? Is the Woods Hole Marine Biological Laboratory a knowledge community? Is the Physics Department of Duke University one? The Democratic Party? A kindergarten class? All the readers of this (or any other) book? Some of those readers? Everyone who hasn't read it? They would also examine whatever tends to cement communities (especially knowledge communities), whatever tends to weaken or dissolve communities, and whatever characterizes a peer in any sort of community.

Second, students would examine the way people go about joining knowledge communities and the criteria that knowledge communities apply in defining a person as knowledgeable. They would learn to apply all kinds of knowledge communities questions such as those Thomas Kuhn has posed:

> How does one elect and how is one elected to membership in a particular community, scientific or not? What is the process and what are the stages of socialization to the group? What does the group collectively see as its goals; what deviations, individual or collective, will it tolerate; and how does it control the impermissible aberration?[6]

To examine how knowledge communities come about would raise a further question crucial to change in knowledge: Once we are in a community of knowledgeable peers, how do we get out of it? *Can* we get out of a knowledge community once we have become a full-fledged member? Is renegotiating our membership a real alternative, and if so, how do we go about doing that? How do knowledge communities change? Do they in fact ever change? If knowledge is socially justified belief, and if the authority of knowledge is established by a community of assent, how do individuals "grow"? Does knowledge "grow"? If so, in what sense and how?

Third, students would consider how the heritage of the past contributes to the present composition of the community of college—or university-educated people and to the satisfactions that the community can provide. To what extent do the language and symbol systems of "the best that Western culture has to offer" constitute that community? To study that heritage for this purpose, students would undertake an archeological examination of the western cultural heritage of the sort implied in Bruno Latour's metaphorical use of the term "black box."

Latour adopts the "black box" as a metaphor for an understanding or concept that we have thoroughly learned or that a community accepts unquestioningly as established. A "black box" is an instrument that scientists regard as neutral relative to the results of an experiment. They do not know, and do not have to know, how the instrument works, what its history is, or how to fix it. For example, a dictionary is a "black box" to most people. So is a car, a telephone, and the color royal blue. A "black box," Latour says, is a routine, an enclosed, unexamined "premise . . . for all further reasonings in the matter" agreed upon by a certain community of knowledgeable peers. To follow the history of something "known" is therefore an "archeological" study. It is to dig down through strata of nested, overlaid, and overlapping "black boxes."[7]

Fourth and finally, students would consider the sense in which science, history, literature, and the arts are not a record of the work of "great" individuals (Rembrandt, Shakespeare, Woolf, Washington, Einstein, Faraday, Nightingale, Darwin, King). They would study the communities that those individuals belonged to, their society and culture, and their political, artistic, and intellectual cohorts. They would examine the role of "great" individuals in helping to create a consensus among members of those communities: ways of seeing, talking with, and hearing one another, ways of writing to and reading one another, and ways of acting in concert. Students would be led to describe the social construction of literary texts in many ways yet to be fully explored, some of which are represented, for example, in Jerome McGann's *Critique of Modern Textual Criticism*. Study of this nature is likely to result in new versions of such traditional academic fields as biography, history, and philology.

Humanists would also engage students in considering the contribution of the past to the composition of current communities by studying more carefully how literature communities are constituted and integrated over space and time. They would study how, with language and other symbol systems, communities transmit from place to place and from generation to generation their socially justified beliefs and their ways of socially justifying them that, as Kuhn puts it, "have withstood the test of group use."[8] And humanists would examine how humanistic texts and other cultural artifacts both reveal us to one another and hide us from one another.

This process would differ considerably from what is known as "sociology of literature," which is concerned with what Harry Levin called "literature as an institution." The sociology of literature is foundational in its phenomenological assumptions and is framed in subject-object terms, assuming as given the inner world of writers and the outer social world they inhabit. Its central issues are how literature "reflects" that world and how writers adapt to it or hope to change it.[9] Examining how literate communities are constituted and integrated would have more in common with a current approach described as the analysis of "narratives of socialization." These are, as Janet Carey Eldred puts it, texts "that chronicle a character's attempt to enter a new social (and discursive) arena," in the process dramatizing "the collision between competing discourse communities, their language conventions, and their inherent social logics."[10]

That is, a nonfoundational social constructionist study of literature of the sort sketched here would focus first on the *intratextual* communities of a text or other symbolic artifact, and of the language-constituted communities dramatized in it. It would identify the languages specific to those communities and the stories or fragments of stories that community members tell each other in order to explain who they are, what's going on, and how things hang together. It would identify changes in community membership that the text renders, how characters choose which communities to join or not to join, how communities choose individuals for membership (and decide to exclude others or eject current members), how members recognize potential new members, how communities reacculturate potential members into full-fledged membership, and what accounts for compatibility among communities, or their incompatibility.

Studies of this sort would also identify *extratextual* communities, membership in communities constituted by the text among those who read it, by virtue of reading and discussing it. Furthermore, some intratextual communities, rendered or implied within the text, would be found to be fictional extratextual communities, constituted by allusions to other texts. Illuminating parallels would be drawn between the way these fictional extratextual communities are constituted within the text and the way the text constitutes extratextual communities among its readers. And there would be a sense in which a text (or other symbolic artifact) "chooses" new members to join the extratextual communities it constitutes, through the nature of its language, its explicit narratives, and the already existing extratextual community of readers it constitutes.

The curriculum I have been sketching here is certainly incomplete and limited in many ways. For example, it does not promulgate the certainties and truths of Western intellectual and artistic accomplishment, and it does not confirm the unity of thought and knowledge. But criticism of that sort is based on foundational assumptions, in terms of which, of course, the whole project announced and carried forth in this book is flawed.

Even as a nonfoundational, social constructionist project, however, the curriculum I have outlined may be criticized from two quite different points of view. One of these is the conservative nonfoundational position perhaps best described, paraphrasing Richard Rorty, as "right-wing Kuhnian." This position is impeccably articulated by Stanley Fish.[11] Fish argues that because knowledge communities give rise to, determine, and control "the thoughts . . . [we] can think and the mental operations [we] can perform," we cannot analyze and understand what constitutes those communities or break through their boundaries and step outside them. All our beliefs are already inescapably "situated" in these historical, social, and ideational contexts. We cannot escape our acculturation.[12]

Any scheme that proposes to help us do that and calls itself "nonfoundational," such as the curriculum I have sketched here, Fish would say, is self-contradictory. It implies that people can leave communities into which they have been acculturated, or at least renegotiate their membership in them, by achieving a "perspective on [their] beliefs . . . from which those beliefs can be evaluated and compared with the similarly evaluated beliefs of others." It therefore manifests what Fish calls "theory hope," a wish to discover a foundational rationale the "consequences" of which are whatever it is one does or wants to do. We fail in these efforts to examine other community languages—other cultures—and to translate them into the languages of our own communities, Fish would explain, because we cannot avoid transforming what we examine or adopt: "The imported product will always have the form of its appropriation rather than the form it exhibits 'at home.'"[13]

Fish's argument identifies conceptual change exclusively with generational change. It is a position that at some level is difficult to gainsay *(plus ça change . . .).* As Max Planck said: "A new scientific truth does not triumph by convincing its opponents . . ., but rather because its opponents eventually die, and a new generation grows up that is familiar with it."[14]

However persuasive this conservative nonfoundational position may seem to be, it has the troubling disadvantage, as the social critic Roberto Unger puts it, of "justify[ing] the authority of existing institutional arrangements or of reigning modes of discourse."[15] It tends to deny the potential to effect change through education. It also masks self-contradiction of its own, as Fish has himself more recently begun tacitly to acknowledge.[16] The "situation" within which Fish believes everyone is unchangeably fixed is itself a social construct. It is some story or other that we tell ourselves about ourselves, about our knowledge, and about our past, present, and future. None of these stories is static. Like oral epic narratives, every such story is constantly undergoing change in the telling and retelling.

As we revise the stories we tell ourselves, moreover, they "enact possibilities." They help us, Unger says, "insert [ourselves] into a social world" other than one to which we are currently acculturated—into other "situations"—and to develop "our capacity to escape or to revise the social and imagination frameworks within which we deal with one another." By telling ourselves old stories, we remain what we are by describing ourselves as we have been. When we tell ourselves new stories, we redescribe who we are, what we are, and what we know, and thus how we learn. With new stories, we translate one "situation" into another, with the result, as Rorty puts it, of having "changed ourselves by internalizing a new self-description." At some point, even Copernicus and those who agreed with him had to become "Copernican" by telling a different story."

To understand knowledge and learning nonfoundationally in this way and to explain collaborative learning as a kind of nonfoundational education is not, however, to adopt a social constructionist "theory" that "grounds" an educational "practice." It is to suggest that nonfoundational social construction and nonfoundational education are two practices related by common assumptions: that knowledge is a constructed, sociolinguistic entity and that learning is an interdependent social process. Social construction assumes that we construct and maintain knowledge not by examining the world but by negotiating with one another, within and among communities of knowledgeable peers. Similarly, a nonfoundational understanding of learning assumes that learning occurs among persons, not between persons and things. These statements do not adumbrate a theory. They provide new speech, new "texts"—language for describing and "speaking differently" about what college and university teachers do, a redescription that can suggest and energize ways of doing it differently.

The curriculum sketched here may also be criticized from a nonfoundational social constructionist point of view that is diametrically opposed to Fish's, namely, the one that Rorty has called the "left-wing Kuhnian" position.[18] From this position, of which Unger and Bruno Latour are perhaps the farthest "left," most attempts to make education nonfoundational that I have been discussing (including my own) share an assumption that Unger calls "modernist" and regards as obsolete. This assumption, Unger would argue, limits their long-run effectiveness.

The "modernist" assumption implicit in all these exercises in curricular speculation is revealed in their tendency to address cultural diversity as a problem in contextuality. Like Barbara Johnson's education in a "plurality of forces and desires" and Lyotard's "worthwhile" class (both discussed in Chapter 11), their purpose is to acknowledge "difference," resolve the differences that are resolvable, discover constructive ways to exploit tensions among other differences, and negotiate a truce among differences that defy resolution. All of them assume that human beings are "contextual beings": our mental and social lives are "shaped by institutional [and] imaginative assumptions" that are socially constructed and historical in nature.[19]

This is the process that the nonfoundational curriculum I have sketched recommends when it asks students to look at, in Unger's terms, "formative contexts," past and present, our own and others', locally and elsewhere: both people's institutional arrangements, such as economic and governmental structures, and their "explanatory or argumentative structure," such as religions, art, literature, music, research agendas, guiding concerns, and standards of sense, validity, or verification.[20] It also resembles the recommendations of most essayists in the Johnson and Nelson volumes (discussed in Chapter 11). The purpose of examining these "formative contexts" is to understand the "mental and social life" that we ourselves and other people are conditioned and limited by; they are the boundaries imposed by cultural conditions. Stanley Fish's belief in the unchangeable "situation" we inhabit is also contextual in this sense.

Traditional, foundational, humanist education assumes the value of understanding great works of the past, regarded as being deeper, richer, older, and more nuanced. "Modernist" educational thought, both foundational and nonfoundational, assumes that, with the skillful and appropriate application of interpretive techniques to significant texts and through "knowledge of the functioning of language, of symbolic structures," human beings—especially young ones—can destabilize, renegotiate, or abandon the contexts that have shaped them and replace them with contexts that seem to them, and perhaps to some others (such as their college and university teachers), more satisfactory.

Unger maintains that trying to cope with cultural diversity in this contextualist way alone, whether our assumptions are foundational or nonfoundational, falls short of our needs. It may even stand in the way of fulfilling those needs, because an exclusive concern with contexts evades what Unger regards as the central fact of human relations. Along with addressing "the problem of contextuality," we should also be addressing what he calls "the problem of solidarity" or what Latour calls "the powers of association."

Contextual and solidarian thought have a good deal in common. They share the nonfoundational assumption that we socially construct human identity, and hence human diversity. But contextual thought begins already a step removed from the direct impact of human relations. It addresses that impact displaced into conceptual and symbolic forms and institutional arrangements. In contrast, solidarian thought begins with the most immediate and direct impact of human relations: our ambivalence to one another, the 'mutual longing and jeopardy," the "unlimited need and . . . unlimited danger" of social life. Unger's most important contribution to educational thought is probably this understanding of radical ambivalence in human relations. It underlies, for example, the difficulties discussed in Chapter 2 that students may encounter when they first begin collaborative learning and go through the two complex "phases of work," dependence and interdependence, involved in adaptation to group work. And it implicitly informs Latour's "performative" definition of power and the study of "associations" that he recommends.[21]

Unger elaborates his notion of social ambivalence in considerable detail, but the basic notion is easy to grasp because it is familiar to everyone. On the one hand, he reminds us, we all need one another's company, support, acceptance, recognition, engagement, and cooperation. Indeed, as Unger puts it, we crave the greater opportunity, the "enlarged possibility in self-expression and reconciliation," that we gain in association with one another. Each of us desires "acceptance and recognition, to be intimately assured that we have a place in the world, and to be freed by this assurance for a life of action and encounter."

On the other hand, in requiring the company of others, Unger reminds us, we submit to the threat of suppression, conformity, and constraint. Thus the inevitable counterpart and unremitting companion of our "unlimited need" for one another is our feeling of "unlimited danger" every time we try to fulfill that need. To satisfy our longing for acceptance, recognition, and freedom, "we must open ourselves to personal attachments and communal engagements whose terms we cannot predefine and whose course we cannot control," attachments and engagements that can lead to "a craven dependence" that may "submerge our individual selves under group identities and social roles." As liberating, productive, and satisfying as interdependence may be, therefore, it also tends to breed "domination and dependence." The freedom and self-realization that we gain in association with one another can always be compromised, and at worst crippled, by the "depersonalization [and] bondage" that results from entrenched, "ongoing, unaccountable, unreciprocal power."[22]

What we call individual "identity," and hence the differences among us, Unger argues, is in large part a product of the ways in which we manage—or fail to manage—to negotiate this ambivalence to interdependence. Like Fish, Felman, Geertz, Latour and others whose work I discussed in Chapter 11, for Unger the means we choose for negotiating that ambivalence is, to adopt Felman's phrase, our "knowledge of the functioning of language, of symbolic structures." But the nature of these linguistic constructs, Unger points out, is such that none of us can even "describe our situation and . . . reflect about ourselves unless we share in specific, historically conditioned traditions of discourse that none of us authored individually." Without this inherited language and without these inherited categories, he says, "the imagination cannot work."[23]

Because our language and categories are inherited, however, we continually feel our identity under threat. We "cannot easily prevent ourselves from becoming the unwitting reproducers" of a trite, conventional, oppressive "shared picture of the world." We risk confinement within this "collective script," and yet we cannot do without it. "If we stray too far or too quickly" from it, "we are left without a way to converse."[24]

The curriculum offered here does not address the educational implications of the deep social ambivalence that Unger contemplates. It does not address the full potential effect of that ambivalence on our primary tools for coping with it, language and other symbolic constructs. But the organization and constraints of collaborative learning, as described in Chapter 2 and Chapter 5, are designed to address them, however imperfectly. To explore the "problem of solidarity" collaboratively is to examine the emotional, social, economic, aesthetic, and political ways that, by trying to satisfy our "unlimited need" for one another, we may "aggravate" our sense of "unlimited danger." It is also to examine the emotional, social, economic, and political ways that, by trying to defend ourselves against the "unlimited danger" implicit in our need for one another, we may intensify that need. If students explore these forces collaboratively, therefore, they may help accomplish the "practical goal" that Rorty and Unger in common recommend: "human solidarity" based on "the imaginative ability to see strange people" both as "fellow sufferers" and as having the same right we have to life, liberty, and the pursuit of happiness.[25]

A step beyond the curriculum sketched here would guide students in reading our traditional treasured texts, as well as the texts in the newer "canon" currently being assembled, as episodes in that negotiation. To do that would be, once again, to read those treasured texts anew.

Cultural Politics and the Curriculum in Postsecondary Education

WILLIAM G. TIERNEY

In this paper the author investigates how culture gets expressed in postsecondary organizations by way of the curriculum. By utilizing a critical framework of educational organizations and the curriculum and analyzing two ethnographic case studies the author argues that how organizational participants come to terms with definitions of knowledge and the curriculum is permeated and shaped by the culture and ideology of the organization. Rather than assume that knowledge exists as a universally shared list of facts and figures, the presentation offers a dynamic view of the form and content of the curricula in higher education in order to explore how the perspectives individuals have of knowledge create curricular differences that have social and political consequences.

* * *

At Women's College (a pseudonym) a faculty member reflects about faculty life and the institution's attempts at curricular overhaul. He says, "People despair so much. No matter how much we try, there is always an air of despair that we are never successful." At a second institution, Entrepreneurial University, a faculty member in the natural sciences of many years talks about his colleagues in other departments and the failure of the institution to overhaul its curriculum:

> They're a bunch of slimy little bastards up on the hill. The tension on this campus will never go away; nothing will get done as long as that large slug of people is here. They're just rabble-rousers. Some of these guys have coffee klatches and all they do is plot against us. It's a constant battle. They just sit around and plot.

Entrepreneurial University's apparent lack of success at academic innovation and the despair of Women's College faculty at curricular overhaul underscore the difficulties involved with curricular change. Previously, authors have often analyzed the problems associated with academic change in postsecondary education by relying on rationalist premises of the organization and the curriculum (Chickering, et al., 1977; Bennett, 1983; Tucker, 1984). In this paper, I will employ a critical framework of an educational organization and the curriculum as developed by Giroux (1983, 1988a, 1988b), Simon (1987), and McLaren (1986, 1989), among others. My purpose will be to highlight how the curriculum may be viewed as a site where oppositional discourses take place about the nature and content of academic knowledge. As I will elaborate, my assumption is that faculty conflict and disagreements that occur at institutions such as Women's College and Entrepreneurial University are not precipitated merely by differences of opinion about curricular decisions or ineffective decision-making structures; instead, conflict often takes place because of competing cultural definitions of what counts for knowledge.

To elaborate on the idea that the curriculum is a site of on-going negotiation and contestation I will view postsecondary organizations as cultures that are socially constructed and invested with dynamic processes. An organizational culture has an ideology that helps determine how knowledge gets defined. I will argue that how we come to terms with definitions of knowledge and the curriculum is permeated and shaped by a cultural politics of the organization. My objectives are two-fold. First, I hope to extend our understanding of how culture gets expressed in academic organizations by way of the curriculum; second, I wish to touch on how the curriculum might be viewed as an empowering agent for students as they become involved in the struggle for democracy in the 21st century.

The data for the paper comes from a year-long research project where I investigated the curricular decision-making processes in seven postsecondary institutions (Author, forthcoming). I visited each institution twice for about a week at a time. Through ethnographic interviews and observations, I analyzed data from over 250 individuals. For the purpose of this paper, I will discuss two of the seven institutions.

The paper has four parts. In Part One, after briefly discussing a rationalist approach to the curriculum and the inherent underlying organizational premises, I will outline a critical approach to the culture of an educational organization. In doing so, I will consider the curriculum as a component of culture. I will then provide additional data from Women's College and Entrepreneurial University in Parts Two and Three. In Part Four I will conclude with a discussion of the applications of a critical view of the organization and the curriculum.

I. Approaches to the Curriculum

A Rational View

In general, previous writers about higher education's curriculum have acted as if only one epistemological position exists about knowledge. From this perspective, knowledge exists "out there," external and independent of the knower. It is as if knowledge is a jigsaw puzzle that can be shaped into multiple parts; even though different representations can be drawn, the pieces of the puzzle are the same to all of the organizational players. For students to become intellectually engaged they must learn the different pieces of the puzzle. As Diane Ravitch argues, "Students cannot learn to ask critical questions or to think conceptually about the past or about their own lives as political actors unless they have sufficient background knowledge" (1988, p. 129). According to Ravitch "background knowledge" concerns particular facts that all students must know for "any kind" of thinking. Her assumption is that knowledge is neutral, a body of facts that wait to be learned.

Previous research investigations about the curriculum in higher education such as those undertaken by Dresser (1971) and Mayhew and Ford (1971) highlight the problems that occur when we assume that although different institutions may call upon different knowledge puzzles, the pieces are the same. Each author has struggled to develop a taxonomy of postsecondary curricular models. In general, the models relate to the explicit emphases institutions have for the curriculum. For example, combining the work of Dressel and Mayhew and Ford, Bergquist (1977) has arrived at the following list of curricular models in higher education:

1. *Heritage Based*: A curriculum designed to inculcate students with a knowledge of the past.

2. *Thematic Based*: A specific problem (such as the environment) is identified and studied in-depth.

3. *Competency Based*: Students learn specific skills such as proficiency in language and mathematics.

4. *Career Based*: The curriculum is designed to prepare students for a specific career.

5. *Experience Based*: Opportunities are created for the student to learn outside of the classroom.

6. *Student Based*: The curricular emphasis is on providing students with opportunities to control what they learn.

7. *Values Based*: The curriculum emphasizes specific institutional values.

8. *Future Based*: The institution divides the curriculum with a concern for what students will need in the future.

Bergquist's work is quite helpful in providing one view of a curricular undertaking. The characteristics undergirding the view are three-fold: (1) the curriculum is ahistorical, (2) participants such as teachers and students do not create the curriculum, and (3) the models are ideologically neutral. That is, it is possible to discuss the curriculum in terms of its immediate context rather than historically; since meaning and definition reside within each model, issues such as class, race and gender of teachers or students are not inherently important. The models are decontextualized from the situations in which they reside so that ideological concerns are of little consequence. The overriding assumption is that issues such as history or ideology and class are germane only in models where they are made important; otherwise one can develop a curriculum that is ahistorical and ideologically neutral.

My concern with such lists is that we overlook how postsecondary institutions and the curriculum serve, reproduce, and challenge the social order of the society in which they reside. The implicit assumption remains: a singular reality exists to which all of the models apply. As opposed to investigating how the curriculum operates as a set of filters through which we define and choose what counts as knowledge, Bergquist's work and much other previous research about higher education's curriculum functions as a unifying epistemological myth about the nature of knowledge; the institution simply arranges the elements of knowledge according to a particular curricular model. I am suggesting that we need to unmask the inherent values of a particular epistemological position and show the conflict that it conceals.

Each of the above curricular models has implicit values that need to be unearthed. A heritage based model, for example, certainly will have different curricular offerings depending upon whose history and whose culture is included. Similarly, a value-based curriculum will look differently in an organization that adheres to conservative religious mores and an organization that premises itself on a theology of liberation. Moreover, each model subscribes to particular views of history and values.

By pointing out that different institutions subscribe to different curricular formulations I am saying more than simply that one institution differs from another. Clearly, the curriculum of Oral Roberts University will differ from that of Stanford University or Evergreen State College. My point is two-fold. First, we must accept that higher education's curriculum is culturally constructed, and as a cultural construction, the curriculum is inherently partisan.

Second, if the curriculum is culturally constructed and partisan, then of necessity we will pay attention to the relationship of the curriculum to knowledge and power. We will investigate an institution's curriculum not from which area in a taxonomic model it fits, but rather from the perspective that curricular structures imply dominant modes of discourse that deny particular groups a voice. To comprehend the curriculum in this manner we must go beyond outlining rationalist models of curricular formations and move toward an understanding of the curriculum that delineates the inherent premises and values of the organization. We must articulate the underlying conflicts of our epistemological positions and trace the hidden geography of an organization's culture.

Such a study will unveil that different institutions have quite different conceptions of knowledge based on their historical situation, the participants who enact the curriculum, and the context where the institution resides. In short, not only the puzzles will be different, but the pieces the organizational players use to put the puzzle together will also differ. In this light, the relative importance of one curricular model or another is not significant. Neither one best curricular model to which all institutions must subscribe will be found, nor will a taxonomy of models adequately describe the curricular universe. Instead, the curriculum becomes problematic and we question the dialogue that takes place around an institution's curriculum. As McLaren notes we ask:

How and why knowledge gets constructed the way it does, and how and why some constructions of reality are legitimated and celebrated by the dominant culture while others clearly are not. Critical pedagogy asks how our everyday commonsense understandings— our social constructions or "subjectivities" get produced and lived out. In other words, what are the social functions of knowledge? (1989, p, 169).

How the organizational participants construct their reality implies that different realities exist. Not only will institutions arrive at different curricular models; the institutions also will begin with differing conceptions of what counts as knowledge. My assumption, then, is that to understand the curriculum in higher education we must investigate the organizations in which the curriculum resides. To comprehend the culture of educational organizations we need to employ a theoretical framework that delineates the relationships among the participants, the organization and society.

A Critical View

The overarching premise of a critical view of the organization is that the organization's culture focuses the participants' understanding of their relationship to society through an organizational web of patterns and meanings that constantly undergo contestation and negotiation. Interpretation and interaction are highlighted. The culture of the organization constitutes human existence to such an extent that both prediction and the ability to reduce organizational meaning to predetermined elements are impossible. Intentionality depends upon the culture's prior histories within which individuals constitute meaning for themselves, the participants' definitions of reality, and the social and political contexts of the organization. Rather than view reality as objective and external to the participants, the critical perspective assumes that reality is defined through a process of social interchange that cannot be readily mapped, graphed, or controlled. There is no one single, simple, unilinear rationality; there are multiple, competing rationalities.

The assumptions of a critical perspective of organizational culture, and hence the curriculum, are four-fold and stand in sharp distinction to rationalist premises. First, culture is not necessarily understandable either to organizational participants or researchers. Since culture is an act of interpretation, what each person observes and interprets varies. A second, related assumption is that organizational actions are mediated by equifinal processes. That is, the construction of meaning does not imply that all individuals interpret reality similarly. Third, it is impossible to codify abstract reality. Fourth, culture is interpretive, a dialectical process of negotiation between the researcher and the researched.

With regard to the curriculum, a critical investigation differs from the more traditional studies referred to in the previous section in four ways. First, in the rational view, everyone has the same pieces of the curricular puzzle; in the critical view the curriculum is a key interpretive element that highlights how knowledge gets defined. Simon is helpful in understanding this point;

> If education is not to be viewed as a process within which knowledge is transmitted or conveyed but rather as a process of production and regulation of our social and physical world, every time we help organize narratives in our classroom we are implicated in the organization of a particular way of understanding the world and the concomitant vision of one's place in that world and in the future (1987, p. 376).

Thus, not only will organizational characters develop different organizational puzzles, but they are also likely to draw upon different peoples to construct a puzzle; and the forms, shapes, and constructs of the puzzles themselves will differ.

Second, a critical understanding of the curriculum also struggles to understand how different constituencies come to terms with and help define their own relations within the organization and within society; the assumption is that different groups interpret curricular formations in manifold ways. Consequently, the organization's participants are at the center of understanding curricular content and meaning. Third, rather than try to create taxonomies of curricular models, the assumption is that the curriculum, as an abstraction, cannot be codified. Finally, the role of the researcher as an interpreter of the curricular landscape takes on increased importance.

Thus, the initial purpose of this paper comes into focus: rather than assume that the curriculum is a static entity that is ideologically neutral, a critical view investigates the curriculum as a politically-charged site where oppositional discourses take place. "Curriculum stands for the relation of the knower to the known," writes Madeline Gramet. "As a teacher I mediate that relation. I stand somewhere between the student and the forms of knowledge, the content of the curriculum" (1978, p. 38). As opposed to Ravitch's idea that knowledge is neutral, proponents of a critical view subscribe to the notion that the curriculum is inherently ideological. Instead of conceiving of teaching as providing students with "background knowledge that all students need in order to think critically," (Ravitch, 1988, p. 129) from the critical perspective the pedagogic struggle is to expose the underpinnings of that which is learned. Participants become active learners who understand their own relationships to one another, the curriculum, knowledge, and ultimately, society.

As opposed to the rationalist preoccupation with developing curricular taxonomies, the critical perspective highlights ideology, defined by Peter Berger "as a set of ideas which is used to legitimate vested interests of sectors of society" (1963, p. 111). Within an organization, ideology is that component of culture which speaks to the establishment and reconstitution of patterns of belief and meaning (Geertz, 1973). By viewing the curriculum through a cultural and ideological lens the critical theorist struggles to unearth the invisible curricular structures which we take for granted. The critical theorist brings into question the discourses that occur around a college's curriculum and tries to come to terms with how the dialogues are more than rational discussions centering around whether one text or course or another is the best curricular choice. Instead, a critical study struggles to come to terms with how the particular discussion on a college campus about its curriculum relates to the interactive relationships among individuals, the organization and society, and in turn, how those relationships determine relations of knowledge and power.

An investigation of ideology seeks to reveal how ideology reflects the organization's culture. The multitude of cultural artifacts that exist in a college or university, such as the manner in which meetings take place, spatial and temporal arrangements, and the organization's structure, are examples of expressive cultural symbols that aid the researcher in coming to terms with institutional ideology. In so doing, a critical investigation looks for cultural artifacts and symbols that not only reinforce and sustain ideology, but also those symbols that contradict the dominant ideology.

As Giroux notes, "Ideology becomes useful for understanding not only how schools sustain and produce meanings, but also how individuals and groups produce, negotiate, modify, or resist them" (1988b, p. 5). As we will see, postsecondary institutions are terrains where conflicting ideologies take place between those who constitute the dominant discourse of the culture, and those individuals or constituencies who reject the overriding assumptions that operate within the culture. The struggle for the researcher is to isolate the beliefs and interpretations that make up ideology and to expose them. That is, researchers try to uncover not only the overriding discourses at work in the organization, but they also seek to unearth those voices which are silent or resist the dominant ideology.

My assumption is that the ideological resistances and silences within the organization are those which lead to cultural conflict. I am suggesting that the culture of an educational organization has a dominant ideology that gets expressed by way of the curriculum. As employed here, ideology concerns both the production and interpretation of meaning through the enactment of culture. The beliefs and values that organizational participants use to shape the curriculum derive in part from the ideology. The importance of understanding the significance of an organization's ideology concerns both the participants' ability to come to terms with how the organization produces meaning, and how the participants support, contradict, or resist those meanings. The comprehension of how ideology works, for example, enables us to investigate the assumptions of the organizational participants' definition of knowledge and what they believe should or should not go into a curriculum.

To expand on these ideas I turn now to a discussion of the two institutions mentioned at the outset of this article. At Women's College we will explore cultural conflict that occurs due to disagreements over how the institution's ideology gets defined. At Entrepreneurial University we will investigate an institution whose participants also have opposing views, yet the conflict occurs because of the lack of any overt ideological definition. At each institution, the discourse and conflict takes place around the curriculum.

II. Women's College

Clark (1987) and Kuh and Whitt (1988) have tried to unearth the archeology of faculty discourse. They have noted how faculty operate in four interdependent cultures that influence a faculty's beliefs and attitudes: (1) the culture of the institution, (2) the culture of the national system of higher education, (3) the culture of the academic profession, and (4) the culture of the discipline. At Women's College I will consider the different cultures of the faculty. In turn, I will consider how those differences create conflict with regard to the mission and curriculum.

At Women's College the culture of the discipline and the institution take prominence. The culture of the discipline refers to assumptions about knowledge, what it means to be a member of a disciplinary profession, and the relationship between society and knowledge. In this light, some faculty members will have more in common with those in their discipline than they do with those outside it, even if they work together on a daily basis. The culture of the institution is both an independent stimulus for shaping faculty behaviors and the main locale where faculty enact the different cultural formations. Each culture is a different layer of meaning that is in constant motion and change so that a faculty member quite often has different, even contradictory stimuli requiring his or her attention that frames present possibilities. And different cultures provide different interpretations about the institution's mission and curriculum.

Women's College, a hundred year old liberal arts institution, has 2,500 students and a student-teacher ratio of ten to one. Students from throughout the nation attend Women's, and faculty positions are actively sought after; nevertheless, some individuals feel that the distinctiveness of Women's has slipped in recent years.

Women's College still remains a single-sex college, but how individuals interpret the mission and curriculum has become a source of heated debate. For example, one traditionally-minded faculty member notes, "The debate . . . is very loud. What does it mean to think of ourselves as a women's college? Some say that it means the curriculum should be different, about women. I think it means women go here. Period." An opposing viewpoint is expressed by an English professor who states, "Our mission should incorporate scholarship on and by women." An African American professor comments, "Our mission is what we are. We create brilliant Christian women in the Euro-centric tradition. If we are serious about cultural diversity—to serve women of all colors—then we need to realize the serious deficiencies." Another professor contradicts that contention: "I think students should have a common body of knowledge. I like Hirsch's book, *Cultural Literacy*, and feel we can do the same for higher education."

Each of the viewpoints has strong cultural dimensions that affect how the speakers view the overriding ideology of the institution. For example, those faculty who identify the mission of the institution as one in which a women-centered curriculum ought to be addressed are trying to create a specific allegiance to the institution. "The battle," says one professor, "is to incorporate scholarship on women, education about women. That's where we should devote our time, teaching our students about women's education." Faculty who adhere to this line of thinking are more likely to declare fidelity to other scholars across disciplines within the institution then to seek disciplinary rewards outside of the college.

On the other hand, a faculty member who believes quite strongly in an institutional orientation toward the disciplines comments, "I don't believe a discipline is an historic accident. The person who is productive here gives little to the college. The discipline is essential. People use commitment to the college as a substitute for being good in the discipline." A second person echoes similar sentiments when speaking about what a new dean should attempt to do. "Respect the autonomy of the departments. What a departmental structure should be is a replication of the discipline. I want departments to tell us what should be done and not some politically-minded group who advocates for a particular point of view." Both speakers reflect the faculty culture of the discipline; their orientation is toward a disciplinary culture rather than an institutional culture (Author, 1989).

The curriculum becomes a cultural clash between the two groups of faculty oriented toward the different cultures. The curriculum takes on added significance not just as a pedagogic tool for inculcating students with particular values, but as the raison d'etre of the college. I am suggesting that institutional culture is not simply imposed on individuals; rather, the interactions of different faculty cultures play an important role in determining the culture of the organization and the form the curriculum ultimately takes. The possibilities for action, and the inability to perceive of solutions, derive from the different strata of meaning that intersect on the surfaces of faculty life.

Often the most innocuous institutional artifacts take on increased cultural importance because of the participants' interpretations. For example, at Women's College people who resist change are known as "dinosaurs." There are young "dinosaurs" and old "dinosaurs." Even the "dinosaurs" use the term about themselves. A young professor has an inflatable dinosaur sitting on his office bookshelf. He explains the term by saying, "The politics of pedagogy is very evident here. If you're not a traditionalist like I am then you think that the lecture is elitist and discussion is central. I believe there is value in lecturing, in getting across the facts to young people." "Someone started a rumor," relates another individual, "that the feminists in the administration building were taking all the lecture podiums out of the classrooms so that the faculty would not be able to lecture any more." Thus, even inert objects such as lecture podiums become highly charged cultural symbols.

Groups relate symbolic objects and discourses to particular images that are in some way tied to the ideological nature of the institution. That is, culture and ideology are interrelated. Cultural symbols such as dinosaurs or lecture podiums reflect ideology. Again, Berger's concept of ideology is that it is a set of ideas used for legitimation. Within the web of culture the participants reaffirm, reconstitute, or resist ideology. The example of a lecture podium or its absence is a cultural artifact that participants use to reaffirm or deny the dominant ideology of the institution. Conversely, with this example, the ideological "idea" concerns pedagogy: what is the legitimate manner to convey knowledge?

In general, previous investigations of the curriculum have not thought about how the curriculum change process is linked to the cultural makeup of the faculty and the institution or the overriding ideologies implicit at the cultural level. The point is not that one can do away with one cultural form or another, or necessarily that one cultural formation is wrong and another right. The first task is to understand how the participants' cultures interact with one another, and how the interactions hinder or hasten each individual's ability to comprehend the cultural web in which they are enmeshed. Once we understand how cultures interact within the organizational web, we can devise strategies that seek to embolden and empower all participants.

III. Entrepreneurial University

My purpose in this section is to bring into focus the confusion and conflict that takes place when no explicit ideology exists to help the participants define the culture of their institution. As opposed to Women's College, Entrepreneurial University does not have a dominant ethos that creates debate about what kind of institution it should become; instead, on the surface we find an institution whose participants believe they lack an overarching ideology.

Entrepreneurial University, almost 150 years old, has a wealthy, articulate student body, a faculty with a strong reputation and a beautiful campus facility. Full-time faculty are about 250, and student FTE enrollment is close to 3,500. Tuition is more than $10,000. Over eighty percent of the freshman class will graduate within four years.

Entrepreneurial University is an institution that operates in what one individual terms, "the entrepreneurial model." She explains, "No, we really don't know what we're about other than what everyone else is about—teaching, research, and service. What we are, what's great, is that people can go out and start something if they want to. It's like starting a small business." Another individual concurs: "There's lots of flexibility here. There are lots of spaces to do things so we can scoot through the cracks. It's like the ad they use for the Army. 'Be all you can be!'"

Entrepreneurial has a potpourri of innovative programs that faculty have devised. However, important curricular changes on an institutional level have not occurred in over two decades; yet departmental initiatives have blossomed and individuals have devised a number of courses or programs that do not need university sanction. The atmosphere of the university encourages individual ideas, but stymies change that attempts to explicitly define an overarching premise of the institution by way of general education requirements and the like.

Consequently, some students spend their freshmen year together studying the same set of courses with a core faculty. Other students choose courses from a more traditional freshmen general education sequence that consists of choices from many different curricular areas. Additional students spend an intensive amount of time in one course. And still other students become immediately involved in their majors to meet the rigorous demands of premedical or engineering degrees. Although Entrepreneurial's faculty do not agree that one body of knowledge must be taught, the faculty are similar to the more traditional, disciplinary oriented faculty of Women's College in the sense that in general they assume that what they teach is value neutral. One individual, for example, comments:

> I'm involved in the freshmen seminar, and it really shakes students up, they really end up questioning what they're all about. But I honestly don't care what they believe. We don't teach one ideological stance here. Students can pick and choose, and we're quite open about it.

I ask four students who turn out to be "political conservatives" if they feel particular political views are being taught. They laugh and nod their heads affirmatively as one student explains:

> In some classes it doesn't matter, like science or engineering. In some classes it does matter, like Latin American studies or Political Science. That's where the really liberal faculty are, but they're very open about what they believe and we're free to disagree and debate them. I like having them tell their side of the story so I can be prepared when I get out in the real world to defeat the kind of crazy ideas they have. So I'd say they have an ideology, but it's not doctrinaire or anything. It's just a typical liberal professor. But they are open to debate.

If we return to the assumptions of the critical approach we need to locate what both individuals say in terms of their underlying assumptions about knowledge. The professor comments that he is value neutral because he does not "care what they believe." The student feels that some classes are ideological—political science—and others are not—science and engineering. Further, the student implies that because faculty are "open to debate" ideology is relatively unimportant. From a critical perspective, by their comments both individuals are interpreting their experiences only on a surface level. They do not see how the structures of knowledge, the way courses are defined and structured, what is taught and what is absent, have strong ideological parameters. A critical perspective also denies knowledge can ever be neutral.

Yet Entrepreneurial's approach to learning is in line with its mission that allows for faculty to define their relationship to the institution in a wide variety of manners. The shared conviction of the participants about the mission is the belief that faculty have the freedom to teach whatever they want; the design and conduct of the curriculum reflects the diversity. Given that the faculty have the freedom of definition, the assumption is that the approaches to learning, and hence knowledge and the curriculum, is diversified and abstract. Unlike Women's College, Entrepreneurial's faculty do not debate what they should teach; instead they have more of a smorgasbord approach to learning. In some courses students are taught to think about their relationship to concepts such as sexism or racism, but in general the curriculum does not have an overarching concern with how knowledge is produced or why particular subjects are studied and others not. Instead, the curriculum fits Ravitch's assumption that what is taught "does not establish a canon of cultural knowledge," (1988, p. 129) but rather teaches students what is "common knowledge."

In part, Entrepreneurial's lack of success at curricular overhaul exemplifies the multiple interpretations the faculty bring to the institution, and the lack of specificity the mission provides. "I won't try anymore," states a music professor. "I put in my time trying to come up with a general education component, and nothing happened." Another individual comments, "We make attempts at change, some of them are very serious attempts, too. But we always fail." A dean concludes, "We have a very good curriculum. Students learn here. But I think most people have given up the expectation that we will reach consensus around a common core of knowledge." One other faculty member agrees with the dean, but sighs and says, "Yet deep down, I think many of us wish we could agree, wish we could find a common core."

"We have very strong disagreements about the nature of knowledge," concludes a long time professor. "At the least, we have reached a peaceful impasse where we agree to disagree." Curricular innovations rarely occur neither because the structure of the decision-making process is too cumbersome, nor because the institution lacks the necessary funds to carry out any changes, but because cadres of people operate from adumbrated institutional ideologies.

Because of the lack of an overarching definition confusion occurs for groups such as new faculty members about their role. Between my visits to the campus three faculty members are denied tenure; the rumor is that they spent too much time on their teaching, and not enough effort on research. A young faculty member comments, "I think we're two-faced. We talk about teaching. The search committee tells you how important teaching is, and as soon as you get here, the terms change. It's not fair." Another new professor comments, "It seems like we're spinning our wheels, wasting our time, when we should be talking about the curriculum. Isn't that what a teaching institution is about?"

The issue goes beyond accounting for whether teaching is more important than research. The tenure denials and the junior faculty's interpretation of them stand as a vivid illustration of how people learn about and redefine institutional ideology. As noted, at Entrepreneurial there is not a narrow definition of what someone can or cannot do. Instead, broad definitions exist; individuals operate within the context of the definitions and provide their own interpretations. When clear examples arrive such as the denial of tenure to someone, the individual reformulates an understanding of the institution. Curiously, the redefinition in this example does not so much promote what Entrepreneurial is, but what it is not. It is not that the institution is for research, but that it does not reward teaching.

In part, the conflict at Entrepreneurial University is not that disagreements arise over what a curriculum should look like, but that no one has a sense of a guiding vision of the institution other than in the broadest of terms. In general, the individualist logic of Entrepreneurial University allows faculty the freedom to construct their own interpretations of the curriculum. Examples such as a tenure denial provide singular interpretations for individuals; nevertheless, an overriding sense of institutional purpose is absent. With its "realist" epistemology, Entrepreneurial does carry out what it says it will do; the shared conviction of the institution is a dictum that one is free to do as he or she chooses. But it appears that individuals want more from the institution. The confusion and conflict arises when new faculty are unsure how to interpret the mission, or when older faculty feel disenfranchised.

IV. Discussion

Given these two case studies, how might we think about the competing voices of the faculty and their disagreements about the curriculum? As Clark asks, "Beyond weakening attachment to attenuating broad principles, is there anything left, any linkage that somehow connects the many parts to the whole?" (1987, p. 141). And given the "weakening attachment," is there any reason to believe that we should expect a curricular coherence in an institution?

I offer two tentative answers. First I will address how we might act in an organizational world that appears beset by loosely affiliated connections. I will then offer one idea about how we might work toward curricular coherence from a critical view.

1. Action in a Cultural Web

From the critical perspective taken here, "anchoring ideologies become a crucial element" (Clark, 1987, p. 144) in orchestrating the diverse interests of the various constituencies toward a common goal. I maintain that individuals in postsecondary organizations need to explicate institutional ideologies and, as Giroux states, "address the reconstruction of social imagination in the service of human freedom" (1988b, p. 120). That is, critical educators first need to accept that all organizations exist in a cultural network where ideologies operate; they then will struggle to construct their organizations based on a concern for social justice and empowerment.

By calling for the explication of "anchoring ideologies" I run the risk of painting organizations as if they are composed of Durkheimian collectivities. Clearly, I am not interested in how a critical or cultural approach to organizations can hold fragmented constituencies together merely "for the good of the order" (Rhoades, forthcoming, p. 29). However, as with others (Giroux, 1988b; McLaren, 1989; Foster, 1989), I am concerned with coming to terms with how those of us who work in educational organizations can be more engaged in promoting democracy and empowerment amongst our constituencies. I maintain that concentrating on the cultures and ideologies in which colleges and universities operate and delineating the ways in which they pose negative and positive moments for various constituencies will provide understandings that allow for the creation of democratic organizations.

As we have seen at Entrepreneurial, academe is a cultural network composed of contradictory groupings of faculty. The faculty often have only tenuous bonds either to one another, within the institution, or across institutions. Clearly, the professor who calls his colleagues "slimy little bastards" has found little in common with faculty in other disciplines at Entrepreneurial. In part, his disappointment and anger stem from the rigor he feels as a scientist, and what he perceives is the academic shallowness of his colleagues in the social sciences and humanities. He continues, "The humanities used to think kids should take whatever they want; now they want to redo the curriculum to meet their agenda. They've never listened to the scientists." The professor's sentiments are also found at Women's College among those who want to sustain the traditional liberal arts curriculum. We heard, for example, one professor speak disparagingly of those who had a "political agenda" as opposed to individuals like himself who were more disciplinary oriented.

However, the analysis of institutional differences should extend beyond merely summarizing the conflicts by political groupings—liberal vs. conservative, young vs. old, disciplinary vs. interdisciplinary, scientists vs. social scientists, and the like. I do not mean to imply that such groupings do not exist. Clearly, they do. As I have argued elsewhere (Author, 1989) culture arises in relation to a number of internal institutional characteristics as well as factors external to the institutional. The struggle is to be able to understand the characteristics and comprehend the cultural differences. Rather than try to ameliorate or ignore the differences, we must confront them and figure out ways to deal with them.

I am suggesting that organizational leaders need to create conditions that allow for an overt ideological commitment on the part of the organization's participants. What I hope I have shown in this paper is that whether or not participants actively commit themselves to a specific ideology, within all cultures ideology is at work. The participants may be conscious of ideology such as some of the faculty at Women's College, or they may be unaware of their ideological stance such as at Entrepreneurial. Nevertheless, to speak of organizational culture, and human action within it, is to speak of the ideologies to which the participants commit themselves. Necessarily, then, organizational participants need to unearth the inherent assumptions that operate in their missions and cultures and create an ongoing reflexive discourse that works toward achieving collective understandings. Such understandings, however, do not imply a Durkheiman unity. Instead, we need to work toward unearthing the positive and negative ideological moments at work in an organization and come to terms with how the various cultural forms give voice to some, and silence others.

My assumption is that when institutional discourse is about common and communal goals, rather than capturing markets or assuming a neutral view of knowledge, then the participants will move closer toward achieving collective understandings that are rooted in the cultures of the organization. I am proposing that as Michael Katz states, "bonds of reciprocal obligation . . . which makes the preservation of the community an object of desire and not merely a matter of prudence or a command of duty" (1987, p. 179) is of central importance as we approach the 21st century.

I do not believe, however, that organizational participants will be able to provide a definitive answer to the question of institutional ideology. The ideology of an institution is a map that undergoes constant reinterpretation due to the cultural web's reconfiguration. Yet simply because we cannot provide an absolute answer to what institutional ideology is, does not mean we should avoid the question. As Denneny states if the answer to ideology, "cannot be solved, (it) can be thought about; one can strive to reach not an answer but perhaps greater clarity about the issue, and in the process better locate oneself in the contemporary world" (1989, p. 16).

2. A Critical View of Curriculum in a Cultural Web

As opposed to rationalist conceptions of the curriculum, I have offered a critical view. A critical perspective disavows a pedagogy that imparts disembodied knowledge. Instead, a curriculum of difference engages students so that they comprehend how what they are learning relates to their own lives, their own experiences. In doing so, I am suggesting that institutional participants need to link their discussions about the curriculum with the ideology of not only what they are, but also what they want to become. This view maintains that vast possibilities exist for administrators, faculty, and students to redefine the nature of the learning experience beyond what "background knowledge" one must have to be considered well-educated. As McLaughlin states:

> Curriculum becomes more than a sequence of decontextualized apolitical skills. It is designed to help the learner connect academic concepts to a problemized world. As the classroom focus shifts from curriculum that is arbitrary to curriculum that scrutinizes problems immediate to the lives of the students, the teacher's role changes. The teacher becomes coach, an expert who can help solve problems. In the process, pedagogy becomes problem-solving, and curriculum becomes cultural politics (1988, p. 20).

By attempting such an approach we ought to be aware of the inherent premises about the curriculum that I am arguing for in this paper. In working from the assumption that a curriculum is a powerful process that helps structure how organizational participants think about and organize knowledge, I reject the idea that the primary purpose of a curriculum is to inculcate youth with the accumulated wisdom of society. Institutional curricula need to be investigated from the perspective of whose knowledge, history, language, and culture is under examination. Conversely, the organization's participants need to uncover those whose voices are not present in a curricular discourse and give life to them.

From this perspective, we cannot consider curricular models divorced from the contexts in which they are situated. Not only must we understand the organizations in which curricula operate, but we must also investigate the cultures that surround the curriculum. By way of excavating cultural artifacts such as the pedagogical practices used to convey knowledge or the decisional processes called upon to decide what counts for knowledge, we gain a fuller understanding of the curriculum's relationship to knowledge and power than if we tried to create decontextualized taxonomies of higher education's curriculum.

In conclusion, I offer some questions we might raise when we study or participate in curricular change in higher education. An investigation of the kind I am suggesting might revolve around questions such as:

- How do we define knowledge?

- What accounts for a knowledgeable individual?

- How has what we defined as knowledge changed over time?

- Whose interests have been advanced by these forms of knowledge?

- Whose interests have been superceded or ignored by such forms?

- How do we transmit knowledge?

- What is the method used to determine what counts for knowledge?

- Who controls the decision-making?

- Who participates and who does not in curricular decisions?

Clearly, these kinds of questions will unearth different answers than many of the current questions in vogue in the higher education community concerning assessment, quality, and excellence. I am suggesting, then, an alternative approach to the study of the curriculum in higher education that utilizes critical theory in the interest of creating educational communities based on notions of democracy and social justice.

References

Bennett, J. B. (1983). *Managing the Academic Department, Cases and Notes*. New York, NY: Ace/Macmillan.

Berger, P. (1963). *Invitation to Sociology*. Garden City, NJ: Longman.

Bergquist, W. (1977). "Eight Curricular Models." In A. Chickering, et al. (Eds.), *Developing the College Curriculum*. Washington, DC: Council for the Advancement of Small Colleges.

Chickering, A., Halliburton, D.; Bergquist, W., & Lindquist, J. (1977). *Developing the College Curriculum: A Handbook for Faculty and Administrators*. Washington, DC: Council for the Advancement of Small Colleges.

Clark, B. (1987). *The Academic Life*. Princeton, NJ: The Carnegie Foundation for the Advancement of Teaching.

Denneny, M. (1989). "Chasing the Crossover Audience." *Out/look*, 1(4), 16–21.

Dressel, P. (1971). *College and University Curriculum*. Berkeley, CA: McCutchan.

Fester, W. (1989). "Toward a Critical Practice of Leadership." In J. Smythe (Ed.), *Critical Perspectives on Educational Leadership*. New York, NY: Falmer Press.

Geertz, C. (1973). *The Interpretation of Cultures*. New York, NY: Basic Books.

Giroux, H. (1988a). *Teachers as Intellectuals*. Gradby, MA: Bergin & Garvey Publishers.

Giroux, H. (1988b). *Schooling and the Struggle for Public Life*. Minneapolis, MN: University of Minnesota.

Giroux, H. (1983). *Theory and Resistance in Education: A Pedagogy for the Opposition*. South Hadley, MA: Bergin & Garvey Publishers.

Grumet, M. (1978). "Curriculum as Theater." *Curriculum Inquiry*, 8(1), 37–64.

Katz, M. B. (1987). *Reconstructing American Education*. Cambridge, MA: Harvard University Press.

Kuh, G., & Whitt, E. (1988). "Using the Cultural Lens to Understand Faculty Behavior." Paper Presented at the Annual Meeting of the American Educational Research Association, New Orleans, Louisiana.

Mayhew, L., & Ford, P. (1971). *Changing the Curriculum*. San Francisco, CA: Jossey-Bass Publishers.

McLaren, P. (1989). *Life in Schools*. White Plains, NY: Longman.

McLaren, P. (1986). *Schooling as a Ritual Performance*. London, England: Routledge.

McLaughlin, D. (1988). "Critical Theory and Literacy Program Development." *Journal of Navajo Education*, 6(1), 10–21.

Ravitch, D. (1968). "A Response to Michael Apple." *Teachers College Record*, 90(1), 128–130.

Rhoades, G. (forthcoming). "Academic Culture and Professional Mandate."

Simon, R. (1987). "Empowerment as a Pedagogy of Possibility." *Language Arts*, 64(4), 370–382.

Tierney, W. (1989a). *Curricular Landscapes, Democratic Vistas: Transformative Leadership in Higher Education*. New York, NY: Praeger.

Tierney, W. (1989b). "Academic Work and Institutional Culture: Constructing Knowledge." Submitted for publication.

Tierney, (1987). "Facts and Constructs: Defining Reality in Higher Education Organizations." *Review of Higher Education*, 11(1), 61–73.

Tucker, A, (1984). *Chairing the Academic Department: Leadership Among Peers.* New York, NY: ACE/ MacMillan.

Narrative, Experience and the Study of Curriculum

D. Jean Clandinin and F. Michael Connelly

The speed with which Schön's (1983, 1987) recent works penetrated the reference lists of teacher education writers has been remarkable. Partly, we can explain the phenomenon as resulting from Schön's work fitting among ongoing lines of inquiry into reflection, practice and their combination. There is another reason, less tangible and more a question of, to borrow a term from Eisner (1979), the educational imagination. We see the practices Schön describes as part of the folklore of teacher education, matters kept alive in staffroom discussion but often referred to negatively outside of schools as the 'telling of war stories' and as accounts of mere 'learning-by-doing'. These accounts are frequently seen by 'scientifically' minded teacher-educators as something to be cleansed from student and novice teachers' minds in an attempt to pave the way for more 'scholarly' norms of teaching. The remnants of these discredited practices remain in the Canadian (and, perhaps, American) imagination as the kind of education that was acceptable in the less scientific days of teacher education gone by. Schön's books, we like to think, gave modern value to these professional memories.

Schön, of course, does not use temporality, history and memory to make his case. Rather, his logic consists of a reasoned case against 'technical rationalism' designed to cleanse the novice professional mind, combined with the presentation of case evidence of good educational practice in the professions. But the explanation of why his rhetorical influence in education is all out of proportion to his argument's substance can be explained narratively. Schön makes it possible for many of us to tell the story of teacher education in a way that runs counter to the technical teacher education we are encouraged to sponsor, and study, and he makes it possible for the story to legitimate our professional memory of reflective practice.

What makes this retelling of the story possible is the sense of reductionism entailed in the idea of technical rationalism. The image of professional practice, held in professional memory and rejected in scholarly discourse, is the thing that has been reduced. A rich whole, for us the professional memory, has been reduced through technical rationalism to a formulated set of rules which "may then be written in a book" (Oakeshott, 1962) (or, we might add, embodied in a master professor or teacher) and taught (or copied through role modeling and education's version of 'coaching') to novices. Johnson (1987), in his recent book *The Body in the Mind*, wrote that "without imagination nothing in the world could be meaningful. Without imagination we could never make sense of our experience" (p. ix). The success of Schön's work, we believe, is precisely that it tapped the professional imagination and permitted a reconstruction of the idea of education. It is not only "that none of the theories of meaning and rationality dominant today offer any serious treatment of imagination" (Johnson, 1987, p. ix), it is also the case that imagination is mostly ignored in studies of education. For Johnson, the set of reasons which account for this state of affairs in philosophy is captured by the term 'objectivism' which he metaphorically defines as the "god's-eye-view about what the world really is like" (p. x). It is a view that implies that no matter what any particular person happens to believe about it, there is a correct and true view of the world. It is a depersonalized notion of truth and meaning. The god's-eye-view, say Oakeshott and Schön, has become, in studies of the practical, technical rationalism. Technical rationalism is:

> the assertion that what I have called 'practical knowledge' is not knowledge at all, the assertion that properly speaking there is no knowledge that is not technical knowledge. The rationalist holds that the only element of knowledge involved in human activity is technical knowledge and what I have called 'practical knowledge' is really only a sort of neoscience which would be negligible if it were not positively mischievous. A sovereignty of 'reason', for the Rationalist means the sovereignty of technique. The heart of the matter is the preoccupation of the Rationalist with certainty. (Oakeshott, 1962)

Johnson sees the way of reuniting what the god's-eye-view and technical rationalism have separated and reduced is by "putting the body back into the mind" (Johnson, 1987, p. xxxvi). A disembodied mind permits the certainty needed by technical rationalism. To put the body back into the mind is to wreck havoc with certainty. Emotion, value, felt experience with the world, memory and narrative explanations of one's past do not stand still in a way that allows for certainty.

The suspicion of experience is not the suspicion born of a scientific mind for, as Oakeshott (1962) shows, science, no less than art, is incapable of being reduced to technique and taught out of a book. Those who argue against the study of practice, and the imaginative and narratively generated diversity that goes with it, often define practice as the execution of skills and, ironically, they often argue that to discover and name the skills is to do science. But it is reductionism, and what Dewey (1938) called the "quest for certainty", that marks the technical rationalist and not the doing of science. The doing of science is compatible with narrative and the study of practice in all of its imaginative complexity.

Oakeshott remarks that "the rationalist has taken an ominous interest in education. He has a respect for 'brains', a great belief in training them, and is determined that cleverness shall be encouraged and shall receive its reward of power" (Oakeshott, 1962, p. 32). It is "ominous" because the technical rationalist "has no sense of the accumulation of experience, only of the readiness of experience when it is being converted into a formula: the past is significant to him only as an encumbrance" (Oakeshott, 1962, p. 2). A person with experience is considered, by the technical rationalist, to have "negative capability" (Oakeshott, 1962, p. 2). If the "tabula rasa has been defaced by the irrational scribblings of tradition-ridden ancestors" (Oakeshott, 1962, p. 5) and, one might add, by the experiences of life to date, then, says Oakeshott, the first educational task of the rationalist "must be to rub the slate clean" (Oakeshott, 1962, p. 5). The technical rationalist's interest in education is ominous not because it ignores experience but because experience is seen as a deterrent to the 'true' skilled education. In a line that might have been written by Dewey (1938) with respect to his idea of the reconstruction of experience as the foundation of education, Oakeshott writes that "as with every other sort of knowledge, learning a technique does not consist in getting rid of pure ignorance, but in reforming knowledge which is already there" (Oakeshott, 1962, p. 12). Schön picks up this theme in his work on professional education by legitimating our professional memory and making it possible to return to experience, not as a black mark on the mental slate, but as a resource for the education of professionals including teachers.

There is another story at work in the rescuing of a professional image of practice, experience and narrative. Schön and Oakeshott permit us to imagine a Johnson retelling of "the body in the mind", and, metaphorically, to return 'upward' to the whole from the technical rationalist's reduced world of skilled practice. There is another retelling of the story 'downward' to the whole from a paradigmatic sociopolitical analysis. Just as reductionism makes the whole into something lesser, sociological and political analysis can also make the whole lesser through the use of abstraction and formalism. The disputes between experientialist wholists and those promulgating formalistic lines of inquiry are no less dramatic, although far less widespread, than those between experiential wholists and technical rationalists. The latter disputes are more widely known throughout the educational literature partly because experiential wholists have imagined technical rationalists as the only, or at least the main, opponent of experience in the study and doing of education. But as the arguments in the curriculum literature between experientialists and formalists make clear, the study of practice, experience and narrative is equally mistrusted in formalism as it is in technical rationalism. Our own work on narrative (Connelly & Clandinin, 1988a, 1988b) has recently come under criticism from both sources, technical rationalism and formalism.

The formalists' argument has been supported from two quite different sources, the study of literature and the philosophy of science. In a discussion of the issues at work, Bernstein (1987) remarks that "it has become increasingly fashionable to speak of our time as a 'postera'— 'postmodernity', 'poststructuralist', 'postempericist', 'postwestern', and even 'postphilosophic'— but nobody seems to be able to properly characterize this 'postera'—and there is an inability and an anxiety in the naming of it" (Bernstein, 1987, pp. 516–517). This confusion of the theoretical mind is "a reflection of what's happening in our everyday lives where there is a spread of almost wild pluralism" (Bernstein, 1987, p. 517). "Wild pluralism" is another way of naming the relativism that troubles Booth (1986) in literary criticism and is an expression of what Popper called the "myth of the framework" (Bernstein, 1987, p. 56). It is a formalistic view; a view that things are never what they are but are, rather, what our framework or point of view or perspective or outlook makes of them. Further, since nothing is as it seems, the only thing worth noticing is the terms, the formal structures, by which things are perceived. One does not teach, one mindlessly reproduces a social structure; one does not have emotionally credited intentions, one has preset expectations; one does not have experiences that are one's own, one merely moves forward by contextual design. Formalists say that the facts of the case, the experience one claims to have, or the data collected by empiricist researchers, have little bearing on their claims. A person, they argue, can never see themselves as they are since they are always something else, specifically, they are whatever social structure, ideology or framework is at work in the inquiry. What we have called the whole (the practical, experience and narrative) is, accordingly, as suspect for the formalist as it is for the technical rationalist. The difference between the two is the place given experience. For the technical rationalist, experience is a black mark on the slate to be wiped clean; for the formalist, experience is something to be ignored. For the formalist, there is, in the end, no agency in experience but only in form. For the formalist, a person merely plays out the hegemonies of politics, culture, gender and framework.

Bernstein's task, it might be argued, is to revivify, in the modern age, Deweyan thought which might, as he says, "through communal critical inquiry" (Bernstein, 1987, p. 511), permit a drawing together of the meanings of both technical rationalism and formalism within a theory of experience. As Bernstein remarks "Dewey had a strong sense of both the historicity and the contextualism of all inquiry and experience" and was opposed to the pluralistic "myth of the framework" which "suggests that 'we are prisoners caught in the framework of our theories; our expectations; our past experience; our language'" (Bernstein, 1987, p. 511). 'Inquiry' into teacher education, in the Bernstein-Dewey view, is, at one and the same time, historical and contextual; likewise, the 'experience' of teacher education is at once historical (and therefore personal) and contextual. A person being educated is a person with an experiential history which a theory of experience neither wipes away nor ignores as irrelevant. A person being educated is all of these things at one and the same time. This is the task of the narrative study of schooling in which we and others are engaged. And because narrative is a way of talking about Dewey's reconstruction of experience or Oakeshott's "reforming knowledge which is already there" (Oakeshott, 1962, p. 12) it is considered ill-advised for study by the technical rationalist. Likewise, because narrative is a reconstruction of a person's experience in relation to others and to a social milieu, it is under suspicion as not representing the true context and the proper "postera" by formalists. With a wry sense of irony, we observe that technical rationalists and formalists are joined in common cause against the study of experience.

Schön's service to professional memory, therefore, reaches beyond his grasp. The practical imagination needed support not only from the losses of reductionism, that is, a loss of wholistic identity in technical rationalism, but also from the losses of the concrete and material, that is, in the excesses of contextualism and formalism.

By writing books which embody a concrete conception of the practical, Schön's reach exceeded his anti-reductionist grasp. Unwittingly, to reverse Johnson's epigram (1987), Schön 'put the mind back into the body'. The narrative study of experience brings body to mind and mind to body; it connects autobiography to action and an intentional future; it connects these to social history and direction; and it links the pluralistic extremes of formalism to the concreteness of specific actions.

Narrative thought, that is, how one goes about thinking narratively, has several possibilities. Traditional fields of inquiry offer paradigmatic narrative modes as, for example, in history, literature, biography, philosophy, psychotherapy and so forth. Ours is but one possibility within several and is in education (Baker & Greene, 1987; Enns-Connolly, 1985; Britzman, 1989; Bruner, 1986). Our own work, perhaps more prosaically 'practical' than most, is to rethink curriculum and teaching in terms of a narrative inquiry which draws on classroom observation and participant observation of the practical, along with the bringing forward of personal experience in the form of stories, interviews, rules, principles, images, and metaphors (Clandinin, 1986; Connelly & Clandinin, 1988a).

The Teacher as Curriculum Topic

In a Dewey (1938) inspired essay on forms of inquiry, Schwab (1962) showed how, in the social and physical sciences, the study of the whole vies for place amid downward (reductionistic) and upward (formalistic) modes of explanation. Our discussion of the study of experience is set forth in order to show where the study of experience fits within what Schwab called the "forms of principles for inquiry" (p. 186) in educational studies. Admittedly, the term 'experience' does not make a study wholistic. But 'experience' designates the principal phenomenon that marks the relevant whole, an individual person being educated. Narrative, which we have defined as "the making of meaning from personal experience via a process of reflection in which storytelling is the key element and in which metaphors and folk knowledge take their place" (Connelly & Clandinin, 1988b, p. 16), is our conception of the whole. Narrative is temporal, past, present and future, and, as in all storytelling, is a reconstruction of experience. It is a putting of 'the mind in the body, and 'the body in the mind'. The whole, for us, is the narrative that each person tells of herself/himself, or that is told through processes of inquiry. This is not the place to detail the quality of narrative or of a narrative except to say that, properly done, it countenances the full implications of what Johnson (1987) intended by putting the body in the mind and its reverse. In narrative inquiry, just as in reading any text, there are multiple possible narratives and/or narrative threads and the judgment of whether or not one is 'telling the truth' has to do with criteria such as adequacy, possibility, depth, and sense of integrity. There is no 'quest for certainty' in the writing of narrative and so there is a basic opposition in principle between the wholistic ends of narrative inquiry, the reductionistic ends of technical rationalist inquiry and the generalized and abstract ends of formalistic inquiry.

Our particular approach to curriculum requires that a further point be made before we bring forward illustrative case material. The so-called commonplaces are widely acknowledged as specifying the 'topics' of curriculum discourse. We know of no argument to deny the forceful legitimacy of subject matter, teacher, learner, and milieu as integral parts of an adequate discussion of curriculum. Some, such as Ben-Perétz (1986), would add to the list but none, to our knowledge, would subtract. Generally speaking, learner, subject matter and milieu are well represented in the literature. But in most of the literature, the teacher as a focus for curriculum discourse tends to be minimized and treated in derivative ways. At the risk of oversimplifying, many milieu curriculum arguments tend to treat the teacher as an unconscious reproducer of inequitable social structures; many subject matter arguments demand rationalistic disciplinary training of teachers; and learner based arguments tend to see the teacher as nurturer. In almost all such curriculum proposals 'teacher retraining' is tacked on to the more central topic. Our work puts the teacher in the forefront and constructs a teacher based curriculum argument. It is an argument which conceptually meshes a curriculum for teacher education with a curriculum for those taught.

Our overall argument is constructed on two assumptions, one of which we assert and the other one of which we shall both argue to and from. We assume that studies of school reform, and resistance to it, yield a view of teacher agency such that curriculum plans, whether of milieu, subject matter or learner, founder or prevail on the activities of the teacher. We assume that in the curricular event, it is teachers that reproduce or revolutionize social structures, communicate or reinterpret curriculum context, and cooperate with, or act in opposition to, the nature of their student charges. In short, we propose to entertain the consequences of adopting a teacher topic for curriculum discourse.

The assumption we propose to argue from, and with, might be defined as the assumption of experience and the uses of narrative. We want to rethink the possibilities and potential in Dewey's (1938) idea of experience. As we reflect on experience it is, to us, a remarkable anomaly that general and rhetorical writings on curriculum, textbooks and the like, make experience a key term; likewise, in our everyday discourse about education, the word experience (Deweyian or otherwise) is so common as to be what Schutz & Luckmann (1973) might call the 'unexamined ground of the natural world view of a curricularist'. Yet, when we turn to curriculum inquiry, especially that branch of curriculum inquiry that refers to teachers, it is as if experience is of little importance to education.

In the remainder of this paper, we bring these two sets of assumptions together. We show how a narratively understood curriculum for teacher education meshes with a curriculum for the teacher's students[1]. In our recent book (Connelly & Clandinin, 1988a), we wrote of this idea as 'the teacher's curriculum as a metaphor for the curriculum of the teacher's students'.

The Internship: Laboratory and Apprenticeship

Oakeshott (1962) argued against a technical-rationalist view that practical knowledge could be formulated as a set of rules, principles, directions and maxims that could be recorded in a book and taught to novices. On the contrary, he says, "it is a characteristic of practical knowledge that it is not susceptible to a formulation of this kind" (Oakeshott, 1962, p. 10). He argues that "practical knowledge can neither be taught nor learned, but only imparted and acquired. It exists only in practice", (Oakeshott, 1962, p. 11). Practical knowledge is learned through apprenticeship to a master. Undoubtedly, such an education has great advantages over 'the book' as an education in practice. But taken to its extreme in teacher education, apprenticeship to a master simply replaces the authority of the technical-rationalist's 'book' with the authority of the cooperating teacher.

The principal criticism of this form of apprenticeship in the education of teachers was advanced by Dewey (1938) in his distinction between the laboratory and apprenticeship in teacher education. For Dewey, the laboratory is an occasion for problem-formulation and solution which permits the novice teacher not only to absorb the norms of practice, as in apprenticeship, but also to think for him or herself, to be reflective and, therefore, to culture the seeds of reform. It is in the laboratory, combined with the best of apprenticeship, that practice is learned as a whole, experientially and with the possibility for reconstruction such that the bonds of biography and culture can be stretched and broken. The potential of the internship for these purposes is seen in the following case study work between Clandinin and an intern teacher, Marie[2], and her cooperating teacher, Ellen.

The Teacher/Participant

At the time field records were made, Marie was in her first year of teaching as part of an internship program. She completed a BEd After Degree in Early Childhood Education following a BA and most of an MA in English literature. Marie lived and was educated in different countries as her family was transferred from place to place. She worked in industry for a period of time and then returned to university to pursue teacher education. She was a student in a teacher education class Clandinin taught. She did her primary division student teaching in a class taught by a woman who did a great deal of classroom drama including choral reading, readers' theatre, improvisation and role playing. This is the student teaching experience about which Marie most often talks. She went back to work with this teacher as a volunteer whenever she had time during the two years of her teacher education program.

Marie's internship was in a small school situated in a upper middle class area in a large urban area. She was assigned to a class and a teacher in a new program which combined grade one and kindergarten students. The grade one students attended the program all day and the kindergarten children attended in the afternoon. The cooperating teacher had not taught grade one previously but had considerable teaching experience in kindergarten. Marie was selected for this internship position because she had particular strength in grade one as judged by her student teaching experience. The program was a 'model' program and was closely monitored by the school board.

Curriculum of Teacher Education

Marie was involved in the internship program in a teacher education setting which had some of the features of what we imagine might be contained in a reflective practicum for teacher education. She worked in a classroom with an experienced classroom teacher. As well, she participated in a collaborative way in a research project with Clandinin which contributed, through its methodology, to growth and change. She learned, for the first time on a full-time basis, how to teach by working in a classroom teaching position. It was an apprenticeship situation with the marks of an internship and a laboratory.

Marie's readiness to depart from the constraints of the apprenticeship is seen in the following set of field notes.

> Marie is in charge of the language arts program in the morning. She recounted one of the stories that she was telling where the students got quite excited. She said that she was glad that Ellen, the cooperating teacher, was not in the room for that. Ellen apparently likes to keep the room quite quiet. Marie likes to let the children get involved in the stories and dramatizations of the stories. . . . One of Marie's concerns is the nonintegrated nature of the day. The subjects are taught as different subject matter and this concerns Marie. She had earlier asked Ellen if they could do a theme on fairy tales. Ellen had said that she did not like themes. Marie sees this as one way of getting some integration into the program. (Notes to file, 11 September 1985)

Marie, of course, was not acting entirely on her own initiative in her readiness to break with Ellen's practices. Her preferences for stories and dramatizations are connected to her student teaching assignments with yet another teacher; with her experiences at the university in teacher education; and with her education in English literature. While it would be easy to say that, therefore, Marie was not thinking independently, her situation of different practices in an apprenticeship was, after all, the world of practice familiar to us all. Inevitably, we are called upon to thread our own practical way through an environment of competing, sometimes conflicting, actions of others. How Marie does this through the reconstruction of her own, and her students' narratives, is the story to be told in this set of field notes.

Literature, Drama and Narrative

Even the short excerpt from the field notes quoted above illustrates the wholistic, experiential concern of the novice teacher. Marie's concern for the language arts program, literature, storytelling and dramatization is held together in her thinking by narrative. She wanted the children to "get involved in the stories and dramatizations" not only, we imagine, because of the added meaning involvement brings to interpretation, but because it is a way to create a meaningful narrative thread in the children's daily program. Like many elementary school teachers, she was concerned at the fragmentation of a day organized according to school subjects. This concern is frequently cast as subject matter in opposition to children but, for Marie, the issue was essentially one of continuity and meaning for the children.

A Reconstruction of Marie's Knowledge

In the first set of field notes, Marie seemed to have little sense of doubt with the possible exception of her concern for the student noise generated by her curriculum. She appeared unworried that her ideas for the language arts program and the use of thematic material were not favoured by Ellen. Her confidence was not only connected to her earlier student teaching placement but also to her theoretical training on the use of thematic material. Her success with themes is illustrated in the following field note.

She said that she is having some trouble choosing themes. She said that she thought it would be easy to choose themes. She talked about one of the assignments last year in a course when they needed to choose themes for a year. She said she had no trouble at all doing that but now she was having trouble choosing themes within which she can provide meaningful learning. She talked about the work she is doing on the Halloween theme. She said she is surprised she is able to do what she is able to do with it. She said for the children in their community, Halloween is a big thing. She said that the children go out trick-or-treating with their parents in the immediate area and then the parents have a party at someone's home for groups of children. She said she has thought about this and sees that Halloween is a significant experience in these children's lives. She talked about being able to link the Halloween theme to ghosts and monsters and how these are the nameless fears of children. She thinks that perhaps that is why it has its power. She said that the children are writing about Halloween in their journals. (Notes to file, 21 October 1985)

Here, the sense of the problematic characteristic of Dewey's 'laboratory' is evident. At first, Marie was simply engaged in the problem of choosing themes but, on reflection, she realized that it was much more difficult for her to choose themes for the class than it was for her to choose themes in the university course. The heart of the issue, again, is narrative. How could she identify thematic material which allowed her curriculum to return children's experience to them in a different way and, hence, for them to tell their own stories in richer and more meaningful ways? A double, or 'parallel', narrative was at work, hers and her students'. As Marie began to rethink the idea of 'theme' in terms of her students' experience, rather than in terms of her own, she fastened on Halloween because of its importance to her students. On the one hand, she was retelling, for herself, the role of theme in teaching. But deeper than this, it was interesting to see that her reconstruction of the Halloween theme for the children was that Halloween permitted children to think through their 'nameless' fears and it was the dealing with these fears, and the power they have in the children's lives, that justified the theme for Marie.

Thus, she was beginning to see things that related to the children's experience, and she was led to different understandings than the one she had in her university class where she chose themes that appealed to her. Now she needed themes that permitted her to build on children's experiences. She found herself working on a Halloween theme which was very much a part of the community and family experience for the children and she was surprised she found something of importance in Halloween. She rethought not only the idea of 'theme' but the particular theme of Halloween in terms of fears and powers in children's lives. Halloween became an important part of the school curriculum as she thought about its use and as the children wrote about it in their journals. The second narrative reconstruction was the children's own.

'Transformers' and Reconstruction

Marie's concern for reconstruction in the children's lives as the focus of her curriculum was seen by contrasting Halloween with the children's 'transformer' toys. Her concern for the transformer toys was evident in the following field records.

She then went back to talking about the blocks. (Marie here is referring to the building block center where children build with large construction blocks objects large enough within which to play). She asked how much she could impose on the children. She asked if she could tell them what to build. She told me that the children had been playing for several days with their transformers. (These are a particular kind of plaything, parts of which can be moved and the toy is then 'transformed' into a totally different play thing. For example, a dinosaur could be 'transformed' into the shape of a car by changing some of the parts. There is also a daily cartoon television show about transformers that plays on a local station and that many of the children watch). She said that it was all right dramatic play but it was not as good and not as constructive as when they had played with Goldilocks and the Three Bears. (They had earlier done some work with that story.) She had suggested that they build a cottage for the three bears. She said she supposed even then that she had been interfering in their play. I used the word extend their play. They had talked about what they needed to have a cottage and the children had gone ahead and made the cottage. She had said they had put a roof on it and everything . . . Apparently, the children, for the first time, had put on a play. They had started to do it with trick or treating around Halloween and Marie had asked them how they were going to end it. They had gone off to work on it and the way they ended was that they came home and ate the candy and got a stomach ache. They wanted to present it to the parents. Now they wanted to do lots more plays. Several more children were asking to be involved. She wants to take the idea of Little Red Riding Hood and get the parents' help in making tapes and so on. (Notes to file, 3 October, 1985)

In the above field note segment, we saw Marie raising questions about the use of the block center and how it fits with children's experience. Marie's focus on children's literature was apparent but she now wondered about children's experience with dramatization and the way it connected with the experience of building props for the dramatizations which she saw happening at the block center. Through the work with the three bears' cottage, the children understood they could create plays of the stories. They began to use their own experiences of Halloween to write a play. It was their experience that became the subject matter for the play.

Essentially, then, Marie rejected the transformer toys, and their television counterparts, in favour of something more thematically connected with the children's lives, Halloween. But she recognized a dilemma since the children were also interested in the transformers. The dilemma was illustrated in the following field

She again expressed concern about the block play. She said that she is not sure how different it is for the children to be replaying the television experiences in the block center or whether she imposes it. She sees that the culture, via television, imposes it one way and she imposes it the other. She said that she finds the play doesn't go anywhere for some of the students. She talked about the "transformer" stations and she is not too interested. She helped them build a haunted house. She said that they talked about things like Poltergeist. She said that the children could make the walls shake and they had done a very good job of doing it. She said that the kindergarten children do it with the Grade 1 children and that is why the kindergarten children are able to do as much as they can. (Notes to file, 21 October 1985)

In the above notes, Marie continued to question her work and connected the Halloween experience to the dramatic block play. Again, she connected Halloween to larger supernatural events such as a poltergeist.

Marie sent them off to get started in the haunted house. She gave the other children their choice of centers and then they walked over and watched the students at the haunted house. They had built a haunted house with the large blocks. They had made a number of masks that were moved up and down. The walls moved which they said was the Poltergeist. They showed this for two or three minutes and the other students clapped. Then they went off to their centers and the children at the block center continued to work on their haunted house. (Notes to file, 22 October 1985)

From the field records, it was not at all clear how Marie resolved the dilemma at a conceptual level. But practically, it is clear that she believed there to be more narrative meaning contained in the Halloween dramatization than in the transformer toys and this was the practical route taken. We might well imagine that to the extent that Dewey's sense of the laboratory continued to pervade the internship Marie will come back to questions such as this just as she reconstructed her idea of a theme and of the particular theme, Halloween. But whether or not this eventually occurred, we see how Marie's own narrative of experience drove her partly to reflect upon and think out the curriculum for her students and to act out a curriculum partly in accordance with what she had thought out, and partly in accordance with the underlying narrative beliefs she had about experience, themes, integration and meaning for her children. Thus, Marie has reconstructed her idea of curriculum, and, therefore, in the humble way possible in the ongoing business of schooling, was able to break the bonds of her own university and apprenticeship experience. She had, in effect, broken away from social, theoretical and personal bonds in rethinking her ideas of curriculum. Meanwhile, the students reconstructed their curriculum by deliberately creating a play—a story—in which they were actors. Thus, they not only lived out the story of Halloween, but they saw themselves as participants in the story. It is in storying ourselves that it is possible to remake experience.

Educational Entailments

When we think of life as a story, we are given a measure, however modest, of control. We gain a measure of freedom from the prisons of biography and social form. This short vignette of Marie's classroom curriculum and Marie's teacher education curriculum exhibits the sense in which it is possible to imagine reform in the school curriculum through reform in the curriculum for teacher education. We see in microcosm the power of narrative and how it is both lived out unconsciously, and is deliberately imagined, thereby yielding reform and reconstruction in our lives. Neither the hegemonies of form nor the constraints of maxim and rule, nor even the bonds of autobiography, are safe from the reconstructions of narrative.

Acknowledgments

This work was supported by the Alberta Advisory Council on Educational Studies and the Social Sciences and Humanities Research Council of Canada.

Correspondence: D. Jean Clandinin, Department of Elementary Education, 551 Education South, University of Alberta, Edmonton, Canada T6G 2G5.

Notes

1. The illustrations for this paper are drawn from a two year narrative study by Clandinin with a beginning teacher.

2. Marie and Ellen are pseudonyms used to protect the anonymity of the two teachers.

References

Baker, A. & Greene, E. (1987) *Storytelling. Art and Technique* (New York, R. R. Bowker Co.).

Ben-Perétz, M. (1986) Time: the fifth commonplace in curriculum deliberations, paper presented at the *Annual Meeting of the American Educational Research Association*, San Francisco, April.

Bernstein, R. (1987) The varieties of pluralism, *American Journal of Education*, 95, pp. 509–525.

Booth, W. C. (1986) Pluralism in the classroom, *Critical Inquiry*, 12, pp. 468–479.

Britzman, D. (1989) Who has the floor? Curriculum, teaching and the English student teacher's struggle for voice, *Curriculum Inquiry*, 19, pp. 142–162.

Bruner, J. (1986) *Actual Minds, Possible Worlds* (Cambridge, MA, Harvard University Press).

Clandinin, J. (1986) *Classroom Practice: teacher images in action* (London, Falmer Press).

Connolly, F. Michael and Clandinin, D. Jean (1988a) *Teachers as Curriculum Planners: Narratives of Experience* (New York, Teachers' College Press).

Connelly, F. Michael and Clandinin, D. Jean (1988b) Narrative meaning: focus on teacher education, *Elements*, 19(2), pp. 15–18.

Dewey, J. (1938) *Logic: the theory of inquiry* (New York, Henry Holt & Co.); *Experience and Education* (New York, Collier).

Eisner, E. W. (1979) *The Educational Imagination: on the design and evaluation of school programs* (New York, Macmillan).

Enns-Connolly, E. (1985) *Translation as interpretive act: a narrative study of translation in university-level foreign language teaching*, unpublished doctoral dissertation, University of Toronto.

Johnson, M. (1987) *The Body in the Mind. The Bodily Basis of Meaning, Imagination and Reason* (Chicago, IL, University of Chicago Press).

Oakeshott, M. (1962) *Rationalism in Politics and Other Essays* (London, Methuen).

Schön, D. A. (1983) *The Reflective Practitioner: how professionals think in action* (New York, Basic Books).

Schön, D. A. (1987) *Educating the Reflective Practitioner* (London, Jossey-Bass).

Schwab, J. J. (1962) The teaching of science as inquiry, in: J. J. Schwab & P. Brandwein (Eds) *The Teaching of Science* (Cambridge, MA, Harvard University Press).

Schutz, A. and Luckmann, T. (1973) *The Structures of the Life world* (Evanston, IL, Northwestern University Press).

Curriculum Possibilities in a "Post"-Future

William E. Doll, Jr.

The art born as the echo of God's laughter [has] created the fascinating imaginative realm where no one owns the truth and everyone has the right to be understood.[1]

It is necessary to rethink the world not in terms of its laws and its regularities, but rather in terms of perturbations and turbulences, in order to bring out its multiple forms, uneven structures, and fluctuating organization.[2]

The great end of education is to discipline rather than to furnish the mind; to train it to the use of its own powers, rather than to fill it with the accumulations of others.[3]

The third statement above has been known in the curriculum field for so many decades it has turned into a cliché. In fact, it has become a shibboleth for progressive educators. Paradoxically, I suspect it may have its origins in Yale president Jeremiah Day's spirited defense of his university's Classical curriculum in the late 1820s.[4] But whatever its origins, the statement assumes the "mind" to be a *thing* (a vessel to be filled) or an *organ* (a muscle to be trained) or a *living being* (a creature with powers to be disciplined). All three of these metaphors have played a role in American thought on curriculum. The Progressive movement, particularly from the 1930s through the 1960s, encompassed each of these trends, as well as the *laissez-faire* approach for which it may be best known—leave the child alone and ability, like a sunflower, will burst forth. The view of mind expressed in these metaphors—oddly both anthropocentric and mechanical—had neither strong intellectual foundations nor a record of practical achievements.[5] I believe it is a view we need to replace, possibly with Dewey's or Whitehead's or Bruner's version of mind as an active, self-organizing, self-abstracting process, a process to which we give the label "mind."[6]

But dealing with mind as anything other than a machine (brain) or an anthropocentric metaphor (vital force) has been almost impossible. The "thingness" of mind, a residue from Descartes' mind body split, stubbornly persists. As a result, we have considered curriculum only in its "thing-ness" sense, only in its noun form (a racecourse to be traversed), and not in its infinitive verb form (*currere*—to run, especially the course). In the latter, the emphasis is on the activity of running or, metaphorically, on the activity of our making meaning from the course—our interpreting, or dialoguing with the course. This *currere* view makes mind "a verb" (to use Dewey's phrase: an active, meaning-seeking and meaning-making verb).[7] The implications of considering mind as a verb are just beginning to receive critical acceptance.[8] At issue is whether or not such acceptance will result in fundamental curricular change.

In the late 1960s, Joseph Schwab pronounced the curriculum field "moribund."[9] Two decades later, Donald Schön said the same thing but in different words, discussing the deadening effect of the "technico-rational" model.[10] The curriculum reform movements of the time, whether structural-Piagetian or behavioral-competence, did little to encourage educators to disagree with

Schwab or to disown Shön. Curriculum remained bereft, without theoretical or practical guidance. Students, teachers, administrators, parents—all evidenced a malaise that is still apparent.

We are now in the midst of a budding new movement, characterized by Schön's "reflective practitioner."[11] Will this be but another passing fad, another in the list of 20th-century educational "reforms"—which themselves inevitably end up being reformed? Or will it, combined with such movements as site-based management, school choice, the decentralization of school control, and a rising entrepreneurial spirit, lead to meaningful curriculum and school change, indeed, to school and curriculum redefinition? It is far too early to answer this question with any confidence; and certainly issues of student achievement, teacher "burn-out," and increasing societal demands on the school do not provide encouraging early indicators. Yet, as we prepare to move into a new century, a new millennium, I see encouraging signs.

The level of curriculum discourse has definitely improved over the past decades. As William Pinar says, curriculum has moved from "an exclusively practice-oriented field to a more theoretical, historical, and research-oriented" one.[12] The increase in quantity and quality of journals, articles, discussions, conversations, research studies, and doctorates of a theoretical nature has given the field an awareness of itself. However, this theoretical and historical awareness has not yet influenced school classrooms; there, curriculum is still very much practice-oriented, with little reflection on these practices. However, a rising groundswell of dissatisfaction—from corporations, parents, community groups, even teachers and administrators—questions how well these practices are working. In short, the time may be right for more fundamental change. Yale president Benno Schmidt's leaving his university post for the Edison Project can be seen in this light. In fact, as one reporter has said: "Mr. Schmidt's career choice reflects a clear judgment: Edison is the future, Yale is history."[13]

Fundamental changes certainly are prominent in a number of other fields as diverse as architecture and theology. In fact, we are currently immersed in a "post" era: post-Communist, post-national, post-industrial, post-patriarchal, post-structural. To cover all these "posts," I choose the overarching term "post-modern" and use the hyphen to indicate that the new era, while breaking with the past, does not negate that past. In fact, as Charles Jencks says, at the heart of post-modernism lies a "paradoxical dualism or double coding which its hybrid name entails: the continuation of Modernism and its transcendence."[14] Thus, the movement is Janus-faced, looking both backward and forward, to the past and to the future. This double or dual coding gives post-modernism its paradoxical and startling power—to honor the past and yet to laugh at it (to ensure that we do not get caught in the hyperbole and hypocrisy such honoring brings); to build for the future and yet to doubt whether such a future will emerge. This is a worldview wherein traditional categories, such as order and disorder, are not diametrically opposed or separated but are entwined, each within the other, each reinforcing and sustaining the other.

Our present curriculum frames those of the Tyler/Taylor rationale, of competency based instruction of Madeline Hunter's "seven steps"—are not constructed to use and welcome paradox and eclectism, indeterminacy, self organization, or satire and play. Yet these qualities inhere in a "post" worldview and define a post-modern perspective—to the degree such a perspective can be defined. To study post-modernism (or any of the other "posts") for curricular implications means to question much of what we have heretofore considered natural or normal. Such *fundamental* questioning, of course, is frightening; we worry about the collapse of stability, of the order we have known, of the values we hold dear. But as post-modern complexity theory shows, the collapse of simple, linear, preset order does not necessarily lead to *disruptive* chaos. Rather, a new kind of order—that labeled "chaotic order"—often emerges.[15] Although the phrase seems oxymoronic, it is not; it refers to the subtle, complex, nonlinear order we now see permeating the universe—an order the Hubble telescope is helping us "see"[16] By modernist standards this order does seem quirky and chaotic, really no order at all; but in a post-modern frame the complexity of chaotic order is both natural and beautiful as shown in those magnificent computer designs of recursive spirals, or in the more natural designs of clouds forming, surf breaking, and smoke curling.[17]

Obviously, this is not the simple, symmetrical, Euclidean order we consider "natural". Instead we find complexity, chaos, and contingency built into this new order. Its complexity appears far more pervasive in nature than do the simple and symmetrical Euclidean shapes modernists favored. The study of this nonlinear, or fractal, order began only in the mid 1970s. Understanding its paradoxical qualities is one of the challenges for post-modernism.

Post-modernism is still too young to define itself, and indeed, it may never, or never want to, do so.[18] For to define the word in our usual, modernist sense of definition is to go against the very spirit of post-modernism; that is, definitions limit and close rather than generate and open. Those working on such a definition or nondefinition range from nihilistic deconstructivists to process theologians.[19] But the issues of paradox, indeterminacy, self-organization, and play, seem appropriate concepts on which to base a working frame for post-modernism. We might begin by looking at each of these four qualities in terms of their curricular implications. Then we might attempt to find criteria for judging a "good" post-modern curriculum. These criteria could possibly serve a post-modern curriculum as Ralph Tyler's criteria served the modernist curricula.

Let us begin with indeterminacy, that bugaboo of all modernists theories. As Dewey pointed out in *The Quest for Certainty*, Western philosophy has sought certainty—through philosophy and mathematics—since the time of Plato.[20] The Forms were permanent and determinative—worldly objects being but imperfect copies of the Forms. Descartes in the 17th century thought he had found *the method* "for rightly conducting reason for seeking truth."[21] Newton, three-quarters of a century later, was believed to have discovered *the principle* (gravity) that held the universe together. Laplace, writing after Newton, called him "the most fortunate" of men who ever lived "inasmuch as there is but one universe, and it can therefore happen to put one man in the world's history to be the interpreter of its laws."[22] Further, Laplace argued, it is possible to determine the course of all future planetary movements by knowing *with precision* the present planetary positions. All one needs to do after the data are collected is "the sums."[23] This procedure has been analogized into a linear, cause-effect relationship, so that we now define the "scientific" approach (that most favored by education and the social sciences) as the collection of data and the placing of that data into a set formula. This mathematical modeling method underlies much of economic forecasting, psychometrics, and numerous doctoral dissertations. It is pervasive enough to be considered a semiparadigm for our "rightly conducting reason for seeking truth."

In the early 1900s, Werner Heisenberg became bothered by the indeterminacy he found in his study of the subatomic world. Movement in this world did not fit the patterns of linear order science had been following since Newton and Laplace. He and Bohr spent long hours arguing with Einstein over the nature and role of indeterminacy in the universe—Einstein always holding that "God does not throw dice." Indeed probability theory was developed to help tame the randomness Heisenberg and others found in nature. Still, doubts lingered, and today with the advent of complexity/chaos theory we not only question God's gender but also have doubts as to whether the dice may not be loaded. Indeterminacy, nonlinearity, and a skewed (or "ordered") randomness seem to be woven into the fabric of the universe. The complexity of this fabric is stunningly beautiful, as the computer-generated recursions show; but understanding this fabric requires us to deal with such post-modern paradoxes as "ordered randomness" and "chaotic order."[24]

In curriculum matters, the metaphysical commitment to certainty has encouraged us to structure the curriculum *only* in sequential linear terms (a step-by-step, explanation-first process) and to consider learning *only* as a direct result of teaching.[25] Such sequential ordering and cause-effect epistemology (based on a metaphysical commitment to determinism and certainty) underlie Tyler's modernist rationale for a well-designed curriculum. As Dewey pointed out well before Tyler wrote his rationale, such a view assumes the learner to be a receiver, not a creator, of knowledge, a spectator who in the most creative of moments can only discover that which already is. A curriculum based on these assumptions emphasizes transmission, linearity, and measurement rather than transformation, nonlinearity, and creation.

As might be expected, post-modernism sees indeterminacy in a positive, not a negative, manner. Once one moves beyond seeking certainty, it is possible to see indeterminacy as that which encourages, indeed entices, us to participate in the generation of meaning. The openness of indeterminacy invites us to dialogue with the situation at hand, to communicate with it and with each other. In Wolfgang Iser's phrasing, indeterminacy (especially in a text) "allows a spectrum of actualizations," actualizations that arise from our dialogue, our creative participation.[26] In this manner we, as makers, initiate *"performances" of meaning*. Such performance, of course, is always influenced by text and teacher (their role is to influence in a dialogical way), but the meaning is ours. Thus, meaning is made, not received. The making of meaning requires, but is not guaranteed by, an open, indeterminate system.

Indeterminacy becomes a meaningful concept only to the degree self-organization is operable. Without self-organization, indeterminacy does not take on the character of "primal soup" from which order arises; rather, indeterminacy remains nebulous or loosely and poorly formed. For indeterminacy to have its own sense of power and being, to be a rich and generative *dissipative structure*, in Prigogine's use of this term, self-organization must be real and operable.[27] Self-organization, with its spontaneous creation of new forms, has been around for as long as life has existed. As Jean Piaget says, auto- or self-regulation is the *essence of life itself*.[28] It is the primary hypothesis of his theory of cognitive development.

Biological evolution, of course raises the issue of self-organization—new species emerging from the competition for survival. But the Darwinian view has paid no attention to purposiveness; the emergent species arise randomly, not willfully. It is in Piaget's and Prigogine's writings that we find this sense of *looser teleology* (one in which intentionality is entwined with chance).

Piaget saw humans developing cognitive structures through interaction with the environment. However, with his set stages and fixed sequences there is little if any role for chance. A strong sense of structuralism overlaps Piaget's constructivism. On the other hand, Prigogine's "dialogue with nature" is a good deal more open-ended. The future is unpredictable, dependent on the eventful interactions that have preceded any moment in time. But both Prigogine and Piaget agree that time does have "an arrow"; the past cannot be rerun. In this arrow of time, new ideas, forms, species arise from the interaction between and among events. In this way chance and purpose become codeterminers.

In terms of curriculum, this means there needs to be *just enough* perturbation, disturbance, disequilibrium (Piaget), or dissipation (Prigogine) built in so that self-organization will be stimulated. The teacher's role is to present the curriculum in just enough of a challenging, controversial, "chaotic" manner so that self-organization will be encouraged. Such a role for curriculum, for the teacher—one wherein the teacher becomes "readily confrontable" by the students—is quite different from what we have developed using the Tyler rationale.[29] The Tyler rationale has led us to emphasize precisely defined, well-articulated, preset goals and a delivery system that matches the clarity of the goal statements. Dissipation and disequilibrium are neither desirable nor necessary. In fact, in the operable curriculum model developed between the 1950s and 1990s evidenced in the behavioral objectives movements, competency-based assessment, and Madeline Hunter's set steps—the student has been looked upon more as a receiver of information than as a constructor or generator of meaning. The issues John Dewey wrestled with, challenged, and fought for in the early decades of this century—centering around the difference between the student as a spectator to others' knowledge or as a personal creator of meaning—remain in this last decade of the century. Educationally, we are mired in modernism.

Playfulness and paradox—indeed, playing with paradox—may present ways of getting out of this bog, of breathing new life into our moribund curriculum. Paradox is very much part of our "post" world; it lies at the heart of quantum reality—a reality that accepts that electrons may be considered either as oscillating waves or particle pellets. The choice is ours. Hence we may legitimately say that electrons are both waves and particles. To explain reality in such contrary and contradictory terms is a paradox that modernist thought cannot fathom.

Some post-structuralists, such as Gilles Deleuze, take paradox beyond the micro world of science into the existentialness of being, to the concept of self.[30] Descartes, one of modernism's fathers, held that self was inherently contained within, and yet existed apart from, the body. He thought self to be the "I" of consciousness, the "I" that defines our being—physical and intellectual. His famous phrase "cogito ergo sum" means "thinking accounts for being." Separated from the body yet paradoxically located in the body, "mind" for Descartes was the essence of conscious being, the "I-ness" or subjectivity that defines human being.[31] This consciousness manifests itself in the human's ability to plan, create purpose, have thoughts. Yet, paradoxically again, these purposes, plans, thoughts, were themselves believed to "mirror" an outer (and static) reality.

Thus, human consciousness was basically to form itself into a receptive mode in which its "mirroring" of the outer reality would be clear, precise, accurate.[32] This is why Descartes worked so hard on founding *the method* "for rightly conducting reason for seeking truth." The method is basically copying, and its pedagogical power has been felt from his day to ours.

Foucault and other post-structuralists argue there is no fixed self, that we need to "erase" such a concept from our discourse.[33] An "I" isolated from "others" and subjects separated from objects render both the I and the subjects meaningless. *Self* is understood only in relation to *other*. Both are needed, each becomes the *sine qua non* of the other. Self without an other is not a self. The same can be said about subject and object; neither exists without the other, neither exists independently and in isolation.

A pedagogy based on Cartesian-modernist separation is either a copy-model pedagogy or, at best, a discovery pedagogy. In the former, curriculum is the fixed truths and procedures to be passed on generation to generation, person to person. It is a transmitted curriculum. The teacher-student separation is simple: the teacher teaches, the learner learns. A discovery pedagogy provides more flexibility and openness; the object is not "to furnish the mind" but "to train it to the use of its own powers." However, the separation between subject and object is still presumed: the discovered is that which is already there. One has gone beyond transmission to a limited form of transformation; the subject undergoes limited, controlled, and predictable change, but the external reality remains dominant, unchanged, and controlling.

A pedagogy based on paradox, a paradoxical pedagogy as it were, shifts the focus from this subject-object split to their integration, conjunction, union. The paradox of subject-object, or teacher-learner, or text-reader is that neither is the other, yet neither is without the other. Each needs the other for its own sense of being. This shifts the focus of curriculum from receiving or developing to *dialoguing, negotiating, interacting*. These are not words or concepts found in either the Tyler rationale or in modernist curriculum thought. They imply (and use) indeterminacy, openness, self-organization. They are the words of a transformative curriculum, a *currere*-oriented curriculum, one focusing not on the external attributes of the racecourse but on the process of traversing the course, of negotiating with self, others, and the course.

Play, is a good medium for developing skills in dialoguing, negotiating, interacting. A transformative curriculum looks to and uses play for the development of these skills. Pre-modern, tribal, and medieval cultures honored play through the roles of the shaman, the fool, the jester. Shakespeare used word play extensively in his comedies, even in his tragedies and histories. However, except in kindergarten—with its origins in German romanticism—play has not been an integral or accepted part of the academic curriculum. As David Hamilton points out, our current, modernist curriculum is well-grounded in Calvinist theology.[34] A strong separation divides work and play. Work is the route to eternal salvation; play (the "devil's work") leads to idleness and damnation.[35]

Play, however, especially intellectual play, has a great deal to offer a post-modern curriculum. Play deals not with the present and foundational, but with the absent and the possible. Its very nature invites dialogue, interpretation, interaction. Its free-following form encourages participation. All of these activities are essential to meaning making; they are key elements in what Bruner calls the "narrative mode" of learning.[36] Whereas the analytic mode (which we use in lectures, textbooks, recitations) is transmittive and preset, the narrative mode is transformative and open-ended. Needless to say, the former mode has a set methodology—as evidenced in most curriculum methods courses. The latter mode asks the teacher and students to be playful—with the material and with each other. This mode (metaphorical rather than logical) also places a great burden on the teacher: to help students develop their play with and metaphoric use of ideas, forms, procedures, and patterns to create productive happenings. This is not an easy task.

Another advantage of play, once one is attuned to its nature, is that its freedom allows challenge and exploration in a nonhostile and nonthreatening way. Rap music at its best does this. At its worst, rap crosses the thin, invisible, imaginary line between productive and destructive happenings. Play, like its counterpart chaos, if it is to develop into creativity, needs a sense of boundary or attraction to an "event" (to use a Whitehead term).[37] Such, of course, will not always happen, and the teacher's role in helping such creativity occur is tenuous and delicate.

Nondirection leaves all to chance—a point that bothered Piaget immensely; over direction robs the event of its spontaneity and uniqueness, resulting in mediocrity—a point that bothered Piaget just as much. Creative development occurs in the tension between chance and direction. This tension, which Kuhn calls "essential," must always be maintained.[38]

The Four R's

The Tyler rationale, with its emphasis on closure—choosing "purposes," "experiences," "methods of organization," and then evaluating to "determine whether these purposes [experiences, methods] are being attained"—is so much a product of modernist thinking that it is hardly appropriate to use it as a set of criteria for a post-modern curriculum.[39] A new educational mindset and curriculum frame require a new set of criteria to determine what constitutes a good or quality post-modern curriculum. Toward this end, I propose using the R's of *richness*, *recursion*, *relations*, and *rigor* as criteria. As the three R's of "reading, 'riting, and 'rithmetic" were foundational to late 19th- and early 20th-century curricula, I propose the four R's as potentially foundational for the last years of this century and the early ones of the next.

Richness

The paramount feature of a post-modern curriculum is openness—defined here as generativity, multiple layers of interpretation, and varied realms of meaning. To achieve openness, the curriculum needs to be *rich*; that is, it needs to be filled with enough ambiguity, challenge, perturbation to invite the learner to enter into dialogue with the curriculum and with those working in the curriculum. Meaning making occurs through dialogue and interaction. Thus, the curriculum needs to be *rich* enough in depth and breadth to encourage meaning making. Both the curriculum and the teacher must be challenging and open enough to invite and encourage participation.

Here is a pedagogic creed I try to follow in dialoguing with students:

> In a reflective relationship between teacher and student, the teacher does not ask the student to accept the teacher's authority; rather, the teacher asks the student *to suspend disbelief in that authority*, to join with the teacher in inquiry, into that which the student is experiencing. The teacher agrees to help the student understand the meaning of the advice given, to be readily confrontable by the student, and to work with the student in reflecting on the tacit understanding each has.[40]

The sort of dialogue advocated here can occur best when the curriculum is rich with problems, perturbations, possibilities.

While richness in the sense of having multiple layers of interpretation, meaning, and problematics does produce an exciting curriculum, it also produces one akin to the current view of the nature of the world in which we live. Descartes' set method for "rightly conducting reason for seeking truth"—a foundation of positivist philosophy—was based on the assumption that the universe we live in (indeed, reality itself) is stable, consonant, and simply ordered. As Newton was fond of saying: "Nature is comfortable to Herself and simple."[41] It is this metaphysical assumption, of course, that encouraged Newton to look for the same order in the movement of the planets (the spheres) that existed in apples falling to the ground. Hence was born the concept of gravity. Today order is also posited, but not Newton's simple uniform order. Now order is seen as complex, self-generative, "lumpy," and inherently unstable. Quantum physics shows us a universe (and reality) born quirky and "quarky." Instead of simple order, we posit complex, chaotic order. From the richness of this milieu comes an order which, as we engage it, transforms both ourselves and itself. This is the nature of our creative universe as we now see it.[42]

A creative curriculum, like a creative universe, emerges through dialogue. The product is not preset but emerges through the process—a favorite point of Dewey's. This is why Rorty advocates we "keep the conversation going."[43] To challenge, then, is to develop a curriculum *rich* enough to keep conversation "going and going and going and going."

Recursion

Recursion means *to return*. It is from the Latin *recurrere* (to run back). The connection with curriculum as *currere* is obvious. A recursive curriculum emphasizes the notion of returning—to look at itself, yet again, in a new light, for the first time. This metaphorical playing happens more easily in the humanities than in the sciences. In mathematics, recursion is synonymous with mathematical iteration—working an equation in a nonlinear way so that the solution y (in an x-y formula) is fed back into the equation as a new x. This is done over and over, each new solution (y) becoming input (x) for the next repetition of the equation. It is these recursions/iterations that make up the marvelous fractal computer graphics one sees in chaos mathematics, the Mandelbrot and Julia sets.

In the humanities, however, recursion has a broader meaning. Here, it refers to the act of a mind or self "looping back," "turning around," or reflecting on itself, and in this way actually creating itself as a conscious self—the highest expression of human awareness. In education, recursion means displaying, to self and others, "what one has thought and then turning around on it and reconsidering it."[44] Through this "turning around" or "reconsidering"—which is akin to Dewey's concept of reflection, a second looking—transformation, growth, development occur. A recursive curriculum, then, leaves room for students (or a class) to loop back on previous ideas, to run back or revisit what has gone before. Such a *nonlinear* approach to curriculum represents a definite departure from the *linear* lesson plans, course syllabi, and textbook constructions educators have worked with and accepted for so long. A recursive curriculum is dialogical; its development is open, dependent on the ongoing interaction among teachers, students, texts, cultures. The art of curriculum construction—no mean feat when these four elements are diverse—consists of coordinating and directing these forces. As with Dewey's concept of growth, this coordination and direction must be neither overemphasized nor underemphasized.

Relations

A linear curriculum has a definite beginning, middle, end. A nonlinear curriculum is more akin to a matrix, maybe even to the computer graphics of a Mandelbrot set. A matrix, sphere, or Mandelbrot blob has no beginning or ending, just an ever increasing middle, a middle filled with connections and interconnections. The heart of the curriculum process calls for adding continuously to these connections, making the overall system deeper, richer, darker. Characterizing curriculum in terms of "dark" systems may be an unfamiliar concept; but as more interconnections are made, the points where they meet become darker, richer, more ambiguous. Shakespeare's poetry has lived for centuries not because of its simplicity but because of the richness of its multiple interpretations. The Newtonian metaphysical idea of simplicity—nature comfortable and simple—is passé.

The Mandelbrot set appears mostly black, with luminescent colors at the fringes. The dark blob—itself almost symmetically ordered—represents an area where the equation generating the set is strong, powerful, "alive" with relations. On the fringes, filled with dynamic luminescence and all sorts of weird and fascinating shapes, the equations border on extinction, wandering off into nothingness. Paradoxically, the borders and fringes display the most visual, mathematical, and aesthetic excitement. Here is where the spirals and swirls for which the set is known occur. Here lie Prigogine's "far-from-equilibrium" situations, the most fragile, the most generative, the most transformative.

At the center of the set, the relations are rich with interpretations, but stable. The fringes reveal relations that are also among the most exciting, but that border on extinction. Transposing this metaphor into classroom teaching and curriculum suggests the teacher needs to help the students deal with the richness of multiple but stable interpretations as well as the excitement of tenuous and "far out" ones. Both types of interpretations exist. Without its fringes, the Mandelbrot set is nothing but a blob; but the fringes could not exist without the stability of the blob, the center and core of the set.

Just as richness applies to more than curriculum, to reality in a cosmological sense, so also do relations. In a cosmology such as that described by Whitehead, Prigogine, or process theology—all of which move away from considering Newton's "hard, massy, impenetrable particles" (atoms) as the ultimate essence of reality—*relations* become foundational or essential. Relations form the heart of these cosmologies. The same can be said of post-modernism or post-structuralism in general—*relations*, not things, become the prime focus. Relations, of course, are far more flexible than "impenetrable particles." Relations require interpretation and dialogue for the assessment of meaning; particles require precise measurement and definition. Such precise measurement and definition are not possible in a quantum world, as both Heisenberg and Gödel have shown. Therefore, a post-modern frame substitute relations for particles as its chief characteristic. The curriculum field, however, has yet to make such a shift. Our current concept envisions curriculum as a prearranged set of linear particles, not as a gathering or matrix of interrelated "occasions." Shifting from particles to relations helps us understand with greater depth Whitehead's statements: "Do not teach too many subjects," but "what you teach, teach thoroughly." "Let the main ideas which are introduced . . . be few and important, and let them be thrown into every combination possible."[45]

Rigor

In some ways *rigor* is the most important of the four R's. If richness most distinguishes a post-modern curriculum, then rigor is what makes richness rich. The problems, perturbations, and possibilities that constitute richness need to be ordered (albeit loosely) if they are to shed new and interesting light on a subject. Without such loose ordering, they become merely a jumbled collection of disconnected perturbations, useful to no one. Rigor molds these into a coherent and dynamic unity; rigor is the struggle to work through the problems, perturbations, and possibilities to achieve a sense of coherence and integration not evident (maybe not present) when the struggle began. Rigor enables coherence to emerge from disequilibrium, chaos, and confusing complexity.

The word *rigor* (from the Latin of the same spelling and *rigere* in the infinitive verb form) means stiffness, severity, strictness. *Rigor mortis* is the obvious and direct carryover from Latin to contemporary usage. In a methodological sense, to be rigorous is to be severe and strict in applying a procedure, with no loose, humanist, personal, subjective infringements. In the deductive sciences, this rigor leads to the closure that logic provides for our "rightly conducting reason"; in the empirical sciences, rigor reduces possible causes to *the one* influential cause. In the Tyler rationale, rigor produces the close (or high) correlation between the purposes intended and the result achieved; this is what educational evaluation is all about.

Moving into a hermeneutic frame or into the narrative or post-modern mode softens rigor's harshness and severity. In those modes rigor means not so much strict conformity to a preset procedure as the careful exploration of multiple possibilities and unstated assumptions. Here one looks deeply, critically, generatively, and even contrarily into the "matter at hand." (It is hard to leave the language of modernism, even to express post-modern thoughts.) One explores thoroughly that which interpretation and metaphor present. Rather than deny the role personalness and subjectivity play in interpretation, one uses personalness and subjectivity to help achieve better, deeper, more comprehensive understanding. If, as humans, we are makers of meaning and not merely discoverers or followers of others' meanings, then rigor in this hermeneutic and heuristic sense needs to be included as a criterion of good curriculum.

It should go without saying that the criteria presented here in the four R's are as far removed from the open and progressive movements as they are from the behavioral movements associated with the Tyler rationale.

Notes

1. Milan Kundera, *The Art of the Novel*, trans. Linda Asher (New York: Grove Press, 1988), p. 164.

2. Josué Harai and David Bell, "Introduction: Journal à Plusieurs Voies," in *Michel Serres' Hermes*, ed. Josué Harai and David Bell (Baltimore, MD: Johns Hopkins University Press, 1983), p. xxvii.

3. Anonymous.

4. Herbert M. Kliebard, *Forging the American Curriculum: Essays in Curriculum History and Theory* (New York: Routledge, 1992), pp. 6–11.

5. Richard Rorty, *Philosophy and the Mirror of Nature* (Princeton, NJ: Princeton University Press, 1980).

6. David Olson, "The Mind According to Bruner," *Educational Researcher* 21 (May 1992): 29–31.

7. John Dewey, *Art as Experience* (New York: Perigee Books, G. P. Putnam's Sons, 1980). Original work published in 1934.

8. Jerome Bruner, *Acts of Meaning* (Cambridge: Harvard University Press, 1990); William E. Doll, Jr., *A Postmodern Perspective on Curriculum* (New York: Teachers College Press, 1992).

9. Joseph Schwab, *Science, Curriculum, and Liberal Education: Selected Essays*, ed. Ian Westbury and Neil Wilkof (Chicago: University of Chicago Press, 1978), pp. 287–321.

10. Donald A. Schön, *The Reflective Practitioner: How Professionals Think in Action* (New York: Basic Books, 1983); Donald A. Schön, *Educating the Reflective Practitioner* (San Francisco; Jossey-Bass, Inc. 1987).

11. Donald A. Schön, *The Reflective Practitioner: How Professionals Think in Action* (New York: Basic Books, 1983); Donald A. Schön, *Educating the Reflective Practitioner* (San Francisco: Jossey-Bass, Inc. 1987); Donald A. Schön, *The Reflective Turn: Case Studies in and on Educational Practice* (New York: Teachers College Press, 1991); James G. Henderson, *Reflective Teaching: Becoming an Inquiring Educator* (New York: Macmillan, 1991); Tom Russell and Hugh Munby, eds., *Teachers and Teaching: From Classroom to Reflection* (London: Falmer Press, 1992).

12. William Pinar, ed., *Contemporary Curriculum Discourses* (Scottsdale, AZ: Gorsuch Scarisbrick, Publishers, 1988), p. 2.

13. "Bye, Bye, Eli," *Walls Street Journal*, May 27, 1992, p. A 14.

14. Charles Jencks, *What Is Postmodernism?* (New York: St. Martin's Press, 1987), p. 10.

15. Katherine Hayles, *Chaos and Order* (Chicago: University of Chicago Press, 1991).

16. Eric J. Chaisson, "Early Results from the Hubble Space Telescope," *Scientific American* 266 (June 1992): 44–51; Richard T. Fienberg, "COBE Confronts the Big Bang," *Sky and Telescope* 84 (July 1992): 34–36; Stephen P. Maran, "Hubble Illuminates the Universe," *Sky and Telescope* 83 (June 1992): 619–625. Obviously, there is nothing new in this "new order." The newness lies in our perceptions, both conceptual and visual.

17. Peter Garrison, "Glued to the Set," *Harvard Magazine* 91 (January–February 1989): 31.

18. Stephen E. Toulmin, *Return to Cosmology: Postmodern Science and the Theology of Nature* (Berkeley: University of California Press, 1982).

19. José G. Merquior, *From Prague to Paris: A Critique of Structuralist and Post-Structuralist Thought* (London: Verso, 1986); David R. Griffin, *The Reenchantment of Science: Postmodern Proposals* (Albany: State University of New York Press, 1988).

20. John Dewey, *The Quest for Certainty: A Study of the Relation of Knowledge and Action* (New York: G. P. Putnam, 1960). Original work published in 1929.

21. René Descartes, *Discourse on the Method*, trans. I. J. Lafleur (New York: The Liberal Arts Press, 1950). Original work published in 1637.

22. Edwin A. Burtt, *The Metaphysical Foundations of Modern Physical Science: A Historical and Critical Essay* (New York: Doubleday Anchor Books, 1955), p. 31. Original work published in 1932.

23. Ibid., p. 96.

24. John P. Briggs and David F. Peat, *Looking Glass Universe: The Emerging Science of Wholeness* (New York: Simon and Schuster, 1984); John P. Briggs and David F. Peat, *Turbulent Mirror* (New York: Harper and Row, 1989).

25. John Dewey, *The Quest for Certainty: A Study of the Relations of Knowledge and Action* (New York: G. P. Putnam, 1960), original work published in 1929; Edwin A. Burtt, *The Metaphysical Foundations of Modern Physical Science: A Historical and Critical Essay* (New York: Doubleday Anchor Books, 1955), original work published in 1932; Richard Rorty, *Philosophy and the Mirror of Nature* (Princeton, NJ: Princeton University Press, 1980).

26. Wolfgang Iser, *The Act of Reading* (Baltimore, MD: The Johns Hopkins University Press, 1978), p. 61.

27. Ilya Prigogine, *From Being to Becoming: Time and Complexity in the Physical Sciences* (San Francisco: W. H. Freeman and Company, 1980); Ilya Prigogine and Isabelle Stengers, *Order Out of Chaos: Man's New Dialogue with Nature* (New York: Bantam Books, 1984).

28. Jean Piaget, *Biology and Knowledge: An Essay on the Relations Between Organic Regulation and Cognitive Processes*, trans. Beatrix Walsh (Chicago: University of Chicago Press, 1971), ch. 1.

29. Donald Schön, *The Reflective Practitioner: How Professionals Think in Action* (New York: Basic Books, 1983), p. 296.

30. Gilles Deleuze, *The Logic of Sense*, trans. Mark Lester and Charles Stivale (New York: Columbia University Press, 1990).

31. René Descartes, "Description of the Human Body," trans. John Cottingham, in *The Philosophical Writings of Descartes*, vol. 1 (London: Cambridge University Press, 1985), pp. 314–324. Original work published in 1664.

32. Richard Rorty, *Philosophy and the Mirror of Nature* (Princeton, NJ: Princeton University Press, 1980).

33. Michel Foucault, *The History of Sexuality, Vol. 1: An Introduction*, trans. Robert Hurley (New York: Vintage Books, 1978); Michel Foucault, *The History of Sexuality, Vol. 2: The Use of Pleasure*, trans. Robert Hurley (New York: Vintage Books, 1985); Michel Foucault, *The History of Sexuality, Vol. 3: The Care of Self*, trans. Robert Hurley (New York: Vintage Books, 1986).

34. David Hamilton, *Toward a Theory of Schooling* (Philadelphia: Falmer Press, 1989).

35. William E. Doll, Jr., *Play and Mastery: A Structuralist View* (paper presented at the Terman Memorial Conference, Stanford, 1978)

36. Jerome Bruner, *Actual Minds, Possible Worlds* (Cambridge: Harvard University Press, 1986), ch. 2.

37. Alfred N. Whitehead, *Science and the Modern World* (New York: Free Press, 1967), original work published in 1925; Alfred N. Whitehead, *The Aims of Education* (New York: Free Press, 1967), original work published in 1929.

38. Thomas S. Kuhn, *The Essential Tension: Selected Studies in Scientific Traditions and Change* (Chicago: The University of Chicago Press, 1977).

39. Ralph W. Tyler, *Basic Principles of Curriculum and Instruction* (Chicago: The University of Chicago Press, 1949), pp. 1–2.

40. Assimilated from Donald Schön, *The Reflective Practitioner: How Professionals Think in Action* (New York: Basic Books, 1983), pp. 296–297.

41. Isaac Newton, *Opticks*, 4th ed. (New York: Dover Publications, Inc., 1952), p. 397. Original work published in 1730.

42. Llya Prigogine and Isabelle Stengers, *Order Out of Chaos: Man's New Dialogue with Nature* (New York: Bantam Books, 1984); Paul Davies, *The Cosmic Blueprint: New Discoveries in Nature's Creative Ability to Order the Universe* (New York: Simon and Schuster, 1988); Paul Davies, *The Mind of God: The Scientific Basis for a Rational World* (New York: Simon and Schuster, 1992).

43. Richard Rorty, *Philosophy and the Mirror of Nature* (Princeton, NJ: Princeton University Press, 1980), p. 377.

44. Jerome Bruner, *Actual Minds, Possible Worlds* (Cambridge: Harvard University Press, 1986), p. 129.

45. Alfred N. Whitehead, *The Aims of Education* (New York: Free Press, 1957), p. 2. Original work published in 1929.

PART II
LISTENING TO DISSENTING VOICES: VIEWS ON KNOWLEDGE/ PEDAGOGY

Introduction

What knowledge is most worth knowing? How should that knowledge be organized and taught in the curriculum? Who should determine what is taught and how? These questions—and many more like them—have fueled curricular and pedagogical debates throughout the history of American higher education. In this section, we explore a range of competing perspectives that have ignited historic and contemporary debates over curriculum and pedagogy. Specifically, we address two interrelated themes. First, we include articles that highlight the myriad purposes that colleges and universities have been expected to fulfill over the years and the subsequent tensions they have generated between liberal and professional education. Second, we draw upon the diverse perspectives of several authors to examine the recent "culture wars" in higher education. In so doing, our intent is to illuminate the contemporary debate over what various groups consider "legitimate" knowledge and "appropriate" pedagogy and to stimulate reader interest in exploring critical intersections between curricula and broader social, economic, cultural and political issues in our society.

In order to spark your historical imagination, we begin this section with a handful of selections that document long-standing tensions between continuity and change in American higher education. John Gallagher's article, in particular, sheds considerable light on the changing purposes we have held for higher education and the indelible imprint that they have left on undergraduate curricula. In Gallagher, as well as in the selections by Laurence Veysey, the *Yale Report of 1828*, and Barbara Scott, you will recall how our nation's colleges and universities—depending upon the socio-political and economic contexts of the time—have been expected, for example, to turn selected groups of men into "educated gentlemen"; to prepare others as productive workers for the nation; to forge out of many a unified citizenry bonded by an understanding of a shared, "common culture;" to produce literate and liberally-educated thinkers; and to provide educational opportunities for all in the interest of ensuring an equitable and democratic society. These readings, particularly when viewed in light of the selections included in section one, invite us to think critically and contextually about the purposes we hold for higher education, how these purposes intersect with our views of what curriculum is and should be, and why understandings such as these are critical to helping us grasp the social, economic, political, and cultural implications of the higher learning in American society.

The majority of readings in this section present contrasting perspectives on the so-called "culture wars" of the late 1980s and 1990s. As the most recent entry in a long line of curricular battles in American higher education, this "war" of sorts has focused broadly on four major themes: debates over the Western canon, arguments over multiculturalism in the curriculum, controversies over political correctness ("PC") on campus, and disputations over "appropriate" pedagogies in higher education. Reduced to its simplest form, the debate has been waged by two groups of individuals: those who embrace traditional perspectives on knowledge, curriculum, and pedagogy—reflected in the writings of William Bennett, George Rouche, and Dinesh D'Souza—and others, such as Henry Giroux, Peggy McIntosh, Kathleen Weiler, and Frances Maher, who view knowledge as a social construct and actively seek to incorporate feminist, multiculturalist, and critical perspectives and pedagogies into the curriculum. In this section we have also included three readings—one by us and others by Judith Eaton and James Banks—that analyze the positions that each group has taken and how their positions relate to reforming the undergraduate curriculum.

In encouraging readers to engage each of these readings critically and to make sense of the issues they raise within the context of one's own settings and experiences, we pose the following questions:

- How are institutions of higher education different from corporations and other for-profit organizations? What implications do these differences have for what we teach and learn in colleges and universities?

- What kinds of knowledge, skills, and attitudes do we want our children and professional colleagues to have? Are these the qualities of "educated persons"? How might these expectations affect what knowledge we include in the collegiate curriculum?

- What kind of society do we want? What role should institutions of the higher learning—and, more specifically, what they teach in them—play in developing such a society?

- What knowledge really is most worth knowing? How should that knowledge be organized and taught? Who should decide matters such as these?

- What political, economic, cultural, and institutional forces influence—and should influence—what knowledge is taught and how it is taught in the academy? How would "traditionalists" and those who embrace "emerging" perspectives on knowledge respond to this question?

To be sure, the diversity of perspectives represented in this section's readings raise many more questions—many of which do not lend themselves to ready-made answers. As such, they invite multiple layers of interpretation and realms of meaning which, we hope, will stimulate you and others to engage in rich and rigorous dialogues about what the purposes of higher education are or should be, how these purposes influence and shape what knowledge is and is not included in the curriculum, how that knowledge should or should not be taught, and who is or should be involved in rendering such decisions. In our experience, conversations of this sort not only provide critical insights into the historical and contemporary debates over the undergraduate curriculum, but they also generate intriguing perspectives on what curriculum is and how it is intimately connected to broader social, economic, cultural and political issues in our society.

The Yale Report of 1828

Yale's leadership in furnishing the largest number of college presidents and, with Princeton, faculty members to the new colleges of the South and West made this the most influential document in American higher education in the first half of the nineteenth century. It was written as the reply of the Yale Corporation and faculty to Connecticut critics of the classical college curriculum who, like exponents of vocations, or "practical" studies elsewhere in the 1820s, were specifically opposing the retention of the "dead" languages. The two authors of the Report, which was somewhat shortened for publication in Benjamin Silliman's famous magazine and to which was added a seven-page endorsement by a committee of the Yale Corporation, were President Jeremiah Day (1773–1867) and Professor James L. Kingsley (1778–1852). Day, who wrote the first part, was officially connected with Yale for sixty-nine years as tutor, professor, president, and member of the Corporation; his successful presidency was marked by its stability, conservatism, and caution. Kingsley, author of the second part, taught at Yale from 1801 to 1851; his outstanding scholarship made him eminent in the fields of classics, mathematical science, and New England history. Their work quieted the critics of the college and intrenched the classics at Yale for the rest of the century. Not until the 1850s did men such as Francis Wayland attempt to soften the impact of the Report in some other institutions by their efforts toward curricular change and expansion.

Modern discussions of the Report can be found in R. Freeman Butts, *The College Charts Its Course: Historical Conceptions and Current Proposals* (New York, 1939), pp. 18–25; George P. Schmidt, *The Liberal Arts College: A Chapter in American Cultural History* (New Brunswick, N.J., 1957), pp. 55–58; and Richard Hofstadter and C. DeWitt Hardy, *The Development and Scope of Higher Education in the United States* (New York, 1952), pp. 15–17.

Remarks by the Editor [Benjamin Silliman]

The following papers relate to an important subject, respecting which there is at present some diversity of opinion. As the interests of sound learning, in relation both to literature and science, and to professional and active life, are intimately connected with the views developed in the subjoined reports, they are therefore inserted in this Journal, in the belief that they will be deemed both important and interesting by its readers.

At a Meeting of the President and Fellows of Yale College, Sept 11th, 1827, the Following Resolution Was Passed

That His Excellency Governor Tomlinson, Rev. President Day, Rev. Dr. Chapin, Hon. Noyes Darling, and Rev. Abel McEwen, be a committee to inquire into the expediency of so altering the regular course of instruction in this college, as to leave out of said course the study of the *dead languages,* substituting other studies therefor; and either requiring a competent knowledge of said languages, as a condition of admittance into the college, or providing instruction in the same, for such as shall choose to study them after admittance; and that the said committee be requested to report at the next annual meeting of this corporation.

This committee, at their first meeting in April, 1828, after taking into consideration the case referred to them, requested the faculty of the college to express their views on the subject of the resolution.

The expediency of retaining the ancient languages, as an essential part of our course of instruction, is so obviously connected with the object and plan of education in the college, that justice could not be done to the particular subject of inquiry in the resolution, without a brief statement of the nature and arrangement of the various branches of the whole system. The report of the faculty was accordingly made out in *two parts*; one containing a summary view of the plan of education in the college; the other, an inquiry into the expediency of insisting on the study of the ancient languages. . . .

Report of the Faculty, Part I

. . . We are decidedly of the opinion, that our present plan of education admits of improvement. We are aware that the system is imperfect: and we cherish the hope, that some of its defects may ere long be remedied. We believe that changes may, from time to time be made with advantage, to meet the varying demands of the community, to accommodate the course of instruction to the rapid advance of the country, in population, refinement, and opulence. We have no doubt that important improvements may be suggested, by attentive observation of the literary institutions in Europe; and by the earnest spirit of inquiry which is now so prevalent, on the subject of education.

The guardians of the college appear to have ever acted upon the principle, that it ought not to be stationary, but continually advancing. Some alteration has accordingly been proposed, almost every year, from its first establishment. . . .

Not only the course of studies, and the modes of instruction, have been greatly varied; but whole sciences have, for the first time, been introduced; chemistry, mineralogy, geology, political economy, &c. By raising the qualifications for admission, the standard of attainment has been elevated. Alterations so extensive and frequent, satisfactorily prove, that if those who are entrusted with the superintendence of the institution, still firmly adhere to some of its original features, it is from a higher principle, than a blind opposition to salutary reform. Improvements, we trust, will continue to be made, as rapidly as they can be, without hazarding the loss of what has been already attained.

But perhaps the time has come, when we ought to pause, and inquire, whether it will be sufficient to make *gradual* changes, as heretofore; and whether the whole system is not rather to be broken up, and a better one substituted in its stead. From different quarters, we have heard the suggestion, that our colleges must be *new-modelled*; that they are not adapted to the spirit and wants of the age; that they will soon be deserted, unless they are better accommodated to the business character of the nation. As this point may have an important bearing upon the question immediately before the committee, we would ask their indulgence, while we attempt to explain, at some length, the nature and object of the present plan of education at the college. . . .

What then is the appropriate object of a college? It is not necessary here to determine what it is which, in every case, entitles an institution to the *name* of a college. But if we have not greatly misapprehended the design of the patrons and guardians of this college, its object is to *lay the foundation of a superior education*: and this is to be done, at a period of life when a substitute must be provided for *parental superintendence*. The ground work of a thorough education, must be broad, and deep, and solid. For a partial or superficial education, the support may be of looser materials, and more hastily laid.

The two great points to be gained in intellectual culture, are the *discipline* and the *furniture* of the mind; expanding its powers, and storing it with knowledge. The former of these is, perhaps, the more important of the two. A commanding object, therefore, in a collegiate course, should be, to call into daily and vigorous exercise the faculties of the student. Those branches of study should be prescribed, and those modes of instruction adopted, which are best calculated to teach the art of fixing the attention, directing the train of thought, analyzing a subject proposed for investigation; following, with accurate discrimination, the course of argument; balancing nicely the evidence presented to the judgment; awakening, elevating, and controlling the imagination; arranging, with skill, the treasures which memory gathers; rousing and guiding the powers of genius. All this is not to be effected by a light and hasty course of study; by reading a few books, hearing a few lectures, and spending some months at a literary institution. The habits of thinking are to be formed, by long continued and close application. The mines of science must be penetrated far below the surface, before they will disclose their treasures. If a dexterous performance of the manual operations, in many of the mechanical arts, requires an apprenticeship, with diligent attention for years; much more does the training of the powers of the mind demand vigorous, and steady, and systematic effort.

In laying the foundation of a thorough education, it is necessary that *all* the important mental faculties be brought into exercise. . . . In the course of instruction in this college, it has been an object to maintain such a proportion between the different branches of literature and science, as to form in the student a proper *balance* of character. From the pure mathematics, he learns the art of demonstrative reasoning. In attending to the physical sciences, he becomes familiar with facts, with the process of induction, and the varieties of probable evidence. In ancient literature, he finds some of the most finished models of taste. By English reading, he learns the powers of the language in which he is to speak and write. By logic and mental philosophy, he is taught the art of thinking; by rhetoric and oratory, the art of speaking. By frequent exercise on written composition, he acquires copiousness and accuracy of expression. By extemporaneous discussion, he becomes prompt, and fluent, and animated. It is a point of high importance, that eloquence and solid learning should go together; that he who has accumulated the richest treasures of thought, should possess the highest powers of oratory. To what purpose has a man become deeply learned, if he has no faculty of communicating his knowledge? And of what use is a display of rhetorical elegance, from one who knows little or nothing which is worth communicating? . . .

No one feature in a system of intellectual education, is of greater moment than such an arrangement of duties and motives, as will most effectually throw the student upon the *resources of his own mind*. Without this, the whole apparatus of libraries, and instruments, and specimens, and lectures, and teachers, will be insufficient to secure distinguished excellence. The scholar must form himself, by his own exertions. The advantages furnished by a residence at a college, can do little more than stimulate and aid his personal efforts. The *inventive* powers are especially to be called into vigorous exercise. . . .

In our arrangements for the communication of knowledge, as well as in intellectual discipline, such branches are to be taught as will produce a proper symmetry and balance of character. We doubt whether the powers of the mind can be developed, in their fairest proportions, by studying languages alone, or mathematics alone, or natural or political science alone. As the bodily frame is brought to its highest perfection, not by one simple and uniform motion, but by a variety of exercises; so the mental faculties are expanded, and invigorated, and adapted to each other, by familiarity with different departments of science.

A most important feature in the colleges of this country is, that the students are generally of an age which requires, that a substitute be provided for *parental superintendence*. When removed from under the roof of their parents, and exposed to the untried scenes of temptation, it is necessary that some faithful and affectionate guardian take them by the hand, and guide their steps. This consideration determines the kind of government which ought to be maintained in our colleges. As it is a substitute for the regulations of a family, it should approach as near to the character of parental control as the circumstances of the case will admit. It should be founded on mutual affection and confidence. It should aim to effect its purpose, principally by kind and persuasive influence; not wholly or chiefly by restraint and terror. Still, punishment may sometimes be necessary. There may be perverse members of a college, as well as of a family. There may be those whom nothing but the arm of law can reach. . . .

Having now stated what we understand to be the proper *object* of an education at this college, viz. to lay a solid *foundation* in literature and science; we would ask permission to add a few observations on the *means* which are employed to effect this object.

In giving the course of instruction, it is intended that a due proportion be observed between *lectures*, and the exercises which are familiarly termed *recitations*; that is, examinations in a text book. The great advantage of lectures is, that while they call forth the highest efforts of the lecturer, and accelerate his advance to professional eminence, they give that light and spirit to the subject, which awaken the interest and ardor of the student. . . . Still it is important, that the student should have opportunities of retiring by himself, and giving a more commanding direction to his thoughts, than when listening to oral instruction. To secure his steady and earnest efforts, is the great object of the daily examinations or recitations. In these exercises, a text-book is commonly the guide. . . . When he comes to be engaged in the study of his *profession*, he may find his way through the maze, and firmly establish his own opinions, by taking days or weeks for the examination of each separate point. Text-books are, therefore, not as necessary in this advanced stage of education, as in the course at college, where the time allotted to each branch is rarely more than sufficient for the learner to become familiar with its elementary principles. . . .

We deem it to be indispensable to a proper adjustment of our collegiate system, that there should be in it both professors and tutors. There is wanted, on the one hand, the experience of those who have been long resident at the institution, and on the other, the fresh and minute information of those who, having more recently mingled with the students, have a distinct recollection of their peculiar feelings, prejudices, and habits of thinking. At the head of each great division of science, it is necessary that there should be a professor, to superintend the department, to arrange the plan of instruction, to regulate the mode of conducting it, and to teach the more important and difficult parts of the subject. But students in a college, who have just entered on the first elements of science, are not principally occupied with the more abstruse and disputable points. Their attention ought not to be solely or mainly directed to the latest discoveries. They have first to learn the principles which have been in a course of investigation, through the successive ages; and have now become simplified and settled. Before arriving at regions hitherto unexplored, they must pass over the intervening cultivated ground. The professor at the head of a department may, therefore, be greatly aided, in some parts of the course of instruction, by those who are not as deeply versed as himself in all the intricacies of the science. Indeed we doubt, whether elementary principles are always taught to the best advantage, by those whose researches have carried them so far beyond these simpler truths, that they come back to them with reluctance and distaste . . .

In the internal police of the institution, as the students are gathered into one family, it is deemed an essential provision, that some of the officers should constitute a portion of this family; being always present with them, not only at their meals, and during the business of the day; but in the hours allotted to rest. The arrangement is such, that in our college buildings, there is no room occupied by students, which is not near to the chamber of one of the officers.

But the feature in our system which renders a considerable number of tutors indispensable, is the subdivision of our classes, and the assignment of each portion to the particular charge of one man. . . .

The course of instruction which is given to the undergraduates in the college, is not designed to include *professional* studies. Our object is not to teach that which is peculiar to any one of the professions; but to lay the foundation which is common to them all. There are separate schools for medicine, law, and theology, connected with the college, as well as in various parts of the country; which are open for the reception of all who are prepared to enter upon the appropriate studies of their several professions. With these, the academical course is not intended to interfere.

But why, it may be asked, should a student waste his time upon studies which have no immediate connection with his future profession? . . . In answer to this, it may be observed, that there is no science which does not contribute its aid to professional skill. "Every thing throws light upon every thing." The great object of a collegiate education, preparatory to the study of a profession, is to give that expansion and balance of the mental powers, those liberal and comprehensive views, and those fine proportions of character, which are not to be found in him whose ideas are always confined to one particular channel. When a man has entered upon the practice of his profession, the energies of his mind must be given, principally, to its appropriate duties. But if his thoughts never range on other subjects, if he never looks abroad on the ample domains of literature and science, there will be a narrowness in his habits of thinking, a peculiarity of character, which will be sure to mark him as a man of limited views and attainments. Should he be distinguished in his profession, his ignorance on other subjects, and the defects of his education, will be the more exposed to public observation. On the other hand, he who is not only eminent in professional life, but has also a mind richly stored with general knowledge, has an elevation and dignity of character, which gives him a commanding influence in society, and a widely extended sphere of usefulness. His situation enables him to diffuse the light of science among all classes of the community. Is a man to have no other object, than to obtain a *living* by professional pursuits? Has he not duties to perform to his family, to his fellow citizens, to his country; duties which require various and extensive intellectual furniture? . . .

As our course of instruction is not intended to complete an education, in theological, medical, or legal science; neither does it include all the minute details of *mercantile, mechanical,* or *agricultural* concerns. These can never be effectually learned except in the very circumstances in which they are to be practiced. The young merchant must be trained in the counting room, the mechanic, in the workshop, the farmer, in the field. But we have, on our premises, no experimental farm or retail shop; no cotton or iron manufactory; no batter's, or silversmith's, or coachmaker's establishment. For what purpose, then, it will be asked, are young men who are destined to these occupations, ever sent to a college? They should not be sent, as we think, with an expectation of *finishing* their education at the college; but with a view of laying a thorough foundation in the principles of science, preparatory to the study of the practical arts. . . .

We are far from believing that theory *alone*, should be taught in a college. It cannot be effectually taught, except in connection with practical illustrations. . . . To bring down the principles of science to their practical application by the laboring classes, is the office of men of superior education. It is the separation of theory and practice, which has brought reproach upon both. Their union alone can elevate them to their true dignity and value. The man of science is often disposed to assume an air of superiority, when he looks upon the narrow and partial views of the mere artisan. The latter in return laughs at the practical blunders of the former. The defects in the education of both classes would be remedied, by giving them a knowledge of scientific principles, preparatory to practice.

We are aware that a thorough education is not within the reach of all. Many, for want of time and pecuniary resources, must be content with a partial course. A defective education is better than none. If a youth can afford to devote only two or three years, to a scientific and professional education, it will be proper for him to make a selection of a few of the most important branches, and give his attention exclusively to these. But this is an imperfection, arising from the necessity of the case. A partial course of study, must inevitably give a partial education. . . .

A partial education is often expedient; a superficial one, never. . . .

But why, it is asked, should *all* the students in a college be required to tread in the *same steps*? Why should not each one be allowed to select those branches of study which are most to his taste, which are best adapted to his peculiar talents, and which are most nearly connected with his intended profession? To this we answer, that our prescribed course contains those subjects only which ought to be understood, as we think, by every one who aims at a thorough education. They are not the peculiarities of any profession or art. These are to be learned in the professional and practical schools. But the principles of sciences, are the common foundation of all high intellectual attainments. As in our primary schools, reading, writing, and arithmetic are taught to all, however different their prospects; so in a college, all should be instructed in those branches of knowledge, of which no one destined to the higher walks of life ought to be ignorant. What subject which is now studied here, could be set aside, without evidently marring the system[?] Not to speak particularly, in this place, of the ancient languages; who that aims at a well proportioned and superior education will remain ignorant of the elements of the various branches of the mathematics, or of history and antiquities, or of rhetoric and oratory, or natural philosophy, or astronomy, or chemistry, or mineralogy, or geology, or political economy, or mental and moral philosophy?

It is sometimes thought that a student ought not to be urged to the study of that for which he has *no taste or capacity*. But how is he to know, whether he has a taste or capacity for a science, before be has even entered upon its elementary truths? If he is really destitute of talent sufficient for these common departments of education, he is destined for some narrow sphere of action. But we are well persuaded, that our students are not so deficient in intellectual powers, as they sometimes profess to be; though they are easily made to believe, that they have no capacity for the study of that which they are told is almost wholly useless.

When a class have become familiar with the common elements of the several sciences, then is the proper time for them to *divide off* to their favorite studies. They can then make their choice from actual trial. This is now done here, to some extent, in our Junior year. The division might be commenced at an earlier period, and extended farther, provided the qualifications for admission into the college, were brought to a higher standard.

If the view which we have thus far taken of the subject is correct, it will be seen, that the object of the system of instruction at this college, is not to give a *partial* education, consisting of a few branches only; nor, on the other hand, to give a *superficial* education, containing a smattering of almost everything; nor to *finish* the details of either a professional or practical education; but to *commence* a *thorough* course, and to carry it as far as the time of residence here will allow. It is intended to occupy, to the best advantage, the four years immediately preceding the study of a profession, or of the operations which are peculiar to the higher mercantile, manufacturing, or agricultural establishments. . . .

Our institution is not modeled exactly after the pattern of *European* universities. Difference of circumstances has rendered a different arrangement expedient. It has been the policy of most monarchical governments, to concentrate the advantages of a superior education in a few privileged places. In England, for instance, each of the ancient universities of Oxford and Cambridge, is not so much a single institution, as a large number of distinct, though contiguous colleges. But in this country, our republican habits and feelings will never allow a monopoly of literature in any one place. There must be, in the union, as many colleges, at least, as states. Nor would we complain of this arrangement as inexpedient, provided that starvation is not the consequence of a patronage so minutely divided. We anticipate no disastrous results from the multiplication of colleges, if they can only be adequately endowed. We are not without apprehensions, however, that a feeble and stinted growth of our national literature, will be the consequence of the very scanty supply of means to most of our public seminaries. . . .

Although we do not consider the literary institutions of Europe as faultless models, to be exactly copied by our American colleges; yet we would be far from condemning every feature, in systems of instruction which have had an origin more ancient than our republican seminaries. We do not suppose that the world has learned absolutely nothing, by the experience of ages; that a branch of science, or a mode of teaching, is to be abandoned, precisely because it has stood its ground, after a trial by various nations, and through successive centuries. We believe that our colleges may derive important improvements from the universities and schools in Europe; not by blindly adopting all their measures without discrimination; but by cautiously introducing, with proper modifications, such parts of their plans as are suited to our peculiar situation and character. The first and great improvement which we wish to see made, is an elevation in the standard of attainment for admission. Until this is effected, we shall only expose ourselves to inevitable failure and ridicule, by attempting a general imitation of foreign universities. . . .

It is said that the public now demand, that the doors should be thrown open to all; that education ought to be so modified, and varied, as to adapt it to the exigencies of the country, and the prospects of different individuals; that the instruction given to those who are destined to be merchants, or manufacturers, or agriculturalists, should have a special reference to their respective professional pursuits.

The public are undoubtedly right, in demanding that there should be appropriate courses of education, accessible to all classes of youth. And we rejoice at the prospect of ample provision for this purpose, in the improvement of our academics, and the establishment of commercial high schools, gymnasia, lycea, agricultural seminaries, &c. But do the public insist, that every college shall become a high school, gymnasium, lyceum, and academy? Why should we interfere with these valuable institutions? Why wish to take their business out of their hands? The college has its appropriate object, and they have theirs. . . . What is the characteristic difference between a college and an academy? Not that the former teaches more branches than the latter. There are many academies in the country, whose scheme of studies, at least upon paper, is more various than that of the colleges. But while an academy teaches a little of every thing, the college, by directing its efforts to one uniform course, aims at doing its work with greater precision, and economy of time; just as the merchant who deals in a single class of commodities, or a manufacturer who produces but one kind of fabrics, executes his business more perfectly, than be whose attention and skill are divided among a multitude of objects. . . .

But might we not, by making the college more accessible to different descriptions of persons, enlarge our *numbers*, and in that way, increase our income? This might be the operation of the measure, for a very short time, while a degree from the college should retain its present value in public estimation; a value depending entirely upon the character of the education which we give. But the moment it is understood that the institution has descended to an inferior standard of attainment, its reputation will sink to a corresponding level. After we shall have become a college in *name only*, and in reality nothing more than an academy; or half college, and half academy; what will induce parents in various and distant parts of the country, to send us their sons, when they have academies enough in their own neighborhood? There is no magical influence in an act of incorporation, to give celebrity to a literary institution, which does not command respect for itself, by the elevated rank of its education. When the college has lost its hold on the public confidence, by depressing its standard of merit, by substituting a partial, for a thorough education, we may expect that it will be deserted by that class of persons who have hitherto been drawn here by high expectations and purposes. Even if we should not immediately suffer in point of *numbers*, yet we shall exchange the best portion of our students, for others of inferior aims and attainments.

As long as we can maintain an elevated character, we need be under no apprehension with respect to numbers. Without character, it will be in vain to think of retaining them. It is a hazardous experiment, to act upon the plan of gaining numbers first, and character afterwards. . . .

The difficulties with which we are now struggling, we fear would be increased, rather than diminished, by attempting to unite different plans of education. It is far from being our intention to dictate to other colleges a system to be adopted by them. There may be good and sufficient reasons why some of them should introduce a partial course of instruction. We are not sure, that the demand for thorough education is, at present, sufficient to fill all the colleges in the United States, with students who will be satisfied with nothing short of high and solid attainments. But it is to be hoped that, at no very distant period, they will be able to come up to this elevated ground, and leave the business of second-rate education to the inferior seminaries.

The competition of colleges may advance the interests of literature: if it is a competition for *excellence*, rather than for numbers; if each aims to surpass the others, not in an imposing display, but in the substantial value of its education. . . .

Our republican form of government renders it highly important, that great numbers should enjoy the advantage of a thorough education. On the Eastern continent, the few who are destined to particular departments in political life, may be educated for the purpose; while the mass of the people are left in comparative ignorance. But in this country, where offices are accessible to all who are qualified for them, superior intellectual attainments ought not to be confined to any description of persons. *Merchants, manufacturers*, and *farmers*, as well as professional gentlemen, take their places in our public councils. A thorough education ought therefore to be extended to all these classes. It is not sufficient that they be men of sound judgment, who can decide correctly, and give a silent vote, on great national questions. Their influence upon the minds of others is needed; an influence to be produced by extent of knowledge, and the force of eloquence. Ought the speaking in our deliberative assemblies to be confined to a single profession? If it is knowledge, which gives us the command of physical agents and instruments, much more is it that which enables us to control the combinations of moral and political machinery. . . .

Can merchants, manufacturers, and agriculturists, derive no benefit from high intellectual culture? They are the very classes which, from their situation and business, have the best opportunities for reducing the principles of science to their practical applications. The large estates which the tide of prosperity in our country is so rapidly accumulating, will fall mostly into their hands. Is it not desirable that they should be men of superior education, of large and liberal views, of those solid and elegant attainments, which will raise them to a higher distinction, than the mere possession of property; which will not allow them to hoard their treasures, or waste them in senseless extravagance; which will enable them to adorn society by their learning, to move in the more intelligent circles with dignity, and to make such an application of their wealth, as will be most honorable to themselves, and most beneficial to their country?

The active, enterprising character of our population, renders it highly important, that this bustle and energy should be directed by sound intelligence, the result of deep thought and early discipline. The greater the impulse to action, the greater is the need of wise and skillful guidance. When nearly all the ship's crew are aloft, setting the topsails, and catching the breezes, it is necessary there should be a steady hand at helm. Light and moderate learning is but poorly fitted to direct the energies of a nation, so widely extended, so intelligent, so powerful in resources, so rapidly advancing in population, strength, and opulence. Where a free government gives full liberty to the human intellect to expand and operate, education should be proportionably liberal and ample. When even our mountains, and rivers, and lakes, are upon a scale which seems to denote, that we are destined to be a great and mighty nation, shall our literature be feeble, and scanty, and superficial?

Stability and Experiment in the American Undergraduate Curriculum

LAURENCE VEYSEY

The history of the American undergraduate curriculum needs first to be placed in the context of the broad pattern of academic development during the past 100 years. Since the main outlines of this pattern have often been obscured by the mere spectacle of quantitative growth, or by a tendency to magnify the impact of very recent changes, the overall chronology must be explicitly set forth. After this, it will be profitable to divide the curriculum into a number of its components so that each may receive closer scrutiny.

* * *

Academic Revolution After 1870

The closing years of the nineteenth century brought about the most sweeping transformation of American higher education ever thus far to occur. The decades between 1870 and 1910 witnessed the only genuine "academic revolution" yet to be experienced in the United States. Most of the fundamental academic practices which continue to be familiar to us were first established in that period, including those which bear upon the undergraduate course of study.

To reassure ourselves that this was indeed the case, it is necessary only to cast a quick backward glance in the direction of the mid-nineteenth-century American college. There, even allowing for certain variations among institutions and for tentative gropings toward reform, the picture is mainly one of extreme homogeneity. The primary aim of these colleges was to promote some version of the Christian religion, both by training a ministry and by infusing conventional moral and religious beliefs into the minds of all undergraduates, no matter what their future occupations. The most direct curricular device to achieve this aim was the course in moral philosophy, commonly including Christian evidences, required of seniors and frequently taught by a patriarchal college president. A secondary and related goal was the "disciplining" of the mental and moral faculties, achieved by enforcing a long series of almost deliberately uninviting exercises in Greek and Latin grammar and mathematics, especially during the first two years of the four-year course. Finally, an unstated but very real aim was the maintenance of a numerically tiny social elite against the hostile pressures of a rising Jacksonian egalitarianism. In curricular terms this last aim was fulfilled by promoting the value of a common group experience, as much social as it was intellectual; the collective struggle over the hurdles of a single prescribed curriculum was believed to foster desirable class loyalties.

Elective choice was not entirely absent from the old-time college curriculum. Particularly during the junior and senior years, a certain number of options were often allowed. Rudimentary courses in such areas as history, economics, and several of the natural sciences commonly existed. But anything like the idea of a "major" in a specific subject was as yet unknown.[1] The dominating atmosphere of the traditional college remained hostile to intellectual specialization. Teaching of the natural sciences had to be carefully balanced by the required philosophy courses which connected every detail of the material world to the serene unfolding of divine law. On the surface, science could be welcomed as long as it remained obediently "in its place"; on a deeper level, and increasingly as time went on, it was to be feared. Although the reigning philosophy was Scottish commonsense realism, the harsher term *scholasticism* does not seem entirely inappropriate as a shorthand label for the pervasive tone in these small, scattered institutions.

This peculiarly uniform promotion of an ethos so uncharacteristic of the larger society may be explained only by contemporary alarm over rapid social and intellectual change. It had two major results. First, the colleges became increasingly unpopular. In some places absolute enrollments declined in the years between 1850 and 1880, more commonly, they remained static, while the American population soared. Thus the colleges retained their integrity at the price of a reduced influence. (The number of congressmen who were college graduates sharply declined between 1875 and 1885.) Moreover, those who still went to college came to take the formal curriculum less seriously. Their lives began to center more and more on good times experienced outside the unreal classroom. Perhaps a gulf of this kind would have opened up in any event, given the increasing worldliness of middle-class American life. But the retention of the old course of study, in which, furthermore, Greek and Latin were not taught as literature but as dreary lessons divorced from all larger meaning, certainly speeded the process. The curriculum began to seem like a prison guarding a subject population.

This brief incursion into an alien landscape helps remind us why the academic revolution of the years after 1870 seemed so powerfully attractive while it was still going on. The revolution, it is well to recall, did not involve merely the natural sciences or the practical subjects; at the time, it promoted serious study of every kind. Professors of English and the other modern languages, for instance, greeted the new curricular plan of Cornell University in 1868 with real enthusiasm, for they too, no less than the scientists and historians, had been stifled by the older academic yoke.

The revolution of the late nineteenth century quite simply created the American university (and the undergraduate college) much as we now know them. The product of a mere trickle from the rapidly rising stream of wealth in the society, the new university nonetheless suddenly acquired a prominent place in the American imagination, and along with this a surprisingly definite (some might say rigid) form. The uniformity of arrangements inside these new or reformed institutions deserves notice, as does the absence of conscious, careful debate (such as might survive in the presidential archives of major campuses) about these structural devices. The numbered course; the unit system for credit; the lecture, recitation, and seminar modes of instruction; the departmental organization of learning; the chain of command involving presidents, deans, and department chairmen; and the elective system of course selection all emerged in an astonishingly short period of time and with relatively little variation from one institution to another. (Among the major universities, only Johns Hopkins, Clark, Yale, and Princeton dared for a long time to be somewhat different, the first two in a Germanic direction, and the last two in a more conservative one.) The smaller colleges, admittedly, were very uneven in the speed with which they surrendered to the elective system in the years between 1870 and 1910, but it was believed that there was only this one direction in which they could move.

This rapid achievement of a new uniformity was by no means a simple matter of imitating the German university. The German pattern remained extremely different from the American one in many fundamental respects, both at the level of course structure and at that of administration. European universities were geared toward preparing students for qualifying examinations. Except in England, these were linked to specific professional fields. Emphasis upon these major examination hurdles permitted greater laxity and traditionalism at the day-to-day level of operation. Lecture series and terms did not have to be of uniform lengths; lectures might be largely ignored in favor of tutorial or even less official forms of preparation. The emerging American university was far more impersonal and bureaucratic at every routine step, a much purer case, in other words, of the kind of structural development which Max Weber talked about as "rationalization." Its growth along these lines paralleled, but was not necessarily unduly influenced by, a similar movement toward clarity of structure in American industrial enterprise. It was a form of organization well suited to largeness of scale. But the exact reasons for its development along these particular lines, with so little self-questioning until after the fact, remain a tantalizing mystery. The basic creation of the American university in these years can indeed be explained by the increasing wealth of the society, by alarm among trustees over static enrollments, by major intellectual changes, and by the appearance of a secular managerial elite strongly interested in (though not slavishly subservient to) European educational trends. But the appearance of such a precise academic structure, with so great a uniformity, cannot be accounted for by these factors alone.

One may speculate that, to a degree at least, this highly rationalized pattern was connected with an insecurity which might well have been secretly present in the minds of early university leaders. American culture was strongly anti-intellectual, at least insofar as it viewed serious, advanced study. Student indifference and student revolt had both been endemic in the old-time college. Highly formal organization guaranteed necessary order. In addition, it had the advantage of permitting interchangeability between many of its functioning parts (such as individual courses, regardless of field and, to a large extent, regardless of institution). As a record of these interchangeable courses accumulated, everyone could know at all times just where everyone stood. Rewards and penalties could easily be assigned with a maximum implication of fairness. An impersonal style of treatment at the day-to-day level appears to have been far more congenial to American educators than to those of England and Germany.

The rhetoric of American academic purpose during this revolutionary period, as distinct from the surprisingly identical institutional results, began rapidly to divide into three quite distinct camps. The first major wave of academic reform, during the decade following the Civil War, was dominated by what may be termed a utilitarian point of view. Men of this persuasion urged most of all the inclusion of practical subjects in the curriculum and favored the elective system of study as a convenient means for achieving this end. Open up "all" worthy fields of study, they liked to say; however, the subjects they found especially congenial were those which promised to connect college graduates with skilled vocations or professions, and therefore with the economic heartland of the American middle class. Spokesmen for this kind of academic reform were not often greatly impressed by European education; toward the German university in particular they remained notably lukewarm. They did not highly value scholarship or intellect for their own sakes. Instead, along with their vocationalism went a firm, continuing commitment to American popular morality, and usually to a liberalized form of Christianity. These men either directly represented the upsurge of commercial and industrial practicalism in nineteenth-century American society or else sought (like Charles W. Eliot of Harvard) to give such impulses benign leadership from "above." Their strong presence on the revolutionary academic scene, among the faculty in many disciplines but even more especially at the level of administration, assured that from the very beginning, the American university would prove notably hospitable, as compared with the academic systems of other societies, to technical training in every field from agriculture to business and, someday, to driver education and film making. (For, though the continental universities did conspicuously prepare their students for specific vocations, these were limited to a few highly traditional professions.) Promoters of this very broad kind of educational reform became especially identified with the state universities in America, but they also gained substantial leverage within the leading private ones. From this particular influence, the new universities received their most characteristically American stamp. It was such an indiscriminately utilitarian tendency which long dominated the overall image of the American university in foreign eyes.

Around the mid-1870s, however, a second notable wave of academic reform began, in a much more specifically Germanic direction. Its spokesmen believed in an ideal of pure science, or inductive, empirical research for its own sake. Unlike the utilitarians. These innovators did not particularly care for the existence of large numbers of undergraduate students, though they were willing to tolerate them as a quid pro quo for the freedom to pursue their own investigations and to develop graduate education in their own fields of study. In terms of institutional policy, their frame of reference was primarily qualitative rather than quantitative. Thus it was often frankly elitist, in contrast to the democratic oratory of the utilitarians. But it was an elitism of an entirely different kind from that represented by the old-time college, founded not upon tacit social distinctions but upon the prestige attached to the discovery of new knowledge. The academic ideal of research tended to exist most strongly at the faculty level; it won few administrators single-mindedly to its service. Its spirit came to dominate a great many of the academic disciplines, especially at the leading universities. Such an ideal could be found not only in the natural and social sciences but also in such diverse fields as English (when this meant the study of philology) and the fine arts. In a pure form, however, the drive toward scientific research never came close to capturing the American university in its entirety. Sorely needed funds continued to be spent on gymnasiums and dormitories at the expense of libraries and laboratories. Publication continued to be regarded as an arduous duty rather than a joy by a large sector of the faculty. Clark University, founded as an all-graduate institution in 1889, was forced to add undergraduates in 1902. Most revealingly, research (when divorced from the promise of immediate practical application) failed to capture the imagination of the wider public. When the logic of it became too openly exposed, it remained faintly deviant in the American cultural context. The collegiate aspect of American higher education continued to be the mainstay of the whole enterprise. By founding graduate schools and heralding research, American universities added a major component to their sphere of operations and profoundly influenced the content of much of the curriculum. But they by no means totally transformed themselves in accord with these particular ideals.

By the 1880s, and more noticeably by the turn of the century, a third major position concerning the purpose of higher education had also come into being. This view embraced what was at first often called "liberal culture," and afterward "liberal" or "general" education. Such a position was always most commonly held by faculty members in the humanities, though occasionally it attracted stray professors from the social and even the natural sciences. Certain college presidents, particularly at Yale, Princeton, and the great mass of small liberal arts institutions, also characteristically adopted it as their own. The origin of this educational outlook is particularly hard to describe because in part it derived from those who remained loyal to many of the ideals of the old-time college. And yet in part it also constituted a genuine revolt against them. But in the latter sense it was a reform philosophy competing with the other two for the control of American higher education entirely within the context of the late-nineteenth-century revolution.

As might be expected, a sharper, less easily bridgeable line of division quickly appeared between the advocates of liberal education and those of the other two reform viewpoints. Militant humanists set themselves squarely against some of the strongest tendencies of the new wave of educational change: research, Germany, specialization, the elective system, and too great an emphasis upon natural science. Sometimes they even attacked democracy, although their ideal of cultivation claimed to be universal in its potential application. In this generation, humanistic reformers were apt to retain an emphasis on the social and the moral as distinct from the intellectual aims of higher education. They continued to define education according to a single desirable formula for everyone. But the model was no longer taken from the classics or, in most cases, the tradition of Christian piety. It was that of the well-rounded gentleman or, sometimes, the citizen and potential leader of his society. A strong civic sense marked this camp of academic spokesmen, but unlike the utilitarians, its members firmly divorced the notion of public service from that of vocational expertise. Rather, they turned to the reviving English universities, particularly Oxford, as their contemporary source of inspiration. Their aim was to produce the kind of dutiful, disinterested national elite which they believed to be embodied in the British civil service. Meanwhile, sometimes they promoted philosophical idealism, if they were philosophers, or dabbled in transcendentalism or aestheticism (while drawing back from their more extreme implications), if they were teachers of literature. In the beginning, the cause of liberal education was quite firmly identified with the so-called genteel tradition in American letters. From this essentially aristocratic perspective, science and commercialism were perceived as twin enemies, and a redefined undergraduate education might serve as an appropriate remedy against their powerful threat. But, alas, it appeared that the universities were already in the hands of men who represented these alien forces, for the believers in liberal education found themselves greatly outnumbered except on the margins of the new academic map.

During the 1890s, leading universities rapidly acquired a standardized form which had little to do with the clear-cut necessities of any of these competing philosophies of higher education. Administrators began to appear, such as Nicholas Murray Butler and William R. Harper, who saw themselves not primarily as agents for any of the individual varieties of academic reform but rather as superintendents of great new institutions in all their diversity. Thus the age of academic managerialism, in its pure form, arrived as the final phase of the academic revolution itself. The term *multiversity* had not yet been coined, but the label *Harper's Bazaar*, which soon attached itself to the University of Chicago, expressed much the same idea with equal pungency.

Meanwhile, as a curve of steady quantitative growth began to form in American higher education, qualitative innovation for a time largely stopped. The pressures of intensified competition among rival establishments placed limits upon risky experiment. In this fashion the ideals of vocational training, research, and liberal education would become rather statically frozen inside the American university, the more vociferous advocates of each continuing to feel less than fully satisfied by the blended and compromised result, but with no real chance that any one of them would ever win out decisively against the other two. Utility and research, in particular entered into an uneasy marriage in which neither partner ever lost its identity, while humanists, decade after decade, labored alone in their peculiar comer, beset by unusually intense internecine strife as well.

By 1910 the academic revolution of the several preceding decades was definitely over. This may be seen not only in the fact that the academic structure had so largely crystallized by this date but even more tellingly in contemporary curricular trends. From the 1870s until shortly after the turn of the century, the elective system of studies increasingly gained ground. (The extreme adoption of it by Cornell in 1896 represented a last major victory of this kind.) By 1905 or 1910 a clear reaction against it had set in.[2] Moreover, the years around 1909 and 1910 marked a distinct season of internal questioning in American academic circles.[3] At the same time, the last of the older generation of innovative university presidents departed from the scene, leaving lesser men to cope with the sudden onset of uncertainty.

Reformers of the Interwar Period

Hindsight reveals that a new major phase in the history of American higher education began around 1910 and lasted until after the Second World War. Quantitatively, the new period was marked by steady upward growth. But the very rise in numbers of students has obscured deeper, more disquieting qualitative tendencies. From a viewpoint which is concerned more with structure and innovation than with bare statistics, the new epoch which universities entered after 1910 may be seen as a long and rather disappointing interregnum. If, to a degree, the faculty won stronger control over curricular matters at the expense of presidents, no earthshaking changes occurred as a result.

From about 1910 until 1945 or even somewhat later, it may bluntly be said that American universities failed to fulfill much of their original promise. This was largely a period of drift, characterized by a sense of letdown, perhaps more than merely symbolized by the tendency of professors' salaries to remain far too small as compared with their own expectations. Much of this time, for one reason or another, faculty positions were hard to come by as budgets were continually stretched. (This was true during both the 1920s and the 1930s.) An atmosphere of scarcity prevailed, despite the rising numbers of students.[4] Philanthropic support, outside Harvard and Yale, did not materialize on anything like the scale that had once been hoped. Universities had won an accepted niche in American society, as the magic of the bachelor's degree (considered a kind of insurance policy against downward social mobility) permeated larger sectors of the middle class. But the flavor of a genuine academic "boom," such as had briefly existed during the 1890s, did not return. In the 1930s, to be sure, an awareness that the American public at large was suffering still more acutely somewhat cushioned these disappointments. But the climate was still not one of confidently expected growth. Meanwhile, the tone of campus life continued to be set by athletics and fraternities to a far greater extent than professors had hoped for during the original academic revolution. A social pattern which was hostile in spirit to the entire curriculum remained the common enemy to be faced by advocates of the three surviving serious academic ideals and by the administrators who juggled them. The constant danger which universities faced was that they would turn out after all to be intellectually mediocre.

A restless demand for curricular reform, especially in the direction of renewed emphasis upon liberal education, took shape during these same years. At first it was heard only on the extreme edge of the academic spectrum, but during the 1920s and even more during the 1930s, it found its way into a scattered but collectively impressive number of actual curricular experiments. In the decades after 1910, the academic landscape thus became divided into a definite mainstream and a series of isolated, often transitory pockets of attempted innovation. The mainstream possessed the remarkably static, blended, compromised quality that has already been described; it defined the malaise which the critics and experimenters sought to remedy. In curricular terms, by 1910 the academic mainstream had evolved into an extremely standard pattern with a major-subject system (still usually somewhat less demanding than it would become after the Second World War); a system of universally enforced breadth requirements, sometimes satisfied only by specific courses but more often already by options among courses; and a survival of the free elective system to fill out the remainder of a student's program. It was against this academic lockstep, and against the continuing divorce of the entire curriculum from the wellsprings of student energy, that a new generation of reformers cried out.

These reformers were often highly interesting, controversial men. Their ideas deserve attention entirely out of proportion to the actual influence they wielded during these generally dreary decades in the history of American higher education. It can at least be said of these men, figures such as Alexander Meiklejohn and Robert Hutchins. That they kept an alternative tradition alive and did this so well that by the end of the 1930s, there seemed far more likelihood of widespread curricular rethinking than at any time during the preceding 30 years. Moreover, reformers of this kind launched many actual innovations which would repeatedly recur in curricular revisions down to the present moment. But in their own day all they could do was to chip feverishly against the granite wall of an unresponsive educational system.

These reformers were further divided among themselves, and in a manner strongly reminiscent of the three-sided debates over educational purpose in the revolutionary years before 1910. The thrust toward reform now presented itself almost entirely in the guise of promoting a return to liberal education. But this label masked several distinct aims and programs.

The followers of John Dewey, in the first place, formed a newly visible element, reaching a peak of prominence during the 1930s. Much of their rhetoric echoed the thinking of the utilitarian-minded reformers of the late nineteenth century. Yet the Deweyans were also at odds with the earlier utilitarians, whose descendants were now so strongly entrenched inside the academic establishment, for they rejected specialized technical training as an appropriate focus for the college curriculum and instead preached an emphasis upon courses which would reflect more universal, organically determined "life needs."[5] Courses centering in social and family adjustment and in marriage and the home, indoctrination in John Dewey's liberal civic philosophy, and courses dealing abstractly with the problem of choosing a vocation (rather than courses that prepared one concretely for a given vocation) were what these reformers put forward. Thus their outlook can be credited with a genuine degree of novelty. But in retrospect the Dewey movement must be judged the least important of the reform crusades. The colleges which it powerfully affected (such as Bennington, Sarah Lawrence, and Stephens College in Missouri) usually happened to be either girls' schools or else truly obscure, only Antioch was a conspicuous exception. Moreover, the adherents of the Dewey persuasion communicated a tone of belligerent sectarian isolation, offering ritual formulas of a low intellectual caliber.

A second group of reformers, who also gathered under the increasingly generous banner of liberal education, really represented an accommodation between the ideal of specialized research and the peculiar needs of undergraduates. For instance. William T. Foster, the first president of Reed, argued as early as 1911 for more specialization rather than less and for greater incentives and opportunities for the brighter and more hardworking students at the expense of the less talented. Honors programs and small seminar and independent study arrangements all bore the stamp of this intellectual elitism, though they were tinged by a certain recognition that the scholarship which addressed itself to undergraduate interests might not always neatly coincide with the narrower scholarship of the graduate school. Such programs aimed at helping students form an intense interest in some topic which lay outside their previous grasp and for which the academic techniques of empirical inquiry were appropriate tools. Honors programs had spread to at least 93 institutions by 1927 and to 116 by the end of the Second World War. Thereafter they expanded still more rapidly.[6] Thus they clearly represented the widest penetration of experiment into the academic mainstream. But to the most pure-minded believers in liberal education, they still suggested entirely too much of the flavor of Germanic scholarship to be acceptable.

The third and last group of reformers in the interwar period were the descendants, somewhat updated, of the older advocates of "liberal culture." These men continued to focus their thinking pointedly on the "college," as distinct from the university, and to insist, as their humanistic predecessors of the turn of the century had, that the undergraduate experience, or at least the first two years of it, must train the mind in an entirely different sense from the way it was trained in either the high school or the doctoral program. The mind, in this view, requires contact with a universal scheme of ideas or values before it can profitably reach out in special directions—and, in fact, between the lines, one could read great doubt as to whether such specialization was ever profitable. As in John Dewey's camp, the talk was about training for action and service in the larger world, even though it carefully insisted that such training must remain traditionally intellectual. Indeed, a much more enthusiastic embrace of the general idea of intellectuality distinguished academic humanists of the 1920s from their predecessors 30 years earlier. Gone was the dilettantish quality of the earlier admiration for English amateurism. Instead, the new tone carried a moral seriousness and a relish for abstract ideas which might even suggest an echo of seventeenth-century Puritanism.

To complicate matters, however, the heroes of this particular group tended to be the Greek and medieval thinkers whose names are most directly associated with scholastic philosophy. Surely one of the most remarkable phenomena of the period was the embrace of the natural-law tradition, with its quasi-Catholic emphasis upon authority and certainty, by a persistent faction of American educational reformers, themselves largely secular and politically somewhat radical in outlook. Yet the famous curricular experiments at the University of Chicago under Hutchins and later at the St. Johns colleges bear this peculiar stamp. The thinking of many other advocates of liberal education, both before and after the Second World War, derives in a broader way from this same perspective, in that the "great ideas" of Western civilization are believed to occupy some uniquely central place in the equipment of every properly educated man or woman. In its milder forms, the resurrection of these texts, taught substantively rather than in the superficial manner of the classics 100 years ago, was to have considerable impact upon undergraduate teaching in several disciplines. But the extreme version of neo-Thomism and the "great books" concept had as much of the flavor of the esoteric cult as Deweyan progressivism did, and in terms of the wide picture of American higher education, it must be judged to have reached a similar dead end.

Faced by an apparent choice between the introduction of courses in family living and the somber revival of Aristotle, most professors and administrators understandably clung to their familiar curriculums, even while acknowledging their defects. It was a great misfortune that so many of the ablest internal critics of the curriculum in the interwar years were believers in these two specific philosophies which struck so many outsiders as crankish affectations, wholly out of touch with the flow of modem life which their adherents sometimes sought to celebrate. As a result of these twin deflecting forces, much valuable energy was lost, and the believers in research and the elective system failed to receive a truly adequate challenge at a time when one was no doubt due. Still, these diverse campaigns in the name of liberal education did help collectively to produce an ever-wider flow of internal criticism and experiment as the 1930s passed. Toward the end of that decade, university catalogs revealed a growing sense of innovation, most often in the direction of interdisciplinary majors, honors programs, and independent study. Well before the war, the cry of the reformers and the urgent sense of social crisis produced by the Depression seemed to assure that the long interregnum in the history of American higher education was coming to an end.

There is, then, a certain arbitrariness about selecting the Second World War as a decisive breaking point in this history. A sense exists in which the First World War unhinged American university faculties and administrations more deeply, for all its brevity, than the Second did, just as was true of American society in general. But in the case of the First World War, the dislocation turned out to be extremely short-lived, and the 1920s brought no basic change to most institutions other than numerical growth. On the other hand, from the late 1930s onward one may observe a series of happenings which, in one way or another, tended to alter the fundamental tone of American academic life.

Shock Waves After World War II

Besides the growing outcry of the academic reformers and the enhanced mood of public seriousness, the 1930s witnessed the beginnings of an extremely important ethnic transformation in the character of American university populations. Specifically, more professors and students with Jewish backgrounds appeared, especially on the better-quality campuses. This change stemmed from two quite unrelated sources: the arrival of increasing numbers of refugees from Nazism and their acceptance, slow as this often was, on American faculties, and the simultaneous appearance at the undergraduate level of ever-larger numbers of immigrant sons and grandsons whom internal discriminatory quotas could no longer effectively cordon. Especially to the extent that Jewish intellectual flair might prove catching among admiring Protestants and Catholics, the American university had thus gained a major new lever for a change of emphasis away from football and fraternities. Indeed, the impact of the presence of an increasing flow of students and colleagues of this more serious kind might be fancifully compared with that of a large salary increase (of an order not for many years forthcoming) in improving the morale of the younger faculty as a whole.

More broadly than this, the rise of Nazism and the entire experience of the Second World War intensified these same tendencies. The flow of refugees of all kinds greatly increased, amounting to an enormous transfusion of fresh European blood into all the fields of science and scholarship. And, regardless of arguments over the effects of war upon basic scientific research, such practical war-related tasks as the development of an atom bomb retroactively conferred a new status upon American science. In these ways, the very facts of Nazism and war helped to redefine the American university as a more formidable kind of institution.

Shooting war in this case led directly to cold war, with an equally powerful and much longer sustained impact. For a series of reasons, many of which were rooted in Soviet-American tension, the impulses toward greater academic dedication already present by 1945 could continue to gain an increasing hold, until by the 1960s they promised to set the basic tone of the undertaking at all important campuses. In the light of our recently growing hopes for a permanent detente among the major powers, there is no doubt something deeply ironic about these incidental domestic effects of the cold war. But at the time, most of the participants believed they were responding to a national need every bit as straightforward as the challenge of Nazism.

The forces encouraging this outcome in American higher education, which in retrospect snowballed with such inevitability, nonetheless remained quite diverse and mutually distinguishable even after the Second World War. At least three distinct shock waves may be discerned. The first, of course, was the sudden inundation of the colleges and universities by the wave of returning veterans after the war, stimulated by the GI Bill of Rights. Here were men who had been away for several years (rather than the brief period of the First World War) and who, regardless of ethnic background, tended to see the world through maturer eyes than many who had stayed at home.

Still, one might argue, the effects of such an invasion were bound to be transitory, and universities might yet have slipped back into the hedonism and mediocrity of the 1920s. The danger of this was especially real in view of the fact that all at once, in the late 1940s, the proportion of the overall American population receiving some form of higher education suddenly mushroomed. The war veterans made up only one segment of this "dramatic increase," which more broadly reflected an awareness within a greatly enlarged sector of the middle and skilled working classes that some version of college was necessary in order to keep economically afloat. One should further pause to recall that a very large share of this statistical increase in enrollment reflected itself in junior college and state college attendance, under conditions which had little to do with the factors promoting quality in the leading institutions.[7] The always-present danger in America that an unbridgeable gap would develop between stronger and weaker forms of higher education thus seemed to magnify in the postwar period. Intense economic and community-oriented pressures made it seem unlikely, for instance, that most junior colleges would drop textbooks and survey courses in favor of paperback readings and seminars, though the present flow of better-trained faculty into some of these institutions (as a result of the recent state of the job market) might yet help turn the tide.

That a falling back into relative mediocrity did not occur, at least in the more prominent institutions, must no doubt be credited largely to the cumulative impact of all these changes of the 1940s. In particular, the cold war prevented the 1950s from ever truly reenacting the public temper of three decades earlier. If it produced a silent generation, silence was at least a more fertile seedbed of classroom productivity than the noisy antics of the "hip flask" era. Moreover, world events such as the Korean War and the continuing threat of the draft acted in a more specific way to ensure a continuing mood of sobriety in the student population. At the better institutions, the faculty was now prepared to take advantage of these states of mind, pushing undergraduate performance as far as one could dare.

Then came the second major shock wave: the nationwide season of fear of Russian technology as a result of Sputnik. This mood of panic, traceable to the thriving spirit of competitive nationalism in the modern world, gave further leverage to professors of newer ethnic backgrounds and more demanding intellectual expectations. Everywhere standards of performance were raised, and actual course requirements were made tougher. Meanwhile, the national temper, as it affected both private endowments and governmental appropriations at state and federal levels, brought about a temporary academic boom (lasting from about 1958 to 1966) whose only parallel had been the boom during the greatest revolutionary period of expansion in the 1890s. Salaries jumped and working conditions improved almost overnight. Scientists luxuriated in a sea of federal research grants. Professors were courted and sought after, especially in the illusory years of the Kennedy administration. Everywhere the new tone of seriousness and imperialistic expansion seemed to triumph.

The exhilaration of this peculiar boom period produced certain undeniable excesses. Giddy statistical projections were made for the long-range future expansion of American higher education which apparently went so far as to misread the birthrate to a serious degree. Universities were seen to be replacing business corporations as the principal handmaidens of a benign technocratic government. The St. Simonian utopianism of Daniel Bell (1968, pp. 70–88), along these lines, reads strangely only a few years later. But the very exaggerations reflected the sudden arrival of the academic world onto a new plateau of genuinely unprecedented resources.

Meanwhile, the predominant curricular effect of the accumulating postwar seriousness of academic tone was the further accentuation of the conventional subject major system. The 1950s brought about a great elevation of the research-centered ideal in American higher education, carrying it far beyond its initial peak of influence in the 1890s. For the first time, research chairs became fairly common, at least toward the top of the academic system. Some would go so far as to say that this change ushered in an entirely new era because it meant that leading professors no longer had to bid for students in order to gain prestige. In any event, as the fraction of undergraduates seeking to go on to graduate school rose, the influence of graduate school norms on the entire curriculum increased. In the minds of a majority of professors at the better-quality institutions, such a trend was indeed identified with the very notion of improved standards. Thus the most popular type of curricular innovation during this period, frequently undertaken (as in the 1930s) in the name of "liberal education," continued to be the expansion of honors and independent study programs, as earlier pioneered by such colleges as Swarthmore and Reed. This had always been the version of reform which linked itself most closely to conventional Germanic scholarship. It resulted in some of the most exciting seminar and tutorial teaching of the age. But it revealed a continuing commitment to a strongly empirical style of inquiry, again somewhat modified by an awareness that not all important ideas must be those generated by narrow controversies among advanced scholars in the disciplines.

At the same time, interest still grew in more drastic forms of experiment in the direction of liberal education. The four-year curriculum remained elastic enough so that majors programs and independent study arrangements could expand simultaneously with other proposals which embodied the conflicting ideal of "well-roundedness." A renewed campaign for "general education," begun at Harvard in 1945, began to prosper somewhat on other campuses in the 1960s. A substantial number of professors felt impelled, either by the climate of the times or for their own intellectual reasons, to orient their teaching less exclusively toward single disciplines. As had happened in the 1930s, a few entire campuses, such as Old Westbury on Long Island, temporarily succumbed to these experimental hopes. From the mid-1960s onward, "colleges" again were often promoted as desirable alternatives to large, impersonal universities. The advocates of research might not be unseated, but they were placed on the defensive once more, surprisingly soon after their greatest victories.

The third and last of the recent shock waves, of course, was generated by the rising student protest movement of the late 1960s, itself occasioned largely by world events. The evaluation of its effects must naturally remain more controversial. It deeply divided the academic community to a degree that none of these other happenings since the 1930s had done. A probable majority of professors interpreted student political and cultural protest not as a further reenforcement of the steadily gaining temper of reason and reflection on leading campuses but, in quite an opposite manner, as a frightening new force which threatened to undo all the positive gains of the Sputnik period.

Yet, aside from certain undeniably destructive episodes, a broader undercurrent revealed itself in the student outcry of the 1960s, one which may legitimately be viewed as a further extension of the serious climate of the whole era since the Second World War rather than as a signal of its breakdown. Student dissatisfaction with the curriculum, though it had its naive aspects, manifested a sense of involvement with purely academic issues which would have been unthinkable in the American university as recently as the 1930s. The call for relevance in course work, no matter how absurd when pushed to a logical limit, nonetheless set in motion a self-searching debate in academic ranks which gave some promise of doing what neither the abstract Aristotelianism nor the Dewey movement of the 1930s could hope to do: produce a widespread reexamination of the academic sense of purpose, of a kind never before consciously indulged in. (In its own way, the arrival of larger numbers of black students on many campuses aided in promoting the same result.) The hopes attached to such a process of rethinking may well prove extravagant. But no one, no matter how deep his loyalty to the genuine greatness of the existing American university, can pretend that it is unneeded or that it can inspire no important improvements. Therefore, beyond any doubt, the often angry (or forlorn) students of the past several years must be thanked for having pushed us all much closer to a new look at fundamentals.

The challenge recently presented to the university by student radicalism divides itself into several distinct aspects, each with its own quite separate impact. First and most dramatic was the effort, spearheaded by certain sectors of the New Left, to shut down the entire university as a preliminary to transforming it *en bloc* into an agency for basic social change. The liberalism of the existing academic climate made universities into tempting targets from the perspective of such a strategy. This move soon failed, though the disruptions that it briefly produced have left deep scars on many campuses. Its failure, the result not only of forceful countermeasures but also of a widely shared loyalty to more conventional conceptions of the university, somewhat clears the air. The jolt that it provided prevents the academic community from as yet lapsing into complacency, but the inability of the radicals to seize control makes it apparent that changes will occur through customary channels of debate, only somewhat widened by student participation. The element of co-optation in the compromises that are achieved will increase as memories of past scenes of violence begin to fade.

By contrast, the other versions of student radicalism, which stop short of violent take-over, possess noticeably greater staying power, since they are bound more deeply into the general cultural and social climate of our times. All of them in one way or another demand changes in the substance of what is being taught. The New Left attacks what it believes to be the subtle but pervasive bias of the social sciences toward *moderate* liberalism; when confined to verbal dialogue, this, it seems to me, can be regarded only as a healthy challenge, on a par with the Beardian revolt against academic "formalism" early in this century. In intellectual terms, New Leftist critiques have already pushed major areas of scholarship in such fields as American history into important new directions.

At the same time, blacks and other minorities have demanded control of academic programs centered entirely in cultural nationalism. Academically suspect (not least on the ground that nationalism is parochial no matter who espouses it), such programs nonetheless pose far less of a threat to academic standards than has often been imagined. At their worst, they are far better than the "majors" created several decades ago in education, home economics, and physical education, which served largely as upward-mobility mechanisms for lower-middle-class whites. If universities survived and improved despite these earlier intrusions, they need not fear the practical effects of certain new ones, which at the same time have the virtue of democratizing the institution in a much more basic way. The bachelor's degree in America has so long been cheapened by the existence of the conventional low-quality fields, and by the similar existence of hundreds of low-quality campuses, that there is some justice in the charge of racism when black studies programs are now singled out for worry of this kind.

A much more genuine cause for concern is the final variety of student assault on the conventional curriculum, namely, that which stems from cultural rather than political revolt on the part of middle-class white students. Here of course I refer to the newer forms of antirationalism, springing from the revival of humanistic psychology. At stake is an entire world view, and therefore a deeply felt objection to the survival of conventional (structured, orderly) teaching in all fields. This objection has penetrated the minds of a small but significant faction among younger instructors, who appear to agree wholeheartedly with a larger share of the new generation of students that the aim of education is to study oneself rather than anything else. A cult has thus come into being, far more deeply hostile to centuries-old traditions of rationality in Western culture than the Dewey movement of the 1930s, which in its own way continued to elevate reason. As with the New Left attack upon social science (which takes its direction from a much more orthodox definition of the human mind), the antirationalist challenge could often be regarded as a stimulating therapy, forcing older professors to take a new look at their own fundamental assumptions. Not least, it has encouraged many on the faculty to experiment with a more spontaneous and informal teaching style; if not carried too far, this amounts to a genuine gain. But the actual transformation of the classroom into an encounter group, if done with relentless consistency, threatens definite dangers to the mental health of the students and might someday have to be outlawed on these grounds alone. And, ultimately, it must be said that the university stands for reason, no matter how earnestly it ought to welcome the counterarguments. Those who carry an irrationalist philosophy to the point of finding no value in conventional classroom exchange may need to be encouraged to set up shop elsewhere.

When all these episodes in the history of American higher education since the 1930s are viewed together, they reveal a surprising degree of continuity, sufficient in all likelihood to give the entire span of years its basic definition. The American university, created with such great hopes in the 1880s and 1890s and then cast adrift to flounder in penury and student hedonism for a generation, in this period finally did begin to fulfill itself. No matter what our anxiety may be over some of the symptoms produced by particular episodes of the recent past, both those involving the ties between the academic community and the military-industrial establishment and those having to do with the problems of student radicalism, this fundamental fact can scarcely be challenged. Never before has the intellectual life of American universities, in a wide variety of disciplines and also among a wide sector of students, been so rich. Controversy of many kinds is connected to this very mood of intensity. If, as appears increasingly likely, such controversy will only seldom become demoralizing, then the greatest age of the American university (and, incidentally, of its curriculum) may lie just ahead.

If so, it will be without benefit of the unusual boom conditions of the years 1958 to 1966. This now seems clear. In financial terms the post-Sputnik period, like the 1890s, was something of a fluke. Certain long-range symptoms of popular indifference and anti-intellectual hostility have reasserted themselves. (Though opinion poll data show continuing support for giving high priority to educational expenditures, they do not differentiate between the willingness of the public to give anyone who wants it some kind of a higher education—for instance, in junior colleges—and a much less evident willingness to expand education of very high quality.) But the momentum of the past 25 years is immeasurably greater than that provided by the boom of the 1890s. Despite a more static financial climate, resources remain large. A relatively wide freedom of action persists, even within the limits of present budgets. In this respect, we must not be misled by the gloom of a temporary economic recession into extremes of doubt which would only reverse the errors of prognostication made during the mid-1960s.

The diverse and seemingly rather confusing climate of these last years has created a fluidity which augurs well for change. Many are talking of a new academic revolution. As always, such a label masks the specific tactical intents of a great many competing parties, from student radicals to faculty humanists to promotion-minded administrators. Those who are realistically concerned about the future of the university in America would do well to remain skeptical about such dramatic labels and instead watch closely what each party is seeking to secure. What is to come is less likely an upheaval than a protracted series of bargaining sessions among these various interests. Out of such bargaining a somewhat altered pattern of American higher education, still qualitatively demanding and yet more responsive to the needs of undergraduates as human beings, may actually emerge.

Components of the Curriculum

This recapitulation of the chronology of American higher education has revealed a discrepancy between pronounced changes in the underlying tone and atmosphere, especially after the Second World War, and a strong tendency toward continuity (despite growing experiments) in many aspects of the curriculum itself. The device of the subject major, for instance, dates from shortly after the turn of the century at most institutions, and it remains even more conspicuous at present. In qualitative ways that really matter, universities appear to change, while their formal curricular structures remain rather less affected. Should such a discrepancy bother us? The rest of this chapter will be devoted to exploring the implications of this paradox and the problems it suggests.

It is important at the outset to distinguish clearly between two meanings of the term *curriculum*. The word may connote either formal structural arrangements or the substance of what is being taught. (To be sure, the relations between form and substance, here as always, are complex.) I shall argue that within broad limits, the structural aspects of the curriculum have much less to do with the quality of an education than is often believed. Quality instead is more importantly linked to matters of substance, which it is the primary purpose of the rest of this volume to explore. My own point, then, is largely a negative one by contrast. By surveying in turn the most highly formal components of the undergraduate course of study, I shall try to reveal some of the areas in which future thinking about the curriculum is likely to be misplaced. In certain cases, excessive time and attention have been paid to these areas by faculties and administrations in the past, leading to an enormous waste of energy. In others, relatively little debate has occurred, but they turn out to involve matters that often seem best left alone after all.

What is the "formal" curriculum, as distinct from the substantive one? It is a highly complicated series of structural arrangements, embodying many separate kinds of routine understandings. There is, to begin with, the very idea of a *course* as a concrete entity, extending over time, with a beginning, an ending, and a postmortem result known as a *grade*. There are also other units of time, known as *terms*, *semesters*, or *quarters*, and conventions associated with the total period required for a bachelor's degree. Beyond this, there are customary modes of presenting courses, such as lectures, recitation and discussion sections, seminars, tutorials, and the like. There are systems of numbering and course credit. There is the question of sponsorship of courses, typically involving departmental structure and, more rarely, interdisciplinary committees or colleges. Then—and these have figured more prominently in the discussions of the past—there are the usual ways of fitting courses together into larger schemes. Involved here are the limits imposed upon absolute freedom of choice in the courses students may select. These limits are of more than one traditional kind, comprising subject majors, distributional requirements, and also (considering their own long history) various forms of experimental restructuring. Also relevant is the total number of courses and major programs being offered in an institution at a given time, for their very availability has often figured in the agonizing decisions made by department chairmen, deans, and presidents.

It is not the case, certainly, that *none* of these formal attributes of a curriculum has any bearing upon educational quality. One may indeed imagine extreme circumstances (such as an eight-year B.A. program, a total absence of seminars and discussion sections, or a similar absence of a department of sociology) in which each of these formal aspects of the curriculum might bear heavily upon the fundamental result. Situations of this kind do rarely occur; Amherst College had no sociology department until 1968. But it is far more important to recognize how little of importance has come from the normal range of debate on these matters in undergraduate faculties over the past several decades, the very years when university education was so greatly improving in this country. A historical examination of these topics can help to show the deceptiveness of much of the apparent change and movement that have occurred. It can also pinpoint the few respects in which the picture of meaningful change is quite genuine.

The Course

Let us begin, then, with the fundamental idea of the course. As a basic device, the course is probably the most durable element in American higher education. Entities which are recognizable as courses already dominated the curriculums of traditional American colleges in the mid-nineteenth century, though they were not so often of equivalent intensity and duration, and their extremely small number made it possible to describe them with much less formality. Thus the entire curriculum for the junior year at Harvard in 1869, when Charles W. Eliot first became president, reads as follows:

- *Required studies*—Physics, three hours a week the whole year. Logic and metaphysics, each two hours a week, half the year.

- *Elective studies*—Latin, Greek, ancient history, mathematics, chemistry, natural history, German, English; each three hours a week, and each student must take two and may take three.

- *Italian and Spanish*, as extras, and as a condition of being allowed to continue the study of them in the Senior year with a mark of 8 (Foster, 1911, pp. 362-363).

The academic revolution of the late nineteenth century had the effect merely of further standardizing the notion of the course; by the 1890s courses were everywhere being given specific identifying numbers. From that point forward, there was almost no further change, though eventually (as at the University of Wisconsin in the 1960s) courses might be numbered in each field on a scale that reached from 1 to 999. In a purely formal sense the course survived almost everywhere unquestioned.[9]

Only slightly less tenacious has been the idea of the grade as the logical way in which to report student achievement in courses. Particular grading schemes might vary from place to place over the decades (involving different kinds of numbers or letters), but only a small fraction of educational radicals, starting in the 1930s, began to argue against all conventional grading systems as part of their attack upon compulsion in the learning process in general. A favorite scheme of experimenters in that decade was to shift weight away from course grades toward comprehensive examinations, sometimes postponed until the end of the senior year. (In this there was a belated imitation of the very core of the European university system.) But it was hard to counter the argument that such examinations, if administered rigorously just prior to expected graduation, were a far crueler form of punishment for many students. And not until the 1960s did even a few educators become so permissive (or so cynical) in their philosophy that they began, like growing numbers of students, to question the meaningfulness of *any* definite terminal statement about performance in a classroom. In these terms, even the idea of "pass-fail," which gained currency toward the end of the decade, represented a compromise, especially when (as at the Santa Cruz campus of the University of California) such grades were accompanied by paragraph-style evaluations that were forwarded to graduate schools.[10]

The course and the grade survived with so little challenge for reasons that were no doubt as much psychological as they were historical. Both were primarily instruments of control. Their constant presence, and the fact that neither Germanic nor English influences ever crucially affected this central aspect of American higher education, hinted at a deep-seated and continuing fear of what it might mean to abandon them. In the American cultural context, at least up until very recent years, such fears were entirely understandable. In a society in which larger and larger numbers of students were being prodded by their parents to obtain a bachelor's degree, and yet in which the culture told them that to take the curriculum too seriously (outside the technical fields) would be to turn themselves into social deviants, coercion was constantly needed to keep hypocrisy within reasonable bounds. (Classroom attendance regulations, naturally, were of the same piece.) In the age of the traditional college, this need had been pronounced because the classical curriculum was so patently meaningless. But when the elective system failed to produce enough of an increase in classroom seriousness, the continuing presence of these mandatory forms testified to the deeper cultural conditions which had already made them appropriate. Ours was an affluent society in which a college education, while socially necessary, articulated far less directly with highly desirable professional careers than was true in Europe. Therefore, the American university remained, as Thorstein Veblen observed, partly penal in character. Whether the student population has recently changed to a degree that makes these sanctions entirely superfluous is extremely doubtful.

Another somewhat less important formal attribute of the American curriculum, the system of unit credit, appeared in the 1890s along with the first course numbering systems. Much bewailed by humanists opposed to the spirit of quantification, this device nonetheless had the effect of modifying the uniformity of individual courses. It enabled courses which met less often than usual, or which involved more marginal subject matter, to continue to be taught, with due recognition of the discrepancy. Thus it encouraged variety and even a certain degree of experiment. When Yale in the 1940s, and Amherst shortly afterward, began attempting to prove that an institution could live without such a system of unit values, the catalog was cleaned up at the price of an undeniable increase in rigidity.

The issue of unit credit, however, opens up for inquiry the entire matter of the course as a standardized unit. Would it be an advantage if uniform course lengths and intensities were dropped in favor of individual series of lectures or discussions tailored to the needs and tastes of each person providing them? In some cases the result might be classes meeting for two hours five times a week for a year, and in others an isolated cluster of three or four such presentations. A complicated system of unit credit could allow each offering to receive its due weight on the transcript. But would this be better than what we have now? It is highly doubtful. Aside from the enormous practical problems of scheduling and of jealousies over "course load," most such courses would inevitably tend to be shorter than present ones, resulting in a far choppier total effect. By being forced to "cover" a substantial length of time, professors are encouraged to put their materials together in a sustained and connected way which is more responsible and usually more challenging. Unit credit can best allow for some middle ground between completely uniform rigidity and chaos.

The division of the school year into terms, semesters, or quarters, and the assumption that four such years equal an undergraduate education, involves a broader range of considerations. No matter how much one talks about "continuing" education as the desirable goal of an entire lifetime, it is clear that all educational systems have to establish beginning and ending points for the students who come and go on campuses. Though these decisions always seem rather arbitrary, a psychological or a cultural explanation for their bare existence would seem entirely out of order. (Only a religious mystic, or a Norman O. Brown, would attack this very notion as an instance of debilitating time orientation in organized society.) On the other hand, the *details* of these arrangements have varied considerably in practice, once in awhile with a visible bearing upon educational quality. For instance, terms of instruction in American universities have always been considerably longer than their English equivalents. This fact no doubt connects with the strongly work-oriented, middle-class expectations of American ministers and managers, as opposed to a more aristocratic ideal. Curiously, pressures of this kind intensified in the 1960s (with the possibly abortive movement toward year-round operation), even though it is common to speak of American society as moving generally in the direction of greater leisure. But resistance to a more insistent factory tone of this kind has remained high, among both faculty and students, and basic change in the duration of the academic year appears neither desirable nor likely.

As to how the academic year is internally divided, the 1960s brought a new wave of experimentation, but mainly along lines which had been pioneered at a small number of prominent institutions for many decades previously. An angry debate accompanied the conversion of the University of California to the quarter system in 1966, but it was too easily forgotten that the University of Chicago had steadily followed this same calendar ever since its founding in 1892 (and Amherst College was on it in 1900). Clearly too much can be made of the issue of quarters versus semesters. A study of the Berkeley catalogs before and after the change reveals that the effects differed widely from one department to another.

Another, more important aspect of the way in which an academic season is divided concerns the number of separate courses which students are expected to take at one time. Here the opportunities for experiment are broader, and, starting in the 1920s, the actual history of experimentation is much richer, although it did not affect the mainstream of American higher education. It began to occur to certain reformers, notably to Alexander Meiklejohn when he founded the Experimental College at the University of Wisconsin in 1927, that interesting results might be achieved by asking students to study one area at a time in great depth rather than take the four or five concurrent courses which had been the standard legacy of the nineteenth century. Undergraduates in his program thus spent their freshman year studying Greek civilization from all aspects and their sophomore year in a similar study of American civilization.[10] (Only optional foreign language courses existed in addition.) Both the 1930s and the 1960s witnessed the revival of such an idea, though in the very different context of field study projects, during which students dropped all their normal work for a quarter or a semester and pursued a single independent project of their own, often away from the campus.[11] While the hopes that were attached to both these forms of concentration were no doubt too utopian, and while the scheduling problem that resulted on a large campus remained great, here was an area in which further change of a meaningful kind might occur. But an intrinsic limitation upon such change lay possibly in the unwillingness of faculty to submerge themselves in extremely intensive courses at the expense of their own day-today intellectual variety and sense of balance. A parallel argument applied to students.

There is, next, the matter of the customary four years required for the degree. Oxford and Cambridge have long imposed a shorter period. At Harvard around the turn of the century, Charles W. Eliot prominently began advocating a three-year degree in order to reduce the pressure from the technical schools which were demanding earlier specialization; it was actually possible for many students there to finish early in this fashion for about a decade (as it was also at Amherst from 1915 to 1932). But the experiment seems to have fallen between two stools: (1) the change did not satisfy the professional schools, which wanted to claim two years of an undergraduate's time, and (2) most faculty members saw the result as weakening the concept of a bachelor's training, since it encouraged students to take even larger numbers of courses simultaneously, thereby making each course experience all the more superficial. The next major proposal of this kind was put forward by Robert Hutchins at the University of Chicago in the late 1930s. Hutchins, unlike Eliot, sought to redefine the entire meaning of undergraduate education away from specialization and therefore found a two-year curriculum of a very particular kind sufficient for the award of the degree. But such a shift appeared to most professors to link the spirit of the college too closely to that of the high school (as was indeed an avowed intent of Hutchins's scheme) and therefore to threaten their intellectual and social dignity as advanced teachers. Rightly or wrongly, they rejected any change in their function which tended toward the model of the drillmaster. And thus the Hutchins plan also collapsed.

Recent interest in reducing the bachelor's course to three years has tended more toward the Eliot than the Hutchins model. Rising standards of preparation in leading high schools have made the elementary subjects of the freshman year seem less necessary; Yale in particular has experimented with admitting a certain number of superior students as sophomores. The effect of this approach is the opposite of the effect of Hutchins's; instructors are freed for additional advanced classroom work. This, and the faster overall pace of a three-year degree, implies a changed concept of undergraduate education in a direction unfriendly to the more ardent advocates of liberal education. Moreover, it threatens to intensify elitism, since not all high schools have improved their standards, and the fourth year has given many students a needed opportunity inconspicuously to catch up. Perhaps most important, a three-year degree threatens the whole idea of the undergraduate years as a distinctive "moratorium" during which a student has leisure to find himself by a process of making false starts (Bell, 1968, pp. 285–287).

Turning to the typical modes of course presentation, we enter a domain with a far richer history but one which is likewise bounded by its own inner logic. In the nineteenth-century college, the principal means of instruction was the recitation section (copied, no doubt, from the schoolroom), although some lecturing even then existed, especially in the junior and senior years. By the end of the century, the lecture had become the dominant form in the new universities, and for rather obvious reasons. Numbers were larger, making this style of teaching economical. Besides, the new scientific spirit no less than the older religious one tended to present knowledge as something fixed and final. It was simply to be imparted, rather than being something which came out of the very process of group effort. The elementary undergraduate course in particular was intended only to summarize the existing state of progress in a given discipline. Finally, there was the example of the prominent role of lecturing in the German university system. Lecturing, for this variety of reasons, was given wide scope, and there is no doubt that American universities became too dependent upon it.

As the twentieth century advanced, three distinct forces converged to make a growing number of educators question the dominance of the lecture mode. In the first place, scientifically oriented professors began increasingly to see that the spirit in which they conducted their own advanced inquiry should be encouraged among undergraduates as well; thus the seminar and the laboratory should be promoted at all levels of university education so that students might gain a sense of what it is like to operate on the frontier of knowledge. This kind of antipathy toward lecturing was entirely compatible with the older positivistic conception of the nature of learning, which had now merely embraced subtler, less openly didactic ways and means. But at the same time, as relativistic attitudes gained headway in certain other areas of intellectual life, lecturing began to be challenged on a more fundamental ground, namely, that the very pose of the lecturer tends to imply more certainty about the existence of truth than is compatible with an education of high quality. The newer viewpoint urged that ideas be actively argued about, on the basis of evidence to be sure, but ideally through a combination of planned readings and discussions. The purpose of education shifted, in this perspective, away from the learning of facts and toward a debate over their implications in which all the intelligent and well-informed were presumed to be equals. Finally, one may detect a third separate source of attack upon the lecture system, though for tactical purposes it sometimes disguised itself in the rhetoric of the second. This was, once again, the upsurge of stridently humanistic criticism of the curriculum which had found its first expression in Woodrow Wilson's preceptorials at Princeton and which became more prominent in the 1930s. Men like Hutchins and Meiklejohn promoted the small class, not out of any belief in relativistic open-endedness, but from a desire (which they could not fully parade) to use it as a device for implanting certain moral and philosophical values in the minds of the new generation. The same may be said of the members of the Dewey movement.

The combined effect of these three quite different pressures in challenging the lecture system was considerable, though, as we are aware, it by no means sufficed to end the domination of the lecture as a classroom form, except in a few of the better small colleges. After the Second World

War, the growing tone of student seriousness encouraged university planners, particularly in leading institutions, to add as many seminars and discussion sections to the course catalogs as resources could possibly allow. The post-Sputnik boom expanded budgets sufficiently to permit these classes to come into existence on a genuinely large scale. (Undergraduate history seminar offerings, for instance, grew beyond all recognition during the early 1960s at such diverse institutions as Berkeley and Yale. An institution as vast as Berkeley was able not merely to guarantee but also to require a semester of seminar work of every history undergraduate and to mount an honors program with its own additional seminars as well.) Seminars were appealing because of their very ambiguity in terms of educational aims. Few professors had become thoroughgoing relativists, and yet to students the seminar seemed to promise an atmosphere of freewheeling egalitarianism and initiative; meanwhile, faculty members who actually retained their basic faith either in scientific knowledge through research or in some specific version of humane values had an unparalleled chance to explore their speciality or to promote their point of view.

Tutorial programs, though their inspiration was English rather than German, tended in America to serve much the same role. These had been put forward conspicuously by A. Lawrence Lowell at Harvard.[12] Again they would emerge on a much wider scale in the 1960s, when budgets for a time at least began to allow them. Tutorials, like seminars, gave a welcome impression of an educational program dovetailed with the needs and interests of individual students, while, only somewhat more wastefully from the professor's point of view, they could also merge with the specialized demands of a discipline. Yet financial considerations would always cause them to remain limited in extent, and it could be argued that they were often less beneficial than seminars because of their narrower intellectual interchange.

In sum, economic constraints probably loom larger than intellectual ones in explaining why, despite the growing diversity of recent years, most undergraduate classes in our universities remain large in size. Lectures still predominate, but few members of the academic community openly celebrate them. To this extent, the verbal climate has genuinely shifted in recent years much closer to the outlook of the curricular innovators. But, for the very reason that economics are so manifestly involved, no clear path to the future lies in this direction. And it must again be emphasized how greatly the fashion of the small class has depended for its vogue upon tacit compromises with the spirit of advanced scholarly research in defining the goal of undergraduate education.

There remains the role played by the body which sponsors the given course—normally the department. Here a major historical question arises: Why did departments (or disciplines) spring so rapidly into dominance in American universities, permitting William R. Harper already to declare at the turn of the century, "The division of the work into technical departments is an artificial and misleading one, but it is so fixed that, like the letter of the sacred Scriptures, it is by many supposed to be a part of the original creation itself" (Harper, 1905, p. 99)?

One answer to this question sees the separate departments simply as an inevitable result of the expansion of knowledge in an age of science and specialization. Certainly there appears to have been no doubt in the minds of academic reformers in the late nineteenth century that such areas of inquiry as English, history, chemistry, and physics deserved to be given formal recognition in the structures of the new universities; indeed, this change was central to the very idea of improvement in quality which they sought. (Such other fields as sociology, physical education, home economics, and dramatic art long failed to be accorded so automatic a degree of esteem.) But when one stops to think about this entire situation from a much later vantage point, one is indeed puzzled by the spectacle of discipline formation, which was so largely a product of two decades, the 1880s and 1890s.[13] Did this indeed reflect the very nature of knowledge, hereby revealing itself at long last after centuries of cover-up by the forces of superstition? Once the academic departments had become powerful, it is easy to understand the basis (in institutional politics) for their tendency to retain and enhance the power they had. But why did they initially become so powerful? Harper's contemporary aside merely whets our curiosity, since he too had assumed that a university characterized by basically strong departments was what he had to build at Chicago. Unfortunately, this is one of the central questions involving the creation of the American university on which the surviving letter files of professors and presidents reveal all too little that is fundamentally relevant.

One must not forget how vivid a picture of the departmentless college remained in the minds of the academic men of that generation. Before the 1880s, scholarly and scientific expertise had been given scant recognition in American higher education. Memories were fresh of the days when retired or temperamentally inadequate clergymen had been given college posts as sinecures. The department led grateful men away from the horrors of such a past.

Yet the key probably lies closer to institutional realities than to intellectual ones. One recalls the firm desire on the part of the early university builders to create a structure with strong inbuilt controls at every turn. Presidents of the 1890s relied upon department chairmen to give them this sense of control in their dealings with the faculty at large. Typically they called in a single man of wide reputation, appointed him chairman, and encouraged him to add a cluster of subordinates in his own image. For this reason, it was an age of notable departmental dictatorships. Then, immediately afterward, presidents began to fear some of the consequences of what they had done (it is in this light that the quotation from Harper may be read). As the chairmen they had appointed grew too deeply entrenched, these same men often turned around and responded favorably to pleas from the junior faculty for greater "democracy," thereby creating a more balanced situation which would be to their own long-run advantage. This does not mean that administrators always retained control of the result. Soon the department began serving as an ideal strategic device whereby professors gained leverage of their own. By pressing for more exclusive charge over the curriculum in particular, and by investing these units called "departments" with great dignity, the faculty ultimately erected a series of stout barricades against outside encroachment. From this point of view, it is small wonder that departments thrived—and perhaps more remarkable that a demand for research professorships under their auspices lagged behind, occurring not in the 1890s but in the 1950s. In any event, it is likely that for this mixture of reasons, initially involving the tactics of administrators and later on those of the faculty, the department gained its rapid hold over American academic life. The consequences were indeed very great. It is not too much to say that the course, inherited from the earlier schoolroom, along with the department, created in something like this fashion, together forged the basic pattern of the American university.

Might it have been better organized in another way? What would a university have been like which rewarded brilliance of achievement without conferring any more specific label upon it?[14] The mind, trying to conjure such a utopia, casts about among twentieth-century examples, both inside and outside the university: perhaps a small group of men such as those at Princeton's Institute for Advanced Study; perhaps a nonacademic circle such as the coterie of critics, writers, and artists who live in New York City. Or one thinks of the faculty who were willing to teach in Meiklejohn's Experimental College, in Hutchins's College at the University of Chicago, or most recently at Old Westbury. From any of these visions does there emerge the necessary combination of creative vigor and willingness to immerse oneself in the routine of teaching? And on a scale large enough to educate the thousands of students who are presently enrolled even at our better-quality colleges and universities? Besides, many of these alternatives are riddled with all the problems of charismatic leadership. The department may have sacrificed something in terms of an ultimate level of enthusiastic intellectual exchange (though even this is not certain), it may also have discouraged some of the more fruitful kinds of undergraduate teaching. But it probably offered the stablest compromise between brilliance and hard classroom work.

One may accept the inevitability of the departmental structure, as, in a less conscious way, most professors of the turn of the century seem to have done, and still leave open the question of how powerful and exclusive the role of these departments should be in setting the terms of the curriculum. In this respect, as will be seen in more detail shortly, the role of the departments has tended to gain over time, most visibly in the 1950s. Only the existence of a leisurely four-year curriculum has in fact enabled their aggrandizement to proceed simultaneously with a growing number of experiments in the direction of liberal education. And if there is now a move to consider reducing the curriculum to three years, the long-muted struggle between the specialists and generalists will no doubt be forced into the open. It seems not hard to predict that the advocates of greater specialization will win out in any such clear-cut contest.[15]

The Major Subject System

Nearly all these elementary aspects of an undergraduate curriculum—the course, the grade, unit credit, the term, the standard course load, the mode of presentation, and departmental sponsorship—have produced a certain amount of controversy during the last few decades, at least at the margins of the American academic world. But the major share of everyday argument about the curriculum has centered in the rules governing how courses may be combined into acceptable educational programs. Here there has certainly been no lack of continuing faculty discussion. The problem of interpretation instead centers upon the degree of meaningfulness in such repeated talk and action.

The central historical point that must be made about most American academic programs of study ever since the turn of the twentieth century is the recurrence of strikingly similar patterns among them, when they are viewed at the broadest level.[16] To be sure, genuine changes in their definition have occurred, but these have been of four rather limited sorts. First, there has been the rising number of experiments since the 1920s in the direction of liberal education, but at most institutions their scope remains peripheral, and they have also involved much internal repetition. Second, one finds a certain increase in the proportion of the total four-year program devoted to the subject major, but this tendency retains its own distinct limits. Third, course proliferation has indeed been real at major universities, especially in the last quarter-century. Finally, a major share of the changes involves seemingly endless back-and-forth movements between freedom and prescription, as far as both campuswide breadth requirements and the internal requirements of major programs are concerned.

The major-subject system has been the most sustained feature of the curriculum. In the late nineteenth century, subject majors had not at first been universal in the new universities, despite their emerging departmental structure. Cornell and Johns Hopkins, in particular, were famous for having promoted an alternative known as the *group system*, whereby a student selected one of a limited number of groups, broader in scope than single major fields. (For instance, there might be planned curriculums in the classics, the natural sciences, the social sciences, and the like.[17]) This idea represented a compromise on the part of educators, such as Daniel Coit Gilman and Andrew D. White, who feared the permissiveness of the completely free elective system which then prevailed at Harvard under Eliot. Eliot's system, under which students could simply pick any 16 courses at will, was never widely adopted at other institutions in its full form (without a subject major) and was abandoned at Harvard in 1910. But it represented a logical extreme of total freedom in the early days of the American university against which most other planners felt they had to react.[18]

By 1910 just about all American colleges and universities had embraced the subject major. The majors of this period differed widely from one another in the amount of course work they demanded. Polling 55 institutions in 1909 with this question in mind, William T. Foster discovered that the percentage of the student's time occupied by the major varied from about 7 percent at one college to about 34 percent at another, with the great bulk falling between 14 percent and 25 percent (Foster, 1911, p. 194). These figures show that although a few universities were even then requiring majors as extensive as those of recent years, the average time spent was distinctly less. Majors were still often deemphasized by the device of requiring "minors," less extensive concentrations in a second or even a third field, in addition.

The evolution of the subject major from that period to the present may be illustrated by what happened at three institutions—Berkeley, Yale, and Amherst.[19] At Berkeley, beginning in 1902, 15 units of advanced work had to be taken in a single department, and the term *major subject* to describe this appeared in 1905. The number of subjects in which one could major (in the arts and sciences colleges) rose from 24 in 1901 to 41 in 1913, when a more or less permanent plateau was reached, though the subjects themselves often changed. At Yale a major in 1906 consisted of three year-long courses of increasing difficulty (which translates to 18 units); every student there had to take no less than *two* majors and *three* minors.[21] Two years later a single major, equaling 24 units, replaced the two; it included freshman elementary courses in the subject, however, Amherst lagged behind, not creating any majors until 1910, when it belatedly moved in Yale's earlier direction, requiring three majors and one minor, with a major defined again as three year-long courses in one field and a minor as two.

Until the Second World War, fairly strong counterpressures at all three institutions prevented any great expansion in the proportion of students' time which a subject major demanded. (Indeed, elsewhere the interwar period sometimes produced a slight but noticeable reduction in departmental autonomy and power; Stanford furnishes a case in point.) At Berkeley, from 1915 to 1958, a major was defined as 24 units, often including a small amount of work in a related discipline, but an option of a group major always existed, permitting as few as 12 units of work in a single field in combination with others. Group major was an old-fashioned term for *interdisciplinary program*, and these majors tended to be promoted faddishly—at Berkeley from around 1915 to 1921, at Amherst in great earnest under Meiklejohn in the early 1920s, and again at all three campuses (as "area studies") in the late 1930s and early 1940s. Meanwhile, at Yale after 1911 a student took only one major along with a minor in a related field, and the major equaled 24 units of upper-division work, identical with Berkeley's. There matters stood until 1946, by which time majors in 33 fields were being offered, all but a handful of them departmental in character. Amherst replaced its three majors and minor with *two* subject majors in 1915, an arrangement lasting until 1930, when it switched to a single major and two minors. But not until 1938 (when the minors were finally dropped) did the major expand to 30 units, 22 of which had to be taken within one department—and freshman courses were now often included in the total. In 1940, Amherst offered 25 departmental programs, though in a few cases with so few courses as effectively to bar a major. The counterpressures at these institutions revealed themselves in upper limits, existing at all three of them in the interwar period, upon the number of courses in a single subject which a student might count toward his degree. A variety of requirements expressed fear that students might concentrate too much. Berkeley even moved backward in 1939, newly establishing the option of a "general (nonmajor) curriculum of 36 upper division units, according to the student's choice, distributed through not more than three departments."

Amherst made no further changes (until 1971, when it actually moved toward deemphasizing subject majors), but the more research-oriented atmosphere after World War II made itself felt in this respect at both Berkeley and Yale. Starting in 1958, the general (nonmajor) alternative at Berkeley was dropped, and even the group-major programs were greatly reduced, forcing nearly every student into the hands of a department. Students were forced into departments earlier, too, for freshman and sophomore programs were integrated more clearly into the majors, and by 1968 the upper limit on courses taken in one department disappeared entirely. Majors never totaled less than 30 units (or 45 quarter-units) and could go much higher. After 1946, majors at Yale also demanded the equivalent of 30 units, 6 of which could be in a related field. In 1953, the total went up to 36 and still excluded freshman courses. As at Berkeley, sophomores were now encouraged to begin a definite concentration, and so, in one special program, were freshmen. Countermoves against excessive specialization had been evident in the catalogs from around 1948 to 1931, but by the mid-1950s the tide was fast moving in the other direction.

By the mid-twentieth century, Berkeley and Yale had seemingly become quite different institutions, the one a vast state university, and the other a private institution of more moderate size. Yet the similarities between them—in their initial movement toward majors during the 15 years after 1900, in the static standoff of the inter-war period, and in the definite expansion of majors more recently—are very striking indeed. Amherst traveled more slowly, arriving in 1938 about where Yale and Berkeley had moved by 1913. Since the Second World War, Amherst has held fast, or perhaps even begun a reversal, which may indicate that pressures from the graduate school are apt to be felt far less even now at colleges which do not offer Ph.D. programs. Both Yale and Amherst, incidentally, have offered highly elitist independent study programs as alternatives to conventional majors in recent years. Finally, however, it is important to remember that even at Berkeley, the subject major still often absorbs no more than a third of a student's overall time and need absorb no more than a quarter.

The history of subject-major programs on a campuswide scale must be supplemented by that of changing requirements within individual majors. For this purpose, the history, philosophy, sociology, and physics programs at Berkeley and Yale (and, in some cases, at Amherst) were studied since the turn of the century. Four general patterns seem to emerge:

1. Some programs are hampered by inadequate staffing and recognition, often in conjunction with too exclusive a domination by a single professor. This has been the case in certain fields at Amherst, where the sparscity of course offerings, despite supplementation in recent years by courses at three nearby institutions, becomes painfully evident when one compares its catalog with those of larger institutions. But sociology (or "social science") at both Yale and Berkeley prior to the 1950s also reflects these peculiar problems. The formal requirements of the major mean little because the main need is simply to mount a rudimentary program. When such a field is suddenly allowed to expand, as with sociology at Berkeley in the 1950s, the result is apt to be a rather wild variation in requirements from year to year as the department gets its bearings.

2. Another kind of program conceives of itself as imparting a very definite, stable body of information to all its students. The discipline of physics, again at both Yale and Berkeley (and in the honors version at Amherst), fills this model. As the years have passed from 1900 to the present, more and more required courses and demanding prerequisites have been added to the major, but little has been dropped. Undergraduate major programs of this type might be compared with the prescribed curriculums of entire American colleges in the nineteenth century, except that they offer knowledge of a kind which is held in greater contemporary regard. The intellectual prestige of the discipline, and of its leading practitioners, has in effect banished all curricular doubts. The parallel between classics 100 years ago and physics today reminds one, however, that the mere existence of such a rigorously structured program says nothing about its intrinsic quality.

3. Still another kind of major program, represented especially well by philosophy at Berkeley, offers extreme stability along with a large degree of elective choice. Ever since 1934 (and, with only slight revision, since 1921) Berkeley's philosophy classes have been divided into three groups: first, "courses concerned with a critical analysis and appraisal of specific human interests such as art, literature, morality, religion, science, and society"; second, "courses dealing with the methods of reflective thinking and the more general features of experience" (metaphysics, logic, epistemology, and the like); and third, "courses dealing with individual thinkers and epochs in the history of ideas." Majors have had to take 6 units from each of these groups, the final 6 may be freely chosen, 3 of them from outside the department. In 1958, specific semester courses in ethics and theory of knowledge were first required of all majors (but still counted toward the 6 units in their respective groups). The department rode out the arrival of the quarter system and survived to 1971 with no further shifts in its program. Apparently its formula for reasonable balance still proved satisfying to everybody. Again, as with physics, one should reflect that such stability has no intrinsic relation to academic quality, especially since many philosophy programs at other campuses have moved in radically different directions.

4. A final pattern in departmental major programs is illustrated by the field of history, again at both Berkeley and Yale. This is a tendency toward frequent, restless tampering with requirements, but along lines which, over the years, embody a fairly regular back-and-forth movement between freedom and prescription, or between encouragement and discouragement of specialization. Thus in the history major at Berkeley the pendulum swung toward freedom in 1900, 1918, 1944, and 1966 and toward more uniform requirements in 1912, 1922, and around 1958. At Yale, after many years of reshuffling the fields of concentration within the major, in 1969 all requirements were suddenly abolished (other than a one-year seminar and a senior essay). Almost total freedom suddenly reigned.

The oscillations illustrated by both these history programs may lead one to doubt whether the energy spent in curricular planning at the departmental level over the years has been very meaningful. (The philosophers may indeed have shown more wisdom.) Clearly in this particular discipline there seem to be disadvantages in both extremes—structuring and free election—producing a countermovement whenever one extreme has been neared; yet programs of both types appear to have functioned well at outstanding universities, and it may not matter much what is the momentary outcome. The very variety of structures and nonstructures over the years argues against any intrinsic relationship between the quality of the program and such internal questions of format.

Breadth Requirements

Campuswide breadth or distribution requirements constitute still another central aspect of the undergraduate curriculum. Again using Berkeley, Yale, and Amherst as examples, one may find a long record of maneuver and countermaneuver in this seemingly important area, almost precisely paralleling the kinds of changes taking place inside the individual departments. Indeed, the history of breadth requirements set forth by the College of Letters and Science at Berkeley might be compared with that of the philosophy major at the same institution, while the breadth requirements established by the faculty of Yale College recall the more restless spirit of the two history departments. The record of Amherst falls somewhere in between.

Required studies at all three institutions in the pre-World War I period were formidable, although Amherst before 1910 was unusually liberal. All Berkeley students at the turn of the century had to take 10 units of English, 6 of mathematics, 12 in the natural sciences (where a wide selection of departmental introductory courses was available), 18 of foreign language, 8 of history or political science, and 5 of military science, for a total of 59 units of the 125 required for graduation. In the next two decades language and natural science requirements declined somewhat, and physical education and "subject A" (English composition) were added. At Yale the requirements were more intricate, and the changes in them far more frequent; by 1921 they amounted to 60 units, including two years of natural science. Compulsory college study of the classics had been abandoned in 1911, restored in 1917, and again discontinued in 1920. At Amherst, classical languages, modern languages, English, and mathematics had to be taken in the freshman year. Until 1910, the upper three years offered almost total elective freedom (recall, further, that no majors existed there in that period). But then many new hurdles were imposed, amounting to a year of mathematics; a year of English; two years of Greek or Latin; two years chosen from biology, chemistry, and physics; a reading knowledge of two modern languages; and substantial work in public speaking and physical education. In 1915 a year of history or philosophy was added, and in 1918 an additional year in English, music, or a foreign language.

The decades that followed brought a mixture of stability and cyclical change at these three institutions. At Berkeley there were few alterations in the breadth requirements from 1920 to 1970. These long comprised 15 units of foreign language in not more than two languages, elementary algebra and geometry if not taken in high school, 12 units of natural science (2 of which could be satisfied by proper high school work), and at least a year course in any three of the following five areas: English or public speaking, additional foreign language, more advanced mathematics, history or social science, and philosophy. There were also requirements in military science (until 1963) and physical education and hygiene (until 1933). An American institutions requirement was imposed by the legislature in 1924. In 1940 a sixth distributional field, fine arts, was added, and after 1945 a year course had to be taken in four out of the six. In 1960 the basic foreign language requirement was reduced to 12 units, the mathematics and natural science requirements were made internally more rigorous, and the four-out-of-six fields distribution requirement was replaced by a simple formula of 12 units in the social sciences and 12 in the humanities, with a wide variety of specific courses listed as eligible. During all these decades in the history of a large, internally diverse institution, marked by finely balanced counterpressures, one imagines that a high value was placed upon not rocking the boat. In 1970, however, all breadth requirements were suddenly dropped, putting Berkeley in much the same position as pre-1910 Amherst.

Meanwhile, at Yale, a clublike senior faculty found apparently endless pleasure in debating these same matters, and the result was an urge toward finicky retouching, so frequent and complex that little of it can be recapitulated here. After many years of back-and-forth changes, eight distributional areas were created in 1922: English, biblical literature, or art; history (European or American); anthropology or economics; psychology, philosophy, education, or mathematics; physics, chemistry, geology, or biology; a second natural science from the same list; Greek, Latin, or classical civilization; and modern languages. Students had to take a year course in all eight areas and two in five of them. After further minor changes in the late 1920s, breadth requirements were greatly reduced in 1931. Only two years of natural science (one year after 1933), an advanced foreign language course, and a year of classical civilization were retained. After a decade of unusual calm, movement began in 1942 back toward formidable breadth requirements. A year course was demanded in six newly defined groups (after 1946, nine, plus a compulsory summer reading program; after 1949, in eight of the nine, making it again possible to take only one year of natural science). The pendulum swung sharply toward simplification again in 1955, with year courses in six closely defined areas, plus another three spread among the three broad divisions (these last were dropped in 1962). In 1959, as a response to Sputnik, a second year of natural science was again enforced, Then in 1966 all distributional requirements were entirely discontinued, though the catalog warned that truly eccentric programs would be disapproved on an individual basis.

At Amherst there were also some astonishing shifts over the decades. Two years of the ancient languages finally dropped to one (and was made alternative to mathematics) in 1933. In 1933 a brief but extreme swing toward freedom occurred; all breadth requirements were abolished except public speaking, physical education, and a reading knowledge of French or German. In 1939 prescription returned with a vengeance: two years of science, two years of social studies or philosophy, and two years of English and humanities, plus 13 units of advanced work outside the division of one's major. The mid-1950s brought a further tightening. English and humanities expanded to 2 1/2 years, and several specific compulsory courses were created to fulfill the freshman and sophomore requirements. Then, in 1966, one-semester courses in each of the three divisions replaced the former two-year sequences in each, but sophomores had to take seven courses outside the major department, distributed among the three divisions and in internally meaningful sequences. The language requirement was somewhat eased in 1970; a few years earlier public speaking had finally disappeared. A further trend toward freedom was perhaps in the offing.

Just how consequential are all these maneuverings (or, for that matter, their comparative absence)? Berkeley, for instance, enormously improved the quality of its educational performance during the decade of the 1950s, while its mechanical formula for breadth went untouched. Yale, on the other hand, underwent almost annual revisions of this kind in certain periods and yet retained a reputation for conservatism of a deeper sort. Amherst may also be termed "conservative" in its basic style of education, and yet it has had two earlier flings with freedom and now seems to be moving toward a third. Taking the three institutions together, one can detect a certain movement toward freedom in the mid-1930s and an even stronger one in that direction very recently. But such freedom existed at Harvard, Amherst, and elsewhere more than 60 years ago, producing an impression of cyclical rather than secular change even on this seemingly fundamental level. The difficulty of correlating these curricular changes with other important academic considerations appears to mount with each example.

Course Proliferation

One further aspect of the curricular mainstream in American higher education remains to be explored. This concerns the multiplication of individual courses in every conceivable field as universities have expanded during the twentieth century—the consequences of course proliferation. For if breadth requirements have promoted a certain degree of uniformity (or at least balance) in the educational experience, opposing arguments have long existed, urging the amount of available variety as an even more important index of quality. Variety, after all, makes it easier for students to form connections with definite interests. Nothing is more quickly perceived than an intellectual or economic parsimony which causes the range and depth of the offerings to disappoint one's whetted appetite.

The topic of course proliferation is uniquely amenable to quantitative treatment. Tables 1, 2, and 3 show the number of separate courses (in semester equivalents) available at Berkeley, Yale, and Amherst, at 10-year intervals since 1900, in 13 disciplines selected for their diversity. Naturally it should be understood that even these figures disguise a multitude of arbitrary decisions made during the counting process, and the totals must be regarded as merely approximate.[21]

The figures clearly reveal several things. First, the discrepancy between disciplines is enormous, not only (as might be expected) in overall offerings, but also in degree of growth. While some fields, such as history and philosophy, spectacularly rise, others, such as physics and French, move upward only slowly and slightly. Still others, such as classics and education, markedly decline (though there has recently been something of a classics revival at Berkeley). Second, these statistics vividly show how static American higher education was during the long period before the Second World War; indeed, as enrollments increased during the 1920s and 1930s while course offerings remained relatively level, there is a deep hint of declining quality during this era. (The history offerings at Yale in the 1920s, as compared with those of 10 years earlier, are appalling.) Course proliferation on a grand scale is a product of the last quarter-century. And, even so, it is relatively absent at a small college such as Amherst, through the new availability of courses at three nearby campuses must here be taken into account. Altogether, the figures emphasize how misleading is the picture of American academic history simply as one of steady growth in all areas and at all times during the twentieth century. Instead the story is one of dynamic processes coexisting with static conditions and with still others where an apparent dynamism conceals equilibrium.

For instance, it might be further noted that the proliferation of courses in recent years has not been paralleled by an equivalent rise in the total number of subjects in which an arts and sciences undergraduate can major. Much has been made of the "knowledge revolution" with its explosion of new subspecialties, particularly in the natural sciences.[22] But, apart from programs in computer science, it is difficult to find many concrete effects of such a change in undergraduate course catalogs; most of the new "disciplines" seem to be confined to the graduate and medical schools. Meanwhile, many areas of engineering, no less than classics, have been involved in an actual decline, while such fields as agriculture and business administration (where they have existed in high-quality universities) appear to survive as peripherally tolerated vested interests. The result is that the number of major subjects has by no means moved upward year after year. Instead it has long remained static, probably amounting to somewhere between 25 and 40 at most large institutions.[23] At Berkeley, steady pressure can be detected to rid the letters and science catalog of inappropriately technical major subjects, so that criminology, journalism, home economics, education, and the like were gradually dropped over the years; only a very few such fields, including physical education and social welfare, managed to survive. Moreover, the unmistakable long-term trend is for premedical and prelaw students to be given increasingly less special treatment in the undergraduate years. The desire of nearly all professional faculties to center their teaching efforts at the graduate level once their fields are firmly established has actually succeeded in removing a great deal of the pressure toward early technical specialization which existed in the opening years of the century. The opponents of the humanists have become largely the "pure" researchers rather than the crass utilitarians as a result.

Table 1
Course offerings at Berkeley, 1900–1910, in selected fields (in semester-course equivalents)

Discipline	1900a	1910, by type ld	ud	hon	fe	1910 total	1920, by type ld	ud	hon	1920 total
Classics[c]	45	28	29	7	i	64	14	33		47
Economics	8	10	28	6	1	45	8	22	4	34
Education	14		12	3	1.5	16.5		30		30
French[c]	23	6	16	2		24	6	23		29
Geology[d]	11	2	10			12	3	11		14
History	22	7	20		4	31	6	24	2	32
Mathematics[e]	27	15	16			31	11	18	1	30
Philosophy[f]	9	5	8	2	3	18	8	14	1	23
Physics[g]	18	8	12			20	6	18		24
Portuguese										
Psychology	6	2	5			7	1	16	2	19
Slavic languages[c]		2	9	1	i	12	9	16	3	28
Sociology[h]							2	3		5

Discipline	1930, by type ld	ud	hon	1930 total	1940, by type ld	ud	1940 total
Classics[c]	12	23		35	10	24	34
Economics	6	32[k]		38	6	31	37
Education		39		39		35	35
French[c]	10	18		28	7	16	23
Geology[d]	3	18		21	3	19	22
History	6	34	2	42	4	49	53
Mathematics[e]	10	20		30	16	20	36
Philosophy[f]	5	19		24	5	19	24
Physics[g]	11	16		27	13	14	27
Portuguese		3		3		3	3
Psychology	2	20	1	23	24	23	27
Slavic languages[c]	9	12		21	6	14	20
Sociology[h]	2	8		10	4	7	11

	1950, by type ld	ud	1950 total	1960, by type ld	ud	hon	1960 total	1970, by type ld	ud	hon	1970 total
Classics[c]	13	18.5	31.5	10	19	3	22	10	29	2	41
Economics	4	35	39	3	34	3	40	2	35		37
Education		39	39		26		26		16		16
French[c]	7	21	28	7	24		31	11	32	1	44
Geology[d]	3	20	23	5	21	1	27	3	29		33
History	8	61	69	10	70	5	85	15[l]	69	7	91[l]
Mathematics[e]	20	42	62	16	44	6	66	15	71	7	93
Philosophy[f]	7	22	29	6	29	1	36	10	45	2	57
Physics[g]	11	17	28	8	18	1	27	13	27	1	41
Portuguese	4	3	7	5	3		8	4	4		8
Psychology	5	39	44	4	38	3	45	5	45	7	57
Slavic languages[c]	11	26	37	12	14		26	25	26	1	52
Sociology[h]	4	23	27	4	27	2	33	2	40	3	45

[a] Upper-division and lower-division courses were not clearly distinguished in 1900.
[b] Quarter courses have generally been counted as the equivalent of semester courses.
[c] Excludes courses with reading in translation. Classics excludes Sanskrit and linguisitics, but includes archaeology.
[d] Excludes courses in mineralogy, but includes courses in geophysics.
[e] Includes courses in statistics, even when these were offered in a separate department.
[f] Excludes courses in psychology before these departments were separated.

ᵍ Excludes courses in optometry and in medical physics.

ʰ Includes courses with this subject matter offered in the social science program: excludes a few courses with this subject matter, offered for many years in the departments of economics and anthropology.

ⁱ 4.5 courses of this type not counted because they involved reading in translation.

ʲ 4 courses of this type not counted because they involved reading in translation.

ᵏ Excludes 39 commerce courses.

ˡ In addition, certain lower division seminars were not described in enough detail to be counted separately as they deserved.

NOTE: *ld* indicates lower division; *ud* indicates upper division: *hon* indicates upper-division honors courses: *fe* indicates free elective (culturally or socially relevant courses intended for nonmajors).

Table 2
Course offerings at Yale, 1900–1970, in selected fields (in semester-course equivalents)

Discipline	1900ᵃ	1910, by type A	B	C	1910 total	1920, by type A	B	C	hon	1920 total	1930ᵃ	1940, by type elemᵇ,ʰ	advᵇ	1940 total
Classicsᶜ	42	8	12	12	32	8	6	16	4	34	35	14	18	32
Economics	16	2	6	11	19	2	2	12		16	23	10	33	43
Education	2	(ungraded)			5	(ungraded)				5				
Frenchᶜ	18	8	6	4	18	6	6	4	1	17	24	4	28	32
Geologyᵈ	5		8	4	12	2	8	2	2	14	16	2	14	16
History	27	2	25	14	41	2	15	6		23	26(2)	12	40	52
Mathematicsᵉ	19	2	8	6	16	2	4	8		14	22	12	16	28
Philosophyᶠ	28	9	4	10	23	5	9		6	20	26(6)	6	30	36
Physics	6	2	4	4	10	4	2	4	4	14	20	14	10	24
Portuguese														
Psychology	11	2	8	4	14	2	8	4	2	16	16(2)	4	16	20
Slavic languagesᶜ	4	(ungraded)			2	2	2			4				
Sociologyᵍ	3		2	4	6		6			6	10	2	10	12

Discipline	1950, by type elemʰ	adv	hon	1950 total	1960, by type elemʰ	adv	hon	1960ʲ total	1970, by typeᵍ elemʰ	adv	1970,ʲ total
Classicsᵃ	9	20		29	6	24		30	7	29	36
Economics	4	28	2	34	2	44	4	50	10	58	68
Education	2	2		4							
Frenchᵃ	6	22		28	6	24		30	6	28	34
Geologyᵈ	5	11		16	5	11		16	5	14	19
History	6	34	6	46	15	58	10	83	12	126ʲ	138ʲ
Mathematicsᵉ	12	15		27	12	15		27	16	20	36
Philosophy	3	25		28	8	17		25	20	50	70
Physics	10	16		26	8	18	2	28	14	16	30
Portuguese	2	4		6	2	4		6	2	5	7
Psychology	6	12	4	22	3	22	5	30	2	56	58
Slavic languagesᵍ	4	8		12	4	16	2	22	4	27	31
Sociologyᶠ	2	24	2	28	2	23		25	7	24	31

ᵃ It is not easily possible to segregate elementary from advanced courses on the basis of the 1900 or the 1930 catalog. The only honors courses offered in 1930 in these fields are shown in parentheses at the right of the total.

ᵇ There were no honors courses in 1940 or 1970.

ᶜ Excludes courses with reading in translation. Classics excludes Sanskrit and linguistics, but includes archaeology.

ᵈ Includes mineralogy; excludes geography and paleontology.

ᵉ Excludes drawing, surveying, and astronomy; includes statistics.

ᶠ Excludes courses in psychology before these departments were separated.

ᵍ Excludes courses at all dates with primarily anthropological content. However, for the period before 1930, this comprises the anthropology listings, which were mainly sociological in content. A few courses in economics with sociological content are shown only under economics.

[h] In general, courses numbered below 30 were considered elementary, those above 30 advanced, unless the individual descriptions indicated otherwise.

[i] Excludes history of science and medicine and courses in economic history.

[j] Cross-listed courses, very common in 1960 and 1970, are never counted more than once: they are assigned to what seems the more appropriate discipline in each case.

NOTE: The letters A, B, and C refer to level of difficulty as designated by the faculty: *hon* indicates courses limited to honors students.

Table 3
Course offerings at Amherst, 1900–1970, in selected fields (in semester-course equivalents)

Discipline	1900[a]	1910	1920	1930[b]		1940[b]		1950[b]		1960[b]		1970[b,c]	
Classics[d]	26	19	24	28	(4)	30	(10)	21	(4)	22	(4)	23	(4)
Economics	3	10	10	12	(2)	20	(12)	21	(5)	19	(2)	22	(2)
Education	1	2						1		1		2	
French	9	12	10	16	(2)	16	(6)	20	(2)	17	(2)	19	(2)
Geology[e]	3	3	4	6		7	(2)	7	(2)	8	(2)	13	(2)
History	6	12	10	16	(2)	26	(14)	26	(4)	22	(3)	37	(2)
Mathematics[f]	13	10[g]	8	18		10	(4)	11	(2)	11	(2)	18	(2)
Philosophy[h]	11	5	12	12		16	(4)	12	(2)	14	(2)	18	(2)
Physics	6	8	6	10		12	(4)	16	(4)	14	(2)	18	(2)
Portuguese						[i]							
Psychology	6	2	2	4		8	(2)	12	(2)	18	(2)	15	(2)
Slavic languages										4		11	(2)
Sociology	[j]	[k]	2[l]	[k]								11	(2)

[a] Amherst was then on the quarter system, with most courses meeting four times a week. Quarter courses are counted as if they were semester courses.

[b] The number of honors courses included in these totals is given in parentheses at the right. Amherst has never clearly distinguished between elementary and advanced courses.

[c] Does not reflect the wide availability of courses at three other nearby institutions.

[d] Excludes courses with reading in translation.

[e] Excludes paleontology and certain courses in mineralogy.

[f] Includes statistics.

[g] Excludes mechanical drawing.

[h] Excludes courses in psychology before these departments were separated. Excludes courses in religion.

[i] Portuguese was offered briefly during World War II.

[j] Some time was devoted to sociological topics within one of the philosophy courses.

[k] Two economics courses had strong sociological content.

[l] Called "Social and Economic Institutions."

But if subject proliferation has not accorded with the prophecies of the technocratic enthusiasts, no one can deny that course proliferation, involving many of the most "liberal" of the disciplines, has been exceedingly real, at least at the larger universities. The question therefore remains: What does this kind of change mean in terms of educational quality? The mainstream of American higher education responds to this issue affirmatively, seeing diversity as intrinsically valuable, and therefore regards the last quarter-century as having brought about a spectacular educational breakthrough. The humanistic critics, represented most boldly by the St. Johns colleges, see only the clutter of an empiricism run riot, and they attack the current curriculum as evidence of an unwholesome domination of undergraduate education by the spirit of the graduate school. Meanwhile, those who (like myself) believe in empirical inquiry tempered by a constant awareness of its humane implications may react to the spectacle in a more moderately favorable fashion. Much of the course proliferation of the 1950s and 1960s, it should be remembered, has permitted the great flowering of seminars and discussion courses in several of the central disciplines. The clash between humanistically oriented students and research oriented professors in these small-group settings may actually give American undergraduate education a large share of its present vitality. If this is the case, then as long as specialization does not go to lengths that are truly absurd, there is every reason to applaud the recent tendency. On many campuses, the late 1960s witnessed course proliferation of a type even more directly relevant to student interests, as seminars were created which catered to the hunger for contemporaneity.

Interdisciplinary Courses

Up to this point our topical survey of the undergraduate curriculum has dealt with issues which have affected just about every existing college and university in the United States. Far more striking are the great variety of radical experiments that have been launched, despite their high rate of failure. Such ventures are usually lumped together under the label *interdisciplinary*, though certain kinds of courses offered by single departments really belong under this category as well. An interesting feature of both the Berkeley and Yale catalogs during the progressive era, for example, was the existence of a number of "free elective" courses in the various fields, obviously designed to appeal to nonmajors who wanted cultural breadth and, in some cases, contemporary relevance. These diverse ventures, which disappeared with the First World War, offer an explicit parallel to the many "college" courses at Yale, Santa Cruz, and elsewhere in our own day.

The characteristic form of the interdisciplinary course in the decades prior to the Second World War was the "survey." Very often it comprehended the natural sciences, social sciences, or humanities at the introductory level. As early as 1902, John Dewey (Thomas, 1962, p. 52) had urged that the broadest function of teaching was to give the student "a survey, at least, of the universe in its manifold training," thereby laying some claim to be considered the founder of the general education movement in this country. In a broad sense, both Woodrow Wilson and A. Lawrence Lowell gave further impetus to ideas of this kind. The earliest actual interdisciplinary survey course I have discovered in a university catalog is one given at Berkeley in 1908 in the natural sciences (for nonscience majors).[24] Previous curricular historians, however, have always pointed to a course in social and economic institutions, introduced at Amherst in 1914 shortly after Meiklejohn became president, as the first such offering. In any event, not until 1919 did the movement toward survey courses really take hold, with the creation of the contemporary civilization program at Columbia, along lines that already emphasized the so-called great books. (Both the great books and Western civilization course concepts go back further in time than has been realized, however, and were notably pioneered at Berkeley.[25]) After the idea of a "great books" approach to the study of Western civilization had gained sway at Columbia, it began to spread more rapidly. Hutchins's innovations at the University of Chicago, starting a decade later, in turn helped to spawn the unique curriculum at St. John's College, which was established in 1937. It depended totally on a reading of 100 "great books" over the entire four-year span.

Meanwhile, other less radical versions of the survey course blossomed during the 1920s. The senior symposiums at Reed College, begun in 1924, were notable for their attempt to draw students back toward an integrated view of knowledge after an immersion in specialization, in a kind of secular counterpart to the nineteenth century senior course in moral philosophy. (The similarity between the Reed program of 1924 and Daniel Bell's recipe for "third-tier" courses at Columbia in 1966 is rather astonishing—Bell, 1968, pp. 213–214, 263–264.) More typically, Dartmouth offered a survey sequence in evolution, and Williams one in American national problems. Chicago, even prior to Hutchins, created courses with such titles as Introduction to Reflective Thinking and The Nature of the World and of Man. By 1925, some 82 such survey or orientation courses were counted in American colleges or universities; 10 years later, the number had increased to at least 125 in 99 institutions (64 of which were liberal arts colleges, and the rest teachers colleges or junior colleges). Minnesota and Oregon became famous for establishing entire subcolleges devoted to liberal education of this type, in the former case for unusually weak students and in the latter case for gifted ones.[26] Survey courses reached their peak in the 1930s; thereafter they faced increasing attack for their alleged superficiality. One historian has speculated that survey courses in contemporary issues gained much of their popularity during the Depression decade because they addressed themselves to the "youth problem": if so, then in large part they represented the same sort of curricular response to the demand for contemporary relevance as the "free electives" courses of the progressive era had (Brubacher & Rudy, 1968, p. 278).

It becomes impossible to judge survey courses as a curricular tactic, so greatly did they differ. At one extreme might be placed a year course in contemporary thought which was offered at Northwestern University for a long period starting in 1923 and which featured lectures to as many as 2,000 students, often given by stray, outside celebrities and repeated in the evening for the townsfolk. The main reading imposed upon this huge captive audience was the professor's own textbook, *The New Universe*, and although the course did divide into sections, these in turn contained from 70 to 90 students apiece.[27] At an opposite pole were the surveys given at the University of Chicago in the Hutchins period. In the social sciences, these were notable for their unusual stress upon the mastery of theory, in direct conjunction with study of the public problems of the day. Though a detailed description of them leaves no doubt that they were slanted in part toward specific left-oriented conclusions, it is also clear that (in comparison, for instance, with their Columbia counterparts) they uniquely transcended the progressive historicism which was then so pervasive as an underlying point of view.[28]

The Deweyan approach to the curriculum in this period meanwhile produced results of two opposite kinds: toward a planned uniform program dealing with "life situations" and toward complete individual freedom. The former strategy is intriguingly illustrated by what happened at Stephens College, a Missouri girls' school, where the entire curriculum was redrawn from scratch after 300 young adult women across the United States had been asked to keep full records of their activities, "intellectual and emotional," in the form of diaries for an entire week. On the basis of the material in these diaries—which presumably revealed how these women were actually spending their lives—seven categories of "human needs" were derived. Courses applying the Deweyan perspective to each of these areas were then invented.[29] Meanwhile, at such colleges as Bennington and Sarah Lawrence, the contrary line was taken: Incoming freshmen were tested and interviewed concerning their own distinctive backgrounds and aptitudes and then were set to work on independent projects which reflected this "inventory" of personal needs and talent.[30] The costliness of this last alternative has already been noted; also important was the danger that such an approach would foster premature specialization.[31]

The one curricular experiment of this era which, more even than Hutchins's, transcended all such telltale categories (whether Deweyan or traditional) and instead looked ahead to postwar innovations was Alexander Meiklejohn's Experimental College at the University of Wisconsin, which existed only from 1927 to 1932. In retrospect, Meiklejohn emerges as an altogether remarkable figure, a man who in many ways was a generation ahead of his time. More than anyone else, he bridged the enormous gap between traditional and progressive versions of liberal education, and in a manner which one can now see was entirely compatible with introducing students to the spirit of advanced inquiry, despite his own unreasoning prejudice against the graduate school. The great virtue of Meiklejohn's approach was that it combined respect for intellectual seriousness, the role of tradition, and contemporary relevance. Assuming realistically that the older religious sources of intellectual unification were now dead, he sought to devise an academic program which would nonetheless enable students to see beyond particulars and gain a strong sense of identification with a larger whole, both at the level of the college and in American society. Rejecting pragmatism for its denigration of theory, Meiklejohn held in careful balance the theoretical and the practical, the critical and the affirmative.[32] The aim of education, he announced, was neither utilitarian skill nor scholarly knowledge; it was "intelligence." This word, he said, meant "readiness for any human situation; it is the power, wherever one goes, of being able to see, in any set of circumstances, the best response which a human being can make to those circumstances." In fact, as he used it, the term implied something very close to wisdom. The first two years of the college course should have as their special function the promotion, through the shrewdest possible curricular devices, of this kind of wisdom. Intelligence was to be fostered by reading a wide variety of books in common and by discussing them in groups. Ambitious field study projects were also included. Mere abstract talk about "life needs," such as the Deweyans indulged in, was rejected, as was the "great books" idea, on the sensible ground that it pulled isolated thinkers out of their cultural contexts.[33] Instead, the college set out to create an atmosphere of critical, open-ended dialogue, buttressed by a constant effort to teach skill of expression that involved use of tutorial methods and occasional lectures.[34]

In its own day, and in that particular region, the program could not survive. It ran squarely into the most vicious forms of Midwestern philistinism, both on the rest of the Madison campus and in the state at large. Fraternities, local politicians, and unfriendly professors hounded the program to death. High schools throughout Wisconsin warned their own graduates against entering it, and so almost none did. The out-of-state students who flocked into it were attacked as Jews, radicals, and misfits.[35] False rumors were deliberately spread that the program was being abandoned. Toward the end, the total number of students enrolled in it was far below capacity.

The fate of Meiklejohn's Experimental College reminds us once again of the enormously different temper of American higher education before the Second World War. It is revealing that the Wisconsin program failed ultimately for lack of students, whereas the problem faced by Joseph Tussman in his similar undertaking at Berkeley in the late 1960s was reluctance of the faculty to commit themselves to it in an age (and at a campus) of much increased specialization. On the whole, the chances for such programs appear to have improved during recent years; they would certainly seem to offer the best alternative to elective freedom.

In a broader sense, Meiklejohn's venture (when divorced from some of its antiempirical overtones) looked ahead to the changing spirit of curricular reform during the 1940s and 1950s. At this time, certain new trends appeared. Innovations no longer centered in surveys but rather (at first) in "area studies" and then in interdisciplinary courses and programs dealing with specific themes or "problems." Both these forms combined breadth and depth in the new way that Meiklejohn (with his study of Greek and American civilization) had first suggested, though they often represented a much more conventional commitment to specialized inquiry than Meiklejohn personally favored.

Area studies were the product of increased American concern with remote parts of the globe, beginning in the late 1930s and expanding to meet the practical need for experts during and after the Second World War. To a certain degree, area studies also reflected the growing penetration of the anthropological concepts of "culture" and "cultural relativism." Yet this basic shift in thinking, important as it has seemed to many people since the 1930s, worked no general revolution in American undergraduate education. Many disciplines remained impervious to the newer outlook, continuing to view the world in terms of universals, whether empirical or metaphysical in origin. Area studies, embodying the rival idea of cultural holism, actually began retreating from view after the 1940s, at least on the undergraduate level. In this instance the rapid victory won by the traditional departments of learning may well have dealt an unfair blow to a promising alternative. The concept of culture has offered one of the clearest and most persuasive rationales for cross-disciplinary fertilization, not least in the highly significant area of comparative studies.

But curricular experiment, especially in the freshman and sophomore years, continued to increase, and it often now involved the selection of particular problems or issues which cut across normal disciplinary lines. (Atomic fission was a notable example seized upon at Sarah Lawrence in the late 1940s because in all its implications it involved natural science, social science, and the humanities.) Again as with the older surveys, the "problems" courses became so various as to defy any single judgment about them. But it is clear that they did represent a closer accommodation to the spirit of empirical inquiry and research than the surveys did, and this tendency made it easier for them to gain footing in the postwar educational climate.

A less conventional variant of the problems course or seminar was one sponsored nondepartmentally, often by a "college." This became fashionable, for instance, at Yale and at Santa Cruz, starting in the mid-1960s. A certain revival of a collegiate image for undergraduate training occurred in America at this time, again making one think back to Alexander Meiklejohn. Older colleges or houses, which had been purely residential units, were now sometimes given peripheral academic functions, in the direction of either traditional liberal education or contemporary social relevance. But the college revival was deceptive because it confused the matter of the organizing unit with that of the intellectual substance of its academic program. Though a conventional department might be understood to stand for narrow specialization of some identifiable kind, the idea of a college connoted nothing so distinct. Thus what seemed to matter most about the college revival was not its rather accidental form (for these colleges never became intimate or holistic enough to function as organic communities in the sense that Meiklejohn would have liked) but rather the platform thereby gained for an expanded portion of the curriculum that was at least somewhat student-oriented and experimental.

In recent years there has been more talk (and also somewhat more action) about curricular change than ever before. Yet, as Paul Dressel and Frances DeLisle (1969, pp. 11, 13-33) have shown in their careful quantitative study of actual alterations in the 10 years between 1957 and 1967, the great bulk of such change, at least down to that date, represented nothing more than random minor tinkering. (Thus the proportion of institutions requiring English composition declined slightly, while the proportion requiring foreign language rose a small amount, and so forth.) To the extent that there has been a general trend since 1967, it is toward relaxing formal requirements and giving more scope to individual student choice and initiative. Yet, as we have seen, this in itself represents only the latest in a series of pendulum swings which began with Eliot's establishment of the free elective system at Harvard. Moreover, our survey of the curriculum in the last 70 years has turned up precedents for just about every currently fashionable form of innovation, usually dating from the progressive era of the 1920s. Thus, when one stands back and looks at the entire pattern of the American curriculum from a distance, the changes (aside from course proliferation) seem usually to mark variations on themes begun long ago. Even the more radical experiments appear to subside and lose their vigor as the years pass. After surveying the post-Hutchins reaction at Chicago, Daniel Bell (1968, p. 198) felt moved to derive the "general institutional lesson" that "all revolutions fade, and after a while look tedious to their successors."

Conclusion

In a more analytical perspective, university catalogs over the years reveal that there can be only three major poles of formal curricular differentiation, along whose axes reforms of all kinds (involving campuswide breadth requirements, subject-major programs, and programs in liberal education) must invariably be placed: (1) the contrast between depth and breadth, (2) the contrast between elective freedom and prescription, and (3) absolute abundance or scarcity of course offerings. These three poles define the intrinsic limits of the curriculum, considered as a formal structural device, in affecting the quality of American higher education. Furthermore, all three poles have been at least loosely related. Advocacy of depth, elective freedom (at least outside the major field), and abundant course offerings defines one position about the nature of a superior education. Advocacy of breadth, minimal elective freedom, and deliberately minimal total course offerings (so as to prevent students from unduly scattering their efforts) defines another.

Ultimately, these two versions of an ideal curriculum may be traced back to conflicting attitudes about the individual's relation to authority.[36] At the St. Johns colleges, and admittedly to some extent in Meiklejohn's thinking as well, one finds a basic distrust of youthful individualism. A style of education is created which will promote a deferential attitude toward certain traditional sources of intellectual authority. In these circles, sharpness of mind is tacitly feared whenever it becomes too irreverent. It is suggestive, for instance, that the discipline of history has been greatly neglected in the "great books" programs, both at St. Johns and at Notre Dame. History is no doubt too intrinsically skeptical and variegated a discipline to be warmly embraced in these particular educational settings (Thomas, 1962, pp. 208, 236). By contrast, the educator who favors diversity and free choice is endorsing the far more characteristic attitude of individualism in American culture; he is encouraging students to make their own mistakes, as they move among diverse catalog offerings trying to choose the most stimulating courses and professors. He is less concerned about the danger that students will choose flippantly, no doubt because he has a genuinely different (and more flatteringly egalitarian) image of the "typical" student in his mind.

The point is that this kind of argument, which really centers on such issues as the worth of deferential submission to the wisdom of elders, has in itself continued in American academic circles throughout the past 100 years, ever since the claims of science (and of modern literature) first began to be presented against the domain held by the classicists. In the twentieth century, advocates of a liberal education have thought up several new and somewhat more attractive versions of the classics, just as the builders of the highly structured physics major have. But the fundamental contrast in attitudes between those who favor freedom and those who favor prescription remains very nearly unaffected. Despite the most recent moves in the direction of freedom, symptoms begin to appear that the faculty is at last worn out by this entire mode of attack upon the problems of education. I am told, for instance, that in the debate at Berkeley which preceded the abolition of breadth requirements there in 1970, both sides appeared remarkably lacking in confidence, reasoned argument, and plain energy.

There is no doubt that the arrangement of courses into formal curricular patterns will nonetheless continue to occupy the attentions of faculty and administration. No educator possessed with an experimental impulse will ever want to leave this aspect of the curriculum entirely alone. To a degree, course restrictions send forth important signals as to the expected quality of the entire academic experience, and "good" teaching is less likely to take place within curricular chaos. The question is one of the emphasis that deserves to be placed upon this particular approach to the attainment of quality.

One returns to the fact that American universities have changed far more noticeably over the years than their formal curricular structures have. Our best institutions have greatly improved in quality during the preceding generation—something that has too often been ignored in the anxious self-searching of the past few seasons. This advance has to an important degree been built upon continuity, which in turn is the result of a stable internal balance of forces, aided by traditions which minimize the effects of outside interference. By and large, the learned community in America has earned the right to this autonomy, most of all because of its considerable willingness to bend gracefully in new directions without sacrificing the core of what has been so gradually and painfully constructed. Thus a good curriculum is always in part traditional, in part experimental. A searching reevaluation may (and probably should) produce a larger number of well-conceived experiments, especially in the direction of bringing the empirical and the humane into closer juxtaposition. But the gains of the last 30 years, achieved by intensifying rather than overturning some of the central efforts of the university builders of the 1890s, are real ones and should continue to figure largely in any overall result.

And in the attempt at rethinking and renewal, it should be realized that the formal structure of the curriculum is only a part, and an often exaggerated part, of the educational landscape. With the experience of the Hutchins epoch at Chicago freshly in mind, Harry Gideonse once injected some common sense into this area of discussion:

> Perhaps the major sin of American education lies in its tendency to exaggerate the importance of administrative detail and to overlook the weaknesses in personnel and the possibilities of improvement in quality in the work done under prevailing administrative arrangements. . . . It is more tempting to the average administrator to take an exciting plunge into some new experiment with new gadgets and talking points, but at the end of every educational debauch of this traditional type lie the same old exasperating questions about the human equation: the quality of our students and, above all, the quality of our faculty (B. L. Johnson, 1937, p. 271).

Still other factors may loom larger than the formal curriculum in defining the worth of a given version of American higher education. It may be seriously argued, for instance, that the paperback revolution of the 1950s did far more to improve academic quality in this country (by inducing an attitude of shame among instructors still visibly using textbooks) than any curricular innovation of the last 70 years. We seem to recognize this relative scale of values in the usual judgments which we make of particular colleges and universities, according considerable respect to both Berkeley and St. Johns, despite their extreme curricular differences, while regarding with varying degrees of pity a host of "low-quality" institutions, even though their catalogs are filled with time-honored (and sometimes apparently imaginative) course and program titles.

In order to make sense of these issues, it becomes necessary to revert to the distinction between the curriculum conceived of purely as a skeletal structure and the curriculum defined instead as the substance of what is being taught. The present chapter has focused largely on the first of these two meanings of the term. Its conclusion, that within broad limits the precise nature of the curriculum seems to be rather unimportant (as long as courses are offered with reasonable continuity by responsible agencies), must be understood as applying only to the formal aspects of the concept. The experience of the last 70 years appears to teach us, first, that the exact shape of the boxes matters relatively little, provided that it allows for an easy articulation among neighbors and provided that there are enough boxes to assure frequent routes for individual maneuver-including both exploration and possible escape. Experience also teaches us that the fashion in which the boxes are glued together may also matter, except in the case of a few highly self-confident disciplines, a lot less than we often think. But the flavor and texture of the contents of each box may, on the contrary, matter enormously. It is in this important sense that 16 or 20 courses clearly do not, of themselves, "equal an education." By calling attention to certain dimensions of the topic which have misleadingly attracted excessive attention in the past, or which may now beguile us with false promises, I have tried to clear the decks for the harder, more baffling questions which do indeed involve the bearing of the curriculum upon education.

References

Bell, Daniel: *The Reforming of General Education*, Anchor Books, Doubleday & Company, Inc., Garden City, N.Y., 1968.

Benezet, Louis T.: "General Education in the Progressive College," *Teachers College Press*, Columbia University, New York, 1943.

Brigham, A. P.: "Present Status of the Elective System in American Colleges," *Educational Review*, vol. 14, 1897.

Brubacher, John S., and Willis Rudy: *Higher Education in Transition*, rev. ed., Harper & Row, Publishers, Incorporated, New York, 1968.

Butts, R. Freeman: *The College Charts its Course*, McGraw-Hill Book Company, New York, 1939.

Dewey, John: *The Educational Situation*, The University of Chicago Press, Chicago, 1902.

Dressel, Paul L., and Frances H. DeLisle: *Undergraduate Curriculum Trends*, American Council on Education, Washington, D.C., 1969.

Foster, William: *Administration of the College Curriculum*, Houghton-Mifflin Company, Boston, 1911.

Fraser Mowat: *The College of the Future*, Columbia University Press, New York, 1937.

General Education in a Free Society, Harvard University Press, Cambridge, Mass., 1945.

Harper, William R.: *The Trend in Higher Education*, The University of Chicago Press, Chicago, 1950.

Hull, Helen: *The Asking Price*, Coward-McCann, Inc., New York, 1930.

The Idea and Practice of General Education, The University of Chicago Press, Chicago, 1950.

Johnson, B. Lamar: *What about Survey Courses?* Henry Holt and Company, Inc., New York, 1937.

Johnson, Roy (ed.): *Explorations in General Education*, Harper & Brothers, New York, 1947.

Jones, Barbara: *Bennington College*, Harper & Brothers, New York, 1946.

Lazarsfeld, Paul, and Wagner Thielens, Jr.: *The Academic Mind*, The Free Press of Glencoe, Inc., New York, 1958.

Meiklejohn, Alexander: *The Liberal College*, Marshall Jones, Boston, 1920.

Meiklejohn, Alexander: *The Experimental College*, Harper & Brothers, New York, 1932.

Meiklejohn, Alexander: *Education between Two Worlds*, Harper & Brothers, New York, 1942.

Meiklejohn, Alexander: *Inclinations and Obligations*, University of California Press, Berkeley, 1948.

Neff, Wanda F.: *Lone Voyagers*, Houghton Mifflin Company, Boston, 1929.

Phillips, D.E.: "The Elective System in American Colleges," *Pedagogical Seminary*, vol. 8, 1901.

Pierson, George W.: "The Elective System and Difficulties of College Planning," *Journal of General Education*, vol. 4, 1950.

Riesman, David: *Constraint and Variety in American Education*, Anchor Books, Doubleday & Company, Inc., Garden City, N.Y., 1958.

Rudy, Willis: *The Evolving Liberal Arts Curriculum*, Teachers College Press, Columbia University, New York, 1960.

Thomas, Russell: *The Search for a Common Learning*, McGraw-Hill Book Company, New York, 1962.

Veysey, Laurence R.: *The Emergence of the American University*, The University of Chicago Press, Chicago, 1965.

ACKNOWLEDGMENT: I wish to thank Hugh Hawkins, Carl Kaysen, and Henry F. May for very helpful readings of this chapter at an earlier stage.

Notes

1. The most convenient place to examine the complete curriculums of representative nineteenth-century American colleges is in Foster (1911, pp. 353–383).

2. For the best contemporary surveys of this situation, see Brigham (1897, pp. 360–369); Phillips (1901, pp. 206–230); see also Butts (1939, pp. 242, 247–248); and Pierson (1950, p. 174).

3. See Veysey (1963, pp. 232–259) and, for a good contemporary summary of it, Foster (1911, pp. 139–165).

4. For revealing novelistic portrayals of the interwar academic atmosphere, see Neff (1929) and Hull (1930).

5. For a characteristic expression of these views, see Fraser (1937).

6. See Brubacher & Rudy (1968, p. 274).

7. The percentage of the college-age group attending college in America stood at 1.7 percent in 1870, 4 percent in 1900, 14 percent in 1940, and 40 percent, in 1964. See Bell (1968, p. 105).

8. David Riesman called attention to the enormous differences between high- and low-quality campuses in *Constraint and Variety in American Education* (1958), as did Lazarsfeld and Thielens (1958). Riesman was probably too optimistic in believing that the lesser institutions were still imitating the better ones in accord with some automatic process.

9. Certain extremely elementary courses, e.g., in languages and mathematics, have been considered dispensable for entering students performing well on examinations. In a much rarer experiment, the University of Michigan in the 1880s released selected upperclassmen from course-work in two or three subjects, though requiring them to take the final exams. The "scholar of the house" program at Yale has allowed a few talented seniors to avoid course work since 1948, and the flurry of similar (if less ambitious) tutorial and independent study programs has at least modified the definition of a course somewhat.

10. Here, as is the case with most other innovations, earlier, almost forgotten precedents may be unearthed. U.C.L.A., for instance, allowed honors students to take as many as four courses on a passed-not-passed basis in the year 1949. Stanford and Michigan had both briefly experimented with abolishing letter grades several decades earlier, out of a democratic conviction that brilliance should not be conspicuous.

11. For a more detailed description of this curriculum, see footnote 35.

12. For a discussion of field study projects of the 1930s, see Butts (1939, pp. 411–412). The unique Antioch curriculum should not be forgotten in this connection.

13. Although the Berkeley catalog of 1910 already listed "German 150A–150B. Special Study. Topics selected with the approval of the department and studied privately under the direction of one of the instructors." A senior thesis program in geology existed there at the same time.

14. By 1902 in the colleges of letters, natural sciences, and social sciences one could major at Berkeley in philosophy, education, jurisprudence, history, political science, economics, linguistics, Semitic languages, Oriental languages, Greek, Latin, English, German, Romanic languages, Slavic languages, mathematics, physics, astronomy, chemistry, botany, zoology, physiology, geology, and mineralogy. What seems striking is how well-rounded the university had already become on a departmental basis.

15. It should be apparent that the label *division* (such as a division of natural sciences) is only slightly less specific than *department* and therefore, in logical terms, constitutes no genuine alternative to the latter. Once one begins to make any use of such labels, it is hard to argue for a certain arbitrary stopping place as peculiarly important.

16. For a concrete example of this at Harvard, see Bell (1968, p. 132).

17. Widely read accounts of the curriculum, such as Bell's (1968, pp. xxiii, 55–36), greatly exaggerate the amount of secular (as opposed to cyclical) change in recent years.

18. These group systems are described in Butts (1939, pp. 187–188, 197).

19. The typical pattern at the weaker colleges around 1901 appears to have been one of relative course proliferation but, at the same time, retention of a large amount of prescription (Butts, 1939, p. 240).

20. These three institutions were selected to demonstrate curricular patterns throughout the next section of the chapter. Their catalogs since 1900 were examined in detail. By setting the Berkeley and Yale data alongside the descriptions of Chicago, Columbia, and Harvard in Bell (1968), one can gain an understanding of conditions at five large universities. However, Columbia and Chicago in recent decades are far less typical of the American undergraduate scene than the others.

21. To avoid confusion, I am describing units or credit hours at Yale in the same terminology that always prevailed at Berkeley.

22. Two-unit courses were usually counted as if they were three-unit courses, as were those of one unit. Courses of more than three units were not given extra weight. Courses listed as omitted for the particular year of the survey were never counted. Graduate courses (even if open to a few undergraduates) were not counted, and neither were courses with extremely specialized functions, such as language courses for engineers. Independent study courses (for instance 199s, which have been common at Berkeley for decades) have been listed as one regular semester course in each case. Wherever courses have been shown with many subsections treating entirely different topics (as in certain discussion seminars in recent years), each subsection has been counted as a course. Multiple-track sections of courses offering identical or nearly identical content have not been counted more than once. The aim in all these decisions has been to reproduce the genuine amount of variety available to students at a given moment.

23. For example, see Bell (1968, pp. 74–83).

24. See the tables showing these figures at 26 institutions between 1903 and 1935 in Rudy (1960, pp. 40–42).

25. It was called a *general science course* and offered one semester in the physical sciences and a second in the biological sciences. It expired very soon. An announcement in the 1910 Berkeley catalog on "the comparative study of literature" revealed further interest in such integration, although no specific courses were offered.

26. English 4 at Berkeley as of the year 1900 was already explicitly titled "Great Books." Taught by Charles M. Gayley, it was still in existence 10 years later. The course description read: "A discussion of certain foreign masterpieces in their bearing upon English literature." The course was clearly intended as a basic "breadth" course for students majoring in far-removed fields. The readings changed greatly from year to year; there was as yet no conception of staying with the "very best" books of all time. Moreover, starting in 1911 Berkeley offered History IA-IB. General History, taught by H. Morse Stephens, which was interdisciplinary in all but name: "Lectures on the growth of western civilization from the earliest times to the end of the nineteenth century. This course is designed as an introduction to the study of history, and for the purpose of affording a general perspective of the development of society, politics, and literature in Europe. No textbook is used. . . . The class is divided into sections in which recitations, examinations, and conferences are conducted by the teaching fellows in history." Clearly the University of California has been underestimated as a pioneer in the field of liberal education.

27. The best accounts of this whole movement are in Thomas (1962, esp. pp. 75–76); Butts (1939, pp. 253–415); Brubacher & Rudy (1968, pp. 268-288); and B. L. Johnson (1937), which contains invaluable detailed descriptions of many such programs.

28. Still, this early course already offered another fashionable teaching device of recent years: students were to maintain journals in the spirit of intellectual autobiographies. But it is not surprising that this course was bitterly opposed by most of the Northwestern faculty. See B. L. Johnson (1937, pp. 313–326). Another course at Iowa in the 1930s was proudly described by its creator as opening "the windows of the mind to the romance of science" (B. L. Johnson, 1937, p. 330).

29. In the two-year sequence titled *Study of Contemporary Society*, changing meanings of words like *freedom*, *property*, and *democracy* were first studied, along with the concept of social change. Next came direct analysis of the impact of industrial change, both in England and in present-day America, stressing growth of the market economy. Economic theory then followed. In the succeeding unit, similar alternation between concepts and practical issues occurred in the realm of anthropology, especially focusing on ethnocentrism. Theories of education, social planning, and government were subsequently analyzed, along with the actual structure of English and American government. The second year began with problem debates in the areas of freedom and authority, progress and stability, anarchy and planning, and interdependence and independence. Typical issues connected with the free enterprise system, such as the business cycle, urbanization, economic nationalism, and the implications of specific

New Deal programs, were taken up. Then, perhaps inevitably, the entire program concluded with a reading of Aristotle's *Ethics and Politics* (B. L. Johnson, 1937, pp. 258–273). For a general history and description of the Hutchins curriculum at Chicago, see *The Idea and Practice of General Education* (1930, esp. pp. 48-255). The two-year social science program that developed at Columbia under Harry J. Carman at the same time dealt with many of these same areas, but had more of a historical orientation within the context of an unexamined progressivism; its much less theoretical tone was closer to the usual spirit of such programs (B. L. Johnson, 1937, pp. 247–257).

30. Brubacher & Rudy (1968, p. 281). See also R. Johnson, ed. (1947, esp. pp. 39–42).

31. However, at Bennington in the 1930s three-quarters of a freshman's program did consist of formal course work, organized under divisions rather than departments. See Jones (1946, pp. 56–57).

32. Ibid., p. 83. For more detailed descriptions of these curriculums, see Benezet (1943).

33. For his general position in social philosophy, see Meiklejohn (1942, 1948).

34. His educational views and plans are contained in his book *The Liberal College* (1920), which reprints his earlier articles and addresses and gives his detailed suggestions for an improved Amherst curriculum, and *The Experimental College* (1932), which recounts the Wisconsin experiment in vivid form and also defends it philosophically.

35. When first inaugurated, Meiklejohn's Wisconsin curriculum devoted the full-time study of its group of freshmen to Athens in the age of Pericles and that of its sophomores to America in the nineteenth century. Thereafter, the work of both years was broadened, in the American case to move up into the contemporary. Athens was chosen to illustrate "an attempt at ordered thinking" in a society, in contrast to the intellectual chaos of the present. (No doubt this assumption tended to impose an artificial degree of unity upon the Athenian scene.) The year spent on Greece began with intellectual history and philosophy—the reading of Plato, Thucydides, and the dramatists. The paper topics encouraged the students to reach their own conclusions about each of the thinkers studied; though some were very demanding in a literal, informational sense, they seldom lost sight of the aim of producing internally derived judgments. Later in the year, students spent a month doing their own artwork or taking photographs of Greek art. During another month, they kept "an informal notebook or diary" of their reading, "in which you may discuss points that interest, please, or puzzle you... include quotations, and make any comments that may appeal to you." These notebooks were brought to half-hour private conferences with the faculty advisers; the conferences, along with half a dozen lectures and discussion groups, were the core of the weekly schedule. (A Monday morning assembly of the whole college helped to foster the sense of community.) Toward the end of the first year, the paper topics encouraged students to see integrative relationships between various aspects of the Athenian experience. Finally, in May, students could choose one aspect of Greek life to explore in detail, thus being allowed a certain degree of specialization even as freshmen.

The sophomore curriculum, as it eventually developed, devoted part of the year (and the preceding summer vacation) to preparing regional or community studies, often of the students' home areas, on an individual basis. (These were obviously somewhat inspired by *Middletown*.) In addition, there were common topics, for instance, Henry Adams, the scientific world view, religion in one's hometown, the writing of an inaugural address as if one had just been elected president or governor; special topics in literature: and, interestingly, a careful reading of John Dewey's *Human Nature and Conduct* (just a bit reminiscent, perhaps, of the role given Aristotle at the end of the Chicago social science sequence). On the whole, the sophomore topics clearly encouraged diversity and variety. Meiklejohn insisted that this curriculum did not aim to present a fixed "scheme of reference" for students to memorize. Grades were given only on the regional study project and on one other major paper, usually a literary one. The training in writing was intensive. Every week throughout the two years each student had to submit a paper, either a draft or a final version, to his adviser. These papers were freely subjected to open criticism. There is no doubt that the natural sciences suffered in this program: a rather unsatisfactory course was supplied for a few weeks in the sophomore year. The main intrinsic weakness of the program, however, was that the faculty had to spend such a large share of its time teaching (or advising) in areas that lay outside the nominal range of competence. To Meiklejohn, and apparently to this particular faculty as a whole, such an objection simply did not matter, for their sights were set on the aim of encouraging self-motivated, yet disciplined thinking, no matter in what area. They probably did not care too greatly if they gave the students some wrong factual information.

36. Of these hostile stereotypes, the anti-Semitic one appears to have been already notably potent (Meiklejohn, 1932, pp. 217–224, 286, 290–291, 299).

37. For Example, see *General Education in a Free Society* (1945, p. 43).

What Is the Purpose of Higher Education in American Society?

JOHN GALLAGHER

The most remarkable, and certainly the saddest, characteristic of the debate about higher education today is what is not being discussed: What is the purpose of higher education in society?

For 45 years, that question has not been debated. There have been countless arguments about core curricula and multiculturalism, the social responsibilities of research, access by minority students to colleges, the spiraling cost of education. The chasms on campus have been the subject of a seemingly endless stream of books and articles. At times it seems that there is hardly a question that has not been asked and answered at least a thousand times.

Except the most fundamental one of all: the question of a university's ultimate purpose. Does college exist to be an agent of social change? Is specialized research a reasonable extension of the belief that knowledge for its won sake ultimately, if indirectly, benefits society? How close a partnership should colleges have with government or with corporations?

Those questions could be answered more satisfactorily, if not more easily, if we knew what higher education was meant to do in society. But while society has changed, and the campus with it, the idea of higher education has not since the end of World War II when colleges, with the help of a Presidential commission, reinvented higher education to absorb unprecedented numbers of students for what the commission called "the self-protection of our democracy."

Since then, higher education has been rocked by enormous crises: the McCarthy era, the youth movement and Vietnam, the growing tension between teaching and research, unparalleled attacks from critics within the institutions themselves, the erosion of civilized discourse. Any one of these problems—let alone the combination of them—would have been sufficient to prompt a sweeping reevaluation of the academy's role in society. But none of them did.

Of course, educational leaders and professors have written copiously about the aims of higher education in the past four decades. However, and with virtually no exceptions, they have concentrated on a description of what they have found higher education already is. Sometimes the description is largely congratulatory, such as Clark Kerr's: at other times, the report sounds more like a jeremiad, such as the one delivered by Allan Bloom.

In these writings, so much time is spend delineating the present role of higher education in society that the more important matter—what is the proper role—is given short shrift. As each new book or article appears, it becomes increasingly clear that higher education has fallen short of its ideal.

But what is that ideal? By focusing on the condition of or abuses in higher education, the writers miss the larger point. "Abuses are always a minor importance," said Jose Ortega y Gassett about Spanish colleges in the 1930s. "For either they are abuses in the most natural sense of the word, namely, isolated, infrequent cases of departure from usage; or else they are so frequent and customary, so persistent and so generally tolerated, that they are no longer to be called abuses. . . . It is something in the usage, the policy, and not the breach of it, which needs our attention."

We have had our attention called before to the problem of defining higher education's purpose. "[W]e found in our study great difficulty sometimes to the point of paralysis, in defining essential purposes and goals," Ernest Boyer, president of the Carnegie foundation for the Advancement of Teaching, said in *College: The Undergraduate Experience in America*. Boyer's experience visiting a range of colleges led him to conclude that there was an urgent need for the constructive debate about the meaning of the undergraduate college.

There have been other invitations for debate, on all levels of higher education, to end the paralysis Boyer described. Howard Bowen called for "a larger vision of where higher education could and should be headed in the twenty-first century" so that educators could make decisions from a sound philosophical basis. Sadly, Bowen noted, "this part of the discourse on the place of higher education in American society is strangely and tragically missing."

Yet another call to debate met with no greater success, even though it came from one of higher education's most visible leaders, the late Yale President A. Bartlett Giamatti. In two speeches in 1987, Giamatti tried to rouse interest in the issue by candidly tracing the public's disillusionment with higher education to the academy's inability to define its purpose.

Said Giamatti: "We hear of the tactics and strategy for this institution or that, but rarely if ever of the nature and purpose of college: What is it for? How is an academic institution different from a government or a for-profit corporation? Why is it important the a college or university be different? What is the price paid when those differences disappear? The most pressing need in higher education in the next ten years is not for management strategies. It is for debate on each campus, led by its leaders, as to what the purposes and goals of each campus are. . . ." Six years later, the debate is even more overdue.

Higher education is lost in a dark wood. If it is ever to leave it, it will have to stop concentrating on how dark the wood is and consider instead what path it wishes to be on. It is only one it knows where it wants to go that it will finally be able to leave the wood behind.

Should Education Be Practical?

One of the longest-standing complaints about higher study is that the end product is too pedantic for society. As long ago as the Renaissance, Francis Bacon was condemning some education as "a kind of adoration of the mind . . . by means whereof men have withdrawn themselves too much from the contemplation of nature, and the observations of experience, and have tumbled up and down in their own reason and conceits." Knowledge, he continued, should "not be as a courtesan, for pleasure and vanity only, or as a bond-woman, to acquire and gain to her masters' use; but as a spouse, for generation, fruit and comfort."

While Bacon's imagery would hardly be used today, his sentiment is still current, prefiguring as it does the dismissive phrase "the ivory tower." Bacon raises the perpetual question: How practical should an education be?

That question is one of the fault lines running beneath higher education, with two great traditions pushing up against each other. One tradition argues that the pursuit of knowledge for its own sake creates fully-rounded men and women with sharp enough minds to succeed at anything they attempt. The other tradition contends that pursuit of practical knowledge, particularly the scientific, sharpens minds as effectively as the study of Greek and Latin, and addresses the broad needs of the people.

The earliest education leaders in this country were clear in their preference. Colleges were meant to be schools for the highest vocation. Cotton Mather said that the pious founders of Harvard foresaw that without "a nursery" for ministers, "darkness must have soon covered the land and gross darkness the people." William and Mary's Charter (1693) noted the need for the Church to "be furnished with a Seminary of Ministers of the Gospel" who would in turn educate American Indians "to the Glory of Almighty God." Yale's charter (1745) expanded the vocation somewhat to include "the service of God in the state as well as in church."

The founding of a republic which separated Church and State did not lessen the practical considerations of higher education. In a report to the Commissioners for the University of Virginia, Thomas Jefferson listed first among the goals of the new institution the formation of "the statesman, legislators and judges, on whom public prosperity and individual happiness are so much to depend." The university students are also expected "to harmonize and promote the interests of agriculture, manufactures and commerce."

Ironically, it took a cleric to offer a scathing dismissal of usefulness as a goal of higher education. "The Philosophy of Utility, you will say, Gentlemen, has at least done it's work," said Cardinal John Newman in a lecture in 1852. "And I grant it—it aimed low, and it fulfilled its aim."

Newman proposed in its place an almost monastic ideal of the college, "a pure and clear atmosphere of thought." There the student would pursue a "Liberal Education," which would lead to "the true and adequate end of intellectual training," "Thought or Reason exercised upon Knowledge."

In other worlds: knowledge as its own end. For Newman, research was the work of other institutions, not college. "If its object were scientific and philosophical discovery, I do not see why a University should have any students," he told his audience in Dublin. Instead, the university was to sharpen the minds of young men (the advancement of women not being among the ideas that Newman himself had cultivated). The goal was nothing less than understanding our intellectual tradition and the principles upon which it rested.

But there would be a practical benefit to such a process, Newman admitted: the training of good members of society. A university training, said Newman,

> ... aims at raising the intellectual tone of society, at cultivating the public mind, at purifying the national taste, at supplying true principles to popular enthusiasm and aims to popular aspiration, at giving enlargement and sobriety to the ideas of the age, at facilitating the exercise of political power, and refining the intercourse of private life. It is the education which gives a man a clear conscious view of his own opinions and judgments, a truth in developing them, an eloquence in expressing them, and a force in urging them. It teaches him to see things as they are, to go right to the point, to disentangle a skein of thought, to detect what is sophistic, and to discard what is irrelevant. It prepares him to fill any post with credit, and to master any subject with facility.

All this, because an educated man has acquired the highest skill of all. He can think clearly.

We are still grappling with Newman's exacting standards, or to put it more fancifully, we are haunted by Newman's ghost. Every discussion about the role of higher education has his spirit hovering in the background. From Robert Hutchins to Clark Kerr and Derek Bok, Newman's presence can be felt in the discussion of the aims of higher education. His forceful apologia for the intellectual life may embarrass us a little now because of its Victorian certainty but its appeal to our nobility still leave us awestruck.

American academics in the early nineteenth century had set forth many of the principles that we now associate with Newman. In 1828, a committee of Yale faculty members produced a report in response to complaints from critics that is classical curriculum was impractical. It was nothing of the sort, the faculty argued. The purpose of the college was "to lay the foundation of a superior education," not to train someone for a career.

"Everything throws light upon everything," the Yale report said. "The great object of a collegiate education, preparatory to the study of a profession, is to give that expansion and balance of the mental powers, those liberal and comprehensive views, and those fine proportions of character, which are not to be found in him whose ideas are always confined to one particular channel."

But even as the Yale Report and Newman were defending liberal education, the example of the German University was leading other scholars to propose a different purpose for higher education, one in which research, particularly scientific, was uppermost. Francis Wayland of Brown University told the University Corporation in 1850 that "Civilization is advancing, and it can only advance in the line of the useful arts." Andrew White, the first president of Cornell, organized that university around the advancement, not merely the conservation, of knowledge. In his inaugural address as president of Harvard, Charles Eliot, the first scientist to hold the position, called for more science and an elective system for courses.

Years after he helped shape the idea of the modern university, Daniel Coit Gilman, the first president of Johns Hopkins, which was itself the first great graduate school in the U.S., reflected on the state of higher education in the 1870s. "When this university began, it was a common complaint, still uttered in many places, that the ablest teachers were absorbed in routine and were forced to spend their strength in the discipline of tyros, so that they had no time for carrying forward their studies or for adding to human knowledge," he recalled.

As the first great graduate school in the U.S., Johns Hopkins set a new level for academic standards, investing not in magnificent buildings but in magnificent faculty. (Early Baltimoreans sometimes confused the university building with a local piano factory, according to John Brubacher and Willis Rudy.) The faculty had complete freedom to pursue whatever research they chose to, and Gilman often took a personal interest in their projects. Along with this "Lehrfreiheit," as the Germans called it, students were given a corresponding "Lernfreiheit" to choose what they wanted to study.

Within 30 years, the innovations forged at Johns Hopkins were considered the standard for the modern university. In the process, universities shifted their loyalty to research, while trying to maintain their respect for liberal education. The reorganization was not without pain. The animosity between the two branches was so great that, for example, at Yale scientific students were segregated from their classmates in chapel. So unlikely was the combination on campuses, said Christopher Jencks and David Riesman, that why it was even attempted is "one of the more puzzling questions about the evolution of higher education in this era."

In part, at least, the question was not voluntarily raised. The Morrill Act, passed by Congress in 1862, was a tremendous advance for applied science on the campus. The bill resulted in the creation of more than three dozen colleges devoted to agriculture and the mechanical arts, a practical application of the proposed theory.

Since then, higher education has been caught in continuing debate about how it best serves society: through practical education or liberal education. Throughout the end of the nineteenth and beginning of the twentieth centuries, supporters of liberal education found themselves on the defensive, pointing out the dangers of practical education while watching their own influence wane.

There were, however, some attempts to unite the two ideas together in a single vision, most notably by Alfred North Whitehead. Unlike Newman, Whitehead readily conceded the importance of the "usefulness in higher education. "Pendants sneer at an education which is useful," said Whitehead. "But if education is not useful, what is it? Is it a talent, to be hidden away in a napkin?"

Whitehead wanted to merge the research and teaching visions of the university and proposed a simple solution. "Do you want your teachers to be imaginative? Then encourage them to research. Do you want your researchers to be imaginative? Then bring them into intellectual sympathy with the young at the most eager, imaginative period of life, when intellects are just entering upon their mature discipline."

Yet, in key ways, Whitehead echoed Newman. "What education has to impart is an intimate sense for the power of ideas, for the beauty of ideas, and for the structure of ideas, together with a particular body of knowledge which has peculiar reference to the life of the being possessing it," said Whitehead some 70 years after Newman delivered his lectures.

Whitehead's sense of utility bore more than a passing resemblance to Newman's sense of liberal education. "Of course, education should be useful, whatever your aim in life," said Whitehead. "It is useful, because understanding is useful."

It is that understanding which is the goal of higher education. "The really useful training yields a comprehension of a few general principles with a thorough grounding in the way they apply to a variety of concrete details," said Whitehead. The student's ability to comprehend something other than facts, to be able to glimpse the sweep of ideas, matters more to Whitehead than anything else.

What the university is meant to do, said Whitehead, is cultivate a mental habit, "a principle that has thoroughly soaked into you." Whitehead suggested that it is almost a Pavlovian response; a mind that has been properly trained will respond with vigor and clarity when it is prodded into activity. (This is not sharpening the mind, as Newman might have argued, since Whitehead believes the mind is always active in any event.)

The mind reaches that state of fitness by understanding how ideas are all linked. Whitehead decried the fragmentation that classes often unwittingly create. Instead, he stressed the need to throw ideas into fresh context with one another, so that they can be seen in different ways and be tested.

But Whitehead did not automatically confine the cultivation of mental habits to the liberal arts. Speaking at a time when Harvard was preparing to open a Business School "on a scale amounting to magnificence," he justified the new enterprise as springing from a long-standing tradition.

"At no time have universities been restricted to pure abstract learning," Whitehead noted. But he also stressed that universities have an obligation to do more than just present facts. Indeed, that is their purpose in society.

"The justification for a university is that it preserves the connection between knowledge and the zest of life, by uniting the young and the old in the imaginative consideration of learning," said Whitehead. "The university imparts information, but it imparts it imaginatively. At least, this is the function which it should perform for society. A university which fails in its respect has no reason for existence" Thus, a business school could—indeed, should—tackle such diverse topics as geography, psychology and government, in order to bring together as originally as possible the practical matters with which a business executive might deal. (One wonders what Whitehead's response might be to the modern MBA program.)

Others were less impressed with the idea of professional education. "[T]here has also come an increasingly habitual inclination of the same uncritical character among academic men to value all academic work in terms of livelihood or earning capacity," Thorstein Veblen wrote in 1918. In 1930 Abraham Flexner, director of the Carnegie Foundation, similarly blasted higher education for its high regard of usefulness. "Why do certain American universities feel themselves under pressure to develop their "service" functions, even to call themselves "public service" institutions?" Flexner asked. He concluded that it was because they need to feel useful, "And when I say useful, I mean directly, immediately useful, for Americans like to see results."

Inevitably, the rising tide of professionalism on campuses led to crusade for correction. The crusade found its leader in Robert Hutchins, the president of the University of Chicago.

"Every group in the community wants the university to spare it the necessity of training its own recruits," he warned in 1936. "They want to get from the university a product as nearly finished as possible, which can make as large and as inexpensive a contribution as possible from the moment of graduation. This is a pardonable, perhaps even a laudable desire. But the effect of it on universities will be that soon everybody in a university will be there for the purpose of being trained for something."

Hutchins proposed a bold reorganization along the lines of the liberal tradition, so that students "will learn what has been done in the past, and what the greatest men have thought," a common knowledge that will unite them. The professional schools themselves would concentrate on theoretical concerns, a proposal also put forth by Flexner. (Veblen was more of a purist; he wanted to ban professional schools from the campus, in order to preserve the research integrity of graduate programs.) The practice for Hutchins' doctrine was to be found in the study of great books, books that are "contemporary in every age," the repository of rational wisdom. The point of the great books was not to stimulate mental exercise, such as Newman suggested. Rather, Hutchins was promoting the life of the mind as the ideal life.

John Dewey immediately criticized Hutchins for authoritarianism, a serious charge at a time when the threat from fascism was growing. "Basically his idea as to the proper course to be taken is akin to the distrust of freedom and the consequent appeal to *some* fixed authority that is now overrunning the world," Dewey said.

". . . President Hutchins' policy of reform by withdrawal from everything that smacks of modernity and contemporaneousness is not after all the road to the kind of intellectuality that will remedy the evils he so vividly depicts."

Hutchins' proposals did find some takers, although his attempts at reform at his own university (e.g., eliminating football, recruiting high school sophomores, allowing students to graduate on the basis of comprehensive exams and not credit hours) generated so much controversy that they did not outlive his tenure. But Hutchins, and his colleague Mortimer Adler, did generate a debate about what higher education was meant to do for society.

The debate was interrupted by World War II, but resumed as the war came to a close. A committee appointed by Harvard President James Bryant Conant surveyed the problems of higher education in the U.S. and concluded that the lack of "common ground of training and outlook" on campuses was working 'against the common good of society."

One point about education was clear, the Report stated: "It depends in part on an inherited view of man and society which it is the function, though not the only function of education, to pass on." The committee summed up that view as "the dignity of man" and the individual's "recognition of his duty to his fellow man."

The committee also noted the perils of specialization, starting that "a society controlled wholly by specialists is not a wisely ordered society," while at the same time noting that specialization had become the means of advancement in society. The issue facing higher education was how to reconcile specialization with general education, "to adapt general education to the needs and intentions of different groups and, so far as possible, to carry its spirit into special education." (Brubacher and Rudy pointed out that the Report did not address just how that might be done.)

The tone of the Harvard Report perfectly matched its era. "The dignity of man" nicely describes the animating principles behind the allied efforts to free Europe and rebuild it. But if the war influenced the tone of the report, it also influence the shape of higher education. With the passage of the GI bill, colleges found themselves flooded with veterans, an influx of new students unmatched in American history.

Realizing that the veterans were reshaping the profile of higher education, President Truman appointed a commission to reexamine the objectives and methods of higher education in the U.S. The resulting six-volume report, issued in 1947 and 1948, provided a new rationale for admissions, urging the removal of any barriers that restricted access to a college education, whether it be race, economic background or even academic past. Any qualified individual should have the opportunity to go to college. To accommodate the new students, more faculty and more colleges would be in order.

But just as importantly, the Commission provided a clear statement of higher education's role in society. "The social role of education in a democratic society is at once to insure equal liberty and equal opportunity to differing individuals and groups, and to enable the citizens to understand, appraise, and redirect forces, men, and events as they tend to strength or to weaken their liberties," the Commission states. The group assigned higher education three explicit goals: "education for a fuller realization of democracy in every phase of living," "education directly and explicitly for international understanding and cooperation," and "the application of creative imagination and trained intelligence to the solution of social problems and to the administration of public affairs."

Moreover, the Commission underscored the need for General Education. "The failure to provide any core of unity in the essential diversity of higher education is a cause for grave concern," the Commission noted. "A society whose numbers lack a body of common experience and common knowledge is a society without a fundamental culture; it tends to disintegrate into a mere aggregation of individuals." A core of common learning would give a student "the values, attitudes, and knowledge, and skills that will equip him to live rightly and well in a free society."

The 28-member commission, headed by George Zook, president of the American Council on Education, was criticized for advocating the decline of academic standards to allow for more college students. Hutchins, who said the report "reads like a Fourth-of-July oration in Pedaguese," denounced its faith in improving the American populace by opening higher education to more students, since he believed the educational system offered no real direction to the students it already had.

Criticisms aside, the Commission's findings, coupled with the Harvard Report, sparked extensive debate in the higher education community, since they both were proposing nothing less than the reorganization of the principles upon which higher education rested. The Commission report, in particular, gave individual a chance to examine specific goals in society for higher education and consider whether or not they were fitting. It was virtually the last time the debate focused on what higher education should do instead of how bad things are.

The Present Confusion

In 1964, Clark Kerr, Chancellor of the University of California, Berkeley, published a series of lectures delivered the year before on the state of the university or, as Kerr preferred to term it, the multiversity. His book, *The Uses of the University,* is a remarkable work, for while it is often a celebration of the condition of higher education, it became the target of severe criticism for its parade of overconfident, unstated and even offensive assumptions, often about the relationship between the university and current government policies.

To be fair to Kerr, he had ample precedent for his beliefs. In a speech titled "Princeton in the Nation's Service," Woodrow Wilson, then a professor of jurisprudence and political economy, said that ultimately "it is not learning but the spirit of service that will give a college a place in the public annals of the nation." Wilson emphasized that he did not mean party politics but instead "the air of the world's transactions, the consciousness of the solidarity of the race, the sense of duty of man toward man, of the presence of men in every problem," which require that "the school must be of the nation." (In fact, the first six American presidents believed in a national university and had urged its creation.)

Moreover, Kerr was writing at the peak of American certainty in the nation's goodness, when unimpeded progress stretched itself out on a limitless horizon. It was not a notable time for qualms. Doubt would follow later.

Kerr reflected that serene self-assurance. The university, he believed, could tackle any problem. "So many of the hopes and fears of the American people are now related to our educational system and particularly to our universities—the hope for longer life, for getting into outer space, for a higher standard of living; our fears of Russian and Chinese supremacy, of the bomb and annihilation, of individual loss of purpose in the changing world," he wrote. "For all these reasons and others, the university has become a prime instrument of national purpose."

It was not an especially unified instrument. Kerr acknowledged the pull of conflicting interests, kept in check by a wise administrator. "A university anywhere can aim no higher than to be as British as possible for the sake of the undergraduates, as German as possible for the sake of the graduates and the research personnel, as American as possible for the sake of the public at large—and as confused as possible for the sake of the preservation of the whole uneasy balance," he remarked.

Kerr presented knowledge as a kind of universal commodity, with the university as prime purveyor. Knowledge "is wanted, even demanded by more people and more institutions than ever before," Kerr boasted. "The university as producer, wholesaler and retailer of knowledge cannot escape service. Knowledge, today, is for everybody's sake."

But most of all, it was for the sake of the nation, "a component part of the 'military-industrial complex.'" The federal government's commitment to higher education, through the funding of key research projects, has already contributed much to knowledge, and will only contribute more.

Kerr may seem like a federal apologist, but he was noteworthy more for his optimism than for his point of view. The university in the nation's employ has been a theme of more than one scholar in the past four decades. Bowen lists ten economic, political, and social problems facing the nation, ranging from unemployment to pressure-group democracy, and stresses the necessity of higher education to address them.

But the most prominent proponent of the university in national service is former Harvard President, Derek Bok. Almost 30 years after Kerr wrote, Bok matter-of-factly accepted the close relationship between government and university although, like Kerr, he has serious reservations about the federal influence on universities. In general, Bok was firmer than Kerr about the need for academic independence. But about the basic requirements of higher education in society, Bok was in no doubt.

"Serving society is only one of higher education's functions, but it is surely along the most important," noted Bok. "At a time when the nation has its full share of difficulties, therefore, the question is not whether universities need to concern themselves with society's problems but whether they are discharging this responsibility as well as they should."

Some of that responsibility is in making sure that the country is getting something for all of its money. Professors receive over $6 billion annually in research and development funds, said Bok, to say nothing of state funding. "How could faculties possibly expect to go on receiving such support from the nation's taxpayers without making efforts to respond to society's needs?" he wondered.

If anything, Bok suggested, universities aren't doing enough for society. "Again and again, universities have put a low priority on the very programs and initiatives that are needed most to increase productivity and competitiveness, improve the quality of government, and overcome the problems of illiteracy, miseducation, and unemployment," he wrote.

Hutchins despised the point of view that Kerr and Bok embraced." [T]he American university is supposed to assist in the solution of any current practical problem that anybody has," Hutchins lamented. "And when there is money in it and good public relations in it, the fact that the project runs counter to the purpose of the university, which is to pursue knowledge for its own sake, does not make the lure of such work any easier to resist. The purpose of the university has long since been changed; it is now regarded as a service station for the community."

Robert Paul Wolf, a philosophy professor at Columbia, was hardly more charitable when he criticized the philosophy in 1969. "When Kerr speaks repeatedly of the multiversity's responsiveness to national needs, he is describing nothing more than its tendency to adjust itself to effective demand in the form of government grants, scholarship programs, corporate or alumni underwriting, and so forth," Wolf charged. "But his language encourages the reader to suppose that the demands to which the multiuniversity responds are expressions of genuine human and social needs, needs which make a moral claim upon the effort and attention of the academy." In fact, said Wolf, there is a significant difference between the real needs of society and the market demand of the nation.

More recently, Page Smith has said that by allying with the military-industrial complex, the universities "sold their souls." The latest wrinkle in the Faustian bargain, the university-corporate contract for research, led Smith to write that what higher education is pursuing "with far more dedication than the truth is big bucks."

Bok fell into the same trap as Kerr, failing to make the distinction between society and the nation while extolling worthy goals. Is the nation the government? The public? Some combination of the two? Is society different from both of them? Exactly whose interests the university is supposed to represent is never entirely clear.

Others have been more cautious. "We need concerned people who are participants in inquiry, who know how to ask the right questions, who understand the process by which public policy is shaped, and are prepared to make informed, discriminating judgments on questions that affect the future," said Boyer. "To fulfill this urgent obligation, the perspective needed is not only national, but global."

Newman offered a similarly broad view. "There is a duty we owe to human society as such, to the state to which we belong, to the sphere in which we move, to the individuals towards whom we are variously related, and whom we successively encounter in life," he said.

The practical application of research had its philosophical complement in the professional schools, where students could be trained to meet the specific needs of the marketplace, and whose very presence served as an irritant to those who saw higher education as the center of knowledge, not vocationalism.

It was a long-standing complaint. "Some great men . . . insist that Education should be confined to some particular and narrow end, and should issue in some definite work, which can be weighed and measured," Newman said. "There is a conflict between one aim of the university, the pursuit of truth for its own sake, and another which it professes too, the preparation of men and women for their life and work," Hutchins said. Barzun ridiculed the idea that there could be such an animal as a professor of "effective living."

But Riesman and Jencks provided an important caveat. "In almost any discussion of higher education, whether with professors, students or the general public, somebody is likely to put forward the idea that the nation's colleges have been corrupted by vocationalism," they wrote. "In the good old days, it will be argued, colleges were pure and undefiled seats of learning. . . . Like other pastoral idylls, this myth serves all sorts of polemical purposes, good and bad. But it is a myth nonetheless."

Student activists in the 1960s took the idea of vocationalism one step further, describing universities as factories producing Establishment men. "The customers for this product are the corporations, government agencies, foundations, military services, and universities whose destructive, repressive, antisocial activities demand an ever-larger supply of loyal and unquestioning workers," Wolf said in summarizing the activists' argument.

Wolf himself believed that any institution tied too closely to the government loses its ability to criticize the government when it is wrong. That is an argument often also used by the student activists of the 1960s against higher education. Pointing to colleges' connections to government waging a war they believed was unjust, the activists accused higher education of being an active part of the military machine. (Kerr's ebullient recognition of the bond between campus and government did not serve him well in this regard at Berkeley.)

Implicit in the students' fiery accusations was another kind of societal role for higher education: reformer of society gone bad. Jencks and Riesman, and Brubacher and Rudy, insisted that at least the early student protests were not aimed at the academic profession, but were directed at society at large.

"What students are saying, in their somewhat incoherent way, is that they no longer have any confidence in government, politics, business, industry, labor, the church, for all of these are hopelessly corrupt," said Henry Steele Commager. "Only the university is left. Clearly it is corrupt, too, but not hopelessly; it can still be saved and if it is saved, it can be made into an instrument to reform the whole society."

In an odd way, the students seemed to believe in the university as a pure and clear atmosphere, much as Newman had hoped it would be, free from the exigencies of the outside world. But, at the same time, the students seemed to have as great a faith in the power of the university to improve society as Kerr did. It was the definition of "improve" that differed. Whereas Kerr saw the university as an agent for national progress, protesters saw it as an agent for social change. Unfortunately, the formulation of higher education philosophy, including a considered appraisal of past traditions, was never really a goal of protesters. To the extent that they relied on a philosophy at all, they usually turned to Marxist principles, a revolutionary approach out of character with higher education's distinctly evolutionary nature.

Not everyone believed that the changes that the students sought were for the better. Bloom for one, said flatly that nothing good came from the sixties. For him it was a time when civilized discourse, respect for the law and academic standards all fled the campus because of the capitulation of milquetoast professors and administrators. Wolf, a self-described leftist, foresaw in the use of higher education for political ends the demise of the academic enterprise.

The two men were not alone in their views. Commager described the student protests as "the most reckless attack upon academic freedom in our history." Sidney Hook warned that the student ideal of higher education as societal reformer would only imperil the independence of institutions and lead to "retaliatory curbs and controls."

But Hook, along with Jacques Barzun, was not a defender of the multiversity. Any attempt to turn higher education into a social service organization filled them with dread; in many ways they were harsher in their criticism of higher education than the students they attacked.

"Let us recall the provinces from which [the university] has abdicated," said Barzun. "The unity of knowledge; the desire and power to match; the authority and skill to pass judgment on what claims to be knowledge, to be a universalist, to be a scholar, to be a basic scientist; finally, the consciousness of what is properly academic—a consciousness which implies the right to decline alike: commercial opportunity, service assignments for industry, the administering of social welfare, and the bribes, flattery, or dictation of any self-seeking group."

In fact, Hook in particular was a long-time critic of higher education's "deficiencies as an instrument of liberal education," echoing Newman and Hutchins, although giving liberal education Dewey's twist of pragmatism.

Liberal education's emphasis on the great texts of the past, even given a contemporary gloss, did not sit well with students demanding relevance, the students' own version of practicality. But their objections did not deter Bowen, who explicitly linked liberal education to practical needs. "A revival of liberal learning for both young people and adults may be an effective means of reorienting the values that propel our economy and our government," he said. "It is only as we improve our people that we can hope to improve our society."

By the time Bowen made his argument in 1980, the skirmishes over the issue had died down for a while, but they emerged with fresh vehemence in the mid-1980s in the debate over core curriculum, particularly as it reflected Western Civilization. The core had staunch defenders, who relied on arguments set out by Hutchins, Hook, the Harvard Report—all the way back to Newman, though without Newman's emphasis on mental exercise.

"It might seem obvious that all students should be knowledgeable about texts that have formed the foundations of the society in which they live," said Lynne Cheney, director of the National Endowment for the Humanities. "But opponents argue that those works, mostly written by a privileged group of white males, are elitist, racist, and sexist."

In fact, says Page Smith, they are probably right, and the insistence on Western Civilization courses in only hypocritical. The university doesn't have "the human resources to do a decent job (a fact now proved over almost a century)," he claimed. "It can never be done properly, and thus shouldn't be done at all until the university has had a change of heart and becomes, in fact as well as name, a university, a genuine universe of learning."

There is a sense in which the core curriculum is the antithesis of social activism, harkening back to the debate over knowledge for it own sake rather than the efficacy of applied (now social) research.

"American colleges and universities are quick to proclaim their duty to address all sorts of things that are wrong in the world, to speak truth to power, to discourse on the most complex social and moral issues beyond their walls, and to instruct political and business and religious leaders on the proper path to follow," argued William Bennett while he was Secretary of Education. "But they have a prior duty, which is to see to the education of young people in their charge."

Cheney made the point more explicitly. "Teaching becomes a form of political activism, with texts used to encourage students, in the words of one professor, to 'work against the political horror of one's time,'" she said.

In fact, teaching as a form of activism is probably the most widely if not most accurately, documented aspect of the current debate in higher education. The most compelling—to say nothing of lurid—of the reports, by Dinesh D'Souza, went so far as to state that the courses consciously promote a negative image of anyone who is white, heterosexual, and male, resulting in an education "in closed-mindedness and intolerance."

D'Souza, Bennet, and Cheney all pointed to the study of the classics as a way of promoting common understanding. Bloom went so far as to call for the return of Hutchins' Great Books scheme, although he clearly does not expect to see anyone follow his suggestions. Others, such as E. D. Hirsch, argued that not only will the classics help students formulate their own values, they will provide a grounding in facts and beliefs that every educated person should know.

Whitehead, however, was wary of the need for lists. "Whatever be the detail with which you cram your student, the chance of his meeting in after-life exactly that detail is almost infinitesimal; and if he does meet it, he will probably have forgotten what you taught him about it," he said. Better for the student to have acquired a spirited mind than a list of facts. More in keeping with Whitehead's belief in the need to link information imaginatively is Boyer's proposal for an "integrated" core, seven themes that cut across the curriculum.

But Boyer's proposal faced an enormous hurdle: the increased specialization in higher education. The freedom under Gilman's standard to pursue research freely has become, by all admissions, a cross of gold upon which faculty are crucified. Instead of a pleasure, research as become a duty. And the research must be original. "We built our universities on the Germanic model with our own particularly nasty twist, the added insistence that universities be judged in terms of their productive output," said George Douglas.

Thus, Gilman's goal of advancing society's knowledge has, in Barzun's word, been "preposterized." "Since the Second world War, as everybody knows, the mania has become endemic: everybody shall produce written research in order to live, and it shall be decreed a knowledge explosion," Barzun wrote. "An explosion it may be, of print and paper pulp, but the knowledge is extensively imaginary."

Cheney found that the explosion is made up of increasingly narrow pieces of research, with no professional incentive to break away. "There is still little vocational encouragement for the scholar to undertake the general investigations that can give pattern and purpose to specialized studies," she said. Indeed, there is substantial reason not to undertake such an investigation. Julius Getman detailed several cases in which tenure was denied to professors whose work was deemed too broad or popular to be "academic."

In fact, the descriptions seem to harken back to the confusion that Kerr described. But now the balance seems to be more lacking than ever. "There is an extraordinary gap between the rhetoric and the reality of American higher education," said Bennett. "The gap is so wide, in fact, that we face the real possibility—not today, perhaps not tomorrow, but someday—of an erosion of public support for the enterprise." It follows that if the gap is so great, then perhaps the rhetoric, and the principles upon which it rest, need to be reevaluated. "From time to time, it's not a bad idea to look at what's really going on, and to ask some hard questions," said Bennett. Unfortunately, the combative tone of some of his questions made them sound more like declarations of war than an attempt to address the philosophical issues.

Fragments Against the Ruins

In the past 25 years, writers have spent a great deal of time surveying the ruins of higher education. As long ago as Kerr, the cracks were evident. The more thoughtful analysts, such as Boyer, have noted that there is still much to celebrate, especially the commitment of many professors to educating undergraduates. But the steady stream of books published in the last seven years that describe a riven, fragmented, politicized campus with few if any commonalities leaves no doubt as to the extent of the problem.

What those reports from the front (which is how Bloom characterized his book) do not do is address in a detailed, comprehensive and equitable way the fundamental question of the role higher education is meant to play in society. "Without a coherent notion of what a university is for—some idea of what it should be and do—we cannot possibly evaluate existing universities," said Wolf.

Wolf did make an effort to rethink the university's purpose in society. It was, he concluded, "a community of learning . . . a community of persons united by collective understandings, by common and communal goals, by bounds of reciprocal obligation, and by a flow of sentiment which makes the preservation of the community an object of desire, not merely a matter of product or a command of duty." It served society best as a center of free inquiry, where scholars could transmit their knowledge to students and further rational discourse.

Wolf's ideal led him to some debatable conclusions. He considered a Catholic university to be "a strict contradiction in terms" because it adherence to doctrine prevented free inquiry. He considered the presence of professional schools to be so inimical to the pursuit of knowledge that he would sever their connection to the university, a move that Flexner also considered. But, as impractical as some of his ideas may sound, Wolf addressed the problems directly and proposed systematic solutions based on a stated ideal of the university's role in society. It is a claim too few can make.

Bowen proposed some questions that higher education needs to ask: "What kind of people do we want our children and grandchildren to be? What kind of society do we want them to live in? How may higher education be guided and shaped to help nurture people of this kind and to help create this kind of society?' He noted that higher education has increasingly relied on "bread-and-butter" arguments to justify its role in society, while downplaying the long-term educational benefits to society.

The debate Bowen envisioned would require a unified effort on the part of the higher education community, something that higher education has never been good at, he admitted. "But the crisis is severe enough, and the basic principles of academic freedom and liberal learning are sufficiently threatened that joint action is surely called for," he said.

Bowen also provided an important corrective to many of the reports on the problems of higher education, from Wolf on. He made his efforts to include the range of institutions. By contrast, other reports are often skewed by their attention to the most visible institutions for examples of the problems. Those institutions are not representative of higher education as a whole, as indeed no small sampling would be. They are usually prestigious research universities. You are far more likely to read about Harvard than you are about San Jose State or the College of New Rochelle, to say nothing of junior or community college.

Yet the students, faculty and administrators at those institutions are as much a part of higher education as their peers in the Ivy League. They bring an entirely different perspective to the debate, one that has, for the most part, been missing. Since many of those institutions were created as a result of the last great reorganization of higher education, their omission is especially glaring. While different institutions may ultimately arrive at different conclusions as to what role they should play in society, they all must engage in the same debate in order to establish their shared values and not merely the ones they do not share.

The debate clearly can no longer be delayed. The current stalemate has resulted in an educational system that is so divided in its aims and so confused in its direction that it benefits to society and to itself are dwindling. Giamatti put it eloquently:

> American colleges and universities do not play the role in our society as centers for independent thought, for the open pursuit of truth, for the protection of minority or dissenting or critical views—they do not serve America—when they mimic governmental institutions or private businesses or allow themselves to be simply holding pens for competing dogmas. American colleges and universities serve neither themselves nor the country if they are unsure of their own principles and purposes or if they cannot convey them to the people at large. The deepest need is for the permanent parts of the place—the members of the faculty and the administration—to reforge common aims, to establish again a common set of goals and values, to lay aside the mistrust that corrodes the capacity to educate the young and to discover and share new knowledge, and to speak to the public of the nature and purpose of education.

Giamatti wanted to see the resurrection of higher education as "free and ordered spaces, for those who live there, for the country at large." His ideal is one that few would disagree with. If it is ever to be realized, we will have to reconsider the most fundamental principles. It is an examination with a single question, from which all others flow: what does society need from higher education?

Trends and Innovations in General Education Reform

Jerry G. Gaff

Although the national debate has not led to agreement about a specific course of action for improving undergraduate education, it has sparked similar debates on college campuses. This is the most important place for such discussion to take place, because only individual colleges, as legal entities, can determine the nature of their instructional programs. At this level, the debates often are more productive, for two reasons. Although the problems, issues, and themes on campuses resonate to their counterparts in the national debate, the particular local context brings abstractions down to concrete reality. Further, curriculum review committees typically make a serious effort to join the issues, address specific problems, avoid unnecessary conflict, and help their colleagues reach broad areas of agreement.

For this reason, more than a national debate is taking place. Talk is leading to action. Hundreds of individual colleges and universities have overcome the substantial barriers to change and taken concrete steps to strengthen their general education offerings. Some of the changes are large and significant, others are more modest, even trivial. But so many institutions are involved, the changes are so central to a student's academic program, and the changes so affect the education of all students in the institutions that they constitute a curriculum reform movement.

Adding to the movement is the fact that the work on college campuses is aided by a wide range of extrainstitutional activities. Foundations and public funding agencies operate programs to support curriculum, course, and faculty development to improve student learning. Educational associations conduct programs to assist reforms, establish model programs, and disseminate results. All sorts of groups offer conferences and seminars on such topics as the teaching of writing and critical thinking, freshman year programs, and assessment, for example. System offices, boards of trustees, and offices of governors and state legislatures search for ways to stimulate improvements on the campus. Books and articles on general and liberal education have multiplied.

Most improvements on individual campuses are made quietly and out of the spotlight. Unlike attacks on the curriculum, which are flashed in the media, curriculum improvements are not particularly newsworthy: another case where good news is no news. As a result, most citizens, even many academics, are unaware of the extent or significance of the changes taking place in the instructional programs. After studying the sweep and shape of the changes, I can only conclude that the character of the college curriculum is changing in a significant way.

Curriculum Trends

On the basis of completing my survey, reading descriptions of hundreds of new curricula, and visiting scores of campuses, I have identified a number of trends that point to the directions of change in the college curriculum. As a group these trends give an overview of the curriculum reform movement. Today's curriculum trends emphasize the following and each will be discussed in some detail.

1. Liberal arts and sciences subject matter

2. Fundamental skills

3. Higher standards and more requirements

4. Tighter curriculum structure

5. The freshman year

6. The senior year

7. Global studies

8. Cultural diversity

9. Integration of knowledge

10. Moral reflection

11. Active learning

12. Extension through all four years

13. Assessment

Before discussing the individual trends, let us be clear about what they actually are: prominent tendencies that can be observed in large numbers of diverse colleges and universities. Some colleges embrace several of the trends, while others may incorporate only one or two. The trends take different shapes in different institutions; to use the example of writing, one college may require more writing courses in the English department and another may increase the amount of writing courses across the curriculum. Finally, one may cite examples that run counter to these trends. Nonetheless, these appear to me to be the dominant changes taking place in today's curriculum. Collectively, they constitute a general description, a kind of road map, of the changes that are bringing about a new general education curriculum.

Liberal Arts and Sciences Subject Matter. Educators are rediscovering the liberal arts and sciences after an infatuation with vocational education during the 1970s and early 1980s. Spurred by the concern for excellence, they are recognizing the importance of understanding history and culture; having a familiarity with science and technology; and knowing principles of human motivation and behavior, logical and critical thinking, clarity of expression, and other aspects of a broad general education. Under the banner of providing this broad general education for all students, the liberal arts are taking a more prominent place in the curriculum, even in professional and preprofessional programs.

The liberal arts were seriously eroded as colleges added a host of new vocationally related programs, and students flocked to them in droves. Colleges that had previously been dominated by a liberal arts ethos found the liberal arts disciplines overtaken by new fields such as business, computing, and communications. Indeed, David Breneman (1990) argues that career-related study has become so pervasive that there are only about 200 private colleges left that can truly be called liberal arts colleges. While there is controversy about some of his assumptions and about his precise list, Breneman's main point about the growth of vocational subjects eclipsing the arts and sciences remains valid. Large numbers of new faculty were hired, often at high, market-driven salaries, which further diminished and demoralized faculty in the arts and sciences. The opportunity to conduct curriculum reviews provided an opportunity to redress the balance.

Leaders in professional programs, too, saw the centrality of the liberal arts to the successful practice of their crafts. Two reports (Holmes Group, 1986; Carnegie Forum on Education and the Economy, 1986) recommended that teacher training programs, for example, abolish the undergraduate major in education and require prospective teachers to earn the baccalaureate degree, including a liberal arts major, before beginning pedagogical training. As the conduct of business changed, business programs, such as the one at the University of Minnesota, gave more emphasis to such subjects as communications, cross-cultural studies, science, ethics, and social science. A report (Task Force on the Future of Journalism and Mass Communication Education, 1989) recommended that future journalists need a broad general education with only about a quarter of their study in professional journalism courses. The Panel on the General Professional Education of the Physician (1984, p. 5) recommended that undergraduate education should be broadened as one way to strike at what it called "the premedical syndrome." "College and university faculties should require every student, regardless of major subject or career objective, to achieve a baccalaureate education that encompasses a broad study in the natural and the social sciences and in the humanities."

These are indications that professionals are seeing greater value in the study of the arts and sciences through general education. Many professionals have concluded that the liberal arts are practical arts. Rather than seeing them as subjects that, in the patronizing language of an earlier time, are "good for students" and make them "better people"—which may be just as true if not so widely believed—more leaders are seeing the arts and sciences as an essential part of professional practice, hence of preprofessional preparation.

The arts and humanities have gained enrollment from more required work in such fields as history, literature, philosophy, religion, and fine arts. Sometimes these are traditional courses taught in the conventional way by regular faculty members. But some colleges have gone further by mandating the use of original texts (rather than predigested textbooks); written assignments as a means of learning to improve expressive abilities and to foster active involvement (rather than passive learning and memorization); or seminars and discussion sections so that students can express, defend, and modify their own ideas (rather than simply accept the ideas of others). Such guidelines are designed not just to emphasize certain important subject matter but to create the conditions of teaching and learning that make the subject *matter* to students.

Other colleges have been even bolder by requiring interdisciplinary core courses. Roanoke College requires three such courses in different chronological time periods focusing on literature, history, and the fine arts. The University of North Carolina at Asheville offers a sixteen-hour humanities core; the courses are The Ancient World, The Rise of European Civilization, The Modern World, and The Future and the Individual. The University of Nevada at Reno has a three-course Western Tradition sequence for all students; students read seminal writers from the Greeks to the twentieth century, as well as study the American experience. Teams of faculty members and teaching assistants meet regularly to plan and teach these core courses.

Like their humanities counterparts, the natural sciences also have been eroded, as the loose distribution system allowed many students to bypass this entire area or to complete a requirement by taking a "gut" course, a watered down course such as Physics for Poets (although there are some very good science courses for nonmajors bearing this same name). A report issued by the American Association for the Advancement of Science (AAAS), *The Liberal Art of Science* (1990) calls for half of the curriculum in both four- and two-year colleges to be devoted to the liberal arts, and a quarter of that to be earmarked for natural sciences. Furthermore, it says science education needs "radical reform." Traditional teaching relies on "lectures, textbooks, and perfunctory laboratory activities." The report (p. 29) states that not only are conventional methods of teaching science ineffective in conveying an understanding of subject matter, but also they create incomplete and inaccurate views of the nature of science and the scientific enterprise, even among high achieving students." Science should be regarded as a liberal art instead of a technical field; be more fully integrated into the general education curriculum; and be broadened to include the aspects of history, philosophy, sociology, politics, and economics of science and technology. Finally, it recommends that science courses should be organized around issues, themes, or problems and taught by professors in small courses rather than in large lectures.

Despite their centrality to modern life and to a solid education, the sciences traditionally have fit uneasily into general education. Their more structured knowledge, reliance on mathematics, and use of the first course as an introduction to advanced work has complicated their role in general education. However, more colleges today are emphasizing science in general education.

Some merely raise graduation requirements and demand one to four courses, usually with at least some laboratory component. Others are making some of the changes suggested by the AAAS report. Columbia College developed a two-semester interdisciplinary science course in the spirit of its long-running humanities core, using original science papers to show what scientists actually do. Robert Pollack (1988) describes the first semester as starting with mathematics "taught from the ground up," including number systems, methods of pattern recognition, and the concept of a mathematical model. It then deals with the discovery of nuclear fission; promotes discussion of papers by such luminaries as Faraday, the Curies, Rutherford, Bohr, and others; and concludes with discussion of two fission papers, accompanied by an on-site demonstration of the fission experiment. The second semester begins with more mathematics, this time emphasizing probability, information processing, and statistics, followed by papers by Mendel, Darwin, and Lederberg leading to Watson, Crick, and the genetic code. Examinations are analyses of other science papers. Pollack reports: "Students are able to summarize and analyze these papers, and they are usually able to propose clever and stimulating next steps in the process. To teach science to a class of scientifically naive students in this way permits us to raise the most serious scientific questions of our day in order to examine the responses of individual scientists. Unanswered questions become the norm, not the exception, since the emphasis is on an open-ended process of model building rather than on the elaboration of a mass of 'known' facts" (1988, p. 14).

A cluster of courses in science, technology, and society is employed at Syracuse University, where students are required to take four science courses. After taking two laboratory courses in biology chemistry, geology or physics, students may opt for two more courses: Introduction to Technology and The Social Impact of Technology. In these they learn about technological innovations that follow from basic science and then examine the social and ethical issues that arise in both science and technology. Hunter College operates a science course for nonscientists by focusing on a few key concepts and infusing a strong historical dimension into the first course of a sequence.

Fundamental Skills. Skills such as writing, speaking, logical and critical thinking, foreign language, mathematics, and academic computing are increasingly emphasized in curricula today. The experience with recent attempts to improve writing is particularly interesting to examine. Writing is an important skill that is central to all of learning, it is the most widespread aspect of general education programs, and it has received a great deal of emphasis during recent years. So what have we learned? That it is very hard to raise achievement levels, but it can be done with a coordinated effort.

The Consortium for the Advancement of Private Higher Education (CAPHE) awarded grants to several colleges to work on the improvement of writing. Whitworth College required a freshman writing course, but the faculty concluded that was not enough. Whittier extended the requirement to two semesters and concluded that was not enough. William Jewell had students take a proficiency test and assigned them to a freshman writing course according to ability level, they were required to take two additional courses with a significant amount of writing, and a writing center was created to assist them. It still was not enough. As one person put it, they tried simply to "stamp out" bad writing and discovered it was not that easy. With the use of (CAPHE funds, each of these colleges subsequently decided on a large and coordinated effort to extend writing across the curriculum and to train faculty with the latest theories and methods of teaching writing. What are those latest methods? Some of the basic tenets of most contemporary approaches are these:

- Writing is like a muscle. It is strengthened with repeated practice and atrophies when not used.

- Writing should be viewed as a process rather than a product; the finished product is a natural consequence of the act of writing.

- Teachers should intervene in the process of student writing by providing useful feedback and expecting corrections to be incorporated in the next draft.

- Coherence, logical development of a line of argument, highlighting main points, and providing supporting evidence are more important than mechanics, grammar, or spelling.

- Writing is an excellent vehicle to teach the skills of critical thinking as well as to promote learning of subject matter in virtually all fields.

- Writing styles vary according to the purpose and audience, and there is no one universal "right way"; students should practice writing for various purposes and audiences.

- Faculty in all departments can learn to give assignments that call for meaningful written responses; to give specific, useful, and constructive feedback to students; and to design tests that involve effective writing.

At the present time large numbers of faculty members at such diverse institutions as Madonna College, Dillard University, Brown University, and LaGuardia Community College employ variations of this approach. The dean at one institution employing these principles said the writing program was the most notable part of the general education program and exulted, "It works!"

Similar strategies are used to teach other skills. Across the curriculum, efforts are being used to teach speaking at Paine College, mathematics at the Evergreen State College, computing at Washington College, and critical thinking at Jackson State University. The argument made by each of these institutions is that their graduates will be seriously deficient if they lack speaking skills, mathematical proficiency, computer facility, or the ability to think critically. For that reason they made a commitment to train and coordinate large numbers of the faculty to teach and reinforce essential skills throughout the curriculum.

A somewhat different approach has been taken in regard to teaching foreign language. Whether or not to require students to acquire a foreign language is one of the most divisive issues regarding the development of skills, with passionate arguments on each side. Proponents assert that one must know a foreign language to get an inside view of another culture, and opponents counter that much language learning is simply memorization and that most students do not go far enough to understand other ways of thinking. And there is the ever-present question of what requiring a foreign language will do for (or against) admissions. Without resolving this eternal academic debate, we can merely note that many colleges adding or raising academic requirements simply set standards (typically facility at the first, second or third year of college-level work) and then offer the courses to implement the program. Several institutions, however, have taken other approaches. Some have adopted the oral proficiency approach, in which most instruction is oral, students get a lot of practice speaking, and professors grade spoken discourse. There is evidence that this technique is effective, and often whole departments receive training as oral instructors and examiners. Another approach was developed at Illinois Wesleyan University, where the language faculty are developing expertise with interactive computer and video systems and developing their own instructional programs. This allows students to obtain more practice, the essential element in acquisition of a skill, without increasing inordinately the amount of time the faculty must spend with them.

Flagship or elite institutions may take other steps. The University of Minnesota College of Liberal Arts established a requirement for students to complete two years of college-level foreign language instruction. Ostensibly a graduation requirement, it functions informally as an entrance requirement, because students may complete part or all of the work in high school and take other courses at the university. On the other hand, students may take the first year of language instruction at the university, but they do not get college credit for it. This policy by the flagship institution is one reason why over two hundred more high schools throughout the state added foreign language courses. It illustrates how a curriculum change by a single institution can help raise the level of education across an entire state.

Higher Standards and More Requirements. College faculties are rediscovering that all courses are not created equal, that some fields of knowledge are more important than others. Some knowledge or skills are regarded as so important that colleges are making them a requirement for graduation. Subjects such as history, literature, mathematics, and science are specified as large numbers of institutions raise their academic standards. Sometimes higher standards are imposed for admission or for advancement to upper-level study. Of course, there is vigorous debate about what standards are proper and whether they should be applied at entrance (where they might assure minimal preparation for college instruction) or at graduation (where they might raise the level of college instruction). Critics fear that higher standards, especially at entrance, might limit access to higher education. There is also disagreement about whether requirements strengthen education by exposing students to areas they might not otherwise take or weaken quality by forcing students into classes they do not want to take. The campus debates are being won by those who favor higher standards and more specific requirements.

Reflecting students' flight to quality during the 1980s, many leading liberal arts colleges have gradually and consistently raised entrance requirements. Macalester College and DePauw University, for example, have seen their applications increase, and they have become more selective. The same phenomenon can be seen in the public liberal arts colleges, including St. Mary's College in Maryland, Northeast Missouri State University, and Mary Washington College in Virginia. The average SAT or ACT scores of their freshmen students have risen dramatically.

The situation is very different in public institutions that have an open-door policy, but even there standards are on the rise. Florida has mandated a "rising junior" examination that students must pass in order to demonstrate they are qualified to pursue upper-level studies, and students in Texas's public colleges must demonstrate proficiency in basic skills—reading, writing, and mathematics—in order to continue their studies. The assumption is that once students recognize they must pass a test to complete their studies, they will master the necessary skills. There is enormous controversy around these new policies, in large part because they raise questions about two opposing ideals: quality and equality. Opponents argue that the policies deny access to students for whom education should be regarded as a right. They also argue that the need for educated people is so great that it is unwise to bar further study from individuals who are enrolled in college. This policy has the greatest impact on minority students, who are the most educationally disadvantaged. The passing rate on the test for Florida's black and Hispanic students is reported to be significantly lower than for white students ("State Notes," 1990). The policy requires those students who, as a group, enter college with less developed skills not only to make the gains expected of more successful students but also to make up all the deficiencies resulting from their prior education.

Although this policy and its rationale are easy to state, they are very difficult to implement. They place an enormous burden on the technical aspects of testing, and there are controversies over which test to use, how to construct a fair instrument, where to set a cutoff point, how many chances a student may have to pass, and what kinds of assistance are provided to help students succeed. Whatever the eventual fate of rising junior exams, mandated testing, or more curricular requirements as a means to increase quality, many proponents sympathize with the sentiment of Robert McCabe, president of Miami-Dade Community College: Higher standards may be the only way to keep the open door open.

The City University of New York is reportedly taking another approach. ("CUNY Officials Propose New Academic Standards," 1991). It intends to raise the level of quality while maintaining its policy of guaranteeing admission to any graduate of the New York City public schools by requiring that applicants complete a college preparatory program. Those who do not meet the requirements will have to complete comparable courses at one of the system's twenty one campuses. The specific requirements are being determined by faculty members from CUNY and the public schools and are expected to be approved by the system's trustees so they may be phased in beginning in the fall of 1992. Currently, about half of the students attending four-year campuses completed a college preparatory program, although a much smaller percentage at the two-year campuses have done so.

Tighter Curriculum Structure. The trend is away from loose distribution requirements that students may satisfy with a large number of courses. Increasingly, colleges are deciding on the qualities they think educated students should possess, and they are designing more purposeful curricula to achieve those goals. Three different mechanisms reflect this principle: (1) specific courses in an academic field, such as Western civilization or American history, that all students must take; (2) a limited set of specially designed courses that meet specific purposes; and (3) interdisciplinary core courses that are taken by all students. In practice, most new curricula use some combination of these mechanisms.

In 1978 Harvard University adopted a set of graduation requirements that were expected to foster "the 'knowledge, skills, and habits of thought' that are of general and lasting intellectual significance." Ten semester courses in five substantive areas are required. In literature and the arts, three courses are specified: literature, fine arts or music, and the contexts of culture; in history, two courses: one on some aspect of the modern world and another on the historical process and perspective; in social and philosophical analysis: one course on social analysis and another in moral and political philosophy; in science and mathematics: one course in physical science and mathematics and another in biological and behavioral science; and in foreign cultures: one course on Western Europe or a major non-Western culture. In addition, proficiency is required in writing, mathematics, and a foreign language. Further, specific criteria established by a college-wide committee and subject matter subcommittees allow them to review course proposals and to approve courses that meet the criteria. In this way students are directed to valued goals and guided through a carefully designed set of courses. Approximately 150 specifically targeted courses constitute the general education curriculum, down from the roughly 2,500 courses among which students previously could select. Despite the continued criticism of the Harvard Plan, the core courses continue to be oversubscribed by the students, suggesting that it plays better with the undergraduates than in the media.

A very different approach to a more purposeful curriculum is Brooklyn College's highly touted model of general education. All students must complete a set of ten interdisciplinary core courses that are designed and taught by teams of faculty members: Classical Origins of Western Culture; Introduction to Art and Music; People, Power, and Politics; The Shaping of the Modern World; Mathematical Reasoning and Computer Programming; Landmarks in Literature; Chemistry and Physics; Biology and Geology; Studies in African Asian, and Latin American Cultures; and Knowledge, Existence, and Values.

During the past decade many colleges have opted for a tighter curriculum. Barbara Hetrick, vice president at Hood College, reported that as a part of the revised curriculum that was implemented in fall 1990, the faculty "adopted learning objectives for the Core and its various subsections. . . . This is important for three major reasons: we can now explain to students, prospective students, and the general community why students are required to take a Core and why they are required to take these particular requirements; they will help ensure that all courses in a category meet the same objectives (it was chaos before); and we have a sound basis for the assessment of the effectiveness of the Core" (personal correspondence, Feb. 13, 1990).

Students at Maryland's Mount St. Mary's College take six interrelated core courses in Western history, literature, and philosophy and then spend a year studying American culture to examine comparisons and contrasts. Many institutions, including Bemidji State University and Catonsville Community College, have tightened their distribution requirements. Often they also provide a clearer rationale for the requirements, establish criteria for general education courses, and empower a college-wide committee to approve courses that meet the criteria. All of this makes for a tighter and more purposeful curriculum.

The Freshman Year. Entering college is an important transition, but until recently colleges have been relatively cavalier about it. They viewed the freshman experience with "a kind of social Darwinism," in the words of John Gardner, the driving force behind this innovation. Today new students are receiving more attention to their intellectual and personal development, stronger advising, and better orientation to college through specially designed freshman seminars and related programs.

There are two basic types of freshman seminars, each of which seems to be effective. The first type follows the tradition of perhaps the best known version, University 101, operated at the University of South Carolina since 1972 and replicated widely. The goal is to foster the overall development of students and assist them to make a good adjustment to the university. The focus is on three topics: themselves, the campus, and higher education. A teacher is expected, first, to create a sense of community among the class, utilize group building activities that promote social interaction and self-disclosure, and create conditions so that students look forward to the course. There are units on such topics as library research methods, planning for the choice of a major and career, learning about campus resources, study skills, getting along with others, and whatever the instructor and group decide upon. A combination of lecturing, discussion, and group activities is encouraged, and students write frequently. Some variations of this model at other institutions make the seminar available to those who want it, and others require it of all freshmen. The amount of academic credit awarded varies from none to regular course credit.

Southwest Texas State University launched a version of this kind of seminar in 1986 with sixteen sections, expanded it to forty sections the next year, and taught the entire freshman class in 1988. The objective of this one-credit course is "primarily motivational" and designed "to create commitment," according to the instructor's manual. Secondary objectives include:

- To focus attention on the process of growing up, establishing an identity, shaping a career and a life

- To raise the question of what constitutes a good life; to help students think through their values and their goals

- To present a comprehensive view of a university education

- To present the rationale for the required courses; to make the case for broad learning

- To explore with our students the points of connection between a university education and a fulfilling life

- To explore the relation between their university study and their informed, well-thought-out personal goals (Gordon, n.d., p. 4)

Instructors are encouraged to play the role of skilled facilitators rather than the usual subject matter experts.

A second, though related, conception is a freshman seminar with a more academic emphasis. The argument for this form is that freshmen often are overwhelmed by veteran students in many of their courses, and it helps to have a course made up of only new students. Further, the usual introductions to the academic disciplines do not provide a broad enough focus to intellectual life; a topical course drawing on a range of disciplinary perspectives constitutes a better introduction to the life of the mind. By concentrating on the close reading of texts, discussion in small groups, and frequent writing of papers, students can develop valuable skills essential to the rest of their study. These groups, too, seek to foster a sense of community, and the instructor may serve as the academic adviser of students in the seminar.

Marietta College introduced a mandatory freshman seminar with a substantive intellectual focus in 1990, as a part of its new general education program. Similar efforts exist at such diverse places as Broome County (Community) College and Seton Hill College, which requires a year-long course.

Although generalizations are difficult because of the variety of programs, there is strong evidence that they work. Fidler and Hunter (1989) reviewed many research reports and concluded that, in general, freshman year programs seem to improve the academic performance, satisfaction, and retention of students. In addition, they seem to increase the knowledge and use of campus services. And they note some evidence that "faculty-student relationships, communication skills, and study habits may also be positively affected" (p. 224). During a time when traditional-age students are more scarce, freshman year programs are a popular way for colleges to serve students better and to maintain enrollment by enhancing retention. Special first-year programs also work for nontraditional students.

The Senior Year. The other major transition for college students is out of college and into the world of work, graduate or professional school, or some other activity. Many institutions expect seniors to take a senior seminar or to complete a significant project that integrates much of their education, demonstrates sophisticated skills, or culminates in a "capstone" experience.

Here, too, there are alternative models. Ohio University adopted a three-tier general education program that deals with skills (tier one), distribution of academic disciplines (tier two), and an interdisciplinary senior synthesis (tier three). Approximately seventy-five senior seminars are offered on a variety of topics. Hope College has a senior seminar that is more personal and seeks to draw out a student's own values as well as to foster intellectual integration. Students are expected to write a "life view" paper that is both disciplined and personal. A Task Force on the

Undergraduate Experience at Northwestern University (1988, p. 28) recommended a senior year project or research experience for all students. Student research and 'senior theses' represent one option for the senior project; other options might include a senior performance or recital, one or more senior seminars, or an extended essay done by the student through independent study of one or more quarters." The report noted that many departments already offer such an opportunity, and it simply recommends broadening it.

A very different approach is utilized at Wheaton College, which established a Center for Work and Learning to assist its liberal arts students to become more familiar with the world of work. According to a grant proposal (1985), the center seeks to "create new links between the liberal arts and the world of work through a program which integrates an explicit learning component into work and internships; develops courses with a required experiential component; creates a program to bring executives, labor leaders, and experts on the world of work to campus; and institutes faculty internships." Although not focused solely on seniors, this is another effective way to assist the transition of students into life after college.

Muhlenburg and Susquehanna Colleges require both freshman and senior seminars. They are regarded as helpful mechanisms to both launch and complete the overall college experience.

Global Studies. Because of the growing interdependence of peoples around the globe in regard to economic systems, environmental protection, national security, and a host of other issues, colleges are stressing the study of other cultures. A study by the Educational Testing Service (Barrows, Clark, and Klein, 1980) identified three aspects of global sophistication: knowledge of other countries, positive attitudes toward international affairs, and empathy for other peoples and cultures. These are in varying degrees goals of many new global studies programs.

In the past, the focus of international programs has been on specialties in international relations or the study of some geographical area of the world. Typically they enroll a few students who major in these programs. The emphasis today is to insert global studies into the general education curriculum taken by all students. This is done primarily by means of two different mechanisms: requirement of a course dealing with other cultures or infusion of global perspectives into courses across the curriculum.

Several institutions require students to take a course on other cultures, most of which deal with Western civilization, the tradition out of which our culture developed. Although such courses provide the ideas, history, and culture of the West, however they are not likely to help students to understand the revolutionary changes taking place in the Soviet Union, the trade barriers between Japan and the United States, the religious fundamentalism in the Middle East, or poverty in Latin America: implicit aspirations of the global studies agenda. More is needed.

Several institutions that have revised their curricula have specified that students study an unfamiliar northwestern culture. Few, however, go as far as Goshen, the Indiana Mennonite college, which requires students to travel to a non-Western country to get a first-hand experience with a radically different way of life. But several, such as Western Maryland College, do require students to take a course on the developing world.

The Consortium for the Advancement of Private Higher Education has provided support to several private colleges for the development of an infusion model. The college of Holy Cross determined the focus of its project would be China. It recruited ten faculty members from as many departments to participate in the program, which included a year-long seminar on the culture and history of China, elementary language learning, a month-long trip to China for sight-seeing and to meet faculty colleagues, in-depth orientation and structured debriefing, and opportunities to integrate knowledge and insights into courses offered the following year. By all accounts, it was a successful effort that strengthened the college's Asian Studies program by infusing it throughout the curriculum.

With minor variations on this theme, St. Joseph's College developed a core course on Mexico, St. Michael's College focused on Japan, and the University of San Diego concentrated on two areas of strategic importance to it, Latin America and the Pacific Rim. The University of the Pacific established a new School of International Studies, drawing largely from faculty members throughout the existing departments. These approaches represent a kind of tightly focused approach to global studies, where a country, region, or particular program is utilized.

More of a shotgun approach was employed by Concordia College (Moorhead, Minnesota). Following a series of lectures and workshops on global studies, faculty members were encouraged to apply for grants to support foreign travel and study leading to the development of new or revised courses reflecting their learning. A total of forty submitted proposals that were subsequently funded. Following their various travels, they taught courses containing the new material. They then participated in a Global Studies Teaching Conference in which each person gave a brief presentation about the changes in their teaching and the apparent effects on the students. According to Peter Hovde, the director, the conference was "a productive opportunity for interdisciplinary communication and cooperation" that brought faculty together in a common endeavor. Because the program involved roughly a quarter of the entire faculty, large numbers of courses, and a sharing of the experiences in a common forum, it had a significant impact on the instructional program.

A recent study by Richard Lambert (1989) indicates that most international studies (apart from foreign language) are not evenly distributed. They tend to consist largely of history and literature courses and to focus on geographical areas, they are heavily Eurocentric, and they are concentrated in four year colleges and universities. Such courses are more likely to be taken by students majoring in the humanities and spurned by those in the natural sciences and career fields. Requiring specific courses in general education or infusing them throughout the curriculum are useful ways to extend global sophistication among all students. Whatever specific mechanisms are utilized, institutions that are revising their curricula are placing greater emphasis on global studies.

Cultural Diversity. Another trend is heightened attention to cultural pluralism in America and the West and the incorporation of new scholarship on these topics into the core curriculum.

As usual, the simplest mechanism is to require a course. For example, the University of California, Berkeley, requires a course on ethnic minorities, not unexpected for a campus in which the majority of students are now non-Caucasian. The University of Tennessee, Knoxville, requires a course selected from an approved list dealing with either gender or racial issues.

Another common approach is to infuse the "new scholarship" in courses across the curriculum, particularly in the core. This stands in opposition to the dominant pattern of the 1960s, when the trend was to create majors in Women's or Ethnic Studies, which functioned like ghettos of the converted. The trend now is to "mainstream" the knowledge and perspectives, so that all students can better understand cultural diversity. For example, San Jose State University adopted a policy that, insofar as possible, all general education courses are expected to address contributions of women and ethnic minority groups, according to Leon Dorosz, associate academic vice president. He notes that evaluation questions given to students in general education courses ask how ethnic/gender issues were addressed. In addition, the university mandates a course on cultural pluralism that deals with comparisons of at least two distinct cultural groups; this requires students to do more sophisticated analysis, comparison, and contrast rather than simply to recognize the issues and contributions of women and cultural groups.

The project on Engaging Cultural Legacies of the Association of American Colleges states in the proposal that colleges should help students "address the complexity that is part of their cultural inheritance; the disparate and often conflicting sources of their traditions; the values, commitments, questions, and tensions that are intrinsic to any rich tradition; the difficulties of framing judgments that draw on inherited values" (Association of American Colleges, 1989, p. 2). The project involves fifty-four diverse institutions working with nine other mentor institutions to create sequences of core courses that deal with the multiplicity of heritages.

Integration of Knowledge. Integration, according to Harlan Cleveland, is what is higher about higher education. Most people agree that students should not simply learn various bits of knowledge but should also make relevant connections between them and with the rest of their lives. Unfortunately, the students are usually left to make such connections on their own. An iron law promulgated by Jonathan Smith of the University of Chicago puts a different light on the matter: "A student shall not be expected to integrate anything that the faculty can't or won't!" What he means is that integration should be a central part of instruction and that professors should both teach and model that kind of thinking. Without explicit training, students are not likely to make relevant connections. Deliberate attempts to integrate knowledge are found in many reformed curricula.

Perhaps the simplest mechanism is a broad-gauge course that includes interdisciplinary perspectives, such as the two-semester sophomore course called Cultures and Traditions used at Wabash College for fifteen years. The first-semester students study the unfamiliar culture of ancient China and then the roots of their own heritage in the ancient Greeks and Hebrews. During the second semester they study Western civilization from the medieval period through the process of "modernization." They end by returning to China and examining its recent attempts to move into the modern world. The course is taught by a cadre of faculty in discussion sections of about fifteen students. Similar approaches have been recently established elsewhere, such as the new humanities course at Utah Valley Community college called Ethics and Ideals.

Some colleges foster integration by linking two or more courses that students take simultaneously. Whittier College offers students the option of satisfying its requirements in World Civilizations and in Contemporary Society and the Individual by either taking pairs of carefully coordinated courses in different disciplines or team-taught courses offered in consecutive semesters. Faculty members must work together to plan and teach jointly these related courses that differ significantly from the usual separate courses. California Lutheran employs a cluster of two regular courses and a third that bridges them—typically an English course that involves students in thinking and writing about the topics of the other two courses. Because the professors plan their work collaboratively, they are able to help students make connections across the courses that would otherwise not be possible.

Another variation on this theme is the use of interdisciplinary core courses or sequences. Hiram College organizes much of its general education "not around traditional departmental questions, but rather, around more universal ideas, problems or issues..." Groups of three or four faculty members from two or more disciplines organize a collegium that studies a substantial topic. Each collegium organizes and teaches three courses, all of which the twenty-five to thirty students take during the year. Sample collegia are The Idea of the West, The Origin of Life, The Progress Paradox, and The Environment: Ecology, Economics, and Ethics.

A more intense educational experience is what might be termed a "learning community." Pioneered by Patrick Hill, former provost at the Evergreen State College, it is based on the observations that learning is an individual (but not necessarily solitary) activity and that it can be more effective when done as a part of a community of learners. LaGuardia Community College annually offers about ten different communities, which constitute the primary responsibility for each of the twenty-six to twenty-eight students and three faculty members. Separate topics are designed to appeal to liberal arts and business majors; for liberal arts students The Concept of Freedom clusters introductory courses in philosophy and a social science with an English writing course. For business students, introductory courses in economics and business and an English writing course are joined. The learning community helps overcome the isolation of students and faculty. Roberta Matthews (1986, p. 46) writes: "Because learning communities encourage continuity and integration in the curriculum, students learn more from courses experienced within the community than they would from taking each course as a discrete entity taught with no outside references.... [Further, they] offer the closest facsimile of dormitory life to commuter students in nonresidential community colleges."

There is empirical evidence to support her contentions. Students taking the composition courses within the cluster have a higher completion rate and half the failure rate, and they receive 10 to 20 percent more "A" and "B" grades. In the business cluster, the completion rate of the economics courses was 5 percent higher and the business course 20 percent higher, and teachers of the two courses assigned 25 percent more "A" and "B" grades than in their discrete courses. Experiences like these are among the reasons the Washington Center at Evergreen State is working with colleges and universities across the state to establish learning communities in all types of institutions. More information about this form of organization may be found in a publication by Gabelnick, MacGregor, Matthews, and Smith (1990).

Several colleges have established whole programs or even subcolleges to create a more integrated education for a small number of students, typically 200 to 500. The Classic Learning

Core at the University of North Texas offers, according to Robert Stevens, the director, "a truly integrated and sequenced curriculum of liberal arts requirements for self-selecting students who are willing to agree to a fairly strict succession of courses" (personal communication, Jan. 16, 1990). The curriculum is organized loosely around the three themes of virtue, civility, and reason. The thirty faculty members from nine departments participate in a two-week summer workshop to discuss ideas and plan courses, and they meet every two weeks during the term to construct a common reading list, discuss common texts, and consider means for unifying the learning of their students. Similar efforts are found at George Mason, Miami (Ohio), and California State Polytechnic universities as well as at Gustavus Adolphus and St. Olaf colleges.

Wesley Brown (1989) has assembled a great deal of evidence that demonstrates the effectiveness of the Paracollege, a subcollege at St. Olaf. The students achieved at high levels on standardized achievement tests, demonstrated a great deal of intellectual and personal growth, enhanced their intellectual interests, gained in thinking and communication skills, and were very satisfied with their education. Indeed, Brown (p. 101) concludes that "something associated with their participation in the Paracollege had an effect on their development not shared to the same degree by other students at St. Olaf or, indeed, by most students at other colleges. . . . "This experience is consistent with others who advocate the integration of knowledge, especially if it takes place within a genuine community of learners.

Moral Reflection. More than technical expertise is expected of the educated person, and colleges that are revising their educational programs are once again starting to emphasize values. Although implementing any of the programs included in these trends is difficult, the emphasis on values and ethics is particularly tricky. With the exception of a few strict religious institutions, the purpose is not indoctrination nor to get students to adhere to a particular belief system or code of behavior. It is to develop and strengthen the abilities of students to think through value-laden issues, to discuss them intelligently, and to develop the ability to make reasoned judgments about alternatives.

The traditional way of addressing this topic is to require a course in philosophy (or theology in some religious colleges) or, more recently, to offer courses in professional ethics. But a number of new ways are coming into being. A required interdisciplinary and team-taught core course is a form employed at Louisiana College, designed to teach students about the nature of values, the process by which they are chosen, and their role in the life of an individual. St. Andrews Presbyterian College requires an interdisciplinary course that deals with a global issue and explores controversies and personal values in relation to it. It culminates in a class position paper that reflects common values concerning the issue that emerge from a semester of study and discussion. Los Medanos, a California community college, has a two-semester requirement, Ethical Inquiry into Societal Issues. During the first semester students examine a limited number of topics, such as equality, population, and the environment; during the second they pursue one topic in greater depth.

Freshmen and senior seminars often raise value conflicts and foster greater awareness of the students' own values. These cornerstone and capstone experiences seek to capitalize on the value challenges inherent in the freshman and senior transitions to increase the sophistication of students in thinking through complex issues.

Albion College prefers not to add a course on ethics but to infuse ethics into courses across the curriculum. Frank Frick, director of the Center for Ethics, encourages faculty members to study values related to their disciplines and to incorporate those topics into regular courses. Alverno and Clayton State Colleges have a competency-based curriculum in which valuing is one of the abilities to be developed and assessed. Earlham supports collaborative student-faculty research on themes central to the character of this Friends college, including peace, justice, and race and gender equality. In these ways, several colleges are seeking to develop an educated heart to go along with an educated mind.

The "New Practicality" Revisited: Changes in the American College Curriculum

BARBARA ANN SCOTT

Thorstein Veblen and Robert Maynard Hutchins, a generation apart, each wrote a book title *The Higher Learning in America* (Hutchins, 1936; Veblen, 1957 [1918]; also see McClure, 1976). The common denominator of both volumes was an indictment of the utilitarian corruption of the college curriculum and an impassioned defense of the pursuit of learning for its own sake. The vocational training vogue, in particular, Hutchins contemptuously labeled a "service station approach" that was threatening to turn the traditional liberal arts colleges into mere "trade schools." To Veblen, universities had become something akin to modern department stores, "competitors for traffic in merchantable instruction" (p. 24).

Apparently, the dilemma was a familiar one two thousand years ago, for Aristotle was moved to ask, "Should the useful in life . . . or should the higher knowledge be the aim of our training?" (Maeroff, 1977, p. C-6). Today, there is fresh urgency to the issue that so troubled these passionate prophets of recent and ancient times. With the vocational vogue now gathering momentum on college campuses, the general education that Hutchins championed at the University of Chicago is more and more losing its allure. As one observer noted: "Young people are inclined to think that in a bad job market, majoring in accounting, electrical engineering, or hospital administration makes more sense than majoring in philosophy, literature, or the classics" (Maeroff, 1977, p. C-6).

A front page story in the *New York Times* summed up the "new practicality" with the headline, "STUDENTS FLOCK TO JOB-RELATED COURSES." Noting the "nationwide trend" of booming enrollments[1] in such fields as business administration, accounting, engineering, agriculture, and mining, the *Times* report explained: "In a quest for better job credentials . . . students are deserting the humanities and many of the social sciences for academic programs that they consider more practical." Among those students stalwart enough to resist the general stampede and remain in liberal arts degree programs, many are nonetheless "seeking vocationally oriented minors to go with their less marketable majors" (Maeroff, 1975, p. C-10).

The "new practicality"[2] among college students is also, it seems, fostering a new parochialism. The American Council on Education reported in 1978 that today only 3% of undergraduates were enrolled in any programs dealing with international affairs, other nation-states, or other cultures. Enrollments in foreign language courses had declined drastically over the previous decade. In the late 1960s, language courses attracted more than 15% of undergraduate students. A decade later, this share had dropped to less than 9%. As of the late 1970s, language requirements for college admissions had been abandoned by all but 10 percent of our 3,200 academic institutions" ("The Future Forsaken," 1978, p. 3).

These trends, however, are not only a matter of student attitudes and choice. The new practicality also gained new promoters among policy planners and new practitioners among academic administrators. Carl Kaysen, vice-chairman of the prestigious Sloan Commission on Government and Higher Education, unambiguously listed as one of the major functions of higher education "the application of knowledge to the solution of practical problems in the wider society" (Kaysen, 1969, p. 7). In the mid-1970s the President's Task Force on Higher Education bluntly criticized a "tendency to concentrate on liberal arts" in many of the public colleges across the nation. This blue-ribbon panel declared: "Occupational training must become more acceptable in the minds of students, their parents and potential employers" ("Great American Dream Freeze," 1975). This was also the explicit goal of former U.S. commissioner of education Sidney P. Marland, Jr., when he enthusiastically explained the federal government's commitment to career education as an effort to "gear all education to the world of work" (cited in O'Toole, 1975, p. 30).

Just how much the new practicality inspired the thinking of academic policy planners is quite clear from the Carnegie Commission on Higher Education's plans for overhauling the college curriculum. Criticizing the "pace and organization" of the learning experience as unnecessarily rigid, and as limiting "the flexibility of colleges in undertaking reforms," the Commission stressed the need for making college education more "adaptable" and "advantageous" to individual students and, at the same time, "more useful" to society (Carnegie Commission, 1973, p. 43).

Among the Commission's many practical proposals were to speed up to the instructional process and to shorten the time in formal education. In this way, a BA degree could be gained in three years, a PhD in four. It also recommended expanding educational credentials so that a degree or certificate would be given to students "at least every two years and in some cases every year." Finally, higher education should be focused more toward work. At the top of the Commission's agenda in this regard was the expansion of vocational education both inside and outside the formal college, the facilitating of work-study arrangements with public and private employers, and the encouragement of "stop-outs" and precollegiate military service and work experience, for which academic credit might be given (Carnegie Commission, 1973, p. 44).

In its policy report on higher education, the Committee for Economic Development (CED) announced a similar set of curricular goals and similar enthusiasm for curricular efficiency as had the Carnegie Commission. Hailing the possibilities of "non-traditional education," especially under the stimulus of government philanthropic initiatives, the CED called upon college executives to "explore the possibilities of new modes of instruction, new types of curricula, new educational timetables and alternative methods of degree granting in order to provide wider diversity of educational opportunities and the greatest possible effectiveness in the use of resources" (CED, 1973, pp. 51–52).

Although the new curricular practicality has many dimensions, academic policy planners clearly have at the top of their curricular agenda the promotion of career education.

Career Education: Vocationalism by Another Name

The latest fad in educational circles, from junior high through college, career education was first conceived and promoted by Sidney P. Marland, Jr., in 1971 when he was the U.S. commissioner of education.[3] It soon became a cornerstone of federal education policies under the Nixon administration and has been generously funded in the years since. Initially, $850 million was authorized over a three-year period for career education at the postsecondary level alone—a generous sum in those days. Despite the budget-cutting fervor of the Reagan administration in its first two years in office, spending increases were authorized for career education of close to $100 million over the $701.4 million appropriated during the final year of the Carter presidency. In the succeeding five fiscal years, again despite substantial cuts in other education programs, spending for career education was held constant at an approximate annual average of $754 million. All told, during the eight years of the Reagan administration, the federal government subsidized career education by more than $6 billion.[4]

The career education movement is, to be sure, more than a byproduct of federal largesse. Since its eventual beneficiaries are, by and large, private employers, it is hardly surprising that corporate and foundation interests feel a strong commitment to its success and a willingness to contribute generously to its support. The American Banking Association, for example, has initiated and financially underwritten a banking program at Texas Southern University; a substantial grant from the Ford Foundation went to establish a graduate school of business at the Atlanta University Center; and a consortium of high-tech companies contributed $6 million to the University of Minnesota to set up facilities for microelectronics, automation, and software design (Newt Davidson Collective, 1973, p. 83; "High Tech and the Schools," 1983, p. 7) Recently, American University found itself at the center of a storm of controversy when it accepted a grant of $5 million from multimillionaire arms merchant Adnan Khashoggi to underwrite construction of a sports and convention center. In addition to having the center named after him, Khashoggi was rewarded for his generosity with a seat on the university's board of trustees (McCarthy, 1987, p. 253). Having first earned international notoriety as a key go-between in the "Iran-Contra" scandal, Khashoggi was, at this writing, under federal indictment for allegedly helping Ferdinand and Imelda Marcos loot the Philippines.

No single private institution demonstrates the corporation/college connection more conspicuously than the Massachusetts Institute of Technology (MIT), whose campus is "dotted with buildings donated by Exxon, Campbell Soup, Texas Instruments" as well as by industrialists Alfred P. Sloan and George Eastman. MIT's ties to Exxon, in particular, were cemented not long ago with an $8 million grant to finance combustion research, while the W. R. Grace Company contributed $8.5 million for commercial applications of microbiology research, two of the largest single corporate contracts (Bouton, 1983, p. 63; Crittenden, 1981, pp. D-1, D-11). In the decade from 1979 to 1988, corporate-financed research there more than quadrupled, outstripped only by the robust investment of the Department of Defense (DOD) in military-related research which in 1987 totaled $408 million, making MIT the number one academic beneficiary of DOD largesse (MIT Alternative News Collective, 1988, p. 59).

Corporations are only too happy to have a strong federal commitment to and sponsorship of programs such as career education, even if most of the funds go to vocational training at the public colleges. The advantages to private business and industry are twofold: first, a supply of technically skilled labor and, second, private occupational training at public expense. Moreover, the colleges that have instituted such vocational training programs appear to be amply accommodating to the needs of area employers. One spokesman for an interest group representing the community colleges said that when "corporate managers . . . announce a need for skilled workers . . . college administrators trip over each other in their haste to organize a new technical curriculum" (Cohen, 1977, p. 6).

Evidence of such academic and corporate cooperation (in alliance, of course, with government) can clearly be inferred from statistics showing that of the more than 9 million students attending community, technical, or junior colleges, two thirds are enrolled in vocational programs, the most popular being electronics, nursing, data processing, secretarial, business, and law enforcement ("Vocational Schools Get Respect," 1983, p. 79). Of course, the vocational vogue at the college level is largely a function of the extensive groundwork laid in the junior and senior high schools. According to the U.S. Department of Education, as early as 1975 (four years after the federal program began) career education was firmly entrenched in 5,000 of the nation's 17,000 school districts ("The Great Training Robbery," 1978, p. 12).

Other centers of career education with more direct and immediate ties to business and industry are the proprietary schools and colleges run by such corporations as ITT, Bell & Howell, R. J. Reynolds Industries, RCA, Holiday Inns, and the Xerox Corporation. At least 18 corporations and industry associations have been authorized to grant academic credentials, ranging from associate of arts degrees to doctorates (Fiske, 1985, p. A-10). One of the oldest, General Motors Institute (GMI), founded in 1919, was the first fully accredited college in the United States owned and operated by an industrial corporation; it offered GM employee-students four majors (in industrial administration and in mechanical, electrical, and industrial engineering). "During their years at GMI," a journalist observed, "most students seem to absorb GM's relentlessly optimistic corporate ethic" (Marbach & Young, 1981, p. 62). In 1982, GM's official proprietorship came to an end, when GMI became incorporated as an independent, nonprofit college (Fiske, 1985, p. A-10).

A 1985 report of the Carnegie Foundation for the Advancement of Teaching, *Corporate Classrooms: The Learning Business*, found that corporate-run education has become a booming $60-billion-a year enterprise, "similar to the cost of the nation's four-year colleges and universities, both public and private," and approaching "the total enrollment of those same institutions - about eight million students" (Fiske, 1985, p. A-10). One recent innovation has been the establishment of satellite universities through the corporate exercise of *cooperative philanthropy*. The first was the National Technological University created in 1985 by IBM, the Westinghouse Corporation, the Digital Equipment Company, and other firms that use "satellites to broadcast courses to corporate classrooms around the country and abroad" (Fiske, 1985, p. A-10).

The patterns of cooperative planning and promotion are as conspicuous as the patterns of cooperative philanthropy undergirding the career education movement. They have helped to coordinate the new vocationalism administratively, give it nationwide momentum, and orchestrate public consensus behind it. *Fortune* magazine explained the necessity for such inter-institutional cooperation by noting that the new programs "obviously cannot be carried on by educators, alone; they require the active collaboration of the business community, which stands to benefit from their success" ("The Great Training Robbery," 1978, p. 12). One of the leading quasi-governmental planning bodies, the National Commission on the Financing of Post Secondary Education, called upon the nation's colleges and universities two decades ago to increase their efforts to secure accurate data on local "work force retirements." Recognizing the need to improve communication and cooperation between corporations and the campus, the commission strongly recommended that all post-secondary institutions "develop a greater capacity for expanding and contracting their professional and occupational training programs according to continuing measures of demand" (Newt Davidson Collective, 1973, p. 81).

Cooperative Education and the Corporate Ethos

In the 1970s and 1980s, a movement to rationalize the corporation-college connection, along the lines recommended by the National Commission, gathered momentum and secured federal sanction under the title *cooperative education*. This, quite simply, is career education pushed to a closer and cosier connection with business and industry. Cooperative education operationalizes the proposals of the Carnegie Commission, the CED, and other planning bodies for "work-study" and "stop-out" arrangements with public and private employers for which academic credit is given for work experience. The Carnegie Commission, in its policy report *Less Time, More Options*, was particularly explicit in urging the expansion of innovative forms of education "outside the formal college, in apprenticeship programs, proprietary schools, in-service training in industry and in military programs; appropriate educational credit should be eligible for federal and state assistance available to students in formal colleges" (Carnegie Commission, 1971, p. 13).

The State University of New York (SUNY) has long championed the cause of cooperative education at its 64 campuses. Its 1972 Master Plan, for example, caught the spirit and substance of the Carnegie policy report by specifying that new cooperative arrangements be made with the state's "industrial plants, government agencies, professional offices, hospitals, clinics, laboratories, courthouses, modern farms, and even shopping centers" New York Board of Regents, 19782, p. 12). Statewide, the cooperative education movement was fueled by the enthusiastic support of SUNY's chancellors. In March 1975, then-chancellor Ernest L. Boyer candidly outlined the State University's hopes and plans for a new University-Industry Task Force: "The University wants very much to help management and labor become more productive and, at this time of unprecedented unemployment, we have a special obligation to retrain individuals in new career fields." One of the first accomplishments of the new task force was to sign a major agreement between SUNY and the state's largest corporation, the New York Telephone Company, aimed at "relating the resources of the University much more closely to the world of work." Under the precedent-setting agreement—intended as a model for cooperative education programs in the state—several of the SUNY colleges were to offer vocational training and retraining courses to the telephone company's 85,000 employees. Upon conclusion of the historic accord, telephone company president William M. Ellinghaus enthusiastically remarked, "This is one of those happy instances where everyone benefits. The University extends its services more widely. Our business gains better trained, more expert personnel which, in turn, benefits the public" ("SUNY, NY Tel. in Major Accord," 1975, p. 1).

Clifton Wharton, Jr., who succeeded Boyer as SUNY chancellor, issued a call for an upgraded "knowledge extension service, whereby the university's research, scholarly and professional resources are made available to industry, commerce, city and state government" (Wharton, 1978, p. 13). He declared that this was in keeping with SUNY's third mission, public service, encapsulated in the university's motto: "To Learn—To Serve."

By the mid-1980s, it has been calculated, at least half of the nation's two- and four-year colleges had contractual arrangements for cooperative education programs with employers— whether corporations, government agencies, or professional associations. According to the *Chronicle of Higher Education:*

> Under the typical contract, the college provides the education or training, which is often tailored to the specific needs of the employer, as well as the faculty members who teach the course. The company usually, but not always, recruits the employees for the program and provides classroom facilities and some administrative assistance. (Watkins, 1984, p. 1)

A few such contracts are for liberal arts courses, but most, understandably, are for business education or technical training. Pace University, for example, set up a special Office of Corporate Education Services (OCES) in 1981 with some 50 different programs offered "off the shelf" on corporate sites. The director of the OCES candidly explained Pace's motive: "We are in the business of serving the corporate community primarily for new markets"—in order to offset, in short, declining numbers of traditional-age students with corporate-commandeered workers. "Colleges and universities (after all)," he went on, are in the educational contracting business primarily to make money" (Watkins, 1984, p. 10).

In Orange County, California, the community college system has joined with 400 nearby firms, many of them top Pentagon contractors, to form the "Technology Exchange Center." Chancellors of the eight colleges in the system sit on a board of directors with corporate chief executive officers "anticipate job openings and plan training programs to fill them. Students use space and equipment at the industry sites and companies get pre-trained employees at low cost" ("Vocational Schools Get Respect," 1983, p. 80).

The new practicality of college administrators and their corporate counterparts has been reinforced by a multimedia blitz directed to present and future educational consumers. Over the past decade and a half, the public has been inundated with newspaper reports, feature articles in magazines, television specials, and paperback best-sellers with such provocative titles as *The Case Against College* and *The Over-Educated American* (Bird, 1975; Freeman, 1976) that defend the new practicality. If one must go to college (and it is not clear that one must), at least make it "career education," these media seem to say. The unmistakable message, according to Jerome Karabel, is that "vocational training is a 'no nonsense' approach which, unlike vaguely directed liberal arts programs, pays off in dollars." In view of the currents of anti-intellectualism in American culture, "this pseudo-populist appeal," Karabel adds, "is quite powerful indeed" (Karabel, 1974, p. 16).

While addressing the question "College, Who Needs It?", *Time* magazine gave its editorial approval to a midwestern college which now offers degrees in automobile body repair and mechanics. Shortly after the federal government announced its plans to underwrite career education, the *Wall Street Journal*, in an editorial praising the new federal initiatives, expressed the hope that a career orientation would give students a greater sense of purpose and reduce the numbers "drifting aimlessly into college," which had heretofore denied "needed skills and talents to the economy" (Karabel, 1974, p. 16). Probably the most potent effort to push the new practicality with the general public was a CBS television special bearing the provocative title (reminiscent of *Time* magazine's), "Higher Education, Who Needs It?" The program's audience was given the distinct impression, according to Jerome Karabel, that "the shortest road to the bread line is by way of the college gate." Sardonically, Karabel summarized the program's not-so-hidden message:

Myths . . . [CBS claims] have caused students to flock to liberal arts programs leading to the B.A. The central myth is that college is the "only stepping stone to high-status careers." Instead, the show informs us, jobs and money are really located elsewhere.

With Ph.D.'s portrayed as parking lot attendants, and a tough-talking Ford executive informing us that at least 80,000 openings are available for automotive mechanics at this very moment, more career education is obviously needed. (Karabel, 1974, p. 17)

The Reagan administration's flamboyant secretary of education, William J. Bennett, offered a version of the "College, Who Needs It?" argument. Commenting more from the perspective of an educational elitist critical of academic mismanagement and deteriorating performance standards, Bennett made headlines by telling the press that if some day his infant son were to ask him for $50,000 to start his own business in lieu of tuition for an Ivy League Education, he might "think that was a good idea." Bennett proposed that $50,000 option, he remarked, to challenge the assumption that "wonderful things must come to pass when you get a degree" (Hechinger, 1985, p. C-1).

The New "Practical" Liberal Arts

The popularizers of the new practicality in the mass media and its promoters on college campuses have helped to stimulate still another trend: the gradual infusion of a "practical" focus into traditional liberal arts courses and curricula. This change has resulted from the self-conscious efforts at fiscal crisis management on the part of college administrators in order to salvage liberal arts programs and reverse the decline in student interest and enrollments. One small liberal arts college in Illinois, for example, "superimposed a Business Preparation Program on top of its liberal arts curriculum" that, the college's administration reported with pride, may be "combined with any major field of study." The program called for a 19-hour sequence of required courses with such titles as: "Career Planning and Human Development," "Case Studies in Business," "Career Entry Seminar," and "Business and Society." Students must also take courses in computer programming, accounting, and marketing. A college brochure explained the rationale behind the new program: "we . . . have a strong belief in the liberal arts background as a sound beginning for a flexible business career. We are aware, however, that it takes more than a degree to land a job" (Maeroff, 1977, p. C-6).

Throughout the academic system, other such efforts to refurbish the liberal arts with the new practicality could easily be found. Music majors at Oregon's Willamette University, the *New York Times* reported in 1975, could "combine their liberal arts preparation with training in music therapy." Penn State's French Department, according to the *Times*, had developed a program with the College of Business Administration. In addition, Eastern Michigan University was training managers for cultural institutions, while Baruch College in New York had a "similar program to give history majors the business expertise to run historical societies" (Maeroff, 1975, p. C-10). Economics departments throughout the country are adding special programs, minors, and major "tracks" in accounting and business administration to supplement their more theoretically-focused traditional curricula. The field of mathematics has experienced a similar transformation from "pure" to "applied" science largely fueled by the boom in computer technology.

But the biggest boom of all seems to be in the rising demand for business courses. "Such courses have become so popular," a *New York Times* report notes "that they are even being offered at the most prestigious liberal arts schools" (Bruno, 1985). In 1985 Wesleyan University introduced the first accounting course in its 153-year history, while at Amherst financial accounting reappeared in the curriculum after a 20-year absence. "Dickinson College in Pennsylvania, rated among the top ten liberal arts colleges by *U.S. News and World Report*, established a policy and management studies major in 1981. . . . At Bryn Mawr, people with business and administrative experience . . . are brought in to teach seminars. At Oberlin, its first 'executive-in-residence,' a vice-president of Equitable Life, taught a two-week business management course for credit" (Bruno, 1985, p. 18). Such curricular trends have, of course, presupposed and fostered the rapid expansion both of career counseling and placement services and of corporate recruiting on campus.

In 1982 an influential policy study, *Global Stakes: The Future of High Technology in America*, made headlines when it argued for a $1 billion "crash program . . . of integrating the humanities with technology education," financed jointly by the federal and state governments and private industry. The $1 billion in start-up funds was to be used to "buy equipment, finance scholarships and research in math, engineering, and computer sciences." Calling it a "modern Morrill Act" (after the legislation which created the federal land grant colleges), the report's authors sought to make high technology central to the college curriculum, even at the tradition-bound liberal arts colleges, in order to "balance the goals of employment and enlightenment" (McQuaid, 1982, p. 8).

Encroachments upon the liberal arts seem destined to spread. This prospect is all the more certain in view of the continuing growth and prosperity of the community colleges—the institutional vanguard of the new vocationalism.

Community Colleges: Academic "Service Stations"

Of all the institutions in the academic tier system, the public community colleges have become the prime laboratories for vocationalizing the academic curriculum and fulfilling higher education's "public service" mission. As a result, they have achieved the dubious distinction of being "service stations" of the academic world.[5] It is not at all surprising that the policy planning literature implicitly views them that way.

The Carnegie Commission, for example, in a well-known policy report, *The Open Door Colleges*, argued for occupational education being given "the fullest support and status within the community colleges." Moreover, the Commission called for "coordinated efforts" at the federal, state, and local levels to "stimulate the expansion of occupational education in community colleges and to make it responsive to changing manpower requirements." A collateral function of the community college, in the Commissioner's view, is the provision of "continuing education" for adults and a second chance, so to speak, for four-year college dropouts. Inasmuch as the "average adult may have to shift (his or her) occupation three or four times" in a lifetime, the easily-accessible, programmatically-updated community colleges offer the best insurance "against educational and occupational obsolescence" (Carnegie Commission, 1970b, p. 20).

The Commission was quite emphatic about the need to specialize the community college curriculum and, in so doing, to differentiate its content more conspicuously from that of the four-year liberal arts colleges and universities. Community colleges, according to the Commission, have a unique role to play and "should be actively discouraged by state planning and financing policies from converting to four-year institutions." The main reason the Commission offers for, in effect, permanently consigning the community colleges to a lowly two-year status is that otherwise "they might place less emphasis on occupational programs and leave an unmet need in the local community" (Carnegie Commission, 1970a, pp. 23, 25).

The American Association of Community and Junior Colleges (AACJC), the leading interest group representing the two-year colleges, has also sought to save local colleges from suffering "unmet needs" through its advice to its member colleges. In a policy report enthusiastically promoting career education, the AACIC argued: "Career education as a concept can be the vehicle through which community and junior colleges undertake a fundamental reformation of their curricula to make them more responsive to emerging needs and less dependent upon their tradition as the lower division of the four-year institutions" (Pincus, 1974, p. 28).

The AACJC has been a consistent champion of practical education ever since its founding in 1920, so it came as no surprise when it further urged its member colleges to "consider the development of occupational education programs linked to business, industry, labor, and government a high priority" (Pincus, 1974, p. 29). To facilitate their cooperation in meeting this objective, AACJC staff researchers periodically prepare brochures and book-length reports advising member colleges on how best to "sell" the new practical curricula.

Just how much of a marketing mentality prevails today among community college administrators was amply evident at a statewide deans conference held in Poughkeepsie, New York. Two local community college administrators who were participant-observers at the conference reported (with considerable dismay) that the overwhelming consensus favored popularizing the new practicality whenever and wherever possible. One of the conference speakers repeatedly stressed the need to "vocationalize" liberal education. He insisted that each college professor justify to each class the "usefulness of his or her course in the job hunt." Another speaker was reported to have claimed that "students have the right to ask of any course, 'How much is this worth? How much can I get for this?'" Evidently, he meant "worth" and what one "gets" in a strictly practical and pecuniary sense (Winn, 1977, p. 10).

An important component of the vocationalizing of the community college curriculum—one that is often overlooked—is that the vocational or career education programs are designed as "terminal" for the students who elect (or, more accurately, are channeled into) them. What is even more overlooked is the role that philanthropy has played in generating this outcome. It is quite clear from recent policy reports that skilled training at these colleges is not designed to facilitate and encourage access to "higher skilling" at the higher tiers of the academic system, still less to a broad-based liberal arts education. On the contrary, provisions of federal vocational legislation such as the Vocational Education Act of 1963 and the Higher Education Amendments of 1972— specifically prohibit the subsidizing of vocational training in baccalaureate degree programs or in college preparatory (or "transfer") programs at two-year institutions (Zwerdling, 1976, pp 60-61).

Moreover, the pattern of federal subsidies for curriculum development has been quite lopsided in favor of vocational programs. For example, of the total funds appropriated in one year for community colleges, $850 million was earmarked for vocational education and less than one-third as much ($275 million) for academic programs (Zwerdling, 1976, p. 60). Such selective and discriminatory dispensing of public philanthropy documents the government's commitment to "universal access" at the so-called open door colleges. According to historian Steven Zwerdling, such unequal funding not only deepens the division between transfer and terminal education at these institutions, but also "leads to separate facilities and separate administrations for academic and vocational education and, ironically, may contribute to the low status currently assigned to vocational programs" (Zwerdling, 1976, p. 61). The tacit promulgation, in short, of a separate-but-equal policy at the community colleges has been the cornerstone of curricular reform.

Elite Colleges: Last Bastions of the Liberal Arts?

In the preceding sections, I called attention to the hegemony of the new practicality in the curricula of the community colleges and its partial infusion into liberal arts courses and degree programs elsewhere in the academic tier system. But how widespread, we might ask, is the eclipse of the higher learning? Have the upper tiers of the academic system—in particular, the doctoral-granting research universities and some of the private four-year colleges been able to resist the vocational vogue and administrative encroachments upon their pursuit of liberal education?

Judging from recent trends and anticipated policy agendas, there is little cause for optimism. If anything resembling a general education in the liberal arts remains in present-day higher education, it is increasingly becoming the curricular monopoly of the elite universities, especially in the private sector. But even within that uppermost tier of the academic system, there are centrifugal tendencies. The experience of Rhode Island's Brown University may provide an interesting case in point.

One of the charter institutions of the elite Ivy League, Brown received nationwide media attention when, in response to the campus struggles of the 1960s and students' demands for "relevance", it instituted a sweeping reorganization of its undergraduate curriculum. Brown abolished distribution requirements and most compulsory course sequences in 1969, made numerical or letter grades optional (permitting evaluation instead on a pass/fail basis), and instituted a variety of innovative, interdisciplinary programs, contract majors, and independent study options. At many institutions, with poorly motivated students and indifferent faculty, such curricular license would have been a disaster and, in practice, often was. At Brown, however, with its first-rate faculty and academically ambitious students, the new curriculum proved an intellectually rigorous, stimulating, and challenging experiment. This was largely attributable, most observers agree, to the success of the so-called "Modes of Thought" courses - a series of seminars which focused upon fundamental concepts and methods of inquiry and took an interdisciplinary approach to the subject matter.

By the mid-1970s, however, as the *New York Times* reported, "the reforms that were hailed as 'the most flexible and progressive undergraduate curriculum to be found in any major American university' [were] struggling for survival against heavy odds" ("At Brown," 1976, p. C-5). The Modes of Thought program, in particular, the *Times* noted, seemed to be "on the rocks". In the "desperate scramble" to get into graduate and professional schools or to legitimize the baccalaureate degree to prospective employers, "more and more students [were] insisting on old-fashioned grades," while only 10% of the students took advantage of the various independent and group study opportunities. The "impassioned spirit" and politicized consciousness of 1969 were being displaced, in short, by new attitudes of pragmatism and preprofessionalism.

A student editorialist explained the shifting definitions of curricular "relevance" at Brown and elsewhere: "For today's career-and-success-oriented students . . . the new strain is more down-to-earth than esoteric, and more likely to help someone earn a buck than discover truth or launch a crusade." The practical brand of relevance was manifesting itself, he reported, in the popularity of Engineering 25, "Mechanical Technology," a course that had now taken its place beside that seeming pinnacle of the new practicality, a course in bartending offered by the Student Employment Office "to train students for jobs." Both courses evidently were "enjoying unmitigated student interest; somewhere in the vicinity of 100 would-be bartenders were turned away [that first semester] due to an enrollment limit for the course."

This anecdote may overstate the depths of which curricular "reform" has sunk in the Ivy League. There are, to be sure, important reservoirs of the old-style relevance as well as academically respectable and rigorous courses in liberal arts disciplines at colleges in both the private and public sectors. Even more important, there are signs of a revival of interest in general education, with its tell-tale distribution requirements and predicable program sequences. The pace has been set by Harvard University, which, more than 30 years after the publication of its pioneering "Redbook," *General Education in a Free Society*, approved a revised distributing requirement in five subject areas (literature and the arts, history, social and philosophical analysis, science and mathematics, foreign languages and cultures), with a tightened core of course from which students choose approximately half of their total degree program (Scully, 1978, p. 1). Other colleges have been following Harvard's lead by reinstating or refurbishing general education programs. Such efforts have won the blessing of many federal and state education officials such as William J. Bennett, secretary of education in the Reagan administration, and leading foundations such as the Carnegie Foundation for the Advancement of Teaching.[6]

There is a second major aspect to the curricular changes taking place among institutions in the upper tier of the academic system. Its primary inspiration stems from the economics of cost-efficiency and the politics of management control. Cost-efficiency in the higher echelons of higher education has had its most conspicuous curricular consequence in the paring down of graduate programs and the limiting of access through such mechanisms as reduced financial aid and fellowships, tougher admissions criteria, and propaganda about the dismal job market for advanced degree recipients.

Claiming to make "more effective use of resources," leading policy planning organizations have resolved to consolidate and centralize the topmost tier. The Carnegie Commission was quite explicit on the matter: "State coordinating councils and similar agencies should develop strong policies . . . for preventing the spread of Ph.D. programs. . . . We also strongly recommend the continuous review of existing degree programs with a view to eliminating those that are very costly or of low quality and the concentration of highly specialized degree programs on only one or two campuses of multi-campus institutions" (Carnegie Commission, 1973, p. 160).

In the guise of "sounding fiscal management," the Academy for Educational Development recommended:

- Abolishing departments or academic programs that have too few students to justify continuation,

- Abolishing language requirements, ultimately abolishing language departments with too few students;

- Eliminating master's degree programs in science and mathematics;

- Requiring the faculty to defend every single academic program now being offered. (Academy for Educational Development, 1973, p. 160).

In the two decades since, state education departments and coordinating agencies have taken many steps to follow the planning commission's directives. The curricular reorganization of American higher education, prodded by private and public philanthropy, has had far-reaching consequences. In a sense, the transformation of the curriculum is but one manifestation of a larger transformation. Specifically, it has been part of a comprehensive stratification strategy, devised by leading centers of policy planning, which has reinforced the structural inequalities of prestige and power among institutions and tiers of the academic system. The expansion of vocational and applied studies at the lowest tiers, together with the concentration in the highest tiers of more theoretical and rigorous liberal arts programs, compounds the polarization between top and bottom. Increasingly, as we have seen, higher learning becomes the curricular monopoly of the elite colleges and universities, while "lesser" institutions devote themselves to more standard-ized, trivialized, and vocationalized programs.

Just as the differential prestige and power of academic institutions affects the life-chances and self-image of their personnel, conversely, the social composition of the institutions reflects and reinforces their location within the tier system. By the same token, the hierarchies of both institutions and personnel reinforce and, in turn, are reinforced by the hierarchy of the curricu-lum. The overall structural consequence, accordingly, has been a reshaping of the form as well as the content of postsecondary education in America.

References

Academy for Educational Development. (1973). *319 ways colleges and universities are meeting the financial pinch.* New York: Academy for Educational Development.

Bird, C. (1975). *The case against college.* New York: David McKay Company.

Bouton, K. (1983, September 11). Grubstake: a radical proposal. *Change.*

Brown Alumni Monthly (1974, May). Providence, RI: Brown University, p. 34.

Bruno, M. B. (1985, January 6). The liberal arts and the world of work. *New York Times,* Section 12, p. 18.

Carnegie Commission on Higher Education. (1970). *The open door colleges: policies for community colleges.* New York: McGraw-Hill.

Carnegie Commission on Higher Education. (1971). *Less time, more options.* New York: McGraw-Hill.

Carnegie Commission on Higher Education. (1973a). *College graduates and jobs.* New York: McGraw-Hill.

Carnegie Commission on Higher Education. (1973b). *A digest of reports.* New York: McGraw-Hill.

Carnegie Council on Policy Studies in Higher Education. (1977). *Missions of the College Curriculum.* New York: McGraw-Hill.

Carnegie Council on Policy Studies in Higher Education. (1980). *A summary of reports.* New York: McGraw-Hill.

Change (1978, October). Editorial: The future forsaken. 10(9).

Chronicle of Higher Education (1985, February 18), 34, 3.

Cohen, A. M. (1977). Stretching pre-college education. *Social Policy,* 2(1), 5–7.

Committee for Economic Development. (1973). *The management and financing of colleges.* New York: Committee for Economic Development.

Crittenden, A. (1981, July 22). Industry's role in academia. *New York Times,* p. 63.

Fiske, E. B. (1985, January 28). Booming corporate education efforts rival college programs, study says. *New York Times.*

Freeman, R. B. (1976). *The over-educated American.* New York: Academic Press. The great American dream freeze. (1975, March). *Dollars and Sense,* pp. 3-6. The great training robbery: Does career education do any good? (1978, November). *Dollars and Sense,* pp. 10-13.

Hechinger, F. M. (1985, February 21). Federal aid and the colleges. *New York Times,* pp. C-1, C-8.

High tech and the schools. (1983, May/June), *Dollars and Sense,* pp. 6–8.

Hutchins, R. M. (1936). *The higher learning in America.* New Haven: Yale University Press.

Karabel, J. (1974). Protecting the portals: Class and the community college. *Social Policy,* 5(1), 14–19.

Kaysen, C. (1969). *The higher learning, the universities, and the public.* Princeton, NJ: Princeton University Press.

Marbach, W. D. & Young, J. (1981, May 11). *Newsweek.*

McQuaid, E. P. (1982, September 15). New Morrill Act sought to generate $1 billion for high technology education. *Chronicle of Higher Education.*

Maeroff, G. (1975, November 3). Students flock to job-related courses. *New York Times,* p. C-10.

Maeroff, G. (1977, June 12). The liberal arts degree and its real value. *New York Times,* p. C-6.

Mills, C. W. (1959). Chapter 4: Types of Practicality. *The sociological imagination.* New York: Oxford University Press.

MIT Alternative News Collective and Science Action Coordinating Committee (1988, November). *How to fathomit: MIT disorientation manual* 1988-89 (second edition). Cambridge, MA: MIT Alternative News Collective.

McCarthy, C. (1987, February 28). Big man on campus. *The Nation,* pp. 253–254.

McClure, P. (1976). Grubstake: A radical proposal. *Change.* 8(5), 36–39.

New York State Board of Regents. (1972). *Master Plan.* Albany: New York State Education Department.

Newt Davidson Collective. (1973). *Crisis at C.U.N.Y.* New York: Newt Davidson Collective.

O'Toole, J. (1975). The reserve army of the underemployed, Part II. *Change.* 7(6). 28–33.

Pincus, F. L. (1974). Tracking in community colleges. *Insurgent Sociologists.* 4(3), 25–30.

Reinhold, R. (1976, February 24). At Brown, trend is back to grades and tradition. *New York Times,* p. C-5.

Scully, M. (1978, May 8). Tightening the curriculum: Enthusiasm, dissent, and "so what else is new?" *Chronicle of Higher Education,* pp. 1, 14.

State University of New York (1975, March). SUNY, NY Tel. in major accord. *The News* (newspaper of the State University of New York), p. 1.

Vocational schools get respect. (1983, March 7). *Newsweek,* p. 80.

Wharton, C. R., Jr. (1978). SUNY's third mission: Public service. *Universitas,* 1(1), 12–14.

Veblen, T. (1957 [1918]). *The higher learning in America.* New York: Hill and Wang.

Watkins, B. T. (1984, June 27). Contracts to provide courses for workers can be a "win/win deal," universities are learning. *Chronicle of Higher Education,* pp. 1, 10.

Winn, J., & Winn, O. H. (1977). *Pre-packaging authoritarianism: Mix business values and community colleges and you don't get democracy.* Unpublished manuscript, Dutchess Community College, Poughkeepsie, New York.

Zwerdling, S. (1976). *Second best: The crisis of the community college.* New York: McGraw-Hill.

Professional Education: Stratifying Curricula and Perpetuating Privilege in Higher Education

GARY RHOADES

In this chapter, I pursue two analytical interests in reviewing two literatures regarding professional education. My first interest is in the general professional discourse of American higher education, in the way that scholars in the general literature on subjects such as curriculum and instruction, and students, address and characterize professional programs. My second interest is in specialized scholarship on professional programs, in the way that researchers in the various professional fields study professional education, the perspectives they adopt, and the questions they pose. With respect to the first issue, I find that scholars tend to stratify curricula, subordinating professional education to liberal education. Professional education is a peripheral and devalued category in the general higher education literature, often characterized as overly narrow, specialized, and focused on skills and training versus general education. With respect to the specialized literature on professional programs, I find that researchers overwhelmingly tend to adopt a functionalist perspective and to pose functionalist questions in studying professional education. Such scholarship serves more to perpetuate and enhance professional privileges than to call into question some of these privileges and seek ways of enhancing the rights and position of nonprofessional individuals and groups vis-a-vis existing professions

The chapter is organized into three sections. In the first section, I review the treatment of professional education in the general higher education literature. Given the standing of the volumes of *Higher Education: Handbook of Theory and Research* as a series of reviews of state of the art research in higher education, I begin by examining how the topic of professional education has been handled in chapters covering various substantive areas. Then I move to a content analysis of leading journals and magazines in higher education over the past five years, examining the extent to which professional education is an explicit focus of research.

In the second section of the chapter, I review the specialized literature on professional education. I do not attempt an exhaustive, descriptive review of the vast literatures in the various professional fields. Instead, I conduct an analytical review that is structured by the research topics that are generally addressed in these fields, and by the kinds of questions researchers are asking, and the conceptual frameworks these questions are derived from.

In the conclusion to the chapter, I synthesize my findings surrounding the two analytical interests that focus my literature reviews, providing a critical analysis of the way professional education is handled and studied in the general higher education and specialized professional education literatures. Then, by way of contrast, I briefly identify and review research on professionals and professional education that comes out of symbolic interactionism and critical professionalization theory in sociology. My aim is to crystallize the professional discourse about professional education, and to inform that discourse with theoretical perspectives that offer new questions and avenues of research.

Before undertaking this formal review and analysis of the treatment of professional education in the literature, as an observer of and participant in the higher education literature I had been struck by what seemed to me to be a preoccupation with liberal arts education. I pursued that observation formally in a content analysis of four recent reform reports on undergraduate education (Rhoades, 1990). What my deconstructionist, interpretive analysis revealed was that each of the reports promoted elements of a liberal education ideal that drew on curricular and other characteristics of elite private colleges and universities. The reports consistently devalued various aspects of vocational, professional and graduate education, which were portrayed as being hostile to quality undergraduate education. In carrying out the analysis for this chapter, I was interested in determining whether some of these same patterns were evident in the general higher education literature. I find the valuation of the liberal arts, a conception of education based on classical culture and on a time when education was for gentleman, intriguing in a country that is marked more than most countries by an explicit concern with access and egalitarian ends. I find the devaluation of the practical and the professional ironic and puzzling in a country that has probably the largest professionalized work force in the world.

In using the term "professional education," I do not wish to define it narrowly. Although I have no particular definition in mind, I want to deal with professional education writ large, including undergraduate and graduate education. I am not, therefore, musing exclusively on professional schools such as medicine and law, but am including programs at the undergraduate level that might fall under the general rubric of professional programs. As a sociologist I make a conscious, theoretically based choice to not objectively define what programs fall within the category of professional education. In the sociology of professions, functionalist scholars have long defined professions as occupations that are characterized by certain objective traits—e.g., a code of ethics, a technical knowledge base, control over certification and entry into the occupation. But there are competing, and long-standing, sociological perspectives on the professions, reflected in the traditions of symbolic interactionism and critical professionalization theory. Scholars in these traditions regard the term profession as a subjective, value laden attribution rather than an objective description.

> It happens over and over that the people who practice an occupation attempt to revise the conceptions which their various publics have of the occupation and of the people in it. . . . The model which these occupations set before themselves is that of the Profession": . . . The movement to "professionalize" an occupation is thus collective mobility of some among the people in an occupation. (Hughes, 1958, p. 44)

Given this view, the analytical focus is on how occupations gain and maintain professional status by convincing the public of their merit and virtue. In the critical tradition, the analysis of the professionalization process more explicitly incorporates conceptions of power and class in the occupation's efforts to gain monopoly over a domain of work (Collins, 1979; Larson, 1977; Slaughter and Silva, 1984). In the conclusion to this chapter, I will explore some of the implications these views of professions have for the study of professional education. Here I am simply establishing that rather than providing my own definition of professional education, I am interested in the way scholars talk about and study professional education, in how they construct and define this category of curricula. Issues such as what is the difference between professional and vocational education are left to the empirical study of whether and how people construct those terms.

Professional Education in the Discourse of Higher Education

How is professional education dealt with and characterized in the general professional discourse of American higher education? That question underlies the two content analyses I conducted for this section of my chapter. The field of Higher Education is marked by the standard features or professional organization that facilitate the examination of professional discourse. It has its own professional journals, and, more recently, an annual review of work in the field. I first look to the way we organize ourselves, albeit loosely, as a field of study. I utilize the *Handbook* as an indicator of the categories into which we subdivide our field, and to its state of the arts reviews of the literature as indicators of the place and treatment of professional education in some of these substantive subdivisions. I then look to some of the arenas in which we conduct much of our public professional discourse. I examine six of the major professional journals/magazines in the field to determine the extent to which professional education is a major topic of study, and to examine the ways in which it is explicitly referred to, if at all, in research on topics such as curriculum and instruction, and students.

Perhaps because of its youth, the field of Higher Education has already demonstrated a penchant for self-examination. For example, within the past five years, there have been several reviews of the field that have focused on topics addressed and methodologies utilized in journal articles, on the *Handbook,* and on the field in general (e.g., Conrad, 1989; special issue of *The Review of Higher Education* 10,2:1986; Keller and Moore, 1989; Kuh et al., 1986; Lincoln and Guba 1989; Mentkowski and Chickering, 1987; Silverman, 1987). In carrying out my content analyses, I draw on some of this literature in assessing the place of professional education in our professional discourse.

Professional Education and the Handbook

Higher Education: Handbook of Theory and Research is more than an annual collection of literature reviews. In the words of its editor and originator, John C. Smart, the *Handbook is* an effort

> to bring order and understanding to the increasingly rich, diverse, and fragmented research findings that are presently available. The need is to pull together and synthesize our increasingly disjointed research findings in order to establish a solid foundation for future advances toward the development of cumulative knowledge. (Volume 1, 1985, p. vii)

Divided into 12 general areas of scholarly and policy inquiry, the *Handbook* orders and reflects the field of higher education. As George Keller and Kay Moore (1989, pp. 124, 129) have noted in commenting on the first four volumes of the *Handbook,* the project of John Smart and his 12 editors/apostles has been to "codify" the available research and shape future research agendas, thus providing readers with "a conscious intellectual artifact of the field of higher education."

The *Handbook,* then, provides definitive statements by leaders of the field regarding the directions research has taken and should take. It is therefore an appropriate source for examining the way professional education is characterized in the professional discourse of higher education scholars. As a starting point, it is useful to consider whether professional education is identified as one of the 12 general areas of inquiry.

In the first three volumes, one of the 12 categories is continuing education for the professions, which represents only a small part of the general area of professional education. Two articles on continuing professional education appeared in those three volumes, "Emerging Perspectives on Continuing Professional Education" (Smutz et al., 1986), and the Organization and Provision of Continuing Professional Education: A Critical Review and Synthesis" (Cevero and Young, 1987). In subsequent volumes of the *Handbook,* the category of continuing professional education is replaced by graduate and professional education. The articles that have been commissioned in this configuration include "Graduate Education as an Area of Research" (Malaney 1988), "The Melancholy of Anatomy: The Personal and Professional Development of Graduate and Professional School Students" (Baird, 1990), "The Federal Role in Graduate Education" (Gumport, forthcoming), and this chapter.

Such categorical labels and changes raise some interesting questions about what is included and/or changed in the way we organize our knowledge (Keller and Moore, 1989). For my purposes here, they also provide some intriguing clues as to what is meant by professional education. For example, does subsuming professional education within the relatively narrow category of continuing professional education suggest that the editors tend to think of professional education as narrow, skills-oriented training? Does the creation of a graduate and professional education category suggest that the editors tend to think of professional education as separate in some fundamental way from undergraduate and graduate education?

In themselves, the categorical labels tell us little about the place and treatment of professional education in the general professional discourse. Is the categorization of professional education indicative of its centrality or its marginality in the field? Is professional education considered in research that deals with topics that touch on education generally? To answer such questions, I turn to an examination of to what extent and how professional education is treated in related substantive areas codified in the *Handbook*—curriculum and instruction, and students. I content analyze individual articles in these areas in the first five volumes of the *Handbook,* focusing on whether professional programs, students, or faculty are mentioned, and how they are characterized. I present the findings as I conducted the analysis, one article at a time, yet organized around the two substantive areas identified above.

Curriculum and Instruction

In the chapters on curriculum and instruction, there are very few references to professional programs. In some cases, there is no mention at all. On the surface, the analysis may either be generic, or not specified to a particular curricula, with the focus on arts and science curricula being implicit in the categories of analysis, or the analysis may explicitly concentrate on liberal and/or general education curricula. In other cases, professional curricula are mentioned, but they are identified as being part of the problem. In general, then, there are few references to professional programs, and such references are not flattering.

In Volume I, Cameron Fincher's chapter, "Learning Theory and Research," offers a generic treatment of the topic, looking for example, at general principles of learning theory. Active learning is preferable to passive learning, and meaningful is preferable to rote learning. But the content of the curricula is not treated as a significant dimension along which types of learning might vary. In talking about learning conditions, the review focuses on individual differences such as ability, preparation, and motivations but not on variation by type of curricula. There is one explicit reference to professional programs that suggests such curricula are skills-oriented, rather than being oriented to conceptual development and broad understanding.

> Learning theory and research suggest a form of conceptual/symbolic/verbal learning that leads to knowledge as an organized structure of information. In much the same manner, theory and research imply a form of skills/proficiency/competency learning that leads to competent or proficient performance in such activities as arts and crafts, athletics, and professional occupations. (Fincher, 1985, p. 89)

In the main, not only is the literature that Pincher reviews marked by an absence of concern with the content of the curricula, Fincher does not direct future researchers to concern themselves with possible variations along curricular lines.

Another chapter in the first volume, by Michael T. McCord (1985), entitled "Methods and Theories of Instruction," makes no reference at all to professional curricula. In opening, McCord notes that there is little research on graduate and professional education. Although he does not explicitly concentrate on arts and science fields, the categories of instruction that he reviews and suggests for future research reflect an arts and social science bias. For example, the "conventional modes of instruction" he examines include lecture, seminar, discussion, and independent study, but exclude modes of instruction such as clinical teaching that are typical of and specific to professional education. McCord even largely excludes lab work, which is typical of the sciences. In closing, McCord poses several questions for future researchers to pursue, none of which refer to professional programs, and one of which assumes a letters and science focus on disciplines—"Do effective questioning strategies differ across disciplines?"

The third chapter in the area of curriculum and instruction in the first volume is by Clifton F. Conrad and Robert T. Blackburn (1985), "Program Quality in Higher Education Review and Critique of Literature and Research." In reviewing research that adopts one of three approaches to studying quality—reputational, "objective" indicators, or quantifiable program characteristics associated with high quality programs—Conrad and Blackburn are critical of the little attention that has been given to professional programs particularly in the latter two approaches. However, in making suggestions for future research Conrad and Blackburn do not speak to the necessity of examining professional programs, or to the potential of developing approaches to evaluating quality that come out of professional education—e.g., evaluating the competence of graduates/ practitioners, as has been done with teacher education.

Conrad also has a chapter on academic programs in the second volume of the *Handbook*, with Anne M. Pratt (1986), "Research on Academic Programs: An Inquiry into an Emerging Field." Throughout, the focus is on liberal, general, and undergraduate education, in the research reviewed and the paths of future research charted. Conrad and Pratt's review is divided into sections on incidents and histories, norms and outcomes, and conceptual frameworks. Whether they are examining cases of innovation, histories, academic change, normative and descriptive statements, studies of effects, or typologies and models of academic programs, Conrad and Pratt concentrate on "work done in the area of general or liberal education." (p. 261)

Another chapter in the area of curriculum and instruction in the second volume is by Jonathan Z. Shapiro (1986), "Evaluation Research and Educational Decision Making." Evaluation and assessment obviously have to do with curriculum. Perhaps not so obviously, in some respects, the mechanisms of evaluation and assessment are most evident in professional fields of study—for example, in professional accreditation. Yet, Shapiro reviews the development, conduct, and utilization of evaluation generically, not specifying it to particular kinds of programs. There are explicit references to the program review that comes out of state coordinating agencies in higher education, and out of voluntary accreditation bodies, but there is no mention of professional programs and accreditation. The third chapter on curriculum and instruction in Volume 11 is by Cameron Fincher, "Trends and Issues in Curricular Development" (1986). Fincher opens by noting the theme underlying reports on undergraduate education issued by the National Institute of Education, the National Endowment for the Humanities, and the Association of American Colleges:

> Each report addresses the decline in liberal or general education and calls for national efforts to strengthen undergraduate programs in community colleges, senior colleges, and universities. The dominant theme of all three reports can be expressed as a belief that the quality of undergraduate education has declined over the past two decades and that quality can be restored by concerted attention to liberal and/or general education. (p. 275)

Although he tries to go beyond the reports in providing direction and guidance for strengthening undergraduate curricula, Fincher sustains the reports' theme of linking liberal or general education to quality education, and regarding professionalizing tendencies in the curriculum as narrow, training oriented and problematic.

> An important conclusion drawn from Dressel and DeLisle's survey is the balance that undergraduate colleges sought between liberal and professional course work. In brief, few colleges were attempting to be exclusively liberal arts and were quite sensitive to the professional or career interests of students and to the admissions requirements of professional or graduate schools. Colleges were still trying to provide breadth, however, by distributional requirements among the humanities, the natural sciences, and the social sciences. (p. 285)

> To many critics and observers, the traditional liberal arts program of four-year colleges no longer has the purpose and value it should have. Many four-year colleges are seen as preprofessional colleges in which the value of the programs is attested to by the number of graduates entering graduate or professional school. The content and substance of their undergraduate courses is seen as more in tune with professional entrance requirements than with the traditional values of a liberal education. Similar arguments are heard concerning general education and the significance or value of undergraduate degrees that do not result in career placement. (p. 295)

Fincher adopts the position of those championing liberal and general education, stating, for instance, that "The fact that the purpose and meaning of a liberal education is again debatable is, by its own evidence, an indictment of higher education in the 1980s." (p. 298) One of the four major trends (all of them negative) he notes in curricular development is "the increased professionalization of education to satisfy the career objectives of students and the requirements of accrediting agencies and professional societies." (p. 279) Finally, Fincher closes with a quote that identifies the development of a viable general education as one of the three most pressing curricular problems of recent generations.

In the next three volumes of the *Handbook,* the area of curriculum and instruction receives reduced attention. With the exception of three chapters on graduate and continuing professional education, there is only Peter T. Ewell's (1988) chapter in Volume IV, "Outcomes, Assessment, and Academic Improvement: In Search of Usable Knowledge." Ewell's chapter provides no discussion and indeed no mention of professional programs. In framing his review of literature on "assessing and improving the outcomes of undergraduate instruction," Ewell concentrates on the so-called "college impact" literature, and looks as well to literature on change. The chapter is organized around discussions of outcomes, the production function by which such outcomes are produced, and the potential for intervention designed to change outcomes. Although he does at one point refer to variation in outcome by "microsetting"—for example, by academic department—Ewell does not develop a discussion of particular types of curricula and outcomes. In closing, Ewell offers an agenda for action research that suggests the importance of disaggregation, such as "using units of analysis that correspond to the actual levels at which such experiences take place: programs and curricula, classrooms, living units, and other identifiable 'microsettings.'" (p. 95) But there is no specification based on previous research of particular curricular divisions that merit consideration.

For obvious reasons, I do not examine the two chapters on continuing professional education. However, in closing the section on curriculum and instruction, I do want to emphasize that the editorial category of graduate and professional education—established in Volume IV—separates (and prioritizes?) the two curricula, a separation that is evidenced in the chapter by Gary D. Malaney (1988), "Graduate Education as an Area of Research. " Malaney takes the category definition seriously. With the exception of some studies of M.B.A.'s, Malaney concentrates primarily on graduate education.

Students

In the chapters on students, as with those on curriculum and instruction, there is little mention of students in professional programs. For the most part, the research examines the effects of college on students. Many variables are controlled for in both the literature and the reviews. But none of the chapters suggest that a critical variable in the analysis of students is systematic patterns of differences among groups of curricula. In some cases, particular professional fields, such as medicine or engineering, are identified. In other cases, scholars point to some variations among students by curricula or by academic major. But the dimension of professional versus arts and science curricula is not featured as a central part of the analysis in research on students.

In Volume I of the *Handbook,* Ernest T. Pascarella's (1985) chapter, "College Environmental Influences on Learning and Cognitive Development," carefully disaggregates data on a number of dimensions, none of which explicitly include professional programs. Utilizing Astin's (1973) two-by-two model of college outcomes (cognitive/affective, psychological/behavioral), Pascarella examines the effects of various independent variables: of college, of different types of institution, and of different types of experience within the same institution. The last variable of differential experience is conceptualized in the literature as different type of subenvironment in the same institution. Studies focus on residential subenvironment (e.g., dormitory versus Greek), interaction with faculty, person/ environment fit, and curricular effects. But curricular effects refer to the effects of particular curricular interventions that are designed to have specific cognitive impacts, rather than to broad curricular categorizations. In gauging the effects of different independent variables, research controls for student characteristics such as academic aptitude, family background, personality, and motivations and aspirations. None of these are operationalized in ways that direct attention to possible variation by professional versus other types of orientations and curricula (the one exception is Astin's (1963) typology of social, enterprising, and realistic orientations, which cross-cut professional and other fields of study).

The other chapter on students in the first volume is by Y.G.-M. Lulat and Philip G. Altbach (1985) International Students in Comparative Perspective." In some respects, this chapter represents an important exception to the standard *Handbook* contribution. Utilizing concepts drawn from political sociology, Lulat and Altbach develop an extended discussion of "International Study as Educational Dependence." They consider the effects of cultural imperialism and cultural colonialism that are expressed in the educational dependence of third world countries on the universities of Western industrialized nations. Power is incorporated into their analysis of relations between educational systems as well as between faculty and students in a way that is atypical of the conventional, functionalist *Handbook* contribution. In this context, Lulat and Altbach occasionally mention the disproportionate presence of international students in American universities in certain fields and departments such as engineering. But they do not incorporate or promote a consistent and systematic analysis of professional programs—for example, on what effects the presence of international students has on professional programs in the United States and on professional practice in third world countries. In this regard, the Lulat and Altbach chapter is much like others on students.

The only chapter on students in Volume II is by Vincent Tinto (1986), "Theories of Student Departure Revisited." Tinto's revisitation is organized around five types of theory—psychological, societal, economic, organizational, and interactional. Variables that are analyzed include personality and motivation, SES and race, costs and benefits, size and organizational goals, and individual/organization fit. Despite the possibility that such variables are related to field of study, no mention is made of curriculum, either in Tinto's review, or in his suggested directions for future research. It is quite possible that rates of and reasons for departure vary by curricular context. Yet the literature does not attend to this central dimension of postsecondary institutions' context.

In Volume III, Larry Nucci and Ernest T. Pascarella (1987) consider another type of college impact in their chapter, "The Influence of College on Moral Development." As Pascarella indicated in his review of literature on college's impact on learning and cognitive development, the vast majority of work on college effects has focused on dependent variables such as values, attitudes, orientations, and moral development. Underlying such research is an assumption that college should contribute to the formation of students' character, that the nonacademic effects of higher education are central. That assumption is clearly acknowledged and expressed by Nucci and Pascarella in opening their chapter.

> [T]he academic curriculum and the entire campus environment clearly viewed the formation of student character as a central mission of the collegiate experience. Consistent with the classical tradition, the liberal arts college believed, as did Plato, "that education makes good men and that good men act nobly." (p. 271)

> Despite these fundamental changes, however, the tradition of liberal education and its attendant concerns with developing the whole individual still hold a prominent place in the ethos at American higher education . . . There continues to be a presumption that the college experience, and liberal education in particular, contributes not only to cognitive development, but also to an expansion of the student's world view and the capacity to apply reasoning and intellect to interpersonal, political and social as well as to purely academic questions. (p. 272)

After reviewing moral development theory, Nucci and Pascarella examine the effects of college, of different kinds of colleges, and of different college experiences in the same institution. As with Pascarella's earlier chapter, the different college experiences in the same institution were discussed largely in terms of student involvement with faculty and residential arrangements. However, Nucci and Pascarella do note that some studies have examined differences in moral reasoning by academic major, with the limited evidence being contradictory as to comparisons of the effects of liberal arts versus scientific and technical majors. The directions for future research that Nucci and Pascarella emphasize include focusing on the effects of different postsecondary institutions (with no mention of the curricular emphasis of the institution) and on the conditional effects of different academic experiences in the same institution. With respect to the latter point, the only focus on curriculum refers to particular curricular or course interventions that are designed to foster better moral reasoning.

A third chapter on students in Volume III is by D. Parker Young and Martha C. Braswell (1987), "An Analysis of Student Academic Rights." What is remarkable about this chapter is that despite the number of court cases reviewed in which litigants were students in professional programs, there is no consideration of the importance of field of study in the analysis. The chapter reviews cases regarding student rights in a range of areas such as disciplinary proceedings, admissions, academic advising, and liability. In several of these areas, a large proportion of the cases involve students in professional programs, particularly in health related areas. Apart from indicating what kind of student was involved (e.g., nursing or medical), Young and Braswell do not incorporate field of study into an analysis of patterns of litigation. In reading the cases, one is tempted to suggest that the corpus of law on student rights has been fundamentally shaped by conditions and students in professional programs of study.

Although there are no chapters on students in the fourth volume of the *Handbook*, there are two chapters in Volume V. The first of these is by Don Hossler, John Braxton, and Georgia Coopersmith (1989), "Understanding Student College Choice." Hossler et al. subdivide their topic into sections on conceptual approaches that have been used to frame investigations of college choice, on fitting diverse research into a three stage model of college choice (predisposition, search, and choice), and on a summary of existing empirical studies. With the exception of some isolated references to a "masculinity/technical orientation" versus a "fine arts orientation," or to "program offerings," in none of these sections is the type of educational programs emphasized. Nor do the authors' "suggested future directions" mention the need to consider college choice in the context of program characteristics and emphases along the lines of professional versus liberal arts orientation.

A second chapter on students in Volume V is by John C. Weidman (1989), "Undergraduate Socialization: A Conceptual Approach." In focusing on the affective dimensions of student outcomes—values, personal goals, aspirations—Weidman notes that the college impact literature tends to look at four general sets of variables—student background characteristics, college characteristics, students' linkage to college environment, and indicators of college effects. Weidman is critical of the field's weak conceptual frameworks and lack of theory development, and he offers a generic conceptual framework for understanding undergraduate socialization. On a couple of occasions, Weidman refers to academic departments and even to specific fields of study.

> These authors argue that the socializing impacts of the department are determined by the expressed goals of the faculty for undergraduate education, which, in turn, determine faculty behavior and expectations for students. They identify three areas of faculty emphasis or goals for undergraduate education: providing a broad, liberal education; providing occupational training; and mixed goals, where both are emphasized. (p. 306)

> It could be argued that the outcomes of undergraduate socialization during any particular time period are as much a function of the characteristics, values, and aspirations of the students as they are of the socialization processes that occur during college. Certainly, there is considerable documentation of the changes in career orientations over the past few decades, with a general increase in students' interest in obtaining specific occupational skills in college rather than a broad, liberal arts education.

In such references, it is evident that professional education, to the extent that it is considered, is cast in rather disparaging terms as narrow, skills-oriented training, as opposed to broad, liberal-oriented education.

For the most part, then, the higher education literature on students, like that on curriculum and instruction, focuses on arts and science undergraduates. In the major research areas of college effects and student retention, there is virtually no consideration of either graduate or professional students and programs. The separation and the focus are intriguing in that much of the writing on undergraduate education decries the effects of graduate education and professional schools—in the form of specialization and vocationalization—on liberal and general education in the baccalaureate years.

Summary

In this review of the review essays in the *Handbook,* I do not intend to call into question the quality of the contributions, which generally are quite high. Rather, I want to direct attention to the way we construct our fields of research in higher education. The *Handbook* represents a forum in which higher education scholars define and direct the state of the art. In examining this forum, I was interested in the centrality or marginality of professional programs as an area of research in higher education. As a rough indicator of position in the field, my content analysis of chapters on curriculum and instruction, and students pursued the question of whether and how professional programs were considered and characterized in research that touches on these general educational topics. I found evidence of marginality in two respects. First, professional education is marginal in terms of the number of times a *Handbook* chapter on that topic appears. Second, the field is marginal in the sense of not being mentioned as a significant consideration in general categorical areas that include professional programs and students. Research on curriculum and instruction, and students, is largely normed on the arts and sciences.

In closing this section on the *Handbook,* it is worth noting that the liberal arts bias I identified in the literature reviews are found as well in two particularly important journal articles focusing on the areas of curriculum and instruction, and students. In an article entitled, "Linking Educators and Researchers in Setting a Research Agenda for Undergraduate Education," Marcia Mentkowski and Arthur Chickering (1987) describe a broad-based dialogue among educators, administrators, and researchers in the American Association for Higher Education and Division J of the American Educational Research Association. Out of this dialogue came a research agenda that included teaching, assessment, learning, critical thinking, liberal education/general education, and voluntary service. Of the dozens of questions that Mentkowski and Chickering pose in these research areas, none make mention of professional programs or of the significance of program area in impacting the topics of the agenda. Similarly, Kuh et al. (1986), in an article entitled, "Changes in Research on College Students Published in Selected Journals Between 1969 and 1983," make no mention of professional programs and students. The analytical focus was on various dimensions of articles on college students or student life published in eleven journals, including topics, sample characteristics, data collection methods, design and analytical techniques, and type of article. The topics included five major categories—behavior, selected characteristics, student development, instruction, and miscellaneous—with none specifying professional programs or students in particular or curricular area in general. In discussing their findings, Kuh et al. are critical of the overriding focus on doctoral granting institutions, with virtually no attention devoted to community colleges and baccalaureate granting institutions. But they do not target curricular area as an important variable in the future study of students.

Professional Education and Leading Higher Education Journals

In the preceding section, I examined the treatment of professional education in the professional discourse of higher education by studying how the field of higher education consciously constructs itself in the organization and chapters of the *Handbook.* In this section, I follow up with a more general review of the field, examining the same issue by looking to leading journals and magazines in the field of higher education. The general question that orients my analysis of this literature is, to what extent is professional education a topic of study in these professional publications?

Academic journals provide, among other things a textual source of professional discourse and academic convention. As the editor of one at the top generalist journals in higher education suggests, editors "sift and certify" knowledge and what counts as knowledge, making journals an authoritative archival source of legitimated professional discourse (Newell, 1990). The ways that a field of study constructs itself, consciously and unconsciously, are embodied in the articles and studies published in that field's professional journals/magazines. Such publications are a principal written forum in which professionals talk to each other. But journals do more than reflect and represent the discourse of a profession; they also shape that discourse. Whether it is in the topical areas that are presented in journals, the structure of the articles, or the categories by which contributors define their subject matter, journals perpetuate and sometimes even create conventional patterns of discourse (Silverman, 1987). As gate keepers of professional dialogue and investigation, through the editorial and peer review and selection process, journals designate what categories of knowledge are meaningful and what those categories mean.

Given my interest in analyzing the treatment of professional education in the general professional discourse of higher education, I selected six core professional journals/magazines in the field. Given my particular interest in the area of students, I included two journals in the field of student affairs. The journals that I analyzed for the years 1985 to the summer issue of 1990 were: *Change* (Ch), *Journal of College Student Personnel* (now *Journal of College Student Development*) (JCSP), *Journal of Higher Education* (JHE), *National Association of Student Personnel Administrators Journal* (NASPA), *Research in Higher Education* (RHE), and *Review of Higher Education* (Rev). Having already established through my review of *Handbook* chapters the treatment of professional education in literature dealing generally with curriculum and instruction, and students, I conducted a quantitative content analysis of the extent to which professional programs and professional students are featured in journal articles. I reviewed all articles in all issues of the above periodicals, focusing on the titles of the articles. The articles about curriculum and instruction were coded into one of the following categories: generic, undergraduate/liberal arts (with liberal arts expressed as a proportion of articles on undergraduates), graduate, professional, womin (women and minorities), and miscellaneous. Within the miscellaneous category were articles on community colleges, summer sessions, and the teaching effectiveness of foreign teaching associates. The articles about students were coded into similar categories: generic, undergraduate/liberal arts (with liberal arts expressed as a proportion of articles on undergraduates), graduate, professional, freshmen, women, minorities, and miscellaneous. Within the miscellaneous category were articles on adult, non-traditional, disabled, international, and other kinds of specified students that did not fit into the preceding categories (e.g., athletes). On a few occasions, articles were double counted—for example, an article on women doctoral students would be coded in two different categories.

In Table 1, the distribution of articles about curriculum and instruction that appeared in four of the six journals/magazines from 1985 to 1990 are presented. For this analysis, after reviewing the journals I decided to drop JCSP and NASPA from the presentation of data because the articles on curriculum and instruction found in these periodicals were fundamentally different from those in the generalist periodicals. In the JCSP, articles in this category were on cocurricular student affairs programs, such as counseling center programs and types of delivery, rather than on academic curriculum and instruction. In the NASPA journal, articles in this category were on either co-curricular programs or on the curriculum and training of student affairs professionals, such as introductory courses for graduate preparation programs or the development of professional education models and professional identity. Such articles would have skewed my analysis of the extent to which professional programs are represented as a focus of study in the generalist literature on curriculum and instruction.

In each of the journals, almost half of the articles on curriculum and instruction were generic. They did not specify a type or level of curricula or teaching, nor did they identify gender or ethnicity as a dimension to be considered. Included in this category were titles such as: "College

Table 1
Number of Articles about Curriculum and Instruction in Selected Journals, 1989–1990

Jrnl	GENER	UND/LA	GRAD	PROF	WOMEN	MISC
CH	12	9/7	—	2	1	—
JHE	18	7/4	1	5	1	3
RHE	15	1	10	5	1	1
REV	14	2/2	2	1	—	1
TOTAL	59	19/13	13	13	3	5

Teachers: Miscast Professionals," "Teaching Teamwork as a Basic Skill," "Beyond Value-Added Education," "Improving Faculty Teaching, and "Research on Teaching and Learning." Overall, more than half of the coded articles were generic.

The category of undergraduate/liberal arts is somewhat misleading. In the case of those articles coded as generic, their texts indicate that they are virtually all about undergraduate education and teaching. It is not clear why in some cases authors choose to specify their focus on the undergraduate level, with titles such as, "Promoting Excellence in Undergraduate Education in Ohio." In many cases, the specification is explained by the concentration on liberal or general education, as in titles such as, "The Skillful Baccalaureate: Doing What Liberal Education Does Best." although only 19 articles are coded in the undergraduate category, as compared with 13 each for the graduate and professional categories, the overwhelming number of coded articles deal with the undergraduate level.

Although I have separated the categories of graduate and professional, sometimes the separation is not clear. On three occasions, the articles were coded as graduate because that was the word utilized in the title, whereas the fields being dealt with—Higher Education and Social Work— were in a professional school. That in itself may say something about how we subordinate professional to academic fields of study. Neither or these types and/or levels of education is accorded much attention in the four journals.

Of those articles coded as professional, half dealt with a specific field of professional study. The narrowness of the focus is revealed by the fact that four of the articles dealt with teacher education. By contrast, in the category of graduate education, the only articles that identified a particular field of study were the three that examined Higher Education and Social Work, professional fields. The articles on graduate education were more broad-based, with titles such as, "Advice to Doctoral Guidance Committees," "Time to Completion of Doctorates," and "Differentiation in Graduate Education."

In Table 2, the distribution of articles about students that appeared in the six journals/ magazines from 1985 to 1990 are presented. A comparison of the totals of Tables 1 and 2 is obviously misleading because of the two additional journals included in the latter table. If we subtract the totals for JCSP and NASPA, we find that there are more than twice as many articles in the generalist higher education journals devoted to students than there are articles on curriculum and instruction (232 versus 100).

As with the substantive area of curriculum and instruction, by far the largest number of articles on students were in the generic category. The articles in this category accounted for over 44 percent of the total articles, nearly three times as many as the next largest category (miscellaneous). Included in this category were titles such as, "Changes in Students' Self-Confidence in College," "Students' Affective Development Within the College Environment," "Student Perceptions of College Quality," "Wellness Needs of Incoming Students," "The Impact of Living Group Social Climate on Student Academic Performance," and "What do Students Want?" In all but one of the journals (CH), the generic category was the largest. In that case, one more article was coded in the category minority than in generic. But those numbers are somewhat misleading. The

Table 2
Number of Articles about Students in Selected Journals, 1989–1990

Jrnl	GENER	UND/LA	GRAD	PROF	FROSH	WOMEN	MIN	MISC
CH	13	1/0	3	1	—	2	14	3
JCSP	115	9/3	5	4	21	45	47	54
JHE	24	5/4	6	1	2	9	7	6
NASPA	73	—	3	2	3	2	5	20
RHE	32	5/0	7	3	3	7	2	9
REV	15	2/0	3	1	1	2	7	4
TOTAL	272	22/7	27	12	30	67	82	96

articles on minorities were clustered in a couple of special issues (in another journal (REV), all the articles coded minority were in one issue).

Apart from the miscellaneous category, the second largest category overall was minority (82 articles) followed by women (67 articles). That represents a significant increase over the number of college student articles on minorities (and women) identified by Kuh et al. (1986–from less than 5 (and 5.2) percent of the total number of articles in Kuh et al.'s sample to over 13 (and 11) percent of the total number of articles in my sample. Well over half of the articles in my analysis were accounted for by one journal (JCSP), which had the largest number of coded articles (200). Titles included the following: "Problems of Minority Students," "Women's Career Assistance," "Minority Students' Involvement," "Reentry Female Students," and "Minority Students' Reasons for Not Seeking Counseling." In this regard, JCSP provides a sharp contrast with the other student affairs journal (NASPA), which had the second largest total number of articles among the six journals, but the fewest number of articles coded minority (5) or women (2).

The remaining categories were relatively small in terms of numbers of articles. Overall, there were more articles on freshmen than on graduate, undergraduate, or professional students, although this pattern was skewed by the student personnel journal. Among the titles were: "Changes in College Freshmen after Participation in a Student Development Program," "Academic Advisement for Freshmen," "Freshmen Retention and Attrition," and "Residentially Based Freshmen." Combining the freshmen and undergraduate/liberal arts category yields a reading of the percentage of articles devoted explicitly to undergraduate education (8.5 percent), nearly twice the percentage of articles devoted explicitly to graduate students (4.4 percent). The numbers on graduate students are up from Kuh et al.'s analysis (up to 4.4 from 1.3 percent). The category with the smallest number of coded articles on students (12) was professional. The reader should keep in mind, however, that as with the articles on curriculum and instruction, virtually all of the articles on students in the generic category were on undergraduates.

The overwhelming emphasis, then, measured by a quantitative count of articles in the substantive fields of curriculum and instruction, and students, is on arts and science undergraduate education. There is an irony in this topical emphasis. Although Kuh et al. (1986) found in their content analysis of research on college students that scholars tend to study students at doctoral granting universities, these scholars do not for the most part study doctoral and professional students. I believe that the message embedded in the title of another article by George Kuh et al. (1987) applies to the subfields of curriculum and instruction, and students, "Student Affairs and Liberal Education: Unrecognized (and Unappreciated) Common Law Partners." For Kuh et al., the partnership lies in the similar goals of student affairs and liberal education, which can be seen as complementing and supporting one another. For higher education scholars, the significance of that shared purpose is expressed in an overriding focus on undergraduate education in the disciplines as opposed to the professions. The emphasis is so pervasive that it is assumed and subsumed in generic treatments of various topics in substantive fields such as curriculum and instruction, and students.

Summary

Professional education is a peripheral category in higher education scholarship. My analyses of selected chapters in the *Handbook,* and of selected journals in the field, provide quantitative and qualitative evidence of such marginality. First, professional programs, instruction, and students are featured much less frequently than other areas of research in the titles of *Handbook* literature reviews and of the periodical literature. My review of the Tables of Contents of six core journals/ magazines in the field of higher education empirically confirmed the rough impressions drawn from the first five volumes of the *Handbook.* Second, professional programs, instruction, and students tend not to be identified as significant considerations in other categorical areas. The omission is remarkable, particularly given the variables that are targeted, such as residential arrangement and involvement with faculty.

The situation of professional education is much like that of class in considering demographic characteristics. In their research on college students, scholars in the United States control for and concentrate on characteristics such as gender, ethnicity, and age, but not social class. If higher education scholars refer to class, it is generally to the level of education, under or upper classmen, rather than to the social relations of production. If higher education scholars refer to family background, it is generally to father's income, or with euphemisms such as first generation college student. Although I have included the category in my tables, professional education is not a central category in the literature. For example, in Halstead's (1984) bibliographic taxonomy of higher education, there is no category for professional programs. Although there is a section entitled "Disciplines," none of the disciplines listed constitute professional areas of study.

Why do I regard the tendency toward generic treatment, and the inherent bias toward liberal arts education, as being problematic? I believe that program area is a significant dimension to consider in understanding some phenomena in the substantive fields of curriculum and instruction, and students, and I believe that professional programs are in many ways different from academic programs. For example, the nature of instruction and learning is likely to vary dramatically between certain academic and professional programs, with the latter often characterized by clinical teaching involving small student/faculty ratios and hands-on, active learning by doing that is rarely found in academic programs. Similarly, I would expect the nature of student/faculty interaction and student involvement to be different in medical school or in an undergraduate nursing program than in a sociology department at the undergraduate and graduate levels. As suggested by research coming out of the Biglan studies (Biglan, 1973a, 1973b; Muffo and Langston, 1981; Roskens, 1983), program area is a variable that needs to be systematically disaggregated.

To the extent that the literature does currently consider program area, it is less as a structural than as an individualistic variable, revealed in different orientations, values, etc. of faculty and students in different fields. I am suggesting that program area is a significant structural variable that differentially shapes a variety of phenomena, and that therefore should be specified and disaggregated rather than treated generically. More than that, however, I also believe that by focusing specifically on professional programs we may draw attention to a range of external variables that are generally overlooked but that profoundly shape curriculum and instruction, and students in a variety of ways. For example, in several professional fields there has been considerable challenge to the profession, sometimes in the form of consumer or client-based social movements. In response to such movements or public criticism, there have also been considerable changes in the curricula of certain professional programs. As Gumport (1988) and Slaughter and Silva (1983) indicate, that broader focus on political and social movements, the forces of political economy, and the involvement of faculty in them, is a critical consideration in explaining curricular innovation and change in academic fields.

Professional Education in the Specialized Literature

How is professional education studied in the specialized literature that concentrates on this topic? What are the topics that are addressed, the questions that are posed, and the conceptual frameworks they are derived from? These are the questions that underlie the content analyses I conducted for this section of my chapter.

The research literature on professional programs is voluminous and fragmented among a variety of journals/publications that are specific to particular fields of professional study. I make no pretense of providing an exhaustive review of this literature, describing the findings of countless investigations into the details of diverse and distinctive fields. Rather, I cast an analytical net that will detail patterns in the focus of research on professional education.

Fortunately, higher education's preeminent scholar of professional education has preceded me into the field. In a relatively recent monograph, Joan Stark et al. (1986a) conducted a massive review of the professional education literature, focusing on 12 fields and fitting articles into a conceptual framework she has generated for the study of preservice professional education. Since Stark and her contingent have reviewed nearly 3,000 journal articles, it makes little sense to try to duplicate or replicate their efforts. Rather, I attempt to build on their work in three respects. First, I review recent editions of some of the journals Stark et al. analyzed, seeking to determine what questions and themes are prominent. Second, I explore the assumptions and theoretical underpinnings of Stark's work, and incorporate my recent review into that framework. Third, I return to the higher education journals, examining studies of higher education and student affairs professionals (the latter in NASPA) and programs as a specialized, professional education literature.

Common Themes in Diverse Settings

The settings of professional education vary dramatically from one field to the next. The nature of the curriculum and instruction, and the characteristics of the students, are quite diverse. Some professional programs are undergraduate, whereas others are graduate. Professional programs are differentially integrated with other academic units on campus. Teaching means quite different things in different professional fields. Programs range widely in terms of whether they have a major clinical component and what it consists of. Students may be contrasted by cognitive skills, preparation, achievement measures, and demographic characteristics.

At the same time, many would say that these diverse fields share common problems and purposes. For example, all professional programs struggle with the problem of integrating theory and practice, with connecting and making abstract, academic knowledge relevant to concrete matters of professional practice. Similarly, all professional programs share the purpose of preparing skilled practitioners who will successfully make the transition to the world of professional work. The problems and purposes are shared, although the particular means by which they are addressed and pursued may vary by professional field.

Stark et al.'s (1986a) literature review works out of the assumptions identified above, and the categorical distinction described in the preceding section between things professional and liberal in education. In opening the monograph, Stark et al. confront the prevailing view that professional programs "are inappropriately narrow and specialized," and that "professional educators concentrate on technical skills and devalue broader aspects of their students' education." (p. iii) By looking at the emphasis that professional educators place on "generic outcomes of professional study" such as competencies and attitudes, Stark et al. explore the validity of criticism regarding the narrowness of professional education. They survey professional educators and conduct an extensive content analysis of the professional education literature. The content analysis covered 14 journals of 12 professional fields (architecture, business administration, dentistry, education, engineering, journalism, law, library science, medicine, nursing, pharmacy, and social work) from January 1979 through December 1984.

In conducting their content analysis, Stark et al. focused on articles that dealt with educational outcomes. However, much of the literature in the selected journals deals with other aspects of professional education. In their executive summary, Stark et al. note that even in those fields where professional educators "express strong interest in fostering attitudes like long-term career awareness, professional identity, and ethical standards," the professional education journals are not necessarily filled with articles articulating and measuring such outcomes. Therefore, rather than simply updating Stark et al.'s review, by content analyzing the same journals over the past six years, I was interested in addressing two somewhat different issues. First, to what extent are outcomes the principal research focus of articles in professional education journals? Second, what are the basic categories into which articles in these journals can be classified? If most scholars are not focusing on outcomes, what are they studying?

Of the 14 journals analyzed by Stark et al., I examined five, plus one journal I added from the area of business, which had been omitted in Stark's study. I tried to select journals that dealt with professional fields having the largest numbers of enrollments and also varied by general curricular area and prestige (e.g., health related, helping, technical, fields and professions). The journals I analyzed were: *Engineering Education, Journal of Legal Education, Journal of Medical Education, Journal of Social Work Education* (formerly *Journal of Education for Social Work),* and *Journal of Teacher Education.* I also analyzed the *Journal of Education for Business,* which was not in Stark et al.'s sample, and which cross-cuts the secondary, postsecondary, and collegiate levels of education. My review for this section of the study was somewhat less formal and extended than it was in the case of the generalist higher education journals. The choice of single journals in a field of professional education does not provide the same kind of coverage that is yielded by analyzing six higher education journals, making any quantitative count of trends more misleading than revealing. I rely then, more on general, tentative impressions than on formal totals and percentages of articles in various categories. For each of the journals, I sampled three years of editions, including one year drawn from the time frame studied by Stark et al. I wanted to be able to determine whether the patterns I found held at the time of their study, or were more recent developments. In presenting the findings, journal by journal, I try to give the reader a flavor of the specialized discourse and of the patterns by topical area and question addressed, and by framework adopted.

Not surprisingly, I found some interesting variations among the journals, along with some continuities. The articles in *Engineering Education* provide the clearest sense of any of the journals of the profession's connection to external developments and societal needs. For example, three articles in a 1988 edition (78/9) deal with the impact of space exploration on engineering programs. Each of the years I sampled also had special editions on pipeline issues, related to faculty and students. Edward Wenk Jr.'s (1988) article, "Social, Economic, and Political Change: Portents for Reform in Engineering Curricula," captures the sensitivity to external influences. Wenk centers his article on the proposition that engineering programs must prepare professionals who are more than technical decision makers. He stresses the impact on the profession of public concerns regarding health, safety, environmental, and natural resource issues, and of interorganizational relations that will involve negotiations surrounding these issues. I categorized articles that adopted such an approach to professional education, looking to client demands and needs, as "external orientation." For all of the journals, this was the category with the fewest number of articles.

Each of the editions of *Engineering Education* has a section entitled, "Ideas in Practice," which conveys one of the central emphases in the journal. The largest number of articles were focused on programs or teaching strategies that had been found effective, many of which addressed creating competencies. I labeled these two categories of articles, "exemplary practices" and "skills."

Some attention was also devoted to matters surrounding "student characteristics." For example, the special issue on the student pipeline examined various demographic characteristics. In general, the category also included articles on questions of admissions, graduation, and career placement.

Finally, a considerable amount of attention was devoted to attitudes, or what I would call professional "values." Several articles dealt with engineering ethics. And a special issue was devoted to the liberal arts. The cover was an adaptation of a Monet painting with the caption, "Different Strokes: can engineering and the humanities paint each other into the picture? Included in the issue were articles such as Samuel Florman's "In Search of a Civilized Engineer."

The same categories of "skills," "student characteristics," "values " "exemplary practices," and "external orientations applied to the articles found in the *Journal of Education for Business* . By far the largest category was "exemplary practices." Articles in this category tended to focus on particular strategies, and involved subjects such as applying certain software to particular classes, utilizing simulation, types of teaching, and a spreadsheet approach to teaching.

Quite a few articles dealt with "skills" and "values." As one would expect, the most commonly mentioned skills had to do with communication and oral presentation. As one would hope, the articles on values had to do with ethics, in a variety of permutations. Some dealt with general ethics education or with courses designed to deal with ethical issues—for example, "Values Issues in Introductory Finance." Other articles focused on particular practices, such as "Reducing Fraudulent Financial Reporting."

Very few articles fell in the categories of "characteristics" or "external orientation." One that focused on externalities concentrated on the profession—"Meeting the Needs of the Accounting Profession." The journal was quite internally focused on improving the skills and values of practitioners, and on effective educational practices.

The *Journal of Legal Education* is marked by a very different presentational format than the previous two journals. It is much more a scholarly journal, with the extended exegesis that one finds in law journals, whereas the engineering and business journal articles were short and almost journalistic in character. As a result, there are far fewer articles in the legal journal, and no sections or short blurbs on exemplary practices.

The issues of the *Journal of Legal Education* are thematic. For the most part, they concentrate on broad curricular issues. For example, in the time frame in which Stark et al. coded the articles, themes included: "The Place of Economics in Legal Education," "Administrative Law in the 1980s," "American Bar Foundation Studies Concerning Legal Education," and "Law Curriculum in the 1990s." The category of exemplary practices, then, was the largest, though somewhat in contrast to the previous two journals the focus was primarily on broad curricular questions and problems rather than on teaching. The smallest categories were skills and external orientation.

Several of the articles dealt with values, having titles such as, "The Moral Development of Law Students." In fact, there was a special issue devoted to "Humanistic Perspectives on Legal Education." Two of these articles adopted a critical perspective in analyzing legal education, breaking with the conventional concern for enhancing effectiveness within the confines of existing practice. In the following subsection of this chapter, when I review Joan Stark's work and examine its conceptual underpinnings, along with the assumptions embedded in most of the specialist professional education literature, I will explore these two articles on legal education in some depth.

Like the legal journal, the *Journal of Medical Education* was scholarly in orientation, reflecting the norms of research in its field. Consequently, its articles tended to be shorter and were likely to be quantitative empirical studies. For example, several articles examined predictors of success in medical school for different kinds of students.

Consistent with the other journals, the exemplary practices category had more articles than any other. Yet the articles were more evenly distributed across the various categories than they tended to be in other journals. There were quite a few articles in the skills, values, and student characteristics categories. Several different sorts of skills were addressed. Unfortunately, though as one might expect, there was only one article that dealt with communicative competence, in contrast to the journal on business education! The articles in the category of values were more wide ranging than was the case in other journals. They dealt not just with medical ethics courses and human values teaching programs, but with such matters as attitudes of medical students towards AIDS patients.

With the exception of the engineering journal, the *Journal of Medical Education* had more articles with an external orientation than the other periodicals. Several had to do with changes in health care systems: "Characteristics and Training Considered Desirable by Leaders of HMOs," "The Changing Medical Care System: Some Implications for Medical Education," and "The Impact of Competitive Health Care Systems on Professional Education." But the external concerns went beyond organizational and economic changes in the workplace, as evidenced in this title, "Medical Education and Societal Expectations: Conflicts at the Clinical Interface."

The editions of the *Journal of Social Work Education* are divided up into various subsections. The titles of these subsections reflect a fairly balanced focus on values, exemplary practices, and student characteristics. Although one article dealt in part with skills, "The Effects Of Graduate Social Work Education on Personality, Values, and Interpersonal Skills," this was not a topical area that was covered very much. Rather, most of the articles addressed issues of values and curriculum. Some of the subsection headings referring to values included, "Ethical Issues in Educational Process," "Social Work Values Among Students," "Ethical Issues," and "Ethics." Articles examined confidentiality, stereotyping, humanistic values, ethical admissions processes, and changing interests of social work students. Some of the subsection headings referring to curriculum and exemplary practices included, "Using Literature to Teach Social Work," "Curricular Content Areas," "Doctoral Education," "The Field Component," "Curricular Reform," "Curricular Inertia," and "Specialization and Core Content."

A few of the articles in the social work journal adopt a more political view of professional education than is found in most of the journals. One of these deals with sexual harassment, "Sexual Harassment in Graduate Schools Of Social Work: Provocative Dilemmas." In looking at the conflictual relations between students and professors in graduate school, this article partly breaks with the conventional focus on socialization, which assumes that faculty are trying to socialize students into the values of the profession. The author is critical of the attitudes and behaviors of the faculty.

Two other articles focus on the external, political involvement of social work professionals, and the connection of the profession to the political process. Although they could be coded in the category of external orientation, in a sense, the articles are about inculcating the values of the profession into future practitioners, since part of the code of ethics of the National Association of Social Workers calls social workers to political action. Yet, as I will explore in some depth in a subsequent section, the articles direct attention to a dimension of professional work that is completely ignored in the other journals. The framework adopted by the authors raises quite different questions from those that drive the overwhelming proportion of the research on professional education.

The last journal I examined was the *Journal of Teacher Education*. Most of the articles in this journal dealt with exemplary practices. Each edition has a theme, and many of these reflected the fundamental concern with improving teacher education through new programming and the structuring of the teacher education program: "Preparing Teachers for Urban Schools," "Teacher Education and Technology," and "Field Experiences and Teacher Education." One of the interesting aspects of the research in this journal was the tendency to draw on studies of teacher thinking and teacher practices to inform the improvement of teacher education. Indeed, many researchers in the field are promoting a case method approach to training teachers, utilizing examples of good teaching to prepare practitioners.

Quite a few articles also dealt with skills and student characteristics. Thematic titles such as "Cognitive Science and Critical Thinking" and "Critical Reflection in Teacher Education" suggest the sorts of critical and reflective skills that are emphasized for teachers. Similarly, the thematic title of, "Selection, Retention, and Recruitment of Minority Teachers," reflects concerns about the characteristics of students.

Although it did not show up in the journal editions I examined, the study of teacher education in general is marked by a concern with the value and attitudinal change experienced by teacher education students as they move through the professional education program and out into the schools. The absence of such process/product studies testifies to the limitations of analyzing one journal per field of professional education.

In a special issue entitled "The Reconceptualists," two articles break out of the conventional framework of examining socialization into the teaching profession. M. Gail Jones, in "Gender Issues in Teacher Education," and Paul Farber, Paul Wilson, and Gunilla Holm in "From Innocence to Inquiry: A Social Reproduction Framework," examine the reproduction of inequality in professional education programs. Jones (1989) examines how gender bias is being reproduced in the classroom interactional patterns of professional education courses. Farber et al. (1989) draw on a social reproductionist view of education to identify practices in teacher education that foster student failure and inequality.

My review of the specialist journals in six fields of professional education suggests that the outcomes approach generated by Stark et al. certainly reflects some of the major concerns of scholars. Much of the literature examined skills and values, or in Stark et al.'s terms, competencies and attitudes. For the most part, articles on such topics did not consist of sophisticated quantitative analyses of the impact of professional education on particular skills or attitudes. But they did address particular competencies and values that were considered important parts of professional practice. So the outcomes variables were focused on in many of the articles, but they did not constitute the principal focus of professional education research in these journals.

Overall, the category into which most articles could be classified was exemplary practices. Whether the topic had to do with curricular programs or teaching and delivery strategies, the emphasis was on providing examples or tips on how to improve professional education. The general, orienting question of how to make the preparation of professionals better was the dominant framework out of which were generated a variety of specific questions.

Consistent with the preceding concerns was an interest in how to fit the profession to changing external realities. In some cases, such realities referred to pipelines issues, with articles focusing on student characteristics. In other cases changing external realities referred to transformations of the workplace, with articles being categorized as having an external orientation.

One category that did not emerge from the data was faculty. Despite the interest in improvement and effectiveness, articles generally did not focus on faculty. At first blush, such an omission seems rather strange. If you want to talk about the skills and values that students are socialized into, how can you not talk in some detail about the socializers, about those who are articulating, modeling, and hopefully transmitting those skills and values. On reflection, the omission makes a good deal of sense, for it is consistent with most of the general literature on socialization. Typically, the study of socialization centers on those being socialized rather than on those doing the socializing. The expertise of the professionals doing the socialization is assumed, and the problem is to figure out the best way to prepare new professionals.

Grounding Theory in a Functionalist Framework

The work of Joan Stark and her colleagues accounts for nearly one-fourth of the articles on professional education that I identified in the six higher education journals. She is virtually the only higher education scholar who has systematically studied professional education as a general field. In this subsection, I explore the topics and questions that Stark addresses, and the analytical framework out of which she derives these substantive concerns. I incorporate my preceding analysis of the specialist literature on professional education into this review of Stark's work.

Several of Stark's articles deal with curricular dimensions of professional programs. In addition to establishing a framework for studying preservice professional programs, Stark has studied perceptions of professional preparation environments and of influences on professional programs. She has also examined accreditation standards. In each of these cases, Stark's focus is comparative, looking at professional education across several fields of study.

In contrast to the specialist literature, much of Stark's work concentrates on the faculty. Three of the five articles I reviewed have the word "faculty" in their titles: "Faculty Roles and Role Preferences in Ten Fields of Professional Study," "Faculty and Administrator Views of Influences on Professional Programs," and "Faculty Perceptions of Professional Preparation Environments: Testing a Conceptual Framework." As is clearly expressed in two of these titles, the ultimate substantive concerns in these analyses come back to the professional programs themselves.

A synopsis of the articles reveals the underlying questions that orient Stark's work. In the main, Stark's questions have to do with the quality of professional preparation that is provided, with various factors that influence the provision of professional education and with how to improve those programs. In a very real sense, Stark examines inputs and outputs of professional education, with the aims of evaluating and making the process more effective.

The article on faculty roles is on the surface perhaps the one that is least connected to programmatic issues. In this paper, Stark, Lowther, and Hageny (1986b) study professional education faculty in much the same way that most higher education scholars have studied faculty in general. That is, how do faculty allocate their time among the diverse and competing roles they play, and what is the relationship between the way they spend their time and the way they would like to spend their time? Although higher education scholars generally neither acknowledge nor deal in depth with the concepts, the implicit theoretical foundations of their questions lie in social psychology, in functionalist conceptions of role and role strain. Roles are seen as objective statuses that have various expectations and responsibilities attached to them. Role incumbents find themselves pulled among the various demands of their role and their preferences. Significant disjunctures between the ways people spend their time by virtue of the demands of the role, and the ways they would like to spend their time, are seen as potentially dysfunctional, or problematic, both for the individuals and for the academic units in which they work. Stark et al. investigate the preferences and time allocation of faculty in ten fields of professional study among teaching, research, consulting, and professional practice.

The focus on programs is more explicit in Stark et al.'s (1987a) article on faculty and administrators' views of influences on professional programs. Again, the analytical focus follows a common approach in the field to the study of faculty, involving comparing the goals of faculty and administrators to determine whether there are inconsistencies that might detract from the effectiveness of the organization. In this case, Stark et al. modify this approach a bit by looking not at goals but at views about different influences on professional programs. Consistency of views is regarded as positive. In asking faculty and administrators about university, society or professional community influences, and internal curricular debates, Stark et al. underscore the importance of professional communities—beyond the academic unit, and within the unit itself—being marked by cohesive, shared values. The sense is that quality in professional education is related to such commonality, to an integrated professional community.

A subsequent study by Hageny and Stark (1989) on accreditation is even more explicit in its concern with enhancing quality. Hageny and Stark consider specialized accreditation in terms of its goal of fostering excellence by developing criteria and guidelines for assessing excellence. In looking at the accreditation standards of ten professional preparation programs, Hageny and Stark "explore relationships between the occurrence of explicit outcome statements in accrediting standards and independently derived faculty perceptions of accrediting rigor." (p. 3) Their ultimate interest is in the quality of the professional programs.

> Currently, it appears there is insufficient evidence to objectively assess the value of making outcomes explicit in accrediting standards. When we compare those few fields with quite explicit standards . . . with those far less explicit, we could identify no association of explicitness with perceived rigor of the accrediting agency, with endorsement of the specified outcomes by faculty in their field, with faculty estimates that outcomes receive greater emphasis in their programs, or with clarity of educational activities assumed to achieve the outcomes. (p. 18)

In a sense, Hageny and Stark, like most of the scholars in the specialist journals on professional education, are searching for exemplary practices that will enhance the quality of professional programs. Unlike most of the contributors to the professional journals, Hagerty and Stark's focus is far above and much broader than the classroom or even the curriculum itself.

Two of the articles by Stark et al. in the generalist higher education journals in the past five years surround the conceptual framework by which she organized her content analysis of specialist journals on professional education. In first presenting this framework, Stark et al. (1986c) indicate that they developed a "generic" framework to guide the study of professional programs, with the intention of helping self study, improving external reviews, and clarifying program goals. I would submit that although Stark et al. claim to have used a grounded theory approach so as not to bias the work with "subjective predispositions," they offer us a functionalist frame for studying and thinking about professional programs. Embedded in this functionalist frame are assumptions and perspectives that lead us to regard some research questions as meaningful and natural, and to not raise some other research questions. Frames can focus and sharpen attention, but they can also serve as blinders.

Questions about exemplary practice, and about the skills and attitudes fostered by professional education, are abundant in the specialist professional education journals, just as they are prominent in the research of Stark and her associates. Such questions seek to improve professional education at the same time that they accept the essential parameters within which professional preparation is currently conducted. In concentrating attention on effectiveness, scholars implicitly suggest that professional education is primarily and even exclusively about preparing competent and ethical practitioners, that it is meritocratic. The kinds of topics and questions that are addressed in the specialist literature and in the work of Stark, do not challenge the current position, role, and practices of professionals in society.

The exceptions demonstrate the power of the conventional rule. Two articles in the *Journal of Legal Education* that break with the functionalist perspective work out of a critical theory framework. Two articles in the *Journal of Social Work Education* that break with the functionalist perspective offer a more politically proactive view of professionals and professional education than is typically found in the literature.

In an article entitled, "Legal Education and the Reproduction of Hierarchy," Duncan Kennedy (1983) analyzes and reinterprets socialization in law school as "ideological training for willing service in the hierarchies of the corporate welfare state." He examines noncurricular practices and the formal curriculum of legal rules and reasoning that "demobilizes" students who come into law school hoping to substantially change society. Along the same lines, Stephen C. Halpern (1982), in an article entitled, "On the Politics and Pathology of Legal Education (Or,

Whatever Happened to that Blindfolded Lady with the Scales?),'' states:

> I will argue that the socialization which occurs has a substantial political dimension to it. Indeed, the first year of legal education is as much political indoctrination and ideology as it is anything else. Ironically, that political indoctrination is made all the more effective and powerful because it ignores or, worse yet, denies the ultimate political character of the law itself. Legal education divorces law from politics. . . . This paper is written in an attempt to help undermine that ideology and to explore the underlying political values and interests which are served by the traditional structure and character of legal education. (p. 383)

The argument is that professional education, by socializing future practitioners into a depoliticized view of the role of that profession, serves the political interests of both the profession and the powerful interests it serves.

Two articles on social work education adopt a more politically proactive than a critical stance in discussing professional curricula. In the first article, "Joining Together: A Faculty-Student Experience in Political Campaigning," Grafton H. Hull Jr. (1987) promotes the active involvement of faculty and students in local politics. He draws on the field's code of ethics, and on a curriculum policy statement issued by the Council on Social Work Education, stating that, "One purpose of social work is 'the pursuit of such policies, services and programs through legislative advocacy, lobbying, and other forms of social and political action, including providing expert testimony, participation in local and national coalitions, and gaining public office.'" (p. 37) That proactive approach to the social work profession is also promoted in an article by Roger Witherspoon and Norma Kolko Phillips (1987), "Heightening Political Awareness in Social Work Students in the 1980s."

> Social workers must participate as members of pressure groups to shape the future of the social welfare system and uphold professional values, including preventing further social deterioration and correcting existing social problems. . . . Social work students need greater awareness of the possibilities and processes of political change. This paper discusses goals of stimulating students' interest in questions of social justice and helping students gain skills for effective social change within the social welfare policy curriculum and classroom experience." (p. 44)

These social work articles offer a view of the practitioner as a political worker not just an expert. They connect the growth and even the purpose of the profession to political activities and goals.

Notwithstanding such exceptions as those discussed above, the work of Joan Stark, like the work that appears in the specialist professional education journals, adopts a functional approach to professional programs. The focus is on improving professional education and practice, on preparing skilled practitioners who have been socialized into the values and beliefs of the professional community. The assumption is that professionals will benefit society by virtue of applying their expertise in a particular domain of work. Professional politics, within or outside professional programs, and the political economy of professional practice, are not addressed.

Preparing Higher Education Professionals: How Do We Study Ourselves?

In this last subsection on the specialist literature, I examine the way that we talk about preparing higher education practitioners. In other words, I treat articles on higher education programs as a specialist literature on professional education. A few of these articles appeared in the generalist journals I reviewed. Several that focused on student affairs practitioners appeared in one of the student affairs journals (NASPA) in which a good deal of attention was devoted to developing the professional field of student affairs. My focus, as with the specialist literature in the other fields of professional education, is on the topics that are addressed, the questions that are asked, and the conceptual framework that underlies this work.

In my sample of higher education journals over the past five years, the articles that dealt with professional education in the general field of higher education appeared in the *Review of Higher*

Education. The first of these to appear was by David Dill and James Morrison (1985), "EdD and PhD Research Training in the Field of Higher Education: A Survey and a Proposal." In this article, Dill and Morrison trace the history of EdD and PhD degrees, and survey higher education programs regarding the objectives and research requirements of their curricula. After finding that the differences between the two degree programs are minimal, Dill and Morrison differentiate and clarify the purposes of each and propose distinctive programs of study that would meet the different needs and objectives of each. The idea is to rationalize and thereby improve graduate education in higher education. In the language of my earlier review of the specialist professional education literature, Dill and Morrison's article falls in the exemplary practices category. At the same time, it addresses skills concerns—for example, it identifies analytical and other skills that academic managers and leaders versus researchers need.

In an article entitled, "A Profile of Higher Education Doctoral Programs," Patricia Crosson and Glenn Nelson (1986) present a descriptive profile of doctoral programs for the study of higher education, with one of the goals being to take stock as well as to enhance and improve the quality of the field. In surveying directors of higher education programs, Crosson and Nelson gather data on program goals, curriculum and degree offerings, organizational structure, faculty and student characteristics, and admissions requirements. The conclusion to the article poses a series of questions: Have higher education programs reached the point of overproduction of doctoral degrees?, Do higher education programs have too many students?, Can higher education programs preserve dynamism among their faculty?, What is the distinction between Ph.D. and Ed.D. programs and degrees?, and Do higher education programs occupy a strong enough position within the schools of education? The questions, coming out of a functionalist frame, relate to efficiency, effectiveness, and quality.

In their article, "Taking Stock: The Higher Education Professoriate," L. Jackson Newell and George Kuh (1989) identify changes in various characteristics of the faculty. Their examination of the age, activities, research methods, and professional values of this faculty group are intended to benefit the field by encouraging a reassessment of priorities. The nature of the reassessment, and the characteristics that are focused on, are not unlike those found in the article by Stark et al. on faculty roles and role preferences.

Barbara Townsend and Stephen Mason (1990), in "Career Paths of Graduates of Higher Education Doctoral Programs," presents survey data on the graduates of 36 programs. Townsend and Mason describe the impetus for their study as follows:

> Prompted by concerns about market saturation and potential enrollment problems in higher education programs, this study is an effort to evaluate these programs by assessing their impact upon graduates' careers and ascertaining graduates' attitudes towards their degrees. The data gathered illuminate some important caveats for faculty and administrators connected with and committed to higher education doctoral programs. (p. 78)

Just as with Karen Gallagher and Don Hossler (1987) who examine graduation rates in higher education doctoral programs, the reason for attending to pipeline issues—the category of student characteristics—lies in providing some perspective and direction for improving the programs. The belief is that such improvement will be generated by the information that is gathered through an ongoing process of monitoring the field.

In the student affairs journal NASPA, there are several articles on in-service training and staff development. In general, such contributions aimed to enhance the quality of professional practice. Four articles concentrate on the graduate education of student affairs professionals. In "Graduate Preparation Programs in College Student Personnel: One Introductory Course," David Meabon and Hilda Owens (1984) survey programs to determine, among other things, what courses are offered. Much like the surveys of higher education programs, in part the objective of such work is to guide the field toward the development of an academic identity, in this case a consistency across programs in terms of the common knowledge that is agreed upon by the profession and transmitted to students. Walter Shaw (1985) conducted a similar sort of survey, regarding the extent to which programs cover the topic of small college administration. Effectiveness and improvement through a rationalization of the connection among ends (program objectives), means (curricula), and outcomes (job placement).

In two cases, student affairs articles go well beyond the analysis and data provided by the articles on professional education in the field of higher education. One article, "Graduate Education for the Student Development Educator: A Content and Process Model," by Robert D. Brown (1984), calls for an end to the process of ad hoc accretion by which student affairs programs have developed. Starting with assumptions about society's and students' needs, Brown proposes a program that is integrated and functional in the way it connects basic knowledge, intervention knowledge, and experiential knowledge. He offers his content and process model as a tool for evaluating programs and planning changes. A more empirically grounded basis of assessment is provided by Robert B. Young (1985) in, "Impressions of the Development of Professional Identity: From Program to Practice." Young analyzes the identity development and commitment of students as they move through student affairs programs.

The literature on the professional education of higher education practitioners is marked by the same functionalist cast that characterizes the specialist literature on professional programs in other fields of study. The topics and questions are oriented to effectiveness and improvement. The perspective that is adopted reflects the viewpoint of those who are in power. Much like was argued in the case of legal education in the two articles that broke with convention, higher education programs treat administrative knowledge and practice as neutral. The politics, professional and otherwise, that underlie such knowledge and practice, or the political economic structures and conditions that make such administrative knowledge meaningful, are ignored and even denied.

The exception, in an article by Sheila Slaughter and Edward Silva (1983), "Service and the Dynamics of Developing Fields: The Social Sciences and Higher Education Studies," reveals the limitations of the rule. Slaughter and Silva offer a sociology of knowledge and curriculum that fundamentally challenges functionalist accounts of how fields of study develop and change. Getting beyond the questions of quality and effectiveness, Slaughter and Silva connect professional practice to the interests of social classes external to the academy. Professionals gain power and privilege by serving the powerful and privileging the privileged. What does that mean in the case of higher education programs? It means that we need to begin to consider how our connections to power affect the kinds of questions we address as scholars and professional educators. It means that we need to begin to consider the extent to which the belief systems that prevail in the political economy are incorporated into our doctoral programs.

Summary

The analytical focus of the specialist literature on professional education is marked by commonality in its topical coverage, the questions it asks, and the conceptual framework in which it is grounded. Three different literatures were examined: six specialist journals on professional education, the work of Stark and her colleagues in higher education, and literature on professional programs in higher education, particularly student affairs. In each case, most of the articles fall into the categories of skills, values, or exemplary practices (some other articles fall into categories of student characteristics or external orientation). The orienting question that drives the bulk of this work is how can we improve professional education.

The commonality that is found in these literatures is not generic; born of natural interests anyone would have in professional education. Rather, the commonality is theoretically and politically derived and inscribed in the acceptance and legitimation of professional privilege. Scholars in these areas work out of a functionalist framework that is oriented toward effectiveness, as defined by those in positions of power. Professional education is understood primarily in terms of forming and preparing expert and ethical practitioners. Research questions therefore revolve around the identification of exemplary teaching practices and programs, and of desirable outcomes in the areas of professional skills and values. The idea is to improve professional practitioners and practices, in effect, to strengthen the profession.

Conclusion: Beyond Functionalism

There is a dual irony to the treatment of professional programs in the general professional discourse of higher education, and in the specialized literature on professional education. First, we generally ignore and devalue a range of curricula that are particularly popular among students and a growth area in postsecondary enrollments, that account for a large proportion of the budgets of postsecondary educational institutions, and that prepare students for a sector of the work force that is growing. Second, when we do specifically focus on professional programs and the professions, we are studying powerful people, but we do not study power. Just as we stratify institutions and students in our general professional discourse, so we stratify and categorize curricula. In my content analysis of chapters on curriculum and instruction, and students, in the first five volumes of the *Handbook,* and of the articles of six higher education journals over the past five years, the marginality of professional education was clear. Professional programs are relatively ignored in the generalist literature. Few articles are devoted to the topic, particularly in a general analysis of issues relevant to professional programs. Articles in general substantive areas such as curriculum and instruction, and students, do not treat professional programs as a significant variable or dimension of education to be considered. Moreover, the research is largely normed on liberal arts undergraduates.

By not studying power, we perpetuate privilege. In my review of journals on professional education in six fields of study, of Joan Stark's work in higher education, and of articles in higher education journals on professional programs in student affairs and higher education, I found few examples of articles dealing with questions of power. Existing patterns of hierarchy and privilege were assumed to be meritocratic and natural. For example, the articles adopt the vantage point of the faculty or of others seeking to socialize students, indicating an acceptance of the distribution of professional power within professional education and in the workplace. Attention was directed almost exclusively to matters of enhancing the quality of professional programs and practitioners. Questions and topics came out of a functionalist theoretical framework.

Do we have to study power? Perhaps not all of us as a field have to study power as directly as I might suggest. Joan Stark and her colleagues, for example, are to be commended for directing sustained attention to the topic of professional programs. There may be nothing wrong with the perspective that they adopt. But that perspective is limited. I believe that the professional discourse about professional programs, and our enactment of professional education, would be enriched and enhanced by drawing on other conceptual frameworks that do study power, that raise questions about existing patterns or power and privilege, and that make current practices and distributions of resources problematic. I also believe it is important that those scholars who pursue functionalist questions of how to improve professional education confront and take seriously the proposition that in attending to questions of quality they are enhancing the legitimacy and power of professionals vis-a-vis non-professionals. By not considering questions of professional power and privilege, such scholars help perpetuate existing patterns of privilege.

Alternative Sociological Frameworks and Research Questions

The sociological literature provides at least two alternatives to the functionalist framework for studying professional programs. First, there is a rich tradition of symbolic interactionist studies of professional education. Second, there is a rich tradition of critical studies of education. Either of these frameworks leads researchers to quite different research agendas from those that have been derived and followed in higher education and in the specialist literature on professional education.

In sociology, the study of the process by which professionals are prepared in formal educational settings has tended to be grounded in either functionalism or symbolic interactionism. In analyzing the higher education literature, I have shown that the functionalist approach has generated questions regarding how to bring about effective professional socialization, how to ensure that future practitioners develop the appropriate skills and values and are properly initiated into the professional community. The viewpoint is top down. The assumption is that professional education is organized and controlled by socializing agents who transmit knowledge, beliefs, ethics, etc., to students so that they may be fit into the professional role. By contrast, the symbolic interactionist approach has generated questions regarding the daily interaction among faculty and students within professional education settings, and the perspectives that students develop in the course of this interaction. The focus is on interaction, not induction. The viewpoint is, if anything, bottom up. Symbolic interactionist scholars have concentrated on the situational perspectives that are developed by students in negotiating and coping with the contingencies of their everyday lives. The assumption is that the meanings that people develop within professional programs are the product of constant interaction, conflict, and interpretation. As a result, the analytical focus goes well beyond the formal curriculum to less formal and explicit dimensions of professional programs.

The two classic examples of these contrasting approaches to professional education are Morton et al.'s (1957), *The Student Physician,* and Becker et al.'s (1961) *Boys in White.* In the past two decades, the clear trend in sociological research, in contrast to the prevailing perspective I have found in the higher education and specialist literatures, has been to adopt the interactionist approach. The most prominent examples of such research in professional fields of study are found in the health sciences (Koff, 1989). The focus of these studies is on students' active negotiation and construction of their experiences in professional education (Freidson, 1970; Light, 1980, 1988; Scully, 1987; Stelling and Bucher, 1973). In the main, such research offers a different and more critical view of the beliefs that students develop in the course of their professional education. For instance, rather than talking about codes of ethics and ideals of service, such research concentrates on how professionals develop strategies for coping with and defining away mistakes, and how professionals develop attitudes about clients, whom they would like to deal with, and what sorts of professional practice they would like to pursue. From this perspective, professional education is not neutral.

The general study of education in sociology has in large part been structured by two theoretical frameworks: functionalism and critical theory. In the case of research on education in general, the functionalist perspective has generated a set of questions and agenda somewhat similar to that found in studying professional education. But while the emphasis is on socialization, and making the transmission of culture to students a more effective process, and while the viewpoint remains top down, the empirical focus is more on students. Sociological researchers examine the extent to which the educational system is functioning properly by studying students and their characteristics and practices more than by studying teachers.

In adopting the perspective of critical theory, an entirely new set of questions and different agenda are generated. I believe these are relevant to the investigation of professional programs. The revisionist critique of education, whether in the "reproduction" or "resistance" traditions of critical theory, directs attention to questions of power, exploitation, struggle, and the reproduction of unequal structures of class, race, and gender. Critical scholars connect schools and schooling to external structures of power such as social class and patriarchy, and examine how power and privilege and struggle are played out in the everyday lives and practices of people in the schools. Consequently, as with symbolic interactionism, the analytical focus goes well beyond the formal curriculum to the so-called hidden curriculum.

In the sociology of education, the clear trend in recent decades has been towards revisionist work that challenges conventional, functional views of education. The classic American statement of the critical approach is found in Bowles and Gintis' (1976) *Schooling in Capitalist America,* which offers among other things, a "correspondence principle" to explain the structure and culture of schooling, connecting it to social relations of production in the workplace. The 1970s were a period in which the revisionist history of American education was advanced from a critical perspective. At about the same time, a "new sociology of education" was being defined in Britain, offering a critical approach to the analysis of education which focused on microlevel processes in the schools, from teacher-student interactions to the curricular content of educational programs (Karabel and Halsey, 1977). In subsequent years, critical scholars have developed a resistance approach that concentrates attention on students' resistance in the schooling process (McRobbie and McCabe, 1981; Willis, 1977). In the higher education literature, there are a few examples of such work (Holland and Eisenhan, 1990); London, 1978; Weis, 1985). From the standpoint of studying professional programs, what is important about the critical approach is that it reveals that educational processes and curricula are not neutral, but rather express and serve the interests of particular classes and status groups.

The study of professional programs should encompass more than the study of professional education. The sociological frameworks of symbolic interactionism and critical theory offer different views of professionals than do functionalists, and these are crucial to developing the broader study of professional programs. Functionalists treat professionals, like professional education, as neutral. What is of interest to functionalists about professionals is the characteristics they have that make them professionals—e.g., technical knowledge, codes of ethics, ideals of service, self-regulation—and the service they provide to society. In recent decades, however, the predominant view of professionals has drawn on the early work of Everett Hughes (1958) and connected it to the political sociology of Marx and Weber to develop a critical view of professionals called professionalization theory. The classic statements of this approach (Collins, 1979; Larson, 1977) offer a view of professionals as a grouping that seeks to establish and maintain a monopoly over a domain of work, and that articulates a conception and enactment of its professional work that resonates with and serves the interests of powerful social groupings in society. Professionals are not neutral. They are consistently engaged and implicated in political action, even in the course of everyday interactions with clients. We might adopt different views of the nature of this political action. For example, in higher education it might be conceived of as a constant negotiation between professional and lay groups, or professionals and clients (Riesman et al., 1970; Rhoades, 1987). It might be conceived of in terms of political economy, connecting professionals to the interests of a social or institutional class (Rhoades and Slaughter, 1991a, b; Slaughter, 1990; Slaughter and Rhoades, 1990; Slaughter and Silva, 1984). Whatever view we adopt, we need to incorporate questions and power and politics into our study of professional programs.

In closing this chapter, I would suggest that two of the most significant developments in American society in recent decades have been the realignment of professional labor and the renegotiation of relations between professionals and non-professionals. The realignment of professional labor is taking place internally, in the organizations in which professionals work, and externally, in relations with external social groups and classes. The professional workforce and workplace are experiencing considerable change. The renegotiation of relations between professionals and non-professionals is part of a general increasing demand for accountability in recent decades and a particular challenge to the power, expertise, and position of professionals.

In my view, research on professional programs needs to address such developments and considerations. In our general professional discourse, we need to incorporate central consideration of professional programs. In the general discourse, and in the specialist discourse on professional programs, we need to explore the connection of professionals to broader social groupings, and we can draw on prevailing sociological frameworks to do that. In stratifying curricula as we do, subordinating professional to liberal education, we obscure the significance of some of the most important programs in colleges and universities, from community colleges to research universities. In working out of a functionalist framework in looking at professional programs, we obscure the relationship between these programs and social classes, structures, and forces within and beyond the academy, thereby perpetuating existing patterns of privilege. If we do not study power, we enlist ourselves in its service.

References

Astin, Alexander. (1963). Further validation of the Environmental Assessment Technique. *Journal of Educational Psychology* 54: 217–26.

Astin, Alexander. (1973). Measurement and determinants of the outputs of higher education. In Lewis Solomon and L. Taubman (eds.), *Does College Matter?* New York: Academic Press.

Baird, Leonard. (1990). The melancholy of analogy: the personal and professional development of graduate and professional school students. In J.C. Smart (ed.), *Higher Education: Handbook of Theory and Research* Vol. VI. New York: Agathon Press.

Becker, Howard; Geer, Blanche; Hughes, Everett C.; and Strauss, Anselm. (1961). *Boys in White: Student Culture in Medical School* Chicago: University of Chicago Press.

Biglan, Anthony (1973a). The characteristics of subject matter in different academic areas. *Journal of Applied Psychology* 57 195–203.

Biglan, Anthony. (1973b). Relationship between subject matter characteristics and the structure and output of university departments *Journal of Applied Psychology* 57: 204–13

Bowles, Samuel, and Gintis, Herbert. (1976). *Schooling in Capitalist America: Educational Reform and the Contradictions of Economic Life.* London: Routledge and Kegan Paul.

Brown, Robert D. (1984). Graduate education for the student development educator: a content and process model. *National Association of Student Personnel Administrators Journal* 22(3): 38–43.

Cevero, Ronald M., and Young, William H. (1987). The organization and provision of continuing professional education: a critical review and synthesis. In J. C. Smart (ed) *Higher Education: Handbook of Theory and Research* Vol. III. New York: Agathon Press.

Collins, Randall. (1979). *The Credential Society* New York: Academic Press.

Conrad, Clifton F. (1989). Meditations on the ideology of inquiry in higher education: exposition, critique, and conjecture. *Review of Higher Education* 12(3): 199–220

Conrad, Clifton F., and Blackburn, Robert T. (1985). Program quality in higher education. In J. C. Smart (ed.), *Higher Education: Handbook of Theory and Research* Vol. I. New York: Agathon Press.

Conrad, Clifton F., and Pratt, Anne M. (1986). Research on academic programs: an inquiry into an emerging field. In J. C. Smart (ed.), *Higher Education: Handbook of Theory and Research* Vol. II. New York: Agathon Press.

Crosson, Patricia H., and Nelson, Glenn M. (1986). A profile of higher education doctoral programs. *Review of Higher Education* 9(3): 335–57.

Dill, David D., and Morrison, James L. (1985). EdD and PhD research training in the field of higher education: a survey and a proposal. *Review of Higher Education* 8(2): 169–92.

Ewell, Peter T. (1988). Outcomes, assessment, and academic improvement: in search of usable knowledge. In J. C. Smart (ed.), *Higher Education: Handbook of Theory and Research* Vol. IV. New York: Agathon Press.

Farber, Paul; Wilson, Paul; and Holm, Gunilla (1989). From innocence to inquiry: a social reproduction framework. *Journal of Teacher Education* 40(1): 45–50.

Fincher, Cameron. (1985) Learning theory and research. In J. C. Smart (ed.), *Higher Education: Handbook of Theory and Research* Vol. I. New York: Agathon Press.

Fincher, Cameron. (1986). Trends and issues in curricular development. In J. C. Smart (ed.), *Higher Education: Handbook of Theory and Research* Vol. II. New York: Agathon Press.

Florman, Samuel. (1988). In search of a civilized engineer. *Engineering Education* 78(3): 162–163.

Freidson, Eliot. (1970). *Profession of Medicine: A Study of the Sociology of Applied Knowledge.* New York: Dodd, Mead, and Company.

Gallagher, Karen S., and Hossler, Don. (1987). Graduation rates in programs of higher education: trends and policy considerations. *Review of Higher Education* 10(4): 369–372.

Gumport, Patricia J. (1988). Curricula as signposts of cultural change. *Review of Higher Education* 12(1): 49–62.

Gumport, Patricia J. (1991). The federal role in graduate education. In J. C. Smart (ed.), *Higher Education: Handbook of Theory and Research* Vol. VII. New York: Agathon Press.

Hagerty, Bonnie M. K., and Stark, Joan S. (1989). Comparing educational accreditation standards in selected professional fields. *Journal of Higher Education* 60(1): 1–20.

Halpern, Stephen C. (1982). On the politics and pathology of legal education (or, whatever happened to that blindfolded lady with the scales?). *Journal of Legal Education* 32(3): 383–394.

Halstead, D. Kent., ed. (1984). *Higher Education: A Bibliographic Handbook,* Vols. 1 and 2. : National Institute of Education.

Holland, Dorothy, and Eisenhart, Margaret A. (1990). *Educating for Romance*. Chicago: University of Chicago Press.

Hossler, Don; Braxton. John; and Coopersmith. Georgia. (1989). Understanding student college choice. In J. C. Smart (ed.), *Higher Education Handbook of Theory and Research*. Vol. V. New York: Agathon Press.

Hughes, Everett C. (1958). *Men and Their Work*. Glencoe, Illinois: The Free Press.

Hull, Grafton H., Jr. (1987) Joining together: a faculty-student experience in political campaigning. *Journal of Social Work Education* 23(3): 37–43.

Jones, M. Gail. (1989). Gender issues in teacher education. *Journal of Teacher Education* 40(1): 33–38.

Karabel, Jerome, and Halsey, A. H. (1977). Educational research: a review and interpretation. In Jerome Karabel and A. H. Halsey (eds.), *Power and Ideology in Education*. New York: Oxford University Press.

Keller, George, and Moore, Kathryn M. (1989). Review essay: reflections on higher education research . *Review of Higher Education* 13(1): 119–36.

Kennedy, Duncan. (1983). Legal education and the reproduction of hierarchy. *Journal of Legal Education*. 32(4): 591–615

Koff, Nancy. (1989). Trainee negotiation of professional socialization in medical education. Doctoral dissertation, Department of Higher Education, University of Arizona.

Kuh, George D.; Bean, John P.; Bradley, Russell K.; Coomes, Michael D.; and Hunter, Deborah E. (1986). Changes in research on college students published in selected journals between 1969 and 1983. *Review of Higher Education* 9(2): 177–92.

Kuh, George D.; Shedd, Jill; and Whitt, Elizabeth. (1987). Student affairs and liberal education: unrecognized (and unappreciated) common law partners. *Journal of College Student Personnel* 28(3).

Larson, Magali Sarfatti. (1977). *The Rise of Professionalism: A Sociological Analysis*. Berkeley: University of California Press.

Light, Donald. (1980) . *Becoming Psychiatrists: The Professional Transformation of Self*. New York: W. W. Norton and Company.

Light, Donald. (1988). Toward a new sociology of medical education. *Journal of Health and Social Behavior* 29: 307–322.

Lincoln, Yvonna S., and Guba, Egon G. (1989). Ethics: the failure of positivist science. *Review of Higher Education* 12(3): 221–240.

London, Howard. (1978). *The Culture of a Community College*. New York: Praeger.

Lulat, Y. G.-M., and Altbach, Philip G. (1985). International students in comparative perspective. In J. C. Smart (ed.), *Higher Education: Handbook of Theory and Research* Vol. 1. New York: Agathon Press.

Malaney, Gary. (1988). Graduate education as an area of research. In J. C. Smart (ed.) *Higher Education: Handbook of Theory and Research* Vol. IV. New York: Agathon Press.

McCord, Michael T. (1985). Methods and theories of instruction. In J. C. Smart (ed.) *Higher Education: Handbook of Theory and Research* Vol. 1. New York: Agathon Press.

McRobbie, Angela, and McCabe, T. (1981). *Feminism for Girls*. London: Routledge and Kegan Paul.

Meabon, David L., and Owens, Hilda F. (1984). Graduate preparation programs in college student personnel: the introductory course. *National Association of Student Personnel Administrators Journal* 22(1): 2–12.

Mentkowski, Marcia, and Chickering, Arthur W. (1987). Linking educators and researchers in setting a research agenda for undergraduate education. *Review of Higher Education* 11(2): 137–60.

Merton, Robert K.; Reader, G.; and Kendall, P. (1957). *The Student-Physician*. Cambridge, Massachusetts: Harvard University Press.

Moore, Kathryn M. (1989). Review essay: reflections on higher education research. *Review of Higher Education* 13(1): 126–136.

Muffo, John A., and Langston, Ira W. IV. (1981). Biglan's dimensions: are the perceptions empirically based? *Research in Higher Education* 15(2): 141–159.

Newell, L. Jackson. (1990). Sifting and certifying knowledge. *Review of Higher Education* 14,1: 1–4.

Newell, L. Jackson, and Kuh, George D. (1989). Taking stock: the higher education professoriate. *Review of Higher Education* 13(1): 63–91.

Nucci, Larry, and Pascarella, Ernest T. (1987). The influence of college on moral development. In J. C. Smart (ed.), *Higher Education: Handbook of Theory and Research,* Vol. III. New York: Agathon Press.

Pascarella, Ernest T. (1985). College environmental influences on learning and cognitive development. In J. C. Smart (ed.), *Higher Education: Handbook of Theory and Research,* Vol. 1. New York: Agathon Press.

Rhoades, Gary. (1987). Higher education in a consumer society. *Journal of Higher Education* 58(1): 1–24.

Rhoades, Gary. (1990). Calling on the past: the quest for the collegiate ideal. *Journal of Higher Education* 61(5): 512–534.

Rhoades, Gary, and Slaughter, Sheila. (1991a). Professors, administrators, and patents: the negotiation of technology transfer. *Sociology of Education,* 64(2) 65–77.

Rhoades, Gary, and Slaughter, Sheila. (1991b). The public interest and professional labor: research universities. In William Tierney (ed.), *Culture and Ideology in Higher Education: Advancing a Critical Agenda.* New York: Praeger.

Riesman, David, Gusfield, Joseph, Gamson, Zelda. (1970). Academic *Values and Mass Education.* Garden City, New York: Doubleday and Company.

Roskens, Ronald W. (1983). Implications of Biglan model research for the process of faculty advancement. *Research in Higher Education* 18(3): 285–297.

Scully, Diana. (1987). Negotiating to surgery. In H. D. Schwartz (ed.), *Dominant Issues in Medical Sociology.* New York: Random House.

Shapiro, Jonathan Z. (1986). Evaluation research and educational decision making. In J. C. Smart (ed.), *Higher Education: Handbook of Theory and Research,* Vol. II. New York: Agathon Press.

Shaw, Walter B. (1985). Graduate student affairs education and the small college. *National Association of Student Affairs Administrators Journal* 22(3): 44–46.

Silva, Edward, and Slaughter, Sheila. (1983). *Serving Power: The Making of the Social Science Expert, 1865-1921.* Westport, Connecticut: Greenwood Press.

Silverman, Robert J. (1987). How we know what we know: a study of higher education journal articles. *Review of Higher Education* 11(1): 39–60.

Slaughter, Sheila. (1990). *The Higher Learning and High Technology: Dynamics of Higher Education Policy Formation.* Albany: State University of New York Press.

Slaughter, Sheila, and Rhoades, Gary. (1990). Re-norming the social relations of academic science: technology transfer. *Educational Policy:* 4(4): 34–61.

Slaughter, Sheila, and Silva, Edward. (1983). Service and the dynamics of developing fields: the social sciences and higher education studies. *Journal of Higher Education* 54(5): 481–499.

Smart, John C. (1985). Preface. In J. C. Smart (ed.), *Higher Education: Handbook of Theory and Research,* Volume I. New York: Agathon Press.

Smutz, Wayne D.; Crowe, Mary Beth; and Lindsay, Carl A. (1986). In J. C. Smart (ed.), *Higher Education: Handbook of Theory and Research,* Vol. II. New York: Agathon Press.

Stark, Joan S.; Lowther. Malcolm A.; and Hagerty, Bonnie M. K. (1986a). *Responsive Professional Education: Balancing Outcomes and Opportunities* . ASHE-ERIC Higher Education Report No. 3, Washington, D.C.: Association for the Study of Higher Education.

Stark, Joan S.; Lowther, Malcolm A.; and Hagerty, Bonnie M. K. (1986b). Faculty roles and role preferences in ten fields of professional study. *Research in Higher Education* 25(1): 3–30.

Stark, Joan S.; Lowther, Malcolm A.; Hagerty, Bonnie M. K.; and Orczyk, Cynthia. (1986). A conceptual framework for the study of preservice professional programs in colleges and universities. *Journal of Higher Education* 57(3): 231–258.

Stark, Joan S., Lowther, Malcolm A., and Hagerty, Bonnie M. K. (1987a). Faculty and administrator views of influences on professional programs. *Research in Higher Education* 27(1): 63–84.

Stark, Joan S., Lowther, Malcolm A., and Hagerty, Bonnie M. K. (1987b). Faculty perceptions of professional preparation environments: testing a conceptual framework. *Journal of Higher Education* 58(5): 530–561.

Stelling, Joan, and Bucher, Rue. (1973). Vocabularies of realism in professional socialization. *Social Science and Medicine* 7: 661–675.

Tinto, Vincent. (1986). Theories of student departure revisited. In J. C. Smart (ed.) *Higher Education: Handbook of Theory and Research.* Vol. II. New York: Agathon Press.

Townsend, Barbara K., and Mason, Stephen O. (1990). Career paths of graduates of higher education doctoral programs. *Review of Higher Education* 14,1 63–82.

Weidman, John. (1989). Undergraduate socialization. In J. C. Smart (ed.), *Higher Education: Handbook of Theory and Research* Vol. V. New York: Agathon Press.

Weis, Lois. (1985). *Between Two Worlds: Black Students in an Urban Community College* Boston: Routledge and Kegan Paul.

Wenk, Edward Jr. (1988). Social, economic, and political change: portents for reform in engineering curricula. *Engineering Education* 78(10):

Willis, Paul. (1977). *Learning to Labor: How Working Class Kids Get Working Class Jobs.* New York: Columbia University Press.

Witherspoon, Roger, and Phillips, Norma K. (1987). Heightening political awareness in social work students in the 1980s. *Journal of Social Work Education* 23(3) 44–49

Young, D. Parker, and Braswell, Martha C. (1987). An analysis of student academic rights. In J. C. Smart (ed.), *Higher Education Handbook of Theory and Research.* Vol. III. New York: Agathon Press.

Young, Robert B. (1985). Impressions of the development of professional identity: from program to practice. *National Association of Student Affairs Administrators Journal* 23(2) 50–60.

Academic Reform:
Compelling Conversations of the 1980s

JUDITH S. EATON

Overview

Three major approaches to academic values and direction were apparent during the 1980s. These were (1) preference for the ideological stance of the Reagan administration, (2) support for the standard practices of the higher-education community as they had been developed during the 1960s and 1970s, and (3) a "third agenda," or significant disagreement with each of the other approaches primarily because these approaches did not adequately address the issues of social change needed for true education reform. Those identified with the first approach were generally called "conservative," while those identified with the second approach may be called "establishment," or part of the national higher education community. Those with a third agenda were sometimes referred to as "radical-education" thinkers. Conservatives sought to return to an era in which schools were homogeneous and orderly. Establishment thinkers sought schools that retained traditional academic structure and values while at the same time were responsive to some social change. Third-agenda thinkers urged that schools reflect a reformed society in which economic and social justice were truly valued.

The 1980s were years in which academic reform was a major higher-education topic, concern, and preoccupation. These years may be contrasted with the 1960s and 1970s, in which equity issues, enrollment growth, and proliferation of institutions dominated the dialogue. In the 1960s we worried about relevance and student choice; in the 1970s we were concerned about diversity and vocationalism. The 1980s saw renewed emphasis on curricular issues, reinvigoration of discussions of academic standards, and, in general, a focus on academic effectiveness. In part this focus was the result of the higher-education community's concern with educational achievement. It was also the result of the community's tendency to sustain important discussions of general education, the liberal arts, and curriculum reform on an ongoing basis. This chapter will consider this important national conversation in two ways: by reviewing the various national reports that emerged during the decade and by discussing some of the thinking of conservative, establishment, and third-agenda educators about the condition of the higher-education enterprise.

Educational Effectiveness and the Establishment: Spokespersons Bok and Boyer

During the 1980s, Derek Bok and Ernest Boyer each offered analysis and evaluation of the role of higher education, its effectiveness, and the social context in which higher education operates. Their works are important as excellent examples of the general features of the approach of those who were considered establishment: members of the Washington-based higher-education associations, presidents of prestigious colleges and universities, and consultants, researchers, and intellectuals involved with association or university work.

Derek Bok, president of Harvard University, comprehensively addressed an agenda for higher education on two separate occasions in the 1980s (1982, 1986). He used these respective opportunities to focus first on higher-education's social responsibilities beyond the academy and then to address issues within the academy itself. Bok's approach to the academic-reform issues of curricular change, general education, and educational quality may be described as sensitive to our strengths and weaknesses and patient about change. Keenly aware of the historic value of the higher-education enterprise to the nation and its individual citizens, Bok seeks to acknowledge the legitimacy of criticisms of higher education while at the same time softening their harshness. Bok is important: not only has he led the higher-education institution considered to the nation's premier university, he is also considered by many to be a thoughtful and resourceful educational thinker and writer.

Bok points out that concerns about curricular effectiveness, whether reflected in the language of the various national reports or the rhetoric of the Reagan administration, are neither unusual nor unique. He notes that the question of what is to be taught is perennial and that the 1960s were not the first era in American higher education in which we relaxed curricular requirements. The decade of discussion in the 1980s was the most recent in a long-standing effort to grapple with the questions of a prescriptive versus elective curriculum, curricular breadth, and curricular integration. The solutions offered most frequently to the challenge of curricular content are (1) a prescribed curriculum such as a "great books" curriculum, (2) emphasis on modes of thought or a curriculum focusing more on method than on a defined body of learning, and (3) distribution requirements. Bok finds little in our latest wave of discussion and deliberation that will move us toward a new vision; curricula have not moved in any clear direction in the twentieth century (1986).

When Bok talks about allegations of deterioration of educational quality in our colleges and universities, he focuses on factors external to specific institutions. He points out that one potential disadvantage of our decentralized, autonomous, and competitive aggregate of higher-education institutions is the survival of institutions of doubtful quality. He refers to the steady drop in academic qualifications of entering freshman resulting, in his view, from more people attending college, the effects of television, the effects of family disintegration, and declining standards in public schools. Bok also notes that the tighter job market has the impact of driving students away from the liberal arts to vocationally oriented studies (1986).

Bok is addressing the question of how well universities educate and how they could do better. After acknowledging the impact on the liberal arts of greater complexity of knowledge, extracurricular opportunities for students, and the changing mix of students, he turns to teaching and learning. Here Bok stresses the importance of focusing faculty attention on common purposes: the shared objectives of liberal education and their relationship to individual courses. He urges that the discussion of quality not be restricted to a consideration of curriculum alone but extend to pedagogy and evaluation. He speaks to the difficulty of rallying faculty to agree to common education aims for an undergraduate experience. Bok stresses the great variety of individual interests and intellectual commitments among faculty. The university is not organized such that faculty will spontaneously come together to develop and pursue common academic objectives. While seeking to preserve faculty individuality, Bok nonetheless urges some attention to shared purposes:

> it is inappropriate and unrealistic to expect professors to subordinate everything to helping students achieve a set of shared objectives. But it is equally wrong for faculties to pay no attention to common goals and to ignore the question of how these aims are realized. (1986, p. 63)

Bok goes on to discuss the impact of knowledge growth, our seemingly intractable national problems, international challenges, and the questioning of traditional values. He sees the tasks before us as long-term and calling for the use of creative energy by students, faculty and administrators.

Underlying Bok's discussion of the university's response to the future is his faith in the current structure, operation, and values of America's colleges and universities. He is calling for more effective use of the potential of higher education to assist in the resolution of individual, community, national and international concerns. He does not see this as requiring radical restructuring of the higher-education enterprise. Bok suggest patience rather than dramatic change. He uses the accurate observation that our problems are not new to justify the more questionable notion that the social, political, and economic *status quo* is adequate as we attempt to resolve these problems. We read in Bok's message no call for major change in social values and behavior.

In *College: The Undergraduate Experience in America* (1987) by Carnegie president Ernest Boyer, emphasis is placed upon constructive debate concerning the undergraduate experience, the meaning of that experience, and our capacity to enrich and revitalize it. "The American college is, we believe, ready for renewal, and there is urgency to the task," Boyer maintains (p. 7). To set the terms for the debate, Boyer cites eight problems or points of tension for the undergraduate college and those it serves. In the academic arena, he identifies the goals and curriculum of education, the conditions of teaching and learning, and the priorities of faculty. More generally, he identifies transition from school and college, quality of campus life, college governance, outcomes assessment, and, in his words, "the connection between the campus and the world" (p. 6). Boyer considers our primary enemy to be fragmentation: in the society, our loss of cultural coherence and commonalities; in the academy, the presence of departmentalism, intense vocationalism, and fragmentation of knowledge. He sees the primary solutions to be connectedness, community, and a sense of wholeness.

What if Boyer were to achieve resolution of the tensions identified in *College*? What type of undergraduate education enterprise would emerge? We would find additional cooperation between schools and colleges to ensure that prospective students are meaningfully informed about a collegiate experience. College-entrance considerations would be dramatically altered in terms of what the institution seeks to learn about prospective students and also in terms of making requirements sensitive to the changing demographics of the elementary and secondary population. Significant additional attention would be paid to orienting students to a collegiate environment, especially part-time students. Students would be exposed to an institution with a clear and vital mission, guided by a vision and goals common to the institution as a whole.

In the academic arena, we would find students who are better prepared because the pre-collegiate educational experience would have been significantly strengthened. Colleges would have greatly increased their respective demands for study that builds reading and writing skills through a variety of English courses. Students would spend significant time in a general-education curriculum, throughout their undergraduate program. Boyer stresses that general education is not a single set of courses but a program with a clear objective that might be achieved in any number of ways. The crucial element is clarity of purpose. Concentration, or the "major," is to be integrated with a general-knowledge program in pursuit of the baccalaureate.

Faculty in a Boyer-influenced institution would retain emphasis on scholarship and research, but they would strengthen their commitment to teaching and their recognition of the importance of quality teaching. The classroom experience would be a collaborative undertaking between students and professor. Boyer asserts, "The central qualities that make for successful teaching can be simply stated: command of the material to be taught, a contagious enthusiasm for the play of ideas, optimism about human potential, the involvement of one's students, and—not least—sensitivity, integrity, and warmth as a human being" (p. 154).

Campus life outside the classroom would also have affected the undergraduate teaching and learning experience. Institutional behavior would reflect institutional values and standards. There would be expectations and rules that are public and clearly understood. An institution, like an individual, can sustain or lack character. Campus life as Boyer sees it, both inside and outside the classroom, would stress the value and importance of service:

> In the end, the quality of the undergraduate experience is to be measured by the willingness of graduates to be socially and civically engaged. . . . Is it too much to expect that , even in this hard-edged, competitive age, a college graduate will live with integrity, civility—even compassion? Is it appropriate to hope that the lessons learned in liberal education will

reveal themselves in the humaneness of the graduate's relationship with others? (pp. 278–279)

It is difficult to disagree with Boyer's vision of a desirable future. Who among us would not wish to achieve many of his goals? We want colleges of quality and colleges of competence. But it is difficult to identify strategies for the resolution of the tensions he outlines, and this limits the likelihood of realization of the higher-education world Boyer and others would like to see. Boyer does us the service of providing us, if we choose it, a common vision. He sets standards that are sensitive to both individual and communal needs. He touches upon the troubled sense many of us have concerning the often fragmented, isolated nature of the world we inhabit. He encourages hope.

Boyer, like so many others, puts a good deal of faith in our ability to achieve the vision he and others articulate. Faith can be powerful, but it may not be enough. The increasingly intractable difficulties both within the academy and outside its walls are not used to test the extent to which Boyer's vision is realistic. If our goals cannot be realized and our institutions and the society continue to suffer, do we continue to sustain our dreams and ignore the problems we are failing to address? We would benefit if Boyer offered some analysis of the likelihood of success for his "good college" in light of the present serious obstacles to realization of many of his goals. Additionally, it would be of value to carefully consider alternatives to that vision if there is reasonably compelling evidence that it is unlikely to be realized.

Yes, the quality of the undergraduate experience may improve if elementary and secondary college-preparatory education improves. Yes, we might enjoy coherent and purposeful general-education programs if more faculty preferred a more intellectual rather than a more political approach to their work. Yes, integrity can abound on the college campus if administrators, faculty, and trustees were insulated from the compromising influences of our society. But how likely is any of this? The challenge here is to address the quality of the undergraduate experience, the presence of general education, and the integrity of campus life in the face of poor preparatory education, a political faculty and administration, and a morally ambivalent society. This means either finding ways to achieve Boyer's goals when his conditions to achieve these goals do not prevail or to change the conditions. Boyer could have provided his readers with a larger exploration of either the likelihood of realization of his vision or practical suggestions to achieve it. He offers neither. We are left with comforting words and respect for our author. We then go back to our classrooms filled with the academically underprepared, our curriculum committees filled with contentiousness, and our campus life filled with interest-group pressures, governmental regulation, and political interference.

A Conservative Agenda

Conservative educators offered a number of preferences about education in the 1980s. They tended to maintain that the problems of education during the decade derived from educational practices encouraged in the 1960s. They contended that schools' failure to educate has more to do with the failure of students than the failure of institutions. They leaned toward educational policies that promoted traditional standards and traditional forms of authority and discipline. To further these policies, they encouraged a school role in promoting values and encouraged moral regulation through the curriculum, a source of power and authority that they consider significant and about which they are astute in their understanding. Conservatives demanded excellence and took strong positions on related issues such as behavior and discipline. They are perceived to have an essentially authoritarian approach to the relationship between students, school officials, and community in which the officials are in charge. They are also perceived as comfortable with education as an adjunct of the labor market in spite of the economic inequities of that market.

Conservative thinking about education is here contrasted with approaches described as "liberal" and "radical." Liberals argue that education offers possibilities for individual development, social mobility, and political and economic power for the disadvantaged. Education is a great equalizer. In this context, they stress individualism, competition, and personal effort and reward. Radical educators question the extent to which it is desirable that schools replicate the existing socioeconomic order of things and the extent to which reliance on individual effort under unequal circumstances can produce change. They disagree that schools should remain the way they are and they disagree that liberal values and approaches are the most viable vehicles for change.

Allan Bloom and E. D. Hirsch

Allan Bloom and E. D. Hirsch are two prominent examples of 1980s conservative thinking about higher education. They are frequently linked with the thinking and preferences of William Bennett and the Republican administration. Publishing in 1987, they were, throughout much of the remainder of the decade, viewed as a conservative response or contrast to the prevailing discussion of academic reform as reflected in the thinking and approaches of the establishment higher-education community. This was especially interesting in the case of Hirsch, who was seen by some to in fact belong elsewhere in the political spectrum. It is Hirsch's emphasis on the importance of content that appears to place him in a "conservative" camp.

Both Bloom and Hirsch offer solutions that are curriculum-based in response to the problems perceived as besetting higher education. Bloom, in *The Closing of the American Mind*, seeks to reestablish the "great books" curriculum; Hirsch, in *Cultural Literacy*, argues for a "national curriculum," or shared knowledge of important people, events, and artifacts of culture. Both men are interested in improvement of education through curricular redesign. In this, they are in the tradition of the National Institute of Education, National Endowment for the Humanities, and Association of American Colleges reports—although their particular curricular solutions differ significantly from the reports and these latter documents do focus on institutional and faculty issues as well. Bloom argues for several major points in addition to his curricular preferences. He wants education to be confined to an academically talented elite. He wants education to focus on the pursuit of intellectual certainty, preferably the certitude of Plato. He questions the value of the feminist movement. He does not like the nature of the black student presence on college campuses in the 1980s. He finds faculty in general unduly influenced by the liberalism of members of the lower middle class, who were able to benefit from earlier educational opportunity in our society, earn doctorates, and become members of the professoriate. He is opposed to affirmative action.

Bloom contends that every educational system has a goal that informs its curriculum:

> Aristocracies want gentlemen, oligarchies men who respect and pursue money, and democracies lovers of equality. Democratic education, whether it admits it or not, wants and needs to produce men and women who have the tastes, knowledge, and character supportive of a democratic regime. (p. 26)

Our educational system and its attendant goal have, in Bloom's eyes, shifted from the vision of the rational, industrious, honest, law-abiding, family-oriented men—who had a powerful attachment to the historical American notion of rights to the democratic man—to the education of openness. The education of openness celebrates relativism and, indeed, makes relativism the "only plausible stance in the face of various claims to truth" (p. 26). Bloom sees the education of openness as discouraging any fundamental agreements and encouraging all kinds of individuals, ideologies, and life-styles. Openness and relativism, according to Bloom, have helped produce the current inadequacy of education. Education in our colleges and universities is no longer a search for truth. Education reflects a lack of conviction that there are "truths" to be comprehended. Education fails to sustain the values of shared thinking required to sustain the society.

Bloom wants several things. He seeks restoration of the "great books" curriculum as a vehicle to establish an alternative to intellectual relativism. He desires political realignment within colleges and universities, of a sort that would diminish the power of academic enclaves while encouraging some shared academic values. Finally, he wants to reestablish higher education as a search for intellectual certitude:

> The real community of man, in the midst of all the self-contradictory simulacra of community, is the community of those who seek the truth, of the potential knowers, that is, in principle, of all men to the extent that they desire to know. (p. 381)

In Bloom's view, we have paid a price for equality: unwillingness and incapacity to make claims of superiority.

Hirsch's work does not reflect the philosophical depth of Bloom's efforts. Hirsch makes several main points: There is a body of information needed by all of us to function effectively in the society. We can determine what that body of information should be. Our failure, to date, to focus on educational content is harmful to students and society. Hirsch decries the teaching of skills at the price of emphasis on shared knowledge; he believes we need the teaching of a national vocabulary in a truly coherent manner (Zemsky, 1989). Hirsch struggles with the difficult issue of how to be prescriptive about the substance of educational experience without impairing individualism and individual differences and without making value judgments about the relative importance of some aspects of culture and society over others. He attempts to persuade us that it is reasonable to determine the content of educational experience provided that one is flexible about change in content. We all need to know an amoebalike aggregate of information.

Hirsch is anxious that education cease backing away from the issue of what its content needs to be: "To suggest that it is undemocratic or intolerant to make nationwide decisions about the extensive school curriculum must not any longer be allowed to end the discussion" (p. 144). Hirsch contends that both Rousseau and Plato were wrong about content: Rousseau was incorrect in his preference to ignore content, and Plato was wrong to insist upon specific content. Rather, Hirsch argues for cultural literacy as an alternative to both: "cultural literacy" constitutes the basic information required to get on well in the modern world, the only certain avenue for the disadvantaged young, "the only reliable way of combating the social determinism that now condemns them to remain in the same social and educational condition as their parents" (p. xiii). Hirsch's cultural literacy is intended to describe the information possessed by literate Americans and therefore of value to most Americans. He claims that we need effective communication, which in turn requires the transmission of specific information.

It was not popular in the 1980s, but one could risk arguing for the plausibility of some of the thinking of both Bloom and Hirsch. What, after all, are they seeking? They want educators to make important decisions about curriculum content. They seek the primacy (not exclusivity) of Western thought as a foundation for education in a Western society. They want demanding standards set for effective academic performance. They contend that colleges and universities have an obligation to assert values and make judgments about the nature of knowledge and critical inquiry. They assert that the judgments of professional educators and academics should be, for the most part, more important than the wishes of students. Why, then, the uproar within the academic community with the publication of these two books? Since the publication of both works in 1987, it has been fashionable in higher education to be deprecatory and derisive about them. Indeed, a position of support for them raises serious questions about one's real values, especially in areas of race, gender, and social change.

The reaction to Bloom and Hirsch did not focus primarily on their suggestions for curricular change. Rather, many members of the higher-education community and some outside this community tended to support or attack Bloom and Hirsch based on the extent to which these authors were viewed as forwarding and agenda consistent with the Reagan administration's agenda. Bloom and Hirsch were judged in terms of ideology and not content. Those who consider themselves liberals in their approach to higher education find Bloom and Hirsch to be barely disguised elitists favoring privileged education for the dominant white population, ignoring the reality of our contemporary racial, ethnic, and gender difficulties, and, at heart, favoring pro-Western, antipopular culture. It was not difficult to move from this description of Bloom and Hirsch to the allegation that their approaches were racist and sexist—that they were apologists for a *status quo* badly in need of change, and committed to an elitism that is hostile to a heterogeneous and democratic society. These critics were chronically unable to find anything of worth and substance in either author's work. Much of what Bloom and Hirsch wrote was considered a barely disguised attack on minorities, women, and the poor in our colleges and universities. Bloom and

Hirsch constituted a major challenge to efforts within the higher-education community to achieve social justice and social equity goals dating back to the 1960s. In addition to these criticisms, there were also more specific challenges to the solutions each man presented. Bloom was attacked for his preference for a Western-focused curriculum and his restoration of Plato. He was criticized for offering nothing new when he urged education through "great books." Hirsch's national curriculum was considered an unworkable suggestion. His concept of literacy was described as superficial.

Bloom and Hirsch were easy targets of criticism. Participants in the higher-education enterprise make a living through articulation and exchange of ideas. One major dimension of this is the capacity for critical analysis. The comparatively few people who write books and articles in the field of academics are evaluated by a much larger academic audience of nonwriters. It is easier to criticize than to create. This tradition continued with the reaction to Bloom and Hirsch. Second, these authors may have unintentionally demonstrated, once again, that timing is everything. Those reacting to Bloom and Hirsch saw their thinking as essentially linked to the Reagan revolution and conservative thinking. It is very difficult to separate a consideration of the ideas of Bloom and Hirsch from the political strengthening of conservativism. If the 1980s saw a second-term President Carter or a President Mondale, might the reaction to Bloom and Hirsch been somewhat muted? Third, quality and authority were unfashionable values, at least in the first half of the 1980s. Those espousing the benefits of either were viewed as really seeking preservation of the *status quo*, which meant they supported social inequity and social injustice, and that they were against change that would be helpful to have-nots. Advocates for quality and authority were not perceived as seeking a better society at all. To the contrary, they were seen as justifying the values and conditions that have produced current social conditions of unfairness, stratification, insensitivity, and indifference to others. Fourth, the educational enterprise was confused in the 1980s. If intellectual relativism was viewed as the solution to economical and social problems in the 1960s, it had come to be viewed as a source of problems in the context of the 1980s. Reassertion of intellectual authority appeared to be a rejection of our commitment to social goals established twenty-five years ago. The higher-education community has not yet been able to strike a workable balance of authority and relativism.

Whatever our response to Bloom, Hirsch, and a conservative agenda, it is important to carefully identify the proposals for academic change that they are submitting and distinguish them from the context in which we are giving them consideration. While the social and economic conditions in which we find ourselves clearly affect our interpretation of suggestions for academic reform, it is still of value to investigate the merits and limitations of recommendations for academic improvement in light of their intrinsic value as well as their social context. Viewed in this manner, assessment of the conservative agenda can be undertaken in less emotional and partisan terms.

A Third Agenda

In contrast to the thinking of the Reagan administration and some conservative ideologues and the positions taken by the higher-education establishment, there are those inside the academy who have seen the needs of the nation and the role of higher education in quite different light. A "third agenda" emerges from the work of some education thinkers and writers who are impatient with the conservative and establishment agendas. They see education at all levels as a tool to perpetuate a social and economic order which is oppressive and undesirable. They perceive the major difference between establishment and conservative educators as being that the former practice benign indifference while the latter are aggressively insensitive. Neither group was genuinely willing to take on the formidable tasks associated with major educational reform. The notion of "third-agenda" thinkers rather than "radical" thinkers is used here to focus on a few themes of those not a part of the conservative or establishment environment while avoiding some of the emotional context in which "radical" may be embedded.

A Third Agenda Critique

Third-agenda thinkers contend that schools at elementary, secondary, and collegiate levels have failed to educate but instead function as adjuncts of the labor market in a manner that perpetuates economic inequity. School knowledge, they argue, is instrumental for the reproduction of capitalist social relations and critical to the preparation for hierarchically arranged occupational and class structures. Schools transmit the discourse of domination. Indeed, the main function of schools are the reproduction of dominant ideology and reproduction of social division of labor. Third-agenda educators do no blame students for educational failure; they blame dominant society. Those educators whose thinking is Marxist-oriented are especially concerned about ideology:

> Marxists take seriously Marx's statement that the ruling ideas of any society are the ideas of the ruling class and that the task of the left is to demystify them through relentless critique. In turn, the left regards school knowledge as an instance of bourgeois ideology. (Aronowitz and Giroux, 1985, p. 6)

Third-agenda thinkers frequently use criticism of conservative approaches to education as a starting point for describing the educational climate they wish to establish. Ann Bastian and the co-authors of *Choosing Equality* (1986) argue that conservatives and neoconservatives seek to achieve through the educational climate system the specific goals of reduction of government responsibility in the area of social needs, reinforcement of competitive structures of mobility, lowering of expectations for security, and popularizing of social Darwinist thinking (p. 14). Conservatives believe that school improvement requires standardization, regimentation, and competition. Conservatives describe the educational crisis as one of the declining achievement of college-bound students that, in turn, will produce a shortage of skilled personnel needed by the economy. This achievement decline is, according to conservatives, the result of permissiveness and changes in attitudes toward authority and quality that can be traced at least in part, to the 1960s. Thus, conservatives seek reform by means of a return to academic basics and rigor. This would take the form of standardized pedagogy, core curricula, increased emphasis on testing and tracking, and reinforcement of the authority of school professionals. Bastian and her colleagues address elementary and secondary education, but their description of the conservative agenda for K-12 education reflects consistency with the thinking of conservatives about higher-education.

In the main, the authors of *Choosing Equality*, as illustrative of third-agenda thinkers, are anxious to shift the responsibility for educational ineffectiveness from the students to the schools and the community. They claim that conservatives are blaming the victim and failing to look at the social, economic, and political conditions surrounding our schools that have helped to produce the problems of the 1980s for elementary and secondary education. They talk about three myths of school performance: (1) that there was an era in which public education was appreciably better, (2) that equity reforms since the 1960s, to the extent that they were successful, occurred at the price of quality and excellence, and (3) that our nation's economic growth and individual mobility require more demanding education standards in an environment that stresses competitiveness. They contend, in contrast to the myths: (1) that education has always been stratified and unequal and especially unsuccessful with the poor and with minorities, (2) that equity reforms enjoyed such limited success that they did not make a dramatic impact either on schools or students and thus did not occur at the price of quality and excellence, and (3) that the relationship conservatives claim exists between education and economy does not exist.

Suggestions for Educational Reform

As early as 1984, Daniel Rossides argued that the fundamental basis from which we attempted to evaluate educational effectiveness needed to be changed. He made several important points. These included his contentions that educational improvement was not possible without changes in social and economic conditions and that educational institutions are used to perpetuate economic and social injustice and inequity. Rossides argued that we have burdened higher education with expectations more appropriately directed to our economy and our political way of life. It is, in his view, foolish to consider change in education independent of change in the society at large:

> A democratic and effective education must ask: what kinds of competence does society need and what social institutions are needed to produce them? To prepare youngsters for concrete skills such as household budgeting, hygiene, home and appliance repairs, sexuality, fathering and mothering, first aid, preparing for death, drawing up a will or closing property deals, would require vast transformation of education. To develop real competence as a consumer, a client, and a citizen would be well-nigh revolutionary, requiring deep alterations not only to education but to power relations in the economy, the professions, and the polity. Education for competence would be truly revolutionary if it brought honesty and science to the main questions of social science. What division of social labor is needed, what are the requirements for each position, and how are people to be selected and trained for social status? How should health-care resources be utilized? The true meaning of these questions cannot be grasped until it is realized that we have not even begun to ask them. (p. 46)

Aronowitz and Giroux agree (1988). They present the 1980s educational-reform agenda as a mechanism for ensuring that educational stratification meets the needs of the economy and is accompanied by the inculcation of values identified with the Western tradition:

> We . . . argue that the real crisis in American schooling can be better understood through an analysis of the rise of scientism and technocratic rationality as a major ideological force in the 1920s; the increasing impingement of state policy on the shaping of school curricula; the anti-communism of the 1950s; the increasing influence of industrial psychology in defining the purpose of schooling; the rise of individualism and consumerism through the growth of the culture industry in which the logic of standardization, repetition, and rationalization define and shape the culture of consumption; the gendered nature of teaching as manifested in the educational labor force and in the construction of school administration and curriculum; the racism, sexism, and class discrimination that have been reinforced through increasing forms of tracking and testing; and the failure of teachers to gain an adequate level of control over the conditions of their labor. (p. 90)

While many have historically viewed education as the vehicle by which we will realize societal change, Rossides (1987) and others insist that the reverse is the case: society determines the condition of education. We cannot expect education to either improve itself or improve society until and unless we address fundamental economic and social issues within our environment. The discussion cannot end with our observations that education is a major contributing factor to preservation of societal inequities. There are two points here. Conservative and establishment educators do not address this third-agenda description of the relationship between society and education. And we need proposals to modify the society-education relationship as well as proposals to change our educational practices.

Rossides (1987) suggests that we start with reconsidering the purposes we are trying to realize through education. He contends that education is of value to us if "it provides the skills, knowledge, and values that managing our personal and public life requires" (p. 408). He urges that we focus less on the individual and more on the society we wish to have. He sees educational thinking and practice dominated by elites who are mainly interested in perpetuating an economic system that Rossides considers to be unfair and inequitable. Other third-agenda educators agree. They are consistent in their construing of the educational system of the United States as a vehicle for preservation of privilege and status. While they do not fully identify any clear plan of action or conceptual framework from which we may reconstruct American education based on principles they consider important, they do speak to the important issues of educating for an effective society, the use of education for desired economic mobility, and the need to sustain standards while being sensitive to changing demographics. And, as with many of their colleagues, they are struggling to provide comprehensive solutions.

Sheila Slaughter (1988) maintains that higher education, instead of providing leadership in educational opportunity that furthers our goal of an equitable society, is sandwiched between competing groups seeking to use higher-education resources in very different ways. There are those who envision higher education as a means of ensuring international competitiveness and military strength and those who envision higher education as a means through which to obtain greater equality, economic security, and social control. Slaughter explores the impact of this struggle on academic freedom and concludes that this freedom is endangered by being grounded in an outdated theory of knowledge. The resource allocation that drives the theoretical work of our universities is limiting some areas of academic inquiry and enlarging others. Slaughter takes this resource limitation to be a compromising of professional autonomy because the limitations are felt in some academic arenas but not others. Specifically, academic work that is not in support of private business interests is at risk. This happens to be the academic work in which one is most likely to find women and minorities, such as publicly funded social service areas. The arena of private business interests, on the other hand, is dominated by white men.

Stanley Aronowitz and Henry Giroux (1985) point out that even the 1960s commitment to open admission failed to democratize education through the disintegration of the higher-education hierarchy. They characterize conservative educational thinkers as focused on economic rather than social concerns: the kind of schooling that will produce workers for jobs rather than an educational enterprise that leads to social equality. They see the conservative emphasis on quality as an effort to reinforce authoritarianism in the schools and contend that conservatives are not justified in their simple assertion of the desirability of standards. They also describe the conservative agenda as seeking to justify education only in terms of economics:

> Educational conservatives have echoed the demand that school knowledge be relevant to students' lives. But they wish to subordinate educational priorities to those of the corporate order on the grounds that this is the relevant social and economic effect of knowledge. (p. 10)

Aronowitz and Giroux urge some alternative thinking about education. They ask us to begin with identifying the purposes we want education to serve. We then need to move to reconsideration of the social and ideological roles of educators. Aronowitz and Giroux seek educators perceived as intellectuals: mediators and producers of ideas who perform a pedagogical function that is political in nature. They argue for multifaceted education leading to autonomy and creativity. This is accomplished in part through stressing the centrality of curriculum and a dedication to promoting critical citizenship and civic courage. Aronowitz and Giroux also ask us to consider a middle group between those (generally conservative) who see education as transmitting high culture and those (generally radical) who see education as needing to transmit popular culture. They urge us to consider curricula forms that deal with both dominant and subordinate cultures. Aronowitz and Giroux are anxious that schools be more than sites of information transmission. Schools should be seen "as active sites of interventions and struggle" (p. 215). Schools are to be engaged in constant redefinition of the norms of literacy and the content of curricula: this means a reconsideration of the role of teachers and administrators.

Bastian and her colleagues (1986) urged that we focus on what they call "democratic schooling." They view the current state of educational inadequacy as a failure that disproportionately affects the poor and minorities, a circumstance not unique to the late twentieth century. The improvement of education will not take place through focus only on students and the creation of more rigorous demands in a competitive environment. Rather, they stress many more factors need to be considered in analyzing educational effectiveness: the school environment, teachers, the community, and governmental responsibility. The authors maintain that each of these elements has a role to play in improving education:

> We have argued that improving instruction for all students involves creating more supportive, flexible, and collaborative school environments and enlarging the commitment to equality of results. Achieving these improvements is primarily a matter of political choices and priorities rather than a problem of technique. (p. 92)

"Democratic schooling" can be described in terms of those practices its advocates oppose and in terms of those practices its advocates find desirable. The concept of democratic schooling specifically rejects the fundamental features of the conservative agenda for schools. It opposes standardization, regimentation, and competitiveness as values that will produce educational success. The argument behind democratic schooling is that schools perpetuate our economic stratification and fail to provide individual mobility. Further, advocates of democratic schooling assert that it is misleading to maintain that schools will drive our future economic well-being as justification for competitive school practices. They urge that equality and quality are not mutually exclusive. Meritocratic practices, they also contend, focus only on student limitations. Proponents of democratic schooling object to the narrow focus of conservatives who maintain that if education is ineffective, it is essentially the student who needs to change.

Advocates of democratic schooling maintain that we should focus particular attention on school improvement for low-income and minority students. The reforms of the 1960s and 1970s produced some gains for these populations, but not enough to significantly deal with unequal education made available to them. We should be attentive to those deficiencies of school culture, funding, and community involvement that produce inferior education. In this context, democratic-schooling advocates urge collaboration among teachers, school administrators, parents, and the community in attempting to improve schools. They point to recent findings concerning the importance of the school culture, of parental involvement, and of teacher-classroom autonomy and flexibility. They stress the importance of educational excellence but urge that there are a variety of ways to measure student performance. They are emphatic in their contention that the schools belong to the community and require significant community involvement and leadership. These advocates also prefer not to endorse any single system or educational paradigm. Rather, they are more comfortable in calling attention to general conditions that need to prevail in order for our schools to improve based on two criteria: the need to enhance student capacity to think critically and acquire social knowledge and the need to provide low-income and minority students with decent schools and skills. They understand educational excellence and quality but disagree with conservative approaches toward realizing these goals. They urge attention to not only pedagogical issues but also to the politics and structures of our schools and of our communities. They stress, again and again, that the reforms of the 1960s and 1970s constituted only a bare beginning for needed changes, in part because such attempts at reform have never been adequately funded or supported.

Curricular Transformations:
Traditional and
Emerging Voices in the Academy

Jennifer Grant Haworth and Clifton F. Conrad

The purpose, content, and meaning of the undergraduate curriculum has been vigorously debated throughout the history of American higher education. From the antebellum debates over the classical curriculum at Yale and William and Mary to the biting critiques recently leveled against "relativism" in higher education (Bloom, 1987), the undergraduate curriculum has served as an historic theater for defining, producing, and legitimating knowledge. In the past decade, the curriculum has been enacted by a wide range of actors who hold a vital stake in higher education—including academics, policy-makers, students, and representatives of the business community (Conrad, 1989). Their perspectives have focused on both a reassertion—and a reexamination—of the centrality of the traditional canon in the undergraduate curriculum. This dynamic interplay between traditional and emerging stakeholder voices has recently contributed to an intriguing transformation of the American undergraduate curriculum.

By curricular transformation, we are referring to those informal and formal procedures through which knowledge within the curriculum is continually produced, created, and expanded by a wide range of stakeholders acting within a broader social and historical context. The recent introduction—and, in numerous cases, incorporation—of emerging modes of inquiry, perspectives, and pedagogical techniques into the undergraduate curriculum suggests that the purpose, content, and meaning of the undergraduate curriculum is in the midst of major reexamination and change. In this essay, we reflect on the various forces transforming the undergraduate curriculum across three lines of inquiry. First, we explore the contemporary context and discuss four informing forces that have catalyzed recent developments in the undergraduate curriculum. Second, given this contextual background, we discuss the knowledge claims recently articulated by two broad groups of stakeholders and examine their consequences for the undergraduate curriculum. In our final section, we investigate how new knowledge claims are being legitimated by stakeholders within the academy and illustrate how this development has led to a transformation of the undergraduate curriculum.

I. The Contemporary Context

In his inaugural presidential address at Harvard in 1869, Charles William Eliot suggested that "the institutions of higher education . . . are always a faithful mirror in which are sharply reflected the national history and character" (Rudolph, 1977, p. 5). From the colonial colleges and land-grant colleges to the movement for equality of educational opportunity during the last three decades, American institutions of higher learning have actively responded to the prevailing trends and social values of the day. Three broad societal changes and one significant change within academe have acted as powerful informing forces on the recent development of the undergraduate curriculum.

Changing Demographics

The ethnic composition of American society has diversified markedly over the past decade, a trend that is expected to continue well into the twenty-first century. By 1996, for example, it is expected that one out of every three 15-24 year olds will be a member of a minority group. The percentage of non-minority white youth aged 15-24 is expected to decline by 12 percent while the number of Hispanic youth aged 15-24 is expected to increase by 44 percent (Wetzel, 1987).

This increasing diversity is reflected in college and university enrollments. Since 1980, there has been a richer blend of age, race, and ethnic backgrounds among college and university students than ever before in American higher education. Between 1978 and 1989, the number of adult students (aged 25 years and older) attending college increased by approximately 24 percent, whereas the number of traditional age college students (18-24 years) grew by only 7 percent over the same time period (NCES, 1989). Similarly, the number of women enrolling in postsecondary education increased 26 percent between 1978 and 1989 (NCES, 1989).

Minority enrollment in higher education has also increased over the past decade. Based on data from the National Center for Education Statistics, approximately 18 percent of all college and university students represented minority groups in 1988, an increase from 16 percent in 1980. This increase occurred, despite the drop in black student enrollment from 9.2 percent in 1980 to 8.7 percent in 1988, because Hispanic and Asian/Pacific Islander student enrollments increased notably over the past ten years (NCES, 1989). Although the modest gains in minority student enrollment are troublesome, four out of every five institutions report that they are currently involved in activities designed to increase minority enrollment and retention (El-Khawas, 1989).

Traditionalist Educational Policy Agenda

With the publication of *A Nation At Risk* in 1983, the first indication of an impending traditionalist policy agenda was recognized on American college and university campuses. Under the bully-pulpit political leadership of then Secretary of Education William Bennett, calls for a return to the fundamentals of the higher learning were stressed by both the popular press and many academics. These fundamentals included greater attention on basic skills acquistion, a renewed emphasis on studying the humanities and the great books of Western civilization, and stronger calls for assessing student learning and development.

The back-to-basics movement in higher education has experienced a revival of interest over the past decade. A number of educational reform reports have suggested that colleges and universities must pay greater attention to strengthening basic writing, mathematics, communication, and logical reasoning skills among undergraduate students (NIE, 1984; AAC, 1985; Boyer, 1987). This renewed emphasis on basic skills appears to have been precipitated by studies indicating the academic underpreparedness of today's college-aged youth. According to one recent study of 250 four-year institutions, one out of every seven freshman students was in need of remedial coursework in English or mathematics (Roueche, Baker, and Roueche, 1985). In response to this growing concern, a large number of institutions have recently instituted mandatory basic skill assessments for students. A 1989 study of 366 two- and four-year institutions, for example, found that basic skills testing was firmly in place at 65 percent of all postsecondary institutions and that another 19 percent had initiated plans for testing (El-Khawas, 1989).

The reassertion of the intellectual and social value of the humanities and the traditional great books canon has likewise found expression on college and university campuses across the nation. Initially promoted by Bennett (1984), Allan Bloom (1987) and E.D. Hirsch (1987) have recently penned best-selling volumes that have argued for the inherent worth of the humanities as a course of study—and the great books as the preferred curriculum—in undergraduate education. Colleges and universities have responded to this call: in 1986, 42 percent of universities, and 35 percent of four-year colleges required that original texts be used in their humanities courses (El-Khawas, 1986).

The call for accountability has likewise spread across American colleges and universities. In the mid 1980s, several national reform reports—including those by the National Institute of Education (1984) and the Association of American Colleges (1985)—recommended that colleges and universities implement systematic student assessment programs to monitor and track student learning outcomes. According to a 1989 American Council of Education survey of 366 two- and four-year postsecondary institutions, approximately 70 percent of the surveyed colleges and universities had institutionalized some form of assessment activity (El-Khawas, 1989). For the most part, these assessments have targeted basic skills (65 percent), higher order thinking skills (25 percent), general education (25 percent), and major subject content areas (26 percent) in the undergraduate curriculum (El-Khawas, 1989).

Increasingly Pluralistic Environment

Over the past fifteen years, an increasingly pluralistic environment has emerged both within and outside of the academy. Grounded in societal demographic changes, the international trend toward a global economic marketplace, and the growing environmental recognition of the world as a global village, pluralistic perspectives have surfaced in the American undergraduate curricular landscape in the form of global, gender, and ethnic studies courses.

A number of stakeholders have recently given voice to this pluralistic perspective. In their reform reports, the Association of American Colleges (1980 and 1988) became one of the first major groups to call for the inclusion of multicultural and global perspectives into the undergraduate curriculum: "The first curricular priority is to implant a strong international dimension into the core of general education requirements. The curriculum should be expanded to introduce students particularly to non-Western cultures" (AAC, 1980, p. 4). Several government agencies and private foundations—including the Fund for the Improvement of Postsecondary Education (FIPSE), the Lilly Endowment, and the Andrew W. Mellon Foundation—have provided funding for implementing global, gender, and ethnic studies into the undergraduate curriculum. The entrance of greater numbers of women and minorities into the professoriate has likewise advanced both feminist and multicultural world views.

These pluralistically-inspired courses and program innovations are generally characterized by both a high degree of interdisciplinarity and the use of perspectives and texts not traditionally represented in the Western civilization canon. Pluralists and educational traditionalists have recently locked horns over the legitimacy of representing multiple world views in the undergraduate curriculum. This debate has been most recently illustrated by the curriculum revision projects at the University of California-Berkeley and Stanford University, where both universities have recently revised their general education requirements to include pluralistic perspectives (Mooney, 1988).

Competing Perspectives in the Academy

The recent dynamic interplay between traditionalist and pluralistic perspectives has generated a spectrum of colorful debates among scholars in academe. The anthropologist Renato Rosaldo has used a militaristic metaphor to describe the recent debate as a "raging battle" where the epithet was the weapon of choice: "Name calling has pitted 'objectivists' against 'relativists,' 'presentists' against 'historicists,' and 'foundationalists' against 'interpretivists'" (Rosaldo, 1989, p. 219). Not unlike the debates at the turn of the century between scientists and liberal humanists, this recent exchange over the legitimacy of competing epistemologies, modes of inquiry, and perspectives appears to cut both across—and within—disciplines and professional fields.

This "raging battle" has largely centered on the validity of the traditional, postivist approach to scholarly inquiry. A growing number of scholars have recently objected to the epistemological view that truth is objective and exists "out there" to be discovered through value-free, neutral, scientific methods (Lincoln and Guba, 1985). The emergence of diverse new perspectives—including interpretivism, feminism, multiculturalism and critical theory—has offered competing epistemologies where truth is viewed as subjective and existing, at least in part, within the realm of an individual's personal and cultural experiences. Because of the constructed nature of knowledge, these scholars argue that new modes of inquiry—such as oral history, ethnography, hermeneutics, and the greater use of interdisciplinary and comparative studies—must be used to achieve not only a critical understanding of their own disciplines, but of the world as well.

As the formal medium for communicating knowledge within the university, the curriculum is heavily influenced by the prevailing events, values, and beliefs of the society in which it is situated. In the past ten years, three broad societal changes—the increasing cultural diversity of American society, the resurgence of traditionalist values and attitudes, and the fuller recognition of pluralistic perspectives—as well as the internal conflict over epistemologies and modes of inquiry within academe, have acted to transform the undergraduate curriculum. These contemporary developments have been facilitated by a diverse group of stakeholders holding multiple perspectives for the purpose, content, and meaning of the undergraduate curriculum. As our next two sections will suggest, these perspectives have contributed to fundamental changes in the undergraduate curriculum.

II. Stakeholder Knowledge Claims on the Undergraduate Curriculum

There have been few periods in the history of American higher education when the purpose, content, and meaning of the undergraduate curriculum has been debated as vigorously or as publicly as in the decade of the 1980s. One diverse group has provided high-pitched critiques of American education, arguing that dramatic changes are needed to revitalize the collegiate curriculum. Their proposals have included pleas for reclaiming the national legacy (Bennett, 1984), restoring curricular integrity (AAC, 1985), re-opening the American mind (Bloom, 1987), and ensuring the cultural literacy of our youth (Hirsch, 1987). A second, highly diversified stakeholder group has argued that the current curriculum is narrowly defined by a myopic world view that has minimized the knowledge claims of various groups, including women, minorities, and non-Western authors (see, for example, McIntosh, 1981; Schuster and Van Dyne, 1984; Andersen, 1987; Rosaldo, 1989; Tierney, 1989b). The diversity and vitality of perspectives generated by these two stakeholder groups has drawn national attention to the purpose and substance of the undergraduate curriculum in our nation's colleges and universities. In this section, we discuss the knowledge claims recently articulated by these two stakeholder groups and briefly examine their consequences for the undergraduate curriculum.

Stakeholder Knowledge Claims: Traditional Voices

As noted above, several individuals (Bennett, 1984; Bloom, 1987; Hirsch, 1987; Cheney, 1989) have recently published policy reports and national best-selling books calling for the revitalization of the undergraduate curriculum. Presenting what is widely considered a traditionalist agenda for curricular reform, these stakeholders have argued that the curriculum has become watered down by "relativistic" points of view, becoming little more than a "supermarket" of electives where the central role of the "humanities has been siphoned off, diluted, or so adulterated that students graduating know little of their heritage" (Bennett, 1984, p. 5). These stakeholders have called for a reinstatement of the liberal arts course of study and the traditional great books canon as two mandatory steps toward restoring the educational integrity of the undergraduate curriculum.

From an epistemological perspective, these "traditional voices" are firmly rooted within a particular view of knowledge—logical positivism—that has been the predominant mode of inquiry within the academy since the beginning of the American research university in the late nineteenth century. This epistemology assumes that knowledge exists "out there" and can be discovered through objective and empirical means. From this perspective, knowledge is viewed as a series of lawlike, absolute, universal truths that exist independent of, and external to, the knower. The scholar's task is to act as a detached observer in the pursuit of truth and knowledge.

This guiding epistemology is revealed in the traditionalist's knowledge claims concerning the purpose and content of—and, to a lesser degree, the pedagogy within—the undergraduate curriculum. Believing that the kinds of "knowledge most worth knowing" in a Western, democratic society are based in those universal truths of Western civilization that have endured the test of time, traditionalists argue that the purpose of the undergraduate experience is to expose students to the time-honored truths of their society. For many in this group, these truths are best revealed in the humanities:

> I would describe the humanities as the best that has been said, thought, written, and otherwise expressed about the human experience. The humanities tell us how men and women of our own and other civilizations have grappled with life's enduring questions: What is justice? What should be loved? What deserves to be defended? ... We should want all students to know a common culture rooted in civilization's lasting vision, its highest shared ideals and aspirations, and its heritage (Bennett, 1984, p. 6).

Many traditionalists further argue that if students are to learn the truths of their common culture, the university must provide programs based upon the "judicious use of great texts" (Blooom, 1987, p. 344) which provoke:

> Awareness of the classic—particularly important for our innocents; an acquaintance with what big questions were when there were still big questions; models, at the very least, of how to go about answering them; and, perhaps, most important of all, a fund of shared experiences and thoughts on which to ground their friendships with one another (Bloom, 1987, p. 344).

These "great texts," according to traditionalist reformers, "embody the best in our culture ... no student citizen should be denied access to the best that tradition has to offer" (Bennett, 1984, p. 29).

Without these fundamental truths, traditionalists maintain that students will lack the requisite knowledge needed to be productive and informed citizens in American society. Diane Ravitch has argued that "students cannot learn to ask critical questions or to think conceptually about the past or about their own lives as political actors unless they have sufficient background knowledge" (1988, p. 129). Through the study of the humanities and the great thinkers of the past, the traditionalist-crafted undergraduate experience is designed to provide students with the requisite "background knowledge" in order to live wisely and well.

The traditionalists' pedagogical approach is likewise deeply rooted within their epistemology. In her discussion of teaching in the undergraduate core curriculum, Lynne Cheney references the pedagogical wisdom of the *Yale Report of 1828*:

> "The two great points to be gained in intellectual culture," an 1828 report from Yale University noted, "are the *discipline* and the *furniture* [her italics] of the mind; expanding its powers, and storing it with knowledge" (1989, p. 14).

When knowledge is viewed as a series of absolute and universal truths that exist independent of, and external to, the knower, the teacher is viewed as a kind of sage whose task is to impart these universal truths to students neutrally. Given that the aim of a college education is to exercise, condition, and strengthen the intellect, the pedagogical element of the traditionalist's epistemology becomes important only insofar as it more fully engages students in the content of their inquiry.

Traditionalist knowledge claims have contributed significantly to the growing conservative policy agenda that has swept over American education during the past ten years. Their influence over the purpose and content of the undergraduate curriculum has been apparent in a number of areas, including recent movements to increase the amount of general education required by undergraduates, the fuller integration of liberal education into professional undergraduate education programs, as well as the new emphases placed on basic skills, humanities, and great books instruction (Conrad and Haworth, forthcoming). Ironically, perhaps the most instrumental goal of the traditionalists—to establish interdisciplinary core curricula—has not experienced much success. According to a recent survey of 284 four-year institutions, only 2 percent had implemented an interdisciplinary core curriculum for their general education program (Locke, 1989).

Although some recent reform reports, such as Bennett's *To Reclaim a Legacy* and Cheney's *50 Hours,* have recommended that universities select their "most distinguished faculty" to teach core courses, traditional stakeholder perspectives have generally made few recommendations to improve pedagogical practices within the undergraduate curriculum. An exception is the recent AAC report, which includes substantive pedagogical suggestions for "reorienting teaching" that go beyond content issues and address the process of teaching (AAC, 1988). Specifically, the report encourages active student learning through an improved understanding of how students "hear, understand, interpret, and integrate ideas" (AAC, 1988, p. 28) and suggests that teachers enlist their students as "coinquirers" in the learning process.

Stakeholder Knowledge Claims: Emerging Voices

A chorus of new voices has recently been heard in the academy. These stakeholders—although expressing diverse points-of-view—have shared a single perspective in common: the belief that knowledge, as it is currently understood in the undergraduate curriculum, is partial, incomplete, and distorted. Calling for an end to the exclusive dominance of the traditional canon in the undergraduate curriculum, these scholars have argued for an expansion of curricular borders in higher education to include various cultural and theoretical perspectives.

While highly diverse in their own scholarly visions, these new voices share the view that knowledge, at least in large part, is a social construct. This perspective is directly antithetical to the traditionalists' epistemology that knowledge is an objective entity that exists "out there," external to, and independent of, the knower. By contrast, in this other, more contingent approach to knowledge, the interaction between the individual and his or her cultural context is critical to the construction of what is—or is not—considered knowledge. As William Tierney has described it, this epistemological view ". . . assumes that reality is defined though a process of social interchange that cannot be readily mapped, graphed, or controlled" (1989b, p. 43). Rather than employ "one single, simple, unilateral rationality," this epistomological perspective maintains that "there are many rationalities" which are contingent upon "the mores of the enterprise, the individuals involved in the organization, and the socio-historical context in which the organization resides" (Tierney, 1989b, p. 43). Given the belief that knowledge is socially constructed, the scholar's task is to articulate these "multiple constructed realities" (Berger and Luckmann, 1973), not through a detached, neutral stance but, instead, through reflexive inquiry that recognizes the dynamic interplay between the researched and the researcher (Rosaldo, 1989).

An array of emerging knowledge claims regarding content and process in the undergraduate curriculum have been expressed recently by these stakeholders. Firmly rooted within the epistomological assumption that there is no one single objective truth, these stakeholders have proposed that the purpose of an undergraduate education should be, in the words of Nannerl Keohane, president of Wellesley College, not to "reclaim a legacy . . . but to build upon it for a fuller understanding of the works of human beings in the present and the future" (1986, p. 88). To achieve this purpose, the traditional canon must be expanded to include a balanced view of multiple—rather than a single—knowledge perspectives. As Renato Rosaldo has explained it, the traditional canon as a "classic norm should become one mode of representation among others . . . allowing forms of writing that have been marginalized or banned altogether to gain legitimacy" within the curriculum (1989, p. 62).

For these stakeholders, newly emerging knowledge claims from interpretivist, feminist, critical theory, post-structuralist, and multicultural scholarship must be integrated into the curriculum to ensure a holistic undergraduate experience for students (see, for example, McIntosh, 1981; Lather, 1984; Andersen, 1987; Conrad, 1989; Rosaldo, 1989; Tierney, 1989b). The study of these diverse perspectives, these stakeholders suggest, enriches students with a broader context in which to place their own personal experiences and root their future inquiries. Likewise, the incorporation of new inquiry and theoretical perspectives into the curriculum provides new vistas from which both students and scholars alike can explore familar and emerging topics.

With respect to pedagogy, this diverse group of stakeholders has offered a number of suggestions for strengthening the quality of instruction in the undergraduate curriculum. Based on the epistemological assumption that knowledge is largely a social construct rooted within the context of individual experience, these stakeholders view the current traditionalist approach to education as inherently limited. One critical theorist, Paulo Freire, has likened the traditional educational approach to banking, where the role of the teacher is to deposit objective, "universal truths" into student minds (Freire, 1971). The problems with this approach, these stakeholders argue, are twofold: first, teachers assume that there is a universal canon of thought to be taught; and second, because a predefined school of knowledge is available, teaching is often little more than a one-way transaction where teachers neutrally deposit knowledge into student "savings accounts." This banking approach "anesthetizes" and "attempts to maintain the submersion of consciousness" in students (Freire, 1971, p. 68).

Feminists and critical theorists, by contrast, do not view knowledge as static and objective. Consonant with their view of knowledge as a social construct, they argue that teachers may be better viewed as midwives than as bankers:

> Midwife-teachers are the opposite of banker-teachers. While the bankers deposit knowl-edge in the learner's head, the midwives draw it out. They assist the students in giving birth to their own ideas, in making their own tacit knowledge explicit and elaborating it . . . they assist in the emergence of consciousness (Belenky, Clinchy, Goldberger, and Tarule, 1986, pp. 217–218).

The role of the teacher in this pedagogical model is to help students unearth their own experiences within the context of the studied material and, within this process, to empower students to recognize their own abilities and to discover their individual "voice" (Shrewsbury, 1987). This pedagogical view suggests that knowledge is not the exclusive property of the teacher whose role is to dole it out to his or her students, but rather an interaction between student and teacher where both equally participate in the "pedagogic struggle to expose the underpinnings of that which is learned" (Tierney, 1989a).

The knowledge claims recently articulated by feminist, critical theorist, and multiculturalist stakeholders have contributed significantly to the growing acceptance of pluralistic points-of-view both within and outside of the academy. The influence of these perspectives over the purpose and content of the undergraduate curriculum has become increasingly apparent in the recent trend to integrate feminist, critical theory, and multicultural perspectives into general education progams previously dominated by the traditional canon of thought and in the rapid expansion of women's and ethnic studies departments and courses across the country (Conrad and Haworth, forthcoming). In addition, a significant number of institutions have recently implemented faculty development programs targeted at integrating many of these emerging theoretical and pedagogical perspectives into the undergraduate curriculum (AAC, 1981; Hoffman, 1986; Conrad and Haworth, forthcoming).

In the past decade, two diverse groups of stakeholders—each subscribing to different episte-mologies—have advanced separate knowledge claims in the undergraduate curriculum. The lively exchange between these two groups has resurrected the continual question of "what knowledge is most worth knowing." Although the consequences of this debate have been visibly evidenced in changes in the content and structure of the undergraduate curriculum, this funda-mental questioning of what counts as knowledge has also yielded an increasingly visible con-sciousness of alternative knowledge perspectives among scholars in the academy. It is at this juncture, perhaps, where Jose Ortega y Gasset's observation may offer a useful starting point for grappling with competing stakeholder knowledge claims in the undergraduate curriculum:

"Reality happens to be, like a landscape possessed of an infinite number of perspectives, all equally veracious and authentic. The sole false perspective is that which claims to be the only one there is" (cited in Conrad, 1989, p. 215)

III. Stakeholder Knowledge Claims and Curricular Transformations

Between 1983 and 1987, 95 percent of American colleges and universities were either currently reviewing their undergraduate curriculum or had completed fundamental revisions of their undergraduate program (El-Khawas, 1987). This latest revisiting of the purpose and content of the undergraduate curriculum lends credibility to the epistemological position that what is defined as (valued) knowledge in the university changes with different cultural and historical contexts. During the 1980s demographic, traditionalist, and pluralistic societal demands have had an influential effect on the contour and texture of the undergraduate curriculum. It appears that what Frederick Rudolph noted about the curriculum almost fifteen years ago remains true today: "Curricular history is American history and therefore carries the burden of revealing the central purpose and driving directions of American society" (1977, p. 20).

The recent clashes between stakeholders voicing traditional and emerging knowledge claims have likewise provoked a fundamental reexamination of how knowledge is defined, approached, and taught within the academy. As faculty have published articles in scholarly journals, presented papers at professional conferences, and restructured their courses around alternate perspectives and modes of inquiry—such as feminism, critical theory, and multiculturalism—the academic community has responded vigorously to their tentative knowledge claims. The recognition, acceptance—and in many disciplines, the legitimation—of these knowledge claims has led to a significant transformation that has expanded the traditionally-defined canon to include a diversity of new theoretical and pedagogical perspectives. In this section, we examine how stakeholders have facilitated this transformation through the integration of these new knowledge claims into both their research and classroom activities.

Integration of Emerging Knowledge Claims in Disciplinary Scholarship

A merging of the old with the new has generated a fascinating mixture of theoretical perspectives within the traditional arts and science disciplines. Catalyzed by a number of faculty and student-driven initiatives—including newly formed interests in exploring traditionally unstudied populations, re-examining old questions from alternate viewpoints, and utilizing interdisciplinary perspectives in scholarly research—feminist, critical theory, and multicultural perspectives have recently entered the mainstream of scholarly activity in the academy. Each of these perspectives and accompanying modes of inquiry is premised on the epistemological view that knowledge is socially constructed within a cultural and historical context.

Feminist thought has generated widespread influence in a number of traditional social science and humanities disciplines, including psychology, sociology, anthropology, economics, history, and English. Although there are many variations of feminist thought (e.g., radical feminism, liberal feminism, neo-Marxist feminism, black feminism), most are firmly grounded in the belief that knowledge is a social construction. As Margaret Andersen explains:

> Including women refers to the complex process of redefining knowledge by making women's experiences a primary subject for knowledge, conceptualizing women as active agents in the creation of knowledge, looking at gender as fundamental to the articulation of knowledge in Western thought, and seeing women's and men's experiences in relation to the sex/gender system (1987, pp. 224–225).

Within disciplines, feminist research has helped scholars to articulate new meanings in familiar topics. For instance, in anthropology, the study of kinship systems has come to include an examination of gender issues (Coughlin, 1987a, p. A12). In history, scholars have not only begun to focus on the influence of women in the historical process, but have also questioned the legitimacy of traditional historical narratives that have been constructed almost exclusively on the historical accounts of heroic white males (Andersen, 1987). The influence of feminist research in psychology has virtually created a subdiscipline in the psychology of women. Among other things, research in this area has identified how women and men often view reality from contrasting epistemological perspectives (Gilligan, 1982; Belenky, Clinchy, Goldberger, and Tarule, 1986). Sociologists have recently begun to explore the gender-structuring of organizations, the economy, and the workplace (Coughlin, 1987a). And feminist research in economics has investigated the economic relationship between public and private markets, suggesting that household work has a significant economic dimension (Andersen, 1987).

The impact of feminist scholarship has also been felt within the literary disciplines. For instance, in addition to studying works by female authors, literature scholars have begun to investigate why thousands of novels by American women have been excluded from the traditional canon of literary classics (McIntosh, 1981). One scholar has suggested that "reentering knowledge within the experience of women unmasks the invisible paradigms that guide the curriculum and raises questions that require scholars to take a comprehensive and critical look at their fields" (Andersen, 1987, p. 237). If this brief sketch is any indication, it appears that the acceptance of feminist perspectives by social science and humanities scholars has led to the revisiting of such traditional cornerstones as historical periodization, political hierarchies, public sphere economics, sex-role behaviors, and literary canonization.

Critical theory has likewise influenced the development of scholarship in the social sciences and humanities. Critical theory, like feminism, has many variations, but all are tied together by a general critique of the functionalist characteristic of positivist thought. As Henry Giroux explains:

> Critical theory [is] tied to a specific interst in the development of a society without injustice. Theory, in this case, becomes a transformative activity that views itself as explicitly political and commits itself to the projection of a future that is as yet unfulfilled . . . Rather than proclaiming a [functionalist] notion of neutrality, critical theory openly takes sides in the interest of struggling for a better world (cited in Tierney, 1989b, p. 40).

Critical scholarship has become an identifiable feature across the disciplinary landscapes of sociology, economics, political science, history, literature, law, education, women's studies, and ethnic studies. For example, in sociology and economics, scholars have begun to redefine the concept of class in terms of cultural and political variables (Winkler, 1986). In political science, scholars are questioning if political power elites mechanically mirror economic interests or if other cultural explanations may be insightful in explaining power within a given society (Winkler, 1986). In recent years, literary critical theorists have incorporated post-structuralist and psychoanalytic insights into their interpretations in an attempt to understand how "capitalism affects cultural life and human consciousness" (Winkler, 1987). Critical theory has also influenced legal scholars, who have investigated how notions of class influence the development of legal decisions (Winkler, 1986). In education, critical theory has examined how the curriculum is shaped by cultural and political factors (Tierney, 1989a). More recently, many critical theorists have begun to incorporate other non-traditionalist oriented theoretical perspectives into their scholarship, including post-structuralism, feminism, psychoanalysis, and neoclassical economics (Winkler, 1986).

Just as scholars have embraced feminist and critical theories within their disciplines, many have likewise extended their inquiry to include multicultural perspectives. Rooted as well in the epistemological view that knowledge is socially constructed, multiculturalists seek to understand how meaning is constructed within a specific cultural context. This approach stands in stark contrast to traditional structural-functional approaches which have attempted to explain cultural differences through a Eurocentric lens. In the discipline of black studies, for example, one recent multiculturalist perspective—Afrocentricity—has sought to understand the experiences of blacks around the world as an extension of African history and culture (Coughlin, 1987b). Some historians have criticized the "one-shot approach" to studying minorities in American history and have, instead, adopted multicultural approaches in their research of Hispanics, blacks, Asian-Americans, and American Indians (Winkler, 1986). In sociology, scholars have begun to expand their scope of inquiry to include a new emphasis on cross-national research (Winkler, 1989). In anthropology, a reverse trend has occured where scholars have become increasingly interested in the study of American society and its many diverse subcultures (Coughlin, 1987a). And, within the literary disciplines, the study of minority and non-Western authors has gained increasing interest over the past decade.

These three perspectives and modes of inquiry—feminism, critical theory, and multiculturalism—have had a profound impact on faculty scholarship in the social sciences and humanities. Tierney has noted that "theory acts as a filter through which we define problems and read answers so that we come to terms with the internal logic of different cultures" (1989b, p. 45). These newly-emergent theoretical perspectives have provided faculty with alternate lenses for understanding how people make sense of reality in a complex, problematic, multicultural world. As faculty have incorporated these perspectives and modes of inquiry into their research, their underlying claim that knowledge is socially constructed has taken on greater legitimacy among scholars in the academy.

Integration of Emerging Knowledge Claims into Classroom Activities

As faculty have expanded their scholarly repertoire to include feminist, critical theory, and multicultural perspectives, they have likewise incorporated these new theoretical views into the undergraduate curriculum. With additional support from the public sector (e.g., private foundation and government agency officials) and from institutional-level and student stakeholders, a number of faculty-driven curricular projects designed to include interpretivist, feminist, critical theory, and multicultural perspectives have been recently integrated into the undergraduate experience at numerous colleges and universities across the country.

Although relatively recent in origin, these curriculum revision/expansion projects have found widespread support from a variety of private foundation and government agencies, including the Ford Foundation, the Andrew Mellon Foundation, the Mott Foundation, the Fund for the Improvement of Postsecondary Education (FIPSE) and the U.S. Office of Education Women's Educational Equity Act (WEEA) Program. In the ten year period between 1975 and 1985, approximately 80 curriculum integration projects were funded by these and other private and public sources; recent trends indicate that institutional support for these projects has increased over the past five years (Andersen, 1987). Similarly, the 48 Centers for Research on Women in the United States have received substantial funding from these stakeholder groups (Hoffman, 1986). These curriculum projects and research centers have sought both to expand the undergraduate curriculum to include feminist, critical theory, and multicultural perspectives and to model a pedagogy that encourages teachers and students to draw upon each other's experiences in the knowledge construction learning process (Hoffman, 1986).

A recent project funded through the New Jersey Department of Higher Education provides a telling indication of the growing support for incorporating diverse perspectives into the curriculum. Declaring 1987 the "inaugural year of integrating the scholarship of women" into the undergraduate curriculum, then New Jersey Governor Thomas Kean awarded $362,500 to the state's 56 public and private colleges for the "New Jersey Project: Integrating the Scholarship on Gender" (McMillen, 1987). The project is designed to provide an impetus to the state's colleges to "revise their courses to reflect a more balanced view of women, as well as minority groups" (McMillen, 1987). At Spelman College, a grant from the Mott Foundation provided funding for the first women's center at a traditionally black women's college. Their recent Ford Foundation funded project, "Integrating Black Women's Studies into the Liberal Arts Curriculum," has led to a fuller integration of race and gender issues in the undergraduate curriculum. Scores of other institutions have likewise received funding from private and public sources to integrate the emerging knowledge claims of women, minorities, and non-Western cultures into undergraduate courses (McIntosh, 1981; AAC, 1981; Hoffman, 1986).

Institutional-level stakeholders have also supported a number of recent initiatives to integrate feminist, critical theory, and multicultural perspectives into the undergraduate curriculum. Primarily driven by student and faculty demands, these changes have been felt at both the institutional and departmental levels. For example, at the University of California-Berekely, where approximately one out of every two students is a member of a minority group, students have pressured faculty and administrators for a more culturally balanced curriculum (Mooney, 1988). Under mounting pressure from its minority student population, Stanford University's Faculty Senate recently replaced the university's year-long Western civilization requirement with a new multicultural general education sequence entitled "Culture, Ideas, and Values" (Mooney, 1988). The new program is designed to give "substantial attention" to race, gender, class, and multicultural perspectives. Similar institutional level efforts are underway at numerous colleges, including Hartwick College, which recently implemented a "gender-balanced" curriculum (Heller, 1988).

At the departmental level, many faculty have made attempts to integrate feminist, critical theory, and multicultural perspectives into their courses. In the area of women's studies alone, more than 500 programs and approximately 39,000 courses have been offered in American colleges and universities since 1970 (AAC, 1988). At Carnegie-Mellon University, English department faculty recently reoriented the focus of the department and created, in the words of the department chair, the "nation's first poststructuralist undergraduate curriculum" (Heller, 1988). At both the University of Illinois-Chicago and Brown University, faculty members have taken the study of socially constructed meanings seriously by introducing courses in hermeneutics and an undergraduate concentration in semiotics (Heller, 1988). And, in a recent development, Cultural Studies departments have begun to appear at institutions all across the country, often drawing upon the theoretical perspectives of feminism, poststructuralism, multiculturalism, and critical theory within their courses.

The anthropologist Clifford Geertz has suggested that the curriculum can be viewed as a cultural artifact of the knowledge valued by a single—or set of—institutions (1983). Patricia Gumport has further suggested that faculty members, as "mediators of intellectual ideas," validate and legitimate new knowledge claims through their activities within the university. As faculty begin to structure their activities around certain knowledge claims, they concurrently redefine what counts as legitimate knowledge within the university. In no small measure, faculty are encouraged to explore, examine, and integrate these knowledge claims into their scholarship and classroom activities vis-a-vis a larger stakeholder network—including public policymakers, institutional level administrators and students (Conrad, 1989).

Gumport (1988) has suggested that curricular change is rooted within "the cultural life of academic organizations in which faculty, adminstrators, and students construct and revise their understandings and in which they negotiate about what counts as valid knowledge in particular and historical settings" (1988, p. 50). Over the past decade, a variety of demographic, conservative, and pluralistic societal demands have helped to facilitate the debate between traditional and emerging knowledge claims in the undergraduate curriculum. As traditionalists have continued to argue for the legitimacy of objective, universal truths, other scholars have suggested that truth is neither universal or objective; rather, what is defined as truth is often the byproduct of a cultural social construction process. The result of this recent debate has been an intense interest on the part of a broad range of stakeholders—including faculty, policymakers, institutional administrators, the popular press, and students—in the legitimacy of competing knowledge claims within the university.

One higher education curriculum scholar recently argued that "history is an interaction between participants' lived internalized experiences, and the ideological momentum that becomes institutionalized over the passage of time" (Tierney, 1989b, p. 44). Recent events have witnessed a rapidly growing and widespread interest on the part of faculty, policymakers, institutional administrators, and students in the "tentative" knowledge claims of feminism, critical theory, and multiculturalism. Undergirding these alternate knowledge claims has been a new epistemology that views knowledge as a social construct. As more stakeholders have embraced this epistemological stance, the "tentative" knowledge claims of feminism, critical theory, and multiculturalism have been slowly acknowledged, integrated, and legitimated into these stakeholders' research and classroom activities. The consequence for the undergraduate curriculum has been a fascinating transformation where these knowledge claims have become recognized features on the undergraduate curricular landscape.

In a recent volume, Denise Shekerjian relates an interesting story about perspective that may be helpful in understanding the negotiation of knowledge in the curriculum:

> A story about Picasso tells of how when he was a schoolboy he was terrible at math because whenever the teacher had him write the number 4 on the blackboard, it looked like a nose to him and he'd keep doodling to fill in the rest of the face. Everyone else in the class saw a number on the blackboard; Picasso perceived a face (cited in the *Chronicle of Higher Education*, March 28, 1990, p. B3).

To recent scholars, the debate between traditional and emerging knowledge claims within the undergraduate curriculum has been viewed as a struggle for the prize of what knowledge is most worth knowing. Among others, Shekerjian has suggested that "creativity . . . requires something new, a different interpretation, a break from the twin opiates of habit and cliche" (*Chronicle*, 1990, p. B3) From our perspective, the introduction of new knowledge claims into the academy has provided stakeholders with a fresh perspective on how *we come to know what we know*. It is this development, we believe, which has at once energized and signalled a recent transformation in the undergraduate curriculum.

References

Andersen, M.L. (1987). "Changing the Curriculum in Higher Education." *Signs: Journal of Women in Culture and Society, 12* (2), 222–252.

Association of American Colleges. (1980). *Toward Education with a Global Perspective: A Report of the National Assembly on Foreign Language and International Studies*. Washington, D.C.: Association of American Colleges.

Association of American Colleges. (1981). "The Study of Women in the Liberal Arts Curriculum." *The Forum for Liberal Education, 4* (1), pp. 1–18.

Association of American Colleges. (1985). *Integrity in the College Curriculum: A Report to the Academic Community*. Washington, D.C.: Association of American Colleges.

Association of American Colleges. (1988). *A New Vitality in General Education: Planning, Teaching, and Supporting Effective Liberal Learning*. Washington, D.C.: Association of American Colleges.

Belenky, M.F.; Clinchy, B.M.; Goldberger, N.R.; & Tarule, J.M. (1986). *Women's Ways of Knowing: The Development of Self, Voice, and Mind*. New York: Basic Books.

Bennett, W.J. (1984). *To Reclaim A Legacy: A Report on the Humanities in Higher Education*. Washington, D.C.: National Endowment for the Humanities.

Berger, P.L., & Luckmann, T. (1973). *The Social Construction of Reality*. London: Penguin.

Bloom, A. (1987). *The Closing of the American Mind*. New York: Simon and Schuster.

Boyer, E.L. (1987). *College: The Undergraduate Experience in America*. New York: Harper and Row.

Cheney, L.V. (1989). *50 Hours: A Core Curriculum for College Students*. Washington, D.C.: National Endowment for the Humanities.

Conrad, C.F. (1989). "Meditations on the Ideology of Inquiry in Higher Education: Exposition, Critique, and Conjecture." *The Review of Higher Education, 12*, 199–220.

Conrad, C.F. & Haworth, J.G. (forthcoming). "Curriculum in Higher Education." In M.C. Alkin (Ed.), *The Encyclopedia of Educational Research (sixth edition)*. New York: Macmillan.

Coughlin, E.K. (1987a, September 2). "Humanities and Social Sciences: The Sound of Barriers Falling." *Chronicle of Higher Education*, pp. A6–A7, A10, A12.

Coughlin, E.K. (1987b, October 28). "Scholars Work to Refine Africa-centered View of the Life and History of Black Americans." *Chronicle of Higher Education*, pp. A6–A7, A12.

El-Khawas, E. (1986). *Campus Trends, 1986* (Higher Education Panel Reports Number 75). Washington, D.C.: American Council on Education.

El-Khawas, E. (1987). *Campus Trends, 1987* (Higher Education Panel Reports Number 76). Washington, D.C.: American Council on Education.

El-Khawas, E. (1989). *Campus Trends, 1989* (Higher Education Panel Reports Number 78). Washington, D.C.: American Council on Education.

Freire, P. (1971). *Pedagogy of the Oppressed*. New York: Seaview.

Geertz, C. (1983). *Local Knowledge: Further Essays in Interpretive Anthropology*. New York: Basic Books.

Gilligan, C. (1982). *In A Different Voice: Psychological Theory and Women's Development*. Cambridge, MA: Harvard University Press.

Gumport, P.J. (1988). "Curricula as Signposts of Cultural Change." *The Review of Higher Education*, 12, 4961.

Heller, S. (1988, August 3). "Some English Departments are Giving Undergraduates Grounding in New Literary and Critical Theory." *Chronicle of Higher Education*, pp. A15–A17.

Hirsch, E.D., Jr. (1987). *Cultural Literacy*. Boston: Houghton Mifflin.

Hoffman, N. (1986). "Black Studies, Ethnic Studies, and Women's Studies: Some Reflections on Collaborative Projects." *Women's Studies Quarterly*, 14, 4953.

Keohane, N.O. (1986, April 2). "Our Mission Should Not Be Merely to 'Reclaim' a Legacy of Scholarship—We Must Expand on It." *Chronicle of Higher Education*, p. 88.

Lather, P. (1984). "Critical Theory, Curricular Transformation, and Feminist Mainstreaming." *Journal of Education*, 166 (1), 49–62.

Lincoln, Y.S., & Guba, E.G. (1985). *Naturalistic Inquiry*. Beverly Hills: Sage.

Locke, L. (1989). "General Education: In Search of Facts." *Naturalistic Inquiry*, 21 (4), pp. 21–23.

McIntosh, P. (1981). "The Study of Women: Implications for Reconstructing the Liberal Arts Disciplines." *The Forum for Liberal Education*, 4 (1), pp. 13.

McMillen L. (1987, September 9). "More Colleges and More Disciplines Incorporating Scholarship on Women in the Classroom." *Chronicle of Higher Education*, pp. A16–A17.

Mooney, C.J. (1988, December 14). "Sweeping Curricular Change is Underway at Stanford as University Phases out Its 'Western Culture' Program." *Chronicle of Higher Education*, pp. A1, A11, A13.

National Center for Education Statistics. (1989). *Digest of Education Statistics, 1989*. Washington, D.C.: National Center for Education Statistics, Office of Educational Research and Improvement, U.S. Department of Education.

National Institute of Education. (1984). *Involvement in Learning: Realizing the Potential of American Higher Education*. Washington, D.C.: National Institute of Education.

Ravitch, D. (1988). "A Response to Michael Apple." *Teachers College Record*, 90 (1), 128–130.

Roueche, J.E.; Baker, G.A.; & Roueche, S.D. (1985). *College Responses to Low Achieving Students: A National Study*. Orlando, FL: Harcourt, Brace, Jovanovich.

Rosaldo, R. (1989). *Culture and Truth: The Remaking of Social Analysis*. Boston: Beacon.

Rudolph, F. (1977). *Curriculum: A History of the American Undergraduate Course of Study Since 1636*. San Francisco: Jossey-Bass and the Carnegie Foundation for the Advancement of Teaching.

Schuster, M., and Van Dyne, S. (1984). "Placing Women in the Liberal Arts: Stages of Curriculum Transformation." *Harvard Educational Review*, 54 (4), 413–428.

Shekerjian, D. (1990). "Uncommon Genius: How Great Ideas Are Born." *Chronicle of Higher Education*, March 28, 1990, p. B3.

Shrewsbury, C.M. (1987). "What is Feminist Pedagogy?" *Women's Studies Quarterly, 15* (3 & 4), 6–13.

Tierney, W.G. (1989a). "Cultural Politics and the Curriculum in Postsecondary Education." *Journal of Education*, forthcoming.

Tierney, W.G. (1989b). *Curricular Landscapes, Democratic Vistas: Transformative Leadership in Higher Education*. New York: Praeger.

Wetzel, J.R. (1987). *American Youth: A Statistical Snapshot*. New York: The William T. Grant Foundation.

Winkler, K. (1986, July 9). "Flourishing Research in Marxist Theory Belies Signs of Its Demise, Scholars Say." *Chronicle of Higher Education*, pp. 4–5, 7.

Winkler, K. (1987, November 25). "Post-structuralism: An Often-abstruse French Import Profoundly Affects Research in the United States." *Chronicle of Higher Education*, pp. A6–A9.

Winkler, K. (1989, January 11). "Dispute over Validity of Historical Approaches Pits Traditionalists against Advocates of New Methods." *Chronicle of Higher Education*, pp. A4–A5, A7.

To Reclaim a Legacy:
A Report on the Humanities in
Higher Education

William J. Bennett

Introduction

Although more than 50 percent of America's high school graduates continue their education at American colleges and universities, few of them can be said to receive there an adequate education in the culture and civilization of which they are members. Most of our college graduates remain shortchanged in the humanities—history literature, philosophy, and the ideals and practices of the past that have shaped the society they enter. The fault lies principally with those of us whose business it is to educate these students. We have blamed others, but the responsibility is ours. Not by our words but by our actions, by our indifference, and by our intellectual diffidence we have brought about this condition. It is we the educators—not scientists, business people, or the general public—who too often have given up the great task of transmitting a culture to its rightful heirs. Thus, what we have on many of our campuses is an unclaimed legacy, a course of studies in which the humanities have been siphoned off, diluted, or so adulterated that students graduate knowing little of their heritage.

In particular the study group was disturbed by a number of trends and developments in higher education:

- Many of our colleges and universities have lost a clear sense of the importance of the humanities and the purpose of education, allowing the thickness of their catalogues to substitute for vision and a philosophy of education.

- The humanities, and particularly the study of Western civilization, have lost their central place in the undergraduate curriculum. At best, they are but one subject among many that students might be exposed to before graduating. At worst, and too often, the humanities are virtually absent.

- A student can obtain a bachelor's degree from 75 percent of all American colleges and universities without having studied European history, from 72 percent without having studied American literature or history, and from 86 percent without having studied the civilizations of classical Greece and Rome.

- Fewer than half of all colleges and universities now require foreign language study for the bachelor's degree, down from nearly 90 percent in 1966.

- The sole acquaintance with the humanities for many undergraduates comes during their first two years of college, often in ways that discourage further study.

- The number of students choosing majors in the humanities has plummeted. Since 1970 the number of majors in English has declined by 57 percent, in philosophy by 41 percent, in history by 62 percent, and in modern languages by 50 percent.

- Too many students are graduating from American colleges and universities lacking even the most rudimentary knowledge about the history, literature, art, and philosophical foundations of their nation and their civilization.

- The decline in learning in the humanities was caused in part by a failure of nerve and faith on the part of many college faculties and administrators, and persists because of a vacuum in educational leadership. A recent study of college presidents found that only 2 percent are active in their institutions' academic affairs.

In order to reverse the decline, the study group recommended:

- The nation's colleges and universities must reshape their undergraduate curricula based on a clear vision of what constitutes an educated person, regardless of major, and on the study of history, philosophy, languages, and literature.

- College and university presidents must take responsibility for the educational needs of *all* students in their institutions by making plain what the institution stands for and what knowledge it regards as essential to a good education.

- Colleges and universities must reward excellent teaching in hiring, promotion, and tenure decisions.

- Faculties must put aside narrow departmentalism and instead work with administrators to shape a challenging curriculum with a core of common studies.

- Study of the humanities and Western civilization must take its place at the heart of the college curriculum.

Why Study the Humanities?

The federal legislation that established the National Endowment for the Humanities in 1965 defined the humanities as specific disciplines: "language, both modern and classical; linguistics; literature; history; jurisprudence; philosophy; archaeology; comparative religion; ethics; the history, criticism, and theory of the arts"; and "those aspects of the social sciences which have humanistic content and employ humanistic methods." But to define the humanities by itemizing the academic fields they embrace is to overlook the qualities that make them uniquely important and worth studying. Expanding on a phrase from Matthew Arnold, I would describe the humanities as the best that has been said, thought, written, and otherwise expressed about the human experience. The humanities tell us how men and women of our own and other civilizations have grappled with life's enduring, fundamental questions: What is justice? What should be loved? What deserves to be defended? What is courage? What is noble? What is base? Why do civilizations flourish? Why do they decline?

Kant defined the essence of the humanities in four questions: What can I know? What should I do? What may I hope for? What is man? These questions are not simply diversions for intellectuals or playthings for the idle. As a result of the ways in which these questions have been answered, civilizations have emerged, nations have developed, wars have been fought, and people have lived contentedly or miserably.

If ideas are important, it surely follows that learning and life are poorer without the humanities. Montaigne wrote:

A pupil should be taught what it means to know something, and what it means not to know it; what should be the design and end of study; what valor, temperance, and justice are; the difference between ambition and greed, loyalty and servitude, liberty and license; and the marks of true and solid contentment.

Further, the humanities can contribute to an informed sense of community by enabling us to learn about and become participants in a common culture, shareholders in our civilization. But our goal should be more than just a common culture—even television and the comics can give us that. We should, instead, want all students to know a common culture rooted in civilization's lasting vision, its highest shared ideals and aspirations, and its heritage. Professor E. D. Hirsch of the University of Virginia calls the beginning of this achievement "cultural literacy" and reminds us that "no culture exists that is ignorant of its own traditions." As the late philosopher Charles Frankel once said, it is through the humanities that a civilized society talks to itself about things that matter most.

How Should the Humanities Be Taught and Learned?

Mankind's answers to compelling questions are available to us through the written and spoken word—books, manuscripts, letters, plays, and oral traditions—and also in nonliterary forms, which John Ruskin called the book of art. Within them are expressions of human greatness and of pathos and tragedy. In order to tap the consciousness and memory of civilization, one must confront these texts and works of art.

The members of the study group discussed at length the most effective ways to teach the humanities to undergraduates. Our discussion returned continually to two basic prerequisites for learning in the humanities: good teaching and a good curriculum.

Good Teaching

Good teaching is at least as essential in the humanities as in other fields of learning. In this connection, it is critical to point out that of all undergraduate credit hours taken in the humanities, 87 percent are taken in the freshman and sophomore years. Because nonhumanities majors account for the largest part of these credit hours, courses taken at the introductory level are the first and only collegiate exposure to the humanities for many students. Therefore, we should want to extend to these students the most attractive invitation to the humanities possible. This requires teachers who can make the humanities live and who can guide students through the landscape of human thought.

Just as students can be drawn to the humanities by good teachers, they can be chased off by poor ones. "Students come to learning through their teachers," wrote Oberlin College Dean Robert Longsworth, "and no list of great works nor any set of curricular requirements can do the work of a good teacher." Although it can take many forms, we all know what poor teaching is. It can be lifeless or tendentious, mechanical or ideological. It can be lacking in conviction. Perhaps most commonly, it can fail to have a sense of the significance of the material it purports to study and teach. It can bore and deaden where it means to quicken and elevate. Giving one example, Harvard Professor David Riesman pointed out that poor teaching can masquerade as good teaching when it "invites students to join a club of sophisticated cynics who are witty, abrasive, and sometimes engrossing; many teachers in the humanities parade and glorify their eccentricities, and only on reflection and at some distance does one realize that they are really lifeless."

What characterizes good teaching in the humanities? First, and foremost, a teacher must have achieved mastery of the material. But this is not enough; there must also be engagement. Professor William Arrowsmith of Emory University described good teachers as "committed to teaching what they have learned to love." In one crucial way, good teachers cannot be dispassionate. They cannot be dispassionate about the works they teach—assuming that they are teaching important works. This does not mean they advocate each idea of every author, but rather that they are moved and are seen to be moved by the power of the works and are able to convey that power to their students. Just as good scholarship is inspired, so must good teaching be.

A Good Curriculum

If the teacher is the guide, the curriculum is the path. A good curriculum marks the points of significance so that the student does not wander aimlessly over the terrain dependent solely on chance to discover the landmarks of human achievement.

Colleges and universities have a responsibility to design general education curricula that identify these landmarks. David Savage of the *Los Angeles Times* expressed the consensus of the study group when he said: "Most students enter college expecting that the university and its leaders have a clear vision of what is worth knowing and what is important in our heritage that all educated persons should know. They also have a right to expect that the university sees itself as more than a catalogue of courses."

Although the study group embraced the principle that all institutions should accept responsibility for deciding what their graduates should know, most members believed that no single curriculum could be appropriate in all places. The study group recognized the diverse nature of higher education under whose umbrella are institutions with different histories philosophies, educational purposes, student body characteristics, and religious and cultural traditions. Each institution must decide for itself what it considers an educated person to be and what knowledge that person should possess. While doing so, no institution need act as if it were operating in a vacuum. There are standards of judgment: Some things are more important to know than others.

The choices a college or university makes for its common curriculum should be rooted firmly in its institutional identity and educational purpose. In successful institutions, an awareness of what the college or university is trying to do acts as a unifying principle, a thread that runs through and ties together the faculty, the curriculum, the students, and the administration. If an institution has no clearly conceived and articulated sense of itself, its efforts to design a curriculum will result in little more than an educational garage sale, possibly satisfying most campus factions but serving no real purpose and adding up to nothing of significance. Developing a common curriculum with the humanities at the core is no easy task. In some institutions, it will be difficult to attain. But merely being exposed to a variety of subjects and points of view is not enough. Learning to think critically and skeptically is not enough. Being well-rounded is not enough if, after all the sharp edges have been filed down, discernment is blunted and the graduate is left to believe without judgment, to decide without wisdom, or to act without standards.

The study group identified several features common to any good curriculum, regardless of institutional particulars:

(1) **Balance between breadth and depth.** A good curriculum should embody both wide reading and close reading. Students should study a number of important texts and subjects with thoroughness and care. They should also become acquainted with other texts and subjects capable of giving them a broader view, a context for understanding what they know well. Excessive concentration in one area however, often abetted by narrow departmentalism, can promote provincialism and pedantry. Conversely, as William Arrowsmith warned, going too far toward breadth could make the curriculum a mere "bus trip of the West" characterized by "shallow generalization and stereotypes."

(2) **Original text.** Most members of the study group believed that the curriculum should be based on original literary, historical, and philosophical texts rather than on secondary works or textbooks. By reading such works, reflecting on them, discussing them, and writing about them, students will come to understand the power of ideas.

(3) **Continuity.** The undergraduate's study of the humanities should not be limited to the freshman and sophomore years. Rather, it should extend throughout the undergraduate career so that continuing engagement with the humanities will complement and add perspective to courses in the major field as well as contribute to students' increasing intellectual maturity as juniors and seniors. Professor Linda Spoerl of Highline Community College said: "The idea that general education requirements should be satisfied as quickly as possible before the student goes on to the 'real' part of education does everyone a disservice."

(4) **Faculty strength.** Because a good curriculum must rest on a firm foundation of good teaching, it follows that the nature of that curriculum should respect areas of faculty

competence and expertise. As David Riesman pointed out, it does little good to require study of Shakespeare if there are no scholars on the faculty who can teach Shakespeare with insight and contagious appreciation. On the other hand, any institution that lacks faculty expertise in the basic fields and work of the humanities should take immediate steps to fill those gaps or to develop such competence in existing faculty.

(5) **Conviction about the centrality of the humanities.** Finally, the humanities must not be argued for as something that will make our students refined, nor should the humanities be presented as a nonrigorous interlude where the young can chew over their feelings, emote, or rehash their opinions. The humanities are not an educational luxury, and they are not just for majors. They are a body of knowledge and a means of inquiry that convey serious truths, defensible judgments, and significant ideas. Properly taught, the humanities bring together the perennial questions of human life with the greatest works of history, literature, philosophy, and art. Unless the humanities are taught and studied in this way, there is little reason to offer them.

Based on our discussions, we recommend the following knowledge in the humanities as essential to a college education:

* Because our society is the product and we the inheritors of Western civilization, American students need an understanding of its origins and development, from its roots in antiquity to the present. This understanding should include a grasp of the major trends in society, religion, art, literature, and politics, as well as a knowledge of basic chronology.

* A careful reading of several masterworks of English, American, and European literature.

* An understanding of the most significant ideas and debates in the history of philosophy.

* Demonstrable proficiency in a foreign language (either modern or classical) and the ability to view that language as an avenue into another culture.

In addition to these areas of fundamental knowledge, study group members recommended that undergraduates have some familiarity with the history, literature, religion and philosophy of at least one non-Western culture or civilization. We think it better to have a deeper understanding of a single non-Western culture than a superficial taste of many. Finally, the study group thought that all students should study the history of science and technology.

What Should be Read?

A curriculum is rarely much stronger than the syllabi of its courses, the arrays of texts singled out for careful reading and discussion. The syllabi should reflect the college's best judgment concerning specific texts with which an educated person should be familiar and should include texts within the competence and interest of its faculty.

Study group members agreed that an institution's syllabi should not be set in stone; indeed, these syllabi should change from time to time to take into account the expertise of available faculty and the result of continuing scrutiny and refinement. The task, however, is not to take faculty beyond their competence and training, nor to displace students' individual interests and career planning, but to reach and inhabit common ground for a while.

We frequently hear that it is no longer possible to reach a consensus on the most significant thinkers, the most compelling ideas, and the books all students should read. Contemporary American culture, the argument goes, has become too fragmented and too pluralistic to justify a belief in common learning. Although it is easier (and more fashionable) to doubt than to believe, it is a grave error to base a college curriculum on such doubt. Also, I have long suspected that there is more consensus on what the important books are than many people have been willing to admit.

In order to test this proposition and to learn what the American public thinks are the most significant works, I recently invited several hundred educational and cultural leaders to recommend ten books that any high school graduate should have read. The general public was also invited in a newspaper column by George F. Will to send me their lists. I received recommendations from more than five hundred individuals. They listed hundreds of different texts and authors, yet four—Shakespeare's plays, American historical documents (the Constitution, Declaration of Independence, and Federalist Papers), *The Adventures of Huckleberry Finn,* and the Bible—were cited at least 50 percent of the time.

I have not done a comparable survey on what college graduates should read, but the point to be made is clear: Many people do believe that some books are more important than others, and there is broader agreement on what those books are than many have supposed. Each college's list will vary somewhat, reflecting the character of the institution and other factors. But there would be, and should be, significant overlap.

I am often asked what I believe to be the most significant works in the humanities. This is an important question, too important to avoid. Some works and their authors have profoundly influenced my life, and it is plain that the same works have influenced the lives of many others as well. In providing a list of these works and authors, it is not my intention (nor is it my right) to dictate anyone's curriculum. My purpose is not to prescribe a course of studies but to answer, as candidly as I can, an oft-asked question.

The works and authors I mention virtually define the development of the Western mind. There are, at a number of institutions, strong introductory courses already in place whose syllabi include such works. These institutions do not expect undergraduates to read most of the major works of these authors. They have learned, however, that it is not unreasonable to expect students to read works by some of them and to know who the others were and why they are important.

The works and authors I have in mind include, but are not limited to, the following: from classical antiquity—Homer, Sophocles, Thucydides, Plato, Aristotle, and Vergil; from medieval, Renaissance, and seventeenth-century Europe—Dante, Chaucer, Machiavelli, Montaigne, Shakespeare, Hobbes, Milton, and Locke; from eighteenth- through twentieth-century Europe—Swift, Rousseau, Austen, Wordsworth, Tocqueville, Dickens, Marx, George Eliot, Dostoyevsky, Tolstoy, Nietzsche, Mann, and T. S. Eliot; from American literature and historical documents—the Declaration of Independence, the Federalist Papers, the Constitution, the Lincoln-Douglas Debates, Lincoln's Gettysburg Address and Second Inaugural Address, Martin Luther King, Jr.'s "Letter from the Birmingham Jail" and "I have a dream..." speech, and such authors as Hawthorne, Melville, Twain, and Faulkner. Finally, I must mention the Bible, which is the basis for so much subsequent history, literature, and philosophy. At a college or university, what weight is given to which authors must of course depend on faculty competence and interest. But, should not every humanities faculty possess some members qualified to teach at least something of these authors?

Why these particular books and these particular authors? Because an important part of education is learning to read, and the highest purpose of reading is to be in the company of great souls. There are, to be sure, many fine books and important authors not included in the list, and they too deserve the student's time and attention. But to pass up the opportunity to spend time with this company is to miss a fundamental experience of higher education.

Great souls do not express themselves by the written word only; they also paint, sculpt, build, and compose. An educated person should be able not only to recognize some of their works, but also to understand why they embody the best in our culture. Should we be satisfied if the graduates of our colleges and universities know nothing of the Parthenon's timeless classical proportions, of the textbook in medieval faith and philosophy that is Chartres cathedral, of Michelangelo's Sistine ceiling, or of the music of Bach and Mozart?

How Well are the Humanities Being Taught and Learned on the Nation's Campuses?

Our experience in higher education and study of empirical data convince us that the humanities are being taught and learned with uneven success. Some institutions do an outstanding job, some a poor one. At most colleges and universities, the humanities are taught both well and poorly, with inspiration in one classroom, excruciating dullness or pedantry in another. Overall, however, both teaching and learning in the humanities are not what they should be or can be, and they are neither taught as well nor studied as carefully as they deserve to be.

Evidence for this decline is compelling. Preliminary findings from a 1984–85 survey by the American Council on Education indicate that a student can obtain a bachelor's degree from 75 percent of all American colleges and universities without having studied European history, from 72 percent without having studied American literature or history, and from 86 percent without having studied the civilizations of classical Greece and Rome. The Modern Language Association reports that both entrance and graduation requirements in foreign languages have been weakened significantly since 1966. In that year, 33 percent of all colleges and universities required some foreign language study for admission. By 1975, only 18 percent required a foreign language, and by 1983 only 14 percent. The picture is similar for graduation requirements. In 1966, 89 percent of all institutions required foreign language study for the bachelor's degree, dropping to 53 percent in 1975 and 47 percent in 1983.

Conventional wisdom attributes the steep drop in the number of students who major in the humanities to a concern for finding good-paying jobs after college. Although there is some truth in this, we believe that there is another, equally important reason—namely, that we in the academy have failed to bring the humanities to life and to insist on their value. From 1970 to 1982, the number of bachelor's degrees awarded in all fields *increased* by 11 percent from 846,110 to 952,998. But during the same period, degrees in English *dropped* not by a few percentage points, but by 57 percent, in philosophy by 41 percent, in history by 62 percent, and in modern languages by 50 percent. Indications are that the decline is continuing. From 1975 to 1983, the number of high school seniors who took the SAT exam and specified an intended college major rose by 14 percent. Over the same eight-year period, the number who planned to major in the humanities fell by 42 percent. Prospective history majors decreased by 60 percent.

If further evidence of students' estrangement from the humanities is required, one need only refer to the American Council on Education's 1983 survey of academic deans at colleges and universities. Two-thirds of those surveyed indicated that the most able entering undergraduates were turning away from the humanities to other fields, mainly professional and technical. This is not merely a rejection of a career in the humanities, but a rejection of the humanities themselves. The former is not a cause for alarm; the latter is.

Impressionistic or anecdotal evidence for the decline of the humanities surfaces every time I talk with college professors, academic officers, and students. Such evidence is familiar: students who graduate from college unable to write lucidly or reason clearly and rigorously; students who are preoccupied (even obsessed) with vocational goals at the expense of broadening the intellect; students who are ignorant of philosophy and literature and know and care little about the history of their nation and their culture. For example, I know of one university philosophy professor who administers a simple test to his students at the beginning of classes each year to determine how much prior knowledge he can presume. The test consists of identifying twenty important names and events from history (such as Shakespeare, St. Augustine, Beethoven, the Protestant Reformation, and Rembrandt). On the most recent test, his students—mainly sophomores and juniors—correctly identified an average of only six of the twenty.

I must emphasize here that our aim is not to argue for more majors in the humanities, but to state as emphatically as we can that the humanities should have a place in the education of all. Our nation is significantly enriched by the breadth and diversity of its professions and occupations and the interests of its citizens. Our universities should continue to encourage instruction in a full variety of fields and careers. But we do argue that, whatever endeavors our students ultimately choose, some substantial quality instruction in the humanities should be an integral part of everyone's collegiate education. To study the humanities in no way detracts from the career interests of students. Properly taught, they will enrich all.

The State of Teaching in the Humanities

If learning in the humanities is in decline, at least some of the blame must be assigned to those who teach the humanities and to academic administrators who determine the allocation of institutional resources. The study group criticized some universities for surrendering the teaching of introductory and lower division courses to graduate assistants or adjunct, part-time faculty. In making these criticisms, the study group recognized that classes taught by adjunct faculty and graduate students allow the institution to serve more students per faculty salary dollar, and that it is necessary to give future professors experience in the classroom. Nevertheless, the study group was concerned that such persons are not, as a group, the *best* teachers—the most experienced, most accomplished, and most intellectually mature. They are not capable of extending the most attractive invitation to the humanities to those lower division students who account for nearly 90 percent of all humanities credit hours taken. If students do not experience the best the humanities have to offer early in their undergraduate careers, they are unlikely to come back for more. University of Chicago Professor Wayne Booth said in his 1982 presidential address to the Modern Language Association:

> We have chosen—no one required it of is—to say to the world, almost in so many words, that we do not care who teaches the nonmajors or under what conditions, so long as the troublesome hordes move on and out: forced in by requirements, forced out by discouragement, or by disgust, or by literal failure. The great public fears or despises us because we hire a vast army of underpaid flunkies to teach the so-called service courses, so that we can gladly teach, in our advanced courses, those precious souls who survive the gauntlet. Give us lovers and we will love them, but do not expect us to study courtship.

> If we had decided to run up a flag on the quad saying that we care not a whit whether our society consists of people who practice critical understanding, so long as we are left free to teach advanced courses, we could not have given a clearer message.

And Frank Vandiver, president of Texas A&M University, recently analyzed the problem this way: "The liberal arts . . . have allowed this to happen to themselves. They have allowed themselves to sit behind ivy-covered walls and say, 'We are the liberal arts and to hell with you.'"

The problem is more than just who does the teaching it is also how the humanities are taught. Too often introductory humanities courses are taught as if they were initial preparation for majors rather than as general education for all students. This often contributes to a fragmented, compartmentalized curriculum instead of an integrated, coherent one. When the humanities are presented as a series of isolated disciplinary packages, students cannot possibly see the interrelatedness of great works, ideas, and minds.

The study group was alarmed by the tendency of some humanities professors to present their subjects in a tendentious, ideological manner. Sometimes the humanities are used as if they were the handmaiden of ideology, subordinated to particular prejudices and valued or rejected on the basis of their relation to a certain social stance.

At the other extreme, the humanities are declared to have no inherent meaning because all meaning is subjective and relative to one's own perspective. There is no longer agreement on the value of historical facts, empirical evidence, or even rationality itself.

Both these tendencies developed in the hope that we will again show students the relevance of our subjects. Instead of demonstrating relevance, however, they condemn the humanities to irrelevance—the first, by subordinating our studies to contemporary prejudices; the second, by implying that the great works no longer have anything to teach us about ourselves or about life. As David Riesman said, some students are captivated by these approaches and think them modern or sophisticated. But the vast majority of students have correctly thought otherwise and have chosen to vote with their feet, stampeding out of the humanities departments. We cannot blame this on an insufficient number of students, or on the quality of students, or even on the career aspirations of students. We must blame ourselves for our failure to protect and transmit a legacy our students deserve to know.

Effects of Graduate Education on Teaching

Instead of aiming at turning out men and women of broad knowledge and lively intellect, our graduate schools produce too many narrow specialists whose teaching is often lifeless, stilted, and pedestrian. In his recent lecture to the American Council of Learned Societies, Yale Professor Maynard Mask took graduate schools to task for failing to educate broadly:

> When one reads thoughtfully in the works by Darwin, Marx, and Freud, what one finds most impressive is not the competence they show in the studies we associate them with, though that is of course impressive, but the range of what they knew, the staggering breadth of the reading which they had made their own and without which, one comes to understand, they could never have achieved the insights in their own areas that we honor them for. Today, it seems to me, we are still moving mostly in the opposite directions despite here and there a reassuring revolt. We are narrowing, not enlarging our horizons. We are shirking, not assuming our responsibilities. And we communicate with fewer and fewer because it is easier to jabber in a jargon than to explain a complicated matter in the real language of men. How long can a democratic nation afford to support a narcissistic minority so transfixed by its own image?

University of Oregon Dean Robert Berdahl described the problem as one of acculturation and unrealistic expectations. Dean Berdahl observed that most of today's college faculty were trained during the 1960s and early 1970s, a period of rapid growth in the academic sector and increasing private and government support for research. As a result, they are oriented more toward research, publication, and teaching graduate students than toward educating nonmajors and generalists. "The successful career to which one is taught to aspire," wrote Dean Berdahl, "is to end up at an institution like that at which one received one's doctorate, where the 'real work' of the profession takes place and where, if one must teach undergraduates, one need only deal with majors or very bright students."

When these former graduate students secure jobs in our college classrooms, they find themselves poorly equipped to teach undergraduates. Again, Robert Berdahl:

> English professors insist that they are not able to teach composition, so that must be left to graduate students or a growing group of underpaid itinerant instructors. Historians who used to be responsible for teaching the entire sweep of Western civilization or the Survey of American History now insist on teaching only that portion of it that corresponds to their specialities. Foreign literature specialists consider it a waste of their talent to teach foreign language classes. Lower division, general education courses are thus often conceptually no different from the upper division courses offered for majors and graduate students; they are only broader. Instead of asking: "What should a student learn from this 'Civ' class or 'Intro to Lit' class if this is the only history or literature class he or she will take in four years?", we ask: "What will best prepare the student to take advanced literature or history classes?"

Graduate education's tendencies toward what Mellon Foundation President John Sawyer called "hyper-specialization and self-isolating vocabularies" often result in a faculty that, even after several years of advanced study, are no better educated than the undergraduates. John Silber, president of Boston University, wrote in a letter to me:

> The Ph.D. is no longer a guarantee that its holder is truly educated. Everyone has seen the consequences of this: How frequently we now meet Ph.D.'s who are incapable of writing correctly or speaking effectively; who are so narrow in their interests that the civilizing effect of the humanities appears to have been entirely lost upon them; who are so jejune in their research interests as to call into question the entire scholarly enterprise.

In a recent article, Harvard Professor Walter Jackson Bate warned that "the humanities are not merely entering, they are plunging into their worst state of crisis since the modern university was formed a century ago in the 1880s." Professor Bate went on to exhort graduate humanities departments to examine their priorities:

The subject matter—the world's great literature—is unrivaled. All we need is the chance and the imagination to help it work upon the minds and characters of the millions of students to whom we are responsible. Ask that the people you are now breeding up in departments, and to whom you now give tenure appointments, be capable of this.

Training good researchers is vital to the humanities and to the mission of every graduate school. But many graduate schools have become so preoccupied with training narrow research specialists that they no longer address adequately the more pressing need of higher education for good teachers, broadly versed in their fields, inspired by the power of their subjects, and committed to making those subjects speak to the undergraduate. Unless our graduate schools reexamine this misplaced emphasis, much of our teaching will remain mediocre and our students indifferent.

The State of the Humanities Curriculum

The past twenty years have seen a steady erosion in the place of the humanities in the undergraduate curriculum and in the coherence of the curriculum generally. So serious has this erosion become that Mark Curtis, president of the Association of American Colleges, wrote: "The chaotic state of the baccalaureate curriculum may be the most urgent and troubling problem of higher education in the final years of the twentieth century." Clark Kerr has called the undergraduate curriculum "a disaster area," and Professor Frederick Rudolph of Williams College has written:

> . . . when the professors abandoned a curriculum that they thought students needed, they substituted for it one that, instead, catered either to what the professors needed or what the students wanted. The results confirmed the authority of professors and students but they robbed the curriculum of any authority at all. The reaction of students to all this activity in the curriculum was brilliant. They concluded that the curriculum really didn't matter.

A collective loss of nerve and faith on the part of both faculty and academic administrators during the late 1960s and early 1970s was undeniably destructive of the curriculum. When students demanded a greater role in setting their own educational agendas, we eagerly responded by abandoning course requirements of any kind and with them the intellectual authority to say to students what the outcome of a college education ought to be. With intellectual authority relinquished, we found that we did not need to worry about what was worth knowing, worth defending, worth believing. The curriculum was no longer a statement about what knowledge mattered; instead, it became the product of a political compromise among competing schools and departments overlaid by marketing considerations. In a recent article, Frederick Rudolph likened the curriculum to "a bazaar and the students [to] tourists looking for cheap bargains."

Once the curriculum was dissolved, colleges and universities found it difficult to reconstruct because of the pressures of the marketplace. All but the most selective institutions must now compete for scarce financial resources— students' tuition and enrollment-driven state subsidies. As a consequence, many are reluctant to reinstate meaningful course requirements for fear of frightening away prospective applicants. (I believe such a fear is misplaced, but more on this later.)

Intellectual authority came to be replaced by intellectual relativism as a guiding principle of the curriculum. Because colleges and universities believed they no longer could or should assert the primacy of one fact or one book over another, all knowledge came to be seen as relative in importance, relative to consumer or faculty interest. This loss was accompanied by a shift in language. The desired ends of education changed from knowledge to "inquiry," from content to "skills." We began to see colleges listing their objectives as teaching such skills as reading, critical thinking, and awareness of other points of view. These are undeniably essential ends to a college education, but they are not sufficient. One study group member said, "What good is knowing how to write if you are ignorant of the finest examples of the language?" Failure to address content allows colleges and universities to beg the question of what an educated man or woman in the 1980s needs to know. The willingness of too many colleges to act as if all learning were relative is a self-inflicted wound that has impaired our ability to defend our subjects as necessary for learning or important for life.

Effects of the Curriculum on Secondary Education

It is not surprising that once colleges and universities decided the curriculum did not have to represent a vision of an educated person, the secondary schools (and their students) took the cue and reached the same conclusion. Vanderbilt University Professor Chester Finn pointed out that college entrance requirements constitute *de facto* high school exit requirements for high school graduates—now nearly six of every ten—who seek postsecondary education. With exit requirements relaxed, college-bound students no longer perceive a need to take electives in English and history, let alone foreign languages. Instead, they choose courses thought to offer immediate vocational payoff. Clifford Adelman described research for the National Commission on Excellence in Education that dramatically illustrates this trend. From 1969 to 1981, the humanities declined as a percentage of total high school credits taken, a decline parallel to that in the colleges. Credits in Western civilization are down 50 percent, in U.S. history down 20 percent, and in U.S. government down 70 percent. My own experience attests to the woeful state of the high school curriculum. Recently I met with seventy high school student leaders—all excellent students—from all over the country. When I asked them how many had *heard* of the Federalist Papers, only seven raised their hands.

As enrollments in basic high school humanities courses fell off, it became more difficult for the schools to justify keeping them. Therefore, many schools dropped humanities courses from the curriculum. When high school graduates enter college, they are poorly prepared in basic knowledge of the humanities as well as in such essential skills as reading and writing. The remedial courses needed by these students cut into the college curriculum, effectively reducing the amount of actual college level course work they can take.

Twenty years ago, William Arrowsmith wrote: "Our entire educational enterprise is . . . founded upon the wholly false premise that at some prior stage the essential educational work has been done." Sadly, this is still true today. The humanities must be put back into the high school curriculum, but this is unlikely to happen unless they are first restored in the colleges. If colleges take the lead in reinstating humanities course requirements, the high schools will surely respond. Evidence of this was related by Professor Noel Reynolds of Brigham Young University, who described how college preparatory course enrollments in Utah's high schools rose after an announcement by the state's two largest universities that preference for admission would be given to students who had completed college preparatory, including humanities, courses. Some Utah secondary schools reported an increase in foreign language enrollments of as much as 200 percent, and only slightly less dramatic increases in English and history.

Bright Spots in the Curriculum

The study group examined in depth the graduation requirements of numerous colleges and universities. The group found enormous variety, ranging from no course requirements of any kind to sequences of highly prescriptive core courses. Types of curricula did not seem to be associated with types of institutions. Some of the least coherent curricula were those of nationally prestigious, highly selective institutions, while some of the most carefully defined were found at less selective local or regional institutions. The most common type of curriculum was the "distribution requirements" model, in which students selected courses from a limited list of regular departmental offerings within a few broad interdepartmental clusters. Typically, "the humanities" is one of the clusters. Often the humanities requirement can be satisfied by taking such courses as speech, remedial writing, or performing arts. Even in institutions where the humanities are defined more rigorously, distribution requirements rarely guarantee that a student will master an explicit body of knowledge or confront a series of important original texts.

A few colleges and universities have rejected this model in favor of a course of studies in which all students share a carefully designed learning experience. Some colleges and universities have been doing this for a long time and have remained steadfast in their commitment. Others have moved in recent years to restore a sound common curriculum. Two of the latter captured the attention of the study group: Brooklyn College and St. Joseph's College.

Brooklyn College, part of the City University of New York system, has about 14,000 undergraduates, many of whom are recent immigrants. Most major in professional fields such as prelaw, accounting, and communications. Yet, since 1981 all bachelor's degree candidates, regardless of major, have taken a sequence of ten core courses, seven of which are in the humanities. Many of the courses emphasize original texts. For example, Core Studies 1, "Classical Origins of Western Culture," requires readings in Homer, Sophocles, Herodotus, Aristophanes, Aristotle, Vergil, and other writers of classical antiquity. Brooklyn's success with the core curriculum has surpassed all expectations. The college reports that its faculty (50 percent of whom teach in the core) are enlivened intellectually by teaching the core courses and that students' writing has improved considerably as a result of a "Writing Across the Core" program. Students, too, are excited by the new curriculum. They say they are able to see relationships among fields, and they talk about a renewed sense of a community of learning, a community that includes faculty, students, and administrators. The administration's commitment to the curriculum can be seen in the fact that both the president and provost teach core courses.

Although it is a very different kind of institution, St. Joseph's College in Indiana has developed a similar curriculum with equally good results. St. Joseph's is a Catholic school of about 1,000 students. Business, finance, and computer science are popular majors. Like Brooklyn College, St. Joseph's requires a sequence of ten core courses. St. Joseph's differs from Brooklyn in distributing these courses over all four years, whereas Brooklyn's core courses are concentrated in the first two. The Brooklyn and St. Joseph's cores also share curricular coherence in the way courses are arranged in logical progression, each course building upon the previous one. All core courses at St. Joseph's involve the humanities. There is tremendous enthusiasm for the core approach among faculty, two-thirds of whom teach core courses. Even more telling is the enthusiasm of St. Joseph's alumni, who frequently write faculty to praise the core as an outstanding feature of their college career.

Among two-year colleges, where vocational training is so important to the institutional mission, some schools have recognized the need for a strong common curriculum in the humanities. Kirkwood Community College in Iowa is a noteworthy example. Kirkwood serves about 6,000 students, half of whom are enrolled in liberal arts degree programs. In 1979, several faculty and administrators formed a Humanities Committee to review the humanities curriculum and recommend improvements. The committee developed and obtained approval for a new twenty-four humanities core requirement. Candidates for the Associate of Arts degree now select from a very limited list of challenging academic courses—in literature, history, philosophy, and languages—which concentrate on reading primary texts and require extensive student writing.

The experience of Brooklyn College, St. Joseph's College, and Kirkwood Community College proves that the drift toward curricular disintegration can be reversed, that colleges and universities—and not just the elite ones—can become true communities of learning, and that it is possible even in this age of skepticism to educate students on the principle that certain areas of knowledge are essential for every college graduate. Their experience also belies the oft-heard fear that students will reject or avoid such a structured curriculum. Intellectually challenging, well-taught courses, whether required or not, will attract good students, and any college that offers a curriculum of such courses will not lack applicants.

The Challenge to Academic Leadership

Revitalizing an educational institution is not easy. Usually it requires uncommon courage and discernment on the part of a few and a shared vision of what can and ought to be on the part of many. Higher education may now be more receptive to decisive leadership than it has been for some time. As University of Puget Sound President Philip Phibbs observed, most colleges and universities sense a crisis on the way and are concerned about the future. Administrators and faculty alike are beginning to perceive that what has traditionally been good for this or that department, one school or another, may be harmful to the institution as a whole and to its overall educational mission.

Recently, educational researchers sought to determine those factors that make some elementary and secondary schools more successful than others. Among the most important was strong leadership from the school principal. Although colleges and universities are more complex institutions than secondary schools, with far stronger fragmenting tendencies, leadership plays the same uncial role.

Curricular reform must begin with the president. In their research on presidential leadership, Clark Kerr and David Riesman found that only 2 percent of the more than seven hundred college and university presidents interviewed described themselves as playing a major role in academic affairs. This is an alarming finding. A president should be the chief academic officer of the institution, not just the chief administrative, recruitment, or fund-raising officer. The president and other principal academic officers (provosts, deans, vice presidents for academic affairs) are solely accountable for all its parts and the needs of all its students. They are ultimately responsible for the quality of the education these students receive.

Members of the study group—which included several deans and presidents—believed strongly that presidents can be an effective force for curricular change only if they define their role accordingly. Bucknell University's Frances Fergusson said that a president's role is to "define, articulate, and defend institutional goals and to redirect the energies of the faculty towards these broader concerns." David Riesman characterized a good president as having "a combination of persuasiveness, patience, ingenuity, even stubbornness." Philip Phibbs said that a president must "have the courage to state and insist upon important, and often uncomfortable, if not initially unacceptable, ideas."

There are a number of concrete steps presidents can take to strengthen the humanities within their institutions. Roland Dille, president of Moorhead State College, said that "in the dozens of speeches that a president makes there ought to be some sign of his having been touched by the humanities." Beyond this, he can set standards for excellence in undergraduate teaching and see that they are met by hiring deans, provosts, and faculty who are committed to those standards. President Hanna Gray of the University of Chicago urged her fellow presidents to "insist on certain priorities" and to "raise certain questions and insist that they be answered." Donald Stewart, president of Spelman College, showed that a president who views himself as all an academic leader can make a real difference. From the beginning of his presidency at Spelman, Stewart sought to cut through the prevalent vocational orientation by stating openly and repeatedly that the humanities are basic to Spelman's mission, and, in so doing, set a new intellectual tone for the institution. Such statements by institutional leaders must, of course, be accompanied by actions. Among these, and not the least important, is rewarding good teaching in hiring, promotion, and tenure decisions.

But as Frederick Rudolph has frequently pointed out, the curriculum cannot be reformed without the enthusiastic support of the faculty. Institutions such as Brooklyn college, St. Joseph's College, and Kirkwood Community College were able to implement strong curricula because their administrators and faculty worked together toward a common goal, not in opposition to one another or to protect departmental turf. Philip Phibbs called upon humanities faculty to recognize their common interests:

> Leadership . . . must also come from the humanities faculty itself. This group must assert itself aggressively within the larger faculty and make its case with confidence and clarity. In too many cases, I think, faculty members in the humanities assume that any intelligent human being, and certainly any intelligent faculty colleague, understands the value of the humanities. It should not, therefore, be necessary to articulate the case. This is a dangerous and misguided assumption.

Concluding Thoughts

The humanities are important, not to just a few scholars, gifted students, or armchair dilettantes, but to any person who would be educated. They are important precisely because they embody mankind's age-old effort to ask the questions that are central to human existence. As Robertson Davies told a college graduating class, "A university education is meant to enlarge and illuminate your life." A college education worthy of the name must be constructed upon a foundation of the humanities. Unfortunately, our colleges and universities do not always give the humanities their due. All too often teaching is lifeless, arid, and without commitment. On too many campuses, the curriculum has become a self-service cafeteria through which students pass without being nourished. Many academic leaders lack the confidence to assert that the curriculum should stand for something more than salesmanship, compromise, or special interest politics. Too many colleges and universities have no clear sense of their educational mission and no conception of what a graduate of their institution ought to know or be.

The solution is not a return to an earlier time when the classical curriculum was the only curriculum and college was available to only a privileged few. American higher education today serves far more people and many more purposes than it did a century ago. Its increased accessibility to women, racial and ethnic minorities, recent immigrants, and students of limited means is a positive accomplishment of which our nation is rightly proud. As higher education broadened, the curriculum became more sensitive to the long-overlooked cultural achievements of many groups with what Janice Harris of the University of Wyoming referred to as "a respect for diversity." This, too, is a good thing. But our eagerness to assert the virtues of pluralism should not allow us to sacrifice the principle that formerly lent substance and continuity to the curriculum, namely, that each college and university should recognize and accept its vital role as conveyor of the accumulated wisdom of our civilization.

We are a part and a product of Western civilization. That our society was founded upon such principles as justice, liberty, government with the consent of the governed, and equality under the law is the result of ideas descended directly from great epochs of Western civilization—Enlightenment England and France, Renaissance Florence, and Periclean Athens. These ideas, so revolutionary in their times yet so taken for granted now, are the glue that binds together our pluralistic nation. The fact that we as Americans—whether black or white, Asian or Hispanic, rich or poor—share these beliefs aligns us with other cultures of the Western tradition. It is not ethnocentric or chauvinistic to acknowledge this. No student citizen of our civilization should be denied access to the best that tradition has to offer.

Ours is not, of course, the only great cultural tradition the world has seen. There are others, and we should expect an educated person to be familiar with them because they have produced art, literature, and thought that are compelling monuments to the human spirit and because they have made significant contributions to our history. Those who know nothing of these other traditions can neither appreciate the uniqueness of their own nor understand how their own fits with the larger world. They are less able to understand the world in which they live. The college curriculum must take the non-Western world into account, not out of political expediency or to appease interest groups, but out of respect for its importance in human history. But the core of the American college curriculum—its heart and soul—should be the civilization of the West, source of the most powerful and pervasive influences on America and all of its people. It is simply not possible for students to understand their society without studying its intellectual legacy. If their past is hidden from them, they will become aliens in their own culture, strangers in their own land.

Restoring the humanities to their central place in the curriculum is a task each college and university will have to accomplish for itself, its faculty and administrators working together toward a common goal with all the vision, judgment, and wisdom they can muster. Every institution has its own unique character, problems, sense of purpose, and circumstances; a successful approach at one school may be impractical at another.

Instead of listing formal recommendations this report concludes with some questions. We believe that if colleges and universities ask these questions of themselves and honestly answer them, the process of reform will have begun.

Questions for the academic community of each institution:

- Does the curriculum on your campus ensure that a graduate with a bachelor's degree will be conversant with the best that has been thought and written about the human condition?

- Does your curriculum reflect the best judgment of the president, deans, and faculty about what an educated person ought to know, or is it a mere smorgasbord or an expression of appeasement politics?

- Is your institution genuinely committed to teaching the humanities to undergraduates? Do your best professors teach introductory and lower division courses? Are these classes designed for the nonmajor, and are they part of a coherent curriculum?

Questions for college and university presidents:

- Do you set an intellectual tone for the institution, articulating goals and ideals?

- Do you take a firm stand on what your institution regards as essential knowledge?

- Do you reward excellent teaching as well as good research in hiring, promotions and tenure decisions?

Questions for humanities faculty:

- Does your teaching make the humanities come alive by helping students confront great texts, great minds, and great ideas?

- Are you as concerned with teaching the humanities to nonmajors as you are with signing up departmental majors?

Questions for graduate humanities departments:

- Are your graduates prepared to teach central humanities texts to undergraduates in addition to being trained as researchers and scholars?

- Are your graduates broadly educated in fields of knowledge other than their primary one? As scholars, are they concerned only with pursuing research of narrow scope or are they able, as well, to ask questions of wide significance?

We conclude with these questions because the spirit of higher education in a free society is the spirit of knowledge and inquiry, the framing of important questions in the vigorous search for good and truthful answers. First, however, we must ask the important questions of ourselves, of our institutions, of our faculties, and of our curricula. We must assure ourselves that the answers we live by are true and valuable. Are we teaching what we should? Are we teaching it as well as we can? No college or university, if it is honest with itself, concerned for its students, and mindful of its largest responsibilities, will reject such questions out of hand or dismiss them with easy affirmatives or conventional excuses.

More than four decades ago, Walter Lippmann observed that "what enables men to know more than their ancestors is that they start with a knowledge of what their ancestors have already learned." "A society," he added, "can be progressive only if it conserves its tradition." The challenge to our colleges and universities, I believe, is to conserve and transmit that tradition, understanding that they do this not merely to pay homage to the wisdom of the past but to prepare wisely for the future.

The College Curriculum and Political Correctness

George Roche

In 1992, Secretary of Education Lamar Alexander issued a report stating that during the previous ten years spending on education, including higher education, had *doubled* and that even after inflation the total was up 40 percent. He noted, however, that college enrollment had risen only slightly and that the results of efforts to improve educational quality and access were disappointing.[1] His proposed solution? It was identical to that of his democratic successor, Secretary of Education William Riley: Spend more money on "changing schools." Is more money the answer? Let us look briefly at what we have paid for so far with billions of state, federal, and private dollars spent on higher education.

The Core Curriculum

For much of American history, the heart of undergraduate education was what was known as the "core curriculum." It consisted of a deliberately sequenced set of rigorous courses in mathematics, science, philosophy, history, languages, and literature that all students must master in order to receive a bachelor's degree. Though not every college or university taught these courses in precisely the same fashion, they were in unquestioned agreement about the nature of what undergraduates should learn. As early as the 1890s, however, a few individual educators began to express doubt about the "relevance" and "efficacy" of the core curriculum. Their main spokesman was university scientist and educational philosopher John Dewey, who viewed higher education's main task not as leading students toward the pursuit of truth, which he saw as a shifting construct rather than as a permanent reality, but toward "socialization" in order that they might be recruited into the intellectual movement to "change the world."

Once challenged, the curriculum was not transformed overnight, but gradually it did change. During the decades of Progressivism, the New Deal, and World War II, Dewey and his disciples on the Left gained influence and power in the academy, and new, rival disciplines like sociology and psychology, once reserved for graduate study, began to intrude upon the core. It was not long before they were joined by "practical" instruction in everything from accounting to shorthand. With so many new majors and courses available, colleges and universities increasingly began to rely on the "elective system" rather than the core because it allowed students to design their own patterns of study after taking a minimal number of required courses. The core was reduced to something to be gotten over or gotten through.

As a kind of smorgasbord approach, the elective system really came into its own during the 1960s under the banner of the student's "right to choose." The net result was not more freedom but the trivialization of learning, says George H. Douglas, professor of English at the University of Illinois and author of *Education Without Impact*. Everything was "pummeled, shrunk, detoothed," as "faculties discovered ways to defreight the traditional curriculum so that students could be bused along to law or professional school or to the job market painlessly and without complaint."[2] Although still considered a useful vehicle for "socialization" and, increasingly for political and ideological transformation, now *all* undergraduate education, not just the core curriculum, became something to be gotten over or gotten through, and a bachelor's degree became a mere useful credential rather than a mark of special academic achievement.

Also in the 1960s, Brown University introduced the "New Curriculum." This quickly became the hottest fad in the nation with countless imitations. As Charles J. Sykes, author of *Profscam*, has pointed out, it was in reality more like a noncurriculum. Students were free to take whatever courses appealed to them, often on a pass/fail basis. At Brown "D"s were also abolished and "F"s were not recorded on transcripts. A Brown dean justified the policy by saying, "I regard recording [failures] for the external world both superfluous and intimidating, or punishing."[3] The courses themselves were specifically designed to cater to adolescent tastes and centered on fashionable intellectual trends rather than time-tested academic subjects. Anything that smacked of the traditional was *boring*. It was also *Establishment*, so it had to be carted off to Madame Guillotine while the liberated citizens of the First Republic On Campus cheered and congratulated themselves on having thrown off the yoke of academic oppression. With a few minor changes, the noncurriculum still dominates higher education, but many of its features seem to have been dreamed up not by the New Jacobins but by Ripley's Believe It or Not. Here are some examples from the early 1990s:[4]

- At San Francisco State University, the humanities requirement could be fulfilled by taking a course in interior design.
- At American University, a course called "Lifetime Fitness" met the social studies distribution requirement.
- At Pennsylvania State University, it was possible to earn a Leisure Studies degree in golf management. Students christened it a "Fore-Year Degree."
- At Michigan State University, one could earn a master's degree in "packaging."
- The University of Pennsylvania granted a Ph.D. for a dissertation on the New England clambake, and the State University of New York granted one for "Women's Shopping: A Sociological Approach."
- At Lehigh University, marketing students could earn class credit for going on a date.
- At Stanford University, an upper division course was called "Black Hair as Culture and History."
- Middlebury College in Vermont had a class devoted, among other things, to the "eroticism, esthetics, voyeurism, and misogyny" of the films of Brigitte Bardot.
- Auburn University had a course called "Recreation Interpretive Services."
- Kent State offered "Camp Leadership" "SocioPyschological Aspects of Clothing," "Basic Roller Skating," and "Dance Roller Skating."
- The University of Illinois offered "Pocket Billiards" and "The Anthropology of Play."
- The University of Massachusetts-Amherst offered "Ultimate Frisbee."
- At Harvard University, students received class credit for "evaluating the nutritional content of their own diets" and for "studying the Harvard football team's offense under the tutelage of the quarterback." One of Harvard's more serious academic courses called, impressively enough, "The Concept of the Hero in Hellenic Civilization," was so undemanding that students regularly referred to it as "Heroes for Zeroes."
- Rutgers University devoted a course for German majors to "The Seduced Maiden Motif in German Literature."
- At Johns Hopkins University, a course on biomedical research was taught using the format of "The Tonight Show."

- Kenyon College's "Biology of Female Sexuality" class used as one of its course texts *Witches Heal,* which asserts, "As lesbians, we . . . must question male medical authority, dare to hear and follow the witches, uncover the old wyve's tales, and heal ourselves."
- Brown University, the pioneer of the noncurriculum and an early proponent of such new, noncore disciplines as women's studies in the 1970s and 1980s, offered in this field: "Seminar on Sexuality," "Feminist Film Criticism," "Writing and Sexual Difference," "Feminism and Drama," "Tough Women and Tender Men in Modern Fiction," "Black Women: Psychological Perspectives," "Social Inequality," "Cold War: Language, Gender, and Representation in the 1950's America," "Behind the Lavender Curtains: Problems in 20th-Century Lesbian and Gay American Drama," "The Social Construction of Sexuality and the Making of the Modern Lesbian/Gay Community," "Comparative Sex Roles," "Psychology of Gender," "The Biology of Gender," and "Society and Behavioral Sciences Selective: Gender and the Health Care Delivery System."

In its 1985 report "Integrity in the College Curriculum," the Association of American Colleges lamented that "almost anything goes" in what passes as a college curriculum and expressed serious reservations about the content and purpose of many courses being taught today.[5] In the late 1980s (and still today, I suspect), it was possible to graduate from *78 percent* of the nation's colleges and universities without taking a course in the history of Western civilization; *38 percent* without taking any history course; *45 percent* without taking an American or English literature course; *77 percent* without taking a foreign language course; *41 percent* without taking a mathematics course; and *33 percent* without studying the natural or physical sciences.[6] Requirements for majors have also been eviscerated. At Duke University, for example, students are not required to read Homer, Dante, Donne, Milton, Eliot, or even Shakespeare in order to graduate with a B.A. in English.[7] And requirements also vary widely from department to department, creating at best a problem in "quality control" and at worst a kind of academic schizophrenia. No single campus authority seems to be able to offer a rationale for it, let alone control it and, as a result, course catalogues have exploded. Many list anywhere between five hundred and nine hundred offerings.

But, as George Douglas earlier pointed out, freedom of choice has hurt, not helped. A 1993 Rand Corporation study reports: "Over one-half of a national sample of college upper class students were unable to perform cognitive tasks at a high school level; three-quarters of the faculty surveyed in a recent poll felt that their students did not meet minimum preparation standards."[8] Thousands of students are graduating from college without acquiring critical thinking skills, let alone such basic skills as reading, writing, and arithmetic. Some are actually illiterate; they cannot read their own diplomas. Rightly, much of the blame has been directed toward the K–12 system, but higher education is also culpable. It has lowered standards and expectations to such an extent that it has given up on helping those who are hard to teach or who are ill-prepared for college.

Even though 30 percent of all college freshmen take at least one remedial course, many public and private campuses are dropping them since, says the *Chronicle of Higher Education,* neither tuition-paying parents nor state legislators like paying twice for students to take high school subjects.[9] But a 1987 Gallup poll of more than seven hundred *college seniors* indicates that perhaps more rather than less remedial education is desperately needed: 24 percent thought Columbus had landed in the New World after 1500; 42 percent could not place the Civil War in the correct half-century; 58 percent did not know that Harry Truman was president when the Korean War began; 55 percent could not identify the Magna Carta; and 23 percent identified Karl Marx's dictum, "From each according to his ability, to each according to his need," as a part of the U.S. Constitution. Fifty-five percent were given the theoretical grade of "F," since they missed more than 60 percent of the correct answers on the test of rudimentary knowledge the pollsters devised.[10] (Many of them, by the way, attended "prestige schools" where their parents assumed they were getting what they were paying for.)

Average SAT scores have declined about *75 points* since the 1960s, but the response of colleges and universities has been to cover up rather than address the problem. When reporting scores for their institutions, they commonly cite the figures on students accepted rather than actually enrolled. This means, as Thomas Sowell points out, that if a student with combined math and verbal skills of, say, 1,400, applies to five schools, all five will count his scores in their official reports. As many as one-quarter of all students also are categorized as "special" or "provisional," and their scores do not need to be counted at all. Naturally, students with the poorest scores are always put in this category.[11]

Colleges and universities have also responded by making entrance exams less of a factor in the admissions process; a *USA Today* survey of nearly five hundred four-year institutions reveals that only 7 percent now rank them as most important. Fifty-eight percent depend on high school grades even while acknowledging that they are highly inflated.[12] Grade inflation is not limited to high schools; colleges and universities award passing and even high marks to thousands of students for substandard and minimal achievement. Charles J. Sykes reports that at the University of Michigan in 1975, the freshman class had the weakest SAT scores in decades but was given the highest grade point average ever. In the same year, 70 percent of all grades at Princeton were "A"s or "B"s, and at Stanford University, the average grade was "A-."[13] Sowell adds that at Harvard University in 1978, 78 percent of the student body made it onto the dean's list, compared with 20 percent in the 1920s and 26 percent in the 1930s. At Yale University, the proportion of "A"s awarded to students in the 1980s never fell below 40 percent.[14] And Douglas notes that at the University of Illinois in the late 1980s, 80 percent of all students enrolled in "Freshman Rhetoric" received "A"s and "B"s, and in some sections 100 percent received "A"s.[15]

Former journalism professor David Berkman gives one reason why this particular brand of academic corruption is so common: "If two-thirds of the students do not possess the skills necessary for professional success, there is no way you can flunk out a number anywhere near that percentage. There is simply too much intimidation in the academic environment. This is especially true for junior—meaning untenured—faculty members. . . . No junior professor who wishes to gain tenure will flunk out 67 percent in an introductory course."[16] But there is another, even more important reason for grade inflation: Professors have lost faith—faith in their students, that is. They simply don't expect more than a handful to excel or to be interested in what goes on in the classroom.

There is, of course, considerable cause for their defeatist attitude. Sowell reports in *Inside American Education* that less than a quarter of all college students put in sixteen or more hours of study per week, and only about 27 percent check at least one book out of the library during the year.[17] And Jacques Barzun relates a story in *Begin Here* that is becoming all too common in academe:

> The screening committee had to interview 150 young people—the three top students from each state—and award ten of them full scholarships, each worth $60,000. One member of the committee asked every candidate this question: "Did you, during the past year, read a book that was not assigned? If so, please tell us a little about that book." Only one student out of 150 was able to comply.[18]

Professors are also under enormous pressure to practice "affirmative grading," i.e., race-norming for minorities, which further lowers expectations and casts even more doubt on student abilities.[19] Defended by many groups, including the National Education Association, the American Bar Association, and the U.S. Departments of Labor and Education, as well as by many prominent college and university leaders, this form of grade inflation is based on the premise that "academically challenged individuals" (a code term for minority students) should not be "discriminated against" in the testing and grading process. University of Texas Professor Emeritus of English James Sledd contends in defense of affirmative grading: "A person (need one say it?) can learn a huge amount without being able to read or write at all. . . . Quite simply, it is a gross injustice to demand a mastery of standard English from students who through no fault of their own have had no chance to master it."[20] Anne Green, an associate professor of English and director of the writing program at Wesleyan University, concurs that too much emphasis is placed on spelling, punctuation, grammar, and "surface features of writing."[21]

But in truth there is nothing that justifies cheating students out of a good education. Chronic writing and mechanical errors by white as well as minority students are only the "tip of an iceberg of ignorance."[22] There are plenty of professors who feel this way and are opposed to the noncurriculum, lowered standards, and affirmative grading. But since they are afraid of creating controversy and jeopardizing their jobs, they remain, for the most part, silent critics. Perhaps they would be tempted to speak up if they recalled the lesson of the miserly farmer, who decided to save money by mixing sawdust with the grain he fed his horse. Gradually he added more and more sawdust, until there was so little grain in the feed that the horse died from starvation.

Political Correctness

While they are at it, today's educators must also decide what is the aim of undergraduate education. Once, they shared a clear consensus (just as they did about the core curriculum and about what should be expected of students) that it was to share with succeeding generations the inherited wisdom of mankind and the historical and moral traditions of their own culture. But for some years many of them have been trying to substitute a new aim known as "relevance" in the 1960s–1970s and "political correctness" in the 1980s–1990s.

Political correctness has three main doctrines. The first: *There are certain ideas, issues, and actions that simply are unacceptable within the academic community, and it is educators' prime responsibility to "reeducate" students so that they will automatically eschew the "incorrect."*

Thus more than two hundred colleges and universities have attempted to enforce speech codes or revised codes of conduct in the last several years. These have been struck down as unconstitutional once at the University of Wisconsin and twice at the University of Michigan, but de facto codes have taken their place and have been given added support by a 1992 Supreme Court decision that makes it legal for administrators to invoke tough penalties for supposedly "bias-motivated" crimes.[23]

Duke University Professor of English Stanley Fish, widely acknowledged as the "high priest" of political correctness, defends outright as well as de facto speech codes by arguing (reminiscent of John Dewey) that free speech is only a "political construct," and that "the First Amendment is the first refuge of scoundrels."[24] But the most common "PC" argument is that the unrestricted right to freedom of speech belongs only to victims of discrimination. Liberal Harvard University law professor Alan Dershowitz, by no means the stereotypical opponent of PC, objects that this line of reasoning has led to an intolerable situation in which women and minorities are entirely free to attack white men "in the most offensive of terms." He continues, "Radical feminists can accuse all men of being rapists, and radical African-Americans can accuse all whites of being racists, without fear of discipline or rebuke. But even an unintentionally offensive parody of women or blacks provides the occasion for demanding the resignation of deans, the disciplining of students, and an atmosphere reminiscent of McCarthyism."[25] Unabashed, however, many colleges and universities have embraced PC fully. In the early 1990s, they went so far as to publish and distribute warnings against certain forms of "politically incorrect" language and behavior:[26]

- The University of Missouri's school of journalism handbook outlawed "'burly' (too often associated with black men, implying ignorance), 'glamorous' (sexist), 'white' (refers to a racist power structure), 'banana' (offensive to Asian-Americans), 'gyp' (offensive to Gypsies), 'mafia' (offensive to Italian-Americans), 'Dutch treat' (offensive to those of Dutch extraction), 'community' (implies a monolithic culture in which people think, act, and vote in the same way), and 'Ugh!' (offensive to Native Americans)."

- Nebraska Wesleyan University, like many schools, forbad "freshman" and "chairman" as sexist.

- Michigan State University's "Fact Sheet on Bias-Free Communications" warned against "culturally deprived," "black mood," "yellow coward," and "he."

- The College of William and Mary disapproved of "kingpin," and suggests substituting "key person."

- The University of Arizona outlawed "nerd."

- Several campuses also included "child-free" instead of "childless" in their PC lexicon.
- At the University of Michigan even "minority" was out; "multicultural," however, was definitely in. The school also dictated use of "sexual orientation" over "sexual preference," "life partner" over "spouse," and (my personal favorite) "personhole" over "manhole."
- Smith College had penalties for "lookism," i.e., discrimination on the basis of physical appearance.
- Duke University prohibited "disrespectful facial expressions or body language."
- Until compelled to reverse its policies, the University of Connecticut banned "inappropriate laughter."

Another popular PC device introduced in the early 1990s was "sensitivity training" on race, gender, and "sexual orientation." Today, many colleges and universities are forcing students and faculty to undergo this particular form of reeducation. Here are just a few recent examples:[27]

- At the University of Tennessee's required sensitivity workshops, trainers betrayed their own lack of sensitivity by publicly berating and humiliating several staff employees for their reluctance to participate.
- A Stanford University neurosurgeon was forced to resign his department chairmanship and undergo a year of "sensitivity training" after being accused of sexism by a colleague.
- At the University of Arizona, the creative writing faculty was ordered to undergo reeducation as the result of unsubstantiated campus rumors that they might be "insensitive."
- At the University of Minnesota, the faculty was informed by the dean of liberal arts that they not only must attend "Mandatory Sexual Harassment Training" but also sign certificates of attendance.
- At the University of Florida, a new policy forced sororities and fraternities to send all new members to a month-long series of sensitivity seminars.
- At Emory University, the entire faculty was told to attend sensitivity workshops after an instructor was accused but found innocent of sexually harassing a student. The Atlanta branch of the Department of Education's Office of Civil Rights insisted on the workshops and warned that less than full cooperation would put the university *in danger of losing all federal funding*. (Look for much more of this kind of federal intimidation in the future.)

The price of being sensitive, as we all know from personal experience, is dear, but perhaps not so dear as it is in higher education. "Sensitivity trainers," though they possess no real credentials, charge as much as $2,500 for a half-day workshop and up to $16,000 for follow-up sessions. Colleges and universities scrambling to show their own high degree of institutional sensitivity are also hiring full-time "diversity directors" and "deans of multicultural affairs," with starting salaries of $35,000–$60,000.[28] (Of course, they must also pay for all the expensive new programs, newsletters, brochures, secretarial help, office space, and equipment that go along with these positions, but they have become ingenious at finding ways to make taxpayers pick up the tab for such things.)

Colleges and universities also mete out stern punishment to the "politically incorrect," which is what occurred at Stanford University in the 1980s when a graduate student was expelled for documenting the government policy of coerced abortions in communist China and at Dartmouth College where conservative student newspaper editors were expelled for confronting a black music professor whose lectures routinely featured obscenities and racial and sexual epithets. Dartmouth also suspended two students who dared appear dressed as Indians at a hockey game after displays of the traditional school symbol had been banned as offensive to Native Americans. (It was a week before the end of the term; the students received no class credit and no tuition refund.)[29]

Yet, in a clear case of double standards, those who persecute the politically incorrect go unpunished. At the University of Pennsylvania in 1993 a group called "Concerned Black and Latino Students" stole fourteen thousand copies of the *Daily Pennsylvanian*. Even though the group readily admitted responsibility, administrators ignored the theft, just as it had largely ignored all verbal threats, physical harassment, and vandalism directed against the conservative student newspaper. Administrations at Massachusetts' College of the Holy Cross, North Carolina State University, Pennsylvania State University, Dartmouth University, the University of California-Berkeley, the University of North Carolina, and the University of Michigan have behaved similarly.[30]

Even classroom debate has been curtailed by PC, as Thomas Sowell documents. At Humboldt State College, a student who disagreed with a professor's antinuclear views was barred from returning to class, and, at the University of Michigan, a student who dared question his professor's statements about Central American politics (made in biology class) was told by the professor that he should go to El Salvador and get blown up. At the State University of New York-Farmingdale, an enraged professor called in security guards to escort a student out of class because he criticized the professor's parodies of Ronald Reagan and the Bible. At the University of Washington, a male student was physically barred from attending the women's studies course in which he had enrolled.[31] But controversial ideas are fine in the classroom as long as they are approved by the campus thought police:[32]

- At the University of Massachusetts-Amherst, one American history professor began the first day of class by announcing, "This class will be consistently anti-American."

- At St. Cloud State University in Minnesota, one course included class credit for protest marching.

- At the University of Texas-Austin, a Marxist economics course syllabus announced that the class "provides you with an opportunity to learn how to view the world from a new point of view and the tests are aimed at evaluating whether and to what degree you have learned to do this."

- At the University of Wisconsin, a course called "Curriculum and Instruction" was taught as a how-to lesson in political protesting and in "interrupting business as usual (that is, social relations of racism, sexism, classism, Eurocentrism as usual) in the public spaces of the library mall and administrative offices."

PC also extends to other issues of "social relevance." A number of schools are now considering imitating the University of Georgia, which requires every student to demonstrate "environmental literacy" before graduation. Haverford College in Pennsylvania has a "social justice" requirement for undergraduates.[33] At the University of Alabama-Birmingham, the art department recently chose to elevate the cultural consciousness of its student body by raising $4,200 to buy a photograph of Andres Serrano's "Piss Christ." (It reveals a plastic statue of Jesus submerged in a jar of urine and cow's blood.) The student government voted ten-to-two to condemn the purchase while the faculty senate voted unanimously in favor of it. President Charles A. McCallum admitted he found the work personally offensive, but that it had "significant artistic and educational merit."[34] An exhibit at Harvard Divinity School in 1992 featured condoms in rainbow colors, covered with beads, fur, yarn, leather, feathers, bracelet charms, filled with honey, alphabet soup, a baby's sneaker, globes, and sunflower seeds. Defenders of the show said this was "serious art," and the acting director of the school opened the exhibit with a dedication ceremony devoted to the cause of AIDS victims.[35]

It is a political rather than an educational agenda that now rules the campus. And the deliberate intention of the politically correct professor is no longer to be neutral but to propagandize and indoctrinate. Andrew Ross, a Princeton University professor, admits freely, "I teach in the Ivy League in order to have direct access to the minds of the children of the ruling classes."[36] Sam Abel, a gay activist and assistant professor of drama at Dartmouth College, says, "Teaching is a form of political action," and adds, "Deconstructing *Moby Dick* can't change the world, but the student who learns to think deconstructively can."[37] Charles Paine, a Duke University teaching assistant, writes in a similar vein in an article in *College English* that students must be taught about "radical visions of the world," and that "the teacher must recognize that he or she must influence (perhaps manipulate is the more accurate word) students' values through charisma or power."[38]

In class, the primary objective is to preach the second doctrine of political correctness: *All differences in ideas, values, and lifestyles are equally valid, and any attempt to prefer one over the other or to devote more attention to one than to the other is an act of prejudice. Moreover, the differences between people—between blacks and whites, men and women, rich and poor, Westerners and non-Westerners—are more important than the qualities they share in common. For that reason, questions of race, gender, class, and power are the real issues that govern human events.*

Because Western culture rejects this doctrine, it is racist, sexist, and oppressive, and the curriculum as it has been taught for the last two hundred or more years is also racist, sexist, and oppressive. History, philosophy, science, the arts—all are invalid because they have not given equal time to nonwhite, nonmale, non-Westerners. But it is literature that comes in for the worst censure. The traditional canon, comprised of the "Great Books" of the Western world, is nothing more than the imposed intellectual domination of dead white males. A representative sample of this view may be found in an anthology used in many introductory freshman composition classes entitled *Racism and Sexism.* Former National Endowment for the Humanities Chairman Lynne Cheney summarizes it:

> This book begins by defining racism as something only white people can be guilty of and sexism as unique to men. It goes on to portray the United States as a country in which racism and sexism pervade every aspect of life. The book offers no comparison with other cultures, no context to show how American ideals and practices measure up against those of the rest of the world or the rest of history. Instead, it paints a picture of unremitting oppression and suggests that any solution will require "fundamental changes in the ways that wealth is produced and distributed"—that is, the abandonment of capitalism.[39]

Rereading America is another popular anthology assigned to college freshmen. It offers essays that argue that "the American dream . . . is governed not by education, opportunity and hard work, but by power and fear," and that "class standing and consequently life chances are largely determined at birth."[40]

Why do college and university leaders tolerate this kind of vicious, ideological axe-grinding, particularly when it is passed off as educational material? Generally it is because they, too, worship at the altar of political correctness. Donna Shalala, for example, the former chancellor of the University of Wisconsin and current secretary of the Department of Health and Human Services, has commented repeatedly: "American society is racist and sexist."[41] There have been other administrators, of course, who object to political correctness. Former Yale University President Benno Schmidt has decried the fact that "universities have become saturated with politics, often of a fiercely partisan kind," and former Harvard University President Derek Bok has warned, "What universities can and must resist are deliberate, overt attempts to impose orthodoxy and suppress dissent."[42] But they have done little or nothing to stop political correctness; indeed, while in office, they presided over its growth.

To cite just one example of capitulation, they, like other college and university leaders, allowed freshman orientation to become "a crash course in the strange new world of university politics" where students are urged to identify themselves as the oppressors or the oppressed. "Within days of arrival on campus" says Heather MacDonald in the *Wall Street Journal*, students "learn the paramount role of gender, race, ethnicity, class, and sexual orientation in determining their own and others' identity." They are told, furthermore, that "bias lurks around every corner" and to suspect all persons and ideas that they will encounter during the next four years.[43]

Specifically, she notes:

- At the University of California-Berkeley, they are informed that the American system perpetuates racism, homophobia, ableism, ageism, sexism, and statusism.

- At Dartmouth College, they are presented with a mandatory program called "Social Issues," which features skits on politically correct responses.

- At Columbia University, they listen to other students read essays on what it is like to be gay or some other kind of "victim of society."

- At Stanford University, they learn about the "Faces of Community" and how previous generations ruthlessly discriminated against them.

- At Bowdoin College, they are hit with the less felicitously titled program, "Defining Diversity: Your Role in Racial-Consciousness-Raising, Cultural Differences and Cross-Cultural Social Enhancers."

- At Oberlin College, they are segregated into different groups to watch performance theatre on race and gender issues—blacks are grouped with blacks, whites with whites, Asian-Americans with Asian-Americans, gays with gays, and so on.

College and university leaders have also allowed political correctness to enter the classroom under the guise of "multiculturalism." Supposedly broadening the curriculum by introducing minority and Third World perspectives, this new fad has gained the support of many who are not in the PC camp but who are generally in favor of vague concepts of "diversity" and "pluralism."

But multiculturalism, as *The New Republic* points out, is "neither multi nor cultural," and it is part of an effort to impose "unanimity of thought on campus."[44] Dinesh D'Souza agrees that multiculturalism "does not present the historical realities of other cultures but instead advocates modern Western political ideologies, using other cultures as no more than masks, distorted and misrepresented to provide as much evidence as is needed for present political purposes."[45] Still, multiculturalism is immensely popular in academe. In 1988, Stanford University's faculty voted to drop its traditional "Western Civilization" course and replace it with "Culture, Ideas, and Values," which is specifically designed to focus on race, ethnicity, gender, and class issues. In the years since, hundreds of schools have followed Stanford's lead and junked their old courses for "new and improved" multicultural ones.

Most of these have a Marxist emphasis. Though largely an extinct intellectual doctrine in other nations, Marxism flourishes in the modern American university. Nearly half of all recent Ph.D.s in literature, for example, say that Marxist approaches to literature influence their teaching of undergraduates.[46] Even *Newsweek* has concluded that the new politically correct/multicultural tilt in the college curriculum is "Marxist in origin in the broad sense of attempting to redistribute power from the privileged class (white males) to the oppressed masses."[47] And those who pooh-pooh the idea that Marxism is a dominant force still admit that "there will always be a little room for a brand of academic theorizing that includes the notions that what we already have is rotten, that old values must be thrown overboard, that tradition should be undermined, that the smug and comfortable world of parents, or of corporate executives, or of liberal education, should be trashed if at all possible."[48]

Even more troubling, however, than all these features of political correctness—its restrictive limits on speech and behavior, its counterfeit multiculturalism, its Marxist, anti-establishment origins—is its third doctrine: *"Truth" does not exist, and it cannot be taught. What has been passed off as "truth" are merely the collective prejudices of the dominant ruling class and culture. Students must be shown how to "deconstruct" what they think is "true."*

If you ask, "How, if truth does not exist, can anyone believe in political correctness?" you have caught on to the contradiction in this doctrine; but academics thrive on contradiction. The politically correct professor freely admits that what he teaches is dogma, like everything else, but he argues that *his* dogma is more compelling, more socially and ideologically acceptable. His first announcement to new students on the first day of the semester invariably is: "This class will challenge everything you always took for granted to be true. It will strip away all your myths and preconceived notions. . . ." To impressionable, young undergraduates who have always suspected that they were "missing the real story" in those boring high school classes where they were expected to memorize dates and facts, this sounds bold, innovative, and "fun," but what they are being offering is a more rigid bunch of stereotypes than any they have encountered before, as in "All white males are. . . . All women are. . . . All blacks are. . . ."

In literature, there is supposedly no truth in language; words are subjective and the real meaning of a text rests in each reader's response, not in the words themselves or in the author's intent. Since different readers will have different responses, no one meaning can be true, and the accumulated insights of previous generations are not to be trusted. The same goes for insights in history, psychology, biology, sociology, religion, political science, economics, and the law: One person's reality is another person's hallucination.

The only "truth" political correctness will admit is that everything—every poem, every book, every historical event or person, every emotion, attitude, or belief, every action—must be viewed in a political context as an instrument of exclusion, oppression, or liberation. This ties in nicely with the first and second doctrines of political correctness, but, as Lynne Cheney warns, it also brings us "perilously close to the world of George Orwell's *1984*, the world where two and two make five, if it's politically useful."[49]

The New Segregation

Jacques Barzun has noted that political correctness does not legislate tolerance; it only organizes hatred.[50] Nowhere can this be seen more clearly than in the "new segregation" on campus. It began as intellectual segregation in the doctrine that white males are oppressors. There are no exceptions; every white male is an oppressor and a racist, "with the only distinction being between those who are overt and those who engage in psychological 'denial.'"[51] For centuries, white males have persecuted their permanent victims—women and minorities—and, according to new "evidence" in politically correct books like *Stolen Legacy* and *Black Athena*, they have even robbed them of credit for the most important developments of civilization. Women and minorities are told, says San Jose State University Professor Shelby Steele, that their real identity lies in their particular grievance against white males. And, accordingly, they are encouraged to demand special entitlements: "No longer is it enough just to have the right to attend a college or a university on an equal basis with others or to be treated like anyone else." Schools must set aside special money and special academic departments just for them, based on their grievance, says Steele.[52]

Intellectual segregation has led to physical segregation. A number of colleges and universities now offer with pride separate dorms, homecomings, yearbooks, and graduations for black students. Separate departments for black studies, Hispanic studies, and women's studies have also become the rule, and they are generally well funded, even when budget cuts are imposed on other departments. (When in rare circumstances they, too, have to absorb cuts, this is regarded as further "proof" of discrimination. As Sykes has pointed out, it is always "easier to blame 'racism' than to allocate scarce resources.")[53]

Three-fourths of all student newspaper editors responding to a *U.S. News & World Report* survey reported that segregation between races is common at their school. Seventy percent of all black undergraduates at the University of Michigan admitted recently that they lived such a segregated existence on campus that they had no close white acquaintance.[54] Higher education has resurrected, say numerous observers, the "separate but equal" world of *Plessy v. Ferguson. It* also has resurrected racial tension and violence:[55]

- At Oberlin College, Missouri Valley College, and North Carolina State University, there have been racial protests involving anywhere from a few hundred to a thousand students.

- At the University of Massachusetts, the Rodney King trial led to protests and violence and what was described as a "dorm rampage."

- At the University of Rhode Island, hundreds of black students staged a sit-in protest because a Malcolm X quotation newly inscribed on the campus library building omitted the words "fighting the white man."

- At UCLA, two hundred black students marched, protesting alleged racism of fraternities.

- At the University of Oregon, students tore down a banner with the message, "You meet the most interesting people in summer school," and painted the word "racism" over the faces of Michelangelo, Plato, Jane Austen, and a number of other well-known historical figures.

- At Georgia State University, a large demonstration was sparked by racist graffiti on a trash can.

- At Iowa State University, a brawl between black and white students required the police to use tear gas.

- At Southern Illinois University, mace was used to halt another race-related fight between students.

- At Harvard University, law school students disrupted commencement exercises to demand more hiring of women and minorities and the resignation of the dean.

- At Olivet College in Michigan, a single alleged racial incident was so sensationalized by the media and political activists that the campus was plunged into a state of emergency and the president eventually resigned.

One of the campuses worst hit by the new segregation is the University of North Carolina-Chapel Hill. John Moody, student body president in 1992, remarked: "Our campus is already largely two separate campuses through all-black or all-white fraternities and sororities; black business, law and preprofessional organizations; self-segregated living arrangements; and extra-curricular activities."[56] UNC's Black Student Movement has demonstrated repeatedly, demanding a new multimillion-dollar cultural center exclusively for their use and threatening black faculty members who do not lend complete support to their cause. On his visit to the troubled school, film director Spike Lee suggested to an audience of five thousand students that black athletes should boycott all athletic events, saying, "There wouldn't be no Final Four, no Rose Bowl. . . ." At the same rally, a representative of Louis Farrakhan called Socrates a "faggot," and added, "We are tired of a blond-haired, pale-skinned, blue-eyed, buttermilk complexioned cracker Christ or peckerwood Jesus." A National Public Radio reporter on the scene could not find any campus official or faculty member willing to go on record protesting these remarks.[57]

Students have been cowed into silence, too. Blacks, for example, who have criticized minority vandalism and harassment directed against whites have been physically threatened by other blacks. Thomas Sowell notes that this also is common at other institutions: "Campus political activists in various groups attempt to stigmatize those students of their own race who do not join their political constituency and share its group think."[58] *Washington Post* columnist William Raspberry adds that it has come down to a stark choice for students bullied by their peers: "Are you gonna hang with us or are you gonna hang with them?"[59] Inevitably, there will be more racial tension and violence on campus in the future—on the part of nonminority students who are resentful of the preferential treatment minorities receive and of the PC attitude that brands them as oppressors—and on the part of minorities, who are taught to resent both real and imagined injustices and to use them as justification for retaliation.

The Victim's Revolution on Campus

Dinesh D'Souza

There are few places as serene and opulent as an American university campus. The students move in small groups, heading for class, the library, or the dining hall, greeting their friends and apparently conscious of being part of a community. At the major universities, gigantic auditoriums, dormitories, and gymnasiums sprawl across the landscape, advertising a tremendous investment of resources. At the prestige schools, such as those of the Ivy League, impressive domes and arches give off a distinct aroma of old money and tradition. Across the lawns the scholars come and go, talking of Proust and Michelangelo. Tributes to the largesse of democratic capitalism, American universities are nevertheless intellectual and social enclaves, by design somewhat aloof from the pressures of the "real world."

For the last decade or so, the larger society has not heard much from the university, certainly little of the truculence and disruption that seemed a campus staple in the late 1960s and early 1970s. The reason for the taciturn university atmosphere of the eighties, commentators generally agree, is that the current generation of young people lacks social consciousness, and cares mainly about careers and making money. Yet in the past few years, the American campus appears to be stirring again. University outsiders have been shocked to hear of a proliferation of bigotry on campus; At the University of Michigan, for example, someone put up posters which said, "A mind is a terrible thing to waste—especially on a nigger." Typically these ugly incidents are accompanied by noisy protests and seizures of administration buildings by minority activists, who denounce the university as "institutionally racist." Both bewildered and horrified, the university leadership adopts a series of measures to detoxify the atmosphere, ranging from pledges to reform the "white male curriculum" to censorship of offensive speech.

Both university insiders as well as informed off-campus observers know that the recent incidents of bigotry have produced a good deal of excess on all sides. Responding to several cases of insensitivity or flagrant bigotry at Michigan, student and faculty activists demanded that all black professors be given immediate tenure, that admissions requirements such as standardized test scores be abolished, and that female and minority students be permitted to conduct hearings to penalize white students whom they find guilty of making racially and sexually "stigmatizing" remarks. In this case, the university administration took each of these demands seriously and partially acquiesced in them, agreeing to give preferential treatment to minority student and faculty applicants over non-minorities with stronger qualifications, and to adopt censorship regulations outlawing speech offensive to "persons of color," as well as women and homosexuals.

It is not always obvious, in these disputes, whose side a reasonable person should take, or whether it is possible, in good conscience, to endorse any side at all. The middle ground seems to have disappeared as a consequence of ideological fracas and polarization; whether it can be restored is an open question. But for those who visit any American campus, peruse the student newspaper, enter the student union and talk with some of the undergraduates, or examine the lectures and workshops listed on the bulletin board, it is clear that the heavily publicized racial confrontations on campus are mere symptoms of much deeper changes that are rapidly under way, with far-reaching consequences for American society.

These are changes in the intellectual and moral infrastructure of the American university, not in its outer trappings. Within the tall gates and old buildings, a new world view is consolidating itself. The transformation of American campuses is so sweeping that it is no exaggeration to call it an academic revolution. The distinctive insignia of this revolution can be witnessed on any major campus in America today, and in all major aspects of university life.

Admissions Policy

Virtually all American universities have changed their admissions rules so that they now fill a sizable portion of their freshman class each year with students from certified minority groups—mainly blacks and Hispanics—who have considerably lower grade point averages and standardized test scores than white and Asian American applicants who are refused admission. Since it is often difficult for minorities admitted on the basis of preferential treatment to compete, most universities offer an array of programs and incentives, including cash grants, to encourage these students to pass their courses and stay in school. The coveted perks of so-called affirmative action policies have sometimes been extended to other groups claiming deprivation and discrimination, such as American Indians, natives of Third World countries, women, Vietnam veterans, the physically disabled (now sometimes called the "differently abled"), homosexuals and lesbians.

- At the University of California at Berkeley, black and Hispanic students are up to twenty times (or 2,000 percent) more likely to be accepted for admission than Asian American applicants who have the same academic qualifications. Ernest Koenigsburg, a Berkeley professor of business who has served on several admissions committees, asks us to imagine a student applicant with a high school grade point average of 3.5 (out of a possible 4.0) and a Scholastic Aptitude Test (SAT) score of 1,200 (out of a possible 1,600). "For a black student," Koenigsburg says, "the probability of admission to Berkeley is 100 percent." But if the same student is Asian American, he calculates, "the probability of admission is less than 5 percent." Koenigsburg, one of the architects of the policy, is satisfied with the outcome. "I suppose it's unjust, in a way, but all rules are unjust."[1]

- At Ivy League colleges, which are among the most competitive in the nation, incoming freshmen have average grade scores close to 4.0 and average SATs of 1,250 to 1,300. According to admissions officials, however, several of these schools admit black, Hispanic, and American Indian students with grade averages as low as 2.5 and SAT aggregates "in the 700 to 800 range."[2]

- A similar pattern can also be found at state schools. Over the past five years, the University of Virginia has virtually doubled its black enrollment by accepting more than 50 percent of blacks who apply, and fewer than 25 percent of whites, even though white students generally have much better academic credentials. In 1988, for example, the average white freshman at the university scored 240 points higher on the SAT than the average black freshman. An admissions dean told the *Washington Post*, "We take in more from the groups with weaker credentials and make it harder for those with stronger credentials."[3]

- At Pennsylvania State University, preferential treatment for black students extends beyond admissions; the university offers financial incentives to induce blacks to maintain minimum grades and graduate. All black students who maintain a grade average of C to C+ during the course of a year get checks from the school for $580; for anything better than that, they get $1,160. This official policy endures for all four years of college; it is not connected with financial aid; it applies regardless of economic need. White and other minority students are ineligible for the cash awards.[4]

- Financial subsidies are also offered elsewhere. Starting in the fall of 1990, as part of a program to increase black enrollment by 50 percent, Florida Atlantic University is offering free tuition to every black student who is admitted, regardless of financial need. President Anthony Catanese said the measure is necessary to demonstrate that FAU is "serious about recruiting.[5] Miami-Dade Community College recruits minority students by promising that, if they do not find jobs in their fields of study after graduation, the college will refund their tuition money. No other students qualify for this money-back guarantee.[6] Earlham College in Indiana has a standing offer restricted to black, Hispanic, and American Indian residents of the state: if they choose to attend, the school will replace their student loans with grants.[7] And the University of Nebraska uses state money to fund special scholarships of $1,500 to $3,995 which Vice Chancellor James Jriesen maintains are essential "to correct a documented under-representation of specified minorities in our student population."[8]

- Sometimes university leaders offer justifications for these preferences. Erdman Palmore, a Duke University professor who serves as chairman of the Committee on Black Faculty, maintains that financial inducements are essential for minority students and faculty whose social contributions have been historically undervalued. "By bidding up the price of blacks," says Palmore, "we are hoping to increase their value."[9] Michael Harris, professor of religious studies at the University of Tennessee, argues for greater preferential treatment for minorities and suspension of academic requirements because "when you see the word 'qualifications' used, remember that this is the new code word for whites."[10]

- Although they are stipulated as the prime beneficiaries, not all blacks feel honored by preferential treatment awards. When Stephen Carter, a graduate of Stanford, applied to the Harvard Law School, he received a letter of rejection. Then, a few days later, two Harvard officials telephoned him to apologize for their "error." One explained, "We assumed from your record that you were white." The other noted that the school had recently obtained "additional information that should have been counted in your favor," namely the fact that Carter is black.

Carter recalled:

Naturally I was insulted by this. Stephen Carter, the white male, was not good enough for the Harvard Law School. Stephen Carter, the black male, not only was good enough, but rated agonized telephone calls urging him to attend. And Stephen Carter, color unknown, must have been white: how else would he have achieved what he did in college? In other words, my academic record sounded too good for a black Stanford undergraduate, but not good enough for a white Harvard Law student. Because I was black, however, Harvard was quite happy to scrape me from what it apparently considered the bottom of the barrel.[11]

- Favorable recruitment and hiring policies are not limited to racial minorities at Columbia University. In 1989, the *Columbia Law Review* announced a recruitment program offering preferential treatment for homosexuals and lesbians. The journal added five extra seats to its editorial board to promote "diversity," including special consideration for "sexual orientation."[12]

In the Classroom

Most American universities have diluted or displaced their "core curriculum" in the great works of Western civilization to make room for new course requirements stressing non-Western cultures, Afro-American Studies, and Women's Studies. Since race and gender issues are so sensitive, the university leadership often discourages faculty from presenting factual material that may provoke or irritate minority students. Several professors who cross the academic parameters of what may be said in the classroom have found themselves the object of organized vilification and administrative penalties. Again, these intellectual curbs do not apply to professors who are viewed as the champions of minority interests—they are permitted overtly ideological scholarship, and are immune from criticism even when they make excessive or outlandish claims with racial connotations. This dogmatism extends to the official policy of academic organizations such as the Modern Language Association.

- In the winter of 1989, at the University of Virginia Law School, Professor Thomas Bergin was conducting his usually sprightly class on property. As students responded to his queries, he shot back rebuttals and jibes, egging them on to more thoughtful answers. It is Bergin's style to employ colloquial jargon; thus when one black student stumbled over a question, Bergin said, "Can you dig it, man?" Some students laughed, the class went on, the bell rang.

  The next class day, Bergin entered the room visibly shaken. "I have never been so lacerated," he said. He read from an anonymous note calling him a "racist" and a "white supremacist" on account of his remark to the black student.

  Bergin did not ask who wrote the note. He did not explain his intentions, and move on with the class material. Rather, he gave the class a lengthy recital of his racial resume: he did *pro bono* work for the civil rights movement, he was a member of Klanwatch which monitored hate groups, he was active in recruiting minorities to the university, and so on. Eventually Bergin's eyes filled with tears. "I can't go on," he said. He rushed out of the classroom, unable to control himself.[13]

- When Princeton University in the early 1980s debated whether to introduce a Women's Studies program, which would study "gender scholarship" outside the traditional departments, Dante scholar Robert Hollander expressed reservations at the faculty meeting. "I did not like the fact that this was not a debate about academic issues but about political sensitivity," Hollander says. "My colleagues were telling me that they didn't think much of the program, but would vote for it anyway. I spoke out because I did not want to respond cynically."

  When he criticized the proposed program for its stated political objectives, however, Hollander remembers being subjected to a barrage of personal attacks. "I achieved instant notoriety. Even now, years later, my speech is the thing that most people remember about me." Hollander was surprised to discover that "colleagues I had worked with for a long time, with whom I got on extremely well, turned on me with incredible savagery. I wanted to say, hey, this is your friend, this is Bob Hollander. But nothing I could say would hold them back."

  When the motion to establish Women's Studies passed, Hollander remembers, "Women were embracing and kissing on the floor. This struck me as odd. Was this an academic discussion or a political rally? Were we discussing ideas or feelings? It confirmed what I had feared about the program."

- New approaches to teaching now enjoy prominence and acclaim on campus. Speaking at an October 1989 conference in Washington, Houston Baker of the University of Pennsylvania argued that the American university suffers from a crisis of too much reading and writing. "Reading and writing are merely technologies of control," Baker alleged. They are systems of "martial law made academic." Instead of "valorizing old power relations," universities should listen to the "voices of newly emerging peoples." Baker emphasized the oral tradition, extolling the virtues of rap music and holding up as an exemplar such groups as Public Enemy and NWA.[14] NWA stands for Niggers With Attitude. The group, among other things, sings about the desirability of violence against white people.[15] Baker himself is regarded as one of the most promising black intellectuals in the country, and a leader of the movement to transform the American academy.

- African American scholar Leonard Jeffries claims that whites are biologically inferior to blacks, that the "ultimate culmination" of the "white value system" is Nazi Germany, and that wealthy Jews were responsible for financing the slave trade. Adopting an evolutionary perspective, Jeffries told his class that whites suffer from an inadequate supply of melanin, making them unable to function as effectively as other groups. One reason that whites have perpetrated so many crimes an atrocities, Jeffries argues, is that the Ice Ages caused the deformation of white genes, while black genes were enhanced by "the value system of the sun."[16] Jeffries is no academic eccentric; he is chairman of the Afro-American Studies department at City College of New York (CCNY), and co-author of a controversial multicultural curriculum on-line for all public schools in New York State. Moreover, such extreme views are now frequently expressed by black scholars and activists.

- Many white students graduate from college with similar ideas. Reflecting several themes now promoted on the American campus, a recent graduate from two of the nation's top universities commented in a national magazine:

I am a male WASP who attended and succeeded at Choate preparatory school, Yale College, Yale Law School, and Princeton Graduate School. Slowly but surely, my lifelong habit of looking, listening, feeling, and thinking as honestly as possible has led me to see that white, male-dominated, Western, European culture is the most destructive phenomenon in the known history of the planet. . . . It is deeply hateful of life and committed to death; therefore, it is moving rapidly toward the destruction of itself and most other life forms on earth. And truly, it deserves to die. . . . We're going to have to bite the bullet of truth. We have to face our own individual and collective responsibility for what is happening—our greed, brutality, indifference, militarism, racism, sexism, blindness. . . . Meanwhile, everything we have put into motion continues to endanger us more every day.[17]

- Frequently the sources of such sentiments are minority studies courses. In a manual for race and gender education, distributed by the American Sociological Association, Brandeis University Women's Studies professor Becky Thompson acknowledges the ideological presuppositions of her basic teaching methodology: "I begin the course with the basic feminist principle that in a racist, classist and sexist society we have all swallowed oppressive ways of being, whether intentionally or not. Specifically, this means that it is not open to debate whether a white student is racist or a male student is sexist. He/she simply is. Rather, the focus is on the social forces that keep these distortions in place."[18]

- It is now familiar practice for professional associations of scholars to adopt political positions to which they lend their academic credibility. In 1987, the Modern Language Association, whose members include humanities scholars from universities across the country, passed the following resolution: "Be it therefore resolved that the MLA will refrain from locating future conventions, not already scheduled, in any state that has criminalized acts of sodomy through legislation, unless that legislation, though still on the books, has been found to be unconstitutional, or the state has been enjoined from enforcing it through decisions rendered by the courts."[19]

Life on Campus

Most universities seek to promote "pluralism" and "diversity" on campus by setting up and funding separate institutions for minority groups; thus one finds black student unions, black dormitories, and "theme houses," black fraternities and sororities, black cultural centers, black dining sections, even a black yearbook. Universities also seek to protect minority sensitivities by imposing administrative sanctions, ranging from forced apologies to expulsion, for remarks that criticize individuals or policies based on race, gender, and sexual orientation stereotypes. Since blacks, feminists, and homosexuals are regarded as oppressed victims, they are usually exempt from these restrictions and permitted considerable license in their conduct.

- For example, graduate student Jerome Pinn checked into his dormitory at the University of Michigan to discover that his roommate had covered the walls with posters of nude men. When the young man told Pinn he was an active homosexual who expected to have partners over, Pinn approached the Michigan housing office and asked to be transferred to another room. "They were outraged by this," Pinn says. "They asked me what was wrong with me—what *my* problem was. I said that I had a religious and moral objection to homosexual conduct. They were surprised; they couldn't believe it. Finally they agreed to assign me to another room, but they warned me that if I told anyone of the reason, I would face university charges of discrimination on the basis of sexual orientation."

- In 1988 the law school faculty of the State University of New York at Buffalo adopted a resolution which warned students not to make "remarks directed at another's race, sex, religion, national origin, age or sexual preference," including "ethnically derogatory statements as well as other remarks based on prejudice or group stereotype." Students who violate this rule should not expect protection under the First Amendment, the faculty rule says, because "our intellectual community shares values that go beyond a mere standardized commitment to open and unrestrained debate." The faculty agrees to take "strong and immediate steps" to prosecute offending students through the university judiciary process, but it will "not be limited solely to the use of ordinary university procedures." The faculty also resolves to write to "any bar to which such a student applies," offering "where appropriate, our conclusion that the student should not be admitted to practice law."[20]

- Censorship regulations at several colleges today are restrictive enough that a typical policy at the University of Connecticut interprets as "harassment" all remarks that offend or stigmatize women or minorities. Examples of violations of the University President's Policy on Harassment, for which the penalty ranges from a reprimand to expulsion, include "the use of derogatory names," "inconsiderate jokes," and even "misdirected laughter" and "conspicuous exclusions from conversation." At the same time, and in apparent contradiction with this policy, U-Conn places no restrictions on the sexual conduct of students; the handbook notes that "the university shall not regard itself as the arbiter or enforcer of the morals of its students."[21]

- When the University of Pennsylvania recently announced mandatory "racism seminars" for students, one member of the University Planning Committee voiced her concerns about the coercion involved. She expressed her "deep regard for the individual and my desire to protect the freedoms of *all* members of society." A university administrator sent her note back, with the word "individual" circled and the comment, "This is a RED FLAG phrase today, which is considered by many to be RACIST. Arguments that champion the individual over the group ultimately privilege the 'individuals' who belong to the largest or dominant group."[22]

- Although male white students are expected, on pain of punishment, to demonstrate tolerance and acceptance of minority sentiments, Gayatri Spivak, Andrew Mellon Professor of English and cultural studies at the University of Pittsburgh, argues that such qualities as tolerance cannot reasonably be expected of minority victims. "Tolerance is a loaded virtue," said Spivak, "because you have to have a base of power to practice it. You cannot ask a certain people to 'tolerate' a culture that has historically ignored them at the same time that their children are being indoctrinated into it."[23]

- A student newspaper funded by Vassar College termed black activist Anthony Grate "hypocrite of the month" for espousing anti-Semitic views while publicly denouncing bigotry on campus. In an acrimonious debate, Grate reportedly referred to "dirty Jews" and added, "I hate Jews." Grate later apologized for his remarks. Meanwhile, outraged that the *Spectator* had dared to criticize a black person, the Vassar Student Association first attempted to ban the issue of the publication, and when that failed it withdrew its $3,800 founding. The newspaper "unnecessarily jeopardizes an educational community based on mutual understanding," the VSA explained.[24]

- Some black students have noticed that the campus environment permits and even encourages a double standard on issues affecting race. Rachael Hammer, a bright and attractive young student at Columbia University, said that a black campus activist accused her of being a racist for refusing to date him. "He said: you are going to go out with me," Hammer recalls. "I said no. He then said I was a racist."

Hammer said that the only overt racism she has encountered at Columbia involves hostility directed against whites. "I am told that as a person of color and a member of a historically persecuted group, I cannot be racist against whites," Hammer said. "But blacks can say anything about whites and Jews." Of her prospective suitor, Hammer said, "I knew him since freshman year. Nobody ever heard of him until he got into a fight with a white guy. He turned it into a racial issue that rocked the campus for weeks." Pretty soon, Hammer said, "he started organizing rallies, writing articles in the student paper. His language changed into a kind of ghetto slang. He got into writing poetry—basically a string of epithets about what it felt like to be a black male."

- Among many young blacks on campus, there are hints of profound estrangement and suspicion toward the larger culture. In early 1989, Howard University's campus newspaper, *The Hilltop*, published an article which advanced an argument not infrequently heard on the campus. In "The White Conspiracy," undergraduate Malcolm Carson writes that "black males are specifically programmed for self-destruction by this society.... Hundreds of thousands of U.S. military troops are called on to wage urban warfare on our people. . . . An avalanche of cheap heroin was unleashed into our communities to lull our people to sleep.... African Americans are beginning to realize that the real enemy is not the brother standing across the street, but the white man in the top floor of the downtown high rise."[25]

- Feminists are capable of equally stern sentiments. Commenting on the problem of sexual harassment in late October 1989, University of Colorado graduate student Kristen Asmus observed, "Let's just face it. The men in our society cannot control themselves." Her solution? "Women will start fighting back. Women will begin to react with as much violence as men have mustered against them. Women will begin to stop talking about castration, and make it a reality. Women will begin to abandon their life-giving, caring inner nature and start carrying guns. Women will begin to kill men if they have to."[26]

- University administrators are not always sure how to deal with minority grievance and protest. In May 1989, thirty-one black and Hispanic students barricaded themselves in the office of Stanford president Donald Kennedy, demanding further action on minority issues. Kennedy issued a statement saying "the university will not negotiate on issues of substance in response to unlawful coercion."[27] The next day, Kennedy broke down under pressure, went on to negotiate with the students, and committed the university to hiring thirty minority professors over the next decade and doubling the number of minority doctoral students within the next five years.[28]

- When minority students forcibly occupied the office of the president of the University of Vermont, Lattie Coor, he agreed to sign a seventeen-point agreement, including the provision that "in no case will the number of minorities hired for faculty positions be less than four each year." Coor explained how he came to negotiate with the students. "When it became clear that the minority students with whom I had been discussing these issues wished to pursue negotiations in the context of occupied offices, I agreed to enter negotiation with them."[29]

- One way in which universities appease minority protesters is by setting up and funding distinctive black, Hispanic, or Third World organizations. For example, although its handbook advocates racial integration, Cornell University supports a host of ethnic and minority institutions, most of which do not admit, and none of which encourage, white students as members: Cornell Black Women's Support Network; Ethos Minority Yearbook; Black Biomedical and Technical Association; Gays, Bisexuals and Lesbians of Color; La Asociaciòn Latina; La Organizaciòn de Latinas Universitarias; Le Club Haitien; Mexican-American Student Association; Minority Business Students Association; Minority Industrial and Labor Relation

Student Organization; Minority Undergraduate Law Society; National Society of Black Engineers; Society of Minority Hoteliers; Students of African Decent United; Uhuru Kuumba; Washanga Simba. In addition, there are nine black and Hispanic fraternities and sororities.[30]

- In some quarters not just whites, but also heterosexuals, are suspect. The University of California at Los Angeles (UCLA) recently granted official recognition to Lambda Delta Lambda, a lesbian sorority. UCLA officials emphasized, however, that the sorority may not ban heterosexual women from joining.[31]

- The difficulties encountered by universities in their effort to define and promote "diversity" are evident in an incident at Yale University a few years ago. In August 1987, taking account of the extremely well-attended and vocal activism of homosexuals at Yale, the *Wall Street Journal* reported that the place was getting a gay reputation.[32] Yale has no less than five gay and lesbian groups, including one just for Chicano lesbians.[33] More than a thousand students attend Yale's annual gay-lesbian ball, and gay activist Sara Cohen asks, "What's wrong with a little bestiality?"[34] Concerned that this flagrancy would upset alumni donors, President Benno Schmidt of Yale promptly sent a letter to two thousand volunteer fund-raisers, denying that Yale was a "gay school" and concluding, "If I thought there were any truth to the article, I would be concerned too."[35] Schmidt's statement caused an eruption at the university. A graduate student announced that he was canceling his course in homosexual rights. Gay activist groups besieged Schmidt and demanded to know: what was wrong with 25 or even 70 percent of Yale students being homosexual? What was wrong with Yale being a gay school? Somewhat chagrined, Schmidt responded that, no, there wouldn't be anything wrong with that, but Yale needed to have a proportionate number of heterosexuals too—for the sake of diversity.[37]

• • •

As these examples suggest, an academic and cultural revolution is under way at American universities. It is revising the rules by which students are admitted to college, and by which they pay for college. It is changing what students learn in the classroom, and how they are taught. It is altering the structure of life on campus, including the habits and attitudes of the students in residence. It is aimed at what University of Wisconsin chancellor Donna Shalala calls "a basic transformation of American higher education in the name of multiculturalism and diversity." Leon Botstein, the president of Bard College, goes further in observing that "the fundamental premises of liberal education are under challenge. Nothing is going to be the same any more."

This revolution is conducted in the name of those who suffer from the effects of Western colonialism in the Third World, as well as race and gender discrimination in America. It is a revolution on behalf of minority victims. Its mission is to put an end to bigoted attitudes which permit perceived social injustice to continue, to rectify past and present inequities, and to advance the interests of the previously disenfranchised. Since the revolutionaries view xenophobia, racism, sexism, and other prejudices to be endemic and culturally sanctioned, their project seeks a fundamental restructuring of American society. It involves basic changes in the way economic rewards are distributed, in the way cultural and political power are exercised, and also in privately held and publicly expressed opinions.

The American university is the birthplace and testing ground for this enterprise in social transformation.

There are two reasons why such changes are worthy of close and careful examination. The first is that universities are facing questions that will soon confront the rest of the country. America is very rapidly becoming a multiracial, multicultural society. Immigration from Asia, Latin America, and the Caribbean has changed the landscape with an array of yellow, brown, and black faces.[38] Meanwhile, European immigration has shrunk from 50 percent of all arrivals between 1955 and 1964 to around 7 percent between 1975 and the present.[39] The recolorization of America is further enhanced by domestic minority birth rates, which exceed that of whites.[40]

The result is a new diversity of pigments and lifestyles. When America loses her predominantly white stamp, what impact will that have on her Western cultural traditions? On what terms will the evanescent majority and the emerging minorities, both foreign and domestic, relate to each other? How should society cope with the agenda of increasingly powerful minority groups, which claim to speak for blacks, Hispanics, women, and homosexuals? These challenges are currently being faced by the leadership of institutions of higher education.

Universities are a microcosm of society. But they are more than a reflection or mirror; they are a leading indicator. In universities, as environment where students live, eat, and study together, racial and cultural differences come together in the closest possible way. Of all American institutions, perhaps only the military brings people of such different backgrounds into more intimate contact. With coeducation now a reality in colleges, and with the confident emergence of homosexual groups, the American campus is now sexually democratized as well. University leaders see it as a useful laboratory experiment in training young people for a multicultural habitat. Michael Sovern, president of Columbia, observes, "I like to think that we are leading society by grappling earnestly and creatively with the challenges posed by diversity."[41]

Since the victim's revolution is transforming what is taught, both inside and outside the American university classroom, the second major reason to examine the changes is to discover what young people are learning these days, particularly on questions of race and gender, and the likely consequences for their future and that of their country.

Numerous books, studies, and surveys have documented the alarming scientific and cultural illiteracy of American students.

- A 1989 survey commissioned by the National Endowment for the Humanities showed that 25 percent of college seniors have no idea when Columbus discovered America; the same percentage confuse Churchill's words with Stalin's, and Karl Marx's ideas with those in the U.S. Constitution. A majority of students were ignorant of the Magna Carta, the Missouri Compromise, and Reconstruction. Most could not link Dante, Shakespeare, and Milton with their major works.[42]

- A recent survey of five thousand faculty members by the Carnegie Foundation for the Advancement of Teaching found general agreement about the "widespread lowering of academic standards at their institutions," a deterioration that was only partially camouflaged by an equally "widespread grade inflation."[43]

- A review of twenty-five thousand student transcripts by Professor Robert Zemsky of the University of Pennsylvania showed broad neglect of mathematics and science courses, especially at the advanced level, and an overall "lack of depth and structure" in what undergraduates study.[44]

- Research indicates that it is possible to graduate from 37 percent of American colleges without taking any courses in history, from 45 percent without taking a course in American or English literature, from 62 percent without studying any philosophy, and from 77 percent without studying a foreign language.[45]

• • •

Parents, alumni, and civic leaders all invest substantial resources of time and money in American higher education. They are justifiably anxious about whether the new changes in universities will remedy these problems, or exacerbate them. Will the new policies in academia improve, or damage, the prospects for American political and economic competitiveness in the world? Will they enrich, or debase, the minds and souls of students? Will they enhance, or diminish, the prospects for harmony among different groups? In short, how well will the new project prepare the nation's young people for leadership in the multicultural society of the future?

The current academic revolution is being conducted at the highest levels of the university establishment. It is what Donald Kagan, dean of arts and sciences at Yale University, calls a "revolution from the top down." This fact distinguishes the contemporary period from the 1960s, when student activists applied pressure to a reluctant and recalcitrant administration. Today's university officials are generally sympathetic and often actively engaged in the victim's revolution. In some cases, they sponsor the changes without any student or faculty demands. These revolutionaries inhabit the offices of presidents, provosts, deans, and other administrators. Thus it is possible to alter the basic character of liberal education without very much commotion; as Kagan says, "Few outside the university have any idea what is going on."

Most university presidents and deans cooperate with the project to transform liberal education in the name of minority victims. This group includes an overwhelming majority of presidents of state universities, and all the presidents of the Ivy League schools. Only two or three college heads in the country have voiced public reservations about the course of the academic revolution.[46]

Here, for instance, are the presidents of four major universities voicing support for the minority agenda. While their statements vary in stridency, all of them diagnose the same underlying inequities, and seek the structural reform of higher education as a solution. Further, they all employ the characteristic vocabulary of the revolution, which we must learn to recognize as a kind of code language for the changes to which they point.

"We can create a model here of how a more diverse and pluralistic community can work for our society," University of Michigan president James Duderstadt said in a letter to students and faculty.[47] He added, "Our university has a moral imperative to address the underrepresentation of racial and ethnic groups. . . . The insights and erudition of hitherto excluded groups can enrich our scholarly enterprise; indeed, it seems apparent that we cannot sustain the distinction of our university in the pluralistic world that is our future without the diversity that sustains excellence."[48]

Stanford president Donald Kennedy told the Academic Council in May 1989 that, "we accept the basic design of the multicultural community, and commit ourselves to the encouragement and preservation of these minority groups. We confirm that many minority issues and concerns are not the special pleadings of interest groups, but are Stanford issues—ones that engage all of us."[49]

Keith Brodie, president of Duke University, said in his convocation address to the freshman class in 1989, "We have come to realize that the naturally broadening and civilizing process of a liberal arts education is not enough, by itself, to accomplish the goals of community we have set before us. We must engage intolerance...openly and publicly, as a community, at every opportunity."[50]

Donna Shalala of the University of Wisconsin remarked, "I would plead guilty to both racism and sexism. The university is institutionally racist. American society is racist and sexist. Covert racism is just as bad today as overt racism was thirty years ago. In the 1960s we were frustrated about all this. But now, we are in a position to do something about it."

These statements are not mere rhetoric. Several colleges have issued internal blueprints outlining a basic transformation of the campus over the next few years. In March 1989 Smith College published its *Smith Design for Institutional Diversity*, endorsed by President Mary Dunn and the board of trustees, which includes a pledge for Smith to more than quadruple minority representation on the faculty to 20 percent.[51] The Stanford admission has accepted most of the 132 provisions of the *Final Report of the University Committee on Minority Issues*, which calls for compulsory ethic studies, graduate programs in Afro-American Studies, further expansion of preferential treatment, and funding for "ethnic theme houses" for blacks, Hispanics, and American Indians.[52] Ohio State operates under the *Ohio State University Action Plan*, which seeks to more than double minority student and faculty recruitment by 1994, regardless of the available pool of qualified applicants.[53] The University of Wisconsin has issued *The Madison Plan*, initiated by the chancellor and now official policy, which includes a timetable for special scholarships for minority students, a minority cultural center, an ethic studies requirement, sensitivity education in race and gender, and the hiring of at least seventy minority faculty in three years.[54] The University of Michigan in early 1990 issued its *Michigan Mandate*, claiming credit for hiring seventy-six minority faculty through affirmative action efforts in two years, for multiplying black and Hispanic scholarships and fellowships, for establishing a multimillion dollar Afro-American studies center, and for allocating $27 million for various minority-related programs.[55]

Other colleges such as Arizona State, Berkeley, Columbia, Cornell, Florida State, Harvard, Miami University of Ohio, Penn State, Princeton, Rutgers, the State University of New York at Albany, Stockton State, Temple, Tufts, Vassar, Wayne State University, the University of Arizona, UCLA, University of Massachusetts at Amherst, University of North Carolina at Chapel Hill, and the University of Pennsylvania have announced ambitious projects to rearrange admissions and curricular requirements to foster such values as "tolerance" and "diversity." Over the past few years, presidents and deans on most campuses have assembled task forces to set their agenda for "multiculturalism" or "pluralism," and have then incorporated several of their recommendations into official policy. Diversity, tolerance, multiculturalism, pluralism—these phrases are perennially on the lips of university administrators. They are the principles and slogans of the victim's revolution.

Among university professors, there are many qualms about the academic revolution under way because it challenges traditional norms of scholarship and debate. But these doubts are dissipating with time, as the composition of the body of American faculty rapidly changes. Older, traditionally liberal professors are retiring and making way for a new generation, weaned on the assorted ideologies of the late 1960s: the civil rights movement, the protest movement against U.S. involvement in Vietnam, and the burgeoning causes of feminism and gay rights. Many of these scholars in the humanities and social sciences have now invested their energies in what sociologist David Riesman of Harvard University calls "domestic liberation movements"; in fact, at a recent conference on liberal education, the *New York Times* found the young academics in agreement that "just about everything...is an expression of race, class or gender."[56]

Speaking with the typical frankness of these newly ascendant activists, black scholar Henry Louis Gates of Duke University remarks, "Ours was the generation that took over buildings in the late 1960s and demanded the creation of Black and Women's Studies programs and now, like the return of the repressed, we have come back to challenge the traditional curriculum."[57] Middlebury English professor Jay Parini writes, "After the Vietnam War, a lot of us didn't just crawl back into our library cubicles; we stepped into academic positions. With the war over, or visibility was lost and it seemed for a while—to the unobservant—that we had disappeared. Now we have tenure, and the work of reshaping the universities has begun in earnest."[58] Annette Kolodny, dean of the humanities at the University of Arizona, says that she was ideologically trained as a leader of the Berkeley protests of the 1960s. "I see my scholarship as an extension of my political activism," she says. As a former worker for Ceasar Chavez's United Farm Worker, Kolodny maintains that her scholarship is designed to expose "the myths and U.S. has always put forward about itself as an egalitarian nation." In fact, she argues, the United States has "taken this incredible fertile continent and utterly destroyed it with a ravaging hatred."[59]

These younger professors are now the bellwethers of the victim's revolution. Already their influence is dominant; soon they will entirely displace the old guard. As it is, most of the senior humanities and social science faculty acquiesce in the changes, and mildly protest only when the issue engages obvious faculty concerns such as intellectual freedom or the preservation of academic standards. Outside the mainstream of the academy, the National Association of Scholars, a small group of faculty crusaders, is launching a bold but somewhat quixotic effort to arrest the pace of the revolution.[60]

Although it began in the humanities and social sciences, the reverberations of the revolution are now being felt in law schools, medical schools, and the departments of the hard sciences which previously considered themselves exempt from campus agitation. Many law school and medical school deans and faculty are already reconciled to routinely extending admission to minority students who are academically less prepared than other applicants who are refused admission. Professor Bernard Davis of Harvard Medical School says that faculty face enormous pressure from the administration to pass black and Hispanic students even when they fail the same exam repeatedly.[61] For the first time, undergraduate and graduate professors in physics, chemistry, and biology are accused by minority activists of practicing "white male science" and operating "institutionally racist" departments. While many continue to resist pressures for preferential minority hiring and the inclusion of minority and especially female "perspectives" in the hard sciences, they seem bewildered about, and mute in responding to, accusations of systematic and methodological racism and sexism; consequently, with administrative and activist pressure, the victim's revolution is beginning its siege of the final bastion of "pure scholarship."

Many students are unable to recognize the scope of the revolution, because it is a force larger than themselves, acting upon them. Thus they are like twigs carried by a fast current. They are well aware that something is going on around them, and they might even squirm and complain, but for the most part students do not shape the rules that govern their academic and social lives in the university. Rather, those rules are intended to shape them. There are, on virtually every campus, organized alliances of minority, feminists, and homosexual students, who generally form the youth corps of the revolution. But they are not its prime movers: their numbers are too small, and they have no power to make the fundamental decisions that change the basic structure and atmosphere of the university.

Iconoclastic student newspapers at a number of universities mount spirited attacks on the revolution. Of the fifty or so publications, perhaps the most famous is the *Dartmouth Review* at my own alma mater. As a former editor of the *Review,* I witnessed first-hand engagement with the administration, although I had graduated long before the newspaper's most notorious show-downs—the 1986 sacking of anti-apartheid shanties by conservative students on the Dartmouth green, and the bitter confrontation between *Review* reporters and a black music professor in 1988.

While these recent episodes are not representative of the content of the *Review* or other papers, they illustrate the temptations to which overzealous undergraduate activists sometimes succumb. No doubt some of these antics are sophomoric, but we must remember that they are largely carried out by sophomores. The result, however, is that the influence of the "alternative student papers" is generally limited to confounding a few professors and deans, offering a therapeutic outlet for a small group of students, and in some cases informing and mobilizing a part of the alumni body. These undergraduate renegades are not powerful enough to stall the victim's revolution; perhaps for this reason, some of their attacks are reflective, ill-considered, unkind, and lacking in historical perspective; thus they become further symptoms, rather than remedies, for campus maladies. Much of the time, they serve as a kind of journalistic tripwire, kicking up issues larger than they are equipped to handle.

Consequently, the current academic revolution on behalf of minority victims moves at a swift pace. Nothing interrupts it or gives it pause; changes are proposed, accepted, and implemented in broad, continuous strokes. It is not that the changes are indefensible, but simply that they are seldom if ever subjected to criticism; thus there is never any need to offer an explanation.

Nevertheless, it is crucial that the arguments for the revolution be made, objections to them offered, and the two sides weighed against one another. Such an approach will ensure that universities define and defend their objectives, that mechanisms are developed to carry out worthy objectives, and that both the ends and the means serve the students for whom the universities exist in the first place.

• • •

In this book, I dramatize the transformation in academia through an examination of six episodes at different universities—Berkeley, Stanford, Howard, Michigan, Duke, and Harvard—which are in the vanguard of the revolution of minority victims. These colleges are leaders in the academy whose policies smaller schools often emulate. In every instance, I supply examples to show that the phenomena I describe are widely experienced on other campuses. Each case study exposes the conflicts and changes which the revolution must face, and reveals kernels of principle upon which priorities have been established and those challenges resolved. Through narrative and firsthand interviews, I seek to give the reader an inside look into how the controversial claims of the new politics of race and sex assert themselves in all areas of campus life, and are debated and adjudicated within the governing framework of the university.

Three basic issues are addressed:

Who Is Admitted?

How are preferential treatment policies justified which treat racial groups differently and admit some students based on academic merit, and others largely or exclusively based on their skin color? Is there such a thing as good discrimination? What effect does "affirmative action" have in the classroom and on campus? What becomes of students who benefit from preferential admissions? What are the arguments of justice and of expediency that warrant such programs?

What Is Studied?

Why are universities expelling Homer, Aristotle, Shakespeare, and other "white males" from their required reading list? Is it true that a study of non-Western and minority cultures will liberate students from ethnocentrism, racism, sexism, and homophobia? What are the merits of overtly ideological scholarship in Afro-American Studies and Women's Studies programs? What totems and taboos attend the teaching of sensitive material in race and gender scholarship? What do students learn from the new curriculum that prepares them for life after college?

Life on Campus

Should universities promote integration or separatism? Why do minority students attack exclusively, yet seem to prefer segregated institutions for themselves? Should universities encourage or allow corresponding all-white groups, and if not, why? Is there a case for university censorship of opinions that trespass on the feelings of blacks, feminists, and homosexuals? Should universities subject students to "sensitivity education" aimed at raising their consciousness of race and gender? Why are there so many racial incidents on campuses in recent years, and why do they happen most frequently at universities which are most resolute in their campaigns to combat bigotry?

While in each case I show what internal and external forces generate the conflicts that universities must face, my emphasis throughout is on how the university leadership deals with its challenges. It is here, after all, that social responsibility for establishing a healthy educational and cultural environment ultimately rests, and it is those in charge who make the rules that either solve problems or make them worse. Since I uncover and document many areas where our current university leadership seems to fall short, in my final chapter I suggest ways in which these issues could be handled more responsibly, so that the revolution of minority victims may more effectively achieve its legitimate aspirations, and all students may be better prepared for the challenges of career and citizenship in the society in which they will find themselves after graduation.

• • •

During my research for this book I discovered a tremendous curiosity, on the part of my sources, about my own background and were I was "coming from." Issues of race and sex are inevitably personal, and detachment is considered difficult, if not impossible. I am usually credited with a "Third World perspective," a term I find unclear and problematic. For readers who are interested, however, I offer a few personal comments which may be helpful in establishing my own interest and viewpoint.

I am a native of India who came to the United States in 1978. India is a democratic country struggling to accommodate enormous religious, tribal, and cultural heterogeneity. From my childhood I have experienced, and wondered about, this struggle, which is a subject of ongoing conversation and debate among Indians. America affords me a rare opportunity to examine questions of ethnocentricity, race, and gender, but from a unique cultural perspective. On questions that are so close to our daily lives, that engage us on both a conscious and subconscious level, I think that an element of critical distance may be helpful and illuminating. It makes possible observations that are more difficult to make when one is too close to, or engulfed by, an issue.

A personal anecdote may clarify why I believe this is so. A month or so after I arrived in the United States and enrolled, as a Rotary exchange student, in a public high school in Arizona, my host parents urged me to take someone from my class to the Homecoming dance. At first I was reluctant, but finally agreed. I approached a pretty young woman who said that she would have to ask her parents but would let me know tomorrow.

The next day I asked, "What did they say?"

She looked at me, "Who?"

"Your parents," I said.

"Say about what?"

At first I was simply astounded, but then I realized, with a sinking feeling, that I had approached *the wrong girl*. It was only later that I realized what my problem was: I thought all white women looked alike.

Later, when I was at Dartmouth and heard a student in the Afro-American Society charge that it was "grossly racist" that she was mistaken for someone else by a white student, I was sympathetic but could not be totally outraged. My own experience helped me understand that, no matter what our skin color or background, it is not easy to transcend our cultural particularity. Provincialism is a universal problem which all groups must confront; it is not a moral deformity confined to whites.

I enrolled as a freshman at Dartmouth in 1979, and graduated in 1983. I spent the next two years at Princeton University, where I edited an alumni magazine. Since then, I have continued to observe and follow goings-on in the American academy. For the past two years I have researched and studied the revolution of minority victims, spending a great deal of time on various campuses, attending classes and interviewing administrators, faculty, and students. As a student, I developed hypotheses that subsequent research has systematized or, in some cases, invalidated. Although I now write from a position more informed, and I hope more mature, than that of my undergraduate days, I believe that my close contact with the university over the past decade has given me a valuable eyewitness position to observe the sweeping changes going on around me.

I found, during my recent campus travels, that I can still pass for a student. I feel a bond with the new generation of young people, and do not agree with those who say that today's students are only interested in personal aggrandizement. Everywhere I observed a strong idealism, a search for principles that transcend expediency and self-interest. I admire this youthful quest and believe that universities should sustain and encourage it.

I especially emphasize with minority students, who seek to discover principles of equality and justice that go considerably beyond the acquisition of vocational skill. Acutely conscious of America's history of exclusion and prejudice, they know that their past victories have not come without a struggle, and they yearn to find their place in the university and in society, to discover who they are, individually and as a people. These are challenges I faced very recently in college, and continue to face as a first-generation immigrant. Thus I feel a special kinship with minority students, and believe that the university is the right location for them to undertake their project of self-discovery.

I believe, as John Henry Newman writes in *The Ideal of a University*, that the goal of liberal learning is "that true enlargement of mind which is the power of viewing many things at once as one whole, of referring them severally to their true place in the universal system, of understanding their respective values, and determining their mutual dependence." This knowledge of ourselves, and of the geographic and intellectual universe we inhabit, is ultimately what liberates and prepares us for a rich and full life as members of society. The term *liberal* derives from the term *liberalis*, which refers to the free person, as distinguished from the slave. It is in liberal education, properly devised and understood, that minorities and indeed all students will find the means for their true and permanent emancipation.

The Vanishing Classics and Other Myths: Two Episodes in the Culture War

Gerald Graff

What follows are two episodes in the culture war over the university. The first exemplifies the distorted way recent changes in the university are seen from the outside; the second suggests how these changes are experienced from the inside, from the perspective of one teacher's classroom. As we will see, there is a certain discrepancy.

"To Hell with Shakespeare," or the Great *Color Purple* Hoax

The story that the classics of Western civilization are disappearing from college reading lists has been told so often and so widely that it has virtually become a commonplace of the current educational debate. A recent book reviewer in the *Chicago Tribune*, for example, writes of how "authors central to the western literary and philosophical traditions" are being "stripped from the curriculum and replaced by vociferous enemies of our common culture."[1] The reviewer cites no evidence that what he describes is, in fact, taking place. He obviously thinks he does not have to; that the classics are going out is presumably as obvious as that tuition fees are going up.

Dinesh D'Souza, in his recent best seller *Illiberal Education* asks, "Why are universities expelling Homer, Aristotle, Shakespeare, and other 'white males' from their required reading list?"[2] Again, the way the question is put makes it as established that the state of affairs being described actually exists. The issue is not whether "white males" are, in fact, being "expelled" from required courses, but why. We well see the kind of evidence on which D'Souza bases his observation.

As it happens, the claim that the classics have been or are in the process of being "expelled" and "stripped from the curriculum" is provably false, as D'Souza and the *Tribune* reviewer might have suspected had they taken the trouble to spend a few minutes in the textbook departments of a few campus bookstores. No doubt the full story will someday be told of how the myth of the vanishing classics could have come to be so uncritically believed and disseminated. For now, however, a look at an exemplary case should tell us a good deal.

Early in 1988 Christopher Clausen, head of the English department at Pennsylvania State University, published an article in the *Chronicle of Higher Education* entitled "It Is Not Elitist to Place Major Literature at the Center of the English Curriculum." The article rehearsed what was already by then becoming a familiar set of charges about the damaging effect of canon revisionism on the college curriculum. What was to make Clausen's article memorable, it turned out, was a comment he dropped almost in passing: Clausen observed that he would be willing to "bet that [Alice Walker's] *The Color Purple* is taught in more English courses today than all of Shakespeare's plays combined."[3]

The alarm that the traditional canon was being tossed out had been loudly sounded in 1984 by William J. Bennett, soon to become secretary of education, in a National Endowment for the Humanities report entitled "To Reclaim a Legacy," and it was sounded again three years later by Allan Bloom in his best seller *The Closing of the American Mind*.[5] By 1988 reports were circulating about a controversy at Stanford University over its Western civilization course, as Bennett and others charged that the great books were being sacrificed at Stanford to a minority political agenda, subsequently to be labeled "political correctness." Only days before Clausen's article appeared in print, both the *New York Times* and the *Washington Post* had run editorials on the theme of the vanishing classics. In the *Post* article Jonathan Yardley wrote as follows:

> [A]ccording to [current] vigilantes of the English departments, literary quality is irrelevant. . . . Makes you want to rush right back to college, doesn't it? To hell with Shakespeare and Milton, Emerson and Faulkner! Let's boogie! Let's take courses in the writers who really matter, the writers whom the WASPish old guard sneers at. Let's get relevant with courses on Gothic novels, bodice-ripper romances, westerns, detective stories—all of which, The Times advises us, "are proliferating" in the English departments.[6]

Shocking as Yardley's comments were, however, they left vague the actual extent of the damage. No one has reduced it to cold, hard numbers until Clausen offered to wager that Walker's novel had achieved parity with "all of Shakespeare's plays combined."

Nor was it any mere outsider talking now, but the head of one of the nation's major English departments. When someone so close to the scene and in a position of such authority makes such a pronouncement, any reporter or other nonacademic is justified in assuming that he must know what he is talking about. And Clausen would not be the only well-placed professor to declare that the situation was desperate.

It is possible that Clausen imagined his article would be read mostly be fellow academics, who would know enough to discount his improbable estimate as a case of facetious professorial exaggeration. But before anyone could determine whether Clausen was serious, much less take him up on his bet, his *Color Purple* remark had become Exhibit A in a trumped-up charge of canonicide in the national press.

Within days of its publication Clausen's remark was quoted in a fresh denunciation of the canon revisionists in the *Wall Street Journal*. In this article, entitled "From Western Lit to Westerns as Lit," journalist David Brooks gave the strong impression that at Duke University and other campuses, popular authors like Louis L'Amour, "Zane Grey novels, movies and even comic books . . ." had virtually superseded Shakespeare and other classic authors.[7]

The following week Secretary Bennett cited Brooks's *Wall Street Journal* article in a widely reported address in which (as the *Chronicle* reported) he charged that colleges "are eliminating classic works from the curriculum and replacing them with 'nonsense' promoted by 'trendy lightweights.'" The *Chronicle* reporter quoted Clausen's *Color Purple* remark, though without saying if Bennett had referred to it.[8]

A few months later Clausen's *Color Purple* remark and Brooks's *Wall Street Journal* editorial (which had quoted Clausen's remark) were adduced once again in an essay entitled "The Canon under Siege" in the neoconservative *New Criterion*. The fiction writer and man of letters Mark Helprin quoted Clausen and Brooks to back up his claim that literature departments were being taken over by "urban guerrillas," who "are not really interested in literature at all" and view it merely "as a tool of oppression (or, at best, a weapon against it), rather than in impartial phenomenon that addresses essential questions beyond and apart from politics."[9] Shortly before Helprin's article, Terry Teachout in *Commentary* had declared that it was the expressed objective of the revisionists "to erase the values of Western culture from the minds of the young by deliberately failing to introduce them to the history and literature in which those values are embodied."[10] Somehow, Teachout neglected to quote Clausen. But by now it was ceasing to matter who was quoting whom.

Clearly a certain picture of reality was forming out of the sheer repetition of the same recycled "evidence" from one overheated account to the next. The next writer to reinforce the picture was Lynne V. Cheney, Bennett's successor as chairman of the National Endowment for the Humanities. Cheney wrote in *Humanities in America*, a report on the state of the humanities "to the

President, the Congress, and the American People," that "viewing humanities texts as though they were primarily political documents is the most noticeable trend in the academic study of the humanities today. Truth and beauty and excellence are regarded as irrelevant," and "questions of intellectual and aesthetic quality" are dismissed.[11] Among the handful of sources for her observation that Cheney cited was Brooks's *Wall Street Journal* article.

All this took place within a few months in 1988. Since then I have seen Clausen's *Color Purple* comment quoted again and again as if it were sober truth. It would take considerable research to track down all these citations, which would be tedious to list in any case, but one of them especially deserves mention: Dinesh D'Souza uses Clausen's comment to nail down the above-mentioned assertion in *Illiberal Education* that universities are "expelling Homer, Aristotle, Shakespeare, and other 'white males' from their required reading list." D'Souza acknowledges that "most colleges still retain a mixture of Western classics and newly introduced texts reflecting the new minority agenda." But the acknowledgment is followed immediately be a warning that the classics' days are numbered. "[T]he late arrivals," writes D'Souza, "are displacing their predecessors as the campaign for curricular diversity gains momentum." D'Souza's evidence? "Perhaps Christopher Clausen, chairman of the English department at Penn State University, reflected the emerging consensus when he remarked, 'I would bet that Alice Walker's *The Color Purple* is taught in more English courses today than all of Shakespeare's plays combined.'"[12]

Did Clausen, D'Souza, or any of the other critics who popularized the *Color Purple* story make any effort to check its accuracy? One might have expected them to, since another part of their complaint was that the very idea of truth was being held in contempt by canon revisionists, who allegedly reduced all knowledge to ideological bias. In fact, it is not difficult to obtain information about the texts being taught in college courses. Most departments now issue course description pamphlets listing the titles and authors to be assigned in the coming semester.

Using such materials myself along with enrollment statistics, I was able in a few hours to make a rough canvass of the texts taught in the Northwestern University English department from the fall of 1986, when Alice Walker's novel was first assigned in a course, to the spring of 1990. Over this four-year period I located two courses in which *The Color Purple* was taught, while I found eight courses that required at least six plays by Shakespeare and eight that required at least two. Shakespeare's dominance became even more visibly one-sided when I totaled the number of students in these courses. The courses assigning at least six Shakespearean plays enrolled 681 students, while the ones assigned at least two enrolled 874, for a total of 1,555 students reading a minimum of two plays. The enrollment in the two courses assigning *The Color Purple* 12.5 read at least two of Shakespeare's plays and 5.5 read six or more. In other words, for every reading of Walker there were approximately *eighty-three* readings of Shakespeare. Shakespeare 83, Walker 1.

There is no reason to think Northwestern is exceptional. According to Duke University Professor Cathy Davidson, the Duke English department, "ostensibly the worst offender at tossing out the classics," requires "a 'Major Writers' course on Chaucer, Shakespeare, Milton, and Pope. (Pope!)"[13] None of the exposés on Duke had mentioned this evidently unnewsworthy fact, as none had mentioned that traditional literary approaches are at least as well represented on the Duke literature faculty as recent innovations.

At Stanford also, the extent of curricular change turns out to have been widely inflated by the critics. D'Souza in his chapter on Stanford draws a scandalous picture in which Plato, Locke, and other canonical figures have given way at Stanford to the likes of Frantz Fanon's *The Wretched of the Earth*. But as John Searle points out in a *New York Review of Books* article that is itself harshly critical of canon revisionism, the revised Stanford program still demands that courses satisfying the humanities requirement assign "the Bible, 'a classical Greek philosopher, an early Christian thinker, a Renaissance dramatist, an Enlightenment thinker,' and readings from Marx and Freud. At least one non-European work must be studied and at some point in each academic quarter 'substantial attention' must be given to 'the issues of *race, gender, and class.*'" Searle judges that only one of the eight courses fulfilling the requirement, a course entitled "Europe and the Americas," represents "a genuinely radical change from the earlier program." And even in this course texts from "the European canon remain, but they are read along with works of Spanish-

American, American-Indian, and African-American authors."[14] Searle concludes that the Stanford "controversy became so fogged by political polemics and by partial and inaccurate reports in the press that the cultural issues, and what actually occurred, were not made clear to the general public." In short, "reports of the demise of 'culture,' Western or otherwise, in the required freshman course at Stanford are grossly exaggerated."[15]

More systematically gathered information about the national picture has been available since 1986, thanks to a Modern Language Association (MLA) sampling of catalog descriptions of eighty-one English programs at four-year colleges and universities in 1984-85. According to a report on the sampling, "the basic configuration of the English major appears to have changed only slightly since 1965-68," the period of an earlier study. Most departments (76 percent) still require "historical coverage. . . ."[16] A more comprehensive MLA study of the English major in 271 departments in 1984-85 reveals a similar emphasis on tradition. "Arranged in their approximate descending order of frequency, the courses most commonly prescribed for the major are British literature survey; American literature survey; Shakespeare; history of the English language, linguistics or comparative grammar; and literary criticism or theory."[17]

The MLA study of course catalogs also indicates that though "new courses—in women and literature, black American literature, popular literature, literary theory—have been added to the general English curriculum, . . . few have found their way into the requirements for the major."[18] The key phrase here is "added to"; the most striking changes have been at the edges of the curriculum, in the elective courses, where new texts and topics have been overlaid without altering the shape of the curriculum as a whole or the bread-and-butter requirements, which remain dominated almost as much as they were a half century ago by the likes of Shakespeare, Austen, and Dickens. The Alice Walker, Toni Morrisons, and Zora Neale Hurstons crop up frequently, but they appears usually as add-ons rather than permanent replacements for the older authors.

This pattern is confirmed by a 1990 MLA survey of texts taught in several upper-division literature courses (i.e., American literature, 1800-1865; the nineteenth-century British novel, preferably the Victorian; and Renaissance literature, excluding Shakespeare). Though the survey was restricted to three courses, its results are nonetheless significant, in part because almost six hundred English faculty members provided information on their courses. According to Phyllis Franklin and her colleagues at the MLA, the findings for nineteenth-century American literature indicate that "respondents give priority to the authors who have long been regarded as major figures of the period"—specifically, Hawthorne, Thoreau, Melville, and Emerson. "A similar pattern exists in courses in the British novel. Major writers of the period—Jane Austen, Charlotte and Emily Brontë, Charles Dickens, George Eliot, Thomas Hardy, and William Makepeace Thackeray—are still being taught and are regarded as important."[19]

Even more to the point than the strong showing of the canonical favorites is the weak one made by their recent challengers. Among authors and works recently added to required readings in nineteenth-century American literature, Harriet Beecher Stowe was the most frequently mentioned noncanonical author. Yet Stowe was listed by only 15 percent of the teachers surveyed. Native American literature has lately been added to required readings by an even more meager 6 percent.[20]

In short, the college literary canon has been changing, as it had for a century, by accretion at the margins, not by dumping the classics. Indeed, no recent revision in the canon has been nearly as abrupt and dramatic as the one that occurred at the end of the nineteenth century, when—in the face of dire predictions by traditionalists that anticipated those of today—the Greek and Latin classics were replaced by English works, which now acquired the title of "the classics."

The state of literature offerings in American high schools is not significantly different from that of the colleges, according to another recent report, by the Center for the Learning and Teaching of Literature at the State University of New York at Albany. The Albany report, written under the chairmanship of the distinguished educational historian Arthur N. Applebee, concludes that as of 1989, "the lists of most frequently required books and authors" are still "dominated by white males, with little change in overall balance from similar lists 25 to 80 years ago." It finds that such figures as Shakespeare, Steinbeck, Dickens, and Twain remain central and that the addition of minority writers seems "to be limited to the margins of the established canon. . . ." The new additions "certainly do not reflect any wholesale rethinking." In fact, in many schools, "there is no evidence of a broadening of the canon to represent a wider spectrum of authors."[21]

My point in producing statistics is not to minimize the changes that have been taking place in the teaching of the humanities, changes we will soon examine more closely. The exposés of political correctness have exaggerated and misrepresented the phenomenon, but they have not made it up. There are those who disregard the norms of democratic debate and seek to turn the entire curriculum into an extension of a radical social agenda, with compulsory reeducation workshops thoughtfully provided for the unenlightened. There are those who justify turning their courses into consciousness raising sessions on the ground that all teaching is inevitably political anyway. This authoritarian behavior is indeed disturbing, and it has been making enemies out of potential friends of the reform movement. But this is hardly an excuse for the critics' apocalyptic descriptions of the entire scene, to whose complications they are oblivious. To put it simply, the critics have not been telling the truth.

Teaching the Politics of *Heart of Darkness*

Since I started teaching in the mid-1960s, a work I have assigned frequently is Joseph Conrad's classic *Heart of Darkness*, published in 1899. When I first assigned the novella in 1966 or 1967, I taught it in much the way it had been taught to me in college in the late 1950s, as a profound meditation on a universal moral theme. I presented Conrad's story of the destruction of the idealistic trader Mr. Kurtz as a universal parable of the precarious status of civilized reason in a world overly confident of its having outgrown the primitive and the irrational.

My reading of *Heart of Darkness* as a universal parable of reason and unreason pointed up something in the novel that I still think is important. But this reading also depended on my not seeing certain things or not treating them as worth thinking about. Of little interest to me were the facts that Conrad set his novella in the Congo in the high period of European colonialism and that he chooses subjugated black Africans to represent the primitive, irrational forces that are Mr. Kurtz's undoing. Conrad, after all, could have chosen any number of ways to symbolize the forces of primitive unreason. That he happened to choose black Africa seemed incidental to his main intention, which was to make a statement about the human condition that would transcend mere questions of nationality and race.

Like Mark Helprin, whom I quoted above from The *New Criterion*, I had been trained to believe that literature is "an impartial phenomenon that addresses essential questions beyond and apart from politics," and I assumed that these transcendent concerns were what the teaching of literature is all about. The subjugation of black Africans was the sort of thing that might interest historians, sociologists, and political scientists, but if the job was to treat literature *as* literature, it was at best of ancillary interest. After all, if God had wanted us to raise political questions in teaching literature, why had he put the departments of English and sociology in separate buildings?

It never occurred to me to ask how a black person might read the story, and the fact that only a small number of black students appeared in my classes helped assure that the question did not come up. Had it come up, however, I would have found it beside the point. What difference did it make who you were and what your history was when you read a literary work? The point of studying literature was to rise above those traces of your upbringing and history. It was Conrad and his vision that mattered, and reflecting on the position from which you read Conrad could only distract attention from his vision to your own narcissistic special interests.

Today I teach *Heart of Darkness* very differently. One critical work that caused me to change my approach was an essay by Nigerian novelist Chinua Achebe, entitled "An Image of Africa: Racism in Conrad's *Heart of Darkness*."[22] Achebe argues that Conrad's presentation of black Africa is thoroughly racist. And he is able to accumulate a painfully large number of quotations from both the novel and Conrad's letters and diaries that do reveal how cruelly stereotyped Conrad's thinking about the black African is. Here, for example, is a part of one of the passages quoted by Achebe in which Conrad's narrator, Charlie Marlow, reflects on the position of himself and his shipmates:

We were wanderers on a prehistoric earth, on an earth that wore the aspect of an unknown planet. We could have fancied ourselves the first of men taking possession of an accursed inheritance, to be subdued at the cost of profound anguish and of excessive toil. But suddenly as we struggled around a bend there would be a glimpse of rush walls, of peaked grass-roofs, a burst of yells, a whirl of black limbs, a mass of hands clapping, of feet stamping, of bodies swaying, of eyes rolling under the droop of heavy and motionless foliage. The steamer toiled along slowly on the edge of a black and incomprehensible frenzy. The prehistoric man was cursing us, praying to us, welcoming us—who could tell?. . . .[23]

Achebe observes that in this passage and often elsewhere in the novel black Africans appear as an undifferentiated mass of eye-rolling, tomtom-beating savages, "a black and incomprehensible frenzy" representing a primitive and "prehistoric" stage of humanity. One is a bit startled to realize that passages of apparent eloquence that have sent chills down the spine of Western readers sound worse than comic when read from Achebe's point of view (though Achebe notes that F. R. Leavis also found the prose of this novel comically bathetic).[24]

Achebe acknowledges that Conrad expresses compassion for the exploited Africans and that he "condemn[s] the evil of imperial exploration."[25] Yet Achebe argues that ultimately Conrad reduces Africa to a mere "foil for Europe," a mere "setting and backdrop which eliminates the African as human factor," and directs the reader's attention instead to the tragedy of the white imperialist Kurtz. More important and disturbing for Achebe than Conrad's stereotyped portrayal of black Africans is his unspoken assumption about whose point of view counts. As Achebe puts it, "Can nobody see the preposterous and perverse arrogance in thus reducing Africa to the role of props for the break-up of one petty European mind?"[26]

In short, according to Achebe, what Conrad does to black Africa at the level of representation is something like what European imperialism was doing to it. Even in the process of satirizing European imperialism, Conrad uses Africa as a "backdrop" for the implied superiority of European civilization. The real question, Achebe says, "is the dehumanization of Africa and Africans which this age-long attitude has fostered and continues to foster in the world. And the question is whether a novel which celebrates this dehumanization, which depersonalized a portion of the human race, can be called a great work of art. My answer is: No, it cannot."[27]

I suspect it would be hard for anyone of whatever political persuasion to read Achebe's essay and still read and teach *Heart of Darkness* in quite the same way he or she did before. I at least found I could not. It was not that Achebe's essay convinced me that *Heart of Darkness* is completely racist; in fact, it did not. What Achebe did convince me was that Conrad's assumptions about race are not, as I had imagined, simply an extraneous or nonliterary element of the novel but something that the novel's literary and aesthetic effort depends upon. It had obviously been far easier for me to suspend disbelief in Conrad's assumptions about race and to turn the story into purely aesthetic experience that it was for Achebe, for whom the way a novel represents black Africans could be truly a matter of life and death.

Then, too, black and third world students were beginning to show up more frequently in my university and my classes—still in pitiful proportions, to be sure, but enough to make it harder for me to take for granted that Conrad's outlook and my own were the natural and normal one. This is not to say that how we read is determined by our color (or gender or ethnic origin). But it would be foolish to deny that the social composition of the students sitting in front of you has an influence on the way you teach. If it did not, we all would be teaching Greek and Latin instead of English and American literature.

Even if Achebe's interpretation of Conrad is unfair, as I think it is, it forced me to rethink my assumptions about art and politics. For according to Achebe, Conrad's novel is not simply a disinterested work of art, but a text that played and may still be playing an active role in constructing the Western image of black Africa. "Conrad did not originate the image of Africa which we find in this book," Achebe writes. "It was and is the dominant image of Africa in the Western imagination and Conrad merely brought the peculiar gifts of his own mind to bear on it. For reasons which can certainly use close psychological inquiry the West seems to suffer deep anxieties about the precariousness of its civilization and to have a need for constant reassurance by comparison with Africa."[28] Achebe's point is one that recent literary and cultural "theory" has been making, though I think with more complications and qualifications; that literary representations are not simply neutral aesthetic descriptions but interventions that act upon the world they describe. This, in fact, is the point underlying many recent critiques of the idea of *objectivity*, critiques that are poorly understood by their critics; the point is not that there is no truth but that descriptions influence the situations they describe, thereby complicating the problem of truth.

In short, I was forced to rethink not just my interpretation of *Heart of Darkness* but my theoretical assumptions about literature. First, I was forced to recognize that I *had* theoretical assumptions. I had previously thought I was simply teaching the truth about *Heart of Darkness*, "the text itself." I now had to recognize that I had been teaching an interpretation of the text, one that was shaped by certain *theory* that told me what was and was not worth noticing and emphasizing in my classroom. I had been unable to see my theory *as* a theory because I was living so comfortably inside it.

When I teach *Heart of Darkness* now, as I have in several undergraduate courses for the last few years, I assign Achebe's essay. I do not simply teach Achebe's interpretation as the correct one, however, but ask my student to weigh it against other interpretations. Nor do I discard my earlier reading of the novel as a contemplation of universal truths about the human soul. I assign another critical essay that argues for that interpretation. I also assign several essays (all these materials are included in the Norton Critical Edition of Conrad's novel) by critics who take issue with Achebe. These critics—and I agree with them—grant Achebe's thesis up to a point about Conrad's racism and colonialism but argue that Achebe ignores or minimizes the powerful critique of racism and colonialism that coexists in the novel with these more sinister attitudes.

After Conrad my class reads Achebe's novel *Things Fall Apart*, which presents a counterview of Africa to Conrad's, as if Achebe were trying to wrest the power to represent Africa away from the great European. I supplement these materials with short essays representing opposing sides in the past and present debate over the place, or nonplace, of politics in the arts, illustrating the fact that the debate has a long history dating back to Plato's founding of the history of criticism in an act of political correctness, his expulsion of the poets from his republic for corrupting the morals of the state. Also included in the reading list are several recent neoconservative polemics, some of which say unflattering things about me, impressing my students that their instructor has been abused by so many prominent people. I also invite conservative colleagues into my class to debate the issues with me and my students. To make sure my students enter the debate rather than watch passively from the sidelines, I assign a paper on it or ask them to prepare class presentations in which they give their views.

In short, I now teach *Heart of Darkness* as part of a critical debate about how to read it, which in turn is part of a larger theoretical debate about how politics and power affects the way we read literature. Without claiming to be neutral or disguising my own leanings, I try to help students adjudicate between competing arguments and make informed choices on the key points of contention: Is literature a realm of universal experience that transcends politics, or is it inevitably political, and in what sense of "political," a word too often brandished today without being defined?

I also raise the question of the extent to which a work like *Heart of Darkness* is itself a conflict of theories. Contrary to their opponents, the point of current politically oriented theorists is not that literary works are simple expressions of racism or colonialism but that literature is an area of conflicting and contradictory social values, a struggle of utopian and dystopian visions.[29] The point needs underscoring: The dominant trend in contemporary theory is *not* to reduce literary works to transparent expressions of ideology, whether for good or bad. This is the impression that has been presented by critics whose dislike of recent theory exceeds their willingness to read it. The most powerful and influential of recent theories argue that literature is a scene of contradictions that cannot be subsumed under any "totalizing" ideology.

The only prominent critic of theory I know who gets this right is Frederick Crews of the University of California at Berkeley. As Crews concisely and accurately sums it up, the primary message of recent theory is "that literature is a site of struggle whose primary conflicts, both intrapsychic and social, deserve to be brought to light rather than homogenized into notions of fixed authorial 'values.'"[30] Crews has provided what seems to me a model of what a scrupulous critique of current theory would look like: He shows how at its worst this kind of theory simply replaces the clichés and predictable readings of earlier critical schools with a new set of clichés and predictable readings, but how at its best it has revitalized whole fields such as Faulkner studies.

Far from debasing the academic standards of my courses, teaching *Heart of Darkness* as I now teach it seems to me to have made my courses considerably *more* challenging than they were previously. For my students now have to be more reflective about their assumptions than they had to be before, and they are now asked to take part in a set of complex debates that I previously did not expect them to. Nor, I think, do the critical and theoretical debates I teach distract students from the close reading of literary works in themselves. When it seemed to me at one point that my students were agreeing too easily with Achebe, I corrected by restating the aesthetic reading of *Heart of Darkness* and the need to return constantly to the verbal particulars of the text.

In the end I think Achebe's critique pushes my students to a closer reading of the verbal and stylistic particularity of *Heart of Darkness* than they would achieve through an exclusively aesthetic approach. Then, too, I think it also enables them to understand more clearly just what an "aesthetic approach" is, since they now have something to compare it with. Before, students would look blank when I used words like "aesthetic" (or "traditional," "humanistic," etc.), as if to say, "'Aesthetic' as opposed to *what?*" Introducing a challenge to traditional values helps students understand what is at stake in embracing or rejecting them.

Was I really being less "political" when I taught *Heart of Darkness* without mentioning the issue of race than I am now when I put that issue in the foreground? In today's climate of hysterical accusation and denunciation, merely to raise the question for debate is for some of us enough to convict a teacher of the crime of political correctness. Yet is seems to me reasonable to argue that something political is at stake in whose representation of black Africa, Conrad's or Achebe's, gets into the debate, just as something political is at stake in whether other representations of the culture war get into the national media besides the ones favored by those who see nothing on the scene but the takeover of "urban guerrillas."

The way of teaching I have described will obviously not recommend itself to all teachers. Not all teachers will be comfortable dealing with political conflicts, nor is there any reason why they should have to. I choose to deal with these political conflicts not because I take them to be the only ones worth teaching but because they do have a good deal of urgency in our culture today and because I think frank discussion of these conflicts is more likely to improve our handling of them than pretending they do not exist.

In this, I like to think I am moving toward a solution to the current controversies that other teachers are also finding today, which is to incorporate the controversies themselves into my reading list and course framework. Instead of choosing between the Western Conrad and the non-Western Achebe, I teach the conflict between their novels and between competing views of literature.

One dividend of this approach I did not expect. Teaching *Things Fall Apart,* I found the novel not only first-rate literature and a source of insight into a culture unfamiliar to me but a means of illuminating *Heart of Darkness* that I had not previously had. When I had taught Conrad's novel as a universal statement, my students seemed to find the concept of universality difficulty and elusive—or perhaps they simply could not see the point of insisting on it. Again, "Universality as opposed to what?" seemed to be their unspoken thought. Once I introduced Achebe, however, with his sharp challenge to the idea that Conrad's world view is the universal one, the concept of universality came into much clearer focus for my students. The "Western" aspect of Conrad suddenly became a less mystifying quality now that students had something to contrast it with. And this led in turn to the question of whether "Western" and "non-Western" are really mutually exclusive.

"I Better Watch My Grammar"

If the flagrant misrepresentation typified by the *Color Purple* case erases the reality of how the humanities are actually being taught today, the reasons for the misrepresentation can only partly be attributed to the organized power of the right over certain sectors of the media. Part of the problem lies also in the peculiar difficulty of representing intellectual developments in the press. A vulgarized version of a theory or critical approach is inevitably easier to describe in the confines of a brief news article than the best, most sophisticated version of the theory or approach. A doctrinaire assault on "dead white males" can be easily summarized in a column inch or two, whereas it would take many pages to describe intellectual movements that are complex, diverse, and rife with internal conflicts. Glib falsifications can always be produced at a faster rate than their refutations.

Then, too, few readers of the popular press are in a position to recognize misrepresentations of academic practices, a fact that relieves anyone who wants to debunk these practices of the responsibility to do their homework. So feminism, multiculturalism, and deconstructionism are understood not as a complicated and internally conflicted set of inquiries and arguments about the cultural role of gender, ethnicity, language, and thought but as a monolithic doctrine that insists, as D'Souza formulates it, "that texts be selected primarily or exclusively according to author's race, gender, or sexual preference and that the Western tradition be exposed in the classroom as hopelessly bigoted and oppressive in every way."[31] Such views may characterize a Leonard Jeffries, the City College of New York Professor whose absurd speculations about "ice people" (Europeans) and "sun people" (Africans) have indeed had a lamentable influence on certain Afrocentric school curricula. But anyone who takes these views to be typical of academic revisionist thinking simply knows nothing of the reality.

I do not deny that others can be found who hold these disturbingly crude doctrines and that some of them see nothing wrong with forcing them on others. But no academic critic of any standing or influence does not repudiate these doctrines, and it is unfair to judge any trend by its least admirable versions. This caricaturing practice has obscured the fact that virtually every major advance in humanistic scholarship over the last three decades is indebted to the movements that are widely accused of subverting scholarly values: feminism, ethnic studies, postcolonialism, deconstruction, and the new historicism. The irony is that these movements have themselves been so concerned about challenging naïve notions of disinterested objectivity that they have failed to emphasize their own objective contribution to our knowledge. The conservatives, on the other hand, who defend scholarly values against politics, have produced little humanities scholarship of interest but a great many political polemics.

There is still another reason why myths about the academy have flourished, however, and this is one for which the academy has itself to blame. Academics have given journalists and others little help in understanding the more difficult forms of academic work. As this work has become increasingly complex and as it increasingly challenges conventionally accepted forms of thinking, the university acquires an obligation to do a more effective job of popularization. Yet the university has been disastrously inept in this crucial popularizing task and often disdains it as beneath its dignity. If the university has become easy prey for ignorant or malicious misrepresentations, it has asked for them. Having treated mere image making as beneath its dignity, the academy has left it to its detractors to construct its public image for it.

Until recently it has been a common joke among English professors that when people meet one of our species at a party, all they can think to say is, "Oh, you teach English? I guess I better watch my grammar." It would not have been so easy to replace this older image of the English professor as a grammatical pedant with the new image of "urban guerrilla" had the discipline thought more seriously about clarifying its concerns to outsiders. This would mean not simply speaking more clearly, however, but also respecting the objections of those whose minds one presumably hopes to change.

This is where the argument of this book comes in: I argue that the poor quality of communication between the academic humanities and the outside world has a lot to do with the poor quality of communication between academic humanists themselves and between sectors of the university in general. If the university is poor at representing itself to the wider student body and the public, the problem lies not just in its notorious proclivity for jargon. It has a deeper source in institutional practices than isolate teachers from one another and prevent conflicting views from entering into clarifying dialogues. In the absence of continuous public discussion and debate, doctrines harden and paranoid myths proliferate—like the myth that *The Color Purple* is replacing Shakespeare or that new academic theories are attempts to destroy Western civilization. By changing these institutional practices, we can clarify the real controversies in the academy and dispel the myths surrounding them.

Decentering the Canon: Refiguring Disciplinary and Pedagogical Boundaries

Henry Giroux

I will begin with what has become a controversial but not insignificant assertion: that the most important questions facing both the liberal arts and higher education in general are moral and political.[1] By invoking the category of the political, I wish to separate myself from a species of neoconservativism that claims that the relationship between the liberal arts and politics is one that taints the scholarship and teaching of those who dare even suggest that such a relationship exists. Nor do I believe that the fashionable but derogatory label of "politically correct" used by liberals and neo-conservatives adequately captures the complex set of motives, ideologies, and pedagogies of diverse progressive and radical scholars trying to engage the relationship between knowledge and power as it is expressed through the history and process of disciplinary canon formation. In fact, the charge that radical scholars are to be condemned for exercising a form of theoretical terrorism appears to be nothing more than a rhetorical ploy that barely conceals the highly charged ideological agenda of neoconservative scholars who refuse to address in any substantive way the political and theoretical considerations currently being raised within the academy by feminists, people of color, and other minority groups.[2]

What is being protested as the intrusion of politics into academic life is nothing less than a refusal to recognize that the canon and the struggle over the purpose and meaning of the liberal arts has displayed a political struggle from its inception. There are no disciplines, pedagogies, institutional structures, or forms of scholarship that are untainted by the messy relations of worldly values and interests.[3] For example, the history, configuration, and legitimation of the canon in the liberal arts cannot be removed from the issue of securing authority. As Gayatri Spivak points out, "canons are the condition and function of institutions, which presuppose particular ways of life and are inescapably political."[4]

More specifically, the various questions that have been raised recently about either defending, reconstructing, or eliminating a particular canon in higher education can only be understood within a broader range of political and theoretical considerations that bear directly on the issue of whether a liberal arts education should be considered a privilege for the few or a right for the vast majority of citizens. This is not merely a matter of deciding who is eligible or can financially afford a liberal arts education; it is fundamentally part of a wider discourse that has increasingly challenged the American public in the last decade to rethink the role of higher education and its relationship to democratic public life.

This debate raises new and important questions regarding the social and political implications of viewing curriculum as a historically specific narrative and pedagogy as a form of cultural politics. What must be asked about these specific narratives is whether they enable or silence the differentiated human capacities that allow students to speak from their own experiences, locate themselves in history, and act so as to create liberatory social forms that expand the possibility of democratic public life.[5] I believe that the current debate on higher education opens up new possibilities for rethinking the role that university educators might play as critically engaged public intellectuals. While neoconservatives generally view the extensive debate about the fundamental place of literature, culture, ethics, and politics in the academy and the wider society as symptomatic of a crisis of authority and an unmitigated assault on Western civilization itself, I would rather view it as part of a great renewal in academic life.[6]

Before I discuss these issues in detail, I want to stress the importance of recognizing that the university is not simply a place to accumulate disciplinary knowledge that can be exchanged for decent employment and upward mobility. Neither is it a place whose purpose is merely to cultivate the life of the mind or reproduce the cultural equivalent of "Masterpiece Theater." I firmly believe that the institutions of higher education, regardless of their academic status, represent places that affirm and legitimate existing views of the world, produce new ones, and authorize and shape particular social relations; put simply, they are places of moral and social regulation "where a sense of identity, place, and worth is informed and contested through practices, which organize knowledge and meaning."[7] The university is a place that produces a particular selection and ordering of narratives and subjectivities. It is, furthermore, a place that is deeply political and unarguably normative.

Unfortunately, questions concerning higher education in general and liberal arts in particular are often discussed as if they have no relation to existing arrangements of social, economic, and political power. Central to this chapter are the arguments that as a social, political, and pedagogical site, the university is a terrain of contestation and that one can neither understand the nature of the struggle itself nor the nature of the liberal arts unless one raises the question of what the purpose of the university actually is or might be. Or, as Jacques Derrida has put it, "To ask whether the university has a reason for being is to wonder why there is a university, but the question 'why' verges on 'with a view to what?'"[8] It is this question of purpose and practice that illuminates what the limits and possibilities are that exist within the university at a given time in history. Putting aside Derrida's own political agenda, this is essentially a question of politics, power, and possibility. As we know, the liberal arts and various other programs and schools within the university presuppose and legitimate particular forms of history, community, and authority. Of course, the question is what and whose history, community, knowledge, and voice prevails? Unless this question is addressed, the issues of what to teach, how to teach, how to engage our students, and how to function as intellectuals becomes removed from the wider principles that inform such issues and practices.

The sphere of higher education represents an important public culture that cultivates and produces particular stories of how to live ethically and politically; its institutions reproduce selected values, and they harbor in their social relations and teaching practices specific notions regarding "what knowledge is of most worth, what it means to know something, and how one might construct representations of [themselves], others, and the social environment." In many respects, the normative and political language taught in the university can be compared to what Ernst Bloch called the utopian impulse of daydreams.

> Dreams come in the day as well as the night. And both kinds of dreaming are motivated by the wishes they seek to fulfill. But daydreams differ from night dreams; for the day dreaming "I" persist throughout, consciously, privately, envisaging the circumstances and images of a desired, better life. The content of the daydream is not, like that of the night dream, a journey back into repressed experiences and their association. It is concerned with, as far as possible, an unrestricted journey forward, so that instead of reconstituting that which is no longer conscious, the images of that which is not yet can be fantasized into life and into the world.[9]

Bloch's analysis points to an important relation between daydreaming and the liberal arts that is often overlooked. As an introduction to, preparation for, and legitimation of social life, a liberal arts education inscribes students in a present informed by a past that presupposes a particular citizen, society, and future. In other words, like the process of daydreaming, the liberal arts is fundamentally involved in the production of narratives of that which is "not yet." As Roger Simon points out, "the utopian impulse of such programs is represented in the notion that without a perspective on the future, conceivable as a desired future, there can be no human venture."[10] In this respect, the language of education that students take with them from their university experience should embody a vision capable of providing them with a sense of history, civic courage, and democratic community. It is important to emphasize that visions are not only defined by the representations they legitimate and the practices they structure, but also by the arguments they embody for justifying why meaning, knowledge, and social action matter as part of the rewriting and remapping of the events that make up daily life as well as the dynamics of the larger world. The question becomes To what version of the future do the visions of our students speak? To whom do such visions matter and why? As a matter of pedagogical practice, students need to take up these questions through a language of obligation and power, a language that cultivates a capacity for reasoned criticism, for undoing the misuses of power and the relations of domination, and for exploring and extending the utopian dimensions of human potentiality. Needless to say, such a language is at odds with the language of cultural despair, conservative restoration, and aristocratic elitism trumpeted by the educational theorists of the New Right.[11]

It serves us well to remember that the visions presupposed in the structure and discourse of the liberal arts are neither ideologically neutral nor politically innocent. Visions always belong to someone, and to the degree that they translate into curricula and pedagogical practices, they not only denote a struggle over forms of political authority and orders of representation, but also weigh heavily in regulating the moral identities, collective voices, and the futures of others.[12] As institutionalized practices, visions draw upon specific values, uphold particular relations of power, class, gender, ethnicity, and race, and often authorize official forms of knowledge. For this reason, visions always have a moral and political dimension. Moreover, they become important not as a signal for a single-minded preoccupation with academic achievement or social status but as a context from which to organize the energies of a moral vision, to believe that one can make a difference both in combating domestic tyranny and assaults on human freedom and in creating a society that exhibits in its institutional and everyday relations moral courage, compassion, and cultural justice. This is, after all, what university life should be all about: the politics and ethics of dreaming, dreaming a better future, and dreaming a new world.

The current debate about education represents more than a commentary on the state of public and higher education in this country, it is basically a debate about the meaning of democracy, social criticism, and the status of utopian thought in constituting both our dreams and the stories that we devise in order to give meaning to our lives. This debate has taken a serious turn in the last decade and now as before its terms are being set principally by extremists and anti-utopians. Critics such as Allan Bloom, Lynne V. Cheney, Roger Kimball, and John Silber have presented an agenda and purpose for shaping higher education that abstracts equity from excellence and cultural criticism from the discourse of social responsibility. Under the guise of attempting to revitalize the language of morality, these critics and politicians have, in reality, launched a serious attack on some of the most basic aspects of democratic public life and the social, moral, and political obligations of responsible, critical citizens. What is being valorized in this language is, in part, a view of higher education based on a celebration of cultural uniformity and a rigid view of authority; in addition, the neoconservative agenda for higher education includes a call to remake higher education an academic beachhead for defending and limiting the curriculum to a narrowly defined patriarchal, Eurocentric version of the Western tradition and a return to the old transmission model of teaching.

Within this new public philosophy, there is a ruthlessly frank expression of doubt about the viability of democracy.[13] What at first sight appears to be a debate about the meaning and purpose of the canon has become a struggle for "the moral definition of tomorrow's elites."[14] Unfortunately, this is not a debate being conducted within the parameters of critical exchange. It is increasingly taking on the shades of McCarthyism rampant in the 1950s in the United States, with those in power using their influence in the press, in well-funded public symposiums, and through highly financed private think tanks to conjure up charges that academics who are questioning the relationship between the liberal arts and the discourse of power and citizenship are to be judged by their motives rather than their arguments. With great burst of melodramatic rhetoric, we are told, for example, by Roger Kimball, the editor of *The New Centurion*, that politically motivated academic radicals, regardless of their particular theoretical orientation, have as their goal nothing less than the destruction of the values, method, and goals of Western civilization. Equating advocates for a multicultural curriculum with the forces of barbarism, Kimball constructs a reductionistic opposition in which conservatives become the defenders of civilization itself. Kimball spares no words on the importance of his messianic struggle:

> The multiculturalists notwithstanding, the choice facing us today is not between a "repressive" Western culture and a multicultural paradise, but between culture and barbarism. *Civilization* is not a gift it is an achievement—a fragile achievement that needs constantly to be shored up and defended from besiegers inside and out.[15]

Critics such as Allan Bloom and John Silber extend the tone and logic of such attacks by arguing that the very nature of Western civilization is under attack by the infusion of critics in the humanities who constitute a monolithic party (surely an embarrassing overstatement given the endless fragmentation and divisions that characterize the American left). There is more at stake here than the rise of a new nativism; there is also the nature of academic freedom as it has developed in the liberal arts in the last few decades. The poison of McCarthyism is once again being used to limit debate and constrain the so-called excesses of democracy. For instance, instead of addressing the complexity of issues being waged over the nature of the liberal arts and the ideological construction of the canon, John Silber, the President of Boston University, has urged fellow conservatives to abandon any civility toward scholars whose work is considered political. Instead of encouraging rigorous debate, Silber has urged his fellow conservatives to name names, to discredit educators who have chosen to engage in forms of social criticism (work the New Right considers political) at odds with the agenda of the New Rights's mythic conception of the university as a warehouse built on the pillars of an unproblematic and revered tradition.[16] In the Bush Era, there are, sadly, few attempts to engage in dialogue about the assumptions that inform the traditional view of the curriculum and canon; on the contrary, the privileged and the powerful in academia and in government positions now openly advocate crude policing functions as a way to regulate university life. So much for the spirit of democracy and academic freedom.

The loss of utopian vision that characterizes this position is no where more evident than in Allan Bloom's *The Closing of the American Mind* and E. D. Hirsch's *Cultural Literacy*.[17] For Bloom, the impulse to egalitarianism and the spirit of social criticism represent the chief culprits in the decay of higher learning. Bloom argues that the university must give up educating intellectuals, whose great crime is that they sometimes become adversaries of the dominant culture or speak to a wider culture about the quality of contemporary politics and public life. He would prefer that the university curriculum be organized around the Great Books and be selectively used to educate students from what he calls the top twenty elite schools to be philosopher-kings. What Bloom appears to suggest by reform is nothing less than an effort to make explicit what women, people of color, and working-class students have always known: The precincts of higher learning are not for them, and the educational system is meant to reproduce a new mandarin class.

Hirsch, like Bloom, presents a frontal attack aimed at providing a programmatic language with which to defend schools as cultural sites; that is, as institutions responsible for reproducing the knowledge and values necessary to advance the historical virtues of Western culture. Hirsch presents his view of cultural restoration through a concept of literacy that focuses on the basic structures of language, and he applies this version of cultural literacy to the broader consideration of the needs of the business community as well as to maintenance of American institutions. For Hirsch, the new service economy requires employees who can write a memo, read within a specific cultural context, and communicate through a national language composed of the key words of Western culture.

Central to Hirsch's concept of literacy is a view of culture removed from the dynamics of struggle and power. Culture is seen as the totality of language practices of a given nation and merely "presents" itself for all to participate in its language and conventions. Not unlike Bloom's position, Hirsch's view of culture expresses a single durable history and vision, one at odds with a critical notion of democracy and difference. Such a position maintains an ideological silence, a political amnesia of sorts, regarding either how domination works in the cultural sphere or how the dialectic of cultural struggle between different groups over competing orders of meaning, experience, and history emerges within unequal relations of power and struggle. By depoliticizing the issue of culture, Hirsch ends up with a view of literacy cleansed of its own complicity in producing social forms that create devalued others. This is more than a matter of cultural forgetting on Hirsch's part; it is also an attack on difference as possibility. Hirsch's discourse also attempts to undermine the development of a curriculum committed to reclaiming higher education as an agency of social justice and critical democracy and to developing forms of pedagogy that affirm and engage the often silenced voices of subordinate groups.

In the most general sense, Bloom, Hirsch, Cheney, Kimball, and Silber represent the latest cultural offensive by the new elitists to rewrite the past and construct the present from the perspective of the privileged and the powerful.[18] They disdain the democratic implications of pluralism and argue for a form of cultural uniformity in which difference is consigned to the margins of history or to the museum of the disadvantaged. From this perspective, culture, along with the authority it sanctions becomes merely an artifact, a warehouse of goods, posited either as a canon of knowledge or a canon of information that simply has to be transmitted as a means for promoting social order and control. In this view, pedagogy becomes an afterthought, a code word for the transmission and imposition of a predefined and unproblematic body of knowledge. For educators like Bloom and Cheney, pedagogy is something one does in order to implement a reconstituted body of knowledge or information. The notion that pedagogy is itself part of the production of knowledge, a deliberate and critical attempt to influence the ways in which knowledge and identities are produced within and among particular sets of social relations, is far removed from the language and ideology of the neoconservatives.

What is at stake here is not simply the issue of bad teaching, but the broader refusal to take seriously the categories of meaning, experience, and voice that students use to make sense of themselves and the world around them. It is this refusal to enable speech for those who have been silenced, to acknowledge the voices of the other, and to legitimate and reclaim student experience as a fundamental category in the production of knowledge that the character of the current dominant discourse on the canon reveals its totalitarian and undemocratic ideology.

Put in Bloch's terms, this new conservative public philosophy represents a form of daydreaming in which tradition is not on the side of democracy and difference, but is a form of the "not yet" expunged of the language of hope and strangled by a discourse in which history and culture are closed. It is a public philosophy in which teaching is reduced to a form of transmission, the canon is posited as a relationship outside of the restless flux of knowledge and power, and intellectuals are cheerfully urged to take up their roles as clerks of the empire.[19]

It is worth noting that Bloom, Cheney, and other neoconservatives have been able to perform a task that humanists and progressives have generally failed to do. They have placed the question of curriculum at the center of the debate about both education and democracy, but they have argued for a view of the liberal arts fashioned as part of an anti-utopian discourse that serves to disconnect the purpose of higher education from the task of reconstructing democratic public life. This is not to suggest that they have not invoked the notions of democracy and citizenship in their arguments. But in doing so they have reduced democracy to gaining access to an unproblematic version of Western civilization and defined learning as the training of good citizens, that is, "willing subjects and agents of hegemonic authority."[20] By refusing to link democracy to forms of self and social empowerment, neoconservatives have been able to suppress the relationship between learning, social justice, and critical citizenship. This new cultural offensive presents a formidable challenge to humanists who have attempted to defend liberal arts education from the perspective of a highly specialized, self-referential discipline that holds up either a plurality of canons or a canon that serves as a model of scientific rigor and sophisticated methodological inquiry. In such cases, the purpose of the liberal arts is defined, though from different ideological perspectives, from within the perspective of creating a free, enterprising, educated, well-rounded individual. Though well meaning, this discourse discounts the most important social relations that are constitutive of what it means to be educated. That is, it ignores the social and political function of particular knowledge/power/pedagogy relations and how they serve to construct students individually and collectively within the boundaries of a political order that they often take for granted.

The liberal arts cannot be defended either as a self-contained discourse legitimating the humanistic goal of broadly improving the so-called life of the mind or as a rigorous science that can lead students to indubitable truths. Similarly, it is insufficient to defend the liberal arts by rejecting technocratic education as a model of learning. All of these positions share the failure of abstracting the liberal arts from the intense problems and issues of public life. Moreover, the defense of the liberal arts as a gateway to indubitable truths, whether through the discourse of Western civilization or science, often collapses into a not too subtle defense of higher education as a training ground for a "dictatorship of enlightened social engineers."[21] This issue at stake is not one of merely creating a more enlightened or scientific canon but of raising more fundamental questions about how canons are used, what interests they legitimate, what relations they have to the dominant society, and how students are constituted within their prevailing discourses and social relations. How we read or define a "canonical" work may not be as important as challenging the overall function and social uses the notion of the canon has served. Within this type of discourse, the canon can be analyzed as part of a wider set of relations that connect the academic disciplines, teaching, and power to more political considerations defined through broader, intersecting political and cultural concerns such as race, class, gender, ethnicity, and nationalism. What is in question here is not merely a defense of a particular canon, but the issue of struggle and empowerment.[22]

The debate over the canon must be refigured in order to address issues of struggle in which power and knowledge intersect to produce and legitimate specific orders of representations, values, and identities. As such, the issue of canon formation must be engaged in terms that address the historical formation of the canon and the pedagogies through which it is taught and how these pedagogies have either provided or excluded the conditions and knowledge necessary for marginal people to recover their own histories and to speak and learn in places occupied by those who have the dominant power to shape policy and act. In other words, the liberal arts should be defended in the interest of creating critical rather than "good" citizens. That is, the notion of the liberal arts has to be reconstituted around a knowledge-power relationship in which the question of curriculum is seen as a form of cultural and political production grounded in a radical conception of citizenship and public wisdom.

By linking the liberal arts to the imperatives of a critical democracy, the debate on the meaning and nature of higher education can be situated within a broader context of issues concerned with critical citizenship, politics, and the dignity of human life. In this view, it becomes possible to provide a rationale and purpose for higher education, which aims at developing critical citizens and reconstructing community life by extending the principles of social justice to all spheres of economic, political, and cultural life. This position is not far from the arguments posed by John Dewey, George S. Counts, C. Wright Mills, and more recently Hannah Arendt and Alvin Gouldner. These theorists fashioned the elements of a public philosophy in which the liberal arts was seen as a major social site for revitalizing public life. Dewey, for example, argued that a liberal education afforded people the opportunity to involve themselves in the deepest problems of society, to acquire the knowledge, skills, and ethical responsibility necessary for "reasoned participation in democratically organized publics."[23] Mills urged intellectuals to define the liberal arts and their own roles through a commitment to the formation of a critical and engaged citizenry. He envisioned the liberal arts as social site from which intellectuals could mobilize a moral and political vision committed to the reclamation and recovery of democratic public life.[24] In the most general sense, this means fashioning the purpose of higher education within a public philosophy committed to a radical conception of citizenship, civic courage, and public wisdom. In more specific terms, this means challenging the image of higher education as an adjunct of the corporation and rejecting those ideologies and human capital theories that reduce the role of university intellectuals to the status of industrial technicians and academic clerks whose political project or, lack of one, is often betrayed by claims to objectivity, certainty, and professionalism. It means challenging the sterile instrumentalism, selfishness, and contempt for democratic community that has become the hallmark of the Reagan-Bush Era.[25] It means recognizing and organizing against the structured injustices in society that prevent us from extending our solidarity to those others who strain under the weight of various forms of oppression and exploitation. It also means enhancing and ennobling the meaning and purpose of a liberal arts education by giving it a truly central place in the social life of a nation where it can become a public forum for addressing preferentially the needs of the poor, the dispossessed, and the disenfranchised.

A public philosophy that offers the promise of reforming liberal arts education as part of a wider revitalization of public life raises important questions regarding what the notion of empowerment would mean for developing classroom pedagogical practices. That is, if liberal arts education is to be developed in relation to principles consistent with a democratic public philosophy, it is equally important to develop forms of critical pedagogy that embody these principles and practices, a critical pedagogy in which such practices are understood in relation to rather than in isolation from those economies of power and privilege at work in wider social and political formations.

Critical Pedagogy as a Form of Cultural Politics

For many educators, pedagogy is often theorized as what is left after curriculum content is determined. In this view, knowledge "speaks" for itself and teaching is often a matter of providing an occasion for the text to reveal itself. Guided by a concern with producing knowledge that is academically correct or ideologically relevant, educational theorists have largely sidestepped the issue of how a teacher can work from sound ethical and theoretical principles and still end up pedagogically silencing students. Put another way, if educators fail to recognize that the legitimating claims they make in defense of the knowledge they teach is not enough to ensure that they do not commit forms of symbolic violence in their pedagogical relations with students, they will not adequately understand the ways in which students are both enabled and disabled in their own classrooms.

Central to the development of a critical pedagogy is the need to explore how pedagogy functions as a cultural practice to *produce* rather than merely *transmit* knowledge within the asymmetrical relations of power that structure teacher-student relations. There have been few attempts to analyze how relations of pedagogy and relations of power are inextricably tied not only to what people know but also to how they come to know in a particular way within the constraints of specific cultural and social forms.[26] Rendered insignificant as a form of cultural production, pedagogy is often marginalized and devalued as a means of recognizing that what we teach and how we do it are deeply implicated not only in producing various forms of domination but also in constructing active practices of resistance and struggle. Lost here is an attempt to articulate pedagogy as a form of cultural production that addresses how knowledge is produced, mediated, refused, and represented within relations of power both in and outside of the university.

Critical pedagogy as a form of cultural politics rejects the reduction of teaching to a narrowly defined concern with instrumental techniques, skills, and objectives. The instrumentalization of teaching erases questions of power, history, ethics, and self-identity. Absent from this discourse is any attempt to understand how pedagogical and institutional practices produce, codify, and rewrite disciplinary practices, values, and social identities in relation to, rather than outside of, the discourse of history, power, and privilege. Critical pedagogy also rejects the notion of knowledge as accumulated capital. Instead, it focuses on the production of knowledge and identities within the specificity of educational contexts and the broader institutional locations in which they are located. Critical pedagogy refers to a deliberate attempt to construct specific conditions through which educators and students can think critically about how knowledge is produced and transformed in relation to the construction of social experiences informed by a particular relationship between the self, others, and the larger world. Rather than reducing classroom practice to forms of methodological reification governed by a pragmatic concern for generating topologies or a reductionist fetish for empirical verification, critical pedagogy stresses the realities of what happens in classrooms by raising a number of crucial questions. These include how identities and subjectivities are produced differently in relation to particular forms of knowledge and power; how cultural differences are coded within the center and margins of power; how the discourse of rationality secures, ignores, or dismisses the affective investments that organize the daily experiences of students; how education might become the practice of liberation and what it means to know something as part of the broader discourses of cultural democracy and citizenship.[27]

The notion of pedagogy being argued for here is not organized in relation to a choice between elite or popular culture, but as part of a political project that takes issues of liberation and empowerment as its starting point. It is a pedagogy that rejects the notion of culture as an artifact immobilized in the image of a storehouse. Instead, the pedagogical principles at work here analyze culture as a set of lived experiences and social practices developed within asymmetrical relations of power. Culture in this sense is not an object of unquestioning reverence but a mobile field of ideological and material relations that are unfinished, multilayered and always open to interrogation. Moreover, this view of culture is defined pedagogically as social practices that allow both teachers and students to construe themselves as agents in the production of subjectivity and meaning. Such a pedagogy transcends the dichotomy of elite and popular culture by defining itself through a project of educating students to feel compassion for the suffering of others, to engage in a continual analysis of their own conditions of existence, to construct loyalties that engage the meaning and importance of public life, and to believe that they can make a difference, that they can act from a position of collective strength to alter existing configurations of power. This notion of pedagogy is predicated on a notion of learned hope, forged amidst the realization of risks, and steeped in a commitment to transforming public culture and life. It is a notion of critical pedagogy that stresses the historical and transformative in its practice.

In the debate about the importance of constructing a particular canon, the notion of naming and transmitting from one generation to the next what can be defined as "cultural treasures" specifies what has become the central argument for reforming the liberal arts.[28] For that reason, perhaps, it appears as though the debate is reducible to the question of the contents of course syllabi. The notion of critical pedagogy for which I am arguing provides a fundamental challenge to this position. For in the great challenges that we confront as university educators, what is called for is a more critical and fundamental argument that transcends the limited focus on the canon. What the issue of critical pedagogy raises in this debate is that the crisis in liberal arts education is one of historical purpose and meaning that challenges us to rethink in a critical fashion the relationship between the role of the university and the imperatives of a democracy in a mass society.

Historically, the liberal arts education was conceived of as the essential preparation for governing, for ruling—more specifically, as the preparation and outfitting of the governing *elite*. The liberal arts curricula, composed of the "best" that had been said or written, was intended, as Elizabeth Fox-Genovese has observed, "to provide selected individuals with a collective history, culture, and epistemology so that they could run the world effectively."[29] The canon, considered a possession of the dominant classes or groups, was fashioned as a safeguard to insure that the cultural property of such groups was passed on from generation to generation along with the family estates. Thus, in these very terms it seems most appropriate that the literary canon should be subject to revision—as it has been before in the course of the expansion of democracy—such that it might also incorporate and reflect the experience and aspirations of the women, minorities, and children of the working class who have been entering the academy.

As conceived above, a radical vision of liberal arts education is to be found within its elite social origins and purpose. But this does not suggest that the most important questions confronting liberal arts reform lie in merely establishing the content of the liberal arts canon on the model of the elite universities. Instead, the most important questions become that of reformulating the meaning and purpose of higher education in ways that contribute to the cultivation and regeneration of an informed critical citizenry capable of actively participating in the shaping and governing of a democratic society. Within this discourse, the pedagogical becomes political and the notion of a liberal arts canon commands a more historically grounded and critical reading. The pedagogical becomes more political in that it proposes that the ways in which students engage and critically examine knowledge is just as important an issue as the choosing of texts to be used in a class or program. That is, a democratic notion of liberal education rejects those views of the humanities that would treat texts as sacred and instruction as merely transmission. This notion of the canon undermines the possibility for dialogue, argument, and critical thinking. Moreover, it treats knowledge as a form of cultural inheritance that is beyond considerations regarding how it might be implicated, as I previously noted, in social practices that exploit, infantilize, and oppress.

The canons we have inherited, in their varied forms, cannot be dismissed as simply part of the ideology of privilege and domination. Instead, the privileged texts of the dominant or official canons should be explored with respect to the important role they have played in shaping, for better or worse, the major events of our time. Moreover, there are forms of knowledge that have been marginalized by the official canons. There are noble traditions, histories, and narratives that speak to important struggles by women, Afro-Americans, minorities, and other silenced groups that need to be heard so that such groups can lay claim to their own voices as part of a process of both affirmation and critical inquiry. At issue here is a notion of pedagogy as a form of cultural politics that rejects a facile restoration of the past and rejects history as a monolog. A critical pedagogy recognizes that history is constituted in dialogue and that some of the voices that make up that dialogue have been eliminated. Such a pedagogy calls for a public debate regarding the dominant memories and repressed stories that constitute the historical narratives of a social order. In effect, a critical pedagogy recognizes that canon formation is a matter of both rewriting and reinterpreting the past, that canon formation embodies the ongoing "process of reconstructing the 'collective reflexivity' of lived cultural experience . . . which recognizes that the 'notions of the past and future are essentially notions of the present.'"[30] Such notions are central to the politics of identity and power and to the memories that structure how experience is individually and collectively authorized and experienced as form of cultural identity.

As a historical construct, critical pedagogy functions in a dual sense to address the issue of what kinds of knowledge can be put in place that enable rather than subvert the formation of a democratic society. On one level, it authorizes forms of counter-memory. It excavates, affirms, and interrogates the histories, memories, and stories of the devalued others who have been marginalized from the official discourse of the canon. It attempts to recover and mediate those knowledge forms and social practices that have been decentered from the discourses of power. Surely, such knowledge might include the historical and contemporary writings of feminists such as Mary Wollstonecraft, Charlotte Perkins Gilman, and Adrienne Rich; Afro-American writers such as W. E. B. DuBois, Martin Luther King, Jr., and Zora Neale Hurston, as well as documents that helped shape the struggles of labor movements in the United States. The pedagogical practice at work here is not meant to romanticize these subjugated knowledges and "dangerous memories" as much as to critically appropriate and renew them as part of the reconstruction of a public philosophy that legitimates a politics and pedagogy of difference.

On another level, critical pedagogy recognizes that all educational work is at root contextual and conditional. This pedagogy refuses the totalizing unity of discourses that expunge the specific, contingent, and particular from their formulations. In this case, a critical pedagogy can only be discussed from within the historical and cultural specificity of space, time, place, and context. A critical pedagogy does not arise against a background of psychological, sociological, or anthropological universals but from within tasks that are strategic and practical, guided by imperatives that are both historical and ethical.

A critical pedagogy also rejects a discourse of value neutrality. Without subscribing to a language that polices behavior and desire, a critical pedagogy aims at developing pedagogical practices informed by an ethical stance that contests racism, sexism, class exploitation, and other dehumanizing and exploitative social relations as ideologies and social practices that disrupt and devalue public life. This is a pedagogy that rejects detachment, though it does not silence in the name of its own ideological fervor or correctness, acknowledges social injustices, and examines with care and in dialogue with itself and others how injustice works through the discourses, experiences, and desires that constitute daily life and the subjectivities of the students who invest in them. That is, it is a pedagogy guided by ethical principles that correspond to a radical practice rooted in historical experience. It is a pedagogy that comprehends the historical consequences of what it means to take a moral and political position with respect to the horror of, for example, the

Gulag, the Nazi holocaust, or the Pol Pot regime, events that not only summon images of terror, domination, and resistance, but also provide *a priori examples* of what principles have to be both defended and fought against in the interest of freedom and life.

Within this perspective, ethics becomes more than the discourse of moral relativism or a static transmission of reified history. Ethics becomes instead a continued engagement in which the social practices of everyday life are interrogated in relation to the principles of individual autonomy and democratic public life—not as a matter of received truth but as a constant engagement. This provides the opportunity for individual capacities to be questioned and examined so that they can serve both to critically analyze and advance the possibilities inherent in all social forms. Community, difference, remembrance, and historical consciousness become central to the language of public life. This particular ethical stance is one that cannot be separated from the issue of how a socialized humanity develops within ideological and material conditions that either enable or disable the enhancement of human possibilities. It moves beyond moral outrage, attempting instead to provide a critical account of how individuals are constituted as human agents within different moral and ethical discourses and experiences. At the heart of such a pedagogy is the recognition that it is important to stare into history in order to remember the suffering of the past and that out of this remembrance a theory of ethics should be developed in which solidarity, compassion, and care become central dimensions of an informed social practice.

Essential to a critical pedagogy is the need to affirm the lived reality of difference as the ground on which to pose questions of theory and practice. Moreover, a critical pedagogy needs to function as a social practice that claims the experience of lived difference as an agenda for discussion and a central resource for a project of possibility. It must be constructed as part of a struggle over assigned meanings, the viability of different voices, and particular forms of authority. It is this struggle that makes possible and hence can redefine the possibilities we see both in the conditions of our daily lives and in those conditions that are "not yet."

A critical pedagogy for the liberal arts is one that affirms for students the importance of leadership as a moral and political enterprise that links the radical responsibility of ethics with the possibility of having those who are not oppressed understand the experience of oppression as an obstacle to democratic public life. Thus, critical pedagogy as a form of cultural politics is a call to celebrate responsible action and strategic risk taking as part of an ongoing struggle to link citizenship with the notion of a democratic public community, civic courage to a shared conception of social justice. Chantal Mouffe argues that a critical conception of citizenship should be "postmodern" in that it recognizes the importance of a politics of difference in which the particular, heterogeneous, and the multiple play a crucial role in the forming of a democratic public sphere:

> The struggle for democratic citizenship is one strategy among others. It is an attempt to challenge the undemocratic practices of neoliberalism by constructing different political identities. It is inspired by a view of politics, which assumes a community of equals who share rights, social responsibility, and a solidarity based on a common belonging to a political community whose political ends—freedom and equality for all—are pursued in participating institutions. This is a long way from . . . a privatized conception of citizenship that intends to whisk away the notion of political community. Democratic citizenship, on the contrary, aims at restoring the centrality of such a notion.[31]

Mouffe's view of citizenship and my view of a critical pedagogy include the idea that the formation of democratic citizens demands forms of political identity that radically extend the principles of justice, liberty, and dignity to public spheres constituted by difference and multiple forms of community. Of course, this is as much a pedagogical issue as it is a political issue. These political identities have to be constructed as part of a pedagogy in which difference becomes a basis for solidarity and unity rather than for competition and discrimination.

If pedagogy is to be linked with the notion of learning for empowerment, it is important that educators understand theoretically how difference is constructed through various representations and practices that name, legitimate, marginalize, and exclude the cultural capital and voices of subordinated groups in American society. Difference in this case does not become an empty marker for registering such differences within the language of harmony and conflict resolution.

On the contrary, difference has to be taken up as a historical and social construction situated within hierarchies of domination and resistance. Hence, differences must be understood historically as part of larger political processes and systems tied to specific forms of exclusion, resistance, and transformation. In this case, difference is about how pedagogical and political practices work within and outside of the university to rewrite, codify, and reshape the practices of some groups within the discourse of privilege, while simultaneously erasing the cultural identities and histories of others.

As part of this theoretical project, a pedagogy of difference must address the question of how representations and practices that name, marginalize, and define difference as the devalued Other are actively learned, internalized, challenged, or transformed. In addition, such a pedagogy needs to address how understanding these differences can be used in order to change the prevailing relations of power that sustain them. It is also imperative to acknowledge and critically interrogate how the colonizing of differences by dominant groups is expressed and sustained through representations: in which the Other is seen as a deficit, in which the humanity of the Other is posited either as cynically problematic or ruthlessly denied. At the same time, it is important for a pedagogy of difference not only to critically unravel the ways in which the voices of the Other are colonized and repressed by the principle of identity that runs through the discourse of dominant groups, but also to understand how the experience of marginality at the level of everyday life lends itself to forms of oppositional and transformative consciousness.[32] This understanding must be based on the Others' reclamation and recreation of their own histories, voices, and visions as part of a wider struggle to change those material and social relations that deny radical pluralism as the basis of democratic political community. For it is only through such an understanding that teachers can develop a pedagogy of difference, one characterized by what Teresa de Lauretis calls "an ongoing effort to create new spaces of discourse, to rewrite cultural narratives, and to define the terms of another perspective—a view from 'elsewhere.'"[33]

What is suggested is a pedagogy in which there is a critical questioning of the omissions and tensions that exist between the master narratives and hegemonic discourses that make up the official curriculum of the university, department, or program and the self-representations of subordinated groups as they might appear in "forgotten" histories, texts, memories, experiences, and community narratives. Not only does a pedagogy of difference seek to understand how difference is constructed in the intersection of the official canon of the school and the various voices of students from subordinate groups, it also draws upon student experience as both a narrative for agency and a referent for critique. This requires forms of pedagogy that both confirm and critically engage the knowledge and experience through which students author their own voices and construct social identities. In effect, we must take seriously, as an aspect of learning, the knowledge and experiences that constitute the individual and collective voices by which students identify and give meaning to themselves and others by first using what they know about their own lives as a basis for criticizing the dominant culture. The student experience has to be first understood and recognized as the accumulation of collective memories and stories that provide students with a sense of familiarity, identity, and practical knowledge. Such experience has to be both affirmed and critically interrogated. In addition, the social and historical construction of such experience has to be affirmed and understood as part of a wider struggle for voice, but it also has to be remade, reterritorialized in the interest of a social imaginary that dignifies the best traditions and possibilities of those groups learning to speak from a position of enablement, that is, from the discourse of dignity and governance. In her analysis of the deterritorialization of women as Other, Caren Kaplan articulates this position well.

> Recognizing the minor cannot erase the aspects of the major, but as a mode of understanding it enables us to see the fissures in our identities, to unravel the seams of our totalities. . . . We must leave home, as it were, since our homes are often sites of racism, sexism, and other damaging social practices. Where we come to locate ourselves in terms of our specific histories and differences must be a place with room for what can be salvaged from the past and made anew. What we gain is a reterritorialization; we reinhabit a world of our making (here "our" is expanded to a coalition of identities—neither universal nor particular).[34]

Furthermore, it is important to extend the possibilities of experience by making it both the object of critical inquiry and by appropriating in a similarly critical fashion, when necessary, the codes and knowledges that constitute broader and less familiar historical and cultural traditions. We need not necessarily indiscriminately abandon the traditions of Western civilization; instead, we need to engage the strengths and weaknesses of such a complex and contradictory tradition as part of a wider effort to deepen the discourse of critical democracy and responsible citizenship.

At issue here is the development of a pedagogy that replaces the authoritative language of recitation with an approach that allows students to speak from their own histories, collective memories, and voices while simultaneously challenging the grounds on which knowledge and power are constructed and legitimated. Critical pedagogy contributes to making possible a variety of human capacities that expand the range of social identities that students may become. It points to the importance of understanding in both pedagogical and political terms how subjectivities are produced within those social forms in which people move but of which they are often only partially conscious. Similarly, it raises fundamental questions regarding how students make particular investments of meaning and affect, how students are constituted within a triad of knowledge, power, and pleasure, and what it is we as teachers need to understand regarding why students should be interested in the forms of authority, knowledge, and values that we produce and legitimate within our classrooms and university. It is worth noting that not only does such a pedagogy articulate a respect for a diversity of student voices, it also provides a referent for developing a public language rooted in a commitment to social transformation.

Another serious challenge of reforming the liberal arts necessitates that university teachers rethink the nature of their role with respect to issues of politics, social responsibility, and the construction of a pedagogy of possibility. Instead of weaving dreams fashioned in the cynical interests of industrial psychology and cultural sectarianism, university educators can become part of a collective effort to build and revitalize critical public cultures that provide the basis for transformative democratic communities. This means, among other things, that they can educate students to work collectively to make "despair unconvincing and hope practical" by refusing the role of the disconnected expert, technician, or careerist and adopting the practice of the engaged and transformative intellectual. This is not a call for educators to become wedded to some abstract ideal that turns them into prophets of perfection and certainty; on the contrary, it represents a call for educators to perform a noble public service, that is, to undertake teaching as a form of social criticism, to define themselves as engaged, critical public intellectuals who can play a major role in animating a democratic public culture.[35] It begs intellectuals to construct their relationship to the wider society by making organic connections with the historical traditions that provide them-selves and their students with a voice, history, and sense of belonging. This view resonates with Gramsci's call to broaden the notion of education by seeing all of society as a vast school. It also resonates with his call for critical intellectuals to forge alliances around new historical blocks.[36]

Educators need to encourage students by example to find ways to get involved, to make a difference, to think in global terms, and to act from specific contexts. The notion of teachers as transformative intellectuals is marked by a moral courage and criticism that does not require them to step back from society but only to distance themselves from being implicated in those power relations that subjugate, corrupt, exploit, or infantilize. This is what Michael Walzer calls criticism from within, the telling of stories that speak to the historical specificity and voices of those who have been marginalized and silenced.[37] It is a form of criticism wedded to the development of pedagogical practices and experiences in the interest of a utopian vision that in Walter Benjamin's terms rubs history against the grain, one that gives substance to the development of a public culture that is synonymous with the spirit of a critical democracy.

Educators must therefore develop a public language that refuses to reconcile higher educa-tion with inequality, that actively abandons those forms of pedagogical practice that prevent our students from becoming aware of and offended by the structures of oppression at work in both institutional and everyday life. We need a language that defends liberal arts education neither as a servant of the state nor as authoritarian cultural ideology but as the site of a counter-public sphere where students can be educated to learn how to question and, in the words of John Dewey, "break existing public forms."[38] This is a language in which knowledge and power are inextricably linked to the presupposition that to choose life, so as to make it possible, is to understand the preconditions necessary to struggle for it. As engaged public intellectuals committed to a project of radical pedagogy and the reconstruction of democratic public life, academics can create forms of collegiality and community forged in social practices that link their work in the university with larger social struggles. This suggests redefining the borders of knowledge-power relationships outside of the limitations of academic specialties so as to broaden the relationship of the university with the culture of public life. Academic interventions can thus provide the basis for new forms of public association, occasions informed by and contributing to moral and political commitments in which the meanings we produce, the ways in which we represent ourselves, and our relation to others contribute to a wider public discussion and dialogue of democratic possibilities not yet realized. This is a call to transform the hegemonic cultural forms of the wider society and the academy into a social movement of intellectuals intent on reclaiming and reconstructing democratic values and public life rather than contributing to their demise. This is a utopian practice that both critiques and transcends the culture of despair and disdain that has characterized education in the Reagan-Bush Era. It also provides a starting point for linking liberal arts education with a public philosophy in which the curriculum is not reduced to a matter of cultural inheritance, but is posed as part of an ongoing struggle informed by a project of possibility that extends the most noble of human capacities while simultaneously developing the potentialities of democratic public life.

Notes

1. Of course, a caveat has to be noted here. For many liberal and left academics, the university is generally regarded as a site constituted in relations of power and representing various political and ethical interests. On the other hand, some neoconservative educators believe that the true interests of the university transcend political and normative concerns and that the latter represent an agenda being pushed exclusively by left-wing academics who are undermining the most basic principles of university life. For example, former Secretary of Education William J. Bennett has argued that most universities are controlled "by a left-wing political agenda" pushing the concerns of feminists, Marxists, and various ethnic groups. The neoconservative argument is often made in defense of an objective, balanced, and unbiased academic discourse. The claim to objectivity, truth, and principle that transcend history and power may be comforting to neoconservative but in reality the discourse of such groups is nothing more than a rhetorical mask that barely conceals their own highly charged, ideological agenda. The neoconservative ongoing attacks against affirmative action, ethnic studies, radical scholarship, modernity, and any thing else that threatens the traditional curriculum and the power relations it supports represent a particularized, not universalized view of the university and its relationship with the wider society. The most recent example of neoconservative "objectivity" and public conscience was displayed in a recent meeting in Washington, D.C., of 300 conservative scholars whose major agenda was to reclaim the universities and to find ways to challenge those left-wing academics, referred to by one of the participants as "the barbarians in our midst" (p. 14), who are challenging the authority of the traditional canon. Underlying this form of criticism is the not so invisible ideological appeal to the "white man's burden" to educate those who exist outside of the parameters of civilized culture; the rhetoric betrays the colonizing logic at the heart of the "reactionary" political agenda that characterizes the new cultural offensive of such groups as the National Association of Scholars. The report on the conference appeared in Joseph Berger, "Conservative Scholars Attack 'Radicalization' of Universities," *New York Times*, November 15, 1988, 14. For a discussion of the conservative offensive in establishing a traditional reading of the liberal arts and the notion of the canon, see William V. Spanos, *Repetitions The Postmodern Occasion in Literature and Culture* (Baton Rouge, 1987); a special issue on "The Politics of Education," *South Atlantic Quarterly* 89:1, (1990); a special issue on "The Politics of Teaching Literature," *College Literature* 17:2/3 (1990); Henry A. Giroux, *Schooling and the Struggle for Public Life* (Minneapolis, 1988).

2. A characteristic form of this type of evasion can be found in John Searle, "The Storm Over the University," *The New York Review of Books* 37:1 (December 6, 1990); Allan Bloom, *Giants and Dwarf: Essays 1960–1990* (New York: Simon and Schuster, 1990), and Roger Kimball, *Tenured Radicals: How Politics has Corrupted Our Higher Education* (New York: Harper and Roe, 1990). All of these books share the lament that progressives and radicals have corrupted the university by politicizing the curriculum. Central to this charge is the assumptions that conservatives are politically neutral and that their call for educational reform is objective and value-free. Searle's claim is a bit more sophisticated, though no less confused. He

alleges that because social critics link university reform with the broader goal of social transformation that they must by necessity engage in forms of political indoctrination. Searle cannot, unfortunately, distinguish between rooting one's pedagogy in a particular set of expectations that serve as a referent for engaging students and a pedagogical approach designed to beat them into ideological submission. In other words, Searle collapses the particular ideological values that educators individually profess and the pedagogy they exercise. While I believe that students should be educated to not simply adapt to the system but be able to change it when necessary, the nature of my pedagogy does not have to be reduced to the inculcation of a specific ideology in the service of social transformation. My immediate goal is to get students to think critically about their lives; the specific objectives and ideologies they choose to address and take up are not something that can be forced upon them. Any pedagogy that acts in the service of only one outcome generally constitutes a form of terrorism.

3. Henry Louis Gates, Jr., "The Master's Pieces: On Canon Formation and the African American Tradition," *The South Atlantic Quarterly* 89:1 (1990), 89–111.

4. Gayatri C. Spivak, "The Making of Americans, the Teaching of English, and the Future of Cultural Studies," *New Literary History* 21:4 (Autumn 1990), 785.

5. Philip Corrigan, "In/Forming Schooling," in David W. Livingstone, Critical *Pedagogy and Cultural Power* (New York, New York: Bergin and Garvey, 1987), 17–40.

6. I am borrowing this idea from Peter Brooks, "Western Civ at Bay," *New York Time Literary Supplement*, January 25, 1991, 5.

7. Roger I. Simon, "Empowerment as a Pedagogy of Possibility," *Language Arts* 64:3 (April 1987), 372.

8. Jacques Derrida, "The Principle of Reason: The University in the Eyes of Its Pupils," *Diacritics* 13:3 (Fall 1983), 3.

9. Ernst Bloch, *The Philosophy of the Future* (New York, 1970), 86–87.

10. The quotes before and after the passage by Bloch are from Roger Simon, "Empowerment, as a Pedagogy of Possibility," 371, 372. I am indebted to Simon for a number of the ideas in this section on Bloch and the relationship between daydreaming and the process of schooling.

11. Leon Botstein illuminates some of the ideological elements at work in the language of cultural despair characteristic of the educational discourse of the New Right:

    In particular, the new conservatism evident in the most influential educational critiques and Jeremiads utilizes the language and images of decline and unwittingly makes comparisons to an idealized American past during which far fewer Americans finished high school. It challenges implicitly (Hirsch) and explicitly (Bloom) the post-World War II democratic goal of American schooling: to render excellence and equity incompatible in reality. In the 1980s, the call for educational reform is not being framed, as it was in the late 1950s (when America was concerned about Sputnik and Harvard's Conant studied the American high school), in terms of what might be achieved. Rather the discussion begins with a sense of what has been lost.

    See Leon Botstein, "Education Reform in the Reagan Era: False Paths, Broken Promises," *Social Policy* (Spring 1988), 7. For a critique of the ideology of cultural decline among universities, see Jerry Herron, *Universities and the Myth of Cultural Decline* (Detroit, 1988).

12. Simon, "Empowerment as a Pedagogy of Possibility."

13. This criticism is more fully developed in Stanley Aronowitz and Henry A. Giroux, *Postmodern Education* (Minneapolis: University of Minnesota Press, 1991); Henry A. Giroux, *Schooling and the Struggle for Public Life*; Stanley Aronowitz and Henry A. Giroux, *Education Under Siege* (Granby, Mass., 1985).

14. Brooks, "Western Civ at Bay," 5.

15. Roger Kimball, *"Tenured Radicals"* As Postscript," *The New Criterion* (January 1991),13.

16. Silber, cited in Carolyn J. Mooney, "Scholars Decry Campus Hostility to Western Culture at a Time When More Nations Embrace Its Values," *The Chronicle of Higher Education*, January 30, 1991, A16.

17. Allan Bloom, *The Closing of the American Mind: How Higher Education Has Failed Democracy and Impoverished the Souls of Today's Students* (New York, 1987). E. D. Hirsch, Jr., *Cultural Literacy: What Every American Needs to Know* (Boston, 1987).

18. Allan Bloom, *The Closing of the American Mind*; E. D. Hirsch, Jr., *Cultural Literacy*; Kimball, *Tenured Radicals*; Lynne V. Cheney, *Humanities in America: A Report to the President, the Congress, and the American People* (Washington, D.C.: National Endowment for the Humanities, 1988).

19. This position is more fully developed in Jim Merod, *The Political Responsibility of the Critic* (Ithaca, 1987); Aronowitz and Giroux, *Education Under Siege*, 1985; Frank Lentricchia, *Criticism and Social Change* (Chicago, 1983).

20. William V. Spanos, *Repetitions*, 302.

21. Christopher Lasch, "A Response to Fischer," *Tikkun* 3:6 (1988), 73.

22. Mas'ud Zavarzadeh and Donald Morton, "War of the Words: The Battle of (and for) English," *In These Times* (October 28–November 3, 1987), 18–19. Hazel Carby, in "The Canon: Civil War and Reconstruction," *Michigan Quarterly Review* (Winter 1989), 36–38, is clear on this point and is worth quoting at length:

   . . . I would argue that debates about the canon are misleading debates in many ways. Arguments appear to be about the inclusion or exclusion of particular texts and/or authors or about including or excluding types of books and authors ("women" and "minorities" are usually the operative categories). It also appears as if debates about the canon are disagreements about issues of representation only. . . . Contrary to what the debate appears to be about, talking about the canon means that we avoid the deeper problem. Focusing on books and authors means that we are not directly addressing ways in which our society is structured in dominance. We live in a racialized hierarchy which is also organized through class and gender divisions. Reducing these complex modes of inequality to questions of representation on a syllabus is far too simple a method of appearing to resolve those social contradictions and yet this is how the battle has been waged at Columbia and Stanford, to take two examples of campuses engaged in debating the importance of canonical works of western culture. What is absurd about these hotly contested and highly emotive battles is that proponents for radical change in canonical syllabi are forced to act as if inclusion of the texts they favor would somehow make accessible the experience of women or minorities as generic types. The same people who would argue in very sophisticated critical terms that literary texts do not directly reflect or represent reality but reconstruct and represent particular historical realities find themselves demanding that the identity of a social group be represented by a single novel. Acting as if an excluded or marginalized or dominant group is represented in a particular text, in my view, is a mistake. . . . Our teaching needs to make connections with, as well as provide a critique of, dominant ideologies and meanings of culture which structure the curricula of departments of English and American studies.

   See also Toni Morrison, "Unspeakable Things Unspoken: The Afro-American Presence in American Literature," *Michigan Quarterly Review* (Winter 1989), 1–34.

23. This particular quote is cited in Frank Hearn, *Reason and Freedom in Sociological Thought* (Boston, 1985), 175. The classic statements by Dewey on this subject can be found, of course, in John Dewey, *Democracy and Education* (New York, 1916) and John Dewey, *The Public and Its Problems* in *The Later Works of John Dewey, Volume 2, 1925–1927*, Jo Ann Boydston, ed. (Carbondale, 1984), 253–372.

24. See, for example, C. Wright Mills, *Power, Politics, and People: The Collected Essays of C. Wright Mills*, Irving Louis Horowitz, ed. (New York, 1963), especially the "Social Role of the Intellectual" and "Mass Society and Liberal Education."

25. For a critical treatment of this issue, see Robert N. Bellah, Richard Madsen, William M. Sullivan, Ann Swidler, and Steven M. Tipton, *Habits of the Heart: Individualism and Commitment in American Life* (Berkeley, 1985); for an excellent analysis and criticism of American life and the decline of community as portrayed in *Habits of the Heart*, see Fredric R. Jameson, "On Habits of the Heart," in Charles H. Reynolds and Ralph V. Norman, eds., *Community in America* (Berkeley, 1988), 97–112.

26. A number of representative essays that deal with pedagogy as a form of cultural production can be found in Henry A. Giroux and Peter McLaren, eds., *Critical Pedagogy, The State and Cultural Struggle* (Albany: SUNY Press, 1988); Henry A. Giroux and Roger I. Simon, eds., *Popular Culture and Critical Pedagogy* (New York: Bergin and Garvey, 1989); Patricia Donahue and Ellen Quandahl, eds., *Reclaiming Pedagogy The Rhetoric of the Classroom* (Carbondale: Southern Illinois University Press, 1989); Aronowitz and Henry A. Giroux, *Postmodern Education*; and Roger I. Simon, *Teaching Against the Grain* (New York: Bergin and Garvey Press, 1991).

27. Democracy, in this case, is linked to citizenship understood as a form of self-management constituted in all major economic, social, and cultural spheres of society. Democracy as it is being used here take up the issue of transferring power from elites and executives authorities, who control the economic and cultural apparatuses of society, to those producers who wield power at the local level.

28. The next two pages draw from Henry A. Giroux and Harvey J. Kaye, "The Liberal Arts Must Be Reformed to Serve Democratic Ends," *The Chronicle of Higher Education*, March 29, 1989, A44.

29. Elizabeth Fox-Genovese, "The Claims of a Common Culture: Gender, Race, Class and the Canon," *Salmagundi* 72 (Fall 1986),133.

30. Gail Valasrakis, "The Chippewa and the Other: Living the Heritage of Lac Du Flambeau," *Cultural Studies* 2:3 (October 1988), 268.

31. Chantal Mouffe, "The Civics Lesson," *New Statesman and Society* (October 7, 1988), 30.

32. bell hooks, "Choosing the Margin as a Space of Radical Openness," *Yearning* (Boston: South End Press, 1990), 145–52.

33. Teresa de Lauretis, *Technologies of Gender* (Bloomington, 1987), p. 25.

34. Caren Kaplan, "Deterritorialization: The Rewriting of Home and Exile in Western Feminist Discourse," *Cultural Critique* 6 (Spring 1987), 187-98.

35. On this point, see Russell Jacoby, *The Last Intellectuals* (New York, 1987); Terry Eagleton, *The Function of Criticism* (London, 1984).

36. Antonio Gramsci, *Selections from the Prison Notebooks* (New York, 1971).

37. Michael Walzer, *Interpretation and Social Criticism* (Cambridge, 1985).

38. John Dewey, *The Public and Its Problems in The Later Works of John Dewey, Volume 2, 1925-1927*, Jo Ann Boydston, ed., (Carbondale, 1984), 253–372.

The Canon Debate, Knowledge Construction and Multicultural Education

James A. Banks

A heated and divisive national debate is taking place about what knowledge related to ethnic and cultural diversity should be taught in the school and university curriculum (Asante, 1991a; Asante & Ravitch, 1991; D'Souza, 1991; Glazer, 1991; Schlesinger, 1991; Woodward, 1991). This debate has heightened ethnic tension and confused many educators about the meaning of multicultural education. At least three different groups of scholars are participating in the canon debate: the Western traditionalists, the multiculturalists, and the Afrocentrists. Although there are a range of perspectives and views within each of these groups, all groups share a number of important assumptions and beliefs about the nature of diversity in the United States and about the role of educational institutions in a pluralistic society.

The Western traditionalists have initiated a national effort to defend the dominance of Western civilization in the school and university curriculum (Gray, 1991; Howe, 1991; Woodward, 1991). These scholars believe that Western history, literature, and culture are endangered in the school and university curriculum because of the push by feminists, ethnic minority scholars, and other multiculturalists for curriculum reform and transformation. The Western traditionalists have formed an organization called the National Association of Scholars to defend the dominance of Western civilization in the curriculum.

The multiculturalists believe that the school, college, and university curriculum marginalizes the experiences of people of color and of women (Butler & Walter, 1991; Gates, 1992; Grant, 1992; Sleeter, personal communication, October 16, 1991). They contend that the curriculum should be reformed so that it will more accurately reflect the histories and cultures of ethnic groups and women. Two organizations have been formed to promote issues related to ethnic and cultural diversity. Teachers for a Democratic Culture promotes ethnic studies and women studies at the university level. The National Association for Multicultural Education focuses on teacher education and multicultural education in the nation's schools.

The Afrocentrists maintain that African culture and history should be placed at the center of the curriculum in order to motivate African American students to learn and to help all students to understand the important role that Africa has played in the development of Western civilization (Asante, 1991a). Many mainstream multiculturalists are ambivalent about Afrocentrism, although few have publicly opposed it. This is in part because the Western traditionalists rarely distinguish the Afrocentrists from the multiculturalists and describe them as one group. Some multiculturalists may also perceive Afrocentric ideas as compatible with a broader concept of multicultural education.

The influence of the multiculturalists within schools and universities in the last 20 years has been substantial. Many school districts, state departments of education, local school districts, and private agencies have developed and implemented multicultural staff development programs, conferences, policies, and curricula (New York City Board of Education, 1990; New York State Department of Education, 1989, 1991; Sokol, 1990). Multicultural requirements, programs, and policies have also been implemented at many of the nation's leading research universities, including the University of California, Berkeley, Stanford University, The Pennsylvania State University, and the University of Wisconsin system. The success that the multiculturalists have had in implementing their ideas within schools and universities is probably a major reason that the Western traditionalists are trying to halt multicultural reforms in the nation's schools, colleges, and universities.

The debate between the Western traditionalists and the multiculturalists is consistent with the ideas of a democratic society. To date, however, it has resulted in little productive interaction between the Western traditionalists and the multiculturalists. Rather, each group has talked primarily to audiences it viewed as sympathetic to its ideologies and visions of the present and future (Franklin, 1991; Schlesinger, 1991). Because there has been little productive dialogue and exchange between the Western traditionalists and the multiculturalists, the debate has been polarized, and writers have frequently not conformed to the established rules of scholarship (D'Souza, 1991). A kind of forensic social science has developed (Rivlin, 1973), with each side stating briefs and then marshaling evidence to support its position. The debate has also taken place primarily in the popular press rather than in academic and scholarly journals.

Valuation and Knowledge Construction

I hope to make a positive contribution to the canon debate in this article by providing evidence for the claim that the positions of both the Western traditionalists and the multiculturalists reflect values, ideologies, political positions, and human interests. Each position also implies a kind of knowledge that should be taught in the school and university curriculum. I will present a typology of the kinds of knowledge that exist in society and in educational institutions. This typology is designed to help practicing educators and researchers to identify types of knowledge that reflect particular values, assumptions, perspectives, and ideological positions.

Teachers should help students to understand all types of knowledge. Students should be involved in the debates about knowledge construction and conflicting interpretations, such as the extent to which Egypt and Phoenicia influenced Greek civilization. Students should also be taught how to create their own interpretations of the past and present, as well as how to identify their own positions, interests, ideologies, and assumptions. Teachers should help students to become critical thinkers who have the knowledge, attitudes, skills, and commitments needed to participate in democratic action to help the nation close the gap between its ideals and its realities. Multicultural education is an education for functioning effectively in a pluralistic democratic society. Helping students to develop the knowledge, skills, and attitudes needed to participate in reflective civic action is one of its major goals (Banks, 1991).

I argue that students should study all five types of knowledge. However, my own work and philosophical position are within the transformative tradition in ethnic studies and multicultural education (Banks, 1988, 1991; Banks & Banks, 1989). This tradition links knowledge, social commitment, and action (Meier & Rudwick, 1986). A transformative, action-oriented curriculum, in my view, can best be implemented when students examine different types of knowledge in a democratic classroom where they can freely examine their perspectives and moral commitments.

The Nature of Knowledge

I am using knowledge in this article to mean the way a person explains or interprets reality. *The American Heritage Dictionary* (1983) defines knowledge as "familiarity, awareness, or understandings gained through experience or study. The sum or range of what has been perceived, discovered or inferred" (p. 384). My conceptualization of knowledge is broad and is used the way in which it is usually used in the sociology of knowledge literature to include ideas, values, and interpretation (Farganis, 1986). As postmodern theorists have pointed out, knowledge is socially constructed and reflects human interests, values, and action (Code, 1991; Foucault, 1972; S. Harding, 1991; Rorty, 1989). Although many complex factors influence the knowledge that is created by an individual or group, including the actuality of what occurred, the knowledge that people create is heavily influenced by their interpretations of their experiences and their positions within particular social, economic, and political systems and structures of a society.

In the Western empirical tradition, the ideal within each academic discipline is the formulation of knowledge without the influence of the researcher's personal or cultural characteristics (Greer, 1969; Kaplan, 1964). However, as critical and postmodern theorists have pointed out, personal, cultural, and social factors influence the formulation of knowledge even when objective knowledge is the ideal within a discipline (Cherryholmes, 1988; Foucault, 1972; Habermas, 1971; Rorty, 1989; Young, 1971). Often the researchers themselves are unaware of how their personal experiences and positions within society influence the knowledge they produce. Most mainstream historians were unaware of how their regional and cultural biases influenced their interpretation of the Reconstruction period until W. E. B. DuBois published a study that challenged the accepted and established interpretations of that historical period (DuBois, 1935/1962).

Positionality and Knowledge Construction

Positionality is an important concept that emerged out of feminist scholarship. Tetreault (1993) writes:

> Positionality means that important aspects of our identity, for example, our gender, our race, our class, our age . . . are markers of relational positions rather than essential qualities. Their effects and implications change according to context. Recently, feminist thinkers have seen knowledge as valid when it comes from an acknowledgment of the knower's specific position in any context, one always defined by gender, race, class and other variables. (p. 139)

Positionality reveals the importance of identifying the positions and frames of reference from which scholars and writers present their data, interpretations, analyses, and instruction (Anzaldúa, 1990; Ellsworth, 1989). The need for researchers and scholars to identify their ideological positions and normative assumptions in their works—an inherent part of feminist and ethnic studies scholarship—contrasts with the empirical paradigm that has dominated science and research in the United States (Code, 1991; S. Harding, 1991).

The assumption within the Western empirical paradigm is that the knowledge produced within it is neutral and objective and that its principles are universal. The effects of values, frames of references, and the normative positions of researchers and scholars are infrequently discussed within the traditional empirical paradigm that has dominated scholarship and teaching in American colleges and universities since the turn of the century. However, scholars such as Myrdal (1944) and Clark (1965), prior to the feminist and ethnic studies movements, wrote about the need for scholars to recognize and state their normative positions and valuations and to become, the apt words of Kenneth B. Clark, "involved observers." Myrdal stated that valuations are not just attached to research but permeate it. He wrote, "There is no device for excluding biases in social sciences than to face the valuations and to introduce them as explicitly stated, specific, and sufficiently concretized value premises" (p. 1043).

Postmodern and critical theorists such as Habermas (1971) and Giroux (1983), and feminist postmodern theorists such as Farganis (1986), Code (1991), and S. Harding (1991), have developed important critiques of empirical knowledge. They argue that despite its claims, modern science is not value-free but contains important human interests and normative assumptions that should be identified, discussed, and examined. Code (1991), a feminist epistemologist, states that academic knowledge is both subjective and objective and that both aspects should be recognized and discussed. Code states that we need to ask these kinds of questions: "Out of whose subjectivity has this ideal [of objectivity] grown? Whose standpoint, whose values does it represent?" (p. 70). She writes:

The point of the questions is to discover how subjective and objective conditions together produce knowledge, values, and epistemology. It is neither to reject objectivity nor to glorify subjectivity in its stead. Knowledge is neither value-free nor value neutral; the processes that produce it are themselves value-laden; and these values are open to evaluation. (p. 70)

In her book, *What Can She Know? Feminist Theory and the Construction of Knowledge*, Code (1991) raises the question, "Is the sex of the knower epistemologically significant.?" (p. 7). She answers this question in the affirmative because of the ways in which gender influences how knowledge is constructed, interpreted, and institutionalized within U.S. society. The ethnic and cultural experiences of the knower are also epistemologically significant because these factors also influence knowledge construction, use, and interpretation in U.S. society.

Empirical scholarship has been limited by the assumptions and biases that are implicit within it (Code, 1991; Gordon, 1985; S. Harding, 1991). However, these biases and assumptions have been infrequently recognized by the scholars and researchers themselves and by the consumers of their works, such as other scholars, professors, teachers, and the general reader. The lack of recognition and identification of these biases, assumptions, perspectives, and points of view have frequently victimized people of color such as African Americans and American Indians because of the stereotypes and misconceptions that have been perpetuated about them in the historical and social science literature (Ladner, 1973; Phillips, 1918).

Gordon, Miller, and Rollock (1990) call the bias that results in the negative depiction of minority groups by mainstream social scientists "communicentric bias." They point out that mainstream social scientists have often viewed diversity as deviance and differences as deficits. An important outcome of the revisionist and transformative interpretations that have been produced by scholars working in feminist and ethnic studies is that many misconceptions and partial truths about women and ethnic groups have been viewed from different and more complete perspectives (Acuña, 1988; Blassingame, 1972; V. Harding, 1981; King & Mitchell, 1990; Merton, 1972).

More complete perspectives result in a closer approximation to the actuality of what occurred. In an important and influential essay, Morton (1977) notes that the perspectives of both "insiders" and "outsiders" are needed to enable social scientists to gain a complete view of social reality. Anna Julia Cooper, the African American educator, made a point similar to Merton's when she wrote about how the perspectives of women enlarged our vision (Cooper, 1892/1969, cited in Minnich, 1990, p. viii):

The world has had to limp along with the wobbling gait and the one-sided hesitancy of a man with one eye. Suddenly the bandage is removed from the other eye and the whole body is filled with light. It sees a circle where before it saw a segment.

A Knowledge Typology

A description of the major types of knowledge can help teachers and curriculum specialists to identify perspectives and content needed to make the curriculum multicultural. Each of the types of knowledge described below reflects particular purposes, perspectives, experiences, goals, and human interests. Teaching students various types of knowledge can help them to better understand the perspectives of different racial, ethnic, and cultural groups as well as to develop their own versions and interpretations of issues and events.

I identify and describe five types of knowledge (see Table 1): (a) personal/cultural knowledge; (b) popular knowledge; (c) mainstream academic knowledge; (d) transformative academic knowledge; and (e) school knowledge. This is an ideal-type typology in the Weberian sense. The five categories approximate, but do not describe, reality in its total complexity. The categories are useful conceptual tools for thinking about knowledge and planning multicultural teaching. For example, although the categories can be conceptually distinguished, in reality they overlap and are interrelated in a dynamic way.

Table 1
Types of Knowledge

Knowledge Type	Definition	Examples
Personal/cultural	The concepts, explanations, and interpretations that students derive from personal experiences in their homes, families, and community cultures.	Understandings by many African Americans and Hispanic students that highly individualistic behavior will be negatively sanctioned by many adults and peers in their cultural communities.
Popular	The facts, concepts, explanations, and interpretations that are institutionalized within the mass media and other institutions that are part of the popular culture.	Movies such as *Birth of a Nation, How the West Was Won,* and *Dances with Wolves.*
Mainstream academic	The concepts, paradigms, theories, and explanations that constitute traditional Western-centric knowledge in history and the behavioral and social sciences.	Ulrich B. Phillips, *American Negro Slavery,* Frederick Jackson Turner's frontier theory; Arthur R. Jensen's theory about Black and White intelligence.
Transformative academic	The facts, concepts, paradigms, themes, and explanations that challenge mainstream academic knowledge and expand and substantially revise established canons, paradigms, theories, explanations, and research methods. When transformative academic paradigms replace mainstream ones, a scientific revolution has occurred. What is more normal is that transformative academic paradigms coexist with established ones.	George Washington Williams, *History of the Negro Race in America,* W.E.B. DuBois, *Black Reconstruction;* Carter G. Woodson, *The Mis-education of the Negro;* Gerda Lemer, *The Majority Finds Its Past,* Rodolfo Acuña, *Occupied America: A History of Chicanos;* Herbert Gutman, *The Black Family in Slavery and Freedom 1750–1925.*
School	The facts, concepts, generalizations, and interpretations that are presented in textbooks, teacher's guides, other media forms, and lectures by teachers.	Lewis Paul Todd and Merle Curti, *Rise of the American Nation;* Richard C. Brown, Wilhelmena S. Robinson, & John Cummingham, *Let Freedom Ring: A United States History.*

Since the 1960s, some of the findings and insights from transformative academic knowledge have been incorporated into mainstream academic knowledge and scholarship. Traditionally students were taught in schools and universities that the land that became North America was a thinly populated wilderness when the Europeans arrived in the 16th century and that African Americans had made few contributions to the development of American civilization (mainstream academic knowledge). Some of the findings from transformative academic knowledge that challenged these conceptions have influenced mainstream academic scholarship and have been incorporated into mainstream college and school textbooks (Hoxie, no date; Thornton, 1987). Consequently, the relationship between the five categories of knowledge is dynamic and interactive rather than static (see Figure 1).

The Types of Knowledge

Personal and Cultural Knowledge

The concepts, explanations, and interpretations that students derive from personal experiences in their homes, families, and community cultures constitute personal and cultural knowledge. The

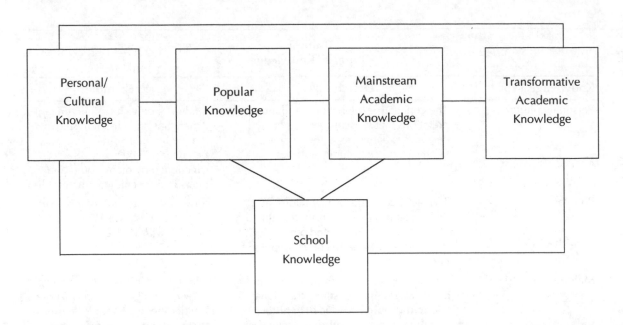

Figure 1

assumptions, perspectives, and insights that students derive from the experiences in their homes and community cultures are used as screens to view and interpret the knowledge and experiences that they encounter in the school and in other institutions within the larger society.

Research and theory by Fordham and Ogbu (1986) indicate that low-income African American students often experience academic difficulties in the school because of the ways that cultural knowledge within their community conflicts with school knowledge, norms, and expectations. Fordham and Ogbu also state that the culture of many low-income African American students is oppositional to the school culture. These students believe that if they master the knowledge taught in the schools they will violate fictive kinship norms and run the risk of "acting White." Fordham (1988, 1991) has suggested that African American students who become high academic achievers resolve the conflict caused by the interaction of their personal cultural knowledge with the knowledge and norms within the schools by becoming "faceless" or by "ad hocing a culture." Delpit (1988) has stated that African American students are often unfamiliar with school cultural knowledge regarding power relationships. They consequently experience academic and behavioral problems because of their failure to conform to established norms, rules, and expectations. She recommends that teachers help African American students learn the rules of power in the school culture by explicitly teaching them to the students. The cultural knowledge that many African American, Latino, and American Indian students bring to school conflict with school norms and values, with school knowledge, and with the ways that teachers interpret and mediate school knowledge. Student cultural knowledge and school knowledge often conflict on variables related to the ways that the individual should relate to and interact with the group (Hale-Benson, 1982; Ramirez & Castaneda, 1974; Shade, 1989), normative communication styles and interactions (Heath, 1983, Labov, 1975; Philips, 1983; Smitherman, 1977), and perspectives on the nature of U.S. history.

Personal and cultural knowledge is problematic when it conflicts with scientific ways of validating knowledge, is oppositional to the culture of the school, or challenges the main tenets and assumptions of mainstream academic knowledge. Much of the knowledge about out-groups that students learn from their home and community cultures consists of misconceptions, stereotypes, and partial truths (Milner, 1983). Most students in the United States are socialized within communities that are segregated along racial, ethnic, and social-class lines. Consequently, most American youths have few opportunities to learn firsthand about the cultures of people from different racial, ethnic, cultural, religious, and social-class groups.

The challenge that teachers face is how to make effective instructional use of the personal and cultural knowledge of students while at the same time helping them to reach beyond their own cultural boundaries. Although the school should recognize, validate, and make effective use of students' personal and cultural knowledge in instruction, an important goal of education is to free students from their cultural and ethnic boundaries and enable them to cross cultural borders freely (Banks, 1988, 1991/1992).

In the past, the school has paid scant attention to the personal and cultural knowledge of students and has concentrated on teaching them school knowledge (Sleeter & Grant, 1991a). This practice has had different results for most White middle-class students, for most low-income students, and for most African American and Latino students. Because school knowledge is more consistent with the cultural experiences of most White middle-class students than for most other groups of students, these students have generally found the school a more comfortable place than have low-income students and most students of color—the majority of whom are also low income. A number of writers have described the ways in which many African American, American Indian, and Latino students find the school culture alienating and inconsistent with their cultural experiences, hopes, dreams, and struggles (Hale-Benson, 1982; Heath, 1983; Ramirez & Castaneda, 1974; Shade, 1989).

It is important for teachers to be aware of the personal and cultural knowledge of students when designing the curriculum for today's multicultural schools. Teachers can use students' personal cultural knowledge as a vehicle to motivate students and as a foundation for teaching school knowledge. When teaching a unit on the Westward Movement to Lakota Sioux students, for example, the teacher can ask the students to make a list of their views about the Westward Movement, to relate family stories about the coming of the Whites to Lakota Sioux homelands, and to interview parents and grandparents about their perceptions of what happened when the Whites first occupied Indian lands. When teachers begin a unit on the Westward Movement with students' personal cultural knowledge, they can increase student motivation as well as deepen their understanding of the schoolbook version (Wiggington, 1991/1992).

Popular Knowledge

Popular knowledge consists of the facts, interpretations, and beliefs that are institutionalized within television, movies, videos, records, and other forms of the mass media. Many of the tenets of popular knowledge are conveyed in subtle rather than obvious ways. Some examples of statements that constitute important themes in popular knowledge follow: (a) The United States is a powerful nation with unlimited opportunities for individuals who are willing to take advantage of them. (b) To succeed in the United States, an individual only has to work hard. You can realize your dreams in the United States if you are willing to work hard and pull yourself up by the bootstrap. (c) As a land of opportunity for all, the United States is a highly cohesive nation, whose ideals of equality and freedom are shared by all.

Most of the major tenets of American popular culture are widely shared and are deeply entrenched in U.S. society. However, they are rarely explicitly articulated. Rather, they are presented in the media and in other sources in the forms of stories, anecdotes, news stories, and interpretations of current events (Cortes, 1991a, 1991b; Greenfield & Cortes, 1991).

Commercial entertainment films both reflect and perpetuate popular knowledge (Bogle, 1989; Cortes, 1991a, 1991b; Greenfield & Cortes, 1991). While preparing to write this article, I viewed an important and influential film that was directed by John Ford and released by MGM in 1962, *How the West Was Won*. I selected this film for review because the settlement of the West is a major theme in American culture and society about which there are many popular images, beliefs, myths, and misconceptions. In viewing the film, I was particularly interested in the images it depicted about the settlement of the West, about the people who were already in the West, and about those who went West looking for new opportunities.

Ford uses the Prescotts, a White family from Missouri bound for California, to tell his story. The film tells the story of three generations of this family. It focuses on the family's struggle to settle in the West. Indians, African Americans, and Mexicans are largely invisible in the film.

Indians appear in the story when they attack the Prescott family during their long and perilous journey. The Mexicans appearing in the film are bandits who rob a train and are killed. The several African Americans in the film are in the background silently rowing a boat. At various points in the film, Indians are referred to as "hostile Indians" and as "squaws."

How the West Was Won is a masterpiece in American popular culture. It not only depicts some of the major themes in American culture about the winning of the West: it reinforces and perpetuates dominant societal attitudes about ethnic groups and gives credence to the notion that the West was won by liberty-loving, hard-working people who pursued freedom for all. The film's narrator states near its end, "[The movement West] produced a people free to dream, free to act and free to mold their own destiny."

Mainstream Academic Knowledge

Mainstream academic knowledge consists of the concepts, paradigms, theories, and explanations that constitute traditional and established knowledge in the behavioral and social sciences. An important tenet within the mainstream academic paradigm is that there is a set of objective truths that can be verified through rigorous and objective research procedures that are uninfluenced by human interests, values, and perspectives (Greer, 1969; Kaplan, 1964; Sleeter, 1991). This empirical knowledge, uninfluenced by human values and interests, constitutes a body of objective truths that should constitute the core of the school and university curriculum. Much of this objective knowledge originated in the West but is considered universal in nature and application.

Mainstream academic knowledge is the knowledge that multicultural critics such as Ravitch and Finn (1987), Hirsch (1987), and Bloom (1987) claim is threatened by the addition of content about women and ethnic minorities to the school and university curriculum. This knowledge reflects the established, Western oriented canon that has historically dominated university research and teaching in the United States. Mainstream academic knowledge consists of the theories and interpretations that are internalized and accepted by most university researchers, academic societies, and organizations such as the American Historical Association, the American Sociological Association, the American Psychological Association, and the National Academy of Sciences.

It is important to point out, however, that an increasing number of university scholars are critical theorists and postmodernists who question the empirical paradigm that dominates Western science (Cherryholmes, 1988; Giroux, 1983; Rosenau, 1992). Many of these individuals are members of national academic organizations, such as the American Historical Association and the American Sociological Association. In most of these professional organizations, the postmodern scholars made up of significant numbers of scholars of color and feminists—have formed caucuses and interest groups within the mainstream professional organizations.

No claim is made here that there is a uniformity of beliefs among mainstream academic scholars, but rather that there are dominant canons, paradigms, and theories that are accepted by the community of mainstream academic scholars and researchers. These established canons and paradigms are occasionally challenged within the mainstream academic community itself.

However, they receive their most serious challenges from academics outside the mainstream, such as scholars within the transformative academic community whom I will describe later.

Mainstream academic knowledge, like the other forms of knowledge discussed in this article, is not static, but is dynamic, complex, and changing. Challenges to the dominant canons and paradigms within mainstream academic knowledge come from both within and without. These challenges lead to changes, reinterpretations, debates, disagreements and ultimately to paradigm shifts, new theories, and interpretations. Kuhn (1970) states that a scientific revolution takes place when a new paradigm emerges and replaces an existing one. What is more typical in education and the social sciences is that competing paradigms coexist, although particular ones might be more influential during certain times or periods.

We can examine the treatment of slavery within the mainstream academic community over time, or the treatment of the American Indian, to identify ways that mainstream academic knowledge has changed in important ways since the late 19th and early 20th centuries. Ulrich B. Phillips's highly influential book, *American Negro Slavery*, published in 1918, dominated the way

Black slavery was interpreted until his views were challenged by researchers in the 1950s (Stampp, 1956). Phillips was a respected authority on the ante-bellum South and on slavery. His book, which became a historical classic, is essentially an apology for Southern slave holders. A new paradigm about slavery was developed in the 1970s that drew heavily upon the slaves' view of their own experiences (Blassingame, 1972; Genovese, 1972; Gutman, 1976).

During the late 19th and early 20th centuries, the American Indian was portrayed in mainstream academic knowledge as either a noble or a hostile savage (Hoxie, 1988). Other notions that became institutionalized within mainstream academic knowledge include the idea that Columbus discovered America and that America was a thinly populated frontier when the Europeans arrived in the late 15th century. Frederick Jackson Turner (Turner, 1989) argued that the frontier, which he regarded as a wilderness, was the main source of American democracy. Although Turner's thesis is now being highly criticized by revisionist historians, his essay established a conception of the West that has been highly influential in American mainstream scholarship, in the popular culture, and in schoolbooks. The conception of the West he depicted is still influential today in the school curriculum and in textbooks (Sleeter & Grant, 1991b).

These ideas also became institutionalized within mainstream academic knowledge: The slaves were happy and contented; most of the important ideas that became a part of American civilization came from Western Europe; and the history of the United States has been one of constantly expanding progress and increasing democracy. African slaves were needed to transform the United States from an empty wilderness into an industrial democratic civilization. The American Indians had to be Christianized and removed to reservations in order for this to occur.

Transformative Academic Knowledge

Transformative academic knowledge consists of concepts, paradigms, themes, and explanations that challenge mainstream academic knowledge and that expand the historical and literary canon. Transformative academic knowledge challenges some of the key assumptions that mainstream scholars make about the nature of knowledge. Transformative and mainstream academic knowledge is based on different epistemological assumptions about the nature of knowledge, about the influence of human interests and values on knowledge construction, and about the purpose of knowledge.

An important tenet of mainstream academic knowledge is that it is neutral, objective, and was uninfluenced by human interests and values. Transformative academic knowledge reflects postmodern assumptions and goals about the nature and goals of knowledge (Foucault, 1972; Rorty, 1989; Rosenau, 1991). Transformative academic scholars assume that knowledge is not neutral but is influenced by human interests, that all knowledge reflects the power and social relationships within society, and that an important purpose of knowledge construction is to help people improve society (Code, 1991; S. Harding, 1991; hooks & West, 1991; King & Mitchell, 1990; Minnich, 1990). Write King and Mitchell: "Like other praxis-oriented critical approaches, the Afrocentric method seeks to enable people to understand social reality in order to change it. But its additional imperative is to transform the society's basic ethos" (p. 95).

These statements reflect some of the main ideas and concepts in transformative academic knowledge: Columbus did not discover America. The Indians had been living in this land for about 40,000 years when the Europeans arrived. Concepts such as "The European Discovery of America" and "The Westward Movement" need to be reconceptualized and viewed from the perspectives of different cultural and ethnic groups. The Lakota Sioux's homeland was not the West to them; it was the center of the universe. It was not the West for the Alaskans; it was South. It was East for the Japanese and North for the people who lived in Mexico. The history of the United States has not been one of continuous progress toward democratic ideals. Rather, the nation's history has been characterized by a cyclic quest for democracy and by conflict, struggle, violence, and exclusion (Acuña, 1988; Zinn, 1980). A major challenge that faces the nation is how to make its democratic ideals a reality for all.

Transformative academic knowledge has a long history in the United States. In 1882 and 1883, George Washington Williams (1849–1891) published, in two volumes, the first comprehensive history of African Americans in the United States, *A History of the Negro Race in America From 1619 to 1880* (Williams, 1982–1983/1968). Williams, like other African American scholars after him, decided to research and write about the Black experience because of the neglect of African Americans by mainstream historians and social scientists and because of the stereotypes and misconceptions about African Americans that appeared in mainstream scholarship.

W. E. B. DuBois (1868–1963) is probably the most prolific African American scholar in U.S. history. His published writings constitute 38 volumes (Aptheker, 1973). DuBois devoted his long and prolific career to the formulation of new data, concepts, and paradigms that could be used to reinterpret the Black experience and reveal the role that African Americans had played in the development of American society. His seminal works include *The Suppression of the African Slave Trade to the United States of America, 1638–1870*, the first volume of the Harvard Historical Studies (DuBois, 1896/1969). Perhaps his most discussed book is *Black Reconstruction in America: An Essay Toward a History of the Part Which Black Folk Played in the Attempt to Reconstruct Democracies in America, 1860–1880*, published in 1935 (1935/1962). In this book, DuBois challenged the accepted, institutionalized interpretations of Reconstruction and emphasized the accomplishments of the Reconstruction governments and legislatures, especially the establishment of free public schools.

Carter G. Woodson (1875–1950), the historian and educator who founded the Association for the Study of Negro Life and History and the *Journal of Negro History*, also challenged established paradigms about the treatment of African Americans in a series of important publications, including *The Mis-education of the Negro*, published in 1933. Woodson and Wesley (1922) published a highly successful college textbook that described the contributions that African Americans have made to American life, *The Negro in Our History*. This book was issued in 10 editions.

Transformative Scholarship Since the 1970s

Many scholars have produced significant research and theories since the early 1970s that have challenged and modified institutionalized stereotypes and misconceptions about ethnic minorities, formulated new concepts and paradigms, and forced mainstream scholars to rethink established interpretations. Much of the transformative academic knowledge that has been produced since the 1970s is becoming institutionalized within mainstream scholarship and within the school, college, and university curricula. In time, much of this scholarship will become mainstream, thus reflecting the highly interrelated nature of the types of knowledge conceptualized and described in this article.

Only a few examples of this new, transformative scholarship will be mentioned here because of the limited scope or this article. Howard Zinn's *A People's History of the United States* (1980), *Red, White and Black: The Peoples of Early America* by Gary B. Nash (1982), *The Signifying Monkey: A Theory of African-American Literacy Criticism* by Henry Louis Gates, Jr. (1988), *Occupied America: A History of Chicanos* by Rodolfo Acuña (1988), *Iron Cages: Race and Culture in 19th Century America* by Ronald T. Takaki (1979), and *The Sacred Hoop: Recovering the Feminine in American Indian Traditions* by Paula Gunn Allen (1986) are examples of important scholarship that has provided significant new perspectives on the experiences of ethnic groups in the United States and has helped us to transform our conceptions about the experiences of American ethnic groups. Readers acquainted with this scholarship will note that transformative scholarship has been produced by both European-American and ethnic minority scholars.

I will discuss two examples of how the new scholarship in ethnic studies has questioned traditional interpretations and stimulated a search for new explanations and paradigms since the 1950s. Since the pioneering work of E. Franklin Frazier (1939), social scientists had accepted the notion that the slave experience had destroyed the Black family and that the destruction of the African American family continued in the post-World War II period during Black migration to and settlement in northern cities. Moynihan (1965), in his controversial book, *The Negro Family in America: The Case of National Action,* used the broken Black family explanation in his analysis. Gutman (1976), in an important historical study of the African American family from 1750 to 1925, concluded that "despite a high rate of earlier involuntary marital breakup, large numbers of slave couples lived in long marriages, and most slaves lived in double-headed households" (p. xxii).

An important group of African and African American scholars have challenged established interpretations about the origin of Greek civilization and the extent to which Greek civilization was influenced by African cultures. These scholars include Diop (1974), Williams (1987), and Van Sertima (1988, 1989). Cheikh Anta Diop is one of the most influential African scholars who has challenged established interpretations about the origin of Greek civilization. In *Black Nations and Culture*, published in 1955 (summarized by Van Sertima, 1989), he sets forth an important thesis that states that Africa is an important root of Western civilization. Diop argues that Egypt "was the node and center of a vast web linking the strands of cultures and languages; that the light that crystallized at the center of this early world had been energized by the cultural electricity streaming from the heartland of Africa" (p. 8).

Since the work by Diop, Williams, and Van Sertima, traditional interpretations about the formation of Greek civilization has been challenged by Bernal (1987–1991), a professor of government at Cornell University. The earlier challenges to established interpretations by African and African Americans received little attention, except within the African American community. However, Bernal's work has received wide attention in the popular press and among classicists.

Bernal (1987–1991) argues that important aspects of Greek civilization originated in ancient Egypt and Phoenicia and that the ancient civilization of Egypt was essentially African. Bernal believes that the contributions of Egypt and Phoenicia to Greek civilization have been deliberately ignored by classical scholars because of their biased attitudes toward non-White peoples and Semites. Bernal has published two of four planned volumes of his study *Black Athena*. In Volume 2 he uses evidence from linguistics, archeology and ancient documents to substantiate his claim that "between 2100 and 1100 B.C., when Greek culture was born, the people of the Aegean borrowed, adapted or had thrust upon them deities and language, technologies and architectures, notions of justice and polis" from Egypt and Phoenicia (Begley, Chideya, & Wilson, 1991, p. 50). Because transformative academic knowledge, such as that constructed by Diop, Williams, Van Sertima, and Bernal, challenges the established paradigms as well as because of the tremendous gap between academic knowledge and school knowledge, it often has little influence on school knowledge.

School Knowledge

School knowledge consists of the facts, concepts, and generalizations presented in textbooks, teachers' guides, and the other forms of media designed for school use. School knowledge also consists of the teacher's mediation and interpretation of that knowledge. The textbook is the main source of school knowledge in the United States (Apple & Christian-Smith, 1991; Goodland, 1984; Shaver, Davis, & Helburn, 1979). Studies of textbooks indicate that these are some of the major themes in school knowledge (Anyon, 1979, 1981; Sleeter & Grant, 1991b): (a) America's founding fathers, such as Washington and Jefferson, were highly moral, liberty-loving men who championed equality and just for all Americans; (b) the United States is a nation with justice, liberty, and freedom for all; (c) social class divisions are not significant issues in the United States; (d) there are no significant gender, class, or racial divisions within U.S. society; and (e) ethnic groups of color and Whites interact largely in harmony in the United States.

Studies of textbooks that have been conducted by researchers such as Anyon (1979, 1981) and Sleeter and Grant (1991b) indicate that textbooks present a highly selective view of social reality, give students the idea that knowledge is static rather than dynamic, and encourage students to master isolated facts rather than to develop complex understandings of social reality. These studies also indicate that textbooks reinforce the dominant social, economic, and power arrangements within society. Students are encouraged to accept rather than to question these arrangements.

In their examination of the treatment of race, class, gender, and disability in textbooks, Sleeter and Grant (1991b) concluded that although textbooks had largely eliminated sexist language and had incorporated images of ethnic minorities into them, they failed to help students to develop an understanding of racism, sexism and classism in American society, and described the United States as a nation that had largely overcome its problems. Sleeter & Grant write:

The vision of social relations that the textbooks we analyzed for the most part project is one of harmony and equal opportunity—anyone can do or become whatever he or she wants; problems among people are mainly individual in nature and in the end are resolved. (p. 99)

A number of powerful factors influence the development and production of school textbooks (Altbach, Kelly, Petrie, & Weis, 1991; FitzGerald, 1979). One of the most important is the publisher's perception of statements and images that might be controversial. When textbooks become controversial, school districts often refuse to adopt and to purchase them. When developing a textbook, the publisher and the authors must also consider the developmental and reading levels of the students, state and district guidelines about what subject matter textbooks should include, and recent trends and developments in a content field that teachers and administrators will expect the textbook to reflect and incorporate. Because of the number of constraints and influences on the development of textbooks, school knowledge often does not include in-depth discussions and analyses of some of the major problems in American society, such as racism, sexism, social-class stratification, and poverty (Anyon, 1979, 1981; Sleeter & Grant, 1991b) . Consequently, school knowledge is influenced most heavily by mainstream academic knowledge and popular knowledge. Transformative academic knowledge usually has little direct influence on school knowledge. It usually affects school knowledge in a significant way only after it has become a part of mainstream and popular knowledge. Teachers must make special efforts to introduce transformative knowledge and perspectives to elementary and secondary school students.

Teaching Implications

Multicultural education involves changes in the total school environment in order to create equal education opportunities for all students (Banks, 1991; Banks & Banks, 1989; Sleeter & Grant, 1987). However, in this article I have focused on only one of the important dimensions of muticultural education—the kinds of knowledge that should be taught in the multicultural curriculum. The five types of knowledge described above have important implications for planning and teaching a multicultural curriculum.

An important goal of multicultural teaching is to help students to understand how knowledge is constructed. Students should be given opportunities to investigate and determine how cultural assumptions, frames of references, perspectives, and the biases within a discipline influence the ways the knowledge is constructed. Students should also be given opportunities to create knowledge themselves and identify ways in which the knowledge they construct is influenced and limited by their personal assumptions, positions, and experiences.

I will use a unit on the Westward Movement to illustrate how teachers can use the knowledge categories described above to teach from a multicultural perspective. When beginning the unit, teachers can draw upon the students' personal and cultural knowledge about the Westward Movement. They can ask the students to make a list of ideas that come to mind when they think of "The West." To enable the students to determine how the popular culture depicts the West, teachers can ask the students to view and analyze the film discussed above, *How the West Was Won*. They can also ask them to view videos of more recently made films about the West and to make a list of its major themes and images. Teachers can summarize Turner's frontier theory to give students an idea of how an influential mainstream historian described and interpreted the West in the late 19th century and how this theory influenced generations of historians.

Teachers can present a transformative perspective on the West by showing the students the film *How the West Was Won and Honor Lost* narrated by Marlon Brando. This film describes how the European Americans who went West, with the use of broken treaties and deception, invaded the land of the Indians and displaced them. Teachers may also ask the students to view segments of the popular film *Dances With Wolves* and to discuss how the depiction of Indians in this film reflects both mainstream and transformative perspectives on Indians in U.S. history and culture. Teachers can present the textbook account of the Westward Movement in the final part of the unit.

The main goals of presenting different kinds of knowledge are to help students understand how knowledge is constructed and how it reflects the social context in which it is created and to enable them to develop the understandings and skills needed to become knowledge builders themselves. An important goal of multicultural education is to transform the school curriculum so that students not only learn how to critically analyze the knowledge they master and how to construct their own interpretations of the past, present, and future.

Several important factors related to teaching the types of knowledge have not been discussed in this article but need to be examined. One is the personal/cultural knowledge of the classroom teacher. The teachers, like the students, bring understandings, concepts, explanations, and inter-pretations to the classroom that result from their experiences in their homes, families, and community cultures. Most teachers in the United States are European American (87%) and female (72%) (Ordovensky, 1992). However, there is enormous diversity among European Americans that is mirrored in the backgrounds of the teacher population, including diversity related to religion, social class, region, and ethnic origin. The diversity within European Americans is rarely discussed in the social science literature (Alba, 1990) or within classrooms. However, the rich diversity among the cultures of teachers is an important factor that needs to be examined and discussed in the classroom. The 13% of U.S. teachers who are ethnic minorities can also enrich their classrooms by sharing their personal and cultural knowledge with the students and by helping them to understand how it mediates textbook knowledge. The multicultural classroom is a forum of multiple voices and perspectives. The voices of the teacher, of the textbook, of mainstream and transformative authors—and of the students—are important components of classroom discourse.

Teachers can share their cultural experiences and interpretations of events as a way to motivate students to share theirs. However, they should examine their racial and ethnic attitudes toward diverse groups before engaging in cultural sharing. A democratic classroom atmosphere must also be created. The students must view the classroom as a forum where multiple perspec-tives are valued. An open and democratic classroom will enable students to acquire the skills and abilities they need to examine conflicting knowledge claims and perspectives. Students must become critical consumers of knowledge as well as knowledge producers if they are to acquire the understandings and skills needed to function in the complex and diverse world of tomorrow. Only a broad and liberal multicultural education can prepare them for that world.

Author's Note

This article is adapted from a paper presented at the conference "Democracy and Education," sponsored by the Benton Center for Curriculum and Instruction, Department of Education, The University of Chicago, November 15–16, 1991, Chicago, Illinois. I am grateful to the following colleagues for helpful comments on an earlier draft of the article: Cherry A. McGee Banks, Carlos E. Cortes, Geneva Gay, Donna H. Kerr, Joyce E. King, Walter C. Parker, Pamela L. Grossman, and Christine E. Sleeter.

References

Acuña, R. (1988). *Occupied America: A history of Chicanos* (3rd Ed.). New York: Harper & Row.

Alba, R. D. (1990). *Ethnic identity: The transformation of White America.* New Haven: Yale.

Allen, P. G. (1986). *The sacred hoop: Recovering the feminine in American Indian traditions.* Boston: Beacon.

Altbach, P. G., Kelly, G. P., Petrie, H. G., & Weis, L. (Eds.). (1991). *Textbooks In American society.* Albany, NY: State University of New York.

The American Heritage Dictionary. (1983). New York: Dell.

Anyon, J. (1979). Ideology and United States history textbooks. *Harvard Educational Review*, 49(3), 361–386.

Anyon, J. (1981). Social class and school knowledge. *Curriculum Inquiry*, 11(1), 3–42.

Anzaldúa, G. (1990). Haciendo caras, una entrada: An introduction. In G. Anzaldúa (Ed.), *Making face, making soul: Haciendo caras* (pp. xv–xvii). San Francisco: Aunt Lute Foundation Books.

Apple, M. W., & Christian-Smith, L. K. (Eds.). (1991). *The politics of the textbook.* New York: Routledge.

Aptheker, H. (Ed.). (1973). *The collected published works of W. E. B. DuBois* (38 Vols.). Millwood, NY: Kraus.

Asante, M. K. (1991a). The Afrocentric idea in education. *The Journal of Negro Education,* 60(2), 170–180.

Asante, M. K. (1991b, September 23). Putting Africa at the center. *Newsweek,* 118, 46.

Asante, M. K., & Ravitch, D. (1991). Multiculturalism: an exchange. *The American Scholar,* 60(2), 267–275.

Banks, J. A. (1988). *Multiethnic education: Theory and practice* (2nd Ed.). Boston: Allyn & Bacon.

Banks, J. A. (1991). *Teaching strategies for ethnic studies* (5th ed.). Boston: Allyn & Bacon.

Banks, J. A. (1991). Multicultural education: For freedom's sake. *Educational Leadership,* 49(4), 39–36.

Banks, J. A., & Banks, C. A. M. (Eds.). (1989). *Multicultural education. Issues and perspectives.* Boston: Allyn & Bacon.

Begley, S., Chideya, F., & Wilson, L. (1991, September 23). Out of Egypt, Greece: Seeking the roots of Western civilization on the banks of the Nile. *Newsweek,* 118 48–49.

Bernal, M. (1987–1991). *Black Athena: The Afroasiatic roots of classical civilization* (Vols. 1–2). London: Free Association Books.

Blassingame, J. W. (1972). *The slave community: Plantation life in the Ante-bellum South.* New York: Oxford University Press.

Bloom, A. (1987). *The closing of the American mind.* New York: Simon & Schuster.

Bogle, D. (1989). *Toms, coons, mulattoes, mammies, and bucks: An interpretative history of Blacks in American films* (new expanded ed.). New York: Continuum.

Butler, J. E., & Walter, J. C. (Eds.). (1991). *Transforming the curriculum: Ethnic studies and women studies.* Albany, NY: State University of New York.

Cherryholmes, C. H. (1988). *Power and criticism: Poststructural investigations in education.* New York: Teachers College Press.

Clark, K. B. (1965). *Dark ghetto: Dilemmas of social power.* New York: Harper & Row.

Code, L. (1991). *What can she know? Feminist theory and the construction of knowledge.* Ithaca, NY: Cornell University Press.

Cooper, A. J. (1969). *A voice from the South.* New York: Negro Universities Press.

Cortes, C. E. (1991a). Empowerment through media literacy. In C. E. Sleeter (Ed.), *Empowerment through multicultural education.* Albany: State University of New York.

Cortes, C. E. (1991b). Hollywood interracial love: Social taboo as screen titillation. In P. Loukides & L. K. Fuller (Eds.), *Beyond the stars II: Plot convention in American popular film* (pp. 21–35). Bowling Green, OH: Bowling Green State University Press.

Delpit, L. D. (1988). The silenced dialogue: Power and pedagogy in educating other people's children. *Harvard Educational Review,* 58(3), 280–298.

Diop, C. A. (1974). *The African origin of civilization: Myth or reality?* New York: Lawrence Hill.

D'Souza D. (1991). *Liberal education: The politics of race and sex on campus.* New York: Free Press.

DuBois W. E. B. (1962). *Black reconstruction in America 1860–1880: An essay toward a history of the part which Black folk played in the attempt to reconstruct democracy in America. 1860–1880.* New York: Athenaeum. (Original work published 1935).

DuBois, W. E. B. (1969). *The suppression of the African slave trade to the United States of America, 1638–1870.* Baton Rouge, LA: Louisiana State University. (Original work published 1896).

Ellsworth, E. (1989). Why doesn't this feel empowering? Working through the repressive myths of critical pedagogy. *Harvard Educational Review, 59*(3), 297–324.

Farganis, S. (1986). *The social construction of the feminine character.* Totowa, NJ: Russell & Russell.

Fitzgerald, F. (1979). *America revised: History schoolbooks in the twentieth century.* New York: Vintage.

Foucault, M. (1972). *The archaeology of knowledge and the discourse on language.* New York: Pantheon.

Fordham, S. (1988). Racelessness as a factor in Black students' school success: Pragmatic strategy or Pyrrhic victory? *Harvard Educational Review, 58*(1), 54-84.

Fordham, S. (1991). Racelessness in private schools: Should we deconstruct the racial and cultural identity of African-American adolescents? *Teachers College Record, 92*(3), 470–484.

Fordham, S., & Ogbu, J. (1986). Black students' school success: Coping with the burden of acting White. *The Urban Review, 18*(3), 176–206.

Franklin, J. H. (1991). Liberal education: An exchange. *New York Review of Books, 38,* 74–76.

Frazier, E. F. (1939). *The Negro family in the United States.* Chicago: University of Chicago Press.

Gates, H. L., Jr. (1988). *The signifying monkey: A theory of African-American literary criticism.* New York: Oxford University Press.

Gates, H. L., Jr. (1992). *Loose canons: Notes on the culture wars.* .New York: Oxford University Press.

Genovese, E. D. (1972). *Roll Jordan roll: The world the slaves made.* New York: Pantheon.

Giroux, H. A. (1983). *Theory and resistance in education.* Boston: Bergin & Garvey.

Glazer, N. (1991). In defense of multiculturalism. *The New Republic, 205*(10), 18–21.

Goodlad, J. I. (1984). *A place called school: Prospects for the future.* New York: McGraw-Hill.

Gordon, E. W. (1985). Social science knowledge production and minority experiences. *Journal of Negro Education, 54*(2), 117–132.

Gordon, E. W., Miller, F., S. & Rollock, D. (1990). Coping with communicentric bias in knowledge production in the social sciences. *Educational Researcher, 14*(3), 14–19.

Grant, C. A. (Ed.). (1992). *Research and multicultural education: From the margins to the mainstream.* Washington, DC: Falmer.

Gray, P. (1991, July 8). Whose America? *Time, 138,* 12–17.

Greenfield, G. M., & Cortes, C. E. (1991). Harmony and conflict of intercultural images: The treatment of Mexico in U.S. feature films and K–12 textbooks. *Mexican Studies/Estudios Mexicanos, 7*(2), 283–301.

Greer, S. (1969). *The logic of social inquiry.* Chicago: Aldine.

Gutman, H . G . (1976). *The Black family in slavery and freedom 1750–1925.* New York: Vintage.

Habermas, J. (1971). *Knowledge and human interests.* Boston: Beacon.

Hale-Benson, J. E. (1982). *Black children. Their roots, culture, and learning styles* (rev. ed.). Baltimore: Johns Hopkins University Press.

Harding, S. (1991). *Whose science? Whose knowledge? Thinking from women's lives.* Ithaca, NY: Cornell University Press.

Harding, V. (1981). *There is a river: The Black struggle for freedom in America.* New York: Vintage.

Heath, S. B. (1983). *Ways with words: Language, life and work in communities and classrooms.* New York: Cambridge University Press.

Hirsch, E. D., Jr. (1987). *Cultural literacy: What every American needs to know.* Boston: Houghton Mifflin.

hooks, b., & West, C. (1991). *Breaking bread: Insurgent Black intellectual life.* Boston: South End.

Howe, I. (1991). The value of the canon. *The New Republic, 204*(7), 40–47.

Hoxie, F. E. (Ed.). (1988). *Indians in American history.* Arlington Heights, IL: Harlan Davidson.

Hoxie, F. E. (no date). *The Indians versus the textbooks: Is there any way out?* Chicago: The Newberry Library, Center for the History of the American Indian.

Kaplan, A. (1964). *The conduct of inquiry: Methodology for behavioral science.* San Francisco: Chandler.

King, J. E., & Mitchell, C. A. (1990). *Black mothers to sons: Juxtaposing African American literature with social practice.* New York: Lang.

Kuhn, T. S. (1970). *The structure of scientific revolutions* (2nd ed.). Chicago: University of Chicago Press.

Labov, W. (1975). *The study of nonstandard English.* Washington, DC: Center for Applied Linguistics.

Ladner, J. A. (Ed.). (1973). *The death of White sociology.* New York: Vintage.

Meier, A., & Rudwick, E. (1986). *Black history and the historical profession 1915–1980.* Urbana, IL: University of Illinois Press.

Merton, R. K. (1972). Insiders and outsiders: A chapter in the sociology of knowledge. *The American Journal of Sociology, 78*(1), 9–47.

Milner, D. (1983). *Children and race.* Beverly Hills, CA: Sage.

Minnich, E. K. (1990). *Transforming knowledge.* Philadelphia: Temple University Press.

Moynihan, D. P. (1965). *The Negro family in America: A case for national action.* Washington, DC: U.S. Department of Labor.

Myrdal, G. (with the assistance of R. Sterner & A. Rose). (1944). *An American dilemma: The Negro problem in modern democracy.* New York: Harper.

Nash, G. B. (1982). *Red, White and Black: The peoples of early America.* Englewood Cliffs, NJ: Prentice-Hall.

New York City Board of Education. (1990). *Grade 7, United States and New York state history: A multicultural perspective.* New York: author.

New York State Department of Education. (1989, July). *A curriculum of inclusion* (Report of the Commissioner's Task Force on Minorities: Equity and excellence). Albany, NY: The State Education Department.

New York State Department of Education. (1991, June). *One nation, many peoples: A declaration of cultural interdependence.* Albany, NY: The State Education Department.

Ordovensky, P. (1992, July 7). Teachers: 87% White, 72% women. *USA Today,* p. 1A.

Philips, S. U. (1983). *The invisible culture: Communication in classroom and community on Warm Springs Indian Reservation.* New York: Longman.

Phillips, U. B. (1918). *American Negro slavery.* New York: Appleton.

Ramirez, M., III, & Castaneda, A. (1974). *Cultural democracy, bicognitive development and education.* New York: Academic Press.

Ravitch, D., & Finn, C. E., Jr. (1987). *What do our 17-year-olds know? A report on the first national assessment of history and literature.* New York: Harper & Row.

Rivlin, A. M. (1973). Forensic social science. *Harvard Educational Review, 43,* 61–75.

Rorty, R. (1989). *Contingency, irony, and solidarity.* New York: Cambridge University Press.

Rosenau, P. M. (1992). *Post-modernism and the social sciences: Insights, inroads, and intrusions.* Princeton, NJ: Princeton University Press.

Schlesinger, A., Jr. (1991). *The disuniting of America: Reflections on a multicultural society.* Knoxville, TN: Whittle Direct Books.

Shade, B. J. R. (Ed.). (1989). *Culture, style and the educative process.* Springfield, IL: Thompson.

Shaver, J. P., Davis, O. L., Jr., & Helburn, S. W. (1979). The status of social studies education: Impressions from three NSF studies. *Social Education, 43*(2), 150–153.

Sleeter, C. E. (1991). (Ed.). *Empowerment through multicultural education.* Albany: State University of New York.

Sleeter, C. E., & Grant, C. A. (1987). An analysis of multi-cultural education in the United States. *Harvard Educational Review, 57*(4), 421–444.

Sleeter, C. E., & Grant, C. A. (1991a). Mapping terrains of power: Student cultural knowledge versus classroom knowledge. In C. E. Sleeter (Ed.), *Empowerment through multicultural education* (pp. 49–67). Albany: State University of New York.

Sleeter, C. E., & Grant, C. A. (1991b). Race, class, gender and disability in current textbooks. In M. W. Apple & L. K. Christian-Smith (Eds.), *The politics of textbooks* (pp. 78–110). New York: Routledge.

Smitherman, G. (1977). *Talkin and testifyin: The language of Black America.* Boston: Houghton Mifflin.

Sokol, E. (Ed.). (1990). *A world of difference: St. Louis metropolitan region, preschool through grade 6, teacher/student resource guide.* St. Louis: Anti-Defamation League of B'nai B'rith.

Stampp, K. M. (1956). *The peculiar institution: Slavery in the Ante-Bellum South.* New York: Vintage.

Takaki, R. T. (1979). *Iron cages: Race and culture in 19th-century America.* Seattle, WA: University of Washington.

Tetreault, M. K. T. (1993). Classrooms for diversity: Rethinking curriculum and pedagogy. In J. A. Banks & C. A. M. Banks (Eds.), *Multicultural education: Issues and perspectives* (2nd ed., pp. 129–148). Boston: Allyn & Bacon.

Thornton, R. (1987). *American Indian holocaust and survival: A population history since 1492.* Norman: University of Oklahoma Press.

Turner, F. J. (1989). The significance of the frontier in American history. In C. A. Milner, II (Ed.), *Major problems in the history of the American West* (pp. 2–21). Lexington, MA: Heath. (Original work published 1894)

Van Sertima, I. V. (Ed.), (1988). *Great Black leaders: Ancient and modern.* New Brunswick, NJ: Rutgers University Press, African Studies Department.

Van Sertima, I. V. (Ed.), (1989). *Great African thinkers: Vol. 1. Cheikh Anta Diop.* New Brunswick, NJ: Transaction Books.

Wigginton, E. (1991). Culture begins at home. *Educational Leadership, 49*(4), 60–64.

Williams, G. W. (1968). *History of the Negro Race in America from 1619 to 1880: Negroes as slaves, as soldiers, and as citizens* (2 Vols.). New York: Arno Press. (Original work published 1892 & 1893)

Williams, C. (1987). *The destruction of Black civilization: Great issues of a race from 4500 B.C. to 2000 A.D.* Chicago: Third World Press.

Woodson, C. G. (1933). *The mis-education of the Negro.* Washington, DC: Associated Publishers.

Woodson, C. G., & Wesley, C. H. (1922). *The Negro in our history.* Washington, DC: Associated Publishers.

Woodward, C. V. (1991, July 18). Freedom and the universities. *The New York Review of Books, 38,* 32–37.

Young, M. F. D. (1971). An approach to curricula as socially organized knowledge. In M. F. D. Young (Ed.), *Knowledge and control* (pp. 19–46). London: Collier-Macmillan.

Zinn, H. (1980). *A people's history of the United States.* New York: Harper & Row.

Curricular Re-vision:
The New Knowledge for a New Age

PEGGY MEANS MCINTOSH

Serious discussion of educating the majority allows us to celebrate not one but two cultural shifts. A majority of Americans of all ethnic and racial groups now have some chance at higher education, and within higher education women have now become the majority within the student population as they are in the population at large. Work, struggle, legislative mandate, and unanswerable demonstrations of ability have won significant access to education for previously excluded groups.

The work toward equal access goes on, but now we must give concentrated attention to the content of the curriculum. For access to education does not ensure educational equity. Access to a sexist and racist curriculum is not sex or race equity. Women, now the numerical majority in college as in U.S. society, still learn from the curriculum that they are a marginal majority. Students who are told they have equal access to higher education sit in classes that day in and day out deliver the message that white Anglo-European males are more real than anyone else. Such courses do not give all students equal access to a sense of identity. They teach students to defer to white Western male authority and thus subtly persuade our future voters, policymakers, parents, and teachers to keep cultural and political power in the hands of those who currently have most of it.

Curricular shifts toward inclusiveness have a long but hidden history, marked by occasional lurches toward democratic rethinking despite resistances and conceptual challenges. The development of women's studies since the early 1970s is a dramatic curricular achievement that would be very hard to wipe out entirely. There are now more than five hundred women's studies programs in the United States, almost half of them offering a major in women's studies as well as elective work. There are more than fifty Centers for Research on Women. The publications emanating from teaching, scholarship, and research on women are astonishing in their volume. Beyond its informational content, the work points to reconceptualizations of knowledge itself, of education, and of societal structures.

Further institutionalization of women's studies is our best present hope for meaningful education of women as well as men, for it is the only area of the curriculum in which women's existence is fully registered, a *thoroughgoing* methodological awareness is encouraged, and there is an attempt to develop frameworks that get beyond implicit metaphors of conflict and conquest for life and learning. Women's studies provides a systematic way to critique our present systems and clarify the ways these systems operate to exclude many people or underreward many of the most constructive functions of human personality and society. The cultural pluralism represented on our campuses today cries out for new and innovative thinking about pluralistic pedagogy and inclusive politics in the classroom. In addition, the violence of individuals and institutions calls for citizens educated to think about life not simply in terms of winning and losing, but in terms of working for the decent survival of all. The classroom is the place to prepare women and men students for the complexity of roles they must play in our society and the world in a nuclear age. To date women's studies, more than any other field, has worked toward systemic visions of our problems and has given permission to students to try to conceptualize a world in which all human beings might survive with dignity.

Such an understanding of women's studies is rare in teachers and administrators, most of whom have seen the area as simply one more narrowly specialized curricular development. We who care about educating the majority will need to continue to make the case for women's studies on our university and college campuses, despite the misunderstandings and antidemocratic reactions which are inevitable. An argument for women's studies based on the ideal of curricular justice does not serve us well, since institutions of higher education have never been particularly concerned with justice. We will do better to argue first on the academy's own grounds, that a curriculum that lacks women's studies suffers from gross scholarly inaccuracy. Likewise, a curriculum for future citizens and voters is dysfunctional if it teaches students to overlook half the population of the nation and the world. Further, a university cannot claim to benefit students' development if its curriculum jeopardizes the mental health of half the students by implying they are not fully real, while inflating the egos of the other half by implying that they are larger than life. Moreover, universities that claim to give students a sense of tradition and history, but fail to teach about women, men of color, working-class people, or daily maintenance of society and psyche, serve to keep the majority of students from a sense that they have been part of history and that it is they who will help to create the future. Finally, we need to urge the university to rethink its work, since education in this troubled age can help us with our problems only if it involves development of many capacities beyond competition and what is called rational analysis.

We who care about educating the majority will need to continue to argue for women's studies as a source of new information and new perspectives which will benefit people of both sexes and of all cultural and racial groups. Far from being the exclusive study of a narrow interest group, women's studies is centered in the experience of the majority and committed to the healthier development of all our political and social institutions as well as our individual female and male psyches in all of their affective and cognitive capacities. Far from being an isolated undertaking, of interest only to women, women's studies promises to alter teaching, thinking, and the role of feeling in every one of the academic fields. Since this author's work has centered on the usefulness of feminist materials and perspectives for changing the rest of the curriculum, her contribution here centers on implications of women's studies for other disciplines and for administrators as they consider how best to use their resources to educate the majority.

It is now clear that research on women—the study not only of the women we are allowed to call "notable" but of women as half the world's population—poses questions for scholars and teachers in each of the academic disciplines. As we came to see the comparative absence of women's experience from the account of reality passed on to students by our present curriculum, we began to ask questions that would help us, as scholars, to fill in the overlooked record of the "other" half of the human race. In the Mellon National Faculty Development Program that this author directed at the Wellesley College Center for Research on Women from 1979 to 1985, faculty from many fields were encouraged to focus on two key framing questions. First, what is the basic content, scope, and methodology of my discipline? Second, how would my discipline need to change in order to reflect the fact that women are half of the world's population and have had half of the world's lived experience?

The initial answers vary from discipline to discipline and thus appear at first to reinforce our sense of the differences between disciplines. But in the end, the answers lead us to perceive that some of the boundaries between disciplines result from the same tendency to compartmentalize that has kept women's experience from being construed as a part of social reality in the first place. Therefore, research on women has come to pose a challenge not only to the epistemological ground rules within disciplines, but also to the very distancing between disciplines, and between people, which our present modes of finding and passing on knowledge enforce and reinforce.

The traditional humanities curriculum has stressed the public sphere: laws, wars, cultural change, public events, individual accomplishment, conflict, and the activity of "the makers and shapers of civilization," or of those who have survived fairly well within cultural systems. But society has been held together by groups of people who are not distinguished by public achievement, public power, or recognized cultural innovation—those who have made and mended the personal and social fabric, living outside of most scholars' fields of vision. The valuable work that such people have done has included taking care of people and systems and maintaining reproduction and production. Many have barely survived; some have prospered; all have lived within worlds we were taught to overlook, those "lower worlds" including that of "women's work." The richness and complexity of their lives, the concerns of their existences, their particular textures of "achievement" and "genius" have yet to be recognized within our academic disciplines or explored for the development of our students' humanity.

If we balance the curriculum, we would diminish the emphasis on those who attained power, "importance," or "excellence" as we have been taught to define them. We would increase the attention given to those women and men, previously invisible in the curriculum, whose lives are equally important, interesting, and revealing for us to study, if we are claiming to "know" about human life and history. We would also increase attention to the functions of personality and society which have provided our daily material and relational matrices.

If transformed, the field of religion would become less centered on theology and public institutions and would suggest the *effects* of religious belief or observance on the daily lives of ordinary people. Intellectual history would balance attention to the thought of recognized individuals and "movements" with the study of platitudes, truisms, and the belief systems that permeate "ordinary" lives. Such givens may not have the cerebral clarity of thought displayed by the thinkers whom we are told shaped intellectual history, and to study them well requires more intellectual rigor than most scholars have realized. History itself, if it reflected the fact that women are half the world's population, would concern itself less with laws and wars and more with the social fabric of most people's lives. A course called "History of France" that omitted women would have to change its name. Historians would attempt to answer more questions like "What was it like to live, to be a human being, especially a woman, in given ages of the world's history, and in a variety of statuses, places, and cultural contexts?" Historians who feel these questions are pointless are those who have not done or studied the research. For richness emerges with the answers. Although women's studies scholars sometimes ask, "What was it like for those at the bottom?" they also begin to doubt whether what we defined as "top" and "bottom" are in fact so high and low, and to ask who wrote those definitions, and whom the definitions serve.

The study of music, art, and architecture is transformed if one goes beyond those works that were made for public use, display, or performance and were supported by aristocratic or institutional patrons. One begins to study quilts, breadloaf shapes, clothing, pots, or songs and dances that people who had no musical literacy or training took for granted. One studies what music meant to audiences as well as to composers. Architecture becomes less the study of the architect's place in a tradition of designers and more the study of human arrangements of space and effects of spaces on those who inhabit them—the effects on daily lives of buildings, pavements, and kitchens. One looks at the same time for the influence that women did have in shaping or resisting their environments and in bringing about architectural and environmental change; we learn what they cared about in their surroundings.

Economics, changed to reflect the fact that women are half the world's population, would put more emphasis on unpaid labor. To consider unpaid, unsought labor as a central part of the economic picture would truly transform economics. In political science, the meaning of "politics" needs to be extended to cover private relationships that do involve power but which are not often acknowledged by scholars in political science: the politics of neighborhoods, of schools of curricula, of families, of bedrooms, of classes, of races, ethnic, and religious groups outside of public institutions, and of all people who are given responsibility without corresponding authority. To see personal relations as having political dimensions is both to make women visible and to reconstrue "politics."

A freshman English curriculum reflecting the fact that women have been half of the world's population may now recognize writing in many modes rather than simply stressing the art of rhetoric, a genre derived from the Greek conventions of persuasion in which one male leader aimed to persuade a group of listeners of his point of view. Women, like most people we do not often study, have chiefly used language to make connections between people, to elicit information, and to carry on daily work. Teachers are beginning to devise ways to give academic credit for forms of communication that do not lend themselves to the argumentative monologue of the expository essay. In literature itself, we need far more descriptive work on writing by women and unread men. Critics are asking how it happens that the genres most used by women—for example, in the United States, the journal, diary, letter, and the short story—are considered marginal or subliterary. Or how thousands of novels by nineteenth-century women have disappeared from accounts of America's literary history. (Editor's note: For examples in science see Harris et al. in Part Three.)

One moves from simple answers to complex answers in addressing the question "How would my discipline need to change in order to reflect the fact that women are half the world's population?" In general, the simple answer involves getting the "women's sphere" added to the subject matter of the discipline. But it is now clear that the discipline itself is not simply enlarged but also challenged in its essential terminology and methodology by the addition. Research on women calls into question Matthew Arnold's conviction that one cultural group can simply identify for all "the best that has been thought and said in the world." Research on women both challenges the definition of "best" and asks who defined what is best, whom the definitions benefited most, and why the student must be called upon to look "up" rather than "down," *around,* and *within* in being taught about the world. Hierarchies and canon-making in the academy were corollary to hierarchies and canon-making in social life, and so it is not a surprise that a thorough study of women also makes visible many men who were not previously featured in the curriculum. In fact, about nine tenths of the world's population suddenly becomes visible when one takes the emphasis off the public lives of white Western men, who are seen as cultural leaders, and includes those who for reasons of sex, race, class, nationality, or religious background were defined as "other" and therefore lesser. One sees that the record of knowledge was not only incomplete but that it was also *incorrect,* and that its errors perpetuated the past balances of power in our societies. In the words of Marilyn Schuster of Smith College, "At first, you study women to fill in the gaps. But then you see that the gaps were there for a reason." Our curriculum and our other societal structures were products of the same social and political construction of reality. So we begin to see, for example, that most affective functions of men's lives were left out of the record, as were most women's activities; this double suppression perpetuates a particular identification of masculinity with cognitive control. The omission, then, has political consequences.

The new scholarship on women has unearthed such tremendous amounts of material that this development of new knowledge cannot be seen merely as a fad. It promises to widen the account of reality that institutions of higher learning pass on to their students, to broaden or challenge the definitions of the "best that has been taught and said [and done] in the world," and to increase students' awareness of the world in which they live. The traditional curriculum was designed for the education of white male Western leaders in a time of Western dominance and economic expansion. A revised curriculum would give both our male students and our female majority a better preparation for a world in which non-Western people of color are the world's majority. The life of Western dominance and expansion should no longer be taken for granted, and the caretaking roles assigned previously to women and other lower-status people are needed on a global scale for human survival.

How can our educational institutions work toward an inclusive curriculum that recognizes and better educates students for a world of interdependence and survival rather than violence in the service of winning? Faculty can do much of the work, and students' interest and gratitude fuels the effort, but support from administrators is essential to the development of inclusive curriculum in all of its forms. In colleges and universities to date, a strong women's studies program with a budget for administration, instruction, and programming has been the most effective starting point, for as indicated here, women's studies is the field that has showed the most coherent concern about inclusive educational content, methods, and ideals. We need far more tenured positions in women's studies. Women's studies programs will continue to be necessary and desirable even if all of the other departments work to bring women and undervalued human capacities into the curriculum, just as English departments will continue to be necessary even if they persuade all other departments to work on the problems of students' writing and reading. Women's studies is the center and source of most of the new interdisciplinary insights that inclusive curriculum projects rely on, and in a number of colleges where inclusive curriculum change projects were undertaken without a women's studies program, a program was eventually developed in response to the need for a theoretical, interdisciplinary and coherent base to aid the work. Faculty development has been a critical component of many women's studies programs. We need college administrations to fund such activity and fully support and reward the participation of all faculty in bringing their knowledge, awareness, and aims for education in line with our needs in the late twentieth century.

For the faculty members doing the work, women's studies is both difficult and gratifying. Administrators will help most if they fund women's studies faculty adequately for their complex interdisciplinary tasks and recognize the degree of effort and innovation involved in keeping up with a tremendously burgeoning interdisciplinary field. With regard to carrying work into other disciplines, administrators will be able to help most if they understand how much emotional and intellectual growth is necessary in all faculty members as they face new scholarship on women and new feminist perspectives on society and learning. New work on women is not simply summer reading. It challenges the intellect and puts stress on the belief systems of the teacher. On the basis of work with college and school teachers on curriculum change over the last decade, here are some of the elements of those stresses and challenges in the faculty development process.

When facing this new scholarship for the first time, most white faculty members of both sexes receive bad blows to the ego. As professors, most of us had learned to think of ourselves as fairly intelligent, fair-minded, knowledgeable, on guard against being politically manipulated, and unique or at least free to be unique in our styles of teaching.

The now-massive new scholarship on women implies that we were not so intelligent or fair-minded if we never learned about women and never noticed the omission, and not so knowledgeable if we knew nothing of the lives or perspectives of the world's majority. We were not only manipulated but were manipulating others in passing on, under the illusion of objectivity, bodies of knowledge that kept most "lower-caste" people's lives and perceptions invisible.

It is hard for us as white teachers, who considered ourselves part of the solution to societal problems of class, race, and sex, to realize that we have instead been part of the problem, insofar as we have been competent teachers of a defective curriculum. Finally, it is a blow to the ego to realize that one's teaching and scholarship were not special but at best merely average, following traditional lines of exclusion and incomplete generalization.

First encounters with work from women's studies, then, tend to undermine the sense of professorial self in the experienced college teacher. If he or she can get past the first natural defensive emotions a process of intellectual and personal development is set in motion that, when fostered, eventually reinstates and renews the sense of professional self on a far firmer grounding than before. That is, one feels truly more intelligent, more fair-minded, more knowledgeable than before, more alert to manipulation and more innovative in one's research and teaching.

But this process of intellectual and emotional development is full of challenges. Most faculty need the support of administrators and colleagues to face the undertaking. Faculty who thought that women's studies was about women's "contributions" or "achievements" learn that, more importantly, it asks who defined contributions and achievements in ways that leave out the lives of most people of the world, including most men. Those who thought it was only about women's "issues" find instead that it is about women's whole existences seen in all of their complex contents.

Those who thought that women's studies was an optional "approach" contributing a new set of data to existing tables learn that it does not merely add new materials and perspectives to the existing bodies of knowledge; it critiques those bodies of knowledge and their unacknowledged political underpinnings. Finally, newcomers to women's studies scholarship learn that it is not the study of a few white women. It aspires to be the multiracial and cross-cultural study of women as half of any population, and at its best it embodies a new aspiration for methodological, emotional, and intellectual awareness in all of the liberal arts disciplines. But one does not learn all of these things at once.

Many faculty seem, in fact, to go through a series of phases as they become involved in the study of women, first seeing women in terms of white Western men, then trying to see women diversely and on their own terms, and as a result reseeing women, men, and society. The work turns out to be conceptually far more difficult than originally anticipated. I attribute the difficulties in part to encountering worlds for which one has not been given names or concepts. We have plenty of words, for example, surrounding the human capacity for competition that has been identified in the West with white males, and has been overrewarded in them, and overdeveloped also in all of our psychological structures, institutions, and learning systems. But we have few words and concepts for the equally important human capacity for collaboration that has been, I think, projected onto women and lower caste males, and then underrewarded and undervalidated in them as in all of our psyches, institutions, and learning systems. Traditional curricula give us models and vocabulary for the vertical ladder-climbing processes in all of the discourses of arts and sciences. Winning and losing are familiar and, sadly, accepted givens. We have not yet fully developed the vocabulary we need to give attention to and validation for the lateral and sustaining functions, and to teach students of both sexes how to develop in themselves both the competitive and the collaborative human skills.

Like other colleagues who have done faculty development work in women's studies, this author has noticed some recurring patterns of changed consciousness and curricula as traditionally trained faculty approach the study of women. I see interactive phases of personal and curricular change occurring in both individuals and courses specifically in conjunction with raised consciousness about vertical and lateral elements in the psyche and the society. Within the development of history courses, for example, this author names Phase I: Womanless History; followed by Phase II: Women *in* History, as exceptions. Next comes the issues-oriented Phase III: Women as a Problem, Anomaly, Absence, or Victim in History. Then comes a radical turn into the study of women's lives on their own terms—Phase IV: Women's Lives *As* History, which reaches toward Phase V: History Redefined and Reconstructed to Include Us All, which this author sees as a one hundred-year project.

Phase II courses bring in a few famous or notorious women, but do not challenge the traditional outlines and winner-focused definitions of those who "made" history. In Phase II, one teaches about heroines, exceptional or elite women, who are seen to have climbed above their group. In Phase III, Issues History, one studies women (or lower-caste men) as victims, as deprived or defective variants of more powerful Anglo-European men, as losers, as "have-nots," or as protesters, with "issues." Women can at least be seen in a systemic context, since class, race, and gender are seen as interlocking political phenomena by faculty who have gotten beyond Phase II. But it is insulting to any individual or cultural group to be defined as having only what this author would call a "deficit identity." We will never make "ordinary" people's experience seem either real or valid if our teaching and research still rest on the categories of analysis which were derived from the experience of those who had the most power, and who saw themselves as the chief models.

In Phase IV, the categories for analysis shift. The faculty member begins to realize that since women have had half of the world's experience, we need to ask what that experience has been and to consider it as half of history. Phase IV takes a positive look at women and at our strategies for coping or thriving, and for maintaining life; it looks also at the lives of many of those men, equally overlooked in the curriculum, who were likewise doing the work on which human survival has depended. It often focuses on *lateral functions of personality and society* more than on discrete individuals or groups of either sex. Phase IV is racially inclusive, multifaceted, and filled with rich variety; it suggests and validates plural versions of reality. It brings in all kinds of evidence and source material that academic people are not in the habit of using. It examines and tries to name the communicative, relational, passionate affiliations and affections. Faculty doing Phase IV work often feel by turns unprofessional and truly engaged in genuine research and teaching for the first time. The teacher becomes less of an expert, the student more of a resource; both can bring the authority of their own (avowedly limited) experience to the alert, empathetic study of diverse phenomena.

We need to move beyond Phase IV, since women and little-studied functions of men's lives are not all of history. Phase V will help students to have that "doubled vision" which the late historian Joan Kelly described: the sense that we are both part of and alien to the dominant culture, the dominant version of history. And when history is seen as a series of constructs to begin with, students are then empowered and invited to create more usable and inclusive constructs that validate a wider sample of life and help us to recognize the human talent for identification and caretaking which is currently projected onto and demanded of too small a group. Phase IV consciousness is still rare in individuals and in institutions. This author thinks Phase V history will be one hundred years in the making, if we live that long. Meanwhile, Phase I versions of history, of politics, of welfare, and of leadership endanger us all.

The Phase I syllabus in every discipline is very exclusive. Phase IV and V syllabi are very inclusive. Individuals and consciousnesses and causes do not exist fixedly in given phases, but show points of dynamic interaction among several of the phases, if the teacher or researcher is conscious of the many forms of the problem of curricular politics. But often superficial curriculum change gets arrested in Phases II and III. The study of women only as exceptions or as victims perpetuates misogyny, so it is important to move individual faculty and their courses through discussion of "role models" or struggles for women's rights to acknowledge also the truly interdisciplinary and genuinely new human-centered scholarship of Phase IV, and to imagine the reconstructed knowledge of Phase V.

How can administrators help? As has been indicated, strong women's studies programs are the best starting point, because at present they have the most inclusively humanistic aims. Reeducating faculty in traditional disciplines is an essential step. Deans can make a real difference not only by strengthening women's studies programs, but also by providing released time, money, colleagueship, and incentives for faculty to retrain themselves to teach about women. They benefit from each other's help as they begin the disconcerting work of reading voluminous scholarship on women and understudied men, seeing from new angles, seeing the present curriculum as a social and political construction, and at least recognizing if not yet correcting exclusive habits of thinking, reading, teaching, and doing research which pervade the traditional academy.

Administrators and tenure and promotion committees together can provide the most important incentives by gradually instituting policies that reward faculty who incorporate the scholarship on women into their teaching, and thereby avoid passing onto students versions of reality which are obsolete. A faculty member who, in 1988, is still wholly incompetent in scholarship on women is a poor candidate for several decades of tenure.

Finally, administrators can insist that discussions of general education include consideration of women's studies. Since women now constitute the majority in college populations as in the population at large, further exclusion of women from the "core" will eventually have to be seen as conscious misogyny on the part of faculty committees. The time is past for the objection that women's studies is political. All curricula are political. A curriculum that leaves women out is highly politicized. Which *forms* of curricular politics the colleges and universities choose now is the question.

An inclusive curriculum stands to benefit, and to change, men as well as women. In the light of our global emergencies, one hopes that the colleges and universities will elect to develop inclusive versions of reality rather than standing by the old exclusive ones. It has become clear that our collective human survival depends on different processes, in women's and especially in men's minds, from the ones we have set in motion in the past. No investment in faculty and curriculum that colleges and universities can now make bears more importantly than women's studies on human futures, individual, and collective.

Freire and a
Feminist Pedagogy of Difference

KATHLEEN WEILER

In this article, Kathleen Weiler presents a feminist critique that challenges traditional Western knowledge systems. As an educator, Weiler is interested in the implications of this critique for both the theory and practice of education. She begins with a discussion of the liberatory pedagogy of Paulo Freire and the profound importance of his work. She then questions Freire's assumption of a single kind of experience of oppression and his abstract goals for liberation. A feminist pedagogy, she claims, offers a more complex vision of liberatory pedagogy. Weiler traces the growth of feminist epistemology from the early consciousness raising-groups to current women's study programs. She identifies three ways that a feminist pedagogy, while reflecting critically on Freire's ideas, also builds on and enriches his pedagogy: in its questioning of the role and authority of the teacher; in its recognition of the importance of personal experience as a source of knowledge; and in its exploration of the perspectives of people of different races, classes, and cultures.

We are living in a period of profound challenges to traditional Western epistemology and political theory. These challenges, couched in the language of post-modernist theory and in postcolonialist critiques, reflect the rapid transformation of the economic and political structure of the world order: the impact of transnational capital; the ever more comprehensive integration of resources, labor, and markets; the pervasiveness of media and consumer images. This interdependent world system is based on the exploitation of oppressed groups, but the system at the same time calls forth oppositional cultural forms that give voice to the conditions of these groups. White male bourgeois dominance is being challenged by people of color, women, and other oppressed groups, who assert the validity of their own knowledge and demand social justice and equality in numerous political and cultural struggles. In the intellectual sphere, this shifting world system has led to a shattering of Western metanarratives and to the variety of stances of postmodernist and cultural-identity theory. A major theoretical challenge to traditional Western knowledge systems is emerging from feminist theory, which has been increasingly influenced by both postmodernist and cultural-identity theory. Feminist theory, like other contemporary approaches, validates difference, challenges universal claims to truth, and seeks to create social transformation in a world of shifting and uncertain meanings.

In education, these profound shifts are evident on two levels: first, at the level of practice, as excluded and formerly silenced groups challenge dominant approaches to learning and to definitions of knowledge; and second, at the level of theory, as modernist claims to universal truth are called into question.[1] These challenges to accepted truths have been raised not only to the institutions and theories that defend the status quo, but also to the critical or liberatory pedagogies that emerged in the 1960s and 1970s. Feminist educational critics, like other theorists influenced by postmodernism and theories of difference, want to retain the vision of social justice and transformation that underlies liberatory pedagogies, but they find that their claims to universal truths and their assumptions of a collective experience of oppression do not adequately address the realities of their own confusing and often tension-filled classrooms. This consciousness of the inadequacy of classical liberatory pedagogies has been particularly true for feminist educators, who are acutely aware of the continuing force of sexism and patriarchal structures and the power of race, sexual preference, physical ability, and age to divide teachers from students and students from one another.

Paulo Freire is without question the most influential theorist of critical or liberatory education. His theories have profoundly influenced literacy programs throughout the world and what has come to be called critical pedagogy in the United States. His theoretical works, particularly *Pedagogy of the Oppressed*, provide classic statements of liberatory or critical pedagogy based on universal claims of truth.[2] Feminist pedagogy as it has developed in the United States provides a historically situated example of a critical pedagogy in practice. Feminist conceptions of education are similar to Freire's pedagogy in a variety of ways, and feminist educators often cite Freire as the educational theorist who comes closest to the approach and goals of feminist pedagogy.[3] Both feminist pedagogy as it is usually defined and Freirean pedagogy rest upon visions of social transformation; underlying both are certain common assumptions concerning oppression, consciousness, and historical change. Both pedagogies assert the existence of oppression in people's material conditions of existence and as a part of consciousness; both rest on a view of consciousness as more than a sum of dominating discourses, but as containing within it a critical capacity—what Antonio Gramsci called "good sense"; and both thus see human beings as subjects and actors in history and hold a strong commitment to justice and a vision of a better world and of the potential for liberation.[4] These ideals have powerfully influenced teachers and students in a wide range of educational settings, both formal and informal.

But in action, the goals of liberation or opposition to oppression have not always been easy to understand or achieve. As universal goals, these ideals do not address the specificity of people's lives; they do not directly analyze the contradictions between conflicting oppressed groups or the ways in which a single individual can experience oppression in one sphere while being privileged or oppressive in another. Feminist and Freirean teachers are in many ways engaged in what Teresa deLauretis has called "shifting the ground of signs," challenging accepted meanings and relationships that occur at what she calls "political or more often micro political" levels, groupings that "produce no texts as such, but by shifting the 'ground of a given sign . . . effectively intervene upon codes of perception as well as ideological codes."[5] But in attempting to challenge dominant values and to "shift the ground of signs," feminist and Freirean teachers raise conflicts for themselves and for their students, who also are historically situated and whose own subjectivities are often contradictory and in process. These conflicts have become increasingly clear as both Freirean and feminist pedagogies are put into practice. Attempting to implement these pedagogies without acknowledging the conflict not only of divided consciousness—what Audre Lorde calls "the oppressor within us"—but also the conflicts among groups trying to work together to name and struggle against oppression—among teachers and students in classrooms, or among political groups working for change in very specific areas—can lead to anger, frustration, and a retreat to safer or more traditional approaches.[6] The numerous accounts of the tensions of trying to put liberatory pedagogies into practice demonstrate the need to reexamine the assumptions of the classic texts of liberatory pedagogy and to consider the various issues that have arisen in attempts at critical and liberatory classroom practice.[7]

As a White feminist writing and teaching from the traditions of both critical pedagogy and feminist theory, these issues are of particular concern to me. In this article, I examine and critique the classic liberatory pedagogy of Paulo Freire, particularly as it is presented in *Pedagogy of the Oppressed*, his most famous and influential text. I then examine the development and practice of feminist pedagogy, which emerged in a particular historical and political moment in the United States, and which as a situated pedagogy, provides an example of some of the difficulties putting these ideals into practice and suggests at the same time some possible theoretical and practical directions for liberatory pedagogies in general. I argue that an exploration of the conflicts and concerns that have arisen for feminist teachers attempting to put into practice their visions of a feminist pedagogy can help enrich and re-envision Freirean goals of liberation and social progress. This emerging pedagogy does not reject the goals of justice—the end of oppression, and liberation—but frames them more specifically in the context of historically defined struggles and calls for the articulation of interests and identity on the part of teacher and theorist as well as student. This approach questions whether the oppressed cannot act also as oppressors and challenges the idea of a commonality of oppression. It raises questions about common experience as a source of knowledge, the pedagogical authority of the teacher, and the nature of political and pedagogical struggle.

The Pedagogy of Paulo Freire

Freire's pedagogy developed in particular historical and political circumstances of neocolonialism and imperialism. As is well known, Freire's methods developed originally from his work with peasants in Brazil and later in Chile and Guinea-Bissau.[8] Freire's thought thus needs to be understood in the context of the political and economic situation of the developing world. In Freire's initial formulation, oppression was conceived in class terms and education was viewed in the context of peasants' and working people's revolutionary struggles. Equally influential in Freire's thought and pedagogy were the influence of radical Christian thought and the revolutionary role of liberation theology in Latin America. As is true for other radical Christians in Latin America, Freire's personal knowledge of extreme poverty and suffering challenged his deeply felt Christian faith grounded in the ethical teachings of Jesus in the Gospels. Freire's pedagogy is thus founded on a moral imperative to side with the oppressed that emerges from both his Christian faith and his knowledge and experience of suffering in the society in which he grew up and lived. Freire has repeatedly stated that his pedagogical method cannot simply be transferred to other settings, but that each historical site requires the development of a pedagogy appropriate to that setting. In his most recent work, he has also addressed sexism and racism as systems of oppression that must be considered as seriously as class oppression.[9] Nonetheless, Freire is frequently read without consideration for the context of the specific settings in which his work developed and without these qualifications in mind. His most commonly read text still is his first book to be published in English, *Pedagogy of the Oppressed*. In this classic text, Freire presents the epistemological basis for his pedagogy and discusses the concepts of oppression, conscientization, and dialogue that are at the heart of his pedagogical project, both as he enacted it in settings in the developing world and as it has been appropriated by radical teachers in other settings.

Freire organizes his approach to liberatory pedagogy in terms of a dualism between the oppressed and the oppressors and between humanization and dehumanization. This organization of thought in terms of opposing forces reflects Freire's own experiences of literacy work with the poor in Brazil, a situation in which the lines between oppressor and oppressed were clear. For Freire, humanization is the goal of liberation; it has not yet been achieved, nor can it be achieved so long as the oppressors oppress the oppressed. That is, liberation and humanization will not occur if the roles of oppressor and oppressed are simply reversed. If humanization is to be realized, new relationships among human beings must be created:

> Because it is a distortion of being more fully human, sooner or later being less human leads the oppressed to struggle against those who made them so. In order for this struggle to have meaning, the oppressed must not, in seeking to regain their humanity (which is a way to create it), become in turn oppressors of the oppressors, but rather restorers of the humanity of both.[10]

The struggle against oppression leading to humanization is thus utopian and visionary. As Freire says elsewhere, "To be utopian is not to be merely idealistic or impractical but rather to engage in denunciation and annunciation."[11] By denunciation, Freire refers to the naming and analysis of existing structures of oppression; by annunciation, he means the creation of new forms of relationships and being in the world as a result of mutual struggle against oppression. Thus Freire presents a theoretical justification for a pedagogy that aims to critique existing forms of oppression and to transform the world, thereby creating new ways of being, or humanization.

Radical educators throughout the world have used *Pedagogy of the Oppressed* as the theoretical justification for their work. As an eloquent and impassioned statement of the need for and possibility of change through reading the world and the word, there is no comparable contemporary text.[12] But when we look at *Pedagogy of the Oppressed* from the perspective of recent feminist theory and pedagogy, certain problems arise that may reflect the difficulties that have sometimes arisen when Freire's ideas are enacted in specific settings. The challenges of recent feminist theory do not imply the rejection of Freire's goals for what he calls a pedagogy for liberation; feminists certainly share Freire's emphasis on seeing human beings as the subjects and not the objects of history. A critical feminist rereading of Freire, however, points to ways in which the project of Freirean pedagogy, like that of feminist pedagogy, may be enriched and re-envisioned.

From a feminist perspective, *Pedagogy of the Oppressed* is striking in its use of the male referent, as usage that was universal in the 1960s, when this book was written.[13] Much more troublesome, however, is the abstract quality of terms such as humanization, which do not address the particular meanings imbued by men and women, Black and White, or other groups. The assumption of *Pedagogy of the Oppressed* is that in struggling against oppression, the oppressed will move toward true humanity. But this leaves unaddressed the forms of oppression experienced by different actors, the possibility of struggles among people oppressed differently by different groups—what Cameron McCarthy calls "nonsynchrony of oppression."[14] This assumption also presents humanization as a universal, without considering the various definitions this term may bring forth from people of different groups. When Freire speaks of the oppressed needing to fight the tendency to become "sub-oppressors," he means that the oppressed have only the pattern of oppression before them as a way of being in a position other than the one they are in. As Freire writes, "Their ideal is to be men; but for them, to be men is to be oppressors. This is their model of humanity."[15] What is troubling here is not that "men" is used for human beings, but that the model of oppressor implied here is based on the immediate oppressor of men—in this case, bosses over peasants or workers. What is not addressed is the possibility of simultaneous contradictory positions of oppression and dominance: the man oppressed by his boss could at the same time oppress his wife, for example, or the White woman oppressed by sexism could exploit the Black woman. By framing his discussion in such abstract terms, Freire slides over the contradictions and tensions within social settings in which overlapping forms of oppression exist.

This usage of "the oppressed" in the abstract also raises difficulties in Freire's use of experience as the means of acquiring a radical literacy, "reading the world and the word." At the heart of Freire's pedagogy is the insistence that all people are subjects and knowers of the world. Their political literacy will emerge from their reading of the world—that is, their own experience. This reading will lead to collective knowledge and action. But what if that experience is divided? What if different truths are discovered in reading the world from different positions? For Freire, education as the practice of freedom "denies that men are abstract, isolated, independent, and unattached to the world. . . . Authentic reflection considers neither abstract man nor the world without men, but men in their relations with the world."[16] But implicit in this vision is the assumption that, when the oppressed perceive themselves in relation to the world, they will act together collectively to transform the world and to move toward their own humanization. The nature of their perception of the world and their oppression is implicitly assumed to be uniform for all the oppressed. The possibility of a contradictory experience of oppression among the oppressed is absent. As Freire says:

> Accordingly, the point of departure must always be with men in the "here and now," which constitutes the situation within which they are submerged, from which they emerge, and in which they intervene. Only by starting from this situation—which determines their perception of it—can they begin to move.[17]

The assumption again is that the oppressed, these men, are submerged in a common situation of oppression, and that their shared knowledge of that oppression will lead them to collective action.

Central to Freire's pedagogy is the practice of conscientization; that is, coming to a consciousness of oppression and a commitment to end that oppression. Conscientization is based on this common experience of oppression. Through this reading of the world, the oppressed will come to knowledge. The role of the teacher in this process is to instigate a dialogue between teacher and student, based on their common ability to know the world and to act as subjects in the world. But the question of the authority and power of the teacher, particularly those forms of power based on the teacher's subject position as raced, classed, gendered, and so on, is not addressed by Freire. There is, again, the assumption that the teacher is "on the same side" as the oppressed, and that as teachers and students engage together in a dialogue about the world, they will uncover together the same reality, the same oppression, and the same liberation. In *Pedagogy of the Oppressed*, the teacher is presented as a generic man whose interests will be with the oppressed as they mutually discover the mechanisms of oppression. The subjectivity of the Freirean teacher is, in this sense, what Gayatri Chacravorty Spivak refers to as "transparent."[18] In fact, of course, teachers are not abstract; they are women or men of particular races, classes, ages, abilities, and so on. The teacher will be seen and heard by students not as an abstraction, but as a particular person with a certain defined history and relationship to the world. In a later book, Freire argues that the teacher has to assume authority, but must do so without becoming authoritarian. In this recognition of the teacher's authority, Freire acknowledges the difference between teacher and students:

> The educator continues to be different from the students, but, and now for me this is the central question, the difference between them, if the teacher is democratic, if his or her political dream is a *liberating* one, is that he or she cannot permit the necessary difference between the teacher and the students to become "antagonistic."[19]

In this passage, Freire acknowledges the power of the teacher by virtue of the structural role of "teacher" within a hierarchical institution and, under the best of circumstances, by virtue of the teacher's great experience and knowledge. But Freire does not go on to investigate what the other sources of "antagonism" in the classroom might be. However much he provides a valuable guide to the use of authority by the liberatory teacher, he never addresses the question of other forms of power held by the teacher by virtue of race, gender, or class that may lead to antagonisms. Without naming these sources of tension, it is difficult to address or build upon them to challenge existing structures of power and subjectivities. Without recognizing more clearly the implicit power and limitations of the position of teacher, calls for a collective liberation or for opposition to oppression slide over the surface of the tensions that may emerge among teachers and students as subjects with conflicting interests and histories and with different kinds of knowledge and power. A number of questions are thus left unaddressed in *Pedagogy of the Oppressed*: How are we to situate ourselves in relation to the struggles of others? How are we to address our own contradictory positions as oppressors and oppressed? Where are we to look for liberation when our collective "reading of the world" reveals contradictory and conflicting experiences and struggles? The Freirean vision of the oppressed as undifferentiated and as the source of unitary political action, the transparency of the subjectivity of the Freirean teacher, and the claims of universal goals of liberation and social transformation fail to provide the answers to these questions.

Calling into question the universal and abstract claims of *Pedagogy of the Oppressed* is certainly not to argue that Freire's pedagogy should be rejected or discarded. The ethical stance of Freire in terms of praxis and his articulation of people's worth and ability to know and change the world are an essential basis for radical pedagogies in opposition to oppression. Freire's thought illuminates the central question of political action in a world increasingly without universals. Freire, like liberation theologians such as Sharon Welch, positions himself on the side of the oppressed; he claims the moral imperative to act in the world. As Peter McLaren has commented in reference to Freire's political stand, "The task of liberating others from their suffering may not emerge from some transcendental fiat, yet it nevertheless compels us to affirm our humanity in solidarity with victims."[20] But in order better to seek the affirmation of our own humanity and to seed to end suffering and oppression, I am arguing for a more situated theory of oppression and subjectivity, and for the need to consider the contradictions of such universal claims of truth or process.

In the next section of this article, I explore feminist pedagogy as an example of a situated pedagogy of liberation. Like Freirean pedagogy, feminist pedagogy is based on assumptions of the power of consciousness raising, the existence of oppression and the possibility of ending it, and the desire for social transformation. But in its historical development, feminist pedagogy has revealed the shortcomings that emerge in the attempt to enact a pedagogy that assumes a universal experience and abstract goals. In the attempt of feminist pedagogy to address these issues, a more complex vision of liberatory pedagogy is being developed and explored.

Feminist Pedagogy, Consciousness Raising, and Women's Liberation

Feminist pedagogy in colleges and universities has developed in conjunction with the growth of women's studies and what is inclusively called "the new scholarship on women." These developments within universities—the institutionalization of women's studies as programs and departments and the challenge to existing canons and disciplines by the new scholarship on women and by feminist theory—are reflected in the classroom teaching methods that have come to be loosely termed feminist pedagogy. Defining exactly what feminist pedagogy means in practice, however, is difficult. It is easier to describe the various methods used in specific women's studies courses and included by feminist teachers claiming the term feminist pedagogy than it is to provide a coherent definition.[21] But common to the claims of feminist teachers is the goal of providing students with the skills to continue political work as feminists after they have left the university. Nancy Schniedewind makes a similar claim for what she calls "feminist process," which she characterizes as "both feminist vision of equalitarian personal relations and societal forms and the confidence and skills to make their knowledge and vision functional in the world."[22]

The pedagogy of feminist teachers is based on certain assumptions about knowledge, power, and political action that can be traced beyond the academy to the political activism of the woman's movement in the 1960s. This same commitment to social change through the transformative potential of education underlay Freire's pedagogy in Brazil during the same period. Women's studies at the university level have since come to encompass a wide variety of political stances and theoretical approaches. Socialist feminism, liberal feminism, radical feminism, and postmodern feminism all view issues from their different perspectives. Nonetheless, feminist pedagogy continues to echo the struggles of its origins and to retain a vision of social activism. Virtually all women's studies courses and programs at least partially reflect this critical, oppositional, and activist stance, even within programs now established and integrated into the bureaucratic structures of university life. As Linda Gordon points out:

> Women's studies did not arise accidentally, as the product of someone's good idea, but was created by a social movement for women's liberation with a sharp critique of the whole structure of society. By its very existence, women's studies constitutes a critique of the university and the body of knowledge it imparts.[23]

Despite tensions and splits within feminism at a theoretical level and in the context of women's studies programs in universities, the political commitment of women's liberation that Gordon refers to continues to shape feminist pedagogy. Thus, like Freirean pedagogy, feminist pedagogy rests on truth claims of the primacy of experience and consciousness that are grounded in historically situated social change movements. Key to understanding the methods and epistemological claims of feminist pedagogy is an understanding of its origins in more grassroots political activity, particularly in the consciousness-raising groups of the women's liberation movement of the late 1960s and early 1970s.

Women's consciousness-raising groups began to form more or less spontaneously in northeastern and western U.S. cities in late 1967 among White women who had been active in the civil rights and new left movements.[24] In a fascinating parallel to the rise of the women's suffrage movement out of the abolitionist movement in the mid-nineteenth century, these activist and politically committed women came to apply their universal demands for equality and justice of the civil rights movement to their own situation as women.[25] While public actions such as the Miss America protest of 1968, mass meetings, and conferences were organized in this early period, the unique organizational basis for the women's liberation movement was grounded in the small groups of women who came together for what came to be known as consciousness raising. Early consciousness-raising groups, based on friendship and common political commitments, focused on the discussion of shared experiences of sexuality, work, family, and participation in the male-dominated left political movement. Consciousness raising focused on collective political change rather than on individual therapy. The groups were unstructured and local—they could be formed anywhere and did not follow formal guidelines—but they used the same sorts of methods because these methods addressed common problems. One woman remembers the first meeting of what became her consciousness-raising group:

> The flood broke loose gradually and then more swiftly. We talked about our families, our mothers, our fathers, our siblings; we talked about our men; we talked about school; we talked about the "movement" (which meant new left men). For hours we talked and unburdened our souls and left feeling high and planning to meet again the following week.[26]

Perhaps the clearest summary of consciousness raising from this period can be found in Kathie Sarachild's essay, "Consciousness Raising: A Radical Weapon."[27] In this article, Sarachild, a veteran of the civil rights movement in the South and a member of Redstockings, one of the earliest and most influential women's groups, presents an account that is both descriptive and proscriptive.[28] She makes it clear that consciousness raising arose spontaneously among small groups of women and that she is describing and summarizing a collective process that can be used by other groups of women. Fundamental to Sarachild's description of consciousness raising is in its grounding in the need for political action. She describes the emergence of the method of consciousness raising among a group of women who considered themselves radicals in the sense of demanding fundamental changes in society. As Sarachild comments:

> We were interested in getting to the roots of problems in society. You might say we wanted to pull up weeds in the garden by their roots, not just pick off the leaves at the top to make things look good momentarily. Women's liberation was started by women who considered themselves to be radicals in this sense.[29]

A second fundamental aspect of consciousness raising is the reliance on experience and feeling. According to Sarachild, the focus on examining women's own experience came from a profound distrust of accepted authority and truth. These claims about what was valuable and true tended to be accepting of existing assumptions about women's "inherent nature" and "proper place." In order to call those truths into question (truths we might now call hegemonic and that Foucault, for example, would tie to structures of power), women had nowhere to turn except to their own experience. Sarachild describes the process of her group:

> In the end the group decided to raise its consciousness by studying women's lives like childhood, jobs, motherhood, etc. We'd do any outside reading we wanted to and thought was important. But our starting point for discussion, as well as our test of the accuracy of what any of the books said, would be the actual experience we had in these areas.[30]

The last aspect of consciousness raising was a common sharing of experience in a collective, leaderless group. As Michele Russell points out, this sharing is similar to the practice of "testifying" in the Black church, and depends upon openness and trust in the group.[31] The assumption underlying this sharing of stories was the existence of commonality among women; as Sarachild puts it, "we made the assumption, an assumption basic to consciousness raising, that most women were like ourselves—not different."[32]

The model for consciousness raising among the Redstockings, as with other early groups, came from the experiences of many of the women as organizers in the civil rights movement in the South. Sarachild, for instance, cites the example of the Student Nonviolent Coordinating Committee, and quotes Stokely Carmichael when she argues for the need for people to organize in order to understand their own conditions of existence and to fight their own struggles. Other sources cited by Sarachild include the nineteenth-century suffragist Ernestine Rose, Mao Zedong, Malcolm X, and the practice of "speaking bitterness" in the Chinese revolution described by William Hinton in *Fanshen*.[33] Both the example of the civil rights movement and the revolutionary tradition of the male writers that provided the model for early consciousness raising supported women's commitment to political action and social change.[34] As Sarachild comments:

We would be the first to dare to say and do the undareable, what women really felt and wanted. The first job now was to raise awareness and understanding, our own and others—awareness that would prompt people to organize and to act on a mass scale.[35]

Thus consciousness raising shared the assumptions of earlier revolutionary traditions: that understanding and theoretical analysis were the first steps to revolutionary change, and that neither was adequate alone; theory and practice were intertwined as praxis. As Sarachild puts it, "Consciousness raising was seen as both a method for arriving at the truth and a means for action and organizing."[36] What was original in consciousness raising, however, was its emphasis on experience and feeling as the guide to theoretical understanding, an approach that reflected the realities of women's socially defined subjectivities and the conditions of their lives. Irene Peslikis, another member of Redstockings, wrote, "When we think of what it is that politicizes people it is not so much books or ideas but experience."[37]

While Sarachild and other early feminists influenced by a left political tradition explored the creation of theory grounded in women's feelings and experiences, they never lost the commitment to social transformation.[38] In their subsequent history, however, consciousness raising and feminist pedagogy did not always retain this political commitment to action. As the women's movement expanded to reach wider groups of women, consciousness raising tended to lose its commitment to revolutionary change. This trend seems to have been particularly true as the women's movement affected women with a less radical perspective and with little previous political involvement. Without a vision of collective action and social transformation, consciousness raising held the possibility of what Berenice Fisher calls "a diversion of energies into an exploration of feelings and 'private' concerns to the detriment of political activism."[39] The lack of structure and the local nature of consciousness-raising groups only reinforced these tendencies toward a focus on individual rather than collective change. The one site in which the tradition of consciousness raising did find institutional expression was in academia, in the growth of women's studies courses and programs stimulated by the new scholarship on women. The founders of these early courses and programs tended to be politically committed feminists who themselves had experienced consciousness raising and who, like Friere, assumed that education could and should be a means of social change.

The first women's studies courses, reflecting the growth of the women's movement in what has come to be called the second wave of feminism, were taught in the late 1960s.[40] In 1970, Paul Lauter and Florence Howe founded The Feminist Press, and important outlet for publishing early feminist scholarship and recovering lost texts by women writers.[41] In 1977, the founding of the National Women's Studies Association provided a national organization, a journal, and yearly conferences that gave feminists inside and outside of academia a forum to exchange ideas and experiences. By the late 1980s, respected journals such as *Signs* and *Feminist Studies* were well established, and women's studies programs and courses were widespread (if not always enthusiastically supported by administrations) in colleges and universities.[42] At the same time, feminist research and theory—what has come to be called "the new scholarship on women"—put forth a profound challenge to traditional disciplines.[43] The growth of women's studies programs and feminist scholarship thus provided and institutional framework and theoretical underpinning for feminist pedagogy, the attempt to express feminist values and goals in the classroom. But while feminist scholarship has presented fundamental challenges to traditional androcentric knowledge, the attempt to create a new pedagogy modeled on consciousness raising has not been as successful or coherent a project. Serious challenges to the goal of political transformation through the experience of feminist learning have been raised in the attempt to create a feminist pedagogy in the academy. The difficulties and contradictions that have emerged in the attempt to create a feminist pedagogy in traditional institutions like universities raise serious questions for all liberatory pedagogies and echo some of the problems raised by the unitary and universal approach of *Pedagogy of the Oppressed*. But in engaging these questions, feminist pedagogy suggests new directions that can enrich Freirean pedagogies of liberation.

Feminist pedagogy has raised three areas of concern that are particularly useful in considering the ways in which Freirean and other liberatory pedagogies can be enriched and expanded. The first of these concerns the role and authority of the teacher; the second addresses the epistemological question of the source of the claims for knowledge and truth in personal experience and feeling; the last, emerging from challenges by women of color and postmodernist feminist theorists, raises the question of difference. Their challenges have lead to a shattering of the unproblematic and unitary category "woman," as well as of an assumption of the inevitable unity of "women." Instead, feminist theorists have increasingly emphasized the importance of recognizing difference as a central category of feminist pedagogy. The unstated assumption of a universal experience of "being a woman" was exploded by the critiques of postmodern feminists and by the growing assertion of lesbians and women of color that the universal category "woman" in fact meant "White, heterosexual, middle-class woman," even when used by White, heterosexual, socialist feminists, or women veterans of the civil rights movement who were committed to class or race struggles.[44] These theoretical challenges to the unity of both "woman" and "women" have in turn called into question the authority of women as teachers and students in the classroom, the epistemological value of both feeling and experience, and the nature of political strategies for enacting feminist goals of social change. I turn next to an exploration of these key issues of authority, experience, feeling, and difference within feminist pedagogy and theory.

The Role and Authority of the Teacher

In many respects, the feminist version of the teacher's authority echoes the Freirean image of the teacher who is a joint learner with students and who holds authority by virtue of greater knowledge and experience. But as we have seen, Freire fails to address the various forms of power held by teachers depending on their race, gender and the historical and institutional settings in which they work. In the Freirean account, they are in this sense "transparent." In the actual practice of feminist pedagogy, the central issues of difference, positionality, and the need to recognize the implications of subjectivity or identity for teachers and students have become central. Moreover, the question of authority in institutional settings makes problematic the possibility of achieving the collective and nonhierarchical vision of early consciousness-raising groups—and emphasis on feeling, experience, and sharing, and a suspicion of hierarchy and authority—continue to influence feminist pedagogy in academic settings. But the institutionalized nature of women's studies in the hierarchical and bureaucratic structure of academia creates tensions that run counter to the original commitment to praxis in consciousness raising groups. Early consciousness-raising groups were homogeneous, antagonistic to authority, and had a commitment to political change that had directly emerged from the civil rights and new left movements. Feminist pedagogy within academic classrooms addresses heterogeneous groups of students within a competitive and individualistic culture in which the teacher holds institutional power and responsibility (even if she may want to reject that power).[45] As bell hooks comments, "The academic setting, the academic discourse [we] work in, is not a known site for truthtelling."[46] The very success of feminist scholarship has meant the development of a rich theoretical tradition with deep divisions and opposing goals and methods.[47] Thus the source of the teacher's authority as a "woman" who can call upon a "common woman's knowledge" is called into question; at the same time the feminist teacher is "given" authority by virtue of her role within the hierarchical structure of the university.

The question of authority in feminist pedagogy seems to be centered around two different conceptions. The first refers to the institutionally imposed authority of the teacher within a hierarchical university structure. The teacher in this role must give grades, is evaluated by administrators and colleagues in terms of expertise in a body of knowledge, and is expected to take responsibility for meeting the goals of an academic course as it is understood within the wider university. This hierarchical structure is clearly in opposition to the collective goals of a common women's movement and is miles from the early structureless consciousness-raising groups in which each woman was an expert on her own life. Not only does the university structure impose this model of institutional authority, but students themselves expect it. As Barbara Hillyer Davis comments: "The institutional pressure to [impart knowledge] is reinforced by the students' well-socialized behavior. If I will tell them 'what I want,' they will deliver it. They are exasperated with my efforts to depart from the role of dispense of wisdom."[48] Feminist educators have attempted to address this tension between their ideals of collective education and the demands of the university by a variety of expedients: group assignments and grades, contracts for grades, pass/fail course, and such techniques as self-revelation and the articulation of the dynamics of the classroom.[49]

Another aspect of institutionalized authority, however, is the need for women to *claim* authority in a society that denies it to them. As Culley and Portugues have pointed out, the authority and power of the woman feminist teacher is already in question from many of her students precisely because she is a woman:

> As women, our own position is precarious, and the power we are supposed to exercise is given grudgingly, if at all. For our own students, for ourselves, and for our superiors, we are not clearly "us" or "them." The facts of class, of race, of ethnicity, of sexual preference—as well as gender—may cut across the neat divisions of teacher/student.[50]

Thus the issue of institutional authority raises the contradictions of trying to achieve a democratic and collective ideal in a hierarchical institution, but it also raises the question of the meaning of authority for feminist teachers, whose right to speak or hold power is itself under attack in a patriarchal (and racist, homophobic, classist, and so on) society. The question of asserting authority and power is a central concern to feminists precisely because as women they have been taught that taking power is inappropriate. From this perspective, the feminist teacher's acceptance of authority becomes in itself liberating to her and to her students. It becomes a claim to authority in terms of her own value as a scholar and a teacher in a patriarchal society that structurally denies or questions that authority as it is manifest in the organization and bureaucracy of the university. Women students, after all, are socialized to be deferential, and both men and women students are taught to accept male authority. It is instructive for students to see women assert authority. But this use of authority will lead to positive social change only if those teachers are working also to empower students in a Freirean sense.[51] As Susan Stanford Friedman argues:

> What I and other women have needed is a theory of feminist pedagogy consistent with our needs as women operating at the fringes of patriarchal space. As we attempt to move on to academic turf culturally defined as male, we need a theory that first recognizes the androcentric denial of *all* authority to women and, second, points out a way for us to speak with an authentic voice not based on tyranny.[52]

These concerns lead to a conception of authority and power in an positive sense, both in terms of women asserting authority as women, and in terms of valuing intellectual work and the creation of theory as a means of understanding and, thus, of changing the world.

The authority of the intellectual raises issues for feminists in the academy that are similar to those faced by other democratic and collective political movements, such as those faced by other democratic and collective political movements, such as those described by Freire. There is a contradiction between the idea of a women's movement including all women and a group of what Berenice Fisher calls "advanced women."[52] Feminists who question the whole tradition of androcentric thought are deeply suspicious of women who take a position of "expert" who can translate and interpret other women's experiences. Fisher articulates these tensions well:

> Who are intellectuals in relation to the women's movement? . . . Are intellectuals sorts of leaders, sage guides, women who give voice to or clarify a broader urge toward social change? Is intellectual work essentially elitist, a matter of mere privilege to think, to write, to create? Is it simply a patriarchal mode of gaining and maintaining power, a way of negating women's everyday experience, a means of separating some women from the rest of the "community?"[54]

Fisher argues that feminist intellectuals are struggling with these questions in their scholarship, teaching, and roles within the universities and the wider women's movement. She does not reject the authority of the feminist intellectual, but she also does not deny the need to address and clarify these contradictions. She, like Charlotte Bunch, is an embodiment of this attempt to accept both the authority and responsibility of the feminist intellectual who is creating theory.

In terms of feminist pedagogy, the authority of the feminist teacher as intellectual and theorist finds expression in the goal of making students themselves theorists of their own lives by interrogating and analyzing their own experience. In an approach very similar to Freire's concept of conscientization, this strategy moves beyond the naming or sharing of experience to the creation of a critical understanding of the forces that have shaped that experience. This theorizing is antithetical to traditional views of women. As Bunch points out, traditionally

> women are supposed to worry about mundane survival problems, to brood about fate, and to fantasize in a personal manner. We are not meant to think analytically about society, to question the ways things are, to consider how things could be different. Such thinking involves an active, not a passive, relationship to the world.[55]

Thus feminist educators like Fisher and Bunch accept their authority as intellectuals and theorists, but they consciously attempt to construct their pedagogy to recognize and encourage the capacity of their students to theorize and to recognize their own power.[56] This is a conception of authority not in the institutional terms of a bureaucratized university system, but rather an attempt to claim the authority of theorist and guide for students who are themselves potential theorists.

Feminist concerns about the authority of the feminist teacher address questions of classroom practice and theory ignored by Freire—in his formulation of the teacher and student as two "knowers" of the world, and in his assertion that the liberatory teacher should acknowledge and claim authority but not authoritarianism. The feminist exploration of authority is much richer and addresses more directly the contradictions between goals of collectivity and hierarchies of knowledge. Feminist teachers are much more conscious of the power of various subject positions than is represented in Freire's "transparent" liberatory teacher. An acknowledgment of realities of conflict and tensions based on contradictory political goals, as well as of the meaning of historically experienced oppression for both teachers and students, leads to a pedagogy that respects difference not just as significant for students, but for teachers as well.

Personal Experience as a Source of Knowledge and Truth

As feminists explore the relationship of authority, theory, and political action, they raise questions about the categories and claims for truth underlying both consciousness raising and feminist pedagogy. These claims rest on categories of experience and feeling as guides to theoretical understanding and political change. Basic to the Freirean method of conscientization is the believe in the ability of all people to be knowers and to read both the word and the world. In Freirean pedagogy, it is through the interrogation of their own experiences that the oppressed will come to an understanding of their own power as knowers and creators of the world; this knowledge will contribute to the transformation of their world. In consciousness-raising groups and in feminist pedagogy in the university, a similar reliance on experience and feeling has been fundamental to the development of a feminist knowledge of the world that can be the basis for social change. Underlying both Freirean and early feminist pedagogy is an assumption of a common experience as the basis for political analysis and action. Both experience and feeling were central to consciousness raising and remain central to feminist pedagogy in academia; they are claimed as a kind of "inner knowing," shaped by society but at the same time containing an oppositional quality. Feeling is looked to as a guide to a deeper truth than that of abstract rationality. Experience, which is interpreted through ideologically constructed categories, also can be the basis for an opposition to dominant schemes of truth if what is experienced runs counter to what is set forth and accepted as "true." Feminist educators, beginning with women in the early consciousness-raising groups, have explored both experience and feeling as sources of knowledge, and both deserve closer examination.

In many ways, feeling or emotion has been seen traditionally as a source of women's knowledge about the world. As we have seen, in the early consciousness-raising groups, feelings were looked to as the source of a "true" knowledge of the world for women living in a society that denied the value of their perceptions. Feelings or emotions were seen as a way of testing accepted claims of what is universally true about human nature or, specifically, about women. Claims such as Freud's theory of penis envy, for example, were challenged by women first because these theoretical descriptions of women's psychology did not match women's own feelings about their lives. As feminist pedagogy has developed, with a continued emphasis on the function of feelings as a guide to knowledge about the world, emotions have been seen as links between a kind of inner truth or inner self and the outer world—including ideology, culture, and other discourses of power.[57] However, as feminist educators have explored the uses of feeling or emotion as a source of knowledge, several difficulties have become clear. First of all, there is a danger that the expression of strong emotion can be simply cathartic and can deflect the need for action to address the underlying causes of that emotion. Moreover, it is not clear how to distinguish among a wide range of emotions as the source of political action. At a more theoretical level, there are contradictions involved in claiming that the emotions are a source for knowledge and at the same time arguing that they are manipulated and shaped by dominant discourses. Both consciousness-raising groups and feminist theorists have asserted the social construction of feelings and their manipulation by the dominant culture; at the same time, they look to feelings as a source of truth. Berenice Fisher points to the contradiction implicit in these claims:

> In theoretical terms, we cannot simultaneously claim that all feelings are socially conditioned and that some feelings are "true." We would be more consistent to acknowledge that society only partly shapes our emotions, leaving an opening where we can challenge and change the responses to which we have been socialized. That opening enables the consciousness-raising process to take place and gives us the space in which to reflect on the new emotional responses that our process evokes.[58]

In this formulation, Fisher seems to be arguing for a kind of Gramscian "good sense," a locus of knowing in the self that is grounded in feeling as a guide to theoretical understanding. Feelings thus are viewed as a kind of cognition—a source of knowledge.

Perhaps the most eloquent argument for feelings as a source of oppositional knowledge is found in the work of Audre Lorde. Lorde, a Black lesbian feminist theorist and poet, writes from the specificity of her own socially defined and shaped life. For her, feeling is the source of poetry, a means of knowing what challenges White, Western, androcentric epistemologies. She specifically ties her own feelings as a Black woman to a non-Western way of knowing. She writes:

> As we come more into touch with our own ancient, non-European consciousness of living as a situation to be experienced and interacted with, we learn more and more to cherish our feelings, to respect those hidden sources of power from where true knowledge and, therefore, lasting action comes.[59]

Lorde is acutely aware of the ways in which the dominant society shapes our sense of who we are and what we feel. As she points out, "Within living structures defined by profit, by linear power, by institutional dehumanization, our feelings were not meant to survive."[60] Moreover, Lorde is conscious of the oppressor within us: "For we have, built into all of us, old blueprints of expectation and response, old structures of oppression, and these must be altered at the same time as we alter the living conditions which are the result of those structures."[61] But although Lorde does not deny what she calls "the oppressor within," she retains a belief in the power of deeper feeling to challenge the dominant definitions of truth and to point the way to an analysis that can lead to an alternative vision:

> As we begin to recognize our deepest feelings, we begin to give up, of necessity, being satisfied with suffering and self-negation, and with the numbness which so often seems like their only alternative in society. Our acts against oppression become integral with self, motivated and empowered from within.[62]

For Lorde, then, feelings are a guide to analysis and to action. While they are shaped by society and are socially constructed in that sense, Lorde insists on a deeper reality of feeling closer in touch with what it means to be human. This formulation echoes the Freirean vision of humanization as a new way of being in the world other than as oppressor and oppressed. Both

Freire and Lorde retain a Utopian faith in the possibility that human beings can crate new ways of being in the world out of collective struggle and a human capacity to feel. Lorde terms this the power of the erotic; she speaks of the erotic as "a measure between the beginnings of our sense of self and the chaos of our strongest feelings," a resource "firmly rooted in the power of our unexpressed or unrecognized feeling."[63] Because the erotic can challenge the dominant, it has been denied as a source of power and knowledge. But for Lorde, the power of the erotic provides the basis for visionary social change.

In her exploration of feelings and of the erotic as a source of knowledge about the world, Lorde does not reject analysis and rationality. But she questions the depth of critical understanding of those forces that shape our lives that can be achieved using only the rational and abstract methods of analysis given to us by dominant ideology. In Foucault's terms, she is seeking a perspective from which to interrogate dominant regimes of truth; central to her argument is the claim that an analysis framed solely in the terms of accepted discourse cannot get to the root of structures of power. That is what her well-known phrase, "The Master's Tools Will Never Dismantle the Master's House," implies. As she argues:

> Rationality is not unnecessary. It serves the chaos of knowledge. It serves feeling. It serves to get from this place to that place. But if you don't honor those places, then the road is meaningless. Too often, that's what happens with the worship of rationality and that circular, academic analytic thinking. But ultimately, I don't see feel/think as a dichotomy. I see them as a choice of ways and combinations.[64]

Lorde's discussion of feeling and the erotic as a source of power and knowledge is based on the assumption that human beings have the capacity to feel and know, and can engage in self-critique; people are not completely shaped by dominant discourse. The oppressor may be within us, but Lorde insists that we also have the capacity to challenge our own ways of feeling and knowing. When tied to a recognition of positionality, this validation of feeling can be used to develop powerful sources of politically focused feminist education.

For Lorde and Fisher, this kind of knowing through an exploration of feeling and emotion requires collective inquiry and constant reevaluation. It is a contingent and positioned claim to truth. Similar complexities arise in the use of experience as the basis for feminist political action. Looking to experience as the source of knowledge and the focus of feminist learning is perhaps the most fundamental tenet of feminist pedagogy. This is similar to the Freirean call to "read the world" to seek the generative themes that codify power relationships and social structures. The sharing of women's experiences was the touchstone of early consciousness-raising groups and continues to be fundamental method of feminist pedagogy. That woman need to examine what they have experienced and lived in concrete ways, in their own bodies, is a materialistic conception of experience. In an early essay, Adrienne Rich pointed to this materiality of experience: "To think like a woman in a man's world means . . . remembering that every mind resides in a body; remaining accountable to the female bodies in which we live; constantly retesting given hypotheses against lived experience."[65] As became clear quite early in the women's movement, claims about experience as a source of women's knowledge rested on certain assumptions about commonalities in women's lives. Women were conceived of as a unitary and relatively undifferentiated group. Sarachild, for example, spoke of devising "new theories which . . . reflect the actual experience and feelings and necessities of women.[66] Underlying this approach was the assumption of a common woman's experience, one reflecting the world of the White, middle-class, heterosexual women of the early feminist movement. But as the critiques of lesbians, women of color, and postmodernist feminist theorists have made clear, there is no single woman's experience to be revealed. Both experience and feeling thus have been called into question as the source of an unproblematic knowledge of the world that will lead to praxis. As Diana Fuss comments: " 'female experience' is never as unified, as knowable, as universal, and as stable as we presume it to be."[67]

Challenges to the concept of a unitary women's experience by both women of color and by postmodern critics has not meant the abandonment of experience as a source of knowledge for feminist teachers. Of course experience, like feeling, is socially constructed in the sense that we can only understand it and speak about it in ideas and terms that are part of an existing ideology and language. But in a stance similar to that of Lorde in her use of the erotic, feminist teachers have explored the ways in which women have experienced the material world through their bodies. This self-examination of lived experience is then used as a source of knowledge that can illuminate the social processes and ideology that shape us. As Fuss suggests, "Such a position permits the introduction of narratives of lived experience into the classroom while at the same time challenging us to examine collectively the central role social and historical practices play in shaping and producing these narratives."[68] One example of this approach is found in the work of Frigga Haug and the group of German feminists of which she is a part.[69] Haug and this group use what they call collective memory work to explore their feelings about their own bodies in order to uncover the social construction of their selves:

> Our collective empirical work set itself the high-flown task of identifying the ways in which individuals construct themselves into existing structures, and are thereby themselves formed; the way in which they reconstruct social structures; the points at which change is possible, the points where our chains chafe most, the point where accommodations have been made.[70]

This collection exploration of "the point where . . . chains chafe most" recalls the Freirean culture circles, in which peasants would take such examples as their personal experiences with the landlord as the starting point for their education or conscientization. Basic to their approach is a belief in reflection and a rejection of a view of people as "fixed, given, unchangeable." By working collectively on "memory work," a sharing and comparison of their own lives, Haug and her group hope to uncover the workings of hegemonic ideology in their own subjectivities. Another example of such collective work can be found in the Jamaican women's theater group, Sistren. Founded in 1977, Sistren is a collaborative theater group made up of working-class Jamaican women who create and write plays based on a collaborative exploration of their own experiences. The life histories of the women of Sistren have been collected in *Lionheart Girl: Life Stories of Jamaican Women*. In the compilation of this book, the Sistren collective used the same process of the collective sharing and analysis of experience that is the basis for their theater work. As the company's director Honor Ford-Smith writes:

> We began meeting collectively at first. Starting with our childhood, we made drawings of images based on such themes as where we had grown up, symbols of oppression in our lives, our relationships with men, our experience with race and the kind of work we had done.[71]

For Haug and her group, the Sistren collective, the early consciousness-raising groups, and the Freirean culture circles, collective sharing of experience is the source of knowledge of the forces that have shaped and continue to shape them. But their recognition of the shifting meaning of experience as it is explored through memory insists on the profoundly social and political nature of who we are.

The Question of Difference

Both women of color writing from a perspective of cultural feminism and postmodernist feminist theorists converge in their critique of the concept of a universal "women's experience." While the idea of a unitary and universal category "woman" has been challenged by women of color for its racist assumptions, it has also been challenged by recent analyses of feminist theorists influenced by postmodernism, who point to the social construction of subjectivity and who emphasize the "unstable" nature of the self. Postmodernist feminist critics such as Chris Weedon have argued that socially given identities such as "woman" are "precarious, contradictory, and in process, constantly being reconstituted in discourse each time we speak."[72] This kind of analysis considers the ways in which "the subject" is not an object; that is, not fixed in a static social structure, but constantly being created, actively creating the self, and struggling for new ways of being in the world through new forms of discourse or new forms of social relationships. Such analysis calls for a recognition of the positionality of each person in any discussion of what can be known from experience. This calling into question the permanence of subjectivities of what Jane Flax refers to as the "unstable self."[73] If we view individual selves as being constructed and negotiated, then we can begin to consider what exactly those forces are in which individuals shape themselves and by which they are shaped. The category of "woman" is itself challenged as it is seen more and more as a part of a symbolic system of ideology. Donna Haraway calls all such claims of identity into question:

> With the hard-won recognition of their social and historical constitution, gender, race, and class cannot provide the basis for belief in "essential" unity: There is nothing about being "female" that naturally binds women. There is not even such a state as "being" female, itself a highly complex category constructed in contested sexual discourses and other social practices. Gender, race, or class consciousness is an achievement forced on us by the terrible historical experience of the contradictory social realities of patriarchy, colonialism, and capitalism.[74]

These analyses support the challenges to assumptions of an essential and universal nature of women and women's experience that have come from lesbian critics and women of color.[75]

Both women of color and lesbian critics have pointed to the complexity of socially given identities. Black women and other women of color raise challenges to the assumption that the sharing of experience will create solidarity and a theoretical understanding based upon a common women's standpoint. Lesbian feminists, both White and of color, point to the destructive nature of homophobia and what Adrienne Rich has called compulsory heterosexuality. As is true of White, heterosexual, feminist educators, these theorists base their analysis upon their own experiences, but those experiences reveal not only the workings of sexism, but of racism, homophobia, and class oppression as well. This complex perspective underlies the Combahee River Collective Statement, a position paper written by a group of African-American feminists in Boston in the 1970s. This statement makes clear what a grounded theory of experience means for women whose value is denied by the dominant society in numerous ways. The women in the Combahee River Collective argue that "the most profound and potentially most radical politics come directly out of our own identity, as opposed to working to end somebody else's oppression."[76] For African-American women, an investigation of the shaping of their own identities reveals the ways in which sexism and racism are interlocking forms of oppression:

> As children we realized that we were different from boys and that we were treated differently. For example, we were told in the same breath to be quiet both for the sake of being "ladylike" and to make us less objectionable in the eyes of white people. As we grew older we became aware of the threat of physical and sexual abuse from men. However, we had no way of conceptualizing what was so apparent to us, what we *knew* was really happening.[77]

When African-American teachers like Michele Russell or Barbara Omolade describe their feminist pedagogy, they ground that pedagogy in an investigation of experience in material terms. As Russell describes her teaching of an introductory Black studies class for women at Wayne County Community College in Detroit: "We have an hour together. . . . The first topic of conversation—among themselves and with me—is what they went through just to make it in the door, on time. That in itself became a lesson."[78] And Omolade points out in her discussion of her teaching at Medgar Evers College in New York, a college whose students are largely African-American women:

> No one can each teach students to "see," but an instructor is responsible for providing the coherent ordering of information and content. The classroom process is one of information-sharing in which students learn to generalize their particular life experiences within a community of fellow intellectuals.[79]

Thus the pedagogy of Russell and Omolade is grounded in experience as a source of knowledge in a particular materialistic way; the knowledge generated reveals the overlapping forms of oppression lived by women of color in this society. The investigation of the experiences of women of color, lesbian women, women whose very being challenges existing racial, sexual, hetero-sexual, and class dominance leads to a knowledge of the world that both acknowledges differences and points to the need for an "integrated analysis and practice based upon the fact that the major systems of oppression are interlocking."[80] The turning to experience thus reveals not a universal and common women's essence, but, rather, deep divisions in what different women have experienced, and in the kinds of knowledge they discover when they examine their own experience. The recognition of the differences among women raises serious challenges to feminist pedagogy by calling into question the authority of the teacher/theorist, raising feelings of guilt and shame, and revealing tensions among students as well as between teacher and students. In classes of African-American women taught by African-American teachers, the sharing of experience can lead to the same sense of commonality and sharing that was true of early consciousness-raising groups. But in settings in which students come from differing positions of privilege or oppression, the sharing of experience raises conflicts rather than building solidarity. In these circumstances, the collective exploration of experience leads not to a common knowledge and solidarity based on sameness, but to the tensions of an articulation of difference. Such exploration raises again the problems left unaddressed by Freirean pedagogy: the overlapping and multiple forms of oppression revealed in "reading the world" of experience.

Conclusion

Both Freirean and feminist pedagogies are based on political commitment and identification with subordinate and oppressed groups; both seek justice and empowerment. Freire sets out these goals of liberation and social and political transformation as universal claims, without exploring his own privileged position or existing conflicts among oppressed groups themselves. Writing from within a tradition of Western modernism, his theory rests on a belief of transcendent and universal truth. But feminist theory influenced by postmodernist thought and by the writings of women of color challenges the underlying assumptions of these universal claims. Feminist theorists in particular argue that it is essential to recognize, as Juliet Mitchell comments, that we cannot "live as human subjects without in some sense taking on a history."[81] The recognition of our own histories means the necessity of articulating our own subjectivities and our own interests as we try to interpret and critique the social world. This stance rejects the universalizing tendency of much "malestream" thought, and insists on recognizing the power and privilege of who we are. As Biddy Martin and Chandra Mohanty comment:

> The claim to a lack of identity or positionality is itself based on privilege, on the refusal to accept responsibility for one's implication in actual historical or social relations, or a denial that positionalities exist or that they matter, the denial of one's own personal history and the claim to a total separation from it.[82]

Fundamental to recent feminist theory is a questioning of the concept of a coherent subject moving through history with a single essential creation and negotiation of selves within structures of ideology and material constraints.[83] This line of theoretical analysis calls into question assumptions of the common interests of the oppressed, whether conceived of a women or peasants; it challenges the use of such universal terms as oppression and liberation without locating these claims in a concrete historical or social context. The challenges of recent feminist theory and, in particular, the writings of feminists of color point to the need to articulate and claim a particular historical and social identity, to locate ourselves, and to build coalitions from a recognition of the partial knowledges of our own constructed identities. Recognizing the standpoint of subjects as shaped by their experience of class, race, gender, or other socially defined identities has powerful implications for pedagogy, in that it emphasizes the need to make conscious the subject positions not only of students but of teachers as well. These lines of theoretical analysis have implications for the ways in which we can understand pedagogy as contested, as a site of discourse among subjects, teachers, and students whose identities are, as Weedon puts it, contradictory and in process. The theoretical formulation of the "unstable self," the complexity of subjectivities, what Giroux calls "multi-layered subjects," and the need to position ourselves in relation to our own histories raise important issues for liberatory pedagogies. If all people's identities are recognized in their full historical and social complexity as subject positions that are in process, based on knowledges that are partial and that reflect deep and conflicting differences, how can we theorize what a liberatory pedagogy actively struggling against different forms of oppression may look like? How can we build upon the rich and complex analysis of feminist theory and pedagogy to work toward a Freirean vision of social justice and liberations?

In the complexity of issues raised by feminist pedagogy, we can begin to acknowledge the reality of tensions that result from different histories, from privilege, oppression, and power as they are lived by teachers and students in classrooms. To recognize these tensions and differences does not mean abandonment of the goals of social justice and empowerment, but it does make clear the need to recognize contingent and situated claims and to acknowledge our own histories and selves in process. One significant area of feminist work has been grounded in the collective analysis of experience and emotion, as exemplified by the work of Haug and her group in Germany or by the Jamaican women's theater group, Sistren. In many respects, these projects look back to consciousness raising, but with a more developed theory of ideology and an acute consciousness of difference. As Berenice Fisher argues, a collective inquiry "requires the slow unfolding of layers of experience, both the contradictory experiences of a given woman and the conflicting experiences of a different woman."[84] Another approach builds on what Bernice Reagon calls the need for coalition building, a recognition and validation of difference. This is similar to what has come to be known as identity politics, exemplified in what Minnie Bruce Pratt is seeking in her discussion of trying to come to terms with her own identity as a privileged Southern White woman.[85] Martin and Mohanty speak of this as a sense of "home," a recognition of the difficulties of coming to terms with privilege or oppression, of the benefits of being an oppressor, or of the rage of being oppressed.[86] This is a validation of both difference and conflict, but also an attempt to build coalitions around common goals rather than a denial of differences.[87] It is clear that this kind of pedagogy and exploration of experiences in a society in which privilege and oppression are lived is risky and filled with pain. Such a pedagogy suggests a more complex realization of the Freirean vision of the collective conscientization and struggle against oppression, one which acknowledges difference and conflict, but which, like Freire's vision, rests on a belief in the human capacity to feel, to know, and to change.

Notes

1. See as representative Henry Giroux, ed., *Postmodernism, Feminism and Cultural Politics* (Albany: State University of New York Press, 1991); Cleo Cherryholmes, *Power and Criticism: Poststructural Investigations in Education* (New York: Teachers College Press, 1988); Henry Giroux and Roger Simon, eds., *Popular Culture, Schooling and Everyday Life* (Westport, CT: Bergin & Garvey, 1989); Deborah Britzman, *Practice Makes Practice* (Albany: State University of New York Press, 1991); Patti Lather, *Getting Smart: Feminist Research and Pedagogy With/in the Postmodern* (New York: Routledge, 1991).

2. Paulo Freire, *Pedagogy of the Oppressed* (New York: Herder & Herder, 1971), p. 28.

3. Margo Culley and Catherine Portugues, "Introduction," in *Gendered Subjects* (Boston: Routledge & Kegan Paul, 1985). For comparisons of Freirean and feminist pedagogy, see also Frances Maher, "Classroom Pedagogy and the New Scholarship on Women," in *Gendered Subjects*, pp. 29–48, and "Toward a Richer Theory of Feminist Pedagogy: A Comparison of Liberation and 'Gender' Models for Teaching and Learning," *Journal of Education, 169*, No. 3 (1987), 91–100.

4. Antonio Gramsci, *Selections from the Prison Notebooks* (New York: International Publishers, 1971).

5. Teresa deLauretis, *Alice Doesn't: Feminism, Semiotics, Cinema* (Bloomington: Indiana University Press, 1984), p. 178.

6. Audre Lorde, *Sister Outsider* (Trumansburg, NY: The Crossing Press, 1984).

7. See, for example, Elizabeth Ellsworth, "Why Doesn't This Feel Empowering? Working Through the Repressive Myths of Critical Pedagogy," *Harvard Educational Review, 59* (1989), 297–324; Ann Berlak, "Teaching for Outrage and Empathy in the Liberal Arts," *Educational Foundations, 3*, No. 2 (1989), 69–94; Deborah Britzman, "Decentering Discourses in Teacher Education: Or, the Unleashing of Unpopular

Things," in *What Schools Can Do: Critical Pedagogy and Practice*, ed. Candace Mitchell and Kathleen Weiler (Albany: State University of New York Press, in press).

8. Freire's method of codifications and generative themes have been discussed frequently. Perhaps the best introduction to these concrete methods can be found in Paulo Freire, *Education for Critical Consciousness* (New York: Seabury Press, 1973).

9. See, for example, Paulo Freire, *The Politics of Education* (Westport, CT: Bergin & Garvey, 1985); Paulo Freire and Donaldo Macedo, *Literacy: Reading the Word and the World* (Westport, CT: Bergin & Garvey, 1987); Paulo Freire and Ira Shor, *A Pedagogy for Liberation* (London: Macmillan, 1987); Myles Horton and Paulo Freire, *We Make the Road by Walking: Conversations on Education and Social Change*, ed. Brenda Bell, John Gaventa, and John Peters (Philadelphia: Temple University Press, 1990).

10. Freire, *Pedagogy of the Oppressed*, p. 28.

11. Paulo Freire, "The Adult Literacy Process as Cultural Action for Freedom," in *The Politics of Education*, p. 57.

12. Freire and Macedo, *Literacy: Reading the Word and the World*.

13. See Simone de Beauvoir, *The Second Sex* (New York: Knopf, 1953), for a more striking use of the male referent.

14. Cameron McCarthy, "Rethinking Liberal and Radical Perspectives on Racial Inequality in Schooling: Making the Case for Nonsynchrony," *Harvard Educational Review, 58* (1988), 265–280.

15. Freire, *Pedagogy of the Oppressed*, p. 30.

16. Freire, *Pedagogy of the Oppressed*, p. 69.

17. Freire, *Pedagogy of the Oppressed*, p. 73.

18. Gayatri Chakravorty Spivak, "Can the Subaltern Speak?," in *Marxism and the Interpretation of Culture*, ed. Cary Nelson and Lawrence Grossberg (Urbana: University of Illinois Press, 1988), pp. 271–313.

19. Freire and Shor, *A Pedagogy for Liberation*, p. 93.

20. Peter McLaren, "Postmodernity and the Death of Politics: A Brazilian Reprieve," *Educational Theory, 36* (1986), p. 399.

21. When definitions of feminist pedagogy are attempted, they sometimes tend toward generalization and such a broad inclusiveness as to be of dubious usefulness. For example, Carolyn Shrewsbury characterizes pedagogy as follows:

    It does not automatically preclude any technique or approach. It does indicate the relationship that specific techniques have to educational goals. It is not limited to any specific subject matter but it does include a reflexive element that increases the feminist scholarship component involved in the teaching/learning of any subject matter. It has close ties with other liberatory pedagogies, but it cannot be subsumed under other pedagogical approaches. It is transformative, helping us revision the educational enterprise. But it can also be phased into a traditional approach or alternative pedagogical approach. (Shrewsbury, "What Is Feminist Pedagogy?," *Women's Studies Quarterly, 15*, Nos. 3–4 [1987], p. 12)

    Certain descriptions of feminist pedagogy show the influence of group dynamics and interactionist approaches. See, for example, Nancy Schniedewind, "Feminist Values: Guidelines for Teaching Methodology in Women's Studies," *Radical Teacher, 18*, 25–28. Methods used by feminist teachers include cooperation, shared leadership, and democratic process. Feminist teachers describe such techniques as keeping journals, soliciting students' responses to reading and to the classroom dynamics of a course, the use of role playing and theater games, the use of self-revelation on the part of the teacher, building leadership skills among students by requiring them to teach parts of a course, and contracting for grades. For accounts of classroom practice, see the articles in the special issue on feminist pedagogy of *Women's Studies Quarterly, 15*, Nos. 3–4 (1987); Culley and Portugues, *Gendered Subjects*; Charlotte Bunch and Sandra Pollack, eds., *Learning Our Way* (Trumansburg, NY: The Crossing Press, 1983); Gloria Hull, Patricia Bell Scott, and Barbara Smith, eds., *But Some of Us Are Brave* (Old Westbury, NY: The Feminist Press, 1982); and numerous articles in *Women's Studies Newsletter* and *Radical Teacher*.

22. Nancy Schniedewind, "Teaching Feminist Process," *Women's Studies Quarterly, 15*, Nos. 3–4 (1987), p. 29.

23. Linda Gordon, "A Socialist View of Women's Studies: A Reply to the Editorial, Volume 1, Number 1," *Signs, 1* (1975), p. 559.

24. A discussion of the relationship of the early women's liberation movement to the civil rights movement and the new left can be found in Sara Evans, *Personal Politics* (New York: Vintage Press, 1980). Based on extensive interviews as well as pamphlets and private documents, Evans shows the origins of both

political goals and methods in the earlier male-dominated movement, particularly the model of Black student organizers and the Black church in the South.

25. While mid-nineteenth century suffragist developed their ideas of human equality and justice through the abolitionist movement, by the late nineteenth century, White suffragists often demonstrated racist attitudes and employed racist strategies in their campaigns for suffrage. This offers another instructive parallel to the White feminist movement of the 1960s. Here, once again, feminist claims emerged out of an anti-racist struggle for civil rights, but later too often took up the universalizing stance that the experiences and issues of White women represented the lives of all women. See bell hooks, *Ain't I a Woman?* (Boston: South End Press, 1981) and *Feminist Theory for Margin to Center* (Boston: South End Press, 1984) for powerful discussions of these issues.

26. Nancy Hawley as quoted in Evans, *Personal Politics*, p. 205.

27. Kathie Sarachild, "Consciousness Raising: A Radical Weapon," in *Feminist Revolution*, ed. Redstockings (New York: Random House, 1975).

28. Redstockings included a number of women who were influential in the women's movement; Shulamith Firestone, Rosalyn Baxandall, Ellen Willis, and Robin Morgan were among a number of other significant feminist writers and activists who participated.

29. Sarachild, "Consciousness Raising," p. 144.

30. Sarachild, "Consciousness Raising," p. 145.

31. Michele Russell, "Black-Eyed Blues Connection: From the Inside Out," in Bunch and Pollack, *Learning Our Way*, pp. 272–284.

32. Sarachild, "Consciousness Raising," p. 147.

33. William Hinton, *Fanshen* (New York: Vintage Books, 1966).

34. See Berenice Fisher, "Guilt and Shame in the Women's Movement: The Radical Idea of Political Action and Its Meaning for Feminist Intellectuals," *Feminist Studies, 10* (1984), 185–212, for an extended discussion of the impact of the methods and goals of the civil rights movement on consciousness raising and the early women's liberation movement.

35. Sarachild, "Consciousness Raising," p. 145.

36. Sarachild, "Consciousness Raising," p. 147.

37. Irene Peslikis, "Resistances to Consciousness," in *Sisterhood Is Powerful*, ed. Robin Morgan (New York: Vintage Books, 1970), p. 339.

38. See, for example, Kathy McAfee and Myrna Wood, "Bread and Roses," in *Voices from Women's Liberation*, ed. Leslie Tanner (New York: New American Library, 1970) for an early socialist feminist analysis of the need to connect the women's movement with the class struggle.

39. Berenice Fisher, "What is Feminist Pedagogy?," *Radical Teacher, 18*, 20–25. See also bell hooks, "on self-recovery," in *talking back, thinking feminist, thinking black* (Boston: South End Press, 1989).

40. Marilyn Boxer, "For and about Women: The Theory and Practice of Women's Studies in the United States," in *Reconstructing the Academy: Women's Education and Women's Studies*, ed. Elizabeth Minnich, Jean O'Barr, and Rachel Rosenfeld (Chicago: University of Chicago Press, 1988), p. 71.

41. See Florence Howe, *Myths of Coeducation* (Bloomington: University of Indiana Press, 1984), for a collection of essays documenting this period.

42. Boxer estimates there were over 300 programs and 30,000 courses in women's studies given in 1982. See "For and about Women," p. 70.

43. The literature of feminist challenges to specific disciplines is by now immense. For general discussions of the impact of the new scholarship on women, see Ellen DuBois, Gail Kelly, Elizabeth Kennedy, Carolyn Korsmeyer, and Lillian Robinson, eds., *Feminist Scholarship: Kindling in the Groves of Academe* (Urbana: University of Illinois Press, 1985), and Christie Farnhum, ed., *The Impact of Feminist Research in the Academy* (Bloomington: Indiana University Press, 1987).

44. See, for example, Diana Fuss, *Essentially Speaking* (New York: Routledge, 1989); hooks, *talking back*; Britzman, *Practice makes Practice*.

45. Susan Stanford Friedman, "Authority in the Feminist Classroom: A Contradiction in Terms?," in Culley and Portugues, *Gendered Subjects*, 203–208.

46. hooks, *talking back*, p. 29.

47. See Alison Jaggar, *Feminist Politics and Human Nature* (Sussex, Eng.: The Harvester Press, 1983), for an excellent discussion of these perspectives.

48. Barbara Hillyer Davis, "Teaching the Feminist Minority," in Bunch and Pollack, *Learning Our Way*, p. 91.

49. See, for example, Eveylyn Torton Beck, "Self-disclosure and the Commitment to Social Change," *Women's Studies International Forum, 6* (1983), 159–164.

50. Margo Culley and Catherine Portugues, "The Politics of Nurturance," in *Gendered Subjects*, p. 12. See also Margo Culley, "Anger and Authority in the Introductory Women's Studies Classroom," in *Gendered Subjects*, pp. 209–217.

51. See Davis, "Teaching the Feminist Minority," for a thoughtful discussion of the contradictory pressures on the feminist teacher both to nurture and challenge women students.

52. Friedman, "Authority in the Feminist Classroom," p. 207.

53. Fisher, "What Is Feminist Pedagogy?," p. 22.

54. Fisher, "Guilt and Shame in the Women's Movement," p. 202.

55. Charlotte Bunch, "Not by Degrees: Feminist Theory and Education," in Bunch and Pollack, *Learning Our Way*, p. 156.

56. See Berenice Fisher, "Professing Feminism: Feminist Academics and the Woman's Movement," *Psychology of Women Quarterly, 7* (1982), 55–69, for a thoughtful discussion of the difficulties of retaining an activist stance for feminists in the academy.

57. See Arlie Russell Hochschild, *The Managed Heart* (Berkeley: University of California Press, 1983), for a discussion of the social construction of emotions in contemporary society. Hochschild argues that emotion is a "biologically given sense . . . and a means by which we know about our relation to the world" (p. 219). At the same time she investigates the ways in which the emotions themselves are manipulated and constructed.

58. Berenice Fisher, "The Heart Has Its Reasons: Feeling, Thinking, and Community Building in Feminist Education," *Women's Studies Quarterly, 15*, Nos. 3–4 (1987), 48.

59. Lorde, *Sister Outsider*, p. 37.

60. Lorde, *Sister Outsider*, p. 34.

61. Lorde, *Sister Outsider*, p. 123.

62. Lorde, *Sister Outsider*, p. 58.

63. Lorde, *Sister Outsider*, p. 53.

64. Lorde, *Sister Outsider*, p. 100.

65. Adrienne Rich, "Taking Women Students Seriously," in *On Lies, Secrets, and Silence*, ed. Adrienne Rich (New York: W. W. Norton, 1979), p. 243.

66. Sarachild, "Consciousness Raising," p. 148.

67. Fuss, *Essentially Speaking*, p. 114.

68. Fuss, *Essentially Speaking*, p. 118.

69. Frigga Haug, *Female Sexualization* (London: Verso Press, 1987).

70. Haug, *Female Sexualization*, p. 41.

71. Sistren Collective with Honor Ford-Smith, *Lionheart Girl: Life Stories of Jamaican Women* (London: The Women's Press, 1986), p. 15.

72. Chris Weedon, *Feminist Practice and Poststructuralist Theory* (Oxford: Basil Blackwell, 1987), p. 33.

73. Jane Flax, "Postmodernism and Gender Relations in Feminist Theory," *Signs, 12*, (1987), 621–643.

74. Donna Haraway, "A Manifesto for Cyborgs," *Socialist Review, 80* (1985), 72.

75. As representative, see Johnnella Butler, "Toward a Pedagogy of Everywoman's Studies," in Culley and Portugues, *Gendered Subjects*; hooks, *talking back*; Hull, Scott, and Smith, *But Some of Us Are Brave*; Gloria Joseph and Jill Lewis, *Common Differences: Conflicts in Black and White Perspectives* (New York: Anchor Books, 1981); Chierrie Moraga and Gloria Anzaldua, eds., *This Bridge Called My Back* (Watertown, MA: Persephone Press, 1981); Barbara Omolade, "A Black Feminist Pedagogy," *Women's Studies Quarterly, 15*, Nos. 3–4 (1987), 32–40; Russell, "Black-Eyed Blues Connection," pp. 272–284; Elizabeth Spelman, "Combating the Marginalization of Black Women in the Classroom," in Culley and Portugues, *Gendered Subjects*, pp. 240–244.

76. Combahee River Collective, "Combahee River Collective River Statement," in *Home Girls*, ed. Barbara Smith (New York: Kitchen Table—Women of Color Press, 1983), p. 275.

77. Combahee River Collective, "Combahee River Collective River Statement," p. 274.

78. Russell, "Black-Eyed Blues Connection," p. 155.

79. Omolade, "A Black Feminist Pedagogy," p. 39.

80. Combahee River Collective, "Combahee River Collective River Statement," p. 272.

81. Juliet Mitchell, *Women: The Longest Revolution* (New York: Pantheon Books, 1984).

82. Biddy Martin and Chandra Mohanty, "Feminist Politics: What's Home Got to Do With It?," in *Feminist Studies/Critical Studies*, ed. Teresa deLaurentis (Bloomington: University of Indiana Press, 1986), p. 208.

83. See, for example, Flax, "Postmodernism and Gender Relations in Feminist Theory"; Sandra Harding, *The Science Question in Feminism* (Ithaca: University of Cornell Press, 1986); Dorothy Smith, *The Everyday World as Problematic* (Boston: Northeastern University Press, 1987); Haraway, "A Manifesto for Cyborgs," *Socialist Review, 80* (1985), 64–107; Nancy Hartsock, *Money, Sex, and Power* (New York: Longman, 1983); Mary O'Brien, *The Politics of Reproduction* (Boston: Routledge & Kegan Paul, 1981); Irene Diamond and Lee Quinby, eds., *Feminism and Foucault* (Boston: Northeastern University Press, 1988); Linda Alcoff, "Cultural Feminism versus Post Structuralism: The Identity Crisis in Feminist Theory," *Signs, 13* (1988), 405–437; Special Issue on Feminism and Deconstruction, *Feminist Studies, 14*, No. 1 (1988); Judith Butler, *Gender Trouble* (New York: Routledge, 1990), Linda Nicholson, ed., *Feminism/Postmodernism* (New York: Routledge, 1990).

84. Fisher, "The Heart Has Its Reasons," p. 49.

85. Minnie Bruce Pratt, "Identity: Skin Blood Heart," in *Yours in Struggle*, ed. Elly Bulkin, Minnie Bruce Pratt, and Barbara Smith (Brooklyn, NY: Long Hand Press, 1984).

86. Martin and Mohanty, "What's Home Got to Do With It?"

87. Bernice Reagon, "Coalition Politics: Turning the Century," in Smith, *Home Girls*, pp. 356–369.

Classroom Pedagogy and the New Scholarship on Women

FRANCES MAHER

Introduction

What are the implications for classroom pedagogy as it relates to the new scholarship on women and the new consciousness of women's issues? This article is an analysis of the factors contributing to the need for particular pedagogies, or ways of teaching, when dealing with women as students and with women's experiences as subject-matter. The word 'pedagogy' is often defined to include curricular choices. Here, however, the focus will be on processes of teaching and learning, and classroom interactions as they relate to what and how people learn.

The assumptions behind this search for appropriate teaching styles for and about women are threefold. One is that, as Adrienne Rich says, 'women's minds and experiences are intrinsically valuable and indispensable to any civilization worth the name' (1979, p. 235). The second is that the public examination of women's lives, those of half the race, has been virtually buried until recently. Thus we need to construct a language, a world view (or views), a research methodology, and a pedagogy to discover, examine and describe a set of experiences which, up until now, did not officially exist.

Thirdly, appropriate teaching styles to recover the female experience can also be applied to the education of all people. Although women have been particularly silent and silenced, 'official' truths and traditional teaching methods have distorted other truths and experiences, as well—such as those of minority and working-class women and men. The traditional mode of university teaching, that of the lecture, presumes that an expert will present to the students an objective, rationally derived and empirically proven set of information. This mode, no matter how complete, can only reflect one version (usually the one dominant in the culture). It does not necessarily hold personal meaning for all students—they may simply memorize it on the teacher's terms, for a grade or career goal. (Thus we have the common distinction of learning 'for yourself' or for 'the test'.) Moreover, this traditional version of education as the wisdom of generations is especially pernicious for women (and other oppressed groups) because its content has often ignored or demeaned them. They are memorizing truths to which their own historical, cultural, and personal experience gives the lie.

A pedagogy appropriate for voicing and exploring the hitherto unexpressed perspectives of women and others must be collaborative, cooperative and interactive. It draws on a rich tradition going back to Paulo Freire, John Dewey, and even Socrates, of involving students in constructing and evaluating their own education. It assumes that each student has legitimate rights and potential contributions to the subject-matter. Its goal is to enable students to draw on their personal and intellectual experiences to build a satisfying version of the subject, one that they can use productively in their own lives. Its techniques involve students in the assessment and production, as well as the absorption, of the material. The teacher is a major contributor, a creator of structure and a delineator of issues, but not the sole authority.

This essay will first describe some sources of such an interactive pedagogy as it applies to women's concerns—namely, the needs and characteristics of women students, the nature of research on women and recent changes in the scholarly disciplines. It will next explain some components of this pedagogy as they may be practiced in classrooms. Finally, it will examine some further possible implications of interactive learning and teaching for women students, and for students as a whole.

Women Students in the Classroom

Women by now are over half the undergraduate population (Perun, 1982). Presumably they receive the same education and have the same college experience as men, including access to all college facilities, courses, and activities. Outside and inside the classroom, however, their experiences are very different from those of their male counterparts. College is a male-dominate hierarchy in which male professors hold social and intellectual sway over other males (their students and disciples) and females in many subordinate roles (their wives, secretaries and female students and disciples). Female professors are fewer in number (even in all-women's colleges they are seldom a majority), usually lower in status, and do not command a similar 'retinue' (see Rich, 1979, p. 137). In this regard, of course, college life reflects accurately many aspects of life in the society at large. Thus women students not only lack enough role models of women as scholars, but are faced with women in a variety of traditional, subordinate, and demeaning roles even as they are presumably enjoying equal educational opportunities and status.

We are most concerned here, however, with the classroom setting. How are women, and women's experiences, devalued *inside* the classroom? Paulo Freire and others have described oppressed peoples in traditional and authoritarian societies as being denied their own voices and experiences by the imposition of the single dominant worldview of 'the oppressor' as the only reality. In the traditional model of education that Freire portrays, the teacher (representing the oppressor) is the sole authority and the 'Subject' (capitalization as original) of the learning process; he chooses the content which the oppressed students passively accept. In essence, he makes deposits of predetermined information into the empty vaults of students' minds (see Freire, 1970, p. 59). The application of this concept of 'banking education' to women in modern American society is striking.[1] Men in general have often been described as the 'subject' for which women are the 'object'. More importantly, women are silenced, objectified and made passive through both the course content and the pedagogical style of most college classrooms.

First, academic disciplines ignore and distort the experience of women as a group by structuring their concepts and subject-matter around male-derived norms. Second, however, the dominant pedagogical style of most classrooms discriminates against women's experience and participation in a variety of ways, all of which reinforce female passivity. Professors—male and, sometimes, female—tend to call on women students less in discussion, to ask them less probing questions, and to interrupt them more often. They make more frequent eye-contact with men and are more attentive to male questions or comments (see Thorne, 1975, quoted in Hale and Sandler, 1982, pp. 7–9). On a deeper level, classroom discussions (as well as lectures) are usually conducted so as to reward 'assertive speech,' competitive 'devil's advocate' interchanges, and impersonal and abstract styles—often incorporating the generic 'he' (*ibid.*, pp. 9, 10). These modes of speech, while perhaps not inherently 'masculine,' seem more natural to men in this culture; women tend to be more tentative, polite, and hesitant in their comments and thus are taken less seriously by teachers. Women who try to be more assertive face a double bind, for they are perceived as 'hostile' females rather than as 'forceful' men. Perhaps as a result of this treatment, as well as the subject-matter, women college students as a group are simply more silent than men. Like Freire's 'oppressed,' they do not speak up; their experiences, their interpretations, their questions are not heard as often.

What are the implications of this analysis for interpreting and changing current classroom practices? At the root of the problem of awakening women students is a recognition of the central validity of their own perceptions in choosing and interpreting their education. In order for the oppressed to be liberated, according to Freire, their experiences under the oppressors must be raised to the level of personal consciousness, recognized and affirmed. Then teachers and students can be equals in a cooperative search for understanding about the experiences of people in their world (Freire, 1970, p. 67).

In this light we can begin to see the primary importance of the inclusion of women's perspectives in the subject-matter disciplines. But we can also reexamine women's patterns of classroom participation and see them as cooperative and constructive, rather than non-assertive and hesitant. Common patterns of competition and argument in discussion came not only from 'masculine' modes of speech, but from traditional notions of learning, wherein we search for objective truth and the single 'right answer' rather than for shared and comparative conclusions about multiple experiences. In fact, Hale and Sandler, in their research on college women's classroom experiences, intimate that 'feminine' styles might be more conducive to a notion of discussion as a 'cooperative development of ideas' rather than as 'competition from the floor.' They describe women's tendency to end questions with a questioning intonation, encouraging the next speaker to elaborate. They quote findings to show more class participation by both sexes in courses taught by women, although women teachers are not immune to the discriminatory practices we have been describing (Hale and Sandler, 1982, p. 10).

Simply in terms of classroom interactions, then, we can suggest that teaching practices which stress cooperative rather than competitive participation may encourage more women students (and more students) actively to question and examine the implications of the material they are learning for their own experience and their own lives, thus better addressing their educational needs and priorities. (For a specific description of a graduate course in sociology using such methodologies, and its effects on students, see Nelson, 1981.) Some components of such an interactive pedagogy are described below; I wish now, however, briefly to indicate several ways in which interactive teaching practices are related to both methodology and content in the field of Women's Studies.

The Nature of Research on Women

In every scholarly discipline wherein the female experience has been explored, the new scholarship on women has challenged not only the scope, the content, and the conclusions of the field, but also the research methods by which the knowledge in the field has been derived in the first place. Scholars concerned with women have evolved, not coincidentally, a methodology which reflects the nature of the information they are now seeking and also the kind of teaching practices described here. This methodology involves a conceptualization of knowledge as a comparison of multiple perspectives leading towards a complex and evolving view of reality. Each new contribution reflects the perspective of the person giving it, each has something to offer. This methodology replaces the search for a single, objective, rationally derived 'right answer' that stands outside the historical source or producer of that answer. Instead, it aims for the construction of knowledge from multiple perspectives through cooperation problem-solving.

What are some components of this 'interactive' research methodology? As said above, in every scholarly discipline concerned with human behavior, generalizations about 'man' have hidden women's experiences—which have often been different, even opposite. Thus, women's roles have been demeaned, ignored, privatized, and/or made the exception. Men have been the subjects of the actions, women the objects. If women's experiences are to be equally represented, then, we must locate and describe these experiences, analyze them, and give them theoretical and conceptual frameworks. Since prior frameworks have hitherto reflected only male perspectives, however, Women's Studies challenges the validity of any *single* 'objectively derived' framework within which to describe our experiences. There are 'women's' version and 'man's,' and 'young black men,' and so on. In this regard, we must acknowledge the subjectivity of the researcher, and the role of his or her perspective in the construction and interpretation of knowledge. We must also replace a search for one universal truth or explanation with a search for shared meanings, for comparative approaches, for what any one of many perspectives has to offer (or challenge) the others.

Thus the study of women calls for a research methodology that acknowledges the multiple context within which knowledge is produced. In fact, as Marcia Westcott says, such a methodological approach 'converges with the interpretive tradition in the social sciences . . . Social knowledge is always interpreted within historical contexts, and truths are, therefore, historical rather than abstract, contingent rather than categorical.' Why does the study of women imply such a methodology? Because 'the (traditional) concept of the human being is only the man writ large . . . The *specificity* of the knower is only revealed when women become subjects of knowledge, because women are not identified with the abstract human being but with particular deviations or negations of this abstracted universal' (Westcott, 1979, pp. 422, 426). In other words, Women's Studies as subject-matter reflects the particularistic, historical and contextual nature of all our conceptualizations of human society. To study women as *subjects*, equal to men, is to recognize that human experiences are multiple and must be multiply interpreted.

A similar conception of methodology has been applied to the natural sciences as well. While acknowledging 'objectivity' as the goal of scientific method, Longino (1981) argues that scientific observations are, in fact, dependent on theoretical formulations which often compete with each other to explain the same facts. Therefore, 'there is no independent field of facts (for recourse); scientists work within logically independent and incomparable world views determined by their paradigms.' Given such disagreement, she reformulates the notion of science as 'something practiced not primarily by individuals but by groups.' Again, knowledge is conceived as the accretion of mutually critical perspectives, each reflecting 'background beliefs which can be articulated and subjected to criticism from the scientific community' (*ibid.*, p. 191).

In another context, Catherine MacKinnon (1982, p. 537) also argues that women's experiences outside the male paradigm allow them to critique the existence of any single paradigm:

> Feminism does not see its view as subjective, partial, or undermined but as a critique of the purported generality, disinterestedness and universality of prior accounts. A perspectivity (or objectivity) is revealed as a strategy of male hegemony . . . Power to create the whole world from (a single) point of view is power in its male form.

The worldview expressed in the traditional disciplines, calling itself universal, in fact only reflect the experiences and purposes of one group, giving them an exclusive power over the definition of knowledge which was denied to everyone else. Going further than Westcott and Longino, MacKinnon then asserts that feminist method, by legitimizing the study of women's experiences, gives women a new means of understanding and coming to terms with their own personal condition. 'Feminist method,' she says, 'is consciousness raising; the collective critical reconstitution of the meaning of women's social experience, as women live through it.' It could also, presumably, include men's experience, as men live through it, if handled in collective and consciousness-raising fashion. In either case, knowledge should be defined, interpreted and created so as to empower different groups of people to understand (and improve) their own lives.

As we have already seen, Freire's concern is for oppressed peoples (males); his approach is consciousness-raising is through pedagogy, no research. Yet he raises similar concerns. In defining the terms of his pedagogy, he calls for a search for 'generative themes' that describe the relations between men and their world. He says that such themes cannot be found 'in men, divorced from reality, not yet in reality, divorced from men . . . [they] can only be apprehended in a man-world relationship.' In this search, research, teaching and learning all become part of the same educative process. Teachers and students become 'co-investigators' both in the discovery of knowledge and the frameworks that give it meaning. Because of this integral relationship between knower and known, 'the methodology proposed requires that the investigators and the people should act as co-investigators. The more active an attitude men take in regard to the explanation of their thematics, the more they deepen their critical awareness of reality and . . . take possession of that reality.' Answering the charge that the people, because searching for personal meaning, will destroy objectivity, he echoes Longino: 'the same objective fact could evoke different complexes of generative themes in different epochs.' (Freire, 1970, pp. 97–8)

Giving students the tools to discover themes for themselves will allow them to understand reality on their own terms. Like MacKinnon, Freire is concerned with knowledge for social change: once able to name, evoke and describe their oppression, people will act to transform it.

Thus, for many scholarly researchers, the study of women involves a major methodological shift. They are moving away from the traditional search for objectivity and towards a multilayered and comparative construction of social realities. In this search they acknowledge their own subjectivity, even as they try to transcend it by listening to, and drawing on, the experiences of others. To go back to the classroom with this perspective is immediately to recognize its relevance to interactive pedagogies, which draw on students' experiences not only for their own learning, but also to enrich the interpretation and materials of the discipline itself.

The Scholarly Disciplines and Women's Studies

Another source of pedagogical change implied by the new research on women is the change in the scholarly disciplines themselves and, therefore, in the content of course offerings. The new scholarship on women has begun to alter the standards of judgment, the concepts and the generalizations in almost every discipline, by enlarging the scope of experiences to be included. While a discussion of all these changes is obviously beyond the scope of this article, we can briefly examine the pedagogical implications of such changes in two disciplines—history and psychology. In history, attention to women has been a means of examining social history and of studying 'ordinary people's lives, both in the public and private spheres. Feminist scholars attempt to examine all aspects of human society as engaged in by both men and women: the family, popular culture, the workplace, and religious, philanthropic, and educational institutions, as well as politics and laws. Even the study of politics has changed; the social root of political movements are explored in the motives and goals of reformers and their followers.

Obviously, the inclusion of women's lives has in itself a liberating effect on the education of female students. They are not learning 'the history of man' while being denied the knowledge of any history of their own. But because women have been not only an ignored but an oppressed group, to describe historical experience from the perspective of female lives is to liberate women (and men) students in another way. If history is not only the story of 'great men,' then students can use and critically evaluate it to locate themselves as 'ordinary people' in historical time and place. They can explore the popular roots of historical change and development in terms of their own position in society. For example, they can investigate the histories in their own families, examining particular occupational and gender roles to illustrate wider social trends. Pedagogically, a history which includes the experiences of women calls for a multiplicity of perspectives and experiences in the past and the present which students can explore.

In psychology the impact of the new scholarship of women has also been profound. The equation of male psychological development with the 'norm,' particularly for Freud and his followers, left women inherently inferior (and silenced), because of their lack of assertiveness, individuation, rationality, and 'objective' standard of moral judgment. The recent work of Chodorow (1978), Gilligan (1982), and others, however, has given us a picture of 'normal' female development as differently staged, toward different ends, than that of males. In these models, the interpersonal and responsive qualities of females are conceptualized not as 'inferior' and failed struggles for a (masculine) autonomy, but as particular strengths. Gilligan, for example, speaks of a female network of caring relationships to complement the hierarchies of moral choices based on male notions of abstract justice (Gilligan, 1982, chapter 2).

For educators, this psychology does more than describe a new perspective. The research illuminates and legitimizes female behavior in classrooms and elsewhere. For example, women in our culture, socialized differently from men, quite often have different speech patterns and ways of expressing themselves. We can say that some of these patterns, such as the hesitation mentioned earlier, come from actual (and perceived) powerlessness; they might also, however, come from a regard for other points of view. In either case, women's modes of expression are not 'less articulate'; they are different. The new psychological research also challenges the whole concept of what behaviors and attitudes constitute 'normal' or healthy development, in much the same way as the new historical research enlarges the concept of legitimate history. In both subjects, the range of legitimate, permissible, and valid experiences expands not simply from one or two, but from one to many. Instead of women as 'inferior' men, or blacks (and black women) as 'inferior' whites, we can perceive and articulate varieties of psychic health in a variety of situations. Third, some scholars have attempted, while exploring the differences between men and women, to locate areas of similarity and complementary as well. Lifting the rigid mantle of contemporary sex-role socialization and gender identification gives us all an expanded emotional and intellectual repertoire. Again, the implications for pedagogy of these changes in the discipline of psychology are obvious. Students, in being encouraged to relate psychological insights to their own experience simultaneously learn and evaluate psychological theories (and their empirical basis), and can contribute to their ongoing formulation. An interactive and cooperative pedagogy, drawing on all the available perspectives in class, is therefore not only appropriate but necessary.

Components of Interactive Pedagogy

The needs of the students, of the research process, and of the disciplines themselves thus all require an interactive pedagogy for the treatment of women's experiences. While women students (and many men) have been silenced in college classrooms, a new process of relating subject-matter to student needs and interests depends upon the active participation of all students, particularly women, whose experiences (and voices) have until recently been considered illegitimate. Such a process also draws on the 'female' modes of collaborative, rather than competitive, interaction. Researchers have turned away from a competitive search for the one best theory or explanation of phenomena (which can then be 'taught to students) towards a collaborative, evolutionary and complementary approach (which can be opened up to include student views). In addition, the content of major disciplines is being reshaped to accept multiple viewpoints as equally valid, particularly those which have been unexpressed and suppressed before. Therefore, student contributions can enrich interpretations in the discipline as well as in their own learning.

What are some concrete and practical aspects of this 'interactive' pedagogy? How does subject-matter presentation change? What are some roles and activities of the teacher and student? How can classes be structured? What issues and problems need further discussion?

Subject-matter Presentation

A subject-mater that denies or contradicts a student's own experience can still be absorbed in several ways. Students may 'learn' it on its own terms, without expecting the content to have any personal relevance or meaning. For instance, many have memorized historical facts and dates, and even used them appropriately in essays, without ever having experiential reference-points for these facts. A second mode of reception is that of misunderstanding. A teacher may describe a law as 'progressive,' a certain family as 'middle class,' or a person as 'depressed.' In each of these cases, students may 'understand' these words in a different sense from the one the teacher intends, and thus perhaps misinterpret course assignments and representations. In either of the above examples, the traditional lecture approach leaves no room for clarification. Obviously, the more distant the students' own experience from the subject-matter as defined by the teacher, the more difficult and alienating this lack of understanding will be (as in women's exclusion from male-derived norms and concepts).

However, training in all disciplines involves the study of unfamiliar terms or terms used in discipline-specific ways. Thus, if we want our students to construct both an accurate and personally meaningful version of our subject-matter—one that can be discussed and built on with the teacher and each other—we must begin with the construction of a common vocabulary and language among teacher and students. Too often we assume that students attach the same attributes to key concepts as we do. In our formulation, we often use one term which is unfamiliar to students to describe another unfamiliar term—leaving them confused and reduced to rote memorization and passive learning (see Maher and Lyman, 1982). Teachers can begin classes by asking students for their *own* meanings for key terms, and then using these in the definitions of new ones. For example, students in an educational psychology class are asked to evaluate the concept of 'intelligence' as it relates to IQ testing. To prepare for this discussion, they write an essay entitled 'How Smart I Am' to express their own experience of this loaded and controversial concept.

For Paulo Freire, this act of naming our experiences is a crucial step in the awakening of the consciousness of the oppressed. The essence of dialogue is the 'word.' By constructing common names and meanings for their realities, people describe and activate the world for each other—and, in doing so, may change it. Once armed with the concept of 'exploitation,' for example, they can begin to define its features and interpret them: 'Dialogue is the encounter between men, mediated by the world, in order to name the world' (Freire, 1970, p. 76). In our terms, *women* need to name and describe our world, to differentiate its terms and meanings from those of male experience, if only to see our commonalities as well. (For example, is 'depression' different for women than for men? How can the two forms be described and compared?) Until teachers explicitly work toward constructing a commonly understood language in their classrooms, the subject-matter concepts will be alien to some students' experiences.

A more fundamental change in subject-matter presentation involves making explicit connections in course topics among the three levels of theory, research, and the students' (and teacher's) own observations and experiences. As students explore different explanatory models for data discussed in courses, they learn that the validity of any strong theory comes from its ability to explain aspects of both learned about and personally experienced reality. They also learn some ways in which different perspectives, including their own, help to determine what data is used and considered important. Thus Bunch (1979) has students compare personal solutions to set discrimination issues with those of feminist theorists. In my educational psychology course the students (all female) contrast a new model of female moral development (Gilligan, 1982) to the more traditional approaches of Kohlberg, Piaget and others. They analyze their own thinking in relation to these theories through class discussions of moral dilemmas. In so doing, they are able not only to challenge a previously held norm, but also to reassess the universal applicability of all such stage theories to explain human development.

In another course, students examine sexism in schools—the controversy over girls and math, discriminatory tracking and counseling practices, and classroom interaction patterns that favor boys. They compare research findings to classroom observations and to their own experiences as females in school. They look at explanatory models for this discrimination from feminist and non-feminist schools of thought. (For example, are girls' minds genetically different, or socially programmed for different interests?) Relating theory, research, and experience in this way, they can begin to think of ways schools might serve not only girls, but a wide variety of students perhaps previously ignored or demeaned by the imposition of a single academic norm.

The Roles of Teacher and Student

Beyond such new treatment of subject-matter topics described above, there are several related ways of transforming our pedagogy to reflect the collaborative and interactive nature of the new scholarship on women. If this work has legitimized the study of ordinary lives from multiple perspectives, and made explicit the connection between the framework of the knower and what is known, then students and teachers can use their own experience in the creation, as well as the illustration, of course topics. One way to do this is by the use of the 'self as subject.' Student educational autobiographies in education courses and family trees and family history in history courses are examples of this approach. In one education course, students analyze the significance for both women's roles and the education profession of the fact that most teachers in America have been women. (See, for example, Grumet, 1981.) In a related discussion of their educational family trees, students in one class found that *every* grandmother who worked was at one time a teacher. This common background, besides giving these education students a strong sense of historical identification and persisting societal norms, also encouraged them to reevaluate their own possible choice of teaching as a career. Central to this inclusion of the self as subject, however, is the teacher's acknowledgment of his or her perspective as, of necessity, a partial one as well. Instead of presenting all course topics and materials as objective truth, the teacher must be explicit about his or her rationale behind the choice of readings, issues and so on.

There is here, as we have said above, an admitted 'intersubjectivity of meaning of subject and object . . . the questions that the investigator asks of the object of knowledge grow out of her own concerns and experiences' (Westcott, 1979, p. 426). Westcott and others see this dialectical relationship between self and material as particularly powerful for women studying women, because 'knowledge of the other and knowledge of the self are mutually informing . . . self and other share a common condition of being women.' However, this paradigm may illustrate any exploration in which aspects of personal identity illuminate the subject-matter—whether workers studying workers, Italians studying Italians, and so on. The interpretation of particular masculine experiences as generalized truths has denied such insights to many groups. Students and teachers using the 'self as subject' can call up and legitimize a variety of hitherto unexplored experiences and themes. (The validly and power of self-examination, and explicit subjectivity, in contributing to a personally meaningful education has also been recently explicated by many modern curriculum theorists. See, for example, Freire, 1970; Greene, 1975; and Mitrano, 1981.)

A second way of empowering students as experts is to use the notion of the 'self as inquirer.' Here, more than in other modes of teaching, we are asking our students not only to answer questions, but to pose them; to become creators and constructors, as well as learners, of knowledge. We can assign them topics to pursue in which they take a particular interest (once again being explicit about the connection between knowledge and knower); their research can then be challenged and enriched by each other's contributions and perspectives. Such assignments can make individuals or groups responsible for constructing components of the course: in a government course, for example, students can research and present the policies of a particular party, country, or pressure group. Or assignments can illustrate or examine course theories: as mentioned above, student field observations in elementary schools can test presumed differences in boy/girl behavior raised in education and psychology classes. Thus, student research into the experiences of particular groups can build on and/or transform theories or hypotheses introduced in class. Such research gives the material personal importance for students, as well as enriching the discipline itself.

The Structure of Classes and Courses

This consideration of students as 'subjects' and 'inquirers' involves, however, the serious inclusion of their contributions in both the presentation and the structuring of our courses. Thus, in interactive and democratic teaching modes the most common form of communication is discussion, not lecture. The teacher (or student) raises a problem from the readings; students explore its meaning and ramifications, relate it to their own experiences, consider solutions and so on. The teacher may have been responsible for the selection of the reading and the framing of the problem, but the discussion legitimizes the experience of all in analyzing it. Hence, both teacher and students can play the role of both experts and learners.

In conducting discussions, teachers need to encourage students to listen and react to each other's statements, and to put student comments on the board for emphasis. To gain maximum participation, discussion on specific topics can be arranged in small groups, with results reported to the class as a whole and emphasized by the teacher. In general, habits of inferiority and passivity, of looking to the teacher for the answer, have to be deliberately challenged to be broken. We can be explicit that a course relies on student contributions and formulations, but we must also arrange classroom discussion so that this reliance is genuine. With women students (especially silenced) and Women's Studies (until recently not considered a legitimate field of inquiry) such new patterns should be particularly emphasized.

Differences among students are often an issue in ongoing class discussions. Some students are more vocal than others: for example, males tend to volunteer more answers than females. Females, and quieter students, need to be explicitly encouraged; to be called on when not volunteering and to be placed in small groups where participation may be easier. Students with differing perspectives may also actively disagree. They may not see each other's perspectives as mutually reinforcing, but as conflicting—which is sometimes the case. For example, in a recent Women's Studies case, working-class white women and upper-middle-class black women argued extensively over the relative weight of class and race in female oppression. Each group had both personal experience and evidence to support their position. More specifically, as Davis points out, 'feminist' students whose consciousness has already been raised may feel uncomfortable with their more traditional sisters. 'However "advanced" their intellectual and emotional grasp of feminist issues, [they] often lack empathy with or respect for the hard choices and important conflicts of traditional women' (Davis, 1981, p. 8).

For differences and divisions like these (and again such differences can come up in any classroom where multiple perspectives are discussed), the teacher can function as a 'simultaneous translator . . . hearing and giving back in other words what another person has just said, and presenting an explanation in another language which will illuminate the issue for a second group without alienating the first' (*ibid.*, p. 9). In such discussions, the prior creation of common definitions for terms and a common language for the group is particularly important. If all agree on what 'social class' means, then unnecessary misunderstanding can be avoided. Furthermore, the teacher can both model and explain the rationale for her translating activities. A more complete view of the world does not come from dichotomizing views into 'good' or 'bad,' 'right' or 'wrong,' but rather using them to build a more complex picture of the problem. This stance does not, and should not, minimize conflict or disagreement: it clarifies it and seeks to put it in a larger context. In addition, students can also be taught to listen to, and to translate, each other's languages and concerns. In this way, they may replace their own search for 'right answers' with a critical understanding and evaluation of their own and others' perspectives.

Second, courses can be structured so as to depend on, and draw from, student research as an integral part of the course work itself (rather than scheduling 'oral reports' at the end). Several students can read and comment on each other's papers before they are presented in class, so that the students can lead a discussion of the paper. Students can research topics that illuminate and build on course themes; such topics can become an integral part of the course syllabus (as in history via family trees, or psychology via biography and autobiography.) A related teacher responsibility may be to train students in the appropriate research and writing skills for successfully completing such assignments. Depending on the level of the students, teachers may hand out guidelines for research papers, for the use of the library and so on. Teachers can also encourage students to help each other on projects. Students may be put in cooperative groups for research as well as discussion purposes (see the work of David and Roger Johnson, 1975).

Related Issues

Classes and courses can thus be deliberately structured to build on, and encourage, active student (and teacher) involvement in a collaborative learning enterprise. Other issues and considerations arise, however. There are differences *among* students, to which we assign relative value in the form of grades. Grading policies vary and are controversial. An interactive pedagogy may imply that students grade themselves, or are involved in the process by which criteria for grades are set. However, teachers who wish to retain these powers of grading can be explicit about the criteria they themselves use. Written guidelines for conducting discussions, for research papers and for projects, as mentioned above, can function as checklists of evaluative criteria which are actually applied to student work. Many teachers also allow rewrites of papers after comments are discussed.

Finally, a word about large classes. This essay has assumed group sizes appropriate for discussions. In classes of forty, eighty, or more, can we use interactive pedagogies? Outside lectures, students can be divided into reading and discussion groups, or task forces for particular assignments and projects. The teacher can occasionally take class time to meet with these groups, and can schedule student-led presentations and discussions, as well. However, the structure of the university, in which large lecture courses are a dominant mode, is a paradigm for the traditional concept of knowledge as a fixed store of information and expertise to be pumped into passive student minds. The content of this knowledge has been masculine experiences, standards, and worldviews; its form is oppressive and exclusive. Even were the content of lectures in this mode to be replaced with a "Women's Studies' content, it has been the thrust of this essay that such *forms* of both research and teaching must be changed to reflect the existence of multiple experiences of the world.

Conclusions

This essay has described some features of classroom pedagogy to fulfill women's needs as students in relation to classroom treatment of the new scholarship on women. The evaluation of female concerns into our consciousness and our curriculum has demonstrated the falsity and incompleteness of previous worldviews. It has imposed on us a search for multiple truths and perspectives, and showed us the integral connection between knower and known. Women's Studies has specifically challenged the teacher/expert-student/novice dichotomy by the inclusion of personal experience, private life, and popular history in our subject-matter—how can we simply 'tell' people about their own lives?

However, throughout this essay there has also been an attempt to link the lessons derived from the creation of a 'feminist' pedagogy to the consideration of pedagogy in general. The powers of creating and dispensing knowledge in our universities are at base only reflections of, and continuing guarantees of, powers in our social institutions at large. Both control over our social institutions and control over our education have been in the hands of white upper-class and middle-class males. Movements for equal voices in the universities, on the part of minorities and women, have always paralleled, supported, and been supported by, movements for social and legal equality in the wider society. Thus, there is a clear connection between the women's suffrage movement and the earliest female PhDs, the civil rights movement and Black Studies, the struggle for Equal Rights Amendment and the new scholarship on women.

The pedagogical implications of this relationship are several. An interactive and democratic approach to knowledge and to pedagogy is appropriate for all oppressed groups seeking consciousness of their own past and future aims and identities. Men, too, can learn to think and learn 'like women.' Second, those forces against a realization of full equality in the wider society have their counterparts in the university. It is of course misleading to view the proponents of 'objective' science, 'great books' and traditional expertise simply as mouthpieces for the political status quo. However, the exclusivity of their hold on the definition of 'worth-while' knowledge must be actively challenged, rather than ignored.

The implications of a full implementation of the educational approaches outlined here are profound. First, we need to conduct research into both interactive and traditional classrooms, dealing with both Women's Studies and traditional subject-matters. What effect does the study of women's experiences in particular have on the cognitive development and personal confidence of female students? Do interactive pedagogies promote greater self-realization than the traditional lecture mode? How does the active involvement of the students with the subject-matter affect the meanings they give to their education? We need studies that further explore both the nature and the effects of the teaching practices outlined above. (For reviews of the current status of research in Women's Studies and teaching effectiveness see Boxer, 1982; and Porter and Eileenchild, 1980. Porter recommends 'an approach to research and evaluation that acknowledges the interaction between students, teacher and the subject matter and seeks to establish relationships between multiple variables that obtain in teaching and learning.') However, there are also implicit assumptions here about the value of interactive teaching and the inclusion of female and minority experiences as a framework for designing courses in all disciplines.

We want to educate women (and men) to realization of the full worth and legitimacy of their own experience, as well as that of others. But can we really imagine a society that takes female voices as seriously as male voices, black voices as seriously as white ones, working-class voices as seriously as managerial ones? Inside the classroom we can dismantle, disperse and democratize the powers of knowledge and the means of acquiring it. However, we also need to examine explicitly the dimensions of the society our students will enter. A recent essay on Women's Studies and the academic disciplines pointed out that 'we especially gain from [the new work on women] many tools for understanding American life, so that we need not perpetuate the tenacious falsehood that in our culture any individual can do whatever he or she wants to do' (MacIntosh, 1982, p. 31). We need to explore the wider political implications of our democratic pedagogy—what it shows us about both our society and the kind of society we desire. Otherwise it will indeed continue to be the case that 'Women's Studies' are peripheral, and not as important as those 'great books' which allegedly prepare us for life in the mainstream.

Notes

1. The relevance of Freire's work for women is ironic because Freire never mentions women. He uses 'people,' sometimes, but usually discussed men: 'It is not surprising that the banking concept of education regards men as adaptable, manageable beings' (Freire, 1970, p. 60).

References

Boxer, Marilyn (1982), 'For and About Women, the Theory and Practice of Women's Studies in the United States,' *Signs: Journal of Women in Culture and Society*, vol. 7, no. 2, summer, pp. 661–95.

Bunch, Charlotte (1979), 'Not By Degrees," *Quest*, vol. 5, no. 1, summer, pp. 7–18.

Chodorow, Nancy (1978), *The Reproduction of Mothering*, Berkeley: University of California Press.

Davis, Barbara Hillyer (1981), 'Teaching the Feminist Minority,' *Women's Studies Quarterly*, vol. 9, no. 4, winter, pp. 7–9. Reprinted as ch. 22 in the present work.

Freire, Paulo (1970), *Pedagogy of the Oppressed*, New York: Continuum, 17th printing, 1981.

Gilligan, Carol (1982), *In A Different Voice, Psychological Theory and Women's Development*, Cambridge, Mass.: Harvard University Press.

Greene, Maxine (1975), 'Curriculum and Cultural Transformation,' *Cross Currents*, vol. 25, no. 2, summer, pp. 175–86.

Grumet, Madeleine (1981), 'Pedagogy for Patriarchy: The Feminization of Teaching,' *Interchange on Educational Policy*, vol. 12, nos 2/3, pp. 165

Hale, Roberta, and Bernice Sandler (1982), *The Classroom Climate: A Chilly One For Women?* Project on the Status and Education of Women, Washington, DC: American Association of Colleges.

Johnson, David, and Roger Johnson (1975), *Learning Together and Alone*, Englewood Cliffs, New Jersey: Prentice-Hall

Longino, Helen (1981), 'Scientific Objectivity and Feminist Theorizing,' *Liberal Education*, fall, pp. 187–95

MacKinnon, Catherine (1982), 'Feminism, Marxism, Method and the State: An Agenda for Theory,' *Signs: Journal of Women in Culture and Society*, vol. 7, no 3, spring, pp. 515–45

MacIntosh, Peggy (1982), 'Warning, the new Scholarship on Women May Be Hazardous to Your Ego,' *Women's Studies Quarterly*, vol. 10, no. 1, spring, pp. 29–31

Maher, Frances, and Kathleen Lyman (1982), 'Definitions of Social Studies Concepts: A Precondition for Inquiry,' unpublished paper, December.

Mitrano, Barbara (1982), 'Feminism and Curriculum Theory, Implications for Teacher Education,' *Journal of Curriculum Theorizing*, vol. 3, no. 2, summer, pp. 5–85

Nelson, Randle (1982), 'Reading, Writing and Relationship: Toward Overcoming the Hidden Curriculum of Gender, Ethnicity and Socio-economic Class,' *Interchange on Educational Policy*, vol. 12, nos 2 and 3, pp. 229–42

Perun, Pamela (1982), *The Undergraduate Woman, Issues in Educational Equality*, Chapter 1, 'The Undergraduate Woman, Theme and Variations,' Lexington, Mass.: D. C. Heath, pp. 3014

Porter, Nancy, and Margaret Eileenchild (1980), *The Effectiveness of Women's Studies Teaching*, Women's Studies Monograph Series, Washington DC: National Institute of Education.

Rich, Adrienne (1979), *On Lies, Secrets and Silence*, New York: Norton

Throne, Barrie, and Nancy Henley (1975), *Language and Sex, Difference and Dominance*, Rowley, Mass.: Newbury House Publishers.

Westcott, Marcia (1979), 'Feminist Criticism of the Social Sciences,' *Harvard Educational Review*, vol. 49, no. 4, November, pp. 422–30

PART III
CONSTRUCTING CURRICULA: PLANNING AND IMPLEMENTATION

Introduction

Up to this point we have explored various frames of reference on curriculum and examined historic and contemporary debates over what knowledge should be included in the undergraduate curriculum and how knowledge should be taught. These understandings provide a philosophical and historical foundation for our next area of inquiry: curriculum planning, development, and change. In this section, we include readings that address various theoretical and applied approaches to developing curricula and also devote space to writings that chronicle the political, intellectual, socio-cultural, and structural dynamics of curriculum change. We do not offer these readings as a definitive "cookbook" for curricular planning and development; to the contrary, our hope is that readers will use these ideas as "thinking devices" to stimulate dialogue about curriculum development and change in their own settings.

Whether planning a formal course, a student affairs workshop, or our own learning plans, all of us have been involved in developing curricula. More than likely, we approached this task from many different starting points. Some of us, for example, probably began by identifying goals and learning objectives and then planned learning experiences designed to achieve those goals. Others may have focused less on purposes and goals and instead sought to make key choices within specific "decision arenas." Still others may have tried to fit their curriculum into a pre-existing plan or model. In each of these instances, those engaged in the planning and development process constructed curriculum; that is, each played an active role in interpreting and defining what the curriculum would look like, how it would be structured, and who it would supposedly serve.

The first four articles in this section discuss various approaches to designing curriculum. William Toombs and William Tierney, for example, begin by casting a wide net on the topic, conceptualizing curriculum planning more as a "problem in design" than as one of "philosophy or technique." Toward this end, they highlight the key role that faculty play in shaping, developing, and refining curricula. From here, Clifton Conrad and Anne Pratt offer a critique of traditional curricular planning models in the literature and then introduce an approach to curriculum development that isolates key variables and interactions that might affect the curricular decision-making process. James Davis emphasizes the importance of establishing goals, clarifying objectives, and identifying "organizing principles" in what many have described as a "rational" approach to planning and designing curriculum. Finally, we offer a "decision-situation" approach that places student and faculty experiences squarely at the center of planning and draws attention to the contextualized and interpretative nature of curriculum development efforts.

After examining various approaches to curriculum development, we include a number of readings that describe how various authors have made sense of and experienced the dynamics of curricular change. For instance, after describing how four institutions grappled with changing their general education curricula, Clif analyzes the various political pressures that often precipitate, confound, and produce academic change. In her article, Patricia Gumport discusses how various cultural factors—such as the changing epistemological and political commitments of faculty—can often lead to the reconstruction of knowledge in the academy. Similarly, Margaret Anderson, Elizabeth Higginbotham, and Johnnella Butler provide intriguing analyses of how changing social, cultural, political, and intellectual attitudes contribute to curricular transformations in various fields of study, including women's studies.

We believe that the selections in this section raise many questions that are surely part and parcel to any discussion of curricular planning and change. Among others, these include:

- What kinds of internal and external developments contribute to curricular change?

- What role should philosophy and mission play in curriculum development? How about purposes, goals, objectives, and outcomes? How important is it that faculty (and others) agree on mission, goals and outcomes?

- What are some key decision-situations that faculty (and others) should consider when designing academic programs?

- What does a college or university need to know about its students and faculty as it develops or revises its overall curriculum?

- Is faculty development an important consideration in curricular decision-making? Why?

- How important is curriculum integration? Who should have responsibility for it?

- Why is curricular change often a slow and arduous process?

Questions such as these, we hope, will encourage readers to explore with one another the intellectual, political, socio-cultural, and economic bases that so often influence and shape how we construct and change curriculum.

Curriculum Definitions and Reference Points

WILLIAM E. TOOMBS AND WILLIAM G. TIERNEY

If the curriculum is to be the instrument of change in education, its meanings and operational terms must be clearer than they are currently. For all its frivolous Latin roots, *curriculum*'s larger meanings do not spring from the literal meaning, a "racecourse," but from the practical, chilly, Calvinist climate of Scotland. Medieval universities and colleges derived their power not from teaching, research, or a coherent program of studies but from the right to certify and examine. Historical accounts show us that studies on the continent and in England were little more than loose congeries of subjects grouped around faculty members. Canon law, theology, and civil law predominated. The period of study was of indeterminate length, with the professor and examiners the arbitrators.

> How long a student remained part of the corporation of "professeurs" depended on a number of factors. . . . The duration depended primarily on student's choice of professor or university, for . . . the period of residence demanded of graduates could vary significantly from faculty to faculty and from institution to institution.[1]

In Spain, students often attended university only a year or two, until they landed a preferment in the hierarchy of civil or church administration.[2] The fortunes, enrollments, and subjects in French and German universities were "continually threatened by the brooding, 'protective' presence of spiritual and temporal powers."[3] Only the Scottish universities adopted the modern usage for curriculum. The earliest recorded reference, at the University of Glasgow in 1643, identifies a "curriculum quinque annorum." The term kept its meaning, and the Glasgow calendar of 1829 refer to "the curriculum of students who mean to take degrees in Surgery to be three years."[4]

Scottish usage did not spread widely or rapidly. In the normal course of events, once a useful concept is introduced, the term is elaborated, invested with specific meanings, and articulated as part of the technical terminology. Those events never quite happened with the idea of a curriculum. It is not accidental that the two settings where the notion of a curriculum did persist were Scotland and the United States. Scottish legends and divines populated the colonial universities in America. They brought with them the influences of the Scottish Enlightenment, stern in its theology and orderly in its views of education.

> The colonial colleges, founded like the lower schools to preserve traditional and transmit culture, had become mildly innovative in spite of themselves. . . . Colonial colleges consequently often looked for precedent and advice to the more lively Scottish universities and the far more innovative Dissenting academies of England.[5]

With "moral philosophy" at the peak of the curriculum, these influences continued well into the 19th century.

It is not hard to understand the conquests of academic America in the early 19th century by the philosophy of Common Sense. It was enlightened, moderate, practical, and easy to teach. It could be used to sustain or validate any set of ideas, but was in fact associated with the Moderate Enlightenment and Moderate Calvinism. It was never anti-scientific nor obscurantist, never cynical, and it opened no doors to intellectual or moral chaos.[6]

In the United States, the development of a *structure* for the curriculum, the macrodimension of the teaching-learning experience, proceeded rapidly. The expansion and differentiation of the natural sciences, the "elective principle [that] led to the gradual elimination of the old curriculum and to the success of the new scholarly disciplines and professional studies," and the more sophisticated organization of American universities all contributed to the evolution of an orderly, phased schedule of studies.[7] Structural features of the curriculum were standardized: the adoption of Carnegie credits in high schools that carried over into colleges, and agreement on course nomenclature, degrees, and academic dress. "Much of the writing on the curriculum . . . in the U.S. was . . . administrative and managerial in emphasis," however.[8]

In contrast to the growth of curricular *structure*, the passage of the *idea*—the concept of what the realm of the curriculum might be—became highly diffused, and two consequences persist. First, the curriculum as a concept, as a discrete idea, is almost without boundaries. It can mean anything from the "bundle" of programs an institution offers to the individual experience of a particular student. Second, systematic description, that is, an orderly, technical terminology that enhances insights on practice and links ideas to application, has not developed. "What we appear to lack . . . is a general vocabulary or framework for understanding the nature of knowledge and skills across university disciplines."[9] Often faculty at work on the curriculum must invent their own labels to describe what they do.

The idea of a curriculum has been differentiated across a wide range of meanings. One basic view is that curriculum is "what is taught."[10] A narrow view holds that curriculum is "the body of courses that present knowledge, principles, values, and skills that are the intended consequences of formal education."[11] The broad view holds that "the curriculum . . . will have to be conceived as the name for the total active life of each person in college."[12] Even the set of choices from which the curriculum can be defined is broad.

Some see a split in the definition:

> It is important at the outset to distinguish clearly between two meanings of the term "curriculum." The word [can] connote either formal structural arrangements or the substance of what is being taught. (To be sure, the relations between form and substance, here as always, are complex.)[13]

Others find evidence of six uses:

1. a college's—or program's mission, purpose, or collective expression of what is important for students to learn
2. a set of experiences that some authorities believe all students should have
3. the set of courses offered to students
4. the set of courses students actually elect from those available
5. the content of a specific discipline
6. the time and credit frame in which the college provides education.[14]

The distinction between structure and concept is important in light of the preemptive administrative interest and faculty neglect of the idea. Most faculty would side with the notion that "the structural aspects of the curriculum have much less to do with the quality of an education than is often believed. Quality instead is more importantly linked to matters of substance."[15] Or they would agree that "all arguments of detail about the curriculum are absolutely pointless. . . . Arguments of principle, centering on what to do instead of lining up courses end to end until graduation, might be helpful."[16]

A result of this diffusion is recorded in faculty interviews showing how difficult it is for faculty members to get much beyond their own courses in thinking about the curriculum.[17] Most analysts find the situation chaotic as well. This disorder is a product of many factors:

The curricular disarray constitutes a major artifact that permits several inferences. It testifies to the loss of confidence among faculty. It testifies to the enlargement of popular functions. . . . And it provides archeological evidence of the vast transformation of the amount and shape of knowledge—what there is to teach-over the past century.[18]

In sum, application of the concept of "curriculum" spread in the United States, but it did not achieve the refined meaning, precise definition, or consensus among professors that standards of professional practice normally require. Those who apply the concepts of the curriculum to real situations must first devise a working definition and then put it into operation. Doing so might not be all bad, for it forces consideration of meanings, and any working definition must allow plenty of room for local initiatives.

Those who are building a working definition fortunately have recent scholarly compilations of definitions to draw on.[19] It is interesting, perhaps a sign of progress, to find that many of the earlier working definitions of, say, 20 years ago tried to incorporate as many dimensions of study as possible, while later definitions have tended to focus on coherence across a more limited scope.

A working definition can be constructed around several common concepts. First, the concept of the curriculum as a *plan for learning* is well developed, based on a comprehensive analysis of the literature on the subject.[20] Further field research among faculty led back to the coarse as the fundamental component of such a plan, not the curriculum. Second, the curriculum can be seen as an *instructional system*, another well-developed approach.[21] Third, the concept of system has been extended to consider the curriculum as a *major subsystem of the university*, thus opening analysis of inputs and outcomes.[22] This approach can be characterized as "systemic curricular planning." Fourth, the idea of the curriculum as a *medium of student development* has been explored and developed in some of the most compelling literature of higher education.[23] Fifth, strong traditional orientations to the curriculum as an *analog to the structure of knowledge* persist in "essentialist" approaches and in contemporary reinterpretations.[24]

Useful but more instrumental or prescriptive aids to defining curriculum also abound in the literature. Perhaps the simplest framework for looking at the curriculum is provided by four penetrating questions about purpose, content, organization, and evaluation.[25] Dressel's 21 "general principles of curriculum construction" examine the curriculum from many positions.[26]

In the best tradition of American pragmatism is the "competency-based" approach to curriculum. A product of the last 20 years, it has been fully articulated at Alverno College. Stated "competence" is also characteristic of programs that lead to external certification of licensing, such as nursing, business, and engineering. The same goal-oriented approach to the curriculum is found in the contemporary emphasis on "outcomes."[27]

In looking for guidance to develop a working definition of the curriculum, one caveat is worth noting. At an early meeting of any committee, study group, or task force, someone will likely recommend that a comprehensive statement of philosophy must precede any detailed consideration. Philosophy in education is tricky business. At the start of a project, philosophical assumptions have to be made, but they are not *the* philosophy. The full meaning the "philosophy of the curriculum, cannot be known until the working components are in place and the program has been operating for a time.

> The history of the curriculum is one in which theories are never realized in the manner they are intended. There are always unintended, unanticipated, and unwilled consequences as theories are put into social action.[28]

Many a curriculum committee has foundered because at the first meeting—and every one thereafter—someone insisted that the philosophy be fully articulated before any action is undertaken.

The Design Approach

Reviews of curricular projects (successful and unsuccessful), observation of curriculum committees and task forces wrestling with issues of the curriculum, and an examination of proposals for overhauling undergraduate studies stimulate an interesting proposition. Effective organizing principles for the curriculum exist at a lower level of abstraction than "theory," "philosophy," or "historical dialectic." The concept and design is just such a principle. It is supported by a sound conceptual framework that is less demanding than a fully formatted theory but easily overcomes the sins of instrumentalism. The heart of this approach is to deal with the curricular sector of practice as a *problem in design*. Once a problem in the realm of practice is defined, all the mature professions have orderly tools of artifacts to deal with it. The artifact of the academy is the curriculum.

The notion of artifacts as the means of meeting problems in design is well developed, leading us to see each program of education as an "artifact," an artificial system intended to fulfill a purpose.

> Fulfillment of purpose or adaptation to a goal involves a relation among three terms: the purpose or goal, the character of the artifact, and the environment in which the artifact performs. . . . An artifact can be thought of as a meeting point, an "interface" in today's terms, between an "inner" environment, the substance and organization of the artifact itself, and an "outer" environment, the surroundings in which it operates. If the inner environment is appropriate to the outer environment, or vice versa, the artifact will serve its intended purpose.[29]

A fundamental distinction here lies between "artificial systems" and the "natural systems" of science, which aim at understanding, systematic understanding, and prediction with respect to phenomena that already exist in nature.

> The artificial world is centered precisely on this interface between the inner and outer environments; it is concerned with attaining goals by adapting the former to the latter. The proper study of those who are concerned with the artificial is the way in which that adaptation of means to environments is brought about, and central to that is the process of design itself.

> Historically and traditionally, it has been the task of the science disciplines to teach about natural things: how they are and how they work. It has been the task of engineering schools to teach about artificial things: how to make artifacts that have the desired properties and how to design.

> Engineers are not the only professional designers. Everyone designs who devises courses of action aimed at changing existing situations into preferred ones. The intellectual activity that produces material artifacts is no different fundamentally from the one that prescribes remedies for a sick patient or the one that devises a new sales plan for a company or a social welfare policy for a state. *Design, so construed, is the core of all professional training;* it is the principal mark that distinguishes the professions from the sciences. Schools and engineering, as well as schools of architecture, business, education, law, and medicine, are all centrally concerned with the process of design.[30]

In light of this conceptualization, revisions to the curriculum, which seem endless to faculty, and the shades of difference that arise among academic programs are not symptoms of confusion, but evidence of vitality.

What process is postulated by the notion of design? In its usual format, design defines a problem and formulates a solution. That solution can never be perfect, only "satisficing" (to use Simon's term)—exactly the case with a curriculum. It is from artists, architects, and engineers that the details emerge. The designer operates with few preconceptions and uses available resources, taking full account of their strengths and shortcoming. The title of a book, *Design: The Problem Comes First*, explicates the pattern.[31] A group of art students offer these defining phrases: "Design is the placing of subject matter so as to put it to its greatest advantage or to have it in the most interesting shape, form, or position possible."[32]

In more esoteric phrases, "a universal process of ordering, evidenced in both the 'physical' and 'mental' spheres, is opening after years of concern with, not beauty, humility, or poetry, but with ELEMENTALS. . . . An epoch of ORDER is opening."[33] The "order" that stands at the center of the concept is not casual. "A good design never comes by chance; it is the product of trained intelligence. . . . By design we mean the creating of relationships. . . ."[34]

One great asset of the concept of design is its comprehensive neutrality. The curriculum designer is free of presumptions, free to examine components on their relative merits; large classes or small, interdisciplinarity or multidisciplinarity, master classes or studio classes—their value is determined by the place in the design. With an approach involving design, questions are moved to a lower level of abstraction, and, consequently, more dimensions of operation can be considered.

This advantage was first observed nearly a century ago: "When we approach the study of design, from whatever point of view, . . . we can hardly fail to be impressed with [the] vast variety and endless complexity of forms . . . the term covers. . . . The range is enormous."[35] The essential process in the application of design involves "inventing things [that] display new physical order, organization, form, in response to function."[36]

To approach change in the curriculum as a problem in design, not philosophy or technique, fixes the responsibility with the inventor—that is, the faculty. Curriculum as design emphasizes invention, intention, and construction.

> The essence of the natural sciences is the discovery of hidden patterns or partially concealed ones *[echoes of developmental psychology!]*. Natural phenomena have an air of "necessity" about them. Artificial phenomena have an air of "contingency" in their malleability by the environment.[37]

It is not surprising that many educational thinkers and writers have touched the edge of the idea of design, for "curriculum theory is about *mix*," and the curriculum is a "social artifact."[38] "Theory is inadequate to the tasks of the curriculum."[39]

A Framework for Design Analysis

If "design" holds advantage over "theory" as the way to invest the curriculum with practical effectiveness, how can it be applied? Any elaboration of the idea should provide boundaries and reasonable specificity; but, most important, the refinement of definitions should not be so detailed that it hampers the judgment of those who have to work with it.

The implications of the preceding subsection can be woven into a comprehensive definition: *The curriculum is an intentional design for learning negotiated by faculty in light of their specialized knowledge and in the context of social expectations and students' needs.* That definition might be a bit stodgy, but it does sharpen the point that a curriculum is an artifact produced by a particular faculty for students at a particular institution. The essential qualities are all there: *faculty responsibility, specialized knowledge, intended outcomes, negotiated relationships,* and a *learning plan for students.*

The components of design as they apply to higher education must be identified. Readily adaptable from art, engineering, and science are the three basic components of design—*context, content, and form* (see Table 1)—and each component can be elaborated to fit higher education. The figure provides an open matrix into which most curricular change can be inserted. Probably the simplest application of these components is as a checklist to describe fully what is contained and implied in a given academic program. The open matrix is also useful for comparing the features of one unit of the curriculum to another. It can function as a planning format that presents current versus intended states. It can aid an evaluation of practice against ideal or intended features. And the order of the major components—context, content and form—can be rearranged to reflect priorities. For example, form might be elevated to a primary position if the design problem focuses on a comprehensive introduction of computer technology across the curriculum.

Such an analytical scheme ensures a complete beginning, not a solution. It has been used in research on curricula dealing with environmental studies programs, professional preparation of athletic trainers, and institutional comparisons."[40] Faculty groups in several settings, including nursing, continuing education, and general education, have adapted it.

Table 1
Components of Curriculum Design: An Open Matrix

1. CONTEXT	*Examples*
Social and Cultural Influences	
• How society defines the functions of higher education; expectations	• Cultivate expert work force, build responsible citizens, sustain elite leadership, provide upward mobility
• Filtering and interpretive influences	• Prevailing cultural waves (free speech in the 1960s, "me-ism" in the 1980s, issues of equity)
	• Political, social, economic events: wars, depressions, civil rights movement
	• Pressures of a "hidden curriculum"
Direct Influences, Environmental Factors	
• Legislation, public policy	• G.I. Bill, NDEA, student loan programs, draft exemptions, civil rights decisions in courts
• Market forces, labor markets, financial markets	• Placement patterns, interest rates
• Demographic trends and events	• Baby boom, immigration, sex ratio, single-parent home
• Value of knowledge-in-use, technology-in-demand	• Post-*Sputnik* emphasis on science, business boom of the 1980s
Organizational/Institutional Climate	
• Institutional features	• Tradition, "saga," culture, administrative structure, faculty ethos
• Community dimensions	• Student cultures and subcultures
	• Ecology of service area

2. CONTENT	
Nature of Significant Knowledge: Epistemology	
• Structure of organized knowledge	• Principles, theories, laws, bodies of information
• Methods of establishing and verifying knowledge	• Styles of inquiry, systems of proof, technique
• Subsets of related knowledge	• Prerequisite and conjunctive disciplines and fields
• "Ideal-typical" role	• Expected role attributes, "knowledge-in-action" behaviors
Nature of Learning Psychology of Field	
• Learning strategies for apprehending the field at higher cognitive levels	• Laboratory, clinical, field experience
• Students' capacities and learning styles; preconditions of maturity, experience, schooling	• Perfect pitch for music, physical vigor and coordination, aptitude for spatial relations, work experience
Affective Domain: Values, Attitudes, Beliefs	
• Helpful personality traits, orienting values, attitudes, beliefs	• Licensed "expertise," orientations toward helping, precision in observations
Consequences of Knowledge Holding: Manifest and Latent	
• Cognitive outcomes, "certain knowledge" of field	
• Patterns of habit and trained behaviors	
• Sensitivities and appreciations	
• Components of skill and technique, competencies	

3. FORM

Distribution of Learning Resources: Time,
Space, Facilities

- Faculty work load

- Contact hours, preparation, course development, advising, in-house, extramural service, research and scholarship

- Faculty expertise: matching talent to learning designs
- Inventory of faculty training, survey of interests
- Student time distribution, weighting credits
- Class/study mix, part-time work, structure of credit
- Budgetary system, allocation methods, priorities, adjustments
- Allocation of physical facilities, space, equipment, services

Instructional Strategies and Prevailing Modes
of Instruction

- Calendar and scheduling system; class size, composition, and sorting processes; instructional strategies; alternatives to formal study
- Challenge exams, advanced placement, credit for life experiences, tutorials, projects

- Integrating learning experiences, applications of knowledge
- Study abroad, honors programs, senior seminars, case studies, internships, voluntary service, field study

Proximate Outcomes and Assessments

- Standardized tests of formal knowledge, external examiners, competency reviews
- GRE, LSAT, MCAT, ACT—Comp; licensing, certification, and accrediting boards; performance portfolios, evaluations of specific skills

- Qualitative assessments
- Student self-reports, situational measures, involvement summaries

- Career development and entry experience, formal grading and reporting procedures
- Alumni surveys, feedback from employers, placement data, policies on grades, transcripts, privacy

A Working Terminology

If the first challenge of curriculum is defining the concept, the second is adding a systematic terminology that will set out workable segments. Once a curricular issue is seen as a "problem in design," the next questions are, What do we look at? How does one designate the scope and dimensions of the problem? The answers determine the nature of resources to be invested. The terminology proposed here is based on operational scope and the level of faculty members' engagement.

In the normal scheme of things, faculty members' day-to-day attention is fully occupied with keeping up-to-date in their fields, holding courses on track, and planning classes. Again and again, faculty report that keeping up with their field is *the* major function.[41] In surveys, interviews, and self-reports, faculty show little appreciation for other aspects of the curriculum.

Ordinarily, much of the curriculum operates as a tacit design, accepted but not fully examined. Only intermittently do academics take the measure of the curriculum, and then only a few at a time.[42] "There is often little collective work on the curriculum. Rather, courses 'belong' to a professor who exercises exclusive control over their content. Thus, in the extreme, hiring decisions determine the curriculum."[43]

But the "course and the "curriculum" are real entities. "Social facts are things," and in this case both course and curriculum are discrete entities. "If you wish to witness instant shock, ask a faculty member to talk about the curriculum. . . . Yet the curriculum lies at the heart of education. . . . Its grand design is a matter of the greatest consequence."[44]

Two lines of systematic search and invention mark the effort to get beyond a fixation with courses into terminology that reflects the wider reach of learning. One is taxonomic, the other functional.

Taxonomic approaches are the most popular. They mirror the process of the natural sciences, examining, describing, sometimes measuring, and sorting according to prominent characteristics cases in the field. These features are then laid out in a hierarchy of family, genus, species, and variety.

A field based inventory stops short of the Carnegie Foundation's full classification.[45] While eight common prototypes or models of curriculum encourage comparative study, the technical precision needed for wide application is limited.[46] Three key elements are necessary to create a curriculum: content, pedagogy, and social purpose.[47]

Functional categories are derived from concepts or premises considered critical to the processes of teaching, learning, or development. An interesting and enlightening common-sense approach uses "course structure, course content, teaching methods, assessment, and industrial experience" to compare the curriculum in chemistry of the Grandes Ecoles of France and British universities.[48] The comparisons clearly describe the differences and open the way to fruitful consideration of the pros and cons of each.

A functional terminology of "six curricular dimensions"—time, space, resources, organization, procedures, and outcomes—can be used to describe a college curriculum in terms of a series of decisions that the college has made about each of these six dimensions.[49] In an interesting application of what might be called "reverse English," respondents are presented with 57 statements in a "curriculum orientation profile" with which they can "agree" or "disagree."[50] The statements are scored according to five categories based on the purpose of education, development of cognitive processes, curriculum as technology, self-actualization, social reconstruction or relevance, and academic rationalization, all abstracted from the literature. Another approach to the problem of terminology postulates a paradigmatic structure to the curriculum.[51] Others emphasize the decision-making qualities reflected by the curriculum, citing the systemic, interactive, and nonlinear attributes of those decisions, or emphasize the division of authority and apply the distinctions to various functions.[52]

Each of these approaches has virtues in helping to understand and describe the complexity of the curriculum as faculty members encounter it day by day. The "design for learning" formulation, with its concentric domains arrayed around curricular functions, goes a long way toward spanning that gap.[53] The gap to practice is closed, perhaps foreclosed, with a tightly knit set of design procedures based on instructional development.[54]

A terminology that combines the emphasis on design with dimensions close to the realities of practice could be even more useful. The value of such a typology is its capacity to establish a focus or scope for curricular change. When confronted with large or pressing issues, people tend to exaggerate the scope to gain emphasis. It is neither necessary nor desirable to mobilize an entire institution around changes in the curriculum to address, for example, quantitative reasoning. A key point in this article is that clear definitions of scope and intentions lie at the heart of effective curricular change.

The terminology developed in the rest of this section takes account of the operating components of the curriculum at five levels: course, pattern, constellation, program, and curriculum (see Table 2). Three of these terms—course, program, and curriculum—are entirely familiar, although the refinement of their meaning might be new. The other two are derived form understanding and use that have gone unlabeled, though teaching faculty often acknowledge them in discussions. Their potential for analytical use is suggested as several critical aspects of each term are pointed out: the nature of the unit is specified; primary interest groups, stakeholders, and actors identified; some major kinds and sources of information noted; and possible mediums of action and modalities of professional practice discussed.

Table 2
A Terminology for Curriculum Analysis

COURSE

What: Basic building block of a curriculum and fundamental unit of professional practice for academics. Can be subdivided into modules or units.

Who: The domain of individual faculty members. Students' role is reactive. Departmental interest is usually tacit.

How: Course reviews best conducted by three-person team from within the department, concentrating on description.

PATTERN

What: Groups of courses related by internal affinities of knowledge, technique, or methodology. Commonality of content in such sets of courses the hallmark.

Who: Faculty members from involved departments plus department heads. Deans hold role of observer/monitor.

How: Interdepartmental communities review plans and practice for coherence and redundancy.

CONSTELLATION

What: Courses related by common goals or objectives, oriented toward similar outcomes.

Who: Deans and/or program directors hold the initiative. Faculty in committees or task forces make decisions. Chief academic officer has supporting role. Aims must be clear to students.

How: Standing committees or commissions have oversight. Specialized staff support might be needed.

PROGRAM

What: An arrangement of courses and learning options that leads to publicly recognized certificates or credentials.

Who: Deans hold a primary interest. External bodies, usually professional associations or licensing boards, participate.

How: External reviews play a major role. Consultants, advisory committees, and self-studies are significant.

CURRICULUM

What: An institution's entire educational program.

Who: Chief academic officer in charge of initiatives. Deans and faculty responsible for operations. Board of trustees has oversight. State could have a formal responsibility.

How: Comprehensive, process-oriented academic plan requiring various working papers and position documents.

Courses

Faculty view their courses as the fundamental unit of practice in the teaching-learning domain and the basic building blocks of the curriculum. The unit is a nearly universal phenomenon bonded to the nature of the discipline,[55] and courses have exhibited their durability throughout history.

> As a basic device, the course is probably the most durable element in American higher education. Entities . . . recognizable as courses already dominated the curriculum of traditional American colleges in the mid-19th century, though they were not so often of equivalent intensity or duration, and their extremely small number made it possible to describe them with much less formality. . . . The course and grade survived with so little challenge for reasons that were no doubt as much psychological as they were historical. Both were primarily instruments of control.[56]

It is at the level of course that the greatest sense of responsibility and commitment to the discipline resides. Few would question the importance held by courses in U.S. education. The difficulty arises when it is necessary to consider other levels of learning.

> The way in which a discipline structures its knowledge provides the best structure for transmitting it to students [is one untenable assumption]. . . . The distinction I wish to make here is between what can be called the logical and epistemological arrangement of subject matter. On the one hand, and the "learning structure" on the other.[57]

The stakeholders and actors are individual faculty members, with students as implicated bystanders. The province of individual faculty members' control over courses had the qualities of a sacred right. To address any curricular issue, however, ways must be found to factor in the external implications of a course as well as its intrinsic qualities. Students exercise their interests at this level largely through veto power—the capacity to reject a given course.

Sources of information for the construction or review of a given course begin with the relationship between the structure of the discipline and the syllabus of the course, then move to more complex relationships. Fortunately, the last 10 years have been marked by widespread attention within the disciplines—chemistry, sociology, and history have been the leaders—to the material to be taught and the method of teaching.

From experience with change in curriculum at Wellesley College come the kind of questions that reach across disciplinary courses and broaden the span of concern: "What are the *shaping dimensions* (content, scope, methodology) of the discipline at present? How would the discipline need to change to reflect the fact that women are half the world's population and have had, in one sense, half the world's experience?"[58]

A second kind of information about courses deals with what might be termed "presentation," these days a bit more palatable than "pedagogy." The concentration is on the appropriateness of relations between the material and the learner, the "learning structure." Often it is easier to stimulate course analysis by opening the prospects of new techniques than to start with content or elusive goals. Workshops or seminars in a nonperspective mode that illustrate a variety of techniques, such as team teaching, collaborative learning, computer-assisted learning, and experiential learning, offer a nonthreatening introduction to review of a course.[59] In recent years, more and more institutions provide special support—release time, grants, summer supplements—to develop courses.

One modality for improvement in this sector of the curriculum is course review. The scrutiny of courses is usually left to the faculty member and no one else. More useful is a departmental review by three-person teams that examine syllabi, texts, classroom techniques, and evaluation. If the courses taught by the teams' members are interrelated, the way is opened to examine relationships among courses. The emphasis is on description, not justification. Because the intellectual harmonics of each course echo across related studies, reviews by collegial teams tend to be very useful. At the outset, participants deserve to be reminded that they are their own experts: at a college or university, no band of curriculum "experts" is waiting in the wings with knowledge demonstrably superior to that of the faculty.

Patterns

Arrangements of related courses constitute the next functional level. The term *patterns* is not in general use, but the idea—groups of courses that are related to each other by virtue of internal affinities of knowledge, skills, and methodology—is readily recognized. Interdependence among courses, a commonality of substance, has long been recognized informally, but systematic attention to the implications of relationships has seldom been explored. Relationships among courses lie at the heart of a thorough analysis of a curriculum.

Three basic structures are possible: sequential, associative, and parallel. Only the first is used with any regularity.

In the natural sciences, strings of prerequisites are the means to expanding, in steps, the understandings students have of the discipline. Other fields have emulated the sequential pattern, often as a matter of convenient scheduling.

In an associative pattern, courses are related in a kind of mosaic: it does not matter which is taken first so long as the whole area is covered. Many student-designed programs have an underlying expectation that an associative pattern will be the final outcome. This assumption is also apparent in fields like literature or history.

The notion of parallel relationships is less developed, although the idea was applied with good results in the cultural studies introduced under the National Defense Education Act of the 1960s. The idea is that students who study, say, 19th-century European history will gain from a tacit exchange of ideas if they pursue courses in Victorian prose and poetry and the Romantic Movement in German literature at the same time.

The actors and stakeholders in pattern analysis are faculty within the disciplinary departments and in closely related fields, often those jointly involved in the preparation of students for professional certification. Students' interests are largely inferred rather than solicited, with the final judgment left to reaction and response.

Currently, several strong lines of interest are best addressed through pattern analysis: writing across the curriculum is prominent among them. The more successful approaches overreach departments.[60] The place of computers in the curriculum can be analyzed at this level, although widespread variation and some confusion about how to deal with this technology still exist.[61] Critical thinking is another phenomenon that cuts across courses and benefits from pattern analysis.[62] Interest is rising rapidly in scientific and technical understanding, again, as it interacts across courses.[63] Options for creative study that link business and languages as preparation for international marketing management, and packages joining statistics and research methodology reflect such thinking. Still other topic that can benefit from pattern analysis are clusters focusing on civic responsibility, leadership, and professional ethics.

A modality for working through these curricular issues is an interdepartmental committee, study group, or task force. The scope of the charge can be made very specific, and beneficial outcomes are usually clear: less repetition of material more varied perspectives on the same phenomenon, supplementary views, or consolidated common insights.

Especially appropriate for dealing with patterns of courses and all the higher levels of analysis of the curriculum is a "two-committee structure." In this approach the exploratory, information-gathering stage is separated from the decision stage. The first committee is charged with surrounding the issue, bringing views froward, and developing alternatives, not decisions. The second committee is charged with recommending a decision and action plan.

Constellations

Another level of focus is those clusters of courses with a distinct shape or form. The term *constellation* is not generally used, but the idea is well understood. Constellations are groups of courses related to one another by their mode of response to some *common aim*, to extrinsic factors rather than intrinsic relationships in the subject matter. Often that aim has a rationale of its own and must be clearly communicated. Major and minor course sets and the general education sector are the prominent examples. It is the proposals for new constellations, however, that today present the most interesting challenges to the curriculum: women's studies; African-American studies; non-Western civilization; emphases on ethnicity and diversity; global studies; science, technology, and society; and so on. A critical issue, as discussed later, is whether these topics affect the entire curriculum or just one sector.

The interest groups, stakeholders, and actors at this level cover a much wider range than for a course or pattern. Students' interest is frequently direct and vocal. Frequently, interest groups outside the university have a stake in the outcome and the process. Even though factual are the source of information and judgment, only the top administration can command and orchestrate the use of the resources likely to be required for a thorough analysis of a constellation. The chief academic officer, the provost, or a vice president necessarily plays a major role as the convening authority—although not necessarily the sponsor.

Sources of information on the topics arising here are likely to be rich and varied. Staff support will probably be required to collect, organize, and distribute materials. Time is a major factor; as much as two academic years might be required for study, communication, and negotiation. At this level, the costs of analyzing the curriculum and the recurring future costs of change rise substantially and can rarely be absorbed into normal operating expenditures. Only a major task force or commission planning for operations over several years is likely to give complete results. Investments in the process itself becomes a matter of prime importance.

Programs

Collections of courses that lead to certification or credentials lie at the heart of institutional accountability, and the complexities are familiar territory to anyone who has participated in regional or professional accreditation. Among the essential features of *programs*, as the term is used in this article, is the requirement for communicability. The public expects that persons certified through an educational program will hold and act on certain knowledge, skills, and understandings.

The stakeholders, interest groups, and actors for programs are extended by one more degree. External parties like licensing boards, advisory bodies, visiting evaluators, professional societies, and even state legislatures are always involved at this level of curricular analysis. The dean holds much of the initiative. The form and substance of review at this level are often prescribed (what has been called the "outside-in syndrome") or, at the very least, must be respected.[64]

A wide range of possibilities exists for program review, and each exercise is tailored to fit the requirements of the particular institution. Not too many years ago, internal program reviews gained wide attention, largely as an instrument of retrenchment. After one or two experiences, most institutions found the process prohibitively time-consuming, costly, and indeterminate. Because the elements of self-study and iteration that go into program reviews are so costly, they are best reserved for evaluations in which the materials can be turned to several uses.

The Curriculum

In this suggested terminology, the term *curriculum* is reserved for an institution's entire educational program. It is the locus of corporate responsibility for learning that engages faculty, trustees, administration, and students. The curriculum encompasses all the sectors of the institution involved with the process of teaching and learning.

Issues appropriately addressed at this level are very few, but they are among the most important for an institution's future—for example, what profile of programs best fits the institution. Issues must be selected and treated with care. It is both a tactical and strategic error to declare an issue to be a problem of the curriculum if it really lies within the realm of a program or constellation.

Leadership among the actors and stakeholders resides with the senior academic officer, provost, or academic vice president. The president's and the trustees' major functions are oversight and support. All of the faculty have a primary stake in the character of the curriculum. Issues that are truly curricular in scope will affect all courses in some way, for the most critical decisions determine the learning environment, define the conditions of professional practice, and change the financial operations of a college, school, or university.

A full review of the curriculum opens so many demands for information that it can seldom be undertaken without a special staff unit charged with coordinating responsibility. The self-study has become the instrument of choice for conducting such a review. Costs are high, and presidents often seek outside funding from friends of the institution or foundations. The amount of time required is also large, taking as much as three or four years to reach implementation.

Notes

1. L. W. B. Brockliss, *French Higher Education in the 17th and 18th Centuries: A Cultural History* (Oxford: Clarendon Press, 1987), p. 55.
2. Richard L. Kagan, "Universities in Castille, 1500–1810," in *The University in Society*, vol. 2, ed. Lawrence Stone (Princeton, NJ: Princeton University Press, 1975), p. 355.
3. L. W. B. Brockliss, *French Higher Education in the 17th and 18th Centuries: A Cultural History* (Oxford: Clarendon Press, 1987), p. 444.

4. *The Compact Edition of the Oxford English Dictionary* (New York: Oxford University Press, 1971).

5. Henry F. May, *The Enlightenment in America* (New York: Oxford University Press, 1976), p. 33.

6. Ibid., p. 346.

7. Joseph Ben David, *American Higher Education* (New York: McGraw Hill, 1972), p. 58, Joseph Ben David, *Centers of Learning* (New York: McGraw Hill, 1977), p. 77.

8. Geoffery Squires, *First Degree: The Undergraduate Curriculum* (Buckingham, England: Society for Research into Higher Education, 1990), p. 1, ERIC document ED 326 168. See also William Reid, "Curriculum Theory and Curriculum Change: What Can We Learn from History?" *Journal of Curriculum Studies* 18 (April–June 1986): 159.

9. J. G. Donald, "Knowledge and the University Curriculum," *Higher Education* 15 (Nos. 3–4 1986): 267.

10. Geoffery Squires, *First Degree: The Undergraduate Curriculum* (Buckingham, England: Society for Research into Higher Education, 1990), ERIC document ED 326 168.

11. Arthur Levine, *Handbook on Undergraduate Curriculum* (San Francisco: Jossey-Bass, 1981).

12. Harold Taylor, ed., *Essays in Teaching* (New York: Harper, 1950), p. 220.

13. Laurence Veysey, "Stability and Experiment," in *Content and Context*, ed. Carl Kaysen (New York: McGraw-Hill, 1973), p. 73.

14. Joan S. Stark and M. A. Lowther, *Designing the Learning Plan: A Review of Research and Theory Related to College Curriculum* (Ann Arbor: Regents of the University of Michigan, 1986), p. 45.

15. Laurence Veysey, "Stability and Experiment," in *Content and Context*, ed. Carl Kaysen (New York: McGraw-Hill, 1973), p. 22.

16. Peter Caws, "Instruction and Inquiry," *Daedalus* 103 (No. 4 1974): 24.

17. Joan S. Stark and others, *Reflections on Course Planning*, Technical Report 88-C-002.2 (Ann Arbor: Regents of the University of Michigan, 1988), p. 85

18. Harold R. Bowen, *Investment in Learning: The Individual and Social Value of American Higher Education* (San Francisco: Jossey-Bass, 1977), p. 413

19. For a comparative analysis, see Clifton F. Conrad, *The Undergraduate Curriculum: A Guide to Innovation and Reform* (Boulder, CO: Westview Press, 1978) and C. F. Conrad, *ASHE Reader on Academic Programs in Colleges and Universities* (Lexington, MA: Ginn, 1985), for a classical work on reconciling tensions, see Paul Dressel, *College and University Curriculum* (Berkeley, CA: McCutchan, 1971); for a discussion of five of the essential conflicts that surface in curricular work, see Elliot W. Eisner and Elizabeth Vallance, *Conflicting Conceptions of Curriculum* (Berkeley, CA: McCutchan, 1974); for the compilation of a range of views around the theme that "the curriculum is a struggle to accommodate many competing issues," see Lewis B. Mayhew and Patrick J. Ford, *Changing the Curriculum* (San Francisco: Jossey-Bass, 1971); for a full review of definitions and the literature that supports them, including a review of the use in kindergarten through grade 12 and an articulated schema of major topics that bear on the curriculum, see Joan S. Stark and M. A. Lowther, *Designing the Learning Plan: A Review of Research and Theory Related to College Curriculum* (Ann Arbor: Regents of the University of Michigan, 1986).

20. Joan S. Stark and others, *Reflections on Course Planning*, Technical Report 88–C-002.2 (Ann Arbor: Regents of the University of Michigan, 1988).

21. See Robert M. Diamond, *Designing and Improving Courses and Curricula in Higher Education: A Systematic Approach* (San Francisco: Jossey-Bass, 1989) for both theoretical and practical aspects of sustaining a highly systematic plan of action.

22. Clifton F. Conrad, *The Undergraduate Curriculum: A Guide to Innovation and Reform* (Boulder, CO: Westview Press, 1978) and C. F. Conrad, *ASHE Reader on Academic Programs in Colleges and Universities* (Lexington, MA: Ginn, 1985).

23. See Arthur W. Chickering, *The Modern American College* (San Francisco: Jossey-Bass, 1981); Arthur W. Chickering, David Hallibuston, William H. Bergquist, and Jack Lindquist, *Developing the College Curriculum* (Washington, DC: Council for the Advancement of Small Colleges, 1977), ERIC Document ED 152 125; K. Patricia Cross and Anne-Marie McCartan, *Adult Learning: State Policies and Institutional Practices*, ASHE-ERIC Higher Education Report No. 1 (Washington, DC: Association for the Study of Higher Education, 1984), ERIC document ED 246 831; Zelda F. Gamson and Associates, *Liberating Education* (San Francisco: Jossey-Bass, 1984); and Nevitt Sanford, ed., *The American College* (New York: John Wiley & Sons, 1962) among others.

24. Daniel Bell, *The Reforming of General Education* (New York: Columbia University Press, 1966); Paul Hirst,

Knowledge and the Curriculum (Boston: Routledge & Kagan Paul, 1974); and Philip H. Phenix, *Realms of Meaning* (New York: McGraw-Hill, 1964).

25. Ralph Tyler, *Basic Principles of Curriculum and Instruction* (Chicago: University of Chicago Press, 1950).

26. See Lewis B. Mayhew and Patrick J. Ford, *Changing the Curriculum* (San Francisco: Jossey-Bass, 1971) for a summary.

27. Ernest T. Pascarella and Patrick T. Terenzini, *How College Affects Students* (Cambridge, MA: MIT Press, 1991). See also William H. Bergquist, Ronald A. Gould, and Elinor M. Greenberg, *Designing Undergraduate Education* (San Francisco: Jossey-Bass, 1981) for a comprehensive inventory of outcomes and a matrix for assessment; and Brenda D. McKelvie, "The University's Statement of Goals," *Higher Education* 15 (No. 1–2, 1986): 151–163, and Carol A. Pazandak, *Improving Undergraduate Education in Large Universities*, New Directions in Higher Education No. 66 (San Francisco: Jossey-Bass, 1989) for a discussion of the value of goals in a large university setting.

28. Thomas S. Popkewitz, "Knowledge, Power: A General Curriculum," in *Cultural Literacy and the Idea of General Education*, 87th Yearbook of the National Society for the Study of Education, part 2, ed. Ian Westbury and Alan C. Purves (Chicago: University of Chicago Press, 1988), p. 69.

29. Herbert F. Simon, *The Sciences of the Artificial* (Cambridge, MA: MIT Press, 1969), p. 6.

30. Ibid., p. 55, emphasis added.

31. Jens Bernsen, *Design: The Problem Comes First* (Copenhagen: Danish Design Council, 1982).

32. Sybil Emerson, *Design : A Creative Approach* (Scranton, PA: International Textbook Co., 1957).

33. Lancelot Law Whyte, cited in Reyner Bantam, *The Aspen Papers* (New York: Praeger, 1974).

34. Ibid.

35. Walter Crane, *The Bases of Design* (reprint; London: George Bell, 1977).

36. Christopher W. Alexander, *Notes on the Synthesis of Form* (Cambridge, MA: Harvard University Press, 1964)

37. Herbert F. Simon, *The Science of the Artificial* (Cambridge, MA: MIT Press, 1969), p. 3, emphasis added.

38. Harry S. Broudy, "Can Curriculum Escape the Disciplines?" in *Curriculum Handbook*, ed. Louis Rubin (Boston: Allyn and Bacon, 1977); Frederick Rudolph, *Curriculum* (San Francisco: Jossey-Bass, 1977).

39. Joseph J. Schwab, "The Practical: A Language for Curriculum," *School Review* 78 (November 1969), 1–23.

40. Joaquin H. Molinari, "Environmental Studies at the Undergraduate Level: Curriculum and the Integration of Knowledge" (doctoral dissertation, The Pennsylvania State University, 1982); Patricia Wentzel, "Approved Athletic Training Programs and the National Certification Exam: A Comparative Study of Performance and Curriculums" (doctoral dissertation, The Pennsylvania State University, 1986); Li Bao Ming, "Collegiate Curricula in China: Stability and Change Under a Centralized System" (doctoral dissertation, The Pennsylvania State University, 1991).

41. Howard R. Bowen and Jack H. Schuster, *American Professors* (New York: Oxford University Press, 1986), p. 283

42. Joan S. Stark and others, *Reflections on Course Planning*, Technical Report 88-C-002.2 (Ann Arbor: Regents of the University of Michigan, 1988), p. 88.

43. Carol A. Pazandak, *Improving Undergraduate Education in Large Universities*, New Directions in Higher Education No. 66 (San Francisco: Jossey-Bass, 1989), p. 18.

44. H. L. Enarson, "The Undergraduate Curriculum: Who's in Charge?" *NASULGC Newsletter* (Toledo: University of Toledo, 1987).

45. Arthur Levine, *Handbook on Undergraduate Curriculum* (San Francisco: Jossey-Bass, 1981).

46. William H. Bergquist and Steven R. Phillips, *A Handbook for Faculty Development* (Washington, DC: Council for the Advancement of Small Colleges, 1977).

47. W. E. Marsden, "All in a Good Cause," *Journal of Curriculum Studies* 21 (November-December 1989), 509–526.

48. H. Sutcliffe, "A Comparison of the Teaching of Chemistry in French Grande Ecoles and British Universities," *Studies in Higher Education* 7 (No. 1 1982): 57.

49. William H. Bergquist, Ronald A. Gould, and Elinor M. Greenberg, *Designing Undergraduate Education* (San Francisco: Jossey-Bass, 1981), p. 5.

50. Patric Babin, "A Curriculum Orientation Profile." *Education Canada* (Fall 1979), 38.

51. Arthur W. Chickering, David Hallibuston, William H. Bergquist, and Jack Lindquist, *Developing the College Curriculum* (Washington, DC: Council for the Advancement of Small Colleges, 1977), ERIC document ED 152 125, et al.

52. Clifton F. Conrad and Anne M. Pratt, "Making Decisions About the Curriculum: From Metaphor to Model," *Journal of Higher Education* 54 (January-February 1983): 16–30; Thomas E. Tellefsen, *Improving College Management: An Integrated Systems Approach* (San Francisco: Jossey-Bass, 1990).

53. Joan S. Stark and M. A. Lowther, *Designing the Learning Plan: A Review of Research and Theory Related to College Curriculum* (Ann Arbor: Regents of the University of Michigan, 1986), p. 7.

54. Robert M. Diamond, *Designing and Improving Courses and Curricula in Higher Education: A Systematic Approach* (San Francisco: Jossey-Bass, 1989).

55. Burton R. Clark, *The Academic Life: Small Worlds, Different Worlds* (Princeton, NJ: Princeton University Press, 1987), p. 184.

56. Laurence Veysey, "Stability and Experiment," in *Content and Context*, ed. Carl Kaysen (New York: McGraw Hill, 1973), p. 62.

57. Robert Glaser, "Ten Untenable Assumptions," *Education Record* 49 (Winter-Fall 1968): 158–169.

58. Peggy McIntosh, "Interactive Phases of Curricular Revision: A Feminist Perspective," Working paper 124 (Wellesley, MA: Wellesley College, 1983), p. 2.

59. Horatio M. LaFauci, *Team Teaching at the College Level* (New York: Pergamon, 1970); John Harris, *Assessment: Providing Quality Assurance for Students, Programs, and Career Guidance*. New Directions for Higher Education No. 57 (San Francisco: Jossey-Bass, 1987).

60. Susan H. McLeod, ed., *Strengthening Programs for Writing Across the Curriculum*. New Directions for Teaching and Learning No. 36 (San Francisco: Jossey-Bass, 1988) and Edward M. White, *Developing Successful College Writing Programs* (San Francisco: Jossey-Bass, 1989).

61. P. A. Cohen, "Computing at Dartmouth: Survey of Faculty and Students," *Journal of Educational Technical Systems* 12 (No. 1 1983): 95–106; R. W. Haigh, "Planning for Computer Literacy," *Journal of Higher Education* 561 (1985): 161–171.

62. Chet Meyers, *Teaching Students to Think Critically* (San Francisco: Jossey-Bass, 1986).

63. Fernand Brunschwig and R. Breslin, "Scientific and Technical Literary: A Major Innovation and Challenge," *Liberal Education* 68 (Spring 1982): 49–62.

64. Carol C. Ferguson, "Inside-out Curriculum," *Educational Leadership* 39 (November 1981): 114–116.

Making Decisions about the Curriculum

Clifton F. Conrad and Anne M. Pratt

Buffeted by external and internal pressures, postsecondary institutions have been forced to make critical decisions affecting long-term and short-term institutional planning in order to develop and maintain distinctive educational programs or, in some cases, simply to survive. As a fundamental component of higher education, undergraduate curricula have always received a fair amount of attention in theory and in practice. Until recently, however, the undergraduate curriculum and the idea of planning have been treated in relative isolation. Since it is clear that curriculum development in colleges and universities can no longer remain sacrosanct, a need exists for comprehensive curriculum planning models that will aid in the process of integrating various theoretical considerations with an array of practical realities.

In recent years, Axelrod [1], Dressel [7, 8], and Mayhew and Ford [14] have developed models for curriculum planning. The models vary according to differential emphases placed upon certain key curricular dimensions and interactions. For instance, the most recent model by Dressel presents six continua as necessary considerations in developing programs. The continua deal with the relationship of teacher to discipline, student to content, practice to theory, flexibility to rigidity, unity to compartmentalization, and continuity to fragmentation. Dressel suggests that the continua (and his concomitant discussion) provide "both a rational and necessary series of steps to arrive at a sound program" [8, p. 79].

While Dressel emphasizes one set of considerations, each of the other models offers an alternative view of curriculum planning. To be sure, some global perspectives of the critical dimensions of curriculum planning surface across the models, but the differing thrusts and directions suggested by each model offer a confusing panorama for curriculum planners. In order to move beyond these general perspectives in an effort to capture the detail essential to effective planning, major points of imprecision, unclarity, and ambiguity require recognition. Five such areas of uncertainty may be critically delineated in these particular models. First, these models give insufficient attention to the relationships between curriculum development and the environment, including the internal environment of the college or university. Second, although all of the models emphasize the importance of a systematic approach to curriculum planning, they tend to deal less with the interaction between various components of the curricular system than with the components themselves. Third, these models are primarily prescriptive rather than descriptive and explanatory. Fourth, none of these models integrates nontraditional curricular arrangements in sufficient detail to aid critical planning decisions. Finally, all three frameworks can be criticized in terms of their applicability to actual curriculum planning. Axelrod's complex conceptual model does not adequately link abstract to pragmatic considerations in curricular decision making, while the other two models seem to reduce curriculum planning to a mechanistic, stepwise process. Other recent models such as those of Bergquist [2] and Conrad [4] focus on the identification of nontraditional curricular structures, but these frameworks are also vulnerable to the other criticisms noted above.

In a pithy article, Toombs [20] critiqued the literature on curriculum design, concluding that the continuing dependence on historical narratives and descriptive essays had not yielded a theory of curriculum. He proposed moving to a lower level of abstraction and applying the concept of design as developed in the arts and engineering. Further, he offered a set of design concepts and a tentative schema for mapping curricula, subsequently applying his schema to a small set of new programs in general education and inviting others to propose alternative frameworks.

In light of Toombs's important suggestion, one might further conclude that a focus on curricular decision making—rather than on curriculum planning—might help to direct curriculum development theory away from the normative and prescriptive approaches predominant in the literature and toward the development of more descriptive, generalizable theoretical constructs. Instead of beginning with a prescriptive framework for curriculum planning, research could be aimed at generating a tentative model of curricular decision making. By isolating the key variables and interactions in decision making, such a framework could, in turn, be used as a planning tool for those involved in curriculum development.

The purpose of this article is to present a conceptual model of curricular decision making that identifies curricular planning variables and clarifies the relationship among these variables. The environmental inputs affecting curricular decision making, the curricular design variables from which decisions evolve, and the relationships implicit in the juxtaposition of input variables with curricular design variables represent the primary considerations that informed the literal and figurative modeling.

In addition, the model represents an integration of many of the more global concepts incorporated in earlier models. In particular, Dresser's concept of curricular "emphases," Axelrod's focus on curricular "system," and Toombs's concern with "content, context, and form" influenced the conceptualization. The work of Conrad [4] and Mayhew and Ford [14] suggested other important considerations that the model addresses. Finally, decision-making theory and models of decision making per se have been incorporated into the design concept so that the emerging model in fact represents a new view of curricular decision making, a new concept of curricular design.

From Metaphor to Model

In *Beyond Culture*, Edward Hall notes that learning is necessary to the survival of an individual. Learning exists as the creative essence that signals the growth or change that ensures human endurance [10]. Decision making, in turn, represents an integral part of learning and of change, both for the individual and for those human extensions, such as curricula, which have been designed to assist in the human endeavor. Indeed, decision making determines the direction and the rate of change or of growth; and decisions made succeed or fail based on how closely the decision process accurately analyzes and approximates perceived human need.

Moreover, decisions will vary based on the ability of the decider(s) to recognize all of the available options and to act. To be useful, then, decision-making models should seek to illuminate those variables, both internal and external to the decider, essential to the decision as well as the processes that impinge upon any deciding action. Two further considerations grounded in the decider appear to be basic to any model that seeks to approximate a complete decision-making process. First, the memory storage and retrieval capability of the decider apparently operates like a hologram, which "does not capture a thingy thing. It captures rules—a harmonic syllogism . . . mathematics in reverse" [10, p. 170]. Decision-making models should reflect the holographic nature of the human deciding mechanism, whose overt manifestations may approach some step-by-step deductive ordering, but whose actual functioning may more closely resemble an instantaneous process, where the entire image is at once captured and reflected in all of its parts. With such a "harmonic syllogism," seemingly diverse parts may interact to produce a whole image. Even as one considers this aspect of a balanced human deciding process, however, one must also consider a second trait of the deciding mechanism: "the physiological organism is deeply altered by experience" [10, p. 167]. Therefore, regardless of the ability of the decider to capture a complete image, decisions will nevertheless be altered by past experience, and completeness will be tempered by that which the decider allows to surface as a complete image. On the one hand, while this aspect of deciding permits one to accept some hard-earned truths of the past without always having to begin anew with each decision, on the other hand, the comfort that resides in the known may obscure available options and processes for the decider.

Turning from metaphor to model, it follows that a useful model for a group decision-making process needs to account for these human characteristics as they affect and effect deciding, despite the acknowledgment that such an expansion of the metaphor redounds in increasingly greater complexity. While one may rationally desire an orderly, sequential process toward curricular decision making, in reality the process rarely resembles such a harmonious procedure. After all, from one holographic perspective, a curriculum is at once the product of a number of decisions made and in the making, using processes (and variables within the processes) that are individually and collectively familiar or acceptable to the decider(s). It may be helpful, therefore, to design decision-making models that delineate the divergence of mental processes underpinning any group decision making, as well as the currently acknowledged variables related to the decisions, in the hope of capturing a more realistic design.

Many existing decision-making models represent linear designs. While the sequential nature of the design is useful for establishing order in the process, linear models fail to account for the behavioral component of deciding. This behavioral factor, which can be referred to as the "political" component of decision making, accounts for the multiple factors that impinge on the decision-making process and the impact of a collectivity on evaluation and consensus. Given an apparent need for a degree of order as well as realism in design, a combination of a linear model (that attempts to outline the acknowledged, essential considerations in some sequential fashion) and a political model (that attempts to consider the interactive, behavioral components of deciding) may prove beneficial.

To effect such a combination, one can begin by noting the basic characteristics that describe a decision-making process. Adaptive decisions appear to occur in four stages: "(a) establishing the purpose or goal whose achievement is to be advanced by the decision, (b) analyzing the information relevant to the decision, (c) synthesizing a solution by selecting the alternative action or actions most likely to lead to the purpose or goal, and (d) implementing the decision by issuing a command signal to carry out the action or actions" [15, p. 100]. Numerous models exist that incorporate these four stages in a linear fashion. Providing a systematic breakdown of the phases of decision making can be useful in several analytical stages of the process because of the need to simplify a complex phenomenon for conceptual purposes. However, if the mind of a decider appears not to proceed in such a linear fashion, it seems unlikely that any group process would be so ordered. Linearity, sequence, and integration represent, therefore, ambitious assumptions [9, p. 6]. Still, despite the absence of realistic description in linear models, a sequential approach does aid in articulating those assumptions acknowledged as rudimentary to deciding.

In contrast, political decision-making models represent, by definition, a group process. Fincher [9] has developed a heuristic model of political decision making that illuminates the behavioral component of group deciding. There are four basic features of Fincher's model (see Fig. 1):

1. There is a centripetal direction of inquiry. The center of the model represents the target of participant interaction and exchange.

2. The center should retain an imprecise location, as well as a neutral and balanced perspective. This effort to remain flexible, adjustable, and adaptable stems from the need for creative tension in the deciding process as a whole. Divergent opinions, pressures, or requirements of participants are not allowed to converge, but rather are returned to the participants/viewers for a view of the perceived consequences of their ideas.

3. Participants will more than likely have indefinite interrelationships with one another and may even retain a certain degree of anonymity. Because participants

interact in ways that are not easily discernible, equality of roles among deciders is difficult to determine. Participant behavior may be described as a process of bargaining, negotiation, or compromise.

4.   The outputs of the deciding process may be described best as "modified inputs" for other decisions, for political decision making never fully satisfies outsiders in definitions given to the problem or its apparent solution. The process "satisfices" under conditions prevailing at the time [9, pp. 11–12].

While Fincher's model provides a useful point of departure for describing the interactive component of deciding, several further observations can be made. Fincher places leadership in the decision-making process at the center of his model, with the leader serving mostly as a mediator. In comparison, Conrad [3] has found that in the change process leadership may surface in a number of representative people or groups so that the designation of a lead mediator at some central position in a model may be unrealistic. A more accurate design might capture the fluctuating nature of leadership in any group-deciding process (regardless of who ultimately receives credit for a decision).

In addition, Fincher notes that the outputs of any group-deciding process will become the modified inputs for future processes; however, yet another crucial observation needs consideration here. The outcomes of any deciding process also involves the modification of any original inputs. Once again a holographic perspective seems necessary to yield a complete image. One may envision "if A then B then C," and simultaneously be "rationally bounded" [12] by the profound alteration of past experience.

It follows, then, that a design for curricular decision making needs to include enough specificity to account for what is known, acknowledged, and acceptable in the process, as well as enough abstraction to allow for reconceptualization and growth. Logical deduction may be an individual preference for progressing toward a decision in a certain manner as well as the collective acknowledgment of using certain procedures and following certain designs. The transactional element may be the "re-" component of any growth process, as divergent "logics" combine to allow for remodeling, redesign, and reconceptualization, both individual and collective. In short, the realistic design needs to account for a three-dimensional process of deciding, which illuminates what *is* as well as what *can be*. The following model describes such an ongoing process using a combination of linear and interactive designs.

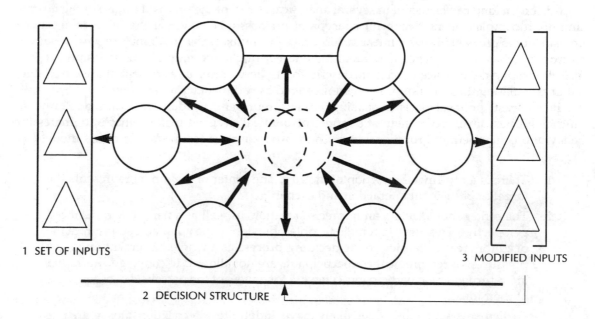

Figure 1 A Heuristic Model for Political Decision Making

Premises of the Model

1. The curriculum operates as an interactive subsystem of the larger college or university system. The curricular process affects and is affected by external influences and the internal institutional environment. Existing states of stability as well as the capacity of the decider(s) to consider risk will impose constraints from within and without [15].

2. Environmental input variables, curricular design variables, and the relationships among these variables appear to be explicitly or implicitly allied in any curricular model. The degree to which a variable or relationship is influential varies according to the particular decision-making situation. To understand differences among colleges regarding the outcomes of individual institutional curricular decision-making processes (i.e., specific curricular designs and educational results), the interrelationships among input variables, curricular design variables, and the decider(s) that manipulates those variables must be taken into account.

3. Curricular decision making usually proceeds in a nonlinear fashion. Although there are numerous variables and curricular components about which decisions are made, there is no specific order in which the decisions occur. Because influential variables shift in relative importance and the strength of relationships varies, the ongoing evaluation of new information—coupled with appropriate adjustments in the curricular design—is an essential part of the process of deciding.

The Model

Although far more linear in concept than are the interactive elements involved in the curricular decision-making process, this design presents a general outline of major curricular variables and the interaction implied by the manipulation of those variables in a decision-making process. Because of the idiosyncratic nature of deciding, for individuals as well as groups, the discussion of the model will deal only with the following broad areas of influence in any decisions about the curriculum (to be more specific would require a case-by-case analysis of the process): (1) environmental inputs over which planners have minimal control; (2) curricular design variables that constitute decision opportunities over which planners have considerable control; and (3) outcome variables that reflect the results of curriculum planning (the specific type of curricular design), and outcome variables that reflect the results of the operation of the curricular system (educational outcomes). Neither the model nor the order of discussion should be taken as a prescribed order for consideration of the variables. The interactive phases (e.g., management perspective, committee perspective, and interest group perspective) in the model reflect transactional possibilities or considerations rather than discrete occurrences in every decision-making process. Decision-making processes can and do vary from place to place and from time to time and are multidirectional. The placement of group interactive phases at certain points in the model represents only a possible arrangement of deciders or groups of deciders.

Environmental Inputs

Environmental inputs are key influence variables that affect decisions about curricula. Their relative importance and the nature of their influence potential fluctuate from institution to institution. These variables can be discussed under three general headings. (1) Societal factors constitute a broad category of the following kinds of influence variables: the expressed and perceived needs of various publics, for example, industrial and business staffing needs, community educational needs, cultural needs, and area and regional economic needs or constraints; the constraints of state or federal governmental guidelines such as those emanating from the Department of Education or state coordinating boards; and the constraints placed on institutions and their programs by various educational and professional certification agencies. (2) Institutional

Figure 2 A Model of Curricular Decision Making

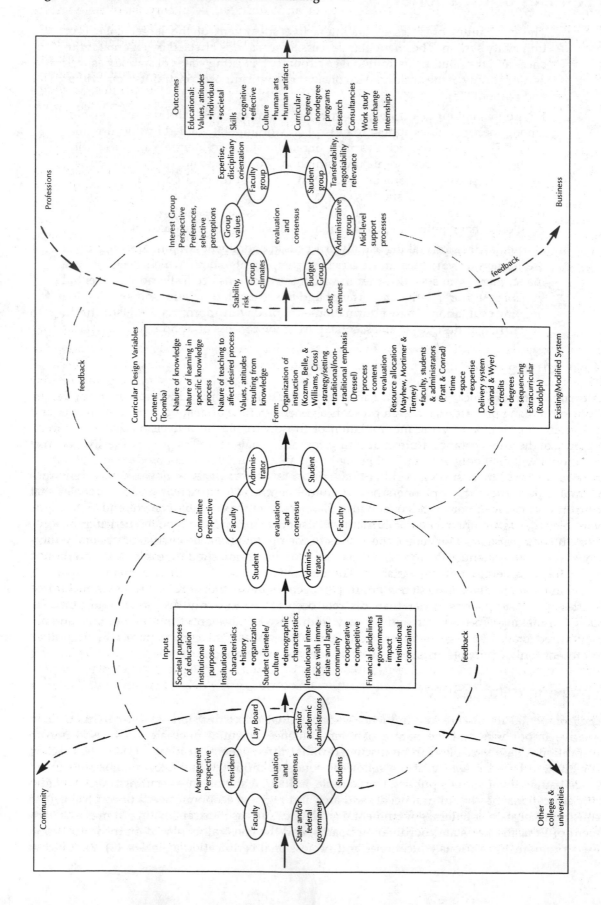

characteristics comprise yet another category of variables related to institutional mission or purpose: the physical and financial resources of an institution, its history, faculty resources, governance structure, management capacity, adaptive capacity, and boundary exchange capacity. As might be expected, the specific nature of the variables under this heading fluctuates considerably across institutions. (3) Student clientele/culture represents a category of basically demographic variables such as projected enrollment population, average age of students, average working status of students, financial capabilities of students and/or their parents, previous academic preparation of students, predominant socioeconomic backgrounds of the student population, and perceived and expressed educational needs of students.

Figure 2 suggests that these environmental variables are not only related to one another, but also have reciprocal relationships with the curricular system. For this reason, while environmental variables are generally found in the model under inputs, these same variables are also dispersed throughout the system (particularly in the feedback loops) to depict the input more realistically. Although environmental variables are considered in the model as elements over which curriculum planners have relatively little control, it should not be assumed that there can be no control over these variables or that the operational curricular system has no impact on them. Curriculum planners can and do manipulate environmental input variables to suit the needs of curricular decision making.

Curricular Design Variables

Decisions made about options within the category of curricular design variables reflect both the interaction of design variables with environmental inputs and the interrelationships among the design variables themselves. This area is the critical decision area for curriculum planners because it is through the analysis of information, the evaluation of relevant relationships, and the selection of appropriate curricular options that curricular designs emerge. In the model, curricular design variables have been divided into two subcategories—content and form.

Content

Societal and institutional goals will inform any decisions about what a curriculum should contain. In turn, this goal-setting will define the scope of the curriculum design and will reflect both general purpose and specific program aims. Goals frequently change during the planning process. Some goals are refined and retained; others are eliminated from the plan and are replaced. Similarly, the projected educational outcomes are reformulated as the emerging curricular design becomes more systematically integrated on the basis of the continuing evaluation of relevant input variables and the selection of curricular options.

Related to all curricular decisions are considerations of the organization or structure of knowledge for the purposes of curriculum design. By far the most commonly accepted structure is that of the traditional academic disciplines. Another perspective views knowledge as it is structured through different ways of knowing about or inquiring into phenomena [17]. Still other perspectives structure knowledge in different ways. For example, phenomenologists explain the structure of knowledge according to the analysis of consciousness; some developmental psychologists, such as Piaget, describe the structure of knowledge in terms of the genesis of its logical complexity.

The epistemological question of the structure of knowledge is one that educational planners usually ignore. Rarely do institutional planners articulate a conception of the structure of knowledge upon which educational programs are based. The reason for this oversight seems to lie in the complexity of the issue and in the predominance of the disciplinary perspective. This dimension of curricular design is included in the model because a more conscious decision about the structure of knowledge may result in curricular designs that exhibit more philosophical coherence, given the simultaneous necessary consideration of teacher and learner behaviors inherent in the various epistemological perspectives. A concomitant result may be the creation of particularly distinctive curricular designs. The central point to be made is simply that in addition to the traditional academic disciplines, there are a variety of alternative conceptions of the structure of knowledge that can be considered in curriculum planning. Without this examination, institutions may uncritically accept an epistemology based on the academic disciplines when an alternative epistemology might be more appropriate.

Form

Organizing and delivering curricular content can be divided into two areas—organizational and instructional. Organizational vehicles represent methods of arranging curricular subject matter to reflect the goals and epistemological perspectives of the decision makers; they provide a form for or structure to curriculum content. Depending upon the particular conception of the structure of knowledge, content can be arranged in a variety of ways. For example, a thematic organizational vehicle could result in the development of courses or experiences related by an underlying theme, such as a futuristic curriculum, a heritage-based program, or a values-oriented curriculum. More traditional vehicles for organizing curricular content include specific academic, career, or professional disciplines. The adoption of a disciplinary organizational vehicle usually results in the development of learning experiences (often departmental or divisional courses) that are discipline-specific—that is, governed in content by the nature of the discipline. On the other hand, if an interdisciplinary organizational approach is used, learning experiences or courses are developed and arranged to focus on the interrelationships among selected disciplines. Since many undergraduate curricula often include several component areas of study (e.g., general education and concentration), each planned by different individuals, it is not unusual to find more than one organizational vehicle underlying a curricular design.

In addition to the organizational vehicles mentioned above, other possibilities include adopting an experiential basis for arranging content, using modes of inquiry as an organizational approach, or applying as an organizational vehicle the "ways of knowing" as suggested by Philip Phenix's [17] six realms of meaning. Of course, each of these organizational vehicles reflects less traditional epistemological perspectives and views of organizing and interrelating curricular content. Even a cursory review of existing curricula suggests that it is rare for a curricular design to be organized around a single, unified, alternative mode of organizing knowledge. The existing need, however, to examine how the relationship between organizational vehicles and their epistemological underpinings affects curricular decision making has been cited repeatedly [7].

At the same time, the effectiveness of any instructional vehicle in fostering learning seems to depend largely on the fit of the mode of instruction with characteristic student and faculty variables. On the one hand, instructional strategies that faculty may employ include lecture; seminar, field, studio, or laboratory experiences; mastery learning strategies, including such approaches as computer-assisted, personalized, and competence-based instruction; team teaching; and independent study. On the other hand, faculty willingness and expertise in the use of these strategies must be a consideration. Varying student interests and abilities will also mediate effectiveness. Further, available physical resources and the means of allocating these resources will influence effectiveness as well as efficiency. The following continua represent the kinds of formative interfaces that need consideration and careful juxtaposition when combining organizational and instructional elements of curricula.

1. Content coverage
   Depth .... Breadth
2. Time dimension
   Past .... Present .... Future
3. Locus of learning
   Campus .... Field
4. Instructional strategies
   Traditional .... Nontraditional

5. Faculty expertise
   Cognitive.. Affective
   Traditional .... Nontraditional
6. Student development
   Cognitive.. Affective
   Traditional .... Nontraditional

In turn, delivery systems should be appropriately matched to organizational and instructional design variables. Delivery systems may be arranged according to some of the following options, again presented as continua.

1. Flexibility of program
   Required .... Distribution .... Elective
2. Design of program sequence
   Faculty .... Contractual .... Student
3. Evaluation procedures
   Faculty .... Mutual .... Student
   Time-based .... Mastery-based
4. Calendar
   Semester/Quarter.. Other
5. Credit options
   Credit by course completion .... Credit by examination

Outcomes

The final portion of the model describes two types of outcomes: (1) educational outcomes—the educational results of the operational curricular process, and (2) curricular outcomes—a reflection of the specific type of curricular design that emerges from the decision process.

The educational outcomes resulting from curricular processes can either be anticipated (in the decision process) and intended (e.g., mastery of Chinese) or unanticipated (e.g., a new translation of Lin Piao). Furthermore, the values, skills, and culture that a particular curricular design educes at once describe the existence and the essence of the entire educational endeavor. As such, educational outcomes affect curriculum planning in two major ways. Treated as formative criteria, they provide information concerning the ongoing effectiveness of specific aspects of the educational process. As summative criteria, they provide information on the general effectiveness of the educational program. In either case, educational outcomes reenter the institutional system, constituting additional variables that influence subsequent curricular decision making. Unfortunately, the values, skills, and culture that are reflected in educational outcomes seem to be indissolubly linked to each other and, thus, represent elusive pieces of information for curricular designers to grasp completely in any concrete fashion because of the difficulty (perhaps, futility) of separating one from the other. Nevertheless, certain anticipated results of the curriculum can be examined for their global ramifications in hopes of providing the requisite foundation from which the anticipated as well as the unanticipated can freely develop. Indeed, outcomes made too specific deny the legitimacy of the diverse human element to which a curricular design must attend [13, pp. 171–72].

Curricular outcomes, in comparison, provide only a glimpse of the working design. Although evaluation and adjustment to a curricular design are an ongoing process, at some point most of the relevant variables have been accounted for and the design emerges. The nature of the emerging design will be in large part determined by the decisions planners made based on their analysis of the importance of input variables, their evaluation of the relationship between these inputs and the various curricular design variables, and their selection of curricular options. Specific degree programs, research orientations, consultancies, and the like will evolve that correspond to the decisions made and the design drawn.

If one considers all possible combinations of variables that might affect curricular decisions, one might conclude that it would be difficult to find two curricula that are alike. Of course, one need only review several existing programs to discover that most curricula are more alike than they are different. Where differences in curricula exist, they can be traced largely to significant institutional differences in key environmental inputs, to specific decisions regarding curricular design options, and to differences in the nature of the anticipated outcome variables.

From Model to Metaphor

Superimposing the metaphor upon the model, this discussion has moved full circle: what the interactive components of the deciding process allow foreshadow any potential curricular designs. Obviously, the attempt has not been to capture a "thingy thing," but rather to illuminate any order or logic that seems apparent, to capture a sense of the impact of history on deciding processes, whether individual or collective, and to describe the illusive transactional element of deciding about curricula.

Neither model nor discussion offer prescriptive guidelines, yet the combination delineates a number of variables and suggests possible interactions of variables in the deciding process to which curriculum planners should be sensitive. In this sense, the concept can have applied uses as well as contribute to an understanding of the evolving curriculum.

References

Axelrod, J. "Curricular Change: A Model for Analysis." *The Research Reporter*, 3 (1968). Berkeley, Calif.: Center for Research and Development in Higher Education, University of California.

Bergquist, W. H. "Curricular Practice." In *Developing the College Curriculum: A Handbook for Faculty and Administrators.* by A. W. Chickering et al., pp. 77–109. Washington, D.C.: Council for the Advancement of Small Colleges, 1977.

Conrad, C. F. "A Grounded Theory of Academic Change." *Sociology of Education*, 51 (April 1978), 101-12.

Conrad, C. F. *The Undergraduate Curriculum: A Guide to Innovation and Reform.* Boulder, Colo.: Westview Press, 1978.

Conrad, C. F., and J. C. Wyer. "Liberal Education in Transition." AAHE-ERIC/Higher Education Research Report No. 3. Washington, D.C.: American Association for Higher Education, 1980.

Cross. K. P. *Accent on Learning.* San Francisco: Jossey-Bass, 1976.

Dressel, P. L. *College and University Curriculum.* Second edition. Berkeley, Calif.: McCutchan, 1971.

Dressel, P. L.. *Improving College Degree Programs.* San Francisco: Jossey-Bass, 1980.

Fincher, C. "Technology Transfer and Political Decision Making: The Conflict in Models." Athens, Ga.: Institute of Higher Education, University of Georgia, 1975.

Hall, E. T. *Beyond Culture.* New York: Anchor Press/Doubleday, 1976.

Kozma, R. B., L. W. Belle, and G. W. Williams. *Instructional Techniques in Higher Education.* Englewood Cliffs, N.J.: Educational Technology Publications, 1978.

March, J., and H. Simon. *Organizations.* New York: Wiley, 1958.

Mayhew, L. B. *Surviving the Eighties.* San Francisco: Jossey-Bass, 1979.

Mayhew, L. B., and J. Ford. *Changing the Curriculum.* San Francisco: Jossey-Bass, 1971.

Miller, J. G. *Living Systems.* New York: McGraw-Hill, 1979.

Mortimer, K. P., and M. L. Tierney. "The Three 'R'S' of the Eighties: Reduction, Reallocation and Retrenchment." AAHE-ERIC/Higher Education Research Report No. 4. Washington, D.C.: American Association for Higher Education, 1979.

Phenix, P. *Realms of Meaning.* New York: McGraw-Hill, 1964.

Pratt, A. M., and C. F. Conrad. "Everyman's Undergraduate Curriculum: A Question of Humanistic Context." *Liberal Education*, 67 (Summer 1981), 168–76.

Rudolph, F. *Curriculum*. San Francisco: Jossey-Bass, 1977.

Toombs. W. "The Application of Design-Based Curriculum Analysis to General Education." *Higher Education Review*, 1 (Spring 1978), 18–29.

The Subject

James R. Davis

Now what I want is Facts. Teach these boys and girls nothing but Facts. Facts alone are wanted in life.
—*Charles Dickens*, Hard Times

Broad and Narrow Definitions

In common usage the term "subject" refers to the content of an academic discipline, such as chemistry, history, or mathematics. This emphasis on content is the narrower definition of subject. A good teacher needs to know the subject. As one teacher put it: "You can't teach without some stuff." Effective teachers know the intellectual turf, and they know it well enough to make complex explanations and take on challenging questions. It is assumed, *a priori*, that before teachers begin to think about selecting teaching strategies, they must know their subject in some depth.

Most of us have spent years learning a specialization in a "subject" major and in academic programs leading to advanced degrees. Sometimes we have also accumulated significant levels of experience with the subject in professional or commercial employment settings. Most of us know how to continue to increase our knowledge of the subject as content. What we often lack, however, is a way of thinking more systematically about the purpose of our subject, that is, what we hope students will learn through the subject.

A broad definition of "the subject" may include not only content (information), but also such things as skills and abilities, thinking processes, and values and attitudes related to the content. Although students today expect and need information, they will need more than that. One might say, the subject is whatever the teacher hopes will be learned and whatever the students are willing to learn. This broader way of looking at the subject is more useful, but it opens a floodgate to a deluge of possibilities. We are then confronted with the question: What should be included?

Establishing Goals

Because no teacher can teach everything, the key question, framed aptly by the nineteenth-century philosopher Herbert Spencer, becomes the following: What knowledge is of most worth?[1] In the information age, when new knowledge is generated at an ever-accelerating rate, Spencer's question takes on new urgency. Conscientious teachers struggle with this question to delineate the subject more precisely for the purposes of instruction. This delineation involves setting goals. Consider how each of the following teachers addresses Spencer's question.

At Mid-West University, Roscoe Meade is one of 16 professors in a department that has a very carefully sequenced curriculum designed to serve undergraduate majors, master's degree students, and doctoral candidates. The goal, throughout the curriculum, is to help students "think like a sociologist thinks"; that is, to expose students to the topics that sociologists study and the ways they go about conducting research. For Professor Meade, the discipline of sociology is extremely useful for "packaging" the knowledge he most wants his students to have.

At Elm Grove College, Edna Wolf wants to expose students to the very best classic works of literature with the hope that her students will not only appreciate the technical craft and aesthetic grace of the writing, but will also gain some deeper vision of the meaning of human existence. She knows that her colleagues in the Humanities Division at Elm Grove share this goal, because together they have carefully selected the "great works of art" most worthy of study in the coordinated series of courses that make up the "core curriculum" in the humanities. For Edna Wolf, the knowledge most worth having is the classical wisdom that addresses ultimate concerns.

When people ask Vicki Hastings what she teaches at Pacific Coast Community College, she replies, "students." Her goal is to get to know each one personally in her wellness classes and to select the kinds of activities and topics that will best meet their individual needs for personal and physical development. For Vicki, the needs of her students play an important role in determining what knowledge is of most worth.

When Nancy Green teaches interior design at the Art Institute of the South, she sometimes feels inexperienced as a teacher, but she knows that she is an expert in her field, because she has lived it for 15 years. Her goal is to teach the skills that she knows will be needed on the job. She hates the thought of sending her students into the field poorly prepared. For Nancy, the knowledge of most worth is the information and skills that will make her students competent designers.

At New England Theological Seminary, Jonathan Wesley wants to help students understand themselves as agents of social transformation by experiencing what it means to change—beginning with their own attitudes, opinions, and beliefs. To help others change, one must first experience the process of transformation within one's own self. For Jonathan Wesley, the knowledge of most worth is that which will enable his students to become effective advocates of social change.

All these teachers answer the question, "What knowledge is of most worth?" in very different ways. They all arrive at different conclusions about goals; and their goals, naturally, determine what will be included in their courses. It is often a painful process, this business of articulating goals, but this is the place to begin, because it is the foundation of all instructional activity. Curriculum specialists—people who do research and write in a sub-field of education known as "curriculum theory"—have provided a number of useful concepts for helping teachers select the "knowledge of most worth" and organize it for instruction.

Clarifying Objectives

The process of clarifying objectives is simply a matter of making goals more specific. A teacher without objectives—some basic plan for what is to be accomplished—is like a traveler without a destination; not only is it hard to get there, it is also difficult to know when you have arrived. Sometimes objectives will be very concrete delineations of what the students will be able to do as a result of learning; at other times objectives may be more open-ended, flexible descriptions of a situation or problem, out of which various kinds of learning might arise. Either way, a teacher needs some clarity about desired learning outcomes—what the student will learn from instruction.

Teachers are often tempted to teach more than can be learned because there is so much "out there" that could be learned. An effective teacher learns to narrow learning outcomes to a manageable list. Usually we are forced into choosing among desirable outcomes of various kinds. *Cognitive outcomes* have to do with thinking and conceptual abilities; *affective outcomes* have to do with attitudes, values, and feelings; and *psychomotor outcomes* have to do with movement or activity, such as the ability to perform a skill.[2] Although all of these outcomes are desirable, forced choices often have to be made in prioritizing the most desirable outcomes.

When effective teachers seek to define objectives, they ask a series of probing questions about the subject.[3] Where does the subject begin and end? This is usually referred to as *scope* in curriculum planning. How much of the delineated subject should be included in instruction? This is usually called breadth in curriculum planning. How deeply should the teacher go into a particular aspect of the subject? This is usually called *depth*. Of the many things to be covered, how much time should be devoted to some things as opposed to others? This is usually called *centrality and balance* in the curriculum. To what extent should students be required to study certain things as opposed to being allowed to pursue their own interests? This is usually called *flexibility* in the curriculum. Which things should be taught first and which second, that is, are there certain topics or skills that are prerequisite to other topics and skills? This is usually referred to as *sequence* in curriculum planning. What is the teacher intentionally leaving out? This is the matter of identifying *gaps* in the curriculum. What is the teacher forgetting to include? This is called the *null* curriculum. What is the teacher unwittingly and unintentionally teaching? This is called the *hidden* curriculum.

As teachers make plans for a class or a course, they must make decisions about all of these matters. These are all difficult questions to answer, and may never be answered fully or finally, but they are useful guides for selecting and organizing the subject for instruction. The answers to these questions help teachers in framing their objectives. Consider the examples presented earlier.

Professor Meade focuses primarily on cognitive outcomes in his upper division course in demographics. He uses a standard textbook and takes up the topics in the order in which they are presented in the book. This is not a "survey" course, so his object is depth and his central focus is on methods of acquiring and interpreting demographic data. Students are permitted some flexibility in selecting a term project topic, but there is also a final exam, along with several quizzes, to ensure that students have a grasp of all the essential information. There is general agreement in the discipline of sociology about what a course in demographics should contain, and it is a fairly self-contained field, so Professor Meade doesn't need to worry much about duplication of material presented in other courses. His colleagues can count on him to cover the essential content and not leave any gaps.

Edna Wolf focuses on affective as well as cognitive outcomes in her literature course, that is, she hopes that students will have opinions and feelings about the classic works of literature she presents. The order of the material is not important; she gave up historical chronology years ago in favor of in-depth study of a few key selected works. Students have no choice of what to study; after all, she and her colleagues have spent considerable time in selecting the most appropriate classics. There is no chance of duplication from course to course this way, and there is little concern about gaps, since chronological survey is not the goal. The central focus is on using great works of literature to help students "examine their unexamined lives." The most important objective is to enable students to gain a deeper vision of the meaning of life in a rapidly changing post-modern society characterized by normlessness.

Vicki Hastings focuses on affective and psychomotor outcomes in her course on wellness. She hopes to help students forge new commitments about eating, mental attitudes, and exercise habits. Because she focuses on the students and their needs, she "covers" various topics when students express interest, not going into much depth on any one subject with the whole group, but conferring after class with students who want to learn more. She knows that she can't teach everything in one course and encourages students to register for the advanced course in the following term. Because her course is not a "talk course," the central focus is on getting people moving, enabling them to experience the new-found sense of well-being that comes with becoming more physically fit by practicing fitness. And above all, Vicki knows that she can't come to class 50 pounds overweight and smoking like a chimney; because if she does, the hidden curriculum" will override everything else she tries to do or say about fitness.

Nancy Green is interested primarily in cognitive outcomes, but she also wants her students to develop the interpersonal skills needed for working as members of a team and for working with clients. She knows that her students must be able to solve "real world" design problems, and that to do so, they must become experts in dealing simultaneously with the functional use of space, with aesthetic concerns, and with financial considerations. This becomes her central focus and these are the topics she wants to include, but she knows that flexibility can be introduced into the course as students work together on a final team project that addresses these topics.

Jonathan Wesley knows that the commitment to social justice is already implanted in his divinity students; his concern is in helping them to understand how people come to change their attitudes, opinions, and values as they make personal and social transformations. To gain this understanding, his students are given the opportunity to experience what it is like to reexamine their own position on various social questions. The focus of the course, therefore, is on affective outcomes, what Wesley calls "the transformation of the heart." He selects a few social issues to study in depth—capital punishment vs. rehabilitation of offenders, "pro-choice" vs. "right-to-life," public vs. private approaches to social welfare— and uses these as the vehicle for exploring where attitudes about public policy come from and how they can be changed. The sequence of the study of these issues is immaterial, and the coverage of all the important current issues is not the goal, because the central focus is on learning firsthand how personal transformation takes place.

Every teacher needs to be able to identify immediate and long-range objectives—for each class and for the course as a whole as the first step toward carrying out instruction. Teaching often breaks down right at the beginning when we have not clarified our primary goals and expressed them as objectives. When we lack a clear sense of the desired outcomes of instruction, we often try to do too much and our teaching gives way to random (often frantic) activity. Effective teachers know what they are trying to achieve, and they consciously select and continually refine their objectives.

Identifying the Organizing Principle

Course objectives are important, but they exist in a broader context. Most courses have their niche within a broader set of organizing principles and educational philosophies. The organizing principle of a course, or set of courses, may or may not be well-articulated; but it is usually there, determining, often in subtle ways, what happens day after day in the classroom.

One place to look for the organizing principle is in the core of required courses that students must take, sometimes referred to as the general education requirements.[4] What is it, if anything, that the institution identifies as essential for all students? In a large, public university this may take the form of a distribution requirement, such as 12 credit hours in each of the areas of the sciences, social sciences, and humanities. Such a requirement sends the message that the academic disciplines are important and that students should be exposed, usually through introductory courses, to several of these disciplines. On the other hand, a small liberal arts college may require that all students take a series of interdisciplinary, often team-taught, courses, especially designed as a core curriculum. Through such courses, the faculty sends the message that a liberal education has at its core certain essential knowledge found through acquaintance with the great books or seminal thinkers of an intellectual tradition. Students are expected to obtain a "general education" or a "common learning" as well as the specialized knowledge that comes through a disciplinary major or professional training. The transfer program of a community college, likewise, may have certain required courses, which are part of an articulated transfer agreement with the public, four-year institutions in the same state. For the occupational programs of a community college or a proprietary school, the core requirements may be in certain basic skills, such as reading, writing, and speaking or in mathematical computation. A theological seminary will usually identify certain courses in the Bible, theology, and church history as "foundational" to all further study. The way an institution identifies its "required core" of studies will often provide some insight into the educational philosophy or key organizing principle of the curriculum in that institution.

It is important, however, to look beyond the core, beyond the general requirements, to identify a more comprehensive principle used to organize subjects for instruction. Five organizing principles may commonly be found in the curricula of postsecondary institutions, and one or more of these principles will surface in most institutions as the key organizing principle or as the "philosophy" of the curriculum.[5]

The most frequently observed principle is the organizational system of the academic disciplines. Most colleges of arts and sciences are organized according to a disciplinary system, and the disciplines usually correspond to departments, such as chemistry, sociology, history, or biology. But what is a discipline? One comprehensive description suggests that a discipline is a community of persons; an expression of human imagination; a domain; a tradition; a syntactical structure and mode of inquiry; a conceptual structure; a specialized language or other system of symbols; a heritage of literature and artifacts and a network of communication; a valuative and affective stance; and an instructive community.[6] A discipline is all of these things, but a simpler definition might be this: A discipline is a specified academic domain with agreed-upon rules for discovering and transmitting knowledge.

Neither the number of disciplines nor their boundaries has ever remained static over time. Old disciplines die out as new disciplines emerge, providing the basis for new methods of inquiry and new knowledge. But at any given point in time, there is general (if not absolute) agreement within a discipline about what is to be studied and how it is to be studied. The professional associations of the major disciplines play a key role in this process of definition.

There are, of course, great advantages to the organizational system of the academic disciplines. As Philip Phenix notes:

> The most impressive claim the disciplines have upon education is that they are the outcome of learning that has actually been successful. A discipline is a field of inquiry in which learning has been achieved in an unusually productive way. Most human efforts at understanding fail. A very few succeed, and these fruitful ways of thought are conserved and developed in the disciplines. Every discipline is simply a pattern of investigation that has proved to be a fertile field for the growth of understandings.[7]

Furthermore, the disciplines provide a common understanding (a lingua franca) for stable interchange among institutions and teachers. A course in introductory sociology is likely to be relatively the same from institution to institution. Most chemists will have at least general agreement about what is taught in organic chemistry.

Although most postsecondary teachers have had a significant exposure to the academic disciplines in their own education—enough to appreciate the value of the disciplinary system— many teachers today raise questions about the predominance of the disciplines as the exclusive organizing principle for the curriculum. While the disciplines may serve well the "academic priesthood," most of life's problems in the information age, both in the world of work and in the society at large, do not come in the tidy packages suggested by the academic disciplines. Students trained exclusively in a system of academic disciplines may be ill-equipped to deal with the problems of the real world. Students often have trouble seeing the relationships among disciplines, and the rigid boundaries and specialized language of the disciplines often hinder communication. Although the academic disciplines provide an excellent framework for the discovery of knowledge, they do not necessarily provide the best (and certainly not the only) means for the transmission and application of knowledge.

Some colleges organize the curriculum around a different principle, using a list of selected "great books."[8] In the earliest colonial colleges of America, students studied (usually in Greek or Latin) the "classics," a series of great works that embodied the roots of Western thought. Proponents of this view today argue that the wisdom of the past is distilled in selected great books that have become classics. Although the knowledge of the world is always expanding, they argue that the important problems confronting human beings have already been dealt with by the great minds through the ages. While the form of the problems may change, the substance will not. Thus, the foundation of learning should be found in the great books or other works of art and music— that represent the best of a long tradition. The great books curriculum helps students to distinguish between genuine knowledge and the superficial accumulation of information. It also addresses directly the problem of normlessness by introducing students to the cultural norms and values that have come to be considered timeless.

The most ardent defenders of the great books organize the entire curriculum around a list of classics. Most often, only a course, or a series of courses (often within the general education curriculum) are organized around the great books theme. In either case, it is in the discussion of these works, usually in small seminars, where the essence of the educational experience lies. The strength of this approach is in the development of critical thinking, speaking, and writing skills—the traditional foundations of liberal learning—and in the humanizing effect of such learning.

It can be argued, however, that a curriculum with such a strong historical orientation shortchanges the study of the present and the future and does little to prepare students to enter the highly specialized and increasingly technical job market of the information age. If there has been a true "system break" with the past, perhaps the extraordinary emphasis on "classics" in the great books approach is dysfunctional for students in the information age. Today, there is also much controversy about the works that truly belong on the list, with some critics of the great books curriculum suggesting that more works from non-Western cultures and more works by women and members of minority groups should be included for study.[9] The widespread and frequent encounter today of diverse groups of people suggests that knowledge of Western culture alone is insufficient.

Another way of organizing the curriculum is to focus on the personal development of students. Here the organizing principle is shifted from the content of the subject to the growth of the individual student. The subject becomes the medium for personal development. Through recent research on human development, particularly (post-adolescent) adult development, key developmental tasks of college-age students (establishing identity, becoming autonomous, etc.) have been identified. Theories of social-emotional, ethical, and cognitive development provide insights into the stages of normal development through which most college students are passing.[10] Advocates of what is often called a "student-centered curriculum" argue that the primary purpose of education is to facilitate human development, and that nothing is truly learned unless it involves the maintenance or enhancement of the self in some way.[11] Courses should include subjects that address students' personal concerns, and the curriculum should not be a series of requirements but a list of opportunities from which students choose those studies that best meet their needs. Through extensive consultation with faculty mentors, students and faculty together design a program of studies— courses, independent study projects, work experience, internships, travel—that facilitates the development of students here and now rather than preparing them for some remote indescribable future.

Although student development as an organizing principle for the curriculum maximizes opportunities for personalizing education, critics argue that the substance of education, particularly the development of academic skills in some depth in a selected field, is often neglected. Students may too easily avoid what is new, difficult, or of future (rather than present) interest or value. They may complete their program of studies lacking the technical knowledge (gleaned through sometimes distasteful discipline) so essential for the information age.

Still another organizing principle for the college curriculum is the development of selected competencies. Proponents of what is often called a "competency-based curriculum" contend that education should be functional and students should be prepared for specific roles, particularly occupational roles, which they will begin to fill upon completion of their studies. Competency-based curricula are most often found in professional schools and in majors designed to prepare students for a specific occupation, but some efforts have also been made to establish competency-based curricula in liberal arts colleges.[12] The most important questions in a competency-based curriculum are the following: What should graduates be able to do? What competencies should they have? What educational experiences will assure specified outcomes? In a competency-based curriculum the starting point is usually some occupational or "real-life" activity or skill. If it is possible to specify what a teacher, nurse, accountant, or parent or citizen, actually does when he or she is doing it well, then it is possible to work backward from those activities to the educational experiences that will produce those competencies. Students work through a series of course and other educational activities that have been carefully designed to develop (and test) selected competencies.

The great strength of a competency-based curriculum is its emphasis on results—specific, testable, clearly defined educational outcomes. Students often are allowed to work at their own pace, focusing on what they really need to learn to become competent. Teachers and students both know the goal and when they reach it. Critics of this approach, on the other hand, argue that the focus is too narrow and too future-oriented. Students fail to gain a sufficient appreciation of their cultural heritage and the ways knowledge comes into being. When the focus is exclusively on pre-selected competencies, the educational experience becomes routine and unimaginative. Students will settle for learning only what they need to know rather than developing a love of learning for its own sake. It is sometimes argued that students in such programs trade away an education for the accumulation of a handful of currently marketable but soon-to-be-outdated skills. As for exploring the deeper meaning of life, the important questions may not even be raised.

A final theme sometimes used as an organizing principle for the curriculum is social change. Here the emphasis is on developing individuals who are able to help build a better society. The assumption, of course, is that the present society is far from perfect, producing too many unresolved social, economic, political, and environmental problems. Some argue that because education is increasingly funded by society, a collegiate education ought to result collectively in the betterment of society. For this to occur, it is necessary to use an interdisciplinary approach and to attack the problems of society by studying those problems directly. In what is sometimes called a "social problems curriculum," courses are organized around problem themes, such as urban problems, environmental issues, criminal justice, or Third World problems. Some institutions even organize into "cluster colleges" or "colleges within a college" where students of similar interests can live and study together.[13] Usually, a challenging out-of-the-classroom internship or service experience is also associated with these programs.

The great advantage to this approach is that by emphasizing the present and the future, a social problems curriculum prepares students to take active roles as citizens in the community and gives them the knowledge and skills they need to become leaders and change-agents in the information age. To the extent that this curriculum also addresses problems from a global perspective, students are also better prepared to grapple with life in the global village. Those who criticize this approach, however, point out that an *a priori* commitment to change seriously threatens education as a "value free" process. The highly desirable academic value known as "objectivity" is often replaced with a conscious nurture of commitment. Furthermore, the study of the historical heritage and great works of the past is often shortchanged in the rush to cast everything as a contemporary problem. By overemphasizing "problem solving," other academic skills are neglected. A preoccupation with social problems, it is argued, leads to an overemphasis on the utilitarian function of education, while neglecting deeper academic values, such as the development of a philosophy of life or the cultivation of the "life of the mind" for its own sake. Consider once again the examples provided earlier.

> Professor Meade's sociology courses are part of a curriculum that uses the academic disciplines as the chief organizing principle. He wants to introduce students to sociology as a discipline and to "socialize" them into the modes of academic inquiry that sociologists use to go about their studies. Edna Wolf's courses in the Humanities Division at Elm Grove College have been organized around the great books theme. She believes that most of the important human concerns have been expressed already in the classics; and she wants her students to share with her and with each other their personal responses to these works. To the extent that Vicki Hastings' courses at Pacific Coast Community College are part of any organized set of offerings, they reside within a student-centered curriculum. Her courses are there for students to choose when they feel a personal need to live happier, healthier lives. Nancy Green's courses at the Art Institute of the South are part of a competency-based program in interior design. As an experienced designer herself, she has a clear concept of what jobs in this field are and what skills are needed to perform these jobs well. She knows that functional, aesthetic, and financial considerations come into all design decisions, and she wants her students to have the competencies to deal effectively with these problems. Jonathan Wesley organizes his teaching around the theme of social change. His course in personal and social transformation at the New England Theological Seminary is designed to provide students with first-hand knowledge of how people come to hold social attitudes and what mechanism can be used effectively to help people reexamine their attitudes.

Most teaching is brought into focus by an organizing principle that governs the "how and why" for the way things are done. The organizing principle does not always appear in its pure form, and in some cases two or more principles are combined in creative ways. Nevertheless, teachers need to become aware of and be able to articulate clearly the dominant organizing principles governing their teaching.

Agreeing to Disagree

Where do these organizing principles come from? Surely they do not appear one day out of thin air! Curriculum themes have their origins, of course, in many places. John Dewey once identified the sources of curricular goals as "the students, the society and organized subject matter."[14] In higher education, these origins take on their own peculiar form, but in general, Dewey's assertion holds.

Students exert their influence directly, as the "peaceful protesters" did in the 1960s, or indirectly, as the "calculating consumers" did in the 1980s. The most important, but perhaps most subtle, influence of students is through the *a priori* decision that the institution has made about what students to serve and how to serve them. By agreeing to serve a particular kind of student, the institution has opened the door to a big influence on the curriculum. The underlying themes and organizing principles usually arise at least in part from the way the institution defines what students to serve and how to serve them.

Societal influences are also important, because the dominant values of society are quickly turned into expectations for education. In the late 1950s, the launching of Sputnik by the Soviet Union produced a wave of anxiety in the United States about training more and better scientists and technicians. In the 1960s, the civil rights and women's movements generated a high level of concern about equal educational opportunity. In the 1970s and 1980s, as the employment market underwent important structural changes, a new emphasis was placed on career education and job preparation.[15] In the years ahead, the emphasis will be on new knowledge, new abilities to derive and manage technical information, and new interpersonal skills necessary for working in a globalized environment. In the United States today, where change is very rapid and there is a frequent turnover in ideas, values, and technology, the curriculum is often strongly impacted by the shifting expectations of a rapidly changing society.

The curriculum is also influenced by the ways in which "subject matter" is conceptualized, formalized, and emphasized. In higher education this takes place chiefly through a host of academic professional associations and accrediting bodies. These are essentially voluntary associations of scholars with similar interests, but they now have a profound influence upon the curriculum through their reports, recommendations, and annual meetings. What would the language curriculum be without the Modern Language Association? How would the business curriculum be different without the American Assembly of Collegiate Schools of Business? What influence takes place through the accrediting processes of the American Psychological Association or the American Chemical Society?

Teachers in postsecondary institutions today must take into account a broad array of outside factors that influence the curriculum. The subject, in the broader sense, involves a balance between what the teacher wants to teach, what someone else wants taught, and what students want to learn. Even in the most prestigious colleges and universities, where the curriculum has long been the sacred prerogative of the faculty, student needs, societal pressures, and changing conceptions of the subject increasingly determine what is taught. The curriculum exists in a social context.

Ultimately, however, the organizing principles of the curriculum have their origins in a "philosophy of education." Whenever choices are made about what to include in instruction or how to go about instruction, values are at stake; and values—what is real, true, good, and beautiful—rest ultimately on one's personal philosophy. Many decisions about what should be included in instruction are governed by philosophical considerations. Differences in curriculum orientation, therefore, ultimately involve disagreements about the underlying purposes of educational.[16] Disagreements about educational purposes, in turn, involve fundamental philosophical controversies about the nature of reality, what constitutes knowledge, and how to define human nature. Is knowledge gained primarily from sense experience? Is the world we see the real world, or is there more to the world than meets the eye? Are human beings more emotional than rational? Is the individual more important than society, or society more important than the individual? Are students naturally good and internally motivated, or are they essentially lazy and perverse? Is there such a thing as progress? These are the great, unanswerable human questions—issues that philosophers have struggled to clarify through the ages—but the tentative answers we provide to these questions determine in large measure how we will organize our subject for instruction.

Sometimes our colleagues will ask, "What evidence is there that the curriculum should include one thing as opposed to another?" Usually this is the wrong question, because "evidence" of the kind that will settle the argument is not forthcoming. Most curricular decisions are based on a commitment to particular values that become the criteria for "what's important." If Roscoe Meade, Edna Wolf, Vicki Hastings, Nancy Green, and Jonathan Wesley were all brought together in the same room, it would not be long before they would be at each other's throats, because they all have different ideas about what is important in their teaching. It is not difficult to predict what would happen if they were all asked to serve on the same curriculum committee. There would be, no doubt, heated arguments about vocational vs. liberal education (the "cash vs. culture" debate), egalitarian vs. elitist education (the "all vs. best" debate), and applied vs. basic education (the "useful vs. theoretical" debate). Hopefully, these teachers would grow to appreciate the strengths and weaknesses of their varying and sometimes opposing viewpoints. Maybe they would be able to generate some creative synthesis of their differences. But more likely they would simply have to agree to disagree. Perhaps it is best that they all teach at different institutions. Agreeing to disagree is what Americans have chosen to do about higher education. That is why there is no national system of higher education, no national examination for entrance, no national university, and so many different kinds of institutions. The great achievement of American higher education is its diversity; it's great challenge will be in generating diverse responses to the demands of a new era.

Will a new curriculum theory emerge for the information age? Will the older organizing principles—the disciplines, the great books, the student-centered approach, the competency-based system, the social problems curriculum—give way to some new organizing principle, based on a yet to be articulated futuristic philosophy of education? In an age of such rapid change, filled with so many surprises, it is imprudent to answer with an unequivocal "no"; but the organizing principles have deep roots, and because education has been a conservative and conserving enterprise, it is unlikely that these principles will suddenly drop out of sight. What is more likely, instead, is that they will take on new forms, become more highly elaborated, differentiated, and synthesized. The disciplines will not go away; to the contrary, there will probably be more of them, but more interdisciplinary studies surely will be elaborated. The list of "great books" will become longer and longer (because truly new knowledge has been generated in the twentieth century), and the list will surely be broadened and integrated to include the great works of other cultures and sub-cultures. There will be many student-centered curricula, based not only on the developmental needs of traditional-age college students, but also on the needs of mid-career adults and senior citizens, and members of different ethnic groups and genders. And so on. Some of the best aspects of the various organizing principles may be connected in creative new ways to overcome the shortcomings of each alone. It may be possible within a disciplinary framework to introduce students to the "great books" of that discipline, or to strike a balance somehow between what a student needs to know (competency-based curriculum) and wants to know (student-centered curriculum).

A new curriculum, better suited to the present and the future, will be a protean curriculum that changes shape to fit the needs of many different subjects being taught to many different kinds of students in a variety of institutional settings. It will be "pluralistic," achieving many goals and connecting in creative and enriching ways the singular strands of earlier organizing principles. The new curriculum will respect (and teach respect for) cultural pluralism within a nation and cultural diversity among many nations. Through the pluralistic curriculum, students will develop an awareness that many kinds of knowledge are of great worth. Greater efforts will be made to connect the learning that occurs in general education with the major and across majors, and more attention will be paid to assessing learning outcomes at all levels.[17] Above all, the curriculum of the new era will reflect diversity—the diversity of the peoples of the world, and the diversity of ways of learning in a world governed less by tradition and more by existential choices growing out of well-articulated needs.

As teachers we need to know what our role is and where we fit in all of this diversity. We are likely to be most effective in a setting where our goals and abilities are relatively compatible with the curriculum we are trying to implement, where there is a high level of correspondence between our philosophy of education and what we can reasonably expect to achieve with the students we teach. Because the philosophical questions are for the most part unresolvable, they keep coming around again and again, like the decorated horses on a merry-go-round. It is important to realize that the significant philosophical issues in education have their historical antecedents.[18] What most people argue about today in education has been argued about many times before. Effective teachers know how and when to take a stand, and they know what their institution stands for; but they also know that reasonable people will disagree about what is most valuable in education, and that certain arguments won't be settled. They know how to get off the issue merry-go-round and get on with their teaching; they know how to keep from going in circles and how to make commitments to what is important in their classroom, at their institution, and for their students. Effective teachers are able to see the subject in perspective.

Conclusions

Before selecting a teaching strategy, we must surely know the subject, not only in the narrow sense of content, but also in the broader and deeper sense of a medium for what is to be learned. In addition, we must be able to think systematically about organizing the subject for instruction. What are the goals? What are the long-range and immediate objectives of instruction? What are the organizing principles upon which goals and objectives are based? What, also, are the deeper, underlying purposes of education? What are the origins of these purposes? What is the educational philosophy undergirding the curriculum? And, above all, we need to ask ourselves these questions regularly and systematically: When I teach, what am I really trying to do? What is my subject and what am I trying to teach *through* my subject?

All serious thinking about teaching appropriately begins with the subject.

Notes

1. Herbert Spencer, *Education: Intellectual, Moral and Physical* (New York: Appleton, 1860); quoted in Daniel Tanner and Laurel Tanner, *Curriculum Development: Theory into Practice*, 2nd ed., (New York: Macmillan, 1980), p. 143. The work by Tanner and Tanner is perhaps the most useful single volume on general curriculum theory and is recommended for those who wish to pursue the subject further.

2. The designation of outcomes into "cognitive," "affective," and "psychomotor" domains is commonly found in curriculum textbooks. Efforts to establish a series of taxonomies of outcomes appear in Benjamin Bloom, *Taxonomy of Educational Objectives: Cognitive Domain* (New York: David McKay, 1956); David Kathwohl, *Taxonomy of Education Objectives: Affective Domain* (New York: David McKay, 1964); and Nita Harrow, *Taxonomy of Educational Objectives: Psychomotor Domain* (New York: Longman, 1972).

3. The concepts for analyzing the curriculum (scope, sequence, breadth, depth, etc.) are found scattered about in the basic standard curriculum texts . This list is a composite developed by the author from William H. Schubert, *Curriculum: Perspective, Paradigm and Possibility* (New York: Macmillan, 1986); Daniel Tanner and Laurel Tanner, *Curriculum Development*, and Paul Dressel, *College and University Curriculum* (Berkeley, CA: McCutchan, 1968). The concept of the hidden curriculum comes from Benson Snyder, *The Hidden Curriculum* (New York: Alfred Knopf, 1971), and the idea of the "null curriculum" is derived from Elliot Eisner, *The Educational Imagination*, 2nd ed., (New York: Macmillan, 1985). For a guidebook on planning courses and curricula in higher education, see Robert Diamond, *Designing and improving Courses and Curricula in Higher Education* (San Francisco: Jossey-Bass, 1989) and William Berquist, Ronald Gould, and Elinor Greenberg, *Designing Undergraduate Education* (San Francisco: Jossey-Bass, 1981).

4. The concept of "general education" has been elaborated in many sources and over a long period of time. The idea has its roots in the early twentieth century and was a response in part to the elective system established under Charles Eliot at Harvard and also a reaction to the apparent "normlessness" of the World War I period. A brief conceptual treatment can be found in a report of the Carnegie Foundation for the Advancement of Teaching, *Missions of the College Curriculum* (San Francisco: Jossey-Bass, 1977), Chapter 8, "General Education: An Idea in Distress," and in Ernest Boyer, *College: The Undergraduate Experience* (New York: Harper & Row, 1987), Chapter 6, "General Education: The Integrated Core." For historical treatments, see especially Daniel Bell, *The Reforming of General Education* (Garden City, NY: Anchor, 1966) and Ernest Boyer and Martin Kaplan, *Educating for Survival* (New Rochelle, NY: Change Magazine Press, 1977). For examples of current programs, see Zelda Gamson and Associates, *Liberating Education* (San Francisco: Jossey-Bass, 1984). For guidelines on curricular change in general education, see Jerry Gaff, *General Education Today* (San Francisco: Jossey-Bass, 1983).

5. The organizing principles developed in this section were originally developed by the author for a course and shared with a colleague. The same structure was used by that colleague, Clifton Conrad, in *The Undergraduate Curriculum: A Guide to Innovation and Reform* (Boulder, CO: Westview Press, 1978). For a fuller treatment of curricular issues in higher education and an interesting collection of source materials, see Arthur Levine, *Handbook on Undergraduate Curriculum* (San Francisco: Jossey-Bass, 1978), the best single-volume work on higher education curriculum.

6. Arthur King and John Brownell, *The Curriculum and the Disciplines of Knowledge* (New York: John Wiley, 1966), p.95.

7. Phillip Phenix, *Realms of Meaning* (New York: McGraw-Hill, 1964), p. 36.

8. The college that uses the great books curriculum in its purest form is St. John's College with campuses in Annapolis, Maryland, and Santa Fe, New Mexico. For a historical treatment of the origin of the great books curriculum and a listing of the classics used for study, see Arthur Levine, *Handbook on Undergraduate Curriculum* (San Francisco: Jossey-Bass, 1978), pp. 356–58 and 592–96.

9. "The Canons Under Fire," *Time*, April 11, 1988, p.66. The article contains a summary of the struggles at Stanford University to revise the list of books used for its Western culture courses.

10. The classic formulation of student development needs appears in Arthur Chickering, *Education and Identity* (San Francisco: Jossey-Bass, 1969). A presentation of the case for a student-centered curriculum is found in Arthur Chickering and David Halliburton, et al., *Developing the College Curriculum: A Handbook for Faculty and Administrators* (Washington, DC: Council for the Advancement of Small Colleges, 1977). A more recent summary of developmental needs of nontraditional as well as traditional age students can be found in Arthur Chickering, *The Modern American College* (San Francisco: Jossey-Bass, 1981), Chapter 1, "The Life Cycle," by Arthur Chickering and Robert Havinghurst. The volume also contains excellent chapters on emerging theories of ego development, cognitive development, and moral development.

11. Carl Rogers, *Client-Centered Therapy* (Boston: Houghton-Mifflin, 1951), Chapter 9, "Student-Centered Teaching." As Rogers puts it: "A person learns only those things which he perceives as being involved in the maintenance of, or enhancement of, the structure of self."

12. Competency-based curricula in teacher education date back to the work of W. W. Travers in the 1920s. The best-known recent effort to establish a competency-based curriculum in a liberal arts college is at Alverno College, Milwaukee, Wisconsin. See Bob Knott, "What is a Competency-Based Curriculum in the Liberal Arts?" *Journal of Higher Education*, 1975, 64, pp. 25–39.

13. The University of Wisconsin, Green Bay, was originally organized around the theme of "environmental problems" and some of the "cluster colleges" at the University of California, Santa Cruz, have social problems themes as their organizing focus. John Dewey is the key resource on education as "social reconstruction." See John Dewey, *Democracy and Education* (New York: Macmillan, 1961).

14. An application of Dewey's model of the forces that shape the curriculum can be found in Denis Lawton, *Social Change, Educational Theory and Curriculum Planning* (London: University of London Press, Ltd., 1973). See also Carnegie Foundation, *Missions of the College Curriculum*, Chapter 3, "External Forces that Shape Curriculum," and Tanner and Tanner, *Curriculum Development*, Chapter 5, "Curriculum Sources and Influences—Society, Knowledge and Learner."

15. For a discussion of the passage of student generations from one era to another see Arthur Levine, *When Dreams and Heroes Died* (San Francisco: Jossey-Bass, 1980).

16. The best single volume for introducing the classical "philosophers of education" is Robert Ulich, *Three Thousand Years of Educational Wisdom* (Cambridge, MA: Harvard University Press, 1954). An excellent

exposition of the relationships of philosophical issues and curriculum theory is found in Robert Zais, *Curriculum: Principles and Foundations* (New York: Harper & Row, 1976).

17. Association of American Colleges, *The Challenge of Connecting Learning*, Vol. I, *Liberal Learning and the Arts and Sciences Major* (Washington, DC: Association of American Colleges, 1991).

18. For those seeking an understanding of the historical roots of contemporary issues in higher education, the following sources are recommended: Frederick Rudolph, *The American College and University: A History* (New York: Knopf, 1965); Frederick Rudolph, *Curriculum: A History of the American Undergraduate Course of Study Since 1636* (San Francisco: Jossey-Bass, 1977); and John Brubacher and Willis Rudy, *Higher Education in Transition* (New York: Harper & Row, 1958). A useful historical chronology and a brief description of 12 important events in the development of the undergraduate curriculum in the United States can be found in Levine, *The Undergraduate Curriculum*, p. 484 ff. and p.538 ff.

Research Findings on the Seven Principles

MARY DEANE SORCINELLI

The Seven Principles for Good Practice in Undergraduate Education grew out of a review of "50 years of research on the way teachers teach and students learn" (Chickering and Gamson, 1987, p. 1) and a conference that brought together a distinguished group of researchers and commentators on higher education. The primary goal of the Principles' authors was to identify practices, policies, and institutional conditions that would result in a powerful and enduring undergraduate education. A second goal was to offer a set of research-based principles that would help sustain debate and action to stimulate reform in undergraduate education.

This chapter takes a step beyond the definitions and examples of the Seven Principles to examine ways in which research on college teaching and learning validates them. The chapter introduces each principle, presents findings of research, and suggests directions for further study.

The task of distilling five decades of knowledge on teaching and learning in higher education into Seven Principles was challenging (Chickering and Gamson, 1987). The task of reviewing the literature over the same span of time and topics is equally formidable. First, as noted by other reviewers, the literature is voluminous, amazingly diverse in content, and highly variable in quality and style (Menges and Mathis, 1988). Second, there are obvious difficulties in trying to generalize from the research findings—applicability may vary across disciplines, methods of teaching, ways of learning, institutional contexts, and the like. Finally, because they are meant to be generalizable, the Principles are painted in broad strokes yet contain subtleties in both their research groundings and practice.

Several difficult decisions had to be made in choosing research that related to each principle. First, at least two distinct strands of research support the Principles. One set of studies focuses on the development of students, looking at both the broad outcomes of college as well as specific dimensions such as intellectual, personality, psychological, and ethical development. Many of these works are longitudinal studies conducted during the 1960s (Becker, Geer, and Hughes, 1968; Chickering, 1969; Feldman and Newcomb, 1969; Heath, 1968; Katz and Associates, 1968; Newcomb, Koenig, Flacks, and Warwick, 1967; Perry, 1970; Sanford, 1962). It should be noted, however, that more recent literature and research on student development also supports the Principles (Belenky, Clinchy, Goldberger, and Tarule, 1986; Chickering and Associates, 1981; Katchadourian and Boli, 1985; Knefelkamp, Widick, and Parker, 1978; Parker and Schmidt, 1982; Richardson, Fisk, and Okun, 1983; Winter, McClelland, and Stewart, 1981).

The second strand of research is on college teaching and the effects of teachers on students. This chapter draws heavily from such research because the Principles point to the commitment of teachers and students as central to the effort of improving undergraduate education (Chickering and Gamson, 1987). And although it is clear that there is a long trajectory of research for many of the Principles, this chapter focuses on more recent research. Care was taken, however, to select publications that reviewed and synthesized older as well as more current studies.

Despite the aforementioned challenges in approaching, reviewing, and selecting studies, this chapter stands as a guide to improving practice. The chapter cites key findings that can help faculty, administrators, and other constituents of higher education understand the conceptual bases for the Seven Principles and their potential for improving undergraduate teaching and learning.

Good Practice Encourages Student-Faculty Contact

Chickering and Gamson (1987) emphasize that professors who encourage student contact both in and out of classes enhance student motivation, intellectual commitment, and personal development. A substantial body of research on effective teaching documents the importance of student-faculty contact. Much of this research has focused on student ratings of classroom teaching, but some studies also have compared student ratings with peer ratings, self-reviews, and other sources (Cohen, 1981; Feldman, 1976; Marsh, 1984; McKeachie, Pintrich, Lin, and Smith, 1986). All have arrived at fairly consistent findings about the characteristics of good teaching. These studies stress command and organization of the subject matter, expressiveness and enthusiasm, and interaction and rapport with students.

When such studies emphasize personal behaviors useful to working with students in the classroom, they describe good teachers as approachable and interested in students, easy to talk to, inviting of student views and discussion, concerned about student progress, and open to helping students with problems (Hildebrand, Wilson, and Dienst, 1971; Murray, 1985; Wilson and others, 1975).

Further, there is evidence that faculty who are most accessible to students in the classroom also encourage high levels of interaction with students outside of class. A growing number of studies serve to highlight the unique and positive impact of student-faculty contact that goes beyond the classroom (Pascarella, 1980; Snow, 1973; Wilson and others, 1975).

Wilson and others (1975) conducted perhaps the most impressive study of the influence of informal contact with individual faculty members on students. Their eight-institution study included faculty members and students and used a range of surveys on views of teaching and faculty impact on students over a four-year span. The researchers found that faculty who were nominated by students and colleagues as especially effective reported more interaction with students beyond the classroom. In addition, students who showed gains in intellectual commitment, certainly of career choice, and satisfaction with academic and nonacademic experiences during their college years reported more contact with faculty, particularly outside of class. Wilson and others (1975, p. 107) concluded that "the relationships that faculty and students develop outside the classroom may well be the part of teaching which has the greatest impact on students."

In a subsequent synthesis of research on the association between student-faculty nonclass contact and various outcomes of college, Pascarella (1980) found similarly promising results. Reviewing research studies dating from the 1950s to the present, Pascarella concluded that student-faculty nonclass contacts were significantly related to such educational outcomes as satisfaction with college, educational aspirations, intellectual and personal development, academic achievement, and persistence in college beyond the freshman year. Moreover, Pascarella pointed out that informal contacts focusing on intellectual, literary, or artistic interests, value issues, or future career concerns appeared to have the greatest impact. Put simply, the most important informal contacts between students and faculty may be those that extend learning in academic programs to students' lives outside of the classroom.

In all, it seems that college and university teachers can derive positive guidance from research on student-faculty contact inside and outside of the classroom. Clearly, more research is needed to understand how student-faculty contact comes about, and how such variables as professorial or student initiative, class size, classroom experience, and institutional size, structure, or policy affect the contact (Pascarella, 1980). Still, the evidence at hand supports the notion that commitment to a reasonably high degree of teacher-student contact characterizes good teaching and helps students attain a number of educational goals.

Good Practice Encourages Cooperation Among Students

The connections between this second principle and the third—Good Practice Encourages Active Learning—are unmistakable. In many ways, the cooperative learning practices described in the second principle can be seen as a large and important subset of the active learning practices described in the third. For example, in summarizing the second principle, Chickering and Gamson (1987, p. 1) note that "working with others often increases involvement in learning." Furthermore, a review of the literature reveals that the terms "cooperative" and "active" are suggestive and commodious rather than precise. There are articles under different rubrics—cooperative, active, collaborative, peer, student-centered—that discuss similar issues, classroom behaviors, and teaching and learning methods.

In what important ways, then, do the two principles come together and stand apart? Despite the range of labels, meanings, and techniques, the Principles share one crucial variable: the active involvement of students as opposed to their passive exposure to a learning task. At the same time, cooperative and active learning do have distinguishing features. While cooperative learning calls for active involvement of students organized into small groups, active learning can be experienced solo. In such instances, active learning can be encouraged through independent study, internships, computer-based instruction, and so on. This section concentrates on syntheses of research on cooperative learning, peer teaching, and other student-centered teaching and learning methods, acknowledging links to other active learning practices where appropriate.

Research support for cooperative learning techniques, in which students work in small groups and receive recognition or rewards based on their group performance rather than on individual achievement, is growing (Johnson and Johnson, 1989). In reviewing the state of the art of cooperative learning in colleges, Johnson, Johnson, and Smith (1990) describe a conceptual approach to cooperative learning that is characterized by five elements (positive interdependence, face-to-face interaction, personal responsibility, collaborative skills, and group processing) and three types of learning groups (informal, formal, and base).

Based on a review of the results of 137 studies on cooperative learning methods at the college level, Johnson, Johnson, and Smith (1990) conclude that the pattern of research findings supports the utility of cooperative learning groups for increasing productivity, developing committed and positive relationships among members, increasing social support, and enhancing self-esteem.

Research on peer teaching, in which students teach students in situations that are planned and directed by a teacher, is equally encouraging (Whitman, 1988). In a review of several peer-teaching models, Goldschmid and Goldschmid (1976) examined discussion groups led by undergraduate students, proctoring (for example, Keller's Personalized System of Instruction [PSI]), student learning groups or pairs, and student counseling of students. They concluded that peer teaching was best used in conjunction with other teaching and learning methods. Given that caveat, however, they did agree that peer teaching "has great potential for both student 'teacher, and student 'learner,' especially if one seeks to enhance active participation and develop skills in cooperation and social interaction" (1976, p. 9). Whitman's (1988) review of peer teaching found that peer teachers and learners gain a better understanding of the subject matter and benefit from the cooperative relationships that peer teaching generates.

A review of empirical support for other student-centered methods by McKeachie, Pintrich, Lin, and Smith (1986) corroborates these conclusions. They compared research on student-led discussions, the learning cell, and a range of studies that compared student-centered methods (for example, group-centered, nondirective discussions) to instructor-dominated methods (for example, lectures). They found that differences in application of concepts, problem solving, attitude, motivation, or group membership and leadership skills all favored student-centered methods. McKeachie, Pintrich, Lin, and Smith (1986, p. 63) concluded that "the best answer to the question of what is the most effective method of teaching is that it depends on the goal, the student, the content and the teachers. But the next best answer is 'Students teaching other students.'"

Good Practice Encourages Active Learning

Research confirms that cooperative and social learning increase involvement in learning. We simply do not have as much data confirming the beneficial effects of other kinds of active learning such as the case method, independent study, and individualized methods (for example, computer-based instruction).

The case method, developed at Harvard Business School, is a case in point. It has a long history of use in business and law schools and, more recently, has been disseminated to a range of disciplines (Christensen 1987). The case method, like games and simulations, embodies many of the attributes of active learning: Students discuss and challenge ideas and analyze and solve problems. Still, despite its promise as a vehicle for active learning, little research has been done on its effectiveness (McKeachie, Pintrich, Lin, and Smith, 1986).

Independent study, too, would seem to be an ideal way of helping students take active responsibility for their own learning. McKeachie, Pintrich, Lin, and Smith (1986) reviewed a handful of studies from the late 1950s and early 1960s, however, and did not find significant differences between the achievement of students working independently and those taught in more traditional courses. Research that demonstrated the effectiveness of independent study did find differences in such dimensions as curiosity and motivation for continued learning. Future research experiments on independent study may be strengthened by recent resources on arranging independent study experiences, developing motivating devices, and measuring outcomes (Boud, 1981; Dressel and Thompson, 1973; Henderson and Nathenson, 1984).

Findings on individualized learning methods are favorable. In syntheses of research studies that compared individualized methods such as audio tutorial instruction, programmed instruction, Keller's PSI, and computer-based instruction with conventionally taught courses, audio tutorials showed small but positive effects on student achievement and satisfaction (Kulik, Kulik, and Cohen, 1980). For students in Keller's PSI courses, the effects were considerably stronger.

Overall, more research is needed on examples of active learning such as the case method and independent and individualized study opportunities. Still, research indicates that teaching methods that encourage student activity and involvement, especially student-to-student interaction, are likely to be superior to more passive methods when higher-level cognitive or affective learning is the goal.

Good Practice Gives Prompt Feedback

Students need prompt feedback on performance to benefit from courses. Such feedback can include diagnosis at the beginning of a semester, frequent tests with prompt feedback throughout the term, and assessments at various points during college.

Recently, several researchers and commentators in higher education have emphasized the importance of providing practice with timely feedback (Cross, 1987; Study Group, 1984; Dunkin, 1986; McKeachie, Pintrich, Lin, and Smith, 1986). After reviewing key resources on instruction, Menges and Mathis (1988) concluded that the content of a classroom presentation is better remembered when it is followed by a test. This finding, which dates back to research conducted early in this century, was not widely known.

Despite the finding's past invisibility, it is clear that use of prompt feedback in college courses shows a clear and positive relation to student achievement and satisfaction (Dunkin, 1986; McKeachie, Pintrich, Lin, and Smith, 1986). Indeed, one persuasive argument for the importance of providing prompt feedback comes from the considerable research on Keller's PSI (Kulik, Kulik, and Cohen, 1980).

Keller's PSI is a system of individualized instruction that features, among other major characteristics, the following: (1) A student works at his or her own pace through a series of topics or units. (2) A student must master each unit by achieving a near perfect score on a test before moving on to the next topic. (3) A student proctor corrects the test, provides immediate feedback to the student, and offers encouragement and remedial help (Keller, 1968).

Dunkin (1986), in reviewing research on a range of individualized teaching methods, reported that the PSI offered statistically significant superiority in student achievement and satisfaction. Most important, Dunkin found that frequent testing, immediate feedback, and mastery on a unit before progression to the next topic were key factors for increased student achievement. He concluded that PSI is clearly superior to other methods with which it has been compared and ranks as the method with the greatest research support in the history of research on teaching.

The most significant conclusion to be reached from research on innovative teaching methods, then, is that immediate, corrective, and supportive feedback is central to learning. Despite the substantial and positive evidence of its importance, however, aspects of prompt feedback are worthy of further exploration. McKeachie, Pintrich, Lin, and Smith (1986) caution that the long-term effects of prompt feedback depend on the quality of the tests (for example, tests for memorization versus critical thinking) and the quality of the feedback (for example, encouraging and informative in terms of pinpointing the source of student errors versus an overall grade or general comment). Also, tests are not the only means for providing a foundation for feedback. Papers, oral presentations, research, and participation in discussions are also important means of providing feedback. Finally, beyond the course level, institutions need to learn much more about the effects of performance assessment at various points in the college career (for example, periodic counseling on progress and future plans, assessment through a portfolio process or standardized tests).

Good Practice Emphasizes Time on Task

The myriad decisions teachers must make in this arena—time allocation, time management, time on task—all affect student learning. Most of the research on the variable of engaged time or time on task has been conducted at the elementary and high school levels (Cross, 1987). At these levels, there is strong empirical evidence of a direct relationship between time allocation (for subject matter areas, levels of learning), time management (after it has been allocated), and time on task, on the one hand, and student achievement, on the other (Berliner, 1984).

One recent set of studies has attempted to measure the variable "academic learning time" (ALT). Defined simply, ALT is the time engaged with materials or activities that result in high student success rates, as measured by instruments such as achievement tests. Students or classes that accrue large amounts of ALT achieve more than do students or classes with lower amounts of ALT (Berliner, 1984).

There is some evidence that effective use of time in the college classroom means effective teaching for faculty and effective learning for students. For example, a large-scale study of student evaluations of teaching showed consistently significant correlations between the effective use of class time and overall ratings of course, instructor, and amount learned (Franklin, in press).

The success of Keller's PSI may also be related, in part, to its emphasis on time on task. As noted in the discussion of the previous principle, the aspects of PSI that most affect achievement are mastery of a unit, frequent testing, and feedback. Strikingly similar in emphasis to ALT, PSI calls for assigning activities related to desired outcomes, seeing that enough time is allocated for students, mastery of a unit, and encouraging success through frequent testing and feedback.

Finally, McKeachie, Pintrich, Lin, and Smith (1986) looked at several studies on time spent in class with a teacher and concluded that college courses requiring more class periods (meeting four times a week rather than once) and longer class periods (periods of fifty-five rather than thirty minutes) proved superior, as measured by student achievement. These findings support Chickering and Gamson's (1987) contention that time on task must be addressed at an institutional as well as course level. How a college defines time expectations for students and faculty also can make a difference in quality of performance of each group.

The general consensus of research is that the more time students are engaged in learning, the greater the amount of their learning. But there are still large gaps in our understanding of time on task. As McKeachie, Pintrich, Lin, and Smith (1986) point out, the larger question concerns not simply the amount of time spent but how it is spent. How do teachers who use class time effectively spend the time? How do such variables as time management, time allocation, pacing, and time on task interact? To what degree are other principles important, such as spending time on articulation of goals, cooperative activities, active learning, frequent testing, and prompt feedback? These questions suggest that we must continue to explore the nature of time on task in the college classroom and its influence on student learning.

Good Practice Communicates High Expectations

Chickering and Gamson (1987) point out that high expectations are important for everyone—for the poorly prepared or motivated as well as for the bright and well motivated. They also suggest that the expectations and efforts of teachers and administrators can permeate an institution, creating an institutional climate that either challenges students or demands little of them.

There is a considerable literature on academic expectations for achievement, but, again, effects have been studied primarily in elementary and secondary classrooms (Brophy and Good, 1974; Cooper, 1979). In general, research shows that if teachers set high but attainable goals for academic performance, academic achievement usually increases. If teachers set low goals, academic achievement usually decreases (Berliner, 1984).

Evidence on the effects of expectations in the college classroom can be found in research on student ratings of teaching. The literature consistently shows, contrary to faculty belief, that students give higher ratings to difficult courses in which they have to work hard (Cashin, 1988; Cashin and Slawson, 1977; Marsh, 1984). For example, Cashin (1988) found that workload/difficulty items such as "amount of reading," "amount of other assignments," "difficulty of subject matter," and "I worked harder in this course than on most courses I have taken" correlated positively with student ratings. Conversely, after reviewing work on teacher expectations of academic performance in the college classroom, Cross (1987) hypothesized that communication of low expectations by college teachers leads to minimal student growth, improvement, and satisfaction.

Finally, in both secondary and postsecondary education, there is evidence that schools and colleges that communicate high expectations enjoy beneficial effects in areas other than academic achievement. Studies suggest that positive effects of high expectations are evidenced in such areas as student attendance and sense of responsibility (Rutter, Maughan, Mortimore, and Ousten, 1979; Cross, 1987).

The practice of setting high but attainable goals for learners has become a central theme of the reform movement in higher education (Chickering and Gamson, 1987; Cross, 1987; Study Group, 1984). There is cause for confidence that this practice is effective in improving learning. Teachers, researchers, and policymakers in higher education must continue to examine the roles of teachers and institutions in affecting academic expectations in positive ways.

Good Practice Respects Diverse Talents and Ways of Learning

The seventh and final principle emphasizes the need to recognize the different talents and styles of learning that students bring to college. In effect, this principle defines a way of viewing the world. And it may be the linchpin that holds the Seven Principles together, for knowledge about learning styles helps faculty to transmit their course content with greater sensitivity to the differences that students bring to the classroom Moreover, faculty who show regard for their students' unique interests and talents are likely to facilitate student growth and development in every sphere—academic, social, personal, and vocational.

While a full exploration of the various lines of research on learning styles is beyond the scope of this chapter, Menges and Mathis (1988) warrants special mention as a key resource on learning, and Claxton and Murrell (1987) stands out as a comprehensive introduction to student learning research at the college level. The latter researchers examine approaches to students' learning styles by ordering students, preferences or orientations at four levels of analysis: personality, information processing, social interaction, and instructional model. They also look at how information about learning styles can be used across diverse settings inside and outside of the classroom (for example, student affairs, jobs, work with minority students).

Researchers readily agree that although students clearly learn in different ways, the concept of "learning style" has proved difficult to define and even more difficult to assess in terms of its implications for teaching practices (Claxton and Murrell, 1987; Stark, Shaw, and Lowther, 1989). Despite inadequacies in our understanding of learning styles, however, cumulative findings of research in this area do provide guidelines for practice. For example, some evidence suggests that when students learn about their own respective styles, they can increase their chances of success in courses. Also, a match between instructional methods and students, learning styles can lead to improved learning. Finally, students can expand their repertoire of learning strategies, which is important to lifelong learning (Claxton and Murrell, 1987).

At one level we need to understand more about the process of learning. At another level we need to understand its connections to other areas such as student goals and motivations intellectual development, academic and social integration, disciplinary perspectives, and the learning styles of women and minority students (Belenky, Clinchy, Goldberger, and Tarule, 1986; Stark, Shaw, and Lowther, 1989; McKeachie, Pintrich, Lin, and Smith, 1986; Tinto, 1987; Green, 1989). At still another level, we need to know how and in what ways the seventh principle is intertwined with the other six. At this point we can only speculate on the potential ways in which student-faculty contact, student cooperation and active involvement, prompt feedback, time on task, and high expectations support diverse talents and ways of learning. These relationships warrant further exploration.

Summary

The research reported in this chapter indicates that the Seven Principles for Good Practice in Undergraduate Education provide substantive research-based advice that can enrich our understanding and practice of teaching and learning at the college level. Results of research on student-faculty contact, prompt feedback, and active involvement in learning are especially encouraging. Admittedly, among the Seven Principles there is the likelihood of variation in applicability across disciplines, teaching methods, learning styles, institutions, and even methods of implementation. Still, the Principles are a first step in an important direction and present bountiful questions for future research and practice.

References

Becker, H. S. Geer, B. and Hughes, E. C. *Making the Grade: The Academic Side of College Life*. New York: Wiley, 1968.

Belenky, M. F., Clinchy, B., Goldberger, N. R., and Tarule, J. M. *Women's Ways of Knowing: The Development of Self, Voice, and Mind.*. New York: Basic Books, 1986.

Berliner, D. C. "The Half-Full Glass: A Review of Research on Teaching." In P. L. Hosford (ed.), *Using What we Know About Teaching* . Alexandria, Va. Association for Supervision and Curriculum Development, 1984.

Boud, D. (ed.) *Developing Student Autonomy in Learning*. New York: Nichols, 1981.

Brophy, J. and Good, T., *Teacher-Student Relationships. Causes and Consequences*. New York Holt, Rinehart & Winston, 1974.

Cashin, W. E. "Student Ratings of Teaching: A Summary of the Research." IDEA Paper No. 20. Manhattan: Center for Faculty Evaluation and Development, Kansas State University, 1988.

Cashin, W. E., and Slawson, H. M. *Description of Data Base, 1976–77*. IDEA Technical Report No. 2 Manhattan: Center for Faculty Evaluation and Development, Kansas State University, 1977.

Chickering, A. W. *Education and Identity*. San Francisco: Jossey-Bass, 1969.

Chickering, A. W., and Associates. *The Modern American College: Responding to the New Realities of Diverse Students and a Changing Society*. San Francisco Jossey-Bass, 1981.

Chickering, A. W. and Gamson, Z. F. "Seven Principles for Good Practice in Undergraduate Education." *AAHE Bulletin*, 1987, 39 (7), 3–7.

Christensen, C. R. *Teaching and the Case Method: Texts, Cases, and Readings.* Boston: Harvard Business School, 1987.

Claxton, C. S., and Murrell, P. H. *Learning Styles: Their Impact on Teaching and Administration.* ASHE-ERIC Higher Education Research Reports, no. 4. Washington, D.C.: Association for the Study of Higher Education, 1987.

Cohen, P. A. "Student Ratings of Instruction and Student Achievement: A Meta-Analysis of Multisection Validity Studies." *Review of Educational Research,* 1981, 51, 281–309.

Cooper, H. "Pygmalion Grown Up: A Model for Teacher Expectation, Communication, and Performance Influence." *Review of Educational Research,* 1979, 79, 389–410.

Cross, K. P. "Teaching for Learning." *AAHE Bulletin,* 1987, 39 (8), 3–7.

Dressel, P. L., and Thompson, M. M. *Independent Study.* San Francisco: Jossey-Bass, 1973.

Dunkin, M. J. "Research on Teaching in Higher Education." In M. C. Wittrock (ed.), *Handbook of Research on Teaching.* (3rd ed.) New York: Macmillan, 1986.

Feldman, K. A. "The Superior College Teacher from the Students' View." *Research in Higher Education,* 1976, 5, 243–288.

Feldman, K. A., and Newcomb, T M. *The Impact of College on Students.* San Francisco: Jossey-Bass, 1969.

Franklin, J. Technical Report No. 2. Boston: Office of Instructional Research and Evaluation, Northeastern University, in press.

Goldschmid, B., and Goldschmid, M. L. "Peer Teaching in Higher Education: A Review." *Higher Education,* 1976, 5, 9–33.

Green, M. F. *Minorities On Campus: A Handbook for Enhancing Diversity.* Washington, D.C.: American Council on Education 1989.

Heath, D. H. *Growing Up in College: Liberal Education and Maturity.* San Francisco: Jossey-Bass, 1968.

Henderson, E. S., and Nathenson, M. B. (eds.). *Independent Learning in Higher Education.* Englewood Cliffs, NJ.: Educational Technology, 1984.

Hildebrand, M., Wilson, R. C., and Dienst, E. R. *Evaluating University Teaching.* Berkeley: Center for Research and Development in Higher Education, University of California, 1971.

Johnson, D. W., and Johnson, R. T. *Cooperation and Competition: Theory and Research.* Edina, Minn.: Interaction Books, 1989.

Johnson D. W., Johnson, R. T., and Smith, K. A. "Cooperative Learning: An Active Learning Strategy." *Focus on Teaching and Learning,* 1990, 5(2), 1–8.

Katchadourian, H. A., and Boli, J. *Careerism and Intellectualism Among College Students: Patterns of Academic and Career Choice in the Undergraduate Years.* San Francisco: Jossey-Bass, 1985.

Katz, J., and Associates. *No Time for Youth: Growth and Constraint in College Students.* San Francisco: Jossey-Bass, 1968.

Keller, E. S. "Goodbye Teacher." *Journal of Applied Behavioral Analysis,* 1968, 1, 79–89.

Knefelkamp, L., Widick, C., and Parker, C. A. (eds.). *Applying New Developmental Findings.* New Directions for Student Services, no. 4. San Francisco: Jossey-Bass, 1978.

Kulik, C. C., Kulik, J. A., and Cohen, P. A. "Instructional Technology and College Teaching." *Teaching of Psychology,* 1980, 7, 199–205.

McKeachie, W. J., Pintrich, P. R., Lin, Y., and Smith, D. *Teaching and Learning in the College Classroom: A Review of the Research Literature.* Ann Arbor: National Center for Research to Improve Postsecondary Teaching and Learning, University of Michigan, 1986.

Marsh, H. W. "Students' Evaluation Of Teaching: Dimensionality, Reliability, Validity, Potential Biases, and Utility." *Journal of Educational Psychology,* 1984, 76, 707–754.

Menges, R. J., and Mathis, B. C. *Key Resources on Teaching, Learning, Curriculum, and Faculty Development: A Guide to the Higher Education Literatures.* San Francisco: Jossey-Bass, 1988.

Murray, H. G. "Classroom Teaching Behaviors Related to College Teaching Effectiveness." In J. G. Donald and A. M. Sullivan (eds.), *Using Research to Improve Teaching*. New Directions for Teaching and Learning, no. 23. San Francisco: Jossey-Bass, 1985.

Newcomb, T. M., Koenig, K. E., Flacks, R., and Warwick, D. P. *Persistence and Change: Bennington College and Its Students After Twenty-Five Years*. New York: Wiley, 1967.

Parker C. A., and Schmidt, J. A. "Effects of College Experience." In H. E. Mitzel (ed.), *Encyclopedia of Educational Research*. (5th ed.) New York: Free Press, 1982.

Pascarella, E. T. "Student-Faculty Informal Contact and College Outcomes." *Review of Educational Research*, 1980, 50, 545–595.

Perry, W. G. *Forms of Intellectual and Ethical Development in the College Years*. New York: Holt, Rinehart & Winston, 1970.

Richardson, R. C., Jr., Fisk, E. C., and Okun, M. A. *Literacy in the Open-Access College*. San Francisco: Jossey-Bass, 1983.

Rutter, M., Maughan, B., Mortimore, P., and Ousten, J. *Fifteen Thousand Hours*. Cambridge, Mass.: Harvard University Press, 1979.

Sanford, N. (ed.). *The American College*. New York: Wiley 1962

Snow, S. "Correlates of Faculty-Student Interaction." *Sociology of Education*, 1973, 46, 489–498.

Stark, J. S., Shaw, K. M., and Lowther, M. A. *Student Goals for College and Courses*, ASHE-ERIC Higher Education Research Reports, no. 6. Washington, D.C.: Association for the Study of Higher Education, 1989.

Study Group on the Conditions of Excellence in American Higher Education. *Involvement in Learning: Realizing the Potential of American Higher Education*. Washington, D.C.: U.S. Department of Education, 1984.

Tinto, V. *Leaving College: Rethinking the Causes and Cures of Student Attrition*. Chicago: University of Chicago Press, 1987.

Whitman, N. A. *Peer Teaching: To Teach Is to Learn Twice*. ASHE-ERIC Higher Education Reports, no. 4. Washington, D.C.: Association for the Study of Higher Education, 1988.

Wilson, R. C., Gaff, J. G., Dienst, E. R., Wood, L., and Barry, J. L. *College Professors and Their Impact upon Students*. New York: Wiley, 1975

Winter, D. G., McClelland, D. C., and Stewart, A. J. *A New Case for the Liberal Arts: Assessing Institutional Goals and Student Development*. San Francisco: Jossey-Bass 1981.

A Grounded Theory of
Academic Change

CLIFTON F. CONRAD

A grounded theory of academic change is offered as an alternative to existing models of academic change. The constant comparative method, an inductive method of discovering theory, is elaborated and applied to the emergence of the theory. The theory is then presented through a series of theoretical statements which relate a series of primarily political concepts and processes. Briefly, the theory identifies several major processes which link pressures for change and a policy decision to change: conflict and interest group pressures followed by power exertion, administrative intervention, faculty leadership exercised through interest group advocacy, and compromises which are negotiated through administrative leadership. Finally, the theory is briefly discussed and compared with alternative models of change, including Baldridge's political model of academic change.

During the past decade, the process of change at the college and university level has been the topic of considerable debate. What is change? How does it come about? What are the major processes involved? Who are the agents of change? All of these are central questions that have been posed by those investigating academic change.

Colleges and universities are frequently discussed in terms of their susceptibility to external and internal environmental pressures. Although much has been written about the ostensible sources of change, little is known about the conditions under which, or the degree to which, "sources of change" are influential upon those who make the decision about whether change will or will not occur.

Four principal models have been developed which have guided research on academic change: the complex organization (Griffiths, 1964; Hefferlin, 1969; Hodgkinson, 1970), diffusion of innovations (Mitchell, 1970; Rogers, 1962), planned change (Lippitt, Watson, and Westley, 1958; Bennis, Benne, and Chin, 1961; Rogers, 1964), and the political (Fashing, 1969; Baldridge, 1971; Lindquist, 1972). Each model has centered upon some particular aspect of change (authority, communication, interest group pressures), but none has provided a satisfactory explanation as to precisely how change occurs or who and what are finally changed at the end of the entire process.

For the most part change has been viewed as some mystical process that is totally unplanned. Kerr (1963:102) characterizes this view:

> When change does come, it may be by the slow process of persuasion, or by subversion as through the inside-outside alliance, or by external decision. The academic community, regardless of the particular process involved, is more changed than changing; change is more unplanned than planned.

There have been, however, few attempts to isolate those factors, external or internal to institutions, which are most critical in originating the change process. Neither has there been much research directed at understanding the dynamics and processes of academic change. Moreover, the relevant literature includes few attempts to generate, much less test, a theory of academic change. The four models have sensitized researchers to different dimensions of the change process and these may prove to offer further insight. But the research has been largely descriptive and seldom centered around identifying critical variables in, and their relationship to, the change process.

The primary purpose of this article is to present a grounded theory of academic change that is based upon research guided by two major research questions: What are the major sources of academic change? What are the major processes through which academic change occurs? For purposes of this paper, grounded theory is defined as theory generated from data systematically obtained and analyzed through the constant comparative method. Because this approach has not been explicated as a major research methodology in the higher education literature, the constant comparative method will be elaborated and applied to the research problem stated above. A grounded theory of academic change, which is based solely on the application of the constant comparative method, will subsequently be presented in a discussion format. The final section examines the theory in light of alternative models of change.

Methodology

Constant Comparative Method

The constant comparative method, an inductive method of discovering theory that has been elaborated most systematically by Glaser and Strauss (1967), served as the major research procedure. In general, the comparative method combines systematic coding and analysis with theoretical sampling to generate a theory that is integrated, consistent, close to the data, and in a form clear enough to be operationalized for testing in quantitative research. Unlike most methods of analysis, which are designed to ensure that two analysts working independently with the same data will achieve the same results, the constant comparative method is designed to permit the kind of flexibility that aids the creative generation of theory.

There are four stages included in the comparative method: (1) comparing incidents applicable to each category; (2) integrating categories and their properties; (3) delimiting the theory; and (4) writing the theory (Glaser and Strauss, 1967:105). First, the analyst codes each datum incident into as many categories of analysis as possible. As categories emerge or as data emerge that fit existing categories, the analyst begins thinking in terms of the theoretical properties of the category: its dimensions, its relationship to other categories, and the conditions under which it is pronounced or minimized. This process includes a continual returning to the data until the categories become theoretically saturated.

The analysis increasingly moves from comparison of incident with incident to comparison of incident with properties of the category that resulted from initial comparisons of incidents. The further refinement of categories (or variables) and their interrelationships gradually leads to the development of theory. The theory is continually delimited as a smaller set of higher level concepts emerges. Finally, when the researcher is convinced that the theory is satisfactorily integrated, the theory is presented either in a discussion form or as a set of propositions.

Theoretical sampling is the process of collecting data for comparative analysis, and it is especially intended to facilitate the generation of theory. Beyond the decisions concerning the initial collection of data, the process of data collection is controlled only by the emerging theory. That is, the emerging theory enables the researcher to select comparison groups (including groups within institutions) on the basis of their theoretical relevance, thus avoiding the collection of a large mass of data of questionable theoretical relevance. Put differently, the universe of data is gradually delimited through the use of theoretical criteria.

The critical question in theoretical sampling is: To what comparison groups does one turn next in data collection? And for what theoretical purpose? The basic criterion governing the selection of comparison groups for discovering theory is their theoretical relevance for furthering the development of emerging categories. The researcher is throughout an active sampler of theoretically relevant data as he/she identifies the central variables of the emerging theory; thus the researcher must continually analyze the data to see where the next theoretical question will lead. When initially generating the basic categories and their properties, the researcher minimizes differences in the comparative groups. Under these conditions, maximum similarity in data leads to: (1) verifying the usefulness of the variables; (2) generating basic properties; and (3) establishing sets of conditions for a degree of variation.

With the emergence of a basic theoretical framework, the researcher turns to maximizing differences among comparison groups. The maximization among comparison groups (by maximizing differences in data) stimulates the generation and further refinement of theoretical properties once the basic framework has emerged. The maximization of the diversity in the data forces: (1) the dense development of the properties of the variables; (2) the delimitation of the scope of the theory. Theoretical sampling of different comparative groups complements the second and third stages of the constant comparative method. The active search for theoretically relevant data, first between similar and different comparison groups, continues until all the critical variables and their interrelationships have been theoretically saturated. The criterion for saturation is that no additional data can be found which further embellish the theory.

To summarize, the comparative method is not built upon a predetermined design of data collection and analysis but represents a method of continually redesigning the research in light of emerging concepts and interrelationships among variables. Using a comparative technique that allows for similarities and later differences between groups, qualitative data are sought from a variety of sources to ensure a rich comparative data base. The comparative method of continual coding and analysis, controlled throughout by the guidelines of theoretical sampling, lends itself to different methods of data collection which yield a diversity of data, but data that are collected and analyzed to the extent that they are in the service of grounded theory.

There are several reasons for the selection of the comparative method. First, it is a methodology which is particularly well-adapted to the task of generating, and not simply verifying, theory. Instead of relying on preselected groups, as in most methodologies which place relative emphasis on verification, it includes the comparison of similar and different groups to facilitate the development of theory. In particular, the maximization of differences between groups promotes the embellishment of the theory. Thus the comparative method provides not a method where different slices of data are seen as a test of each other but rather different modes of knowing which must be explained and integrated theoretically by adding slices of data to qualify the theory. Coupled with theoretical sampling, the comparative method encourages a multifaceted investigation in which there are no limits to the techniques of data collection, the way they are used, or the types of data acquired except for the requirements of theoretical saturation.

Second, the constant comparison of variables (including their properties and their interrelationships with each other) results in a type of "development" theory. The grounded theory is constantly being delimited and modified in light of the phenomena under investigation. The comparative method especially facilitates the generation of theories of process and change through the joint process of coding and analysis until theoretical saturation is reached.

Sample Selection

According to the guidelines of theoretical sampling, comparison groups or institutions should be selected on the basis of their theoretical relevance. In the case of this particular research problem only institutions that had changed their curriculum met that criterion. But the comparative method also calls for the minimization and the maximization of differences between comparative groups. In this study, that criterion was satisfied by choosing institutions which had utilized different vehicles to realize change. For example, formal curriculum committees were used in some institutions, while on other occasions ad hoc groups were employed.

Four institutions were selected which met the sample criterion. Two of the schools, the University of Rochester and Ohio State University, were selected primarily because the vehicle of change was the formal curriculum committee. Aquinas College and Western Michigan University were selected because the vehicle of change was an ad hoc group.

Procedure

During the initial visit to each of the four schools, data collection was guided by a general organizational and sociological perspective. An extensive range of qualitative data was obtained, including interviews and documents.

Interviews were the main source of data. In the early stages of the research, as the researcher was struggling to make sense out of the data, an open-ended interview form guided the discussion. Its main value was in systematizing the inquiry around a broad set of questions. It was carefully employed to avoid forced responses. In the latter stages of the research, as the theory gradually began to emerge, the form was restricted almost entirely to a device for recording the data.

In addition to interview data, a considerable amount of primary and secondary material was gathered at each of the four institutions: (1) membership lists and minutes from the appropriate committees, ad hoc groups, and faculty senates; (2) personal files of committee members; (3) campus newspaper articles; (4) published and unpublished reports; (5) personal letters; (6) speeches; (7) published articles; and (8) tapes of faculty meetings. These documents were extremely valuable in interpreting data gathered from interviewees and constituted an excellent check on the other data.

The investigator was confronted by a large body of data during and immediately following the initial field visits. The collected data were examined in detail from all four of the universities during and following the visits. At the same time, however, the researcher immediately began thinking of the emerging variables, including their central properties and conditions under which they were maximized and minimized, their consequences, and their relation to other variables. Theoretical properties gradually emerged from the data as concepts were first developed and relationships first recorded.

The University of Rochester was the first institution to be visited. The evidence at Rochester early suggested that while underlying conflict seemed to be a precondition of change, conflicts became visible only when external or internal pressures threatened the status quo. Several major pressures for change were suggested by the evidence: curriculum practices at other institutions, faculty subcultures, and organizational turnover. It is useful to indicate how one pressure—curriculum practices at other institutions was identified as a major source of change.

The evidence was compelling that the major pressure for change was curricular innovation concurrently being implemented at institutions that Rochester considers in its peer group. For example, examination of a number of documents, including faculty minutes, revealed that the Rochester faculty was sensitive to changing academic practices at selected Ivy League institutions, including Columbia, Yale, and Princeton. Moreover, interviews with a wide variety of faculty and administrators supported the generalization that a major reason for reviewing the curriculum was that certain Ivy League institutions had modified their curricula. The Dean of the College of Arts and Science, who served as the major agent of change, admitted that academic changes at Princeton were a major impetus to change. Thus on the basis of the initial visit to Rochester, one tentative proposition was: Curriculum Practices at Institutions Perceived as Peer Institutions are a Major Source of Change. Like many propositions in the emerging theory, this generalization was later modified because additional evidence disconfirmed the importance of the emphasis initially placed on peer institutions; the modified proposition that curriculum practices at other institutions are a major impetus to change was eventually incorporated into the final theory because of strong supporting evidence from each of the sample institutions.

The evidence at Rochester tentatively suggested a political perspective of the change process, and relationships between interest group pressures, conflict, and change were initially explored. But one aspect of the change process emerged as central: the role of an administrative agent who provides the impetus for the reexamination of the academic program by selecting a controlling mechanism for change.

The Rochester evidence clearly indicated that the Dean of the College was the central agent in the change process. For example, every single interviewee, except the Dean himself, admitted that curriculum reexamination probably would not have been seriously entertained without his involvement. More than one interviewee recalled the Dean's judicious use of information as a tool for promoting change.

The critical role of the administrative change agent was first suggested by the evidence gathered at Rochester. At the same time, however, it is important to note that the researcher also sought explanations for emerging concepts and propositions, for grounded theory must not only be induced on the basis of evidence; it must also include plausible explanations for purported relationships. In this case, there were two such explanations. First, administrators are likely to have an overall perspective of their institutions because of their formal position. At many institutions, sensitivity to pressures for change, *sine qua non*, is essential for maintaining an administrative position. Second, the administrative leadership has a vested interest in identifying and responding to pressures for change. The maintenance of their positions is at least partly dependent upon the accommodation of formal and informal component parts of their respective institutions. It is often in the interests of the administrative leadership to control or guide those pressures by initiating the process of curriculum change, regardless of individual preferences either for or against change.

This discussion of the gradual emergence of a theory of academic change, based on evidence from Rochester, emphasizes the role of both evidence and explanation in the development of grounded theory. At the same time, to insure that additional or alternative explanations of curriculum change were not overlooked, a concerted effort was made throughout the field visits to avoid the early delimitation of a theory which would, in turn, lead only to the collection of data supporting, disconfirming, or modifying that set of explanations.

This caveat notwithstanding, the researcher adopted a broad interpretative framework, which especially guided the interview process, as he subsequently visited Aquinas College, Western Michigan University, and Ohio State University. This framework consisted of a broad set of questions which, based on the earlier data-collection, increasingly guided the research. Especially during the initial visits, the processual and dynamic character of this framework cannot be overemphasized. Not infrequently, for example, variables that seemed important in one setting were irrelevant in another and were omitted from the guiding framework. The role of an outside Advisory Board at Aquinas College is a case in point. Because outside consultants were not included in the change process at the other institutions, there was insufficient evidence to suggest that consultants are a necessary component of curriculum change.

To illustrate the ongoing dynamic between discovery and verification, it is instructive to briefly review some of the evidence from Aquinas College, the second institution visited during the initial round of field visits. It was at Aquinas that the political image of academic change assumed a more prominent place in the emerging framework. Based upon a large number of interviews, the evidence supported the interpretation that prior to the initiation of efforts to bring about curriculum change, conflicts concerning the academic program had been emasculated. But increasingly the Aquinas community became divided over the issue of change in general and curriculum change in particular. The circumstances leading to the selection of a new president committed to curriculum change helped to illuminate a relationship between an increasingly fragmented social structure and administrative intervention in the process of academic change. Interview evidence revealed that the emergence of quasi-interest group sentiment for academic change was the most critical underlying factor leading to the selection of a president committed to change. As one interviewee put it: "We wanted somebody who would shake the institution to its political roots." An influential group of senior lay faculty and many younger faculty viewed Aquinas as a static institution. In particular, they viewed educational innovation as a way of addressing impending financial problems and responding to the trend toward major curricular innovations at other liberal arts institutions. Because they were unwilling to seize the initiative under the heavy-handed leadership of the former president, however, it was not until his retirement that an opportunity existed for change. The subsequent selection of a president who would accept the position only under the condition that the college would engage in a self-study is an indication of the strong sentiment for change at Aquinas. Thus while the new president served as the visible agent, the hidden criterion for his selection was tied to quasi-interest group pressure for change. Without pressures for change, the new president might not have been selected under such unusual conditions. This interpretation was strongly supported by seven of nine interviewees. In any case, the new president was hardly unaware of this sentiment for change and, coupled with his commitment to self-study when he accepted the position, it proved to be a powerful rationale for embarking at once on a major reexamination of the academic program.

Regardless of interest group pressures for change, curriculum reexamination would not have come about without the new president. All fourteen persons interviewed at Aquinas, including the president himself, agreed that he was the agent of change.

The political image of the change process emerged as a useful analytical device in explaining the process of change at Aquinas following the completion of the self-study process. More specifically, the concept of power exertion, as opposed to more static notions such as "power holding" or the innocuous term "power," became a critical variable in accounting for the decision to change the academic program. An interpretation of the evidence at Aquinas suggests that power exertion by an interest group favoring change is important for two reasons. First, it forces the appropriate decision-making body to consider seriously the recommendations submitted by the ad hoc committee. Second, power exertion by interest groups favoring change combines advocacy with a power base which, if used resourcefully, may be sufficient to bring about a decision to change curriculum. In any event, the evidence at Aquinas revealed a compromise decision between competing interest groups, but one in which the changes in the curriculum—both in terms of direction and magnitude reflected the interests of the group exerting the most power.

The emphasis on discovery, as much as verification, guided the data collection process as subsequent visits were made to Western Michigan University and Ohio State University. Thus numerous alternative explanations of the change process were investigated as the researcher resisted the tendency toward premature closure. Indeed, several new concepts, such as "structural reorganization" as a major pressure for change, were added to the framework. Interestingly, however, most of the concepts and relationships derived from the visits to the first two institutions were confirmed by evidence from Western Michigan University and Ohio State; still, the evidence from the latter two schools led to a considerable refinement of several of the concepts and their relationship to academic change. Increasingly rigorous and potentially more useful definitions were developed as concepts were continually revised based upon the ongoing interpretation of the data.

Following the first field visits, the interview data were formally recorded and a lengthy analytic summary sheet was prepared for each institution. The broad interpretative framework, which had been continually revised during the visits, was systematized in these lengthy summaries. By the conclusion of the first round of field visits, a primitive theory of curriculum change was outlined.

During the second phase of field visits, the constant collecting, coding, and analysis conformed more closely to the guidelines of theoretical sampling. Two comparison groups were selected for their theoretical relevance on the basis of preliminary analysis that the process of curriculum change was related to the vehicle of change. The University of Rochester and Ohio State University, which had used a formal curriculum committee, were compared and contrasted with Aquinas College and Western Michigan University where ad hoc groups had been utilized. This maximization of differences between comparison groups stimulated the further refinement of the theory.

A return visit was made to all of the schools except the University of Rochester. During this second phase, the emerging theory guided the process of data collection and the universe of data was gradually delimited. Interviews were oriented toward testing, elaborating, and refining the theory. As a technique for achieving closure at each institution, the researcher asked several interviewees about propositions that were being tested. This technique required courage, but its dividend for validation is immense. If there was agreement that the propositions were a reasonable interpretation of the process, the visit was concluded. If there was some disagreement, then it was necessary to conduct additional interviews until a revised interpretation received validation.

Following the second field visits, the analytic summary sheets were amended in light of the new data. After further analysis, including validation of certain evidence, the researcher concluded that no additional data could be found which further embellished the theory.

An Illustration of the Research Procedure

The sheer volume of the data collected during the investigation, as well as a substantial number of institutional peculiarities at each of the four sample schools, precludes a thorough discussion of the richness, complexity and movement that characterized the application of the constant comparative method to this investigation. However, the reader might gain greater insight into the dynamic of discovery and verification by an illustration of how one concept was abandoned and another was modified during the second field visits.

As the investigator began the second round of visits, the concept of faculty leadership in an ad hoc mechanism during the policy-recommending process had been incorporated into the primitive theory. The concept had been first developed during the initial visit to Western Michigan University where a preliminary analysis of events surrounding the ad hoc group suggested that the chairman and another faculty member exercised an important role in the change process. Five interviewees had indicated that the chairman was the single most instrumental person in realizing a recommendation for change. Following the establishment of the primitive theory, the investigator concluded that the concept should be further tested at Western Michigan: more important evidence should be obtained from the other institution (Aquinas College) utilizing an ad hoc mechanism in order to support, disconfirm, or modify the tentative proposition regarding faculty leadership.

The return visit to Western Michigan yielded data which tended to disconfirm the importance previously placed on faculty leadership. In particular, interview data suggested that the composition of the ad hoc group and the commitment to change accompanying an ad hoc vehicle, together with a policy-recommending process relatively free of interest group pressures, were far more responsible for the recommendation to change than faculty leadership. In the testing of this proposition, however, data were collected which shed further light on the developing theory. At Western Michigan, the concept of "collegiality" was further developed and modified as the investigator attempted to verify the concept of faculty leadership. It was verified that the chairman of the ad hoc group promoted the myth of collegiality to mold apparent consensus by accommodating differences throughout the process and during the writing of the final committee report. Thus while the concept of faculty leadership was disconfirmed, an important variable in explaining the policy-recommending process in ad hoc groups was further refined. The concept of collegiality was defined as brokerage leadership by the chairperson whereby potentially dissatisfied interest groups are persuaded not to exert power to realize their preferred goals.

The return visit to Aquinas College and the collection of additional data further disconfirmed the earlier proposition regarding faculty leadership. Indeed, no single faculty leader of the three visible Aquinas faculty was agreed upon by interviewees as having exercised an indispensable role in the self-study. At the same time, however, pinpointed observations revealed that the leaders of several study groups comprising the larger ad hoc group at Aquinas had exercised an important role in accommodating substantial differences within their respective groups. The leaders of study groups on Teaching Resources and Learning Resources, for example, accommodated differences of opinion that would have otherwise split the groups over proposed changes in general education. Thus the evidence from Aquinas, like Western Michigan, mandated that chairpersons of ad hoc groups are essential components of the change process in the brokerage sense of accommodating differences; in particular, the myth of collegiality is judiciously employed by power brokers to delegitimize deviants and mold apparent consensus for academic change.

This illustration provides an instructive example of how one concept was disconfirmed while another was modified through the gradual delimitation of the theory during the second round of field visits. At the very least, it illustrates the dynamic process of theory construction in the research setting. The theory which had been gradually developed and refined throughout the entire research process, is presented below.

A Grounded Theory of Academic Change

Premises of the Theory

1. Conflict is a natural process in colleges and universities which may or may not lead to change. Change, on the other hand, will invariably include some conflict between old and new social conditions and their proponents. Moreover, change must also involve the exercise of power by a group(s) favoring change.

2. Colleges and universities are splintered into divergent social groups having various interests. That is, they are made up of a loose assemblage of formal and informal parts, with varying degrees of integration. Although the goals of colleges and universities, as in the area of general education, may be stated so broadly as to be acceptable to nearly everyone in an institution, how these goals are to be achieved and precisely how they are to be interpreted is a major source of conflict between various interest groups.

3. Colleges and universities are not characterized by an authority structure which is centralized vis-a-vis academic policy. They are fragmented into interest groups and potential power blocs, each attempting to influence policy so that its values and goals are given consideration. Insofar as it is possible, there is a tendency for interest groups with power to exclude others with less power, such as administrators excluding students from the decision-making process.

4. Although power is diffuse, there are elements of formal authority in colleges and universities, and a recognizable decision-making process does exist. Administrators are agents of academic change, though they are not as frequently advocates of change as they are providers of an impetus to the reexamination of the academic program and the negotiators of compromises between interest groups.

5. To understand change, the goals and values of administrators must be taken into account because administrators are the most frequent interpreters of organizational goals.

The Theory

1. Conflict exists in the college or university to the extent that all interest groups believe that they are participating in the decision-making process. Those interest groups in the social structure of colleges and universities that do not believe they are in a position of power or influence or are not benefiting equally from the academic reward system tend to be agents of conflict and agitation against the status quo. Administrators may be seen as either the facilitators of academic change or the "establishment" holding the power and unwilling to change. They may not merely be "brokers" during the process of conflict. In the college and university, how and by what methods administrators are influenced by power groups largely determines whether or not change will occur.

2. Although underlying conflicts may be embedded in the social structure of colleges and universities, they become visible when one or more external and/or internal pressures threaten the status quo. Structural reorganization, for example, may lead to changes in the distribution of power which in turn lead groups to reevaluate their preferred goals. Other major internal pressures include organizational turnover and the development of faculty subcultures; major external pressures include fluctuating financial conditions, new faculty and students, and curriculum practices at other institutions.

3. Conflict is often heightened through the clash of vested interests; groups with conflicting values and goals seek to find means for the translation of these goals into

effective influence in order to initiate action by the appropriate policy-recommending body.

4. The administrative leadership, in the person of an agent, responds to interest group pressures for change by selecting a mechanism for the reexamination of academic policy and thereby provides an immediate impetus for change.

5. As interest groups exert power to achieve their own goals, quasi-interest groups join together for common purposes as power is exerted and countered until there are only two major interest groups involved in power exertion. Conflict is transformed into policy in the direction of the group exerting more power. Thus it is the group or groups that either singularly, or in concert, exert the greatest amount of power upon/against the administrators due to their numbers or the voice they have in the academic community that is/are most likely to have their interests and goals articulated through policy changes. If the policy-recommending body is an ad hoc group, however, then power is not exerted until the recommendations to change reach the appropriate legislative body. Under these conditions, chairpersons of ad hoc groups promote collegiality by persuading potentially dissatisfied interest groups to accept a carefully orchestrated proposal for academic change.

6. Although decisions do not necessarily take the form of bureaucratic orders, administrators may indeed exercise a brokerage role between competing interest groups. In particular, certain myths such as collegiality are used by power brokers to mold apparent consensus and delegitimize deviants. On the other hand, the faculty at large serve as advocates for interest groups and for change proposals emanating from policy-recommending bodies.

7. Once the process has proceeded past the policy-making stage, a new academic policy is the official climax to interest groups' pressures for change, administrative intervention and brokerage, faculty advocacy, and power exertion by interest groups favoring change. The new academic policy may in turn create controversy, alienate certain interest groups, and engender another power struggle and movement for change.

8. Competent administrators, when aware that such a struggle exists within the college or university environment, may facilitate the process of change, make it less divisive and, at times, less destructive by providing channels of communication between varying interest groups and by attempting to establish university goals and values in concert with the entire university environment. However, one group or another will periodically attempt to exert its power to the maximum extent possible within its particular academic environment.

Discussion

Four different models have guided research on academic change: complex organization, planned change, diffusion of innovation, and political. This section evaluates the utility of the first three models in light of the theory developed here. Because Baldridge's political model most closely approximates the theory, it will be discussed in the concluding summary section.

A Comparison with Alternative Models of Change

Proponents of a complex organization perspective view change as a response to pressures and demands from the environment. When an institution is threatened by stresses and strains, it acts to protect itself by initiating compensatory actions which often lead to changes in the program or structure of the organization. Put simply, change is viewed as a result of minor adjustments by the organization to disruptive forces. Although this model emphasizes external sources of change, it does not ignore internal sources; change is imposed on the organization and is essentially unplanned and unintentional.

Viewed in terms of the grounded theory discussed above, the complex organization model is particularly useful as a tool to sensitize researchers to the underlying sources of change, because academic change is initially more unplanned than planned and more the result of impersonal forces than intentional actions. At the same time, however, the model assumes that pressures are nearly automatically accommodated within the institution as minor changes are made. Because the model does not focus on the problematic outcome of pressures for change, it fails to explain how pressures are linked to a decision to change the academic program. This lack of attention to the dynamic process is compounded because the formal bureaucratic structure is emphasized at the expense of informal processes. For example, the model does not satisfactorily account for conflict, interest group formation, the interaction between groups, and informal power relationships.

The planned change perspective suggests that the impetus for change comes from within an organization with a change agent serving as a catalyst; the greater emphasis, however, is on the process of change, where change is viewed as rational and intentional. The search for the common good of the institution—when accompanied by interpersonal trust, communication, and participation—invariably leads to change.

The planned change model is especially useful in explaining the immediate impetus to change in the person of a change agent, and it is also a good tool for understanding the policy-recommending process when an ad hoc group is appointed to review the academic program of an institution. The policy-recommending phase can fruitfully be analyzed through using this approach. But the model falls short with regard to explaining the sources of change and the dynamics of the final decision-making process. Although the process may appear rational, it is misleading to infer that the impetus to change is the "conscious, deliberative, and collaborative effort to improve the operation of a system through the utilization of scientific knowledge" (Bennis, Benne, and Chin, 1961:3). Moreover, the assumption that the final decision is consensually reached represents a normative prescription rather than a heuristic framework for grappling with the empirical world. The model cannot account for the informal processes which prompt the intervention of the change agent and which, in the decision-making stage, lead to a decision to change the academic program.

The diffusion of innovations approach views change as a result of the diffusion of innovative educational practices. However, the focus is more on the process than the antecedent sources of academic change. The diffusion paradigm is useful in alerting the researcher to the role of interpersonal influence in the communications process: Who (source) says what (message) to whom (receiver) through what channels (medium) to what effect (consequences). But the model provides an incomplete picture of the process of academic change. Although diffusion of outside innovations serves as a major source of change, there are other external and internal sources. More important, the diffusion model assumes that interpersonal influence and communication are sufficient to bring about change. The model cannot account for other informal processes which first prompt the reexamination of the academic program and subsequently lead to a decision to change the program.

All three of these models offer insights into the sources and dynamics of academic change. But taken individually or collectively, they fail to account for the problematic outcome of change without distinctly political pressures and processes. They also fail to investigate the nature of academic power in the change process.

Summary and Conclusions

To summarize briefly, the theory follows five overlapping stages:

1. *Social Structure.* External and internal social structural forces, which frequently threaten the status quo, are the underlying sources of academic change.

2. *Conflict and Interest Group Formation.* In response to one or more of these pressures for change, quasi-interest groups emerge as preexisting conflicts are forced into the open. Conflict is often heightened through the clash of vested interests as groups with conflicting values and goals seek to find means for the translation of these goals into effective influence.

3. *Administrative Intervention.* In response to interest group pressures for change, an administrative agent provides the impetus for the reexamination of the academic program by selecting a controlling mechanism for change.

4. *Policy-Recommending Stage.* A recommendation is made to change the existing academic program.

5. *Policy-Making Stage.* Finally, policy will be determined in the appropriate decision-making body.

Throughout stages four and five, power is exerted and countered through faculty advocacy until there are only two major interest groups involved in power exertion. Administrators then enact a brokerage role between the remaining groups as a compromise decision is reached to change the academic program in the direction of the group exerting more power.

The theory has many similarities with a political model of academic change. In its generally accepted usage, a political model focuses explicitly on the political dimensions surrounding the process of academic change, giving special attention to the formation of interest groups and the ways in which these groups attempt to utilize power and influence in the shaping of new policy. The theory can fruitfully be contrasted with Baldridge's (1971) insightful political paradigm of academic change and governance.

While power is exerted during all five stages, it is stage three that becomes the critical stage in the theory. It is there that the administrator becomes either the facilitator for change or resists change. Thus the understanding of the administrative role not only as a "brokerage role" in the process of academic change; as Baldridge's model suggests, but also as a vested interest group with a substantial amount of power is a critical element in the process of change. The appropriate choice by the administrative agent of a vehicle for change will then account for a change in policy in stages four and five. It is this aspect of the theory, the understanding of who has power within the academic arena, and how that power is used to influence administrators in their selection of a policy-recommending body, that most clearly distinguishes this perspective from Baldridge's political model. The focus shifts from the mere "process of change" to how power is exerted to influence administrators, and the subsequent outcome of that influence.

The theory is a potentially useful tool of analysis because it appears to explain the processes through which most decisions are reached in colleges and universities concerning academic change. It offers a tested framework for understanding those changes. Baldridge's use of political concepts such as interest groups, conflict and compromise—has alerted researchers to the dynamic process of academic change. The grounded theory, however, suggests a set of relationships between political concepts that Baldridge's model neglects. Accordingly, the theory may better explain the processes through which continually changing internal and external pressures lead to academic change.

To summarize briefly, by viewing change as either planned and rational or simply the accommodation of stresses and strains within an institution, the existing literature fails to account for the processes through which pressures are translated into permanent program changes. The grounded theory identifies several major processes which link pressures for change and a policy decision to change: conflict and interest group pressures followed by power exertion, administrative intervention, faculty leadership exercised through interest group advocacy, and compromises which are negotiated through administrative leadership.

The theory outlined here is offered as an alternative to existing perspectives, especially Baldridge's political model. This grounded theory of academic change, generated from data systematically obtained and analyzed through the constant comparative method, now requires further testing through the application of verification methodologies. At the very least, it offers a tested approach to guide research on academic change.

References

Baldridge, J. V. 1971. *Power and Conflict in the University.* New York: Wiley.

Bennis, W. G., K. D. Benne, and R. Chin (eds.) 1961. *The Planning of Change: Readings in the Applied Behavioral Sciences.* New York: Holt, Rinehart and Winston.

Fashing, J. J. 1969. *The Politics of Educational Change: Experimental Education in the College and University*. Doctoral dissertation, University of Oregon.

Glaser, B. G., and A. L. Strauss. 1967. *The Discovery of Grounded Theory: Strategies for Qualitative Research*. Chicago: Aldine.

Griffiths D. E. 1964. "Administrative theory and change in organizations." In M. B. Miles (ed.), *Innovations in Education*. New York: Bureau of Publications, Teachers College, Columbia University.

Hefferlin, J. B. 1969. *The Dynamics of Academic Reform*. San Francisco: Jossey-Bass.

Hodgkinson, H. L. 1970. *Institutions in Transition: A Profile of Change in Higher Education*. New York: McGraw-Hill.

Kerr, C. 1963. *The Uses of the University*. Cambridge, Massachusetts: Harvard University Press.

Lindquist, J. D. 1972. *Political Life in the State University: A Systems and Community Power Analysis*. Doctoral dissertation, University of Michigan.

Lippitt, R., J. Watson, and B. Westley 1958. *The Dynamics of Planned Change*. New York: Harcourt and Brace.

Mitchell, W. G. 1970. *Communication of an Education Innovation in an Institution of Higher Learning*. Doctoral dissertation, Michigan State University.

Rogers, E. M. 1962. *Diffusion of Innovation*. New York: The Free Press.

Rogers, I. L. 1964. *The Process of Institutional Change, with Particular Reference to Major Curriculum Change in Selected Colleges*. Doctoral dissertation, University of Michigan.

Master's Programs and Contextual Planning

Clifton Conrad and Jennifer Grant Haworth

From 1970 to 1990 the number of master's degrees awarded by U.S. universities annually increased 48 percent. So large has been the growth that more than one-half of all earned master's degrees in the history of U.S. higher education were conferred during these 20 years. In the past five years about 300,000 master's degrees have been awarded in America each year. Master's degree education has been a major growth sector of higher education.

Yet few scholars have studied master's level education, especially from the experiences of master's program participants. So between 1989 and 1991 we conducted a national study of master's education (Conrad, Haworth, and Millar 1993). Our focus was on how people involved in master's degree education interpreted and made sense of their experiences. We used an open-ended, multi case study design that was grounded in the perspectives of six "stakeholder" groups: program administrators, faculty, university administrators, current students, master's program graduates, and employers of the graduates. We looked at 47 master's programs distributed across 11 fields of study: five established professional fields (business, education, engineering, nursing, and theater), four emerging fields (applied anthropology, computer science, environmental studies, and microbiology), and two fields in the arts and sciences (English and sociology). The 47 programs represented 31 colleges and universities in 19 states.

What we learned has considerable implications for academic planning. We found that most stakeholders do not make decisions based on mission or purposes but on "decision-situations," or the specific choices that surround persons when they need to decide. That is, persons decide largely on the basis of five major areas of appraisal.

We therefore suggest that planners, especially academic planners, look closely at a new decision-situation approach rather than the traditional mission-objectives-options-decision approach. Such an approach has four major consequences. One is that the experiences of participants in the program move smartly to the heart of the decision-making process. Two, faculty members and university administrators can concentrate their choices and resource allocations on key decision-situations, not on long-range goals. Three, it makes education planning less generic and more institution-specific. And four, the approach makes pedagogy and institutional support as important as curriculum. In a nutshell, we believe that a decision-situation approach to planning offers new possibilities for enhancing not only master's degree programs, but also all the academic programs at an institution.

The High Five

When we interviewed persons about their master's experiences, we found they overwhelmingly portrayed them in terms of five types of decision-situation questions:

1. What kind of approach is there to teaching and learning?
2. What is the orientation of the program: academic or professional?
3. How does the academic department or professional school regard its master's degree programs?
4. What support and encouragement does the college or university provide for its master's programs?
5. What is the student culture, the connections among students, in the program?

For a detailed description of the five decision-situations, see Table 1.

The most important decision-situation for many of the faculty and students we interviewed was the approach to teaching and learning used in the master's program. Faculty and program administrators usually emphasized one of three approaches: didactic, facilitative, or dialogical.

Those who preferred a didactic approach generally embraced an authoritative view of knowledge whereby faculty transmitted knowledge to students. Faculty conveyed their expert knowledge and skills to students who were expected to receive, master, and store it for later use. Many faculty we interviewed expressed their belief that this approach to teaching was, as one put it, "the way for students to get in-depth knowledge." The faculty who used a didactic approach relied mostly on lectures and lecture-discussions, and saw laboratory, clinical, and fieldwork experiences as supplemental.

Faculty and program administrators in a second set of cases preferred a facilitative approach to teaching and learning, where the master's program was an opportunity for students not only to acquire knowledge but also to develop their capacities as generators of knowledge. They embraced a more contigent view of knowledge with knowledge continually being discovered, constructed, and scrutinized by people in specific settings. As teachers, those faculty allowed more participation and felt they were "mentoring" or "apprenticing" students, and they emphasized intensive hands-on learning in experimental settings. As one professor told us, "We try to get our students prepared for Ph.D. work."

In the third set of cases, faculty and program administrators chose a dialogical approach. They often organized their teaching around collegial or collaborative settings, viewing students as less experienced colleagues and co-learners. One faculty member said, "There are no teachers and students here. We are all learning." In these master's programs there were more seminars, colloquia, hands-on experiential learning, and informal out-of-class discussions.

Question of Orientation

The second decision-situation was the orientation of the master's program. For some it was academic, for others professional, and for still others connected.

Faculty and administrators who saw their graduate program as academic accentuated those skills valued in the academic culture: research, problem-solving, and written communication. One nursing brochure stated that the master's program "set forth an integrated body of knowledge with primary emphasis on presenting principles and theories rather than on developing skills and techniques for immediate practical application." Indeed, many of the programs in the academic set did not incorporate technical or practical knowledge, nor did most of the faculty have experience in professional workplace settings.

In the second set we found that faculty and administrators chose a more professional orientation, combining theoretical and applied knowledge with practical knowledge. They stressed the skills of the workplace, including field-specific professional practice skills, analytical and problem-solving skills, and oral as well as written skills. This set often hired full-time faculty who had professional experience, and hired professional practitioners as adjunct faculty.

Table 1
Five Decision-Situations

Decision-Situation One: Approach to Teaching and Learning

Choices	I. DIDACTIC	II. FACILITATIVE	III. DIALOGICAL
Overview	Faculty didactically transmit knowledge to students, emphasizing student mastery of knowledge.	Faculty facilitate knowledge transfer and generation, emphasizing student involvement in the rediscovery and generation of knowledge.	Faculty and students dialogically engage in questioning throughout knowledge transfer and generation processes, emphasizing mutual (faculty and student) generation of knowledge and meaning.
View of Knowledge	Authoritative	Authoritative/Contingent	Authoritative/Contingent
Model of Communication	Transmission	Interactive	Interactive
View of Teacher and Teaching	Hierarchical: Teacher is viewed as "authoritative expert" whose role is to transmit didactically to students "expert" knowledge and skills.	Participative: Teacher is viewed as "expert guide" whose role is to assist students in acquired knowledge and skills through an apprenticeship approach.	Collaborative: Teacher is viewed mostly as "colleague" whose role is to interact dialogically with students in the teaching and learning of knowledge and skills.
View of Learner and Learning	Students are seen as "receivers" of didactically transmitted knowledge whose role is to acquire and "store" knowledge for future use.	Students are viewed as "apprentices" whose role is to understand, test, and apply knowledge to learn their craft.	Students are viewed as "colleagues" with ideas to contribute, whose role is to interact dialogically with faculty and other students.
Focus of Teaching and Learning Experiences	Primary learning experiences occur in the classroom where faculty rely heavily on lectures and lecture-discussions to transfer knowledge to students. Laboratory, clinical, and field-work settings are viewed as supplementary learning experiences.	Primary learning experiences occur in the laboratory or field where faculty use a variety of "hands-on" activities to apprentice students in the knowledge and skills of their craft. Classroom activities (lectures, seminars, discussions) are viewed as supplementary learning experiences.	Primary learning experiences occur within the context of a tacit "learning community" where mutual dialogue between faculty and students as co-learners is encouraged through activities such as classroom seminars; laboratory, clinical and field experiences; and out-of-class learning experiences.

Decision-Situation Two: Program Orientation

Choices	I. ACADEMIC ORIENTATION	II. PROFESSIONAL ORIENTATION	III. CONNECTED ORIENTATION
Knowledge Emphasized	Specialized theoretical knowledge	Specialized theoretical and applied knowledge	Generalized and specialized theoretical and applied knowledge (knowledge is viewed in "connected." dynamic terms)
Skills Emphasized	• Research skills • Analytical and problem-solving skills • Communication skills (primarily written)	• Technical, field-specific, professional practice skills • Analytical and problem-solving skills • Communication skills (oral and written)	• "Big Picture" skills • General and technical-specific, professional practice skills • Analytical and problem-solving skills • Communication skills (oral and written)

Table 1 (continued)

Primary Faculty	Full-time, Ph.D. faculty with minimal non-university professional work experience.	Combination of full-time Ph.D. faculty with some non-professional work experience and part-time adjunct faculty with significant non-university professional work experience.	Full-time, Ph.D. faculty, many with significant non-professional work experi-ence, and part-time adjunct faculty.

Decision-Situation Three: Departmental Support

Choices	I. WEAK	II. STRONG
Conditions of Support	Master's program not viewed as significantly enhancing financial or human resources, reputation, and mission of the department.	Master's program viewed as enhancing financial and human resources, reputation, and mission of the department.
Kinds of Support	Weak financial and symbolic support; weak faculty commitment to master's students.	Strong financial and symbolic support; strong faculty commitment to master's students.

Decision-Situation Four: Institutional Support

Choices	I. WEAK	II. STRONG
Conditions of Support	Master's program not viewed as greatly enhancing financial or human resources, reputation, or mission of the institution.	Master's program viewed as enhancing financial and human resources, reputation, and mission of the institution.
Kinds of Support	Weak financial and symbolic support to master's program, including nonsupportive faculty reward policies.	Strong financial and symbolic support to master's program, including supportive faculty reward policies.

Decision-Situation Five: Student Culture

Choices	I. INDIVIDUALISTIC	II. PARTICIPATIVE	III. SYNERGISTIC
Views of Peers and Peer Learning	Relatively isolated learners who have little to contribute to one another's learning.	Participative learners who can contribute to one another's learning.	Community of interdepen-dent and collegial learners who synergistically contri-bute to one another's learning.
Interaction Patterns with Peers	Individualistic peer relation-ships characterized by either highly competitive or isolated interactions.	Cooperative peer relationships characterized by frequent and cordial interactions.	Collaborative peer relation-ships characterized by frequent, synergistic interac-tions where the "whole" is valued more than "indivi-dualistic parts."
Involvement in Outside-of-Class Activities	Little to no student involve-ment in program; students occasionally form study groups with the intention of improving their own performance.	Moderate student involve-ment in program activities, including study groups, student-run social clubs, and student government associations.	Heavy student involvement in program activities based on strong commitment among students to a vital student learning community.

Note: This table is taken from *A Silent Success: Master's Education in the United States,* which will be published by the Johns Hopkins University Press in 1993.

In contrast to those campuses that had academic or professional orientations in their master's programs, a third set elected to connect the theoretical and applied, the academic and the professional. For example, one professor told us that his program sought to develop a connected view of knowledge analogous to a "soufflé [which] provides an opportunity for synthesis. You put these ingredients together, and it rises and becomes a new entity." Faculty devoted to this orientation emphasized that it helped students see the "big picture."

The third of the five decision-situations was whether or not the department or school provided strong support to its master's program. For the most part, faculty, department chairs, and deans made this decision by evaluating the contribution that the master's program made to their resource base, to their reputation, and to their overall mission. Support was expressed through allocation of financial resources to the master's program, faculty rewards, and assignments to faculty.

In one set, there was weak support for the master's program. Faculty and administrators in this set told us that, while the program contributed to needed resources, it was the baccalaureate and doctoral programs that really mattered. Consequently, minimal budget, space, and faculty support was provided.

A second set, however, provided strong support to their master's programs, allocating financial and human resources and providing assistantships and scholarships to the master's students. A distinguishing feature of this set was the faculty's commitment to master's level education.

The fourth decision-situation we discovered was the degree of upper-level college and university support for master's programs. One set clearly felt these programs did not bring in money, enhance the institution's reputation, or contribute much to the institution's mission. As the administrator at a national institution told us, "The doctoral program is really responsible for our reputation. The master's program only contributes insofar as it provides a screen for the most capable to move on to the Ph.D." A professor reported, "There is no financial or political incentive here for a faculty member to be involved with the master's program."

But a second set of schools we visited chose to provide strong support for their master's degree programs. At these campuses, administrators provided budgetary support, space, and symbolic and rhetorical boosts, as well as counting faculty commitment to excellent master's programs in promotion and tenure decisions. One senior administrator boasted that the college had "gained a great deal of statewide visibility because of its master's programs."

What About the Students?

Many students told us that the student culture—how students interact with each other—greatly affected their learning in the master's program. Across our 47 case studies, we learned that students chose an individualistic, participatory, or synergistic student culture.

One cluster of cases in our sample had students who described themselves as doing best "on their own." Students in this individualistic culture tended to be more competitive or, if not competitive, relatively isolated. They seldom became involved in out-of-class activities and rarely chose to socialize with each other. One student who wanted to interact with her peers said, "I would meet people in class and start talking with them, but then they'd say they had to run off to a job or work on their own."

In a second set of master's programs, the students worked at establishing a participatory culture. These learners engaged in frequent discussions with each other, participated in out-of-class study groups, and joined in student-run organizations. They enhanced each other's understanding of the course material. However, those in the participatory student culture viewed faculty knowledge and perspectives as more valuable than that of their fellow students.

In the third set of cases, students preferred a synergistic student culture in which they actively sought to teach and learn from each other. As an alumna of a program with a synergistic culture told us, "There's no doubt in my mind that I learned as much, if not more, from my peers than I did from the faculty." A faculty member said, "They teach each other as much as we teach them."

Students in synergistic student cultures often establish student clubs, invite speakers, and sponsor social events and academic events. In some programs, they help recruit students and serve as counselors to new students. And graduates of programs with a synergistic culture told us they remain active in networking, recruiting, and placement activities.

A Decision-Situation Approach to Planning

We think the five decision-situations we found offer a novel matrix for planning and evaluating master's degree programs and experiences. Colleges and universities planning a master's degree program, or wishing to improve an existing one, would do well to examine these five process-related decisions in relation to participants' experiences.

This approach contrasts sharply with conventional goal-based planning, which usually ignores the everyday decisions and actions that shape the character of faculty and student learning. The decision-situation approach places the students and their experiences squarely in the center of the decisionmaking process. And it does not reify planning but puts planning and evaluation decisions in their contextual reality.

One more thing. Involving stakeholders in the planning process provides faculty with an enhanced understanding of the experiences that students, alumni, and employees have with their programs. Many faculty in our study told us that these other stakeholders often illuminated decisions that had been made formally or unintentionally and provided valuable feedback for their teaching.

Master's degree programs have grown in size and importance and they deserve greater attention. It would help if that attention—and the planning for better master's programs—used the decision-situation approach.

Reference

Conrad, C., J. Haworth, and S. Millar. 1993 (forthcoming). *A Silent Success: Master's Education in the United States.* Johns Hopkins University Press.

Curricula as Signposts of Cultural Change

PATRICIA J. GUMPORT

Recent approaches to studying higher education reflect a new view of higher education organizations as cultural constructions (Masland 1985; Lincoln 1986; Tierney 1987). Using the concept of culture as a root metaphor, some researchers have suggested that analyzing academic life may reveal the complex ways in which shared systems of beliefs and meanings emerge and evolve among organizational participants (Smircich 1983). This view of academic culture may include many levels of higher education, such as specific campuses and institutions (Clark 1970; Dill 1982), disciplinary cultures (Becher 1984), class cultures within the academic profession (Ryan and Sackery 1985), and national systems of higher education (Clark 1983).

Applying this analytical lens to curricula and curricular change shifts our attention away from such conventional measures as resource allocations courses, degree requirements, and syllabi and toward the cultural life underlying these artifacts. Rather than indicating fairly stable, shared understandings about what constitutes academic knowledge and what knowledge is most worth transmitting, curricula may be only signposts of evolving commitments.

I propose a fluid view of curricula as academic knowledge that is always in process or under construction by organizational participants. In this article I focus primarily on faculty. Underlying the courses and syllabi that they produce and revise are the intellectual, social, and political lives of faculty members that not only shape their scholarly interests but also frame their sense (i.e., meanings and beliefs) about what counts as legitimate knowledge.

Calling attention to the dynamics of knowledge construction is usually noted only when curriculum is changed, for example, when establishing a new major or revising distribution requirements. These occasions of change mark the creation—or re-vision—of academic knowledge.

I believe that we may *always* be re-visioning knowledge. Ralph Tyler has suggested that the academic disciplines should be viewed as "not simply a collection of facts . . . but (as) an active effort to make sense out of some portion of the world or of life" (in Ford and Pugno 1964, 4). Similarly, curricula may be seen as that part of the cultural life of academic organizations in which faculty, administrators, and students construct and revise their understandings and in which they negotiate about what counts as valid knowledge in particular historical and social settings. This paper examines one aspect of the dynamic foundation on which curricula rest: the changing scholarly commitments of faculty and the ontological foundations of such commitments.

I will review briefly some previous ways of viewing academic knowledge and present an alternative conception of knowledge as socially constructed. My views are based on a case study of a new area of academic knowledge—feminist scholarship. During the past two years, I have interviewed seventy-five faculty and administrators in twenty colleges and universities about the challenges posed by feminist perspectives in academia—both in disciplinary canons and in individual academic programs.[1]

Rather than focusing here on the interview data, I describe the conceptual framework that I used for understanding academic knowledge as an ongoing process at the core of organizational cultural life. This framework more accurately captures the complexity of our scholarly lives, including the ways in which some of our interests may crystallize into visions for academic change. It also uncovers potential tensions within organizational life, such as the difficulty in sustaining social cohesion in higher education organizations.

Previous Views

Many higher education researchers and practitioners now consider curriculum a dynamic rather than a fixed component of organizational life. Accounts of curricular change in higher education have ranged from historical descriptions that illuminate centuries of changing purposes and interests (Rudolph 1962, 1981) to normative indictments that equate relativism with a loss of standards (Bloom 1987). Organizational theorists have provided especially valuable descriptions and analyses of changes in the content and organization of academic knowledge, usually by identifying and isolating factors involved in creating new academic domains. Some of these include available material resources (Hefferlin 1969), a decentralized organizational structure (Blau 1973), student demands (Ross 1976), compatible values between the innovation and the host organization (Levine 1980), and profitability for the host organization (Levine 1980).

Studies derived from these kinds of organizational analyses tend to view formal organizational structures as determinative features and antecedents to change; they seldom capture the ongoing, dialectical tensions in knowledge production. According to these studies, organizational participants are severely constrained by the structural features of their contexts.

In addition to those studies that attribute curricular change to specific structural features, other studies explore how faculty members act on their own behalf in establishing new academic areas, including faculty as initiators and advocates (Hefferlin 1969), the importance of a critical mass of faculty (Blau 1973), and faculty aspirations to achieve upward mobility and to resolve role conflict (Ben-David and Collins 1966).

However, even the analyses that place faculty at the center as initiators and advocates of change are deficient in at least two ways. First, these studies fail to explore the interdependence between intellectual content and social-structural features. For example, some scholars who trace the interweaving of intellectual and social aspects of knowledge production, disagree about the sequence of developing a new academic area. Does successfully establishing an organizational form (e.g., course, major, department) depend on a group's ability to achieve a well-articulated point of view (Pfeffer 1981) or, as Oberschall found for sociology, does the organizational form precede the development of distinctive intellectual content (Wood 1979, 33–34)?

More important, however, is understanding the interactive and non-linear nature of knowledge production, how a new academic area is institutionalized simultaneously as scholarly ideas *and* social networks of scholars who pursue those ideas are being developed. Furthermore, the interactions vary in different organizational settings and in different historical time periods, which leads to my next point.

A second shortcoming of these studies is that they neglect the interdependence between academic knowledge and the wider historical and cultural context (Hefferlin 1969, 142; Nelson 1974). Nearly two decades have passed since Hefferlin called for an analytic approach to curricular change that acknowledges the involvement of "a constellation of factors . . . a whole network of factors—attitudes, procedures, mechanisms, pressures" (1969, 189). Hefferlin pointed out the need for a comprehensive framework to trace the mechanisms that bring "environmental" pressures from the outside to colleges and universities. Even recent theoretical advances in organizational culture tend to "stress the internal, rather than look to the external, societal, cultural context in which organizations are embedded" (Jelinek, Smircich, and Hirsch 1983, 338).

In sum, we need to trace scholarly ideas as they are developed by people in particular social-historical locations. Selznick has identified the significance of internal interest groups. From the standpoint of leadership, he pointed out, "They represent sources of energy, self-stimulated, not wholly controllable by official authority. They may subvert the enterprise or lend it life and strength" (1957, 93). Similarly, Clark has noted the growing importance of faculty subcultures as well as the increased separation of faculty and administrative cultures (1983, 89).

Leaving organizational theory of higher education aside for a moment, noteworthy contributions to conceptualizing academic knowledge have been made within other branches of sociology. Sociologists of knowledge and sociologists of science frequently see curricular change as reflecting a larger, complex process of knowledge production. Scholars in these traditions have explored the development of knowledge (or scientific thought) in its immediate social context. Analytic approaches include viewing knowledge production as a social system (Barber 1952; Storer 1966) and as a cultural activity (Whitley 1974; Foucault 1973).

Sparked by the landmark contribution of Kuhn (1962), one fruitful line of inquiry within sociology of science has been to investigate the emergence of research areas, cognitive cultures, and invisible colleges (Crane 1969, 1972). Empirical investigation of the emergence of new scholarly subcultures is based on the assumption that we can measure knowledge growth (e.g., by publications), demarcate boundaries between groups, and discover membership in networks (e.g., through patterns of citations and authorship). Only recently have scholars' political commitments been considered influential in determining intellectual choices (Mok and Westerdiep 1974).

In spite of dramatic conceptual and empirical advances from these scholarly traditions, we have yet to develop a *holistic* understanding of curricular change and of the underlying changes in the content and organization of systems of academic thought they represent. According to Geertz (1983, 152, 154, 157), we can consider academic thought as a cultural artifact; in so doing, it is worthwhile to explore how intellectual villages develop and how their thought frames change. As I understand Geertz, we should develop a conceptualization that places knowledge and its carrying groups at center stage.

A Cultural View

Building on Clark's (1983) idea of knowledge as the oftentimes invisible material around which action takes place and knowledge bundles as the basic organizing principles of academic activities, we can explore how current organizational structures define, but only in part, what counts as knowledge. Organizational participants may redefine, expand, delete, or reorganize legitimating structures.

Current course offerings, majors, and departments both reflect what is currently legitimate and frame future possibilities. If something is legitimate, it is accepted, recognized, or taken for granted by members of an organization. As Spender argues:

> While all human beings may generate "explanations" of the world, may devise schemata for organizing the objects and events of the world, not all of them become legitimated and acceptable explanations; there is a selection process at work and it has a power dimension. It can also be a self-perpetuating power dimension for those who have power to validate their own models of the world, can validate their own power in the process (1981, 1).

If knowledge is continuously constructed and evolving, then legitimacy is relative and contingent, not absolute or static.

Using a cultural view requires us to expand our definition of academic knowledge to include scholarly interests and ideas that may not yet be identified as "bundles." Thus, knowledge is more an ongoing activity among individuals engaged in revisions and less the products of scholarship.

New knowledge, then, becomes valid and legitimate through the efforts of individuals working to formulate and revise their visions for change. We can explore more precisely how new knowledge bundles develop and struggle for legitimacy by seeing faculty as mediators, propelled by their commitments for academic change. Our attention shifts from structural constraints within organizational life to the power of scholarly ideas and the actual experience that informs those ideas.

Faculty, then, may be considered not only as knowledge carriers but also as "re-visioners." Their expertise and loyalty to particular bundles of knowledge dominate their academic lives— their social interactions as well as their teaching, writing, and thinking.

All faculty manipulate knowledge: in "varying combinations of efforts . . . [they] discover, conserve, refine, transmit and apply it"; grouped according to their bundles of knowledge in departments and disciplines, faculty function as knowledge-bearing groups (Clark 1983, 12, 6).

But the manipulation of knowledge is also where faculty diverge; increasingly they are fragmented by expertise (Clark 1983, 36). Faculty have multiple memberships in different levels of the academic profession and speak to shifting audiences which may cut across lines of formal organizational structure and academic culture.

Moreover, informal networks may dramatically influence the development of new knowledge, as appears to have been the case in feminist scholarship (Gumport 1987; Simeone 1987, 99). Such networks create a space in which to formulate and discuss new questions, thereby providing a new scholarly community to stimulate ideas outside the traditional boundaries of "legitimate" disciplinary discourse.

In summary, faculty are mediators who negotiate a complex set of organizational and cultural influences, all of which influence the academic knowledge that they create and revise. By examining the social networks in which faculty participate, it becomes clear which scholarly interests and interpretations are reinforced as worthwhile academic pursuits. New commitments—or shared understandings—may develop, thereby bringing faculty together as a distinctive subculture of proponents working for a new bundle of knowledge.

I cannot understate the significance of commitment. According to Clark (1983, 10), the division of labor in academic organizations is based on division of commitment. I want to expand this concept by examining the basis for new scholarly commitments.

I have already described the view that curricula, the institutional embodiment of individual and organizational commitments to certain academic understandings, reflect what curriculum counts as legitimate academic knowledge. Curricular change, then, signifies changes in a faculty's underlying assumptions about what counts as knowledge, what knowledge is (most) worthy of transmitting, and what organizational form is appropriate (i.e., whether as department or teaching program, as major or just course offerings, or as a nonteaching unit such as a research center).

It is the scholarly commitments of faculty and the subcultures they produce, that constitute curricula's dynamic foundation. Underlying choices about the content and organization of the curriculum lies a complex web of commitments, values, and experiences that comprise the cultural life of our academic organizations. Let me elaborate on two of these notions: commitments and experiences.

Commitments

Scholars have studied how organizations can generate or enhance commitment. According to Pettigrew, commitment, purpose, and order within an organization are generated through the feelings and actions of people as well as through "the existing amalgam of beliefs, ideology, language, ritual and myth (1979, 579). Kanter (1968) and Buchanann (1974) have also explored commitment within organizations.

My research examines the ways in which scholarly commitments have been influenced by political commitments *external* to the academy. In the case of feminist scholarship, a new scholarly agenda grew out of efforts by a generation of academic women to resolve tensions between their political and academic interests. The commitments to develop new academic knowledge apparently rested on two values: an intellectual conviction of the importance of scholarship and a serious interest in bringing a politically informed perspective to academic understandings. (Ironically, it may have been the lack of investment in their academic organizations that enabled some scholars to take such risks in their scholarly innovations; at least in the early years, some scholars were willing to subordinate their academic interests to their political agendas.)

Experiences

In the case of feminist scholarship, political/personal experiences seemed to energize the newly emerging feminist scholarly commitments.

As women questioned their prescribed natures and roles in society, they introduced a new way of understanding that included recognizing ways in which women were systematically omitted and/or devalued. In some cases, women scholars translated this new way of interpreting their experiences directly to their academic work. Realizing that women were worthy of inclusion, for example, one scholar I interviewed stated, "I felt that I had something to say, because there was this whole reality that was left out. Here was sociology allegedly explaining the social world, and the social world I lived in had just been ignored and overlooked."

Many people I interviewed reinforced this link between actual experience and the drive to revise academic understandings. Some feminist critiques of the canon and curriculum were even more far-reaching. They formulated new visions of an academic order emphasizing empowerment and relatedness while minimizing dominance, competition, and hierarchy.

Underlying various feminist visions for change is a consistent premise: The perspective for understanding the world is necessarily rooted in one's experience of the world. (This fact is often referred to as "the social location of the knower.") As one's experiences expand and shift, so does one's drive to alter academic knowledge and one's motivation to form new cultural groups. Having a "shared history of experience" actually binds a group, as Schein has pointed out (1985, 8).

But if shared experiences are essential, what about academic organizations in which people experience different social realities because of their gender, class, race, and ethnicity—to mention a few factors? A picture of academic life becomes one of cultural fragmentation. A source of this fragmentation is clearly ontological.

As experiences inform people's world views, people are motivated to search for academic understandings that reflect their world views. The tendency is particularly evidenced in disciplines in which the focus is on theorizing about human societies. (For example, note the agenda of feminist anthropologists as described in the introduction to Rosaldo and Lamphere 1974.)

The result of changing world views inside an organization is "a web of conflict and tension" created by competing subcultures, each promoting and protecting its distinctive system of meaning and values (Sergiovanni 1984, 8).

Thus, exploring the experiential basis of scholarly commitments illuminates a crucial consideration: to what extent is there a shared vision for academic organizations, and within that vision, how is the organization of academic knowledge (i.e., curriculum) even sustained?

Implications and Summary

We take it for granted that academic knowledge is valued differentially. I am less concerned with the changing knowledge base of truth and fact than with the process by which certain ideas even become contenders for inclusion in curricula. This process of knowledge construction is highly imbued with value and commitments—both by the participants (faculty, students, and administrators) and by the organizations themselves (campuses and disciplines). Both have vested interests in deciding what knowledge is worth pursuing in research and what knowledge is most worth teaching to students.

The view of curricula that I propose points to the complex core of the cultural life of academic organizations calling attention to issues of social cohesion in which researchers and administrators of higher education are interested. In particular, this conceptualization clarifies three important dimensions of academic life.

First, we all know that the scholarly interests of faculty members are influenced by commitments that extend beyond their immediate organizational contexts and disciplines. The conceptualization that I propose views faculty as mediators of intellectual ideas, local organizational opportunities and political commitments rooted in a broader cultural movement; consequently, it shows how those influences become (passionately) linked with academic work.

Second, this perspective enables us to explore the ways in which emerging subcultures of scholars potentially conflict with conventional academic understandings. By examining the commitments and experiential basis of those commitments, we may better understand the points of contention and the impetus for challenging a range of academic norms, including emotional neutrality, political neutrality, competitiveness, individualism, and universalism.

Finally, this framework highlights the problematic task of organizing academic knowledge. Rather than viewing knowledge as having an objective, independent existence, this perspective sees knowledge as dynamic, as intimately connected to human experience and human interaction. Current knowledge bundles may not truly reflect commitments of organizational participants. As new areas of academic discourse emerge, so do subcultures of proponents. While this ongoing process of change indicates scholarly creativity, it also points to the problem of sustaining organizational cohesion: How do we sustain a shared sense of community within an organization when these subcultures compete for legitimacy within a system that may have finite capacities for expansion?

I have intended in this paper to propose a working conceptual framework for understanding curricula and the cultural life it embodies. Organizational analyses (which focus on structural opportunities and constraints) can be enriched by recognizing knowledge as an ongoing process of social construction that is historically bounded, with knowledge at the center and people pursuing interests and developing commitments that correspond to their lived experiences.

From this perspective, empirical investigation of changes in academic knowledge is an ambitious task, as Clark has observed: "Change in systems organized around bundles of knowledge and their carrying groups will remain uncommonly disjointed, incremental and even invisible"; knowledge is a "peculiarly slippery and even invisible substance" (1983, 186). Since I have suggested focusing our attention on commitments of participants, then one natural empirical anchor is the subjective understandings held by those participants. Hagstrom (1965) used scholars as expert "informants," and other scholars have attempted "to *discover* academic knowledge as a segment of culture already defined by the actors themselves" (Barnes 1974, 100).

A cultural view of curricula enables us to take into account both the subjective understandings of organizational participants and the shared systems of meaning and values among subcultures within an organization. This attention to the cultural features of organizational life complements attention to such structural features as resources, size, and centralization. A cultural approach enables both researcher and manager in higher education to interpret curricula as emerging out of faculty commitments.

It has been suggested that administrators of academic programs work among different tribal groups, each with different and competing tribal stories; these tribal stories constitute the curricula (Burlingame 1984, 298). Using the perspective proposed here enables administrators to better understand what has happened (retrospectively) and to anticipate or diagnose tensions among tribal stories and their proponents. In particular, faculty subcultures that potentially challenges a current curriculum become evident. We can explore which scholarly commitments are shared and where they diverge. In so doing, we can also see potential alliances among like-minded faculty members (e.g., feminist scholars across disciplines) as well as among like-minded faculty subcultures (e.g., ethnic studies and women's studies). These are patterns of cultural life in our academic organizations; they include ideas, social relations, and the sharing of commitments—an amalgam of factors that has thus far remained elusive to organizational theorists.

Notes

1. For details of this study, see Gumport 1987. I conducted in depth interviews with seventy-five faculty and administrators in twenty colleges and universities of varying size and prestige. Faculty interviews include retrospective accounts of intellectual biographies and career histories, primarily within disciplines of sociology, history, and philosophy. This paper focuses on only one of three generations of women faculty, the pathfinders who initially developed feminist scholarship; I have not discussed here the generation of pathtakers who followed nor the forerunners who preceded.

   It is important that I note the limitations of this study. Feminist scholars are only one subculture to emerge in a particular historical period and within particular organizational contexts. Obviously, I hope rather to offer a starting point for achieving greater empirical understanding of the emergence of a subculture with scholarly commitments to revise what counts as valid academic knowledge and to change curricula.

References

Barber, Bernard. *Science and the Social Order.* New York: Collier Books, 1952.

Barnes, Barry. *Scientific Knowledge and Sociological Theory.* London: Routledge and Kegan Paul, 1974.

Becher, Tony. "The Cultural View." In *Perspectives on Higher Education: Eight Disciplinary and Comparative Views,* edited by Burton R. Clark, 165–198. Berkeley and Los Angeles: University of California Press, 1984.

Ben-David, Joseph, and Randall Collins. "Social Factors in the Origins of New Science." *American Sociological Review* 3 (August 1966): 451–65.

Berger, Peter, and Thomas Luckmann. *The Social Construction of Reality.* Garden City, New York: Doubleday, 1966.

Blau, Peter M. *The Organization of Academic Work.* New York and London: John Wiley and Sons, 1973.

Bloom, Allan D. *The Closing of the American Mind.* New York: Simon and Schuster, 1987.

Buchanan, Bruce. "Building Organizational Commitments: The Socialization of Managers in Work Organizations." *Administrative Science Quarterly* 19, (1974): 533–46.

Burlingame, Martin. "Theory into Practice: Educational Administration and the Cultural Perspective." In *Leadership and Organizational Culture,* edited by Thomas J. Sergiovanni and John E. Corbally, 295–309. Urbana and Chicago: University of Illinois Press, 1984.

Clark, Burton R. *The Distinctive College.* Chicago: Aldine, 1970. *The Higher Education System.* Berkeley and Los Angeles: University of California Press, 1983.

Crane, Diana. "Social Structure in a Group of Scientists: A Test of the Invisible College Hypothesis." *American Sociological Review* 34 no. 3 (June 1969): 335–52.

_____. *Invisible Colleges: Diffusion of Knowledge in Scientific Communities.* Chicago: University of Chicago Press, 1972.

Dill, David. "The Management of Academic Culture: Notes on the Management of Meaning and Social Integration." *Higher Education* 11 no. 3 (May 1982): 303–20.

Ford, G. W., and Lawrence Pugno, eds. *The Structure of Knowledge and the Curriculum: A Conference.* Chicago: Rand McNally, 1964.

Foucault, Michael. *The Order of Things: An Archaeology of the Human Sciences.* New York: Vintage Books, 1973.

Geertz, Clifford. *Local Knowledge: Further Essays in Interpretive Anthropology.* New York: Basic Books, 1983.

Gumport, Patricia J. "The Social Construction of Knowledge: Individual and Institutional Commitments to Feminist Scholarship." Ph.D. diss., Stanford University, 1987.

Hagstrom, Warren O. *The Scientific Community.* New York: Basic books, 1965.

Hefferlin, J. B. Lon. *Dynamics of Academic Reform.* San Francisco: Jossey-Bass, 1969.

Jelinek, Mariann, Linda Smircich, and Paul Hirsch. "Introduction: A Code of Many Colors." *Administrative Science Quarterly* 28, no. 3 (1983): 331–38.

Kanter, Rosabeth Moss. "Commitment and Social Organization: A Study of Commitment Mechanisms in Utopian Communities." *American Sociological Review* 33, no. 4 (1968): 499–517.

Kuhn, Thomas S. *The Structure of Scientific Revolutions.* Chicago: University of Chicago Press, 1962.

Levine, Arthur. *Why Innovation Fails: The Institutionalization and Termination of Innovation in Higher Education.* Albany: State University of New York Press, 1980.

Lincoln, Yvonna S. "A Future-Oriented Comment on the State of the Profession." *The Review of Higher Education* 10 (Winter 1986): 135–42.

Masland, Andrew T. "Organizational Culture in the Study of Higher Education." *The Review of Higher Education* 8, no. 2 (Winter 1985): 157–68.

Mok, A., and A. Westerdiep. "Societal Influences on the Choice of Research Topics of Biologists." In *Social Processes of Scientific Development*, edited by Richard Whitley, 210–23. London: Routledge and Kegan Paul, 1974.

Nelson, B. "On the Shoulders of the Giants of the Comparative Historical Sociology of Science—in Civilizational Perspective." In *Social Processes of Scientific Development*, edited by Richard Whitley, 13–20. London: Routledge and Kegan Paul, 1974.

Pettigrew, Andrew M. "On Studying Organizational Cultures." *Administrative Science Quarterly* 24 no. 4 (December 1979): 570–81.

Pfeffer, Jeffrey. "Management as Symbolic Action: The Creation and Maintenance of Organizational Paradigms." *Research in Organizational Behavior* 3 (1981): 1–52.

Rosaldo, Michelle Z., and Louise Lamphere, eds. *Women in Culture and Society*. Stanford, Calif.: Stanford University Press, 1974.

Ross, R. Danforth. "Academic Innovations: Two Models." *Sociology of Education* 49 (April 1976): 146–55.

Rudolph, Frederick. *The American College and University: A History*. New York: Vintage Books, 1962.

_____. *Curriculum: A History of the American Undergraduate Course of Study Since 1936*. San Francisco: Jossey-Bass, 1981.

Ryan, Jake, and Charles Sackery. *Strangers in Paradise: Academics from the Working Class*. Boston: South End Press, 1985.

Schein, Edgar H. *Organizational Culture and Leadership*. San Francisco: Jossey-Bass, 1985.

Selznick, Philip. *Leadership in Administration: A Sociological Interpretation*. 1957 Reprint. Berkeley and Los Angeles: University of California Press, 1984.

Sergiovanni, Thomas J. "Cultural and Competing Perspectives in Administrative Theory and Practice." In *Leadership and Organizational Culture*, edited by Thomas J. Sergiovanni and John E. Corbally, 1–12. Urbana and Chicago: University of Illinois Press, 1984.

Simeone, Angela. *Academic Women: Working Toward Equality*. South Hadley, Mass: Bergin and Garvey, 1987.

Smircich, Linda. "Concepts of Culture." *Administrative Science Quarterly* 28, no. 3 (1983): 339–58.

Spender, Dale, ed. *Men's Studies Modified: The Impact of Feminism on the Academic Disciplines*. Oxford: Pergamon Press, 1981.

Storer, Norman W. *The Social System of Science*. New York: Holt, Rinehart and Winston, 1966.

Tierney, William. "Facts and Constructs: Defining Reality in Higher Education Organizations." *The Review of Higher Education* 11 (Autumn 1987): 61–74.

Whitley, Richard. "Cognitive and Social Institutionalization of Scientific Specialties and Research Areas." In *Social Processes of Scientific Development*, edited by Richard Whitley, 65–95. London: Routledge and Kegan Paul, 1974.

Wood, Diane. "Women's Studies Programs in American Colleges and Universities: A Case of Organizational Innovation." Ph.D. diss., Vanderbilt University, 1979.

Changing the Curriculum
in Higher Education

M ARGARET L. A NDERSON

In Susan Glaspell's short story, "A Jury of Her Peers," a man is murdered, strangled in his bed with a rope. The victim's wife, Mrs. Wright, formerly Minnie Foster, has been arrested for the crime. The men investigating—the sheriff, the county attorney, and a friend—think she is guilty but cannot imagine her motive. "It's all perfectly clear, except the reason for doing it. But you know juries when it comes to women. If there was some definite thing—something to make a story about. A thing that would connect up with this clumsy way of doing it," the county attorney says.[1]

When the three men go to the Foster house to search for evidence, two of their wives go along to collect some things for the jailed Minnie Foster. In the house the men laugh at the women's attention to Minnie's kitchen and tease them for wondering about the quilt she was making. While the women speculate about whether she was going to quilt it or knot it, the men, considering this subject trivial, belittle the women for their interest in Minnie's handwork. "Nothing here but kitchen things," the sheriff says. "But would the women know a clue if they came upon it?" the other man scoffs.[2] The three men leave the women in the kitchen while the search the rest of the house for important evidence.

While in the kitchen, the women discover several things amiss. The kitchen table is wiped half-cleaned, left half messy. The cover is left off a bucket of sugar, while beside it sits a paper bag only half filled with sugar. Mrs. Hale and Mrs. Peters see that one block of the quilt Minnie Foster was making was sewn very badly, while the other blocks have fine and even stitches. They wonder, "What was she so nervous about?" When they find an empty bird cage, its door hinge torn apart, they try to imagine how such anger could have erupted in an otherwise bleak and passionless house. Remembering Minnie Foster, Mrs. Hale recalls, "She—come to think of it, she was kind of like a bird herself. Real sweet, and pretty, but kind of timid and—fluttery. How—she—did—change."[3] When the women pick up her sewing basket, they find in it Minnie's dead canary wrapped in a piece of silk, its neck snapped and broken. They realize they have discovered the reason Minnie Foster murdered her husband. Imagining the pain in Minnie Foster's marriage to Mr. Wright, Mrs. Hale says, "No, Mr. Wright wouldn't like the bird, a thing that sang. She used to sing. He killed that too."[4]

Soon the men return to the kitchen, but the women have tacitly agreed to say nothing of what they have found. Still mocking the women's attention to kitchen details, the men tease them. The country attorney asks, "She was going to—what is it you call it, Ladies?" "We call it, knot it, Mr. Henderson."[5]

"Knot it," also alluding to the method of murder, is a punning commentary on the relative weights of men's and women's knowledge in the search for facts and evidence. Women's culture—"not it" to the men—is invisible, silenced, trivialized, and wholly ignored in men's construction of reality. At the same time, men's culture is assumed to present the entire and only truth.[6]

Glaspell's story suggests the social construction of knowledge in a gender-segregated world. In her story, women's understandings and observations are devalued and women are excluded from the search for truth. How might the truth look different, we are asked, were women's perspectives included in the making of facts and evidence? What worlds do women inhabit and how do their worlds affect what they know and what is known about them?

The themes of Glaspell's story are at the heart of women's studies, since women's studies rests on the premise that knowledge in the traditional academic disciplines is partial, incomplete, and distorted because it has excluded women. In the words of Adrienne Rich, "As the hitherto 'invisible' and marginal agent in culture, whose native culture has been effectively denied, women need a reorganization of knowledge, of perspectives and analytical tools that can help us know our foremothers, evaluate our present historical, political, and personal situation, and take ourselves seriously as agents in the creation of a more balanced culture."[7] Women's studies was born from this understanding and over the past two decades has evolved with two goals: to build knowledge and a curriculum in which women are agents of knowledge and in which knowledge of women transforms the male-centered curriculum of traditional institutions.[8] Curriculum change through women's studies is, as Florence Howe has said, both developmental and transformative: it is developmental in generating new scholarship about women and transformative in its potential to make the traditional curriculum truly coeducational.[9]

Since women have been excluded from the creation of formalized knowledge, to include women means more than just adding women into existing knowledge or making them new objects of knowledge. Throughout this essay, including women refers to the complex process redefining knowledge by making women's experiences a primary subject for knowledge, conceptualizing women as active agents in the creation of knowledge, including women's perspectives on knowledge, looking at gender as fundamental to the articulation of knowledge in Western thought, and seeing women's and men's experiences in relation to the sex/gender system. Because this multifaceted understanding of "including women in the curriculum" is an integral part of the new scholarship on women and because we have not developed language sufficient to reflect these assumptions, readers should be alert to the fact that phrases like "scholarship on women," "including women," and "learning about women" are incomplete but are meant to refer to the multidimensional reconstruction of knowledge.

Women's studies has developed from feminists' radical critique of the content and form of the academic disciplines, the patriarchal structure of education, the consciousness education reproduces, and the relation of education to dominant cultural, economic, political, and social institutions. Women's studies seeks to make radical transformations in the systems and processes of knowledge creation and rests on the belief that changing what we study and know about women will change women's and men's lives.[10] Hence, curriculum is understood as part of the political transformation of women's role in society because all teaching includes political values. As Florence Howe has written,

> In the broadest context of that word, teaching is a political act: some person is choosing, for whatever reasons, to teach a set of values, ideas, assumptions, and pieces of information, and in so doing, to omit other values, ideas, assumptions, and pieces of information. If all those choices form a pattern excluding half the human race, that is a political act one can hardly help noticing. To omit women entirely makes one kind of political statement; to include women as a target for humor makes another. To include women with seriousness and vision, and with some attention to the perspective of women as a hitherto subordinate group is simply another kind of political act. Education is the kind of political act that controls destinies, gives some persons hope for a particular kind of future, and deprives others even of ordinary expectations for work and achievement.[11]

This discussion raises important questions about how we define women's studies in the future and how, especially in this conservative political period,[12] the radicalism of women's studies can be realized within institutions that remain racist and sexist and integrally tied to the values and structures of a patriarchal society. But, as Susan Kirschner and Elizabeth Arch put it, women's studies and inclusive curriculum projects are "two important pieces of one work."[13] Feminists in educational institutions will likely continue working for both women's studies and curriculum change, since both projects seek to change the content and form of the traditional curriculum[14] and to contribute to social change through curriculum transformation. It is simply impossible, as Howe has put it, "to move directly from the male-centered curriculum to what I have described as 'transformation' of that curriculum into a changed and co-educational one—without passing through some form of women's studies."[15]

Building an Inclusive Curriculum

Peggy McIntosh estimates that since 1975 there have been at least eighty projects that, in various ways, examine how the disciplines can be redefined and reconstructed to include us all.[16] This estimate gives some idea of the magnitude of the movement to create new curricula that include women. Moreover, according to McIntosh, although fewer projects are now being funded through sources external to the institutions that house them, internal funding for such projects seems to be increasing.

Curriculum-change projects in women's studies have varied widely in their purposes, scope, institutional contexts, and sources of funding. For example, projects at Wheaton College and Towson State University (both funded through the Fund for the Improvement of Post Secondary Education [FIPSE]) are university-wide projects engaging faculty in the revision of courses across the curriculum. Other projects involve consortia of several campuses, such as those at Montana State University, the Southwest Institute for Research on Women (SIROW) at the University of Arizona, and the University of Massachusetts-Amherst.

The SIROW project has several dimensions, including course development and revision at the University of Arizona and a three-year project for integrating women into international studies and foreign language courses at several universities in Arizona and Colorado. Funded by the Women's Educational Equity Act Program (WEEA), the Montana State project began as a two-year faculty development project intended to reduce bias in the curriculum; it was later renamed the Northern Rockies Program on Women and was expanded to develop curriculum resources in a twenty-five school consortium in Montana, Utah, Wyoming, and Idaho. The project "Black Studies/Women's Studies: An Overdue Partnership," funded by FIPSE, includes faculty from the University of Massachusetts, Smith College, Hampshire College, Mount Holyoke College, and Amherst College; twenty-nine faculty from this project met to create new courses and build theoretical and curricular connections between black studies and women's studies. The Mellon seminars at the Wellesley College Center for Research on Women, funded through the Andrew W. Mellon Foundation, have drawn together faculty from the New England area to apply feminist scholarship to curriculum transformation.

At the University of Delaware, the university provided funds for a development project for faculty in the social sciences who were revising introductory and core courses to make them inclusive of gender and race; faculty in the project met in an interdisciplinary faculty seminar on feminist scholarship, followed by a day-long conference on curriculum change and a one-year program for visiting consultants who gave public lectures and advised faculty on the reconstruction of their courses. The Women's Research and Resource Center at Spelman College, funded by the Ford Foundation, has emphasized curriculum revision in freshmen courses in English, world literature, and world civilization with the purpose of building a cross-cultural perspective that would illuminate both the contributions and experiences of Afro-American women and women in the Third World. Still other projects are designed primarily for resource development, such as the project of the Organization of American Historians that produced curriculum packets designed to integrate women in the United States and Europe into survey courses at both the college and secondary school level. The Geraldine R. Dodge seminars also focus on the secondary school level. Involving teachers from public and private secondary schools in three regions of the country, these seminars are intended to help teachers become better acquainted with feminist scholarship and to develop high-school curricula that reflect women's history, experiences, and perceptions.

There are so many of these projects that it is impossible to describe all of them here. These few example do, however, give an idea of the range of activities and the different institutional contexts of inclusive curriculum projects. All of them rest on the concept of faculty development since building faculty knowledge of new interdisciplinary scholarship from feminist studies is an integral and critical part of curriculum transformation.

Directors of these projects typically begin with the recognition that women's studies scholarship has not fully made its way into the "main" curriculum of colleges and universities and that, without programs designed to bring the new scholarship into the whole curriculum, most students—male and female—will remain untouched by scholarship on women and therefore unprepared to understand the world. Elizabeth Minnich suggests that, though liberal arts advocates claim that a liberal arts education instills in students the perspectives and faculties to understand a complex world, instead, students learn about a detached and alienating world outside their own experiences. Were we honest about traditional education, she says, we would teach them the irony of the gap between stated educational missions and actual educational practices. Schools do not typically teach a critical view of the liberal arts we have inherited; we seem to have forgotten that, historically, liberal arts education was an entrée into ruling positions for privileged males. Liberal arts education taught privileged men the language of their culture, its skills, graces, principles, and intellectual challenges, modeled on one normative character. It thus emphasized sameness over differences, even in a world marked by vast differences of culture, race, class, ethnicity, religion, and gender.[17] Consequently, there is now entrenched in the liberal arts a curriculum claiming general validity, that is, however, based on the experience, values, and activities of a few.

Curriculum-change projects designed to bring the scholarship on women into the whole curriculum have been variously labeled "mainstreaming," "integrating women's studies into the curriculum," and "gender-balancing the curriculum." There are problems with each of these labels, since they may imply that curriculum change through women's studies follows some simple programmatic scheme when women's studies cannot be merely assimilated into the dominant curriculum. McIntosh says the label "mainstreaming" trivializes women by implying that we have been out of, and are only now entering the mainstream. The term implies that there is only one mainstream and that by entering it, women will be indistinguishable from men. It makes the reconstructive work of curriculum change seem like a quick and simple process, whereas women's studies builds its understanding on the assumption that there are diverse and plural streams of women's and men's experience.[18]

The use of the terms "integration" and "balance" to describe these projects is also problematic. Feminist scholarship has rested on the assumption that the exclusion of women leads to distorted, partial, and false claims to truth, yet "balancing" may imply that all perspectives are equally accurate or significant. Certainly, women's studies instructors do not want room in the curriculum for all perspectives, thereby including those that are racist, anti-Semitic, ethnocentric, class-biased, and sexist. Furthermore, liberal calls for balance often cloak an underlying appeal for analyses that are detached and dispassionate, as if those who are passionately committed to what they study cannot be objective. Gloria Bowles and Renate Duelli-Klein, among others, argue that it is unrealistic to seek a balanced curriculum in a world that is unbalanced.[19] Their concern reflects the understanding that most educational curricula mirror the values and structure of the dominant culture, yet they may underestimate the power of education to generate change.

Similarly, "integration" implies that women's studies can be assimilated into the dominant curriculum, when women's studies scholarship demonstrates that women cannot be simply included in a curriculum already structured, organized, and conceived through the experience of men. Critics of curriculum-integration projects, including Bowles and Duelli-Klein, caution that these projects might dilute the more radical goals of the women's studies movement by trying to make women's studies more palatable to those who control higher education. Integration is inadequate if it means only including traditionally excluded groups in a dominant system of thinking. So, if integration is interpreted as assimilation, these critics are right, but the history of the black protest movement in America indicates that the concept of integration cannot be dismissed merely as assimilation. Advocates of integration in the black protest movement understood that integration required a major transformation of American culture and values, as well as radical transformation of political and economic institutions. In the development of black studies, integration and separatism have not been either/or strategies, though they do reflect different, yet complementary purposes. If we take its meaning from black culture and politics, integration is a more complex idea and goal than assimilation; movements for integration in black history reflect a broad tolerance for diverse efforts to make radical transformations of educational institutions and the society at large.[20]

This controversy is more than a semantic one because the debate about terminology reflects political discussion among feminists who sometimes disagree about the possibilities and desirability of including women's studies in the curriculum. Because women's studies rejects the assumptions of the dominant culture and finds the traditional compartmentalization of knowledge inadequate for the questions women's studies asks, both the language and the work of curriculum change by necessity must maintain that what is wrong with the dominant curriculum cannot be fixed by simple addition, inclusion, and minor revision.[21] Feminist critics of curriculum-integration projects fear that these projects change the primary audience of women's studies to "academics who wish to reform the disciplines but see no need to challenge the existing structure of knowledge based on the dominant androcentric culture."[22] Other feminists criticisms reflect a concern that the political radicalism of feminism will be sacrificed in order to make women's studies scholarship more acceptable to nonfeminists.[23] As Mary Childers, former associate director at the University of Maine at Orono project, states it, curriculum-integration projects may transform feminist work more than they transform the people at whom the projects are directed.[24]

The debate about women's studies and curriculum-change projects has been described as a debate between autonomy and integration,[25] and it reflects the origins of women's studies as both an educational project and as a part of broader societal efforts for emancipatory change. Those who argue for autonomy worry that integration projects compromise women's studies by molding it to fit into patriarchal systems of knowledge. Developing women's studies as an autonomous field is more likely, they argue, to generate the new knowledge we need because it creates a sustained dialogue among feminists working on common questions and themes.[26] Integrationists see a dialectical relationship between women's studies and inclusive curriculum projects and recognize that curriculum-revision projects are not a substitute for women's studies.[27] They see curriculum projects as both growing out of women's studies and fostering its continued development (pointing out that on many campuses where inclusive curriculum projects preceded women's studies, the projects resulted in the creation of women's studies programs). Developers of inclusive curriculum projects know that the projects cannot replace women's studies programs and research. Moreover, the presence of inclusive curriculum projects in institutions has typically strengthened women's studies programs.[28]

Projects to balance the curriculum also raise the question of what it means to have men doing feminist studies, since curriculum-revision projects are typically designed to retrain male faculty. Elaine Showalter discusses this in the context of feminist literary criticism where a number of prominent men have now claimed feminist criticism as part of their own work. She asks if men's entry into feminist studies legitimates feminism as a form of academic discussion because it makes feminism "accessible and subject to correction by authoritative men."[29] And, does it make feminism only another academic perspective without the commitments to change on which feminist studies have been grounded? The radical shift in perspective found in women's studies stems, in large part, from the breach between women's consciousness and experience and that of the patriarchal world.[30] Merely having men study women as new objects of academic discourse does not necessarily represent a feminist transformation in men's thinking. Showalter concludes that in literature, only when men become fully aware of the way in which they have been constituted as readers and writers by gender systems can they do feminist criticism; otherwise, she says, they are only engaging in a sophisticated form of girl-watching. By further implication, transforming men through feminist studies must mean more than their just becoming aware of new scholarship on women or understanding how their characters and privileges are structured by gender; it must include their active engagement in political change for the liberation of women.

For women and for men, working to transform the curriculum through women's studies requires political, intellectual, and personal change. Those who have worked in curriculum-revision projects testify that these are mutually reinforcing changes—all of which accompany the process of curriculum revision through women's studies.[31] Understanding the confluence of personal and intellectual change also appears to help women's studies faculty deal with the resistance and denial—both overt and covert—that faculty colleagues in such projects exhibit.[32] Women's studies scholarship challenges the authority of traditional scholarship and, as a consequence, also challenges the egos of those who have invested their careers in this work. Revising the curriculum is therefore also a process of revising our personalities since our work and our psyches have been strongly intertwined with our educations.[33]

The reconstruction of the curriculum through women's studies is occurring in a context of significant change in the demographic composition of student populations. Women now represent a majority of the college population, and by the year 1990 it is projected that minorities will constitute 30 percent of the national youth cohort.[34] In a report to the Carnegie Foundation, Ernest Boyer and Fred Hechinger conclude that "from now on almost all young people, at some time in their lives, need some form of post-secondary education if they are to remain economically productive and socially functional in a world whose tasks and tools are becoming increasingly complex."[35]

At the same time, current appeals for educational reform threaten to reinstate educational privilege along lines determined by race, class, and sex. Various national reports conclude that there is a crisis in education defined as the erosion of academic standards, and the collapse of traditional values in education. In all of these appeals, the decline of academic standards is clearly linked to the proliferation of scholarship and educational programs in women's studies and black studies.[36] And, though seemingly different in tone and intent, conservative academic arguments about the need to "return to the basics" and to reclaim the legacy of "the classics" are actually attempts to reinstate patriarchal authority.[37] The assumption is that, if we do not reclaim the classical legacy of the liberal arts, we will lose the academic rigor on which such forms of education are seen as resting.[38] By implication, women's studies and black studies are seen as intellectually weak and politically biased, while study of the classics is seen as both academically rigorous and politically neutral.

One of the goals of women's studies is to insure that education becomes democratic. Women's studies practitioners know that the skills acquired through education cannot be merely technical and task-oriented but must also address the facts of a multiracial and multicultural world that includes both women and men. Case studies from universities that have had inclusive curriculum projects show that students do learn through women's studies to enlarge their world views and to integrate academic learning into their personal experience even though this process by which this occurs is full of conflict, resistance, and anger.[39] Other research shows that, following women's studies courses, students report increased self-esteem, interpret their own experiences within a larger social context, increase their identification with other women, expand their sense of life options and goals, and state more liberal attitudes about women.[40] Moreover, faculty in inclusive curriculum projects often report that students are most captivated by the material that focuses specifically on women and gender; students in these projects also report that their classmates and their instructors are more engaged in class material where women are included as agents and subjects of knowledge.[41]

However, given the brief history of inclusive curriculum projects and the fact that balanced courses are still a small percentage of students' total education, evaluating student responses to such projects reveals only part of their significance. Equally important are the opportunities for revitalizing faculty when faculty positions are threatened by budget cuts, retrenchment, and narrowed professional opportunities.[42] Faculty in inclusive curriculum projects report new enthusiasm for their work and see new research questions and directions for their teaching as the result of this work.[43] After her review of inclusive curriculum projects around the country, Lois Banner reported to the Ford Foundation that the projects are also particularly impressive in the degree to which participants discuss and share course syllabi, pedagogical problems and successes, attitudes about themselves, and the changes they are experiencing. She finds this especially noteworthy since college faculty do not ordinarily share course materials with ease and regard their teaching as fundamentally private.[44]

The Phases of Curriculum Change

Several feminist scholars have developed theories to describe the *process* of curriculum change. These are useful because they provide a conceptual outline of transformations in our thinking about women and because they organize our understanding of curriculum critique and revision as an ongoing process. These phase theories also help unveil hidden assumptions within the curriculum and therefore help move us forward in the reconceptualization of knowledge.[45]

An important origin for phase theories is Gerda Lerner's description of the development of women's history.[46] Lerner describes the theoretical challenges of women's history as having evolved in five phases. The first phase was the recognition that women have a history, which led to the second phase, conceptualizing women as a group. In the third phase, women asked new questions about history and compiled new information about women. In the fourth phase, women's history challenged the periodization schemes of history that had been developed through the historical experiences of men, leading them, in the final phase, to redefine the categories and values of androcentric history through consideration of women's past and present.

Lerner's description of the evolution of feminist thought in history showed feminist scholars in other disciplines that scholarship on women was evolving from simply adding women into existing schemes of knowledge into more fundamental reconstructions of the concepts, methods, and theories of the disciplines. She was not the first to see this, but her articulation of these phases of change provided a map for the process through which women were traveling.

McIntosh has developed an analysis of phases in curriculum change that is unique in that it relates patterns of thought in the curriculum to human psyches and their relation to the dominant culture.[47] McIntosh calls phase 1 in the curriculum "womanless" (for example, "womanless history," "womanless sociology," or "womanless literature"). Only a select few are studied in this phase of the curriculum, and highly exclusionary standards of excellence are established. Since the select few in a womanless curriculum are men, we come to think of them as examples of the best of human life and thought. In turn, the curriculum reproduces psyches in students that define an exclusive few as winners and all the rest as losers, second-rate, or nonexistent.

Phase 2 of the curriculum change maintains the same worldview as phase 1, since women and a few exceptions from other excluded groups are added in, but only on the same terms in which the famous few have been included. McIntosh defines this phase as "women in history," "women in society," or "women in literature," to use examples from the disciplines. In this phase of curriculum change the originally excluded still exist only as exceptions; their experiences and contributions are still measured through white, male-centered images and ideas. This phase can suggest new questions about old materials, such as, What are the images of women in so-called great literature? Also, this phase raises new questions like, Who were the best-selling women novelists of the nineteenth century? However, while this phase leads to some documentation of women's experience, it tends to see a few women as exceptions to their kind and never imagines women and other underclasses as central or fundamental to social change and continuity.

McIntosh calls the third phase of curriculum change "women as a problem, anomaly, or absence." In this phase, we identify the barriers that have excluded so many people and aspects of life from our studies, and we recognize that, when judged by androcentric standards, women and other excluded groups look deprived. As a result this phase tends to generate anger, but it is also the phase in which feminist scholars begin to challenge the canons of the disciplines and seek to redefine the terms, paradigms, and methods through which all of human experience is understood. Thus, it leads to more inclusive thinking in which class, race, gender, and sexuality are seen as fundamental to the construction of knowledge and human experience. Moreover, we recognize that inclusive studies cannot be done on the same terms as those preceding, thereby moving us to phase 4—"women on their own terms."

Phase 4, exemplified by "women's lives as history" or "women as society," makes central the claim that women's experiences and perspectives create history, society, and culture as much as do those of men. This phase also departs from the misogyny of the first three phases wherein women are either altogether invisible or are seen only as exceptional, victimized, or problematic relative to dominant groups. Phase 4 investigates cultural functions, especially those involving affiliation; understudied aspects of men's lives, such as their emotional lives and nurturant activities, become visible in this phase. In phase 4, according to McIntosh, boundaries between teachers and students break down as the division between the expert and the learner evaporates and teachers and students have a new adjacent relationship to the subjects of study. This phase also leads to a search for new and plural sources of knowledge.

Phase 5, McIntosh says, is harder to conceive because it is so unrealized—both in the curriculum and in our consciousness. She imagines this as a radical transformation of our minds and our work, centered on what she calls "lateral consciousness"—attachment to others and working for the survival of all.

Marilyn Schuster and Susan Van Dyne see curriculum change evolving from recognizing the invisibility of women and identifying sexism in traditional knowledge, to searching for missing women, then to conceptualizing women as a subordinate group, and, finally, to studying women on their own terms.[48] Through these first steps, women's studies poses a challenge to the disciplines by noting their incompleteness and describing the histories that have shaped their developments. Schuster and Van Dyne add women's studies as a challenge to the disciplines to their phase theory and define the last phase as one that is inclusive of human experience and appropriates women's and men's experience and the experiences generated by race and class as relational. The final phase of curriculum transformation, therefore, would be one based on the differences and diversity of human experience, not sameness and generalization. Schuster and Van Dyne identify the implied questions, incentives for change, pedagogical means, and potential outcomes for each of the six phases they identify, and they ask what implications each phase has for changed courses. They also provide a useful index of the characteristics of transformed courses.

In another analysis of curriculum change, Mary Kay Tetreault defines the phases of feminist scholarship as male scholarship, compensatory scholarship, bifocal scholarship, feminist scholarship, and multifocal or relational scholarship.[49] The first phase she identifies, like the first phases described by McIntosh and by Schuster and Van Dyne, accepts male experience as universal. Phase 2 notices that women are missing but still perceives men as the norm. The third phase, bifocal scholarship, defines human experience in dualist categories; curricula in this phase perceive men and women as generalized groups. This phase still emphasizes the oppression of women. Tetreault calls phase 4 "feminist scholarship"; here women's activities, not men's, are the measure of significance, and more attention is given to the contextual and the personal. Sex and gender are seen within historical, cultural, and ideological contexts, and thinking becomes more interdisciplinary. Tetreault's fifth phase, multifocal scholarship, seeks a holistic view in which the ways men and women relate to and complement each other is a continuum of human experience. In this phase, the experiences of race, class, and ethnicity are taken fully into account.

Tetreault suggests that understanding these different phases of curriculum change can be useful for program and course evaluation since they provide a yardstick for measuring the development of feminist thinking in different disciplines. Nevertheless, none of the authors of phase theories intends them to represent rankings or hierarchies of different kinds of feminist scholarship, and it is important to note that these phases have fluid boundaries and that their development does not necessarily follow a linear progression. Still, organizing women's studies scholarship into phases demonstrates how asking certain kinds of questions leads to similar curricular outcomes. As one example, adding black women into the history of science can reveal patterns of the exclusion of black women scientists and can then recast our definition of what it means to practice science and to be a scientist; this shows the necessity of seeing science in terms other than those posed by the dominant histories of science.[50] Furthermore, Showalter points out that different phases of thinking can coexist in our consciousnesses,[51] so for purposes of faculty development, it is important to recognize that certain phases are appropriate as faculty awareness progresses in different institutional, disciplinary, and course contexts.

Finally, identifying the phases of curriculum change is helpful in developing feminist pedagogy. Drawing from work by Blythe Clinchy and Claire Zimmerman[52] on cognitive development among undergraduate students, Francis Maher and Kathleen Dunn[53] discuss the implications of different phases of curriculum change for pedagogy. Clinchy and Zimmerman describe the first level of cognitive functioning for college students as dualist, meaning that students posit right and wrong as absolute and opposite. Maher and Dunn say the pedagogical complement to this phase of student development is the lecture format in which students are encouraged to see faculty members as experts who impart truth by identifying right and wrong.

Multiplism is the second phase in Clinchy and Zimmerman's analysis. This phase of cognitive development describes knowledge as stemming from within; in this phase, students discover the validity of their own experience. According to Maher and Dunn, this produces among students a highly relativistic stance—one in which they accept the legitimacy of different worldviews and experience, thus opening themselves up to experiences that vary by class, race, and gender but seeing all experiences and perspectives as equally valid. Contextualism is the third phase of cognitive development identified by Clinchy and Zimmerman; according to Maher and Dunn, we can encourage this phase of student development through the creation of a pluralistic curriculum in women's studies.

Like those who have articulated phase theories of curriculum change, Maher and Dunn see the ultimate goal of women's studies as developing a curriculum that is inclusive in the fullest sense—taking gender, race, class, and sexuality in their fullest historical and cultural context and developing an understanding of the complexities of these experiences and their relatedness. Such a curriculum would no longer rest on the experiences and judgment of a few. Since phase theories help us move toward this goal, they are an important contribution to faculty and student development through women's studies.

Critique of the Disciplines

The new enthusiasm that participants in women's studies faculty development projects report for their work is a sign that the insights of feminist scholarship are on the theoretical and methodological cutting edge of the disciplines. Working hard to build a balanced curriculum has renewed faculty and brought them and their students a new level of awareness about women in society, culture, and history. In fact, the revisions in the disciplines that this literature stimulates are so extensive that it is reasonable to conclude that "whether or not you are in women's studies, its scholarship will affect your discipline."[54]

As Schuster and Van Dyne argue,[55] there are invisible paradigms within the educational curriculum that represent tacit assumptions that govern what and how we teach, even when we are unaware of these ruling principles. The feminist movement exposes these unexamined standards by showing their relation to the ideology, power, and values of dominant groups, who in our culture most often are white, European-American men. Thus, although women's studies is often accused of being ideological, it is the traditional curriculum that is nested within the unacknowledged ideology of the dominant culture. The more coherent and tacitly assumed an ideology is, the less visible are the curricular paradigms that stem from it and the more unconsciously we participate in them.

Feminist criticism is generated by the fact that women are both insiders and outsiders to the disciplines; the contradictions imposed by their status create a breach between their consciousnesses and their activity, generating critical dialogue and producing new sources of knowledge.[56] Feminist criticism across the disciplines reveals that what is taken to be timeless, excellent, representative, or objective is embedded within patriarchal assumptions about culture and society. Consequently, recentering knowledge within the experience of women unmasks the invisible paradigms that guide the curriculum and raises questions that require scholars to take a comprehensive and critical look at their fields.

Creating an inclusive curriculum means more than bringing women's studies into the general curriculum because it also means creating women's studies to be inclusive so that women's studies does not have the racist, class, heterosexist, and cultural bias that is found in the traditional curriculum.[57] Feminist curriculum change, then, must not exclude the voices of women of color in posing the research questions, defining the facts, shaping the concepts, and articulating theories of women's studies. How would the work be enriched, both cognitively and emotionally, by listening to the voices and fully including the experiences of women of color? What kind of knowledge is made by ignoring not only class and gender but also race as origins for and subjects of scholarship? If the curriculum—both inside and outside of women's studies—is focused on white cultures, it will continue to define women of color as peripheral and to see white experiences as the norm and all others as deviant or exceptional. It will, in effect, reproduce the errors of classical education.[58]

Esther Chow[59] suggests three strategies for incorporating the perspectives of women of color into courses: the comparison method, special treatment, and mainstreaming. The comparison strategy brings materials on women of color into courses for purposes of comparison with the dominant group experience, and it exposes students to a wide range of materials by examining women's experiences from different perspectives. Chow suggests, however, that it can perpetuate the marginality of women of color by leaving white women at the center of the major paradigm for analysis. Alternatively, the special-treatment approach makes women of color the topic of general survey courses, special topic courses, or independent reading. The advantage to such courses is that they allow for in-depth understanding of the themes in the lives of women of color, although, since these courses tend to be electives, they do not make an impact on a wide range of students. The mainstreaming strategy incorporates materials on women of color into existing courses so that they appear throughout, not just in segregated areas of courses or the curriculum. Chow is careful to point out that the substance of these courses should not be divided along clear racial and gender lines. And she concludes that the effectiveness of these different strategies is dependent on the needs and goals of particular courses, the institutional setting, and interaction between teachers and students of various racial-ethnic backgrounds.

Creating an inclusive curriculum both within women's studies and within traditional disciplines is initiated by asking two questions: What is the present content and scope and methodology of a discipline? and How would the discipline need to change to reflect the fact that women are half the world's population and have had, in one sense, half the world's experience?[60] Those who work in women's studies know that women's studies scholarship cannot be simply added into the existing curriculum, as it challenges the existing assumptions, facts, and theories of the traditional disciplines, as well as challenging the traditional boundaries between the disciplines. The identification of bias in the curriculum is the first step in analyzing the multiple implications of the fact that women have been excluded from creation of formalized knowledge.[61] But as feminist scholarship has developed, more fundamental transformations can be imagined.

Several volumes specifically address the impact of feminist scholarship on the disciplines[62] and, were this essay to review fully the whole of women's studies literature would need to be considered. Of course, this essay cannot possibly do this; instead, it addresses the major themes that emerge from consideration of curriculum change effected through women's studies.

The Arts and Humanities

Feminist criticism shows that the arts and humanities have in the past created and reinforced definitions of life that exclude the experiences of, deny expression to, and negate the creative works of the nonpowerful, even though the humanities claim to take the concerns of all humanity and the human experience as their subject matter.[63] Women have been excluded from literary and artistic canons on the grounds that their work does not meet standards of excellence,[64] though, as Paul Lauter suggests, "standards of literary merit are not absolute but contingent. They depend, among other considerations, upon the relative value we place on form and feeling in literary expression as well as on culturally different conceptions of form and function."[65]

The exclusion of women from literary and artistic canons suggests that the canons themselves are founded on principles embedded in masculine culture, even though many literature teachers and critics will say that great literature and art speak to universal themes and transcend the particularities of sociocultural conditions like race, class, and gender. In tracing the development of the canon of American literature, Lauter has shown that the exclusion of white women, blacks, and working class writers from the canon of American literature was consolidated in the 1920s when a small group of white elite men professionalized the teaching of literature and consolidated formal critical traditions and conventions of periodization.[66] Since then, the aesthetic standards of the canon have appeared to be universal because without revealing their history, the learned tastes and common experiences of certain academic men are exaggerated as universal. And, as Annette Kolodny argues, once a canon is established, the prior fact of canonization tends to put works beyond questions of merit.[67]

Other feminist critics in the arts and humanities have identified the chronological presentation of materials as deeply problematic. Natalie Kampen and Elizabeth Grossman, for example, say that the idea that time is fundamentally linear and progressive—fundamental in the study and teaching of art history through chronology—produces accounts of the development of human culture that are more linear than the actual historical evolution of the culture has been. Chronological presentation also assumes competition as a part of human creativity and suggests that hierarchical arrangements are inevitable in all organization of cultural reality.[68]

Including women in the curriculum has been especially difficult in fields like the history of philosophy where the canon is fixed and relatively small. Even in ethics, where it is more difficult to ignore variations in human values, the subject tends to be studied from the vantage point of those in power, lending the impression that only elites can understand cultural norms.[69] In the humanities, when women do appear in texts and as artistic objects, their own experiences are seldom primary. In American literature, for example, women, native Americans, and blacks sometimes "inhabit" texts but are rarely given primary voices within them. This reveals a deep sex, class, and race bias in the teaching of the arts and humanities.

Were we to begin study in the arts and humanities through the experience of traditionally excluded groups, new themes would be revealed. Gloria Hull, for example, in her account of reading literature by North American women of color, identifies several themes that arise from immersion in this literature on its own terms.[70] An acute awareness of racial and sexual oppression pervades this literature, but so do themes of bicultural identity (especially expressed through language), alternative understandings of sexuality, and the importance of preserving cultural tradition in forms of expression.

History, like literature and the arts, has tended to focus on the historical experience of a few. Because historians tend to concentrate on heroes, they ignore the lives of ordinary men and women. Thus, much of the impact of feminist scholarship in history has been to expand the "characters" of historical accounts. But, more than adding in new characters, feminist scholarship in history shows how the traditional periodization of historical accounts is organized through the experience of bourgeois men.[71] From a feminist perspective, including women means not only including those who have been left out but rethinking historical paradigms to generate new frameworks in which women are agents of history and that examine the lives of women in their own terms and bring them into accounts of historical change. Feminist revisions of history do more than expand the subjects of history; they introduce gender relations as a primary category of historical experience. So, although the narrative style of history has tended to produce singular tales of historical reality, feminist scholarship in history produces accounts that reflect the multiple layers of historical experience.[72] As one example, in American studies, scholars have focused on a singular myth of the physical and metaphysical frontier of the new world as a place to be conquered and possessed. In contrast, Kolodny's work on women's consciousness and westward expansion shows that women imagined the frontier as a garden to be cultivated.[73]

Feminist scholars suggest how excellence is produced and defined by literary and cultural institutions should become part of the study of the arts and humanities. This requires methodological self-consciousness, asking, for example, what social conditions are necessary for certain female images to emerge? Whose interests are served by these images? How do they affect women? And what are the varieties of women's tastes, working methods, and experiences?[74]

These questions help us identify bias in the curriculum and ultimately reveal more deeply embedded habits of thought. In her analysis of foreign language textbooks, Barbara Wright shows that the texts ignore most social classes, except for educated, upper middle-class surgeons, professors, and businessmen.[75] She identifies several phases of critique of the curriculum in foreign language instruction by examining the images of women and girls in textbooks, then studying women's place in the culture being presented, and, finally, developing a critical look at language itself. This last phase of questioning helps us see the value judgments that inform decisions to include or exclude certain semantic and syntactic possibilities in the language and, therefore, reveals ways in which gender, class, and race are embedded in the language of a culture and in our language teaching. Feminist criticism understands that the "circumstances in which culture is produced and encountered, the functions of culture, the specific historical and formal traditions which shape and validate culture—these all differ somewhat from social group to social group and among classes. In this respect, the problem of changing curriculum has primarily to do with learning to understand, appreciate and teach about many varied cultural traditions."[76]

Carolyn Heilbrun writes, "The study of literature cannot survive if it cannot . . . illuminate human experience; and human experience cannot today be illuminated without attention to the place of women in literature, in the textuality of all our lives, both in history and in the present."[77] From feminist work in these fields we begin to see past and present cultures as "multi-layered, composites of men's and women's experiences, and rich in complexity and conflict."[78] This vision of cultural multiplicity explored through feminist scholarship would help the humanities to present a full account of human experience.

The Social Sciences

As in the arts and humanities, the exclusion of women from the social sciences leads to distortion and ignorance of their experience in society and culture.[79] Whereas the social sciences claim to give accurate accounts of social reality, the exclusion of women's experiences and perspectives has produced concepts and theories that, while allegedly universal, are, in fact, based on gender-specific experiences, and so these theories often project the assumptions of masculine, Western culture into the social groups under study.[80]

As a result, feminist scholars suggest that core concepts in the social sciences are gender biased. As one example, the assumed split between public and private spheres is reproduced in social science concepts that tend to be grounded in public experience and that ignore private experience and the relation between public and private dimensions of social life. Focus on the public sphere as the primary site for social interaction omits women's experience and much of men's.[81] Economic activity, for example, is defined as taking place only in the public sphere, leading to the total omission of household work as a measurable category of economic activity in economics. Thus, caring for the sick, elderly, or young is productive economic activity when performed for wages but not when performed by persons in the privacy of the household. Moreover, by assuming white Western male experience as the norm, mainstream economists assume that economic activity is based on rational choice and free interaction. A feminist approach, however, would develop economic analyses that identify constraints on choice and the process of choosing.[82]

Likewise, in political science, textbooks describe political activity only as it occurs in formal public political structures. The representation of women and minority groups in elected offices is typically included, as is some recognition of federal legislation on civil rights. But always omitted are such topics as women's and minority groups' participation in community politics, ethnic identity as a dimension of political activity, or sexuality as the basis of organized political movements. Were we to rely on these texts for our understanding of political systems and behavior, as do most faculty and students, the virtual omission of race, sex, gender, class, and ethnicity would lead us to believe that none of these has been significant in the development of political systems and behavior.[83]

The location of social science concepts within the public and masculine realm reflects the dichotomous thinking that prevails in both social science content and method. Dorothy Smith's work in the sociology of knowledge investigates the implications of the fact that men's experience in the public world has been segregated from that of women in the private sphere. She posits that men are able to become absorbed in an abstract conceptual mode because women take care of their everyday, emotional, and bodily needs. As a result, concepts in the social sciences, as they have been developed by men, are abstracted from women's experience and do not reflect their realities or worldviews.[84] Others have also argued that social science research methods polarize human experience by forcing respondents into either/or choices to describe their social experiences and attitudes. This is especially the case in experimental and survey research and in research on sex differences.[85] Furthermore, research methods in the social sciences routinely isolate people from the social contexts in which they are studied. And, in empirical research, race and sex, if mentioned at all, are treated as discrete categories and are reported as if they were separate features of social experience. It is an exceptional study that even presents data by race and by sex, and, when this is done, race and sex are most often reported separately. For example, sociologists comparing income by race and by sex typically report blacks' and whites' incomes and, in another table, compare men's and women's incomes, In reporting race and sex separately, the particular experiences of black women, white women, black men, and white men disappear from view. This practice produces false generalizations, perpetuates the invisibility of women of color, and denies that women of color have unique historical and contemporary experiences.

One of the greatest obstacles to curriculum change in the social sciences is the disciplines' search to establish themselves as sciences. The scientific method, as adopted in the social sciences, generates hierarchical methodologies in which the knower is seen as expert in the lives of others and produces research methodologies that deny that social relationships exist between researchers and those they study. Since the relationship between the knower and the known is part of the knowledge produced through research, denial of this relationship distorts the accounts produced by social science. Judith Stacey and Barrie Thorne conclude that, in sociology, positivist epistemology prohibits the infusion of feminist insights because positivism sees knowledge in abstract and universal terms that are unrelated to the stance of the observer. Feminist transformation has been more possible, they argue, in disciplines where interpretive methods are used. Interpretive methods are reflexive about the circumstances in which knowledge is produced and see researchers as situated in the action of their research; thus, they are better able to build knowledge in the social sciences that takes full account of social life.[86]

Feminist methodologies in the social sciences begin from the premise that the relationship between the knower and the known is a socially organized practice. The assumed detachment of scientific observers from that which they observe is, as feminists see it, made possible through organized hierarchies of science where, for example, women work as bottle washers, research assistants, or computer operators.[87] Moreover, feminists argue that the assumption of scientific detachment and rationality is a masculine value, one that is made possible by ignoring the role of women in the practice of science. Additionally, Shulamit Reinharz suggests that feminist research in the social sciences should see the self-discovery of the researcher as integral to the process of doing research; consequently, it is ludicrous in her view to imagine the act of "data gathering" as separate from the act of "data analysis."[88]

In response to the preoccupation with scientific method in the social science disciplines, feminist scholars suggest that critiques of the scientific method should be a primary concern in feminist revisions of social science courses. In developing, for example, a feminist approach for teaching methods of psychology, Michelle Hoffnung suggests including a variety of approaches and methods and investigating in each case their assumptions about scientists' relations to the worlds being investigated.[89] Similarly, in teaching courses like the history of psychological thought, we need to recognize that women are more active in the history of psychology and social science disciplines than texts lead us to believe. When texts focus only on the internal development of a science, histories of the discipline wrongly ignore the external social and historical conditions that create scientific investigations.[90] As in the arts and humanities, putting women into social scientific courses requires this more reflexive approach—one that puts women and men in the full context of their historical and cultural experiences and that does not assume the universality of concepts, theories, and facts.

Science and Technology

Of all the disciplines, the natural and physical sciences have the closest connections to political and economic structures, yet they make the strongest claims to academic neutrality. For feminist scholars in the sciences, seeing how scientific studies reflect cultural values is a good starting point for understanding the interwoven worlds of science, capitalism, and patriarchy.

To begin with, scientific descriptions project cultural values onto the physical and natural world. Ruth Hubbard explains that kingdoms and orders are not intrinsic to the nature of organisms but have evolved in a world that values hierarchy and patrilineage.[91] Though it is often claimed that scientific explanations run counter to the widely shared beliefs of society, it is also true that scientific explanations are often highly congruent with the social and political ideology of the society in which they are produced.[92] Research on brain lateralization, for example, reflects a seeming intent to find a biological explanation for sexual differences in analytical reasoning, visual-spatial ability, and intuitive thought that cannot itself be clearly and consistently demonstrated in scientific investigations.[93] And perhaps nowhere else are culturally sexist values so embedded in scientific description and analysis as in discussions of sexual selection, human sexuality, and human reproduction.[94]

The feminist critique of science, as in the humanities and social sciences, looks at cultural dualisms associated with masculinity and femininity as they permeate scientific thought and discourse.[95] Some question whether the scientific method is even capable of dealing with collective behavior due to the fact that it parcels out behaviors, cells, categories, and events. In science, like the humanities and social sciences, explanations thought to be true often do not stand up when examined through women's experiences. For example, whereas medical researchers have typically described menopause as associated with a set of disease symptoms, new research by feminist biologists finds that the overwhelming majority of postmenopausal women report no remarkable menopausal symptoms.[96]

The feminist critique of science can be organized into five types of studies: equity studies documenting the resistance to women's participation in science; studies of the uses and abuses of science and their racist, sexist, homophobic, and class-based projects; epistemological studies; studies that, drawing from literary criticism, historical interpretation, and psychoanalysis, see science as a text and, therefore, look to reveal the social meaning embedded in value-neutral claims; and feminist debates about whether feminist science is possible or whether feminists seek simply a better science—undistorted by gender, race, class, and heterosexism.[97]

Building the feminist critique of science can therefore begin from several questions, including: Why are women excluded from science? How is science taught? What are the scientific research questions that, as feminists, we need to ask? How is difference studied in scientific institutions? Or, how is the exclusion of women from science related to the way science is done and thought? Some of these questions are similar to those asked in social studies of science. But feminist discussions of science specifically examine what Evelyn Fox Keller calls the science/gender system—the network of associations and disjunctions between public and private, personal and impersonal, and masculine and feminine as they appear in the basic structure of science and society. Keller argues that asking "how ideologies of gender and science inform each other in their mutual construction, how that construction questions in our social arrangements, and how it affects men and women, science and nature" is to examine the roots, dynamics, and consequences of the science/gender system.[98]

Science bears the imprint of the fact that, historically, scientists have been men. Therefore, asking how and why women have been excluded from the practice of science is one way to reveal deeply embedded gender, race, and class patterns in the structure of scientific professions and, consequently, in the character of scientific thought. As a consequence, while encouraging the participation of women in science is an obvious question of equity, it also reaches deeply into the social construction of science and provides insights about why some concepts gain legitimacy in science while others do not. So, important as it may be, women's experience is excluded from biological theory because it is considered to be subjective and therefore is considered to be outside the realm of scientific inquiry. Moreover, since it cannot be measured in scientific ways, the topic, not the method, is seen as illegitimate.[99]

Collectively, the work of feminist scientists raises new possibilities for the way science is taught[100] and conceived. By making us more conscious of the interrelatedness of gender and science, this work underscores the connection between science and the sex/gender system. Moreover, a feminist view of science would take it as only one of a number of ways to comprehend and know the world around us so that the hegemony of science as a way of knowing would be replaced with a more pluralistic view.

Resource Materials in the Disciplines

New scholarship on women does not automatically get translated into new teaching within the disciplines. Therefore, several of the professional organizations have sponsored projects that have produced guidelines for integrating new material on women into courses in the disciplines. These are especially valuable for assisting faculty teaching core courses in the disciplines and teaching new courses about women. The series published by the American Political Science Association[101] is a five-volume set with review essays, sample syllabi, field exercises, and suggested reading. The authors review explanations for the underrepresentation of women as public officials and examine sex discrimination against women as attorneys, judges, offenders, and victims. Moreover, they examine the traditional assumption that women are apolitical by looking at the political activity of women in community organizations and grassroots movements that are organized around such issues as sexual harassment, women's health, and violence against women.

Other professional groups have developed materials that focus particularly on integrating the study of women into the introductory curriculum; such materials are available in sociology, psychology, American history, and microeconomics.[102] These collections typically include a sample syllabus for introductory courses, with suggestions for new topics, examples, and reading in the different areas usually included in introductory courses. One collection from Feminist Press, *Reconstructing American Literature*, contains sixty-seven syllabi for courses in American literature. The American Sociological Association has recently published an excellent collection that includes syllabi for courses on sex and gender with suggested student assignments and exercises, lists of film resources, and essays on teaching women's studies, dealing with homophobia in the classroom, integrating race, sex, and gender in the classroom, and the experience of black women in higher education.[103]

The appendix of Schuster and Van Dyne's book, *Women's Place in the Academy: Transforming the Liberal Arts Curriculum*, is especially useful because it is organized by disciplines and separates suggested readings into those for classroom use and those more appropriate for teacher preparation. Faculty working to integrate scholarship on women into their courses would be wise to consult the various review essays published in *Signs* that summarize major research and theoretical developments in the academic fields and to consult the papers on curriculum change in the working papers series published by the Wellesley College Center for Research on Women. Newsletters from campuses with inclusive curriculum projects often include essays on revising courses written by faculty who are working to revise their courses.[104] Finally, women's caucuses within the professional associations of the disciplines can typically provide bibliographies and other resources designed to assist in the process of curriculum change.

A wealth of other materials are available to assist faculty specifically in the process of integrating women of color into the curriculum of women's studies and disciplinary courses. Gloria Hull, Patricia Bell Scott, and Barbara Smith's collection, *All the Women Are White, All the Blacks Are Men, But Some of Us Are Brave* is a classic and invaluable source. It includes not only essays on different dimensions of black women's experiences and contributions to knowledge and culture but also a superb selection of syllabi incorporating the study of women of color into courses and bibliographies and bibliographic essays of print and nonprint materials by and about black women.[105]

The Center for Research on Women at Memphis State University publishes a bibliography in the social sciences that is an excellent review of research about women of color;[106] their other projects include summer institutes on women of color and curriculum change, a visiting scholars program, faculty development seminars, and a working papers series. Maxine Baca Zinn's review essay in *Signs* includes an excellent bibliography for including Chicana women in the social sciences,[107] and *Estudios Femeniles de la Chicana* by Marcela Trujillo includes a proposal for Chicana Studies and course proposals and outlines that are useful for curriculum development.[108] Anne Fausto-Sterling and Lydia English have produced a packet of materials on women and minorities in science that is a collaborative project by students enrolled in a course at Brown University on the history of women and minority scientists; their collection includes essays written by the students about their experiences in science. In addition, Fausto-Sterling and English have printed a course materials guide that is an extensive bibliography of books, articles, bibliographies, visual aids, and reference works on the subject of women and minorities in science.[109]

The journal *Sage* is also an invaluable resource for scholars. *Sage* publishes interdisciplinary writing by and about women of color; recent issues have highlighted the topics of education, women writers, and mothers and daughters.[110] Other journals have published special issues devoted to studying women of color.[111] In addition to this growing primary research literature by and about women of color, there are numerous review essays that provide a guide to this important area of research.[112]

Such a wealth of material about women of color invalidates teachers' claims that they would include material on and by women of color if it were available. It also underscores the need to reeducate by recentering toward the lives of those who have been excluded from the curriculum and to do so by changing the materials and experiences we use in constructing classroom contents. Including the study of women of color in all aspects of the curriculum is rooted in a fundamental premise of women's studies: that there is great variation in human experiences and that this diversity should be central to educational studies. Although, as Johnella Butler notes, reductionist habits in the classroom make teaching about multiplicity difficult,[113] if the classrooms are more pluralistic both teachers and students will be better able to understand the pluralistic world.

Materials to assist in the process of curriculum change are abundant—so much so that one of the problems in faculty development projects is that faculty who have not followed the development of feminist scholarship over the past two decades must now learn an entirely new field of scholarship. Obviously, this cannot be accomplished quickly and, although we may sometimes feel discouraged by the magnitude of the needed changes, it is useful to remember that we are trying to reconstruct systems of knowledge that have evolved over centuries. Small changes, while obviously incomplete, do introduce larger changes—both in course content and in the political, intellectual, and personal transformations that this process inspires. Although it is also sometimes difficult to imagine what a revised curriculum would look like, Butler reminds us that working to build an inclusive curriculum requires a willingness to be surprised.

All of the materials reviewed above help us assess the climate for change in particular disciplines and devise appropriate strategies for the different fields in which we work and teach. With this information in mind and with the underlying philosophies of different projects specified, we can better analyze the context for curriculum change in various disciplines and imagine multiple ways of accomplishing educational change within them.

Conclusion

Adrienne Rich pointed the way to curriculum change through women's studies when she distinguished between claiming and receiving an education. Receiving an education is only "to come into possession of, to act as receptacle or container for; to accept as authoritative or true," while claiming an education is "to take as the rightful owner; to assert in the face of possible contradiction."[114] For women, Rich said, this means "refusing to let others do your thinking, talking, and naming for you."[115]

For women's studies to realize Rich's vision means we must develop women's studies itself to be inclusive curriculum. Inclusive curriculum means both working to build women's studies into the curriculum and doing the work and thinking that makes women's studies multicultural and multiracial. These two dimensions will also strengthen women's studies as a field of its own, since they ask us to examine our own assumptions, methods, and relationship to the society in which we live. In this sense, changing the curriculum has three dimensions: changing our selves, changing our work, and changing society.

These are sobering times for women's studies scholars who seek through education an end to the injustices and patterns of exclusion that have characterized our culture. In the current political climate, one in which we are experiencing a serious backlash in educational change, women's studies and the feminist movement will meet new resistance.[116] Current appeals to return to the basics and to stabilize the curriculum threaten once again to exclude women, people of color, and gays and lesbians from the center of our learning, but Howe provides us with hope for change when she writes, "It is essential to revelatory learning to see the opposition clearly. . . . In a period when the opposition will be most visible, we may be able to do our best work.[117]

Department of Sociology
University of Delaware

Notes

This essay has been developed through the many discussions I have had with people working in women's studies curriculum projects around the country. I am particularly grateful for having been able to participate in the Mellon seminars at the Wellesley College Center for Research on Women. Although I cannot name all of the participants in these seminars, their collective work and thought continuously enriches my thinking and teaching; I thank them all. I especially thank Peggy McIntosh, director of these seminars, for her inspiration and ongoing support for this work. She, Valerie Hans, Sandra Harding, and the anonymous *Signs* reviewers provided very helpful reviews of the earlier drafts of this essay. And I appreciate the support of the Provost's Office of the University of Delaware for providing the funds for a curriculum revision project in women's studies at the University of Delaware; working with the participants in this project contributed much to the development of this essay.

1. Susan Glaspell, "A Jury of Her Peers," in *The Best American Short Stories*, ed. Edward J. O'Brien (Boston: Houghton Mifflin Co., 1916), 371 83.

2. *Ibid.*, 376.

3. *Ibid.*, 381.

4. *Ibid.*, 383.

5. *Ibid.*, 385.

6. Building from Simone de Beauvoir's work, Catherine MacKinnon discusses this point. De Beauvoir writes, "Representation of the world, like the world itself, is the work of men: they describe it from their own point of view which they confuse with the absolute truth" (cited in MacKinnon, 537). MacKinnon continues the point by saying that "men create the world from their own point of view which then becomes the truth to be described." As a result, the male epistemological stance is one that is ostensibly objective and uninvolved and does not comprehend its own perspectives; it does not take itself as subject but makes an object of all else it looks at. See Catherine MacKinnon. "Feminism, Marxism, Method, and the State: An Agenda for Theory." *Signs: Journal of Women in Culture and Society* 7, no. 3 (Spring 1982): 515-44, esp. 537.

7. Adrienne Rich, "Toward a Woman-centered University," in *On Lies, Secrets, and Silence* (New York: W.W. Norton & Co., 1979), 141.

8. Betty Schmitz, *Integrating Women's Studies into the Curriculum* (Old Westbury, N.Y.: Feminist Press, 1985).

9. Florence Howe, *Myths of Coeducation* (Bloomington: Indiana University Press, 1984).

10. Marilyn J. Boxer, "For and About Women: The Theory and Practice of Women's Studies in the United States," *Signs* 7, no. 3 (Spring 1982): 661–95.

11. Howe, 282–83.

12. Deborah Rosenfelt, "What Women's Studies Programs Do That Mainstreaming Can't." in "Special Issue: Strategies for Women's Studies in the 80s," ed. Gloria Bowles, *Women's Studies International Forum* 7, no. 4 (1984): 167–75.

13. Susan Kirschner and Elizabeth C. Arch, "Transformation of the Curriculum: Problems of Conception and Deception," in Bowles, ed. 149–51.

14. Florence Howe, "Feminist Scholarship: The Extent of the Revolution," in *Liberal Education and the New Scholarship on Women: Issues and Constraints in Institutional Change: A Report of the Wingspread Conference*, ed. Anne Fuller (Washington, D.C.: Association of American Colleges, 1981), 5–21.

15. Howe, *Myths of Coeducation*, 280.

16. The 1985 directory of such projects from the Wellesley College Center for Research on Women is reprinted in Schmitz. Although such a directory is quickly outdated, it is useful for seeing the diversity of projects that have been undertaken on different campuses across the country, as well as by professional associations. *Women's Studies Quarterly* periodically publishes reports from various projects:

see vol. 11 (Summer 1983) and vol 13 (Summer 1985). See also Peggy McIntosh, "The Study of Women: Processes of Personal and Curriculum Re-vision," *Forum* 6 (April 1984): 2–4; this issue of *Forum* and the vol. 4 (October 1981) issue of *Forum* also contain descriptions of curriculum-change projects on twenty-six campuses. *Forum* is available from the Association of American Colleges, 1818 R Street N.W., Washington D.C. 20009.

17. Elizabeth Kamarck Minnich, "A Feminist Criticism of the Liberal Arts," in Fuller, ed., 22–38.

18. Peggy McIntosh, "A Note on Terminology," Women's Studies Quarterly 11 (Summer 1983): 29–30.

19. Gloria Bowles and Renate Duelli-Klein, eds., *Theories of Women's Studies* (Boston: Routledge & Kegan Paul, 1983).

20. Margaret Andersen, "Black Studies/Women's Studies: Learning from Our Common Pasts/Forging a Common Future," in *Women's Place in the Academy: Transforming the Liberal Arts Curriculum*, ed. Marilyn Schuster and Susan Van Dyne (Totowa, N.J.: Rowmann & Allanheld, 1985), 62–72.

21. Johnella Butler, "Minority Studies and Women's Studies: Do We Want to Kill a Dream?" in Bowles, ed., 135–38.

22. Bowles and Duelli-Klein, eds., 9.

23. Marian Lowe and Margaret Lowe Benston, "The Uneasy Alliance of Feminism and Academia," on Bowles, ed. (n. 12 above), 177–84.

24. Mary Childers, "Women's Studies: Sinking and Swimming in the Mainstream," in Bowles, ed., 161–66.

25. This debate can be best reviewed in Bowles, ed. (n. 12 above).

26. Sandra Coyner, "The Ideas of Mainstreaming: Women's Studies and the Disciplines," *Frontiers* 8, no. 3 (1986): 87–95.

27. Peggy McIntosh and Elizabeth Kamarck Minnich, "Varieties of Women's Studies," in Bowles, ed., 139–48.

28. See Myra Dinnerstein, Sheryl O'Donnell, and Patricia MacCorquodale, *How to Integrate Women's Studies into the Traditional Curriculum* (Tucson: University of Arizona, Southwest Institute for Research on Women [SIROW], n.d.); JoAnn M. Fritsche, ed., *Toward Excellence and Equity* (Orono: University of Maine at Orono Press, 1984); and Schmitz (n. 8 above). See also Betty Schmitz, *Sourcebook for Integrating the Study of Women into the Curriculum* (Bozeman: Montana State University, Northwest Women's Studies Association, 1983); and Bonnie Spanier, Alexander Bloom, and Darlene Boroviak, eds., *Toward a Balanced Curriculum: A Sourcebook for Initiating Gender Integration Projects* (Cambridge, Mass.: Schenckman Publishing Co., 1984).

29. Elaine Showalter, "Critical Cross-Dressing: Male Feminists and the Woman of the Year," *Raritan* 3 (Fall 1983): 130–49; quotations are from Gayatri Spivak, "Politics of Interpretations," *Critical Inquiry* 9 (September 1982): 259–78, cited in Showalter, 133.

30. Marcia Westkott, "Feminist Criticism of the Social Sciences," *Harvard Educational Review* 49 (November 1979): 22–30.

31. Peggy McIntosh, "WARNING: The New Scholarship on Women May Be Hazardous to Your Ego," *Women's Studies Quarterly* 10 (Spring 1982): 29–31; and McIntosh, "The Study of Women," (n. 16 above).

32. Dinnerstein et al.

33. Peggy McIntosh, "Interactive Phases of Curricular Re-Vision: A Feminist Perspective," Working Papers Series, no. 124 (Wellesley, Mass., Wellesley College Center for Research on Women, 1983).

34. Marilyn Schuster and Susan Van Dyne, "Curricular Change for Twenty-first Century: Why Women?" in Schuster and Van Dyne, eds. (n. 20 above), 3–12.

35. Ernest L. Boyer and Fred M. Hechinger, *Higher Learning in the Nation's Service* (Washington, D.C.: Carnegie Foundation for the Advancement of Teaching, 1981), 28.

36. Michael Levin, "Women's Studies, Ersatz Scholarship," *New Perspectives* 17 (Summer 1985): 7–10. *New Perspectives* is published by the U.S. Commission on Civil Rights.

37. The Family Protection Act proposed by the New Right and introduced to Congress on September 24, 1979, would prohibit "any program which produces or promotes courses of instruction or curriculum seeking to inculcate values or modes of behavior which contradict the demonstrated beliefs and values of the community" or any program that supports "educational materials or studies … which would tend to denigrate, diminish, or deny role differences between the sexes as it has been historically understood in the United States" (Senate Bill 1808, 96th Congress, first session, title 1, sec. 101; cited in Rosalind

Petchesky, "Antiabortion, Antifeminism, and the Rise of the New Right," *Feminist Studies* 7 [Summer 1981]; 225). The Family Protection Act would return moral authority to the heterosexual married couple with children and would eliminate women's studies and any other educational programs that suggest homosexuality as an acceptable lifestyle; it would also severely reduce federal jurisdiction over desegregation in private schools.

38. Nan Keohane, "Our Mission Should Not Be Merely to 'Reclaim' a Legacy of Scholarship—We Must Expand on It," *Chronicle of Higher Education* 32 (April 2, 1986): 88.

39. In Fritsche, ed. (n. 28 above): Christine L. Baker, "Through the Eye of the Storm: Feminism in the Classroom," 224–33; Jerome Nadelhaft, "Predictable Storm in the Feminist Classroom," 247–55.

40. Karen G. Howe, "The Psychological Impact of a Women's Studies Course," *Women's Studies Quarterly* 13 (Spring 1985): 23–24, In addition to a discussion of her own research, Howe includes an excellent review of literature on this topic.

41. Betty Schmitz, Myra Dinnerstein, and Nancy Mairs, "Initiating a Curriculum Integrating Project: Lessons from the Campus and the Region." in Schuster and Van Dyne, eds., 116–29.

42. Marilyn Schuster and Susan Van Dyne, "Placing Women in the Liberal Arts: Stages of Curriculum Transformation," *Harvard Educational Review* 54 (November 1984): 413–28.

43. Dinnerstein et al. (n. 28 above).

44. Lois Banner, "The Women's Studies Curriculum Integration Movement: A Report to the Ford Foundation" (New York: Ford Foundation, March 1985, typescript).

45. For a discussion of phase theories see Mary Kay Thompson Tetreault, "Women in the Curriculum," 1–2; Peggy McIntosh, "Women in the Curriculum," 3; Peggy McIntosh, "Convergences in Feminist Phase Theory," 4; all in the vol. 15 (February 1986) issue of *Comment*. *Comment* is available from RCI Communications, 680 West 11th Street, Claremont, Calif. 91711.

46. Gerda Lerner, "The Rise of Feminist Consciousness," in *All of Us Are Present*, ed. Eleanor Bender, Bobbie Burk, and Nancy Walker (Columbia, Mo.: James Madison Wood Research Institute, 1984), and "Symposium: Politics and Culture in Women's History," *Feminist Studies* 6 (Spring 1980): 49–54.

47. Peggy McIntosh, "Interactive Phases of Curricular Re-vision" (n. 33 above).

48. Schuster and Van Dyne, eds. (n. 20 above), 27–28.

49. Mary Kay Thompson Tetreault, "Feminist Phase Theory," *Journal of Higher Education* 56 July/August 1985): 363–84.

50. Evelyn Hammonds, "Never Meant to Survive: A Black Woman's Journey: An Interview with Evelyn Hammonds by Aimee Sands," *Radical Teacher* 30 January 1986): 8–15. Evelyn Fox Keller, *Reflections on Gender and Science* (New Haven, Conn.: Yale University Press, 1985).

51. Elaine Showalter, *A Literature of Their Own Princeton*, N.J.: Princeton University Press, 1977).

52. Blythe Clinchy and Claire Zimmerman, "Epistemology and Agency in the Development of Undergraduate Women," in *The Undergraduate Woman: Issues in Educational Equity*, ed. Pamela Perun (Lexington, Mass.: D.C. Heath & Co., 1982), 161-81.

53. Frances Maher and Kathleen Dunn, "The Practice of Feminist Teaching: A Case Study of Interactions among Curriculum, Pedagogy, and Female Cognitive Development," Working Papers Series, no. 144 (Wellesley, Mass.: Wellesley College Center for Research on Women, 1984).

54. F. Howe, *Myths of Coeducation* (n. 9 above), 256.

55. Schuster and Van Dyne, "Placing Women in the Liberal Arts" (n. 42 above).

56. Westkott (n. 30 above)

57. Patricia Bell Scott, "Education for Self-Empowerment: A Priority for Women of Color," in Bender, Burk, and Walker, eds. (n. 46 above): 55–66.

58. Maxine Baca Zinn, Lynn Weber Cannon, Elizabeth Higginbotham, and Bonnie Thornton Dill, "The Costs of Exclusionary Practice in Women's Studies," *Signs* 11, no. 2 (Winter 1986): 290–303.

59. Esther Ngan-Ling Chow, "Teaching Sex and Gender in Sociology: Incorporating the Perspective of Women of Color," *Teaching Sociology* 12 (April 1985): 299–312.

60. McIntosh, "Interactive Phases of Curricular Re-vision" (n. 33 above).

61. Mary Childers, "Working Definition of a Balanced Course," *Women's Studies Quarterly* 11 (Summer 1983): 30 ff.

62. See Ellen Carol DuBois, Gail Paradise Kelly, Elizabeth Lapovsky Kennedy, Carolyn W. Korsmeyer, and Lillian S. Robinson, eds., *Feminist Scholarship: Kindling in the Groves of Academia* (Urbana: University of Illinois Press, 1985); Diane L. Fowlkes and Charlotte S. McClure, eds., *Feminist Visions: Toward a Transformation of the Liberal Arts Curriculum* (University: University of Alabama Press, 1984); Elizabeth Langland and Walter Gove, eds., *A Feminist Perspective in the Academy: The Difference It Makes* (Chicago: University of Chicago Press, 1981); Julia A. Sherman and Evelyn Torton Beck, eds., *The Prism of Sex: Essays in the Sociology of Knowledge* (Madison: University of Wisconsin Press, 1979); Eloise C. Snyder, ed., *The Study of Women: Enlarging Perspectives of Social Reality* (New York: Harper & Row, 1979); Dale Spender, ed., *Men's Studies Modified: The Impact of Feminism on the Academic Disciplines* (New York: Pergamon Press, 1981); Marianne Triplette, ed., *Women's Studies and the Curriculum* (Winston-Salem, N.C.: Salem College, 1983).

63. Elizabeth Abel, ed., "Writing and Sexual Difference," *Critical Inquiry* 8 (Winter 1981): 173–403.

64. Lillian Robinson, "Treason Our Text: Feminist Challenges to the Literary Canon," Working Papers Series, no. 104 (Wellesley, Mass.: Wellesley College Center for Research on Women, 1983).

65. Paul Lauter, ed., *Reconstructing American Literature* (Old Westbury, N.Y.: Feminist Press, 1983), xx.

66. Paul Lauter, "Race and Gender in the Shaping of the American Literary Canon: A Case Study from the Twenties," *Feminist Studies* 9 (Fall 1983): 435–64.

67. Annette Kolodny, "Dancing through the Minefield: Some Observations on the Theory, Practice, and Politics of a Feminist Literary Criticism," in Spender, ed., 23–42.

68. Natalie Kampen and Elizabeth Grossman, "Feminism and Methodology: Dynamics of Change in the History of Art and Architecture," Working Papers Series, no. 121 (Wellesley, Mass.: Wellesley College Center for Research on Women, 1983); and Norma Broude and Mary Garrard, *Feminism and Art History: Questioning the Litany* (New York: Harper & Row, 1982).

69. Linda Gardiner, "Can This Discipline Be Saved? Feminist Theory Challenges Mainstream Philosophy," Working Papers Series, no. 118 (Wellesley, Mass.: Wellesley College Center for Research on Women, 1983).

70. Gloria Hull, "Reading Literature by U.S. Third World Women," Working Papers Series, no. 141 (Wellesley, Mass.: Wellesley College Center for Research on Women, 1984).

71. Joan Kelly-Gadol, "The Social Relations of the Sexes: Methodological Implications of Women's History," *Signs* 1, no. 4 (Summer 1976): 809–24.

72. Susan Armitage, "Women and Western American History," Working Papers Series, no 134 (Wellesley, Mass.: Wellesley College Center for Research on Women, 1984).

73. Phyllis Cole and Deborah Lambert, "Gender and Race in American Literature: An Exploration of the Discipline and a Proposal for Two New Courses," Working Papers Series, no. 115 (Wellesley, Mass.: Wellesley College Center for Research on Women, 1983); Annette Kolokny, *The Land before Her: Fantasy and Experience of the American Frontiers, 1630–1860* (Chapel Hill: University of North Carolina Press, 1984).

74. Broude and Garrard.

75. Barbara Drygulski Wright, "Feminist Transformation of Foreign Language Instruction: Progress and Challenges," Working Papers Series, no. 117 (Wellesley, Mass.: Wellesley College Center for Research on Women, 1983).

76. Lauter, ed., *Reconstructing American Literature*, xxi.

77. Carolyn G. Geilbrun, "Feminist Criticism in Departments of Literature," *Academe* 69 (September-October 1983): 14.

78. Carroll Smith-Rosenburg, "The Feminist Reconstruction of History," *Academe* 69 (September–October 1983): 26–37.

79. Marcia Millman and Rosabeth Moss Kanter, eds., "Editorial Introduction," *Another Voice* (Garden City, N.Y.: Doubleday & Co., Anchor Press, 1975); Margaret L. Andersen, *Thinking about Women: Sociological and Feminist Perspectives* (New York: Macmillan Publishing Co., 1983); Carolyn Sherif, "Bias in Psychology," in Sherman and Beck, eds., (n. 62 above), 93–134.

80. Rayna Reiter, ed., *Toward an Anthropology of Women* (New York: Monthly Review Press, 1975).

81. Millman and Kanter, vii–xvi.

82. Barbara Bergmann, "Feminism and Economics," *Academe* 69 (September-October 1983): 22–25.

83. James Soles, "Recent Research on Racism," (paper presented at the University of Delaware, 1985 Lecture Series on Racism, Newark, January 1985).

84. Dorothy Smith, "Women's Perspective as a Radical Critique of Sociology," *Sociological Inquiry* 4 (1974): 7–13, and "Toward a Sociology of Women," in Sherman and Beck, eds., 135–88; Sandra Harding and Merrill B. Hintikka, eds., *Discovering Reality: Feminist Perspectives of Epistemology, Metaphysics, Methodology and Philosophy of Science* (Dordrecht: D. Reidel Publishing Co., 1983).

85. Michelle Hoffnung, "Feminist Transformation: Teaching Experimental Psychology," Working Papers Series, no. 140 (Wellesley, Mass.: Wellesley College Center for Research on Women, 1984); Sherif, 93–134.

86. Judith Stacey and Barrie Thorne, "The Missing Feminist Revolution in Sociology," *Social Problems* 32 (April 1985): 301–16.

87. Marian Low and Ruth Hubbard, eds., *Woman's Nature* (New York: Pergamon Press, 1983).

88. Shulamit Reinharz, "Experiential Analasis: A Contribution to Feminist Research," in Bowles and Duelli-Klein, eds. (no. 19 above), 162–91.

89. Michelle Hoffnung.

90. Laurel Furumoto, "Placing Women in the History of Psychology Courses," Working Papers Series, no. 139 (Wellesley, Mass.: Wellesley College Center for Research on Women, 1984).

91. Ruth Hubbard, "Feminist Science: A Meaningful Concept?" (paper presented at the annual meeting of the National Women's Studies Association, Douglass College, New Brunswick, N.J., June 1984).

92. Ruth Hubbard, "Have Only Men Evolved?" in *Biological Women: The Convenient Myth*, ed. Ruth Hubbard, Mary Sue Henifin, and Barbara Fried (Cambridge, Mass.: Schenckman Publishing Co., 1982), 17–46; Ethel Tobach and Betty Rosoff. eds., *Genes and Gender, vol. I* (New York: Gordian Press, 1979); also see the four subsequent volumes of *Genes and Gender*.

93. Ruth Bleier, *Science and Gender* (New York: Pergamon Press, 1984).

94. Mina Davis Caulfield, "Sexuality in Human Evolution: What Is 'Natural' about Sex?" *Feminist Studies* 11 (Summer 1985): 343–63.

95. Helene Longino and Ruth Doell, "Body, Bias, and Behavior: A Comparative Analysis of Reasoning in Two Areas of Biological Science," *Signs* 9, no. 2 (Winter 1983): 206–27; Nancy Hartsock, "The Feminist Standpoint: Developing the Ground for a Specifically Feminist Historical Materialism," in *Money, Sex and Power*, ed. Nancy Hartsock (New York: Longman, Inc., 1983), 231–51; Elizabeth Fee, "Woman's Nature and Scientific Objectivity," in Lowe and Hubbard, eds., 9–28.

96. Anne Fausto-Sterling, *Myths of Gender; Biological Theories about Women and Men* (New York: Basic Books, 1985), 117.

97. Sandra Harding, *The Science Question in Feminism* (Ithaca, N.Y.: Cornell University Press, 1986).

98. Keller (n. 50 above).

99. Patsy Schweickart, lecture presented at Mellon Faculty Development Seminar, Wellesley College Center for Research on Women, Fall 1985.

100. Dorothy Buerk, "An Experience with Some Able Women Who Avoid Mathematics," *For the Learning of Mathematics* 3 (November 1982): 19–24; Anne Fausto-Sterling, "The Myth of Neutrality: Race, Sex, and Class in Science," *Radical Teacher* 19:21–25, and *Myths of Gender*; see also the special issue, "Women in Science," ed. Pamela Annas, Saul Slapikoff, and Kathleen Weiler, Radical Teacher, vol. 30 (1986) for several excellent pieces evolving from the feminist critique of science.

101. American Political Science Association, *Citizenship and Change: Women and American Politics*, 9 vols. (Washington, D.C.: American Political Science Association, 1983).

102. Judith M. Gappa and Janice Pearce, "Sex and Gender in the Social Sciences: Reassessing the Introductory Course: Principles of Microeconomics" (San Francisco: San Francisco State University, 1982, mimeographed); Barrie Thorne, ed., *Sex and Gender in the Social Sciences: Reassessing the Introductory Course: Introductory Sociology* (Washington, D.C.: American Sociological Association, 1983); Nancy Felipe Russo and Natalie Malovich, *Sex and Gender in the Social Sciences: Reassessing the Introductory Course: Introductory Psychology* (Washington, D.C.: American Psychological Association, 1982); Bonnie Lloyd and Arlene Rengert, "Women in Geographic Curricula," Journal of Geography 77 (September-October 1978): 164–91; Organization for American Historians, *Restoring Women to History: Materials for U.S. I and II*, 2 vols. (Bloomington, Ind.: Organization of American Historians, 1983).

103. Barrie Thorne, Mary McCormack, Virginia Powell, and Delores Wunder, eds., *The Sociology of Sex and Gender: Syllabi and Teaching Materials* (Washington, D.C.: American Sociological Association Teaching Resources Center, 1985).

104. See especially newsletters from the Center for Research on Women, Memphis State University, and "Re-Visions," the newsletter from the Towson State curriculum project funded by the Fund for the Improvement of Post-Secondary Education.

105. Gloria Hull, Barbara Smith, and Patricia Bell Scott, eds., *All the Women Are White, All the Blacks Are Men, But Some of Us Are Brave* (Old Westbury, N.Y.: Feminist Press, 1983).

106. Memphis State University Center for Research on Women, "Selected Bibliography of Social Science Readings on Women of Color in the U.S. " (Memphis, Tenn: Memphis State University Center for Research on Women, n.d.).

107. Maxine Baca Zinn, "Mexican-American Women in the Social Sciences," *Signs* 8, no. 2 (Winter 1982): 259–72.

108. Marcela Trujillo, *Estudios Femeniles de la Chicana* (Los Angeles: University of California Press, 1974).

109. Anne Fausto-Sterling and Lydia L. English, *Women and Minorities in Science: Course Materials Guide.* Pamphlet and other materials are available from Anne Fausto-Sterling, Department of Biology, Brown University, Providence, R. I. 02921.

110. *Sage: A Scholarly journal on Black Women*, Box 42471, Atlanta, Ga. 30311.

111. See *Journal of Social Issues*, vol. 39 (Fall 1983); Conditions, vol. 5 (1979); *Spelman Messenger*, vol. 100 (Spring 1984); *Sinister Wisdom*, vols. 22–23 (1983).

112. Marilyn Jimenez, "Contrasting Portraits: Integrating Materials about the Afro-Hispanic Woman into the Traditional Curriculum," Working Papers Series, no. 120 (Wellesley, Mass.: Wellesley College Center for Research on Women, 1983); Baca Zinn (n. 107 above).

113. Johnella Butler, "Complicating the Question: Black Studies and Women's Studies," in Schuster and Van Dyne, eds. n. 20 above), 73–86.

114. Adrienne Rich, "Claiming Education," in *On Lies, Secrets, and Silence* (n. 7 above), 231.

115. *Ibid.*, 231.

116. Banner (n. 44 above).

117. F. Howe (n. 9 above), 28.

Designing an Inclusive Curriculum: Bringing All Women into the Core

Elizabeth Higginbotham

To be successful, transforming the curriculum involves three interrelated tasks. The first is to gain information about the diversity of the female experience. The second task is to decide how to teach this new material, a process that typically involves reconceptualizing one's discipline in light of a race, class, and gender based analysis. Often this means learning to move typically marginal groups into the core of the curriculum. Furthermore, efforts can be made to present issues on people of color in their complexity, rather than in stereotypic ways. The third task is to structure classroom dynamics that ensure a safe atmosphere to support learning for *all* the students. This paper will discuss each of these tasks. It begins with a critique of the traditional curriculum in light of its treatment of people of color.

Marginal in the Traditional Curriculum

When I consistently see many bright and respected scholars failing to take steps to bring women of color into their teaching and research, I look for social structural explanations. A sociological perspective can help us to understand the roots of racist thinking and the many forms it takes in traditional disciplines and women's studies. This approach is more productive than blaming these scholars—or simply attacking them as racists. The search for the social structural roots of the marginalization of people of color in scholarship and education takes me back to my early schooling.

As a Black person in a society dominated by whites, I was always an outsider—a status that Patricia Hill Collins (1986) argues has advantages and costs. I was cognizant even as a young child that the experiences of Black people were missing in what I was taught in elementary school. This pattern was later replicated in junior high and high school, then in college, and later in graduate school. But while I had been critical all along, not until I entered graduate school could I debate with others about the content of courses.

Throughout my whole educational career, agents of the dominant group attempted to teach me the "place" of Black people in the world. What was actively communicated to me was that Black people and other people of color are on the periphery of society. They are marginal. I learned that what happens to people of color has little relevance for members of the dominant group and for mainstream thinking.

Early in school, when we were studying the original thirteen North American colonies, I was exposed to the myths about who we were and are as a nation. One of the first lessons was that America is a land that people entered in search of freedom—religious freedom, the freedom to work as independent farmers, freedom from the privileged nobility and the hierarchical stratification of Europe, and freedom from the rapid industrialization of Europe. Colonists, and later white immigrants, wanted change in their lives, and they took the risk to begin life anew in this budding but already glorious nation. The fact that they were seeking their "freedom" while enslaving others (principally Native Americans and Africans) was not viewed as a contradictory activity, but just "one of those things" the United States had to do to build a great and prosperous nation.

New York, where I grew up and received much of my education, prided itself on being a progressive state, and required schools to devote time to the Negro experience (as it was called). We discussed slavery in the South, and during Negro History Week we learned about Harriet Tubman, Booker T. Washington, Frederick Douglass, and George Washington Carver. We were explicitly taught that Black people did not share the same history as whites. African people had been forced to come to North America against their will, and instead of finding freedom, they had to work as slaves.

The experiences of Afro-Americans never informed the standard characteristics of the society: even the slave experience of Africans and Afro-Americans did not alter the image that America was a land in which people found freedom. As a student, I had to master the myths and accept them as part of my socialization into the political system. I also learned that the information I accumulated about Black people—and later other people of color—was nice to know for "cultural enrichment." Exposure to the experiences of Afro-Americans, Puerto Ricans, and others was useful to develop tolerance for difference and make us better citizens, but this information was never meant to identify concepts, to develop perspectives, or to generate images or theories about the society as a whole.

I was in school to learn the experiences of the dominant group (which was also very male, as well as white and affluent)—and that would be the basis for an understanding of the system. If I learned that, I could go to college and perhaps do more interesting work than my parents did.

In spite of the intended message, it was hard for me to understand why the experiences of Black people were not incorporated into our images of who we are as a nation. At the time there was no mention of Asian Americans, Chicanos, or Native Americans. But I came to understand the practice. Whatever happened to Black people was an exception to the rule—we were a deviant case—just like using "i" before "e" except after "c." since the experiences of Black people did not have to be included in our search for the truth, they were not the material from which theories and frameworks were derived.

As I reflect on my early educational experiences, I see that the messages I received as a child, an adolescent, and an adult blamed the victim. For example, we were taught that the African people who "came" to America were not civilized; therefore, they could not pursue the American dream as initial settlers and white immigrants had been able to do. The lack of Black participation in mainstream American society was attributed to lesser abilities, defective cultures, lack of motivation, and so froth. To make a "victim-blaming" attribution, teachers did not actually have to say that Black Americans were lazy, ignorant, or savage—although that would surely do the trick. Instead, victim-blaming was subtly encouraged in classes where images of America as the land of freedom and opportunity were juxtaposed with the Black experience, without any reconciling of the contradictions through a structural explanation. Students then relied on prevailing myths and stereotypes to explain the Black "anomaly."

As a young Black girl, I found these messages problematic, and throughout my life I have sought answers to questions about the experiences of Black people at different historic moments. As a scholar, I still struggle with how best to use the knowledge I have gained. Thus, I approach the issue of curriculum integration with a fundamental critique of the traditional curriculum. I did not begin by discovering that women were missing from the curriculum—instead I have always perceived schools as foreign institutions. The information taught in schools was alien to me, to my family, to my neighborhood, and in a certain respect to the city, New York, in which I lived. Yet, in order to move to the next educational level and succeed in society, I had to master this information and pass tests. In my view, you were smart if you could pass the tests, but you had to look elsewhere for information to help you survive in the real world.

Today's wave of curriculum reforms presents an opportunity to restructure education, to alter the environment which was alien to me and many others. Such a remedy would include in the curriculum all the people in the classroom and the nation. Instead of focusing solely on the experiences of dominant group members, faculty members would teach students to use and value many different experiences in order to develop conceptions of life in this country and around the world.

I began by discussing my early experiences, because these experiences are common to many. Although we learn these lessons as members of either privileged or oppressed groups, they are similar lessons. If we are clear about the origins of practices that exclude people of color, we can dispense with blaming ourselves and each other for the difficulties we face in trying to change the curriculum. We are swimming upstream against the intellectual racism that flows through American ideology. The *disregard* for the experiences of Black people and other people of color is part of the American creed. To create a multicultural curriculum we must "unlearn" the ideology which marginalizes all but a tiny elite of American citizens.

Curriculum transformation has the potential for changing our traditional visions of education in American society. Yet, it can also replicate old biases. This is especially likely to occur in situations where the integration process is envisioned as a minor tune-up to an educational system that is fundamentally solid. From my perspective, however, our curriculum needs a major overhaul. It needs much more than the addition of women. It must incorporate the men who are omitted—especially working-class men and men of color. Elizabeth Minnich (1990) reminds us that fundamental change is not possible unless we first understand why these groups were excluded. Enlightened by such a critique, we can decide how we want to change and what we will teach. We can then select the path that leads to a restructuring of the curriculum toward inclusiveness across many dimensions of human experience.

Curriculum Change Starts with Faculty Development

Integrating the diversity among women into the curriculum is difficult. Most faculty members are just learning about women through recent exposure to feminist scholarship few of them are knowledgeable about and at ease with material on women of color. This is understandable. No one mentioned women of color when most contemporary college faculty pursued their degrees, yet the lack of correct information is a major contributor to the limited and inadequate treatment of women of color in courses and in research projects.

As the products of educational experiences that relegated people of color and women to the margins of their fields, faculty members need to compensate for the institutionalized biases in the educational system. They can work to eliminate this bias by gaining familiarity with the historical and contemporary experiences of racial-ethnic groups, the working class, middle-class women, and other groups traditionally restricted to the margins. The first step is to acknowledge one's lack of exposure to these histories.

Structural difficulties make learning new information about women and people of color problematic. It is often hard for faculty members to compensate for the gaps in their knowledge when they are faced with heavy teaching responsibilities and the pressure to publish. College administrators can encourage efforts with release time, financial support for workshops and institutes, and the like. Even without such resources, faculty members can develop long and short term strategies—for example, by organizing seminars to explore the new scholarship. All that is needed is a commitment and a shared reading list.

Another difficulty is the interdisciplinary nature of women's studies. Most faculty members are trained to research a specific discipline. Fortunately, over the years, more resources and tools have become available to help navigate this interdisciplinary field. The Center for Research on Women at Memphis State University has been a pioneer in this area; other research centers and curriculum projects have produced bibliographies, collections of syllabi, essays, and resources to assist with curriculum change. Some resources specifically include race, class, and gender as dimensions of analysis.

Institutionalized racism and sexism are structured into both the commercial and academic publishing markets, thus making it more difficult for scholars studying women and people of color to publish their work. Women's studies centers have initiated projects to help faculty identify relevant citations and locate new research and the development of women's studies and racial-ethnic studies journals has helped a great deal, but structural barriers persist that impede access to research on certain populations, particularly women of color, working-class women, and women in the southern and western regions of this nation. Thus, the very resources college faculty need about women of color are difficult to locate.

Learning to identify myth and misinformation about people of color is a critical task in course and curriculum revision. It is a process that alters teaching content and classroom dynamics. For example, with new knowledge faculty members can teach students in ways that appreciate human diversity. Faculty members will also be better prepared to interrupt and challenge racist, sexist, class-bias, and homophobic remarks made in the classroom.

My own area of specialization have given me information on the experiences of different racial and ethnic groups in this society. I often forget that everyone is not familiar with how most of the Southwest became part of the United States; with the Chinese Exclusion Act of 1882; with the implications of the Immigration Act of 1924 for people of color; with the internment of Japanese-American citizens during World War II; and with the fact that Puerto Ricans are citizens, not immigrants, and cannot be considered undocumented workers. One has to remember that most dominant-group faculty and students are not nearly as familiar with these histories as are student who belong to specific ethnic and racial-ethnic groups. The history of oppression is part of the oral traditions in ethnic and racial-ethnic communities as well as religious groups. Afro-American, Latino, Asian American, and Native American students enter our classrooms with at least a partial awareness of the historic struggles of their people. They frequently feel alienated in educational settings where their teachers and other students relate to them without awareness of their group's history. For example, a faculty member or student who talks about how Japanese Americans have *always* done well in this country denies the reality that racism has severely marred the lives of both Japanese immigrants and Japanese Americans. For much of this century Japanese aliens were denied the opportunity to become citizens. During World War II they were removed from the West Coast and placed in internment camps, primarily because Anglos resented their economic success. Non-Japanese American faculty and students may be unaware of this history. The lack of correct information on the part of the faculty members has consequences for what happens in the classroom: to the Japanese American student, Anglo ignorance of these issues is symptomatic of the persistent denial that racism is an issue for this group (Wong, 1985).

With new information, faculty can challenge myths and begin to interrupt racism in the classroom. The mastering of new information is a key ingredient in combating the feelings of powerlessness many faculty members experience in the face of the racist and sexist attitudes of their students. Once we acknowledge our lack of information, we can use the many resources available to learn about the experiences of women, people of color, working-class people, and other traditionally marginalized groups.

What Do I Do with New Information?

A key issue faced by many faculty is finding a "place" for working-class women, Black women, and other women of color in the curriculum. How do we challenge established practices of marginalizing these populations and truly develop a different educational process? How do we weave this new information on women and specifically women of color into a course on the family, the labor market, the sociology of education, the introduction to political science, and so forth? This is where many faculty learn by trial and error.

Revising the content of one's course requires the clarification of personal goals and educational aims (Andersen, 1987). This is not an issue that faculty approach lightly. One cannot introduce a reading or a lecture where minority women are covered and then merely assume that the goal has been achieved. Curriculum transformation requires much more. Yet, as we move toward that goal, our individual educational philosophy and commitment to our discipline will play a key role in how we resolve these issues.

It is common practice to begin initial integration efforts with one or two lectures on women of color. Faculty who stop at that level of inclusion find that their course is not transformed and that this addition has little impact on students. In fact, this approach can generate new problems. An instructor who performs the obligatory lecture often encounters opposition from students. For example, a Black woman colleague of mine taught a traditional course on the family and included a unit on the Black family. A few vocal students were quick to remind her that they had signed up for a course on the family, not the "Black family." Had she incorporated material on the Black family in every unit throughout the course, the "Black family" would not have appeared to be anomalous, but an integral part of the study of the family.

Yet, this additive approach is problematic. If faculty introduce material on Black women or women of color as interesting variations on womanhood, such actions indicate that readings and lecture materials on these populations are not part of the "core" knowledge covered in the class. Students can tolerate certain amounts of cultural enrichment, but if this material exceeds more than one or two lectures, they lose their patience because they think the instructor is deviating from the core. This reaction can be avoided if material on white working-class women, Black women, and other women of color (as well as men of color and working-class people) is integrated throughout the course. The diversity of experiences should be presented as knowledge that students are responsible for learning and will be evaluated for covering.

Approaches that keep women of color on the margins or peripheral to the course materials fail to address critical issues of racism, sexism, and classism. Faculty who use such approaches tend to introduce material on white middle-class people as the norm, and then later ask for a discussion on the variations found among working-class whites and people of color. This approach does a great deal to foster ideas that blame the victim. Students may even use such discussions as opportunities to verbalize the racism they have learned from the media and other sources. Such interactions tend to polarize a class, and then the faculty member has an additional battle to wage.

In sociology, where attention is given to norms, ideal types, and the like, women of color are often incorporated as deviant cases. Peripheral treatment of groups are obvious to students; furthermore, these approaches complement students' previous learning about racial-ethnic groups. Often when an instructor is about to begin the one obligatory lecture on the Black family, the Black woman, Latinas, working-class women in the labor market, or whomever, a student will ask the question all students want answered, "Are we going to be tested on this?" This also tends to happen when a guest speaker who is a racial minority or a female is invited to class. Students may listen politely but not feel compelled to write anything down or remember what was said.

Students carry old lessons into the classroom. They have already learned that what happens to people of color (or to women) does not count. This has been evident in their learning prior to college and continues in most college courses. Learning about different groups is treated as cultural enrichment, not as a part of the basic scholarship of a field. These are essentially correct impressions on the part of the students. The core material is still about affluent white men; the historical experiences, social conditions, and scholarly contributions of people of color and women are marginal to the disciplines.

Beyond a Universal Model of Gender. In many curriculum integration efforts in social science teaching, the marginalization of women of color takes two forms. Women of color are addressed either as tangents to the "generic" woman or as the "exceptional" women of color. In the first case, African American, Asian American, and Native American women and Latinas are present, but their experiences are not critical to the development of theory or paradigms. This teaching strategy is often linked with the view that gender relations are the foundation for universal experiences. Within this framework, other sources of inequality, particularly race and class, might be acknowledged, but they are clearly less important than gender. As a result, scholarship on women of color in both women's studies and curriculum integration efforts is marginalized (Baca Zinn et al., 1986). Faculty tend to rely upon the experiences of white, middle-class, heterosexual Americans as the norm and view all others as merely exceptions to the rule.

Sandra Morgen (1986) is very critical of this universalist stance. She identifies how looking at the experiences of women of color expands our understanding of critical issues for women and gives a feminist perspective greater depth. Morgen examines how we can develop deeper appreciations of motherhood, the feminization of poverty, and women and resistance by examining the historical and current situations of women of color.

With regard to motherhood, Morgen identifies the way that most white, middle-class feminist scholars see the nuclear family as normative. In a discussion of Dinnerstein's *Mermaid and the Minotaur* (1976), Adrienne Rich's *Of Woman born* (1976), and Nancy Chodorow's (1978) *The Reproduction of Mothering,* Morgen argues that much feminist scholarship about "the" family

> presumes that working women are a relatively recent phenomenon, and that working mothers are even newer, and that the normative family is mom, dad and the kids, and that mothers live with their children and are the primary, if not near exclusive force in their socialization. These assumptions are problematic when explaining the historical and contemporary experiences of many poor and working-class women, and of many women of color. These women have as a group been in the labor force for a much longer period of time, and in situations like slavery, sharecropping, domestic work or unregulated industrial production that did not allow for the kind of full-time motherhood, or the specific mother-child relations which are presumed in Chodrow, Dinnerstein, and Rich (Morgen, 1986, p. 12).

The impact of racial oppression on the mothering behavior of women of color in the 19th century is a theme in the work of Bonnie Thornton Dill (1988). She describes how racial oppression not only shaped the productive roles of African American, Latina, and Asian immigrant women, but also influenced the reproductive labor of these women. Dill's and Morgen's works demonstrate that much can be gained by using the experiences of women of color to develop new theories about women's experiences. Such approaches sharply contrast with those that fit the experiences of women of different classes and races into a universal model.

Morgen (1986) also describes how an analysis of the feminization of poverty can be informed by looking at the circumstances of women who are not new to poverty. She is joined by other scholars who have discovered that not all women are a husband away from poverty. While many middle-class white women experience a significant decline in their social status when they sever their attachment to middle-class white male, many working-class women and women of color find themselves attached to men and still poor (Burnham, 1987). Their poverty is not only a gender issue but is related to a legacy of class and racial discrimination (Higginbotham, 1987).

We can also see beyond approaches which focus on women as victims by learning how working-class women and women of color resist class and racial oppression (Morgen, 1986). Rather than a continuum from accommodation to rebellion, Morgen sees diverse personal and protracted struggles against oppression. These women actively resist the limitations placed on their lives by gender, class, and racial oppression. Denied access to many public spheres, they do not protest by voting or writing letters to congressmen; instead, they are involved in grassroots organizing, efforts to improve public schools and other neighborhood institutions, jobs actions, and the like. Morgen's book (co-edited with Ann Bookman) *Women and the Politics of Empowerment* (1988) incorporates much of the new research on women and resistance, research which is primarily on working-class women. Rich examples of resistance are also found in the new scholarship on women in domestic work (Clark-Lewis, 1985; Rollins, 1985).

If we abandon the practice of keeping working-class women and women of color on the margins in our teaching and our research, and seek ways to incorporate the diversity of women's experiences, we are more likely to involve students and challenge their racist assumptions. We can also move students beyond seeing women of color and working-class women as victims.

Addressing the Lives of Ordinary Women of Color. A second way that women of color are introduced into the curriculum is by a brief look at a few "exceptional" examples. This method is very common in history and the social sciences, where "exceptional" Black women such as Sojourner Truth, Harriet Tubman, Ida B. Wells, and Mary McLeod Bethune are discussed. In contrast to marginal treatments of women of color, described above, where the population of women of color is seen as an undifferentiated mass, this approach holds up a few models—non-victims—for admiration. In the case of Black women, this is often done under the guise that racism has not been terribly difficult for them. The subtle message to students is that if successful Black women could achieve in the face of obstacles, other Black women failed to attain the same heights because of faulty culture, lack of motivation, and other individual deficits. A faculty member might not intend to reinforce the individualistic lessons of the American ideology, but students interpret the material in this way because it is a common theme in our history. The "exceptions" approach fails to depict the larger social system in which the struggles of women of color, whether successful or not, take place.

In "The Politics of Black Women's Studies," by Barbara Smith and Gloria Hull, which is the introductory essay in *But Some of Us Are Brave: Black Women's Studies,* the authors warn of this practice:

> A descriptive approach to the lives of Black women, a "great Black women" in history or literature approach, or any traditional male identified approach will not result in intellectually groundbreaking or politically transforming work. We cannot change our lives by teaching solely about "exceptions" to the ravages of white-male oppression. Only through exploring the experiences of supposedly "ordinary" Black women whose "unexceptional" actions enabled us and the race to survive, will we be able to begin to develop an overview and analytic framework for understanding the lives of Afro-American women (1982, pp. xxi–xxii).

To do otherwise is to deceive ourselves. The experiences of a few exceptional Black women, as typically portrayed in the classroom, serve to deny the reality of oppressive structures. This approach does not help students develop an appreciation for the role of race, class and gender in people's lives. As we attempt to bring women of color out of the margins, we must be prepared to challenge students' tendency to romanticize a few heroines.

These two practices, teaching about women of color as tangents to the "generic" woman and examining the lives of exceptional women of color, work to justify and perpetuate the marginalization of women of color in women's studies scholarship. Approaches such as these retard the field of women's studies and complicate the task of integrating women into the high school and college curricula. While these approaches might represent a step or phrase in the process of changing curriculum, we must also remain clear on the larger goals and objectives of curriculum transformation. As pointed out earlier, each step in transformation brings its own set of problems and contradictions into the classroom. If we are not clear about our ultimate goal, we may become discouraged and retreat before new problems. In the end, we seek a curriculum that teaches an awareness and appreciation of the diversity of human experiences as well as the commonality of the human condition.

If a course is structured around the dominant group experience and people of color are marginalized, faculty members lose the opportunity to critically address social structure—that is, the ways in which the institutions of society shape our opinions and influence our behavior. Transforming the curriculum requires explicit discussion of the roles of gender, race, and class in shaping the lives of everybody. This is accomplished by exploring the diversity of the experiences of men and women in the United States and around the world. For example, being female means privileges and the accompanying restrictions of dependency for some women, while for others it means poverty and the burden of supporting themselves and dependents.

Within this framework, no norm or modal case is taken for granted. If one teaches the sociology of the American family, it is with an eye on examining the diversity of family forms and lives. In family studies, only a minority of today's families fit the supposed norm of the 1950s and 1960s, of a full-time-employed father and a mother at home with children. Therefore, it is easier and more accurate to look at the variations of family forms and discuss which factors obstruct or support specific types of family structures. Faculty members might even find that students, who are well aware of the variety of families, might be motivated to explore the factors behind this diversity. This perspective is the core of a recent textbook about the sociology of the family, *Diversity in American Families,* by Maxine Baca Zinn and D. Stanley Eitzen (1987). The book, which elaborates how race and class, major structures of inequality, affect specific family forms, is well received by students because it does not hold up any single type as the norm by which all other families are judged.

Racism, Diversity, and Classroom Dynamics

Racism is a pervasive classroom problem that has to be addressed. One approach is to inform students that racism often takes the form of misinformation about racial-ethnic groups. Discussions of how misinformation is systematically taught in the schools and the media, and in informal ways from friends, parents, and the like, may relieve individual students from feeling guilty for holding racist notions. Students should be encouraged to think critically about the information they get regarding their own group and others' groups, so that they will learn to question broad generalizations like "All whites are middle class" and "All blacks are poor." Information that sheds light on the diversity within a group is more likely to be corrected.

Students should be encouraged to think critically about information that devalues or dehumanized members of specific groups. For example, any idea that some people (usually Blacks, Latinos, or Native Americans) are more comfortable with hunger, poverty, and the like than other groups (usually white Americans) implies that the former are "less than human." Any information that students received which has the effect of dehumanizing a group can be identified as racist and therefore not a fact of the social world.

These are just a few ideas to help faculty think about combating racism in the classroom. Correct information and changing teaching methods will do a great deal to challenge the racism embedded in our educational system—where there are a limited number of legitimate lines of inquiry and where "inquirers are only allowed to ask certain questions" (Spelman, 1982, p. 15).

The manner in which material on "new" populations is introduced into a classroom can either challenge students' racism or confirm it. Faculty members often interpret students' resistance to material about racial-ethnic groups as a lack of interest in the unique experiences of Afro-Americans, Asian Americans, and other groups. Indeed, students might have little specific interest in these unique experiences, but they can learn the value of a race, class, and gender analysis. As they enhance these skills, they may begin to grasp how structural barriers that shape life options for people of color may also affect their own lives.

How faculty develop an appreciation of diversity will depend upon where they teach. The institutional setting is a key ingredient. An approach might work very will in one setting and then fail miserably in another. If one's institution accepts the challenge of curriculum change, there may be structural supports which would be lacking in an institution that has reconfirmed its commitment to the traditional curriculum. Faculty members must consider the specific agendas and resources of their college or university and gauge their actions accordingly.

A plan for action should also be informed by the racial, class and ethnic backgrounds of the students and other faculty, as well as by the gender composition of the classrooms and the institution's geographic location. An instructor can teach the same course in different institutions and experience very different classroom dynamics (Chow, 1985). Faculty in homogeneous liberal colleges where there are few people of color and the working-class students are very quiet may need to use methods which differ from those who teach in public institutions with more heterogeneous student bodies.

For example, when teaching an undergraduate urban sociology course at Columbia University, I used the urban environment to challenge students' stereotypes and misinformation. I took my entire class on a walking tour of Harlem, the black community down the hill from Columbia. On the tour they could see middle-class housing, both single-family dwellings and apartment complexes, as well as stable working-class housing and deteriorating housing. They could also see Harlem's cultural institutions, such as libraries, churches, community centers, and the like. This tour worked wonders in shaking up the unquestioned "fact" that Harlem is a slum. It also opened students up to questioning other "facts" about the world that they had so readily accepted. A walking tour of a Black community is not an option for faculty located in a small college town who may face students with the same stereotypic notions. Such faculty will have to develop different resources, such as films, speakers, and reading materials that capture the lives of human beings living in Black communities. (One resource is Bettylou Valentine's (1978) *Hustling and Other Hard Work*, a report of five years of field research that challenges standard misinformation and communicates the ways that human beings struggle to survive.)

Plans for curriculum changes are also shaped by the interpersonal dynamics in the courses you teach. Do you depend solely upon the lecture or do you encourage discussions? Do all your students participate in discussions? Is your class a chilly one for women? (Hall, 1982). Do your Black students and other students of color participate in the classroom discussions? (Moses, 1989). Are the people of color in your classes likely to challenge stereotypic or racist comments made by white students? In general, are you pleased with the classroom atmosphere?

Many faculty members who bring a central perspective on women into the classroom find that they abandon their dependency on lectures, which helps to promote lively discussions in class. Yet, this is not a smooth path. Some students, especially those who have enjoyed privilege, might be the most vocal, while students from traditionally disadvantaged populations are more likely to remain silent. It is also possible for students from the majority group to be silent in the face of shifting expectations on them as students. There can be many reasons for students' silence, Vicky Spelman (1982) reminds us. It can reflect a lack of concern; fears, especially about saying the wrong thing; lack of knowledge about the material; or even resistance to the material. Spelman encourages faculty to carefully address the conditions under which discussions take place. We must take precautions to insure that we develop an atmosphere where all class members are full participants.

The routes individual faculty members take to enhance classroom dynamics will vary widely, but there can be some goals we all share. Part of the task of the college instructor is to create an environment where there can be an honest and open exchange about the material and where students can do what they are rarely asked to do—learn from each other.

Conclusion

Curriculum transformation is a challenge in which all faculty can participate. As we pursue short and long term goals it is important to be mindful of the several tasks involved in the process: securing information, integrating material into our teaching, and establishing a supportive classroom. Do not become discouraged by the slow progress. Establishing support for faculty can be critical in the success of projects. Join with other colleagues in learning new materials and experimenting in the classroom. The presence of support groups can help faculty members reflect on their progress and motivate them to take new risks. Faculty who attempt this new challenge may find a rejuvenated interested in teaching their students.

References

Andersen, Margaret. 1987. "Curriculum Change in Higher Education." *Signs: Journal of Women and Culture in Society* 12 (winter): 222–54.

Andersen, Margaret. 1988. "Moving Our Minds: Studying Women of Color and Reconstructing Sociology." *Teaching Sociology* 16 (April): 123–32.

Baca Zinn, Maxine, Lynn Weber Cannon, Elizabeth Higginbotham, and Bonnie Thornton Dill. 1986. "On the Costs of Exclusionary Practices in Women's Studies." *Signs: Journal of Women and Culture in Society* 11 (Winter): 290–303

Baca Zinn, Maxine, and D. Stanley Eitzen. 1987. *Diversity in American Families*. New York: Harper and Row.

Bookman, Ann, and Sandra Morgen, eds. 1988. *Women and the Politics of Empowerment*. Philadelphia: Temple University Press.

Burnham, Linda. 1986. "Has Poverty Been Feminized in Black America?" In *For Crying Out Loud: Women and Poverty in the United States*, ed. Ann Withorn and Rochelle Lefkowitz. New York: Pilgrim Press. Pp. 69–83.

Chow, Esther Ngan-Ling. 1985. "Teaching Sex and Gender in Sociology: Incorporating the Perspective of Women of Color." *Teaching Sociology* 12 (April): 299–311.

Clark-Lewis, Elizabeth. 1985. "'This Work Had A End': The Transition from Live-in to Day work." Southern Women: The Intersection of Race, Class and Gender, Working Paper #2. Center for Research on Women, Memphis State University.

Collins, Patricia Hill. 1986. "Learning from the Outsider Within: The Sociological Significance of Black Feminist Thought." *Social Problems* 33 (December): S14–32.

Dill, Bonnie Thorton. 1988. "Our Mothers' Grief: Racial-Ethnic Women and the Maintenance of Families." *Journal of Family History* 13: 412–31.

Hall, Robert M. 1982. "The Classroom Climate: A Chilly One for Women?" Project on the Status and Education of Women, Association of American Colleges, Washington, D.C.

Higginbotham, Elizabeth. 1986. "We Were Never on a Pedestal: Women of Color Continue to Struggle with Poverty, Racism and Sexism." In *For Crying Out Loud: Women and Poverty in the United States*, ed. Ann Withorn and Rochelle Lefkowitz. New York: Pilgrim Press. Pp. 97–109.

Hull, Gloria T., Patricia Bell Scott, and Barbara Smith. 1982. *But Some of Us Are Brave: Black Women's Studies*. Old Westbury, N.Y.: Feminist Press.

Minnich, Elizabeth Kamarck. 1990. *Transforming Knowledge*. Philadelphia: Temple University Press.

Morgen, Sandra. 1986. "To See Ourselves, To See Our Sisters: The Challenge of Re-envisioning Curriculum Change." A publication from the Research Clearinghouse and Curriculum Integration Project, Memphis State University, Center for Research on Women.

Moses, Yolanda T. 1989. "Black Women in Academe: Issues and Strategies," Project on the Status of Education of Women, Association of American Colleges, Washington, D.C.

Rollins, Judith. 1985 *Between Women: Domestics and Their Employers*. Philadelphia: Temple University Press.

Spelman, Vicky. 1982. "Combating the Marginalization of Black Women in the Classroom' *Women's Studies Quarterly* 10 (Summer): 15–16.

Valentine, Bettylou. 1978. *Hustling and Other Hard Work*. New York: Free Press.

Wong, Eugene F. 1985. "Asian American Middleman Minority Theory: The Framework for an American Myth." *Journal of Ethnic Studies* 13 (Spring): 51–88.

Transforming the Curriculum: Teaching About Women of Color[1]

Johnnella E. Butler

Until very recently, teaching about women of color and incorporating material on women of color into the curriculum has been virtually ignored. At best, attention was paid to women of color from a global, culturally different perspective; however, due to various national and state efforts, race, class, gender, and ethnicity within the United States are getting serious attention. Central to this curricular revision are U.S. women of color. I see the resulting methodology and pedagogy of this cross-ethnic, multiethnic endeavor as rooted in the method of critical pedagogy developing in this country and influenced by Brazilian educator and activist Paulo Friere, and evolving from feminist pedagogy as well as the pedagogy implicit in Ethnic Studies. This chapter provides a conceptual framework, an appropriate starting point for teaching about women of color, which, I demonstrate, is at the core of transforming the curriculum.

Why "Women of Color?"

The phrase "women of color" has come into use gradually. Its use immediately brings to mind the differences of race and culture. It also makes clear that Black women are not the only women of color. In an ostensibly democratically structured society, with a great power imbalance signified by race and class privilege, labels representative of reality for those outside the realm of power are difficult to determine. This power imbalance is both cultural and political and consequently further complicates labelling. Selecting the phrase "women of color" by many women of American ethnic groups of color is part of their struggle to be recognized with dignity for their humanity and their racial and cultural heritage as they work within the Women's Movement of the United States. Furthermore, it signals a political coalescence, implying the particular sameness among U.S. women of color while still allowing for their differences. This effort of women of color to name themselves is similar to attempts by Afro-Americans and other ethnic groups to define with dignity their race and ethnicity and to counter the many stereotypical names bestowed on them. Because we tend to use the word "women" to be all-inclusive and general, we usually obscure both the differences and similarities among women.

With the decline of the Civil Rights Movement of the 1960s, the Women's Movement in the second half of the twentieth century got under way. Not long after, Black women began to articulate the differences they experienced as Black women, not only because of the racism within the Women's Movement or the sexism within the Black community, but also because of their vastly differing historical reality. One major question posed by Toni Cade's pioneering anthology, *The Black Woman*, remains applicable: "How relevant are the truths, the experiences, the findings of White women to Black women? Are women after all simply women?" Cade answers the question then as it might still be answered today: "I don't know that our priorities are the same, that our concerns and methods are the same, or even similar enough so that we can afford to depend on this new field of experts (White, female). It is rather obvious that we do not. It is obvious that we are turning to each other."[2] This anthology served as a turning point in the experience of the Black woman. Previously, White males, for the most part, had interpreted her realities, her activities, and her contributions.[3]

Although we are beyond the point of the complete invisibility of women of color in the academic branch of the Women's Movement—Women's Studies—Black women must still demand to be heard, to insist on being dealt with from the perspective of the experiences of women of color, just as they did in 1970, as the blurb in the paperback *The Black Woman* implies: "Black Women Speak Out. A Brilliant and Challenging Assembly of Voices That Demand to Be Heard." By the latter part of the 1970s, the logic of a dialogue among women of color became a matter of course. We find, as in Cade's *The Black Woman*, women of color speaking to one another in publications such as *Conditions: Five, The Black Women's Issue*, and *This Bridge Called My Back: Writings by Radical Women of Color*.[4] The academic community began to recognize American women of color who identify with the Third World, both for ancestral heritage and for related conditions of colonization; in 1980 we see for example, the publication of Dexter Fisher's anthology *The Third Woman: Minority Women Writers of the United States*.[5]

The most familiar ethnic groups of color are the Asian Americans, Afro-Americans, Hispanic Americans, and Native Americans. Yet within each group there are cultural, class, and racial distinctions. These ethnic groups can be further delineated: Asian Americans consist of Chinese Americans, Japanese Americans, Filipino Americans, and Korean Americans, in addition to the more recent immigrants from Southeast Asia. Afro-Americans consist of the U.S. Afro-American and the West Indian or Afro-Caribbean immigrants. The number of African immigrants is most likely too small to consider as a group; however, their presence should be accounted for. Hispanic Americans, or Latino Americans as some prefer, are largely Puerto Rican, Chicano, and Cuban. The American Indian is made up of many tribal groups such as Sioux, Apache, Navajo, and Chicahominy.

The phrase "women of color" helps women of all these groups acknowledge both their individual ethnicity and their racial solidarity as members of groups that are racial minorities in the United States, as well as a majority in the world. The concept also acknowledges similarity in historical experiences and political position in relation to the White American. In addition, the use of the phrase and the concept "women of color" implies the existence of the race and ethnicity of White women, for whom the word "women' wrongly indicates a norm for all women or wrongly excludes other women of color.

What We Learn From Studying Women of Color

When we study women of color, we raise our awareness and understanding of the experiences of all women either implicitly or directly. Quite significantly, because of the imbalanced power relationship between White women and women of color, information about one group tends to make more apparent the experiences of the other group. It is well known, for example, that ideals of beauty in the United States are based on the blond, blue-eyed model. Dialogue about reactions to that model ultimately reveals that White women often judge themselves by that model of beauty. White women also serve simultaneously as reminders or representatives of that ideal to women of color and, most frequently, to themselves as failures to meet the ideal.

Another way of stating this is that a way of understanding an oppressor is to study the oppressed. Thus, we come to another level of awareness and understanding when we study women of color. We see clearly that White women function both as women who share certain similar experiences with women of color and as oppressors of women of color. This is one of the most difficult realities to cope with while maintaining viable dialogue among women and conducting scholarship. White women who justifiably see themselves as oppressed by White men find it difficult to separate themselves from the effects of and shared power of White men. White women share with White men an ethnicity, an ancestral heritage, a racial dominance, and certain powers and privileges by virtue of class, race, and ethnicity, by race and ethnicity if not class, and always by virtue of White skin privilege.[6] When we study women of color, we raise our awareness and understanding of the experiences of all women, either explicitly or implicitly.

Once we realize that all women are not White, and once we understand the implications of that realization, we see immediately the importance of race ethnicity, and class when considering gender. Interestingly, some scholarship that intends to illustrate and analyze class dynamics is blind to racial and ethnic dynamics. In similar fashion, much scholarship that illustrates and analyzes racial dynamics and class dynamics fails to see ethnic dynamics. Other scholarship gives short shrift to, or even ignores, class. We have begun to grapple with the connectedness of the four big "-isms"—racism, sexism, classism, and ethnocentrism. Much scholarship in Women's Studies, however, fails to work within the context of race, class, ethnicity, and gender and their related "-isms," which modulate each other to a greater or lesser extent. Elizabeth V. Spelman illustrates how the racist equating of Blackness with lustfulness in Western culture modulates sexism toward Black women.[7] One resulting stereotype is that the Black woman has a bestial sexuality and, as such, deserves or expects to be raped. This racism is also modulated by an ethnocentrism that further devalues the Black woman, thereby justifying the sexism. Classism may also modulate this sexism if the perpetrator is of a higher class status than are most Black women. However, if this cannot be claimed, racism, ethnocentrism, or both will suffice. Nonetheless, each is operative to some degree. Lower-class Whites or Whites of the same economic class as Blacks can invoke skin privilege to differentiate within the common denominator of class. The categories of race, class, ethnicity, and gender are unified; likewise their related "-isms" and their correctives.

Attention to race makes us aware of the differing perspectives that women have about race and skin color—perceptions of what is beautiful, ugly, attractive, repulsive: what is ordinary or exotic, pure or evil, based on racist stereotypes; the role that color plays in women's lives; and the norms by which women judge themselves physically. Attention to race also brings us to a realization that White women too are members of a race with stereotypes about looks and behavior. These realizations lead us to more sophisticated analyses of institutional racism. Attention to race in women's lives, with the particular understanding that race has a function for White women and within the context of the connectedness among women due to the playing out of the varying gender roles, as well, reveals the oppression of racism, both from the point of view of one oppressed and of one who oppresses or participates in oppression by virtue of privilege.

Attention to class reveals, among other things, that because of different historical experiences, class means different things to different groups. Not necessarily measured by financial status, neighborhood, and level of education, class status frequently is measured by various ways in which one approximates the Anglo-American norm of middle to upper class. Our society encourages such behavior to a great extent, as shown by the popularity of the Dynasty model, the Yuppie, and the Buppie. Simultaneously, our society insists on formally measuring class status by economic means. Yet for the woman of color, as for the man of color, the dynamic of social class becoming a measure for success is particularly insidious, threatening to destroy the affirmation and utilization of ethnic strengths. Chinese Americans who have reached a high education level may move from Chinatown, feel compelled to adhere to Anglo-American norms that dictate certain dress, foods, and lifestyle, and embrace the cultural imperative of the superiority of the Anglo values. This, in turn, may threaten or seriously distort the sense of a sustaining identity that can recognize and negotiate racism and ethnocentrism. Ties to family and friends may be questioned, and the very historical reality and understandings that provided the source of strength for coping in the White world may be devalued and discarded. Poverty, for example, quickly becomes shameful, and the victim is easily blamed for not being a rugged enough individual.

Ethnicity, as a category of analysis, reveals the cultural traditions, perspectives, values, and choices that shape women's lives and their position in society, ranging from hairstyles and jewelry adornment to modes of worship and ways of perceiving a divine force, from moral values to the perception of women's and men's roles. Ethnicity, our cultural and historical heritage, shapes our perception of race and racism, sex, sexism and heterosexism, class and classism.

The element of power or lack of power has a great deal to do with the benefits or deficits of race and ethnicity. Similar to the example regarding classism, ethnic traditions, kinships, and values that are sustaining in the context of an ethnic group that is a minority, and thus, powerless, may become deficits when interacting with the majority or dominant society. On the other hand, when one becomes secure in one's ethnic identity, deficits of powerlessness and the moves to various levels of success (access to limited power) can be negotiated through variations on those strengths. Kinship networks, for example, are of primary importance to people of color for cultural reasons and for survival. Women's friendships have particular significance specifically friendships of younger women with elder women. The structure of the larger American society does not make allowances for such friendships. Most of us do not live in extended families or in neighborhoods near relatives. Women of color frequently insist that they maintain such relationships over great distances. Time spent with family, especially extended family, must have priority at various times during the year, not just for tradition's sake but for maintaining a sense of rootedness, for a dose of shared wisdom, a balanced perspective of who you are, and often, simply for that affirmation that Momma or Aunt Elizabeth loves you. Ethnicity tells us that women of color celebrate who they are and where they come from, that they are not simply victims of ethnocentrism and other "-isms."

Ethnicity is important in women's lives. Most importantly, ethnicity reveals that besides the usually acknowledged European American ethnic groups, White Anglo-Saxon Protestants are an ethnic group. Even though it is an ethnicity that boasts a defining dominance that makes it unnecessary to name itself, it is an ethnicity. That it is an ethnicity to which many Whites have subscribed, rather than one to which they belong by birth, frequently is cause for confusion. However, it is no less an ethnicity for this reason.

The presence of Anglo-American ethnicity within the ethnicity of ethnic groups of color is often cause for confusion. Nonetheless, American ethnic groups of color manifest ethnicities that constantly balance, integrate, and synthesize the Western European Anglo-American, with what has become, with syncretism over the years, Chinese American, Japanese American, Afro-American, Chicano, American Indian, and Puerto Rican American. In a similar fashion, the English who came here syncretized with the values that emanated from being on this continent and became English Americans. They maintained a position of power so forceful that other Europeans syncretized to their English or Colonial American culture and eventually began to be called Americans. The assumption that people living in the United States are called Americans and that those living in other nations in the hemisphere are Latin Americans, Caribbean Americans, or Canadians attests to this assumed and enforced position of power.

Religion is closely related to ethnicity. Its values are sometimes indistinguishable from ethnic values. Ethnicity as a category of analysis therefore reveals sources of identity, sources of sustenance and celebration, as well as the cultural dynamics that shape women's experience. It makes even more apparent the necessity of viewing women pluralistically.

Gender roles may assume differing degrees of importance. By virtue of the modulation of the other categories, women may see gender or sexism to be of lesser or greater importance. Furthermore, the kind of gender roles or sexism may vary according to the influence of other categories. Attitudes towards homosexuality are most frequently shaped by ethnicity (and by religion, which is closely tied to it), as is the depth and form of homophobia.

Gender roles for women of color are more apparently designated, determined, or modulated by ethnocentrism, racism, and sexism. It should not be surprising that women of color argue that racism most frequently assumes primary importance as an oppressive force with which to reckon. The Black woman, harassed in the workplace because she wears her hair in intricate braids and wears clothes associated with her African heritage, receives harsh treatment because of racism, not sexism. Racism also caused Black women to be denied the right to vote after White women gained suffrage rights. The sexism experienced by women of color within their communities is frequently tied to the racist, classist, and ethnocentrist power relationships between men of color and White America. The sexism experienced in the larger society is affected by this relationship as well as by racism, classism, and ethnocentrism directed specifically to the woman of color.

Women of Color: The Agent of Transformation

In dealing with the commonalities and differences among women, a necessity in teaching about women of color, I am reminded that the title of Paula Gidding's work on Afro-American women is taken from Anna J. Cooper's observation: "When and where I enter, then and there the whole . . . race enters with me."[8] Repeated in many forms by women of color, from the nineteenth-century struggle for the vote to the present-day Women's Movement, this truth ultimately contains the goal of transformation of the curriculum: a curriculum that reflects all of us, egalitarian, communal, nonhierarchical, and pluralistic. Women of color are inextricably related to men of color by virtue of ethnicity and traditions as well as by common conditions of oppression. Therefore, at minimum, their struggle against sexism and racism is waged simultaneously. The experiences and destinies of women and men of color are linked. This reality poses a special problem in the relationship between White women and women of color. Moreover, in emphasizing the commonalities of privilege between White men and women, the oppressive relationship between men of color and White men, women of color and White men, and men of color and White women—all implied in Anna J. Cooper's observation—the teaching about women of color provides a natural pluralistic, multidimensional catalyst for transformation.[9] As such, women of color are agents of transformation.

This section defines transformation and provides the theoretical framework for the pedagogy and methodology of transformation. The final section discusses aspects of the process of teaching about women of color, which, though closely related to the theoretical framework, manifest themselves in very concrete ways.

A review of feminist pedagogy over the past fifteen years or so reveals a call for teaching from multifocal, multidimensional, multicultural, pluralistic interdisciplinary perspectives. This call, largely consistent with the pedagogy and methodology implied thus far in this chapter, can be accomplished only through transformation. Although many theorists and teachers now see this point, the terminology has still to be corrected to illustrate the process. In fact, we often use the words "mainstreaming," "balancing," "integration," and "transformation" interchangeably. Mainstreaming, balancing, and integration imply adding women to an established, accepted body of knowledge. The experience of White, middle-class women has provided a norm in a way that White Anglo-American ethnicity provides a norm, and all other women's experience is added to and measured by those racial, class, ethnic, and gender roles and experiences.

Transformation, which does away with the dominance of norms, allows us to see the many aspects of women's lives. Understanding the significance of naming the action of treating women's lives through a pluralistic process—transformation—leads naturally to a convergence between Women's Studies and Ethnic Studies. This convergence is necessary to give us the information that illuminates the function and content of race, class, and ethnicity in women's lives and in relation to gender. In similar fashion, treating the lives of people of color through a pluralistic process leads to the same convergence, illuminating the functions and content of race, class, and gender in relation to lives of ethnic Americans and in relation to ethnicity.

We still need to come to grips with exactly what is meant by this pluralistic, multidimensional, interdisciplinary scholarship and pedagogy. Much of the scholarship on, about, and even frequently by women of color renders them systematically invisible, erasing their experience or part of it. White, middle-class, male, and Anglo-American are the insidious norms corresponding to race, class, gender, and ethnicity. In contrasting and comparing experiences of pioneers, White males and females, when dealing with American Indians, for example, often speak of "the male," "the female," and "the Indian." Somehow, those of a different ethnicity and race are assumed to be male. Therefore, both the female and the male Indian experience is observed and distorted. They must be viewed both separately and together to get a more complete view, just as to have a more complete view of the "pioneer" experience, the White male and White female experiences must be studied both separately and together. Thus, even in our attempts to correct misinformation resulting from measurement by one norm, we can reinforce measurement by others if we do not see the interaction of the categories, the interaction of the "-isms," as explained in the previous section. This pluralistic process and "eye" is demanded in order to understand the particulars and the generalities of people's lives.

Why is it so easy to impose norms, effectively erasing the experience of others? I do not think erasing these experiences is always intentional. I do, however, think that it results from the dominance of the Western cultural norms of individuality, singularity, rationality, masculinity, and Whiteness at the expense of the communal, the plural, the intuitive, the feminine, and people of color. A brief look at Elizabeth Spelman's seminal work, "Theories of Race and Gender: The Erasure of Black Women," explains the important aspects of how this erasure comes about.[10] A consideration of the philosophical makeup of transformation both tells us how our thinking makes this erasure happen and how we can think to prevent it from happening.

Spelman gives examples of erasure of the Black woman, similar to the examples I have provided. She analyzes concepts that assume primacy of sexism over racism. Furthermore, she rejects the additive approach to analyzing sexism, an approach that assumes a sameness of women modelled on the White, middle-class, Anglo-oriented woman. Spelman shows that it is premature to argue that sexism and racism are either mutually exclusive, totally dependent on one another, or in a causal relationship with one another. She discusses how women differ by race, class, and culture or ethnicity. Most important, she demonstrates that Black does not simply indicate victim. Black indicates a culture, in the United States the African-American culture. She suggests, then, that we present Women's Studies in a way that makes it a given that women are diverse, that their diversity is apparent in their experiences with oppression and in their participation in United States culture. To teach about women in this manner, our goal must not be additive, that is, to integrate, mainstream, or balance the curriculum. Rather, transformation must be our goal.

Essentially, transformation is the process of revealing unity among human beings and the world, as well as revealing important differences. Transformation implies acknowledging and benefiting from the interaction among sameness and diversity, groups and individuals. The maxim on which transformation rests may be stated as an essential affirmation of the West African proverb, "I am because we are. We are because I am." The communality, the human unity implicit in the proverb, operates in African traditional (philosophical) thought in regard to human beings, other categories of life, categories of knowledge, ways of thinking and being." It is in opposition to the individualistic, difference-is-deficit, European, Western pivotal axiom, on which integration, balancing, and mainstreaming rest (as expressed through the White, middle-class, Anglo norm in the United States): "I think; therefore, I am," as expressed by Decartes.

The former is in tune with a pluralistic, multidimensional process; the latter with a monolithic, one-dimensional process. Stated succinctly as "I am we," the West African proverb provides the rationale for the interaction and modulation of the categories of race, class, gender, and ethnicity, for the interaction and modulation of their respective "-isms," for the interaction and modulation of the objective and subjective, the rational and the intuitive, the feminine and the masculine, all those things that we, as Westerners, see as either opposite or standing rigidly alone. This is the breakdown of what is called variously critical pedagogy, feminist pedagogy, or multifocal teaching, with the end result being the comprehension of and involvement with cultural, class, racial, and gender diversity; not working simply toward tolerance, but rather toward an egalitarian world based on communal relationships within humanity.

To realize this transformation, we must redefine categories and displace criteria that have served as norms in order to bring about the life context (norms and values) as follows:

1. Non-hierarchical terms and contexts for human institutions, rituals, and actions

2. A respect for the interaction and existence of both diversity and sameness (a removal of measurement by norms perpetuating otherness, silence, and erasure)

3. A balancing and interaction between the individual and the group

4. A concept of humanity emanating from interdependence of human beings on one another and on the world environment, both natural and human-created

5. A concept of humanity emanating from a sense of self that is not abstract and totally individually defined (I think, therefore, I am), but that is both abstract and concrete, individually and communally defined (I am we; I am because we are; we are because I am).

Such a context can apply to pedagogy and scholarship, the dissemination and ordering of knowledge in all disciplines and fields. Within this context (the context in which the world does operate and against which the Western, individualistic, singular concept of humanity militates) it becomes possible for us to understand the popular music form "rap" as an Americanized, Westernized version of African praise singing, functioning, obviously, for decidedly different cultural and social reasons. It becomes possible to understand the syncretization of cultures that produced Haitian voodoo, Cuban santeria, and Brazilian candomble from Catholicism and the religion of the Yoruba. It becomes possible to understand what is happening when a Japanese American student is finding it difficult to reconcile traditional Buddhist values with her American life. It becomes possible to understand that Maxine Hong Kingston's *Woman Warrior* is essentially about the struggle to syncretize Chinese ways within the United States, whose dominant culture devalues and coerces against syncretization, seeking to impose White, middle-class conformity.

Thinking in this manner is foreign to the mainstream of thought in the United States, although it is alive and well in American Indian traditional philosophy, in Taoist philosophy, in African traditional philosophy, and in Afro-American folklore. It is so foreign, in fact, that I realized that in order to bring about this context, we must commit certain "sins." Philosopher Elizabeth Minnich suggested that these "sins" might be more aptly characterized as "heresies," since they are strongly at variance with established modes of thought and values.[12] The following heresies challenge and ultimately displace the ways in which the Western mind orders the world.[13] They emanate from the experiences of people of color, the nature of their oppression, and the way the world operates. Adopting them is a necessity for teaching about women of color. The conceptualization and the emerging paradigms implied in these heresies surface when we study women of color and lead naturally to the transformation of the curriculum to a pluralistic, egalitarian, multidimensional curriculum.

Heresy 1:   The goal of interaction among human beings, action, and ideas must be seen not only as synthesis, but also as the identification of opposites and differences. These opposites and differences may or may not be resolved; they may function together by virtue of the similarities identified.

Heresy 2:   We can address a multiplicity of concerns, approaches, and subjects, without a neutral or dominant center. Reality reflects opposites as well as overlaps in what are perceived as opposites. There exist no pure, distinct opposites.

Heresy 3:   It is not reductive to look at gender, race, class, and culture as part of a complex whole. The more different voices we have, the closer we are to the whole.

Heresy 4:   Transformation demands an understanding of ethnicity that takes into account the differing cultural continua (in the United States, Western European, Anglo-American, African, Asian, Native American) and their similarities.

Heresy 5:   Transformation demands a relinquishing of the primary definitiveness of gender, race, class, or culture and ethnicity as they interact with theory, methodology, pedagogy, institutionalization, and action, both in synthesis and in a dynamic that functions as opposite and same simultaneously.

A variation on this heresy is that although all "-isms" are not the same, they are unified and operate as such; likewise their correctives.

Heresy 6:   The Anglo-American, and ultimately the Western norm, must be seen as only one of many norms, and also as one that enjoys privilege and power that has colonized, and may continue to colonize, other norms.

Heresy 7:   Feelings are direct lines to better thinking. The intuitive as well as the rational is part of the process of moving from the familiar to the unfamiliar in acquiring knowledge.

Heresy 8:   Knowledge is identity and identity is knowledge. All knowledge is explicitly and implicitly related to who we are, both as individuals and as groups.

Teaching About Women of Color

The first six heresies essentially address content and methodology for gathering and interpreting content. They inform decisions such as the following:

1. Not teaching Linda Brent's narrative as the single example of the slave experience of Afro-American women in the nineteenth century, but rather presenting it as a representative example of the slave experience of Afro-American women that occurs within a contradictory, paradoxical world that had free Black women such as Charlotte Forten Crimke and abolitionist women such as Sojourner Truth. The picture of Black women that emerges, then, becomes one that illuminates their complexity of experiences and their differing interactions with White people.

2. Not simply teaching about pioneer women in the West, but teaching about American Indian women, perhaps through their stories, which they have "passed on to their children and their children's children . . . using the word to advance those concepts crucial to cultural survival." The picture of settling the West becomes more balanced, suggesting clearly to students the different perspectives and power relationships.

3. Not choosing and teaching separate biographies of a White woman, an Asian American woman, and an Afro-American woman, but rather finding ways through biography, poetry, and storytelling to introduce students to different women's experiences, different according to race, class, ethnicity, and gender roles. The emphases are on the connectedness of experiences and on the differences among experiences, the communality among human beings and the interrelatedness among experiences and ways of learning.

The last two heresies directly address process. After correct content, process is the most important part of teaching. Students who learn in an environment that is sensitive to their feelings and supports and encourages the pursuit of knowledge will consistently meet new knowledge and new situations with the necessary openness and understanding for human development and progress. If this sounds moralistic, we must remember that the stated and implied goal of critical pedagogy and feminist pedagogy, as well as of efforts to transform the curriculum with content about women and ethnicity, is to provide an education that more accurately reflects the history and composition of the world, that demonstrates the relationship of what we learn to how we live, that implicitly and explicitly reveals the relationship between knowledge and social action. Process is most important, then, in helping students develop ways throughout their education to reach the closest approximation of truth toward the end of bettering the human condition.

The key to understanding the teaching process in any classroom in which teaching about women of color from the perspective of transformation is a goal, is recognizing that the content alters all students' perceptions of themselves. First, they begin to realize that we can never say women to mean all women, that we must particularize the term as appropriate to context and understanding (for example, White middle-class women, Chinese American lower-class women, or Mexican-American middle-class women). Next, students begin to understand that using White middle-class women as the norm will seem distortingly reductive. White women's ethnic, regional, class, and gender commonalities and differences soon become apparent, and the role in oppression of the imposed Anglo-American ethnic conformity stands out. Student reactions may range from surprise, to excitement about learning more, to hostility and anger. In the volume *Gendered Subjects*, Margo Culley details much of what happens. Her opening paragraph summarizes her main thesis:

> *Teaching about gender and race can create classrooms that are charged arenas. Students enter these classrooms inbred with the values of the dominant culture: they believe that success in conventional terms is largely a matter of will and that those who do not have it all have experience a failure of will.* Closer and closer ties between corporate American and higher education, as well as the "upscaling" of the student body, make it even harder to hear the voices from the margin

within the academy. Bringing those voices to the center of the classroom means disorganizing ideology and disorienting individuals. Sometime, as suddenly as the fragments in a kaleidoscope rearrange to totally change the picture, our work alters the ground of being for our students (and perhaps even for ourselves). When this happens, classrooms can become explosive, but potentially transformative arenas of dialogue.[14]

"Altering the ground of being" happens to some extent on all levels. The White girl kindergarten pupil's sense of the world is frequently challenged when she discovers that heroines do not necessarily look like her. Awareness of the ways in which the world around children is ordered occurs earlier than most of us may imagine. My niece, barely four years old, told my father in a definitive tone as we entered a church farther from her home than the church to which she belongs, "Gramps, this is the Black church." We had not referred to the church as such; yet, clearly, that Catholic congregation was predominantly Black and the girl's home congregation predominantly White. Her younger sister, at age three, told her mother that the kids in the day school she attended were "not like me." She then pointed to the brown, backside of her hand. Young children notice difference. We decide what they do with and think of that difference.

Teaching young children about women of color gives male and female children of all backgrounds a sense of the diversity of people, of the various roles in which women function in American culture, of the various joys and sorrows, triumphs and struggles they encounter. Seeds of awareness of the power relationships between male and female, and among racial, ethnic, and class groups are sown and nurtured.

Teaching about women of color early in students' academic experience, thereby bringing the voices of the margin to the center, disorganizes ideology and ways of being. Furthermore, however, it encourages an openness to understanding, difference and similarity, the foreign and the commonplace, necessary to the mind-set of curiosity and fascination for knowledge that we all want to inspire in our students no matter what the subject.

Culley also observes that "anger is the energy mediating the transformation from damage to wholeness," the damage being the values and perspectives of the dominant culture that have shaped opinions based on a seriously flawed and skewed American history and interpretation of the present.[15] Certain reactions occur and are part of the process of teaching about women of color. Because they can occur at all levels to a greater or lesser extent, it is useful to look for variations on their themes.

It is important to recognize that these reactions occur within the context of student and teacher expectations. Students are concerned about grading, teachers about evaluations by superiors and students. Frequently fear of, disdain for, or hesitancy about feminist perspectives by some students may create a tense, hostile atmosphere. Similarly, fear of, disdain for, or hesitancy about studying people different from you (particularly by the White student) or people similar to you (particularly by the student of color or of a culture related to people of color) also may create a tense, hostile atmosphere. Student expectations of teachers, expectations modulated by the ethnicity, race, class, and gender of the teacher, may encourage students to presume that a teacher will take a certain position. The teacher's need to inspire students to perform with excellence may become a teacher's priority at the expense of presenting material that may at first confuse the students or challenge their opinions. It is important to treat these reactions as though they are as much a part of the process of teaching as the form of presentation, the exams, and the content, for indeed they are. Moreover, they can affect the success of the teaching of the material about women of color.

Specifically, these reactions are part of the overall process of moving from the familiar to the unfamiliar. As heresy #7 guides us, "Feelings are direct lines to better thinking." Affective reactions to content, such as anger, guilt, and feelings of displacement, when recognized for what they are, lead to the desired cognitive reaction, the conceptualization of the facts so that knowledge becomes useful as the closest approximation to the truth. As Japanese American female students first read accounts by Issei women about their picture bride experiences, their reactions might at first be mixed.[16] Raising the issue of Japanese immigration to the United States during the late nineteenth century may challenge the exotic stereotype of the Japanese woman or engender anger toward Japanese males, all results of incomplete access to history. White students may respond with guilt or indifference because of the policy of a government whose composition is essentially White, Anglo-oriented, and with which they identify. Japanese American male students may become defensive, desirous of hearing Japanese American men's stories about picture bride marriages. Afro-American male and female students may draw analogies between the Japanese American experience and the Afro-American experience. Such analogies may be welcomed or resented by other students. Of course, students from varied backgrounds may respond to learning about Issei women with a reinforced or instilled pride in Japanese ancestry or with a newfound interest in immigration history.

Teacher presentation of Issei women's experience as picture brides should include, of course, lectures, readings, audiovisuals about the motivation, the experience, the male-female ratio of Japanese Americans at the turn of the century, and the tradition of arranged marriage in Japan. Presentations should also anticipate, however, student reaction based on their generally ill-informed or limited knowledge about the subject.[17] Discussion and analysis of the students' initial perspectives on Issei women and of how those perspectives have changed, given the historical, cultural, and sociological information, allows for learning about and reading Issei women's accounts to become an occasion for expressing feelings of guilt, shame, anger, pride, interest, and curiosity, and for getting at the reasons for those feelings.

Understanding those feelings and working with them to move the student from damage, misinformation, and even bigotry to wholeness sometimes becomes a major portion of the content, especially when anger or guilt is directed toward a specific group—other students, the teacher, or perhaps even the self. Then it becomes necessary for the teacher to use what I call pressure-release sessions. The need for such sessions may manifest itself in many ways. For example,

> The fear of being regarded by peers or by the professor as racist, sexist or "politically incorrect" can polarize a classroom. If the [teacher] participates unconsciously in this fear and emotional self-protection, the classroom experience will degenerate to hopeless polarization, and even overt hostility. He or she must constantly stand outside the classroom experience and anticipate such dynamics. . . . "Pressure-release" discussions work best when the teacher directly acknowledges and calls attention to the tension in the classroom. The teacher may initiate the discussion or allow it to come about in whatever way he or she feels most comfortable.[18]

The hostility, fear, and hesitancy "can be converted to fertile ground for profound academic experiences. . . . 'Profound' because the students' knowledge is challenged, expanded, or reinforced" by a subject matter that is simultaneously affective and cognitive, resonant with the humanness of life in both form and content.[19] Students learn from these pressure-release sessions, as they must learn in life, to achieve balance and harmony in whatever pursuits; they learn that paradoxes and contradictions are sometimes resolved and sometimes stand separately yet function together (recall heresy #1).

Teaching about women of color can often spark resistance to the teacher or cause students to question subject veracity. Students often learn that the latter part of the nineteenth century and the turn of the century was a time of expansion for the United States. Learning of the experiences of American Indian and Mexican women who were subjected to particular horrors as the United States pushed westward, or reading about Chinese immigrant women whose lives paralleled those of their husbands who provided slave labor for the building of the railroads, students begin to realize that this time was anything but progressive or expansive. Teaching about Ida Wells-Barnett, the Afro-American woman who waged the anti-lynching campaigns at the end of the nineteenth century and well into the twentieth century, also belies the progress of that time. Ida Wells-Barnett brings to the fore the horror of lynchings of Black men, women, and children; the inhuman practice of castration; the stereotyped ideas of Black men and women, ideas that were, as Giddings reminds us, "older than the Republic itself—for they were rooted in the European minds that shaped America."[20] Furthermore, Wells-Barnett's life work reveals the racism of White women in the suffragist movement of the early twentieth century, a reflection of the racism in that movement's nineteenth-century manifestation. The ever-present interaction of racism and sexism, the stereotyping of Black men and women as bestial, the unfounded labelling of Black men as rapists in search of White women, and the horrid participation in all of this by White men and women in all stations of life, make for difficult history for any teacher to teach and for any student to study. The threat to the founding fathers and Miss Liberty versions are apparent. Such content is often resisted by Black and White students alike, perhaps for different reasons, including rage, anger, or shame that such atrocities were endured by people like them; indifference in the face of reality because "nothing like that will happen again"; and anger, guilt, or shame that people of their race were responsible for such hideous atrocities. Furthermore, all students may resent the upsetting of their neatly packaged understandings of U.S. history and of their world. The teacher must know the content and be willing to facilitate the pressure-release sessions that undoubtedly will be needed. Pressure-release sessions must help students sort out facts from feelings, and, most of all, must clarify the relevance of the material to understanding the world in which we live and preventing such atrocities from recurring. Also, for example in teaching either about the Issei women or about the life of Ida Wells-Barnett, teachers must never let the class lose sight of the vision these women had, how they dealt with joy and sorrow, the triumphs and struggles of their lives, the contributions to both their own people and to U.S. life at large.

In addition to variations on anger, guilt, and challenges to credibility in learning about women of color, students become more aware of the positive aspects of race and ethnicity and frequently begin to take pride in their identities. As heresy #8 states, "Knowledge is identity and identity is knowledge. All knowledge is explicitly and implicitly related to who we are, both as individuals and as groups." The teacher, however, must watch for overzealous pride as well as unadmitted uneasiness with one's ethnic or racial identity. White students, in particular, may react in a generally unexpected manner. Some may predictably claim their Irish ancestry; others may be confused as to their ethnicity, for they may come from German and Scottish ancestry, which early on assumed Anglo-American identity. Students of Anglo-American ancestry, however, may hesitate to embrace that terminology, for it might suggest to them, in the context of the experiences of women and men of color, an abuse of power and "all things horrible in this country," as one upset student once complained to me. Here, teachers must be adept not only at conveying facts, but also at explaining the effects of culture, race, gender, and ethnicity in recording and interpreting historical facts. They also must be able to convey to students both the beautiful and the ugly in all of us. Thus, the Black American teacher may find himself or herself explaining the cultural value of Anglo-American or Yankee humor, of Yankee precision in gardening, of Yankee thriftiness, and how we all share, in some way, that heritage. At whatever age this occurs, students must be helped to understand the dichotomous, hierarchical past of that identity, moving toward expressing their awareness in a pluralistic context.

Now that we have explored the why of the phrase "women of color," identified the essence of what we learn when we study women of color, discussed the theory of transformation, and identified and discussed the most frequent reactions of students to the subject matter, we will now focus more on the teacher.

Teaching about women of color should result in conveying information about a group of people largely invisible in our curricula in a way that encourages students to seek further knowledge and ultimately begin to correct and reorder the flawed perception of the world based on racism, sexism, classism, and ethnocentrism. To do so is no mean feat. Redefining one's world involves not only the inclusion of previously ignored content, but also the revision, deletion, and correction of accepted content in light of missing and ignored content. As such, it might require a redesignation of historical periods, a renaming of literary periods, and a complete reworking of sociological methodology to reflect the ethnic and cultural standards at work. This essay, then, is essentially an introduction to the journey that teachers must embark on to begin providing for students a curriculum that reflects the reality of the past, that prepares students to deal with and understand the present, and that creates the basis for a more humane, productive, caring future.

The implications of teaching about women of color are far-reaching, involving many people in many different capacities. New texts need to be written for college-level students. Teacher education must be restructured to include not only the transformed content but also the pedagogy that reflects how our nation and the world are multicultural, multiethnic, multiracial, multifocal, and multidimensional. College texts, children's books, and other materials need to be devised to help teach this curriculum. School administrators, school boards, parents, and teachers need to participate and contribute to this transformation in all ways that influence what our children learn.

For college professors, high school and elementary teachers, and those studying to teach, the immediate implications of a transformed curriculum can seem overwhelming, for transformation is a process that will take longer than our lifetimes. Presently, we are in the formative stages of understanding what must be done to correct the damage in order to lead to wholeness. I suggest that we begin small. That is, decide to include women of color in your classes this year. Begin adding some aspect of that topic to every unit. Pay close attention to how that addition relates to what you already teach. Does it expand the topic? Does it present material you already cover within that expansion? Can you delete some old material and still meet your objectives? Does the new material conflict with the old? How? Is that conflict a valuable learning resource for your students? Continue to do this each year. Gradually, other central topics will emerge about men of color, White men, White women, class, race, ethnicity, and gender. By beginning with studying women of color, the curriculum then will have evolved to be truly pluralistic.

Once embarked on this journey, teachers must be determined to succeed. Why? Because all the conflicting emotions, the sometimes painful movement from the familiar to the unfamiliar, are experienced by the teacher as well. We have been shaped by the same damaging, ill-informed view of the world as our students. Often, as we try to resolve student conflicts, we are simultaneously working through our own. Above all, we must demand honesty of ourselves before we can succeed.

The difficulty of the process of transformation is one contributing factor to the maintenance of the status quo. Often we look for the easiest way out. It is easier to work with students who are not puzzled, concerned, overly romantic, or angered by what they are studying. Teachers must be willing to admit that while we do not know everything we do know how to go about learning in a way that reaches the closest approximation of the truth. Our reach must always exceed our grasp, and in doing so we will encourage the excellence, the passion, the curiosity, the respect, and the love needed to create superb scholarship and encourage thinking, open-minded, caring, knowledgeable students.

Notes

1. A version of this chapter originally appeared in *Multicultural Education: Issues and Perspectives,* ed. James A. Banks and Cherry M. Banks (Boston: Allyn and Bacon, 1989), 145–65. Reprinted with permission.

2. Toni Cade, *The Black Woman: An Anthology* (New York: New American Library, 1970), 9.

3. The Moynihan Report of 1965, the most notable of this scholarship, received the widest publicity and acceptance by American society at large. Blaming Black social problems on the Black family, Moynihan argues that Black families, dominated by women, are generally pathological and pathogenic. In attempting to explain the poor social and economic condition of the Black lower class, Moynihan largely ignores the history of racism and ethnocentrism and classism in American life and instead blames their victims. His study directly opposes the scholarship of Billingsley and others, which demonstrates the organizational differences between Black and White family units as well as the existence of a vital Afro-American culture on which to base solutions to the social problems Moynihan identifies. See Daniel Moynihan, *The Negro Family* (Washington, D.C.: U.S. Dept. of Labor, 1965); Joyce Ladner, ed., *The Death of White Sociology* (New York: Vintage, 1973); Andrew Billingsley, *Black Families in White America* (Englewood Cliffs, N.J.: Prentice-Hall, 1968); Harriet McAdoo, ed., *Black Families* (Beverly Hills, Calif.: Sage Publications, 1981).

4. *Conditions: Five, The Black Woman's Issue* 2, no. 3 (Autumn 1979); Cherrie Moraga and Gloria Anzaldua, eds., *This Bridge Called My Back: Writings by Radical Women of Color* (Watertown, Mass.: Persephone Press, 1981).

5. Dexter Fisher, ed., *The Third Woman* (Boston: Houghton Mifflin, 1980).

6. See "On Being White: Toward a Feminist Understanding of Race and Race Supremacy," in *The Politics of Reality: Essays in Feminist Theory* by Marilyn Frye (Trumansburg, N.Y.: The Crossing Press, 1983), 110–27. Also see "Understanding Correspondence Between White Privilege and Male Privilege Through Women's Studies Work," unpublished paper presented by Peggy McIntosh at the 1987 National

Women's Studies Association Annual Meeting, Atlanta, GA. Available through Wellesley Center for Research on Women, Washington St., Wellesley, Mass., 02181. These works illuminate race and class power relationships and the difference between race and skin privileges. They emphasize not the rejection of privilege but the awareness of its function in order to work actively against injustice.

7. Elizabeth V. Spelman, "Theories of Gender and Race: The Erasure of Black Women," *Quest: A Feminist Quarterly* 5, no. 4 (1982): 36–62. Also see Renate D. Klein, "The Dynamics of the Women's Studies Classroom: A Review Essay of the Teaching Practice of Womens' Studies in Higher Education," *Women's Studies International Forum* 10, no. 2 (1987): 187–206.

8. Paula Giddings, *When and Where I Enter: The Impact of Black Women on Race and Sex in America* (New York: William Morrow, 1984).

9. See Lillian Smith, *Killers of the Dream* (New York: Norton, 1949, 1961). Smith provides a useful and clear description of the interaction between racism and sexism and its legacy.

10. Elizabeth V. Spelman, "Theories of Gender and Race," 57–59.

11. See John Mbiti, *Introduction to African Religion* (London: Heineman, 1975); Basil Davidson, *The African Genius* (Boston: Little, Brown, 1969). For a discussion and explication of Western cultural imperatives, see George Kent, *Blackness and the Adventure of Western Culture* (Chicago: Third World Press, 1972).

12. I began to conceptualize this framework while doing consulting work with college faculty to include Black Studies and Women's Studies content in their syllabi at The Conference on Critical Pedagogy at the University of Massachusetts, Amherst, in February 1985. The concept of heresy here implies a reworking of the way that Westerners order the world, essentially by replacing individualism with a sense of communality and interdependence.

13. See also Paulo Friere, *Pedagogy of the Oppressed* (New York: Seabury, 1969); *Education for Critical Consciousness* (New York: Seabury, 1973).

14. Margo Culley, "Anger and Authority in the Introductory Women's Studies Classroom," in *Gendered Subjects: The Dynamics of Feminist Teaching*, ed. Margo Culley and Catherine Portugues (Boston: Routledge and Kegan Paul, 1985), 209.

15. Ibid., 212. See also in same volume, Butler, "Toward a Pedagogy of Everywoman's Studies," 230–39.

16. "Sei" in Japanese means "generation." The concepts of first-, second-, and third-generation Japanese Americans are denoted by adding a numerical prefix. Therefore, Issei is first generation; Nisei, second; and Sansei, third. Most Issei immigrated to the United States during the first quarter of the twentieth century to provide cheap, male, manual labor, intending to return to Japan after a few years. However, their low wages did not provide enough money for them to return. In 1900, out of a total of 24,326 in the United States, 983 were women. Through the immigration of picture brides by 1920, women numbered 38,303 out of a population of 111,010. Because of racist, anti-Japanese agitation, the U.S. government helped bring these brides to the United States. For a complete discussion, see the Introduction and "Issei Women" in Nobuya Tschida, ed., *Asian and Pacific American Experiences: Women's Perspectives* (Minneapolis: University of Minnesota Press, 1982).

17. An important rule in the scholarship of critical pedagogy is that the teacher should build on the ideas and feelings that students bring to a subject, helping them understand how they might be useful, in what ways they are flawed, correct, or incorrect. Sometimes this simply means giving the student credit for having thought about an idea, or helping the student become aware that he or she might have encountered the idea, or aspects of material studied, elsewhere. Generally this process is referred to as moving the student from the familiar to the unfamiliar.

18. Butler, "Toward a Pedagogy," 236.

19. Ibid.

20. Giddings, *When and Where I Enter*, 31.

PART IV

Learning from Participants' Experiences: Curriculum-in-Practice

Introduction

In this final section of the text, we attempt to connect theory with practice in order to sketch living portraits of how those most directly involved in curriculum—faculty and students—make sense of and evaluate their lived experiences with/in academic programs. Toward this end, we have included case studies that document in rich detail students' perspectives on their general education course work (Twombly), faculty and students' interpretations of effective teaching and learning (Belenky, et al.), students' reactions to feminist, multicultural, and critical perspectives on knowledge in the classroom (Gardner), and faculty resistance to curricular reform (MacCorquodale, et al.).

We include these selections because they cast yet another perspective on curriculum—this time as it is constructed and experienced-in-practice by those who participate in academic programs. From our perspective, too many of us forget that it is human beings—not inanimate planning models or philosophical theories—that animate and breathe life into "curriculum." From our perspective, the readings included in this section challenge us to turn an attentive ear to the stories of those who are at the center of the curricular experience. By listening carefully to their words, perhaps we will begin to (re)vision our understandings of curriculum in higher education.

Student Perspectives on General Education in a Research University: An Exploratory Study

Susan B. Twombly

The meaning students attach to curriculum is a sadly neglected area of study. Perhaps it is because faculty typically hold responsibility for and the authority to determine the curriculum that most literature on undergraduate curriculum is written from a faculty perspective. Most would agree that faculty should determine curricula. After all, how are students to know what constitutes a sound general education curriculum or a sound major course of study? It is more difficult to explain why scholars and administrators ignore students' views of the curriculum when studying or planning curricula. Students are the ones who experience the curriculum as designed by institutions and enacted in classrooms and are in the best position to describe how they interpret and experience the curriculum they are required to take. The premise underlying this exploratory study is that insight into students' understandings and interpretations of the curriculum they experience (specifically, general education) provides knowledge essential to the improvement of the quality of undergraduate education. Therefore, serious effort to improve undergraduate education must take students' views into account.

Two recent trends reinforce the need to examine student views on the curriculum with a particular focus on general education. First is the growing acceptance of a cultural view of the curriculum. Brought to our attention by feminist scholars (e.g., McIntosh 1983; Howe 1984; Andersen 1987) and critical theorists (e.g.. Giroux 1988: Tierney 1989), this view emphasizes the subjective, interpretive, and political nature of the curriculum. These viewpoints have typically focused on knowledge and power—the ideological nature of curriculum. In so doing, they have also legitimized the notion that competing stakeholders shape the curriculum. Feminist scholars in particular draw attention to models of teaching based on students as active learners and collaborators in the teaching and learning process (e.g., Belenky, Clinchy, Goldberger, & Tarule 1986). Richardson (1983, 42) described a negotiation process by which students and faculty determine classroom interaction and assignments. By implication, students can be viewed as active collaborators in the total educational process, interpreting their situations and developing strategies for approaching their education. Although this study is not a critical study in that race, ethnicity, gender, sexual orientation, and class are not expressly taken into consideration, it does recognize that students, as a group, are one of the most important stakeholders in the learning process and that their experiences with the curriculum should be examined.

Second, despite skepticism surrounding the student outcomes assessment movement, experienced observers (e.g., Hutchings 1990; Wright 1990) point to the importance of understanding how students experience the curriculum as both a prerequisite to and an outcome of meaningful assessment activities. These authors also recognize the legitimacy of student experiences in informing meaningful curricular change, particularly for general education. In a recent example, Richard Light, director of the Harvard Assessment Seminars (1991, 6), notes with some surprise the importance of listening to what students have to say as a means of learning about the Harvard educational experience. Light comments: "Students have thought a lot about what works well for them. We can learn much from their insights. Often their insights are far more helpful, and more subtle, than a vague 'common wisdom' about how faculty members can help students to make good decisions at college."

General education is that component of the curriculum that is least owned and agreed upon by faculty, has high educational expectations placed on it, and receives the greatest criticism in times of perceived educational crisis. Despite the fact that the importance of general education, broadly defined, is almost universally espoused, success in achieving general education goals is far from universal. If general education goals for student learning are to be accomplished, faculty and administrators must focus on how students experience the general education portion of their curriculum.[1] With this in mind, the objectives of this study were (1) to identify the perspectives, or the coordinated set of ideas and strategies (academic behavior), that students develop about and toward general education, and (2) to examine the effect of intended major on those perspectives. For the purposes of this study general education was defined broadly as the nonmajor set of requirements common to all students in a particular major or professional school.

Conceptual Framework

This study was concerned with perspectives students have toward general education. Perspective is the analytical concept used by Becker, Geer, and Hughes (1968, 5) to describe the collective action of college students: the form behavior takes, the conditions under which it arises, and its consequences. The notion of perspective is rooted in the symbolic interaction school of sociology, which assumes that all human experience is mediated by interpretation and that it is the meaning attributed to an experience that actually constitutes the experience. Furthermore, interpretation is a collective act, shaped by the acts and meanings of others. More specifically, a perspective is a coordinated set of ideas and actions a person uses in dealing with some problematic situation, but it results from group members sharing common goals and ideas in a common situation (Becker et al. 1968, 5). Perspectives are influenced by the various characteristics of the environment, including other networks of collective action such as faculty or administrators. Under given conditions, groups of individuals work out collective modes of action or perspectives.

The specific case considered in this study was concerned with the perspectives college students created with respect to general education under the conditions of college life in general, but particularly under the general education requirements of the school or college to which they desired admission. The assumption guiding this research is that faculty and administrators give meaning to goals and objectives for general education through the requirements they establish and the courses they teach. Students also interpret and give meaning to this component of the curriculum aided by other students, family, and faculty, to name a few potential influences. These meanings will, in turn, affect academic behavior.

There are many aspects of the college environment that contribute to the development of perspectives about general education. One of these is the degree of emphasis on general versus professional education. Building on the work of Sagen (1973; 1979), Stark, Lowther, Hagerty (1986) and Marsh (1988), this study intentionally focused on the relationship of professional education to general education. Professional education programs are often criticized for giving insufficient attention to general education, while liberal arts majors are criticized for not relating to the needs of contemporary professionals (e.g., Spear 1988). Each of the authors mentioned above has suggested in one way or another that general education goals can more effectively be accomplished within the context of professional education or at least with some specific relationship to work. Within research universities there are several program conditions that affect general education-professional school curricular relationships: general education is taken concurrently with professional education; general education is taken during the first two years in an arts and science college, and students then apply for admission to a professional school at the end of the sophomore year; general education is taken in the liberal arts and science college, and the intended major is an arts and science field; and finally, general education is taken at a community college and credits are transferred to the university.

Relevant Literature

Among the few studies to consider students perspectives about their academic experience, *Making the Grade,* an extensive year-long study of undergraduate education conducted by sociologists Howard Becker, Blanche Geer, and Everett Hughes (1968), stands out as a rare exception. In their study of academic behavior at a large midwestern university they found student academic behavior was dominated by what they termed a grade point average perspective. Few students had what they called a "liberal arts orientation" (126), and even this orientation was not contradictory to the dominant grade point average perspective that seemed to motivate most students. In 1968 when *Making the Grade* was published, the grade point average perspective was so pervasive and powerful as to obscure career as a significant orientation as well. Perhaps the most significant contribution of this study is the more general conclusion that students do respond to curriculum, and they do so in ways that may not be intended, valued, or even known by faculty.

More recently, Gaff and Davis (1981) and Johnston, Jr., Reardon, Kramer, Lenz, Maduros and Sampson, Jr. (1991) examined student views about general education specifically. The latter study pieces together these views of general education from a myriad of studies mostly conducted for other purposes. These two studies and their inferences about students' views about general education provide an important base for the study reported here. Gaff and Davis (1981) directed their attention to students' views of general education specifically. They surveyed students in 10 representative institutions to determine whether general education was an important goal for students, their opinions of the current program, and what changes they would suggest. The Gaff and Davis study reported that students wanted to learn effective communication skills, thinking skills, and interpersonal skills. Gaff and Davis concluded that students value a broad general education, particularly if they can relate general education to other goals such as knowledge about themselves and career preparation. However, as might be expected, they also found students to be critical of general education courses (116). This study is particularly important because, as Gaff and Davis themselves note, "These are hardly radical notions. Indeed, they are similar to the concerns of many faculty members and administrators who are attempting to strengthen general education" (122).

In their comprehensive literature review Johnston Jr., et al. (1991) pieced together student views about general education from a variety of items from numerous national surveys. These items were largely forced-choice items on surveys conducted for other purposes than expressly determining students views on the curriculum. From this review they (and we) learn much about the importance students attach to general education. But they say: "We can essentially only speculate about what students do have in mind when they support a general education and how they think and feel about its individual components" (11). To begin an answer to this question Johnston, Jr., et al. cite the Gaff and Davis study discussed above and a study conducted by Lucile Newman (in Johnston. Jr., et al., 188). Newman found that students' expectations of general education clustered around cognitive development, interactive competence, and personal growth (in Johnston, Jr. et al., 188). Johnston, Jr. et al. conclude their review by saying that "the need for research that would give us a better information on student views is clear enough. Colleges and universities need the capacity to respond more comprehensively and constructively to the perceptions students bring with them to our programs—reinforcing their accurate and productive perceptions and addressing their areas of ignorance and misunderstandings. To do that, however, they need to know far more about what those perceptions and misperceptions are" (195). To this admonition should be added: Faculty and administrators must believe that student views are valid sources of information about the teaching-learning process.

Importance of the Study

This study has both practical and research implications. First, curriculum may be experienced by students in a very different way from what faculty intend. True reform efforts or assessment activities are hampered by lack of understanding of the ways in which students experience the curriculum. Second, the results of this study contribute "data" to the "general education for its own sake" versus "professional education as a vehicle for general education" debate. To date this debate has largely been expressed from the faculty point of view (e.g., Stark et al. 1986). Third, most of the information on students' views of general education has been provided by responses to forced-choice survey items (although according to Johnston, Jr., the Newman study was an exception). This study moves away from that research strategy in order to begin to provide answers to the question of what students have in mind when they discuss general education and its various components. Finally, as an exploratory study this research raises many questions, not the least of which is whole area of fit between institutional general education objectives and individual faculty interpretations of these goals through their teaching.

Research Method and Data Source

The research for this study was carried out during the 1989–90 academic year at a major research university in the midwest and at a nearby community college. Multiple sources of data were used, including university catalogs, brief questionnaires given to student participants, and interviews with significant groups identified by students. The central source of data for this study was focus group interviews (Krueger 1988) with freshman and sophomore students.

The Institution

The university enrolls approximately 20,000 undergraduates in its College of Liberal Arts and Sciences and 10 professional schools. Several aspects of the university are important to this study. First, all new students (exceptions noted below) enroll in the College of Liberal Arts and Sciences for their first two years. Students wishing to pursue majors in professional schools of education, business, journalism, nursing, allied health, and social welfare must apply for admission to the appropriate school during their sophomore year. The schools of fine arts, engineering, and architecture admit students directly as new students. Consequently, all of the professional schools have selective admissions while the College of Liberal Arts and Sciences (CLAS) operates under an open admissions policy. There are no university-wide general education requirements. In fact, it was only during the 1989–90 academic year that schools were required to put their general education goals down on paper. All curricular decisions, including general education requirements, are made by the faculty of each school and the college. Entering new students typically take the general education requirements specified by the school to which they aspire. Requirements are met through courses offered by the College of Liberal Arts and Sciences. Although these differing requirements may include the same courses, there is wide diversity both in the amount and the range of general education required of students. Another important point is that neither faculty nor students at this university typically recognize the term "general education." That is, "general education" is not a term used to describe the breadth component of the curriculum. The only exception to this is the School of Business. As a result, there are four typical patterns of enrollment potentially affecting students' perspectives: (1) students enter CLAS and remain there to major, (2) students enter CLAS and transfer to one of the professional schools at the end of their sophomore years, (3) students enter a professional school directly, or (4) students begin at a community college and transfer to the university.

General Education Requirements

General education requirements varied widely among the schools included in this study, as did the language used in the university catalog to describe general education. Some of the descriptive phrases that appear in the "Aims" of CLAS degrees include "understanding the past"; "Breadth of knowledge is necessary, but risks superficiality"; "Depth is equally important, but risks over-specialization"; "Liberal education presupposes intensive study of the sciences, the humanities, and the social sciences"; "Liberal education embodies both theory and practice" (Catalog, 24). It must be noted that these are aims of a liberal arts degree and not just the general education component of the degree. As might be expected, CLAS has the most lengthy list of "common degree requirements" (Catalog, 25) necessary to earn the bachelor of arts and bachelor of general studies degrees.[2] Each of these degrees has unique "additional requirements" (Catalog, 26) to round out degree requirements. Requirements common to both degrees include three English courses (two specified and one chosen from a short list), one course in oral communication/logic, college algebra and one additional math course, two semesters of Western civilization and one course in a non-Western culture chosen from a list of approved courses. In order to earn a bachelor of arts degree students must take four semesters of one foreign language and nine courses to fulfill the "B.A. Principal Course Distribution Requirement" (Catalog, 29). These nine courses must be selected from a list of approved principal courses and distributed equally over the humanities, natural sciences, and mathematics, and social sciences and over subtopics within each area. B.A. students must take a laboratory science course. Candidates for the bachelor of general studies degree are not required to take a foreign language and have to complete two courses selected from the approved principal course list in each of the humanities, natural sciences and mathematics, and social sciences. These students must also take a minor concentration consisting of three junior/senior level courses in a department outside of their major. Perhaps tellingly, each of these requirements is discussed separately in the university catalog. Requirements for the bachelor of science degree are determined by individual departments but must include basic mathematics and English and 47 hours outside of the major department (Catalog, 33).

The School of Engineering is one of the few schools in the university to admit students in their first year, and it introduces its undergraduate degree requirements with the following statement: "The development of the student's professional competence in his or her chosen engineering discipline is of primary importance, but breadth of experience is also emphasized to make students aware of the social and human impact of technological solutions" (Catalog, 189). Each of the nine separate degree programs within the school includes courses in basic sciences, communications, humanities, and social science as well as general and specialized engineering courses. All programs require some course work in communication and literature. General distribution requirements consist of at least one humanities and one social science course and two courses from one department in either the humanities or social sciences. Some engineering programs require additional humanities and social science courses. So at a minimum engineering students would be required to take six courses excluding the basic sciences courses. In the listing of requirements for each degree program, the humanities and social sciences requirements are referred to as electives (see, for example, Catalog, 192).

The School of Nursing takes a different approach, admitting students in their junior year. The catalog states that "the educational components of the School of Nursing undergraduate program are a broad foundation in the liberal arts and sciences and a concentration in the nursing major" (232). Prospective nursing students are expected to complete "Prenursing Requirements" (233) before they are admitted to the school. These requirements include 6 hours in English, 3 hours of oral communication, 3 hours of mathematics, 26 to 28 hours of natural sciences to be chosen from a specific list, 9 to 10 hours of social sciences to be chosen from a specific list, and 6 hours of humanities to be chosen from a specific list. Foreign language and Western civilization are not required for a bachelor of science degree in nursing but can be used as electives.

In the School of Business, which also admits students as juniors, "The strength of the program is based not only on the quality of professional course offerings, but also on the offerings of other units in the university, particularly in the social science, the natural science, and the humanities"

(Catalog, 158). The School of Business actually does refer to general education requirements. These include three English courses, six to ten hours of mathematics, one specific computer science course, three humanities and three natural science courses, and two psychology courses chosen from a specific list. The business school also requires an external coherent area of study, which can either consist of four semesters of a foreign language, four courses in one area studies program (i.e., Latin American studies), a combination of the first two options, or a nonbusiness concentration.

At the community college, description of general education is complicated by the fact that general education requirements are listed for the associate of arts degree, typically considered to be the appropriate degree for transfer, and yet many hopeful transfer students do not intend to earn the associate of art degree. These students tend to view general education requirements as extras because some of their intended major areas at the university do not require all of the general education courses required for the associate degree. These students are guided by what will transfer rather than by the philosophy of a general education at the community college even though the courses are often identical. The community college catalog describes the associate of arts degree as meeting the educational needs of students through the completion of general education distribution requirements. These include 9 hours of communication courses, 6 hours of humanities/arts courses, 6 hours of social sciences or economics courses, 9 hours in science and mathematics to include one laboratory science, and 1 hour in health or physical education. The requirements are fulfilled by taking courses from a specific list. No more than one course from each subarea within the humanities, social sciences, and natural sciences and mathematics can count toward the general education distribution requirement. In contrast to the university catalog, the community college catalog contains a couple of "goal statements" for general education. For example, the catalog states, "Those receiving the Associate Degree are expected to demonstrate the ability to think and to communicate clearly and effectively both orally and in writing; to use mathematics; to understand the modes of inquiry of the major disciplines including the sciences and technologies; to be aware of our culture and of other cultures and times; to achieve insights gained through experience in thinking about ethical problems to develop the capacity for self-understanding and problem-solving; and finally, to gain sufficient depth in some field of knowledge to contribute to society" (52).

Data Collection

Focus groups were used as the main vehicle for gathering student perspectives. Focus groups (Krueger 1988) are carefully planned discussions designed to obtain perceptions on a defined area of interest in a permissive, nonthreatening environment. Several factors are key to the success of focus groups. First, the ideal group consists of 7 to 10 participants chosen for a shared characteristic relevant to the purpose of the study—in this case intended major was the relevant characteristic used to form groups. For the purposes of this study one group of freshman and sophomore engineering students was randomly selected to represent the case in which students enter the professional school directly from high school. A second and third group consisted of randomly selected students who intend to apply to the schools of nursing and business, respectively, at the end of their sophomore year.[3] These groups represent the condition in which general education is completed in the first two years followed by professional study. However, students often begin taking some introductory professional courses in their first year. Three other groups represented first- and second-year students who intend to major in the broad areas of the humanities, social sciences, and natural sciences, respectively. A final group consisted of community college students who intended to transfer to the university. With the exception of the community college group, students were randomly selected and invited to participate in the focus groups. The community college participants were identified by an administrator. Actual group participation ranged from 5 in one group to 12 in another. On average 7 students participated in each interview.

Each student was asked to provide some general demographic and academic information about themselves. Students ranged in age from 19 to 22 with the exception of the community college students, who were older than their university counterparts. There was likely some self-selection, as grade point averages ranged from 2.4 to 4.0. Only one student had a grade point average under 2.0. Two, one engineer and one humanities student, had perfect 4.0 grade points. Engineering students, as a group, were better students. In part that is due to the selective admissions policy that operates in that school. Despite its open admissions policy, the university has a reputation for drawing largely middle- to upper-middle-class students. Students were not asked to report race and ethnicity, and there did not appear to be any minority students in the pool of selected students with the exception of one international student. The engineering group consisted of all men and the nursing group of all women. The CLAS groups more evenly mixed. Several of the community college students planned to complete the associate degree, but many did not.

Each focus group met once and was led through a series of questions pertaining to general education based on the language used by the relevant school and requirements specific to their intended major. Interviews consisted of six or seven specific questions designed to initiate conversations that would reveal students' perceptions of general education and lasted from 1 to 1-1/2 hours. Interview sessions were flexible and allowed pursuit of topics specific to each group. Questioning was done by the principal investigator assisted by a graduate assistant who took copious notes, recorded each session, and kept track of which student made each comment so that we could determine individual as well as group responses. All interviews were taped and transcribed. The names of the students have been changed in the interest of confidentiality.

Focus groups offered several advantages for this study. Students generally felt comfortable talking about general education with their peers, although there were some differences among groups in communication patterns. It appeared to be more difficult for students to talk about the topic of general education individually than in a group. The smaller groups required much more direct questioning and prompting than larger groups. The larger the group, the more talkative students seemed to be. Engineers, humanities, and natural science majors volunteered their opinions quite freely. Prospective nursing students and social science majors required more prompting. Within the professional school groups, students seemed to be basically in agreement. There was more disagreement, less of a uniformly held perspective, among the social science and humanities groups. The community college group was somewhat different in character than the university groups. These students had been gathered by an administrator, and most were involved in some sort of student activities. They were similar to their university counterparts in that they were traditional college-age students. However, this group differed in that a variety of intended majors was represented. These students were generally very participative in the group discussion but seemed to be somewhat confused about what I, the interviewer, wanted to hear. Halfway through this interview, we returned to the first question: What is the purpose of general education from your point of view? Although they had responded quite appropriately the first time, after hearing each other talk for 20 minutes they wanted to try again.

Because this research assumed that perspectives are shaped by others, social interaction prompted by focus groups was appropriate and facilitative rather than contaminating as long as students were free (and were encouraged) to express all viewpoints. Focus groups have high face validity. The results seem believable and are expressed in the participants own words. Focus groups entail low cost and allow the researcher to increase the number of participants.

Limitations of this method include having less control than in an individual interview; complexity of analysis may be increased because of the group nature of comments and the necessity of having two facilitators—one to direct conversation and the other to take notes (Krueger 1988). A further limitation of this study is its restriction to one university. However, because a wide range of academic conditions exist for students on this campus (i.e., some enter the College of Liberal Arts and Sciences and some enter the professional school directly from high school), the results are more generalizable to other similar institutions than would be the case were all new students subject to the same academic conditions (for example, if all new students entered professional schools directly from high school). In hindsight, the variability in terminology used to describe general education and in the amount of requirements would make a larger, multi-institution study difficult. Another potential limitation is that any group interview could be dominated by one individual or idea. In this case, the researchers made extra effort to draw quiet students into the conversation and to encourage diverse viewpoints. Consequently, all students did participate. One might expect this because the students made the effort to meet the interviewers and actually showed up to be interviewed. Finally, although the students were selected randomly to participate in the focus groups, the study can not be considered representative. In an attempt to compensate for the relatively small number of students interviewed, participants were asked to talk about the views of other students they knew.

Interviews were reviewed for emerging themes and patterns reflective of the major objectives of the study following the guidelines suggested by Bogdan and Biklen (1982). Analysis also permitted identification of unintended responses or trends. Specific themes identified early in the interviewing were "tested," in the form of open-ended questions, with succeeding groups.

Findings are discussed in terms of four major areas: purposes, influences, expectations of general education courses, and strategics. To the extent possible, findings are reported in the words of the students themselves. Quotes have been edited slightly to eliminate distracting phrases such as "I mean" and "you know" when these phrases obviously had no bearing on the response.

The Purposes of General Education

Students' interpretations of the purposes of general education fell into four categories: educational, instrumental, personal, and negative.

Educational

By far the most frequently cited purpose of general education was to make students well-rounded. The following quotes are illustrative of responses to the question of why students thought they had to take courses outside of their major.

> I don't know. I guess to be more well-rounded (Laura, Nursing).

> Just to get you well-rounded, I guess. Instead of just concentrating on engineering (James, Engineering).

> That's part of what a liberal arts education is—getting all those different subjects along with your major (Peter, Natural Sciences).

> What's "getting" them? (Interviewer).

> Being exposed to different subjects than you would normally take (Sam, Natural Sciences).

The well-rounded purpose came up frequently in all of the groups. However, some students articulated more specifically what well-rounded meant to them. Getting along with or being able to talk to different people was an important benefit of well-roundedness that emerged frequently during interviews. To many students well-rounded seemed to mean being able to carry on an intelligent conversation and relate to others.

> But the point of humanities is to broaden your base so you're not so narrow minded. . . . most of your life is interaction with people and if you can't interact with people and know what's going on in the surroundings around you then you're really lost, and it doesn't matter how much engineering you know. . . . Who cares how many semesters of math you've had. It doesn't make any difference. What makes a difference is whether you can get along with people and get along well . . . (John, Engineering).

> Because when you finally graduate you find that you are not going to work in isolation. There are so many relationships in life and somehow you get involved in a diverse environment and somebody who is narrowly focused won't appreciate problems as much as somebody who is broadly minded. Even if that knowledge is shallow, the fact that you know a little bit of it will put at more advantageous positions than somebody who doesn't know it at all . . . (Steve, Natural Science).

> Just carrying on everyday conversations with people or just current events stuff. . . . to carry on a conversation about current events you have to know history and other things like that too. . . I want to be able to hold at least a decent conversation with her [roommate] about what I do know instead of saying . . . "oh, look at that cloud" and she's talking about a painting and we can't even relate to each other . . . (Mary, Natural Sciences).

A few students were more cynical about the well-rounded purpose of general education. Partially joking, one student said, "it helps when you're playing "Jeopardy." (laughter) There's always some subject there that you don't know (Todd, Natural Sciences). When pressed, this student explained his comment: "You kinda know a little bit about everything, instead of just focusing all your time and energy on, like, engineering. . . ."

These sentiments were shared by other students in the humanities and social sciences as well. One humanities major compared distribution requirements to another game of the 1980s, *Trivial Pursuit*.

As suggested by John in a quote above, students also understand general education as providing a foundation for further study or their life's work.

> In teaching it [general education] will be useful because it gives me a better knowledge of things around me (Jerry, Community College).

> Things that I can apply to my daily life, or somehow carry toward my major (Gloria, Humanities).

> It's a solid foundation to carry on your studies either for an A.A. or a Bachelor's. It means you know the basics plus more (Mora, Community College).

Nurses were somewhat more specific about the relation of general education to their intended profession and future course work.

> Basic knowledge . . . you use—well, math—I mean you're going to use when you have to figure out how many cc's a person needs. . . . (Jenny, Nursing).

> It's just to give you a background . . . just the basics so you can build on it when you get to the Med Center (Laura, Nursing).

> Like the ethics course? That's basic for any kind of medical profession with . . . the topics of euthanasia coming up . . . (Laura, Nursing).

Nurses were less certain of the purposes behind other requirements but had faith that if they had to take a course there must be a reason. Jenny said:

> Oh, I'm sure there's a reason, otherwise they wouldn't. . . . (laughter) I mean there's gotta be. . . . there are some courses that you need to take just for basic knowledge . . . like a history class. You really won't use history of the U.S. in [nursing]. I could see we would use history of medicine more than we would history of the U.S. But [history] is just basic. . . . That's just the kind of basic knowledge that everyone should know, I guess.

Engineers responded similarly, also making a connection to their future lives.

> It gives you a base, or something like that. Gives you some kind of a ground to start, to begin your engineering work on. It's like a foundation—or something like that. . . . I think it's good because as far as an English class goes . . . with some of the papers that have to be written, a lab write-up or something like that in an engineering class—that really helps. It really helps to know how to structure things when you're trying to get a point across . . . (John, Engineering).

For James and Perry general education was important because, in their minds, engineering careers involve more than science.

> Engineering is so quantitative. You know it's all numbers and manipulations and it doesn't really—to me—it doesn't deal with the real world. You know there's people and there's interaction between people and, you know, that's by far the more percentage of your life is not in electrons and stuff like that, but other stuff (James, Engineering).

Definitely, my Dad, he was telling me about this. He went to Vanderbilt University and got his bachelor of science in electrical engineering. He stayed around and got his master's and doctorate in electrical engineering. . . . And I go, "how much do you use," now he's been out, in the work world for about thirty years. He [says], "not one ounce. I manage people." Maybe for the first five or ten years in engineering you're dealing with hands-on stuff.

Pretty soon you get up in the management level and you need to be able to work with people. For as much as they make you study engineering, you'd think you'd be in it a lot more, but I'd say maybe less than one half of your career is going to be engineering. It's going to be working with people (Perry, Engineering).

General education was also attributed with helping students understand history and human processes.

[In] the history courses . . . you learn kind of the phases that people have gone through, throughout different time periods, you can kind of understand why people did something why people reacted a certain way to this and what event happened in history and what another person's reaction was and what happened in government and I think that's where you can take that into developing something in relation to other people in the time that you live in right now (Perry, Engineering).

If they shortened—I've got to take 12 hours of physics—if they shortened that to four or even five, I could . . . take a political science or take a history class. Because the big thing about history is you learn from your mistakes and/or other people's mistakes. That's why I think you ought to take a history class so we don't repeat the same mistakes again. I think it just goes in cycles, because people don't realize this has happened before. Let's avoid this, let's change it so we can make a better world instead of finding the coefficient of some incline plane (Perry, Engineering).

Instrumental Purposes

Students in all programs identified what I called instrumental purposes of general education. These had more to do with outcomes such as confidence and discipline rather than knowledge. Instrumental purposes seemed to be particularly prevalent among community college students.

It's experience for the real world. Teachers put deadlines on you for papers and your job will have deadlines too. Learn how to handle it in school, handle pressure dealt with deadlines, do research (Linda, Community College).

They [general education courses] give you an idea of what else is out there. People change their minds four times during a college career. Also if the boss asks, you can do the extras (Randy, Community College).

It's . . . a proving ground. If you make it through, then you can go ahead and take your major courses (Sara, Community College).

Study habits. It think it's more useful to students at four-year universities. They have to make it there away from home. Transfer students are like being freshmen and junior at the same time. Here they just teach you that you need to study, you need to go to class. I don't know how that will transfer when I move to [university town] (Sara, Community College).

This semester I'm taking a couple of electives in the humanities . . . something that maybe I can build on, and maybe get some confidence in myself to . . . so that when I get really into the meat of the curriculum I can go . . . you know, I've had this semester of this and I did pretty well, and I should be able to do better, or just as well, in something else. And maybe I'll apply myself better (John, Engineering).

They try to do it [include a humanities course] every semester just kind of as a break from the rest of the engineering stuff. . . . And whether it's intended or not, I kind of use it as a break from everything else (Larry, Engineering).

> You also meet people from other schools . . . and see what they do at college, the classes they like . . . (Greg, Engineering).

> I think it helps the ones that don't know what they want to do. Don't know what they want to major in . . . it makes them take a variety of courses and I mean they probably wouldn't think of taking something like geography but they might like it if they take it (Dona, Humanities).

> Also, you won't get so burned out . . . in your major if you're taking these courses (Mary, Natural Sciences).

This last sentiment was shared by the engineers in particular.

General education also serves as a safety net as suggested by Evan, a humanities major who had recently changed to sciences: "Nobody can be 100 percent sure what they're going to be doing in the future." One student majoring in the social sciences even suggested that general education makes a liberal arts major seem more legitimate and rigorous.

> Everybody kind of laughs and thinks that the College of Liberal Arts and Sciences is so easy, but . . . it kind of makes it more respectable to take a wide variety because . . . I don't have to take really tough math or really tough chemistry, so everyone thinks it's so easy. But at least, you know you have to take some stuff that's hard . . . (Kate, Social Sciences).

> It's looked better upon, I guess. I mean a B.A. is better than a B.S. because you are more well-rounded (Sam, Natural Sciences).

Personal

Personal benefits were also cited, but to a lesser extent.

> General ed courses give me a better understanding of myself—a better understanding of what goes on around me (Barbara, Community College).

> It's not as . . . they don't beat you to death and it's not as structured, and I'm somewhat more able to express myself (Larry Engineering).

> I took Psych 104 my first semester up here and there were some things they discussed that helped . . . like stress—chapters on stress and coping, time management . . . (Gloria Humanities).

Negative

There were several expressly negative purposes attributed to general education.

> I'm an older student in a hurry to get my degree. These extra courses are obstacles that get in the way. Courses I'm not really interested in but somebody else thinks I need to take. I've been out there. I know what I want to do. Now I just need to get it done (Jerry, Community College).

> The extra baggage that doesn't affect me directly. How well I know Mayan culture isn't really going to affect how I design airplanes (Jack, Community College).

> I haven't thought about it really . . . I just thought it was something you had to get in (Brad, Business).

Several students also talked about general courses negatively because they detracted from their overall GPAs.

Influences

There were two general categories of factors that seemed to influence students' understanding of the purposes of general education: (1) perceptions of need or use (or lack thereof) in future job, program, or life, and (2) people. Many of the quotes already cited reflect the way in which students view general education in relation to their futures. These are reinforced by the following examples, which demonstrate linkage to future work or, as in the case of some liberal arts majors, perceptions of what they will not need based on a relatively vague notion of future careers.

> Psychology you're going to need, especially if you're going to work up on the Psych Ward as a nurse (Jenny, Nursing).

> You're going to have to write reports as a nurse (Laura, Nursing).

> I don't think I'll use calculus in any job I'm in (Kerry, Humanities).

> I was agreeing with her [another student] that . . . you should be able to take some sort of proficiency exam and not have to take any [math courses] here. Because I found they just lowered by GPA and it's something that I'm not going to need (Kerry, Humanities).

> You need math, but I think that the second math course, 115 [calculus], I just don't see how it's applicable for anyone that isn't going into a math-related field (Jeff, Humanities).

> Well, there's a lot of stuff that you think you'll probably never use . . . . I have to take four semester of Spanish and I don't think I'll probably ever use it (Kate, Social Sciences).

This sense of need (and lack of need) also affected students' strategy for approaching general education—choosing courses and the amount of effort they devote to courses. This is discussed in greater detail below.

A variety of people were reported to have influenced students' understanding of general education. They included the self, parents, siblings, and to a lesser extent advisers and teachers.

> One might think parent, but that's not true. It's self-understanding—knowing what's right and what's wrong (Mora, Community College).

> A sense of maturity. I sat out a semester and then came back. I worked in a restaurant and didn't want to work there for the rest of my life. I heard conversations going on around me I couldn't relate to. Now when a conversation happens, I can say, "I know something about this—I can put in an intelligent bit or two" (Linda, Community College).

> Students. You can say to yourself. "It's not just me. Everybody else is going through this too" (Randy, Community College).

> Definitely, my dad, he was telling me about this. He went . . . (Perry, Engineering).

> I think my Mom drilled it in my head a lot. I think I asked those questions before I came up here. I went to a college prep high school—so maybe I got it from there also (Roberta, Social Sciences).

> I just use my older brother as an example. He's a civil engineer and he's working for this company and he's always got to write up—he designs huge treatment plants and he's got to write manuals and things . . . (Todd, Natural Sciences).

Community college students were generally more positive about the role of teachers and advisers in shaping their ideas about general education. Advisers provided important information that guided course selection.

> Teachers. I didn't think they would be as personable as they are (Linda, Community College).

> Teachers. I took an honors project which was one on one with a teacher. He taught me a lot about general ideas. I worked with him on modern art history. I had an interest in it but I didn't want to pursue it. I'm still not going to take more classes in it, but that's when I began to realize that not everything has to go toward my major (Barbara, Community College).

University students did not directly mention teachers as influencing their understanding of general education, and when asked if advisers had any influence students typically reported a negative response:

> Well-rounded. That's the one thing they say. That's the only thing they say. They say, next subject. . . (Sam, Natural Sciences).

> Mine never really say anything (Mary, Natural Sciences).

It became clear that faculty do exert a strong influence on the attitudes that students develop toward general education requirements, although in this particular study that influence was exerted through the ways in which general education classes were taught and advising was done. This issue is discussed elsewhere (Twombly, in progress).

Expectations of General Education Courses

For the most part students did not have very sophisticated expectations of general education courses. They expected to learn very broad, general knowledge but in many instances reported being subjected to many facts, which they often felt were unnecessarily detailed. Furthermore, they expected general education courses to be easier than their major courses and they were often surprised when they were not.

> Todd (Sciences): Just to have a broad overview. I don't remember too many particulars.

> Sam (Sciences): Easier level. Well, compared to other classes like organic chemistry. By the labels of the classes you'd think they were easier, but that's not always . . . the grade point's the same. Three hours is three hours. Those classes can kill you just as bad as the other ones.

> Kate (Social Sciences): I figure it's very general, you know, introductory.

> Roberta (Social Science) Oh, general knowledge of whatever the class is supposed to be in.

> Bob (Social Science): I expect to get a rudimentary knowledge of that subject and to be able to . . . read a newspaper, know something about the subject if I have any other contact with the subject. Some basic vocabulary, have an outline of what's going on, what the conversation might be about, what material I might need to know to carry on his conversation.

> Larry (Engineering). I think the main thing is just seeing how everything fits together and cause and effect type of thing.

> I don't like having to take PASCAL, but l m going to get something out of it. Because that will help me with problem solving . . . so I'm getting stuff out of it (Jeff, Humanities).

Strategies

In this study I was interested not only in the perspectives held by students about general education but also about the effects of these perspectives. In other words, what strategies did students develop toward general education, how did they choose courses, and how did they study?

Choosing Courses

Several value premises guided choice of general education courses. They included: attempt to find the easiest, desire to get the requirement out of the way, interest, availability, estimates of work load, and structure of major.

> But I took geology just because I needed a five-hour lab science and it was the easiest one. I mean, that's the sole reason I took that—because it's an easy class. . . . It turned out to be a halfway interesting class. . . . it's a waste of my time (Bob, Social Sciences).

> Actually, l take them just to get the requirement out of the way. I either try to pick what's most appealing or easiest.

> That's what I do. I'm not going to pick some really hard class just to get a requirement out of the way and have it lower my GPA (Bob, Social Sciences).

> If you'd have a use for them later. . . . if you know you re going to go to Russia, then take a Russian history class (Kate, Social Sciences).

Well, because for me personally, if I'm interested in something it'll be easy, whereas no matter how easy the course is if I don't like it I don't usually do very well (Roberta, Social Sciences).

What I am interested in (Jeff, humanities).

Dad's always encouraging me, if I'm interested in something to take it. It's just that I don't want to be here for seven years. (laughter) I wouldn't mind doing it if I had extra time . . . waste a whole year or something (Todd, Natural Sciences).

Pin it up and throw a dart at it (Evan, Humanities).

Get 'em out of the way. Take it but get on to your major (Randy, Community College).

I look at the course description catalog. Ones I'm interested in. I don't like to read much so if Western civ has a lot of reading and history doesn't have as much. . . . Talk to other students about instructors and teaching methods (Jerry, Community College).

Some students reported making choices about general education courses in reference to their entire workload.

You pick your sciences classes first, get those set in your schedule. Those are the hard ones. Those are the ones I'm going to concentrate on. Then you just fill in off the distribution list. No problem, these classes are easy. Then you get to the first day and the syllabus is five times longer for this distribution class than for your biology class (Sam, Natural Sciences).

Well, depending on what your load is, you don't want to take something you don't really have to have—something really hard—that's going to bring your grade down in anatomy (Kathy, Nursing).

You want to take something easier [like philosophy or logic] when you're already taking anatomy and chemistry during the same semester (Laura, Nursing).

Some students were able to take advantage of multiple degree options to avoid one of their least favorite requirements: foreign language. Todd's comment was indicative of much hostility toward having to take four semesters of one foreign language.

In my major you can take a B.G.S. or a B.A. The difference is to get the B.G.S. you don't have to take the four foreign language courses. And that's what I've done. I've gotten around it (Todd, Natural Sciences).

For engineering students the strategy for choosing courses was structured by their curriculum.

I have a very structured . . . I have a two-page sheet that says you will take this in this semester and the following spring you will take these five classes. It's not extremely rigid, but hey, would like you to adhere it? And it makes them a lot happier if you go in with your enrollment card and have written out what they want you to take instead of what you would rather take. If you don't put down what's on the curriculum sheet, they ask you why. Ask you when you're going to pick up the stuff you should be taking now, that kind of thing (Perry, Engineering).

More or less, you have to take what they have written if you want to graduate in four years (Perry, Engineering).

To get a break because engineering is really difficult. A lot of these other humanities aren't as demanding. That's one of the reasons. Plus, just other interests you have (James, Engineering).

"What you can get into" frequently determined what general education courses these students chose. A sense of frustration resulted from not being able to get into general education courses, accompanied by a sense of falling behind.

Usually what you can get into and what sounds good to you (Jeff, Humanities).

Yeah, that's what I did last semester. I just made a big list of all the requirements I needed and put it on my alternative list and whatever was the first one I could get into was what I got (Dona, Humanities).

For me it's generally which course I can get into. You make a list and then . . . (Gloria, Humanities).

And then they require you to take a course that they only provide a certain amount of room for and you can't get . . . Western civ is required and I really want to take it, but I've tried for three semesters to get in there and can't get in it (Dona, Humanities).

It bothers you that you are behind (Gloria, Humanities).

For community college students, the knowledge of counselors was important to making "correct" choices of general education courses. "Correct," as one might expect, referred to transferability of course work.

Counselors are great. They have the right information (Mora, Community College).

That's the key—the right info. I've taken 9 hours that won't transfer on the recommendation of the counseling center (Sara, Community college).

Strategies for Studying

Although students generally reported studying for general education courses, they typically did not spend as much time studying for those courses as they did for courses in their major.

Study time? I usually go in with the intention of trying to get an A and take it from there. So, I do study a lot. I mean some classes take a lot (Bob, Social Sciences).

I don't know . . . I usually read, well sometimes I read what I'm supposed to and usually spend a lot of time studying like right before the test. That's not as much as I should I guess (Kate, Social Sciences).

Depends on how tough it is. I can't skip class. I get more out of going to class than reading the book. By the time I read the book it doesn't help much (Bob, Social Sciences).

I spend less time on them than I do on my biology courses. Mostly because you're wanting to learn more so you know more later. And plus, it's more interesting to you. If someone was majoring in history they'd probably spend more time on their history than math (Jenny, Nursing).

I work more on what I think I need to, like, I worked more on anatomy than I did on geography of human survival. That's probably why I did do bad in the class (Kathy, Nursing).

As far as time—if I have a test to study for in gen ed and one to study for in my major, gen ed is going to get blown off (Randy, community college).

Because I work, I have to prioritize. There are classes where I think I can take a C in that class and it is not going to matter 10 years from now (Sara, community college).

An exchange among science students reflects student feeling about spending study time on general education courses.

It irritates me that I have to spend more time on my history class than on my meteorology class (Mary).

You have to concentrate (Sam).

Yeah . . . I'd rather spend more time on my major classes than something in distribution (Mary).

You have to learn it all for the tests. You can't get around that . . . but, what you retain . . . (Sam).

You remember it for the test and then you're not under any pressure to remember it (Todd).

Especially if it's the last class you've got to take (Sam).

So what kinds of things do you remember for the tests (Interviewer)?

Junk (Todd).

It's mostly facts and not theories and stuff. Like history, you know dates and people and after my mid-term I don't think I could go back to my mid-term and name those people again. I mean I probably could, but if it was last semester that I took it I don't think I could (Mary).

It's all memorization. I mean that's all it really is. There are not theories . . . it's like, it's just facts. So it's a different kind of learning. In science, you can't memorize. If you can, you have a good memory. (laughter) You have to understand a lot of stuff. These other classes, you don't have to understand, you just have to be able to put it on paper. That's all you have to do (Sam).

Others, such as Jeff, an honors humanities student, had more positive attitudes and acknowledged the importance of assuming some of the responsibility for what he learned himself.

You try to get interested and get something out of it. . . . I took chemistry 184 and 188 and that's been my only class that was huge lecture type and a lot of people complained about that, but see I got a lot out of those classes too. . . . you can either be a passive person where you expect the instructor to tell you something, where he's the only one that's going to be able to teach you versus an active learner. Not so much active in class. I mean you read your stuff and everything.

In summary, students interviewed for this study understood that the intentions of general education were to make them into well-rounded individuals who know a little bit about a lot of things and who can carry on intelligent conversations with people around them. Students did not expect or want too much detail in their general education courses, but detail was what they indicated they received. General education was only somewhat facetiously described by some students as good preparation to play the games *Jeopardy* or *Trivial Pursuit*. Further, students reported being rewarded for memorizing material rather than for solving problems or thinking critically. Although a variety of factors were credited as having contributed to students' perspectives, teachers were noticeable by their absence in the reports of university students. Community college students were much more likely to attribute their perspectives, in part at least, to teachers. Strategies for choosing general education courses and for studying were very similar across majors and were not surprising. Perhaps stemming from the belief that the purpose of general education is to make one well-rounded, the most important criteria for choosing courses was interest. Only in two cases did students indicate that they assessed their own strengths and weaknesses and made choices of courses in order to compensate for the gaps. Both the students were somewhat unusual. Jeff, an honors humanities major, had a straight 4.0 GPA, and the other student, a prospective business major, was described by his professor as very atypical.

Discussion and Recommendations for Further Study

In this exploratory study I set out to identify students perspectives toward general education. That is, how did students at one university understand, interpret, and give meaning to general education; and what academic strategies did they use to approach general education? Additionally, because perspectives are influenced by various institutional conditions such as the actions of faculty and the major, I was particularly interested in whether major seemed to affect perspectives. In this section I will first discuss students' perspectives, focusing particularly on students' understandings of general education and their strategies for dealing with this component of the curriculum. Throughout this discussion the effects of major will be noted. Then I will discuss student-identified influences on their perspectives as well as institutional influences.

Although students understood general education as having educational, instrumental, personal, and negative purposes, it was clear that the educational purposes—namely, to make them into well-rounded, more broadly educated people—were the most widely held and valued by university students. Regardless of major, most students seemed to recognize the importance of having some basic and general knowledge that would enable them to communicate with other people. This study provides preliminary support for the argument that prospective major has an impact on students' views about the purposes of general education. In part at least this seems to be related to students' conceptions of their future lives as professionals.

Notes

1. In his discussion of general education, David D. Levine (1989, 96) suggests institutional purposes and goals for general education that were not specifically considered in this study.

2. Despite the greater flexibility of the bachelor of general studies degree only 25 percent of the graduates from CLAS earn this degree, compared to 65 percent who earn the B.A. and 10 percent who earn the B.S. degrees.

3. One of the unintended findings from this study was just how difficult it is to solicit student participation in such a body. Few business students participated and although a few quotes from them are included in this paper there was not enough information to draw any conclusions about the relationship between general education and a business major.

References

Andersen, Margaret. (1988). "Changing the Curriculum in Higher Education." In E. Minnich, J. O'Barr, and R. Rosenfeld (eds.), *Reconstructing the Academy*. Chicago: University of Chicago Press, 1988.

Baxter-Magolda, Marcia. (1991). "A Gender Inclusive Model of Epistemological Development." Paper presented at annual meeting of AERA, Chicago.

Becker, Howard, Blanche Geer, and C. Everett Hughes. (1968). *Making the Grade: The Academic Side of College Life*. New York: John Wiley and Sons.

Belenky, Mary F., Blythe Clinchy, Nancy Goldberger, and Jill Tarule. (1986). *Women's Ways of Knowing: The Development of Self, Voice, and Mind*. New York: Basic Books.

Bogdan, Robert, and Sari Biklen. (1982). *Qualitative Research for Education*. Boston: Allyn and Bacon.

Gaff, Jerry, and Michael Davis. (1981). "Student Views of General Education," Liberal Education Summer: 112.

Giroux, Henry. (1988). *Schooling and the Struggle for Public Life*. Minneapolis University of Minnesota Press.

Hefferlin, J. Lon. (1969). *The Dynamics of Academic Reform*. San Francisco: Jossey-Bass.

Howe, Florence. (1984). *Myths of Coeducation*. Bloomington: University of Indiana Press.

Hutchings, Pat. (1990). "Learning Over Time: Portfolio Assessment." *AAHE Bulletin*, 42, 8:6–8.

Johnston, Joseph Jr., Robert Reardon, Gary Kramer, Janet Lenz, Alexandra Maduros, and James Sampson, Jr. (1991). "The Demand Side of General Education: Attending to Student Attitudes and Understandings. *Journal of General Education* 40: 180–200.

Kimball, Bruce. (1988). "The Historical and Cultural Dimensions of the Recent Reports." *American Journal of Education* 98: 293–322.

Krueger, Richard. (1988). *Focus Groups*. Beverly Hills, Calif: Sage Publications.

Levine, David. (1986). *The American College and the Culture of Aspiration, 1915–1940*. Ithaca, N.Y.: Cornell University Press.

Light, Richard. (1992). The Harvard Assessment Seminars: Second Report. Cambridge: Harvard University.

Marsh, Peter. (1988). *Contesting the Boundaries of Liberal and Professional Education*. Syracuse, N.Y.: Syracuse University Press.

McIntosh, Peggy. (1983). "Interactive Phases of Curricular Re-vision: A Feminist Perspective." Working Paper Series, no. 124. Wellesley, MA: Wellesley College Center for Research on Women.

Richardson, Richard, Elizabeth Fisk, and Morris Okun. (1983). *Literacy in the Open-Access College*. San Francisco: Jossey-Bass.

Sagen, Bradley (1979). "Career, Competencies, and liberal Education. *Liberal Education* 65: 150–66.

Sagen, Bradley, (1973). "Education for the Professions: A Neglected Model for Undergraduate Education." *Liberal Education* 59: 507–19.

Spear, Karen, (1989). "Sources of Strain in Liberal Education." *The Review of Higher Education* 12: 389–401.

Stark, Joan, and Malcolm Lowther. (1990). "Exploring Common Ground in Liberal and Professional Education." In C. Conrad and J. Haworth (Eds.), *Curriculum in Transition: Perspectives on the Undergraduate Experience.* ASHE Reader Series, Needham Heights, Mass.: Ginn Press.

Stark, Joan, Malcolm Lowther, and Bonnie Hagerty. (1986). *Responsive Professional Education.* ASHE-ERIC Reports No. 3, Washington, D.C.: Association for the Study of Higher Education.

Tierney, William. 1989. "Cultural Politics and the Curriculum in Postsecondary Education." In C. Conrad and J. Haworth (Eds.), "Curriculum in Transition: Perspectives on the Undergraduate Experience." ASHE Reader Series. Needham Heights, Mass.: Ginn Press.

Wright, Barbara. (1990). "But How Do We Know It'll Work?" *AAHE Bulletin* 42(8): 14–17.

Connected Teaching

Mary Field Belenky, Blythe McVicker Clinchy, Nancy Rule Goldberger and Jill Mattuck Tarule

It is time for the voice of the mother to be heard in education.

—Nel Noddings, *Caring*

Sharing the Process

Paulo Freire describes traditional education as "banking": The teacher's role is "to 'fill' the students by making deposits of information which the teacher considers to constitute true knowledge" (1971, p. 63). The student's job is merely to "store the deposits."

The banking concept distinguishes two stages in the action of the educator. During the first, he cognizes a cognizable object while he prepares his lessons in his study or his laboratory; during the second, he expounds to his students about that object. The students are not called upon to know, but to memorize the contents narrated by the teacher. Nor do the students practice any act of cognition, since the object towards which that act should be directed is the property of the teacher. (pp. 67-68)

Although none of the institutions in our sample adhered closely to the banking model, our interviews contain poignant accounts of occasions on which teachers seemed trapped against their will into the banker role. The teacher who invited Faith and her classmates to "rip into" his interpretation of *The Turn of the Screw* is a case in point. It is easy to feel compassion for this beleaguered man. He has probably toiled much of the previous night over his interpretation. He is excited about it and imagines that the students, too, will get excited. He imagines hands waving, voices raised in passionate debate. Instead, he sees rows of bowed heads, hears only the scratching of twenty-five pencils. The teacher does not wish to deposit his words in the students' notebooks, but the students insist upon storing them there. They treat his words as sacrosanct. He cannot understand why they will not risk a response.

But the teacher himself takes few risks. True to the banking concept, he composes his thoughts in private. The students are permitted to see the product of his thinking, but the process of gestation is hidden from view. The lecture appears as if by magic. The teacher asks his students to take risks he is unwilling—although presumably more able—to take himself. He invites the students to find holes in his argument, but he has taken pains to make it airtight. He would regard as scandalous a suggestion that he make the argument more permeable. He has, after all, his "standards," the standards of his discipline, to uphold, and he is proud of the rigor of his interpretation. The students admire it, too. It would seem to them an act of vandalism to "rip into" an object that is, as Freire might say, so clearly the teacher's private property.

A woman needs to know, one alumna said, that her own ideas can be "very good" and "thoroughly reliable," that a theory is "something that somebody thought up, and that's all that a

469

theory is. It's not this mysterious thing only Einstein could figure out." Because they are in positions of power, teachers who speak in their own voices risk turning their students' voices into echoes of their own. On the other hand, the utterly objective, "disembodied" voice carries its own dangers. Rich quotes a university teacher of psychology:

> It seems to me that the form of many communications in academia, both written and verbal, is such as to not only obscure the influence of the personal or subjective but also to give the impression of divine origin—a mystification composed of syballine statements—from beings supposedly emptied of the "dross" of the self. (1979, p. 144)

So long as teachers hide the imperfect processes of their thinking, allowing their students to glimpse only the polished products, students will remain convinced that only Einstein—or a professor—could think up a theory.

The problem is especially acute with respect to science. Science is usually taught by males and is regarded as the quintessentially masculine intellectual activity. And science is taught—or, at least, it is heard by students in most introductory courses—as a series of syballine statements. The professor is not indulging in conjecture; he is telling the truth. And, in one of the most shocking statements in all our hundreds of pages of transcripts, a student concluded that "science is not a creation of the human mind."

Simone, one of our most sophisticated science students, said in an interview during her first year at college that you had to "accept at face value" anything a chemistry professor said. By her senior year Simone had come to realize that the professors had been talking not about facts but about models, although they presented the information as if it were fact. "Why do they do that?" we asked. "I don't know," Simone replied. "Maybe they think you wouldn't believe them otherwise. Maybe they do tell you that it's a model, and you just say, 'Oh, well, it must be true,' because a professor is telling you. I mean, he has a Ph.D. Who am I to argue?"

Simone was wise enough to wonder if she might have misheard the professors, but her story suggests that it is especially critical that teachers of science do all that they can to avoid the appearance of omniscience. Between the scientific expert and the layman, says the feminist scholar Elizabeth Fee, there is rarely any dialogue: "The voice of the scientific authority is like the male voice-over in commercials, a disembodied knowledge that cannot be questioned, whose author is inaccessible" (1983, p. 19).

The revelation that professors are not omnipotent, that "they're groping too" comes to Perry's hero at the end of the developmental story. After years of struggling to compose term papers worthy of his professors' praise, the student realizes that the process the professor goes through in writing his books—and even, perhaps, his lectures—resembles closely the process he himself undergoes in writing a term paper. The path that Perry traces, laid out by Harvard, is a tortuous one: Our teachers appear to us first in the guise of gods and are later revealed to be human. We think the revelation might occur sooner if those of us who teach could find the courage—and the institutional support—to think out loud with our students.

It can be argued, of course, that students need models of impeccable reasoning, that it is through imitating such models that students learn to reason. But none of the women we interviewed named this sort of learning as a powerful experience in their own lives. They did mention the deflation of authority as a powerful learning experience. Recall Faith, who learned, through catching her high school teacher in an error about Mount Everest, that teachers' words should not be accepted at "face value." Another student said she felt emancipated when she told her teacher she could not understand a book she was reading and the teacher replied, "Oh, yeah, I know the guy who wrote it. He's an asshole." The student had not realized that authors could be people, let alone assholes, and she was pleased to be disillusioned.

Women have been taught by generations of men that males have greater powers of rationality than females have. When a male professor presents only the impeccable products of his thinking, it is especially difficult for a woman student to believe that she can produce such a thought. And remember that in the groves of academe, in spite of the women's movement most of the teachers are still male, although more than half of the students are now female. Women students need opportunities to watch women professors solve (and fail to solve) problems and male professors fail to solve (and succeed in solving) problems. They need models of thinking as a human, imperfect, and attainable activity.

The Teacher as Midwife

None of the women we interviewed wanted a system in which knowledge flowed in only one direction, from teacher to student. Even those who were most respectful of authority wished to be treated at least as containers of knowledge rather than empty receptacles. The community college student who said she "needed to listen to an instructor from the beginning right through to the end" added in the next breath, "I don't really think that anybody can really put something into someone that isn't there. It has to be there."

Many women expressed—some firmly, some shakily—a belief that they possessed latent knowledge. The kind of teacher they praised and the kind for which they yearned was one who would help them articulate and expand their latent knowledge: a midwife-teacher. Midwife-teachers are the opposite of banker-teachers. While the bankers deposit knowledge in the learner's head, the midwives draw it out. They assist the students in giving birth to their own ideas, in making their own tacit knowledge explicit and elaborating it.

"Banking education anesthetizes," Freire says; it "attempts to maintain the *submersion* of consciousness" (1971, p. 68). When anesthesia is administered to a woman in childbirth, the woman becomes, as McMillan says, "a passive spectator" of the birth of her child. She cannot participate actively because she cannot feel the contractions in the uterus. The physician "usurps the woman's natural role during childbirth as *he* now 'gives birth' to the baby with the aid of an array of technological devices" (1982, p. 135). Midwife-teachers do not administer anesthesia. They support their students' thinking, but they do not do the students' thinking for them or expect the students to think as they do.

Like Freire's partner-teachers, midwife-teachers assist in the emergence of consciousness. They encourage the students to speak in their own active voices.

> She helped me to be able to say what I wanted to say and not worry about whether it was getting too personal. Last semester I started having troubles with being too vague in my papers and using the passive voice a lot, and she hit it right on the head that I was being afraid to come out and say it, say "I believe that this and this and this happened in 1692," or whatever.

In "maternal thinking" Ruddick (1980) says the primary concern is preservation of the vulnerable child. The midwife-teacher's first concern is to preserve the student's fragile newborn thoughts, to see that they are born with their truth intact, that they do not turn into acceptable lies.

The second concern in maternal thinking is to foster the child's growth. Connected teachers support the evolution of their students' thinking.[1] A strikingly high proportion of the women's accounts of teachers who had helped took this form. The teacher said to the student something like Faith's teacher said to her: "What you're thinking is fine, but think more." The teacher did not tell Faith to replace her thought with a different thought but only to "think more," to let the thought grow.

Deborah's high-school English teacher praised her poetry. "She just let me do what I wanted to do and helped me do it, and pushed it further." Deborah's teacher helped her make her private words public; she put her in connection with the culture. She urged Deborah also to "send it someplace, see what they'll do with it. 'Will they give you a prize for it? Will they publish it?' That was when I first began to realize that what I was writing was worth something, that it wasn't just something I did to stay sane."

Midwife-teachers focus not on their own knowledge (as the lecturer does) but on the students' knowledge. They contribute when needed, but it is always clear that the baby is not theirs but the student's. A senior at one of the experimental colleges told us about her thesis adviser, who, she said, "epitomizes the school." The adviser never told her what to do. She read what the student wrote, discussed the writing with her, and suggested something she might want to read. "It's sort of worked back and forth like that. I've followed up her suggestions, which have given me new ideas, but it's been mostly my own work which has been generated in each step." The cycle is one of confirmation-evocation-confirmation. Midwife-teachers help students deliver their words to the world, and they use their own knowledge to put the students into conversation with other voices—past and present—in the culture.

Midwife-teachers encourage students to use their knowledge in everyday life. Women spoke often of their need for "practical" information, ranging from the most obviously and immediately useful (facts on child rearing, how to dress for a job interview) to seemingly remote matters. A Greek drama read and only dimly understood in college rested in one woman's memory for years, rising to offer her solace upon the death of her child. A community college student, veteran of the streets of Spanish Harlem, credited a philosophy course with saving her from being mugged. "There was this teenager ready to mug me. I remember thinking so fast. I could do one of three things. I could scream, which is no good; no one's going to hear me. I could run away, but he'd catch me in a minute. Or I can face up to him. That's exactly what I did." She pretended she had a weapon, talked a fast line of street talk, and convinced the boy to let her alone. "If I hadn't been taking philosophy at that time I wouldn't even have said I had three choices. The whole course was about choices."

Connected Classes

In Freire's "problem-posing" method, the object of knowledge is not the private property of the teacher. Rather, it is "a medium evoking the critical reflection of both teacher and students." Instead of the teacher thinking about the object privately and talking about it publicly so that the students may store it, both teacher and students engage in the process of thinking, and they talk out what they are thinking in a public dialogue. As they think and talk together, their roles merge. "Through dialogue, the teacher-of-the-students and the students-of-the-teacher cease to exist and a new term emerges: teacher-student with students-teachers" (1971, p. 67).

Several women cherished memories of classes in which such dialogue had occurred. Bess described an English course that the teacher usually conducted in the banking mode: "He just hands you his thoughts." On one memorable occasion, however, he allowed a discussion to erupt.

> We were all raising our hands and talking about I forget what book, and some of the students brought up things that he hadn't thought about that made him see it in a whole different way, and he was really excited, and we all came to a conclusion that none of us had started out with. We came up with an answer to a question we thought was unanswerable in the beginning, and it just made you all feel really good when you walked out of class. You felt you had accomplished something and that you understood the book. And he was pleased, too.

Rushing eagerly into the classroom at the next meeting, Bess found to her dismay that the professor had returned to his podium. "I guess he doesn't like that method," she said.

At this traditional, elite institution the students had to adapt to whatever method the teacher chose. Another, older sophomore in an experimental adult program told us quite a different story about a "stern" new teacher who tried to lecture. The students soon set him straight. "We really wanted to be very involved and we wanted to talk as much as he did, and it took him a while to understand that. He kind of rebelled at that because he felt that the other way would be better. He was good after that, but it took a while."

Once the midwife draws a woman's knowledge out into the world, the third concern of maternal thinking becomes central. Ruddick writes, "The mother must shape natural growth in such a way that her child becomes the sort of adult that she can appreciate and others can accept." Typically, the mother "takes as the criterion of her success the production of a young adult acceptable to her group" (1980, p. 107). If a woman is to consider herself a real knower she must find acceptance for her ideas in the public world. Bridget's bleak praise of her college comes to mind.

> In a very unusual way, perhaps it was the right place for me to go. The first time I ever was not a wonder child, a superachiever, the apple of everybody's eye, the blue-ribbon kid, was

when I got there. I never realized until I got there how I had based my own sense of worthiness on everybody else's estimation of what I was. Suddenly it was like that support that I had used was whisked out. I didn't have everybody else's approval, so it had to come from some other source. Myself. So in a way, it was probably the most valuable place I could ever have gone to, because it forced that kind of individual growth. But it's not a goal of the school.

The connected class provides a culture for growth—as Elbow (1973) says, a "yoghurt" class, as opposed to a "movie" class (in which students are spectators). The connected teacher tries to create groups in which members can nurture each other's thoughts to maturity. A college senior told us about an art seminar in which each student was to arrive at approaches to art that seemed most useful to her. The senior tried to define the atmosphere the teacher had established that made the seminar so special. "It's allowing everyone to voice things that they think are uncertain. It's allowing people to realize that they're not stupid for questioning things. It's okay to say 'Why?' or 'How?' or 'What?' I think it's important to let everybody voice their uncertainties."

In a connected class no one apologizes for uncertainty. It is assumed that evolving thought will be tentative. Spacks, writing about feminist criticism, argues that women can mimic a masculine authority rooted in "a universal systematic methodology" and therefore speak with certainty, but we can also try to construct a different sort of authority, based on personal individual experience and acknowledging "the uncertainties implicit in an approach which values the personal" (1981, p. 16).[2]

The discussion that erupted in Bess's English class was not a debate between finished interpretations. It was a conversation in which teacher and students collaborated in constructing a new interpretation. It is this sort of class that women remember with pleasure. Marilyn Rands, who teaches at a women's college, encourages students in her innovative social psychology course to use a variety of formats in making their presentations. Not one student has ever chosen the debate.[3] In a "woman-centered university," Adrienne Rich says, more courses would be conducted in the style of community, fewer in the "masculine adversary style of discourse," which has dominated much of Western education (1979, p. 138).

In a community, unlike a hierarchy, people get to know each other. They do not act as representatives of positions or as occupants of roles but as individuals with particular styles of thinking. A first-year undergraduate remarked that her editing group composed of three classmates in a writing course was not working.

> We just talk about commas and junk like that. I had a peer editing group in high school, and it was terrific. But we all knew each other inside out, so you knew what each person was trying to do in her writing and you knew what kinds of criticisms helped her and what kind hurt her feelings. You can't really help if you don't know people.

Unless she knew the critic personally and the critic knew her personally, she found criticism of her work "hurtful but not helpful"; and she found the concept of "blind grading" simply incomprehensible.

Our vision of a connected class follows directly from our conception of connected epistemology. Norman Holland, a teacher of literature who shares our epistemological assumptions, describes the epistemological assumptions underlying many literature courses.

> People often speak as though the literary work or, in general, some other existed in all its fullness, while I perceive that fullness imperfectly, subtracting out certain aspects. It is as though my perception of the other equaled the other minus something. . . . Thinking this way leads to images like the prison of the self or the limits of what I can see, or the risk, even the peril of interpreting wrongly. All such discomfort proceeds from the debilitating assumption that each of us experiences something imperfectly and someone else knows just how imperfectly. (1975, pp. 281–82)

Given such a model, students in such a class must inevitably "measure their words" in an attempt to avoid disgrace. The model is, as Holland says, both "confusing and discouraging," because "we cannot suddenly know more" (p. 282). We cannot stop being ourselves or step out of ourselves. As one woman told us, "I live within myself. I know only through myself."

"All this confusion and sense of limitation and loss," Holland says, "comes from positing a literary work or, in general, an other which is full and complete and from which we subtract" (p. 282). Suppose that instead of asking what readers fail to see (what they subtract from the text in constructing their own experience of it), we start not with the text but with the students and ask, as Holland suggests, what they are adding to themselves by the act of reading. When teachers and students learn to ask this question of each other, to respect and to enter into each other's unique perspectives, the connected class comes into being.

The connected class recognizes the core of truth in the subjectivist view that each of us has a unique perspective that is in some sense irrefutably "right" by virtue of its existence. But the connected class transforms these private truths into "objects," publicly available to the members of the class who, through "stretching and sharing," add to themselves as knowers by absorbing in their own fashion their classmates' ideas.

The connected class constructs truth not through conflict but through "consensus," whose original meaning, Holland reminds us, was "feeling or sensing together," implying not agreement, necessarily, but a "crossing of the barrier between ego and ego," bridging private and shared experience (p. 291).

Objectivity in Connected Teaching

Connected teachers try to discern the truth inside the students. It is essential that the search be disinterested. A fifty-four-year-old mother of six in her second term at an adult program said,

> I keep discovering things inside myself. I see myself for the first time through the eyes of others. In the past, whenever I've seen myself through the eyes of others it's been another that I cared a great deal about, who had the power to destroy me, and usually did. Now I see myself through the eyes of others who matter, but not that closely. I'm not entwined with them emotionally. I feel that it's a truer thing that I'm getting back from these people.

Several women spontaneously remarked that in this adult program they were able for the first time since childhood to initiate a conversation, because they knew that they would be listened to in their own terms. "Everyone wants what's best for me," said one.

Connected teachers welcome diversity of opinion in class discussion. Many of the women we interviewed spoke with appreciation of teachers who refrained from "inflicting" (a common term) their own opinions on the students. Elizabeth remembered a Bible course as "just great."

> We had Baptists and we had Jews in there and we had atheists in there. We had people with just absolute disregard for humanity in there. And all of us could contribute and learn something and gain something because he could tolerate so many different views. I think that's a mark of excellence, the ability to accept dissent from your own opinion.

Objectivity in connected teaching, as in connected knowing, means seeing the other, the student, in the student's own terms. Noddings contrasts separate and connected (in her terms, "caring") approaches to teaching.

> Suppose, for example, that I am a teacher who loves mathematics. I encounter a student who is doing poorly, and I decide to have a talk with him. He tells me that he hates mathematics. I do not begin with dazzling performances designed to intrigue him or to change his attitude. I begin, as nearly as I can, with the view from his eyes: Mathematics is bleak, jumbled, scary, boring, boring, boring. From that point on, we struggle together with it. (1984, pp 15-16)

In traditional separate education, the student tries to look at the material through the teacher's eyes. In contrast, the caring teacher "receives and accepts the student's feeling toward the subject matter; she looks at it and listens to it through his eyes and ears." She acts "as if for herself," but in the interests of the student's projects, realizing that the student is "independent, a subject"

(Noddings 1984, p. 177). In the developmental story Perry tells, the student becomes an independent thinker through executing the teacher's projects in the teacher's own terms. Connected education follows a straighter path: The student is treated from the start not as subordinate or as object but as "independent, a subject."

Teaching can be simultaneously objective and personal. There is no inherent contradiction, so long as objectivity is not defined as self-extrication. Connected teachers use a technique similar to the "participant-observation" method anthropologists use. Participant-observers maintain "a dynamic tension" between the separate stance of an observer and the connected, "subjective" stance of a participant, being "neither one entirely" (Wilson 1977, p. 250).[4] Reinharz (1984) found the participant-observation method uncomfortable for precisely this reason; investigating friendships among patients in a mental hospital she felt herself to be in an anomalous position, neither truly attached nor truly detached from her subjects, a stranger in their midst. In a subsequent field project in an Israeli town she and her colleagues on the research team coined the phrase "temporary affiliation" to describe their modification of the participant-observation method. This term, Reinharz thinks, better captures the "human mutuality" that should characterize the relationship between researchers and their informants. The researchers act as "short-term partners" who give the informants a chance to be heard and provide feedback to them. For a brief period, researcher and subject meet on common turf, each "truly being with the other."

Noddings describes the relation between caring teachers and their students in similar terms. "I do not need to establish a lasting, time-consuming personal relationship with every student. What I must do is to be totally and nonselectively present to the student—to each student—as he addresses me. The time interval may be brief but the encounter is total" (p. 180).

Portrait of a Connected Teacher

Candace remembered an English professor at the women's college who could serve as an ideal prototype of a connected teacher. Candace was "moved" by this woman's "rigorous" approach to teaching. "You had to assume that there was a purpose to everything the writer did. And if something seemed odd, you couldn't overlook it or ignore it or throw it out." This teacher was thoroughly "objective" in treating the students' responses as real and independent of her own.

> She was intensely, genuinely interested in everybody's feelings about things. She asked a question and wanted to know what your response was. She wanted to know because she wanted to see what sort of effect this writing was having. She wasn't using us as a sounding board for her own feelings about things. She really wanted to know.

She was careful not to use the students to "develop her own argument."

Candace recalled with special vividness an occasion when the teacher became embroiled in a real argument with a student and stubbornly refused to hear the student's point.

> And she came in the next day and said, "You know, my response to this student was being governed by my own biases." And she learned from that, she said, how she really did feel about something, and then she related it actually to the work we were studying. And it was just so wonderful, so amazing that somebody would realize—in this theater of the classroom—that she was fully engaged in what was going on.

This teacher managed not only to present herself as a person while retaining her objectivity but to present objectivity as a personal issue. By her actions as well as her words she made it clear that to overlook or ignore or throw out a piece of data or another person's words was a violation of her own person. And the violation itself became another piece of data not to be overlooked or ignored or thrown out. Instead, it had to be acknowledged in full view of the class, understood, and even used to illuminate the material the class was studying. The personal became the professional; the professional became the personal. And subjectivity and objectivity became one. The anthropologist Mary Catherine Bateson, attempting to define the method of participant-observation, writes,

These resonances between the personal and the professional are the source of both insight and error. You avoid mistakes and distortions not so much by trying to build a wall between the observer and the observed as by observing the observer—observing yourself—as well, and bringing the personal issues into consciousness. (1984, p. 161)

Investigators who use this sort of method, whether they label it "participant-observation" as Bateson does or "experiential analysis" as Reinharz (1984) does, practice a sophisticated form of connected knowing, a "technique of *disciplined* subjectivity" (Erikson 1964) requiring that they "systematically empathize with the participants" (Wilson 1977, p. 259). They participate in the enterprise they are studying in order to undergo experiences similar to those of the other participants, placing themselves in a better position to understand the experiences of the other participants. They use their own reactions to formulate hypotheses about the other participants' reactions.

Candace's English teacher behaved in a similar way. She did not treat her own experience of the material under study as primary, and she did not assume that her students experienced the material as she did; this would be undisciplined subjectivity or, in Elbow's words, "projection in the bad sense" (1973, p. 171). She really wanted to know how the students were experiencing the material. As a teacher, she believed she had to trust each student's experience, although as a person or a critic she might not agree with it. To trust means not just to tolerate a variety of viewpoints, acting as an impartial referee, assuring equal air time to all. It means to try to connect, to enter into each student's perspective.

But, again, subjectivity is disciplined. Like the participant-observer, the connected teacher is careful not to "abandon" herself to these perspectives (Wilson 1977, p. 259). A connected teacher is not just another student; the role carries special responsibilities. It does not entail power over the students; however, it does carry authority, an authority based not on subordination but on cooperation.

Belief, Doubt, and Development

Connected teachers are believers. They trust their students' thinking and encourage them to expand it. But in the psychological literature concerning the factors promoting cognitive development, doubt has played a more prominent role than belief. People are said to be precipitated into states of cognitive conflict when, for example, some external event challenges their ideas and the effort to resolve the conflict leads to cognitive growth.[5] We do not deny that cognitive conflict can act as an impetus to growth; all of us can attest to such experiences in our own lives. But in our interviews only a handful of women described a powerful and positive learning experience in which a teacher aggressively challenged their notions. The midwife model was much more prominent.

This could be interpreted to mean that the midwife model was more prominent than the conflict model in the institutions we sampled, but we do not think so. Women did tell of occasions when teachers challenged their ideas—and we have retold some in this book—but they did not describe them as occasions for cognitive growth. On the whole, women found the experience of being doubted debilitating rather than energizing. Several women said that they and their friends left school as soon as they legally could, married, and got pregnant (not necessarily in that order) "so that we wouldn't have to put up with being put down every day."

Because so many women are already consumed with self-doubt, doubts imposed from outside seem at best redundant and at worst destructive, confirming the women's own sense of themselves as inadequate knowers. The doubting model, then, may be peculiarly inappropriate for women, although we are not convinced that it is appropriate for men, either.

Both the authoritarian banking model and the adversarial doubting model of education are, we believe, wrong for women. Freire says that if we abandon the banking model in favor of the problem-posing model, we will "undermine the power of oppression" (1971, p. 62). If we replace the separate with the connected model, we can spare women the "alienation, repression, and division" their schooling currently confers upon them (Jacobus 1979, p. 10). Education conducted on the connected model would help women toward community, power, and integrity. Such an education could facilitate the development of women's minds and spirits rather than, as in so many cases reported in this book, retarding, arresting, or even reversing their growth.

Women's Development as the Aim of Education

Some years ago, in a now classic paper called "Development as the Aim of Education," Kohlberg and Mayer suggested that the proper purpose of education was to assist students in moving toward more mature stages of intellectual, epistemological, and ethical development. They argued that this sort of education did not entail indoctrination, because it merely stimulated children in the "natural directions" of development (1972, p. 475).

We found this argument compelling at the time, and we still believe in development as the aim of education; but parts of the Kohlberg-Mayer argument now make us uneasy. It turns out, of course, that those "natural directions" in which all human beings supposedly head are toward principled moral judgment and an epistemology based on standard (and separate) "principles of scientific method" serving "as the basis of rational reflection" (p. 475).

Along with many of our colleagues, we believed at the time that psychologists such as Piaget and Kohlberg had established through empirical investigation that these were the universal and natural trajectories in human development. And we believed that they had discovered effective strategies for "moving" students to more advanced levels, such as instigating moral arguments among students at varying stages (the adversarial model) and exposing students to real or fictional people making statements at a slightly more sophisticated stage ("plus-one-model"). Most of the research on these matters had, of course, been done by and "on" males.

Since the publication of Kohlberg's paper, research by, with, and for women has increased. (We like to think less work is being done "on" women.) This research suggests that the directions then assumed to be natural do not come naturally to many women. Gilligan (1982) and Lyons (1983) have demonstrated that an ethic of responsibility may be more "natural" to most women than an ethic of rights. We believe that connected knowing comes more easily to many women than does separate knowing.

We have argued in this book that educators can help women develop their own authentic voices if they emphasize connection over separation, understanding and acceptance over assessment, and collaboration over debate; if they accord respect to and allow time for the knowledge that emerges from firsthand experience; if instead of imposing their own expectations and arbitrary requirements, they encourage students to evolve their own patterns of work based on the problems they are pursuing. These are the lessons we have learned in listening to women's voices.

Notes

1. Freire writes, "Problem-posing education affirms men as beings in the process of *becoming*—as unfinished, uncompleted beings" (1971, p. 72).

2. Catherine Stimpson, a pioneer in the development of women's studies, writes, "We need to find a judicious balance between the claims of personal authority and the waste of reinventing the wheel that occurs when non-personal authority is rejected" (1978, p. 17).

3. Personal communication, October 1984.

4. Those who believe that the social sciences should mimic the natural science stance of "objective outsider" criticize participant-observation for its subjectivity. But in a sense the participant-observer is less subjectivist than is the traditional empiricist. The sociologist Sylvaner Bruyn points out that "the traditional empiricist considers himself (as a scientist) to be the primary source of knowledge, and trusts his own senses and logic more than he would trust that of his subjects. The participant observer, on the other hand, considers the interpretations of his subjects to have first importance" (1966, p 12)

5. On the role of cognitive conflict in learning see Cantor (1983), Langer (1969), Moessinger (1978), Murray (1983a, 1983b), Zimmerman and Blom (1983a, 1983b). For critical commentary on the "disequilibration studies" of moral development, see Rest (1983). For recent theory and research on the effect of conflict among peers on psychological growth, see Berkowitz (1985).

References

Bateson, M. C. (1984). *With a Daughter's Eye*. New York: William Morrow.

Berkowitz, M. 5. (Ed.). (1985). *Peer Conflict and Psychological Growth*. San Francisco: Jossey-Bass.

Bruyn, S. (1966). *Human Perspective in Sociology*. Englewood Cliffs, NJ: Prentice-Hall.

Cantor, G. (1983). "Conflict, Learning, and Piaget: Comments on Zimmerman and Blom's 'Toward an Empirical Test of the Role of Cognitive Conflict in Learning.'" *Developmental Review, 3,* 39–53.

Elbow, P. (1973). *Writing Without Teachers*. London: Oxford University Press.

Fee, E. (1983). "Women's Nature and Scientific Objectivity." In M. Loew and R. Hubbard (Eds.), *Woman's Nature: Rationalizations of Inequality* (pp. 9–27). New York: Pergamon Press.

Freire, P. (1971). *Pedagogy of the Oppressed*. New York: Seaview.

Gilligan, C. (1982). *In a Different Voice: Psychological Theory and Women's Development*. Cambridge, MA: Harvard University Press.

Holland, N. N. (1975). *Five Readers Reading*. New Haven: Yale University Press.

Kohlberg, L., & Mayer, R. (1972). "Development as the Aim of Education." *Harvard Educational Review, 42,* 449–496.

Langer, J (1969). "Disequilibrium as a Source of Development." In P. Mussen, J. Langer, & M. Covington (Eds.), *Trends and Issues in Developmental Psychology*. New York: Holt, Rinehart & Winston.

Lyons, N. (1983). "Two Perspectives on Self, Relationships and Morality." *Harvard Educational Review, 53,* 125–145.

McMillan, C. (1982). *Women, Reason, and Nature*. Princeton, NJ: Princeton University Press.

Moessinger, P. (1978). "Piaget on Equilibration." *Human Development, 21,* 255–267.

Murray, F. B., (1983a). "Equilibration as Cognitive Conflict." *Developmental Review, 3,* 54–61.

Murray, F. B. (1983b). "Learning and Development Through Social Interaction and Conflict: A Challenge to Social Learning Theory." In Liben, L. (Ed.), *Piaget and the Foundations of Knowledge*. Hillsdale, NJ: Lawrence Erlbaum.

Noddings, N. (1984). *Caring*. Berkeley, CA: University of California Press.

Reinharz, S. (1984). *On Becoming a Social Scientist*. New Brunswick, NJ: Transaction.

Rest, J. (1983). "Morality." In J. H. Flavell and E. M. Markman (Eds.), *Cognitive Development*: Vol. 3. of P. H. Mussen (Ed.), *Handbook of Child Psychology* (4th ed.). New York: John Wiley & Sons.

Rich, A. (1979). *On Lies, Secrets, and Silence: Selected Prose—1966–78*. New York: Norton.

Ruddick, S. (1980). "Maternal Thinking." *Feminist Studies, 6,* 70–96. Reprinted in A. Cafagna, R. Peterson, & C. Staudenbaur (Eds.). (1982). *Child Nurturance: Volume 1, Philosophy, Children, and the Family*. New York: Plenum Press.

Spacks, P. (1981). "The Difference It Makes." In E. Langland and W. Gove (Eds.), *A Feminist Perspective in the Academy* (pp. 7–24). Chicago: University of Chicago Press.

Stimpson, C. (1978, May). "Women's Studies: An Overview." *Ann Arbor Papers in Women's Studies* (Special Issue), pp. 14–26.

Wilson, S. (1977). "The Use of Ethnographic Techniques in Educational Research." *Review of Educational Research, 47,* 245–265.

Zimmerman, B J., & Blom, D.E.(1983a). "On Resolving Conflicting Views of Cognitive Conflict." *Developmental Review, 3,* 62–72.

Zimmerman, B. J., & Blom, D. E. (1983b). "Toward an Empirical Test of the Role of Cognitive Conflict in Learning." *Developmental Review, 3,* 18–38.

Responding to Differences in the Classroom: The Politics of Knowledge, Class, and Sexuality

SAUNDRA GARDNER, CYNTHIA DEAN, AND DEO MCKAIG

Learning to recognize and value the diversity of women's lives has become a central theme of women's studies. In this article, the authors examine this issue by analyzing the responses of faculty members and students to differences in a variety of feminist classrooms. The analysis suggests that when differences in knowledge, class, or sexuality arise, a hierarchical mode of conceptualizing and responding to differences typically emerges. The authors discuss why this pattern of response occurs and offer suggestions for changing it.

A contemporary challenge to women's studies, as well as to the feminist movement, is to recognize and appreciate the diversity of women's experience (Baca Zinn et al. 1986; Bunch 1985; Cole 1986; Cruikshank 1982; Hooks 1984; Lorde 1984; Moraga and Anzaldua 1981). This shift from an emphasis on commonalities among women to a perspective that also includes differences among them has necessitated a rethinking of feminist theory and has forced many women to explore critically how they and others respond to the issue of difference in their daily lives, including the classroom.

This article examines the personal and interpersonal struggles that arise when differences in knowledge, class, and sexuality become visible in the feminist classroom.[1] We assume, as have others (Bunch and Pollack 1983; Culley and Portugues 1985; Fisher 1982; Geiger and Zita 1985), that the goals and dynamics of such a classroom are to encourage nonhierarchical, mutually supportive, and empowering modes of though and behavior. However, the patterns of interaction that emerge often conflict with this ideology. This schism is intricately tied to how students and faculty members respond to differences that often reinforce patriarchal values rather than those commonly associated with feminism.

Framework

Our analysis of this classroom dynamic is based on Lorde's (1984) framework for redefining differences. In essence, Lorde argued that all people learn to respond to differences out of what may be called a patriarchal consciousness. This mode of thinking is dualistic and hierarchical. Specifically, it "conditions us to see human differences in simplistic opposition to each other: dominant/subordinate, good/bad, up/down, superior/inferior" (Lorde 1984, p. 114). As a consequence, people respond to differences with fear and often deny or distort the meaning of them. Those who are different become outsiders whose experiences are devalued and often ignored or erased.

Thus, for Lorde, it is not differences that divide people but how differences are conceptualized and responded to. To homogenize differences or pretend that everyone is alike will not alter this patriarchal dynamic or create bonds of sisterhood among women. Such changes depend, instead, on the ability to reclaim and redefine differences, which entails learning to view difference as a source of strength, creative energy, and personal power. Only then will women be able to appreciate their differences, learn from them, and use them as a source of collective power for creating social change. However, women must first learn to relate as equals to others who are different. To do so requires that patriarchal consciousness and oppression, both external and internal, be challenged. To root out these internalized patterns of oppression, women must be willing to name and struggle with that "piece of the oppressor which is planted deep within each one of us" (Lorde 1984, p. 123).

The following sections represent our responses to Lorde's challenge. To preserve the differences among us, we wrote the article in three voices. The first section, on differences in knowledge, was written by the first author, who is a faculty member; the second and third sections, on differences in social class and sexuality, were written by the second and third authors, respectively, who are a graduate student and an undergraduate student. The author of each section describes and analyzes her experiences with differences in feminist classrooms. She also recommends changes that will foster new patterns of relating across differences and that will strengthen the integration of theory and practice in these classrooms.

Differences in Knowledge

As teachers, we often find that students vary in their familiarity with the subject of or specific issues presented in a course. My initial experience teaching an introductory course on women's studies was no exception. The class consisted of 35 students, the majority of whom had a strong background in feminism and women's issues. Most had taken two or more women-centered courses, many had been reading about feminism for a number of years, and several were political activists.[2] Although many might think (and, indeed, I did) that teaching a class in which the majority of students are feminists is a dream come true, it soon became painfully clear that this was yet another illusion. Instead of creating excitement and enthusiasm among students, this skewed distribution of "feminist knowledge" created divisions. However, my expectations for the course, as well as how I initially defined my role in the classroom, were equally responsible for the problems that arose.

I entered the course relieved that I did not have to spend a significant part of the semester explaining why it was legitimate and important to study women's experiences. Since I assumed that the students would offer little, if any, resistance to feminism, I envisioned the class as a semester-long discussion of women's lives characterized by mutual excitement and support. In addition, because this was my first officially designated women's studies course, I thought it had to be "truly feminist" in content and form. Consequently, I was more concerned than usual with the structure and dynamics of the classroom. Even though I had always strived to create a classroom environment that empowered students, I began to view these efforts as only approximations of the "real thing."

The more I contemplated what a "truly feminist" classroom environment might entail, the more my thoughts began to mirror the dualistic thinking so accurately described by Lorde (1984). For example, if professional authority and expertise were emphasized in the traditional classroom, then these qualities would be devalued or absent in a "true feminist" classroom. Instead of being *the* source of knowledge and socially distant, I would become a peer and facilitator of knowledge. Thus, I perceived, as have others (Friedman 1985; Kaye 1972; Mumford 1985), that the "truly feminist" classroom is one in which I would give up my official trappings, merge with the class, and, in the classic sense of "instructor," become invisible.

By playing such a passive role, I helped set the stage for the following dynamic that emerged early in the semester. The feminist majority, or those students with a strong background in feminism, began to use their knowledge as a source of power. As a group, they were articulate and dominated the class discussions. They often talked *at* rather than *with* the other students and, as a consequence, effectively silenced the nonfeminist minority. Thus, rather than sharing ideas and learning from each other, the students used differences in knowledge to create a distinct hierarchy in the classroom, with knowledge being a source of power *over* others. In other words, the feminist majority defined the class as *their* class and soon became the new caste of "men," while the remaining "women" sat passively, accepting their subjugation (Kaye 1972, p. 70). These dynamics polarized the class.

My initial response to these patterns of interaction was confusion. Given my idealized expectations of the course, I had not anticipated such behavior and thence was not prepared to deal with it. Having abdicated my professional authority, I was uncertain about whether or how I should intervene. On the one hand, I was hesitant to "take control," since doing so would have been inconsistent with my conceptualization of a feminist classroom. In addition, I did not want to silence or put down those students who had finally found a safe place to speak their "feminist truths" (Geiger and Zita 1985; Kaye 1972). On the other hand, I knew that my passivity was contributing to the problem and could not continue. The question was, How could I intervene without taking control? Ideally, I wanted all of us to discuss and analyze the patterns of classroom interaction that had emerged. However, given the polarization of the class, I thought such a discussion could not take place unless I created a way for the students to express their concerns "safely." Thus, I asked the students to write about their perceptions of the overall dynamics of the class, as well as my role in the classroom. The following comments were typical:

> There seems to be a definite division within the class with one group not daring to say anything, yet either opposing or at least questioning many of the comments being made. I'm sure they feel intimidated in class. As for myself, some of the comments in class make me furious because of their judgmental edge, yet others make me reevaluate my opinions.

> We are all on different levels with regard to feminism. Some of us have been into the movement for years, some since this class began. Sometimes I have a very difficult time understanding, let alone relating to, what is being said. I feel some women in the class are very condemning of the other women who aren't quite as "into" it as they are. It is turning me off from the movement (and the class) more than encouraging me.

> Class dynamics? It appears to be a case of the "haves" and "have-nots," those who are free, able and willing to speak and others (me included) who can't or *won't*. In my view, the class reflects many aspects of the dominant culture. Those who have the education and self-confidence to speak to the concepts and course content do not realize that they achieved this with a lot of help from many people and resources. We say we want to learn from women's diversity, yet when we discussed Alice Walker's definitions of womanism, she was labeled divisive. The dominant group has to realize that the world is defined from their viewpoint and if they *really* want to learn from other races, classes, etc. they will have to take a look at where they are and *how* they got there. I believe that feminists have a big job to do within their ranks. Theory without practice is useless.

> I never feel like I belong. Even though we all talk about appreciating difference and diversity, I don't feel as if we act on it. Especially "the feminists" in the class. I'd often see them in the Union and they wouldn't even acknowledge me—they'd kind of look right past me. Well, so much for sisterhood.

It is clear that many students were acutely aware of the disparity between theory and praxis in what they defined as a "feminist classroom." In sum, many felt angry, alienated, devalued, and silenced by others. The patterns of domination that had become an integral part of the classroom interaction caused many of the students to perceive themselves as "outsiders" rather than peers. Furthermore, the students suggested that I become "more visible" and assertive and that I provide more structure, synthesize ideas and comments more often, and "wrap things up more tightly." Thus, they wanted me to reclaim my professorial authority and share my expertise, or, as one member of the class commented, "You need to act more like a teacher and less like one of us."[3]

To initiate what Butler (1985, p. 236) referred to as a "pressure-valve-release" discussion,[4] I shared these comments with the class. The more traditional students expressed relief at finally having their reality validated, but the feminist majority initially responded with strong feelings of guilt. They had not been aware of how their behavior had affected others in the class or the ways in which it reinforced the patriarchal dynamics they were so committed to changing. Although these responses could have polarized the class even more, by suggesting that one group of students (the feminist majority) was solely responsible for what had occurred, they did not. By taking an active role in the discussion and highlighting our collective responsibility for group dynamics, I managed to avoid such scapegoating. Thus, we were able to acknowledge how we had each contributed to the classroom dynamics that now divided us: the traditional students by their silence, the feminist majority by their dominance, and I, by abrogating my power and thus my responsibility (Geiger and Zita 1985).

After much discussion and brainstorming about what might be done to alter our patterns of interaction, we decided to incorporate several changes. The first, suggested by a student, was to have the class form two concentric circles. The smaller or inner circle consisted of 3–4 students who would discuss their reactions to a specific reading assignment. Each student was allotted 5–10 minutes in which to speak.[5] During that time, members of the larger or outer circle were not permitted to interrupt or ask questions; their task was to concentrate on what was being said. After each member of the inner circle had spoken, others were invited to comment on their remarks. However, such comments had to be directed to the substantive content of what had been said in the small circle. This "rule" was designed to discourage the pontificating that had earlier plagued the class.

The second change was in my role in the classroom. I provided more structure for the class by contributing concise introductions to new material or sections of the course and periodically "pulling together" or synthesizing ideas that emerged from the discussion, as well as illustrating how these ideas were directly linked to the other key themes of the course. Initially, I also acted as a bridge among the students. When I sensed that some members of the class were confused or did not understand what another student was saying, I would ask the speaker to clarify or explain her ideas more fully. Often the speaker would have to define a particular concept that she had assumed everyone understood (such as compulsory heterosexuality) or identify a particular person (Mary Daly or Ellie Smeal, for example), or describe a specific event (the Nairobi conference, for instance).[6]

The effects of these changes were remarkable. The "legitimated silence" created by the small-circle concept broke the cycle of verbal domination by the feminist majority. The students realized they could *learn much from each other*, regardless of how much they "knew." They also discovered that knowledge could be a means of empowerment, rather than a source of *power over* others. My more active role in the classroom also produced some positive results. Students reported feeling less confused and lost. They thought that my introductory comments or mini-lectures provided a foundation that increased not only their understanding of the material but their willingness to speak in class. By pulling together seemingly disparate ideas and comments during class discussions, I increased their ability to make important theoretical connections or to see "how the pieces of the puzzle fit together." The greater self-confidence and altered perceptions of difference induced by these changes (particularly among the nonfeminist minority) initiated another change: The students began to make an active effort to ensure that their comments were accessible to others in the class. This change was crucial if the students were to speak with, rather than at, each other. For successful communication to occur, it was also imperative that the listeners ask questions or seek clarification when they did not understand what was being said. As each student assumed these reciprocal responsibilities, my role as a bridge among the students became obsolete.

The mutual respect engendered by the restructuring of the classroom enabled all the students to take more responsibility for their learning and, perhaps what was more important, to appreciate and respond to differences in a radically new way. By exposing and challenging hierarchical modes of responding to differences and by confronting that "piece of the oppressor within [them]" (Lorde 1984, p. 123), the students developed a new pattern of relating to each other as equals—at least for the remainder of the semester. They were able to do so, in part, because the feminist majority began to realize that:

> . . . it is as important for feminists to learn to listen as to be heard—to understand the
> complexity of traditional women's lives as to present the alternatives of their own. Other-
> wise, no one is "advanced," we are still in first grade (Hillyer Davis 1985, p. 248).

The shifts in my role also afforded some valuable insights. I learned that to define a "truly feminist" classroom as one devoid of any authority is a great disservice to the instructor as well as to the students. As Culley (1985, p. 207) pointed out:

> It is only in accepting her authority—by this I mean the authority of her intellect, imagina-
> tion, passion—that the students can accept the authority of their own like capacities. The
> authority the feminist teacher seeks is authority with, not authority over.

It took me some time to realize *experimentally* what Culley meant. "Authority" can, indeed, be a source of empowerment. As I learned to accept mine within the classroom, the students learned to accept theirs, and we all benefited. Our learning experience was richer, and we managed to create a new pattern of relating across the hierarchical differences imposed by the structure of higher education.

Differences in Class

Divisions among women because of their social-class background have been prevalent in the feminist movement. Even though feminism is frequently thought to include the experiences of all women, the experiences with which it deals often are those of white middle-class heterosexual women (Baca Zinn et al. 1986; Cruikshank 1982; Dill 1983). In the feminist classroom, which is a microcosm of the feminist movement, the lives of working-class women have been ignored or treated as far removed from the lives of the students. This section explores how the issues of social class becomes visible in the classroom, the students' and instructor's responses to it, and the possible reasons for these reactions. Since my background frames my analysis, I will briefly summarize it as well as the assumptions with which I first entered feminist classrooms.

I grew up in a French, Catholic, working-class family in rural Maine. Both my parents worked in local factories, and their employment was fairly stable, except for occasional layoffs and labor strikes. We were what Rubin (1976) referred to as a "settled living" working class family. I was always conscious that my environment was different from that of my middle-class friends—that I was, indeed, an "outsider."

As a child, I was not exposed to art, literature, or music. My parents did not read much—other than the Bible and *Reader's Digest*—or value education. Thus, although my grades were high, I received no encouragement or support from them to continue my education beyond high school. Fortunately, someone outside my family saw my potential and urged me to apply to the state university.

The letter of acceptance to the university signified more than just acceptance into school. I was now "good enough" and no longer the "other" (Lorde 1984). My class background was erased; I had suddenly become middle class. However, I discovered, much to my disappointment, that the reality of the university was not much different from what I had left behind. Divisive class lines were still drawn. I was, once again, the "other" and felt that I did not belong. Inside the classroom, these feelings intensified.

It was within a traditional course on introductory sociology that I first heard my class background discussed. In that class, "the working-class experience" was presented as an object to be studied, rather than as a possible experiential reality for students in the room. I felt not only invisible but dehumanized. Rather than remain passive, I decided to share some of my experiences as a member of the working class. When I did, a curious silence fell over the room. It became clear that I had broken two unspoken rules of this middle-class academic setting: I had spoken experientially in an environment that values "objective knowledge" and I had revealed my class background. Since the students and the professor did not respond to my comments, I was silenced. I did not speak again in that class or share my personal experience in another class until I started taking women's studies courses.

When I first entered a women's studies class, I expected it to be different. I assumed that since women's studies is concerned with the lives of all women, my experiences would matter and be heard. However, once again, I found that the experiences of working-class women were often invisible or invalidated.

When the lives of working-class women were discussed, three approaches were used. The first was to include social class as a separate, "special" topic, rather than a topic that was integral to the course. This approach is much like the "add women and stir" approach discussed by McIntosh (1984). The second approach was to incorporate a social-class analysis of each topic, thereby making students cognizant that social-class issues are an integral part of women's experience. The third approach was for students, usually working-class students, to challenge the middle-class assumptions made in class by the instructor or the other students.

Of these three methods, the third created the most resistance among the students and instructor. Here the patriarchal consciousness described by Lorde (1984) was most evident and the responses to differences in social class included silence, distancing, guilt, and fear. In contrast, the method that produced responses more closely associated with feminism, such as validation, support, and mutual learning, was the inclusion of a class analysis in each topic. The following example illustrates how patriarchal consciousness operates with respect to social-class differences among women.

The instructor of one women's studies course presented issues, both for discussion and throughout the readings, that involved only the concerns of white middle-class heterosexual women. These issues included dual careers for women, career advancement for professional women, and the "new" issue of child care and housework for women who work outside the home. When I challenged the instructor about her failure to present an analysis of social class and racial issues, she replied that she would love to incorporate these perspectives but they were beyond her students! Although she was unwilling to include these perspectives, she encouraged me and several other concerned students to add such analyses to the discussions in class. She even went so far as to say that we were responsible for teaching the others about these issues. Thus, she implied that it was the responsibility of the subordinate or oppressed group to teach or raise the consciousness of those who are more privileged than themselves. This pattern also allows the privileged to maintain their position and evade responsibility for their actions (Lorde 1984).

During one disturbing discussion about the lack of good child care and the fears about the sexual abuse of children in day care centers, which ignored the realities of working-class women, one student stated that she did not consider these issues to be a social problem, since one could just hire a nanny. In following the instructor's suggestion, I challenged the student's assumption that all working women can afford to hire a nanny and asked her to consider who is supposed to take care of the nannies' children. Both the instructor and the students responded with an uncomfortable silence. They may have felt uncomfortable for a variety of reasons. Given the low level of class consciousness in American society (Mantsios 1988), any comment that highlights class differences (regardless of how it is presented), will challenge both middle- and working-class students' assumptions about the world. Thus, the middle-class students may have felt uncomfortable (and perhaps guilty) because my remarks directly challenged their biases and privilege. Although this would account for the silence of the middle-class students, I believe that the working-class students were silent for different reasons.[7] If they had publicly agreed with me or raised working-class issues, they would have risked being exposed as working class and hence defined as outsiders.

The silence served to invalidate my point and exacerbated the differences between me and the other students. Over time, the students came to define class issues as "my issue or problem." By individualizing an issue that affects millions of women, they were able to discount the social significance of class.

In another women's studies course, the response to social-class differences among women was more congruent with my expectations of a feminist classroom. Instead of fear and silence, there was validation, encouragement, and mutual learning. Many self-identified middle-class students acknowledged their class privilege and the wide range of feelings (including guilt) this awareness provoked. By doing so, *all* the students felt free to share their experiences and ideas openly. I credit this atmosphere to the way in which the instructor presented social-class issues. She incorporated a social-class analysis into every topic and continually emphasized and affirmed the importance of diversity. This approach created an environment that enabled the working-class students to express themselves and the middle-class students to recognize their privilege.

My experience suggests that a number of factors account for the negative responses to social-class issues described here. They include the denial of one's working-class background, guilt associated with class privilege, and the fear of difference. Working-class students who have internalized middle-class values often view their class background as a source of shame or personal inadequacy and, as a consequence, frequently deny their heritage. For them, silence is the safest, and perhaps the only, response that will ensure their anonymity. In contrast, middle-class students are more likely to express guilt once they realize that their privileged status depends on the exploitation and oppression of others. Guilt about class privilege often keeps people paralyzed. They try to relieve their guilt by ignoring and denying class differences or by refusing to accept their own privilege. Both denial and guilt reinforce the fear of difference. However, as long as women fear those who are different from themselves, that fear will be a barrier to understanding. Instead, all women need to become aware of the assumptions they make about others and then challenge those assumptions. If we allow our fear of differences to divide us, we will not be able to work together to change the social conditions that oppress us all.

Differences in Sexuality

Sexual preference is one of the most emotionally charged areas of difference in this society. Usually, it remains hidden through denial and repression by heterosexuals and homosexuals alike. When the subject of lesbianism does emerge, however, reactions are typically judgmental and dualistic. For example, heterosexuals often characterize lesbianism as inferior, bad, sick, disgusting, dangerous, and sinful, while lesbians may be more likely to view their sexual preference as superior, highly evolved, visionary, and a source of pride. Such patterns of polarization and denial not only alienate women from each other, but reinforce a way of thinking about differences that has historically contributed to the oppression of women.

In a university, these responses to difference in sexual preference are perhaps most evident in the traditional classroom. Given the androcentric assumptions and hierarchical structure of such classrooms, it is not surprising that assumptions about sexual preference are rarely addressed. But what about the feminist classroom? Instructors and students have different expectations about the visibility of differences here. It is tacitly assumed that the nontraditional structure and emphasis on process found in the feminist classroom will encourage the exploration of theoretical and experiential differences among women. In this woman-centered environment, surely sexual preference will be one of the differences that is critically examined. How well are these expectations met? What are the responses to differences in this context?

The feminist classroom would seem to be a safe place for students to challenge lifelong assumptions. But challenging assumptions, especially about lesbianism, can be frightening and unsettling. The lesbian who contemplates "coming out" in the classroom may fear rejection or reprisal. The other students, many of whom may have been upset by feminist challenges to their taken-for-granted patriarchal world view, may perceive the subject of lesbianism as an additional threat. They may worry, Is lesbianism a disease? Can I catch it? If I listen to or agree with any of these new ideas, will my life have to change? Will I still like men? Other responses may include disinterest, curiosity, silence, approval, defensiveness, deference, bonding, and envy (Beck 1982; Bulkin 1982; McDaniel 1985; McNaron 1982).

The variety of responses are as disparate as the individuals who express them. However, some factors can minimize or exacerbate the fear of differences. For example, if the instructor is comfortable with the subject, she is more likely to create a climate that facilitates open discussion. If the class is small, it is easier to establish the climate of trust so necessary for honest sharing. Another important factor is whether the lesbians in the class are also feminists. Those who are not may send out nonverbal messages of discomfort, maintain a rigid silence, or try to change the subject, thus increasing the others' fear of differences. To clarify these issues, I will discuss some of my experiences regarding lesbianism in feminist classroom.

In the first feminist class I attended, the subject of lesbianism was introduced through the readings. For the most part, the discussions were theoretical; the students agreed or disagreed with the lesbian authors on intellectual grounds but had few experiential referents. We personally distanced ourselves from the topic, communicating primarily with the instructor rather than with each other. However, in the class discussions, some of the students' enthusiasm for the readings seemed personal as well as academic. Others communicated their fear and dislike of the theories and the personal implications associated with them. Though potentially divisive, these differences did not create a schism in the classroom, since neither the lesbians nor the heterosexuals bonded into groups.

A different dynamic emerged in my second feminist course. Although lesbianism was not explicitly a part of the syllabus, it became a topic of discussion as the semester progressed, mainly because of the climate of acceptance and exploration in the class. Lesbians came out of the closet and challenged discussions as well as in the reading materials. In doing so, of course, they clearly reinforced the patriarchal dynamic referred to by Lorde (1984): that of the oppressed group (lesbians) taking responsibility for raising the consciousness of those defined by society as the superordinate group (heterosexuals). Initially, this dynamic took the form of an "us" versus "them" mentality among some of the lesbians. Their unspoken assumption that lesbianism is a politically correct lifestyle, coupled with their greater knowledge of feminism, helped to create this divisive dynamic. It is ironic and unfortunate that in breaking the silence of denial and invisibility, so characteristic of lesbian life, some lesbians contributed to the silencing of other classmates.

Once the issue of difference in relation to lesbianism became an explicit topic of discussion, the heterosexual students began to express defensiveness. They had a difficult time moving beyond the security of their attachments to specific males in their lives to a more global vision of the possible value of women-centered lives. Gradually, this response gave way to a greater curiosity about and a greater awareness of lesbian experiences. As the mutual sharing of heterosexual and homosexual lived experiences increased, the importance of differences in formal feminist knowledge diminished. All the students were learning about difference and trust through open discussions of sexual preference, race, and class.

My experience in another course was a vivid demonstration that even in a classroom with a self-identified feminist instructor who espoused a feminist approach to the course content, a dualistic and hierarchical consciousness can still operate. As was similar to the case of the students in the course on introductory women's studies discussed in the first section, the lesbian students in the class had a more formal knowledge of feminism. However, unlike the instructor in the introductory course, this instructor exploited the us-versus-them potential. She gave undue deference, and therefore more power, to the lesbians in the class for two reasons. First, I suspect that she was entranced at meeting real out-of-the-closet lesbians. Second, she held the naive belief that all lesbians are highly evolved feminists. By deferring to us as true feminists and enlisting our help as teachers of the others, she reinforced the initial tension and conflict in the class.

These hierarchical dynamics were established at the beginning of the semester and would have continued if personal journals were not used as a pedagogical tool. The lesbians in the class used their journals to vent their impatience with the attitudes of the other students and the instructor; the nonlesbians used them to express their discomfort with the gap in knowledge and their reactions to the presence of lesbians in the class.

This acknowledgment of feelings by all members of the class, albeit in a private communication, led to a breakthrough. In the midst of all the theoretical analysis, the class discussions became experiential. Heterosexuals expressed their curiosity about lesbian stereotypes, and lesbians spoke of the joys of lesbian life and the pain of living as outsiders. This sharing culminated in a small-group presentation that focused on the lesbian continuum discussed by Rich (1980). The participants were three lesbians and two women who were in heterosexual primary relationships yet were deeply cognizant of the depth of their feelings for other women. This panel enhanced the ability of class members to move from their narrow vision of sexism and heterosexism to a broader vision of these forms of oppression as manifestations of patriarchy.

In my current seminar on women's studies, the topic of lesbianism was introduced in a combination of ways: by the instructor, by the students, and through the reading list. The students' responses have ranged from fear to interest to approval. From the first session, all patriarchal assumptions were challenged, and differences were acknowledged through discussions of many isms: sexism, classism, racism, ageism, and heterosexism.

The underlying fear of differences was addressed, primarily through a discussion of Rich's (1980) article "On Compulsory Heterosexuality." In the present seminar, theory was combined with feelings, and resistance was examined—resistance to change, feelings of threat to one's heterosexual assumptions and lifestyle, the fear that strong emotional bonds to women may really mean one is a latent lesbian, the fear of becoming a more conscious feminist and still not being as "legitimate" as is a lesbian if one continues to relate to men sexually, and the discomfort of questioning the concept of choice. These issues were examined from a micro and a macro perspective and validated all our selves and our places along the woman-identified continuum discussed by Rich (1980).

I believe that the more openly the issue of differences is dealt with in the classroom, the greater the opportunity for clearer and more in-depth analyses of feminist issues and women's experiences. Initially, the discussion of differences may cause students to distance themselves from the material, both emotionally and intellectually. Later, it may create a maelstrom of feelings and reactions. However, out of all this potential conflict, students and faculty members alike can gain the clarity necessary for growth, increased understanding, and new feminist visions of the world and our classrooms. The probability of their doing so will increase significantly if the following changes are incorporated (for additional suggestions, see Bulkin 1981; Fontaine 1982; Haney 1985).

- Include a separate unit on lesbianism in the class syllabus and incorporate the subject throughout the course. This change will make differences and responses to differences integral to all the discussions in the course.

- In the required reading list, include some first-person accounts by lesbians, especially about the process of coming out. The best stories are graphic dramatizations of the experience of being different.

- Schedule a lesbian to speak with the class about her life (preferably one who is articulate, intelligent, and humorous). There's nothing like a dose of reality to undermine the fear of the unknown and counteract stereotypical thinking and reactions.

- Form a panel of women of various beliefs and behaviors to encourage bonding within and across groups in the classroom and to take the pressure to perform off any one person or group. If the students are not willing or able to speak about their experiences, assign various roles to them, such as lesbian, bisexual, or feminist, that they must research and present to the class. As an extension of the panel, ask class members to spend a day acting as if they were black, native American, lesbian, working class, and so on and report on their experiences.

- Structure a panel discussion to cover the most prevalent theories of feminism, emphasizing the groups that are likely to subscribe to each. Such a panel would ensure that the radical lesbians separatist position would be presented, as well as the involvement of lesbians in liberalism, socialist feminism, and other movements.

- Assign students to write journals, encourage personal communication, and promise confidentiality. Journal writing frees the students to examine their thoughts and feelings in safety and encourages them to assume responsibility for their intellectual and emotional growth.

- Since the openness of the instructor sets the tone of the classroom, check your attitude and that of other instructors who will be involved in the course. Are all willing to question and challenge their homophobia? In addition to creating an atmosphere in which students will feel free to explore differences and their responses to differences, the openness of the instructors will create a safe space for lesbian students in the class who decide to come out.

Conclusion

We have examined responses to difference within a variety of feminist classrooms. Regardless of whether our focus was on differences in knowledge, class, or sexuality, hierarchical modes of responding to the diversity of women's lives emerged. Differences were used by the superordinate group to gain power over others or were ignored or denied. Each of these responses divided the women in the class. As a consequence, their ability to acknowledge, respect, appreciate, and learn from differences was radically reduced. These classroom dynamics were, in large part, the part of a patriarchal consciousness that "conditions us to see human differences in simplistic opposition to each other" (Lorde 1984, p. 114). In an effort to create new patterns of relating, we offered specific suggestions for transforming how we think about as well as respond to differences in the classroom.

Such changes also have significant implications for the women's movement. Teachers, as well as students, are or will be among those who work to change women's lives. To be an effective agent of social change, one must be aware of both the commonalities and differences among women. An awareness of commonalities enables us to recognize women's oppression as a class, but it is only through an acknowledgment of differences that we learn that all women do not experience this oppression in the same way. By discussing our differences and our responses to them, we are forced to confront our oppressive attitudes and behaviors. Such a confrontation is the beginning of change and necessary prerequisite if we, as women, are to move beyond a patriarchal conceptualization of differences that views us all as "the other." According to Lorde (1984), such a transformation is essential for our future survival.

As teachers and students, we can contribute to this process by working to create a classroom environment in which differences among women are not only acknowledged but valued. Only then will it be possible to "devise ways to use each others' difference to enrich our visions and our joint struggles" (Lorde 1984, p. 122). As Conlin, da Silva, and Wilson (1985, pp. 11–12) noted:

> The things that divide us can define us and help us claim ourselves; they can also be used against us, as ways of keeping us separate from each other and powerless. Only by writing and talking of our differences can we begin to bridge them.

Notes

1. These differences were chosen because they were most salient to our experiences in the classroom. We do not consider them to be more significant or less significant than are other differences among women, such as race, ethnicity, age, and religion.

2. Given the introductory nature of this course, one might have expected students with a strong background in feminism to be in the minority. However, since the University of Maine does not have a formal women's studies program, relatively few women-centered courses are available. Consequently, students often enroll in every such course that is offered, regardless of their background in feminism.

3. This desire for a more "traditional" teaching style is frequently expressed by students in feminist classrooms (Friedman 1985; Kaye 1972; Mumford 1985).

4. Once divisions have emerged in the classroom, Butler (1985) advised making such issues the focus of class discussions. Doing so works best when "the teachers directly acknowledges and calls attention in the classroom" (p. 236). After "naming" the problem, the class discusses why it occurred, possible solutions, and the like.

5. Students could discuss their intellectual and emotional responses to the material. All relations were considered legitimate, and great care was taken to emphasize that there was no "politically correct" response to the reading.

6. Hillyer Davis (1985) described a similar technique for fostering more effective communication in this regard. She suggested the teacher function as a "simultaneous translator," "giving back in other words what person has just said, and presenting an explanation in another language which will illuminate the issue for a second group without alienating the first" (p. 250). A key difference between this role and the one described here is that the *students* are expected to assume responsibility for the "translation."

7. Since a significant proportion of those enrolled at the University of Maine are first-generation college students, I suspect that there were others in the course who shared my class background. However, I was not sure just how many there were, since working-class students often attempt to deny their class background by "passing" as middle class.

References

Baca Zinn, M., L. W. Cannon, E. Higginbotham, and B. T. Dill. 1986. "The Costs of Exclusionary Practices in Women's Studies." *Signs* 11:290–303.

Beck, E. T. 1982. "Teaching About Jewish Lesbians in Literature: From *Zeitl and Rickel* to *The Tree of Begats*." Pp. 81–87 in *Lesbian Studies: Present and Future*, edited by M. Cruikshank. Old Westbury, NY: Feminist Press.

Bulkin, E. 1981. "Heterosexism and Women's Studies." *Radical Teacher* 17:25–31.

_____. 1982. "'Kissing/Against the Light': A Look at Lesbian Poetry." Pp. 32–54 in *Lesbian Studies: Present and Future*, edited by M. Cruikshank. Old Westbury, NY: Feminist Press.

Bunch, C. 1985. *Bringing the Global Home*. Denver, CO: Antelope Publications.

Bunch, C., and S. Pollack, eds. 1983. *Learning Our Way: Essays in Feminist Education*. Trumansburg, NY: Crossing Press.

Butler, J. E. 1985. "Toward a Pedagogy of Everywoman's Studies." Pp. 230–239 in *Gendered Subjects: The Dynamics of Feminist Teaching*, edited by M. Culley and C. Portugues. Boston, MA: Routledge & Kegan Paul.

Cole, J. B., ed. 1986. *All American Women: Lines That Divide, Ties That Bind*. New York: Free Press.

Conlon, F., R. da Silva, and B. Wilson. 1985. *The Things That Divide Us*. Seattle, WA: Seal Press.

Cruikshank, M., ed. 1982. *Lesbian Studies: Present and Future*. Old Westbury, NY: Feminist Press.

Culley, M. 1985. "Anger and Authority in the Introductory Women's Studies Classroom." Pp. 209–217 in *Gendered Subjects: The Dynamics of Feminist Teaching*, edited by M. Culley and C. Portugues. Boston, MA: Routledge & Kegan Paul.

Culley, M., and C. Portugues, eds. 1985. *Gendered Subjects: The Dynamics of Feminist Teaching*. Boston, MA: Routledge & Kegan Paul.

Dill, B. T. 1983. "Race, Class and Gender: Prospects for an All-Inclusive Sisterhood." *Feminist Studies* 9:131–150.

Fisher, B. 1982. "What Is Feminist Pedagogy?" *Radical Teacher* 18:20–24.

Fontaine, C. 1982. "Teaching the Psychology of Women: A Lesbian Feminist Perspective." Pp. 70–80 in *Lesbian Studies: Present and Future*, edited by M. Cruikshank. Old Westbury, NY: Feminist Press.

Friedman, S. 1985. "Authority in the Feminist Classroom: A Contradiction in Terms?" Pp. 203–208 in *Gendered Subjects: The Dynamics of Feminist Teaching*, edited by M. Culley and C. Portugues. Boston, MA: Routledge & Kegan Paul.

Geiger, S. and J. N. Zita. 1985. "White Traders: The Caveat Emptor of Women's Studies." *Journal of Thought* 20:106–121.

Haney, E. H. 1985. "Incorporating Lesbian and Other Woman-Identified perspectives into Courses." Pp. 144–149 in *Toward Excellence and Equity: The Scholarship on Women as a Catalyst for Change in the University*, edited by J. Fritsche. Orono: University of Maine Press.

Hillyer Davis, B. 1985. "Teaching the Feminist Minority." Pp. 245–252 in *Gendered Subjects: The Dynamics of Feminist Teaching*, edited by M. Culley and C. Portugues. Boston, MA: Routledge & Kegan Paul.

Hooks, B. 1984. *Feminist Theory: From Margin to Center*. Boston, MA: South End Press.

Kaye, M. 1972. "'Diving into the Wreck': The Woman Writer in the Twentieth Century." Pp. 68–78 in *Female Studies VI*, edited by N. Hoffman, C. Secor, and A. Tinsley. Old Westbury, NY: Feminist Press.

Lorde, A. 1984. "Age, Race, Class, and Sex: Women Redefining Difference." Pp. 114–123 in *Sister Outsider*, by A. Lorde. Trumansburg, NY: Crossing Press.

Mantsios, G. 1988. "Class in America: Myths and Realities." Pp. 56–68 in *Racism and Sexism*, edited by P. Rothenberg. New York: St. Martin's Press.

McDaniel, J. 1985. "Is There Room for Me in the Closet? Or, My Life as the Only Lesbian Professor." Pp. 130–135 in *Gendered Subjects: They Dynamics of Feminist Teaching*, edited by M. Culley and C. Portugues. Boston, MA: Routledge & Kegan Paul.

McIntosh, P. 1984. "Interactive Phases of Curricular Revision." Pp. 25–34 in *Toward a Balanced Curriculum*, by P. McIntosh. Cambridge, MA: Schenkman Publishing Co.

McNaron, T. A. H. 1982. "A Journey into Otherness: Teaching the Well of Loneliness." Pp. 88–92 in *Lesbian Studies: Present and Future*, edited by M. Cruikshank. Old Westbury, NY: Feminist Press.

Moraga, C. and G. Anzaldua, eds. 1981. *This Bridge Called My Back: Writings by Radical Women of Color*. Watertown, MA: Persephone Press.

Mumford, L. S. 1985. " 'Why Do We Have to Read All This Old Stuff?' Conflict in the Feminist Theory Classroom." *Journal of Thought* 20:88–96.

Rich, A. 1980. "Compulsory Heterosexuality and Lesbian Existence." *Signs* 5:631–660.

Rubin, L. B. 1976. *Worlds of Pain: Life in the Working Class Family*. New York: Basic Books.

Integrating Women into the Curriculum: Multiple Motives and Mixed Emotions

Patricia MacCorquodale and Judy Lensink

In the past two decades, women's studies faculty pursued two directions: one promoted the creation, organization and growth of women's studies programs and departments; the other fostered curriculum integration, i.e., efforts to include material on women in already existing courses and disciplines. Some campuses have concentrated on one of these directions while others have followed both. The Women's Studies program at the University of Arizona is a leader on both fronts. This essay will analyze what factors led us to begin our extensive curriculum integration projects, what the outcomes were for students and faculty involved, and what have been the costs and consequences in terms of the Women's Studies program.

Background

In the 1970s, teaching women's studies in the United States was a time of exhilaration; the field was expanding rapidly. The number of women's studies courses rose from 16 in 1969 to over 15,000 by 1980; over half of the 300 programs offered minors, majors or graduate degrees (Stimpson, 1980). The National Women's Studies Association was founded in 1977; *Signs*, a prestigious new interdisciplinary women's studies journal, published its first volume in the fall of 1975.

The atmosphere at University of Arizona was not unlike that on other campuses. Women's Studies began offering courses in 1971 and added a minor in 1979; by 1980 there were thirty courses. Our research component, the Southwest Institute for Research on Women (SIROW), was established in 1979.

In 1979, we were able to enhance our curriculum through a National Endowment for the Humanities (NEH) Pilot Grant. The grant supported an introductory women's studies course, interdisciplinary senior seminars, and faculty workshops. We evaluated the Pilot Grant through teaching evaluations which compared students in women's studies with students in humanities courses. The results of the student questionnaires were both confirmatory and shocking. Women's studies faculty were rated as excellent teachers, who not only expanded Students' understanding of humanities, but touched students' lives. Students found women's studies courses rigorous and demanding in the amount of material covered and in their development of writing and analytic skills. We were shocked, however, to realize how few of the students surveyed were exposed to a women's studies perspective. Only seven percent of those in humanities courses had taken women's studies. The comparison of women's studies classes to humanities classes revealed clear-cut differences: the humanities courses did not include material on women's roles, status or achievements, or motivate students to get involved in women's issues, or apply the materials to their own lives. The new scholarship on women that had transformed and enriched our own research and teaching had not been incorporated into the traditional humanities curriculum. Thus, most students were not learning about women in the humanities nor were they enrolling in women's studies courses to get their perspective (Auchmuty, Borzello, and Langdell, 1983).

We came to the conclusion that if we wanted to reach those students who would not enroll in women's studies courses, we needed to bring the new scholarship into the traditional curriculum. Hence, our attention turned to curriculum integration, and we entered a debate that continues to this day: should women's studies build its own relatively independent program or should it work to assure that materials on women are included broadly across the curriculum? This is not an either/or choice, but given finite energy and resources, the pursuit of one strategy necessarily sets limits on the other.

Curriculum integration is important for several reasons. The college student body is becoming increasingly female. In the 1960s, women's presence on college and university campuses returned to its prewar level; by 1982, more women than men received bachelor's degrees for the first time in American history (National Center for Education Statistics, 1987). Yet research consistently revealed, for example, that women's self image and self esteem decline during the college years (Astin and Mvint, 1971; Zigili, 1985). The discouragement of women is particularly evident in male dominated fields (Armstrong, 1980; Gornick, 1983; Ware and Steckler, 1983; Reyes and Padilla, 1985). Curriculum integration might make the college experience as well as traditionally male dominated fields more responsive to women's needs.

We wrote and received a multi-year NEH implementation grant to support our efforts in curriculum integration. The primary emphasis was to integrate materials on women into humanities courses by encouraging faculty to revise the curriculum to include materials by and about women. Participating faculty received a stipend. We chose to work with tenured faculty who taught basic courses in humanities and social sciences.[1] Our strategy was to use summer workshops as a forum for discussing interdisciplinary feminist scholarship while participants read intensively in their own fields and prepared annotated bibliographies that dealt with material on women.[2] By the end of the summer, faculty had revised the syllabus for at least one of their courses and agreed to participate in student evaluations of their revised course.

Over the four years of the project, 47 faculty members participated in curriculum integration, although five were involved only marginally for various personal reasons. Because of our decision to work with tenured faculty and because of the structure of the university, the vast majority (91 percent) were male. In terms of disciplines, two-thirds of the participants were from the 'social sciences,' a broad area at our university which included history, psychology, social anthropology, and political theory, while the remaining third were from the humanities, primarily literature and philosophy.[3]

A core group of five women's studies faculty (only one of whom was tenured) designed and led the intensive seminars and served as consultants throughout the year to faculty participants from their own or related disciplines. Although one of us was the 'official' leader of the intensive seminar, we all attended and participated.

Motivations: The Fork in the Road

The women's studies core group felt a sense of mission on behalf of our students because we had seen the impact of women's studies materials in our own classrooms. These materials can motivate and interest students, particularly women, in subjects and materials that they previously dismissed. The materials can help students understand forces in their own lives in ways that provide a new understanding or an impetus to change. Material on women raises aspirations and often provides strategies to overcome barriers. Although students can also be angered or depressed when confronted with the extent of women's oppression, we generally had positive experiences when exposing students to this material. (Recent studies of the impact of women's studies have corroborated our beliefs. Stake and Gerner (1987) found that women's studies students of both genders experienced gains in agentic self esteem, job motivation, and job certainty; that these effects vary by year in college is suggested by Zuckerman (1983). Vedovato and Vaughter (1980) found that women's attitudes became less traditional and their self images more androgynous after taking a women's studies course.) Our initial mood therefore, was optimistic. While there were doubts about how extensively the participants would understand and accept feminist scholarship, we approached the project with the belief that we could convince our colleagues to pursue women's studies.

In order to give us an understanding of the participants' motivations and viewpoints on the project, and to assess changes in their attitudes, we hired an interviewer to talk with each participant. These interviews, based on a series of open-ended questions, were conducted before their participation in the project began and after their year of official involvement ended. What follows is an analysis of participants' motivations before entering the project. It is important to note that while we have categorized the participants' perspectives, the categories are not mutually exclusive. Many people had more than one motive for participating in the project and had multiple reactions to it. What follows is a *post hoc* analysis of data collected as part of the project evaluation. Because we did not set out to study motivations, we did not ask people to rank or prioritize their motives. The categories were created by us after reading and re-reading the interviews. Where patterns appear in the interviews, e.g., motives that often appear together, they will be identified.

Although usually not explicit, one motivation for our colleagues was *financial*, for unlike most curriculum integration projects across the country, ours had external support that enabled us to pay summer stipends.[4] Because resources are very limited and highly competitive in the humanities, most faculty teach summer school; if they spend the summer on their own research, it usually means no salary. To offer faculty the equivalent of what they would have made teaching one summer school course was a powerful incentive. Although external incentives can be powerful motivators, there is a trade-off between external and internal incentives; as one participant explained, 'some of the [participants] look at this as another way to get money and they won't commit to it.' Another said, 'I'm a little embarrassed and guilty. They're paying me money . . . I plan to sit and think for five weeks. The thing is, I'm not convinced my classes will be substantially changed by this project.'[5] In other cases, internal and external motivations were mutually reinforcing. As one participant commented: 'The idea of getting paid for receiving training that's going to make you a better instructor is marvelous; I think that I would be willing to do it regardless of what the rewards were in terms of monetary [rewards].'

We characterized the most common, explicit motivation of participants as a moral and/or intellectual obligation to include material on women. As one professor said, 'many [female authors] have been excluded . . . and it is wrong, very wrong, to exclude one-half of all intellectual contribution. Intellectual honesty demands inclusion and redress." We refer to these professors as the *good liberals*; they wanted to include women because it is the 'right' thing to do. As another professor put it, 'A responsible person would have done it anyway. I feel very open-minded about the whole idea." Many entered the project with a certain amount of guilt about having previously ignored this material. 'My experience has been that of having good intentions and very little execution.' For some, their liberalism was the latest in a series of causes: 'When I was involved in civil rights, I discovered that I was racist. And I think it was an important discovery because once you get a cognitive handle on what's going on inside of you, you can alter your behavior in ways that you don't otherwise do. I suspect that there are similar feelings in respect to women.'

Ironically, the second most common motivation, also a political rationale, which often co-existed with the good liberal approach, was the desire to incorporate material on women in order to eliminate the need for women's studies. We characterize these participants as *anti-separatists*. As one explained emphatically: 'But I will say the *only* reason I'm in the project is that the mainstreaming idea is precisely what I support. I am vehemently opposed to the idea that Women's Studies should be a separatist, isolating thing.' For many, this position was as much a moral obligation as that of the good liberals: 'I am a non-separatist as a matter of conscience.' They believed that 'self-destruction should be the goal so we could see People's Studies, not Men's or Women's Studies.' Many felt, however, that these changes would not be forthcoming in their lifetimes or that there would still be the need for a 'permanent, women's studies resource center.'

The anti-separatists were not the only ones concerned with how women's studies should be organized. Opinions as to any need for a separate women's studies program were sharply divided. Some faculty felt they needed more exposure to women's studies material for informed decision making. 'At some point people will probably have to make hard decision about whether (women's studies) constitutes an academic field that you fund in the long term [with] standard positions.' Other participants saw a long-term future for a flourishing women's studies program: 'As a kind of unit, it has a number of uses that probably won't vanish if materials on women are incorporated into the curriculum.'

A third motivation was pedagogical. We call this group the *teachers*[6]: 'I will learn more as a teacher and become better educated,' said one participant before the project began. Another expected new material to 'make the course more interesting and for the students, both more relevant and more timely to what they're going to be doing.' Within this group, different events had triggered their interest. For some, their students had begun the process of curriculum integration by asking questions about gender and bringing materials to the professors. One faculty member had used as class material a play in which the major female character's over-riding ambition is to be a 'faithful shadow' in supporting the male protagonist. This professor was surprised when students questioned the gender dynamics in this example, and made him begin to question his practice with regard to material on women. Another told students they couldn't read material about women because it didn't exist; students began bringing articles on the new scholarship about women and created a bibliography 'that was the biggest launching pad I've had for starting to read in this area intensively myself.' Some were impressed by students' reactions to material on women that they had already used in their courses. 'I don't ever want to hear again my student's comment: "It was so neat to study a woman author; I didn't know there were any."' Several professors saw curriculum integration as an opportunity to change students' orientations: 'Basically, [what interests me the most] is the idea of getting women into my field; I think my students will enjoy and accept the new material,' one commented. Another saw the issue more broadly: 'I'd wish it [an integrated perspective] to be a way of life for all students . . . We can defeat discrimination with each crop of better-educated students.' The *teachers* saw the transformative potential of women's studies materials. One told the story of a bright, young woman who 'would have dropped out of school had she not found women's studies when she was on campus.' Women's studies gave her 'a focus' and 'confidence' to begin a professional career and later return to law school.

A fourth motivation was the intellectual stimulation that some participants hoped to find in the new scholarship on women.[7] These faculty, who we term *intellectuals*, differed from the other participants in two ways: first, they were more familiar with feminist writings and second, this familiarity usually stemmed from their active involvement in ongoing research. Because they already had some exposure to women's studies, they hoped feminist theory would provide 'new paradigms and new perspectives of how women should be studied.' As one professor said, 'the whole feminist enterprise has given us a new perspective on [the study of literature].' For some, these intellectual motivations extended into the classroom: 'My teaching winds up being an extension of my research.' Or, as another professor said: 'I have been jogged into a new point of view from which I have been teaching. I think it is healthy for anybody who has been teaching for ten years or more every once in a while to be stimulated.'

Finally, cross-cutting all of these motivations were *personal* interests and experiences. Approximately one-third of the participants were married to feminists, most of whom were also in the academy. 'To be honest,' one professor confided, 'my wife is the greatest stimulus for me. It is through her that I have had the most exposure to women's materials.' Another felt 'my wife has also encouraged my interest through her teaching and experiences.' Other family connections also motivated participants; 'I've a daughter coming to the university next year . . . [By participating] I'd have a better idea of what problems she might face.' Although these personal motivations provided some sensitivity to gender issues, the majority of the participants did not see structural discrimination at the university and claimed it no longer existed.

When we read these interviews before the project began, we primarily focused upon the participants' prior exposure to women's studies material and their initial conceptions of curriculum integration, i.e., did they see it as a major transformation or as a process of merely adding some material. What we failed to focus upon at the time were the ways in which these diverse motives would shape resistances to our efforts.

Resistances: One Step Forward, Two Steps Back

The task of integrating material on women into the curriculum asked the participants to value perspectives and materials that are culturally devalued (Aiken, Anderson, Dinnerstein, Lensink, and MacCorquodale, 1987). This proved to be the most common and greatest difficulty, for the new scholarship on women asks its readers to reexamine assumptions, values, and practices from a new perspective that challenges taken-for-granted viewpoints. For most of the *teachers*, who sought such fresh insights to enliven their classrooms, the resistances were minor. For others, the project asked them to scrutinize their intellectual, emotional and academic beliefs; the majority found this task too threatening and developed strategies of resistance based in part upon their initial motivations. The *good liberals*, for example, were torn between believing they should give feminist scholarship a chance and wanting to avoid association with what they characterized as 'second class' work. Their concern with the quality of the scholarship focused upon the perception that '[women's studies material] doesn't quite fit into the mainstream of the scholarship or the disciplines . . . and it's something that people do 'cause they can't, they're not as competitive in terms of the discipline.' They approached curriculum integration by asking 'are these journals as good as regular journals, is the research as significant as other kinds of research?' Another noted, 'feminist [scholarship] is pretty applied and peripheral so just on straight-forward grounds, it would be thought of as less important.'

For the *intellectuals* and some of the *teachers*, this issue of the quality and centrality—the canon—takes the form of questioning what to cut from a course if you want to include new materials on women. 'I don't anticipate, frankly, that we'll put a lot of new things in because that would mean taking the old things out that still *have* to be there.' Another saw this as 'cutting back on the [scholars] that stand out in history . . . who will always be written about as major talents.' For those in the humanities, the canon carries particular weight. As one literature professor remarked, 'when you get to the question of primary materials, it becomes more difficult, because [incorporating new materials] raises the question of the canon, it raises questions of aesthetic value.'

Even the external incentives, time and money, created their own resistances. For those who entered the project reluctantly, the external incentive was accompanied by an uncomfortable sense of obligation: 'I'm given a course off in order to take the seminar, I'm under some kind of an obligation to [incorporate women's material]. That's the hope that [women's studies faculty] have, but I'm not sure that they could actually, physically impose it [integrating women's studies material] upon me to do so.' Others saw the issue in terms of academic freedom. 'My peers,' one believed, 'see it as an encroachment upon academic freedom; women's studies is now telling us what and how we should teach.'

The *good liberals* were extremely troubled by the issue of what is 'objective knowledge.' They described their disciplines as rational and scientific and viewed women's studies as ideological and political. One went so far as to suggest that 'feminist scholarship' was a contradiction in terms. Another professor did not like that fact that 'quite obviously some of the issues that were touched on [in the seminars] were not just objective, intellectual issues, they were emotional issues as well. People responded emotionally.' For another participant, the workshop readings 'had more of a rhetorical purpose than a scholarly one' and feminist scholarship displayed an unnecessary 'tension between advocacy and research.' By dismissing a feminist perspective as 'unobjective,' they minimized their engagement with new materials.

Liberalism itself, with its attention to group rights, afforded another strategy of resistance in that some participants, whether good liberals or not, argued that there were many oppressed groups. The uniqueness of women's position and experience was obscured by deflecting the discussion to other groups who experience discrimination (e.g., blacks, the impoverished, the untenured, even 'the ugly'). One participant felt that his status as the only unmarried member of a department 'set[s] me aside in a way and affects people's treatment of me much as they might have reacted if I were the only female or the only black.' Another believed, 'it will probably be difficult for me to incorporate that kind of material because even when women are different from men, the differences are far, far less than similarities . . . men are also outsiders . . . and men face problems that arise from similar kinds of factors.' The curriculum interests of liberals were not enduring; they tended to move on to other 'causes,' i.e., integrating materials on Native American or Black men.

The *good liberals* were particularly bothered by our efforts to keep the focus to women's experience; they reminded us that 'we're the good guys.' Another reflected that 'men [in the project] are sensitive in the first place . . . and what men want coming into something like this is credit for how far they've come so far, before they get pushed down the road any farther.' Liberals did not want to re-think their positions; they used countless personal examples ('I feed the baby, I let my wife pay all the bills') to demonstrate that they were 'liberal and on the right side on in all these matters' and simply wanted a quick-fix for their courses.

Anti-separatists' resistances were even more extensive than the liberals. If the *anti-separatists* recognized the quantity and high quality of women's studies scholarship, their antagonistic position vis-a-vis the program would have been called into question. This group resisted curriculum integration in two ways. The first strategy was to search for socio/biological differences to explain sexism. One participant argued that older, white men's power, wealth, and 'sexual prowess' enabled them to have sequential marriages with younger wives. These marital patterns, he believed, ensured that these 'patriarchs' would pass along their genes resulting in a genetic disposition for women to prefer older men as sexual partners. Male dominance, therefore, could be seen as 'natural' and outside of the realm of the humanities and social sciences.

The second strategy was to define their own areas of interest so narrowly that women's studies scholarship was not applicable. One said, 'It's a problem of scarcity [of women's materials in my field].' This stance made the interdisciplinary nature of the project problematic. One participant was disappointed because the workshop 'raised lots of issues in areas that are outside of my area of expertise.' Another felt 'what made [the workshop] frustrating is trying to communicate with people who don't speak the same language.' Many of the participants, but especially the *anti-separatists*, did not acknowledge the differences among women; they treated women, including the women's studies faculty, as a homogeneous, unified group. As one commented, 'it was never made very clear that within the feminists, there is a great divergence of opinion.' For another, 'somehow you feel that you are encountering a monolithic ideology that's pushing you hard . . . and that in starting some of these materials [there] is the appearance that men are all alike.'

These resistances were accompanied by peer pressure. Both male and female participants reported during the interviews that they were subjected to criticism from their colleagues, which ranged from accusations of being 'on a cream-puff project' and 'pokes and giggles' to antagonistic criticism. These comments occur repeatedly through the interviews and are pervasive. As one participant painfully recalled: 'a colleague with whom I've worked in [another department] was very upset and said he wouldn't work with me anymore; he said I was selling my soul; that I wasn't professional. In my own department, l received numerous knowing looks, pokes, and giggles.' Another found that 'male colleagues are resistant to the idea. They put on a nice academic front but in day to day conversation you hear all kinds of snide remarks.' Participants took these remarks seriously and saw them as reflections of 'very real resistance,' 'very real bias,' and 'actual viciousness beneath the light matter.' Most professed that 'it doesn't bother me personally,' but one admitted, 'I guess I don't like it much, my colleagues behind my back saying more than they would to my face. It makes me uncomfortable.' A few reacted defensively and redoubled their commitment to the project; for most, the criticism (and 'having to explain and maybe defend what I'm doing') had a more pervasive, enduring effect of dampening their enthusiasm and limiting their involvement in the project.

Outcomes: Baby Steps and Giant Steps

Judging the successes and failures of the project depends, in part, upon the outcomes expected. The core women's studies faculty hoped that exposure to feminist scholarship would be as transformative for the participants as it had been in our own careers. We varied in our assessments of whether anything less than a transformative change could be defined as success, i.e., a significant alteration of the content, structure, and pedagogy of their courses and an almost paradigmatic shift in the questions they raised in and out of the classroom. For many participants, the expectation of extensive change was threatening. After completing the project, one participant, a self-described 'skeptic,' recalled our opening statement '"we hope, and our experience in the past has shown, that this [experience] will change your life,"' and insisted: 'I'm still the same person I was, with the same qualities and flaws. It hasn't changed radically my perception of the world or what academic inquiry should be . . . It hasn't been a 'religious transformation' for me, as I had the impression some people would expect there would be.'

Outcomes, however, are relative; they must be judged against starting points. As one participant aptly put it, 'a lot of [us] have a much further way to go than others. And there was great variety, at least in our group, where people had only baby steps to take, others had giant steps to take.' As the women's studies faculty looked back over the four-year project, we observed that approximately half of the participants were affected positively. These faculty found materials on women, judged the quality of those materials to be good, and subsequently made changes in their courses, referred to as targeted courses. 'I am very impressed with the development in feminist scholarship from the '60s to the current day. It is much more sophisticated, more solid on an academic basis . . . [The] program has introduced me to . . . material which I find fascinating and intriguing, well-argued and very convincing.'

Of this half, one-quarter experienced profound changes in their personal or professional orientation which markedly altered their teaching, research, and politics.[8] These participants understood that integration required them to rethink both the structure, content and process of their courses; for them, exposure to feminist scholarship was a transformative experience affecting their theoretical perspectives, research interests, academic politics and personal lives. '[Women's studies scholarship] is a necessary angle of literary interpretation . . . and for literary history. It's a major expansion in all aspects of our discipline and it's got to be there from now on,' concluded one literature professor. Another participant described the challenge of transformation: 'You know values are called into question when you start something like this. This is *not* an intellectual exercise. It is an exercise or reassessment of your commitment on a major part of your life. That can really be unsettling.'

Of the half who were positively affected, the other quarter met the 'official' goals of the project by incorporating new materials on women into their courses; there was great variation in the amount of materials incorporated and the manner in which it was included. These faculty understood that in an integrated course format they 'shouldn't be cuing people by saying "here we have a little lecture on women today." They believed that 'you can't just add something about women.' Consideration of gender became a regular aspect of their courses.

The remaining half were relatively unchanged in our judgment. Some clearly misunderstood or did not accept the goal of integrating material on women throughout their courses; as one commented, 'I guess I introduce a general topic . . . [and put] women in the examples.' Another wanted to 'spend one whole class period or two surveying just the major aspects of what women do' or fifteen to twenty minutes on male and female sensibilities 'if there's anything remarkable about them.' For some, the extensive change that would be caused by truly integrating women into the curriculum became an excuse. For example, after spending a semester in the project, one participant concluded that 'it will take me a while to think because if I do it properly I would have to re-structure the course far more radically than I was prepared to do on such a short notice.' A few genuinely understood and shared the goal of integration, but were overwhelmed because the task appeared 'beyond [their] capabilities:' 'They are fundamental problems in the basis of [the discipline] that need to be looked at . . . Going through that experience I realized how much [my field] is not about women. But if [it] is not about women, who is it about? . . . some mythical animal that doesn't exist.'

The *good liberals* and the *anti-separatists* had the greatest number of strategies of resistance and changed the least. Skeptical as to the quantity and quality of feminist scholarship, they used their strategies of resistance to minimize successfully the amount of material 'appropriate' for their courses: 'I feel women's issues are very peripheral to [the focus of my course].' This professor summarized the effect of the project as 'simply affording me the opportunity to shore up my lectures and my professional understanding of the material.' They limited their involvement; several admitted doing 'virtually no reading' or finding materials but 'making no major changes in [course] readings at this time.' Another 'rearranged my lectures and in doing that I went through a lot of my old material and found sexist remarks or sexist material. So I removed some of it.'

The *teachers* took the task of curriculum integration seriously, making changes in both the course that they had agreed to alter, targeted courses, and other non-targeted courses. 'It has caused me to reassess my values in teaching. It's exciting. [But also] I am a bit apprehensive,' one observed. For many of the *teachers* '[the project] has had an almost greater effect on a non-targeted course . . . [where] I was pretty well free to do what I wanted to do.' The *teachers* were also affected by ideas about feminist pedagogy: 'the experience will affect my teaching style in any class I teach regardless of subject matter.'

A natural outgrowth of curriculum integration is feminist pedagogy; changes in what we teach are more effective when we also change how we teach. Many participants expressed a desire for more information on feminist pedagogy or wished 'we could have had the pedagogical session first.' One particularly observant participant concluded, 'watching or experiencing the interaction among seminar participants made me aware . . . of just how much resistance there is to feminist thinking in the classroom, and how women bring certain socialized feelings of inadequacy or lack of confidence to a competitive, aggressive, traditionally male-dominated academic setting.' Other participants reported that their interactions with students, especially graduate students, were altered by their new perspective. 'I've become more aware of some of the problems that women in academia have, especially female TA's, who I had always assumed were fairly interchangeable with male TAs . . . Because they are women, they are facing a very different situation in the classroom' and need 'more training and preparation in giving them confidence in themselves and knowing how to meet these situations.' Many believed that working with graduate students was particularly important because 'they will carry this into their own role as teaching assistants.' Others moved beyond changing their curriculum to advocacy. One participant found a list of fellowships and financial assistance available to women and distributed it to all female graduate students in the department. 'I probably wouldn't have done that the year before . . . I think that would relate back to heightened awareness and concern,' he concluded. Another found that 'I am very much more an advocate for the women graduate students than I was before . . . Now I seek them out and I say okay, if you are going to make it through this, this is what you have to do. I feel more radical about making sure that the system works for them.'

The *intellectuals* experienced the most transformation, especially when they saw teaching and research as inseparable. One professor found that 'my participation was greater than expected because what I am teaching links so closely to my research work.' *Intellectuals* were willing to give serious consideration to different, often alien ideas. As one faculty member remarked, 'there are materials that strike me from left field, in the first place, but they do raise issues, important issues, and ones that I hadn't really thought about before.' The professor urged us to concentrate 'more direct attention on [participants'] research . . . because for most college professors, your research leads your teaching rather than the other way around . . . I'm not going to stop. I'll be writing on this for the next twenty years.' For another, 'the seminar experience was a real eye-opener. It made me realize the extent to which traditional conceptions of males and females, and male-type behavior versus female-type behavior or attributes informs the broad field in which I work . . . My experience in the seminar has radically changed the way I see my field of study and will affect both the way I talk about it in my classes and the way I actually conduct my research.'

There were also personal and political outcomes.[9] Many found new colleagues across disciplines. As one participant poignantly remarked, 'We have so little contact among faculty members, particularly across disciplines, or even within disciplines, where you sit down and actually talk about ideas; that was very valuable.' Many commented favorably on the women's studies faculty. One participant was struck by 'their enthusiasm and sincerity . . . It was the first remark I made to my wife—last summer was the first summer that I really enjoyed.' Another found that 'one of the major strengths is the [women's studies faculty] involved in the project . . . I felt I was working together with them rather than opposed to or against them.' One of the benefits to the program and to female faculty was an increased sensitivity to the problems women face in academia; increased sensitivity and respect for female faculty had political outcomes when some participants moved into administrative posts and began 'pressing these kinds of issues as far as departmental policies and activities.'

Student Reactions

The evaluation design compared students in classes that had been revised to include more material on women (targeted classes) with similar courses that had not been revised (control classes).[10] We asked students to evaluate how often they encountered works by women authors and material on women in their assigned readings, syllabus topics, lectures by the instructor, and class discussions. We also provided a series of statements about students' reactions to the materials. Students could agree or disagree, for example, with the statement 'I do not intend to do reading by or about women in the future.'[11] The next set of statements focused on the effect of the materials on students' lives. For example, 'Since taking this course, my feelings about women have changed in 1) a positive way 2) no change 3) in a negative way.' The last few questions asked about the overall quality of the course and whether the instructor's treatment of materials about women was positive, neutral, negative or hostile.

This evaluation instrument reached over 3500 students during the six semesters. The results revealed marked differences between the courses targeted in our project and those selected as controls.[12] Faculty participants were required to submit a revised syllabus and a narrative description of their course to demonstrate that they had integrated material on women into the course. We were pleased that in all five types of classroom materials—assigned readings, syllabus topics, lectures, class discussion, and works by women authors—students in the targeted classes reported more materials on women than students in the control classes. In targeted classes, a quarter to a third typically said that materials on women were included frequently; in contrast, over half of the students in the control classes observed that material on women was not included at all compared to seventeen percent in the targeted classes. This 'bottom line' measure of the success of curriculum integration - the presence of information about women in a course—proved successful.

We were also interested in assessing effects of curriculum integration on students in subsequent courses. Although students from targeted classes were more likely than students from control classes to report using the materials on women to reevaluate the content of other courses, when we probed further, the results were disappointing. We expected students from targeted classes to show more 'curricular activism'—the desire by students to have other courses contain materials on women. The data, however, did not support our expectations. Those from the control classes were *more* likely than those from the targeted classes to say that they would object if other courses omit materials on women or contain biased information. Students from both types of classes were indistinguishable in terms of wanting other courses to contain materials on women or desiring more of these materials in the curriculum. How can we explain these unexpected results? It may be that having attended courses in which there is virtually no information on women throughout their university experience, when students in the targeted group receive some information on women, they believe that it is sufficient. Alternatively, insofar as courses have not included materials on women in the past, all students may believe that these topics belong in specialized courses, such as those offered in the women's studies program. One professor reflected this view in his characterization of student attitudes toward material on women: 'the other [two-thirds] were ambivalent about it. I think they thought, 'What's the point of women's studies in [this course]? I am not paying for women's studies.' Further research is needed to explore students' desire for greater curriculum integration. Although curriculum integration did not increase students' desire for more material on women in the curriculum, the results were encouraging nevertheless; half of both groups would strongly object to classes without materials on women.

Finally, we turn to the issue of how participants' courses were evaluated. Student evaluations are often seen as popularity contests; they measure students' reactions to the professor and the course rather than what students learned or how challenged they were by the course material. Some would argue that the more unsettling and challenging a course is, the more learning occurs (Elbow, 1986). Many faculty participants, however, were quite anxious as to whether their ratings would drop when they included materials and issues on gender. In terms of how the classmates responded to the materials about women, students from control classes rated their classmates as neutral. Students from participants' classes saw fellow students as more positive, more negative, and more hostile. The range of ratings is not surprising, given the controversial issues raised by women's studies material. The controversial nature of the material is reflected in the overall ratings of the quality of the courses. Control courses were more likely to be rated excellent than participants' courses.

Controversy, however, can have a positive effect on students' participation. One faculty member who purposely used controversial issues reported, 'I've noticed that I got more participation . . . not merely from the bright, talkative students, which is easy, but from a wide range of students.'

One question of interest is whether male and female students have different reactions to the inclusion of materials on women. Prior research indicates that male students' attitudes change less than female students' after taking a psychology of women course (Vedovato and Vaughter, 1980). Male students' resistance to materials on women has led some to argue for teaching 'men-free' women's studies courses (Klein, 1983; Mahoney, 1983). Faculty who participated in the project believed that women students responded more favorably to the targeted course.[13] One professor observed, 'Women in the course were very very positive about it. The men were almost nonverbal on many topics during the whole semester.'

Analyses by gender focused on changes in students' self-image and reactions to the instructors. Three-quarters of students from both targeted and control classes did not change their self-image. Twice as many men in the targeted classes (4%) felt more negative about themselves than those in the control classes. Among women, the same proportion (1.4%) felt more negative in both types of classes. Both male and female students felt more negative about women in the targeted classes (4.6%) than in the control classes (3%). Similarly, among the small proportion who began to feel more negative about relationships, men from the targeted classes were twice as likely as women to have this reaction. These results indicate that the consequences of learning about women influence men more negatively than women.

Women, not surprisingly, find course material on women more attractive. Women from both target and control classes were twice as likely as men to want future classes to contain material on women and to intend to do more reading about women. Female students were more likely than male students to perceive the participants' attitude toward the material as positive and three times as likely as men to rate the course as excellent if the professor's attitudes were positive. Male students in targeted classes were three times more likely than female students to see the instructors as hostile.

In many ways the reaction of the male students parallel the resistances we observed among the participants in the project (who were mostly male). Feminist theory precipitates major re-evaluations that are painful for everyone, but especially threatening for men. Given the underlying sexism in contemporary American society, it is not surprising that men are particularly threatened by this material. Men's discomfort in confronting sexism, women's desire for and positive reaction to this material, and increasingly female enrollments on university campuses validate and reaffirm our belief in the necessity of curriculum integration.

Conclusions: The End of the Road?

The curriculum integration project has been over for several years, but it is still difficult to sift and weigh our reactions. At some level we continue to believe in curriculum integration: we have expanded our efforts to community college faculty and women's studies faculty in a four-state area, with an emphasis on international and cross-cultural perspectives. We serve as consultants, speakers, and writers on the topic. Given our experiences with faculty at Arizona, we now work more with younger faculty and with more women, including women's studies faculty. We rely less upon external incentives and more upon internal motivations. Both these factors enable us to find faculty who are more knowledgeable, more motivated, and more interested in learning about women. The greatest benefit to the women faculty and to the women's studies program was the bonds between the core faculty that were strengthened and tested over the years as we worked together. These bonds have enabled us to go on to new projects despite the enormous burn-out and emotional fatigue we experienced during curriculum integration.

However, participation in the curriculum integration program forced us to make trade-offs. Although the number of colleagues sensitive to women's studies was increased by the faculty who underwent extensive intellectual transformations, we might have gained as many sympathetic colleagues if we had focused our efforts upon recruiting specialists in women's studies. The 'success' of the curriculum integration project was used to argue against a campus-wide requirement that all courses include materials on gender and we had to expend energy mobilizing support to have the requirement passed. On the one hand, we gained politically by having more faculty members who had an exposure to women's studies when we came up for promotion and tenure. On the other hand, our careers might have progressed more smoothly and quickly if we had spent the inordinate number of hours devoted to curriculum integration on our own scholarship. Our choice to work with tenured faculty gave us exposure to those in power, but we might have been able to accomplish more change in the academy if we had worked with junior faculty. While focusing upon the undergraduate curriculum, we devoted less time to training and mentoring graduate students.

In many ways, what we experienced was a microcosm of academia: those on the margins, who are most willing to change, often remain marginal, while those within the powerful center—of the canon, the discipline, the androcentric society—are fairly intransigent. What we learned were insights into the structure and process of the university that will be central to future feminist transformations of the academy.

Notes

1. As part of the granting process, we were required to demonstrate institutional commitment to our project. We chose to work with faculty who taught large, basic, introductory courses in our belief that they were more likely to continue teaching at the University than untenured faculty. The unanticipated result of this decision was the exclusion of many younger faculty members who had some familiarity and interest in women's studies.

2. External funding brought the necessity of evaluation. In our zeal for the project, we designed an ambitious, multi-method approach which included interviews with participants before and after their involvement, formative evaluations of the workshops, seminars and project, consultations and feedback from women's studies faculty about each participant's work, and student evaluations of revised courses. Faculty interviews and student evaluations provide the rich and varied information used in this essay.

3. Because of the small number of participants from particular disciplines, we have decided not to link examples and quotations in this essay to specific fields in order to assure the anonymity of our colleagues. We have examined the information presented in this chapter to search for relationships between discipline and participation, and there do not appear to be significant differences by field. We hesitate to generalize about differences between male and female participants because there were so few female participants in the project.

4. Ironically, we did not design the project to provide equivalent support for the women's studies faculty. The grant provided summer salary for only one women's studies faculty member, and the university provided release time for one person during the fourth year. Since we saw the project as collaborative and interdisciplinary, we all participated fully. Very few of the participants understood the differences between their economic support and ours, but upon entering the project one explained, 'the women [the women's studies faculty] who participate in it are doing so out of a sense of desire to do so; that is, you don't have to buy their time, you don't have to twist their arms; so those women who are involved are doing a commitment that is really important.' Many of the questions that remain as to whether the project was worth the time and effort that the women's studies faculty devoted are rooted in the enormous personal and professional costs to the core faculty.

5. Our structuring of expectations about the project changed over time in response to our experiences with participants who did not share our goal of actively changing the curriculum. During the first year. Several participants entered the project with the belief that they would read materials to see *if* they were appropriate for their courses. Starting in the second year, we structured the project in terms of a contractual situation, expected participants to decide not if, but how, they were going to change their courses, and required a revised course syllabus and an annotated bibliography of the material they read.

6. As discussed above, people are not unidimensional with single motivations driving their behavior. Rather they are motivated by various intentions simultaneously. *Teachers* were divided into two

subgroups. One group primarily directed their energy toward teaching. The other combined their enthusiasm for teaching with productive research agendas.

7. As discussed earlier, faculty participants were not unidimensional with single motivations driving their behavior. Rather they often expressed various intentions for their involvement in the project. Thus, some of the researchers were also motivated by their teaching interests, which they saw as going hand-in-hand. Like most large universities, our faculty vary in their involvement in research. Those participants who were not actively involved in scholarly activities were unlikely to have intellectual motivations for joining the project. Some participants who did research did not study areas that lend themselves to feminist analyses or *did not see* the connection of their work to women's studies scholarship. Therefore, in spite of their own scholarly activities, these faculty are not motivated by research interest and are not included in this category.

8. Women who participated in the project had various motives: they were *liberals, anti-separatists,* and *teachers.* That they were unfamiliar with women's studies scholarship before joining the project reflected a conscious choice on their parts to avoid this kind of research. The material, therefore, was new and revelatory for them, much as it had been for us when we discovered it. In terms of outcomes, the consequences of participation on their personal lives were much greater than for the men. Needless to say, the materials and issues raised in women's studies have profound ramifications for understanding women's lives in and out of academia. Women, therefore, are over-represented among those who underwent a clearly transformative change. For more information on the effects of participants' gender, see Leslie Flemming's essay 'New visions, new methods: The mainstreaming experience in retrospect'. In: Aiken *et al.* (1988).

9. Although we became aware of many profound personal transformations during the project, we were unable to assess adequately the level of personal changes and whether they were actually caused by the project.

10. During the first year, we used the Attitudes toward Women scale (Spence and Helmreich, 1972), which focused upon women's roles and status in society. This scale was given at the beginning and the end of the semester to assess attitudinal change. After the first year, we jettisoned this attitudinal survey because there was not significant change in students' attitudes during the semester. There were three problems in measuring attitude change. First, there was a ceiling effect because the majority of students were strongly liberal at the beginning of the semester, and, therefore, their attitudes would not become more liberal on our scale. Second, attitude changes during one semester are often very small, even in courses that are intended to change attitudes [see Brush, Gold and White (1978)]. Third, gender socialization has long term effects that are difficult to alter in one semester.

11. The directionality of the statements was varied in order to avoid students falling into a response pattern, e.g., agreeing with all statements.

12. Faculty participating in the project identified a faculty member in their departments who taught a course at the same level with similar enrollment. Although faculty could pick an instructor with a bad reputation in order to make themselves look good, few did. Nearly everyone sincerely wanted to know what difference integrating material on women made. They often picked instructors they admired. A few people had us evaluate their courses before their participation in order to serve as their own controls.

13. One faculty member's belief that only certain students would be interested in these materials summarized this sentiment: 'I think the ones who already had an interest in problems of women or problems of gays were confirmed in that interest.' Similar arguments often advance 'self interests' to explain the greater prevalence of female scholars than male scholars researching gender.

References

Aiken, S. H., K. Anderson, M. Dinnerstein, J. Lensink. and P. MacCorquodale. (1987). 'Trying transformations: Curriculum integration and the problem of resistance.' *Signs* 12: 255–275.

Aiken, S. H., K. Anderson, M. Dinnerstein, J. Lensink, P. MacCorquodale (1988). 'Changing our minds: The problematics of curriculum integration.' In: *Changing Our Minds,* pp. 134–163. Albany, NY: State University of New York Press.

Armstrong, J. M. (1980). *Achievement and Participation of Women in Mathematics: An Overview.* (Report 10-MA-00). Denver, CO: Education Commission of the States.

Astin, H. S. and T. Mvint. (1971). 'Career development of young women during the post-high school years.' *Journal of Counseling Psychology* 18: 369–393.

Auchmuty, R., F. Borzello, and C. D. Langdell (1983). 'The image of women's studies.' *Women's Studies International Forum* 3: 291–298.

Brush, L. R., A. R. Gold, and M. G. White. (1978). 'The paradox of intention and effect: A women's studies course.' *Signs* 3: 870–883.

Elbow, P. (1986). *Embracing Contraries.* New York: Oxford University.

Gornick. V. (1983). *Women in Science.* New York: Simon and Schuster.

Klein, D. D. (1983). 'The men-problem in women's studies: The expert, the ignoramus, and the poor dear.' *Women's Studies International Forum* 6: 413–421.

Mahoney, P. (1983). 'Boys will be boys: Teaching women's studies in mixed-sex groups.' *Women's Studies International Forum* 6: 331–334.

'National Center for Educational Statistics (1987). *Digest of Educational Statistics.* Table 150 'Earned degrees conferred by institutions of higher education, by level of degree and sex of student: United States, 1969–70 to 1986–87.' p. 172. Washington, D.C.: Office of Educational Research and Improvement, U.S. Department of Education.

Reyes, L. H. and M. J. Padilla. (1985). 'Science, math and gender.' *The Science Teacher* 52: 46–47.

Spence, J. T. and R. L. Helmreich (1972). 'The attitudes toward women scale: An objective instrument to measure attitudes toward the rights and roles of women in contemporary society.' *Journal Supplement Abstract Service Catalogue of Selected Documents in Psychology* 2: 66.

Stake, J. E. and M. A. Gerner (1987). 'The women's studies experience.' *Psychology of Women Quarterly* 11: 277–284.

Stimpson, C. R. (1980). 'The new scholarship about women: The state of the art.' *Annals of Scholarship* 1, 2: 2–14.

Vedovato, S. and R. M. Vaughter. (1980). 'Psychology of women courses changing sexist and sex-typed attitudes.' *Psychology of Women Quarterly* 4: 587–590.

Ware, N. and N. Steckler (1983). 'Choosing a science major: The experience of men and women.' *Women's Studies Quarterly* XI: 12–15.

Zigli, B. (1985). 'College hurts self-esteem of bright women.' *USA Today,* April 2: 10C.

Zuckerman, D. M. (1983). 'Women's studies, self-esteem and college women's plans for the future.' *Sex Roles* 5: 633–642.

Curriculum and Conversions of Capital in the Acquisition of Disciplinary Knowledge

Jan Nespor

Bourdieu (1986) suggests that students' social skills and cultural orientations are forms of 'capital' that can be converted into other forms of capital, such as high school of college performance or educational credentials. The argument developed in this paper is that within educational institutions curricular structures create pressures and constraints on such conversions of capital, in particular, on conversions of social capital into academic capital. The focus will be two undergraduate programmes—physics and management—at a major research university in the US. I examine the interplay of students' academic and social experiences in the two programmes and show how the curricular structures create opportunities and pressures for particular kinds of social relations that, in turn, influence how students perform the academic tasks embedded in the curricula.

In this analysis the term 'curricular structure' refers to the *network organization of pedagogical contexts* within disciplines. I introduce this term as a partial corrective to the practice of conceptualizing curricula as school-sanctioned repositories of knowledge—textbooks, examinations, and classroom materials—or as enacted knowledge—the knowledge accepted as legitimate in classroom interaction (e.g., Anyon 1981, Keddie 1971, cf. Whitty 1985). The analytical focus of such frameworks is curriculum as 'textualized' knowledge that can be 'deconstructed', critiqued in terms of the information it includes and excludes, examined for the implicit messages carried by a rhetorical form, or analysed in terms of the ways it values different conceptions of knowledge and its uses. But such analytic accomplishments are achieved at the price of an implicit endorsement of the basic assumption underlying existing curricula: the idea that learning takes place through students' encounters with knowledge in particular classrooms; that subject matter is learned, or not learned, or learned in particular ways, as the result of what happens in discrete classroom settings. What is ignored are the organizational structures of curricula, the patterning of students' academic careers through these structures, and the cumulative growth of students' knowledge over the course of their academic careers (see Nespor 1986, 1987).

An alternative conception of curricula begins with the premise that student learning takes place over long periods of time (months, years) as students move through systems of courses and contexts. From this perspective, academic learning would be a function of students' *academic careers* through curricula, and these curricula would be viewed as *sequences of organizational contexts* distributed over time. These contexts—courses, for the most part—would be said to consist of sets of 'activities' or 'tasks' analysable into four basic components: 'goals', objects or 'resources' that can be used to achieve those goals, 'operations' or actions that can be used to transform resources to achieve goals, and 'constraints' on permissible lines of action for achieving goals (see Doyle 1983, Nespor 1986). In particular tasks, or in particular courses, students may define task components in ways quite different than their teachers expect, but these task definitions are *not* idiosyncratic, nor do they merely 'reflect' differences among students. Rather, *students's ways of defining tasks are products of their cumulative experiences in curricula* (Nespor 1987), and, at least in curricula with the kinds of structures discussed here, task definitions are powerfully influenced, indeed are created, by means of 'conversions' of students' social and cultural 'capital' onto 'academic capital'. It is this process that I shall try to describe.

The first part of the study describes the structures of the undergraduate physics and management curricula at the university in which this study was conducted. The second part analyses the kinds of social practices students in the two fields develop to negotiate the demands of the curricula. The research reported here comes from a field study of four undergraduate majors (physics, management, sociology, and secondary science education) that differed markedly in curricular structure (see Nespor 1988). I need to note that only physics and management possessed the kind of curricula 'tightness' (defined below) that seemed to produce conversion processes of the kind described here.

The fieldwork was conducted at a large, state-supported research university during the 1986-87 academic year and consisted of 116 interviews with students, faculty, and administrators; over 100 observations of class sessions; the collection and analysis of course syllabi, catalogues, textbooks, and students' class-notes; analyses of 225 transcripts of recent graduates in the fields; and ethnographic observations and interviews with students outside the classroom. In the following analysis I rely most heavily on college catalogues for the discussion of curricular structure, on interviews with seniors in physics and management for discussion of how students experienced the curricula (14% and 12%, of the seniors [fourth year students] in the two majors were interviewed), and on course syllabi, classroom observations, and interviews with faculty for the comments about the task structures in the courses of the curriculum.

Curricular Structure

The curricular structures of the two programmes can be compared along three basic dimensions: density, tightness, and interlocking. *Density* refers to the proportion of the students's undergraduate course requirements accounted for by courses within the major field of study. *Tightness* refers to the proportion of the required courses (or hours of course credit) that are 'completely determined' (in the sense that the specific courses to be taken, whether or not they are in the major field, are prescribed and named). Finally, *interlocking* refers to the linkage and sequencing of courses in the major by prerequisites. When describing interlocking I shall speak of 'interlocked strings', the number of courses (or hours) linked by prerequisites. Table 1 shows the variation across these dimensions in the two fields.

Physics was a dense, tightly-organized, and highly-interlocked major. From their first through to their final semesters, physics majors moved through a sequence of courses that were completely structured by prerequisites. Figure 1 depicts the structure of the curriculum (I use generic labels instead of actual course titles to preserve anonymity).

Table 1
Course requirements in physics and management

	Physics	Management
Total hours for the Bachelors	126	120
Hours in the major	40	21
Completely determined hours	66-69	53
Longest string of interlocking hours	52	15

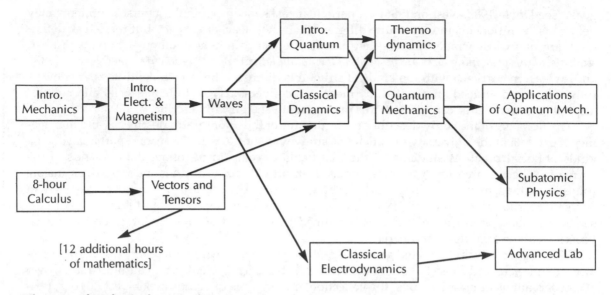

Figure 1 The physical curriculum.

Management, by contrast, had a low density (only 21 hours in the major), but a tight organization (49% of the undergraduate coursework is completely determined). As figure 2 shows, the curriculum derived its tightness from the large number of general business courses, or 'core courses', required of students majoring in the field: six hours each in economics, accounting, and finance; three hours each in statistics, data processing, business law, and marketing. By contrast, there were only nine completely-determined hours in management itself; no management courses were taken until the junior (third) year, and interlocked strings of courses were short.

These figures do not describe the actual course-taking patterns of the students, or even show all of the completely-determined courses students had to take (omitted are the nine credit hours of English, and the four hours each of government and history required for both majors). Rather, they show the curricular structures that formed the skeletons and musculature underlying students' idiosyncratic academic careers. These structures placed powerful constraints on academic careers by limiting the courses students could take, how many they could take, and when they could take them. Less obvious perhaps is the way these structures created pressures for particular kinds of learnings to take place. This is the topic I turn to now.

Conversions and Transformations of Capital in Physics

The undergraduate physics curriculum I studied was part of a longer physics curriculum that began in high school and continued to the graduate level. Students decided to major in physics while in high school, usually taking physics, and mathematics at least to the pre-calculus level. Indeed, the long sequence of prescribed courses beginning in the freshman (first university) year almost required students to have committed to a major in physics prior to entering college (the alternative being a significant extension of one's college career).

What the high school physics and mathematics courses did, then, was recruit and sort students, crating a small clientele for the physics programme, while preparing those students for undergraduate study. The high school physics courses introduced students to some of the basic concepts that they would encounter in Introductory Mechanics (and to lesser extent, Introductory Electricity and Magnetism). However, in addition to a more sophisticated reworking of subject matter already familiar to the students, the two introductory courses did three things.

First, they forced students to work more intensely and for much longer periods of time than they had in high school. The work itself might not have been especially difficult, but there were vastly greater amounts of it. As a student explained:

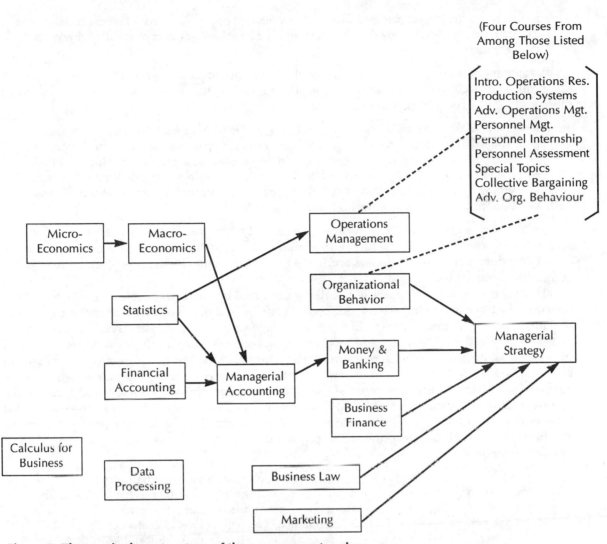

Figure 2 The curriculum structure of the management major.

One of the things you get out of your early classes is you get used to doing a lot of homework. That may sound kind of funny, and it is, but it's true. I mean, when I was in high school I whipped through homework in five minutes towards the end of class. . . . So when I got here I wasn't used to, like, spending most of the night doing problems and getting three or four hours of sleep. And the massive quantities of homework they tend to give you in initial classes teaches you that you're going to have to do that, if not through difficulty then just through sheer volume.

A second and related function of the introductory courses, articulated for the most part by faculty, was to weed out students without the necessary knowledge and willingness to work. About 30% of the students were expected to fail in each of the introductory courses.

Finally, the introductory courses gave students a 'feel for the phenomena'. As one student explained, they provided:

a better intuitive grasp for what's going on. By the time you've gotten into classical dynamics or classical electrodynamics the math is so powerful—it's just amazing to be able to solve these problems that you had to slave over in earlier courses just in one line. But if your introduction to these concepts . . . is through this very powerful mathematics you're going to lose touch with what's going on behind the math, with the physics. And so you develop, perhaps, your intuitive grasp of the real world in the introductory courses, as well as just an ability to comprehend this mathematics and apply it. . . . Its a levels process. In graduate school I'll take exactly the same thing (e.g., mechanical), except at a higher level of mathematics.

As this statement suggests, the physics curriculum was interlocked in a cycling, recursive fashion (a 'spiral' approach, one professor called it, 'where you circle around and bury into the tissue more and more'). As one student explained:

> After you've taken a course and you're onto the next level, you see how that course really help you to get to where you are now. And you do each step of the way. As you're actually taking it you're basically trying to get through the course, pass, get a grade, and . . . I find that I don't understand it as much while I'm taking it as I do *afterwards*, when I've seen everything. Then I see how it all sort of fits together and intertwines. So I find it more and more interesting as I get into the higher and higher levels.

But seeing how it all 'fits together' did not come easily, nor was it in most cases an individual achievement. Rather, understanding both within and across courses was a function of a *group effort* to produce a consensual understanding of the subject matter—students working together to accomplish course tasks.

This group effort was shaped and partially produced by curricular pressures. The density of the coursework in the major, the interlocking of courses, and the 'weeding out' that took place in the introductory courses, meant that by the beginning of the upper-division (third year) coursework (Classical Dynamics and Modern Physics) classes were small (about 20 students) and the students in them knew each other from past courses. In the lower-division (first and second year) courses students had begun experimenting with joint work in groups growing out of lab partnerships. These study groups crystallized in the upper division courses, and through the many hours spent together in and out of classes, physics students began to form close friendships with one another, often to the exclusion of other friendships (the female students were an exception, having friends unconnected to physics in addition to a core of physics friends). As a senior explained:

> Since there's a core set of courses, you usually go through them at the same time. There turned out to be some courses that you weren't taking with your other friends—depending on how they arranged their schedules it was sometimes different, but usually there was at least one person in your class that you had in a class with before. . . . I studied for maybe a year to two years with just the same people . . . you get to be real comfortable around them and you get to know them very well. And we've all become pretty good friends.

According to another senior, working in groups was a conscious strategy for academic success:

> I think either you're extremely bright or you're a fool if you don't get in a study group. Because you save so much time, simply because when you sit there, even if you're trying to explain a problem that you already understand to someone, you learn it that much better by explaining it. And you find out what you don't know while you're trying to explain it. Also, if you're having a problem with something, then someone else might have a different viewpoint on it so they might understand it a little better. And there's also the fact that you're not sitting by yourself for five and six hours on end, pounding over a problem. Instead you sit in groups of four or five and pound over them for four or five hours.

But group work was not merely a more efficient way of learning something that could be learned in solitude. As a senior explained, learning as part of a group was different than learning on one's own:

> If you just try to always think about it or write about it I don't think you ever know what you knew. You need to talk about it, you need to be able to put it into words, what you know. Because if you can't, then you really can't understand it. Working with other people forces you to put it into words, to say what you think, to say why you think your answer is right and his is wrong.

One reason why talking about problems was important was that the kinds of problems students were asked to work changed from the introductory to the upper-division courses. In the former, problems were routine, with well defined goals, operations, constraints, and resources. The emphasis was on learning to work. With the Waves course the emphasis shifted. Only a handful of problems were assigned each week, but they were less well-defined, providing ambiguous specifications of goal states and partial sets of resources (givens). Students could not simply 'solve' them, they had to refine their understandings of the goal and discover the relevant operations. In accomplishing this other students became key resources. As the student just quoted described the process:

> We work, just . . . basically solving problems. And we would just take turns. Each getting up to the blackboard and writing the next equation, and arguing about how things are, and why we believe the answer is this, and there were a lot of things that we found we didn't understand and we argued through some of them.

The instructors reinforced the emphasis on understanding by giving substantial credit for *how* problems were solved. As a senior explained:

> [The professors] don't tell you how to solve a problem. If you solve it in a valid method they have to give you credit for it, even though they may tell you, 'Well, that's not the way we wanted it done'. Most of the time they will give you at least partial credit. . . . They'll leave a note on your paper like 'Not exactly what I had in mind.' Lots of time . . . if you're wrong because of something you don't know about . . . they will give you most of the credit and say like, 'Excellent argument, however, see . . .' and they'll reference a book as to why this can't be done.

The formation of academically-oriented friendship and work groups among physics students thus produced shared understandings of physics, qualitatively different conceptions of the subject matter than would have developed among students working individually. It also had academic consequences. All of the interviewed students who worked in groups had above a B average in physics, the cut-off criterion for admission to graduate school in physics, while all of the interviewed students who worked individually had less than a B average. Although there were undoubtedly exceptions to this pattern, it seems clear that group work influenced grades, and through grades, one's chances of a career in physics.

Why then did four of the 11 seniors interviewed choose to work alone? There was no indication that groups excluded students. Rather, solitary work seemed to be a consequence of one of two factors: strong friendship networks outside physics (and students' entry into the programme in the upper-division), or working-class backgrounds that shaped the outlooks of students in ways that made them reject group study.

One of the four students, for example, had family ties in the area that monopolized his time outside the classroom. With no friends among the physics students, he failed several physics courses, and ultimately abandoned his plans to go to graduate school in physics.

Another student had joined a fraternity (during the summer before he began coursework at the university) and had found his time monopolized by fraternity activities. After making good grades in the lower-division physics courses he began to fail the upper-division physics courses.

> The first physics class . . . I did really well in that, but I'm sure that's because I'd had two years of it in high school. And the same kind of thing happened with my sophomores (second) year, taking the other two lower division physics classes. I didn't do as well, just because the stuff we'd had in high school wasn't quite up to the same level, but still I spent almost no time doing it, I spent a lot of time at the fraternity. And so my grades started to go down. . . . And then first semester junior year was rock bottom.

During his senior year, this student decided to go into secondary school science teaching.

Social class effects on students' orientations to group work were more complex. One of two students with working-class backgrounds had finished 'about 10th from the bottom of the class' in high school. Interested in science from childhood, he earned a degree from a state technical institute, but found himself dissatisfied with work as a technician. He came to the university and began at the bottom of the curriculum in the introductory courses, several years older than his classmates. His prior training did, however, help him find a place in a professor's laboratory as a device-maker. As he described his situation:

> I'm much ahead of my contemporaries, just by the fact that I've got a two-year degree and can design electronics. In physics there's not a lot of coursework designed to familiarize people with electronics. There's one course in the undergraduate curriculum, maybe two, but they're mickey mouse, by and large. . . . And so I can design things, and that's helped me out immensely.

This niche enabled him to survive in the major with a grade point average barely above a C. He still hoped to go to graduate school in physics, but was already pursuing other science-related jobs. He had no friends among the undergraduate physics students, he explained, 'because they have a very unsophisticated view of physics. They haven't ever done it.' More than this, he saw himself as having a fundamentally different approach to life than the physics undergraduates:

> I try to experiment and get things that are really outside of the physics train of thought, just because you can become, and this happens time and time again . . . people are so completely monomaniacal that they're just geeky idiots that know nothing about anything but how to solve the Schroedinger equation or something like that. And they're not able to carry on a conversation to people that are outside of their field. And I think that's really a shame. They're just not well-rounded.

The other working class student I interviewed, the son of a truck driver, used similar terms to describe other physics students:

> Most of my friends are not physics students. . . . [Most physics students] are very introverted and like all they think about is physics, all they want to think about is physics, apparently. You can't strike a conversation up with them about much else. They seem to be quiet and just basically boring. . . . They sit in libraries with books and read and that's boring to me. There's a whole world out there and you've got to try and experience it, in my opinion, to be a well-rounded person.

These students were not unaware of the benefits of group work, but they rejected it as an approach to learning. As the device-maker put it:

> I never work with other people. . . . It's not because I'm full of scruples or anything like that. I just feel that it's a personal endeavour for me. It's just a matter of thinking about things. That's the way I solve the problems. . . . Sometimes talking to other students, your classmates, helps, and a lot of people do that, rely on that, but I don't. And I'm certainly doing myself a big injustice, I think, because, well, it would just make things easier, but I've never been one to address things easy.

This student simply went over and over problems, spent enormous amounts of time on them, and often, by his own admission, failed to find the right path to the solution. The other working class students quoted here also did most of his work alone, though on occasion he sought advice from professors (which was somewhat unusual for an undergraduate).

Both students agreed that the kind of learning one got from working problems alone was qualitatively different from what one would get working in groups. One saw the results of group work as a shallow understanding of physics.

> The key to learning . . . is to understand what's going on, the basics, I mean, why it is happening. If you don't understand that a rock falls because masses attract each other, then you may be able to tell people, if you drop it from this tower it will be moving this fast when it hits the ground. But if someone perturbs the problem and makes it odd so that your formulas don't work exactly and you have to change them, unless you understand why it works, you don't know how to change your formulas. . . . You have to try to teach it to yourself. And some people, myself included sometimes, have a hard time doing it. . . . It's not a very pleasant thing to sit there for hours on end confusing yourself endlessly. And that's just the way you feel about it, you know. I don't feel that a lot of [the students who

work in groups] are worried about it. I don't think they have the right attitude. A lot of them are just interested in getting A's.

The device-maker put it another way, suggesting that the students working in groups acquired an artificial conception of physics.

As a student—what do you know when you know physics?—you know how to solve problems. Which is kind of nothing really to it—that's kind of a lie, it can be very complex, but you just know rules of mathematics, you know some logical thought, you know how to think. . . . So solving problems is just that, it's just something that you have to do. But in the real world situation [in the lab]—what do you know when you know physics?—well, I'll know nuclear physics, which is how, more or less, fundamental particles interact with one another at specific energies. I'll know electronics to design apparatuses. I'll know how my apparatuses work, and I'll know how to write computer programs to analyze my data because it's too complex to do by hand. And then I'll know what it means when I get it out. And so it's much more thorough, yeah, thorough. Academic problem-solving is very mindless in a way. I really have a lot of problems with academic problem-solving—not problems doing it, just problems motivating myself. It's so completely removed from what you have to do, ultimately. I mean, you're never going to have to have to sit and figure out how a penny spins and show it mathematically. And on top of that, everything is set up for you. It's so completely orthogonal to real life situations.

The group *versus* individual work split thus had fateful consequences not only for students' chances of continuing in the field, but for the approach to doing physics that they developed. Figure 3 depicts the curriculum/social organization/academic performance relations described above.

What the physics curriculum did, then, was create a structural pressure for the development of friendships or 'strong ties' (Granovetter 1983) oriented around the performance of academic tasks. Students' responses to these pressures were shaped by their social backgrounds and positions in alternative systems of strong ties. In the language of 'capitals', the curriculum functions as a 'converter' of one form of 'embodied cultural capital' (general tastes, modes of interacting, leisure-time preferences; see Bourdieu 1986) into a narrow and focused kind of social

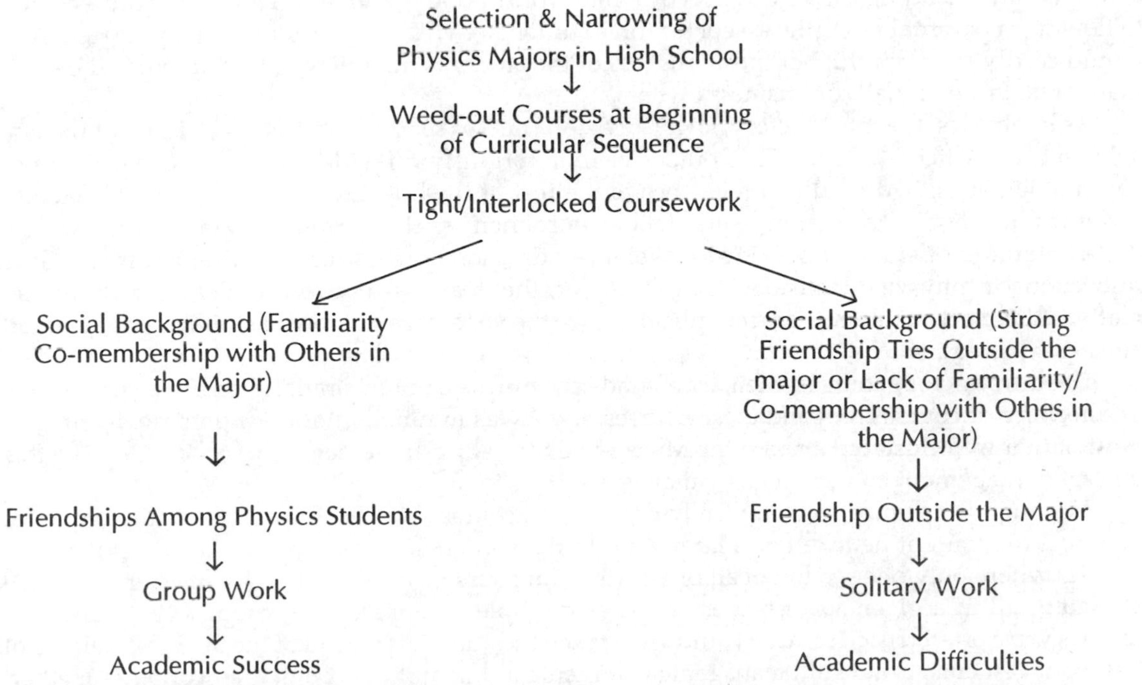

Selection & Narrowing of
Physics Majors in High School
↓
Weed-out Courses at Beginning
of Curricular Sequence
↓
Tight/Interlocked Coursework

Social Background (Familiarity
Co-membership with Others in
the Major)
↓
Friendships Among Physics Students
↓
Group Work
↓
Academic Success

Social Background (Strong
Friendship Ties Outside the
major or Lack of Familiarity/
Co-membership with Othes in
the Major)
↓
Friendship Outside the Major
↓
Solitary Work
↓
Academic Difficulties

Figure 3 Conversions of capital in physics.

capital (friendship groups organized around physics problem solving and studying). This did not occur if students had different kinds of background capital, or if alternative social networks short-circuited the conversion. The students who did make the conversion were then able to convert their new form of social capital into a different form of embodied cultural capital (oriented to the kind of social skills needed for participation in the study groups). This cultural capital could then be converted in turn into academic capital through the process of group work. Ultimately, this academic capital could be converted into a kind of institutional capital in the form of admission to a prestigious graduate programme.

Indeed, although the study reported here did not extend to the graduate level, other research suggests that in some respects academic success can be seen less as a form of valuable capital in itself and more as a kind of institutional certification of students' possession of the narrow form of social capital. Ziman (1987: 63), for example, quotes one participant from his study of practising scientists as presenting the representative view that:

> You only use about 3-5% of your undergraduate training at postgraduate-level, anyway, even if you stay in nominally the same field of physics, and I think if you've got a scientific and technical training you can pick up the other 3-5% in another scientific or technical field . . . very quickly indeed, in a matter of months.

The inference to be drawn is not that the particular field of undergraduate education is unimportant. Rather, it is that the scientific knowledge and skills that students acquire as under-graduates are perhaps no more important than the way they learn them and the social and embodied cultural capital that they acquire in the course of learning them. Team research seems to be the norm both at the graduate and professional levels in physics (Kleppner 1985, Memory *et al.* 1985). This learning to work as the member of a team may be more than a strategy for academic success; it may be an accomplishment that begins to shape students' capacities for participating in the dominant forms of social relations in the professional work of the field.

Generation and Conversions of Capital in Management

Instead of looking at undergraduate education as a preparation for graduate study, management students saw it leading directly to the corporate world upon graduation. This aspiration seemed to flow from parental example: except for three students (two managers returning for degrees that would certify them for 'higher' positions), all of the students interviewed had parents who were managers, professionals, or business owners.

As in physics, the introductory, lower-division courses seemed aimed at weeding out the less able and motivated students. The courses were notoriously difficult, and some, like economics and mathematics, had no direct relevance to the rest of the business curricula. Business faculty had introduced various other measures to limit enrolment, such as a minimal grade point average (GPA) required of students seeking to take upper-division business courses (there were no GPA restrictions in physics). Unlike physics, however, the goal was not to produce a small, highly motivated cohort of students, but simply to reduce the very large number of students who wanted business degrees.

The introductory courses, then, were academic hurdles, not the initial stages in a substantive interlocking of courses. Beyond these courses, there was minimal interlocking in the major, and most of that was clustered around the Managerial Strategy class (essentially serving to make this the last management course taken by management majors).

Although the number of completely-determined courses was fairly large, then, the sequence in which they might be taken was largely up to the students. Moreover, unlike the situation in physics where only one section of an upper-division course was offered each semester (if it were offered at all in a given semester), in business multiple sections of the completely determined courses were offered each semester, and were taken by students from all of the business fields, not just management. As a result, management students did not pass through their courses together.

The lack of interlocking and group passage through the curriculum meant that management students did not form academically-based friendships with their classmates. Indeed, the friendship networks of most of the interviewed students centred not on business students, but on people from hometown schools, dormitories, or boyfriends or girlfriends.

The absence of friends in classes went along with the fact that students did not work together. All of the interviewed students rejected group work as a viable strategy, and it was a major source of dissension in courses where it was required (as in the Managerial Strategy class).

Finally, because the required courses were drawn from a wide range of business fields, and were only minimally interlocked, there was little consistency in the kinds of academic tasks students encountered as they moved through the curriculum. Task types were course-specific rather than general to the discipline. Unlike the 'problem'-based task structure of the physics curriculum, some business courses used large group lecture formats and required only that students pass multiple-choice tests (e.g., marketing), while other courses were oriented around problem-solving (e.g., accounting, operations management), research-based term projects (a number of the elective courses), or case analyses (e.g., business law, Managerial Strategy).

As a result, faculty could not assume that students taking their courses were familiar with the types of tasks they were to be presented with. This forced faculty to make the goals, operations, and constraints of the tasks highly explicit and well-defined. Even in Managerial Strategy it was necessary to review or reteach past lessons and explicitly relate them to the tasks at hand. As a teacher of the course put it:

> Like the accounting—many of them had the [Managerial Accounting] course, they normally would take it in the second semester of their sophomore year. For most of them that's two years back, and for some maybe three or four. It's way back in the recesses of their mind. . . . It's something when I lecture on it or go through examples, it stirs old memories, but it's clearly something that's right at their fingertips.

Despite the number of prerequisites for the course, then, students in Managerial Strategy needed only a rudimentary acquaintance with accounting, finance, and marketing to perform the tasks of the course (e.g., interpreting simplified balance sheets and calculating simple financial ratios), and most of the necessary knowledge was reviewed and provided in the course itself.

However, though there were no academically-oriented friendship groups among management students, no group study activities, and no curriculum-wide task types that would have allowed students to benefit from group study, there *were* several senses in which social networks were of extreme importance to management students.

First, because the students had to take specific courses but had control over when and from whom to take them, a premium was placed on information about courses and professors. Fraternities, sororities, and other student associations played important roles in the distribution of this information. As a student described the process:

> With the sororities and fraternities, what they do is like they . . . put them all into alphabetical order. They put 'Money and Banking' and they'll put 'Dr—' beside it, and they'll have a list. They'll have a 'good list' and a 'bad list'. And the bad list are usually professors that are incoherent . . . or something is not kosher. And then you have put your name under the stuff you wrote down. That means that people can come to you and ask you 'why didn't you like this class?' Like people will come to me and they're going to ask me' . . . why didn't you like Business Finance with Dr—?' And I'm going to go 'basically because of my attitude, I didn't care. I wanted a grade, I wanted out of that class. I studied for it. It was just frustrating, because I tried and I couldn't do it. And therefore I don't like the class.' And they're going to go, 'Oh, okay'. And I'll go, 'But, you know, if you're a finance major and you get into economics and accounting, then that's fine, you'll love the class. But for me, uh uh'. . . . it's what people want, it's not just good or bad.

Often student organization meetings were arranged specifically for the purpose of allowing students to counsel each other:

> This next coming Tuesday, the Management Association is going to have a [meeting] about—we're just all going to get together and help each other out on who to take/who not to take. Or, if you want to take this, this is what you're going to have to do. So people know

what to expect. It makes you feel like—maybe it makes you feel like you have a jump on the next guy—and you probably do.

All but three of the interviewed students used these kinds of advising networks (two of the three had outside jobs, and selected courses on the basis of what would fit into their schedules, the third 'researched' courses by sitting in on the first class session, looking over the course outline and the teacher, and then formally adding the works to his/her programme later).

A second use of the social networks was the distribution of task resources. The well-defined character of course tasks, along with the fact that students belonging to the networks took the courses at different points in time, meant that students became task 'resources' for each other. Most often, resource distribution took the form of circulating notes, test, and papers done for a class to students about to take the class. As one student explained:

> I save all [my notes], I have them all up on a shelf. Some people I know, younger, I've given them to, and I've gotten a lot of notes from people.... You might have an old test or two and you see how they're doing it. It helps a lot to study off of those.

Notes thus were passed down across generations of students

> A lot of people . . . they come and ask 'did you have such and such a class?' 'Yeah.' 'What were the tests like?' 'Well here's my test, my old test, my old notes and stuff'. I mean, I got all these notes from other people, they just keep getting passed down the line. So, I mean, I have them all, and I had a lot of them I've given away. So they've come in helpful, like me using other peoples' notes, cause I mean, it's the same class, but they'll get stuff out of it, maybe, that I wouldn't have . . . that's been really useful.It's just another set of notes that I would coincide with my notes, which I would then coincide with the outline of the chapters to try to get the basic ideas, the main points of the course.

Tests and writing projects (term papers) were also circulated. As one student explained:

> I'd say it's real prevalent in writing projects, as being passed on and somewhat amended in different areas to change it a little bit. So you've got a 20 page project that's due for professor X, and you've got a friend that says 'Hey, I had Professor X, I did this project, let me give it to you.' I think there's a lot of that going on. . . . Either that, or modeling it after another. Which would save a lot of time.

In many cases the stockpiling of tests became an organizational function. As one student, an officer in a service organization, explained; 'I save tests—I try to save many tests as I can. And I put them in the [organization's] test file for other people, to help them'.

Participation in social networks thus clearly had academic benefits, but these were by no means so clear-cut as in physics. Some of the students who participated in the networks had GPAs below the B level, while two of the three students who did not participate were well above the B level. In other words, participation in the social networks was neither necessary nor sufficient to ensure academic success, though by all accounts it improved performance.

Moreover, it would be misleading to suggest that joining fraternities, sororities, service organizations, or student associations was an *academic* strategy. Rather, the initial decision to join seemed to be a function either of 'social strategies' or 'career strategies'. By social strategy I mean a way of finding a friends or getting access to social activities. The physics curriculum supplied its students with a stable block of fellow majors with whom one moved from class to class. That, and the group study format, allowed students to form friendship groups that overlapped with academic groups. The lack of interlocking precluded this in management, but the tightness of the curriculum created shared interests and concerns, and outside organization provided a source of friends with whom one shared similar career goals.

For the most part, however, management students did not join organizations to find friends. Rather, organizational participation was a form of 'career strategy'. Put simply, it was commonly believed that job recruiters placed a premium on membership and activity in student organizations. Not only were the groups important for recruitment—as a form of social certification—they could also serve as means of access to jobs and employers, as introductions to job networks. As one student explained: 'Definitely one of the main advantages of [belonging to groups] is that it looks good to a future employer, I think, being involved, not just being a student'. Others echoed these sentiments:

> I'm in the management association and the marketing association here. I've also been in IASBCE, International Association of Students of Business, Commerce, and Economics. But I was only in that for a semester. [Nespor: Why did you join those?] Well, I hate to say it, but a lot of it had to do with resumes. Towards the end you say 'I've got to make that resume look better'. And while that's not a very good reason for starting it, I've really enjoyed my experiences with these associations, and thought that they've been very beneficial. Although I didn't get into them for maybe the right reasons or whatever.

Sometimes membership could lead directly to a job:

> I found a lot of friends in the business school just because I think you're so aware of 'networking' (laughs). And you want to make these friends, and it's just something that you do consciously. . . . I joined [the Management Association] because I was getting worried about getting a job and I wanted to have more contacts. And it worked. [The group's sponsor] got me a job.

As these statements suggest, many of the organizations' activities centred on making connections and learning job-getting skills:

> Like [in a service organization], you learn things that will help you in your business career. We have top business people come talk from all over. We fly them in and they speak to us and give us pointers. We have like executive cocktail parties. We don't drink at it but we have like 250 executives from all over fly in. We've had resume workshops.

The interplay of curriculum and capitals is thus in some ways more complex in management than in physics. In the first place, the associations and organizations that functioned as networks of 'weak ties' (Granovetter 1983) were stable entities that preexisted the student cohorts that participated in them. Unlike physics, where work groups were formed afresh by each class of students (most of whom were unaware of such groups among their predecessors), the fraternities, sororities, and associations were already there for the management students. Second, management students did not join these groups because of curricular pressures. Rather, they joined them for the most part to build up social capital. Indeed, the idea that business recruiters are interested in students' social accomplishments and organizational memberships was to a great extent signalled to new students in the business programme by the very existence and high visibility of such organizations. It was only when students joined the organizations that they discovered that the groups provided valuable information for negotiating the curriculum. That is, the structure of the curriculum made valuable such information as the groups possessed (knowledge about professors, information about tasks that will be encountered in particular classes). Figure 4 depicts these relationships.

The curriculum in management education, through the way in which it immersed students in the peculiar social world of the business school, thus seemed to act as a *generator* of social capital in the form of group memberships. This social capital could be converted in two ways: directly into another, broader form of social capital spanning the boundaries of the institution (i.e., job networks and 'contacts'), and indirectly into academic capital through the circulation of information about courses and resources for the performance of course tasks.

This dual conversion seemed to stem from the different role that academic performance played in business as opposed to physics. In physics academic performance was a direct reflection of both students' knowledge and their social and cultural capital. In management academic success could be the result of many factors and carried no clear implications about students' social or cultural capital. Moreover, there was a congruence between the academic world of undergraduate physics education and the academic world of graduate physics education that was lacking in the relationship between the academic world of the business school and the world of business. Indeed, good grades alone could have negative meanings for employers in certain areas of business. As one student explained:

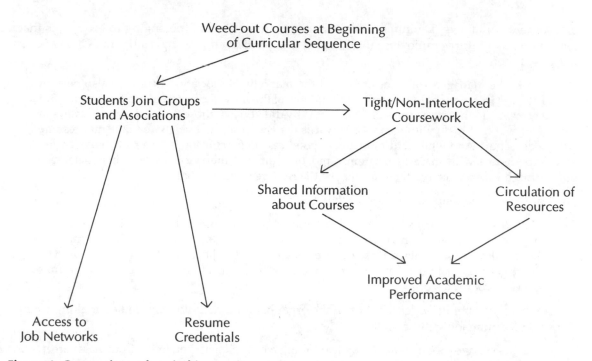

Figure 4 Conversions of capital in management.

> To accounting firms [good grades are] worthwhile, to engineering-type firms it's worth-while—quantitative-type businesses. In marketing and advertising and many other fields [including management], [my high GPA] probably go against me. [Nespor: Go against you? Why?] I would have to prove myself. I would have to show them that I didn't spend the last four years of my life locked up in a room with a book.

Paradoxically, then, in some instances (where a person had a particularly high GPA), social capital might well have functioned to offset the academic capital into which it had previously been converted.

Conclusions

By looking at curricular structure as organizational instructions and resources for activity spread out in time, the approach adopted here focuses attention on the consumption or use of curricula rather than its production. The concepts of 'capitals' and conversion processes represent one way of talking about these uses. Taken together, attention to the curricular structure and capital emphasizes the temporal dimension of educational experiences and moves away from the preoccupation with specific classrooms, focusing attention instead on interactions across a network of classrooms and other contexts. The approach also allows us to talk with some specificity about the interplay of social and academic activity, though as presently formulated it may seem to stray unpleasantly close to economistic, rational choice models of action. This is not my intent. Instead, I am trying to develop a way of talking about curriculum as practice rather than treating it as a text to be picked apart through some sort of hermeneutics.

One 'problem' with looking at curriculum as the product of students' academic careers is that it undercuts our usual way of talking about curriculum. Rather than talking about 'the physics curriculum' or 'the management curriculum' we have to talk about 'the academic careers of physics students' and so forth (although I think it is still useful to talk about 'curricular structure' in the strictly organizational sense used in this paper). In a sense this article has taken the easy path in looking at two fields where particularly 'tight' curricular structures produced group effects that overlapped with organizationally-defined majors. By contrast, a discussion of sociology students, majors in a field with a very loose and thin undergraduate curricular structure, would have revealed an agglomeration of idiosyncratic academic careers among majors in the field. This is not to say that there were no conversion processes going on among sociology majors, simply that they were unrelated to sociology's curricular structure.

As this implies, curricular structure is not the only factor influencing or serving as a medium for conversions of capital. Social groupings organized along a number of lines—from athletic teams to groups of ethnic minority students to members of residential cooperatives—sometimes worked together and shared information and resources even though they may have been majoring in a variety of fields. Group perspectives may have emerged, but they did not correspond to particular disciplines or fields of study.

It is for that reason that disciplines such as the two described here deserve special scrutiny—for they involve the production of the people who will inherit the positions and institutional apparatuses of disciplines that control or influence important domains of everyday life.

This point raises the question of how curricular tightness and interlocking are related to disciplinary power and status. Although there is clearly a need for much more work in different fields and different kinds of institutions, from the evidence presented here one could speculate that fields preparing students for positions of power and status are structured so as to produce cohorts of graduates with shared outlooks, ambitions, definitions of reality, and strategies for acquiring and using knowledge. The curricular structures of the fields produced pressures for and served as resources for the problem solving in physics ad the 'networking' in management. Both kinds of activities can be looked at as kinds of normalizing technologies (Foucault 1977) suppressing difference and 'deviation' and insuring social and cultural 'reproduction' in spheres of power. The content of courses is of secondary importance. It is the structuring of social and academic experiences that accounts for the reproduction of paradigms.

The tight curricular structures of power-linked disciplines do not produce 'better' or 'more powerful' forms of knowledge than other fields. Rather, systems of power are created simultaneously with and interweaved with systems of knowledge in processes that spread out over years, pushed and shaped by organizational structures that become effectual only when experienced by people with certain backgrounds.

References

Anyon, J. (1981) Social class and school knowledge. *Curriculum Inquiry*, 11: 3–42.

Bourdieu, P. (1986) The forms of capital. In J. Richardson (ed.) *Handbook of Theory and Research for the Sociology of Education* (New York: Greenwood Press), 241–258.

Doyle, W. (1983) Academic work. *Review of Educational Research*, 53: 159–199.

Foucault, M. (1977) *Discipline and Punish* (new York: Pantheon).

Granovetter, M. (1983) The strength of weak ties: A network theory revisited. In R. Collins (ed.) *Sociological Theory 1983* (San Francisco: Jossey-Bass), 201–233.

Keddie, N. (1971) Classroom knowledge. In M. F. D. Young (ed.) *Knowledge and Control* (London: Macmillan), 133–160.

Kleppner, D. (1985) Research in small groups. *Physics Today*, 38 (3): 79–85.

Memory, J. D., Arnold, J. F., Stewart, D. W., and Fornes, R. E. (1985) Physics as a team sport. *American Journal of Physics*, 53: 270–271.

Nespor, J. (1986) Theoretical notes: On students' experiences across the grade levels. *Anthropology and Education Quarterly*, 17: 203–216.

Nespor, J. (1987) Academic tasks in a high school English class. *Curriculum Inquiry*, 17: 203–228.

Whitty, G. (1985) *Sociology and School Knowledge* (London: Methuen).

Ziman, J. (1987) *Knowing Everything About Nothing* (Cambridge: Cambridge University Press).

Institutional Topography: The Curriculum

William G. Tierney

The etymology of curriculum derives from "curricle," a two-wheeled carriage or racing chariot. Originally intended to define a racecourse, the word has been appropriated to connote a course of study or training. How educators have defined what the course of study or training should be has varied remarkably throughout the history of American higher education. In *The Reforming of General Education*, Daniel Bell stated the question in the following manner: "Is it the task of the university to be a clerisy, self-consciously guarding the past and seeking assertively to challenge the new? Or is it just a bazaar, offering Coleridge and Blake, Burckardt and Nietzsche, Weber and Marx as antiphonal prophets, each with his own call?" (1967, p. 348).

What counts for knowledge and how organizational participants decide what knowledge to include in the curriculum are the focal points of this chapter. By looking at the nature of knowledge and how definitions of knowledge do or do not get incorporated into the curriculum, we will consider whose interests the curriculum reflects as well as those who are not heard with regard to curricular change.

Knowledge, Culture, and the Curriculum

This section will further delve into the curriculum and construction of knowledge at Cutting Edge College and Entrepreneurial College. First, however, we will discuss an institution with a quite different conception of what accounts for knowledge from both Cutting Edge and Entrepreneurial. The institutions has a long history of teaching "the classics." By and large, the *Classics College* (CC) faculty do not conduct research; teaching is paramount. Classics has prided itself on its student body; although competition to get into the college is not terrifically competitive, the student makeup ranks Classics as one of the best in the country. Established over 80 years ago, half of the students graduate within four years. Retaining the other students has become a major concern. Student enrollment is slightly over 1,000, and FTE faculty is around 100. However, faculty fear that they are not getting the kind of students they once had.

Over the years Classics has had several difficult periods balancing the budget; but they seem to have weathered the storm, primarily through the president's fund-raising efforts and slightly larger class sizes. The administration is small, and the faculty wish it were smaller. After a long tenure at Classics, the president is about to step down, and the AVP will retire soon after. Rumors abound that the new president will want an academic vice president from the outside—a departure from tradition. Several "living legends" of the faculty will also soon retire. Retirements may mean that the purpose of Classics will change, and change has been adamantly resisted by the faculty. The purpose of the institution has always been clear to most of the faculty: "We believe we are an educational institution," mentions one long-time faculty member, "and not a social hostel,

adds, "What's really special about Cutting Edge is the frequency with which we drop in on one another and discuss what we're doing, our ideas, our concerns." People constantly refer to how they "drop in on" and talk with one another about their courses and intellectual dilemmas. Another person confirms the interdisciplinary nature of Cutting Edge: "The institution gives you the freedom and space and help to make connections across boundaries. Your concerns and interests affect you on a curricular level, on what you teach."

What kind of coherence can be made out of a curricular structure that looks on the face of it as if it exists by whim or fancy? At Classics College, for example, professors have intellectual "buckets" that guide the kind of curriculum that will be developed. A biochemistry professor at Classics explains, "The nature of my discipline, the knowledge in it, is being developed so fast. We don't do interdisciplinary things here because just to keep up in my discipline is next to impossible." Although the professor is in a discipline that many look upon as a hybrid—biology and chemistry—the individual speaks quite clearly about what guides his thinking about what kind of knowledge needs to inform the curriculum. Faculty members identify with their discipline, which in turn defines what will be taught. The assumption follows Bloom's line of thinking; students need to be socialized—"there are certain things one must know"—and the discipline defines what those "things" are.

What guides Cutting Edge's curricular process? Various faculty members speak about the purpose of their curriculum in terms that are antithetical to the notion of knowledge as facts and figures. "We need to explode the myth that someone can master a concrete entity called 'knowledge,'" adds another. One longtime faculty member adds, "I think we should take the curriculum apart every few years, totally start over, so that we don't fool ourselves." Another individual comments:

> The curriculum is fragmented, purposefully so. People need to cut it up into different pieces, take knowledge apart and put it back together again. We want students to make the synthesis and connections for themselves. Somewhere after World War II it became impossible to think of all knowledge existing in one paradigm. We're in a different world now and we want to enable our students to grasp onto the power structures. Our purposes isn't just to teach Caribbean literature, but to teach people how to read.

Although most who teach at Cutting Edge agree with the curricular goals, some people are also concerned that not enough structure exists. "I'm dissatisfied with the process," admits one individual. "The curriculum is not coherent because we start out with faculty preference and then leave it up to the students to make the connections. That's not good." Says another, "I don't believe in rigid formulations, but this is too loose sometimes, and the student who is not in command of his or her life gets lost."

A new faculty member speaks about the difficulty that occurs with this curricular approach by talking about her teaching: "We call it 'mode of inquiry,' because we don't lecture, we want discussion. In general I like it, but I worry sometimes that they're missing something. I think my students should know about the Licensing Act of 1737, but how do I get that across?"

Presumably the speaker's concern is not only that students learn about a law concerning the theater, but also about other information as well. Her concern is similar to that of the science professor at Classics College: "What do students need to know?" The difference in curricular formulas between Classics and Cutting Edge is that the former assumes all well-educated people must know certain data, whereas the latter denies the assumption that knowledge is ever neutral. Furthermore, Classics College assumes that until one masters particular information one will not be able to think independently. The outcome of an education is the ability to think. At Cutting Edge College, conversely, they assume that mastery of knowledge is a subjective task that must be understood as a political undertaking. Critical inquiry is the subject of learning.

In one way, Entrepreneurial College is similar to Classics' conception of knowledge. Entrepreneurial has a potpourri of innovative programs that faculty have devised. Some students spend their freshman year together studying a particular set of courses. Other students take a more traditional body of courses. Additional students spend an intensive amount of time in one course. And still other students become immediately involved in their majors to meet the rigorous demands of premedical degrees or engineering and the like. Although the faculty do not agree that one body of knowledge must be taught, the faculty are similar to Classics in the sense that in general they work from the assumption that what they teach is value-neutral. One individual, for example, says: "I'm involved in the freshmen seminar, and it really shakes students up, they really end up questioning what they're about. But I honestly don't care what they believe. We don't teach one ideological stance here. Students can pick and choose, and we're quite open about it."

In the spring I interview four students who turn out to be "political conservatives." I ask them if they feel particular points of view are being taught. They laugh and nod their heads as one student explains:

> In some classes it doesn't matter, like science or engineering. In some classes it does matter, like Latin American Studies or Political Science. That's where the really liberal faculty are, but they're very open about what they believe and we're free to disagree and debate them. I like having them tell their side of the story so I can be prepared when I get out in the real world to defeat the kind of crazy ideas they have. So I'd say they have an ideology, but it's not doctrinaire or anything. It's just a typical liberal professor. But they are open to debate.

Entrepreneurial College's approach to learning is in line with its mission that allows for faculty to define their relationship to the institution in a wide variety of manners. The shared conviction of the mission is the belief that faculty have the freedom to teach whatever they want; the design and conduct of the curriculum reflects the diversity. Given that the faculty have the freedom of definition, the assumption is that the approaches to learning, and hence knowledge and the curriculum, is diversified and abstract. Like Classics and unlike Cutting Edge, Entrepreneurial's faculty do not have an overriding ideology that governs what they teach; instead, they have more of a smorgasbord approach to learning. Unlike Classics, the faculty at Entrepreneurial do not believe that all students must learn a particular canon of knowledge.

The way the faculty knows at Classics College if a student has mastered his or her subject matter is through a senior thesis. In general the thesis is discipline-based, and interaction occurs between the student and one thesis advisor. A long-time faculty member points out, "It's nice to know that the rest of the world is catching on to what we've been doing. People like Boyer now say that a senior thesis is a good form of assessment."

Cutting Edge College has no cultural literacy test for its students. In fact, faculty and administrators seem relatively unconcerned with an overall assessment. Instead, they believe that constant monitoring and advising of students, different thesislike projects during a student's career, and the interaction students have in classes and with their committees provided good evidence about what the student has or has not learned. The projects are in some ways the *anti*-thesis of Classics projects. The projects must cross disciplines, and work occurs not just with one professor but a small team. Interestingly, both Classics and Cutting Edge have final products that are similar to honor's or thesis papers; the process each institution takes to reach the goal of a final paper, however, is radically different, which in turn, effects the purpose of the goal. Classics' goal is to show that a student has mastered a specific body of knowledge, whereas Cutting Edge's goal is to enable the student to understand the underpinnings of the social construction of knowledge. Entrepreneurial College has a more traditional approach to the assessment of learning. Different faculty have different conceptions of what to test student on, and final exams and term papers provide ongoing analyses; there is no unified attempt to have all students either write a senior thesis or undertake a particular project.

Another way to think about assessing what students learn is to also think about what student do not learn. What kind of learning occurs at Classics College that does not take place at Cutting Edge College or Entrepreneurial? What is similar? How do the different faculties account for the other?

As already noted, at Classics the curriculum is prescribed and based on Western civilization, or "Eurocentric," as the student commented. "Women don't fit in our curriculum," notes one student. "Sexism is a problem we won't own up to," comments another. "Male teachers teaching male texts. And guess who gets called on most in class?" A male student acknowledges that men dominate class discussion but says, "Everybody's free to speak up, speak out. That's what is great about our seminars. I don't like sexism, but what can you do? We didn't invent it; we can't solve it."

Pieces of the knowledge puzzle begin to fit together at Classic College. Knowledge is objective and students are made to think about how they can best understand it. Because of the knowledge explosion within each discipline there is much emphasis on disciplinary rigor. Students are not taught to see themselves as part of the process which they study. Sexism, Eurocentrism and the like are acknowledged, but they are not brought into a discourse that links what the student learns with how the world is built.

Similarly, at Entrepreneurial students are taught in some courses to think about concepts such as sexism or racism; but the curriculum does not have an overreaching concern with how knowledge is produced or why particular subjects are studied and others not. Instead, Entrepreneurial follows its general mission that allows for a diversified approach to learning where students come into contact with quite different conceptions of faculty beliefs about what counts for knowledge. Some of Entrepreneurial faculty would fit well in Classics College, and others would be more suited to Cutting Edge.

At Cutting Edge College, people acknowledge that students can graduate from the institution without having come into contact with certain subjects or authors. A professor ruminates, "Does it bother me that a student can graduate without enough coursework in the sciences, or that a kid might not have dabbled enough in the quantitative area? To be honest with you, yes, it bothers me. Should we do anything about it, such as change requirements, absolutely not." Other faculty concur with the professor. "A curriculum will never be a hundred percent error-free," comments one. "A curriculum is a philosophy, and because we don't always achieve it, doesn't mean we should abandon it," adds another. In general, the feeling seems to be that because a student misses an opportunity to broaden his or her horizon does not mean that the process is flawed; if anything, it means that a better advising system is needed.

From the standpoint of the faculty and the students, all institutions need better advising systems. "Advising is terrible," grumbles a student at Classics College, "you can never find your adviser and when you do he doesn't know any more than you do." A student at Entrepreneurial complains: "Faculty don't care about advising. They don't know how to do it, spend the time, actually counsel people. It's especially bad for freshmen. There's so much to take here, but you never learn how to do it." A student at Cutting Edge adds, "It's hit-and-miss. It can take you a long time to find the person who's right for you. And because we work closely with faculty on the exams, it can be frightening."

An area where Classics and Cutting Edge and, to an extent, Entrepreneurial converge is that of the method of instruction. Unlike Women's College where lecture podiums have caused a stir, Classics and Cutting Edge place a high premium on seminars with maximum student interaction. As might be expected, at Entrepreneurial some faculty feel the lecture is the best method and others believe seminars are better. The difference between the pedagogic styles of Classics and Cutting Edge concerns the overall goals of the curriculum at both institutions. At Classics College a student says excitedly, "You get going in one of those seminars and boy it's fantastic! They really make you think in there. You really feel great ideas are being discussed and you're part of the debate."

One night at Cutting Edge I have supper with a student in a campus restaurant; he greets me at the front door dressed in a bright red beret, a faded T-shirt and jeans. As we sit at the rooftop cafe he speaks of his life at the college:

> I'm made to question where I fit in the grand scheme of things. I constantly am brought back to myself, to my relationship to what we're learning. I never thought it would be so lonely. . . . The way it's structured you work incredibly hard on your own. Work. Work. Work. I'm always in the library, or perhaps talking to a professor. It's not an easy life, but I'm learning a lot. What this place teaches you is how to get your hands on the knowledge, to access knowledge.

Again, the inherent differences of each approach come out. The seminar at Classic encourages students to objectify knowledge and see if they can make sense of the knowledge they are taught. The Cutting Edge seminar tries to make students see how what is being discussed impacts on their lives. At Classics College whether the knowledge is referentially linked to the student's life is serendipitous. At Cutting Edge College knowledge is always contextual. At Entrepreneurial students may be exposed to both forms of learning, but as the individual stated above, knowledge is not viewed as ideological. Thus, the curriculum is removed from unearthing the underpinnings of what counts for knowledge. Students may be taught different theories or political viewpoints, but in general they still come to see knowledge as objective.

The student's comment about loneliness should also be mentioned. Each of the institutions value the intellect, but the manner in which the participants manifest the value differs between Cutting Edge and Classics on the one hand, and Entrepreneurial on the other. At Classics and Cutting Edge words like "rigor," "intense," and "standards" continually crop up in conversations with the different constituencies. As opposed to many other institutions in America, and at Entrepreneurial, not much effort is expended toward a student's socio-emotional needs at Cutting Edge of Classics. At Classics they disdain it—"we're not a social hostel," commented the professor. At Cutting Edge their energies are directed elsewhere. A new student services administrator comments, "People say there's no community here; that there are a lot of isolated individuals. To a certain extent that's true. We don't put enough emphasis on the emotional side of things."

In many respects the culture of Cutting Edge and Classics has created what the participants view as legitimate knowledge. "It's important for us to be cutting-edge," says an individual at the institution, pointing out one of the key precepts of the college. Institutional culture highlights particular pieces of knowledge which the participants seek to legitimate and, as importantly, subsumes other knowledge forms that remain hidden or discredited. Because Entrepreneurial has a diffuse culture as derived from the mission, what gets defined as legitimate knowledge is also diffuse. At Entrepreneurial some students join fraternities and the football team—the antithesis of student life at Cutting Edge and Classics—and other students disdain such activities. Entrepreneurial values the intellect, but not to the exclusion of students' socio-emotional needs that extend beyond the classroom.

Working from the notion of culture developed in Chapter 2, I have tried to point out how ideology is enacted through curricular formations. Three institutions where the fit between ideology and discourse is relatively tight have been considered. Although the ideologies and the curricular formations of each institution are quite different, within the culture a relatively high degree of consistency exists. We turn now to a discussion of how curricular decisions get made. . . .

As we conclude the second part of this book, a brief review is in order. We have deliberated over two key words that concern the culture of an academic institution—mission and curriculum. The mission and the curriculum have been discussed from the perspective of seven institutions. Women's College is engaged in a quite serious—sometimes acrimonious—debate about what it means to be a single-sex institution. Testimony State College is a public institution that has a distinctive mode of teaching—"seminaring"—which creates a unique bonding and culture among the participants. Cutting Edge College eschews disciplines and fosters interdisciplinary learning. Entrepreneurial College allows faculty to create a wide array of curricular programs and approaches to learning. A recent tenure denial has created confusion on the part of new faculty about the mission of the institution; attempts at collegewide change have rarely succeeded. Working Class State College is undergoing the possibility of curricular change in a community beset by unemployment. Classics College teaches the curricular canon and the faculty assume that one can attempt to master disciplinary knowledge. Finally, Christian University bases its curriculum on the teaching of the church. Clearly, each institution has a quite different way of perceiving its mission and enacting it by way of the curriculum.

The purpose of Part II has been to highlight and contrast different people's experiences and reflections of their institutions. There have been no heroes or villains. There have been no grand gestures and symbols of academic life to come to terms with an institution's mission or curricular structure. Instead, we have seen how people—administrators, faculty, parents, and students—experience and talk about their institutions on a daily level.

The cultural life of an institution has been portrayed as a pastiche of competing knowledge and practices. And the pastiche is not always mellifluous, as witness the comment at Cutting Edge: "We were set up as a large Italian, Jewish family—lots of good fights, shouting." Further, the participants neither uniformly interpret the mission not the curriculum. Some faculty at

Classics question whether they should still teach the canon, as do some faculty at Christian. Even though both faculty have different conceptions of what the canon is, groups currently question what it should be. At Entrepreneurial, people appear to have given up any hope of reaching consensus about what the curriculum should be, and instead create individual programs. Individuals at Testimony bring their own interpretations to the institution and help the institution revise its conception of itself; and at Women's the debate and discord is out in the open.

By investigating the day-to-day experiences of different participants, I am trying to develop a sensitivity to the cultural aspects of the organization. Once we understand how the operations and perceptions of culture work in an organization, once we accept that an institution's mission is more than a tool for effectiveness, once we comprehend how the curriculum is more than a device for enabling students to become marketable or enriched by static knowledge, we will be able critically to examine the organizational formations that have constrained democratic action by not allowing us to imagine alternative ways of conceptualizing our ideological status.

Giroux notes, "Human beings not only make history, but they also make the constraints; and needless to say, they also unmake them. It needs to be remembered that power is both an enabling as well as a constraining force" (1983, p. 38). A study of the critical words of a postsecondary organization's culture has enabled the reader to see how organizational participants have made their history and their constraints. Part II provided the curricular topography of the institutions, and we have traversed several different curricular routes. But we must go further.

Part III directs the reader's attention to the voices at these institutions and to the faculty and administrators. We consider more systematically the enabling and constraining forces of power. Other voices also will be heard, principally those of the students. The culture of these same seven institutions is viewed from a different perspective. Rather than look at how participants give meaning to the topography of the institution, we will consider the participants themselves and hear their voices borne along the landscapes of their institutions. How are the actors liberated or constrained by the powers behind the ideologies? What do they do, or fail to do, with their own power?

An Experiment in Curriculum Reform

Donald A. Schön

In Nathan Glazer's "schools of the minor professions" (which, as I have pointed out, his "major" schools of business, medicine, and law increasingly resemble) there is a high degree of ambiguity and instability in what counts as professional knowledge. Disciplines are often imported to enhance the prestige of the school, each professor tends to advocate his own discipline as a basis for professional knowledge, and curriculum tends to shift with shifting ideas in good currency in the larger professional field. Faculty members on opposite sides of the dilemma of rigor or relevance—high-ground and swamp-dwellers—tend to disagree about the proper course of professional education. And in this context, conflicts inherent in university culture sometimes reach a state of perceived crisis favorable to educational reform.

This description applies to university-based schools of city planning like the Department of Urban Studies and Planning at M.I.T., where I have taught for the past fourteen years.

Our department has endured frequent changes in curriculum, roughly coincident with changes in the national climate of city-planning practice, and it has initiated some changes in practice and curriculum that have spread to other university-based schools. Since 1972, I have been a part of these changes. My interests in professional practice and education have led me to study what the department was doing and, increasingly, take an active role in shaping its curriculum.

The story I want to tell here is about an effort, undertaken by a small group of faculty members between 1981 and 1984, to restructure the first-semester core curriculum required of all students in the Master of City Planning (MCP) program.

The question of a core curriculum for the professional planning degree had been with the department from its origins. Until the early sixties, required courses reflected the clearly defined subject matter—plan making for the physical city—around which the department had won its independence from the School of Architecture. But with the emergence in the Kennedy and Johnson administrations of an "urban crisis" and the ferment of the civil rights, youth, and peace movements, the field of planning exploded. The earlier core curriculum was discarded by a new generation of faculty disenchanted with the obsolescence of earlier required courses and daunted by the challenge of making a core out of the new subjects—economics, sociology, psychology, anthropology, law—that had begun to proliferate in the department. The students were glad to see the old core go, resenting—in those heady times—any restrictions on their freedom of choice.

By the early seventies, however, freedom of choice had begun to be perceived as anarchy. There was a drive, as the new chairman of the department said, to "put some order back in the place." Under the general rubric of knowledge useful for planning practice, four main subjects were identified—economics, statistical methods, the planning process, and institutional analysis—each of which became a focus of debate. Eventually, the first three courses in this list were agreed upon. They were set out, as one faculty member put it, to represent "The department's view of useful planning knowledge." The courses were required, and students took them, always with some resentment and dissatisfaction.

In 1978, when a new department chairman came in, the makeup of MCP students and faculty had become fairly well established. A significant number of the students—among about forty entering each year—were preoccupied with questions that had become salient in the sixties: social justice, especially for racial minorities, women, and the poor. About half the students were women. Many students had come from careers in community development and advocacy. The department made valiant, if increasingly unsuccessful, efforts to recruit members of ethnic minorities. And many students preoccupied with issues of social justice were also concerned about their prospects for employment, which they tended to translate into an interest in learning "hard skills" like financial analysis, statistics, and computer programming.

The faculty consisted of about thirty full-time members, many of whom had graduated from the department. Some had links to traditions of architecture and environmental design; some had backgrounds as practicing planners; some were social scientists who had joined the department in the explosion of the sixties and early seventies. Like other faculty members in a research university, they tended to prize their freedom to conduct research and practice in the areas of their choice. Many identified with their original disciplines, or practice specialties, rather than with "planning." Research and practice were highly valued; teaching was taken very seriously but ranked second to research and practice; and administration tended to be regarded as an unavoidable and onerous duty.

When the new department chairman an took over in 1978, he assumed the burden of coordinating the courses that make up the core. Nevertheless, students continued to resist required courses and, by 1980, had begun to express their dissatisfaction more overtly. Most of them accepted the idea that there should be a body of required knowledge but objected to the core as it then existed. They found it fragmented, divorced from an understandable context. They resented their isolation from faculty members, missed an emphasis on issues of fairness in public policy (expressed in shorthand as issues of "race, class, and sex"), and felt that they were treated in core courses as though they had no prior knowledge or experience.

The student protest led the MCP committee to form a Core Review Committee, which consisted of three faculty members—myself among them, as chairman—and seven first-year MCP students.

The atmosphere of the review was contentious and, as one student put it, "a little scary." But it also generated a great deal of energy.

In the spring of 1981, the committee carried out its work in a very public way, continually submitting products for the inspection of the larger student and faculty group—like "the planning process of old times," as one committee member put it:

> You had everybody in there. There was an extraordinary number of people. It was amazingly drawn out, a democratic process, which made a real effort to canvass . . . students and faculty.

The committee worked by sketching broad scenarios of possible future directions for the core. Debates centered on conflicting conceptions of the planning profession, the contents and levels of subject matter useful for practitioners, and the relationships of academic course work to practice. An important division of opinion arose between those who favored a "conceptual core"—a way of "teaching you to think," as one student participant said—and those who wanted to give priority to technical skills. An environmental designer on the committee proposed that the new core should be organized around a practicum:

> Somewhere along the line, the idea of a studio, or a case, emerged as . . . a shared context. It came partly out of some of my experience working with very diverse groups. . . . We all decided that we were talking different languages and that one thing we should do is have some common pieces to look at. And the conversation became more interesting. We decided, "That's what we need!"

> We would imbue in people the idea of playing, sketching, thinking things out loud through extremes . . . sort of, "What if we did this?" And it teaches you a lot about thinking process, a way of attacking problems.

The committee's final report proposed an "ideal" scenario that included a "conceptual" approach to course content, supplemented by skill-building sequences, some compromise on issues of "coherence versus flexibility," contexts in which students had greater access to faculty members, "time for reflection" in smaller groups, pass/fail grades, and a recommendation that the "controversial issues" be included as a top priority.

By this time, several things has happened that can be seen, in retrospect, as having set the stage for the year and a half of planning that was to follow. Two students, young women, had emerged as committed participants—in the words of one faculty member, "very special people who had a lot of energy and a lot of imagination and staying power," I had urged one of these to continue to devote time to the process, arguing that she should consider it a prototype of the kind of leadership role she hoped to take in the future.

One of the faculty members most admired by the students, the environmental designer who had proposed the "studio" idea, agreed to take over the leadership of the committee—having determined, as he said, that the other members of the group were prepared to "hold up their end."

In the summer of 1981, we set up a study group that included the three faculty members previously involved, the two students, and two new faculty members who were expected to teach in the new core. Our group included the environmental designer, an institutional economist, an advocate planner, and two of the instructors in the existing quantitative methods course.

We created three basic courses surrounding a central, studiolike project. The three courses were new versions of the earlier set. "Economics" became "Political Economy for Planners," combining institutional economic history with units in micro, urban, and welfare economics. "Quantitative Methods" became "Quantitative Reasoning," organized around data analysis, estimation, modeling, and experiment design. The earlier "Planning Process" and Institutional Analysis" courses were combined in one, "Planning and Institutional Processes," which examined some of the main traditions of city-planning theory and practice, placing programs and methods in the institutional contexts of their application. The studio project eventually settled on the problems of a region in Boston, a corridor beginning with Copley Square, where a massive new development project was going on, and proceeding up Blue Hill Avenue, a blighted neighborhood inhabited mostly by blacks and Hispanics.

As we continued to meet during the next academic year, we developed our own planning "traditions." We worked at listening to one another. At my instigation, we slowed the process down whenever necessary, to make listening possible. We tried to make our disagreements as clear and sharp as we could. We paid attention to the process by which we tried to surface and resolve our conflicting ideas, and increasingly, over time, we thought of ourselves as engaged in an experiment in collective inquiry.

The process was, as one participant described it, "burdensome and stressful" but also exciting. The professor of political economy later described it as follows:

> I know something was going on at the point at which we weren't just using it as a forum for our own positions but started listening to each other. . . . The sense of being a part of something larger—that was very exciting. Early on, certainly Don and I knew, because we talked about it, that this activity was going to make the professional program the center of the department, and that was a good thing to do. . . . We joked sometimes about Don experimenting in terms of group process, trying different things out. We were all doing that, trying things out on one another, trying to teach one another about what we did. That fact in itself was very exciting.

A teacher of writing, who had been working for some years in the department, joined the planning group. She observed

> how thrilling it was to sit around the table to see people actually question how they could teach something best.

And one of the students felt we had made "incredible progress":

> To have started a process basically as a student issue and to have it become legitimate and have it become ongoing, having it become something that there was a commitment to on

the part of the school. And to have it, in a sense, be a model process for them to do other things.

Not everyone shared her enthusiasm, however. One senior professor, a veteran of some twenty-five years in the department, expressed his skepticism about the very idea of required courses. In his view, no matter how enthusiastically they were begun, they tended to end up dry and uninspiring, unsuited to changing student interests. And the department chairman, who had managed the earlier core, though impressed with the energy and commitment devoted to the new venture, doubted that "one giant experience . . . made any sense at all." But he decided, as he said,

> Look, you want to do it a different way? You should do it.

Lessons from the Experiment

The date of the first delivery of the new core was fall 1982, and in spring of 1983, we evaluated it through interviews with faculty members and students who had participated.

Some of our intentions for the core were very clear. We had tried to achieve some, but by on means all, features of the ideally coherent curriculum described in the previous chapter.

We had tried to design our three courses so as to make their conceptual underpinnings clearer than they had been before and more clearly connectable both to one another and to the Copley Place/Blue Hill Avenue project. As part of this effort at integration, we had agreed to attend one another's classes.

We had tried, in the "Political Economy" and "Quantitative Reasoning" courses, to make a workable synthesis of broad, conceptual material and technical content. We wanted to stimulate intellectually interesting and personally meaningful reflection on values important to planning practice, especially values related to the "controversial questions" of race, class, and sex.

We wanted to help students develop "generic competences," some of which we described as follows:

- To take dirty data and make something sensible out of them.
- To write clearly about complicated issues.
- To deal with people who see the world very differently and get something productive to happen.
- To be able to live through hard interpersonal and political issues and hang onto important ideas.
- To be able to deal with people who disagree with you in a productive way.

We wanted our studiolike practicum to serve several functions. We wanted to use it as a prism through which to see the utility of ideas and methods presented in the courses. We wanted it to be, in addition, a vehicle for student and faculty reflection on the process of framing problems in messy, conflictual situations drawn from actual planning practice—a setting where students would reflect on the tacit theories they brought to their project solutions and try out their newly acquired methods of quantitative description and analysis. However, we had not tried to use the practicum as a setting for coaches' demonstration and public reflection on their own planning practice. We had not, in any significant degree, tried to bring into the practicum the organizational experiences of planning practitioners. Nor had we tried to teach our disciplines so as to reveal methods of research that students could use as prototypes of reflection-in-action.

Some of our intentions were fully realized; others, marginally or not at all.

We discovered exciting conceptual connections among disciplines previously treated as intellectual islands. For example, the professor of quantitative reasoning, who had been initially skeptical about the benefits of faculty members attending one another's lectures, later expressed "genuine disappointment at certain times at the end of the semester when certain faculty members were not there on certain days." He gave an example of the kind of insight into conceptual connections that became possible when other faculty members joined his class.

Thinking back about QR, one of the most extraordinary classes . . . actually happened early on when I was trying to explain the difference between a case and a variable, and I had about thirteen pages worth of lecture notes and I got through a page and a half. And that was . . . at the time very frustrating for me. Because it was a lecture which led to a lot of comments by Don, a lot of comments by [other faculty members], and a lot of comments by a lot of students about different ways to approach the question of research about that particular problem, and leaving that, I felt very frustrated and had a long conversation with Don about that. And Don persuaded me that that was a very important conversation to have had, and in fact, in our discussions, that has sort of become a model for [what] is possible with several faculty members present at the same time. Rather than the sort of thing that is costly. . . . But it is interesting how your immediate impression is different from your long-run impression.

In the session to which he referred here, he had asked the class what "cases" and "variables" they would choose for quantitative study if they had to describe deteriorating housing in a center city slum. One faculty member proposed to study entire *blocks* of housing, because of their significance for environmental design and the "contagion" of disrepair. The political economist claimed that it would be essential to study patterns of *ownership*. A practicing planner argued that the choice of cases and variables must reflect the kinds of *actions* that might be taken as a result of the analysis. It became clear to what extent the choice of things to count—the very starting point of quantitative reasoning—depends on disciplinary and political-economic perspectives.

It was clear, to faculty and students alike, that discussion of race, class, and sex had been "too stylized," too much dominated by the views of white, male instructors; inadequate in its treatment of women in planning; insufficiently attentive to the vexed question of race in the history of planning in Boston. Many of the students felt that these questions, which they saw as central to the planning profession, had not become integral to the core.

The professors of "Political Economy" and "Quantitative Reasoning" felt constrained by the limited time available to them for the technically challenging components of their courses.

As to the practicum, the Copley/Blue Hill Avenue project raised issues linked to the core courses and drew on course-related methods of analysis, data gathering, and design. But faculty members had found it difficult to define a level of realism and difficulty that matched the time allocated for project work. Some of them described the small groups as a "tremendous drain of energy" that "may not have been worth it." They felt that the small groups gave them an opportunity to get to know a few students well, but they also felt overwhelmed by the multiple, inadequately defined objects of the exercise—as practicum, time for reflection, and forum for discussion of the "controversial issues." As the environmental designer put it, "You can't do a studio out of three hours a week." And he added,

The irony is that we put as much time into it as into any other piece of the core and I think in many ways it was the least successful.

Some students spoke positively about the experience of working with other students to achieve a shared understanding of a complex and vaguely defined situation. They liked the idea of working with other students of different backgrounds to produce a product in a limited amount of time. As one of them said,

It got you to personally figure out some difficult things: working in groups, struggling with how you define something. These are things you can't really teach someone. There is a lot of anxiety. How can we think we are capable of deciding how to approach this problem? It was not easy; it was good. There are dilemmas you must experience.

But others reacted negatively to these very features of the experience. They found it frustrating to try to get a shared view of a problem about which they all had different ideas. They objected to the vagueness of the task. Some felt they had come to the work with inadequate experience, understandings, and tools of the trade. They didn't know how to tell, as one of them put it, whether "we were in the ball park, hitting a home run, or . . . in the bleachers."

Quite apart from the question of our success in realizing our intentions, we became aware of several unintended consequences. These seemed, if anything, *more* important than some of our intentions.

A practicum more nearly like the experiences described in earlier chapters of this book, was the design of the core itself. The small group of faculty members and students who criticized the old core, planned for the new one, and taught it for the first time were self-consciously engaged in a design process. Over a three-year period, as they familiarized themselves with one another's research and practice, they learned, by doing, to construct a new curriculum. They created an environment for intellectual debate about teaching and, in the process, also created an intellectual community—thereby discovering how much they had missed belonging to one. There was a serious side to their occasional, humorous acknowledgment that the core meant more to them than to the students for whom it was intended!

Moreover, as their comments reveal, members of the core committee were aware of some features of the process by which they had built their reflective practicum. The long-term, "old-time planning process in which everyone participated" and the pressures generated by student dissatisfactions and expectations helped to create an environment of high energy and involvement. Gradually, members of the group had been able to test out one another's commitment to the stringent demands of the design task. Competition and bickering characteristic of normal curriculum planning gradually dissipated as individuals learned to listen to one another with greater attention and critical appreciation. Norms for discussion and ways of resolving conflicts were established, with surprising rapidity, as "traditions."

Those who taught the core courses found it intensely burdensome to sit in on one another's courses and participate in directing the small groups. They doubted whether such intense involvement could be sustained. But they also found extraordinary rewards in the experience of teaching together. One of the younger faculty members remarked,

> I thought it was really good to have other professors in the room. There were certainly occasions when I was nervous or would think twice about what I was going to do, but then I realized it was really good . . . students should see us criticizing one another.

Another faculty member talked about the benefits of mutual accountability:

> If something goes wrong, everybody knows about it quickly. It has to be dealt with; it can't be pushed away. Just the fact of having to be accountable to one another provided a really good discipline.

> [You see yourself] in a situation where your own personal success depends on the success of the group. That is the point at which you transcend your individual competitiveness and move on to something else. And that happened for us a long time ago, even before the first class. It really did, and we had fun!

Nevertheless, the very success of the Core Committee's reflective practicum—its cohesiveness and excitement—gave rise to problems.

Some of these had been predicted by faculty members opposed to the new core. The Core Committee "in-group" helped to create an "out-group" of other faculty members who regarded the new core with disinterest or suspicion. After the first three years, as the usual patterns of faculty discontinuity reasserted themselves, it became difficult to sustain the climate of intense, collective involvement. Still, it proved feasible to attract new faculty members to teach in the core, especially in the small groups. For the most part, new faculty members found the climate of the core refreshing and contributed new skills and points of view. With each passing year, more student "alumni" of the core participated in the new year's core, bringing to it a feeling for the traditions of previous years. And a few members of the original group sustained their commitment to the enterprise. Hence, faculty discontinuities were damaging but not fatal.

There was a more significant, unexpected, and intractable dilemma inherent in the very idea of the core; the curriculum design created through the faculty's reflective practicum showed a very strong tendency to drive out the students' reflection.

It was not as though our students did not have a significant *capacity* for a reflection on their experience. Indeed, a study I had done in the early seventies (Schön, 1973) suggested that students in city planning at M.I.T. had a considerable ability to reflect-in-action on their own professional education. At some point in their careers, many of them learned how to stage a dialogue between their field and classroom experiences and used this discovery to direct and control their own learning. Seeing their courses as pieces of a larger educational puzzle, they used their movement between classroom and field to build up a sense of the practice competencies they wanted to acquire. They sized up what they needed to learn and weighed the value for professional practice of the knowledge they were getting at school. Similarly, they used the movement between field and classroom to test their career goals and their visions of the practice they planned to enter. In their discovery of the possibilities inherent in the dialogue of field and academic careers—limited, to be sure, by their understandings of both—they created a reflective practicum of their own. And according to my informal observations of students over a decade, there were always some who continued to make this discovery.

But in spite of the students' capacities for reflection and the fact that the core was a reflective practicum for those who designed it, the experience of *taking* the core led many students to feel like passive recipients of other people's knowledge. One student complained of having

> no time to think . . . just time to prepare projects, keep up with the reading and get to class and keep from falling asleep. The pace almost killed me.

Another pictured

> little slides of my life: so many hours spent in the reading room, staying up all night to type . . . a lot of physical pain from not sleeping or eating . . . can't believe all the time people spent doing all that work.

And one faculty member described the student experience as a "marathon." adding,

> There ought to be spaces in it, where people can just go off somewhere and try to think.

For some students, the core seemed to take over their lives, becoming their whole world. They found themselves preoccupied with absorbing information, getting problem sets right, passing examinations. Some of them felt they were being drawn into beliefs in spite of themselves. The experience of being continually lectured at made them "feel like an audience."

Other students denied that the totality of the core experience drove out reflective thought. They spoke of their excitement about

> getting practical . . . sitting with a group of people to come up with a definition of a problem . . . and showing that it works.

Some found, as they went on to courses in the following semester, that "we did synthesize some things and are using them now." They were to "see the efforts of what we have learned." Others spoke of their discovery that

> no matter how many models you build, you really have to deal with every day differently, because so many unexpected things come up.

Nearly all the students and several of the faculty members mentioned the strong sense of intimacy and cohesiveness the students seemed to feel with one another. One faculty member commented on

> how remarkable it was that a group of forty people sort of thrown together at random had developed [early in the semester] that kind of cohesiveness and respect for one another and affection for one another. How it was created, how it could be created again, is completely mysterious to me.

But solidarity also had its negative aspects. The sense of membership in a community could be seen as a trap. As one of the students put it,

> We were in an environment that was almost like a bubble within the university.

Coda

When evidence of students' capacity to manage their own education is juxtaposed with their experience in the core, where many of them felt overwhelmed by the very completeness of the curriculum design, it raises an important question: Is it possible to combine a coherent professional curriculum with the conditions essential to a reflective practicum? For the more we integrate in a curriculum the knowledge and skills that students, in our judgment, need to learn, the more we make it difficult for them to function as reflective designers of their own education.

In part, this dilemma has to do with time, or the perception of time, The densely packed core left insufficient time for the practicum we tried to build into it—a practicum that might have given students the opportunity to explore questions of competence, satisfaction, learning, trust, and identity that underlay the self-managed movement of earlier students across field and academic careers. But the problem was not only one of time.

During the period since 1982, as we continued to teach the core and learn from our earlier mistakes, we tried, in various ways, to reduce pressures on the students. We redefined group work and reduced our expectations for student projects. We allowed each group to address a different task. In a number of areas, we cut back on readings, assignments, and requirements. But our results were paradoxical. Cutting back on requirements does not seem to have reduced the students' feelings of pressure—which suggests that the sense of overload may be, at least in part, of their own making.

Those who felt overloaded to the point of "having no time for reflection" may have adopted, with our unintentional help, a passive stance. They may have suffered from a paucity of prior, practice-related experience on which to reflect. And this, if true, suggests that a reflective practicum of the sort we tried to create may most appropriately occur, not at the beginning of a student's professional career, but in the midst of it, as a form of continuing education.

However, it remains to be seen whether, through a curriculum designed based on a better understanding of conflicting demands, we can achieve, at least at threshold level, conditions essential both to a coherent professional curriculum and to a reflective practicum. We may be led to a positive view if we focus—as we have been trying in recent years to do—on timing, pace, and direction. If the entire experience is long enough to allow free time for reflection on course work, if simulated practice occurs when students are equipped to use it to try out ideas and methods they have learned in the classroom, and if we create opportunities for students to connect classroom knowledge to their prior experience, then we may be able to combine faculty-generated ideas about what students need to learn with student's active management of their own learning.

From the perspective of faculty participation, the results of our experiment in curriculum redesign are highly suggestive. They suggest that it is possible, at least over a period of several years, for a small group of faculty members to become committed to collective inquiry into teaching and learning. It is possible to create surprisingly durable "traditions" that channel faculty and student interactions in new ways. Faculty members can find it exciting, even liberating, to make their own teaching into a subject for mutual exploration. And whey they do so, their substantive research interests are engaged.

Most important, many faculty members thirst for an intellectual community. When such a community presents itself as a real possibility, it taps a powerful source of energy for reflection-in-action in curriculum redesign.

The core experiment also suggests how a reflective practicum can become a first step toward remaking the larger curriculum. The base of faculty participation can be sustained even in the face of the discontinuities inherent in academic life. The development of a reflective practicum can join with new forms of research on practice, and education for it, to take on a momentum—even a contagion—of its own.

Bibliography

Abelson, P. (1906). *The seven liberal arts: A study in medieval culture.* New York: Teachers College Press.

Ackerman, J. S. (1973). The arts in higher education. In C. Kaysen (Ed.), *Content and context: Essays on college education* (pp. 219–261). New York: McGraw-Hill.

Adelman, C. (1992). *Tourists in our own land: Cultural literacies and the college curriculum.* Washington, DC: United States Department of Education.

Aiken, S. H., Anderson, K., Dinnerstein, M., Lensink, J. N., & MacCorquodale, P. (1987). Trying transformations: Curriculum integration and the problem of resistance. *Signs: A Journal of Women in Culture and Society, 12,* 255–275.

Aikin, S. H., Anderson, K., Dinnerstein, M., Lensink, J. N., & MacCorquodale, P. (Eds.). (1988). *Changing our minds: Feminist transformations of knowledge.* Albany, NY: State University of New York Press.

Aisenberg, N., & Harrington, M. (1988). *Women in academe: Outsiders in the sacred grove.* Amherst, MA: University of Massachusetts Press.

Alkin, M. C., & Fitz-Gibbon, C. T. (1975). Methods and theories of evaluating programs. *Journal of Research and Development in Education, 8,* 2–15.

Allan, G. (1986). The canon in crisis. *Liberal Education, 72,* 89–100.

American Association of Community and Junior Colleges. (1988). *Building communities: A vision for a new century.* Washington, DC: American Association of Community and Junior Colleges.

Andersen, M. L. (1988). Moving our minds: Studying women of color and reconstructing sociology. *Teaching Sociology, 16,* 123–132.

Anderson, M. L. (1987). Changing the curriculum in higher education. *Signs: A Journal of Women in Culture in Society, 12,* 222–254.

Angelo, T. & Cross, P. (1993). *Classroom assessment techniques: A handbook for college teachers.* San Francisco: Jossey-Bass.

Apple, M. W. (1982). *Education and power.* Boston: Routledge & Kegan Paul.

Apple, M. W. (1979). *Ideology and curriculum.* Boston: Routledge & Kegan Paul.

Arns, R. G., & Poland, W. (1980). Changing the university through program review. *Journal of Higher Education, 51,* 268–284.

Association of American Colleges. (1991) *Liberal learning and the arts and sciences major: The challenge of connected learning* (Vols. 1 & 2). Washington, DC: Author.

Association of American Colleges. (1988). *A new vitality in general education.* Washington, DC: Author.

Association of American Colleges. (1985). The decline and devaluation of the undergraduate degree. In *Integrits in the college curriculum: A report to the academic community* (pp. 1–39). Washington, DC: Author.

Astin, A. (1977). *Four critical years: Effects of college on beliefs, attitudes, and knowledge.* San Francisco: Jossey-Bass.

Astin, A. W. (1993). *What matters in college?: Four critical years revisited.* San Francisco: Jossey-Bass.

Astin, A. W. (1989). Moral messages of the university. *Educational Record, 70,* 22–25

Astin, A. W. (1982). Why not try some new ways of measuring quality? *Educational Record, 63,* 10–15.

Banks, J. A. (1991). A curriculum for empowerment, action & change. In C. Sleeter (Ed.), *Empowerment through multicultural education* (pp. 125–157). Albany, NY: State University of New York Press.

Banta, T., & Associates. (1994). *Making a difference.* San Francisco: Jossey-Bass.

Bar-Haim, G., & Wilkes, J. M. (1989). A cognitive interpretation of the marginality and underrepresentation of women in science. *Journal of Higher Education, 60* (4), 371–387.

Barak, R. J. (1981). Program evaluation as a tool for retrenchment. In J. R. Mingle & Associates (Eds.), *Challenges of retrenchment* (pp. 212–225). San Francisco: Jossey-Bass.

Baxter Magolda, M. B. (1992). *Knowing and reasoning in college: Genderrelated patterns in students' intellectual development.* San Francisco: JosseyBass.

Belenky, M. F., Clinchy, B. M., Goldberger, N. R., & Tarule, J. M. (1986). *Women's ways of knowing: Development of self, voice, and mind.* New York: Basic Books.

Belknap, R. L., & Kuhns, R. (1977). *Tradition and innovation: General education and the reintegration of the university.* New York: Columbia University Press.

Bell, D. (1966). *The reforming of general education: The Columbia College experience in its national setting.* New York: Columbia University Press.

Benson, G. D., & Griffith, B. E. (1991). The process of knowing in curriculum. *Journal of General Education, 40,* 24–33.

Bergquist, W. H., Gould, R. A., & Greenberg, E. M. (1981). *Designing undergraduate education: A systematic guide.* San Francisco: Jossey-Bass.

Berlak, A. (1994). Antiracist pedagogy in a college classroom: Mutual recognition and a logic of paradox. In R. A. Martusewicz & W. M. Reynolds (Eds.), *Inside out: Contemporary critical perspectives in education* (pp. 38–60). New York: St. Martins Press.

Beyer, J. M., & Snipper, R. (1974). Objective versus subjective indicators of quality. *Sociology of Education, 47,* 541–557.

Blackburn, R., Armstrong, E., Conrad, C., Didham, J., & McKune, T. (1976). *Changing practices in undergraduate education.* Berkeley, CA: Carnegie Council on Policy Studies in Higher Education.

Blackburn, R. T., & Conrad, C. F. (1986). The new revisionists and the history of higher education. *Higher Education, 15,* 211–230.

Blackman, E. B. (1969). General Education. In R. L. Ebel (Ed.), *Encyclopedia of educational research* (4th ed., pp. 522–537). New York: MacMillan.

Bloom, B. (1956). *Taxonomy of educational objectives: The cognitive domain.* New York: David McKay.

Bok, D. (1974). On the purposes of undergraduate education. *Daedalus, 103,* 159-172.

Bonwell, C. C., & Eison, J. A. (1991). *Active learning: Creating excitement in the classroom.* ASHE-ERIC Higher Education Report No. 1. Washington, DC: Association for the Study of Higher Education.

Booth, W. C. (1991). *The vocation of a teacher.* Chicago: University of Chicago Press.

Booth, W. C. (1967). Is there any knowledge that a man must have? In W. C. Booth (Ed.), *The knowledge most worth having* (pp. 128). Chicago: University of Chicago Press.

Bouwsma, W. J. (1975). Models of the educated man. *The American Scholar, 44,* 195–212.

Boyer, C. M., & Alghren, A. (1987). Assessing undergraduate patterns of credit distribution: Amount and specialization. *Journal of Higher Education, 58,* 430–442.

Boyer, C. M., & Ahlgren, A. (1982). "Visceral priorities" in liberal education: An empirical assessment. *Journal of Higher Education, 53,* 207–215.

Boyer, E. L. (1987). *The undergraduate experience in America.* New York: Harper and Row.

Bragg, S. (1977). St. Olaf and the paracollege: A case study of planned curriculum and organizational change in higher education. *Journal of Higher Education, 48,* 152–171.

Brann, E. (1979). *Paradoxes of education in a republic.* Chicago: University of Chicago Press.

Braxton, J. M. (1993). Selectivity and rigor in research universities. *Journal of Higher Education, 64,* 657–675.

Braxton, J. M., & Nordvall, R. C. (1985). Selective liberal arts colleges: Higher quality as well as higher prestige. *Journal of Higher Education, 56,* 538–554.

Brick, M., & McGrath, E. J. (1969). *Innovation in liberal arts colleges.* New York: Teachers College Press, Columbia University.

Bromwich, D. (1992). *Politics by other means: Higher education and group thinking.* New Haven, CT: Yale University Press.

Brookfield, S. D. (1986). *Understanding and facilitating adult learning.* San Francisco: Jossey-Bass.

Brubacher, J. (1977). *On the philosophy of higher education.* San Francisco: Jossey-Bass .

Brubacher, J. S., & Rudy, W. (1976). *Higher education in transition* (3rd ed.). New York: Harper and Row.

Bruffee, K. A. (1993). *Collaborative learning: Higher education, interdependence, and the authority of knowledge.* Baltimore, MD: Johns Hopkins University Press.

Burke, C. B. (1982). *American collegiate populations: A test of the traditional view.* New York: Columbia University Press.

Butler, J. E. (1991). The difficult dialogue of curriculum transformation: Ethnic studies and women's studies. In J. E. Butler & J. C. Walter (Eds.), *Transforming the curriculum: Ethnic studies and women's studies* (pp. 1–19). Albany, NY: State University of New York Press.

Butler, J. E. (1991). Transforming the curriculum: Teaching about women of color. In J. E. Butler & J. C. Walter (Eds.), *Transforming the curriculum: Ethnic studies and women's studies* (pp. 67–87). Albany, NY: State University of New York Press.

Butler, J. E., & Walter, J. C. (Eds.). (1991). *Transforming the curriculum: Ethnic studies and women's studies.* Albany, NY: State University of New York Press.

Butts, R. F. (1939). *The college charts its course.* New York: McGraw-Hill.

Callahan, D. (1978). Ethics and value education. *Liberal Education, 64,* 134–143.

Carlson, D. L. (1993). Literacy and urban school reform: Beyond vulgar pragmatism. In C. Lankshear & P. McLaren (Eds.), *Critical literacy: Politics praxis and the postmodern* (pp. 217–246). Albany, NY: State University of New York Press.

Carlson, D. L. (1988). Curriculum planning and the state: The dynamics of control in education. In L. Beyer & M. Apple (Eds.), *The curriculum: Problems, politics and possibilities* (pp. 98-118). Albany, NY: State University of New York Press.

Carlson, D. L. (1985). Curriculum & the school work culture. In P. Altbach, G. Kelly & L. Weis (Eds.), *Excellence in education: Perspectives on policy & practice* (pp. 171–182). Buffalo, NY: Prometheus Press.

Carnegie Foundation for the Advancement of Teaching. (1990). *Campus life: In search of community.* Princeton, NJ: Carnegie Foundation for the Advancement of Teaching.

Carnegie Foundation for the Advancement of Teaching. (1977). *Missions of the college curriculum: A contemporary review with suggestions.* San Francisco: Jossey-Bass.

Carr, W., & Kemmis, S. (1986). *Becoming critical: Education, knowledge, and action research.* Philadelphia: The Falmer Press.

Chamberlain, M. (1988). Enriching the curriculum: Women's studies. *Thought and Action, 4,* 21–28.

Cheit, E. F. (1975). *The useful arts and the liberal tradition.* New York: McGraw-Hill.

Cheyney, L. V. (1989). *50 hours: A core curriculum for college students*. Washington, DC: National Endowment for the Humanities.

Chickering, A. W., & Associates. (1981). *The modern American college*. San Francisco: Jossey-Bass.

Chickering, A. W., & Gamson, Z. (Eds.). (1991). *Applying the Seven Principles for Good Practice in Undergraduate Education*. New Directions for Teaching and Learning. (No. 47). San Francisco: Jossey-Bass.

Chickering, A. W., Halliburton, D., Bergquist, W. H., & Lindquist, J. (1977). *Developing the college curriculum: A handbook for faculty and administrators*. Washington, DC: Council for the Advancement of Small Colleges.

Chu, J. (1986). Asian American women's studies course: A look back at our beginnings. *Frontiers, 8* (3), 95–101.

Clandinin, D. J., & Connelly, F. M. (1990). Narrative, experience, and the study of curriculum. *Cambridge Journal of Education, 20,* 241–253.

Clandinin, D. J., & Connelly, F. M. (1988). *Teachers as curriculum planners: Narratives of experience*. New York: Teachers College Press.

Clark, M. J., Hartnett, R. T., & Baird, L. L. (1976). *Assessing dimensions of quality in doctoral education: A technical report of a national study of three fields*. Princeton, NJ: Educational Testing Service.

Clark, T. N. (1968). Institutionalization of innovation in higher education. *Administrative Science Quarterly, 13,* 1–25.

Cohen, A. M. (Ed.). (1979). *Shaping the Curriculum*. New Directions for Community Colleges. (No. 25). San Francisco: Jossey-Bass.

Collins, P. H. (1986). The emerging theory and pedagogy of black women's studies. *Feminist Issues, 6,* 3–17.

Collins, P. H. (1991). On our own terms: Self-defined standpoints and curriculum transformation. *NWSA Journal, 3,* 367–381.

Conrad, C. F. (1978). *The undergraduate curriculum: A guide to innovation and reform*. Boulder, CO: Westview.

Conrad, C. F. (1978). A grounded theory of academic change. *Sociology of Education, 51,* pp. 101–112.

Conrad, C. F. (1982). Undergraduate instruction. In H. E. Mitzel (Ed.), *Encyclopedia of educational research* (5th ed., pp. 1963–1973). New York: MacMillan.

Conrad, C. F. (1980). Initiating and implementing institutional change. In J. G. Gaff (Ed.), *General education: A guide to resources* (pp. 102–116). Washington, DC: Association of American Colleges.

Conrad, C. F. (1983). *At the crossroads: General education in community colleges* [Horizons Issue Monograph Series]. Washington, DC: Council of Universities and Colleges, American Association of Community and Junior Colleges; Los Angeles: ERIC Clearinghouse for Junior Colleges.

Conrad, C. F., & Millar, S. M. (1992). Graduate curriculum. In B. R. Clark & G. Neave (Eds.), *Encyclopedia of higher education* (6th ed., pp. 1557–1566). New York: Pergamon.

Conrad, C. F., & Eagan, D. J. (1989). The prestige game in American higher education. *Thought and Action, 5,* 5–16.

Conrad, C. F., & Blackburn, R. T. (1986). Current views of departmental quality: An empirical examination. *Review of Higher Education, 9,* 249–265.

Conrad, C. F., & Haworth, J. G. (1992). "Undergraduate Curriculum." In M. C. Alkin (Ed.), *Encyclopedia of educational research* (pp. 411–459). New York: Macmillan, 1992.

Conrad, C. F., Haworth, J. G., & Millar, S. (1993). *A silent success: Master's education in the United States*. Baltimore, MD: Johns Hopkins University Press.

Conrad, C. F., & Pratt, A. M. (1983). Making decisions about the curriculum: From metaphor to model. *Journal of Higher Education, 54,* 16–30.

Conrad, C. F., & Pratt, A. M. (1981). Measure for measure: Liberal education and the fine arts--A delicate balance. *Review of Higher Education, 4,* 47–58.

Conrad, C. F., & Blackburn, R. T. (1985). Research on program quality: A review and critique of the literature. In J. C. Smart (Ed.), *Higher education: Handbook of theory and research* (Vol. 1, pp. 283–308). New York: Agathon.

Conrad, C. F., & Blackburn, R. T. (1985). Correlates of departmental quality in regional colleges and universities. *American Educational Research Journal, 22,* 279–295.

Conrad, C. F., & Wyer, J. C. (1980). *Liberal education in transition.* ASHEERIC/Higher Education Research Report No. 3. Washington, DC: American Association for Higher Education.

Conrad, C. F., & Eagan, D. J. (1989). Achieving excellence: How will we know? In C. H. Pazandak (Ed.), *Improving undergraduate education in large universities* (pp. 51–63) New Directions in Higher Education, No. 66. San Francisco: Jossey-Bass.

Conrad, C. F., & Pratt, A. M. (1986). Research on academic programs: An inquiry into an emerging field. In J. C. Smart (Ed.), *Higher education: Handbook of theory and research* (Vol. 2) (pp. 235–273). New York: Agathon.

Conrad, C. F., & Wilson, R. F. (1985). *Academic program review.* ASHE-ERIC/Higher Education Research Report No. 5. Washington, DC: Association for the Study of Higher Education.

Conrad, C. F., & Pratt, A. M. (1985). Designing for quality. *Journal of Higher Education, 56,* 601–622.

Cranton, P. A., & Legge, L. H. (1978). Program evaluation in higher education. *Journal of Higher Education, 49,* 464–471.

Cremin, L. A. (1971). Curriculum-making in the United States. *Teachers College Record, 73,* 207–220.

Cross, K. P. (1976). Accent on learning: Improving instruction and reshaping the curriculum. San Francisco: Jossey-Bass.

Culley, M., & Portuges, C. (Eds.) (1985). *Gendered subjects: The dynamics of feminist teaching.* Boston: Routledge and Kegan Paul.

D'Souza, D. (1991). *Illiberal education: The politics of race and sex on campus.* New York: Free Press.

Davis, B. G. (1993). *Tools for teaching.* San Francisco: JosseyBass.

Davis, J. R. (1993). *Better teaching, more learning: Strategies for success in postsecondary settings.* Phoenix, AZ: American Council on Education and Oryx Press.

Deegen, W. L., Tillery, D., & Associates. (1985). *Renewing the American community college.* San Francisco: Jossey-Bass.

Dewey, J. (1967). *Democracy and education.* New York: Free Press. (Original work published in 1929)

Diamond, R. M. (1989). *Designing and implementing courses and curriculum in higher education.* San Francisco: Jossey-Bass.

Dill, D. C., & Friedman, C. P. (1979). An analysis of frameworks for research on innovation and change in higher education. *Review of Educational Research, 49,* 411–435.

Donald, J. G. (1986). Knowledge and the university curriculum. *Higher Education, 15,* 267–282.

Donald, J. G. (1983). Knowledge structures: Methods for exploring course content. *Journal of Higher Education, 54,* 31–41.

Dressel, P. L. (1968). *College and university curriculum.* Berkeley, CA: McCutchan.

Dressel, P. L., & DeLisle, F. H. (1969). *Undergraduate curriculum trends.* Washington, DC: American Council on Education.

Drew, L. A. (1978). The Greek concept of education and its implications for today. *Liberal Education, 64,* 302–319.

Drew, D. E., & Karpf, R. (1981). Ranking academic departments: Empirical findings and a theoretical perspective. *Research in Higher Education, 14,* 305–320.

Egan, K. (1978). What is curriculum? *Curriculum Inquiry, 8,* 65–72.

Ewell, P. T. (1987). Establishing a campus-based assessment program. In D. F. Halpern (Ed.), *Student outcomes assessment: What institutions stand to gain* (New Directions for Higher Education, No. 59, pp. 9–24). San Francisco: Jossey-Bass.

Ewell, P. T. (1986). Outcomes, assessment, and academic improvement: In search of usable knowledge. In J. C. Smart (Ed.), *Higher education: Handbook of theory and research* (Vol. 4, pp. 53–108). New York: Agathon.

Feasley, C. E. (1980). *Program evaluation.* AAHE-ERIC/Higher Education Research Report No. 2. Washington, DC: American Association for Higher Education.

Feldman, K. A., & Newcomb, T. M. (1970). *The impact of college on students* (Vol. 1). San Francisco: Jossey-Bass.

Final Report of the Study Group on the Conditions of Excellence in American Higher Education. (1984). *Involvement in learning: Realizing the potentials of American higher education.* Washington, DC: National Institute of Education, U.S. Government Printing Office.

Firestone, W. A. (1977). Participation and influence in the planning of educational change. *Journal of Applied Behavioral Science, 13,* 167–183.

Flax, J. (1990). Postmodernism and gender relations in feminist theory. In L. J. Nicholson (Ed.), *Feminism/post-modernism* (pp. 39–62). New York: Routledge, Chapman & Hall.

Ford, G. W., & Pugno, L. (Eds.). (1964). *The structure of knowledge and the curriculum.* New York: Rand McNally.

Fuhrmann, B. S., & Grasha, A. F. (1983). *A practical handbook for college teachers.* Boston: Little, Brown.

Furst, E. J. (1981). Bloom's taxonomy of educational objectives for the cognitive domain: Philosophical and educational issues. *Review of Educational Research, 51,* 441–453.

Gabriel, S. L., & Smithson, I. (1990). *Gender in the classroom.* Urbana, IL: University of Illinois Press.

Gaff, J. G. (1991). *New life for the college curriculum.* San Francisco: Jossey-Bass.

Gaff, J. G. (1980). Avoiding the potholes: Strategies for reforming general education. *Educational Record, 61,* 50–59.

Gaff, J. G. (Ed.). (1980). *General education: Issues and resources.* Washington, DC: Association of American Colleges.

Gamson, Z. F. (1989). *Higher education and the real world: The story of CAEL.* Wolfeboro, NH: Longwood.

Gamson, Z. F. (1984). Politics of creating change. In Z. Gamson & Associates, *Liberating education* (pp. 131–152). San Francisco: Jossey-Bass.

Gamson, Z. F., & Hill, P. J. (1984). Creating a lively academic community. In Z. Gamson & Associates, *Liberating education* (pp. 83–94). San Francisco: Jossey-Bass.

Gardner, D. E. (1977). Five evaluation frameworks: Implications for decision making. *Journal of Higher Education, 48,* 571–593.

Gardner, S., Dean, C., & McKaig, D. (1989). "Responding to differences in the classroom: The politics of knowledge, class, and sexuality. *Sociology of Education, 62,* 64–74.

Gardner, S., Dean, C., & McKaig, D. (1992). Responding to differences in the classroom: The politics of knowledge, class & sexuality. In J. Wrigley (Ed.), *Education and gender equality* (pp. 131–145). Bristol, PA: Falmer Press.

Gates, H. L., Jr. (1992). *Loose canons: Notes on the culture wars.* New York: Oxford University Press.

Geismar, K., & Nicoleau, G. (Eds.). (1993). Teaching for change: Addressing issues of difference in the college classroom. *Harvard Educational Review* Reprint 25.

Giroux, H. (1991). Liberal arts education and the struggle for public life: Dreaming about democracy. In D. Gless & B. Herrnstein Smith (Eds.), *The politics of liberal education* (pp. 119–144). Durham, NC: Duke University Press.

Giroux, H. (1988). *Teachers as intellectuals: Toward a critical pedagogy of learning.* Granby, MA: Bergin & Garvey.

Giroux, H. A. (1983). *Theory and resistance in education.* South Hadley, MA: Bergin and Garvey.

Giroux, H. (1992). *Border crossings: Cultural workers and the politics of education.* New York: Routledge.

Glazer, N. (1975). The social sciences in liberal education. In S. Hook, P. Kurtz, & M. Todorovich (Eds.), *The philosophy of the curriculum: The need for general education* (pp. 145–158). Buffalo, NY: Prometheus.

Glazer, N. Y. (1987). Questioning eclectic practice in curriculum change: A Marxist perspective. *Signs: A Journal of Women in Culture in Society, 12*, 293–304.

Goode, W. J. (1960). Encroachment, charlatanism, and the emerging professions: Psychology, sociology, and medicine. *American Sociological Review, 25*, 903–914.

Goode, W. J. (1957). Community within a community: The professions. *American Sociological Review, 22*, 194–200.

Gooler, D. D. (1977). Criteria for evaluating the success of nontraditional postsecondary education programs. *Journal of Higher Education, 48*, 78–95.

Graff, G. (1992). *Beyond the culture wars: How teaching the conflicts can revitalize American education.* New York: W. W. Norton.

Graff, G. (1987). *Professing literature: An institutional history.* Chicago: University of Chicago Press.

Grant, G., & Associates. (1979). *On competence: A critical analysis of competence-based reforms in higher education.* San Francisco: Jossey-Bass .

Grant, G., & Riesman, D. (1975). American higher education: Toward an uncertain future. *Daedalus, 104*, 166–191.

Grumet, M. (1994). Conception, contradiction, and curriculum. In L. Stone (Ed.), *The education feminism reader* (pp. 149–170). New York: Routledge.

Guba, E. G., & Lincoln, Y. S. (1989). *Fourth Generation Evaluation.* Newbury Park, CA: Sage.

Guba, E. G., & Lincoln, Y. S. (1981). *Effective evaluation: Improving the usefulness of evaluation results through responsive and naturalistic approaches.* San Francisco: JosseyBass.

Gumport, P. J. (1993). The contested terrain of academic program reduction." *Journal of Higher Education, 64*, 283–311.

Gumport, P. J. (1988). Curricula as signposts of cultural change. *Review of Higher Education, 12*, 49–61.

Gumport, P. J. (1991). E pluribus unum? Academic structure, culture, and the case of feminist scholarship. *The Review of Higher Education, 15*, 9–29.

Hackman, J. D., & Taber, T. D. (1979). Patterns of undergraduate performance related to success in college. *American Educational Research Journal, 16*, 117–138.

Hall, J. W. (1982). *In opposition to core curriculum: Alternative models for undergraduate education.* Westport, CT.

Halpern, D. F., & Associates. (1994). *Changing college classrooms: New teaching and learning strategies for an increasingly complex world.* San Francisco: Jossey-Bass.

Harding, S. (1990). Feminism, science and the anti-enlightenment critiques. In L. J. Nicholson (Ed.), *Feminism/post-modernism* (pp. 83–106). New York: Routledge, Chapman & Hall.

Haworth, J. G., & Conrad, C. F. (1993). Master's programs and contextual planning. *Planning for Higher Education, 21*, 12–18.

Haworth, J. G., & Conrad, C. F. (1992). Conformity or subversiveness: Alternative Approaches to professional master's programs in regional colleges and universities. *Metropolitan Universities, 3*, 8–19.

Haworth, J. G., & Conrad, C. F. (1991). Liberating education in modern metropolitan universities. *Metropolitan Universities, 2*, 21–30.

Heath, D. H. (1976). What do the enduring effects of higher education tell us about a liberal education? *Journal of Higher Education, 47*, 173–190.

Heath, D. H. (1968). *Growing up in college.* San Francisco: Jossey-Bass.

Hefferlin, J. L. (1969). The dynamics of academic reform. San Francisco: Jossey-Bass.

Helms, L. B., Hahn, C. W., & Engel, R. E. (1984). Curriculum reform: Applications from organizational theory. *Journal of Research and Development in Education, 17,* 46–58.

Heppner, F. (1991). Why Robert Burns was right about best-laid plans or what's wrong with the curriculum the way it is? *Change,* 43–48.

Higginbotham, E. (1990). Designing an inclusive curriculum: Bringing all women into the core. *Women's Studies Quarterly, 15,* 7–23.

Himmelfarb, G. (1994). *On looking into the abyss: Untimely thoughts on culture and society.* New York: Knopf.

Hirst, P. H. (1974). *Knowledge and the curriculum: A collection of philosophical papers.* Boston: Routledge and Kegan Paul.

Hook, S., Kurtz, P., & Todorovich, M. (Eds.). (1975). *The philosophy of the curriculum: The need for general education.* Buffalo, NY: Prometheus.

Houle, C. O. (1980). *Continuing learning in the professions.* San Francisco: Jossey-Bass.

Howe, F. (1980). Three missions of higher education for women: Vocation, freedom, knowledge. *Liberal Education, 66,* 285–297.

Hughes, E. C. (1963). Professions. *Daedalus, 92,* 655–668.

Hunkins, F. P., & Hammill, P. A. (1994). Beyond Taylor and Taba: Reconceptualizing the curriculum process. *Peabody Journal of Education, 69,* 4–18.

Hursh, B., Haas, P., & Moore, M. (1983). An interdisciplinary model to implement general education. *Journal of Higher Education, 54,* 42–59.

Hutchins, R. M. (1936). General education. In R. M. Hutchins, *The higher learning in America.* New Haven, CT: Yale University Press.

Jacoby, R. (1994). *Dogmatic wisdom: How the education and cultural wars have misled America.* New York: Doubleday.

Jaeger, W. (1939). *Paideia: The ideals of Greek culture.* New York: Oxford University Press.

Johnson, B. L. (Ed.). (1982). *General education in two-year colleges.* New Directions for Community Colleges No. 40. San Francisco: Jossey-Bass.

Johnson, D. W., Johnson, R. T., & Smith, K. A. (1991). *Cooperative learning: Increasing faculty instructional productivity.* ASHE-ERIC Higher Education Report No. 4. Washington, DC: Association for the Study of Higher Education.

Kanter, S., London, H., & Gamson, Z. (1991). The implementation of general education. *Journal of General Education, 40,* 119–132.

Katz, J., & Sanford, N. (1962). The curriculum in the perspective of the theory of personality development. In N. Sanford (Ed.), *The American college* (pp. 418–444). New York: John Wiley.

Keeton, M. T., & Associates. (1976). *Experiential learning: Rationale, characteristics, and assessment.* San Francisco: Jossey-Bass.

Kegan, D. L. (1977). Using Bloom's cognitive taxonomy for curriculum planning and evaluation in nontraditional educational settings. *Journal of Higher Education, 48,* 63–77.

Keller, G. D., Magallan, R. J., & Garcia, A. M. (1989). *Curriculum resources in Chicano studies.* Tempe, AZ: Bilingual Review/Press.

Keller, P. (1982). *Getting at the core: Curricular reform at Harvard.* Cambridge, MA: Harvard University Press.

Kimball, B. A. (1988). The historical and cultural dimensions of the recent reports on undergraduate education. *American Journal of Education, 98,* 293–322.

Kimball, B. A. (1986). *Orators and philosophers: A history of the idea of liberal education.* New York: Teachers College Press.

Kimball, R. (1990). *Tenured radicals: How politics has corrupted our higher education.* New York: Harper & Row.

Klein, M. F. (1990). Approaches to curriculum theory and practice. In J. T. Sears & J. D. Marshall (Eds.), *Teaching and thinking about curriculum: Critical inquiries* (pp. 3–14). New York: Teachers College Press.

Kliebard, H. M. (1992). *Forging the American curriculum: Essays in curriculum theory and history.* New York: Routledge.

Knight, W. E. (1993). An examination of freshmen to senior general education gains across a national sample of institutions with different general education requirements using a mixed effect structural equation model. *Research in Higher Education, 34,* 41–54.

Knox, A. B., et al. (1986). *Helping adults learn: A guide to planning. implementing and conducting programs.* San Francisco: Jossey-Bass.

Kolb, D. A. (1984). *Experiential learning: Experience as the source of learning and development.* Englewood Cliffs, NJ: Prentice-Hall.

Kramarae, C., & Spender, D. (Eds.). (1992). *The knowledge explosion: Generations of feminist scholarship.* New York: Teachers College Press.

Kuh, G. D., & Ransdell, G. A. (1980). Evaluation by discussion. *Journal of Higher Education, 51,* 301–313.

Kuh, G. D. (1981). *Indices of quality in the undergraduate experience.* AAHEERIC/Higher Education Research Report No. 4. Washington, DC: American Association for Higher Education.

Kurfiss, J. G. (1988). *Critical thinking: Theory, research possibilities.* ASHE-ERIC Research Report No. 2. Washington, DC: Association for the Study of Higher Education.

Ladd, D. R. (1970). *Change in educational policy: Self-studies in selected colleges and universities.* New York: McGraw-Hill.

Langland, E., & Gove, W. (Eds.). (1981). *A feminist perspective in the academy: The difference it makes.* Chicago: University of Chicago Press.

Lather, P. (1984). Critical theory, curricular transformation, and feminist mainstreaming. *Journal of Education, 167,* 49–62.

Lattuca, L. R., & Stark, J. S. (1994). Will disciplinary perspectives impede curriculum reform? *Journal of Higher Education, 65,* 401–426.

Lawrence, J. K., & Green, K. C. (1980). *A question of quality: The higher education ratings game.* AAHE-ERIC/Higher Education Research Report No. 5. Washington, DC: American Association for Higher Education.

Lawson, J. M., Ladd, A. H., & Newell, L. J. (1983). The Utah plan: College freshmen in an experimental liberal studies program. *Journal of General Education, 35,* 136–153.

Lee, C. B. (1966). Knowledge structure and curriculum development. *Educational Record, 47,* 347–360.

Lee, W. A., & Gilmour, J. E., Jr. (1977). A procedure for the development of new programs in postsecondary education. *Journal of Higher Education, 48,* 304–320.

Leslie, L. L. (1976). *Updating education for the professions: The new mission.* In G. L. Anderson (Ed.), Land-grant universities and their continuing challenge (pp. 237–265). Lansing, MI: Michigan State University Press.

Levine, A. (1978). *Handbook on undergraduate curriculum.* San Francisco: Jossey-Bass.

Levine, A., & Weingart, J. (1973). *Reform of undergraduate education.* San Francisco: Jossey-Bass.

Levine, A. E. (1980). *Why innovation fails: The institutionalization and termination of an innovation in higher education.* Albany, New York: State University of New York Press.

Lewis, M. (1990). Interrupting patriarchy: Politics, resistance, and transformation in the feminist classroom. *Harvard Educational Review, 60,* 467–488.

Lewis, M., & Simon, R. I. (1986). A Discourse not intended for her: Learning and teaching within patriarchy. *Harvard Educational Review, 56,* 457–472.

Lindquist, J. (1978). *Strategies for change.* Berkeley, CA: Pacific Soundings Press.

London, H. B. (1978). The culture of a community college. New York: Praeger.

Longino, H. E., & Hammonds, E. (1990). Conflicts and tensions in the feminist study of gender and science. In M. Hirsch & E. F. Keller (Eds.), *Conflicts in feminism* (pp. 164–183). New York: Routledge.

Lowther, M. A., Stark, J. S., & Martens, G. G. (1989). *Preparing course syllabi for improved communication.* Ann Arbor, MI: National Center for Research to Improve Postsecondary Teaching and Learning.

Luke, C., & Gore, J. (Eds.). (1992). *Feminisms and critical pedagogy.* New York: Routledge.

Lukenbill, J., & McCabe, R. (1978). *General education in a changing society.* Dubuque, IA: Kendall/ Hunt.

MacCorquodale, P., & Lensink, J. (1991). Integrating women into the curriculum: Multiple motives and mixed emotions. In G. P. Kelly & S. Slaughter (Eds.), *Women's higher education in comparative perspective* (pp. 297–314). Dordrecht, Netherlands: Kluwer Academic Publishers.

MacCorquodale, P., & Lensink, J. (1990). Curricular reform and gender. In G. Kelly & S. Slaughter (Eds.), *The role and status of women in higher education in international perspective.* Amsterdam, Netherlands: Kluwer Press.

Manns, C. L., & March, J. G. (1978). Financial adversity, internal competition, and curriculum change in a university. *Administrative Science Quarterly, 23,* 541–552.

Martin, J. R. (1982). Excluding women from the educational realm. *Harvard Educational Review, 52,* 133–148.

Martin, W. B. (1982). *College of character: Renewing the purpose and content of college education.* San Francisco: Jossey-Bass.

Martorana, S. V., & Kuhns, E. (1975). *Managing academic change.* San Francisco: Jossey- Bass .

May, W. (1991). Constructing history in a graduate curriculum class. *Curriculum Inquiry, 21,* 163–191.

Mayhew, L., Wick, D. L., & Hoffman, M. J. (1984). Beyond breadth: General education in the research university. *Liberal Education, 70,* 383–400.

Mayhew, L. B., & Ford, P. J. (1971). *Changing the curriculum.* San Francisco: Jossey- Bass .

McCutcheon, G. (1982). What in the world is curriculum theory? *Theory into Practice, 21,* 18–22.

McGrath, E. (1976). *General education and the plight of modern man.* Indianapolis: Lilly Endowment.

McIntosh, P. M. (1989). Curricular re-vision: The new knowledge for a new age. In C. S. Pearson, D. L. Shavlik, & Touchton, J. G. (Eds.), *Educating the majority Women challenge tradition in higher education* (pp. 400–412). New York: American Council on Education & Macmillan.

McIntosh, P. (1981). The study of women: Implications for learning in the later years. *Alternative Higher Education, 5,* 18–29.

Melchiori, G. S. (1982). *Planning for program discontinuance: From default to design.* AAHE-ERIC/ Higher Education Research Report No. 5. Washington, DC: American Association for Higher Education.

Mentkowski, M. (1991). Creating a context where institutional assessment yields educational improvement. *Journal of General Education, 40,* 255–283.

Meyers, C., & Jones, T. B. (1993). *Promoting active learning: Strategies for the college classroom.* San Francisco: JosseyBass.

Meyerson, M. (1974). Civilizing education: Uniting liberal and professional learning. *Daedalus, 103,* 173–179.

Miller, J. L. (1993). Solitary spaces: Women, teaching, and curriculum." In D. Wear (Ed.), *The center of the web: Women and solitude* (pp. 245–252). Albany, NY: State University of New York Press.

Miller, J. L. (1990). *Creating spaces and finding voices: Teachers collaborating for empowerment.* Albany, New York: State University of New York Press.

Minnich, E., O'Barr, J., & Rosenfeld, R. (Eds.). (1988). *Reconstructing the academy: Women's education and women's studies.* Chicago: University of Chicago Press.

Moore, W. E., & Rosenblum, G. (1970). *The professions: Roles and rules.* New York: Russell Sage.

Morris, J. S. (1978). The place of the humanities in the liberal arts. *Liberal Education, 64,* 44–54.

Morrison, J. (1973). *The rise of the arts on the American campus.* New York: McGraw-Hill.

Murchland, B. (1979). Reviving the connected view. *Commonweal, 106,* 42–48.

Musil, C. M. (Ed.). (1992). *The courage to question: Women's studies and student learning.* Washington, DC: Association of American Colleges and National Women's Studies Association.

Nespor, J. (1990). Curriculum and conversions of capital in the acquisition of disciplinary knowledge. *Journal of Curriculum Studies, 22,* 217–232.

Newcombe, J. P., & Conrad, C. F. (1981). A theory of mandated academic change. *Journal of Higher Education, 52,* 555–577.

Newell, L. J. (1985). Shall the twain meet? Liberal education and nursing education. *Journal of Professional Nursing, 1,* 253–254.

Newell, L. J. (1984). A catalyst and a touchstone: Involvement in learning. *Change, 16,* 7–10.

Newell, L. J. (1982). Among the few at Deep Springs College: Assessing a seven-decade experiment in liberal education. *Journal of General Education, 34,* 120–134.

Newell, L. J., & Spear, K. I. (1983). New dimensions for academic careers: Rediscovering intrinsic satisfactions. *Liberal Education, 69,* 103–116.

Newman, J. H. (1959). *The idea of a university.* Garden City, NY: Image Books. (Original work published in 1853).

Nichols, J., & Gamson, Z. (1984). Modifying course content to encourage critical awareness. In Z. Gamson & Associates, *Liberating education* (pp. 113–129). San Francisco: Jossey-Bass.

Nordvall, R. C. (1982). *The process of change in higher education institutions.* AAHE-ERIC/Higher Education Research Report No. 7. Washington, DC: American Association for Higher Education.

Nyre, G. F., & Reilly, K. C. (1979). *Professional education in the eighties: Challenges and responses.* AAHE-ERIC/Higher Education Research Report No. 8. Washington, DC: American Association for Higher Education.

Oleson, A., & Voss, J. (1979). *The organization of knowledge in modern America. 1860–1920.* Baltimore, MD: Johns Hopkins University Press.

Olscamp, P. J. (1978). Can program quality be quantified? *Journal of Higher Education, 49,* 504–511.

Orozco, C. E. (1990). Getting started in Chicana studies. *Women's Studies Quarterly, 1 & 2,* 46–69.

Pace, C. R. (1979). *Measuring outcomes of college: Fifth years of findings and recommendations for the future.* San Francisco: Jossey-Bass.

Parker, C. A. (1980). The literature on planned organizational change: A review and analysis. *Higher Education, 9,* 429–442.

Parlett, M., & Deardon, G. (1977). *Introduction to illuminative evaluation.* Cardiff-by-the-Sea, CA: Pacific Soundings Press.

Pascarella, E. T., & Terenzini, P. T. (1991). *How college affects students.* San Francisco: Jossey-Bass.

Perry, W. F. (1968). *Forms of intellectual and ethical development in the college years.* New York: Holt, Rinehart, and Winston.

Phenix, P. H. (1971). Transcendence and the curriculum. *Teachers College Record, 73,* 271–283.

Phenix, P. H. (1964). *Realms of meaning.* New York: McGraw-Hill.

Phenix, P. H. (1971). Transcendence and the curriculum. *Teachers College Record, 73,* 271–283.

Pinar, W. F. (Ed.). (1975). *Curriculum theorizing: The reconceptualists.* Berkeley, CA: McCutchan Publishing.

Popham, W. J. (1975). *Educational evaluation.* Englewood Cliffs, NJ: Prentice-Hall.

Pratt, A. M., & Conrad, C. F. (1981). Everyman's undergraduate curriculum: A question of humanistic context. *Liberal Education, 67,* 168–176.

Radzialowski, T. (March 1981). The future of ethnic studies. *The Forum for Liberal Education, 3,* 1–3.

Read, J., & Sharkey, S. R. (1985). Alverno college: Toward a community of learning. In J. Green & A. Levine (Eds.), *Opportunity in adversity: How colleges can succeed in hard times* (pp. 195–214). San Francisco: JosseyBass.

Reeves, G., & Jauch, L. R. (1978). Curriculum development through delphi. *Research in Higher Education, 8,* 147–168.

Report of the Commission on the Humanities. (1980). *The humanities in American life.* Berkeley: University of California Press.

Report of the Harvard Committee. (1945). *General education in a free society.* Cambridge, MA: Harvard University Press.

Rhoades, G. (1991). Professional education: Stratifying curricula and perpetuating privilege in higher education. In J. C. Smart (Ed.), *Higher education: Handbook of theory and research* (Vol. 7, pp. 334–375). New York: Agathon Press.

Rhoades, G. (1990). Calling on the past: The quest for the collegiate ideal. *Journal of Higher Education, 61,* 512–534.

Riesman, D., Gusfield, J., & Gamson, Z. (1975). *Academic values and mass education.* New York: McGraw-Hill.

Riesman, D., & Stadtman, V. A. (Eds.). (1973). *Academic transformation: Seventeen institutions under pressure.* New York: McGraw-Hill.

Roche, G. (1994). *The fall of the ivory tower: Government funding corruption, and the bankrupting of American higher education.* Washington, DC: Regnery Publishing.

Rosser, S. (1989). Creating an environment that is conducive to learning for the majority. *Journal of the Freshman Year Experience, 1*(1), 53–63.

Rossi, P. H., & Freeman, H. A. (1982). *Evaluation: A systematic approach.* Beverly Hills, CA: Sage.

Rossides, D. (1987). Knee-jerk formalism: The higher education reports. *Journal of Higher Education, 58,* 404–429.

Rothenberg, P. (1988). Integrating the study of race, gender, and class: Some preliminary observations. *Feminist Teacher, 3,* 37–42.

Rudolph, F. (1977). *Curriculum: A history of the American undergraduate course study since 1636.* San Francisco: Jossey-Bass.

Rudy, W. (1960). *The evolving liberal arts curriculum: A historical review of basic themes.* New York: Bureau of Publications, Teachers College, Columbia University.

Ryan, M. P., & Martens, G. G. (1989). *Planning a college course: A guidebook for the graduate teaching assistant.* Ann Arbor, MI: National Center for Research to Improve Postsecondary Teaching and Learning.

Sagen, H. B. (1979). Careers, competencies, and liberal education. *Liberal Education, 65,* 150–166.

Sagen, H. B. (1973). Education for the professions: A neglected model for undergraduate education. *Liberal Education, 59,* 507–519.

Salner, M. (1985). Women, graduate education, and feminist knowledge. *Journal of Education, 167,* 46–58.

Schein, E. H. (1972). *Professional education.* New York: McGrawHill.

Schlesinger, A. M., Jr. (1991). *The disuniting of America: Reflections on a multicultural society.* New York: W. W. Norton.

Schmidt, G. P. (1957). *The liberal arts college.* New Brunswick, NJ: Rutgers University Press.

Schmitz, B. (1985). *Integrating women's studies into the curriculum: A guide and bibliography.* Old Westbury, NY: The Feminist Press.

Schmitz, B. (1985). *Integrating women's studies into the curriculum: A guide and bibliography.* Old Westbury, CT: The Feminist Press.

Schmitz, B., Dinnerstein, M., & Mairs, N. (1985). Initiating a curriculum integration project: Lessons from the campus and the region. In M. Schuster & S. Van Dyne (Eds.), *Women's place in the academy: Transforming the liberal arts curriculum.* Totowa, NJ: Rowman and Allanheld.

Schon, D. A. (1987). *Educating the reflective practitioner: Toward a design for teaching and learning* in the professions. San Francisco: JosseyBass.

Schuster, M., & Van Dyne, S. (Eds.) (1985). *Women's place in the academy: Transforming the liberal arts curriculum.* Totowa, NJ: Rowman and Allanheld.

Schuster, M. R., & Van Dyne, S. R. (1985). Stages of curriculum transformation. In M. Schuster & S. Van Dyne (Eds.), *Women's place in the academy: Transforming the liberal arts curriculum* (pp. 13–29). Totowa, NJ: Rowman & Allanheld.

Schuster, M., & Van Dyne, S. (1985). Stages of curriculum transformation. In M. Schuster & S. Van Dyne (Eds.), *Women's place in the academy: Transforming the liberal arts curriculum* (pp. 1329). Totowa, NJ: Rowman and Allanheld.

Schuster, M., & Van Dyne, S. (1984). Placing women in the liberal arts: Stages of curriculum transformation. *Harvard Educational Review, 54,* 413–28.

Schwab, J. J. (1951). Dialectical means vs. dogmatic extremes in relation to liberal education. *Harvard Educational Review, 21,* 37–64.

Schwab, J. J. (1964). Structure of the disciplines: Meanings and significances. In G. W. Ford & L. Pugno (Eds.), *The structure of knowledge and the curriculum* (pp. 232–255). San Francisco: Jossey-Bass.

Schwab, J. J. (1949). The nature of scientific knowledge as related to liberal education. *Journal of General Education, 3,* 1–22.

Scott, R. A. (1981). The curriculum as covenant. *College Board Review, 121,* 20–23, 28.

Scott, B. A. (1992). The 'new practicality' revisited: Changes in the American college curriculum. *Journal of Education, 174,* 87–103.

Scriven, M. (1973). Goal-free evaluation. In E. R. House (Ed.), *School evaluation: The politics and process* (pp. 319-328). Berkeley, CA: McCutchan.

Seeley, J. (1981). Program review and evaluation. In N. L. Poulton (Ed.), *Evaluation of management and planning systems* (pp. 4560). New Directions for Institutional Research No. 31. San Francisco: Jossey-Bass.

Seymour, D. T. (1988). *Developing academic programs.* ASHE-ERIC Higher Education Report No. 3. Washington, DC: ASHE-ERIC.

Shapiro, A. (1991). *Creating a conversation: Teaching all women in the feminist classroom.* NWSA Journal, 3, 70–80.

Shirley, R. C., & Volkwein, J. F. (1978). Establishing academic program priorities. *Journal of Higher Education, 49,* 472–488.

Shor, I. (1992). Education is politics: An agenda for empowerment. In I. Shor (Ed.), *Empowering education* (pp. 11–30). Chicago: University of Chicago Press.

Stark, J. S., Shaw, K. M., & Lowther, M. A. (1989). *Student goals for college and courses: A missing link in assessing and improving teaching and learning.* Washington, DC: ASHE-ERIC Higher Education Report No. 6.

Statham, A., Richardson, L., & Cook, J. A. (1991). *Gender and university teaching: A negotiated difference.* Albany, NY: State University of New York.

Stufflebeam, D., & Associates. (1971). *Educational evaluation and decision making.* Itasca, IL: Peacock.

Taba, H. (1962). *Curriculum development: Theory and practice.* New York: Harcourt, Brace, & World.

Terenzini, P. T. (1989). Assessment with open eyes: Pitfalls in studying student outcomes. *Journal of Higher Education, 60,* 644–664.

Tetrault, M. K. T. (1985). Feminist phase theory: An experience-driven evaluation model. *Journal of Higher Education, 56,* 363–383.

The Yale report of 1828. (1961). In R. Hofstadter & W. Smith (Eds.), *American higher education: A documentary history* (Vol. 1, Pt. 4, No. 11, pp. 275–288). Chicago: University of Chicago Press.

Thomas, K. (1990). *Gender and subject in higher education.* Buckingham, England: SHRE & Open University Press.

Thomas, R. (1962). *The search for a common learning: General education. 1800–1960.* New York: McGraw-Hill.

Tierney, W. G. (1990). *Curricular landscapes, democratic vistas: Transformative leadership in higher education.* New York: Praeger.

Tierney, W. G. (1989). Cultural politics and the curriculum in postsecondary education. *Journal of Education, 171,* 72–88.

Toombs, W., Amey, M. J., & Chen, A. (1991). General education: An analysis of contemporary practice. *Journal of General Education, 40,* 102–118.

Toombs, W. (1978). The application of design-based curriculum analysis to general education. *Review of Higher Education, 1,* 18–29.

Toombs, W., & Tierney, W. G. (1991). *Meeting the mandate: Renewing the college and departmental curriculum.* Washington, DC: ASHE-ERIC Higher Education Report No. 6.

Trimbur, J. (1986). To reclaim a legacy, cultural literacy, and the discourse of crisis. *Liberal Education, 72,* 109–119.

Trowbridge, H. (1958). Forty years of general education. *Journal of General Education, 11,* 161–169.

Twombly, S. B. (1992). Student perspectives on general education in a research university: An exploratory study. *Journal of General Education, 41,* 238–272.

Tyler, R. W. (1950). *Basic principles of curriculum and instruction.* Chicago: University of Chicago Press.

Van Doren, M. (1959). *Liberal education.* Boston: Beacon Press. (Original work published 1943).

Vars, G. F. (1982). Designs for general education: Alternative approaches to curriculum integration. *Journal of Higher Education, 53,* 216–226.

Verduin, J. R., Miller, H. G., & Greer, C. E. (1986). *The lifelong learning experience.* Springfield, IL: Charles C. Thomas.

Veysey, L. (1973). Stability and experiment in the American undergraduate curriculum. In C. Kaysen (Ed.), *Content and context* (pp. 1–63). New York: McGraw-Hill.

Veysey, L. R. (1965). *The emergence of the American university.* Chicago: University of Chicago Press.

Vollmer, H. M., & Mills, D. L. (Eds.). (1966). *Professionalization.* Englewood Cliffs, NJ: Prentice-Hall.

Walsh, C. E. (1991). *Pedagogy and the struggle for voice: Issues of language, power, and schooling for Puerto Ricans.* South Hadley, MA: Bergin & Garvey.

Weathersby, R. P., & Tarule, J. (1980). *Adult development: Implications for higher education.* AAHE-ERIC/Higher Education Research Report No. 4. Washington, DC: American Association for Higher Education.

Webster, D. S., & Conrad, C. F. (1986). Using faculty research performance for academic quality rankings. In J. W. Creswell (Ed.), *Measuring faculty research performance* (pp. 43–57). New Directions for Institutional Research No. 50. San Francisco: Jossey-Bass.

Wee, D. (1981). *On general education: Guidelines for reform* (Report from the Project on General Education Models). New Haven, CT: Society for Values in Higher Education.

Wegener, C. (1978). *Liberal education and the modern university.* Chicago: University of Chicago Press.

Weiler, K. (1991). Freire and a feminist pedagogy of difference. *Harvard Educational Review, 61,* 449–474.

Weiler, K. (1988). *Women teaching for change.* South Hadley, MA: Bergin & Garvey.

Weiss, C. H. (1972). *Evaluation research: Methods for assessing program effectiveness.* Englewood Cliffs, NJ: Prentice-Hall.

Westbury, I., & Wilkof, N. J. (1978). *Science, curriculum, and liberal education: Selected essays.* Joseph J. Schwab. Chicago: University of Chicago Press.

Whitehead, A. N. (1969). *The aims of education and other essays.* New York: Free Press. (Original work published in 1929)

Wilensky, H. L. (1964). The professionalization of everyone? *American Journal of Sociology, 60,* 137–158.

Wilson, R. F. (Ed.). (1982). *Designing academic program reviews.* New Directions for Higher Education No. 37. San Francisco: Jossey-Bass.

Wingspread Group on Higher Education. (1993). *An American imperative: Higher expectations for higher education.* Racine, WI: Johnson Foundation.

Winter, D. G., McClelland, D. C., & Stewart, A. J. (1981). *A new case for the liberal arts.* San Francisco: Jossey-Bass.

Winter, D. G., & McClelland, D. C. (1978). Thematic analysis: An empirically derived measure of the effects of liberal arts education. *Journal of Educational Psychology, 70,* 8–16.

Wolf, D. B., & Zoglin, M. L. (Eds.). (1988). *External influences on the curriculum.* New Directions for Community Colleges, No. 64. San Francisco: Jossey-Bass.

Wolff, R. P. (1969). *The ideal of the universality.* Boston: Beacon Press.

Wood, L., & Davis, B. G. (1978). *Designing and evaluating higher education curricula.* AAHE-ERIC/ Higher Education Research Report No. 8. Washington, DC: American Association for Higher Education.

Worthen, B. R., & Sanders, J. R. (1973). *Educational evaluation: Theory and practice.* Worthington, OH: Charles A. Jones.

Yllo, K. (1989). How the new scholarship on women and gender transforms the college curriculum. *American Behavioral Scientist, 32*(6), 658–667.

Zaltman, G., & Duncan, R. (1977). *Strategies for planned change.* New York: Wiley.

Zinn, M. B., Cannon, L. W., Higginbotham, E., & Dill, B. T. (1986). The cost of exclusionary practices in women's studies. *Signs, 11,* 290–303.

Zumeta, W., & Solmon, L. C. (1982). Professions education. In H. E. Mitzel (Ed.), *Encyclopedia of educational research* (5th ed.) (pp. 1458–1467). New York: MacMillan.